AUSTRALIAN DICTIONARY
OF BIOGRAPHY

General Editor
BEDE NAIRN

AUSTRALIAN DICTIONARY OF BIOGRAPHY

VOLUME 6 : 1851-1890

R-Z

Section Editors

GEOFFREY SERLE
RUSSEL WARD

MELBOURNE UNIVERSITY PRESS

First published 1976
Reprinted 1988
Printed in Australia by
Griffin Press Limited, Netley, South Australia, for
Melbourne University Press, Carlton, Victoria 3053
U.S.A. and Canada: International Specialized Book Services, Inc.,
5602 N.E. Hassalo Street, Portland, Oregon 97213–3640
United Kingdom, Ireland and Europe: Europa Publications Limited
18 Bedford Square, London WC1B 3JN

National Library of Australia Cataloguing-in-Publication
entry
Australian dictionary of biography.
Volume 6. 1851–1890, R–Z.
ISBN 0 522 84108 2.
ISBN 0 522 84236 4 (set).

1. Australia—Biography—Dictionaries. 2. Australia—
History—1851–1890. I. Nairn, Bede, 1917-   .
920'.094

PREFACE

This volume of the *Australian Dictionary of Biography* is the fourth of four for the 1851-1890 section. The first three volumes of this section and the two for 1788-1850 have already been published; six have been planned for the third section 1891-1939. This chronological division was designed to simplify production, for about 7000 articles are likely to be included. A general index volume will be prepared when the three sections are completed.

The placing of each individual's name in the appropriate section has been generally determined by when he/she did his/her most important work (*floruit*). For articles that overlap the chronological division, preference has usually been given to the earlier period, although most of the important Federationists will appear in the third section.

The selection of names for inclusion in the *Dictionary* has been the result of much consultation and co-operation. After quotas were estimated, Working Parties in each State prepared provisional lists, which were widely circulated and carefully amended. Many of the names were obviously significant and worthy of inclusion. Others, less notable, were chosen simply as samples of the Australian experience. Some had to be omitted through lack of material, and thereby joined the great anonymous mass whose members richly deserve a more honoured place; however, many thousands of these names are accumulating in the Biographical Register at the *Dictionary* headquarters in the Australian National University.

Most authors were nominated by the Working Parties, and the burden of writing has been shared almost equally by university historians and by members of historical and genealogical societies and other specialists.

The *Dictionary* is a project based on consultation and co-operation. The Australian National University has borne the cost of the headquarters staff, of much research and of some special contingencies, while other Australian universities have supported the project in various ways. Its policies have been determined by the National Committee, composed mainly of representatives from the Departments of History in each Australian university. At Canberra the Editorial Board has kept in touch with all these representatives and with the Working Parties, librarians, archivists and other local experts, as well as overseas correspondents and research assistants in each Australian capital. With such varied support the *Australian Dictionary of Biography* can truly be called a national project.

ACKNOWLEDGMENTS

Special thanks are due to Professor J. A. La Nauze for his helpful guidance as chairman of the Editorial Board. Those who helped in planning the shape of the work have been acknowledged in earlier volumes.

The *Dictionary* is grateful for many privileges extended by the Australian universities, especially the Australian National University.

For assistance overseas thanks are due to David Barron and Ivan Page, Liaison Officers of the National Library of Australia in London, and to their staff; to the archivists and librarians of: the Honourable Society of the Middle Temple, London, Cambridge University Library, University of Durham Library, University of London Library and its King's College Library, and the University of Manchester Archives; the National Library of Scotland, St Andrews University Library, King's and Marischal Colleges, Aberdeen University Library, Edinburgh University Library, University of Glasgow Archives, and the Andersonian Library, University of Strathclyde, Glasgow; Trinity College Library, University of Dublin, King's Inn's Library, Dublin; the National Library of Wales; the Alexander Turnbull Library and the National Archives, New Zealand; the Public Archives of Nova Scotia, Canada, and the Mauritius Archives Department; Emeritus Professor Stephen Welsh, Sheffield, England, J. T. Lloyd, University of Glasgow, Dr Lewis Lloyd, Harlech, Wales, Ms Alice Gay, Paris, and Dr F. Sellheim, Rumbeck, West Germany; the officials of the General Register Office, Edinburgh, the Public Record Office, London, and County Record Offices; Monsignor Cavalleri, Rome, many other clergy and others who have answered calls for help.

The *Dictionary* deeply regrets the death of such notable contributors as Charles Bateson, Keast Burke, S. G. Claughton, L. J. Duffy, W. Hudson Fysh, F. C. Green, M. F. Hardie, W. R. Jewell, A. A. Morrison, H. Z. Palmer, C. C. Singleton, Clive Turnbull, M. J. L. Uren, G. P. Whitley and C. T. Wood who, in their several capacities, greatly assisted the work of this and previous volumes.

Within Australia the *Dictionary* is greatly indebted to many librarians and archivists in Canberra and each State; to the secretaries of many historical and genealogical societies; to the historical research officers of the Australian Post Office; to the Registrars-General of Births, Deaths and Marriages, and of Probates, in the various States, whose generous co-operation has solved many problems. Warm thanks for the free gift of their time and talents are due to all contributors and all members of the National Committee, Editorial Board, and the Working Parties, including past chairmen, H. J. Finnis, F. C. Green*, R. B. Joyce, A. A. Morrison* and G. D. Richardson. For particular advice the *Dictionary* owes much to Professor J. J. Auchmuty, P. L. Brown, Professor K. J. Cable, Rev. S. G. Claughton*, Miss H. Curnow, Frank Cusack, G. L. Fischer, Professor B. Gandevia, A. J. and Nancy Gray, Rev. Dr L. B. Grope, Dr N. Gunson, A. Hicks, R. F. Holder, Rev. Dr M. Lohe, Dr J. A. Merritt, Professor J. N. Molony, Dr H. S. Patterson, J. Potts, A. Warrington Rogers, Dr F. B. Smith, Mrs Frances Stephens, David Symon, George Tibbits, Sir S. Douglas Tooth, G. P. Walsh and J. B. Windeyer.

Grateful acknowledgment is also due to the director and staff of Melbourne University Press; to the editorial staff: Nan Phillips, Martha Campbell, Sally O'Neill, Suzanne Edgar, Deirdre Morris, Chris Cunneen, H. J. Gibbney and Ann-Mari Jordens; to Ruth Frappell, Michael Bosworth and Susan Johnston in Sydney, Noeline Hall and Neil Stewart in Brisbane, Joyce Gibberd and Marlene Cross in Adelaide,

ACKNOWLEDGMENTS

Wendy Birman in Perth, Beth McLeod in Hobart and Margery Walton in New Zealand and to the administrative staff, Dorothy Smith, Norma Gregson, Jill Wright and Ivy Meere.

* deceased

COMMITTEES

COMMITTEES

WORKING PARTIES

Newcastle
J. P. S. Bach; B. W. Champion; E. Flowers; Elizabeth Guilford; W. G. McMinn (Chairman); C. E. Smith; E. M. Travers*.

New South Wales
J. M. Bennett; K. J. Cable; F. K. Crowley; C. Cunneen; R. F. Doust (Chairman); R. Else-Mitchell; F. Farrell; B. H. Fletcher; Hazel King; Beverley Kingston; W. G. McMinn; B. E. Mansfield; B. A. Mitchell; Heather Radi; J. A. Ryan; G. P. Walsh; J. M. Ward.

Queensland
R. J. N. Bannenberg; Jacqueline Bell; Nancy Bonnin; F. S. Colliver; D. K. Dignan; R. Evans; D. Gibson; J. C. H. Gill; S. G. Gunthorpe; Noeline Hall; J. R. Laverty; D. J. Murphy (Chairman); Mary O'Keeffe; S. Routh; June Stoodley; N. Stewart; P. D. Wilson.

North-Queensland sub-committee
D. W. Hunt; K. H. Kennedy; J. N. Moles (Convener); M. J. Richards; R. Sullivan.

South Australia
D. A. Dunstan; R. Gibbs; P. A. Howell; Helen Jones; J. Love; J. M. Main; J. D. Playford (Chairman); J. M. Tregenza.

Tasmania
G. P. R. Chapman; Elizabeth McLeod; Mary McRae; I. Pearce; J. Reynolds (Chairman); O. M. Roe; G. T. Stilwell.

Victoria
W. A. Bate; G. N. Blainey; L. J. Blake; S. M. Ingham; A. W. Martin; S. Murray-Smith; J. R. Poynter (Chairman); J. Rickard; A. G. Serle; F. Strahan; J. Thompson.

Western Australia
O. K. Battye; D. Black; Wendy Birman; G. C. Bolton (Chairman); B. K. de Garis; Rica Erickson; Alexandra Hasluck; J. H. M. Honniball; L. Hunt; D. Hutchinson; Mollie Lukis; Toby Manford; Margaret Medcalf; D. Mossenson; C. T. Stannage; A. C. Staples; Mary Tamblyn; Merab Harris Tauman; M. J. L. Uren*.

Armed Services
M. Austin; F. H. Brown; C. Clark; R. Clark; Jean Fielding; A. Hill; J. McCarthy; R. J. O'Neill (Chairman); B. N. Primrose.

Pacific
W. N. Gunson; D. A. Scarr; Dorothy Shineberg; F. J. West.

* deceased

DOUGLAS HENRY PIKE (1908-1974), station worker, clergyman, historian and editor, was born on 3 November 1908 at Tuhshan, China, son of Douglas Fowler Pike and his wife Louisa, nee Boulter, Australian-born Baptist missionaries with the China Inland Mission. He was educated at the Inland Mission School at Chefoo and arrived in Australia in 1924 where he worked until 1926 as a teacher in the Victorian Department of Education and attended the University of Melbourne. Next year for family reasons he went to New South Wales and became a station overseer successively on several properties, including Collaroy, in the Cassilis-Merriwa district. For a time he managed a religious printery in Sydney, but soon went back to the land. In September 1938 he returned to Melbourne and until 1940 trained for the ministry at the Church of Christ College, Glen Iris. On 25 November next year he married Olive, daughter of Rev. T. Hagger.

Following ordination, Pike worked from 1942 as a Church of Christ clergyman in Adelaide and enrolled at the University of Adelaide, completing his course in 1947 with first-class honours in history and the Tinline [q.v.] scholarship (B.A., 1948; M.A., 1951; D.Litt., 1957). After a temporary lectureship in history at the university, he became a lecturer at the University of Western Australia in 1949, but returned to Adelaide as reader late in 1950. Appointed to the chair of history at the University of Tasmania in 1960, he became foundation general editor of the *Australian Dictionary of Biography* on 31 January 1962, commuting between Hobart and Canberra until December next year; he settled in Canberra on 1 January 1964 as a professor in the Research School of Social Sciences of the Institute of Advanced Studies at the Australian National University.

The *Dictionary* had been mooted in the 1950s and by 1961 a small staff had been engaged on preliminary work for it, but no firm plans had been made for its production. With characteristic energy and foresight Pike set about organizing the project. He soon discovered that a general editor required the skills of a manager and the tact of a diplomat as well as the qualities of an historian and biographer—as he often remarked, his country pioneering stood him in good stead. He needed his diverse range of experience as he consolidated the administrative structure, comprising section editors, National Committee, Editorial Board and Working Parties, and began the task of producing the first two volumes, 1107 entries, covering 1788-1850. Volume 1 appeared in 1966 and Volume 2 in 1967.

By that time Pike had put into shape a complex and efficient production system. His natural courtesy and firm belief in the value of the *Dictionary* had enabled him to obtain the co-operation of a great variety of people: his office staff, who helped in administration, research and checking; senior academics, who assisted in the broad aspects of editing, in the listing of entries and the allocation of authors, and very many writers (about 300 for each volume), from a wide range of occupations and locations. All of these, except the office staff, were unpaid. The principle of honorary national collaboration was firmly established, stemming from the history departments of all the Australian universities, through local historical and genealogical societies, State and National libraries and archives, to many individuals throughout the continent. Not the least of Pike's achievements was to gain the support of registrars of births, deaths and marriages and probates. He was warmly appreciative of all this willing help.

Volumes 1 and 2 established the scholarly base of the *Dictionary* and its social and educative value. Pike had acquired a distaste for adjectives and adverbs—of course, many of them escaped his net, but he was always sadly aware of it—and had developed a flair for lean prose. He was a great raconteur and more than once claimed that when a minister he could always reduce his sermons to one sentence as he ascended the pulpit. He did not overtly expect his authors to do the same with their articles, but often gave the impression that he wanted something like it; some of them objected, but reconciliations were nearly always reached, and each volume won renown (as he might have put it) for succinct restatement of what was well known and much compact presentation of what was new. This high repute was mainly attributable to Pike's skill and industry, but he never tired of acknowledging the teamwork that went into the *Dictionary*.

Pike's sympathetic and effective teaching and his publications, especially *Paradise of Dissent: South Australia 1829-1857* (1957) and *Australia: The Quiet Continent* (1962), had established him as one of Australia's most distinguished historians; his work on the *Dictionary* revealed him as incomparably the country's best academic editor. He was quietly spoken, with a dry but genial sense of humour, leavened by the wisdom that flowed from his innate generosity and his spacious experience and fertile memory; his personal qualities complemented his erudition to enable him to grasp the total substance of the *Dictionary* as well as the significance of every article and its relationship to the whole. He was conscious of the constraint to keep volumes and articles within the allotted word lengths, but was equally aware of the individuality of each author and the uniqueness of each entry. As successive volumes appeared in 1969 and 1972 they revealed how he had mastered the complex task of harmonizing concise biographical writing, virtually all of it new, with the occasionally conflicting demands of contributors and publishers. The Ernest Scott Prize in 1969 and the Britannica Australia Award in 1971 provided appropriate recognition for his great achievement.

In 1973 there were signs that his health was suffering, at least partly from his intense editorial efforts, but by the latter part of the year he had Volume 5 substantially prepared. Pike was to retire on 31 December and had been invited to carry on in order to complete Volume 6, the last of the 1851-1890 series. But he suffered a cerebral thrombosis on 11 November and was admitted to Canberra Hospital where he died on 19 May 1974, survived by his wife and two sons.

B. N.

EDITORIAL ARRANGEMENTS FROM 1973

Following the illness of Professor Pike in November 1973, Bede Nairn became acting general editor of the *Dictionary* project and, specifically, general editor of Volume 6. In 1975 Mr Nairn and Dr A. G. Serle were appointed joint general editors to bring out the six volumes (7-12) covering the 1891-1939 period.

ABBOTT, G. J.:
Woore.
ALDERMAN, A. R.:
Tate.
ALLARS, K. G.*:
Rodd.
ALLINGHAM, E. M.:
White, W.
ALMANZI, Helen K.:
Whitworth.
ANDERSON, Hugh:
Thatcher.
ANDREWS, B. G.:
Ryan; Traill; Turner, C.
ATCHISON, John:
White, R.
AUBREY, Keith H.:
Turner, J.

BADGER, C. R.:
Strong, C.
BARKER, Theo:
White, C.
BARNARD, Alan:
Robertson, A.; Rowan.
BARRETT, Bernard:
Tait, J. McA.; Walker, H.
BASSINGTHWAIGHTE, S. D.:
White, W.
BATE, Weston:
Rede; Smith, W. C.; Steinfeld.
BATTYE, O. K.:
Shenton, A.; Stirling, E.
BAUER, F. H.:
Uhr.
BAXTER, Rosilyn:
Reeve; Rowe, R.; Wilkes.
BEALE, Edgar:
Turner, A.
BEARDWOOD, J. C.:
Stewart, J. jnr.
BEEVER, E. A.:
Ritchie, S.
BENNETT, J. M.:
Simpson, G.; Sleigh; Smith, F. V.
BENNETT, Scott:
Searle.
BENSON, Jean Caswell:
Stacy.
BERGMAN, George F. J.:
Samuel.
BICKERTON, Ian J.:
Reynolds, C.; Sheil.
BIRMAN, Wendy:
Sholl.
BLACK, Alan W.:
Thompson, J. L.; Wallace, D.
BLAESS, F. J. H.*:
Strempel.

BLAINEY, Ann:
Rusden, G.
BLAINEY, Geoffrey:
Smith, F. G.
BLAKE, L. J.:
Stephens, E.; Wilson, S.; Wright, W.
BOLAND, S. J.:
Vaughan, E.
BOLGER, Peter:
Reibey; Salier; Smart, T. C.
BOLTON, G. C.:
Randell, G.; Scott, W. J.; Sellheim;
Swallow; Whish.
BORCHARDT, D. H.:
Tenison-Woods.
BOWD, D. G.:
Town.
BRADSHAW, F. Maxwell:
Ramsay, A.
BRANAGAN, D. F.:
Selwyn, A. R.; Stutchbury.
BRIDGES-WEBB, Charles:
Webb, C.
BROWN, P. L.:
Russell, P. and T.; Wilson, J. Bracebridge.

CABLE, K. J.:
Rossi; Scott, W.; Sladen, D.; Stephen,
A. H.; Sutherland, J.; Taylor R.; Woolley;
Woolls.
CAHILL, A. E.:
Vaughan, R.
CAMPBELL, Jean:
Skipper.
CHAPMAN, G. P. R.:
Smith, J. W.; Webster.
CHISHOLM, A. H.:
Ramsay, E.; Wheelwright.
CLAUGHTON, S. G.*:
Young, R.
COCKBURN, S.:
Thomas, R.
COHEN, B. C.*:
Waylen.
COMBE, Gordon D.:
Reynolds, T.; Tennant.
COPE, Graeme:
Shaw, W.
CORBETT, Arthur:
Russell, P. N.; Warren.
CORRIS, Peter:
Wawn.
COULLS, A.:
Rasp.
COWAN, Peter M.:
Venables.
CRANFIELD, Louis R.:
Wardill.

CREW, Vernon :
  Walker, W.
CRIBB, Margaret Bridson :
  Thomas, L.
CRITTENDEN, Victor :
  Ward, F.
CROCOMBE, Marjorie Tuainekore :
  Ruatoka.
CROWLEY, F. K. :
  Robinson, W.; Windich.
CUNNEEN, Chris :
  Rolleston; Smith, R. Burdett; Trickett, W.;
  White, S.
CURRY, N. G. :
  Ramsay, R., solicitor.
CUSACK, Frank :
  Watson, J. B.

DALEY, Louise T. :
  Schurr; Yabsley.
DAVIS, Rex :
  Selwyn, A. E.
DEASEY, Denison :
  Warburton.
DE GARIS, B. K. :
  Shenton, G.
DENHOLM, David :
  Ranken; Walker, F.; Walsh, W.;
  White, J. C.
DENHOLM, Zita :
  Tyson.
DOUGAN, Alan :
  Steel; Thomson, A.
DOWLING, Austin :
  Smith, A. M.
DUFFY, C. J. :
  Sheridan, J.; Torreggiani.
DUFFY, L. J.* :
  Tully.
DUNBAR, Donald James :
  Tayler.

EADE, Susan :
  Spence, C.
EASTWOOD, Jill :
  Smith, A. K.; Smith, J. T.; Suffolk;
  Summers, C.; Thomson, R.; Topp, A.;
  Watson, G.; Wood, J.; Woods; Wrixon;
  Young, E.
EDGAR, Suzanne :
  Read, C.; Richards, T., printer; Robey;
  Salomons; Scott, E.; Stephen, W.;
  Thomas, R.; Turner, W.
ERICKSON, Rica :
  Timperley.
EUNSON, Warwick :
  Whyte, P.

FEATHERSTONE, Guy :
  Smith, L.

FEENEY, Alan :
  Rees, R.
FINDLAY, Marjorie* :
  Simpson, A.; Smith, R.; Waite, P.
FINLAY, E. M. :
  Supple; Walstab.
FINLAY, H. A. :
  Rogers, J. W.
FIRTH, S. :
  Schleinitz.
FORSTER, Frank M. C. :
  Tracy.
FRANCIS, Charles :
  Stawell; Webb, T.
FREDMAN, L. E. :
  Zox.
FREELAND, J. M. :
  Rowe, T.

GANDEVIA, Bryan :
  Thomson, W.
GEEVES, Philip :
  Saywell.
GELLIE, G. H. :
  Way.
GIBBNEY, H. J. :
  Ranken; Strachan; Thompson, J. M.;
  Walsh, W.; Young, H.
GILL, Peter :
  Topp, C.
GITTINS, Jean :
  Sinclair; Sullivan, T.
GRANT, James :
  Sladen, C.; Stretch; Vance.
GRAY, Nancy :
  Scott, A. W.
GREEN, F. C.* :
  Smith, F. V.
GREEN, R. M. :
  Ritchie, W.
GREVILLE, P. J. :
  Ward, E. W.
GRIFFIN, James :
  Verjus.
GROSS, Alan* :
  Sturt.
GUILFORD, Elizabeth :
  Wisdom.
GUNSON, Niel :
  Ridley; Schirmeister; Waterhouse, J. B.,
  J. and S.; Williams, T

HADGRAFT, Cecil :
  Stephens, J. B.
HAENKE, Helen :
  Thorn.
HALL, A. R. :
  Wallen.
HALL, Noeline V. :
  Raff; Tooth, W.
HARTWIG, Mervyn :
  Tietkens.

HAYMAN, Noel:
Ross, R.
HENNING, G. R.:
Smith, W. H.
HIRST, Christine:
Tinline.
HIRST, J. B.:
Ward, E.
HOARE, Michael:
Smith, John, professor; Smyth; Thomson, A. M.; Ulrich; Wilkinson; Wright, H.
HOBAN, Ruth:
Sutherland, S.
HOLDER, R. F.:
Smith, Shepherd.
HOLMES, J. H.:
Waite, J.
HOLROYD, J. P.:
Robertson, G.
HONE, J. Ann:
Robertson, W.; Simson; Taylor, W., pastoralist; Wettenhall; Willis, E.; Winter, J. and Winter-Irving; Winter, S. P.; Wyselaskie; Yuille.
HORNER, J. C.:
Richards, T., author.
HOSIE, John:
Rocher.
HOWE, Renate:
Symons; Watsford; Waugh.
HUTCHISON, Noel S.:
Sani; Simonetti.
HYAMS, B. K.:
Young, J. L.

ILBERY, Jaki:
Salter; Seppelt; Smith, Samuel.

JAENSCH, Dean:
Strangways; Townsend.
JENKIN, G. K.:
Taplin.
JOHNSON, Robert:
Young, J., contractor.
JONES, Dorothy:
Sheridan, R.
JORDENS, Ann-Mari:
Shillinglaw; Smith, James, journalist; Stenhouse; Templeton, J.; Tucker; Vaughn.
JOYCE, R. B.:
Scratchley; Trollope.

KEENAN, A. I.:
Treacy.
KENNEDY, B. E.:
Vogel.
KIERS, Dorothy:
Thomson, G.
KINGSMILL, A. G.:
Walker, R. C. C.

KRAEHENBUEHL, Darrell N.:
Waterhouse, F.
KUNZ, E. F.:
Wekey.

LACK, Clem*:
Swan.
LACK, John:
Robb.
LANGDON, Robert:
Romilly.
LANSBURY, Coral:
Spence, W.
LARACY, Hugh:
Rays.
LAZARUS, Mary:
Rusden, G.
LEA-SCARLETT, E. J.:
Rotton; Wright, J.; Younger.
LEGGE, J. S.:
Standish.
LENEHAN, Marjorie:
Rouse, R. and R. jnr.
LEVI, J.:
Rintel.
LEWIS, Miles:
Terry, L.
LINANE, T. J.:
Slattery.
LOCKLEY, G. L.:
Wight.
LOUCH, T. S.:
Weld; Wrenfordsley.
LOWNDES, A. G.:
Ross, J. G.
LYONS, Mark:
Raphael; St Julian; Stewart, J.; Taylor, H.; Wearne; Wilson, J. Bowie.

McCALLUM, Austin:
Sutton; Withers.
McCALLUM, C. A.:
Tulk.
McCALMAN, Iain:
Turner, H.
McCARTHY, Susan:
Shackell; Webb, W.
McDONALD, D. I.:
Serisier; Wardell.
McDONALD, Lorna L.:
Reid, W.
MACKNIGHT, C. C.:
Using.
McLAREN, Ian F.:
Wills, W.
McMINN, W. G.:
Young, J. H.
McNICOLL, Ronald:
Riddell.
MANDLE, W. F.:
Wills, T.

MANTON, G. R.:
Strong, H.
MARSDEN, Gillian:
Renard.
MATHESON, Ian:
Soares; Sowerby.
MAUDE, H. E.:
Smith, C.
MAYO, J.:
Tolmer.
MELLOR, Suzanne G.:
Rogers, J. W. F.; Rolando; Ross, J., co-
operative; Russell, J.; Sutherland, G.;
Willoughby.
MIDDELMANN, Raoul F.:
Schomburgk.
MILLER, Robert:
Webb, G.; Williams, E. & H.
MINCHAM, Hans:
Stirling, E. C.
MITCHELL, Ann M.:
Turriff; Youl, R.
MITCHELL, Bruce:
Sly; Wood, H.
MORGAN, E. J. R.:
Thomas, Morgan.
MORRIS, Christopher:
Spofforth.
MORRIS, Deirdre:
Sherwin; Stuart, J.; Torpy.
MORRISON, A. A.*:
Swan.
MORRISSEY, Sylvia:
Singleton.
MULLINS, Helen R.:
Worsnop.
MURRAY-SMITH, S.:
Selfe.

NAIRN, Bede:
Robertson, J.; Robinson, H.; Salomons;
Spence, W.; Stuart, A.; Talbot; Trouton.
NICHOLAS, R. J.:
Whinham.
NORTHCOTT, P. H.:
Sutherland, A.
NORTHEY, R. E.:
Thornton, S.
NOTHLING, Marion:
St Julian.

O'DONNELL, Dan:
Tighe.
O'DONOGHUE, Eileen M.:
Whitty.
O'KELLY, G. J.:
Strele.
O'NEILL, Sally:
Savage.
ORLOVICH, Peter:
Roper.

PALMER, H. Z.*:
Sixsmith.
PARNABY, Joy E.:
Vale.
PEARCE, Helen R.:
Smith, E.
PEMBERTON, Gregory J.:
Richardson, J. S.
PEREZ, E.:
Serra.
PETERS, Merle:
Terry, F.
PHILLIPS, Nan:
Rae.
PHILLIPS, Walter:
Roseby; Short, B.
POTTS, Annette:
Williams, J.
POTTS, E. Daniel:
Train.
POWELL, J. M.:
Skene.
PRIMROSE, B. N.:
Tryon.
PROEVE, H. F. W.:
Rechner.
PUGH, Ann:
Russell, P. N.; Warren.

QUAIFE, G. R.:
Sullivan, J.

RADFORD, Joan T.:
Smith, John, professor.
RADIC, Maureen Thérèse:
Siede; Zelman.
RATHBONE, R. W.:
Weekes.
RAYNER, K.:
Tufnell.
REID, Elgin:
Stephens, T. B.
REYMOND, M. B.:
Reymond.
REYMOND, N.:
Reymond.
REYNOLDS, John:
Rule.
REYNOLDS, Patricia:
Rowe, G.
RICHARDS, Eric:
Solomon; Tomkinson; Vosz.
RICHARDSON, G. D.:
Walker, R. C.
RICKARD, John:
Sargood; Walch, G.
ROBERTS, Alan:
Young, J., contractor.
ROBERTSON, J. R.:
Yelverton.
ROE, Michael:
Taylor, A. J.

Ross, D. Bruce:
Stow.
Rowland, E. C.:
Stanton.
Royle, Harold:
Zouch.
Rundle, J. H.:
Rees, J.; Walsh, J.
Rutherford, J. E. L.:
Rutherford; Webb, E.
Rutledge, Martha:
Redmond; Renwick; Richardson, J.; Richmond; Riley; Roberts, A. & C. J.; Ross, A.; Stephen, A. & M. H. & M. C. and S.; Stuart, A.; Tait, J.; Taylor, A. G.; Thornton, G.; Titheradge; Tooth, R. L.; Watson, J.; White, J.; Wright, F.; Young, C.
Ryan, J. A.:
Wise, E. & G.
Ryan, Lyndall:
Trugernanner.

Saclier, M. J.:
White, G.
Saffin, N. W.:
Smith, T., trade unionist.
Saunders, David:
Reed.
Sayers, C. E.:
Syme, D. & E.; Windsor.
Scott, Belinda F.:
Scott, H.
Serle, Geoffrey:
Service; Smith, R. M.; Turner, M.; Westgarth; Wilson, E.; Winter, S. V. and J.
Shanahan, Mary:
Sheehy.
Shannon, R. B.:
Whitfield.
Shaw, A. G. L.:
Verdon.
Shaw, Mary Turner:
Shaw, T.; Synnot.
Shearer, John:
Shearer.
Shineberg, D.:
Towns.
Sierp, Allan:
Sweet.
Singleton, C. C.*:
Shellshear; Whitton.
Smith, Bertha Mac.:
Smith, John, sheepbreeder.
Smith, F. B.:
Rusden, H.; Symes; Terry, W.; Walker, T.
Smith, Neil:
Sandford; Scott, J.; Stephens, T.; Strahan; Trugernanner; Walch, C.; Walker, J.; Whyte, J.; Wilson, J. M.; Youl, J.
Smith, Ronald E.*:
Smith, James, explorer.

Staples, A. C.:
Rose.
Stephens, S. E.:
Watson, M.
Stevens, Robin S.:
Summers, J.; Torrance.
Stewart, D. F.:
Stewart, J. jnr.
Stewart, J. L.:
Trickett, E.
Stewart, Neil:
Seymour.
Stilwell, G. T.:
Tindal.
Sturkey, Douglas:
Withnell.
Symes, G. W.:
Ross, J., explorer; Todd.

Teale, Ruth:
Smith, T., clergyman; Suttor, F. & W.; Ten; Tyrrell; Waters.
Templeton, Jacqueline:
Templeton, W.
Thorn, Barbara:
Thomas, Mesac.
Tibbits, George:
Tayler; White, F.
Tipping, Marjorie J.:
Sinnett; Smith, B.; Strutt; Thomas, Margaret; Woolner.
Tolley, John C.:
Randell, W.
Townley, K. A.:
Selwyn, A. R.
Tregenza, Jean F.:
Waterhouse, G.
Trevaskis, J.:
Read, H.
Turnbull, Clive*:
Stephens, J.; Thompson, J.; Troedel; Whitehead.
Turney, Cliff:
Stephens, W.; Wilkins.

Vallance, T. G.:
Stutchbury.
Van der Poorten, Helen M.;
Rignall; Williamson.
Van Dissel, Dirk:
Reynell; Short, A.; Smith, R. Barr.
Venn, Michael:
Speight.

Walsh, G. P.;
Ritchie, R.; Roberts, C. F.; Rowntree; Rundle; Russell, H.; Sands; Smart, T. W.; Soul; Spring; Strickland, E.; Terry, S.; Toohey; Tooth, R., E. and F.; Vicars; Vickery; Watt; Willis, J.; Wilshire; Wolseley.

REFERENCES

The following works of reference have been widely used but have not been listed in the sources at the foot of the articles:

D. Blair, *Cyclopaedia of Australasia* (Melbourne, 1881)

B. Burke, *A Genealogical and Heraldic History of the Colonial Gentry*, 1-2 (London, 1891-95)

J. A. Ferguson, *Bibliography of Australia*, 1-7 (Sydney, 1941-69)

H. M. Green, *A History of Australian Literature*, 1-2 (Sydney, 1961; 2nd ed 1971)

J. H. Heaton, *Australian Dictionary of Dates and Men of the Time* (London, 1879)

F. Johns, *An Australian Biographical Dictionary* (Melbourne, 1934)

P. Mennell, *The Dictionary of Australasian Biography* (London, 1892)

E. M. Miller, *Australian Literature . . . to 1935*, 1-2 (Melbourne, 1940), extended to 1950 by F. T. Macartney (Sydney, 1956)

Mitchell Library (NSW), *Dictionary Catalog of Printed Books* (Boston, 1968)

W. Moore, *The Story of Australian Art*, 1-2 (Sydney, 1934)

P. C. Mowle, *A Genealogical History of Pioneer Families in Australia* (Sydney, 1939)

P. Serle, *Dictionary of Australian Biography*, 1-2 (Sydney, 1949)

Australian Encyclopaedia, 1-2 (Sydney, 1925)

Australian Encyclopaedia, 1-10 (Sydney, 1958)

Dictionary of National Biography (London, 1885-1971)

also:

British Museum, *General Catalogue of Printed Books*

Library of Congress, *National Union Catalog*

National Library of Australia, *Annual Catalogue of Australian Publications* (1936-60); *Australian National Bibliography* (1961-)

ABBREVIATIONS

A.A.Co.	Australian Agricultural Company	G, Geog	Geographical
Ac no	Accession number	GB	Great Britain
ACER	Australian Council for Educational Research	Gen	Genealogical, Genealogists
		gen ed	general editor
ACT	Australian Capital Territory	GO	Governor's Office
Adel	Adelaide	Govt	Government
Adm	Admiralty	HA	House of Assembly
Agr	Agriculture, Agricultural	HC	House of Commons
AMA	Australian Medical Association	Hist	History, Historical
ANU	Australian National University, Canberra	HL	House of Lords
		HO	Home Office, London
ANZAAS	Australian and New Zealand Association for the Advancement of Science	Hob	Hobart
		HRA	*Historical Records of Australia*
		HRNSW	*Historical Records of New South Wales*
A'sian	Australasian		
Assn	Association	IAN	*Illustrated Australian News*
Aust	Australia, Australian	Inst	Institute, Institution
		ISN	*Illustrated Sydney News*
Basser Lib	Adolph Basser Library, Australian Academy of Science, Canberra	J	*Journal*
Battye Lib	J. Battye Library of West Australian History, Perth	LA	Legislative Assembly
		LAN	Land Administration Board (Queensland State Archives)
BHP	Broken Hill Proprietary Co. Ltd	LaT L	La Trobe Library, Melbourne
bibliog	bibliography	Launc	Launceston
biog	biography, biographical	LC	Legislative Council
BM	British Museum, London	Lib	Library
Brisb	Brisbane	LMS	London Missionary Society
		LSD	Lands and Surveys Department (Tasmanian State Archives)
Canb	Canberra		
CAO	Commonwealth Archives Office	Mag	*Magazine*
cat	catalogue	Melb	Melbourne
Cmd	Command	MDHC	Melbourne Diocesan Historical Commission, Catholic Archdiocesan Offices, East Melbourne
CO	Colonial Office, London		
Col Sec	Colonial Secretary		
Com	Commission		
CON	Convict records (Tasmanian State Archives)	MJA	*Medical Journal of Australia*
		ML	Mitchell Library, Sydney
CRS	Crown Solicitor's Office (Queensland State Archives)	MS	manuscript
		mthly	monthly
CSD	Chief Secretary's Department (Tasmanian State Archives)	nd	date of publication unknown
CSIRO	Commonwealth Scientific and Industrial Research Organization	NL	National Library of Australia, Canberra
		no	number
CSO	Colonial Secretary's Office	np	place of publication unknown
CSR	Colonial Secretary's Records (Battye Library, Perth)	NSW	New South Wales
		NSWA	The Archives Authority of New South Wales, Sydney
cttee	committee		
Cwlth	Commonwealth	NT	Northern Territory
		NZNA	New Zealand National Archives
ed	editor, edition		
Edinb	Edinburgh	OD	Outward Dispatches
encl	enclosure		
Fr	Father (priest)	p	page, pages
		PAH	*see* RPAH

PD	*Parliamentary Debates*	SAA	South Australian Archives, Adelaide
PMB	Pacific Manuscripts Bureau, Research School of Pacific Studies, ANU	SCT	Supreme Court (Queensland State Archives)
PNGA	Archives Office of Papua and New Guinea, Port Moresby	Sel	Select
		SLSA	State Library of South Australia
PP	*Parliamentary Papers*		
PRGSSA	*Proceedings of the Royal Geographical Society of Australasia (South Australian Branch)*	SLT	State Library of Tasmania
		SLV	State Library of Victoria
		SMH	*Sydney Morning Herald*
priv print	privately printed	Soc	Society
PRO	Public Record Office, London	SPCK	Society for Promoting Christian Knowledge
Procs	*Proceedings*		
pt	part, parts	SPG	Society for the Propagation of the Gospel in Foreign Parts
PTHRA	*Papers and Proceedings of the Tasmanian Historical Research Association*	supp	supplement
		Syd	Sydney
Q	*Quarterly*	TA	Tasmanian State Archives, Hobart
QA	Queensland State Archives, Brisbane		
		Tas	Tasmania
Qld	Queensland	T&CJ	*Australian Town and Country Journal*
[q.v.]*	cross reference		
RAHS	Royal Australian Historical Society (Sydney)	tr	translated, translation
		Trans	*Transactions*
rev	revised, revision	Univ	University
RGS	Royal Geographical Society		
RHSQ	Royal Historical Society of Queensland (Brisbane)	VA	Public Record Office, Melbourne (State Archives)
RHSV	Royal Historical Society of Victoria (Melbourne)	V&P	*Votes and Proceedings*
		VDL	Van Diemen's Land
Roy	Royal	VHM	*Victorian Historical Magazine*
RPAH	Royal Prince Alfred Hospital	v, vol	volume
RWAHS	Royal Western Australian Historical Society (Perth)	Vic	Victoria
1st S	First Session	WA	Western Australia
2nd S	Second Session	Well	Wellington, New Zealand
2nd s	second series	wkly	weekly
SA	South Australia	WO	War Office

* The note [q.v.] accompanies the names of individuals who are the subjects of entries in the *Dictionary*.

N.B. Articles on royal visitors, governors, lieut-governors and Colonial Office officials are included, but [q.v.] is *not* shown against their names.

R

RAE, JOHN (1813-1900), public servant, author and painter, was born on 9 January 1813 at Aberdeen, Scotland, son of George Rae, banker, and his wife Jane, née Edmond. Educated at Aberdeen Grammar School and Marischal College, University of Aberdeen (M.A., 1832), he was articled to a firm of solicitors then continued his law studies and literary interests in Edinburgh. Deciding to migrate to Australia in 1839 he became secretary and accountant to the North British Australasian Loan and Investment Co., and arrived in Sydney in the *Kinnear* on 8 December. Because of unwise land investments the company had almost expired by December 1843.

Sydney's first municipal council meeting was held on 16 November 1842 with a part-time town clerk, C. H. Chambers. Rae, who had declined a similar position in Melbourne, became the first full-time town clerk on 27 July 1843 at a salary of £400, reduced to £300 in December. He was required to be secretary, administrator and chief adviser to the council; he was also legal officer, pioneering the interpretation of the City of Sydney Incorporation Act, and the framing of by-laws and regulations. With substandard office accommodation and inadequate staff, Rae faced a major programme designed to overcome long and serious civic neglect, with the council short of funds, subject to press and public criticism and plagued by 'the fetish for investigation by select committees'. In 1850 the Legislative Council amended the Sydney Corporation Act and provided funds for a specified works programme. In 1843-50 Rae made valuable reports, and at an 1854 inquiry he was regarded as the only constructive witness on public health administration. That year he published a comprehensive index of the Act and amendments.

In 1852 (Sir) Charles Cowper [q.v.] sought another select committee into the state of the council. Rae supported the appointment of a city commission, and in December 1853 three commissioners were appointed: G. Eliott [q.v.] as chief, F. O. Darvall, and Rae who took over the office routine. The commissioners worked hard on an extensive programme, but again they could not satisfy press or public. Charges of mismanagement and neglect led to more select committees and highly debatable reports, but in 1857 the Legislative Assembly decided to dismiss the commissioners and return to a corporation. Rae stood for election to the new council but lost and did not run again. Refusing an inspectorship for warehouses, he sought compensation for his curtailed commissionership or an equivalent appointment.

On 25 July 1857 Rae became secretary to the railway commissioners at a salary of £550; in 1859 he also became accountant under Commissioner B. H. Martindale [q.v.]. On 15 January 1861 Rae was appointed under-secretary for public works and commissioner for railways at a salary of £800. As commissioner he served under seven different ministers, including J. Sutherland [q.v.]; he supported J. Whitton [q.v.] and wanted a standard gauge throughout the colonies. By 1878 many lines had been built and politicians were seeking extensions in their electorates, but Rae was not amenable to pressure. The increasing volume of traffic had outgrown the original administration and he was succeeded as commissioner on 29 January by C. A. Goodchap [q.v.], but continued as under-secretary for public works. He had not received additional salary for his dual post but parliament later showed its appreciation of his work by voting him a gratuity of £800. Rae's annual reports had included a profit and loss account, the first for any railway system; they received international recognition. Granted leave of absence on full pay to go overseas for twelve months from March 1879, Rae visited America and Europe where, as in England, he was well received and given a free pass on all the railways; the Germans provided a special train and staff.

In 1880 Rae also became chairman of the Board for Public Tenders (Works). As a witness before an inquiry into the civil service in 1872, he wanted to improve working conditions and strongly supported the service as a career training school. He clung to office until 31 March 1889, retired on a pension of £543 14s. and became a member of the Civil Service Board at a salary of £1000 until his final retirement in 1893. As an important and impartial public servant Rae had contributed much to the evolution of responsible government through all the turmoil of eighteen ministries. The press gave him the affectionate tag of 'The Admirable Crichton'.

On his arrival in Sydney Rae had become interested in the new Mechanics' School of Arts and in 1841 lectured on 'Taste', 'The English Language', and Robert Burns. In 1842 he wrote the letterpress for J. S. Prout's [q.v.] *Sydney Illustrated*, issued as a single publication in 1844. While town clerk he wrote a long 'serio-comic' poem about the first mayoral fancy dress ball, given by J. R. Wilshire [q.v.]. In 1853 he published *The Book of the Prophet Isaiah, rendered into English Blank Verse; with Explanatory Notes.* Self-taught, he printed and bound his *Gleanings from my Scrap Book* in two separate series which appeared as one volume in 1869, with a third part in 1874. His last literary work was the editing and publication in 1898 of *Thirty-five years on the New South Wales Railways,* a biography of John Whitton. A keen bibliophile, he had a catholic library of over 2000 volumes.

Rae was also a talented amateur artist. He painted water-colours of Sydney streets which earned respect. He taught himself photography and used it to record details for later paintings and his *camera obscura* contributed to his panorama of Sydney Harbour. He also produced large panoramas of Wollongong, Newcastle and part of the Murray Valley. His 'sketches of colonial scenes in the olden time' were sent to the Calcutta Exhibition in 1883 and to the Centennial International Exhibition, Melbourne, in 1888; they gained very favourable comment. In 1900 the *Bulletin* praised his keen artistic perception and considered his collection of views of old Sydney as one of the best extant; twenty-six are now in the Dixson Gallery, Sydney. Perhaps his best-known work was his water-colour in 1850 of the turning of the first sod for the first railway.

Rae both wrote and painted for his own pleasure and his quiet sense of humour is revealed in his work. A man of high principles and integrity he was unobtrusive and retained his preference for urban life. Active in retirement, he owned the Peoples Palace and a natatorium and was a director of the Australian Gaslight Co. On 17 December 1845 he had married Elizabeth Thompson (d. 1877); in 1854 he built his home, Hilton, in Liverpool Street, Darlinghurst. He died on 15 July 1900 and was buried in the Anglican section of Waverley cemetery, survived by four sons and two daughters. His estate was sworn for probate at £60,987.

Dept of Railways, *The railways of New South Wales 1855-1955* (Syd, 1955); D. S. Macmillan, *The debtor's war* (Melb, 1960); H. E. Maiden, *The history of local government in New South Wales* (Syd, 1966); F. A. Larcombe, *The origin of local government in New South Wales 1831-58* (Syd, 1973); F. A. Bland, 'City government by commission', *JRAHS*, 14 (1928); *SMH*, 16 Nov 1842, 28 July, 1 Aug 1843, 9 Jan 1899, 16 July 1900; *Sydney Mail,* 14 Jan 1899; *Bulletin,* 21 July 1900; K. W. Knight, The development of the Public Service of New South Wales 1856-1895 (M.Ec. thesis, Univ Syd, 1955); I. M. Laszlo, Railway policies and development in northern New South Wales 1846-1889 (M.A. thesis, Univ New England, 1956); Parkes letters (ML); MS and printed cats (ML).   NAN PHILLIPS

RAFF, GEORGE (1815-1889), merchant, sugar-grower and politician, was born on 15 April 1815 in Forres, Morayshire, Scotland, son of James Raff, farmer, and his wife Margaret, née Cumming, whose mother was Lesley Baillie, the 'Bonnie Lesley' of Robert Burns's poem. Raff reached Sydney on 2 January 1839 in the *Earl Durham* and probably found employment with Lamb [q.v.], Parbury & Co. In 1842-43 he held Tarwin station, Gippsland, and on 14 April 1843 married Harriet Sealy, daughter of Robert Bourne, a retired missionary with whom he was associated in Gippsland.

Raff returned to Sydney and in January 1851 moved to Brisbane, probably representing Lamb, Parbury & Co. but soon established George Raff & Co. He also founded the Queensland Mercantile and Agency Co. and in 1861 became a director of the Queensland Steam Navigation Co. The direct wool trade between Brisbane and London was mainly due to his efforts. At Morayfield plantation near Caboolture he experimented with sugar and other crops and contributed to a prize for commercial sugar production. He employed Kanaka labour but was commended for his treatment of the men by Rev. J. D. Lang [q.v.] and gave influential evidence to a select committee on Pacific islands labour in 1869. On Inverness plantation near Mackay he found some gold from which he sent his sister in Scotland a gold brooch.

Raff worked hard for the separation movement and in 1859 represented Brisbane in the first parliament. Next year he was appointed to the Board of National Education and to the Exhibition Commission. When Macalister [q.v.] resigned as premier in July 1866 Sir George Bowen invited R. G. W. Herbert [q.v.] and Raff to form a temporary committee to keep government moving. This unorthodox decision was most unpopular and the entire House moved to the Opposition benches. Raff served as minister without portfolio in later Herbert and Macalister ministries until 16 November 1866 and resigned from parliament in June 1867. He contested Moreton in 1870, but lost.

At his house, Moraybank, in New Farm, Raff lived a happy family and social life until 1879 when his wife died. On 7 September 1883 at Sydney he married Eliza Jane Molle, née Lord, a 40-year-old widow with a family; as a result Raff was estranged from most of his seven surviving sons. In 1882 he had formally joined Parbury, Lamb & Co. (as it was then) and it became Parbury, Lamb and Raff. The partnership was wound up in 1886 and a new company, Raff, Graham & Co. Ltd, was registered in April. Raff died on 28 August 1889 leaving an estate valued for probate at £5038.

Though nominally a political liberal, Raff's opposition to government extravagance made him suspect in some liberal circles, but few denied his consistency, sincerity, patriotism and attachment to principle.

W. F. Morrison, *The Aldine history of Queensland* (Syd, 1888); N. Bartley, *Opals and agates* (Brisb, 1892); C. A. Bernays, *Queensland politics during sixty years* (Brisb, 1919); E. W. Docker, *The Blackbirders* (Syd, 1970); family reminiscences by a grandson (Fryer Lib, Univ Qld); Crown land commissioners, Gippsland itineraries (NSWA); CO 234/10/34.

NOELINE V. HALL

RAMSAY, ANDREW MITCHELL (1809-1869), Presbyterian minister, was born on 5 March 1809 at Shettleston, Scotland, son of Robert Ramsay and his wife Margaret, née Mitchell. With distinctions in classics, philosophy and science at the University of Glasgow in 1825, he entered the Theological Hall of Relief Church in 1828. Licensed by the Relief Presbytery of Glasgow in 1832, he was ordained as minister of Allars Relief Church, Hawick, on 29 May 1833. He resigned on 17 February 1846. Religious revivals had followed services he conducted in 1839 at Denholm near Hawick. In 1840 he married Isabella Milne.

Ramsay reached Melbourne in the *Anne Milne* on 4 January 1847 with his wife and two children, a son having died on the voyage. Within a month a meeting of Presbyterians asked Ramsay to form a congregation in Melbourne 'unconnected with the state'. He supplied the pulpit of the Scots Church, Melbourne, from March to May but soon began his own services in Little Collins Street, later in the Temperance Hall, Russell Street, and at the end of 1848 in the Protestant Hall in Exhibition Street. On 22 January 1850 with three other ministers he formed the Synod of the United Presbyterian Church of Victoria. He obtained ministers from Scotland and helped to found at least a dozen congregations in the 1850s. St Enoch's was built for his congregation in Collins Street and opened on 30 March 1851. In April 1855 Rev. James Ballantyne was inducted as Ramsay's colleague but by August 1856 disputes between them left Ramsay on his own with a depleted flock. In the ensuing controversy in the United Presbyterian Church two breakaway groups were formed in 1856 and 1857. Ramsay went overseas in April 1858 seeking replacements and returned in February 1859. His synod was again disrupted in April when he and two other ministers refused to be parties to the union that resulted in the Presbyterian Church of Victoria. The United Presbyterian Church was received into the united body in 1870.

Ramsay sought to build up a denomination of voluntaries and to combat all forms of state aid. He was the power behind the Society for the Repeal of the Fifty-Third Clause of the New Constitution, launched in November 1855, and was prominent at every voluntary meeting in the mid-1850s. In 1856 he published a pamphlet, *How the Money Goes*. An able organizer, he was often so occupied that it was 'with the greatest difficulty that he could command sufficient time for study and pulpit preparation'. Short, with a pale and thoughtful face, he was not a 'popular' preacher but could rise to heights of oratory and, according to Garryowen [q.v. Finn], 'You could not soon forget the speaker, so intense was his earnestness and so thoroughly did he throw himself into his subject'. Though pugnacious, he was also disinterested, generous and unselfish.

Survived by his wife, his son Robert [q.v.], another son and a daughter, Ramsay died of a stroke on 31 December 1869 and was buried in the Melbourne general cemetery.

R. Hamilton, *A jubilee history of the Presbyterian Church of Victoria* (Melb, 1888); F. M. Bradshaw, *Scottish seceders in Victoria* (Melb, 1947); R. I. Cashman, Nonconformists in Victoria in the 1850s (M.A. thesis, Monash Univ, 1963); A. M. Ramsay diaries and United Presbyterian Church of Vic, Synod and Melbourne Presbytery minutes (Presbyterian Church Assembly Hall, Melb).

F. MAXWELL BRADSHAW

RAMSAY, EDWARD PIERSON (1842-1916), ornithologist and zoologist, was born on 3 December 1842 at Dobroyd (Ashfield), New South Wales, son of Dr David Ramsay [q.v.] and his wife Sarah Ann, daughter of Simeon Lord [q.v.]. Educated at Macquarie Fields under G. F. Macarthur [q.v.] he entered St Paul's College, University of Sydney, in 1863 to study medicine but left in 1865 without a degree. Interested in natural history from boyhood, at 17 he corresponded with Governor Denison on conchology. He had briefly visited New Zea-

3

land in 1861 and next year was founding treasurer of the Entomological Society of New South Wales where he exhibited specimens.

Elected to the local Philosophical Society in 1865, Ramsay devoted himself mainly to bird-collecting. In 1866 he went to the Clarence and Richmond rivers to get specimens of the recently discovered Rufous Scrub-bird, Atrichornis rufescens. On 20 December he became a corresponding member of the Zoological Society, London, where he began publishing. He was in close contact with prominent European zoologists, including John Gould [q.v.] and Sir Richard Owen. In December 1867 Ramsay opened the Dobroyd New Plant and Seed Nursery on his share of the Dobroyd estate that he had inherited in 1862. Next year he went to Queensland, bought the Iindah sugar plantation in the Maryborough district and worked it for some years with indifferent success.

Ramsay's connexion with the Australian Museum had begun in 1860 but Gerard Krefft [q.v.] saw him 'as an enemy of mine of long standing on account of my refusing to purchase the rubbish he used to offer'. In 1874 Ramsay emerged as the trustees' protégé and on 22 September they illegally confirmed his appointment as curator, but his position was not confirmed by the government until 1876. As curator in 1874-94 Ramsay built up the museum's collections, corresponded with many scientists, contributed to taxonomic literature and exhibited his work before the local Linnean Society, of which he had been a founder in 1874. He added some 17,600 bird skins, including the Dobroyde Collection made by the Ramsay brothers. He also built on the foundations of Australian lithology laid by W. J. Macleay [q.v.] and published over thirty ichthyological papers, mostly in the Proceedings of the local Linnean Society. Between 1876 and 1894 his Catalogue of the Australian Birds in the Australian Museum at Sydney appeared in four parts and in March 1890 he began publishing the Records of the museum.

A trustee of Hyde, Phillip and Cook parks from 1878 and of the Zoological Station, Watsons Bay, from 1879, Ramsay served on the royal commission into the fisheries in 1880 and in 1882 became a member of the fisheries commission. From 1878 he served on exhibition commissions for New South Wales and won repute for his exhibits and photographic arrangements of colonial produce and phenomena. In March 1883 he visited London as official representative for New South Wales and Tasmania at the Great International Fisheries Exhibition and inspected 'the most important of

the museums, aquaria and zoological gardens in Great Britain and the Continent'. He learnt new techniques, arranged exchanges and negotiated the purchase of Dr Francis Day's collection of Indian fishes. He visited Naples in 1884 and was made a knight of the Crown of Italy.

A councillor of the local Royal and Linnean societies, Ramsay contributed to botany, herpetology and mammalogy and continued Krefft's and A. M. Thomson's [q.v.] work of exploring the caves and rivers of New South Wales. He dredged extensively in Port Jackson, sometimes with Nicholas Maclay [q.v.]. For his part in arranging David Berry's [q.v.] bequest to the University of St Andrew's, he was made LL.D. in 1886. Ramsay was a fellow of the Linnean Society of London, the Royal Society of Edinburgh and the Royal Geographical Society of London and a member of the Royal Irish Academy. In Melbourne in January 1890 he presided over the Biology Section of the Australasian Association for the Advancement of Science.

In 1893 Ramsay took extended sick leave, visited New Zealand and resigned on 31 December 1894. Companionable and competent, he was consulting ornithologist to the museum till 1909. He died of carcinoma of the stomach at Croydon Park on 16 December 1916 and was buried in the Presbyterian cemetery, Haberfield. He was survived by his wife Ellen Eliza, daughter of Captain H. T. Fox [q.v.], whom he had married at Burwood in 1875, and by four daughters and two sons, of whom John Simeon Pierson became a well-known ornithologist, specializing in photography.

H. M. Whittell, The literature of Australian birds (Perth, 1954); V&P (LA NSW), 1883-84, 7, 1231, 1885-86, 4, 481, 1889, 6, 431; R. Etheridge, 'Obituary notice', Aust Museum, Records, 11 (1917); A. H. Chisholm, 'The story of the Scrub-birds', Emu, 51 (1951); G. P. Whitley, 'A survey of Australian ichthyology', Linnean Soc NSW, Procs, 89 (1964); Sydney Mail, 10 Mar 1883; Australasian, 6 Dec 1884, 5 Jan 1895; G. P. Whitley, History of the Australian Museum (Basser Lib, Canberra); Gould letters and papers and Mathews collection (NL); Mueller letters and Ramsay letters (ML); Minute books 1863-74, 1874-79 (Aust Museum, Syd); Philosophical Soc NSW, Minute book 1856-65 (Roy Soc NSW, Syd).

A. H. CHISHOLM

RAMSAY, ROBERT (1818-1910), pastoralist and politician, was born in London on 19 March 1818, eldest son of Captain Robert Ramsay (1787-1846), 14th Regiment, and his wife Margaret, née Cruikshank.

Educated in Edinburgh and at Harrow, he reached Sydney probably in the *Indus* on 13 February 1839. After pastoral experience in New South Wales and Queensland he took up Rosalie Plains on the Darling Downs in April 1848. In July he was joined by Louis Hope [q.v.] and they acquired Cooyar, Lagoon Creek Downs, Kilcoy and other stations in the Burnett District. The partnership was dissolved in 1866 when Ramsay bought a share in Hodgson's [q.v.] Eton Vale run near Toowoomba. In 1897 this property, now freehold, was divided, Ramsay renaming his 35,000 acres Harrow. In London on 18 April 1855 he married Susan, daughter of William Fullerton Lindsay Carnegie of Spynie, Forfar, Scotland, and his wife Lady Jane, daughter of the 7th earl of Northesk.

Ramsay again visited England in 1858-59. On his return from another trip in 1864-65 Eton Vale was secured against selection by use of the pre-emptive right and provisions of the Leasing Act of 1866. He entered parliament in 1867 as member for Western Downs seeking 'the utmost security of tenure possible for Crown lessees', massive auction sales of land, restricted small selection and state aid for religious instruction. In the debates on the 1867-68 land bill, he 'did not agree that Crown Lands should be handed down to posterity when there was such an immense debt to be redeemed'. He always deplored 'the growth of class against class feeling' and blamed it on towns that 'produced nothing, even in the shape of manufactures'. Ramsay was colonial treasurer in the Palmer [q.v.] government from 3 May 1870 to 28 March 1871 and minister without portfolio until January 1874. He had resigned as M.L.A. on 6 November 1873 and was appointed to the Legislative Council on 2 January 1874, but till he retired on 14 June 1877 he was mostly in England, supervising the education of his sons and living the life of a country gentleman.

Though conservative Ramsay never provoked personal animosity. Invariably courteous, kind to his inferiors, generous and fair, his calm and cultivated mien disarmed opposition. Many liberals considered him 'not an extremist but a considerate and moderate representative' who was 'almost a political necessity at these times'. He opposed new principles of land tenure but provided some protection for struggling farmers. His political career was facilitated by weak opposition rather than by his own merits.

In 1883 Ramsay retired to Howletts near Canterbury, England, where he died on 5 July 1910 leaving an estate of £65,211. Five of his six sons and three daughters survived him. A parish and school near Toowoomba are named after him.

H. S. Russell, *The genesis of Queensland* (Syd, 1888); *Toowoomba Chronicle*, 5 June 1867; *Pastoral Review*, 15 Oct 1910; newspaper indexes (ML); Crown land commissioners, Itineraries (NSWA); run registers (QA).

D. B. WATERSON

RAMSAY, ROBERT (1842-1882), solicitor and politician, was born on 16 February 1842 at Hawick, Roxburghshire, Scotland, eldest son of Andrew Mitchell Ramsay [q.v.] and his wife Isabella, née Milne. Ramsay came to Victoria in 1847 with his parents and was educated at Robert Campbell and John Macgregor's school in St Kilda and at Scotch College. Articled in 1859 to John Macgregor junior, later M.L.A., he studied law at the University of Melbourne, graduating in 1861 with second-class honours. Admitted as a solicitor in 1862, he helped to found the firm of Macgregor, Ramsay and Brahe in 1866. As a young man he wrote about the beauties of the Australian bush for the *Argus*.

In 1870-82 Ramsay represented East Bourke in the Legislative Assembly. In 1872-74 he was a member, without office, of the Francis [q.v.] ministry, postmaster-general in the Kerferd [q.v.] ministry in 1874-75, minister of public instruction and postmaster-general in the McCulloch [q.v.] ministry in 1875-77 and chief secretary and minister of education, without salary, in the Service [q.v.] ministry in 1880. He represented Victoria at the telegraph cable conference in Sydney in 1877, was a prominent member of the Law Institute and of Chalmers Presbyterian Church, East Melbourne, vice-president of the Board of Management of the Melbourne Hospital, and a founder of the Old Scotch Collegians' Society in 1879.

Ramsay had a firm belief in National education and the separation of church and state. He was a moderate free trader and though conservative, opposed the ratepayers' roll and plural voting. An efficient minister, as postmaster-general he saved money by replacing annual with long-term contracts; as chief secretary he contributed to the capture of the Kelly [q.v.] gang; and as minister of public instruction he coped with problems of country schools, appointment of teachers and the compulsory clause of the 1872 Education Act. He also laid a firm foundation of adherence to the secular provisions of the Act and in 1876 insisted on a special Victorian edition of the Nelson series of school readers which omitted any reference to the name of Christ.

On 16 April 1868 at Yangery, near Warrnambool, Ramsay had married Isabella Catherine Urquhart; they had two sons and two daughters. Always subject to severe bronchitis, he died of pleurisy at his home in Gipps Street, East Melbourne, on 23 May 1882 and was buried in the Melbourne general cemetery. He left an estate worth some £40,000, including shares in Nanjee station, New South Wales, and an interest in Mount Margaret station in the Warrego District of Queensland.

H. M. Humphreys (ed), *Men of the time in Australia, Victorian series*, 1st ed (Melb, 1878); A. Henderson (ed), *Early pioneer families of Victoria and Riverina* (Melb, 1936); *Age*, 24 May 1882; *Argus*, 24 May 1882; S.M. Ingham, Some aspects of Victorian liberalism 1880-1900 (M.A. thesis, Univ Melb, 1950).

N. G. CURRY

RANDELL, GEORGE (1830-1915), businessman and politician, was born on 5 October 1830 at Milton, Hampshire, England, son of James Randell, cordwainer, and his wife Jane. He married Jane Hyde on 8 April 1850, migrated to Western Australia and prospered quietly as a carpenter and mechanic, later becoming a produce merchant. In 1863, in partnership with Solomon Cook [q.v.], he started the first regular steamship service on the Swan River, plying between Fremantle and Guildford; in 1876 he failed to prevent a proposal for a competing railway, and after the death of his second wife Mary Louisa, née Smith, whom he had married on 14 October 1869, he sold his shipping interests and in 1878 went to England. Returning in 1880, he reinvested in shipping and retained his interest at least until 1900, when the ferry and cruising trade had been boosted by the post-gold rush population.

Randell entered civic politics in 1870 as a member of the Perth Town Trust; he was chairman in 1874 and mayor in 1884-85. In 1875-77 he represented Perth in the Legislative Council and became a nominated member in 1880. He entered the first Legislative Assembly in 1890, representing Perth, and was chairman of committees from 1891 till he resigned his seat in 1892. Next year he was again nominated to the council. In June 1894 he returned to the assembly as member for Perth, and was elected leader of the Opposition but resigned after twelve months. In 1897 he did not seek re-election for Perth; he was elected to the council and in 1898 became government spokesman, colonial secretary and minister for education. He retired from these offices at the 1901 election but remained in the council until 1910.

For sixty years Randell was the mainstay of Perth's Congregational Church and held every lay office; *Who Was Who*, 1916, said

of him, 'with the exception of the two years' visit to England, practically no recreation'; he advocated church disestablishment and secular education. A member of the Central Board of Education from 1871, he campaigned successfully in 1876 for the Perth High School, and in 1894-95 led the successful opponents of state aid to churches.

A self-made businessman, Randell distrusted government intervention especially where it involved money. Despite liberal attitudes on early closing and women's suffrage, he was notable as an inveterate defender of last ditches; cautious and conciliatory, he opposed responsible government, Forrest's developmental policies, and Newton Moore's programme of agricultural expansion. Yet he remained popular because of his sweet temper and reliability. A master of detail, he served on many select committees and royal commissions. In 1889 he originated the colony's first Act to regulate life assurance, and as minister for education he initiated the Claremont Teachers' Training College, the first in Western Australia. He was also president of the Perth Working Men's Association, chairman of the Australian Mutual Provident Society, a director of the Western Australian Bank and a trustee under the 1904 Act for the Endowment of a State University.

Randell died in Perth on 2 June 1915, survived by his third wife Lucy Jane James, née Francisco, whom he had married on 26 January 1881, and by five children. His estate was sworn for probate at £18,094.

J. S. Battye (ed), *Cyclopedia of Western Australia*, 1 (Adel, 1912); *In memoriam: booklet issued at the service of the Hon. George Randell*, J.P. (Perth, 1915); D. Mossenson, *State education in Western Australia* (Perth, 1972); *West Australian*, 29 Apr 1898, 3 June 1915.

G. C. BOLTON

RANDELL, WILLIAM RICHARD (1824-1911), paddle-steamer owner and politician, was born on 2 May 1824 at Sidbury, Devon, England, eldest son of William Beavis Randell and his wife Mary Ann. With his family he migrated with free passages to South Australia in the *Hartley* and arrived at Glenelg on 20 October 1837. The family lived in primitive conditions till his father, who was general stock manager for the South Australian Co., first built a house near Hackney Bridge and soon took up land at Gumeracha, where he erected a flour-mill.

Educated at Exeter, England, and at Adelaide, Randell later held land with his father along the banks of the Murray; it was here, while minding cattle, that he 'became determined to be the first man to put a steamboat on the river'. With his brother John he rented his father's flour-mill; in 1852, aware of the gold-diggings, he 'thought it time to start the steamboat' though he had never seen one and his father opposed it. Carpenters and his brothers Thomas and Elliott cut timber for the hull at Gumeracha and the frame was carted by bullocks over the hills to Mannum. The engine was built in Adelaide by a German engineer and a blacksmith made the boiler to Randell's novel design. The hull, 56 feet long, was completed in February 1853 and in March the steamboat *Mary Ann*, having cost about £1800, made a successful trial run. Randell's first trading voyage began on 25 March but low water below Lake Bonney forced him to return to Mannum. On 25 August he set off again with about twelve tons of stores. Near Swan Hill the *Mary Ann* was overtaken by Francis Cadell's [q.v.] *Lady Augusta* with Lieut-Governor Sir Henry Fox Young and his party on board. Continuing further upstream than the *Lady Augusta* Randell reached Maiden's Punt (Moama) in New South Wales. For his feat the South Australian government gave him £300. A further £400 and a testimonial were later awarded him by citizens who felt that he had been insufficiently rewarded.

In 1854 Randell extended the *Mary Ann* to 75 feet but it was still not big enough for his purposes. Next year he joined it with a new hull, mounted the single paddle-wheel between the two hulls and renamed it *Gemini*. In this unconventional vessel he sailed up the Murrumbidgee River to Lang's Crossing (Hay) where he established a trading store. On later voyages up the Darling River he went as far as Walgett, 1650 river miles from the sea. He then gave up milling and built a house at Mannum.

In 1855 Randell married Elizabeth Ann Nickels and they made their home at Gumeracha. Later he moved to Wentworth to supervise his trading as well as his growing fleet. In 1861 he was appointed a justice of the peace for New South Wales. In the 1870s he returned to South Australia; he lived first at Mannum, where he installed a dry dock, and later at Gumeracha in the family home, Kenton Park, with a redecorated dining room resembling a paddle-steamer saloon. In 1873 he became a justice of the peace for South Australia. He controlled his various activities until 1899 when he handed over to his son, Murray. His most serious loss, costing £6000, occurred in 1863 when his paddle-steamer *Bunyip* and its barges were destroyed by fire on the Murray River; Randell was lucky to escape with his life.

In 1883 Randell became first chairman of the Gumeracha Butter Factory. In 1893-96 and 1896-99 he represented Gumeracha in the House of Assembly. In parliament he favoured water conservation and irrigation, village settlements, working-men's blocks and women's suffrage and opposed protection and taxation change. He was not a prolific debater. Though the oldest member of the House he was still agile, travelling each week from Gumeracha while parliament was in session.

In 1910, in failing health, Randell moved to North Adelaide with a testimonial from the people of Gumeracha. He died on 4 March 1911 survived by five sons and four daughters, leaving an estate sworn for probate at £9000. The No. 1 weir and lock at Blanche Town on the Murray River in South Australia was named in his honour.

J. E. Monfries (ed), *A history of Gumeracha and district . . . 1839-1939* (Adel, 1939); M. M. Kinmont, *Family portrait of William Richard Randell* (Adel, 1951); I. Mudie, *Riverboats* (Adel, 1961); PD (SA), 1893-99; PP (SA), 1853 (96); *Honorary Magistrate*, Jan 1911; *Advertiser* (Adel), 19 Mar 1893, 2 May 1903; *Pictorial Australian*, 1893; *Observer* (Adel), 27 May 1893, 18 July 1896, 27 Nov 1909; *Register* (Adel), 20 June 1896, 6 Mar 1911; H. B. Hoskins (ed), *A historical . . . survey of Mannum*, no 1516 (SAA); J. C. Tolley, Notes on the history of the River Murray system (held by author).

JOHN C. TOLLEY

RANKEN, GEORGE (1827-1895), surveyor, pastoralist, public servant and writer, was born on 17 July 1827 in Ayrshire, Scotland, eldest child of Thomas Ranken, solicitor, and his wife Jean Campbell, née Logan, and nephew of George [q.v.] and Arthur Ranken of Bathurst. Educated at Ayr Academy and trained as a surveyor, he arrived in Victoria in 1851 and served as a gold-buyer in the Ovens district for the Bank of New South Wales in 1853.

Ranken and William Landsborough [q.v.] occupied three runs in the Wide Bay and Burnett districts of Queensland in 1855. The partnership was dissolved in 1858 when Ranken left for Scotland where, in 1859 at Ayr, he married Fanny Sarah Shaw (d. 1918). He returned later that year and settled in Rockhampton, becoming an officer in the Rockhampton Volunteer Rifle Brigade. In 1863-64 he partnered William Rea in an auctioneering and commission agency firm. He became commissioner of crown lands for Port Curtis in March 1868, transferring to Leichhardt District in September. In August 1869, driven by jealousy, he fired a revolver near Rea, but next month was acquitted of a charge of attempted murder.

Discharged from the public service, Ranken moved to Sydney and joined his brother John Logan Campbell Ranken and

J. B. Wilson [q.v.] in a city stock and station agency. About 1876 he settled in East St Leonards as an estate agent, becoming an alderman, and mayor in 1886. He wrote for the *Sydney Morning Herald* on land questions under the pseudonym 'Capricornus'. Some of his pieces were republished as pamphlets and a novel, *The Invasion*, was published pseudonymously (W. H. Walker) in 1877. Another novel, *Windabyne*, serialized in the *Australian* in 1878-79, was published in England after his death. In 1891 he published *The Federal Geography of British Australasia* (Sydney).

In 1879 Ranken was invited to join a royal commission into the Lands Department and on 8 January 1883 he was commissioned with Augustus Morris [q.v.] to inquire into the land laws of the colony. The report presented in May aroused controversy. Sir John Robertson [q.v.], whose land legislation was attacked, described Morris as 'leaky as an old sieve' and the commissioners as 'these two useless, incapable men'. J. S. Farnell [q.v.], secretary for lands, ordered the withdrawal of parts of the report, but it provided the framework for the Crown Lands Act of 1884. Long accepted by historians as a faithful picture of the times, the report has now been shown to have its share of defects.

Ranken joined his brother in a surveying business at Young about 1888. He became a justice of the peace and a member of the local Land Board and was an active member of the Phoenix Literary and Debating Society. On 6 May 1895 he died at Nestle Brae, Young, leaving a wife and four sons. He was buried in the Presbyterian section of the Young cemetery.

G. L. Buxton, *The Riverina 1861-1891* (Melb, 1967); T. A. Coghlan, *Labour and industry in Australia*, 3 (Melb, 1969); *PD* (NSW), 1883, 1926; *V&P* (LA NSW), 1883-84, 11, 786; *Port Denison Times*, 7 Aug, 2 Oct 1869; *Morning Bulletin*, 30 Sept 1869; *Brisbane Courier*, 6, 11 Oct 1869; *Burrangong Argus*, 8 May 1895; Board minutes 1853-62 (Bank of NSW Archives, Syd); run registers (QA).   DAVID DENHOLM
                                        H. J. GIBBNEY

RAPHAEL, JOSEPH GEORGE (1818-1879), politician and philanthropist, was born on 16 February 1818 in London, son of Phillip Raphael, merchant, and his wife Grace, née Raphael. Arriving in Sydney in 1839 he sold ribbons, but was soon a partner in a drapery and by 1842 owner of a general dealer's business and seamen's registry agency. Business prospered and by the late 1850s he was an active shareholder in several banks and insurance companies. He had also

devoted himself to philanthropy and by 1860 was a director of the Society for the Relief of Destitute Children and the Benevolent Asylum of which he later became treasurer. In 1866 he joined the board of the Sydney Infirmary and Dispensary and in evidence to the 1873 royal commission on public charities criticized Lucy Osburn [q.v.]. In 1857 he had sought in vain one of the two auditorships for the reconstituted Sydney Municipal Council. He won the position in 1859, resigned next year and was elected an alderman but by resigning he had broken a provision of the Sydney Corporation Act and was fined. He represented Bourke Ward until 1866 and in 1870-72.

In 1860-65 Raphael was proprietor of the Sydney and Melbourne Hotel. In 1869 he became a partner in a cabinet-making and furniture importing business, and retired from active commercial life in 1872 when he was elected to the Legislative Assembly for West Sydney. He generally supported John Robertson [q.v.] but lost his seat in the 1874 elections. Raphael's public life was characterized by independence, the product of a prickly consciousness of his race and lowly origins. In politics he was disputatious, even violent. Quick to attribute base motives to others, he was often accused himself; once he was called by a slandered opponent 'the foulest-mouthed man in Sydney'. He won repute for philanthropy, but his was a harsh charity based on a belief that its recipients' plight was their own fault. Frequently critical of what he claimed were 'cliques' running the charities, in the early 1870s he aligned himself with a group of Orangemen, but became bitter when they ousted him from one of his directorships. Canon Stephen [q.v.] discerned Raphael's benevolence despite 'all his peculiarities'.

Active in Jewish affairs he was, in the late 1850s, treasurer of the Sydney Synagogue. In 1859 he helped form the break-away Macquarie Street Synagogue and was a member of its committee until 1876. On 30 December 1840 he had married Maria H. Moses of Yass. He died on 2 February 1879 of gastro-enteritis and hepatitis and was buried in the Jewish cemetery, Rookwood, which he had helped purchase. Survived by his wife and four daughters, he left £7000 in goods and a number of city properties.

Jubilee history of the Great Synagogue, Sydney (Syd, 1928); *V&P* (LA NSW), 1861-62, 2, 1025, 1873-74, 6, 187, 1875-76, 6, 126; E. S. Marks, 'Joseph G. Raphael', Aust Jewish Hist Soc, J, 1 (1939-43) pt 10; *Empire*, 28 Apr 1857, 28 Nov 1862, 3 Dec 1870; *Freeman's J* (Syd), 15 Mar 1870, 29 Apr 1871, 17 Feb 1872; *SMH*, 21 Mar 1871, 30 June 1872; *Sydney Mail*, 8 Feb 1879; *T&CJ*, 8 Feb 1879.   MARK LYONS

RASP, CHARLES (1846-1907), prospector, was born on 7 October 1846 at Stuttgart, Duchy of Württemburg, where he was educated. A clerk in a chemical firm, he later trained as an edible-oil technologist with a large chemical manufacturing company in Hamburg, where he worked in the export department as he was fluent in English and French. Rasp was delicate and the bitter winter of 1868 brought on a serious lung weakness, so he decided to leave Germany for a warmer climate.

Rasp arrived in Melbourne in 1869 and found work pruning vines. After two years on agricultural properties he tried the Victorian goldfields but the days of the big strikes were over and the slushy diggings gave him a hacking cough. On advice from friends he moved to New South Wales. He worked on Walwa station, then wandered from place to place until engaged as a boundary rider on Mount Gipps station in the Barrier Ranges in the far west. After discoveries of silver at Silverton and Day Dream every station-hand in the area searched for indications of the metal.

When his duties led him to the 'hill', Rasp often examined the outcrop. No geologist, he was observant and on 5 September 1883 pegged the first block on the 'Broken Hill', which he thought was a mountain of tin. On advice of the Mount Gipps manager, George McCulloch [q.v.], a 'syndicate of seven' was formed and seven blocks pegged to include the whole ridge. Each member subscribed £70 to the unregistered 'Broken Hill Mining Co.' and paid £1 a week towards working the claim.

The syndicate had little success for some months and the Adelaide analysts' reports were disappointing as they only tested for tin. The discovery of rich silver ore in 1885 led to the formation of the Broken Hill Proprietary Co., with capital of 16,000 £20 shares, 14,000 of which went to the syndicate, and to a rapid growth of the mining industry at Broken Hill. Within five years Rasp had made a fortune.

He was prominently connected with Broken Hill for some years. With a large number of shares in the company, he moved to Adelaide when dividends were declared; he married Agnes Maria Louise Klevesahl there on 22 July 1886. They bought a house, Willyama, where his wife entertained in the grand manner. Rasp preferred his library of French and German books. For some years he had mining interests in Western Australia.

Leaving an estate of £48,000, Rasp died suddenly from a heart attack at his residence on 22 May 1907 and was buried in North Road cemetery, Adelaide. He was childless. In 1914 his widow married Count von Zedtwitz and died in Adelaide in 1936. Oil paintings of Rasp and his wife are in the Charles Rasp Memorial Library, Broken Hill.

J. J. Pascoe, History of Adelaide and vicinity (Adel, 1901); R. Bridges, From silver to steel (Melb, 1920); A. Coulls, Charles Rasp: founder of Broken Hill (Broken Hill, 1952); W. S. Robinson, If I remember rightly, G. Blainey, ed (Melb, 1967); Argus, 19 Aug 1905; Barrier Miner, 23 May 1907; Aust Worker, 30 May 1907; information from Mrs M. K. Fowler, Aldgate, SA.   A. COULLS

RAYS, MARQUIS DE (1832-1893), speculator and romantic, was born on 2 January 1832 at the family château at Quimerc'h in Finistère, France, and baptized Charles Marie Bonaventure, son of Charles du Breil, nobleman, and his wife Marie, née Prevost. Inheriting his father's title in 1838, de Rays developed an inordinate taste for the grandiose. In his youth he sought, but failed to find fortune and greatness in the United States, Senegal, Madagascar and Indo-China, and returned to his estates in Brittany. On 22 September 1869 he married Emilie Labat, by whom he had five children, including at least one son, Eugène Paul Emile.

The sad state of France after the Franco-Prussian war of 1870 and the journals of some navigators stirred de Rays to return to youthful goals and to attempt to restore the ancient glory of France and of the Catholic Church. He sought a personal empire in the Pacific. In 1877 he declared himself 'King Charles of New France', an area that extended from eastern New Guinea to the Solomon Islands, unclaimed by European powers. With newspaper advertisements, posters, meetings and in his own journal, Nouvelle France, he expounded his plans for colonizing his allegedly fertile and healthy domain and for converting its inhabitants. On the basis of R. P. Lesson's account in Voyage autour du monde . . . (Paris, 1839) of Duperry's 1823 visit to southern New Ireland, he planned to begin by founding the Colonie Libre de Port Breton at Port Praslin. Governments denounced his scheme; but the promise of cheap land, cheap labour and an assured market for tropical produce, and the offer of a new life with houses, schools, roads, factories, a hospital and even a cathedral, appealed to credulous people in Europe.

In 1880 and 1881 de Rays's ships the Chandernagore, Gentil, India and Nouvelle Bretagne brought about 570 colonists to Port Breton, mostly French, German and

Italian. Supplies were inadequate, malaria was rife, the death rate was high. Most of the colonists soon fled to Australia, New Caledonia and the Philippines. De Rays did not go to Port Breton and was arrested in Spain in July 1882; extradited, he was sentenced by a French court to six years for criminal negligence. After several other dubious ventures, he died near Rosporden, France, on 29 July 1893.

'New France' contributed to Australian sensitivity to the dangers of a northern threat, culminating in the declaration of the British New Guinea Protectorate in 1884: the 240 Italian colonists, most of whom eventually settled at New Italy on the Richmond River in New South Wales, were rumoured to be part of an expeditionary force to New Guinea under Menotti Garibaldi. The scheme also brought the Catholic Church back to New Guinea from which it had withdrawn in 1855. Two chaplains had accompanied the settlers and in 1881 the Missionaries of the Sacred Heart took over the vacant vicariates of Melanesia and Micronesia. The successful traders, Thomas Farrell and 'Queen' Emma Coe, got from the colony much of their initial equipment. A millstone in Rabaul remains a memorial to 'New France'.

A. Baudouin, *L'aventure de Port-Breton et la colonie libre dite Nouvelle-France* (Paris, 1883); M. H. Vermont, *Le procès de marquis de Rays* (Marseille, 1884); J. Lucas-Dubreton, *L'Eden du Pacifique* (Paris, 1929); A. Dupeyrat, *Papouasie: histoire de la mission, 1885-1935* (Paris, 1935); Prime Minister's Dept, Cwlth of Aust, *Official handbook of the Territory of New Guinea* (Canberra, 1937); J. H. Niau, *The phantom paradise* (Syd, 1936); R. W. Robson, *Queen Emma* (Syd, 1965); E. and H. Laracy, *The Italians in New Zealand and other studies* (Auckland, 1973); P. Biskup (ed), *The New Guinea memoirs of Jean Baptiste Octave Mouton* (Canberra, 1974).   HUGH LARACY

READ, CHARLES RUDSTON (1818-1854), naval officer and adventurer, was born on 16 May 1818, probably at Hayton, Yorkshire, England, fifth surviving son of Rev. Thomas-Cutler Rudston-Read and his wife Louisa, née Cholmley. At 13 he entered the navy, passed his examination on 5 October 1838 and first visited Australia in that year. In the *Conway* off the coast of China he assisted in the attacks on Canton and was promoted lieutenant on 8 October 1841. In 1842-45 he served in the *Frolic* on the Brazilian and Pacific stations and in 1845-47 in the *Asia* at Sheerness. He failed to gain promotion in the *Maeander* in 1848, but had two further postings, in *Inconstant* and *Alecto*, before travelling to New Zea-

land late in 1849. He had intended farming but instead journeyed alone through that country; often sleeping out, he covered thousands of miles in eighteen months.

In September 1851 Read reached Newcastle, New South Wales, in the *Halcyon* and went by steamer to Sydney where gold-fever led him to the Turon diggings. With a partner he dug for gold at Thompson's Point until 'sandy blight' forced him to abandon the attempt and return to Sydney in January 1852. There the heightened excitement, this time emanating from Mount Alexander, Victoria, sent him to Melbourne where he found both work and accommodation scarce. Finally he was introduced to Lieut-Governor La Trobe who appointed him, on 20 May, assistant commissioner of crown lands at Forest Creek in the gold district of Castlemaine, at a salary of £500 with rations and forage. He issued licences, detected defaulters, guarded fees and gold, settled disputes and maintained an orderly field. Humane, popular, and understanding, he later wrote critically of the licence-fee system and the police on the diggings.

In June 1852 Read was transferred to Bendigo and on 28 August was appointed a police magistrate. He headed the out-station, Myers Creek, for four months with a clerk, sergeant and nine foot police under him. He spent the day riding over his district, doing the book-work at night.

In 1853 Read resigned, returned to England in the *Statesman* and published, with the aid of private subscriptions, *What I heard, saw, and did at the Australian Gold Fields* (London). Intended as a realistic emigrants' guide, it is a colourful and humorous account of his adventures in which lively, detailed reporting of conditions and methods of digging alternates with comical vignettes of scenes observed. Illustrated by fourteen of his own excellent lithographs of life on the diggings, the book declines in the final section to generalized second-hand information.

Read was approached frequently for advice on emigration; he planned to return to Australia but died in 1854.

W. R. O'Byrne, *A naval biographical dictionary* (Lond, 1849); G. Serle, *The golden age* (Melb, 1963); Sel c'ttee on the ... goldfields, *V&P* (LC Vic), 1852-53, 2, 1853-54, 3 (D8a); *Government Gazette* (Vic), 1852, 2, 519, 933; *Argus*, 3 Jan 1853.   SUZANNE EDGAR

READ, HENRY (1831-1888), Anglican clergyman, professor of classics and medical practitioner, was born at Manchester, Lancashire, England, and baptized on 26

October 1831, son of William Read, tobacco manufacturer and later Anglican clergyman, and his wife Demeride, née Kaye. He was educated at Manchester Grammar School, Huddersfield College and St John's College, Cambridge (B.A., 1855; M.A., 1860), where he was three times an exhibitioner and seven times a prizeman; he also seems to have pursued some medical studies there.

On 3 June 1855 Read was ordained deacon by the bishop of Guiana, and was curate of St Philip's and classical tutor to Bishop's College, Georgetown, in 1855-58. At New Amsterdam, British Guiana, on 4 August 1859 he married Elizabeth, youngest daughter of Thomas Lawrence of Brecon, South Wales. In 1859-61 he was a Society for the Propagation of the Gospel missionary at All Saints, Berbice, and in 1862-64 curate of St Mary's, Antigua. He was appointed inspector of schools in British Guiana and St Kitts but ill health forced his return to England in 1866.

Next year Bishop Augustus Short [q.v.] appointed Read rector of Holy Trinity, Lyndoch, South Australia. He arrived in Adelaide in May 1867. Two years later he became rector of St Michael's, Mitcham, and in 1872 classics tutor to Union College. In 1874, while still rector, he was appointed first Hughes professor of classics and philology at the University of Adelaide where he was twice elected dean. In 1877 he published *Modern Pronunciation of Latin and Greek as Adopted in Universities of Melbourne and Adelaide*.

In June 1878, while his wife was visiting England, Read was required to resign his rectorship and his chair apparently because of a personal scandal; shortly afterwards he sailed with his family for Newcastle, New South Wales. Next year he graduated M.D. from the Medical College of the Pacific, University College, San Francisco. In 1883 he became a licentiate, and a licentiate in midwifery, of the Royal College of Physicians, Edinburgh, and of the Faculty of Physicians, Glasgow, and registered those qualifications later that year in Victoria where he lived for about two years. Soon after going to Brisbane he died of heart disease on 24 March 1888 survived by his wife, two sons and a daughter. He was buried in the Anglican section of Toowong cemetery.

Though an undistinguished holder of his chair, Read was able and courageous, and fluent in French, Italian and Spanish. Generous to his church at Mitcham he recovered well from his trouble at the University of Adelaide and it was a considerable achievement to obtain his medical qualifications in middle age.

St Michael's Church, Mitcham jubilee festival (Adel, 1902); *Illustrated Adel News*, June 1875; *Advertiser* (Adel), 29 May, 3, 5 June 1878; *Register* (Adel), 3 June 1878; *Brisbane Courier*, 26 Mar 1888; Union College, Presbyterian Church records (SAA).

J. TREVASKIS

RECHNER, GUSTAV JULIUS (1830-1900), Lutheran pastor, was born on 29 December 1830 at Liegnitz, Silesia, eldest child of Friedrich Rechner, cloth-weaver, and his wife Wilhelmine, née Maiwald. He studied for teaching but was apprenticed to a clothier and then assisted his father as a clerk. He decided to migrate before military call-up, and arrived at Port Adelaide in the *Victoria* on 7 November 1848. His parents and two surviving sisters followed in 1854.

After a variety of work in the Tanunda district, in June 1850 Rechner became schoolteacher and cantor of the Lights Pass church under Rev. A. L. C. Kavel [q.v.] of Langmeil. He took services on three nights of the week and evening classes in English on three nights for children and adults. He won renown as a teacher and the Lights Pass school grew from 45 to more than 100 pupils. On 23 October 1850 he married Josepha Louise Bertha Bergmann of Liegnitz.

Doctrinal differences between Kavel and his fellow-pastor, G. W. Staudenmayer, came to a head after Kavel's death in February 1860. Rechner, responsible to Staudenmayer for his school but holding to Kavel's views, resigned and became a clerk of George Fife Angas [q.v.]. Twenty-five families seceded from Staudenmayer in November and called Rechner as their pastor. His ordination by J. C. Auricht [q.v.] on 3 February 1861 was initially opposed by all other groups of the Lutheran Church in Australia.

An energetic and able organizer, Rechner often worked an eighteen-hour day. For forty years he ministered in three churches: Strait Gate (Lights Pass), Grünberg (Moculta) and North Rhine (Keyneton); as members of these churches moved in the 1870s to more remote, newly-opened areas of the colony, he organized churches and served them till additional ministers arrived. In 1874-1900 he was president of the Evangelical Lutheran Immanuel Synod of South Australia.

Rechner maintained a lifelong interest in the Aboriginals. In 1863-1900 he was treasurer of the Mission Committee; also chairman in 1874-1900, with confident trust he encouraged his branch of the Church to open or take over a number of areas: Bethesda or Killalpaninna Mission, Cooper's Creek, among the Dieri in 1866; Bloomfield Mission, south of Cooktown, Queensland, in 1883; and Hermannsburg Mission, Central Australia, among the Aranda in 1894.

Rechner died on 21 August 1900 at Lights Pass, survived by his wife, four sons and two daughters; seven children predeceased him.

Gustav Julius Rechner, ein Erinnerungsblatt (Tanunda, 1903); Th. Hebart, *The United Evangelical Lutheran Church in Australia*, J. J. Schultz ed (Adel, 1938); Rechner papers and autobiog (Lutheran Church Archives, Adel).   H. F. W. PROEVE

REDE, ROBERT WILLIAM (1815-1904), goldfields commissioner and sheriff, was born on 13 July 1815 at Ashman's Hall, Beccles, Suffolk, England, the seat of his ancient county family, son of Thomas William Rede, naval officer, and his wife Anne (Mary), née Mills. He was privately educated in England and spent nine years in Paris. He abandoned his medical studies, travelled throughout Europe for many years and was reputedly a queen's messenger to Greece. He arrived at Port Phillip in November 1851, and joined the rush to Bendigo where he dug with some success. Dabbling in medicine he became popularly known as 'the little doctor'. His family background was probably a passport to employment in the Goldfields Commission, which he joined in October 1852. He served at Bendigo and then Mount Korong where he was rapidly promoted to resident commissioner.

In May 1854 Rede took charge at Ballarat. Even more than Governor Charles Hotham, he might have prevented the Eureka rebellion of December. He sympathized with the mining population, but became the object of their hostility over a miscarriage of justice. He was publicly humiliated during the burning of Bentley's hotel, and his pride determined him to teach the miners 'a fearful lesson' if they resisted the arrest of the incendiaries. Backed by military reinforcements he used the hated licence hunts, which he had earlier opposed, to bring about a confrontation; while in Melbourne he conferred with the governor and arranged to communicate with him by cypher if an emergency developed. Although Hotham counselled caution and legality, he gave Rede ample scope for initiative. As early as 28 November, Rede advised that the agitation should be crushed and two days later he provoked resistance by hunting for licences. Intending to split the disaffected from the law-abiding, he forced the Irish and other extremists into open rebellion and justified an attack on them; but he also alienated the majority, whose reaction to the storming of the Eureka stockade on 3 December showed how far Rede and the governor had misread the situation. 'I should be sorry to see them return to their work', declared Rede on the night before the assault, but when the government victory turned into a moral defeat he had to be removed from Ballarat.

Rede was let off lightly by the royal commission into the goldfields administration, and was kept on full pay until late in 1855 when Hotham arranged for his appointment as deputy-sheriff of Geelong and commandant of the Volunteer Rifles. He became sheriff of Geelong in 1857, Ballarat in 1868 and Melbourne in 1877, and major and later colonel of various volunteer detachments. In 1878 he was second-in-command in the colony. Public-spirited, he became a member of the Ballarat and Melbourne clubs and a vestryman at St John's Church of England near his home in Toorak. He retired in 1889.

In 1859 Rede had married Isabella, daughter of J. F. Strachan [q.v.]; she died in 1862 leaving a son. On 9 January 1873 he married Geraldine Margaret, daughter of Dr George Clendinning of Ballarat; they had three sons and three daughters. He died of pneumonia in Melbourne on 13 July 1904 and was buried in St Kilda cemetery.

H. M. Humphreys (ed), *Men of the time in Australia: Victorian series*, 1st ed (Melb, 1878); V&P (LA Vic), 1857-58, 1 (D23); *Government Gazette* (Vic), 1852, 1854, 1857, 1877; *Australasian*, 7 Dec 1889; *Argus*, 14 July 1904; Goldfields Commission letters (PRO, Vic); family information (Melbourne Club Archives).

WESTON BATE

REDMOND, JOHN EDWARD (1856-1918) and WILLIAM HOEY KEARNEY (1861-1917), Irish nationalists, were born on 1 September 1856 and in 1861, at Ballytrent, County Wexford, Ireland, the eldest and second sons of William Archer Redmond, M.P., and his wife Mary, née Hoey. John was educated at Clongowes Wood College by the Jesuits, and in 1874-76 at Trinity College, Dublin. In 1876 he joined his father in London and became a clerk in the House of Commons to which he was elected in 1880 for New Ross. William was also educated at Clongowes. In 1881 under the Irish Coercion Act he was imprisoned in the Kilmainham gaol, Dublin, with Charles Parnell.

On 25 February 1882 John wrote to Hugh Mahon about a visit to Australia as the delegate of the Irish National League to advocate Home Rule and raise funds. He arrived in Adelaide in February 1883 in the *Siam* with William. They held a successful meeting, founded a local branch of the league and went to Sydney. Their reception was hostile because of allegations of the Irish Land League's connexion with the Phoenix Park murders and of the embezzlement of its funds. John denied the charges in the *Sydney Morning Herald* and accused the press of being misinformed about Irish affairs. He had difficulty hiring halls for his meetings, sedition and criminality were freely imputed by the press and in parliament, and many prominent Catholics withheld their support. Early in March the Redmonds toured western New South Wales and at Orange were entertained by James Dalton [q.v.].

In Sydney on 6 March, at a meeting to express loyalty to the Queen, Sir Henry Parkes [q.v.] in 'forcible' language protested against the Redmonds' visit and was assailed by 'a number of roughs' when the meeting ended. At the St Patrick's Day celebrations John addressed a 'remarkably orderly gathering' at Botany and was presented with a gold watch and chain but the banquet was marred by Henry Copeland's [q.v.] 'state of intoxication'. In April the Redmonds went to Brisbane then toured Queensland with less tension.

John's eloquence and moderation won over the rank and file Irish. In May he spoke with great success in southern New South Wales and went to Melbourne, where the press had already stirred up controversy. Both the *Age* and the *Argus* attacked them as extremists in the guise of moderates. John's three main lectures were published as a pamphlet, *Ireland's Case Stated*. Embarking on a strenuous country tour he spoke at forty-two centres. In July William was elected *in absentia* to the House of Commons for Wexford.

In Sydney, on 4 September at St Mary's, North Sydney, John married Jo(h)anna Mary, half-sister of James and Thomas Dalton. She bore him a son and two daughters and died on 12 December 1889. The wedding eve was enlivened by a fracas at Pfhalert's Hotel when William overheard Thomas Curran, the licensee, tell J. G. O'Connor [q.v.], in language worse than that of the 'lowest *navvy*' that John was 'only an adventurer who had come to look for a wife and a fortune'; he challenged Curran, who struck him and ordered the 'scrubbers' out.

The Redmonds toured New Zealand; they returned to Melbourne for the convention of delegates from the National League branches before sailing from Sydney for San Francisco in the *Zealandia* on 7 December 1883. Governor Loftus repeatedly told the Colonial Office that the 'mission of Messrs Redmond to this Colony has been a complete failure' but £15,000 was remitted to the National League in Ireland and they raised only the same sum in America.

The Redmonds remained loyal to Parnell in the split in the Irish Party that followed the O'Shea divorce, and on his death in 1891 John became leader of the Parnellites in the House of Commons; in 1900 he became chairman of the re-united Irish Party. His dignity, moderation, magnanimity and total rejection of violence, strengthened by his Australian connexions, helped him lose touch with Ireland's mood and the 1916 Easter Rebellion took him by surprise. He died suddenly on 6 March 1918; in 1899 he had married Ada Beazley.

On 24 February 1886 in London William had married Eleanor Mary, eldest daughter of James Dalton; they made several visits to Australia. He published *A Shooting Trip in the Australian Bush* (Dublin, 1898) and *Through the New Commonwealth* (Dublin, 1906). Always more fervent than his brother he represented East Clare in the House of Commons in 1891-1917. On the outbreak of World War I he volunteered and became a captain in the Royal Irish Regiment. Promoted major, he was killed in action on 7 June 1917 on Wytschaete Ridge, Belgium, and was buried in the garden of the hospice at Locre. His wife returned to Orange and died in Sydney on 31 January 1947, predeceased by their only son.

D. R. Gwynn, *The life of John Redmond* (Lond, 1932); *PD* (LA NSW), 1883, 8, 573, 848-49, 1545, 1548; *Australasian*, 22 Dec 1882, 17, 24 Feb, 24 Mar, 9 June, 8 Dec 1883; *SMH*, 21, 22, 24, 27 Feb, 9, 19 Mar, 18 Apr, 19 May 1883, 26 Oct 1891; *Sydney Mail*, 24 Mar, 7 Apr, 19 May, 2 June 1883, 19 July 1884; *Argus*, 1, 2, 6-8, 11, 14 June 1883; G. M. Tobin, The sea-divided Gael: a study of the Irish Home Rule movement in Victoria and New South Wales, 1880-1916 (M.A. thesis, ANU, 1969); Mahon papers (NL); J. E. Redmond papers (microfilm, Univ NSW Archives); CO 201/598.

MARTHA RUTLEDGE

REED, JOSEPH (1823 ?-1890), architect, was probably the child baptized in the parish of Constantine, Cornwall, England, on 23 February 1823, son of Nicholas Reed, landowner, and his wife Amy, née Hitchins. He arrived in Melbourne in July 1853 and in January 1854 won the competition to design the Public Library. The same year he designed the Bank of New South Wales in Collins Street (the façade was re-erected in 1938 at the University of Melbourne) and the Geelong Town Hall. In 1856 he was the first elected member of the short-lived first Victorian Institute of Architects.

In 1858 Reed became university architect, succeeding F. M. White [q.v.]. At about the same time he designed the Wesley Church, Lonsdale Street, and the premises in Victoria Street that later became the Royal Society of Victoria building. In 1862 he added the classical portico to the Collins Street Baptist Church and took as partner Frederick Barnes (1824-1884); together they drew plans for the National Museum at the university.

Reed visited Europe in 1863. He returned in October to introduce to Melbourne with enthusiasm the brick architecture of Lombardy that is evident in three 1866 designs, the Collins Street Independent Church, St Jude's, Carlton, and the National school in Carlton, and in the 1868 design for F. T. Sargood's [q.v.] Rippon Lea, at Elsternwick. For the Melbourne Town Hall they returned to the classicism of the Second Empire mode, while the inspiration of their Menzies Hotel (1867) was said to be sixteenth-century châteaux although the treatment was Italianate.

In 1864 Reed and Barnes had successfully competed for Government House but the job was transferred to the Public Works Department under W. Wardell [q.v.]. Reed bitterly recalled it at the royal commission into the department in 1873. That year Reed, as president of the revived Institute of Architects, led deputations to the minister in an attempt to seek open competition for major public works.

In the next ten years the styles of the many buildings designed by Reed and Barnes ranged from astylar Italianate for The Gums at Caramut (1875-76) and the plastered classic of both the Trades Hall (1873) and the Exhibition Building (1879-80) to the widely admired Gothic of Wilson Hall (1878-82) and the Scottish baronial of Ormond College (1879). In February 1877 they resigned from the Institute of Architects, probably because they ignored its directive not to enter a limited competition conducted by the Melbourne City Council for the Eastern Market. Early in 1883 Barnes retired and Reed was joined by A. M. Henderson and F. J. Smart. The firm continued work on St Paul's Cathedral, Melbourne, in 1884 after the distinguished London architect William Butterfield had resigned. In 1890 Henderson withdrew after disagreements and N. B. Taplin joined the firm. The office later became Bates, Peebles and Smart,

and exists today as Bates, Smart and Mc-Cutcheon.

Reed shared a common interest in music with Hannah Elliot Lane; they were married on 26 March 1885 and next day left for an eighteen months tour of Europe. By 1890 Reed was in financial difficulties and that year took seriously ill. He died on 29 April 'of inanition and exhaustion'. His estate included several violins by Stradivarius. His widow remarried in England, becoming Mrs Boase, and had a son whom she named Joseph Reed Stradivarius. She later left her husband in India and brought the boy to Melbourne where she died in 1946.

Although Reed's work varied in quality he dominated the architectural profession in Melbourne, mainly because of his many competition successes and his constant commissions for public and prominent private buildings. Probably his best works were Wilson Hall and the city churches, Scots (1873), Wesley and Independent. The Exhibition Building displays his skill in controlling large volumes in an extensive landscape, while the Bank of New South Wales shows satisfying enrichment of a small-scale building. Retaining for a lifetime several important clients, he successfully ran his large office, the city's first major private architectural office, although David Ross of The Gums wrote in 1876, 'The more I see of Reed the less I think of him as a business man'. One employee remembered him as 'an Australian terrier; liable to snap up at you, with sudden violence, then forget all he had said and be helpful and kind'. Another recalled him as 'practical and decisive, an aggressive little fellow but very kindly'.

. D. Saunders, *Joseph Reed . . . his life and work* (Melb, 1950); R. Boyd, *The Australian ugliness*, rev ed (Ringwood, 1968); J. M. Freeland, *Architecture in Australia; a history* (Melb, 1968) and *The making of a profession* (Syd, 1971); V&P (LA Vic), 1873 (73); R. Boyd, 'Joseph Reed of Melbourne', *Architecture*, 40 (1952) no 4; *Argus*, 30 Apr 1890; David Ross journal (held by Miss S. Agar, Caramut, Vic).

DAVID SAUNDERS

REES, JOHN (1825-1917), farmer and politician, was born on 19 March 1825 at Lower Knowle, Bristol, England, son of John Rees, mechanic, and his wife Mary, née Graves. Educated locally, he worked in a lawyer's office before migrating to Geelong in 1849 with his wife Harriett, née Banfield, whom he had married at Bristol in 1848, and his brother Phillip. Successful on the Ballarat and Bendigo goldfields in 1851-52, he bought land at Little River in the Corio Shire in 1852, naming his property Lower Knowle. With other crop farmers threatened by cheaper South Australian imports, Rees supported the Geelong tariff protection campaign in 1856 and advocated grazing commons for farmers to fatten livestock. He was a delegate at the 1857 Land Convention which endorsed the commons principle and it was included in the 1860 Nicholson [q.v.] Land Act to cover one million acres. Rees later supported farmers who wished to select commons land put up for sale on easy terms.

From August 1866 to July 1891 Rees was a councillor and twice president of the Corio Shire; as an admirer of William Cobbett he persistently attacked squatter 'landlords' in local politics. In 1871 he called a conference of local councils to change the basis of shire taxation from improvement to the 'natural value ... as judged by its sheep carrying capacity'. He welcomed the revival of the Geelong Protection League in 1876 and formed the Little River branch which supported Graham Berry's [q.v.] 'stonewall' opposition to Sir James McCulloch's [q.v.] 'iron hand' ministry. In favour of the National Reform League's proposal for a progressive land tax, he initiated a local branch in February 1877, chaired meetings in the Primitive Methodist Chapel and, backed by Berry, successfully contested the Grant electorate on a joint ticket with Peter Lalor [q.v.] at the May elections for the Legislative Assembly.

Rees voted for the Berry ministry's land tax, payment of members, and constitutional reform proposals in the 1877-80 parliament. After serving on the wattle bark board of inquiry in 1878, he toured Victoria as a tireless member of the crown lands commission of inquiry, 1878-79, and in 1884 was a member of the royal commission on water supply. Attentive to the usual 'roads and bridges' claims from his electorate as 'a delegate of the sovereign power', he also backed improvement for rural Victoria, supporting moves for water trusts, the Dookie State Farm and forest conservation. Favouring high protection for agriculture, he defended the Victorian stock tax, attacked attempts to lower grain duties and spoke out for country millers and maltsters. Seeing intercolonial free trade proposals as solely in the interest of Melbourne men, he warned city protectionists in 1885 that unless they acted 'honestly towards the farmers' they would one day 'find themselves without their support'. With other 'country party' members he remained critical of the Deakin-Gillies [q.v.] ministry and joined the Victorian Farmers' Protection Association in 1887, firmly convinced that 'the miners and farmers should govern the country not the moneyed men of Melbourne'. A pastoralist beat him

narrowly at the 1889 elections after forty of his Mount Egerton supporters had neglected to vote; he again lost in 1892.

Rees remained active in local affairs, was a forceful lay preacher, and for thirty-four years superintendent of the Methodist Sunday school. Rugged strength and a determined manner found expression in his religion, 'a passion to do what his hands found to do and to do it with all his might'. He died on 10 May 1917 having, his mourners claimed, amply fulfilled his favourite text : 'With long life will I satisfy Him and show Him my salvation'. He had ten children by his first wife, and four by his second, Emily Catherine, née Thomson, whom he had married in 1887 at Little River.

A. Sutherland et al, *Victoria and its metropolis*, 2 (Melb, 1888); J. M. Powell (ed), *Yeomen and bureaucrats* (Melb, 1973); *Argus*, 8 July 1876, 17, 18 Aug 1888; *Bacchus Marsh Express*, 31 Mar, 27 Apr, 12 May 1877, 9 Feb 1878; *Age*, 10 May 1917; *Werribee Shire Banner*, 10, 24 May, 14 June 1917; information from Mrs M. Bates, Little River, Vic.   J. H. RUNDLE

REES, ROWLAND (1840-1904), architect and politician, was born on 25 September 1840 at Gibraltar, eldest son of Rowland Rees, officer, Royal Engineers, and later mayor of Dover, England. Educated in Hong Kong and at Wesley College, Sheffield, he trained in civil engineering and architecture with H. E. Kendall, a founder of the Royal Institute of British Architects.

Rees arrived in Adelaide in December 1869 and was in partnership with Thomas English for three years. On 23 November 1870 he married Ada Caroline, eldest daughter of William Sandford, an Adelaide solicitor. The Moonta Methodist Church (1873) and Essenside, Glenelg (1873), established his architectural reputation, while Kither's Buildings in Rundle Street (1879), a three storey shop and office complex in King William Street (1884) and the St Peters Town Hall (1885), now altered, showed his skill in designing ebullient Italianate façades, apparent also in several of his large houses and in his interior decoration. He designed the Lobethal Woollen Mills (1883) and Fulton's Foundry, Kilkenny (1885-86) and was the engineer for the railway from Adelaide to Glenelg (1879-80). His best surviving work is in hotel design : the unadorned British (1883) contrasting with the elaborate Huntsman (1882), Oxford, Cumberland Arms, and Newmarket (1884). His work was identified by careful attention to detail, the bold structure of his chimneys, pronounced hood-moulds, decorative pilasters and capitals, use of parapets with baroque pediments and expert siting of buildings.

From 1878 Rees was on the South Australian Institute Board. In 1880 he helped to select paintings at the Melbourne Exhibition as the nucleus of South Australia's state collection. He served on the Fine Arts Committee of the Public Library, Museum and Art Gallery Board in 1884-96 and was commissioned to select the first addition to the collection in 1888.

As member for Burra in 1873-81 and Onkaparinga in 1882-90 in the House of Assembly Rees advanced liberal ideas and supported payment for members in 1874-75. For six days in 1878 he was minister of education in William Morgan's [q.v.] ministry. He was always eloquent on education, notably in his advocacy of free education, abolition of payment by results, and curriculum reform. In 1879-88 he wanted gambling regulated rather than banned, and in debating the divorce law extension bill in 1883 he argued strongly that women should have equal rights to sue for divorce. In 1889 his long-promoted outer harbour bill was passed, though never put into practice. The public gallery was full in 1889 when he advocated in vain an architects' registration bill. His oratory was both praised and ridiculed and he was once satirized as 'The Ornate': 'There are only two orators in Australasia', he reputedly said, 'myself and my cousin in New Zealand'.

Reported in 1886 to be £6100 in debt, Rees was generously treated by his creditors. His practice declined and he sought work in Western Australia in 1896-99, but returned to Adelaide in 1903. Survived by his wife, he died in Parkside Mental Hospital on 13 October 1904, and was buried in St Jude's Anglican cemetery, Brighton.

G. E. Loyau, Notable South Australians (Adel, 1885); W. H. Bagot, Some nineteenth century Adelaide architects (Adel, 1958); Advertiser (Adel), 15 June 1886; Australasian, 19 June 1886; Government record group 19 (SAA).
ALAN FEENEY

REEVE, EDWARD (1822-1889), writer, museum curator and police magistrate, was born on 15 December 1822 at Locking, Somerset, England, fourth son of Lieutenant John Andrewes Reeve, R.N., and his wife Mary, née Morell. Educated at Bristol College he reached Sydney in the Earl Grey on 25 February 1840. On 21 March 1847 at Christ Church St Laurence, he married Margaret Hennessy, who bore him two sons and two daughters. In 1848 after 'more than eight years of uninterrupted employment and misery as a teacher in New South Wales', Reeve became a clerk in the Immigration Department; he transferred to the Police Department in 1854 and by 1857 had found a 'perfectly congenial' position as a reporter for the Sydney Morning Herald.

Reeve wrote at times under the pseudonym of 'Yorick'. In 1863 his blank verse play, Raymond, Lord of Milan; A Tragedy of the 13th Century (Sydney, 1851), was performed for four nights at Sydney's Victoria Theatre. William Walker [q.v.] described the play as 'the most successful drama which has been produced in this colony' but G. B. Barton [q.v.] thought it 'suffered greatly from the negligence with which it was put on the stage. Intoxicated actors and giggling ballet girls did their best to ruin it'. Reeve's wide-ranging interests were reflected in his journalism. He wrote a series of articles on education in New South Wales for the People's Advocate and, as a member of the New South Wales Professional Literary Association, contributed to its journal, Australian Era. He was associated with the Month, a literary magazine of his friend Frank Fowler [q.v.]. After he retired from active journalism he continued to contribute to Sydney papers and his long romance 'Friends and Foes; or, The Bride of Bernback', was published in the Sydney Mail from January to May 1882. Set in England with local interest provided by a visiting Australian cousin, it is fluently written, with a well-knit plot; its characters, though cast in the romantic convention, often achieve individuality. He compiled a 'Gazetteer of Central Polynesia' for Charles St Julian's [q.v.] Official Report on Central Polynesia (Sydney, 1857), became his secretary and succeeded him as Hawaiian consul-general in 1872. In 1876 he was made a knight commander of the Royal Order of Kalahaua I.

In 1860 Reeve had also become first curator of the Nicholson [q.v.] Museum at the University of Sydney, and compiled and printed a Catalogue of the Museum of Antiquities of the Sydney University (Sydney, 1870). In 1871 he was a founder and honorary secretary of the New South Wales Academy of Art; in his opening speech he stressed that 'our flora and fauna are an inexhaustible store for novelties of beauty and design, of which the old world knows nothing whatever and these suggestive types we must learn to utilize in what we have to do'.

Failing in health, Reeve left the Herald and became police magistrate at Gosford and coroner at Brisbane Water in 1875; he transferred to Port Macquarie in 1887, retired on a pension the next year and resumed his position as curator of the Nicholson Museum. He died on 13 May 1889 and was buried in the Anglican section of Waverley cemetery, survived by his second wife Catherine, née McVeigh, whom he had married in Sydney in 1854, and by three sons and three daughters of their nine children.

G. B. Barton, *Literature in New South Wales* (Syd, 1866); J. S. Moore, *The life and genius of James Lionel Michael* (Syd, 1868); *People's Advocate* (Syd), 1851; *Southern Cross* (Syd), 19 Nov 1859; *T&CJ*, 18 May 1889; Senate minutes (Univ Syd Archives); family papers (held by Harold Reeve, Balgowlah Heights, NSW).
ROSILYN BAXTER

REIBEY, THOMAS (1821-1912), clergyman, farmer and politician, was born on 24 September 1821 at Entally House, Hadspen, Van Diemen's Land, son of Thomas Haydock Reibey, merchant, and his wife Richardie, née Allen, and grandson of Mary Reibey [q.v.]. Educated at W. G. Elliston's school in Longford, Thomas and his brother James were sent to England to be coached for university and holy orders. He was barely equal to his parents' aspirations, being remembered at Trinity College, Oxford, more for his rowing and vigour in the hunt than for academic success. On 28 October 1842 at Plymouth he married Catherine Macdonald Kyle. Though he returned to Tasmania without a degree his prestige, wealth and sociability amply repaired this omission. At a ceremony performed by Bishop Nixon [q.v.] in 1844, Reibey became the first native Tasmanian ordained in his homeland. On 22 October 1853, while in England with his wife, he received an honorary M.A. from the archbishop of Canterbury.

Reibey was an excellent cleric, popular with his parishioners as rector of Holy Trinity, Launceston, and the church at Carrick. The Anglican synod also liked him, for he needed no stipend from the faltering Sustentation Fund or its successors but endowed Carrick with land, church and rectory and would have done the same at Hadspen but for disagreements with Bishop Bromby [q.v.]. In May 1858 Reibey was created archdeacon and in 1863-68 he and his wife again visited England. As adviser to the widow of James Cox [q.v.] and trustee of the Clarendon estate he was drawn into a family quarrel about the division of property among the daughters. In 1868 Cox's son-in-law, H. W. Blomfield, in a letter to synod, accused Reibey of attempts to seduce his wife Margaret. Reibey unsuccessfully sued for libel and the ensuing scandal rocked the colony. He resigned in 1870.

Still vigorous, the failed archdeacon languished as a farmer for a year or two. Yet colonial society was mobile and scandals were commonplace. In 1874 Reibey campaigned for the House of Assembly seat of Westbury, a district in which he owned the Oaks estate, and was returned by an enthusiastic majority which he sustained until 1903. From July 1876 to August 1877 the man the *Mercury* had labelled 'the ecclesiastical debauchee' was premier of Tasmania. He had a progressive public works policy, including purchase of the privately-owned railways, but was frustrated by the Opposition. He was colonial secretary in 1876-79, Speaker of the House in 1887-91 and was on the Executive Council in 1894-99 while minister without portfolio in Braddon's government.

Reibey's greatest sporting interests were hunting and horse-racing. With his all rose colours he won the Launceston Cup in 1882 with Stockwell. He bred Malua, winner of the 1884 Melbourne Cup. He was president of three local racing clubs at Carrick, Rosedale and Newnham as well as the Northern Agricultural Society. He also bred stags and dogs. He died on 10 February 1912 at Entally, predeceased by his wife. They had no children.

A full report of the great libel case: *Reiby v. Blomfield* (Launceston, 1870); *Cyclopedia of Tasmania*, 1 (Hob, 1900); K. R. von Stieglitz, *Entally 1821: pageant of a pioneer family 1792-1912* (Hob, 1950); F. C. Green (ed), *A century of responsible government 1856-1956* (Hob, 1956); *Hobart Town Gazette*, 2 Nov 1822; *Hobart Town Courier*, 7 Mar 1846; *Mercury*, 9 June 1870, 12 Feb 1912; *Examiner* (Launceston), 16 June 1870; *Argus*, 12 Feb 1912.
PETER BOLGER

REID, DAVID (1820-1906) and ROBERT DYCE (1829-1900), pastoralists and politicians, were the first and third sons of David Reid [q.v.], naval surgeon, and his wife Agnes, née Dyce. David was born probably at Plymouth, England, in December 1820 and came to New South Wales on 24 October 1823 in the *Mariner* with his parents and two sisters. The family settled at Inverary Park, near Bungonia. At first educated at home, he attended J. D. Lang's [q.v.] Australian College from 1831 and The King's School from its foundation in 1832. Leaving school at 16, he took charge of his father's run in the Maneroo (Monaro) District but after meeting the overlander John Gardiner [q.v.] he decided to look for land south of the Murray River. Equipped by his father with some 500 head of cattle,

2 bullock wagons and teams and 6 assigned servants, he reached the Ovens River on 8 September 1838 the same day as Rev. Joseph Docker [q.v.]. David settled at Currargarmonge, near Wangaratta, held at first in his father's name and after 1840 as a family partnership; despite an attempted attack by Aboriginals he harvested the first wheat crop in December 1839. At the end of 1843 he took up land near Yackandandah. After his marriage to Mary Romaine Barber on 29 February 1844 at Marulan, New South Wales, he left the partnership and in 1847 took up a section of the family run of which Woorajay (Wooragee) formed a part. He built the first water driven flour-mill in the district on his Yackandandah run in 1845; his woolclip of 1848 was one of the first to be handled by R. Goldsbrough [q.v.] and was claimed to come from sheep descended from stock imported in the 1820s from George III's flock.

In 1852 gold was discovered in the May Day Hills, and the Ovens gold rush settlements of Beechworth, El Dorado, Woolshed, Sebastopol and Reid's Creek developed on Reid family land, ruining its pastoral value. For a time David sold meat to the miners and ran the mill, a store and a gold-buying business, but in 1853 sold his runs and turned profitably to cattle and horse-dealing and general trading between Melbourne and the Riverina and the diggings. In November 1856 he bought the lease of Barnawatha, south of Albury and built the Hermitage but much of the property was resumed for smallholdings. Going into politics, he held the Legislative Assembly seat of Murray from October 1859 to May 1862. At a recount after the 1861 election he was disqualified and did not stand again. In the early 1860s he bought Thelangerin on the Lachlan River, near Hay, financed an expedition to the north of Bourke and took up Delalah on the Paroo River. Foreclosed about 1864 he was forced to sell when land values were at their lowest. Near ruin, he took up his brother Robert's offer of land at Moorwatha near Howlong, New South Wales, and farmed there from 1865.

A magistrate for New South Wales from 1847, David was a foundation member of many local organizations in the Wangaratta and Albury districts. He was first president of the Agricultural and Pastoral Association in 1857 and in 1859 was a committee-man and trustee of the Ovens and Murray Agricultural and Horticultural Society. In the 1880s he was active in the formation of the farmers' union at Burrumbuttock and in 1893 was first vice-president of the Farmers and Settlers' Association of New South Wales. Always interested in racing, he was foundation president of the

first race club in Albury and owned many horses; his bay Medora won at the first meeting held at Flemington, Melbourne, in March 1840. He was a Freemason. He died at Moorwatha on 7 May 1906 and was buried at Howlong, survived by his wife, six of their seven sons and two of their three daughters.

Robert Dyce was born on 3 August 1829 at Inverary Park. At 17 he joined the family in the Wangaratta district and later acquired Moorwatha in the Riverina. With his brothers he was involved in many local organizations and was the first vice-president of the Wangaratta Hospital committee. In 1874 he sold out before leaving for a tour of Europe. In a farewell address the residents of El Dorado affirmed their admiration for him as 'a man and a gentleman' who had always been 'more ready to assist than obstruct the Miner and the Free Selector'; who had accorded his services as magistrate with equal justice and faithfulness; whose views as president and councillor (from 1868) of the North Ovens Shire were sought and valued; and who had been active in encouraging outdoor amusements, 'more especially that of Racing, where so often we have with pleasure seen your colours in the front'.

After his return Robert made his home in Melbourne and in November 1876 was elected unopposed as member for Eastern Province in the Legislative Council. He 'affected to be a radical' and was minister without office in the Berry [q.v.] government from 5 August 1880 to 9 July 1881 and piloted the reform bill through the Upper House. On the defeat of Berry he resigned from the council to contest West Bourke in the Legislative Assembly. He won the seat of Fitzroy in February 1883 but was defeated in 1889, and represented Toorak from October 1894 to his retirement in September 1897. He was a member of the royal commissions on asylums (1884) and banking laws (1887). He died on 5 September 1900 at Armadale, Victoria, survived by his wife Caroline Esther, née Shadforth, and five daughters.

JOHN, second son of David Reid and his wife Agnes, was born at Inverary Park in 1825 and joined the family partnership in the early 1840s. With Dr George Edward Mackay he built the first steam driven flour-mill in Wangaratta in 1856 and later took up Tabratong on the Bogan River in New South Wales. He married Mary Edith Smallman; they had three sons and two daughters. His home was at St Kilda, Victoria, and he died in Sydney on 1 February 1882 aged 62.

CURTIS ALEXANDER, youngest son of David Reid and his wife Agnes, was born at Inverary Park in 1838 and was in the family partnership. He made wine under the Reidsdale label. A good cricketer, he was the first paid secretary of the Melbourne Cricket Club in 1877-79. He married Sophie Dight. Aged 48, he died in Melbourne on 1 July 1886.

Their sister Agnes Cruickshank married Sir Francis Murphy [q.v.] and died in Melbourne on 27 January 1906 aged 88; and Emma Juana, born at sea in 1822, married A. B. Balcombe [q.v.] and died in Melbourne on 3 June 1907.

A. Joyce, *A homestead history*, G. F. James ed (Melb, 1942); W. A. Bayley, *History of the Farmers and Settlers' Association of N.S.W.* (Syd, 1957); D. M. Whittaker, *Wangaratta* (Melb, 1963); North-Eastern Hist Soc, *Newsletter*, Apr 1968, Aug 1969; *Australasian*, 10 July 1886, 8 Sept 1900, 19 May 1906; *Syd Stock and Station J*, 11 May 1906; *T&CJ*, 16 May 1906; W. J. Griffiths, Surgeon David Reid, R.N., and his descendants in Victoria (Melb, 1951, Gen Soc of Vic); D. Reid, Notes of the early times in Australia . . . by an old pioneer *and* David Reid papers (LaT L).

DAVID MAXWELL WHITTAKER

REID, WALTER BALLANTYNE (1834-1911), merchant, was born on 26 July 1834 at Wilton near Hawick, Roxburghshire, Scotland, son of Walter Reid, mason, and his wife Elizabeth, née Ballantyne. Educated at the village school, he worked in Hawick's leading drapery store and, perhaps drawn by the goldfields, migrated to Melbourne, arriving in the *Hibernia* in October 1852.

Employed at Buckley [q.v.] and Nunn's store, Reid left Melbourne in 1862 attracted by gold finds near Rockhampton, Queensland. By March 1864 he had established his own retail business in East Street, but moved to larger premises in Quay Street in 1868, with wholesale trade in wine, spirits, and general merchandise to supply increasing hotel and station demand. Having consolidated his firm in the conservative British tradition he entered shipping in 1878 by running lighters down the Fitzroy River to unload overseas ships at Port Alma.

Reid's character typified the Scottish virtues: a dutiful justice of the peace, industrious and methodical and generous to the needy. Despite a suggestion of aloofness, until 1883 he remained a fashionably dressed bachelor, attractive to the ladies. While visiting Britain he married on 5 February, in a Roman Catholic church, Janie Evangeline Stewart; they returned to Australia in 1884. He had sold out to McIlwraith, McEacharn & Co. in 1881 for £60,000; the original name was retained and within twenty years the business had become a limited liability company with an annual turnover exceeding £500,000. Ironically, this was the situation when Reid returned to Rockhampton in January 1898 to set up a new business in a futile attempt to recover losses incurred during the economic depression of the 1890s.

While Walter Reid & Co. Ltd entered the twentieth century on a wave of expansion which was to make it one of Australia's leading wholesalers, Reid quietly left Rockhampton, broken in health and spirit, to spend the last three years of his life in the Hospital for the Insane, Gladesville, Sydney. He died on 12 January 1911 and was buried in the Anglican section of Waverley cemetery, survived by two of his four children. A portrait is in the firm's board room at Rockhampton.

Alcazar Press, *Queensland, 1900* (Brisb, nd); J. T. S. Bird, *The early history of Rockhampton* (Rockhampton, 1904); J. G. Pattison, *'Battler's' tales of early Rockhampton* (Melb, 1939); *Centenary review of Walter Reid & Company Limited* (Rockhampton, 1962).

LORNA L. McDONALD

RENARD, JULES (1833-1898), woolbroker and merchant, was born at Verviers, Belgium, son of Clement Renard, woolmerchant, and his wife Marie Josephine, née Lennarz. The family later moved to Antwerp, where the sons were trained for the wool trade. Educated at the Athénée and Ecôle Supérieure de Commerce, Antwerp, Renard won a scholarship enabling him to gain business experience in a foreign country and he went to London.

In 1852 he went to Australia in charge of stud Rambouillet sheep for S. P. Winter [q.v.] of Murndal, near Hamilton, Victoria. He remained some years in the Western District, gaining experience and contributing his technical knowledge of the wool industry. He is reputed to have helped control scab in the area and contracted to build sheep dips. Later he overlanded stock, drove wool teams and was a wool-buyer in Sydney for a short period, before joining Gustave Beckx & Co. in 1862. About 1865 he set up his own business and in 1867 with his brother Arthur formed Renard Bros & Co. in Melbourne, with branches in Antwerp, London, Sydney, Brisbane and Adelaide. They bought wool in Melbourne and Sydney for export and also imported goods. Renard advocated sending Australian wool to the Antwerp sales rather than solely to London. In 1874 his company, with the backing of Winter and other Western District growers, made the first shipment of wool direct to Belgium, opening a new market to Australian wool and general trade.

In 1870-95 Renard was Belgian consul in Melbourne, after which he took over his company's Sydney business, and was granted the title honorary consul for life. His services to Belgium, including regular trade reports to Brussels on Victoria, were recognized by his appointment to chevalier of the Order of Leopold on 4 February 1878 (officier, 1892). A commissioner for the Melbourne International Exhibitions of 1880 and 1888, and for the Bordeaux Wine Exhibition in 1882, Renard also represented the Belgian government when he accompanied Sir Henry Parkes [q.v.] to Belgium that year.

Well above average height, Renard was handsome as a youth but became very heavy in old age. On 22 February 1866 at Richmond, Victoria, he had married Fanny, daughter of William Hardcastle, a wool-merchant and staunch Congregationalist, who had migrated from Bradford, Yorkshire. She died of cancer on 25 November 1897; her long illness had signalled Renard's gradual retirement from public and business life and absorption in literature and religion, but he remained a member of the Chamber of Commerce and read a prescient paper on 'Long Distance Telephony' to the conference of Australasian Chambers of Commerce in Sydney in May. He died of pneumonia, aged 65, on 27 August 1898 at Stavelot, Glebe Point; although apparently Catholic by birth, he was buried with his wife in the Congregational section of the Waverley cemetery. Seven children survived them. All three sons, educated in Melbourne and Belgium, were trained for the wool trade and the eldest, Clement William, Melbourne partner of a Bremen-based wool firm, was appointed permanent acting consul on 4 January 1893.

W. A. Brodribb, Results of inquiries . . . in regard to the wool trade (Melb, 1875); Renard Bros & Co., Antwerp versus London as a market for Australian wool (Melb, 1875); J. Smith (ed), Cyclopedia of Victoria, 1 (Melb, 1903); A. Barnard, The Australian wool market, 1840-1900 (Melb, 1958); Melb C. of E. Grammar School, Liber Melburniensis, 4th ed (Melb, 1965); Hamilton Spectator, 16, 26 Sept 1874; Winter-Cooke papers (some copies, LaT L); ML printed cat under Renard; private information from Belgian Embassy, Canberra, and Renard family.   GILLIAN MARSDEN

RENWICK, SIR ARTHUR (1837-1908), physician, philanthropist and politician, was born on 30 May 1837 at Glasgow, Scotland, son of George Renwick, bricklayer, and his wife Christina, née Condie. On 21 July 1841 he reached Sydney with his parents, bounty immigrants, in the Helen. Educated at the Redfern Grammar School, in 1853 he matriculated at the University of Sydney (B.A., 1857). He studied medicine at the University of Edinburgh (M.B., 1860; M.D., 1861) and became a fellow of the Royal College of Surgeons, Edinburgh. After further research courses in Glasgow, London and Paris, in 1862 he returned to Sydney and lived at Redfern. On 26 March 1868 he married Elizabeth, daughter of Rev. John Saunders [q.v.], at the Redfern Congregational Church in the presence of George Allen and John Fairfax [qq.v.].

Renwick soon established a growing practice and was skilled in forensic surgery. In 1862-77 he was visiting medical officer for the Benevolent Society of New South Wales, in 1866-75 an honorary physician at the Sydney Infirmary and Dispensary, medical officer for the Australian Union Benefit Society and examiner in medicine of the University of Sydney. He twice sought nomination to the Medical Board and in July 1873 told Henry Parkes [q.v.] 'I do not know any other medical gentleman who has superior claims'. Appointed to it on 20 August he later became president.

In the 1870s Renwick became a director and honorary consulting physician at the Sydney Infirmary and Dispensary and honorary surgeon to the New South Wales Institution for the Deaf and Dumb and the Blind, and president in the 1880s. In 1878 he succeeded Deas Thomson [q.v.] as president of both the Infirmary and the Benevolent Society. In the 1880s he was the first president of the New South Wales branch of the British Medical Association. In the 1890s he was also a director of the Royal Prince Alfred Hospital, a trustee of the Carrington Centennial Hospital for Convalescents and an honorary physician to the Hospital for Sick Children and the Thirlmere Home for Consumptives.

Elected to the Senate of the University of Sydney in 1877, Renwick was defeated by Edmund Barton for the university seat in the Legislative Assembly in August 1879; but in December, with the support of the Orange and temperance movements, he won East Sydney at a by-election and held it till 1882. An able debater, in 1881-83 he was secretary for mines in the Parkes-Robertson [q.v.] ministry and carried the Ad eundem Degrees Act, an act establishing an anatomy school in the university and the Sydney Hospital Incorporation Act. In an abusive and vain campaign against Henry Copeland [q.v.] in East Sydney in 1883, Renwick disclosed that he had strongly opposed Robertson's land bill in cabinet but had had to yield to his colleagues. His relationship with Parkes deteriorated further in June 1883 when he threatened to sue Parkes for the recovery of £500. In 1885-87 he represented Redfern and was minister of public instruction under Sir Patrick Jennings [q.v.] in 1886-87. On 30 December he was appointed to the Legislative Council. A contemporary described him as 'a very ambitious little gentleman' with 'an enlarged idea of his own political worth'. In November 1889 he refused Parkes's offer of the vice-presidency of the Executive Council.

Renwick was absorbed by his charitable works. An able and efficient administrator, he set the pace in improving conditions at the Benevolent Asylum, especially in standards of care for women and children, and worked for a separate lying-in hospital. In 1881-1901 Renwick was president of the State Children's Relief Department; he established the boarding-out system for orphans and greatly extended the department's legal powers of guardianship of state children. He supervised the planning and erection of the Deaf and Dumb and the Blind Institution's building, Darlington, the main front blocks of Sydney Hospital, the Royal Hospital for Women, Paddington, and State Children's Relief Department's farm homes at Mittagong. In 1896 Renwick drew up the manifesto of the Old-Age Pensions League and became its president. In evidence to a Legislative Assembly select committee he hoped old-age pensions would relieve overcrowding in the Benevolent Asylum.

Renwick remained on the Senate of the University of Sydney until 1908 and was vice-chancellor in 1889-91, 1900-02 and 1906-08 and several times acting dean of the faculty of medicine. In 1877 he had given £1000 for a scholarship in natural science 'with especial reference to Comparative Anatomy' and told the chancellor of his great 'gratification in being permitted to be the first graduate of the University to give sensible expression to the gratitude I feel for the invaluable benefit conferred on me when a humble student'. He also donated the west window of the hall in the Medical School building.

Renwick was a New South Wales commissioner for the Melbourne International Exhibition in 1880, a vice-president of the commission for the Amsterdam Exhibiton in 1883, vice-president and later president of the commission for the Adelaide Jubilee International Exhibition in 1887 and a New South Wales representative commissioner at the World's Columbian Exposition, Chicago, in 1893. In 1897 he failed to be elected to the Australasian Federal Convention.

Associated with various commercial enterprises Renwick was a director and chairman of the Australian Widows' Fund, Mutual Life Assurance Society and the Industrial Building Society. He reputedly amassed a large fortune only to suffer severe losses from mining ventures. Knighted in 1894, he died at his home at Burwood on 23 November 1908 of heart disease and was buried in the Congregational section of Rookwood cemetery. He was survived by his wife, five sons and a daughter to whom he left an estate sworn for probate at £7711.

Lady Renwick was an energetic charity worker and helped her husband in the State Children's Relief Department. She was president of the Young Women's Christian Association and the New South Wales Bush Missionary Society and connected with the National Council of Women of New South Wales, the Sydney Ladies' Sanitary Association, the Australian Trained Nurses Association and the Women's Suffrage League of New South Wales. She died on 17 March 1918.

A bust of Sir Arthur Renwick by Simonetti [q.v.] is owned by the University of Sydney.

Ex-M.L.A., *Our present parliament, what it is worth* (Syd, c1886); *Cyclopedia of N.S.W.* (Syd, 1907); V&P (LA NSW), 1858, 2, 435, 1873-74, 6, *passim*, 1881, 3, 1001, 4, 1033, 1875-76, 6, 916, 1896, 5, 20; *A'sian Medical Gazette*, 21 Dec 1908; *Bulletin*, 3 July 1880; *T&CJ*, 22 Oct 1881, 25 Nov 1908; *Freeman's J* (Syd), 2 Dec 1882; *SMH*, 20, 24 Jan 1883, 24 Nov 1908; *Pastoral Review*, 15 Feb 1894, supp 10; B. Dickey, Charity in New South Wales, 1850-1914 (Ph.D. thesis, ANU, 1966); Parkes letters (ML); Univ Syd Archives.

MARTHA RUTLEDGE

REYMOND, JOSEPH BERNARD (1834-1918), miller and politician, was born on 3 May 1834 in the village of Chabaud, near Orcières, France, son of Etienne Bernard Reymond, farmer, and his wife Elizabeth Charrière, née Rond. After graduating bachelor of letters, in 1854 he became a professor at the College of Gap and taught English. In 1856 he met Augustus Nicolas, recently returned from the Californian and Victorian goldfields with stories of new lands and gold that made Reymond dissatisfied. In October 1856 he took a year's leave and with Nicolas went to Paris and London; in the *Swiftsure* they reached Melbourne early in March 1857. They had brought some general goods and made a half-hearted attempt to rent a shop, but the lure of the goldfields was too strong.

In 1857-62 they prospected at Emu Flat, Ararat, Great Western, Pleasant Creek (Stawell), Ballarat and at Chiltern where

Reymond met Margaret Kerr and married her at Wahgunyah on 13 August 1861. When the Lachlan gold rush started they sold their payable claim and in June 1862 went to Forbes where they built a substantial sawmill and set up in partnership as sawmillers and general merchants. Soon the population fell from some 30,000 to about 500 and they made machines to cut shingles and felloes for markets in Orange and Bathurst. About 1865, with the rediscovery of gold at Forbes, they successfully grew hay and vegetables.

In 1866 Reymond took up a 320-acre selection on the Lachlan River near Forbes, which he named Champsaur. He moved his family there and in 1866-70 worked it of an evening after spending the day at the sawmill. Experiments in wheat-growing in 1866 decided Reymond and Nicolas to build a flour-mill as the nearest was eighty miles away at Orange; it was completed in 1873 and Reymond installed the first reticulated water system in Forbes. Trade became slack again, so they turned to building bridges, gaols and police barracks and worked as farmers, sawyers, engineers, contractors, millers, book-keepers, engine drivers, fruitgrowers and vignerons. By 1875 they had established a second flour-mill and sawmill at Condobolin later taken over by Nicolas.

Reymond established a vineyard and a very large orchard at Champsaur. In 1886 he built a substantial wooden cellar and began the commercial production of wine that has continued to the present day. In its heyday the vineyard produced between 60,000 and 80,000 gallons a year. In 1895 Reymond wrote an article in *Agricultural Gazette of New South Wales* (July-December) on phylloxera. In 1875-84 he was an alderman of the Forbes Municipal Council and was mayor in 1883-84; he had many trees planted in the town and initiated the laying out of the botanical gardens. He was largely responsible for the town's first water supply when a weir across the Lachlan River was built for £117 in 1884. In June 1901 his partnership with Nicolas was dissolved; he carried on alone until J. B. Reymond and Sons Pty Ltd was incorporated in September 1909.

In 1895-1904 Reymond represented Ashburnham in the Legislative Assembly as an independent and was the only Frenchman elected to the New South Wales parliament. In 1900 he led a deputation to Sydney that resulted in the building of Forbes Hospital of which he was one of the three original trustees. He died on 20 September 1918 at his home, The Olives, South Forbes, and was buried in the Catholic cemetery. He was survived by four daughters and three sons. His second son, Ralph Etienne

Bernard, became a solicitor in 1900, was mayor of Forbes in 1904-05 and 1906-07 and served on many local organizations.

Forbes Municipal Council, *Centenary . . . 1870-1970* (Forbes, 1970); Country Promotion League, 'Forbes, N.S.W.', *Immigration and land settlement*, no 8 (Syd, 1922); *Forbes Times*, 7 Aug 1875, 9 Mar 1901; *Sydney Mail*, 16 Jan 1897; *SMH*, 23 Sept 1918; Illustrated history of Forbes, 1915 (ML); Nicolas and Reymond papers, 1866-1893 (ML); J. B. Reymond diaries, 1893-1915 (ML); letters, letter-books and papers (held by authors).   M. B. REYMOND
                       N. REYMOND

REYNELL, JOHN (1809-1873), pastoralist and vigneron, was born on 9 February 1809 at Ilfracombe, Devon, England, son of Henry Reynell and his wife Lydia, née Fagg. At 16 he went to Egypt, returned to England four years later, then spent some time trading in wheat and other cargo in America and Europe, and later went back to Egypt. In October 1838 he arrived in Adelaide in the *Surrey*, and in December took up Reynella Farm where he grew wheat and potatoes and bred sheep and cattle. On 31 January 1839 he married Mary Anne (d. 1867), daughter of Francis Lucas of Ireland. That year he was one of fifty settlers who formed the Agricultural and Horticultural Society of South Australia. Although scab was a constant worry his pastoral pursuits flourished; he introduced Southdown and Saxon rams from Van Diemen's Land, and in 1842 was shearing 4000 sheep.

Observations in Italy and southern France convinced Reynell that the vine, olive and fig could be cultivated in South Australia; in 1841 he planted the first vineyard with 500 cuttings from Tasmania, and made wine in 1843. That year he was declared bankrupt when his pastoral enterprises collapsed during an economic recession. He lost £4000 but was generously treated by his creditors and received a loan from his brother Henry in Calcutta.

In 1844 Reynell planted half an acre with cuttings from G. A. Anstey [q.v. Thomas Anstey], next year four and a quarter acres with shiraz and grenache cuttings from (Sir) William Macarthur [q.v.] and in 1847-48 ten acres with cuttings from E. J. Peake of Clarendon. He pioneered the export of claret and burgundy to New Zealand. Appointed a justice of the peace in 1850, in 1852 he went to the Victorian diggings and won a little gold; in 1854 he sold about forty acres of Reynella Farm for the township of Reynella with ninety-four allotments bringing him nearly £3000. He died on 15 June

1873 survived by a son and two daughters and left an estate of £4000.

His son WALTER (1846-1919) was born on 27 March 1846 at Reynella Farm. Educated at the Collegiate School of St Peter, he helped his father develop the vineyards. At 21 he spent two years on Beltana station working for (Sir) Thomas Elder [q.v.]. He was later part-owner of Tolarno station on the Darling, and for many years ran a land agency business in Adelaide. On 16 May 1877 at Adelaide, he married Emily, daughter of William Bakewell, a lawyer of Pavneham. In 1883 he became manager of Elder Smith [q.v. R. Barr Smith] & Co., supervising the stock business of the firm and its numerous branches. In 1910 he retired to Reynella and with his son Carew he tended the vineyards. He was a member of the Pastoralists' Association of South Australia and West Darling, the South Australian Vinegrowers' Association, and director of Elder Smith & Co. and of the South Australian Brewing Co. He died on 8 April 1919 at Reynella, survived by one of his two sons and three daughters. He left an estate of £28,000.

H. T. Burgess (ed), *Cyclopedia of South Australia*, 1 (Adel, 1908); R. Cockburn, *Pastoral pioneers of South Australia*, 2 (Adel, 1927); H. M. Martin, 'History of viticulture in South Australia', *Aust Brewing and Wine J*, 20 Aug 1923 *and* D2847 (SAA); *Register* (Adel), 1 Apr 1919; Reynell family letters 1841-45 (NL) *and* papers (SAA).   DIRK VAN DISSEL

REYNOLDS, CHRISTOPHER AUGUSTINE (1834-1893), Catholic archbishop, was born on 11 July 1834 in Dublin, son of Patrick Reynolds and his wife Elizabeth, née Bourke. Educated by the Carmelites at Clondalkin, Dublin, he later came under the influence of the Benedictines when he volunteered for the Northern Territory mission of Bishop Salvado [q.v.], and was sent to Subiaco near Rome to train for the priesthood. He left after three years and went to Swan River with Bishop Serra [q.v.] to continue his training at New Norcia, arriving at Fremantle in May 1855. Probably because of poor health, he left the Benedictines and in January 1857 went to South Australia; completing his training under the Jesuits at Sevenhill, he was ordained in April 1860 by Bishop Geoghegan [q.v.]. He was parish priest at Wallaroo (where he built the church at Kadina), Morphett Vale and Gawler. When Bishop Sheil [q.v.] died in March 1872, Reynolds was appointed administrator of the diocese of Adelaide; on 2 November 1873 in Adelaide he was consecrated bishop by Archbishop Polding [q.v.].

Reynolds had a large diocese and in 1872-80 travelled over 52,000 miles in South Australia. The opening up of new agricultural districts, an increase in Irish migrants and diocesan debts had produced a grave shortage of clergy. But his most urgent problem was conflicts between and within the clergy and laity over education, especially the role to be played by the Sisters of St Joseph. He supported the Sisters, reopened schools closed by Sheil and, though opposed by the Bishops Quinn [qq.v.], helped the Superior, Mother Mary McKillop [q.v.], secure Rome's approval for autonomy for her Sisterhood.

Reynolds was not a good administrator and his strenous efforts to extend Catholic education after the Education Act of 1875 incurred alarming debts. In 1880-81 he visited Rome. On his return, increasingly concerned with finances, disturbed at the prospect of losing St Joseph nuns and, to some extent misled by jealousy and intrigue, he dramatically reversed his policy towards the Sisterhood and on 14 November 1883 relieved Mother Mary of her duties as Mother Superior. Though the Plenary Council of the Bishops of Australasia, held in Sydney in 1885, supported him, in 1888 Leo XIII decreed a central government for the Sisterhood, to be located in Sydney. The council requested that Adelaide be raised to an archiepiscopal and metropolitan see and on 11 September 1887 Reynolds was invested archbishop by Cardinal Moran.

His health was never robust and after a two-year illness he died on 12 June 1893 in Adelaide, where he was buried. Although he was austere and hard-working, he left his successor church debts of over £56,000. A particularly fine preacher, Reynolds was widely respected for his missionary zeal and for an ecumenical spirit unusual for his time.

P. F. Moran, *History of the Catholic Church in Australasia* (Syd, 1895); O. Thorpe, *Mary McKillop* (Lond, 1957); Dom Ximenes, 'Notes', *A'sian Catholic Record*, 33 (1956), p 70; *Freeman's J* (Syd), 15 Nov 1873, 17 June 1893; *Observer* (Adel), 17 June 1893; Roman Catholic Archives (Syd).   IAN J. BICKERTON

REYNOLDS, THOMAS (1818-1875), politician, was born in England in 1818. Brought up by his uncle as a grocer in London, he was invited to South Australia in 1840 by his brother who had a large draper's shop in Hindley Street, Adelaide. With his brother dead when he arrived, he opened a grocery and ran it for many years with much success, though he left it temporarily for the gold diggings in

Victoria in 1851. He later retired and pioneered the jam-making industry in South Australia. Among the first to attempt large-scale fruit drying, he had at Wattleville one of the earliest sultana plantations.

An active Wesleyan worker and preacher both in London and Adelaide, Reynolds withdrew in 1847 opposing state aid. He later became a Congregationalist, was an active member of the Union Committee and as a lay preacher often rode great distances to conduct services. Long associated with temperance societies, he was known as 'Teapot Tommy'.

In 1854 Reynolds became an alderman in the Adelaide City Council. Stung by Lieut-Governor Robe's attitude towards an anti-state aid deputation, he plunged into political life and was elected for West Torrens to the Legislative Council in July 1854. A prominent reformer, he sought an elective Upper House and manhood suffrage in a liberal constitution. He attacked the abused system of open elections, and was one of those responsible for the vote by secret ballot in South Australia. With responsible government, Reynolds held Sturt in the House of Assembly in 1857-60 and was commissioner of public works in Hanson's [q.v.] cabinet in 1857-58. He resigned because of the position occupied by the premier's brother on the Railways Board.

In parliament Reynolds developed as a financial expert and on 2 May 1860 his no-confidence motion brought down Hanson's government. A week later, as member for the City of Adelaide, he formed a ministry as treasurer, and announced a policy of retrenchment. Next year he resigned but was commissioned to form another cabinet which remained in office till October 1861. His government's troubled career included difficulties over Judge Boothby's [q.v.] questioning of certain laws passed by the South Australian parliament. In 1861-62 Reynolds was treasurer for four months in the second Waterhouse [q.v.] ministry. Charged with having misused his power as a minister he resigned from the government and from parliament. The matter came before the Supreme Court in a libel action. His friends believed he vindicated himself, and in May 1862 his constituency returned him unopposed. He was treasurer in several ministries in 1865-68 and commissioner of crown lands in 1872-73. He represented East Adelaide in 1864-70 and Encounter Bay in 1871-73.

Early in 1873 Reynolds visited Darwin and witnessed the confusion caused by the gold rush. He tried to restore order, and returned to Adelaide where he reported favourably on the mineral resources of the north. Disagreeing with the resumption of free immigration, he resigned from parliament on 28 August 1873, and later settled in Darwin with his wife Anne, née Litchfield, whose three brothers had been early settlers in South Australia. Unsuccessful there, he was returning to Adelaide in the *Gothenburg* when it was wrecked on the Barrier Reef on 25 February 1875 and he and his wife were drowned; they were survived by two sons.

Reynolds was shrewd in business and for nearly twenty years was a director of the South Australian Insurance Co., but his public career impeded his private profession. He was not a great lawmaker but his influence was continually felt in the general course of legislation. Few men laboured more earnestly or with greater self-sacrifice for South Australia. Reynolds Range in the Northern Territory was named after him.

E. Ward, *The vineyards and orchards of South Australia* (Adel, 1862); J. Blacket, *History of South Australia*, 2nd ed (Adel, 1911); F. W. Cox and L. Robjohns, *Three-quarters of a century* (Adel, 1912); G. D. Combe, *Responsible government in South Australia* (Adel, 1957); *Register* (Adel), 8 Mar 1875.

GORDON D. COMBE

RICHARDS, THOMAS (1800-1877), author, was baptized on 10 July 1800 at Dolgellau, Merioneth, North Wales, son of Thomas Richards (d. 1808), attorney, and his wife Elizabeth. Educated at Christ's Hospital, London, in 1809-15, he was then apprenticed to a medical practitioner and attended clinics at St Bartholomew's Hospital. Granted the licentiate of the Society of Apothecaries in 1823, for the next nine years Richards probably practised both medicine and freelance journalism. He claimed to have contributed to the *Monthly Magazine and British Register* and other literary journals.

In April 1832 with his wife Hannah Elsemere, née Adams, and infant son, he sailed from London in the *Princess Royal* as ship's surgeon; he reached Hobart Town in October to encounter criticism about the control exercised over the free female migrants, nearly 200, on board. He set up as a surgeon at Elizabeth Town (New Norfolk). Richards edited for a while and contributed to Henry Melville's [q.v.] *Hobart Town Magazine* from its appearance in March 1833 to its demise in August 1834. Moving to Hobart about July 1833 he succeeded Henry Savery [q.v.] as editor of the *Tasmanian* after Savery had been wrongfully convicted of libel for an article that Richards admitted writing. In October Richards quarrelled with Melville and resigned.

Although he remained on the list of medical practitioners until 1836, Richards was clerk of the Town Surveyor's Department from 1834 to 1837 when he became involved in a dispute between R. W. F. L. Murray [q.v.], co-proprietor of the *Tasmanian*, and Alexander Murray, the town surveyor. Assistant editor of the *Hobart Town Courier* in 1837, for the next ten years he worked as a senior journalist for J. C. Macdougall's [q.v.] *Colonial Times*. In 1847-48 he visited England. In 1852 he was again listed as a doctor, but returned to journalism late in life as reporter and reader for the Hobart *Mercury*, remaining there till his death.

The greater part of Richards's identifiable literary work was published in the *Hobart Town Magazine*; at least half of its contents were his poems, essays, reviews, sketches and short stories. His verse is slight in both quantity and quality, introspective and sentimental pieces, disciplined but uninspired, strongly influenced by the Wordsworthian school of nature poets. His prose was much more significant. He wrote with good control of vocabulary, clarity of expression and a nice feeling for prose rhythms. He drew on his medical experiences and training, his contact with local politics and his knowledge of the Tasmanian countryside.

Richards was one of the first and the most substantial of early colonial short story writers, at a time when the literary output from Sydney was slight. His better stories and many that are incomplete are set in his well-remembered native Wales. His importance is as an enthusiastic pioneer of what was to develop into a distinctive Australian literature.

Survived by his wife, a son and three daughters he died at Portsea Place, Hobart, on 18 July 1877.

E. M. Miller, *Pressmen and governors* (Syd, 1952), and for bibliog.   J. C. HORNER

RICHARDS, THOMAS (1831-1898), government printer, was born on 21 December 1831 in Pitt Street, Sydney, son of James Richards, builder, and his wife Mary, née O'Brien. He was baptized a Catholic. His parents died in his infancy and he was reared by his aunt, the daughter of a sergeant-major in the First Fleet, and educated at Ebenezer on the Hawkesbury River. Having answered an advertisement 'for an intelligent youth', on 1 January 1845 he was engaged as an apprentice in the Government Printing Office, where he advanced as clerk, proof-reader, compositor, pressman, overseer and, in 1854, superintendent. In June 1859 he became government printer and inspector of stamps at a

salary of £500, which had been reduced from his predecessor's £850, but was raised to £600 in 1863; he had a staff of seventy. As he lacked 'London experience' his appointment was unpopular. From 1 July 1879 he was also registrar of copyright.

During Richards's innovative administration, with increasing volume of work, the office expanded its functions and techniques. In 1863 he introduced photolithography and, after he had observed plant in Victoria in 1864, he added stereotyping and electro-typing. In 1868 following the establishment of extra branches a new fast process of photo-lithography was invented by John Sharkey whose experiments were encouraged and assisted by Richards. The *Sydney Morning Herald* praised the 'gems of photo-lithographic art' the Printing Office displayed at the 1870 Intercolonial Exhibition at Sydney. Later Richards initiated helio-type or photomechanical printing, introduced a perforating machine and invented a method of drying stamps with heat from gas. He devised an arithmotype bars system for numbering debentures which was adopted in all the colonies and England; he alleged the Bank of England took the patent without acknowledgment.

Frequently working long hours, Richards was criticized by some politicians for his administration and his publication of documents of allegedly 'limited public interest'. He defended himself adequately before the 1870 select committee on the Government Printing Office, resisting suggestions of reductions in salaries and praising his men for the 'finest examples of the modern technique of photo-lithography' seen in the colonies; and he admitted ambitions to produce an Australian geography and natural history, a year-book and dictionary of names for New South Wales. Looking back in 1891 he wrote, 'I had opposed to me a truculent minister, a truculent under-secretary and a truculent newspaper proprietor . . . I beat them but came out of the fray wounded in mind body and estate'. He also had trouble with trade unions in difficult industrial times for heads of government departments and in 1875 antagonized the Trades and Labor Council by threatening 'to close the Office against all union men'.

In 1877 Richards represented the government on an English committee to celebrate the quatercentenary of Caxton's introduction of printing. With twelve months' leave he also studied advanced methods and bought new machinery. At the 1878 Paris Universal Exhibition he won a silver and two bronze medals and at the 1880 Melbourne International Exhibition he won five high diplomas for printing, bookbinding and photography. The 1883 Amsterdam Exhibition awarded him a gold and a silver medal, and the Printing Office was commended at other important exhibitions from 1862 to 1886. In 1882 Richards compiled, edited and printed the highly regarded *New South Wales in 1881*, which was translated into French; next year the office produced *An Epitome of the Official History of New South Wales*.

On 23 April 1861 Richards had joined the Volunteer Rifles as a second lieutenant. A good shot and member of the New South Wales Rifle Association, in 1885 he became lieut-colonel of the first regiment, Volunteer Infantry; he resigned next year. In November 1886, because of rapidly failing eyesight, Richards retired as government printer on a pension of £480; he left a staff of 400 and an office with sixty-one new departments. On 31 August 1898 he died at Manly and was buried in the Anglican cemetery there. On 29 January 1865, with Anglican rites, he had married Zara Bell, by whom he had three daughters and two sons who survived him.

V&P (LA NSW), 1870-71, 2, 1137, 1213, 1879-80, 2, 740, 4, 1007, 1881, 3, 981, 1883-84, 11, 615; A'sian Typographical J, Dec 1876, Sept 1898; SMH, 8, 10, 15, 26 Nov 1886; Daily Telegraph (Syd), 1 Sept 1898; Sydney Mail, 10 Sept 1898; Thomas Richards papers and MS cat (ML); Trades and Labor Council minutes 1875 (ML); Govt Printing Office papers, 1/234-36, 1/269 (NSWA).   SUZANNE EDGAR

RICHARDSON, JOHN (1810-1888), storekeeper and politician, was born at Freuchie Manse, Fifeshire, Scotland, eldest son of Rev. John Richardson, United Presbyterian minister, and his wife Grace, née Pratt. Educated at parish schools in Freuchie and Pitlessie and at Cupar Academy, at 16 he was apprenticed to a linen draper in Kirkcaldy and from 1835 worked in London. In April 1837 he reached Sydney in the *Caroline*; he worked with R. Bourne & Co. for four years.

About 1842 he set up as a store-keeper in Brisbane and was one of the first to import goods direct from England. He moved between Sydney and Brisbane and on 10 June 1847 at the Scots Church, Sydney, married Janet, sister of P. N. Russell [q.v.]. About 1850 Richardson built a wharf and warehouse in Brisbane and confined himself to a wholesale commission and shipping agency. In January at a meeting in Ipswich he opposed 'cheap labour' whether convict or coolie. He was an agent for some of Rev. J. D. Lang's [q.v.] migrant ships, defended him against attacks in the press and worked with him for the separation of Queensland.

In 1851 he was appointed to the Steam Vessels Inspection Board, Moreton Bay, and in September was elected to the New South Wales Legislative Council for the County of Stanley. A radical, he supported J. B. Darvall [q.v.] and voted against the second reading of W. C. Wentworth's [q.v.] Constitution bill. In July 1854 he vacated his seat to visit Britain; on his return in 1855 he won a by-election for Stanley Boroughs and in 1856-59 represented it in the new Legislative Assembly. In June 1859 he won Brisbane but ceased to sit when Queensland was separated in December.

In 1857-58 Richardson, with H. W. Coxen [q.v.], took up three runs on the Darling Downs and six in the Maranoa District which they added to before their partnership was dissolved in 1863. He held these runs alone until Shepherd Smith [q.v.] joined him in 1866. In 1865 he took up four runs in Leichhardt and in 1866 two in South Kennedy. Richardson and Smith sold most of their runs in 1872 and two more in 1875-76, but they held Gideon Land on the Darling Downs until 1883. In 1871-74 he sold his Leichhardt runs but in 1878-82 with George Loder held nine in the Warrego District and one on his own in Mitchell. In 1882 he added two more in Mitchell but soon sold them. Reputedly he lost heavily on these speculations.

Soon after his return from England in 1868 Richardson was appointed to the Legislative Council by James Martin [q.v.] and sat until 1887. In 1869 he was auditor of the Bank of New South Wales; a magistrate, he was also a councillor of St Andrew's College, University of Sydney, and a committee-man of the Home Visiting and Relief Society. In 1872 he bought John Moore's general store in Armidale and, as John Richardson & Co., he and his sons built up a flourishing business. As 'Universal Providers' it became one of the biggest firms outside Sydney. They also ran a flour-mill and a furniture and upholstery factory.

Survived by his wife, five sons and two daughters, Richardson died in his house Mavorna, Armidale, on 22 December 1888 and was buried in the Anglican cemetery, Armidale. His estate was valued for probate at almost £30,000.

Armidale Citizens' C'tte, Jubilee souvenir of the Municipality of Armidale (Armidale, 1913); Armidale; diamond jubilee souvenir, 1863-1923 (Armidale, 1923); SMH, 19 Dec 1849, 17, 31 Jan 1850; Empire (Syd), 2 Apr 1856; Bulletin, 5 Nov 1881; press cuttings on cricket (ML); MS cat (ML).   MARTHA RUTLEDGE

RICHARDSON, JOHN SOAME (1836-1896), soldier, was born on 16 March 1836 at

Heydon, Norfolk, England, son of John Richardson, estate manager, and his wife Eleanor, née Soame. Educated at Rugby School, he became an ensign in the 72nd Highlanders in November 1854 and was commissioned lieutenant in November 1855. In the Crimea, he was at the siege and fall of Sebastopol and received the Crimean Medal and Clasp.

Richardson joined the 12th Regiment in England and came to Australia in 1858 in the *Saldanha*. In June 1860 he was appointed adjutant and the same year went to New Zealand where he served in the Taranaki and Waikato campaigns of the Maori wars. Promoted captain in July 1863, he left the imperial service in September 1864 and returned to New South Wales. Having gained his majority, he became inspecting field officer of the Volunteer Forces on 17 February 1865 with the rank of lieut-colonel at a salary of £500. A thorough professional, he several times reorganized the forces and initiated the system of part-paid volunteers which helped achieve efficiency within the shortcomings of the units. He established the reserve rifle companies, but his plans were frustrated as the necessary finance and ministerial sanctions were withheld. After the withdrawal of the British troops in 1870, Richardson was appointed president of the new commission on defence from foreign aggression and of the board for inspecting and maintaining the supply of colonial warlike stores. On 1 August 1871 he became commandant of the permanent and volunteer military forces of New South Wales and was promoted to colonel on 26 August 1876. In 1881 he was a member of the royal commission on military defences; he defended the payment of volunteers and urged the formation of a permanent Australia-wide defence reserve. In France in 1882 despite poor health he inspected the battlefields of the Franco-Prussian war in order to gain an appreciation of changes in warfare.

On 11 February 1885, partly at the instigation of Sir Edward Strickland, W. B. Dalley [qq.v.] offered a New South Wales contingent to Britain for the Sudan campaign. Richardson was appointed to command Australia's first expeditionary force of 750 men. They left Sydney in the two troopships *Australasian* and *Iberia* amid great enthusiasm on 3 March and reached Suakin on the 29th, where they were honoured by being brigaded next to the Guards. The contingent saw little action and was affected by fever, but took part in the advance on Tamai and Richardson was mentioned in dispatches. They returned to Sydney on 23 June.

On 15 August 1885 Richardson was raised to major-general; he was made C.B. and was awarded the Sudan Medal and Khedive

Star. On 3 January 1889 in his inaugural address to the United Service Institution, founded for the higher education of officers, he said 'we must ... demonstrate that we ... are not unmindful or careless of the sacred trust confided to us by New South Wales as her defenders, that we do not wear her uniform for purposes of mere display, but that we rather attach a deeper, more patriotic value to the commissions we have the honor to hold'. However, Richardson had to contend with many problems including failing health, the government's indifference to his proposed reforms, and the enmity of Colonel C. F. Roberts [q.v.]. Amiable and kind-hearted, he was a committee-man of the Union Club and the Australian Jockey Club.

Richardson retired on 9 December 1892 and after some time in a private mental hospital was admitted to the Hospital for the Insane, Callan Park, on 20 May 1894, where he died on 9 June 1896; he was survived by his wife Jeannie Strachan, née Dickson (d. 1935), whom he had married in Sydney on 14 May 1862, and by their two sons and two daughters. Probate of his estate was sworn at £8233. His burial in the Waverley cemetery with full military honours not only indicated the deep respect accorded him at the time, but also symbolized his great contribution to the founding of the Australian military tradition.

V&P (LA NSW), 1872-73, 1, 1355, 1877-78, 3, 307, 1880-81, 1, 325, 1882, 4, 29, 1883-84, 1, 177, 587, 6, 328, 1887 (2nd S), 1, 162; *Bulletin*, 18 Feb 1882; *ISN*, 14 Mar 1885; *SMH*, 10 June 1896; *T&CJ*, 20 June 1896; Parkes letters (ML); CO 201/603/417, 515, 604/347, 369.

GREGORY J. PEMBERTON

RICHMOND, JAMES (1834-1923), sheepbreeder, was born on 1 November 1834 at Southdean, near Jedburgh, County Roxburgh, Scotland, son of Rev. John Richmond, Presbyterian minister, and his wife Catherine, née Mitchell. He was educated at Madras College, St Andrews, and entered United College, University of St Andrews in 1849. Missing out on a cadetship in the Indian army he decided to take up sheep-farming in Australia and on 17 December 1851 sailed for Melbourne in the *Wellington* which ran aground entering Port Adelaide. He worked for A. Scott on Mount Buninyong in the Portland Bay District and Warracknabeal in the Wimmera, and then became a partner of William Halliday [q.v.] in several stations.

In 1860 Richmond visited Scotland where on 3 September 1862 he married Margaret Hunter (d. 1877), who bore him a son and two daughters. After his return in 1863 he built a house, Southdean, in Toorak, Melbourne. He was a member of the Melbourne Club and the Australian and Union clubs in Sydney. By the mid-1860s he owned two runs, Coreen and Pimpana, near Corowa, New South Wales, and found that big, plain-bodied, medium-woolled merinos were the best paying and hardiest. He was a sheep director for Corowa in the 1870s.

In 1873 he bought Haddon Rig, 271,000 acres on the Macquarie River near Warren devoid of improvements. Between visits to England in 1875, 1877 and 1878 he built a 66-stand woolshed, fenced the property, and put in many tanks and dams before he stocked it with sheep. In 1876 he began to convert it to freehold. In 1882, planning to breed his own rams, he founded a stud with 30 Peppin [q.v.] Rambouillet merino rams and 1900 aged ewes bought from Austin [q.v.] and Millear at Wanganella. He later paid high prices for another 8 rams and 2500 stud ewes from the same stud and in 1884 paid 410 guineas for the champion Wool King. He avoided the popular Vermont strain. From the 1880s he also owned Gingie with E. Scott. Although Richmond never lived at Haddon Rig, visiting it only for classing and shearing, he chose capable managers; later the stud became famous. Richmond exported some frozen meat and suggested in 1881 that the company should set up in London its own shops, with a cold store, 'for the sale of Australian frozen meat only'.

A member of the New South Wales Commercial, Pastoral and Agricultural Association, Richmond was an enthusiastic supporter of the Pastoralists' Union, and a member of the Pastoralists' Association of Victoria and Southern Riverina which he represented on the Pastoralists' Federal Council of Australia. He opposed the 1890 shearing strike and refused to shear on union terms. Despite a guard of 30 policemen at the homestead the Haddon Rig woolshed was burnt with some 2000 ewes. Richmond brought shearers from New Zealand to complete shearing. In 1910 Richmond was deeply satisfied when Sir Samuel McCaughey [q.v.] bought all the sheep Haddon Rig could sell him. In September 1916 he sold Haddon Rig to F. S. Falkiner's [q.v.] son; Gingie was sold at the same time.

Visiting England again in 1886-87, Richmond returned there to live in 1893 and came to Australia for the last time in 1895. An elder of St Columba's Church, London, he rented Monzie Castle, Perthshire, Scotland, where he indulged his love of shooting. About 1918 he bought Kincairney House, Perthshire, where he did much for the Red Cross and nursing. He died there on 6 August 1923 and was buried at Caputh. He was survived by his second wife Mary, née Leslie, whom he had married on 17 June 1880, one of their two sons and their four daughters. Richmond's third son was killed in action in World War I and a grandson at Gallipoli. His second son George bought Mogila, Goodooga, New South Wales, in 1908, now the home of Richmond's grandson, James.

75 years progress at Haddon Rig (Syd, nd); NSW Sheepbreeders' Assn, The Australian merino (Syd, 1955); R. M. Brennan, Across the black soil plains (Warren, 1972); Pastoral Review, 15 Sept 1894, 13 Sept 1923; letter-books and diaries (held by James Richmond, Mogila).

MARTHA RUTLEDGE

RIDDELL, JOHN CARRE (1809-1879), pastoralist and politician, was born on 4 June 1809 at Linthill, Roxburghshire, Scotland, third son of Thomas Riddell, of Camieston, and his wife Jane, née Ferrier. (The name is pronounced Riddle). He was educated at the High School, Edinburgh, and at the University of Edinburgh. With his cousin T. F. Hamilton [q.v.] he reached Sydney in the Abberton on 20 August 1839, and next month rode to Melbourne. They went first to the Western District and were briefly with Niel Black [q.v.] before buying, in early 1840, the stock and depasturing licence of the Mount Macedon run, northwest of Melbourne.

They survived the depression of 1843. In 1845-50 Riddell was in charge while Hamilton visited Scotland. By 1846 their run amounted to thirty square miles, but in August 1850 they lost a great deal of it to W. J. T. Clarke [q.v.], whose freehold purchase of 28,000 acres took even their woolshed and sheepwash. The partners reconstituted their run as Cairnhill and Turitable and turned to cattle-raising and farming. When they dissolved partnership in 1861 Riddell owned much land nearer Melbourne and in the Gisborne district.

In 1847 Riddell had declined election to the Legislative Council in Sydney but in 1852 he was appointed a non-official member of the Victorian Legislative Council. In 1860-77 he held West Bourke in the Legislative Assembly. In parliament he spoke rarely and briefly, disapproving of 'long speeches which were frequently to no purpose'. In the 1860s he supported the ministries of Nicholson, O'Shanassy and, especially, McCulloch [qq.v.]. When McCulloch resigned in March 1868 Riddell, as a respected moderate, was asked to form a government but could not persuade his friends to leave the former premier. He broke with Mc-

Culloch in June 1871. Riddell was a liberal, favouring compulsory and secular education and the reduction of state aid to religion. A moderate free trader in 1864, he had become a moderate protectionist by 1877. He was not at ease in the turbulent assembly, and might well have been happier in the Upper House. As the Argus said, 'He was distinguished for gentlemanlike bearing and high character rather than for political activity or demonstrativeness'.

Riddell was an early member and in 1852 president of the Melbourne Club. From 1866 he lived in his large house Cavers Carre in Elsternwick. He had married on 22 October 1846 Marianne Sibella Stephen (d. 1890), whose sister later married T. F. Hamilton. Of their six children, three daughters and two sons, including Walter John Carre (1859-1930), survived him when he died at Elsternwick on 22 December 1879. He was buried at Gisborne in what has become the family cemetery; the town of Riddell bears his name.

A. Henderson (ed), *Early pioneer families of Victoria and Riverina* (Melb, 1936); *Argus*, 18 Apr 1877, 23 Dec 1879; *Herald* (Melb), 18 Apr 1877, 23 Dec 1879; R. R. McNicoll, Memoir on John Carre Riddell *and* Riddell papers (LaT L).

RONALD McNICOLL

RIDLEY, WILLIAM (1819-1878), Presbyterian minister, was born on 14 September 1819 at Hartford End near Chelmsford, Essex, England, son of William Ridley, miller, and his wife Maria, née Dixon. Reared in a prosperous Dissenting family, he was educated at King's College, University of London (B.A., 1842), and put aside a legal career for conscientious reasons. Rejected by the London Missionary Society because he had once held Plymouth Brethren beliefs, in 1849 he was recruited by Rev. J. D. Lang [q.v.] and arrived at Sydney in the *Clifton* on 19 March 1850. He hoped to work with the Aboriginals, but was persuaded to become classics professor at the Australian College.

In 1850 Ridley was ordained in the Scots Church by Lang and on 11 April married Isabella, daughter of Rev. J. R. Cotter, rector of Donoughmore, Cork, Ireland. In 1851 he was appointed to Dungog where friendship with an Aboriginal, Harry of Bungulgully, and the failure of Lang's Grafton mission led him to reconsider Aboriginal work and in May 1853 he began a widespread itinerant ministry in the New England district. In 1855 he extended his mission to Moreton Bay, formed the Moreton Bay Aborigines Friends' Society in February and itinerated through the Darling Downs. His *Report* . . .

of a *Journey along the Condamine, Barwan and Namoi Rivers* (Sydney, 1855) was reprinted by Lang in 1861. He published *Gurre Kamilaroi: or Kamilaroi Sayings* in Sydney in 1856. The same year he refused to be re-ordained by Bishop Barker [q.v.] and his proposed mastership of an Anglican Aboriginal institution lapsed.

Frustrated and indigent, Ridley resumed parish work in 1857 with the United Presbyterian Church of Victoria at Portland. Next year he returned to pastoral work in Sydney because of his wife's health and in 1861 became a journalist. As assistant editor of the *Empire*, and then editor of the *Evening News* in 1873, and the *Australian Town and Country Journal*, he won repute for his writing and 'English liberal' political views. He also helped to edit the *Australian Witness* for two years and wrote for the *Sydney University Magazine*.

Ridley served on committees of the Presbyterian Church, founded a Presbyterian cause at Kogarah, and preached most Sundays until his death. In 1864 he gained an M.A. at the University of Sydney; in 1867 he helped to found St Andrew's College there and became a theological tutor in 1875. A competent linguist, he had learnt Gaelic and, in 1877, Chinese in order to take charge of the Chinese Mission in Sydney, but devoted much of his time to his Aboriginal studies. With Dr R. Steel [q.v.] he obtained government aid for the Maloga mission. Besides contributions to learned societies Ridley published *Kamilaroi, Dippil, and Turrubul: Languages spoken by Australian Aborigines* (Sydney, 1866), revised and enlarged as *Kamilaroi and other Australian Languages* in 1875: it won him the acclaim of ethnologists, notably Professor Max Müller. He also contributed to the works of R. B. Smyth and E. M. Curr [qq.v.] and several of his sermons and lectures were published.

Ridley treated all men with equal consideration and earned a reputation for transparent goodness. Even-tempered, his friendship with Lang was 'never once broken by a quarrel'. Always delicate, he succumbed to overwork, died of apoplexy at Paddington on 26 September 1878 and was buried in the Devonshire Street cemetery, survived by his wife, two sons and four daughters. His journal, which he kept as a young man, was published in Sydney in 1892.

J. D. Lang, *Queensland, Australia* (Lond, 1861); J. J. Westwood, *The journal of . . .* (Melb, 1865); G. King, *Reminiscences* (Syd, 1887); A. D. Gilchrist (ed), *John Dunmore Lang*, 1-2 (Melb, 1951); J. Greenway, *Bibliography of the Australian Aborigines . . . to 1959* (Syd, 1963); N. Gunson, *Australian reminiscences and papers of L. E. Threlkeld*, 2 (Canberra, 1974); V&P

(LA NSW), 1883, 3, 930; *Syd Univ Mag*, Oct 1878; *Life* (Syd), 2 Oct 1878; *T&CJ*, 5 Oct 1878; *Sydney Mail*, 12 Oct 1878; J. D. Lang papers (ML); Col Sec papers, special bundles 1871-75 (NSWA).   NIEL GUNSON

RIGNALL, GEORGE RICHARD (1839-1912), actor-manager, was born at Birmingham, Warwickshire, England, son of William Rignall, provincial theatre manager, and his wife Patience, née Blaxland, actress. They used Rignold as a professional name. George and his brother William started as violinists in theatre orchestras. Later George complained of the squalor and hardship of the provincial theatre, but in 1857 he played the messenger in *Macbeth* at short notice and continued to play bit parts in anything from pantomime to tragedy. On 28 September 1865 at Brighton he married Marie Braybrooke Henderson, comic actress, and noted in his diary 'very pleasant etc'.

From 1870 Rignold played roles ranging from Romeo to Caliban at the Queen's Theatre, Long Acre, London. Back in the provinces, he accepted the offer of American managers A. M. Palmer and Jarrett to play Henry V at the Booth Theatre, New York. They bought costumes and scenery from Charles Calvert's lavish 1872 production and in 1875 presented the play. Women fought over the handsome Rignold and even wore red roses to indicate that they were 'Rignoldites'. He toured the United States and Canada in 1875-76 and with his wife sailed from San Francisco for Sydney. From 28 August 1876, with another overwhelming response from audiences, his run of twenty-four successive performances of *Henry V* was the first 'long run' of a Shakespearian play in the Australian theatre. After engagements in America and the English provinces, Rignold became sub-lessee of London's Drury Lane Theatre, and in November 1879 presented his opulent version of *Henry V*; it excited audiences and puzzled critics who panned Rignold for his carelessness and gabbling but forgave him because of his good looks. Staffordshire replicas of Rignold as the king on horseback were made. In 1880-87 Rignold toured America and Australasia. In 1887-95 he partnered James Allison at Her Majesty's Theatre, Sydney, and opened on 10 September with *Henry V*. He settled down to the serious business of becoming a grand man of the theatre. He wrote a flattering retrospective diary, brought out his own acting editions of Shakespeare and made lengthy speeches to his audiences; and while living at Paddington he bought a property at Middle Harbour, called Braybrook, and flew Henry V's standard whenever there.

In 1889 Rignold played Mark Antony in *Julius Caesar* and Bottom; next year he played Macbeth and was Ford to the Falstaff of his brother William in *The Merry Wives of Windsor*. He mixed spectacular Shakespeare with melodramas such as *Lights o' London*. From 1895 he toured Victoria, Queensland and South Australia with melodramas, and returned to play Othello and Falstaff in the *Merry Wives* in Sydney at the Criterion Theatre from March 1899. Physical dominance and presence were his main assets as an actor, but his stormy Criterion season forced him to admit that he was a little out-of-date. The *Bulletin*, 18 November 1899, complained of his arrogance, slow-wittedness, unpleasantness back-stage with minor actors, impatience with stage-managers and interminable 'farewell' performances.

In private life Rignold had many friends and admirers. His wife's failing health prevented them from returning to England early in 1900, and when she died on 25 February 1902 he withdrew to partial seclusion at Middle Harbour. Once a week he collected provisions in Sydney, saw friends at the Athenaeum Club, attended the theatre and gave interviews to reporters. On 3 October 1907 at Neutral Bay he married Georgina Harriet Don (d. 1911), daughter of George Coppin [q.v.].

Despite mismanagement and unhappy years wasted in cheap melodramas, Rignold succeeded largely in persuading his public that he was the great Shakespearian actor he had wished to be. The lavishness of his spectacles brought the pictorial approach to theatre in Australia as far as it could go. He died childless on 16 December 1912 of empyema and cardiac angina at Charlemont Private Hospital, Darlinghurst, and was buried in the Anglican section of Waverley cemetery. He left the residue of his estate, valued for probate at over £11,000, to the Royal General Theatrical Fund.

P. McGuire et al, *The Australian theatre* (Melb, 1948); *Era* (Lond), Nov 1879; *Barrier Weekly Post*, Oct 1898; playbill collection (Shakespeare Memorial Lib, Birmingham); MS and printed cats under Rignold (ML).

HELEN M. VAN DER POORTEN

RILEY, ALBAN JOSEPH (1844-1914), draper and politician, was born on 8 June 1844 at Balmain, Sydney, son of Alban Joseph Riley, softgoods merchant, and his wife Juliana, née Lyons. About 1850 his family moved to Maitland where he was educated at a private school with (Sir) Samuel Griffith. In 1859 he was apprenticed to Farmer [q.v.] & Co. in Sydney and attended logic and Greek classes conducted by Dr Woolley [q.v.] at the School of Arts. He became chief clerk and gained experience in drapery and in the counting-house. About 1868 he and his brother Philip, who had been with David Jones [q.v.] & Co. for many years, set up as drapers in Sydney and Goulburn as Riley Bros. They opened branches in Bathurst and in 1874 at Maitland. Their '£5 Bale system' of delivering goods throughout the colony enlarged their operations. On 4 October 1870 Alban had married Eleanor Harriet Birkenhead.

Riley was active in the Drapers' Early Closing Association and in 1874 agreed to close at 7 p.m. He was also an organizer of the Saturday half-holiday. In 1878 he visited India, Palestine, Europe and England where he established an export drapery business as A. J. Riley & Co. with a branch in George Street, Sydney, and engaged in indenting. Next year he handed over the retail side of Riley Bros to his brothers.

A magistrate from 1883, Riley was nominated by Governor Loftus in 1885 to fill an extraordinary vacancy on the Burwood Municipal Council. In October he failed to win the parliamentary seat of Canterbury but in 1885-91 represented Cook Ward in the Sydney Municipal Council. He sought to reform the finances of the council and had a committee appointed to investigate its book-keeping and auditing systems which exposed the 'notorious Bradford frauds'. In 1887 he was mayor and was elected as a free trader to the Legislative Assembly for South Sydney but was defeated in the 1889 elections. On 24 March 1891 he was appointed to the Legislative Council but was forced to resign on 16 November 1893 after he became bankrupt. His debts were proven at £98,156 and in August 1894 the judge claimed that Riley had continued to trade and obtain credit for at least three months knowing himself to be bankrupt, had given undue preference to one creditor, his wife, and had been guilty of manipulating his balance sheet. His estate was not wound up until 1946.

In the 1880s Riley had been a committee-man of the School of Arts, a director of Sydney Hospital and the Benevolent Asylum, a special commissioner for the Centennial Celebrations and a New South Wales commissioner for the Adelaide Jubilee International Exhibition, 1887, and the Centennial International Exhibition, Melbourne, 1888. His wife was a committee member of the Sydney University Women's College, the Queen's Jubilee Fund, the National Council of Women, and the Girls' Friendly Society. Riley died at Burwood on 24 July 1914 from uraemia and was buried in the Anglican section of Rookwood cemetery. He

was survived by five sons and five daughters and by his wife to whom he left his estate of £1676. Her estate was sworn for probate at £6787 after her death in 1922.

E. Rigby (ed), *Australian men of mark*, 1 (Syd, 1889); *Maitland Mercury*, 7 July 1874; *ISN*, 15 Feb 1887; *SMH*, 25 July 1914; Newspaper cuttings, vol 135 (ML); Insolvency file 7503/5 (NSWA).   MARTHA RUTLEDGE

RINTEL, MOSES (1823-1880), Jewish minister, was born in Edinburgh, son of Myer Rintel, rabbi of the Jewish community, and his wife Sara. Rintel was educated in Scotland and London and was authorized by Rabbi Solomon Herschell, chief rabbi of London, to officiate as a *shochet* (slaughterman for kosher food) and minister. His first post was in Brighton.

In 1844 Rintel migrated to New South Wales, where he established the Sydney Hebrew Academy. He went to Melbourne in 1849 to take charge of the newly established Hebrew Congregation in Bourke Street as 'reader' of the religious services, teacher of the children, and *shochet*. On 22 August 1849 Rintel married Elvina, daughter of John Hart.

After many disputes, Rintel resigned from the Melbourne Hebrew Congregation in 1857 and established the Mikveh Israel Melbourne Synagogue at the eastern end of the city. The second congregation in size and status, it received a grant of land from the government and built a synagogue at the corner of Exhibition Street and Little Lonsdale Street. In 1877 the congregation dedicated a new synagogue in Albert Street, East Melbourne.

Though the East Melbourne Synagogue was known as 'Rintel's Shool', it was many years before he received a salary for his pastoral work. His marriage and his family connexions brought him a small private income which enabled him to be financially independent. He was trustee, secretary and minister of the synagogue's Board of Management and, while officiating at the congregation as reader, opened an associated school for Jewish boys. Rintel helped to established the first authorized rabbinical court (Beth Din) in the British Empire outside London and eventually became its chairman. In 1868 after a dispute with the rabbi of the Melbourne Hebrew Congregation, the chief rabbi named Rintel senior minister of the Melbourne Hebrew community.

Rintel's career was marked by endless quarrels with his community about proselytes and the children of mixed marriages. He was active in communal and philanthropic affairs and was a distinguished

Freemason. Well known throughout Victoria, he died on 9 May 1880 of tuberculosis, from which he had suffered for many years. He was survived by his wife and eight children and left an estate valued at £3831.

L. M. Goldman, *The Jews in Victoria in the nineteenth century* (Melb, 1954); *Jewish Herald*, 21 May 1880.   J. Levi

RITCHIE, ROBERT ADAM (1836-1891), manufacturer and politician, was born on 18 October 1836 at Paisley, Renfrewshire, Scotland, son of John Ritchie (d. 1861), dyer, and his wife Barbara, née Henderson (d. 1878). In 1848 the family joined an elder brother John, a shipwright and engine-smith, in Sydney. Robert worked for his brother and in 1849-51 at J. and W. Byrnes's [q.v.] woollen mill at Parramatta where his father was manager. After eighteen months at the Turon River diggings he was apprenticed to Joseph Whiting, blacksmith, in Parramatta. In 1857 he took over Whiting's business in Phillip Street and soon expanded it by making agricultural implements including the celebrated 'Ritchie Plough'.

In the 1860s Ritchie moved to George Street, Parramatta. In 1876 he contracted to supply the government with 150 railway trucks worth £70 each and next year successfully tendered for the construction of first-class carriages. In 1879 he opened a branch works at Wickham near Newcastle. By June 1880 Ritchie employed sixty men and was one of the biggest contractors for government rolling stock: his works could make 200-300 railway wagons a year and produced 300 ploughs and a wide variety of general engineering and smithing annually. Ritchie's valuable railway contracts continued and in 1883 he merged with Hudson Bros [q.v.], becoming managing director of their Clyde works. In 1884 he retired from the firm and became a director of Mason Bros Ltd, merchants and importers, of Kent Street, Sydney.

Ritchie was connected with many benevolent and social movements; active in local government, he was an alderman of Parramatta for Anderson Ward from 1877 and chairman of the works committee in 1879, president of the Central Cumberland Agricultural and Horticultural Association, chairman of the Auburn Progress Association and one of the original members of the Parramatta volunteers. He was also a Freemason and a councillor of the Agricultural Society of New South Wales. A staunch free trader, in 1889-91 he represented Central Cumberland in the Legislative Assembly. In the assembly Ritchie was an excellent speaker and shrewd critic; diligent and fair-minded he was mainly interested in local issues, but municipally, according to the *Cumberland Argus*, he was 'more the captious and destructive critic' than the constructive man of action'.

Ritchie died of peritonitis on 16 August 1891 at his residence in Auburn Road, Auburn, and was buried in the Presbyterian cemetery, Parramatta. His will was sworn for probate at under £18,355. He was twice married: on 25 March 1859 at Parramatta, to Jemima Fergus Douglas (d. 1868); and on 6 June 1868, at Sydney, to her sister Clara (d. 1925). Three sons and a daughter of the first marriage and four sons and three daughters of the second survived him.

ISN, 12 June 1880, 22 Feb 1888; T&CJ, 20 Apr 1889, 22 Aug 1891; *Sydney Mail*, 22 June 1889; *Cumberland Argus*, 17 Aug 1891; SMH, 19 Aug 1891, 5 Oct 1892; *Cumberland Times*, 14 Nov 1901.   G. P. Walsh

RITCHIE, SAMUEL SEXTUS (1825-1879), company manager, was born at Greenwich, England, son of William Ritchie, merchant, and his wife Sarah, née Pitcher. He arrived in Victoria from Gravesend in the *Norfolk* on 29 June 1857 and set up as a merchant in Melbourne; by 1860 he had a wine, spirits and general importing business in Elizabeth Street. In London and Melbourne Ritchie gained much knowledge and experience of food preserving, especially meat. In 1867-68 he promoted the Melbourne Meat Preserving Co. which, operating the first successful meat cannery in extensive works of solid bluestone at Maribyrnong, inspired many later ventures; it also provided an essential boost to Victoria's export trade and to a depressed livestock market. As manager Ritchie contributed greatly to the company's success; he received one-fifth of profits after payment of a 10 per cent dividend, which earned him a small fortune in the boom years at the start of the 1870s, but later proved a major source of friction for discontented shareholders. Ritchie accumulated many shares in the company. In 1877 he was prominent in the outcry against a proposed duty on all imported livestock which endangered the company's cheap sources of supply; the same year he contributed the greater part of a pamphlet, *The Property Tax on Livestock*, which attacked the tax.

Although suffering for some time from bad health, Ritchie's death at Maribyrnong on 8 March 1879, aged 53, was unexpected. Only months earlier he had invented canning machinery claimed to be far superior to that used in the United States. At the time of his death he still actively managed the company; he was also a justice of the peace and president of the Braybrook Shire Council, a position that he had held for several years.

Ritchie had married Emma Matilda Windsor on 25 April 1867 at Christ Church, South Yarra; they had three sons and two daughters.

Australasian, 11 Apr 1868, 15 Mar 1879; *Argus*, 10 Mar 1879; E. A. Beever, A history of the Australian meat export trade, 1865-1939 (Ph.D. thesis, Univ Melb, 1968).

E. A. BEEVER

RITCHIE, WILLIAM (1832-1897), solicitor, was born on 31 August 1832 at Scone, near Perth, Van Diemen's Land, sixth son of Captain Thomas Ritchie [q.v.] and his wife Hannah, née Harris. Educated at Rev. W. L. Gibbon's school, Launceston, and Christ's College, Bishopsbourne, he worked in the office of Melbourne solicitor W. D. Wickham before going to England where he studied law and was called to the Bar at the Middle Temple on 26 January 1857. In 1858 Ritchie returned to Tasmania and went into partnership with William Douglas, after whose death he became a partner with Robert John Parker. In 1862-64 they were associated with J. W. Gleadow [q.v.]. By 1884 the firm was doing most of the land conveyancing in northern Tasmania; it still operates as Ritchie and Parker Alfred Green & Co.

Ritchie was interested in the mineral development of the colony and in 1873 floated the Mount Bischoff Tin Mining Co., acquiring James 'Philosopher' Smith's [q.v.] claim for cash and shares. For a number of years he was chairman of the board. He was also interested in the Back Creek goldfield and other prominent mining companies. He strongly favoured widespread legal reform: in 1883 when questioned as to the working of the Land Titles' Office he criticized the Real Property Act as founded on false principles which caused the system to be costly, complicated, dilatory and unreliable. In 1884-85 he wrote over forty letters to the editor of the Launceston *Daily Telegraph* and later had them reprinted in three pamphlets: *Letters on Fiscal and Land Law Reform*, *Letters on the Decay of Agriculture in Tasmania* and *The Assessment of Real Property in Tasmania*. He argued for a larger colonial population, taxation on capital value and free trade.

On 20 December 1860 Ritchie had married Margaret Bowman, daughter of John Fawns of Launceston; they had six sons and three daughters. He died on 4 April 1897 after a long illness.

J. Foster, *Men-at-the-Bar* (Lond, 1885); E. A. Beever, *Launceston Bank for Savings 1835-1970* (Melb, 1972); V&P (HA Tas), 1884, 3 (n.s.) (69); *Examiner* (Launceston), 5 Apr 1897.

R. M. GREEN

ROBB, JOHN (1834-1896), contractor, was born in Londonderry, Northern Ireland, son of Arthur Robb, gentleman, and his wife Sarah, née Bird. He arrived in Victoria about 1854, visited various goldfields and turned to contracting, first with Best Overend as Overend and Robb, and on his own after Overend's death in 1877. Their first large government contract was in 1863 for the removal of Bátman's Hill to make way for Spencer Street railway station in Melbourne. In 1868 the firm constructed the Launceston and Western Railway in Tasmania. For a few years their contracts in Victoria were for water-supply and drainage but from 1874 they concentrated on railways, building the Wangaratta–Beechworth line, sections of the Geelong–Colac line and the Ararat–Hamilton line. In 1877 in South Australia they built the railway from Kapunda to the Murray River.

In 1880 Robb built the Victor Harbour breakwater and a section of the Adelaide sewers. He also constructed the first section of the Fremantle to Guildford railway in Western Australia; when the governor opened the line in September 1880 he said that 'not a single case of dispute between the Works Department and the contractors had been brought to his notice'. Other contracts held by Robb in Victoria included the Morwell–Mirboo (1884), Footscray–Bacchus Marsh (1884-87), Murtoa–Warracknabeal (1885-88) and Moe–Narracan (1886-88) lines.

Constantly on the move, at various times Robb had mining interests in Ballarat, Rutherglen and Tasmania. He was a founding director of the Federal Bank in 1881 and of the Melbourne Hydraulic Power Co. in 1887. Robb's Buildings (1885) on the corner of Collins and King streets was reputedly the highest structure in Melbourne. By 1889 he held valuable freeholds and leaseholds in Victoria and South Australia and had £30,000 invested in the Cudgen Sugar Plantation on the Tweed River in New South Wales. In 1881-82 he had bought Talawanta and Toulby stations in the Warrego district of New South Wales in partnership with James Blackwood's [q.v.] son, Arthur.

Robb's 1887 contract for the second section of the Cairns–Herberton railway led to litigation with the Queensland government. Robb claimed in excess of £250,000, was awarded £20,800 and incurred costs of

£28,000. By mid-1893 the case had been settled, but he was in serious financial trouble with large rural losses and the collapse of the inflated value of his real estate at the end of the Victorian land boom. The Federal Bank closed and an investigation in 1893 disclosed Robb's part in prodigal milking of funds by its directors. Robb had an overdraft of £21,000. Insolvent in October 1894 by £680,000 and supported by relations, he eventually paid 1s. 6d. in the pound.

For many years Robb lived at Coonac, Toorak; aged 62 he died suddenly on 18 May 1896 of apoplexy while on business in the city. He was survived by his wife Elizabeth, née Stranger, three of their eight sons and three daughters. The funeral cortège was joined at Princes Bridge by two hundred of his workmen, who marched in two lines to the Melbourne general cemetery. When the news of his death reached Adelaide, the flag was flown at half-mast from the Royal Exchange. A Presbyterian, Robb had 'a quiet and effective way' and a 'distinct talent for managing men'. He left personalty of £2000.

J. Smith (ed), Cyclopedia of Victoria, 3 (Melb, 1905); M. Cannon, The land boomers (Melb, 1966); J. W. Collinson, 'Building the Cairns Range railway', JRHSQ, 5 (1955); West Australian, 3 Sept 1880; A'sian Sketcher, 14 Jan 1885; Australasian, 13 May 1893; Age, 14 Oct 1893, 7 Apr 1894, 19 May 1896; Argus, 13 Oct 1894, 19, 21 May 1896; Register (Adel), 20 May 1896; Insolvency papers (PRO, Vic).

JOHN LACK

ROBERTS, SIR ALFRED (1823-1898), surgeon, was born in Finsbury Circus, London, son of John Roberts, surgeon. He was educated at St Paul's School and Guy's Hospital and in 1844 became a member of the Royal College of Surgeons and a licentiate of the Society of Apothecaries. He practised for some years with his father in London, then set up in Rye, Sussex, where in 1850 he married Susan Eliza Spencer. In 1854 he arrived in Sydney and from February 1855 to 1870 was an honorary surgeon at the Sydney Infirmary and Dispensary and later a consulting surgeon.

Worried by the inefficient nursing at the Infirmary, Roberts appealed to Henry Parkes [q.v.], who in 1866 asked Florence Nightingale to select a lady superintendent and nurses to train other young women. She sent Lucy Osburn [q.v.] but Roberts clashed with her and told the 1873 royal commission on public charities that Miss Nightingale was disappointed with Miss Osburn and that he thought she had failed. Parkes intervened and wrote to Miss Nightingale that 'Mr Roberts is a respectable professional man ... but he is ... a fussy, officious dilettante in all matters of sanitary reform, who spoils his own efforts to be useful by his desire to be the authority on all occasions'.

Roberts was a director and honorary secretary of the Prince Alfred Hospital Fund from its inception in 1868. In October 1871 he visited England and Europe with a view to designing a model hospital. He had favoured adding a 'Prince Alfred' wing to the Sydney Infirmary but changed his mind. Due to his 'zeal and assiduity' the Royal Prince Alfred Hospital was opened in 1882; he remained a director and honorary consulting surgeon until 1898 and in August supervised the renovation of the operating theatre.

In 1858 Roberts had become an elective trustee of the Australian Museum; he was a councillor of the local Philosophical (Royal) Society to which he read three papers. He was honorary surgeon to the Society for the Relief of Destitute Children and to the Clergy Daughters' School, Waverley; a member of the Official Board of Visitors to Hospitals for the Insane, and president from 1876; medical advisor to the Railway Department of New South Wales; a member of the Board of Health; chief medical officer for the Liverpool and London and Globe Insurance Co.; member of the committee of management of the Technological Museum; examiner in medicine of the University of Sydney; a member and later chairman of the City of Sydney Improvement Board; a New South Wales commissioner for the Melbourne International Exhibition in 1880; a committeeman of the Charity Organization Society and honorary secretary and vice-president of the Carrington Convalescent Hospital. He was also responsible for the construction of the Coast Hospital, Little Bay, for contagious diseases, helped establish the Hospital for Sick Children and designed hospitals for Glen Innes and Mudgee. In 1881 he combated a smallpox epidemic and told cabinet that he favoured compulsory vaccination.

Friend and physician of Parkes and the Macarthurs [qq.v.], Roberts was a member of the Australian Club. Knighted in 1883, he died at Wentworth Falls in the Blue Mountains on 19 December 1898, aged 75, of heart disease and was buried in the Anglican section of Waverley cemetery. His estate was valued for probate at almost £19,500. He divided his multifarious goods and chattels among his family and friends and their children.

F. MacDonnell, Miss Nightingale's young ladies (Syd, 1970); V&P (LA NSW), 1870, 2, 554, 569, 1881, 4, 1051, 1882, 1, 69; A'sian Medical

Gazette, 20 Jan 1899; R. S. Skirving, 'Surgery and surgeons in . . . Sydney over forty years ago', *MJA*, 13 Mar 1926; *Bulletin*, 7 Oct 1882; *Sydney Mail*, 24 Dec 1898; *T&CJ*, 24 Dec 1898; Parkes letters (ML); MS and printed cats (ML).
                                    MARTHA RUTLEDGE

ROBERTS, CHARLES FYSHE (1837-1914), soldier, was born on 20 August 1837 at Ickwell, Bedfordshire, England, son of Captain Charles Roberts, 59th Regiment, and his wife Emma Gertrude, née Hornsby, a connexion of Thomas Fyshe Palmer [q.v.]. Educated at Carshalton House School, he entered the Royal Military Academy, Woolwich, on 23 August 1852 and was commissioned second lieutenant on 28 February 1855. A lieutenant in April, he was sent to the Crimea where he served in the siege of Sebastopol. Personally commended in June by Lord Raglan, he was severely injured on 15 November, but was mentioned in dispatches and awarded the Sardinian Order of Military Valour. In October 1858 he went to India, served at Fort William, Calcutta and Dacca and from January to April 1861 commanded the artillery with the Sikkim Field Force under Colonel Gawler. He was promoted second captain in September 1862 and major in January 1863.

In 1865-68 Roberts served with the Royal Artillery in Sydney and was acting aide-de-camp to Governor Young. On half-pay from July 1869 he retired on an annuity of £110 on 28 September 1871. In January 1873 he became secretary to the New South Wales agent-general in London at £400 a year, but resigned and returned to New South Wales in mid-1874. On 28 August 1876 he was appointed colonel commanding all the artillery forces in the colony at £500 a year; in the same year he was appointed to the commission on defence from foreign aggression and to the board for inspecting and maintaining the supply of colonial warlike stores. In 1881 as one of the royal commissioners inquiring into the military defences of the colony he favoured a permanent artillery force, a small nucleus of permanent infantry supported by unpaid volunteers on the English model, and advocated forming an Australian federal regiment of artillery.

In 1885 he assumed command of all the military forces in the colony when Colonel J. S. Richardson [q.v.] led the Sudan Contingent. In 1887-88 he quarrelled with Richardson over his treatment when the artillery was placed under the general staff. In letters to Sir Henry Parkes [q.v.], a close friend, in February and August 1888 he set out his complaint and his disagreements with Richardson on rearranging the defence forces. In November, though he had misgivings, he asked Parkes to be considered for the proposed new office of secretary for defence. In 1890-91 he twice visited England. In April 1892 he became military secretary of the new Defence Department at £800 a year and in June and July was examined at length by a royal commission into the military service of New South Wales which found the defence system unsatisfactory.

Roberts retired in 1902. In 1905 the royal commission on the claims of members of the New South Wales contingents in South Africa noted that there was some friction between Roberts and General Sir George French and suggested that Roberts had neglected to settle the great confusion over the soldiers' pay. Roberts was absent from the state and did not give evidence.

A competent and very popular officer, he helped form the Australian military tradition. Honorary aide-de-camp to three sovereigns Roberts had been made C.M.G. in 1885. He was a member of the Union Club. He died on 9 September 1914 at his residence, Valensole, Lower Ocean Street, Double Bay, and was buried in the South Head cemetery. He was survived by his wife, Alice Caroline (d. 10 February 1932), youngest daughter of William Bradley [q.v.], whom he had married at Goulburn on 15 November 1866, and by a son and four daughters.

W. H. Askwith (ed), *Kane's list of officers of the Royal Regiment of Artillery . . . to 1899, with notes on officers' service*, 4th ed (Lond, 1900); J. R. J. Jocelyn, *The history of the Royal Artillery: Crimean period* (Lond, 1911); V&P (LA NSW), 1881, 4, 664, Roy Com, Evidence, 1892-93, 7, 28-46, 1906, 3, 30; *T&CJ*, 9 Jan 1892; *Sydney Mail*, 16 Jan 1892; *Bulletin*, 11 Mar 1892; *ISN*, 4 June 1892; *SMH*, 10, 12 Sept 1914; Parkes letters (ML), WO 76/368.
                                        G. P. WALSH

ROBERTS, CHARLES JAMES (1846-1925), publican and politician, was born on 29 March 1846 at Oxford Street, Sydney, eldest son of Charles Warman Roberts, publican, and his wife Annie, née Marsden. He was educated at St James's Grammar School and in 1857-62 was one of the first pupils at the Sydney Grammar School under W. J. Stephens [q.v.], where he excelled at classics. He preferred business to a legal career and became a licensed victualler. On 9 April 1867 at St James's Church he married Lucretia Abrahams, daughter of a well-known chemist. That year Roberts bought from his father the Crown and Anchor Hotel on the corner of George and Market streets. In 1888 he demolished it and built the five-storied Roberts' Hotel on the site. He also developed a wholesale wine and spirits business.

In 1877-80 Roberts was an alderman for Macquarie Ward on the Sydney Municipal Council. He was mayor in 1879 and became a justice of the peace and a metropolitan transit commissioner. With the council bankrupt he persuaded the government to guarantee an overdraft of £75,000 and stressed the urgency of increased endowment and powers for it. He presided over most council meetings, reorganized and reduced the staff but completed more work and co-operated zealously with the health officer to improve the city's sanitary system. As mayor, Roberts and his wife entertained on a grand scale, with a fancy dress ball in the Exhibition Building for 2000 guests, and banquets for J. J. Casey, John Lucas [qq.v.] and Governor Loftus. A commissioner for the Sydney International Exhibition, he fêted the visitors it brought to Sydney. He could boast that 'no man ever departed from an entertainment of his sober who wanted to be otherwise'.

Roberts wrote to Sir John Robertson [q.v.] in August 1880 asking for his support at the forthcoming general election. A free trader and supporter of the 1880 Education Act, Roberts lost after opposing the influx of Chinese and any tax on wool or coal. In December 1882 he won the Hastings and Manning seat; in 1885 he was re-elected though in England. He spoke seldom in parliament but was known for his common sense and courtesy and was 'apt to absent himself when an adherence to party duties would cause him to sit up all night'. As postmaster-general in Parkes's [q.v.] fourth ministry (1887-89) he showed much administrative ability; in Sydney in January 1887 he chaired the Intercolonial Postal Conference; he arranged the ocean mail service contract with the Peninsular and Oriental and the Orient steamship companies, and reduced telegraph rates with South Australia. In 1888 he apologized for seeming to disregard Parkes's 'strict injunction' that only the premier should communicate with the premier of another colony.

In 1879-86 Roberts was a director of the Sydney Infirmary and Dispensary (Sydney Hospital from 1882) and a committee-man of the Industrial Blind Institution and the City Night Refuge and Soup Kitchen. In 1880-81 he had been a commissioner for the Melbourne International Exhibition and in 1882 was created C.M.G. He was a commissioner for the Amsterdam Exhibition in 1883, the Calcutta Exhibition in 1883-84, the Colonial and Indian Exhibition in London in 1886 and the Centennial International Exhibition, Melbourne, in 1888. On 13 March 1890 he resigned from parliament to visit England and in London that year was appointed a commissioner for the Inter-

national Exhibition of Mining and Metallurgy, and also for the World's Columbian Exposition, Chicago, 1893. In April 1890 he had been appointed to the Legislative Council and in 1894-98 was a member of the parliamentary standing committee on public works. In 1895 he helped Parkes against George Reid in the election for Sydney-King.

Roberts was a director of the Colonial Mutual Life Assurance Society Ltd and its chairman in 1909-25. In 1919 the Roberts' Hotel was sold to Farmer [q.v.] & Co. and was demolished, but Roberts acquired the premises of Smart's Hotel on the corner of Pitt and Market streets, and renamed it Roberts' Hotel. Genial and even-tempered, he enjoyed cricket, sailing and rowing and was patron and president of numerous sporting clubs. He and his wife entertained 'on a princely scale' at their home Chatsworth, Potts Point. A diabetic, Roberts died of cerebral arteriosclerosis and uraemia on 14 August 1925 and was buried in the Anglican section of the South Head cemetery. Predeceased by his wife in 1922, he was survived by their only son and five daughters. His estate was sworn for probate at over £70,500.

J. Plummer, A mayoral year (Syd, 1885); Ex-M.L.A., Our present parliament, what it is worth (Syd, c1886); Cyclopedia of N.S.W. (Syd, 1907); V&P (LA NSW), 1889, 1, 8, 130; Sydney Mail, 27 Feb 1879; T&CJ, 1 Mar 1879, 29 Jan 1887, 14 June 1890; Bulletin, 21 Feb, 16 Oct 1880, 7 Dec 1889; SMH, 6, 11, 16, 18 Nov 1880; Aust Worker, 19 Aug 1925; James Inglis letter-books (held by Inglis & Co., Syd); Parkes letters (ML); newspaper cuttings, vol 166 (ML).
                                        MARTHA RUTLEDGE

ROBERTSON, ALEXANDER WILLIAM (1831-1896), coachline proprietor and pastoralist, was born on 16 January 1831, possibly at sea between Scotland and Canada. He was the eldest son and fourth of ten children of Farquhar Robertson and his wife Catherine, née MacIver, from Glenelg, Inverness-shire, Scotland, who migrated to Hawkesbury, Ontario. Alexander arrived in Victoria in 1853, spent some time on the goldfields, and then started as a carrier. By 1859 Robertson, Simpson & Co. was operating a daily wagon service between Melbourne and Bendigo. In 1860 he formed the Ovens Stage Co., but its Melbourne to Beechworth passenger service competed in vain with existing lines and the same year he became manager of the Bendigo Stage Co.

The firm of Robertson and Wagner, for many years identified with the name of 'Cobb [q.v.] & Co.', was created in the summer of 1861-62. In 1861 Robertson and John F. Britton, a coach driver with the original Cobb & Co., won the 1862 Melbourne–Bendigo mail contract and bought the coach service run by the former contractors; within months John Wagner, also a Canadian and ex-carrier, took Britton's place; then a syndicate including Robertson, Wagner, James Rutherford [q.v.] and Walter Russell Hall bought the name and business. The new firm of Robertson and Wagner traded as Cobb & Co. Robertson ran Victorian operations from Castlemaine and developed a near-monopoly of coach services and mail contracts in the north-central and north-west districts. In 1871 the Victorian business, at its peak, became the property of Robertson and Wagner.

On 26 November 1861 Robertson married Emily, daughter of Western District pastoralist Samuel John Davidson; she died in 1866, leaving a daughter. On 1 October 1867 he married Hannah Elizabeth Goldsbrough, daughter of Hugh Parker, brother-in-law and partner of R. Goldsbrough [q.v.]; she died in 1881, leaving three sons and two daughters.

Coaching declined as the railway network spread. Robertson widened his profitable pastoral interests, held through various partnerships with Goldsbrough, Wagner and his brother John (d. 24 June 1899). In 1881 he became a director, in 1886-93 chairman, of R. Goldsbrough & Co. Ltd. In 1882-88 he was also a director of the Squatting Investment Co., an offshoot of the Goldsbrough firm. Robertson was competent but did not provide strong leadership in the difficult years that preceded the 1893 financial collapse; he preferred to enjoy his wealth. A committee-man of the Victoria Racing Club from 1867, he was a keen sportsman. With a son at Cambridge and daughters at a finishing school in Paris, in the later 1880s he travelled extensively to England, the Continent and Canada. He entertained lavishly at Perricoota station near Moama, New South Wales, where the duke of Edinburgh visited, in London where Melba performed for his guests in June 1890, and in the opulent mansion, Ontario, which he built in Caulfield in 1890. He died at Caulfield on 16 July 1896 after a long illness and was buried in Boroondara cemetery, Kew.

K. A. Austin, The lights of Cobb and Co. (Adel, 1967); Australasian, 18 July 1896; Pastoral Review, 15 Aug 1896; Goldsbrough Mort & Co. records and Squatting Investment Co. papers (ANU Archives); information from Mr N. R. G. Robertson, Vic.   ALAN BARNARD

ROBERTSON, GEORGE (1825-1898), bookseller and publisher, was born on 5 July 1825 at Glasgow, Scotland, son of Rev. William Robertson, Congregational minister and city missioner, and his wife Sarah, née Stee. In 1829 the family moved to Dublin. Robertson left school at 12 and was apprenticed to William Curry, jun. & Co., booksellers; S. Mullen [q.v.] worked there later and the two became friends. Robertson joined Curry's manager, James McGlashan, when he began his own bookshop in 1846.

In 1852, with no prospects in Ireland, Robertson migrated to Victoria in the Great Britain, taking a supply of books. He reached Melbourne with Mullen on 12 November; E. W. Cole [q.v.] arrived the same day. With not enough money for a cab to the city, Robertson sold a case of books on the wharf. He opened at 84 Russell Street but in March 1853 moved to larger premises in Collins Street East and Mullen became his manager. Ordering large stocks some six months in advance, Robertson met education orders, opened a library and supplied retailers throughout Australia and New Zealand. With generous credit he helped other booksellers to set up on their own. In 1857 Robertson sent Mullen to London to open a buying office but before he arrived Robertson had given the post to his own brother William. They never spoke to each other again.

With trade increasing, Robertson built a large warehouse in Elizabeth Street in 1860. He opened in Sydney and appointed a resident traveller in New Zealand. In 1862 he quit Sydney but restarted there in 1875 and opened at Adelaide and Brisbane soon after. In 1872 he concentrated on wholesaling and moved to a large warehouse in Little Collins Street. In 1883, at the suggestion of his friend David Syme [q.v.], he made the business a public company, giving shares to senior employees. An individualist, Robertson was soon irked by the board of directors; after four years he bought out the company and resumed control with his sons as partners.

Robertson issued elaborate literary, educational and medical catalogues and in 1861-91 distributed his Monthly Book Circular. He opposed the admission of American pirated editions of British novels. His first publication, a sermon by Rev. Macintosh Mackay, appeared in 1855. He built up an important publishing list and was the first in Australia to set up a separate publishing department. His authors included James Bonwick, A. L. Gordon, Henry Kendall, W. E. Hearn, Marcus Clarke, Rolf Boldrewood (T.A. Browne), G. G. McCrae [qq.v.] and Brunton Stephens. He issued over six hundred titles, including many textbooks and practical works, taking the risk on his principal books; his best publications were reprinted or distributed in Britain. He installed a lithographic plant and bindery and imported the stereotype plates of overseas books for which he had secured the local rights. Robertson imported books from the United States and also printed local editions of leading American writers. He was the only bookseller to have his name as a distributor on the title-page of Raffaello Carboni's [q.v.] *The Eureka Stockade* (1855). He sponsored a biography of C. J. Don [q.v.] and brought out a local edition of the novel by the Irish convict J. B. O'Reilly [q.v.].

In ill health, Robertson retired in 1890 and died on 28 March 1898 at the St Kilda mansion he had built in 1865; he was buried in the St Kilda cemetery and is commemorated by a tablet in All Saints' Church, East St Kilda. He was survived by three sons and three daughters of his first wife, Lavinia Lydia, née Baxter (d. 1879), whom he had married at St Paul's, Melbourne, on 4 July 1857, and by his second wife, Nora Parsons, née Harding, whom he had married on 3 February 1881, and their two sons and two daughters.

Although he lost heavily on his shareholdings during the financial collapse of the 1890s, Robertson left an estate valued at £117,477. After his retirement, his second son, Charles Melbourne, took over the firm, but his sons, who had always deferred to him, were not good businessmen. Reserved and dour, Robertson never sought public honours but was generous to his employees and to charities. An excellent mentor, at various times he employed such notable men as W. Dymock, David Angus, George Robertson (1860-1933), F. W. Preece, and G. B. Philip. The rival firms established by Robertson and Mullen were merged in 1921.

Notices of the book & stationery warehouse . . . erected for George Robertson (Melb, 1860); *Correspondence between Associated Booksellers of Aust . . . and the Publishers' Assn of Great Britain* (Syd, 1926); J. Holroyd, *George Robertson of Melbourne* (Melb, 1968); L. Slade, 'Melbourne's early booksellers', VHM, 15 (1935); *Age*, 24 Mar 1898; *Argus*, 24 Mar 1898.

J. P. HOLROYD

ROBERTSON, SIR JOHN (1816-1891), land reformer and politician, was born on 15 October 1816 at Bow near London, third son and fourth child of James Robertson (1781-1868), watchmaker and pastoralist, and his wife Anna Maria, née Ripley (1784-1868), who were married at Stepney, London, in 1809. James was a friend of Governor Sir Thomas Brisbane and on his advice migrated with his family to New South Wales, arriving in Sydney in the *Provi-*

dence on 8 January 1822. Appointed general superintendent of government clocks he also worked as a watchmaker and silversmith; with an 86-acre grant he moved from Castlereagh Street to Robertson's Point (Cremorne) on Sydney Harbour and acquired property in the Hunter River district.

At first John went to Mr McLeod's school in Phillip Street, then to J. Bradley's school; in 1826 he became the first pupil enrolled at Dr J. D. Lang's [q.v.] primary school and remained close to him until his death in 1878. He completed his education with J. Gilchrist and W. T. Cape [q.v.]. By the age of 16 he had an intimate knowledge of the streets and environs of Sydney and with affectionate skill had mastered sailing on its beckoning harbour; he had been adopted by the vital native-born, whose youth and patriotism blurred class distinctions between the children of those who had been transported and of those who had come free to the colony. Because of a cleft palate his speech was abnormal; it had retarded neither the growth of his command of language nor the unfolding of his love of life, but it had provoked some juvenile ridicule and remained a tempting butt for hostile adults for most of his life; and it had helped to attract a loyal group of young friends who warmed to his personality and found a ready response.

Robertson's adventuresome taste for the sea overcame parental objections and financial problems in 1833 when he worked his passage to England in the *Sovereign* under Captain McKellar. Among many letters to deliver he had one from one of his father's convict servants, James Day, to his mother, who was a friend of Lord Palmerston. He called on Palmerston, spent three days at his country estate and was given a letter recommending him to Governor Sir Richard Bourke, which he later simply posted. Robertson told his relations that while he had been 'an English infant . . . as a man I am an Australian!' He took a course in navigation, studied farming techniques and visited several coastal towns, including Portsmouth where he inspected the dockyard. He also went to Scotland and France, and on his way back to New South Wales called at Brazil and other parts of South America.

Although still drawn to the sea, in 1835 Robertson joined his father on the land at Plashett, Jerry's Plains, on the Hunter River, and gradually acquired much country experience as a station manager and minor explorer of the north-west, traversing the Liverpool Plains to the Namoi and down the Darling to the site of the future town of Bourke. He responded to the harsh demands of the bush and, in becoming a squatter, did not reject their claims for more sympathetic understanding from the government in Sydney; but he never forgot that by depasturing licences and leases they had the use of land that belonged to the community. In 1838 he represented the Namoi pastoralists in Sydney and called a meeting at the Royal Hotel of about fifty squatters, including Alexander Busby and (Sir) Saul Samuel [q.v.], to protest successfully against Governor Sir George Gipps's prohibition of further north-west expansion beyond the boundaries of location. Next year his decision to remain on the land was confirmed when, in Sydney on 9 May, he married Margaret Emma (Madge) Davies, niece of Thomas Barker [q.v.], according to Presbyterian rites, and settled down as a wheat-grower on freehold land near Scone in the Upper Hunter district; in 1840 he was licensee of Arrarrowme, 20,000 acres in the Liverpool Plains District. Bankruptcy forced him to sell his 320-acre farm at Jerry's Plains in 1843.

Robertson was a chief supporter of Richard Windeyer [q.v.] when he won the County of Durham seat at the first elections for the Legislative Council in 1843, and named his first son (b. 1851) after him. Robertson now appreciated the complexity of the land question, becoming increasingly aware of the inferior legislative position of farmers and of the class bias of some wealthy squatters. He was also uneasy about the power of the governor and of the interference of the British government. He therefore supported the squatters in 1844 against Gipps's arbitrary regulations, campaigning in Muswellbrook, Scone, Singleton, Jerry's Plains and Maitland and framing petitions to the council and Westminster. But he rejected their extreme claims to security of tenure and other privileges, and refused to join the Pastoral Association of New South Wales and to endorse the work of Archibald Boyd [q.v.]. By the mid-1840s Robertson's political views were based on his appreciation of rural problems, which he saw as revealing the vital issue of the time: the need for responsible government for the colony, based on equal electorates, with a democratic franchise to control both the exorbitant pretensions of the squatters and the power of the imperial authorities, local as well as British. So he held aloof from any connexion with the existing forms of government, though he shared many of the objectives but not the style of the 'Constitutional Party', which included, with varying degrees of cohesion and political ideas, (Sir) Charles Cowper, Sir Charles Nicholson, Robert Lowe, W. C. Wentworth [qq.v], Lang and Windeyer. In 1848 at a Maitland meeting against Lord Grey's constitution he had an amendment accepted that the colony did not want a House of Lords or a bench of bishops.

Robertson emerged as the most representative New South Wales colonist of the 1850s, moulded by his personal and perceptive experience of the main forces that had shaped colonial society and politics: the competing claims of convict and non-convict elements, as moderated by the role of the native-born; the complex movement for representative government; and the demands of the squatters for security of tenure with the help of the British government and at the expense of the majority of colonists. No other politician had such sympathetic insight into the texture and subtleties of the radical needs of the times: some belonged to the past order of social snobbery and imperial control, such as (Sir) Stuart Donaldson, (Sir) Edward Deas Thomson, and (Sir) Henry Watson Parker [qq.v.]; others were hindered in their understanding by their family connexions, such as Cowper; or by their English formation, such as (Sir) Henry Parkes [q.v.]; or by their social ambitions, such as (Sir) James Martin [q.v.]. Only Wentworth might have rivalled Robertson, but his day was over, his radicalism dimmed by age and wealth. Above all, none, with the minor exception of William Forster [q.v.], had anything like Robertson's familiarity with the Australian outback, and land dominated the politics of the late 1850s and remained a major question for the rest of the century. But if he led enlightened social and political opinion he was not acceptable to polite society. By 1850 his peculiar voice gave authority to a comprehensive repertoire of profanity and he had an enviable capacity to take and hold his liquor; his bushman's clothes were crumpled by constant riding; but he was handsome, with reddish-brown hair and beard, sparkling blue eyes, 'slightly above the middle height, his figure...slim and well-made, not strong nor robust, although . . . apparently very healthy'.

Robertson was affronted by Thomson's Electoral Act of 1850, which redistributed seats in New South Wales after the separation of Victoria, on the basis of 'the great interests' with the towns (mercantile and trading) having 11 members (population 75,000), the counties (agricultural and pastoral) 17 (80,000), and the pastoral districts 8 (30,000). This Act and a restricted franchise convinced Robertson that the squatters, now led by Wentworth, had combined with the local officials to maintain a monopoly of land. Next year at the council elections for the seat of the Counties of Phillip, Brisbane and Bligh he began to campaign for Lang who, however, retained Sydney. When Wentworth's conservative committee submitted its responsible government Constitution bill in 1853 with the remark that it had 'no wish to sow the seeds of a future democracy', Robertson readily accepted the challenge, joined the Constitution Committee, which sought to liberalize the Constitution, and became its most radical member. He wrote to Lang criticizing the committee for its deference to the British Constitution which it saw as 'an answer for everything that could be said against the iniquity of Wentworth's attempt to saddle us with a hereditary upper house . . . and all the paraphernalia of attendant rascalities'.

Robertson saw the British Constitution as vague, aristocratic and largely inapplicable to colonial conditions. As 'a mere denizen of the bush', in long letters to the *Empire* (November, December 1853) from Yarrundi, Scone, he urged petitions to the Queen and British parliament and to the governor for the dissolution of the council, and elections to test the feelings of the voters; he attacked Martin for asserting that 'the franchise was a mere matter of convenience' and argued for universal adult suffrage, though he reluctantly quoted the Bible to exclude women and children; electorates should be based on equal population 'without reference to the locality . . . or the business in which they are engaged', except that the seat of government should have fewer members because it would have several residents elected for country seats; he wanted only one House, elected biennially, but, in accepting two because public opinion favoured it, he required the Upper House of twenty-five to be 'elected by the members of the . . . Assembly, five to go out by rotation every two years'. In 1854 his petition against the nominee Upper House, the two-thirds majority for amendment and the electoral distribution clauses of the Constitution was adopted at a public meeting in Sydney and forwarded to Lowe for presentation to the British parliament; but, despite modifications made in London, the Constitution of 1855 was far from his ideal and his intense opposition to it had contributed to a decline in his health; his voice seemed to be failing completely and his heart weakening. In 1856 he was invited to run for the seat of Phillip, Brisbane and Bligh at the first parliamentary elections and, although he took no active part in the campaign, he won.

Robertson's electoral platform was manhood suffrage, vote by secret ballot, equal electoral districts on population, abolition of state aid to religion, National education, free trade, and free selection of crown lands before survey. Much of this programme was shared by other liberals, but only Robertson was an uninhibited radical determined to overcome the novel parliamentary problems in the manner in which he had come to terms with the sea and the bush. The key to basic social reform was change in land policy, with the colonial legislature and government accepting the need that settlers, mainly agricultural and with minimum capital, should have ready access to land, even that occupied by lease-holding squatters. Constitutional and electoral reform was comparatively easy to effect. The events of 1856-61 showed how Robertson dominated colonial politics as his unique insight and determination led him to implement land reform. In 1856 he changed the reactionary tenor of the Masters' and Servants' Acts continuation bill when he had a select committee appointed, and became one of three members of a sub-committee that drafted a new liberal bill. In 1857 he sat on the select committee on secondary punishment, and opposed strongly Parker's electoral bill, which he described as 'ten times worse than any that was ever before the country'.

In 1855 Robertson had told the old Legislative Council's select committee on the state of agriculture that the government's policy had actually depressed agriculture, with farmers excluded from leasing and generally in a much inferior position to pastoralists; he urged that the balance be redressed, though he insisted that he was not 'hostile, to the pastoral interest . . . [because] one interest should support the other, for complete prosperity can never reach either until both are in a satisfactory state'. This stress on the interdependent rights of both farmers and graziers remained an essential part of his land policy. In 1856 he opposed the Donaldson government's crown lands' sale bill; next year he rejected the Parker ministry's bill and tried to amend the Cowper government's bill by moving for selection either of 'surveyed or unsurveyed' land at a fixed minimum price, on condition that the selectors resided on the land and improved it; at first only D. H. Deniehy [q.v.] supported him and only nine members later; but he was responsible for the bill's discharge on 10 December. He was now recognized as the outstanding land reformer and Cowper, who led the moderate liberals, accepted him on his terms as secretary for lands and works on 13 January 1858. He retained his seat at the general election in February.

Robertson at once set about reforming and extending the infant Department of

Lands. His regulations of 22 February provided that all current and future applications for pastoral runs would be subject to whatever decision parliament should make on land policy. On 12 August he successfully brought down his pastoral lands assessment and rent bill which set rents on runs in the intermediate and unsettled districts and increased rents in the settled district, parliament's initial step to balance the competing land interests. His first major land legislation was the crown lands alienation in certain cases bill; introduced on 2 September it lapsed when the House was counted out on 16 September, a typical parliamentary device. Meanwhile, he had played a strong part in the success of Cowper's electoral law amendment bill, which brought in adult male franchise, increased seats from 54 to 80, plus 1 provisionally for the University of Sydney (the seats were reduced to 72, plus 1, when Queensland was separated in 1859); and he carried the main roads management bill.

At the June 1859 general election Robertson explained the difficulties he was having with his land legislation, and retained his seat, now the Upper Hunter. The Cowper ministry remained in office. Public works was taken from his portfolio, and as secretary for lands he reorganized the Surveyor-General's Department. On 28 September he brought down three bills, crown lands sales, crown lands occupation and leased lands occupation; the last one was defeated 27 to 20 and he withdrew the others. Robertson disagreed with Cowper on the details of the public education bill; the ministry was defeated on it on 22 September and resigned on 26 October, with Cowper resigning his seat the next day. Robertson became leader of the Opposition as Forster formed a new ministry that fell in February 1860; Robertson arranged his first cabinet, as secretary for lands, on 9 March, with Cowper, now in the council, as colonial secretary. By September he had his new land legislation ready and brought down the crown lands alienation bill and the crown lands occupation bill, embodying free selection before survey; both bills passed their second reading, but in committee in October the vital clause was defeated 33 to 28. With his parliamentary resources exhausted Robertson obtained a dissolution and prepared to fight a general election on the issue in December. The New South Wales political crisis received Australia-wide publicity.

It was clear that Robertson had manipulated events to bring radical land reform manifestly before the electors, the first time that they had been asked to decide any political issue. The elections were keenly fought, with excited meetings throughout Sydney and the country. The question of state aid to Churches was also involved and its abolition was probably Robertson's first priority after land reform. He received much help from liberals of varying shades including Cowper, who was returned for East Sydney. The momentum of reform had crystallized much variegated support from town and country, but the elections were a personal triumph for Robertson and a tribute to his radical leadership. Of 53 candidates who said they favoured his land bills, 35 were elected and, of these, 25 wanted abolition of state aid; all 14 candidates who openly opposed the bills were defeated. Although there were no firm party lines it was obvious that the 'new democracy' had endorsed his policy, and that he had contributed to the dissolution of the old conservative, official order.

To concentrate solely on the problem of carrying his legislation in both assembly and council he retired on 9 January 1861 from the premiership, which Cowper resumed. The Sydney Morning Herald was now calling him 'the Dictator'. He resubmitted his bills on 16 January; both were sent up to the council on 27 March; he resigned the next day, and on 3 April was appointed to the council, where he stubbornly refused to compromise with conservative amendments; and he prevailed on Cowper to advise the governor, Sir John Young, to swamp the council, or cabinet would resign. With the end of the first five-year appointments imminent the governor agreed, but nineteen angered conservatives led by President Sir William Burton [q.v.] resigned on 10 May and left the council without a quorum. In the compromise over its reconstruction Robertson was reappointed on 24 June but on a technicality could not reintroduce his legislation; Cowper presented it in the assembly on 18 September and assent was given to both bills on 24 October.

Some historians have seen Robertson's great land reforms as necessary for the triumph of the 'middle classes', including owners of freehold land and urban liberals, over the squatters, with no sincere intention of concentrated land settlement. But colonial society did not lend itself to this over-simplification. Many urban residents, of diverse occupations and financial and political interests, were squatters; many rural residents were neither freeholders nor squatters, and many were liberals. Robertson himself reflected the social and political complexity: he was a country freeholder, but held squatting leases and leased land to tenant farmers, and he was the most radical of the liberals. He certainly saw his gruelling campaign as an honest and balanced attempt to compose the long-standing land problem for the benefit of all colonists, not least the landless country people. He was the great apostle of social equilibrium through land justice and he tapped city and country resentment, built up over a generation, to become one of the great land reformers of the nineteenth century: a result of his individuality and integrated colonial formation. Only he could have responded to the deeply-rooted levelling cry for easy access to land for all who wanted it, and he saw in agriculture a dual opportunity for land settlement and economic differentiation. Virtually none of his parliamentary supporters understood the complexities of his proposals; all of them were dragged along by the force of his personality and his relentless energy to accept the propositions that unsurveyed land could now be selected and bought freehold in 320-acre lots at £1 per acre, on a deposit of 5s. per acre, the balance to be paid within three years, an interest-free loan of three-quarters of the price; and that wealthy people would find it hard to speculate because bona fide residence was stipulated. He had formulated the greatest social theme in nineteenth century Australian history.

Robertson's endearing stubbornness shaded into vanity and he found it hard to comprehend that politics was much wider than the land problem, that voters and politicians were fickle, and that pioneering administration was intricate and burdensome. John Garrett, father of his close friend Thomas Garrett [q.v.], resigned the seat of Shoalhaven to allow him to return to the assembly on 7 January 1862. He lost some popularity the same month when he not only allowed the promoters of the first English cricket team to charge admission to a match on the Sydney Domain, but also arranged a free stand for parliamentarians; but he supplied necessary stiffening for the passage of Cowper's grants for public worship prohibition bill in October. By then Robertson was the centre of a group of admiring followers and he had a few electoral agents, but in no sense a political party; his giving of complete loyalty was distinguishing him from ambitious and devious politicians like Martin and Parkes. He never quite lost the style of the blunt, simple, optimistic countryman. The management of colonial finances was proving difficult for the Cowper government and in October 1863 it lost office to Martin to begin a period of 15 years in which 11 ministries were formed, shared by Martin, 3, Cowper, 2, Parkes, 2, Robertson, 3, and J. S. Farnell [q.v.], 1. Robertson contributed to this political instability and was affected by it.

To meet a balance of payments deficit Martin proposed a mild protective tariff and the ensuing 1864-65 general election raised the fiscal issue for the first time. Robertson had always been a keen free trader, but had subordinated economics to land; now he headed the poll at West Sydney, the chief centre of working-class voters and a strong free-trade area. He became secretary for lands again on 3 February 1865 in the new Cowper government; but the financial problem predominated and the necessity of implementing Martin's fiscal policy shattered the liberals' 1850s dream of prosperity through a new order based on free trade and rational policies on land, religion, railways and education. Robertson found that the Lands Department could not be expanded and reorganized quickly enough to cope with increasing work and complexity; moreover, he had financial problems of his own: his political career had ended his control of his Upper Hunter property and he speculated in squatting in north Queensland; by 10 October these investments demanded his attention and he resigned from parliament; but an equivocal letter to his supporters reflected the great pull politics had on him and they urged him 'to devote such portion of his time and attention . . . to watch and defend [his] great measures of reform'; they renominated him and he regained the seat again on 18 October. By the end of the year he was again active in the assembly, but his finances had not been restored, and some apparent flaws in his 1861 legislation had been revealed.

Four years operation of the land Acts had helped to solve some of the problems of country life, but while settlement and agricultural output had expanded, the pastoral industry was still pre-eminent and run lessees remained vocal and powerful. Some unprecedented agrarian tension suggested the need for an overhaul of legislation and administration. Even if political conditions and his personal affairs had been favourable, Robertson would probably have not admitted that changes were necessary; but the decomposition of the liberals and his own troubles made further reform impossible. On 1 January 1866 Cowper tried to arrest his group's political decline by bringing Robertson back as secretary for lands. In the campaign for his re-election following acceptance of the office Robertson faced opposition that showed the extent of the general disillusionment. Following an electoral meeting at which he was shouted down, the critical Sydney Morning Herald remarked 'that his incomparable eloquence no longer had power to charm'. Specifically, he was blamed for the policy of his predecessor in office, W. M. Arnold [q.v.], of reserving from selection certain land until it was surveyed for water supply or other public purposes. This was interpreted, especially by working-class voters, as yielding to pressure from the squatters. In vain did Robertson tell them and the *Herald* that this procedure was based on a clause of the Land Alienation Act, that it was part of his general policy to protect the public interest, as well as that of selectors and squatters. He lost West Sydney on 17 January and the ministry resigned on 21 January.

Part of the *Herald*'s attack on him had been that he was 'the President of the Fenian Society'; in denying it and explaining that he was sympathetic with the Irish [National] League, 'which upheld Ireland's just claims and requirements', he showed that he had responded to a powerful demand on colonial politicians: discreet adjustment to various sectarian pressures. He was president of the local branch of the league in 1864-65 but, a Freemason, he nicely combined independence, open-heartedness and tolerance, and was never controlled by any organization. He returned to the House at a by-election as member for the Clarence on 27 August and gave vital support to Parkes's public schools bill, though he argued that it conceded too much to denominational prejudices.

Robertson was now living in a fine house, Clovelly (Robertson Park), Watsons Bay, and his personal and political problems did not dampen his spirits. In the House his 'voice [remained] the loudest, his language the most violent and his attitudes the most distorted'. In 1867 A. A. P. Tighe [q.v.] remarked 'He may be a great man in the club-houses, at the street-corners, and in the tap-room; but in this House he is no more than myself'; and Martin compared him to Tiberius Sempronius Gracchus 'in that both advocated the cause of free selection, both hit upon the same amount of land for each individual . . . [and] both had been the idols of the people . . . [and] deserted by the people'. When the Martin government disintegrated in 1868 Robertson formed his second ministry on 27 October, and he won West Sydney at the 1869-70 general election; but both his financial difficulties and the parliamentary torpor intensified; none of his own bills succeeded, including one to reduce parliament's term to three years. On 13 January 1870 Cowper took over as premier and Robertson resigned his seat on 22 February because of his bankruptcy. He had invested in 'very large' Queensland sheep and cattle stations with J. G. Macdonald, and 'for several years . . . incompetent and unfruitful agents' had mismanaged the properties while his parliamentary work had prevented his active control: £168,873 was owing to (Sir) Alexander Stuart and R. Towns [qq.v.], but his final deficiency was £6746.

A reformed social equilibrium, combining elements both of the 'new democracy' and the old establishment, was revealed by the way in which colonists responded to help Robertson. Garrett and Lang rallied his close friends and the movement spread to two public meetings in March at which a wide cross-section was represented, including Sir William Manning [q.v.], a pre-1856 official who said, 'There was a time when I did not hold [him] in such high esteem; but as his public character became developed I learnt to appreciate him'; a committee of twenty-eight was formed to raise and invest money 'for the permanent benefit of Mr. Robertson's family'. He regained his seat on 2 March 1870, was discharged from bankruptcy in August and returned as secretary for lands. But the social absorption of the liberals could not disguise their political dismemberment; after Cowper's acceptance of the post of agent-general in London, his government resigned on 15 December; and next day Robertson shocked many of his friends by joining Martin's ministry as colonial secretary, a decision that revealed the renovated flexibility of colonial politicians and ushered in a decade of sterile exchanges of governments by Robertson and Parkes.

Robertson did nothing to relieve the chronic legislative inertia of the Martin ministry. By early 1872 only seven of eighteen non-financial ministerial bills had been carried and the government had annoyed Victoria and inflamed the Riverina over its failure to re-negotiate the border duties agreement of 1867. Robertson engaged in a lively correspondence with (Sir) Charles Gavan Duffy [q.v.] and spoke strongly about what he saw as Victoria's rapacity. But public opinion was against the government and at the 1872 general election only three of the six ministers, including Robertson at West Sydney, were returned. Parkes became premier on 14 May and Robertson became a peppery leader of the Opposition. In 1874 he incensed Sir Hercules Robinson by his criticism of the governor's language in his Executive Council minute on the public reaction to the release of the bushranger Frank Gardiner [q.v.]. When the Parkes ministry fell on the issue, Robertson won West Sydney in February 1875 and seemed to have collected the most supporters at the general election; after the governor had at first refused to commission him, as colonial secretary he formed his third ministry on 9 February, including W. B. Dalley [q.v.], one of his native-born admirers of the 1850s. He left the accumulating land problems to Garrett who expertly set up new courts under the Lands Acts Amendment Act, 1875, but the Legislative Council had been almost immovable on the bill and no renovation of the laws was attempted.

Elements of farce, disquieting to Governor Robinson, now deranged colonial politics. Robertson's government fell in March 1877 and Parkes was in office until August, when Robertson returned, only to obtain a dissolution in October. Although made a K.C.M.G. and known as 'the Knight of Clovelly', his backing in Sydney was less than in 1866. At his nomination at West Sydney on 23 October 1877 the booing stifled the cheering and he was counted out; he lost his seat, but remained popular in the country and was returned for two electorates, East Macquarie and Mudgee, and sat for Mudgee. Farnell formed a stop-gap ministry on 18 December with parliament divided into at least three loose groups and several independents. Assisted by Governor Robinson, events began to swirl around Robertson and Parkes, compelling the two knights into a latter-day partnership that would consummate the remaining liberal aspirations of the 1850s. Robertson had never got on with Parkes; his deviousness was seasoned with an amiably expressed sense of fun, notably lacking in Sir Henry; and his ambition was far less devouring and self-distorting. Robertson made several cronies out of his many friends. Parkes had few friends. Now they were about to combine in the strongest pre-1894 colonial government.

Farnell's government made an attempt to amend the land laws, but was defeated on 5 December 1878. The governor refused a dissolution and asked Robertson to form a ministry. It was clear to Sir Hercules that the only viable government was one that would include Robertson and Parkes, but he was made aware that Robertson would never make the first move to coalesce when he selected a cabinet of his own friends; at least one of these, James Watson [q.v.], also shared the governor's view. Robertson soon saw that his proposed ministry could not function, and that parliament was rapidly becoming unworkable. He judged that if he were out of the way he would not have to jettison any of his friends in a coalition cabinet, and that Parkes would attract sufficient of his supporters to organize an effective government. On 13 December he resigned his seat in a characteristic fusion of stubborn pride, solidarity, and self-sacrifice; it was not part of a pre-arranged plot with Parkes but it facilitated a meeting of his and Parkes's followers to elect Sir Henry as leader of the Opposition, and the defeat of Farnell on 18 December. In order to consolidate his inchoate support, Parkes offered Robertson the positions of vice-president of the Executive Council and representative of the government in the Legislative Council, on salary; he accepted on 21 December. The governor reported correctly to the British government that the coalition had been conditioned by his procedure of refusing Farnell a dissolution and first asking Robertson rather than Parkes to form a ministry.

The new government repaired more than a decade's neglect of pressing legislation. Its term of office saw an unprecedented rate of introduction and success of public bills by ministers: of 131 brought down, 85 (15 supply bills) were passed. For the first time in parliamentary sessions ministerial bills exceeded private members' bills. Necessary reforms were effected in electoral law, education and hotel licensing, and significant changes in land, mining and aspects of local government. To the governor's relief financial legislation was cleared on time. The coalition increased its support at the 1880 general election. Robertson played a vital part in its success, adapting skilfully to the unique methods of the council and in May adding the portfolio of the first minister of public instruction to his posts. But he resigned from the ministry on 10 November 1881 because of Parkes's antagonism to his friends E. A. Baker [q.v.] and Garrett on the report of the Milburn Creek Copper-Mining Co. royal commission.

By 1880 rising demand for basic reform of Robertson's original land legislation could no longer be ignored. The hard facts of geography, transport and markets had ensured that agriculture was still inferior to the pastoral industry; consequently, the substantial increase in land settlement and wheat acreage, which reflected the significant achievement of Robertson's Acts, had contributed to serious conflict between selectors and squatters, with much litigation and some agrarian lawlessness that had to be stopped. Robertson refused to agree that fundamental change was needed, and he had influenced the partial repairs provided by James Hoskins's [q.v.] Lands Acts Further Amendment Act, 1880; but claims of increasing law-breaking continued, even free selectors' organizations urged greater security of tenure for squatters under certain conditions; and, after Robertson's resignation, cabinet decided that this would be granted. At the same time Parkes's health was failing; he planned a visit overseas and asked Robertson to take over the government. He agreed with alacrity and became acting premier on 29 December 1881.

Hoskins resigned to allow Robertson to become secretary for lands and S. H. Terry [q.v.] resigned for him to regain Mudgee on 13 January 1882. He left no doubt that he would reverse the government's new land policy. When he brought down his crown lands bill on 19 October it reflected his domination over the cabinet, including Parkes who had resumed as premier on 20 August: it consolidated the 1861 law, free selection before survey remained and security of tenure was not granted. Robertson had clung grimly to his great radical ideas of the 1850s, but he was clearly out of touch with the needs of the 1880s and his nostalgic obstinacy destroyed the coalition's cohesion. The bill failed to pass its second reading; a dissolution was granted, the government lost the election and resigned on 4 January 1883. Robertson retained his seat.

He contributed much to the exhausting year it took the Stuart government to pass a new Crown Lands Act, 1884. The travail marked the effective end of his great political work and exposed the renewed confusion of the legislature. He held Mudgee at the general election of October 1885, which confirmed a babble of parliamentary groups, responding unpredictably to a financial crisis that indicated the need for basic political and fiscal reform. He attacked (Sir) G. R. Dibbs's [q.v.] multiform ministry over its financial policy and when it fell he formed his last cabinet on 22 December. He had hoped to include Parkes in a revitalized attempt to restore the old order, but Sir Henry sensed his decline and uncandidly refused, 'So that he might bucket me the first chance he had'. Parkes and others soon took the opportunity and Robertson's government collapsed on 25 February 1886. Later he injured his leg while working in the National Park, south of Sydney: he was chairman of its trustees and had been responsible for its reservation. The accident compounded his dejection and, with his finances low, he resigned his seat on 18 June. The colony agreed with the Jennings [q.v.] government's decision to grant him £10,000 in recognition of his thirty years service to parliament.

In October 1879 Parkes had been having second thoughts about the advantages of Robertson as a partner, and offered him the post of agent-general. In shrewdly declining, he remarked that he had just returned from a 600-mile journey to the north-west, eighty miles on horseback: Parkes had probably never ridden a horse. Despite Robertson's strenuous and gratifying activities he had generally enjoyed robust health. By 1880 his beard and hair, worn long, had whitened; his shoulders had stooped, his nose curved closer to his chin, and a sly glint replaced the spark in his eyes. In becoming more handsome with age he had reached patriarchal status. He was the most representative Australian of the 1880s, a genial, sagacious and incomparably experienced countryman, assimilated to the city.

In Melbourne in 1875, in proposing a toast of 'Prosperity to Victoria', he had said, 'I have never had any miserable objection or petty feeling against Victoria ... I claim to be an Australian'. With reservations that was true. His idea of Australia was the original New South Wales; he had never forgotten that the separation of the Port Phillip District in 1850 and the Moreton Bay District in 1859 had, as he saw it, destroyed the opportunity of great national development. He resented Victoria's failure in 1867 to join a proposed Federal Council to control overseas mail to Australia; he saw its protection policy as selfish and isolationist; when Victorian colonists moved into the Riverina in the 1860s and 1870s and Victorian politicians and publicists spoke of annexing it, his worst fears seemed about to be realized. He interpreted James Service's [q.v.] statements about New Guinea and the Pacific at the 1883 Intercolonial Convention as predatory and dangerous to Britain's interests, and exploded when Service spoke contemptuously of New South Wales politicians on his return to Melbourne. The Sydney Morning Herald summed up his reaction in 1884, 'he pricks the pride of [Victoria's] public men ... [and] sees bumptious pretenders to pre-eminence strutting about in a cabbage garden'.

In 1884 Dalley recalled Robertson's 1875 submission to the British government stressing the urgency of Britain occupying New Guinea and its adjoining islands. Robertson's view of Britain's role was part of his objections to national union. He influentially opposed New South Wales joining the Federal Council in 1884 and in 1884-85 took every opportunity in parliament to criticize Federation. He articulated not only the colony's provincialism but also its well-founded suspicions of Victoria's self-interest in promoting the movement. In the late 1880s he peppered the Sydney newspapers with letters on the subject, some cogent, others violent and irrational. Unlike Parkes, he was unable to grasp the essential need for, and advantages of Federation that transcended any local gains or losses involved; but he helped to prepare public opinion for serious and detailed study of the movement in the 1890s. He scorned the embryonic free-trade political organization in 1887: 'Associations!', he said, 'That is the way they do it in France'.

Lady Robertson chose not to share her husband's public life; she died on 6 August 1889 at Watsons Bay, leaving two of her three sons and five of her six daughters; another daughter died before Robertson's death of heart disease on 8 May 1891 at Watsons Bay. He was buried beside his wife in the Presbyterian section of the near-by South Head cemetery. Public subscriptions paid for the erection over the grave of a forceful stone obelisk, exquisitely carved by J. H. Hunt [q.v.]: statues are in the Sydney Domain and at the Lands Department. Of the abounding anecdotes about Robertson's geniality and conviviality, many related to his presidency of the Reform Club in 1877-82, perhaps the most revealing is his reported reaction to the death of James Day who fell into a well at Clovelly: 'When Robertson found out he started swearing in the full vigour of his manhood. He had kept the man from the days of his laghood, and now when he had b—— well got him to a home where he could end his days in comfort he must go and b—— well drown himself. Robertson gave him a b—— good funeral and was chief mourner'.

D. Buchanan, *Political portraits of some of the members of the parliament of New South Wales* (Syd, 1863); P. Loveday and A. W. Martin, *Parliament factions and parties* (Melb, 1966); *V&P* (LC NSW), 1855, 3, 311-16, (LA NSW), 1879-80, 2, 673; J. Main, 'Making Constitutions in New South Wales and Victoria, 1853-1854', *Hist Studies*, no 28, May 1957; D. W. A. Baker, 'The origins of Robertson's Land Acts', *Historical Studies: selected articles*, J. J. Eastwood and F. B. Smith eds (Melb, 1964); N. B. Nairn, 'The political mastery of Sir Henry Parkes', *JRAHS*, 53 (1967); C. Karr, 'Mythology vs. reality: the success of free selection in New South Wales', *JRAHS*, 60 (1974); *Empire* (Syd), 14 May 1856; *SMH*, 17 Oct 1865, 23 Jan 1866, 9 May 1891; *T&CJ*, 12, 26 Mar 1870; *Syd Q Mag*, June 1886; G. C. Morey, The Parkes-Robertson coalition government, 1878-1883: a study (B.A. Hons thesis, ANU, 1968); C. N. Connolly, Politics, ideology and the New South Wales Legislative Council, 1856-72 (Ph.D. thesis, ANU, 1974); Cowper and Lang papers (ML); Parkes letters (ML); Sir John Robertson scrapbook (NL); CO 201/518, 538, 559, 585.   BEDE NAIRN

ROBERTSON, WILLIAM (1798-1874), pastoralist, was born on 7 October 1798 at Alvie, Inverness-shire, Scotland, son of Duncan Robertson, sheep-farmer, and his wife Christian, née MacBean. Educated at Baldow School, he was trained in sheep-breeding by his father. In 1822 with his brother John he sailed in the *Regalia* to Van Diemen's Land. Their brother Duncan had preceded them and Daniel and James followed. William and John were granted 1400 acres near Campbell Town and they also took up a large cattle run. In 1832 they sold the Campbell Town property, acquired a run near Melton Mowbray and became merchants in Hobart Town. William was a leader of the Anti-transportation League. In 1834 he married Margaret Whyte of Berwick, Scotland, and they had four sons and three daughters.

In 1835 William joined the Port Phillip Association and contributed much to the cost of Batman's [q.v.] first expedition. In 1836 he sailed with J. T. Gellibrand [q.v.] in the *Norval* to Westernport. They overlanded to Melbourne and with William Buckley [q.v.] as their guide explored west of Corio Bay, a rugged trip which was easily met by Robertson's great physical strength and endurance. Robertson returned to Hobart but on another trip to Port Phillip in 1837 he acquired 6000 acres near Colac and 7000 acres at Bolinda (Sunbury) on Deep Creek. In 1843 he bought some of the Bolden [q.v.] brothers' stud and by 1847 had acquired Foster Fyans's [q.v.] run and herd in the Colac area. In 1849 he acquired the 40,000-acre Ondit run, north of Colac. In 1852 he retired from the Hobart business but did not make Victoria his permanent home until 1865. Meanwhile he had visited Britain and selected Herefords and Shorthorns for his Colac property, The Hill, by then one of the best cattle studs in Victoria. Robertson died on 18 January 1874, predeceased by his wife and a daughter; his extensive Colac property was divided equally between his sons, John (1837-1875), William (1839-1892), George Pringle (1842-1895) and James (1848-1890).

Working their properties in conjunction as Robertson Bros with James as managing director, they continued and improved their father's work. Continuing to specialize in breeding Shorthorns they also bred Clydesdales and light horses for the Indian market. Their most important innovation was the annual sale of stud cattle, the first in November 1874. Later described as 'not necessarily great breeders but great organizers and born salesmen', they had five main sales in 1874-78 for a return of £95,000. They issued a herd book in 1875 which contained the names of 189 bulls alone and for a time they were selling three-quarters of all the Shorthorns disposed of in Victoria. In 1875 the brothers bought the Mount Derrimut Stud herd of thirty-seven animals for £27,000. In January 1876 their most notable sale realized some £31,000. The boom in cattle broke at the end of the 1870s; George, William and

James dissolved the partnership in 1885 and turned to sheepbreeding.

WILLIAM, the second son, was born on 29 March 1839 and educated at the High School, Hobart, and Wadham College, Oxford (B.A., 1862) and in 1861 rowed in the winning crew against Cambridge. In 1863 he was called to the Bar at the Middle Temple, before returning to Melbourne where he was admitted to the Victorian Bar in 1864 and practised until 1876. On 24 April 1863 at Tunbridge Wells, he had married Martha Mary Murphy of Melbourne, by whom he had two sons and three daughters.

In 1871-74 William held the seat of Polwarth and South Grenville in the Legislative Assembly. In 1876-77 he visited Europe and North America. He won the seat again in 1880 and supported the Service [q.v.] reform bill but lost at the July elections; he held the seat in 1881-86. In July 1886 he was elected to the Legislative Council for South Western Province but took little part in debates. He had leave of absence from August 1887 and retired by rotation next year.

William was a Colac Shire councillor from 1877 and president in 1880-81. An active supporter of the Colac Agricultural Society, he was a promoter of the 1879 Colac Regatta and its first president. A staunch Presbyterian, he supported the Colac Presbyterian Church and also other denominations. He inherited the splendid stone mansion, The Hill, where he lived the life of a 'hospitable and sport-loving country gentleman'. He died in an operation for cancer of the throat on 23 June 1892, leaving an estate worth £50,000.

A. Sutherland et al, Victoria and its metropolis, 2 (Melb, 1888); M. H. Ellis, The beef shorthorn in Australia (Syd, 1932); A. Henderson (ed), Australian families, 1 (Melb, 1941); M. L. Kiddle, Men of yesterday (Melb, 1961); J. N. Chapman, Historic Homes of Western Victoria (Colac, 1965); Argus, 25 June 1892; Colac Reformer, 26 June 1892.   J. ANN HONE

ROBEY, RALPH MAYER (1809-1864), merchant and politician, was probably born in England, son of William Robey and his wife Elizabeth. After the death of his first wife Mary Ann, née Leese, Robey left Liverpool with his five children in the Larne, arriving at Sydney on 8 November 1841. On 21 October 1842 he married Louisa Townsend. By 1843 he was selling sheep, guns, china, drugs and earthenware in a wholesale store and ironmongery in George Street. He was an assessor in 1844 and an alderman in 1847-51 for Brisbane Ward, Sydney Municipal Council; he was on the lighting and finance standing committees.

Robey's business expanded to include importing, exporting and a shipping agency and he was chairman of the Sydney and Melbourne Steam Packet Co. by 1855. An early advocate of railways, Robey was appointed to the 1846 provisional railway committee to investigate their feasibility; he was a shareholder in the Sydney Railway Co. which continued the project from 1849. A director of the Sydney Fire Insurance Co., by 1853 he was a shareholder in the Bank of New South Wales, and from 1858 a director of the Australasian Steam Navigation Co. and the Newcastle Coal and Copper Co.

In 1847 Robey was chairman of directors of the Australasian Sugar Co. with Edward Knox, Clark Irving [qq.v.] and his brother James; dissension among the partners led to dissolution in 1854. Meanwhile, in 1850 with Thomas Mort [q.v.] and others he had promoted a company to grow sugar at Moreton Bay. Regarded as an influential merchant, he was one of ten shareholders who on 1 January 1855 formed the Colonial Sugar Refining Co. with James Robey as manager. After disputes in 1857 James left and Robey with his son-in-law, George Dibbs [q.v.], formed the rival Messrs Robey & Co. and built a factory costing £30,000 on the North Shore.

A shareholder and director of the Australian Joint Stock Bank, Robey arranged in November 1858 to lodge his company's account with it on assurance of an overdraft to £12,000, not to be altered without six months notice. On 2 August 1859, allegedly on the instigation of Irving, a fellow director, the bank curtailed credit without the stipulated notice. Seriously embarrassed, in October Robey sold out to the C.S.R. at a loss. He claimed that Irving had manipulated the sugar transactions of firms trading at the bank. He sought redress at a meeting of shareholders and circulated a pamphlet, To the shareholders of the Australian Joint Bank, in July 1861. The bank asked both men to resign, suggesting that their long-standing antipathy would be better settled in a boxing ring. Robey retorted that he had had 'fifteen years of litigation and carried it through satisfactorily'. On 22 February 1862 Irving sued him for libel and won with costs; on 27 February Robey sued Irving for breach of contract and was awarded £3500 in damages.

In the 1840s Robey had been active in the Australasian League for the Abolition of Transportation. A magistrate from 1855, he lost Cumberland Boroughs narrowly at the 1856 Legislative Assembly elections. He was a member of the Legislative Council in 1858-61 and was reappointed for life in 1861 although E. D. Thomson [q.v.] opposed it, asserting that he lacked 'social standing'. He supported the Cowper [q.v.] liberals on all their major legislation but was more tolerant than they on Chinese immigration.

An absentee pastoralist, Robey accumulated twenty stations in New South Wales and Queensland. He was an Anglican and a member of St Andrew's Parochial Association. Robey left Sydney in 1863 and died, aged 55, of apoplexy at Gower Street, Longton, Staffordshire, England on 1 April 1864; in December his estate, with liabilities of £86,499, was sequestrated by George Dibbs. He was survived by a large family and his wife who cut her throat on 20 September 1889.

Report on the proceedings of the shareholders of the Joint Stock Bank (Syd, 1861); H. T. E. Holt, An energetic colonist ... Hon. Thomas Holt (Melb, 1972); V&P (LC NSW), 1851 (2nd S), 2, 5, 1858, 143; SMH, 8 Nov 1841, 24 Oct 1842, 27 May, 2 July, 2 Nov 1844, 6 Feb, 9 May 1850, 22, 27 Feb 1862, 16 June 1864; Empire (Syd), 3, 7, 8 Apr 1856, 21 June 1864; C. N. Connolly, Politics, ideology and the New South Wales Legislative Council 1856-72 (Ph.D. thesis, ANU, 1974); Macarthur papers (ML); newspaper indexes under Robey (ML); Insolvency file 6917 (NSWA).   SUZANNE EDGAR

ROBINSON, SIR HERCULES GEORGE ROBERT, 1ST BARON ROSMEAD (1824-1897), governor, was born on 19 December 1824 at Rosmead, County Westmeath, Ireland, second son of Admiral Hercules Robinson and his wife Frances Elizabeth, née Wood. Educated at Sandhurst he joined the 87th Regiment (Royal Irish Fusiliers) as second lieutenant in 1843; he was promoted first lieutenant next year, but the enforced sale of the family estates compelled him to resign in 1846 and until 1849 he supervised relief works for victims of the Irish famine. On 24 April 1846 he married Nea Arthur Ada Rose D'Amour, fifth daughter of Arthur Annesley Rath, Viscount Valentia. In 1852 he was chief commissioner inquiring into Irish fairs and markets. In 1854 he became president of Montserrat and next year lieut-governor of St Christopher (St Kitts), a near-by island of the West Indies, with a dormant commission as governor-in-chief of the Leeward Islands. He was knighted in 1859 and became governor of Hong Kong; he negotiated the annexation of Kowloon and in 1863 was a member of a commission inquiring into the finances of the Straits Settlements. In 1865-72 he was governor of Ceylon and his success led to a K.C.M.G. in 1869 and, on his departure, to a discerning judgment by a local resident: astute and fond of power, a just and efficient administrator and 'an indefatigable worker'; a 'capital' writer and speaker, shy

in public, 'fonder of the desk and ... hard work in travelling, inspecting, and maturing schemes of improvement'. Lady Robinson was summed up as 'fond of gaity and society, and ... majestic-looking'. Gazetted as governor of New South Wales in February 1872, he reached Sydney on 3 June.

Robinson arrived within a month of (Sir) Henry Parkes's [q.v.] first cabinet, formed after a confused election that had followed a dissolution without supply: it was the fourth ministry since October 1868. He stated at once that he would not be a mere figure-head, and later asserted 'that the masses ... instead of ... resenting the outspoken sentiments of a governor on great questions, welcome them'. Aware of the deference that his office commanded in colonial society and of his power as a senior imperial officer, he quickly assessed the popular uneasiness with political instability, and played a valuable role in the evolution of responsible government in New South Wales. But despite his achievements and popularity he was essentially disdainful of colonial institutions and people. Aided by his wife he projected an image of hearty sociality but it was based on an assumption of paternalism more suited to a crown colony than a semi-independent democracy.

Writing to Parkes in October 1873, Robinson observed that the premier's abolition of ad valorem duties would 'not only ... supply a clearly defined principle for parties to contend over, but ... by making this the cheapest place to live in ... eventually result in a Confederation of which NSWales will be the centre and Sydney the metropolis'. The letter suggested both the patronizing style that he reserved for politicians and his feeling for the colony that found a popular response. His relations with the Legislative Assembly were strained by the Rossi case, which raised the constitutional issue of whether the assembly could interfere in the administration of the Volunteer Defence Forces, of which the governor was commander-in-chief. In October the House adopted the report of a select committee that recommended the dismissal of Captain F. R. L. Rossi [q.v.]; in a strong minute to the Executive Council Robinson denied that the parliamentarians had any right to interfere; and when Parkes tabled the papers the governor's views were criticized as an attack on the assembly's powers and privileges. The government survived a censure motion, and the governor received press and popular support.

In 1874 Robinson revealed further his propensity to antagonize parliament. In 1872 he had received petitions for the release of F. Gardiner [q.v.], a bushranger who had served eight years of a thirty-two years sentence. The exercise of the prerogative of mercy in non-capital cases rested with the governor and in 1874 he approved Gardiner's release, subject to exile. Public and political uproar followed the decision and in June Robinson, in another Executive Council minute, referred to the widespread objections as 'unreasonable and unjust clamour'. Parkes's tabling of the minute precipitated another crisis and the ministry fell in November after assertions that the governor had not only slighted parliament but had also opposed the right of petition. By this time the governor had several powerful parliamentary critics, including (Sir) John Robertson, D. Buchanan and W. Forster [qq.v.]. When Parkes lost the elections the governor refused at first to commission Robertson in 1875.

In September 1874 Robinson's stature as an imperial officer and his local prestige had increased when he negotiated the cession of the Fiji Islands from King Thakombau, which resulted in the award of G.C.M.G. in 1875. During his absence in Fiji Chief Justice Sir James Martin [q.v.] was aggrieved when he was not sworn in as colonial administrator. Martin had already sensed the equivocal condescension of Sir Hercules and Lady Robinson, and next year his resentment reached boiling point when the House of Lords papers on Gardiner reached Sydney; they included Robinson's claim that the chief justice had supported his release of the bushranger. ·Martin denied it in angry letters to the *Sydney Morning Herald* and Robinson replied similarly. Implicit in Martin's argument was his belief that the governor was behaving as if he were unaware that New South Wales had a system of responsible government.

Robinson's popularity remained undiminished. Balding and rotund, he had developed a flair for public speaking in which he extolled the merits of manly sport, especially cricket, the Anglo-Saxon spirit, and the advantages of New South Wales. In 1875 with some friends he owned four of the £500 shares in the Jervis Bay Property Association formed to exploit Parkes's coal-bearing land in the Illawarra. He urged his ministers on to a more rapid rate of railway building, rebuked them for slow correspondence and advised them when necessary. He was an enthusiastic race-goer in Sydney and Melbourne and collected a string of outstanding horses, including Kingsborough, which won the Australian Jockey Club Derby in 1874 and St Leger in 1875. At first he wagered heavily, but abandoned it; he became the

patron of the A.J.C., the Northern Jockey Club and the Hawkesbury Racing Club, and did much to improve the tone and administration of horse-racing. In August 1878 when his daughter Nora Augusta Maud married A. K. Finlay (Harrow and Trinity, Cambridge) at St James's Church, Sydney, 'the crushing and screaming ... were almost continuous'. The bride's travelling dress featured her father's racing colours.

Robinson's dispatches to the Colonial Office had always been models of concise and perceptive information. On 19 September 1878 his report on the political situation was based on a confidential minute in which he analysed the paralysis of government and parliament that had resulted from the colonial practice of voting supply in instalments; he pointed out that in twenty-one years of responsible government only two Appropriation Acts had been passed on time. His remedy was to refuse dissolutions unless supply was guaranteed. As a result, after Robertson's government fell in March 1877, two more ministries were formed that year before a general election was held, and it produced J. S. Farnell's [q.v.] stop-gap government. Robinson decided that the only way to effect a degree of stability was to induce Parkes and Robertson to coalesce. When Farnell was defeated in December 1878 he refused a dissolution and commissioned Robertson; he knew that Sir John was unlikely to succeed in forming a cabinet, but hoped that his failure would produce conditions in which Parkes might attract sufficient of Robertson's followers to arrange a viable coalition. Events fell out as the governor had predicted and the Parkes-Robertson government proved to be the strongest between 1856 and 1894.

Robinson left New South Wales on 19 March 1879 to become governor of New Zealand. In August next year he became governor of Cape Colony and high commissioner of South Africa; on his way there he called at Sydney to a rapturous welcome and a special race-meeting. In South Africa he had to contend with complex conflict between the Boers, British and native races. His comparative success led to a privy councillorship in 1883 and an extension of his term in 1887. He left the Cape on 1 May 1889 and became a director of the London and Westminster Bank and in 1891 was created a baronet. In 1895 he was recalled to South Africa and next year negotiated in Pretoria for the release of the Jameson raiders. On leave later in the year he was made Baron Rosmead of Rosmead, Ireland, and of Tafelberg in South Africa. Back at the

Cape he had the difficult task of reconciling the Boers and British but ill health caused his retirement on 21 April 1897. He died in London on 28 October survived by a son and three daughters.

Speeches delivered by ... Sir Hercules G. R. Robinson (Syd, 1879); H. Parkes, *Fifty years in the making of Australian history* (Lond, 1892); V&P (LA NSW), 1872-73, 1, 2, 4, 335, 534, 1873-74, 3, 131, 1875, 2, 1, 3, 5; T&CJ, 3 Feb 1872; SMH, 13 July 1872, 21 July 1875; ISN, 10 Mar 1875, 10 Oct 1876; *Australasian*, 19 Oct 1878, 6 Nov 1897; N. I. Graham, The role of the governor of New South Wales under responsible government, 1861-1890 (Ph.D. thesis, Macquarie Univ, 1973); Parkes letters (ML); Governor's papers 4/874.2, 4/1166, 4/1667 (NSWA); CO 201/570, 573-74, 577, 579, 583-84, 585.   BEDE NAIRN

ROBINSON, SIR WILLIAM CLEAVER FRANCIS (1834-1897), governor, was born on 14 January 1834 at Rosmead, County Westmeath, Ireland, fourth son of Admiral Hercules Robinson and his wife Frances Elizabeth, née Wood. Educated at the Royal Naval School, New Cross, Surrey, he entered the colonial service in 1855 as private secretary to his elder brother Hercules, lieut-governor of St Kitts. In 1859 Hercules was appointed governor of Hong Kong, and he accompanied him there. In 1862 William received his first vice-regal appointment, as president of Montserrat in the West Indies. In April that year he married Olivia Edith Deane, fourth daughter of Thomas Stewart Townshend, bishop of Meath. In 1865 he administered the government of Dominica and in May 1866 was appointed governor and commander-in-chief of the Falkland Islands; he later described the colony and its tiny population as 'a remote settlement at the fag end of the world'. In July 1870 he was made governor of Prince Edward Island, which he administered during the discussions that culminated in its union with Canada in July 1873. That year he was created C.M.G. In 1874 he was governor of the Leeward Islands and in January 1875 assumed the administration of Western Australia. He remained there until September 1877, during which time he carried out the instruction of the Colonial Office to discourage the colonists' attempt to seek responsible government and independence from Britain in internal affairs.

In 1877 Robinson was appointed governor of the Straits Settlements, with headquarters at Singapore, and created K.C.M.G. Next year he led a diplomatic mission to Bangkok in order to invest the King of Siam with the insignia of the Knight Grand Cross of St Michael and St George; in return he was invested with the Grand Cross of the Order of the Crown of Siam. He was then appointed governor of Natal, but the British government replaced him before he took up the position and in April 1880 he was re-appointed governor of Western Australia. During his second period he acquired a reputation for careful and economical administration, as well as for lengthy and pedantic correspondence with his superiors in London. He found the system of representative government hard to manipulate. He did not have the power and authority of the governor of a Crown colony; nor did his senior advisers have the confidence of the elected majority in the legislature, as would have been the case had the system of responsible government been in operation. He was expected to govern the colony, and to carry out the policy of his superiors in London, and yet he was confronted by a permanent non-official elected majority in the Legislative Council, which could impede his legislative programme or put a brake on government expenditure. This intermediate form of government he thought was 'neither flesh, fowl, nor good red-herring', and he told his colleagues, 'Let no man take charge of such a form of government who is not as patient as Job, as industrious as a Chinaman, and as ubiquitous as a provincial mayor in France'. His devotion to music changed the character of the social round in Government House, and he did much to uplift Perth's cultural life.

Robinson's success as an administrator and his personal qualities led in February 1883 to his appointment as governor of South Australia, the occasion being marked by the public performance of his own composition 'Unfurl the Flag'. He exerted a moderating influence over the vigorous contests amongst local politicians for place and position, but as the parliamentary system centred effective political power in the office of premier and his supporters in the Legislative Assembly, the governor's role was chiefly social and symbolic. Furthermore, the second half of the 1880s was politically uneventful, and he was not called on to face a major crisis of politics or finance. He associated with musical, literary and educational groups, and played a part in establishing a chair of music in the University of Adelaide. Music was the passion of his life and many of the songs which he had composed during earlier years became popular throughout Australia, especially 'Remember me no more', 'I love thee so', 'Imperfectus' and 'Severed'. A comic opera which he composed was later performed at the Princess Theatre, Melbourne. He played the violin and piano, and sang well. He helped in the celebration of the colony's jubilee in 1886, and of the Queen's jubilee in 1887, and was said to have entertained more people at Government House than any previous governor. In Adelaide in 1884 he had published *On Duty in Many Lands* and in 1886 his paper *The Physical Geography of the South-West of Western Australia*, which had been read before the South Australian branch of the Geographical Society of Australasia. He was a polished public speaker on a variety of topics, he travelled widely and established good relations with all sections of the upper classes.

In May 1887 Robinson was promoted G.C.M.G. and in the same year declined the governorship of Hong Kong, not wishing to endure its climate. From March to November 1889 he was acting governor of Victoria. He was not permanently appointed though both he and the local politicians expected it; to his chagrin, the British government had adopted a 'new departure' of appointing inexperienced noblemen to prestigious gubernatorial posts.

Robinson declined the governorship of Mauritius, and was then chosen to inaugurate parliamentary government in Western Australia. Before he left London he assisted the colony's delegates and the Colonial Office with the Constitution bill, and took the new Constitution to Perth in October 1890. His arrival as governor for the third time was widely acclaimed. The enactment of the Constitution had marked the end of a lengthy period of political struggle, and the departure of Governor Broome had seen the end of incessant imbroglios amongst the colony's senior officials. Robinson was welcomed because he knew and understood more about Western Australia than any other imperial officer. He arranged for the first elections for the Legislative Assembly; he chose the first premier, John Forrest, whom he had earlier recommended to the position of surveyor-general; and he nominated the members of the Legislative Council. Thereafter his practical role in politics diminished, partly because of constitutional conventions, and partly because Forrest soon established his personal dominance over both cabinet and parliament. Forrest did not take kindly to official advice or admonitions from Robinson, especially when the premier was determined to secure local control over the Aboriginals, which had been the only significant power not transferred to the new legislature and executive.

In 1891 Forrest offered Robinson appointment as the colony's first agent-general in London but, after some hesitation, Robinson declined and retired in March 1895. He then returned to London and accepted

several company directorships. He was the senior member of the colonial service, and although the officials of the Colonial Office had a high opinion of his ability and efficiency, he was not offered further employment. Throughout his career Robinson had been in the shadow of his better-known brother; he was probably as able and as successful an administrator, but he was not as genial or as warm in his official relationships, and it was his lot to manage the lesser of the remote colonies of the Empire. The *Bulletin*, 16 December 1882, had described him as 'tall and slight, with an intellectual cast ... by no means an enthusiast in sporting matters ... a thorough red-tape ruler ... He has a genius for music ...' For twenty years he had done much to further the interests of Western Australia and South Australia, and he was sincerely missed in the role of their unofficial ambassador when he died in South Kensington on 2 May 1897. Survived by his wife, three sons and two daughters, he left estates of £74,558 in England, £8600 in Western Australia and £900 in Victoria.

E. Hodder, *The history of South Australia*, 2 (Lond, 1893); W. B. Kimberley, *History of West Australia* (Melb, 1897); J. S. Battye, *Western Australia* (Oxford, 1924); F. K. Crowley, *Australia's western third* (Lond, 1960) and *Forrest: 1847-1918*, 1 (Brisb, 1971); P. J. Boyce, 'The governors of Western Australia under representative government, 1870-1890', *Univ Studies in History*, 4 (1961-62) no 1; *The Times*, 3 May 1897.

F. K. CROWLEY

ROCHER, JEAN-LOUIS (1809-1894), Marist Father, was born on 29 May 1809 at La Primatiale, Lyon, France, son of Jean-Pierre Rocher and his wife Françoise, née Battex. After a commercial career, Rocher studied for the priesthood at the minor seminary of Largentière, then at the major seminary of St Irenaeus, Lyon. Professed as a Marist on 3 September 1839 he was ordained priest on 21 December by Bishop Devie at Belley. In 1844 he was appointed to assist Fr Antoine Freydier-Dubreul and lay brother Auguste Leblanc to found a supply base in Sydney for extensive Marist Pacific missions. On 12 April 1845 they reached Sydney with a letter of introduction from the cardinal prefect of the Propaganda Fide, Rome. Archbishop Polding [q.v.] feared that the Marists would complicate his plan to make Sydney an 'abbey-diocese' for his own Benedictine Order, and his attitude caused them to consider leaving Sydney. In May 1846 Debreul returned to Europe leaving Rocher in charge.

Rocher reported to the superior-general that deaths from massacre and tropical diseases made the future of the mission off New Guinea very uncertain, and a threatened massacre of missionaries in New Caledonia had been narrowly averted by evacuating them to Sydney where they stayed at a house near Hunter's Hill, which Rocher had bought in May 1847. In 1853 he bought a block of land near by to which the Marists later transferred; he organized the Villa Maria Procure house to help the Pacific missionaries, maintaining communications and supplies by available shipping and chartered vessels; sick missionaries came to Sydney for rest. Other French people also settled in Hunter's Hill which came to be known as 'the French village'.

Rocher, aided by the friendship of Archdeacon McEncroe [q.v.], improved the strained relations with the Benedictines. In 1856 Polding offered him and the Marists the care of the parish of St Charles's, Ryde. He proved an energetic parish priest, completing a church and a school by 1858. He got on well with his people, including the controversial J. K. Heydon [q.v.].

In late 1857 Fr Victor Poupinel [q.v.] was made higher superior in Sydney; he planned an expansion of the functions of Villa Maria and recalled Fr C. M. Joly from Samoa to assist Rocher. In 1859 he visited Europe. After coming back he was appointed acting Pacific superior while Poupinel visited Rome. Asthmatic attacks were weakening him and when Poupinel returned he was repatriated in 1864. He worked in London and then in his native Lyon as mission procurator general. After a gentle retirement he died from inflammation of the lungs on 26 January 1894 and was buried in the cemetery of St Foy-les-Lyon.

Rocher was a simple man, very efficient on behalf of the needs of the missionaries, and in keeping the books. Cautious and tactful in the delicate Sydney situation, he helped the Marists from shaky beginnings to firm establishment in Australia.

J. Hosie, 'Founded upon a rock', *Harvest*, May 1970; J. Hosie, The French mission: an Australian base for the Marists in the Pacific to 1874 (M.A. Hons thesis, Macquarie Univ. 1971); J. K. Heydon letters (ML); Rocher and Poupinel letters (Marist Archives, Rome, microfilm ML and NL).   JOHN HOSIE

RODD, BRENT CLEMENTS (1809-1898), solicitor, was born on 10 December 1809 at Barnstaple, Devonshire, England, son of John Tremayne Rodd, hydraulic engineer, and his wife Bridget (Lucy), née Burnell. After the death of his wife, John with his three young sons reached Hobart Town in January 1822 in the *Tiger* and arrived in Sydney in April in the *Castle Forbes*. He was superintendent of convicts at Newcastle and became a successful pastoralist on the Hunter.

Brent was a store-keeper for Thomas Icely [q.v.] but by 1829 was articled to Edward Keith and was admitted a solicitor on 28 September 1833. In 1829 Rodd had applied for a land grant and claimed to own £500 in sterling, 12 horses and 60 head of cattle. In 1830 he bought land and town lots in Newcastle, Bathurst, Raymond Terrace, Clarence Town and various blocks on the Wollombi Creek. In 1838 he bought fifty acres of the Five Dock Estate, Sydney, from Samuel Lyons [q.v.] and built his house, Barnstaple Manor. On 8 May 1839 he married Sarah Jane, sister of (Sir) John Robertson [q.v.]. In 1842 he complained in vain to Governor Gipps that he had been troubled by shell-gathering trespassers on the mud flats surrounding his land at Rodd Point.

Successful in his profession, Rodd for a time specialized in debt collection and till the early 1860s was the senior partner in Rodd and Dawson. Thereafter he practised on his own at 132 Pitt Street. Among his clients were Edward Smith Hall and Henry Parkes [qq.v.]. Parkes became a lifelong friend and in 1849 invited Rodd to form 'a political association' with Robert Lowe [q.v.] and others. In the early 1850s Rodd worked behind the scenes for Parkes and Rev. J. D. Lang [q.v.]. In 1824 when employed by Icely and Hindson, Rodd had accidentally discharged a pistol into Joseph Underwood's [q.v.] premises and, panicking, had thrown the pistol down a well. In June 1857 he explained his action to Lang, who had tried to use a distorted version of the affair to discredit Icely.

In 1851 Rodd had been on the management committee of the Australasian Botanical and Horticultural Society. He retired in the 1870s and added to his large and catholic library, managed his Barnstaple estate and exchanged photographs of the 'old hands'. W. M. Manning [q.v.] thought Rodd's portrait 'like a Hogarth or Rembrandt who from love of art has himself become a picture'. Rodd died at Barnstaple, Five Dock, of heart disease on 26 November 1898 and was buried according to Presbyterian rites in the family vault; his remains were later reinterred in Rookwood cemetery. Predeceased by his wife who died on 30 December 1896, three sons and two daughters, he was survived by five sons and two daughters. His estate was valued for probate at almost £58,000.

K. G. Allars, 'The Five Dock farm', JRAHS, 34 (1948); SMH, 29 Nov 1898; Parkes letters (ML); MS cat under B. C. Rodd (ML).
                                        K. G. ALLARS*

ROGERS, CHARLES (1844-1909), cabinet maker and merchant, was born on 18 November 1844 at 17 Sweet Apple Court, Hackney Road, Middlesex, London, son of Charles Rogers (1805-1864), furniture maker, and his wife Margaret, née Edmundson (1812-1870). After some elementary schooling he began training as a cabinet maker. About 1859 Rogers arrived in Australia with his family. They settled at Goulburn, New South Wales, where his father set up a small cabinet-making business and Charles continued to learn his trade. On 8 March 1866 he married Elizabeth Johnston, daughter of a veterinary surgeon; she died suddenly on 26 March 1877. On 12 April 1878 at Newtown he married Agnes Hair.

Rogers prospered and the cabinet-making factory employed thirty workers. He had his own network of horse-drawn vans to supply furniture to his agents dispersed from Cooma to Wagga Wagga. Also a retailer and importer, he established a sixty-horse coachline between Goulburn and Yass and ran a livery stable. A great lover of horses, he took pride in driving his own four-in-hand and enjoyed the good things of life. In 1879 he moved into new premises known as the Goulburn Arcade in Auburn Street, designed and built under his own meticulous supervision, and there he became the 'universal provider'. The reputed value of the building, site and stock-in-trade was £90,000. From 1885 his business enterprises expanded south with the railway.

Liberal and public spirited, Rogers helped all charities and religions. A Methodist, he became a trustee of North Goulburn Methodist Church in 1884, and a magistrate next year. He often criticized the local council and others where the interests of Goulburn and his own business were concerned. In the 1880s he led a deputation to the secretary for public works on the vexed question of differential railway freight rates. In 1908 he was president of the local branch of the Rating on Unimproved Values League.

Rogers visited England and made other sea voyages. In March 1900 in the Yass Evening Tribune he published a twenty-five chapter description of his tour to the Western Pacific islands. Rogers died of cirrhosis of the liver at Colombo, Ceylon, on 17 May 1909 while on a cruise. Buried in the Ceylon general cemetery, his body was reinterred in the Methodist section of the old Goulburn cemetery on 10 October 1909. He was survived by two sons and two daughters of his first wife, by his second wife and their three sons, who conditionally inherited his business and estate valued for probate at almost £35,000. They traded as Charles Rogers & Co. until 1947 when the department store was sold to Burns Philp & Co. Ltd. Known as Mates [q.v.] Ltd it still operates on the second site in Auburn Street.

E. Digby (ed), Australian men of mark, 1 (Syd, 1889); R. T. Wyatt, The history of Goulburn, N.S.W. (Goulburn, 1941); Southern Argus (Goulburn), 18 July 1885; family information.   JOHN WOOLLEY

ROGERS, JOHN WARRINGTON (1822-1906), barrister and judge, was the son of John Warrington Rogers of London, and his wife Rebecca. His father and grandfather were solicitors. Rogers entered Magdalen Hall, Oxford, in 1844 (M.A., 1854); he was a member of the Middle Temple from June 1843 and was called to the Bar on 20 November 1846. In 1848 with Henry Riddell he compiled an index to public statutes, and in 1850 published in London a work on the County Court Extension Act.

Described as having 'a character without reproach and [of] perfect competency' Rogers was offered in November 1854 the post of solicitor-general of Van Diemen's Land at a salary of £600. Despite good prospects in England he accepted, probably because of impressions of the colony 'imbibed, when a Boy from an Uncle who made a fortune there'. He arrived at Launceston on 4 August 1855 via Melbourne, took his seat in the Legislative Council as an official nominee and was admitted to the Tasmanian Bar on 7 August. On 19 December he accepted the consolidated posts of solicitor-general, crown solicitor and clerk of the peace on condition that it was a permanent appointment free of political changes; he took up duties in March 1856 but in September won Launceston in the new House of Assembly. He was solicitor-general in the Champ [q.v.] ministry, but in February 1857 declined office in the new government. He continued to be vocal in parliament but settled in Melbourne and in October resigned his seat.

Rogers was admitted to the Bar in Victoria and on 7 January 1858 was appointed a County Court judge and judge of the Court of Mines for the Ballarat district at a salary of £1500. In January 1878 he was a victim of Berry's [q.v.] 'Black Wednesday' retrenchments but in early February he was reappointed, only to resign at the end of June when the ministry refused to make the tenure of office for the County Court same as for the Supreme Court. As a judge he was remembered as 'dignified and refined'. On 2 July he became a Q.C., practised at the Victorian Bar and in 1880 was a member of the royal commission into the constitution of the Supreme Court. He published articles, mostly on legal topics, in the *Melbourne Review* and the *Victorian Review*.

Active in Anglican affairs Rogers was also interested in education. In 1869-70 he had drafted the constitution of the Ballarat School of Mines and served as its first vice-president in 1870 and as trustee and council member in the 1880s. He was a member of the Council of the University of Melbourne in 1861-81 and in 1881-93 lectured on the doctrines of equity and the general principles of procedure. In 1881 he was appointed to the royal commission on education, serving as chairman from December 1881 until February 1884 when he went to Hobart to act as puisne judge of the Supreme Court. His draft report, submitted before he left Melbourne, was so amended by some of the commissioners that Rogers dissociated himself from it and made a separate report with special recommendations for Roman Catholic schools. Neither report was acted on.

After a year in Tasmania Rogers returned to the Victorian Bar. His public lecture at the Wilson Hall in October 1888 on imperial federation was published in pamphlet form. In September 1893 he retired to England, where he died at Ealing on 10 February 1906. He was survived by his wife Eliza, née Carter, whom he had married on 10 July 1856 at New Town, Tasmania, five sons (all then living in Australia) and four daughters.

J. L. Forde, *The story of the Bar of Victoria* (Melb, 1913); A. Dean, *A multitude of counsellors* (Melb, 1968); V&P (LA Vic), 1884, 3 (47); *A'sian Sketcher*, 16 May 1882; *Advocate* (Melb), 17 Feb 1883; *Argus*, 14 Feb 1906; *The Times*, 13 Feb 1906; GO 1/95/14 (TA).

H. A. FINLAY

ROGERS, JOHN WILLIAM FOSTER (1842-1908), educationist and politician, was born on 16 July 1842 at Leeds, Yorkshire, England, son of Thomas George Rogers [q.v.], and his wife Sarah, née Smyth. John, his five brothers and sisters were sent by friends to Port Phillip in January 1850, but after some schooling in Melbourne, John attended Stonyhurst College, Lancashire, England, from 1852.

In 1862 Rogers returned to Victoria and in 1864 founded a 'private' Catholic collegiate school for boys in Ballarat. The school enjoyed Dr Goold's [q.v.] patronage and it prospered until the mining collapse of 1869. He conducted a grammar school in Carlton about 1873 and was headmaster of the Melbourne Hebrew School in 1878 and of St Kilda High School in 1881. In 1883 he

published in Melbourne, Sydney and Adelaide a treatise on *Grammar and Logic in the Nineteenth Century as seen in A Syntactical Analysis of the English Language*; it gained good reviews in Melbourne and overseas, but, to Rogers's annoyance, the University of Melbourne refused to prescribe it.

In 1883 Rogers was appointed first lay inspector of schools under the Catholic Board of Education in Sydney, but when the system of inspectors was abolished in 1886 he was summarily dismissed. After a lawsuit he was awarded £2500 in lieu of five years' salary. Turning to publishing, Rogers visited London in 1887 for the successful first issue of *The Australasian federal directory of commerce, trades and professions*. Conceived and edited by him, it contained informative articles and data on the Australasian colonies as well as a classified occupational directory. Rogers published in Melbourne further volumes that were useful propaganda for Federation. He was sometime editor and a regular writer for the Roman Catholic monthly *Austral Light*, first issued in January 1892, and wrote for the *Advocate*. With publishing stagnant in the depression, he became member of the Legislative Assembly for South Yarra in 1894-97; he contested East Melbourne in 1902 without success. His surplus wealth tax plan roused much comment but little came of it. In 1906 *The Church and the fine arts* by Rogers was published in Melbourne by the Australian Catholic Truth Society.

Rogers married first Catherine Mary Shanahan on 24 June 1867; they had two sons. By his second wife Letitia Catherine Craig, née Morony, whom he had married on 1 October 1881, he had two sons and a daughter. He died in his house at Malvern on 2 December 1908 survived by his wife and five children.

R. Fogarty, *Catholic education in Australia 1806-1950* (Melb, 1959); *Table Talk*, 10 Feb 1888; *Advocate* (Melb), 5 Dec 1908.

SUZANNE G. MELLOR

ROLANDO, CHARLES (1844-1893), artist, was born in Florence, Italy, son of an artist. He showed early ability in painting and studied in Florence. In 1870 he went to England and set up in Liverpool where his commissions included frescoes for a Roman Catholic church. At 30 he married Frances, sister of George Alfred John Webb (b. 1861), a portraitist, who later lived in Adelaide and Melbourne; they had one daughter.

In 1883 Rolando and his wife left for Australia but in Cape Town he gained first prize in an art competition with his landscape of Table Mountain. He stayed for two years, busy on commissions that resulted from his win. He arrived in Melbourne in mid-1885 bringing with him 'warm recommendations on the part of Sir Hercules Robinson' and several South African landscapes which drew immediate attention. In August he opened a studio in Grey Street, East Melbourne, and was soon painting assiduously, chiefly landscapes of the Watts River and Gippsland Lakes country. By January 1886 he had completed five oil paintings of the country around Fernshaw for the Colonial and Indian Exhibition in London and in April contributed three large studies of the Watts River to the Victorian Academy of Arts exhibition. He became a member of the Australian Artists' Association in 1886.

In 1887 Rolando exhibited in Melbourne and major country towns his collection of twenty-eight oils and ten water-colours as well as sketches. He auctioned them in September for £900, with many of the works being sold to local galleries. He then conducted a fashionable art school at studios in Enfield Street, St Kilda. He hung paintings at the Victorian Artists' Society autumn exhibition in May 1888 and at the Melbourne Centennial International Exhibition in August. In his last years he collaborated with J. H. Scheltema (1861-1938), painting the landscape backgrounds to Scheltema's cattle and horses. Critics complained that Rolando was inclined to 'dash off landscapes with such haste as to result in ... unequal work'. But at his best he showed a 'rapid and facile touch, great dexterity of execution, a fine sense of colour, and a feeling for atmosphere and light, combined with unusual skill in discerning and discriminating with various forms and tints of Australian foliage'.

Delicate in health and suffering for the last two years of his life from chronic bronchitis, Rolando was regarded as something of a recluse from the artistic society of Melbourne. Aged 49, he died of pneumonia on 8 July 1893 at his home Riseda, Jackson Street, St Kilda, and was buried in the Melbourne general cemetery. He was survived by his wife.

W. Moore, *The story of Australian art*, 1 (Syd, 1934); *Australasian*, 29 Aug 1885, 4 Aug 1888; *Argus*, 6 Sept 1887, 10, 11 July 1893.

SUZANNE G. MELLOR

ROLF BOLDREWOOD; *see* BROWNE, THOMAS ALEXANDER

ROLLESTON, CHRISTOPHER (1817-1888), public servant, was born on 27 July 1817 at Burton-Joyce, Nottinghamshire, England, second son of John Rolleston, Anglican clergyman, and his wife Elizabeth, née Smelt. After working in a Liverpool mercantile house he went to Sydney and in 1838 bought land on the Allyn River near Paterson, where he farmed with his younger brother Philip. Lack of success led him to apply, through his father, for a government post and in December 1842 Governor Gipps, seeking only 'persons of very active habits ... single men without encumbrance of any sort' as commissioners of crown lands, appointed Rolleston to the frontier district of Darling Downs. His activities as an autocrat on horseback pleased his Sydney superiors and the local squatters. He reported a 'decidedly hostile disposition towards European settlers' among Aboriginals, but later attributed better relations partly to his distribution of blankets, flour and tobacco in winter months. Granted leave of absence to visit England in 1853, he received a silver salver and 125 guineas from the squatters.

On 20 September 1854 at Foller, Aberdeenshire, Scotland, Rolleston married Katherine, daughter of William Leslie, ninth laird of Warthill, and sister of Patrick Leslie [q.v.] formerly of the Darling Downs. In December he brought her to Sydney, reputedly having declined the presidency of Montserrat, in the West Indies, and in January 1855 became private secretary to the governor-general, Sir William Denison. On 10 December he was appointed registrar-general at a salary of £700 and in 1856 he launched the compulsory registration of births, deaths and marriages, based upon statistical principles introduced earlier in Victoria by W. H. Archer [q.v.]. The details required on the new registration forms put the records among the fullest and most useful in the world. Despite obstacles such as 'the indifference of our public men to statistical knowledge', he reported in 1857 that the new system was 'in easy and quiet operation'. Referring in his second report to persisting 'misapprehension', he argued that 'enlightened persons will not object to the apparent exposure of their family history when satisfied that the only object is the promotion of the public welfare, nor will they think inquiries impertinent which, although *seemingly* minute and unimportant, have been recommended by the united experience of the ablest statisticians in Europe'.

Influenced by the growing interest in science fostered by Denison, Rolleston joined the Philosophical (later Royal) Society of New South Wales in 1856 and was sometime treasurer, vice-president and president. He delivered papers and occasionally public lectures on the history of savings banks, statistics and sanitation, and contributed monthly figures on the 'Health of Sydney' to its journal. From 1858 his annual *Statistical Register* was published as a parliamentary paper. In evidence to a parliamentary select committee that year he recommended reforms in land title registration similar to those of R. R. Torrens [q.v.] and, after the 1862 Real Property Act, the new system devolved upon him.

On 10 November 1864 Rolleston became auditor-general at a salary of £900. When the Audit Act was amended in 1870 his office became responsible to parliament alone and he asserted vigorously his duty 'to maintain a check upon the expenditure of the Government'. Though he retired in 1883 he was appointed in 1887 to the royal commission of inquiry into the civil service.

Capital acquired under his marriage settlement and his connexion with the Leslie family and vice-regal dealings helped Rolleston in his financial dealings. From 1860, with Louis Hope [q.v.] and Alfred Denison, he acquired extensive runs in the Leichhardt district of Queensland centred upon his head station, Springsure, near the present town of Rolleston. He was a director of the European Assurance Society, the Mercantile Bank of Sydney and the Australian Gaslight Co. and vice-president of the Savings Bank of New South Wales. A magistrate from 1842, he was active in public affairs. He was superannuation fund commissioner, president of the 1869 imperial royal commission into alleged kidnapping of natives of the Loyalty Islands, a trustee of the Australian Club and an official trustee of the Australian Museum. A prominent Anglican layman he was on the Sydney diocesan synod. He also devoted much time to charity and was chairman of the Government Asylums Board for the Infirm and Destitute and a committee-man of the Institution for the Deaf and Dumb and the Blind. In 1872 he was elected to the Senate of the University of Sydney vice W. C. Wentworth [q.v.]. That year he sought in vain to become agent-general in London. In 1875 he was on the commissions for the Philadelphia International and Melbourne Intercolonial exhibitions, and next year attended Philadelphia as a representative commissioner.

Rolleston's career in the civil service was notable for his steady devotion to duty and his avoidance of political controversy. His work contributed to the orderly growth of responsible government in New South Wales. He was made C.M.G. in 1879. A pillar of the colonial community, he died on 9 April 1888 of chronic Bright's disease at his home, Northcliff, Milsons Point, Sydney, survived by his wife and four of their six children and was buried in the Anglican cemetery, Willoughby. His estate was sworn for probate at £16,763.

HRA (1), 21-26; Reports of registrar-general and auditor-general, V&P (LA NSW), 1856-83; Roy Soc NSW, Procs, 22 (1888); T&CJ, 7 June 1879, 14 Apr 1888; *Australasian*, 14 Apr 1888; W. H. Archer papers (NL); Leslie letters (Oxley Lib, Brisb); Parkes letters (ML); MS cat (ML); run registers (QA); information from Miss A. M. H. Rolleston, Syd. CHRIS CUNNEEN

ROMILLY, HUGH HASTINGS (1856-1892), administrator, author and explorer, was born on 15 March 1856 in London, son of Colonel Frederick Romilly and his wife Elizabeth Amelia Jane, née Elliot, daughter of the earl of Minto. Educated at a Winchester private school and Repton College, he entered Christ Church, Oxford, in 1874 but left without taking a degree to join Melly & Co. of Liverpool.

Prompted by Lady Gordon, in 1879 he joined the staff of Sir Arthur Gordon, governor of Fiji and high commissioner for the Western Pacific. A voyage to Tonga and Rotuma provided material for his first book, *A True Story of the Western Pacific* (London, 1882). He later served in Fiji as a magistrate and private secretary to Gordon. Following Britain's decision to annex Rotuma, Romilly went there as deputy commissioner in September 1880. In March 1881 he began 'an ambulatory mission of inspection of British beachcombers' in New Britain, New Ireland and New Guinea but soon returned to England dangerously ill.

On a second cruise in May 1883 one of his duties was to explain what the islanders could expect if they went to work in Queensland. In October 1884 Romilly went to Port Moresby in H.M.S. *Harrier* to help to establish a British protectorate in New Guinea. He mistakenly hoisted the flag prematurely and the ceremony was later repeated by Commodore Erskine [q.v.]. Romilly was administrator until Sir Peter Scratchley [q.v.] arrived in August 1885 and again for three months after he died in December. On sick leave Romilly supervised the New Guinea exhibits at the Colonial and Indian Exhibition in London and published his second book *The Western Pacific and New Guinea* ... (London, 1886). In July 1887 Romilly, now C.M.G., returned to New Guinea as deputy to John Douglas [q.v.], bitterly disappointed at having been passed over for the top post. With naval help he patrolled the Papuan coast in the yacht *Hygeia* investigating and punishing murderers and wrote *From My Verandah in New Guinea* ... (London, 1889).

After Sir William Macgregor proclaimed the colony of British New Guinea in September 1888 Romilly became British consul for the New Hebrides, but in January 1890 the office was abolished and he returned to England. Offered no further employment, he resigned from the Colonial Office to lead a prospecting expedition to Mashonaland, Africa. On contracting fever, he returned to London where he died unmarried on 27 July 1892. Romilly's *Letters from the Western Pacific and Mashonaland*, written between 1878 and 1891, were published by his brother Samuel in 1893. In an introduction Lord Stanmore (Sir Arthur Gordon) described Romilly as an 'attractive personality' with a quick intelligence, great physical strength, an easy temper and the ability both to obey and command.

D. A. Scarr, *Fragments of Empire* (Canberra, 1967); British New Guinea, *Annual reports*, 1884-89; *T&CJ*, 6 Aug 1892.

ROBERT LANGDON

ROPER, JOHN (1822-1895), explorer and civil servant, was born at Gayton Thorpe, Norfolk, England, son of Edward Roper and his wife Elizabeth, née Flower. He migrated to New Zealand and from June to November 1842 was employed by Willis & Co. of Wellington. Hoping for better prospects in Sydney and to meet his 'cousin Flower' of Flower, Salting [q.v.] & Co., he arrived in Sydney in the *Bright Planet* on 25 January 1843.

Employed by A. W. Scott [q.v.] on Ash Island, Roper met Ludwig Leichhardt [q.v.] and attached himself to his Port Essington expedition. The party left Sydney in the *Sovereign* for Moreton Bay on 13 August 1844 and Jimbour, the furthest out-station on the Darling Downs, on 1 October. Brash, no bushman and 'at all times foolhardy' according to John Gilbert [q.v.], Roper got lost in the bush more than once and on 10 May 1845 was kicked in the chest while trying to catch his horse by its tail. On 28 June he was wounded and lost an eye when the party was attacked by Aboriginals. They reached Port Essington on 17 December and returned to Sydney in the *Heroine* on 25 March 1846. Roper and J. S. Calvert [q.v.] each received £125 from the government. Leichhardt told his brother-in-law that 'Roper was an inexperienced and limited young man who seemed to consider it beneath his dignity to obey me'.

In 1847-53 Roper was clerk of Petty Sessions at Albury and for a time postmaster and registrar of the Court of Requests. He began to acquire land in and near Albury and on 1 July 1857 he became a magistrate. Active in the town's affairs, he was a founding alderman on the Albury Municipal Council in 1859, a member of the provisional committee of the Albury Co-operative Storekeepers' Association, president of the Albury and Murray River Agricultural and Horticultural Society, vice-chairman of the Albury Hospital committee and president of the Albury Jockey Club. In 1860 W. A. Macdonagh tried to get him struck off the roll of magistrates for 'living in a state of undisguised and shameless adultery' with his housekeeper but the police magistrate claimed that their 'improper intimacy' had not affected his social position; the housekeeper was discharged. On 18 December 1861 Roper wrote to his brother William that he had 'just completed a very handsome store' which he hoped would have an annual turnover of £10,000.

Mayor of Albury in 1862, Roper was forced to resign from the council on 29 October and, 'as a landowner and farmer', was declared bankrupt. His estate was not released until 1873. On April 1868 he became a sheep inspector at Merriwa at £250 a year.

Roper claimed to have kept a log on the Port Essington expedition but was unable to produce it or any other papers when pressed to do so by the Geographical Society of Australasia in 1884. In 1888 he complained to J. F. Mann [q.v.] of Leichhardt's conduct and character and said that he had never heard whether any profits had accrued from the publication of Leichhardt's journal, which did 'not accord with my idea of honour'.

After six months' leave of absence Roper retired on 6 October 1893 with a pension of £120 4s. 'Genial, hearty, vigorous' in old age, he died on 15 September 1895 aged 73 at his home Roseberry Park near Merriwa and was buried in the Anglican cemetery. He left his estate of £708 to his housekeeper, Lydia Anne Witney. Leichhardt named Roper's Peak, in the Peak Range, and the Roper River after him.

A. H. Chisholm, *Strange new world* (Syd, 1941); M. Aurousseau (ed), *The letters of F. W. Ludwig Leichhardt* (Cambridge, 1968) and for bibliog.   PETER ORLOVICH

ROSE, ROBERT HENRY (1833-1909), farmer, was born on 26 November 1833 at Stanton, Suffolk, England, eldest son of Robert Henry Rose, farmer of Stanton Hall, and his wife Elizabeth, née Canler. In 1837 his father aged only 32 died of tuberculosis. Rose, also prone to the family weakness, planned in 1851 to escape the Suffolk climate and accompany his sister Mary Ann, wife of Rev. James Leonard, to Western Australia but was delayed by a serious bout of measles. He reached Fremantle in the *Merope* on 25 May 1852, followed next year by his mother, brother, sister and cousin Thomas Hayward [q.v.].

In August 1854 Rose opened a butcher's shop in Perth, but soon, under the supervision of his mother, took up land with Hayward to run cattle, first near the road between Mandurah and Bunbury and then on the Wedderburn estate near Brunswick. In 1855 he obtained the Parkfield grant near Leschenault Inlet, and on 26 March 1857 married Ann Bishop (d. 1864), daughter of John Allnutt of Australind. He increased his holdings to 9000 acres after purchasing cheaply 3000 acres of the defunct estate of the Australind settlement (Western Australian Co.), other blocks from its shareholders who remained in England and J. S. Roe's [q.v.] 2180-acre grant. He also held extensive crown leases.

On land that he proved unsuitable for sheep, Rose was among the first in the higher rainfall districts to demonstrate the most appropriate land use in contrast to the small-farming Australind proposals. At Parkfield he had a large and profitable dairy herd, while cattle from the out-stations were driven to Perth for slaughter. Butter, salted in barrels, was sent north by schooner or sold in Bunbury. A ready market for Parkfield produce, including swamp potatoes, was provided by the townsfolk and the convict road gangs. Men and women immigrants, ticket-of-leave men and Aboriginals provided the farm work force.

Rose was a committee-man and chairman for eighteen years of the Wellington Roads Committee, a member of the local agricultural society and a justice of the peace. Tall, lean and black-bearded, he was an experienced horseman and a keen supporter and captain of the Wellington Mounted Volunteers. In 1892, afflicted by increasing deafness, he moved to Moorlands near Bunbury where he died on 30 November 1909 and was buried in the Anglican section of the Picton cemetery. He was survived by four sons of his first wife, by his second wife Elizabeth, née Teede, whom he had married on 22 July 1865, and their four sons and six daughters. His estate was sworn for probate at £7423.

West Australian, 1 Dec 1909; Rose diaries (Battye Lib, Perth); family papers and notes (held by Miss E. Rose, Bridgetown, Mr B. Rose, Morley, Mrs T. Sanders, Bunbury, and Mrs E. Kerr, Australind).   A. C. STAPLES

ROSEBERY, EARL OF; *see* PRIMROSE, ARCHIBALD PHILIP

ROSEBY, THOMAS (1844-1918), Congregational minister, was born on 8 April 1844 in Sydney, third son of Thomas Roseby (d. 1867), stonemason, and his wife Ann, née Lowes. His father, a Wesleyan Methodist, was a temperance advocate and lay evangelist. Associated with the Pitt Street Congregational Church, Roseby decided to enter the Congregational ministry. He began his training under Barzillai Quaife [q.v.] and at Camden College in 1864. In 1866 he went to the University of Sydney (B.A., 1869; M.A. and LL.B., 1871; LL.D., 1873) and won several scholarships and a gold medal.

Roseby was ordained on 3 October 1867 in Petersham Congregational Church, and inducted as its first minister. On 11 April 1871 he married Sarah Hooworth. In 1872 he became minister of the Moray Place Congregational Church in Dunedin, New Zealand, where he exercised an influential ministry. He helped the temperance movement in New Zealand and was grand worthy chief templar in 1879-80. Keenly interested in education, Roseby was a member of the Senate of the University of New Zealand in 1878-85. In 1884 he helped form the Congregational Union of New Zealand and was chairman-elect when he accepted a call to the Dawson Street Church in Ballarat, Victoria. It prospered under his care from 6 December 1885 but he and his wife found the climate disagreeable and in October 1888 he returned to Sydney to the Marrickville church from which he retired in 1911. Recognized as a leading churchman, he remained active in religious affairs until well into his retirement.

Roseby was chairman of the Congregational Union of New South Wales in 1891 and 1903, represented it at the first International Congregational Council in London in 1891, and preached at the union's jubilee in 1916. Editor of the *Australasian Independent* for nine years, he was also chairman of the Congregational Union of Australasia in 1913-16. Although 'a pronounced Congregationalist' he was also an advocate of Protestant Church union and in 1900 he was elected first president of the Evangelical Council of New South Wales. Warm and friendly, with a 'rather unctuous style' in the pulpit, Roseby won repute for his liberal theology. An advanced thinker, he welcomed higher criticism as 'a rediscovery of the Bible' and saw no basic conflict between religion and science; his 1888 lectures on 'The Genetic Unity of Nature Viewed in a Theistic and Christian Light', the first of the Livingstone Lectures at Camden College, revealed his broad and sympathetic acquaintance with modern science. As early as 1876 he had held that evolution was not inconsistent with Christian belief but 'simply a question of Divine *method*'.

Roseby also espoused radical social ideas. A stern critic of *laissez faire*, he was convinced that a more humane order was emerging. He advocated the co-operative movement and land nationalization in many papers and addresses. His co-religionists found his temperance views more acceptable than some of his revolutionary social teaching, but he remained vague and somewhat pious as to the implementation of a more Christian social order. A strong supporter of trade unionism, in the maritime strike of 1890 he sympathized with the employees and headed an abortive conciliation committee. A member of the Federal Co-operative Association of Australasia, he was honorary secretary of the board of control of the Pitt Town Co-operative Settlement. He was also a member of the Old-Age Pensions League formed in 1896 and was on the Unemployment Advisory Board in 1898. A member of the Sydney branch of the Peace Society established in 1889, he was one of the few clergymen to oppose the Boer war.

Roseby had an active interest in astronomy and botany. With his observatory at Marrickville and later at Mosman he often gave educational evenings to church groups and students. He lectured in New Zealand and contributed a paper, 'The Transit of Venus, Dunedin' in the *New Zealand Journal of Science* (Vol. 1, 1882-83) and in 1896 'Elliptical Orbit of Comet *b* 1894 (Gale)' in the *Monthly Notices* of the Royal Astronomical Society, and was elected a fellow. President of the New South Wales branch of the British Astronomical Association in 1901-02 and 1914, he joined the Royal Society of New South Wales in 1913.

Roseby died from pneumonia at Mosman on 16 December 1918 and was buried in the Congregational section of the Gore Hill cemetery. He was survived by his wife, five sons and four daughters, the eldest of whom, Gertrude Amy, was principal and owner of Redlands School, Neutral Bay, in 1911-45. He left an estate worth £1211 to his wife. The church at Marrickville is now known as the 'Roseby Memorial Church'.

His eldest brother JOHN (1835-1898), monumental mason, was baptized in Stanhope, County Durham, England, on 29 November 1835. He became a magistrate in 1871, was an alderman for Cook Ward in the Sydney Municipal Council in 1870-72 and represented Shoalhaven in the Legislative Assembly in 1877-83. He was active in the temperance cause and in charitable agencies. A director of the Benevolent Society of New South Wales in 1876-98, he was its treasurer in 1898. He was also a director of the Destitute Children's Asylum,

Randwick, and a trustee and custodian of the City Night Refuge and Soup Kitchen. In 1890 he was at the Australasian Conference on Charity in Melbourne and later was elected a public charities' representative on the Metropolitan Charities Association. In 1896 he was a committeeman of the Old-Age Pensions League. He was active in the Protestant Political Association and was deputy grand master of the Loyal Orange Institution in 1870 and grand master in 1885. A member of the Public School League in 1874 he later supported the Bible in Schools League.

On 18 July 1860 Roseby had married Ann Hooworth, elder sister of his brother's wife. She was the first president of the Australasian Woman's Christian Temperance Union. Bankrupted in 1885 with debts of over £7000, his estate was not released until 1897. He died on 22 April 1898 at his home in Hyde Park, survived by his wife, six sons and three daughters. He was buried in the Wesleyan section of Rookwood cemetery. His eldest son, Thomas J., was the first secretary of Sydney's Water and Sewerage Board.

W. A. Stewart (ed), *Early history of the Loyal Orange Institution*, N.S.W. (Syd, 1926); J. A. Garrett and L. W. Farr, *Camden College, a centenary history* (Syd, 1964); J. D. Bollen, *Protestantism and social reform in New South Wales 1890-1910* (Melb, 1972); *Congregationalist* (Syd), 1 Jan 1919; Roy Soc NSW, *Procs*, 53 (1919); *Otago Daily Times*, 18 Nov 1885; *SMH*, 23 Apr 1898, 17, 18 Dec 1918; W. W. Phillips, Christianity and its defence in New South Wales circa 1880 to 1890 (Ph.D. thesis, ANU, 1969); M. Lyons, Aspects of sectarianism in New South Wales circa 1865-1880 (Ph.D. thesis, ANU, 1972).   WALTER PHILLIPS

ROSS, ANDREW (1829-1910), medical practitioner and politician, was born at Carbello, Muirkirk, Ayrshire, Scotland, fourth son of David Ross, farmer, and his wife Mary, née Kerr. Educated at the local parish school and in Edinburgh, he studied medicine at the University of Glasgow (M.D., Ch.M., 1852). He practised in Muirkirk and London and became an assistant medical officer in West London. As an assistant sanitary inspector for the City of London he published several works on the housing of the poor. For a short time he was assistant surgeon in the 68th Cambridgeshire Militia. In 1857 he arrived in Sydney as medical officer of an immigrant ship and within a few months set up in practice in Molong where his brother William had been since 1847. On 29 June 1857 he was appointed district registrar for births, deaths and marriages and for much of the 1860s and

1870s was coroner, government medical adviser, medical officer and public vaccinator.

Ross gradually acquired considerable property' and identified with Molong's residents, winning their trust by his skill and humanity. A magistrate by 1861, Ross resigned from the bench on 9 July 1869 after a dispute and legal action with the local schoolmaster Lewis Chandler. In October 1872 Rev. J. D. Lang asked Henry Parkes [qq.v.] to reinstate him on the bench : 'I have long had a strong interest in Dr. Ross . . . an able and most benevolent man whose excess of philanthropy had led him into difficulties from which he could not extricate himself & had therefore suffered most severely'. In 1873 Ross twice appealed to Parkes about it and later wrote to him on a separate electorate for Molong, the siting of the post office and, as honorary secretary of the Railway League, for the extension of the western line via the town. In December 1878 he urged Parkes in vain to include John Sutherland [q.v.] in his new ministry. An alderman on the Molong Municipal Council from 1881, Ross was mayor in 1882.

Defeating John Smith, Gamboola, he was elected to the Legislative Assembly for the new seat of Molong in 1880 and held it until 1904. Although a convinced protectionist he supported Parkes in the interests of economic government and became 'a distinct personage in Parliament'; 'eccentric', Ross was accepted as 'honest and sincere . . . according to his lights'. He was the scourge of the Public Works Department 'in consequence of [its] neglect of portions of his constituency', and in 1896-1900 four times failed to carry a bill to suppress juvenile smoking. In 1889 and 1894 he wrote scathingly to the Australian Star on the 'political crisis—or the age of bungling and blundering'.

In 1893 Ross founded the Molong Argus but soon sold it. In his 1894 electoral address he advocated retrenchment, the establishment of a national bank, liberal mining laws, an elective Upper House and both income and absentee landowners' taxes. Believing that Federation was premature, in the 1890s he criticized the draft Constitution bill as 'financially unworkable'. He strongly objected to equal representation in the senate and the 'inelastic and drastic' character of the Constitution. In January 1898 he petitioned the Australasian Federal Convention to keep the united colonies free of 'ribbons, stars and garters' and to give the Federal parliament impeachment powers to control fraud and corruption.

Ross contributed many articles to the New South Wales Medical Gazette, some of which he reprinted as pamphlets. In 1882 his paper, On the Influence of the Australian Climates and Pastures upon the growth of Wool (Sydney, 1883), won a prize of £25 from the Royal Society of New South Wales. An 'enthusiastic botanist' he contributed 'The Healing Medicinal Value of the Eucalyptus Foliage' to Mueller's [q.v.] Eucalyptographia . . . (1884). In 1887 he thanked Parkes for a copy of his poems and offered his 'candid opinion' on the work, although he had 'no claim to be considered as a "critic" of poetic worth only [of] such effusions as enlist the pathos and sentiments of my own heart and taste'.

A prominent Freemason and a high knight templar of the Knights of Malta, Ross died aged 81 at his house in Albion Street, Surry Hills, on 29 January 1910 and was buried with Presbyterian rites in Waverley cemetery. He was survived by his wife Frances Ann, née Genn (d. 1923), whom he had married at Molong on 7 November 1881, and by their son and daughter. His estate was valued for probate at £6427.

Ex-M.L.A., Our present parliament, what it is worth (Syd, c1886); Echo (Syd), 24 July 1883; T&CJ, 26 Mar 1887; SMH, 31 Jan 1910; Parkes letters (ML); Andrew Ross papers (NL); Col Sec in-letters (NSWA).   MARTHA RUTLEDGE

ROSS, JOHN (1817-1903), explorer and station manager, was born on 17 May 1817 at Bridgend, on the north shore of Cromarty Firth, Scotland, eldest son of Alexander Ross, millwright and farmer, and his wife Sarah. He arrived in Sydney on 31 August 1837 in the Earl Durham and worked as a shepherd for George Macleay [q.v.]. In 1838 he joined Charles Bonney [q.v.] in the first cattle drive from the Goulburn River to Adelaide.

Ross successfully treated scabby sheep, drove stock and explored various parts of South Australia. In the early 1850s he managed stations for C. B. Fisher [q.v.] and J. Hope and was then associated with J. H. Angas [q.v.] at Mount Remarkable, near Melrose. In 1868-70 he worked for Thomas Elder [q.v.] and in 1869 took 30,000 sheep from his station, Umberatana, 300 miles to the Macumba River. Whilst there he explored the Stevenson River to Eringa and Mount Humphries. He named mountains after his children, Sarah, Rebecca, Alexander and John; they remain on maps as a curious group of names in a remote and lonely region.

Ross's recounted experiences led Elder to recommend him to Charles Todd [q.v.] who in July 1870 appointed him leader of the advance exploration party for the overland telegraph line to blaze a route with water and sufficient timber for the telegraph poles. He followed J. M. Stuart's [q.v.] tracks except through the MacDonnell Ranges. With a party of four he penetrated the Simpson Desert, discovering the Todd River, the Phillipson and Giles creeks and the Fergusson Ranges, which he crossed thrice without finding a suitable route, though he significantly narrowed the search area.

Ross started again in March 1871 and this time passed through a gap between the MacDonnell and Fergusson ranges at Alice Springs, only to find that W. W. Mills had preceded him. Continuing northwards without a surveyor he shortened the route of the line and met the northern telegraph party near the Katherine River. He went on to Darwin, completing his third and most successful expedition, and became the second to cross the continent through the centre.

At 57 Ross was engaged by Elder to lead an expedition to explore west of the Peake and to go on to Perth. Struggling against sandhills and mulga scrub he reached the South Australian border but barren country and brackish water forced him back. After a spell of sheep-farming he sought work in Victoria and eventually reached Roma in Queensland where he drove cattle but returned to central Australia. Later he lived at Norwood with his daughter-in-law. He was almost blind, deaf and destitute when a newspaper appeal for 'a little practical help . . . [as] a deserving tribute to a worthy man' came too late. He died on 5 February 1903 after a fall.

In the early 1850s he had married Rebecca McKinlay Affleck (d. 1869), who bore him three daughters and two sons. In October 1869 he married Georgina Strongitharm by whom he had two daughters. Alexander, his elder son, accompanied him in 1874 and was also a member of the successful Giles [q.v.] expedition in 1875-76. Ross was an excellent bushman with an uncanny 'nose' for water. Opportunities came too late in life to be grasped to the full, but his exploits proved him to be an able explorer and a sagacious and energetic leader.

B. Threadgill, *South Australian land exploration 1856-1880*, 1 (Adel, 1922); 'Letter from Mr. John Ross, concerning the country northwest of Cooper's Creek, Australia', Roy Geog Soc, Procs, 1871, p96; G. W. Symes, 'The exploration and development of the northern part of South Australia . . . and the early life of John Ross', PRGSSA, 58 (1956-57) and 'John Ross—a refutation and a chronology', PRGSSA, 59 (1957-58) and 'Exploring in the Macdonnell Ranges 1870-1872', PRGSSA, 61 (1959-60); A. V. Purvis, 'Forgotten Explorer', North Aust Mthly, June 1958; Register (Adel), 3, 6 Feb 1903; biog notes on John Ross (SAA).

G. W. SYMES

ROSS, JOHN (1833-1920), co-operative and radical, was born on 25 April 1833 at Kingussie, Inverness-shire, Scotland, eldest son of John Ross, farmer, and his wife Christina, née McPherson. His strict Calvinist upbringing caused him in his youth the 'greatest mental agony'. His brother James (1837-1892) became an eminent physician in England. Ross arrived in Victoria in 1862 and in 1866 set up in Melbourne as a wine merchant selling colonial wine.

In the late 1860s Ross associated with Melbourne's leading radicals. An early member of the Eclectic Association he was its vice-president in 1871-72 and president the next year. He was president of the Sunday Free Discussion Society in 1872. A member of the Unitarian Church, in the late 1860s he became interested in the harmonial philosophy of spiritualism, in 1875 he was president of the Melbourne Spiritualist and Freethought Association and in 1880 president of the Victorian Association of Spiritualists.

In 1872 Ross became the first president of the radical Democratic Association of Victoria and in July at one of its public meetings spoke on free trade and protection in relation to labour. He first became acquainted with the principles of co-operation when friends in the Democratic Association introduced him to G. J. Holyoake's writings. He chaired public meetings promoting the co-operative movement and when the Victorian Co-operative Association was set up he became its first president in June. A co-operative store initiated by him operated in 1872-74.

In August 1873 Ross may have taken up farming in the Warrandyte district but about 1876 he joined the Singer Sewing Machine Co., probably through his friend T. W. Stanford. He was also interested in land reform and in 1873 corresponded with J. S. Mill. His debate with A. Sutherland [q.v.] on the unearned value of land was published in the *Melbourne Review* in 1885. In 1887 he founded the Economic Permanent Building Society. A well-known advocate of currency reform, he gave evidence in July 1895 to the royal commission on state banking, and a copy of his articles to the *Age* on 17, 18 and 19 June, reprinted as *The Currency Question and the Demands for a State Bank*, was used as an appendix to the report. Another article to the *Age* on 23 March 1901 was reprinted in pamphlet form as *Federal and State Banks and Currency Reform*. Ross remained a proponent of co-operation and his article on its benefits to the working classes in the January 1881 issue of the *Melbourne Review* won editorial favour in the *Australasian*. He became adviser and later director of the Civil Service Co-operative Society, remained active in its affairs from 1903 to 1913 and wrote for its newspaper, the *Federal Co-operative News*. In 1906 he was a director of a proposed Labor daily, *Progress*. That year he published in Melbourne *From competition to co-operation; or, socialism in the making*. He maintained an interest in the language and literature of the Scottish Highlands and in 1900 was president of the United Council for Women's Suffrage.

Ross died at his home in Beaconsfield Road, Auburn, on 1 February 1920 and was buried in the Melbourne general cemetery. He had married first Isabella Kennedy and second Ann Stevenson, who survived him together with a daughter of the first marriage and two sons and three daughters of the second.

H. Mayer, *Marx, Engels and Australia* (Syd, 1964); *Harbinger of Light*, Nov 1875, Dec 1904, Mar 1920; *Federal Co-operative News*, 27 June 1905; D. H. McKay, History of co-operation in south eastern Australia, 1860-1940 (M.A. thesis, Univ Melb, 1946).

SUZANNE G. MELLOR

ROSS, JOSEPH GRAFTON (1834-1906), company manager and director, was born on 9 June 1834 at Kidderminster, Worcestershire, England, son of Rev. Robert Ross [q.v.] and his second wife Sarah, née Grafton. Ross reached Sydney with his family on 25 February 1840 in the *Earl Grey*. His father took charge of the Pitt Street Congregational Church and became a close friend of David Jones and John Fairfax [qq.v.].

In 1850 Ross joined the Australasian Sugar Co. as a junior clerk under the manager, Edward Knox [q.v.]. When the company went into liquidation and Knox founded the Colonial Sugar Refining Co. on 1 January 1855, he became secretary and manager. With Knox's full confidence Ross was left in charge of the company during his visits overseas. He worked very long hours supervising the buying of overseas sugar and selling the company's refined sugar, the purchase and installation of new equipment and the activities of the technical staff. He showed special competence in financial control and spent much time at the new sugar mills on the northern rivers of New South Wales. He combined hard-headed business methods with the very strict standards of his religious upbringing.

In 1870 he became first general manager of the company and in 1878-80 was a director.

On 29 March 1855 at the Pitt Street Congregational Church he had married Emily, only daughter of John Fairfax, who bore him a son and two daughters. On 28 October 1871 she was killed when she jumped from her father's runaway carriage. Ross became prominent in commercial and charitable circles. In the 1870s he was chairman of the Trade Protection Society of New South Wales, a director of the Australian Gaslight Co., the Mercantile Bank of Sydney and the Australian General Assurance Co. and served on the committee of the Chamber of Commerce. Already a director of the Sydney Infirmary and Dispensary, in 1868 he was a convener of the public meeting that resolved to found a hospital in thanksgiving for the recovery of the duke of Edinburgh. He was honorary secretary of the Prince Alfred Hospital Committee and later a director of the hospital. He also served on the committees of the Sydney Ragged Schools, the Society for the Prevention of Cruelty to Animals, the Charity Organization Society and the National Shipwreck Relief Society of New South Wales. A member of the Royal Society of New South Wales from 1865, he was a committee member of the Union Club and the Royal Sydney Yacht Squadron and honorary treasurer of the Rifle Association.

In 1879 Ross resigned from the Colonial Sugar Refining Co. though the directors tried to dissuade him. In March 1880 he returned to England and never came back to Australia. When E. W. Knox was in London in 1887 he consulted Ross who successfully advised him that the company should limit its liability before issuing debentures or increasing its capital. Ross married a widow, Joanna Trotter Crawley, whom he had known in Australia. They made several visits to Europe and one to the United States and lived at such fashionable spas as Cheltenham and Bournemouth. Ross died at his home, Foxcote, Bournemouth, on 4 July 1906. His estate in New South Wales, valued for probate at £43,000, was left to his surviving daughter, the widow and children of his son and his 'much loved stepson', F. H. Crawley.

V&P (LA NSW), 1859-60, 2, 914, 1872-73, 2, 1227; *Empire* (Syd), 31 Oct 1871; Material on the Ross and Jones families (microfilm FM4/2271, ML); family papers (held by J. Fairfax Ross, London); Colonial Sugar Refining Co. Archives (Syd).

A. G. LOWNDES

ROSS, SIR ROBERT DALRYMPLE (1827-1887), army officer and politician, was born at St Vincent in the West Indies, son of John Pemberton Ross, Speaker of the House of Assembly at St Vincent, and his wife, the only daughter of Dr Alexander Anderson. Educated in England he joined the Commissariat Department of the British army as a temporary clerk in 1855 and was sent to the Turkish contingent in the Crimea. On 1 April 1856 he was commissioned; he then volunteered for service on the West Coast of Africa, and was senior commissariat officer at Cape Coast Castle until September 1859. He was also a member of the Gold Coast Legislative Council. When acting colonial secretary in 1858 he took the lead in suppressing a native uprising.

After short periods of service in England and China, Ross was appointed to South Australia in 1862 as head of the Commissariat Department and was briefly aide-de-camp to Governor Daly. He served in the New Zealand Maori war in 1864-65. On 10 August 1865 in Adelaide he married Mary Anstice (d. 1867), daughter of John Baker [q.v.], and bought Highercombe at Gumeracha. In 1869 he went to England, stopping in India to discuss the possible establishment in South Australia of a remount service for the Indian cavalry. He went to Ireland in 1870 to fight the Fenians and a little later resigned his commission to return to Australia.

In 1875 after being defeated for Gumeracha, Ross entered the House of Assembly for Wallaroo and from June 1876 to October 1877 was treasurer in the Colton [q.v.] ministry. In 1881-87 he was Speaker of the assembly. He represented Gumeracha in 1884-87 and was knighted in 1886.

Ross actively supported schemes to lay a cable from England to Australia and to build a transcontinental railway from Adelaide to Darwin. He sought to develop foreign markets for South Australian produce and in 1879 told a commission on liquor laws that wine would become a most important industry of the colony. He carried out experiments at Highercombe in growing olives and vines, in cider making and in fruit drying. President of the Royal Agricultural and Horticultural Society of South Australia, he gave papers on agriculture, scrub land cultivation and wine and brandy. He was a governor of the Collegiate School of St Peter, Adelaide, a member of the University Council and chairman of the Adelaide Steamship Co. He was also a promoter and guarantor of the Adelaide jubilee exhibition. Described as a 'model colonist' he had wide interests and was always available to give help and advice to others; he was a man of action, noted for his courtesy, dignity and firmness.

Aged 60, Ross died in hospital at North Adelaide on 27 December 1887 and was buried, after a state funeral, in St George's cemetery, Woodforde. He left an estate of £12,000 to his son and daughter. A portrait hangs in Parliament House, Adelaide.

E. Ward, *The vineyards and orchards of South Australia* (Adel, 1862); PP (SA), 1869-70, 2 (43), 1879, 3 (34); *Advertiser* (Adel), 28 Dec 1887; *Australasian*, 7 Jan 1888; S. Newland, An appreciation (SAA); records held by E. A. Ross, Adel; CO 448/2.   NOEL HAYMAN

ROSSI, FRANCIS ROBERT LOUIS (LEWIS) (1823-1903), landowner, was born on 19 February 1823 at Port Louis, Mauritius, elder son of Captain Francis Nicholas Rossi [q.v.], general superintendent of convicts, and his wife Antoinette Geneviève, née Sornay. He reached Sydney with his family in the *Hercules* on 7 May 1825, was educated at The King's School, Parramatta, and declined an army commission in order to work with his father. On 15 December 1847 at St Saviour's, Goulburn, he married Jane Hannah, eldest daughter of Rev. William Sowerby [q.v.]. In 1851 he inherited Rossiville, near Goulburn.

Rossi was proud of his membership of a noble Corsican family (he succeeded his uncle as comte de Rossi in 1896). He was also solicitous about his position as a colonial squire, extending and improving Rossiville, which was robbed by Ben Hall and John Gilbert [qq.v.] in 1864, and playing with enthusiasm and some success the role of the hospitable country gentleman. He was a magistrate and from 1866 a sheep director for Goulburn.

On 7 July 1870 Rossi became captain of the Goulburn Volunteer Rifles. His overbearing conduct aroused public protest and led in 1873 to a recommendation for his removal by a Legislative Assembly select committee; but Governor Robinson ordered a military inquiry and precipitated a constitutional crisis in 1874. Rossi was relieved of his command and enlisted as a private. He was temporarily reinstated when the governor left in 1879.

A devout Anglican and first registrar of the diocese, Rossi was trustee of much Church property. As in other dioceses, dispute and litigation arose about the parish church when it was given cathedral status. The incumbent, Archdeacon A. T. Puddicombe, the parishioners and Bishop M. Thomas [q.v.] were the chief disputants but Rossi became heavily involved. In 1884-94 court actions, newspaper controversies and synod debates confused motives and legal rights. Rossi's alleged position as sole trustee of the cathedral property gave him a key role which he used to the full. Piqued because Bishop Thomas refused to allow a family tablet to be re-erected in the new cathedral, in 1887 Rossi placed it there and kept guard over it; later it was removed and in 1891, amid scenes of great scandal and public excitement, he occupied the building with a group of men. Even after the trusteeship was resolved in 1894, he remained absorbed in proceedings about the episcopal residence and the West Goulburn parish. His role, though sometimes played with popular backing and always with a show of legalism, generally created additional confusion.

From 7 August 1870 Rossi served as registrar of the District Court at Goulburn. In 1871 his salary was reduced and he began a long paper war with the government; in 1902 he sued in vain for £10,000 compensation, a sign of his financial difficulties. In 1890 he had sold Rossiville for over £15,000 to the government for a lunatic asylum. A near-by property, Kenmore, had been acquired already for this purpose; the mix-up led to an official investigation and seemed to symbolize the later stages of Rossi's career.

In 1883 he left his wife and ceased to support her; in November 1892 she divorced him for desertion under Sir Alfred Stephen's [q.v.] new Act. On 29 September 1894 Rossi was married by the Presbyterian minister W. Dill Macky to Florence Jane Hayley of Bowral. Bishop W. Chalmers [q.v.] of Goulburn refused to admit them to the Holy Communion and the Rossis began, but left off, a suit for damages. Rossi died childless at Sydney on 12 November 1903 and was buried in Waverley cemetery. His second wife pressed their unsettled property claims against the diocese of Goulburn with unabated energy.

Rossi's chosen vocation as a local worthy had begun well and he always retained some popularity. But everything went wrong. Sometimes unfortunate, he was occasionally obliged by straitened resources to make discreditable claims. His lofty disregard for convention, his pertinacity in seeking redress of grievances and his dramatic flair caused constant turmoil and irritated both church and state. If there was any way of making a difficult situation worse, Rossi would invariably find it.

R. T. Wyatt, The history of the diocese of Goulburn (Syd, 1937) and The history of Goulburn, N.S.W. (Goulburn, 1941) and 'The Comte de Rossi and the Goulburn Cathedral dispute', JRAHS, 24 (1938); V&P (LA NSW), 1873-74, 3, 131, 1883-84, 6, 31, 77, 1887-88, 2, 143, 897, 1085, 1890, 7, 283; ISN, 15 Apr 1865; SMH, 30 Dec 1873, 2 July 1890, 27 Jan 1892; Daily Telegraph (Syd), 25 June 1897; Goulburn Evening Penny Post, 9 Aug 1902; Diocese of Goulburn, Synod procs, 1891-92, 1894 (Diocesan Registry, Syd); Rossi papers (ML); CO 201/574/620, 628, 577/4, 54, 73.   K. J. CABLE

ROTTON, HENRY (1814-1881), pastoralist, was born at Frome-Selwood, Somersetshire, England, son of Gilbert Rotton, solicitor, and his wife Mary Caroline, née Humphries. Failing to enter the navy, he joined a merchant ship that was wrecked in the West Indies. After rescue he was landed in Africa where he contracted yellow fever. In 1836 he reached Kangaroo Island, South Australia, as second mate in the Emma and soon made his way to Sydney. In February 1839 he took over the licence of the Queen Victoria Inn at Solitary Creek near Rydal. That year he married Lorn Jane Macpherson, who died on 11 September 1843. In 1843-48 he was licensee of the Queen Victoria Inn, Bathurst.

In 1849 Rotton became a mail-coach proprietor and in 1850 had a four-horse service three times a week to and from Sydney, Parramatta, Penrith and Hartley, and many twice-weekly two-horse coaches to near-by towns. In 1851 Deas Thomson [q.v.] wrote to Governor FitzRoy from the goldfields that 'Rotton is anxious to buy the gold carriages as his carriages are nearly all broken down from the immense traffic and dreadful state of the roads'. He prospered from the gold rushes and in 1853 bought Blackdown, an estate at Kelso, near Bathurst, where he became a successful horse and cattle breeder with imported stock. He also acquired Gungalman in the Lachlan District and other pastoral interests.

As a supporter of John Robertson [q.v.], in January 1858 he was elected to the Legislative Assembly for Western Boroughs, despite A. T. Holroyd [q.v.] 'sticking at nothing to obtain pledges'. Defeated for Bathurst in 1859 and 1860 because of his support for the abolition of state aid to religion, he represented Hartley in 1859-64. He opposed free selection before survey and from 1860 voted against Cowper [q.v.]-Robertson ministries. In 1861 Rotton opposed the extension of the southern railway at the expense of the western and northern lines.

At 2 a.m. on Sunday, 25 October 1863, Rotton was woken by his daughter Caroline asking for £500 as ransom for her husband, H. M. Keightley, being held at their Dunn's Plains station by Ben Hall [q.v.] and his gang. Rotton took the ransom money in marked notes and after the release of Keightley went on to Rockley to report the incident. In 1866 he became a sheep director for Bathurst and was chairman of the Bathurst Sheep Board in 1869-81. A zealous supporter of the Baptists, he was a member of the local public school board from 1868 and chairman from 1874. In 1872 he adjudicated in an important squatting case.

Aged 67, Rotton died on 11 October 1881 at Mynora, a property he owned near Moruya occupied by the Keightleys, and was buried in the Baptist cemetery, Bathurst, with Anglican rites. He was survived by a son and daughter of his first wife, and by five sons and six daughters of his second wife, Anne Ford, whom he had married on 18 March 1844. His personalty was valued for probate at £29,000.

E. Digby (ed), *Australian men of mark*, 1 (Syd, 1889); C. White, *History of Australian bushranging*, 2 (Syd, 1900); V&P (LA NSW), 1861, 1, 213, 221, 229, 238; J. MacPherson, 'Henry Rotton, H. M. Keightley, and the bushrangers', JRAHS, 23 (1937); SMH, 1 Jan 1850; *Bathurst Times*, 12 Oct 1881; Parkes letters (ML); information from Mr G. L. Milne, Glenelg, SA, and Mrs L. S. Cash, Parramatta, NSW.   E. J. LEA-SCARLETT

ROUSE, RICHARD. (1842-1903) and RICHARD junior (1843-1906), pastoralists and stud-breeders, were first cousins and grandsons of Richard Rouse [q.v.] of Rouse Hill. Richard was born on 2 January 1842 at Guntawang, near Mudgee, New South Wales, eldest son of Edwin Rouse, grazier, and his wife Hannah Terry, née Hipkins. Educated at Dr Woolls's [q.v.] school at Parramatta, in 1861 he managed Guntawang, 4000 acres on the Cudgegong River near Mudgee and inherited it on the death of his father the next year. Using the 'Crooked R' brand made famous by his grandfather, Rouse bred pedigree carriage horses, cattle and merino sheep and Guntawang became noted for its lavish hospitality. He also held other runs.

In 1870 gold was discovered in the district and Gulgong was founded. In March 1872 Rouse became the principal shareholder in the Guntawang Freehold Gold Mining Co., which was moderately successful. He represented Mudgee in parliament in 1876-77 and in 1879. In 1895 he published *The Australian Horse Trade*, an address to the United Service Institution, in which he stressed the breeding advantages of the 'Yorkshire coach-horse'. He was a magistrate and regularly sat on the bench, first president of the Gulgong Turf Club in 1871, mayor of Gulgong in 1876

and 1899-1903 and a member of the Union Club. On 25 July 1865 in Hobart Town he married Charlotte Emily (d. 1902), daughter of James Barnard [q.v.]. Rouse died at Guntawang on 2 March 1903, survived by three sons and a daughter. His estate was sworn for probate at over £12,400.

Richard junior was born on 15 May 1843 at Jericho, near Windsor, New South Wales, son of George Rouse (d. 1888) and his wife Elizabeth, née Moore. He was educated at The King's School, Parramatta, and then learnt wool-classing. In 1867 he managed the Biraganbil stud flock near Mudgee, founded by his father in 1864 with rams and ewes bought from N. P. Bayly [q.v.] of Havilah and later from E. K. Cox [q.v.] of Rawdon. He kept careful pedigree records and bred sheep with fine strong wool of abnormal elasticity and won many prizes at the Mudgee, Dubbo and Warren shows. He was also noted for breeding race-horses, including the champion, Marvel, and was reputed one of the best judges of horses in the colony. He inherited Biraganbil in 1888 and held three other stations.

In May 1872 Rouse had 1000 shares in the new Biraganbil Gold Mining Co. Ltd. He was a councillor of the Agricultural Society of New South Wales, sometime president of the Gulgong Hospital, chairman of the Mudgee Pastures and Stock Board, a sheep director for Mudgee, a member of the Australian Jockey Club and a magistrate, although he rarely sat on the bench. He died at Biraganbil on 12 February 1906 and was buried in the Anglican section of Mudgee cemetery. He was survived by his wife Mary Helena (d. 1922), daughter of Charles Bland Lowe of Goree, Mudgee, whom he had married on 29 July 1869, and by two sons and two daughters. His estate was valued for probate at nearly £24,000. His eldest son Leslie, solicitor, was an Australian Jockey Club stipendiary steward and keeper of the *Australian Stud Book*.

C. McIvor, *The history and development of sheep farming from antiquity to modern times* (Syd, 1893); V&P (LA NSW), 1878-79, 1, 263, 2, 33; *Government Gazette* (NSW), 1872, 1876; *Sydney Mail*, 5 Aug 1865, 14 Aug 1869, 15 Apr 1871; T&CJ, 7 Jan 1871, 21 Feb 1906; *Gulgong Guardian*, 25 Mar, 1 Apr 1871, 30 Mar, 13 Apr, 25 May, 12 Oct 1872; *Mudgee Guardian*, 16 Feb 1900; *Mudgee Liberal*, 22 Mar 1900, 14 Feb, 20 May 1901; SMH, 4 Mar 1903, 14 Feb 1906.   MARJORIE LENEHAN

ROWAN, ANDREW (1840-1910), merchant, company director and pastoralist, was a son of James Rowan, landed proprietor of Fort Hill, County Down, Ireland, and his wife Ann Elizabeth, née Dodd. He came to Australia with his brother James about 1861; by 1869 he was a merchant in Melbourne providing station supplies to pastoralists and in 1878 opened a Sydney branch.

In 1879 Rowan became a partner of Hubert de Castella [q.v.] in the St Hubert vineyard near Lilydale, Victoria. They fell out in 1886 and Rowan bought de Castella's share in 1890. He was a tireless publicist of St Hubert's prize-winning wines, helped the showing of Victorian wines at the 1882 Bordeaux Exhibition and attended it himself; he opened a London agency in the late 1880s. He also invested in several pastoral properties including, in Queensland, Darrwater and Darr River Downs in the Mitchell District, first held with S. and M. H. Baird from 1876 and transferred, in part, to five of his children in 1906; Weribone and Talavera in the Maranoa District from 1882, the former initially with his brother Thomas, a Melbourne doctor; Malvern Downs and Talagai, and Echo Hills in the Leichhardt District; and in western New South Wales, Thurloo Downs.

Described as 'a man of great force of character ... always the master mind in any business he took in hand', Rowan was a large shareholder in, and in 1884-90 an active director of, R. Goldsbrough [q.v.] & Co. Ltd. Management and personal differences that developed between him and J. S. Horsfall [q.v.], sole survivor of the old Goldsbrough partnership, became notorious in 1889 with the publication in Melbourne of his pamphlet, Letter from Andrew Rowan to the shareholders, Goldsbrough, Mort & Co. Ltd (1889) and of Horsfall's answer; both were forced from the board. Rowan was a director in 1888-1909 of the Squatting Investment Co. Ltd. In 1886 a syndicate including Rowan and George Fairbairn [q.v.] bought the assets of the Central Queensland Meat Export Co. including its Lakes Creek freezing works. Technically and economically the meatworks performed well until overtaken by financial stringencies in the late 1890s; in 1901 the company passed to an English syndicate.

Rowan, like many others, depended on credit for his investments. He speculated, sometimes spectacularly, in stocks and shares and was involved with F. B. Clapp, William McCulloch [qq.v], T. S. Hall and W. G. Sprigg in major raids on the shares of the Melbourne Tramway and Omnibus Co. in 1889-90 and was left with a very large parcel. Great financial ingenuity and agility kept him from ruin in the 1890s,

even though his 1902 balance sheet still showed a deficiency of some £400,000.

Conservative, with free-trade leanings, Rowan was an active member of the Constitutional Association in 1877. He was married on 22 December 1873 by the bishop of Melbourne at St Mary's Church, Caulfield, to Margaret Annie, eldest daughter of a well-connected city lawyer, Francis J. Stephen. After a stroke in 1909, he died on 22 September 1910 while visiting Perth, Scotland, and was survived by his wife and their six sons and three daughters.

J. S. Horsfall, To the shareholders of Goldsbrough, Mort & Co. Limited (Melb, 1889); J. Flanagan, A sample of the commercial & financial morality (?) of Melbourne (Melb, 1898); J. T. Critchell and J. Raymond, A history of the frozen meat trade (Lond, 1912); F. de Castella, 'Early Victorian wine-growing', VHM, 19 (1941-42); Table Talk, 7 Aug 1891; Australasian, 1 Oct 1910; Pastoral Review, 15 Oct 1910; Goldsbrough Mort & Co., Squatting Investment Co., and Central Queensland Meat Export Co. papers (ANU Archives).

ALAN BARNARD

ROWE, GEORGE (1796-1864), artist and lithographer, was baptized on 8 July 1796 at St Sidwell's Parish Church, Exeter, Devon, England, son of George Rowe and his wife Elizabeth. Brought up in Exeter, as a young man he won much repute with his topographical lithographs of resorts in Cornwall, Somerset, Devon and Sussex. He taught drawing in Exeter where in 1828 he married a pupil, Philippa Curtis, the daughter of a major in the British army. In 1834 he moved to Cheltenham and practised as an 'Artist and Drawing Master', aided by his wife and later his daughter. With George Norman, his partner in a printing and publishing business, he was also joint proprietor of the weekly Cheltenham Examiner, first issued in 1839. At an exhibition he reputedly created great interest with his demonstrations of the new 'tinted' style of lithography. He published Illustrations of Cheltenham and its vicinity (c.1840), and Rowe's Illustrated Cheltenham Guide (1845, 1850), interesting for its lithographed vignettes.

In the early 1850s Rowe suffered a severe loss through the default of a partner and sought to recoup his fortunes on the Victorian goldfields. Leaving his family in England he arrived at the Bendigo diggings in 1853 and was joined in November by his eldest son George, and in 1854 by two younger sons Thomas and Sandford. He failed as a gold digger, and also as a storekeeper at Long Gully, Bendigo, but finally succeeded with his water-colours of the

Bendigo and Castlemaine diggings. Fifty of his works were exhibited in an art union at Bendigo in 1857, and next year he lithographed a well-known panoramic *View of the City of Melbourne, from the Observatory.*

About 1858 he returned to England and settled in Exeter. In 1862 his eight watercolours shown in the Victorian section of the London International Exhibition won him a medal for 'faithful and beautiful delineation of the country, workings, and other relations of the gold-fields'. Several of these paintings are in the Dixson Library, Sydney, and he is represented in the National Library of Australia and in the Bendigo Art Gallery. His surviving works are of considerable historical interest, those of Bendigo being among the earliest visual records of the locality, while his letters to his wife and daughter, now held in the La Trobe Library, give absorbing details of his day-to-day life on the diggings. He died at Heavitree, Exeter, on 2 September 1864, survived by his wife, five sons and five daughters.

His eldest son GEORGE CURTIS was born in Exeter on 24 July 1832 and began his theatrical career as George Fawcett at Bendigo in 1853. He was known as an 'excellent actor of eccentric characters' and a talented mimic. He went to England in the late 1860s, added Rowe to his professional name, and became well known there and in the United States as an actor and producer. He adapted many works for the stage, notably *David Copperfield* in 1862. He died in New York on 29 August 1889 and was buried in the actors' plot of the Evergreen cemetery.

Harry Emmet's theatrical holiday book (Melb, 1885); J. R. Abbey, *Scenery of Great Britain and Ireland in aquatint and lithography, 1770-1860* (Lond, 1952); G. Pycroft, 'Art in Devonshire', *Devonshire Assn for the Advancement of Science, Literature, and Art,* 14 (1882); *Bendigo Advertiser,* 15 May 1857; *Argus,* 15 July 1857, 30 Apr, 12 July 1858; *Examiner* (Melb), 13 Sept 1862; *Australasian,* 30 Jan 1869, 7 Sept 1889; *New York Times,* 1 Sept 1889.   PATRICIA REYNOLDS

ROWE, RICHARD (1828-1879), journalist and tutor, was probably born on 9 March 1828 at Spring Gardens, Doncaster, England, son of Thomas Rowe, Wesleyan minister. His father died while he was very young and with his mother and his sister he moved to Colchester where he attended Mr Bradnack's school, and later worked as an usher after it moved to Bath.

In 1853 Rowe came to Australia and in 1856 wrote to Nicol Stenhouse [q.v.] from Bengalla, Muswellbrook, where he was a tutor. Stenhouse lent him books and helped him with German translations which he contributed to the *Freeman's Journal.* In 1857 he was arrested for drunkenness and Stenhouse befriended him in prison and arranged for his rehabilitation in Wollongong. Rowe suffered deep depression and complained 'my dislike of scribbling now amounts to loathing. In no other way, however, can I earn a crust. I detest teaching, have no head for accounts, couldn't stoop to greedy trade and it is too late in the day to think about a profession'.

To raise his fare to England Rowe, helped by Stenhouse, collected his work and published it in *Peter 'Possum's Portfolio* (1858), dedicated to his benefactor. The book gives valuable evidence of the background and education of a member of Sydney's literary coterie. Daniel Deniehy [q.v.] praised it extravagantly, but it is uneven; the essays are competently and often humorously written but the truncated novel 'Arthur Owen, an Autobiography', previously published in the *Month,* verges on melodrama. The original poems, though several appeared in subsequent anthologies, are unremarkable. Rowe belonged to the Frank Fowler, William Wilkes, Sheridan Moore [qq.v.] circle and was an important contributor to Fowler's *Month* and to Wilkes's *Sydney Punch.* He also wrote regularly for the *Sydney Morning Herald* and *Freeman's Journal,* sometimes under the pseudonym 'A Sassenach Settler'. Henry Halloran's [q.v.] enthusiastic verse in the *Empire* urging 'Possum to give up the 'Circe-cup' and become the 'satirist of the age' infuriated 'Q', believed to be Charles Harpur [q.v.], who attacked Rowe in the *Empire* as one

Whose 'moral Waterloo' were best achieved
O'er his insensate passion. Hideous sight
When sottishness obscures with leprous blight
The gifts of Providence—so ill received.

The *Portfolio* sold well and Rowe returned to England in 1858, but kept up a lifelong correspondence with Stenhouse. He rented de Quincey's old rooms in Edinburgh and with the aid of introductions from Stenhouse became assistant editor of the *Scotsman.* He married Mary Ann Yates in 1860 and by 1863 had moved to Glasgow as principal leader writer of the *North British Daily Mail.* That year Fowler died and Rowe collected a selection of his work and published *Last Gleanings* in 1864 to raise money for Fowler's destitute family.

In the same year Rowe was dismissed from the *North British Daily Mail* and lived in poverty in London writing for the *Scotsman* and doing freelance work. By 1868 he had established himself as a contributor to *Fraser's Magazine, Argosy, Chamber's Journal, Cassell's Magazine, Good Words* and other journals and was able to write cheerfully to Stenhouse. He also wrote for Australian papers. He published about twenty books in England; many were adventure stories for boys, three at least with Australian settings, but some of his best works were *Episodes in an Obscure Life* (1871), *Friends and Acquaintances* (1871) and other carefully researched accounts of life among the London poor. 'Edward Howe' and 'Charles Camden' were pseudonyms used by him.

Rowe died on 9 December 1879 in Middlesex Hospital, after an operation for cancer of the tongue. He left a wife, a son, three daughters and a total estate of £20.

Empire (Syd), 24 Mar 1858; *Day of Rest*, Feb 1880; *Bulletin*, 7 Feb 1880, 7 May 1881; *Sydney Mail*, 7 Feb 1880; A. M. Williams, Nicol Drysdale Stenhouse: a study of a literary patron in a colonial milieu (M. A. thesis, Univ Syd, 1963); Stenhouse letters (ML).

ROSILYN BAXTER

ROWE, THOMAS (1829-1899), architect, was born on 20 July 1829 at Penzance, Cornwall, England, eldest son of Richard Rowe and his wife Ursula, née Mumford. Educated at Barnes Academy, Penzance, at 15 he entered his father's building business as a draftsman. The family sailed for Sydney late in 1848 and Thomas worked for local builders till 1851. After the discovery of gold he prospected at Sofala with much success till his partner decamped with their gold. About 1853 with his brother Richard (1831-1909), he set up a building business in Pitt Street mainly for speculative domestic work. Between 1857 and 1895 he practised as an architect in Sydney with W. B. Field, Sydney Green and Alfred Spain as successive partners.

Rowe's practice, mainly in Bathurst, Orange, Newcastle, Goulburn and Sydney, was one of the biggest in New South Wales. It was said in 1890 that one could walk Pitt Street and always be opposite one of his buildings. Often successful in competitions he built commercial premises, large houses and churches, mainly Methodist. Among his best known buildings are the Presbyterian Church, Bathurst (1871), the Jewish Synagogue in Elizabeth Street, Sydney (1874), Sydney Hospital in Macquarie Street (1879, completed by John Kirkpatrick after 1891), Newington College, Stanmore (1878), Sydney Arcade and Vickery's [q.v.]

Building, Pitt Street, Sydney (1874) and warehouses for Hoffnung [q.v.] & Co. in Charlotte Street, Brisbane (1879) and Pitt Street, Sydney (1881).

The sheer quantity of Rowe's work had a significant effect on New South Wales cities and towns in the late nineteenth century. He progressed from a certain simplicity to an elaborate showiness in his larger and later works, and became excessively ornate after he visited Europe in 1884 and was strongly impressed by Venice. But his work was always marked by a heavy hand, a ponderous, unimaginative mind and a leaden, even dull, expression.

Rowe was superintendent of the Dowling Street Wesleyan Sunday school in 1860-90 and was active in the Paddington and Waverley Methodist churches. A justice of the peace from 1874, he was latterly a warden at St Mark's Church of England, Darling Point. He was a founder in 1871 of the Institute of Architects of New South Wales and its president in 1876-89 and 1895-97. He was an alderman for Bourke Ward on the Sydney City Council in 1872-76. First mayor of Manly in 1877, he set up and became captain of the Manly Fire Brigade, the first municipal brigade in Australia, and initiated the planting of the Norfolk Island pines that became the distinctive feature of the Manly beach fronts. A founder of the United Services Institution of New South Wales, he served on other civic bodies and was a trustee of the Rushcutter Bay Park. A first lieutenant in the Engineer Corps in 1872, he became lieut-colonel in 1886, and was a member of the commission on defence from foreign aggression. In 1888 he became president of the Metropolitan Board of Water Supply and Sewerage.

At the peak of his career in 1890 Rowe was reputedly worth £70,000 with an income of £14,000. He lost nearly all in the 1893 depression with the collapse of a syndicate, formed to build a natatorium in Pitt Street. Virtually penniless, he died of cancer on 14 January 1899 at his lavishly furnished home Mona, Darling Point. Buried in the Anglican section of Waverley cemetery, he was survived by two daughters of his first wife Charlotte Jane (d. March 1877), daughter of Captain Piper [q.v.], whom he had married on 21 May 1857, and by his second wife Sarah Selina Cornish, whom he had married in July 1877, and by their seven sons and three daughters. To pay his debts and bring up her children his widow had to take in boarders and run art unions with Rowe's valuable pictures as prizes, including a Constable landscape. Rowe Street in Sydney is named after him.

J. M. Freeland, *Architect extraordinary* (Melb, 1971) and *The making of a profession* (Syd, 1971); M. Berry, A history of Col. Thomas Rowe . . . (B. Arch. thesis, Univ NSW, 1969).

J. M. FREELAND

ROWNTREE, THOMAS STEPHENSON (1818-1902), master mariner and ship-builder, was born on 7 July 1818 at Sunderland, County Durham, England, son of William Rowntree, marine captain, and his wife Mary, née Dodds. Apprenticed at 14 to a shipwright he went to sea at 20 as a ship's carpenter. In 1842-52 he commanded vessels in the English, Baltic and Mediterranean trades. With John Webber he built the 206-ton *Lizzie Webber* for the Australian coastal trade, sailed from Sunderland with his family and other passengers on 1 August 1852 and reached Melbourne on 4 December. His trading was affected by new port regulations and he settled at Balmain, New South Wales.

In 1853 Rowntree sold his ship to lay down a patent slip. With T. S. Mort [q.v.] and J. S. Mitchell, as Rowntree & Co., he acquired more land at Balmain and formed the Waterview Dry Dock Co. The dock was opened in 1855 and Rowntree, with eighteen sixty-fourths of the stock, leased it for shipwrighting until the Peninsular and Oriental Co. took it over in 1858, leaving him as sub-lessee. An official undertaking that the proposed new Fitzroy Dock would not be available for private use was not kept and Rowntree's business slackened. In 1860 he petitioned Governor Denison for relief against 'ruinous competition'. Rowntree withdrew from the company in 1861, did not renew his sub-lease and it was taken over by John Cuthbert [q.v.].

In 1855-57 he testified at parliamentary select committees on marine and related matters. He built several steamships at Waterview Bay and in 1864 took sixteen men and a sawmill in his boat *Caroline* to New Zealand. From the Hokianga district he exported timber including kauri to Sydney. He returned with his family in 1869 and resumed building and repairing ships at Balmain. In 1872, with financial assistance from Robert Towns and (Sir) Alexander Stuart [qq.v.], he bought the floating dock at Darling Harbour but sold it in 1880 and restarted business at Balmain.

Popular and community-spirited, Rowntree was closely identified with the progress of his district: he was an alderman and mayor of Balmain, helped found the local School of Arts in 1850 and was a magistrate and electoral returning officer for many years. He was a member of the Marine Board of New South Wales. A founder of the Royal Sydney Yacht Squadron, he revived the Anniversary Day Regatta and in 1858-64 enjoyed racing, winning seven trophies with his boats *Annie Ogle, Lenan* and *Leisure Hour.*

Rowntree lived in Northumberland House, Darling Street, Balmain, and died there on 17 December 1902; he was buried in the Anglican section of Balmain cemetery. Probate of his estate was sworn at £9126. He was survived by three daughters of his first wife Elizabeth, née Potts, whom he had married in Sunderland in 1839, and by his second wife Annie, née Ogle, whom he had married in Sunderland in 1847, and by their two sons and two daughters. His younger son Cameron Sutcliffe opened a large and successful general store at Quirindi, New South Wales, and his daughter Adelaide married Felix Randle, chairman of the Sydney Stock Exchange. There is a monument to Rowntree at Balmain.

E. Digby (ed), *Australian men of mark*, 1 (Syd, 1889); A. Barnard, *Visions and profits* (Melb, 1961); V&P (LC NSW), 1855, 3, 235, Sel c'ttee on the Hunter River, (LA NSW), 1856-57, 3, p 32 of report; *ISN*, 31 Aug 1872; *T&CJ*, 24 Dec 1902.

G. P. WALSH

RUATOKA (1846 ?-1903), missionary, was born in Tamarua, Mangaia Island, Cook Islands, about 1846. The status of his parents is unknown, but they were Christian converts. Taught by William Wyatt Gill [q.v.] he went about 1868 to Takamoa Theological College, Rarotonga, then under James Chalmers [q.v.].

Ruatoka became one of six Polynesians chosen to convert New Guinea and with his wife, Tungane, left Rarotonga with his five colleagues and Gill in mid-1872 and reached Somerset, Cape York, on 11 October. On 25 November with their wives and one child the missionaries landed at Manumanu on the coast of Papua with a supply of food, some medicine, trade goods and a small boat; in February 1873 they left the station, decimated by fever, and were taken to Somerset by Captain John Moresby [q.v.].

Five months later Ruatoka and three colleagues sailed for Port Moresby. The Motu people, who often traded with Manumanu, recognized him and invited them to stay at Elevara and Hanuabada in Port Moresby. Ruatoka was never appointed leader of the party but clearly took command. The English missionaries depended on him to interpret, advise and supervise when they were away. He was an efficient and dependable guide; short journeys with W. G. Lawes [q.v.] in 1876 and Chalmers in 1877 and a major trip with Chalmers in 1880 behind the Owen Stanley Range made Ruatoka well known on the Papuan coast.

In the 1878 Laloki River gold rush Ruatoka and Tungane nursed sick miners in their own home. Ruatoka once carried a patient for ten miles on his back; no native would help for fear of evil spirits. The miners presented him with a testimonial, not only for his kindness but also for his work as a mediator in land disputes. The Queensland government gave him a fine shotgun. After his first wife died, he married the Papuan widow of another teacher. His children died young, but an adopted son, Teina Materua, served the colonial government for years.

Ruatoka was an effective mediator and a successful evangelist but his teaching was described as 'vigorous ineffectiveness' by one English missionary. When Chalmers was murdered in 1901 Ruatoka offered to go to the same village to take over the work, but he was too old. He died in Port Moresby on 12 September 1903 and was buried there. His name is used in Ruatoka Road, Port Moresby, Ruatoka College, Rigo, Papua, and for the married student quarters in the Pacific Theological College of Suva, Fiji. His most enduring memorials are the stories still current about him in both New Guinea and the Cook Islands.

V. A. Barradale, *Pearls of the Pacific* (Lond, 1907); M. T. Crocombe, 'Ruatoka: a Polynesian in New Guinea history', *Pacific Islands Mthly*, Nov-Dec 1972, and for bibliog; LMS, South Seas journal, Papua reports 1871-1900 (microfilm, NL); M. Crocombe and Ako Toua, Oral tradition records (Univ PNG, Port Moresby, 1967).   MARJORIE TUAINEKORE CROCOMBE

RUDALL, JAMES THOMAS (1828?-1907), surgeon and ophthalmologist, was born at Crediton, Devon, England, son of James Rudall, naval paymaster, and his wife Penelope, née Mackay. After apprenticeship he studied at St Thomas's Hospital, London (L.S.A., M.R.C.S., 1854; F.R.C.S., 1857). In 1854 in H.M.S. *Talbot* he took part in the Arctic search for Sir John Franklin. After working at St Pancras Infirmary and practising in London, in 1858 he sailed for Port Phillip as surgeon in the *Queen of the Seas* and arrived on 14 July. His 1858 diary, which includes the voyage, gives valuable details of the medical practice of the time.

In Melbourne Rudall at first entered general practice, including autopsies for the coroner and at the Yarra Bend Asylum. He was on the honorary surgical staff of the Melbourne Hospital in 1865-75, and briefly

next year was hospital pathologist. In 1887-1901 he was an honorary surgeon at the Alfred Hospital, and was a consultant till 1907. He was an examiner in pathology and physiology of the University of Melbourne and in 1866-1901 honorary oculist to the Victorian Asylum and School for the Blind. He was also honorary surgeon to the Deaf and Dumb Institution. Rudall was one of the few Australian members of the Royal Ophthalmic Society, and he became first vice-president, then president, of the Melbourne Ophthalmological Society on its formation in 1899. In his later years Rudall's practice was largely confined to diseases of the eye, and also of the ear, nose and throat.

Rudall was elected a member of the Medical Society of Victoria in 1865 and served on its committee. He was a founding member of the Victorian branch of the British Medical Association in 1879, a member of the first council, later vice-president and president in 1884-85. In 1881 he represented the branch during a tour of America and Europe. He was a councillor of the Royal Society of Victoria in 1869-90 and also held office in the Medical Benevolent Association. A musician of ability, he was vice-president of the Melbourne Liedertafel in 1880 and president in 1882-85. With F. Mueller's [q.v.] help he had translated from the German and published in Melbourne in 1869 J. L. C. S. van der Kolk's *The Pathology and Therapeutics of Mental Diseases*. He gave evidence to the royal commissions on asylums for the insane and the inebriate (1886) and charitable institutions (1892).

Rudall retired in 1901 for health reasons and died of cardiac and cerebral vascular disease on 4 March 1907. In 1862 he had married Georgiana Gordon Scott (1830-1910). Of the two of their seven children who reached adulthood, James Ferdinand (1864-1944) became an ophthalmologist and honorary medical officer to the Victorian Eye and Ear Hospital.

Rudall contributed over sixty papers to medical journals, mostly Australian, including several translations of important European articles. An accomplished and innovative surgeon he was a founder of ophthalmology in Australia and a leading pathologist. An energetic worker for the welfare of the many institutions with which he was connected, he remained dignified in controversy, and retained a human interest in a brandy and cigar.

D. A. Williams, 'Eyes, surgeons and sociality in Australasia', Ophthalmological Soc of Aust, *Trans*, 7 (1947); B. Gandevia, 'James Thomas Rudall . . . his life and journal for the year

1858', *MJA*, 25 Dec 1954; documents (Vic Medical Soc, Melb).

RULE, JAMES (1830-1901), educationist, was born on 28th July 1830 at Mill Farm, Norham, Northumberland, England, youngest son of Thomas Rule (1787-1878), hereditary slater, and his wife Mary, née Eadington. Educated at the village school, he served an apprenticeship in the family trade and entered St John's College, Battersea, as a trainee teacher. Graduating in 1851 he immediately accepted appointment as headmaster in a large county-controlled school in Monmouthshire. He took an active part in Chartist demonstrations; his father and four elder brothers were involved in radical political movements and he remained closely in touch with his brothers all his life. In 1854 he migrated to Victoria in the *Queen of the East*. After a few weeks at the Ballarat diggings at the time of Eureka he left for Van Diemen's Land.

Failing to find employment as a teacher or slater, Rule became a constable in the Hobart Town Police Force. His first employment as a tutor was with the Morrisby family, farmers in the south-east of Tasmania. In 1855 he joined the Tasmanian Council of Education as headmaster of Hamilton State School. On 12 August 1857 at Kangaroo Point he married Sarah Anne Grimley. She was a certificated teacher and acted as his assistant; for fifteen years Rule was in charge of a number of country schools and in 1870 became headmaster of Battery Point Model School, Hobart, the top school of the colony. Though many of his far-sighted recommendations to a select committee in 1875 were not implemented, next year he was promoted inspector of schools and in 1886 became senior inspector in the colony; in the next eighteen years he established schools in all the new mining settlements in the west and north-eastern districts.

In 1894 he was appointed director of education. It was an inopportune time for a man with a progressive attitude to education, as depression and the failure in 1891 of the Bank of Van Diemen's Land meant the starving of public education by governments. In an official report Rule charged that 'the present system is to prepare children for pauperism not for useful citizenship', and although he set up an organized system of teacher-training at Trinity Hill State School, Hobart, he failed to implement state secondary education.

Rule also took an active part in the development of tertiary education; he was one of the founders and an early councillor of the University of Tasmania. As a fellow of the Royal Society of Tasmania he delivered many addresses on literary and social subjects. A leading member of A. I. Clark's [q.v.] intellectual circle, the Minerva Club, he contributed prose and verse to its journal the *Quadrilateral*. He retired in 1900, doyen of the Tasmanian public service, a 'genial old gentleman brimming with educational lore', having substantially influenced the colony's educational development. He died of phthisis in Hobart on 4 May 1901.

Cyclopedia of Tasmania, 1 (Hob, 1900); V&P (HA Tas), 1867 (44), 1875 (39, 70), 1882 (106); Education Dept Reports, 1895-1901; *Examiner* (Launceston), 5 May 1901; *North West Post*, 5 May 1901; *Mercury*, 6, 7 May 1901; personal records (held by author).   JOHN REYNOLDS

RUNDLE, JEREMIAH BRICE (1816-1893), squatter, merchant and businessman, was born in Cornwall, England, son of Jeremiah Brice Rundle, farmer, and his wife Elizabeth, née White. He arrived in Australia about 1835 and by 1838 was a storekeeper at Murrurundi, New South Wales. In the depressed early 1840s Rundle survived and prospered by boiling down stock for tallow and foreclosing a number of mortgages on runs. Later he and R. C. Dangar (1817-1866) set up as merchants and commission agents, styled Rundle, Dangar & Co., Sydney, and Dangar & Co., London. In 1855 F. H. Dangar [q.v.] joined the firm which also included Edward Chapman: the partnership was dissolved on 31 March 1859. Rundle was also in partnership with Henry Richards, F. H. and H. C. Dangar [q.v.] at Brisbane.

In the 1850s Rundle held Doondi on the Balonne River, Yallaroi, in the Gwydir District and, in partnership with F. H. and R. C. Dangar, 600,000 acres at Walcha in the New England District. In September 1860 Rundle was on a deputation of pastoralists to the colonial secretary to procure a bill for the suppression of cattle stealing, and in November was appointed to the general committee of the New South Wales Constitutional Association. In 1864 with (Sir) John Robertson [q.v.] he was connected with attempts to set up an agricultural college. By 1867 he held over 490,000 acres in the Liverpool Plains and Bligh districts, over 240,000 acres in the Warrego country of Queensland and, in partnership with J. R. Young and J. L. Montefiore [q.v.], 16,000 acres on the Darling Downs.

Examined before a Legislative Assembly committee in February 1878, Rundle criticized stock saleyard facilities in Sydney and supported the idea that new yards should be erected near Homebush and the abattoirs. In December 1881 he was appointed to the Legislative Council; though a frequent attender his only speech was a brief comment on the rabbit nuisance bill in 1883. Rundle was also a director and chairman of the Australian Joint Stock Bank, a director of the Sydney Meat Preserving Co. in 1870-93, the Moruya Silver Mining Co., and the United Fire and Marine Insurance Co. He was a magistrate for the City of Sydney, a trustee of the Victoria Club and one of the earliest members of the Royal Sydney Yacht Squadron.

Aged 77, he died of cancer on 6 March 1893 at his residence, Pomeroy, Potts Point, survived by his wife Mary (d. 1906), née Simond, whom he had married at St James's Church, Sydney, on 18 March 1848, and by four sons and two daughters of their eleven children. He was buried in the family vault in the Anglican section of Rookwood cemetery. His estate was sworn for probate at £62,884.

A. D. Fraser (ed), This century of ours (Syd, 1938); V&P (LA NSW), 1861, 2, 914, 1877-78, 2, 860; T&CJ, 2 Apr 1870; SMH, 9 Mar 1893.

G. P. WALSH

RUSDEN, GEORGE WILLIAM (1819-1903), historian, educationist and civil servant, was born on 9 July 1819 at Leith Hill Place, near Dorking, Surrey, England, son of Rev. George Keylock Rusden (1784-1859) and his wife Anne, née Townshend, and older brother of Henry Keylock [q.v.]. In 1833 Rev. G. K. Rusden had to leave his spacious home and private school at Leith Hill Place and migrated with his wife and ten of his children to New South Wales to join his eldest son Francis. They arrived at Sydney in the James Harris on 1 May 1834 and Rusden took up the parish of Maitland. On the voyage George had been befriended by (Sir) Charles Nicholson [q.v.], and within seven years was managing his property at Mingay, near Gundagai, and soon took over others in the Lachlan and Goulburn districts. By 25 Rusden was a seasoned pastoralist but he despaired of making money from the land: to him New South Wales was a 'cruel' country.

At 28 Rusden sailed to China where his brother-in-law, Ellis Gilman, had commercial interests. Although exulting in the adventure that he found, he did not realize his dream of quick riches. He worked as a clerk in Gilman's factory at Canton and spent some time with his brother Alfred, a tea-taster in Shanghai. He failed in attempts to visit India and Borneo and returned reluctantly to Sydney early in 1849, determined to study for the Bar and

still hoping to make enough money to set up his family in England.

Rusden never began law. Probably through Nicholson, he was appointed on 4 July 1849 agent for the National schools, first at Port Phillip and later at Moreton Bay. He threw himself into his work and in his several tours rode 10,000 miles as far south-west as Portland and as far north as Brisbane, taking in the Hunter Valley and Armidale. An ardent Anglican, he was unusual in his support of state-directed education; but his National Education (Melbourne, 1853) shows that he was much influenced by the ideas of Dr Arnold of Rugby.

By October 1851 Rusden had accepted from La Trobe the post of clerk in the Victorian colonial secretary's office and next year became clerk of the Executive Council. He continued in education as a member of the Board of National Education in 1853-62. In 1856 he took on the post of clerk of the parliaments (being also the clerk of the Legislative Council) at a salary of £1000 and was a weighty adviser to the councillors in their clashes with the assembly. In 1856-57 he was on the board of inquiry into the reorganization of the civil service. He was a member of the Council of the University of Melbourne from its foundation to 1886; he was on the Brighton Municipal Council for five years between 1860 and 1873 and was mayor for three years; he was also a member of the Acclimatisation Society. One of the colony's leading Shakespeare enthusiasts, in 1860-64 he helped to found a Shakespeare scholarship at the university and Shakespeare prizes for children. He was also remembered as the 'finest billiard player in the colony'.

On leave in 1862 he again visited China, probably with the view of taking permanent employment in Gilman's firm, but his Melbourne activities now prevailed and an illness, caught soon after his arrival in Shanghai, possibly made a convenient pretext for a quick departure. While in China Rusden witnessed the relief of Ka Ding held by the Tai Ping rebels, and was deeply impressed by his acquaintance with General Charles Gordon. After Gordon's death at Khartoum in 1885, Rusden became his fanatical champion; W. E. Gladstone, not surprisingly, was Rusden's bête noire.

In 1882 Rusden retired to England on a pension of £500. He settled to a life of writing, travelling in Europe, enjoying his many friendships and meticulously managing his investments. In 1884-92 he was on the executive of the Imperial Federation League in England. By 1883 Rusden was already well known, both under his own name and his pseudonym 'Yittadairn', as the author of many articles, pamphlets and lectures on subjects political, religious and literary. As early as 1851 he had published in Maitland his poem *Moyarra: An Australian Legend, in Two Cantos*, then *The Discovery Survey and Settlement of Port Phillip* (Melbourne, 1871) and in 1874 *Curiosities of Colonization* (London). In that year he visited England to gain support for a history of Australasia, turning especially to his friend Anthony Trollope [q.v.]. In 1878 and 1882 he visited New Zealand, collecting information, and in 1883 the *History of Australia* and the *History of New Zealand* were published in London, each in three volumes. Both works received adverse criticism.

In the *History of New Zealand* Rusden had fiercely and indiscreetly attacked the minister for native affairs, John Bryce, for his part in the Maori wars, relying mostly on the hearsay account of Bishop Hadfield of Wellington. Bryce sued for libel and the action dragged on in London in 1884-87. Rusden appealed against the first verdict in March 1886; he ably defended himself and retracted his statements at the re-hearing in June 1887. Damages were reduced to about half the original £5000 but the whole affair drained him both financially and emotionally.

The *History of Australia* was scathingly reviewed by A. Sutherland [q.v.] in the *Melbourne Review* and David Blair [q.v.] in the *Victorian Review*; while Deakin wrote a memoir partly to refute a work which was 'as untrustworthy as a partisan pamphlet well can be without deliberate dishonesty'. Rusden's personal knowledge of events gave strength to his work but it was often inaccurate and violently prejudiced. Nevertheless with their breadth of scale his histories were a major cultural achievement of the colonial period, particularly notable for his belief that the history of Australasia did not begin with Europeans. He had deep knowledge of and sympathy with the native peoples of Australasia and was, according to D. B. W. Sladen [q.v.], 'a violent Tory on everything except where natives were concerned ... even more violent as an advocate for coloured people'.

An asthmatic, Rusden returned to Melbourne on medical advice in January 1893 and lived quietly at his South Yarra home, Cotmandene, working on his study of *William Shakespeare; his life, his works, and his teaching* (Melbourne, 1903). His interest in his family and friends remained undimmed and his letters to them reveal him as affectionate, amusing, dutiful and generous. He had been very fond of his sister Georgina Mary, who kept house for

him till her death in 1868. Rusden loved celebrated acquaintances; he was a friend of W. E. H. Lecky and knew Carlyle and Millais. His genuine kindness and sense of responsibility redeemed many such relationships from snobbery, and his penchant for bishops was more than outweighed by his personal piety and his devotion to the Church of England. His help in the 1860s for Alfred and Edward, sons of Charles Dickens [q.v.], earned their father's gratitude. In the last decade of his life Rusden struck his contemporaries as 'a quaint old world figure' whose 'unique personality constituted a link between the old and the new order'. On his death on 23 December 1903 an obituarist farewelled him: 'cheery and worthy... with his pleasant crab-apple face and long legs ... as peculiar a gentleman as one will encounter in a lifetime. We don't know any Australian resident so distinctively English ... What a delicious bundle of prejudices was Rusden! A walking Westminster Abbey. And honest as the day'.

Rusden never married. His estate was worth some £18,000 and equal portions were left to the children of his four surviving sisters and his brother Henry. His house went to the Church of England (he had already given £8000 to St Paul's Cathedral and the Bishop of Melbourne's Fund in 1889) while his books and papers were bequeathed to Trinity College (University of Melbourne) and the Church of England Grammar School.

H. M. Humphreys (ed), *Men of the time in Australia: Victorian series*, 1st ed (Melb, 1878); D. B. W. Sladen, *Twenty years of my life* (Lond, 1915); A. Deakin, *The crisis in Victorian politics, 1879-1881*, J. A. La Nauze and R. M. Crawford eds (Melb, 1957); A. G. Austin, *George William Rusden and national education in Australia, 1849-1862* (Melb, 1958); MS cat (ML and Alexander Turnbull Lib, Wellington, NZ); uncat MSS (Trinity College Lib, Melb, and RHSV).

ANN BLAINEY
MARY LAZARUS

RUSDEN, HENRY KEYLOCK (1826-1910), public servant and polemicist, was born at Leith Hill Place, near Dorking, Surrey, England, fourth son of Rev. George Keylock Rusden and his wife Anne, née Townshend. In 1834 he arrived in New South Wales with his family, including his brother George [q.v.]. At 15 he left home and found various jobs in the Riverina. He then joined the gold rushes in New England and Victoria. In 1853 Rusden forsook the diggings for Melbourne and joined the public service. He became an accountant in the Police Department where he stayed until his retirement in August 1891, respected for his punctiliousness. On 5 June 1858 he had married Anna Spence.

Outside the office Rusden was an autodidact who relished disputation. He was a founder of the Eclectic Society in 1867 and remained a member until it disbanded in 1894; he was also a founder of the open, more plebeian, Sunday Free Discussion Society in 1870. Both groups debated political economy, calendar reform, free-thought, divorce, family limitation and eugenics, often under Rusden's leadership. He described himself in the 1870s as 'an atheist in theology', although his eight children who survived infancy were raised as Anglicans, 'a determinist in philosophy, a Malthusian and radical in sociology and an ultra free-trader'. His motto was 'Thorough'. Aroused by a problem in aerodynamics, he made his own boomerangs, although his observation of their flight was hampered by eyes damaged years before by a solar eclipse.

His universe comprised an ineluctable net of causation, in which every entity was subject to law and every human act and natural event had necessary, measurable consequences. Morality, therefore, was determinable by science. Rusden advocated sterilization and experimentation on criminals and the 'socially unfit', defended suicide on compassionate grounds and as a means of removing social liabilities, denounced religious beliefs because they obscured rational moral choices, and looked forward to the sexual and economic emancipation of women and the decay of the nuclear family. Rusden's numerous pamphlets (several under the pseudonym 'Hokor') are collected in the State Library of Victoria. There are papers by him in the *Proceedings* of the Royal Society of Victoria for 1867, 1868, 1872, 1874, 1893, 1895. His intellectual boldness and range were combined with organizational skill: he was elected to the council of the Royal Society of Victoria in 1867-68, 1874, 1876, was secretary in 1870-73 and 1877 and vice-president in 1891-1900. He was also secretary to the Yorick Club and the Cremation Society. The first Australian legalization of cremation, in Victoria in 1903, proceeded from his labours, but he was buried in St Kilda cemetery after his death on 10 April 1910.

F. B. Smith, Religion and freethought in Melbourne, 1870-1890 (M.A. thesis, Univ Melb, 1960).

                                    F. B. SMITH

RUSSELL, HENRY CHAMBERLAIN (1836-1907), astronomer and meteorologist, was born on 17 March 1836 at West Maitland, New South Wales, second son of Bourn Russell (1794-1880) and his wife Jane, née Mackreth. Bourn Russell, born at Rye, Sussex, England, was part-owner and commander of ships on the India, China and South Sea runs and surveyed parts of Sakhalin Island, the north coast of Japan, the Solomon Islands, the Louisiade Archipelago, Dampier Strait and New Guinea. He arrived in Sydney in 1826 and after some whaling ventures opened a store at West Maitland in 1835. Elected to the first Legislative Assembly of New South Wales in 1856, he was later disqualified; in 1858-80 he was in the Legislative Council.

Educated at West Maitland Grammar School and the University of Sydney (B.A., 1859), Henry joined the Sydney Observatory under Rev. W. Scott [q.v.]. In 1862-64 he was acting director and succeeded G. R. Smalley [q.v.] as government astronomer on 12 July 1870 with a salary of £555. Russell reorganized the observatory for systematic work on star positions and observations of double stars and star clusters; he also re-established the meteorological stations discontinued by Smalley. In 1871 with R. L. J. Ellery [q.v.] he organized an expedition to Cape Sidmouth to observe a total eclipse of the sun. In 1874 he sent parties to Woodford, Goulburn and Eden, while in Sydney he observed the transit of Venus; next year he went to England to present his results to the Royal Astronomical Society and to buy instruments for trigonometrical survey. His photographs of the transit were thought 'the best and most complete' and contributed much to the final analysis of data. Russell met leading astronomers and technicians in Europe and America and ordered a six-inch transit instrument, which was also used to determine longitudes for the survey. In 1881 he organized parties to observe the transit of Mercury, but bad weather frustrated his plans to observe the transit of Venus in 1882.

He increased the number of weather stations from 43 in 1870 to 50, plus 210 observers, in 1882; by 1898 there were 1600 observers, using equipment often designed by Russell. He invented and made many instruments including telescope mountings and self-recording meteorological devices: one of his portable anemometers is in the Science Museum, London. He exchanged weather data by wire and set up a system of forecasting with Ellery and Charles Todd [q.v.] and from February 1877 released a daily weather map to the press. In Sydney that year he published his *Climate of New South Wales: Descriptive, Historical, and Tabular* in which he adverted to periodicity.

In 1879 he presided over the first Intercolonial Meteorological Conference held in Australia, began river records and published a seminal paper on artesian water in the Darling basin. His *Physical Geography and Climate of New South Wales* first appeared in 1884. Russell was a pioneer of the global approach to meteorology and 'the first to think comprehensively about the southern hemisphere', his greatest contribution being the radical suggestion that the movement of anticyclones was a hemispheric phenomenon.

In 1887 Russell attended the International Astrophotographic Congress in Paris where Sydney Observatory was allotted the region from −52° to −64° to chart; he then visited other Continental observatories. By 1893 he had remeasured all the principal stars in J. F. W. Herschel's *Results of Astronomical Observations . . . at the Cape of Good Hope* (London, 1847) and discovered 500 new double stars. He was also a dedicated natural historian, interested in terrestrial magnetism, underground water, the growth rate of trees, the effects of vegetation upon climate, the artificial production of rain and the measurement of tides and *seiches*. He was one of the world's pioneer limnologists. He published over 130 papers, 69 in the local Royal Society journal.

Russell was elected a fellow of the Royal Astronomical Society in 1871 and of the Meteorological Society and a member of the Royal Colonial Institute in 1875. In 1886 he was the first graduate of the University of Sydney to be elected a fellow of the Royal Society. Three times president of the local Royal Society, in 1888 he was the first president of the Australasian Association for the Advancement of Science. Made C.M.G. in 1890, he was a founder of technical education in the colony and a vice-president of the Board of Technical Education from 1883. He was a fellow of the Senate of the University of Sydney in 1875-1907 and vice-chancellor in 1891-92.

Russell suffered a severe illness in 1903 and after a year's leave of absence retired on a gratuity of over £2300. Survived by his wife Emily Jane, née Foss (d. 1923), whom he had married in Sydney in 1860, a son and four daughters, he died at the observatory on 22 February 1907 and was buried in the Anglican section of Waverley cemetery.

Vigorous and striking, Russell was often forthright with his staff though kind to them in times of trouble and often sympathetic with their claims for better pay and conditions. In 1877 a bomb had been sent to him at the observatory and in 1889 he was attacked by one of his workmen. His relations with his colleagues Ellery, P. Baracchi and J. Tebbutt [q.v.] were cordial. He was one of the most eminent men of science in Australia in the nineteenth century and the closing words of his 1885 presidential address to the Royal Society of New South Wales sum up his life and work. Reflecting on the contrast between nature's slow change through aeons and man's brief lot, Russell said that the lesson to the scientist is that he must be 'patient in investigation, accurate in measurement, cautious in accepting results, content to stand one in a long series who, for the good of humanity, are striving to interpret the laws of Nature'.

H. W. Wood, *Sydney Observatory, 1858 to 1958* (Syd, 1958); V&P (LA NSW), 1871-72, 2, 959, 1885-86, 6, 552, 582; Roy Astronomical Soc, *Monthly Notice*, 68 (1908); Roy Soc, *Procs* (1908); C. H. B. Priestley, 'The global atmosphere: a memorial to H. C. Russell', *Search* (Syd), 2 (1971) no 8; T&CJ, 15, 22 Sept 1877, 23 Dec 1903; ISN, 13 Oct 1877, 17 June 1893; SMH, 31 Dec 1898, 23 Feb 1907; Russell papers (ML); printed cat under H. C. Russell (ML).

G. P. WALSH

RUSSELL, JAMES (1829-1889), merchant and politician, was born at Falkirk, Scotland, son of William Russell, carter, and his wife Marion, née Duiguid. He arrived in Victoria in 1853 and went to the Creswick goldfield. From his gains as an original shareholder in the old Temperance mine at Little Bendigo, he set up as a produce and grocery merchant in Humffray Street, Ballarat East, in 1869. From about 1882 he also partnered Joseph Foster in a timber business.

In 1871-78 and 1882-89 Russell was a councillor of Ballarat East and mayor in 1874-75 and 1886-87. A supporter of G. Berry [q.v.], in 1877 he failed to win Ballarat East in the Legislative Assembly; in 1880 he defeated D. Brophy [q.v.] for the seat but lost in July after parliament had been dissolved. He held the seat again in 1883-89. A total abstainer, he based much of his support on the temperance and Orange movements. He attended the International Temperance Convention in Melbourne in November 1888.

Always a strong advocate of local industry, Russell was an early shareholder and for some years a director of the Ballarat Woollen Mill Co. A lay preacher and senior steward at the Barkly Street Wesleyan Methodist Church he was an active member of the Wesleyan Local Preachers' Association. He was a leading Rechabite and Freemason and as a justice of the peace he was noted for his sound judgments and desire to reform by kindly measures. He was a committee-man of the Public Library and of many local charitable institutions including the town mission and the Ballarat Orphan and Benevolent asylums. He was also vice-president of the local brass band. In October 1887 he was appointed to the Ballarat Water Commission.

Russell was a member of the royal commission on gold-mining in 1889 but took ill and died of acute hepatitis on 17 October, aged 60. His funeral procession to the Ballarat cemetery was attended by many Freemasons, Orangemen, members of the Old Colonists Association, Rechabites and members of other temperance organizations. On 17 March 1860, aged 26, he had married at Creswick Creek near Ballarat, Elizabeth Jane Nankervis, who survived him together with two of their four sons and four of their seven daughters. His estate was valued for probate at £8503.

G. Serle, *The rush to be rich* (Melb, 1971); *Age*, 18 Oct 1889; *Ballarat Star*, 18 Oct 1889; *Argus*, 21 Oct 1889; J. Oldmeadow, Ballarat Methodism 1870-1877 (B.A. Hons thesis, Monash Univ, 1969).   SUZANNE G. MELLOR

RUSSELL, SIR PETER NICOL (1816-1905), ironfounder and benefactor, was born on 4 July 1816 at Kirkcaldy, Fife, Scotland, second son of eleven children of Robert Russell, ironfounder, and his wife Janet, née Nicol. His father and uncle, Alexander Russell, operated the Kirkcaldy Foundry and Engineering Works. When his sons were old enough to enter the business, Robert dissolved the partnership and established the Phoenix Foundry and Engineering Works. Peter went to the Kirkcaldy Grammar School and then worked for his father. A severe financial depression in 1830 decided the family to migrate to Canada, but a friend persuaded them to settle in Van Diemen's Land. In the *Anne Jamieson* they arrived in Hobart Town in June 1832.

Robert sold his 2000-acre grant, which was too densely timbered to be cleared, and, assisted by his sons Robert, Peter and John, started a general engineering and foundry business which grew for six years. Because of limited opportunities the family moved to Sydney in 1838, leaving Peter to wind up the business. After Robert retired his sons established Russell Bros in Queen's Square, with works built on the banks of the Tank Stream. They benefited from Robert's experience and advice until he died on 25 December 1840; his widow retained a financial interest in the firm. Russell Bros expanded quickly and soon moved to Macquarie Place, where new workshops were erected and stores acquired in Bridge Street.

In 1842 when Robert and John refused an offer to buy James Blanche's foundry Peter decided to take it over. His brothers stipulated that he take only a little of his share of the family capital, and with assistance from his mother he bought the business for £2000 on three-year terms and quickly opened under the name of The Sydney Foundry and Engineering Works. Within two years he had paid off the purchase price and was receiving many orders. He won contracts for the ironwork for Victoria Barracks at Paddington, Darlinghurst Gaol and the Newcastle and Maitland gaols. He had contracts for all the ironwork required by the New South Wales government and the Sydney Municipal Council as well as some private work. He also supplied his brothers with brass and iron castings. They had now branched out into shipbuilding, but a financial collapse resulted in the winding up of Russell Bros and great loss to The Sydney Foundry. Robert went to the Philippines to install plant and equipment and died there in 1849. John assisted Peter for a time then with his financial aid traded in the Pacific, but eventually returned to Sydney.

In 1855 a five-year partnership was formed as P. N. Russell & Co. In 1859 Peter was the resident partner in London, with John Russell and J. W. Dunlop (who had been works foreman) in Sydney and George Russell in Melbourne. The firm flourished as 'Engineers, Founders and Importers'. New premises were built in Pitt Street and workshops extended over a large waterfront area at Darling Harbour with a warehouse in George Street through to York Street. Contracts were received for railway bridges, rolling stock, steam dredges, quartz crushers and flour-mills, also gunboats for the New Zealand government for use in the Maori wars

In 1859 Peter married Charlotte, eldest daughter of Dr Alexander Lorimer, deputy-inspector-general of hospitals at Madras, and returned to Sydney with her. Next year they went back to London where he continued to act as the firm's representative. In Sydney Dunlop was in control until 1863 when he resigned to form a partnership with Norman Selfe [q.v.]. After much industrial unrest in 1873-74 P. N. Russell & Co. was closed. John arranged for the sale of the engineering warehouse section and went to London where he died in 1879. Greatly upset by the firm's closure, Peter visited Sydney in 1877 to settle legal matters, but soon returned to England. In 1885 he sold his extensive property in Brisbane and in 1886 visited Australia for the last time.

On 16 December 1895 the Senate of the University of Sydney accepted Russell's gift of £50,000 to the school of engineering and his condition that it be called the 'Peter Nicol Russell School of Engineering'. In 1904 he offered to provide a further £50,000 for engineering scholarships on the agreement of the government to make available £25,000 for additional accommodation. Knighted in June 1904, he died childless on 10 July 1905 at his home in Porchester Gate, London, survived by his wife. His estate in New South Wales was valued for probate at £98,648. He left £13,000 to charitable organizations in Sydney, as well as £3000 to the Engineering Association of New South Wales. On the foundation of the Institution of Engineers, Australia, in 1919 it established the Peter Nicol Russell memorial medal, awarded annually to a member for a notable contribution to engineering in Australia.

Russell's portrait by Sir William Orchardson, R.A., is in the possession of the University of Sydney.

A. H. Corbett, *The Institution of Engineers, Australia* (Syd, 1973); 'Sir Peter Nicol Russell, a great engineer . . . ', *A'sian Engineer*, Aug 1941; P. N. Russell, 'Sir Peter Nicol Russell', *JRAHS*, 50 (1964-65); A. Pugh, 'One hundred years ago', *Inst of Engineers, Aust, J,* July-Aug 1970; *SMH*, 12, 13 July 1905; *The Times*, 12 July, 10 Aug 1905.   ARTHUR CORBETT
ANN PUGH

RUSSELL, PHILIP (1822 ?-1892) and THOMAS (1828-1920), flock-masters and politicians, were sixth and seventh sons of the fourteen children of James Russell (1768-1839), tenant of Kincraig farm, Fife, Scotland, and his wife Elizabeth, née Couper. They were cousins of Philip and George [qq.v.], William, Rev. Robert and Alexander Russell who had all migrated to Australia by 1842.

In August Philip Russell, who had farmed at Beanston East Lothian, sailed for Hobart Town in the *Calcutta* with his cousins Robert Simson [q.v.] and Philip Russell senior who was returning to the colonies in charge of his 11-year-old niece Annie Lewis. In early 1843 they crossed to Port Phillip as partners and in March, at a Melbourne auction, for £950 cash they bought from the insolvent estate of J. D. Baillie 3500 sheep with lambs given in, and the right to Carngham station, 30,000 acres south of Lake Burrumbeet. Such prosperity dawned that Simson spent most of 1848-49 in Britain, returning with his younger brother John [q.v.] and with Thomas Russell. In January 1851 the new chums and Philip Russell, who had remained at Carngham, bought from James Austin [q.v.] what became the Barunah Plains station, west of Geelong. John Simson and Philip Russell soon withdrew, but three British-based Russell brothers became constituents of Thomas Russell & Co. Early in 1857 Thomas acquired the adjoining Ponds or Wurrook station, which became his headquarters.

Philip Russell and Simson designed their Carngham cottage for two couples. Both married in 1851 when Russell took his bride Annie Lewis to Scotland, while Simson took charge at Carngham. In 1853 the partners separated and Philip Russell took Carngham over.

On 23 August 1860 at Berriedale, Tasmania, Thomas Russell married Anna Louisa Parsons. He was elected councillor and first president of Leigh Shire in 1862, and in 1868-73 was member for Grenville in the Legislative Assembly. In 1869-75 and 1880-86 Philip held the seat of South Western Province in the Legislative Council. Both brothers were prominent Presbyterians.

In January 1873 Thomas left with his wife and six children in the *Baroda* for England. He returned to Victoria about 1887 and in 1889 contested South Western Province, but from about 1900 settled in England permanently, where he died on 6 July 1920 as owner of Haremere Hall, Hurst Green, Sussex. His English estate was valued at £77,474 and his estate in Victoria at £61,368. He had been elected F.R.G.S. in 1875.

Philip Russell gravitated to Melbourne, where his wife died at Chiverton, St Kilda, on 22 June 1869 leaving two sons: James, who inherited Carngham, and George, who inherited Langi Willi station (acquired by his father in 1859) and was member for Grenville in the Legislative Assembly in 1892-1900. In 1877 at Kilrie, Fifeshire, Scotland, Philip married a distant cousin, Mary Ann Carstairs Drysdale, niece of Anne Drysdale [q.v.]; she died on 28 March 1878, a week after the birth of their only son Philip, who was later killed in the Boer war. Philip (father) was a breeder of stud sheep, specializing in growing fine merino wool, and was for six years president of the Ballarat Agricultural and Pastoral Society. He became physically handicapped but maintained efficient control of station affairs. He died at Carngham on 14 July 1892 leaving an estate sworn at £219,000.

P. L. Brown (ed), *The narrative of George Russell* (Lond, 1935) and *Clyde Company papers*, 3-7 (Lond, 1958-71); *Argus*, 8 Sept 1860, 14 July 1920; *Ballarat Courier*, 16 July 1892, 9 May 1914; *Table Talk*, 22 July 1892; *IAN*, 1 Aug 1892; *Pastoral Review*, 16 June 1914.

P. L. BROWN

RUTHERFORD, JAMES (1827-1911), pastoralist and coach proprietor, was born on 24 October 1827 at Amhurst, New York, United States of America, second son of James Rutherford and his wife Hetty, née Milligan. He became a schoolteacher, but decided to join his brother on the Californian goldfields. Finding no ship available he sailed in the *Akbar* for Melbourne arriving on 20 June 1853. After mining briefly near Bendigo he won a contract to cut timber near Ferntree Gully. He later sailed to Queensland and on his way back to Melbourne started the short-lived goldfield at Oban, New South Wales, and bought horses. After two more unprofitable trips he retired to Melbourne ill and almost penniless.

In 1857 Rutherford managed Cobb [q.v.] & Co. for some months but returned to his travelling and trading. In 1861 with several partners he bought the company, became its general manager and next year extended it to New South Wales, driving the leading coach when in June the convoy reached Bathurst, which became the company headquarters. In 1863 at Taradale, Victoria, he married Ada Nicholson. Rutherford soon became involved in Bathurst affairs; mayor in 1868 he resigned before the end of his term. A staunch Anglican, he was a trustee of the Church of All Saints for over forty years and served as a lay member of the synod. For thirty years he was treasurer of the Agricultural, Horticultural and Pastoral Association and later a vice-president. An early trustee of the District Hospital, he was president in 1886-1911; a committeeman of the School of Arts he was president in 1872-1911. He became a magistrate in 1872, was active in the society formed to expedite the railway and served on almost every committee formed for charitable purposes or for the betterment of the town. In the late 1870s Rutherford bought Hereford, near Bathurst, where he built a fine residence and invented an entirely new type of sheep dip.

Cobb & Co. bought its first station property in 1864 and expanded to Queensland in 1865. Victoria withdrew from the partnership in 1871 and Rutherford supervised the firm's great growth over the next forty years: in coaching, its factories and workshops in Bathurst, Goulburn, Hay, Bourke and Charleville, and in property and stock ownership particularly in the Warrego District of Queensland. He also acquired and managed stations on his own account. In 1873 with John Sutherland [q.v.] and others he started the Eskbank Ironworks at Lithgow. After a visit to America in 1876 he had to rehabilitate the company but the

works were leased in the late 1880s and sold to William Sandford in the early 1890s. This experience and the continued entry of cheap iron, often as ballast, confirmed him as a protectionist, and led him in 1889 to co-found and manage the Bathurst *National Advocate* newspaper. The Parkes [q.v.] letters indicate that Rutherford may have considered entering parliament; a member of the protectionist National Club, in 1894 he became president of the Bathurst Protection League.

The 1890s brought great difficulties and the firm had to be reorganized after the death of the last partner, W. F. Whitney, in 1894. Coaching had ceased in New South Wales by 1900 but was still widespread in Queensland. In 1902 the company suspended operations because of the drought but was again restructured with Rutherford as general manager, the largest shareholder and chief guarantor. He apparently accepted personal liability for the station properties to enable the company to carry on as a coaching firm. He made regular tours of inspection and, returning from the far north in 1911, he became ill and was landed at Mackay where, survived by his wife, four of his five sons and six daughters, he died from acute bronchitis and heart failure on 11 September. His body was brought back to Bathurst for burial.

A superb organizer and manager, Rutherford was one of the great country entrepreneurs. In his lifelong travels his rather delicate and slight figure developed into a thickset frame that reflected his great strength and endurance. Although quick-tempered he kept on excellent terms with his employees and was very generous, especially to anyone in difficulties. He was strongly attached to his wife and family. His estate was valued for probate at over £128,000.

J. E. L. Rutherford, *Cobb & Co.* (Bathurst, 1971); *Bulletin*, 12 June 1880, 30 July 1881; *Australasian*, 28 Sept 1889; *National Advocate* (Bathurst), 2 Dec 1892; *Pastoral Review*, 15 Aug 1899; *T&CJ*, 7 Sept 1910, 20 Sept 1911; Parkes letters (ML); H. P. Steel, Family papers, vols 1-4 (ML); MS cat under James Rutherford (ML).

J. E. L. RUTHERFORD

RYAN, JAMES TOBIAS (1818-1899), butcher, pastoralist, politician and sportsman, was born on 4 January 1818 near Penrith, New South Wales, son of John Michael Tobin Ryan, printer, and his wife Mary (1791-1872). His mother was the daughter of Anthony Rope and Elizabeth Pulley (Powley), First Fleet convicts, who in May 1788 were among the first to be

Ryan

married in the colony. John Ryan reached Sydney in 1815 in the *Indefatigable* with a life sentence and in 1827 took over the Rope farm at South Creek.

After a year at boarding school, James worked with his father until 1835 when he was involved in an altercation with police after a house-warming party in Penrith. Forced to flee to the Hunter River, he spent two years as a timber-getter, ploughman, milkman and horse-breaker, then overlanded cattle to Port Phillip before settling in the Nepean district in 1838. In 1840 he became a butcher in Penrith; as the business flourished, he also became an auctioneer, financed a toll-bridge over the Nepean River and in 1850-51 was a registered spirits merchant. Later he ran cattle on Buttabone, Mumblebone and Maryinbone on the Macquarie and Castlereagh rivers. By 1852 he had built Emu Hall, an impressive home on the Emu Plains side of the Nepean, where he entertained visiting politicians and dignitaries. In 1860-72 he represented the Nepean in the Legislative Assembly. Never a contender for ministerial rank, he was a popular and amusing back-bencher with earthy, if impractical, solutions to the problems of government.

But it was as a sportsman that 'Toby' Ryan was best known. Large and rugged of frame, he was in his youth a good boxer and later a crack pigeon shot: he defeated the New Zealand champion H. Redwood and in the early 1860s was president of the short-lived Metropolitan Pigeon Club which met at Charles Beal's hotel in Sydney. He also bred pigeons for shooting and was a successful race-horse owner and breeder. He raced Traveller, a famous performer at bush meetings, who reputedly defeated F. Gardiner's [q.v.] Don't You Know at Forbes in 1862, and several horses that did well on metropolitan tracks. In 1873 Benvolio won the Australian Jockey Club Derby for him, Kingfisher the Epsom Handicap and Leo the Australasian Champion Stakes. Ryan claimed to wager heavily, sometimes spectacularly, on his horses and his betting probably contributed to his decline in fortune. Harassed by bankruptcy in 1871, he

was forced to dispose of most of his property and in 1879-80 was licensee of the Crown Hotel in George Street. When bankrupted in 1885 he and his son Edwin were asphalters. By 1887 he was a valuator and in the 1890s he and his wife ran a boarding-house in Francis Street.

In his *Reminiscences of Australia* (Sydney, 1895), Ryan claimed to have met Bold Jack Donohoe [q.v.], to have been working near by at the time of the Myall Creek massacre, to have associated with Edward Hargraves [q.v.] and to have owned the pistols used in the Sir Thomas Mitchell-Stuart Donaldson [qq.v.] duel. This kind of exaggeration, not without some basis in truth, is one of three characteristics of his book; the others are a simple warmth, generosity and tolerance, and an eccentric prose style reminiscent of his parliamentary speeches. Ryan's language, 'unmistakably vigorous', 'rudely eloquent', but 'nearly always opposed to the rules of the grammarians', is a useful reminder that he was a genuine character, a self-made man proud of his descent from emancipist stock.

Ryan died in penurious circumstances at Woolloomooloo on 17 October 1899 and was buried in the Anglican section of the Emu Plains cemetery. He was survived by four sons and three daughters of his first wife, Mary Dempsey (1817-1864), whom he had married on 16 August 1838; by his second wife Sarah Hadley (d. 1923), whom he had married on 16 September 1866, and by their son and three daughters. A Freemason for fifty-six years he was, in December 1862, the first worshipful master of Queen's Lodge 982, Penrith, under the English constitution.

D. M. Barrie, *Turf cavalcade* (Syd, 1960); J. Cobley, *Sydney Cove, 1788* (Lond, 1962) and *Sydney Cove, 1791-1792* (Syd, 1965) and *The crimes of the First Fleet convicts* (Syd, 1970); V&P (LA NSW), 1859-60, 3, 587, 1875, 2, 237; SMH, 23 Apr 1850, 16 Mar, 6, 20 Apr 1868, 27 Feb, 24 Apr 1871, 18 Oct 1899; *Nepean Times*, 21 Oct 1899; MS cat under Ryan (ML, NL); Insolvency files 10600/7, 20175/12 (NSWA).

B. G. ANDREWS

S

ST JULIAN, CHARLES JAMES HERBERT DE COURCY (1819-1874), journalist and chief justice, was born on 10 May 1819 probably in France, son of Thomas St Julian, a French army officer, and his wife Marian, née Blackwell. Educated in London, he was skilled in carving ivory and wood, but by his own account joined an expedition up the Niger, volunteered as a junior officer in the Circassian contingent and then fought for the Queen of Spain in the Carlist wars. He arrived in Adelaide on 15 May 1838 as Charles Trout, turner, an assisted immigrant in the *Trusty*, and joined the staff of the *South Australian Gazette and Colonial Register*. He moved to Sydney in August 1839 and on 26 November at St Mary's Cathedral married Eleanor Heffernan. He wrote for W. A. Duncan's [q.v.] *Australasian Chronicle* and in 1841 became editor and principal reporter of the *Commercial Journal*, which later became the *Sydney Free Press*. When it failed in 1842 he was engaged by the *Sydney Morning Herald* as parliamentary reporter. In May 1847 he became editor and proprietor of the *Sydney Chronicle* with his friend E. J. Hawkesley. On 2 October 1848 he started the *Daily News* but by next January was bankrupt and rejoined the *Herald* as chief law reporter.

On 29 April 1848 St Julian had begun a regular correspondence with R. C. Wyllie, Hawaiian minister of foreign relations. In 1853 he became King Kamehameha III's commissioner to the independent states and tribes of Polynesia to encourage the development of governments on the constitutional pattern of Hawaii, with a view to forming a confederation under the auspices of the kingdom of Hawaii. As 'Cecrops' St Julian wrote regularly on Pacific matters for the *Australian Era*. Many of his articles were later published in Sydney as books or pamphlets, including *Notes on the Latent Resources of Polynesia* (1851), *The Productions, Industry, and Resources of New South Wales* (1853) with E. K. Silvester, and the *Official Report on Central Polynesia* with a gazetteer by Edward Reeve [q.v.] (1857). By then St Julian had become consul-general for Hawaii and advised Governors FitzRoy and Denison on Pacific affairs. Several of his recommendations for greater British diplomatic representation in the Pacific were forwarded to London. Disappointed in his hopes of becoming British consul at Tonga, he became disillusioned with the Hawaiian

connexion and his correspondence with Wyllie lapsed in 1861.

Of middle height, stout and rather pompous, St Julian was again bankrupt in December 1862; he stated the cause as sickness in the family and the death of his wife on 28 August 1861 and a daughter in November. With debts over £500 he had few assets, but received £5 10s. a week from the *Herald* and £100 a year as correspondent for a Melbourne paper; he had no income as commissioner for affidavits. On 10 January 1863 he married Eliza Winifred Hawkesley, daughter of his former partner. His Catholicism had steered him towards working for Duncan and Hawkesley, and like them he favoured the liberal cause in religion and politics. After initial scepticism he championed the National system of education and his support of (Sir) Henry Parkes's [q.v.] 1866 public schools bill provoked the displeasure of the Church.

Supporting local government, in 1859 St Julian was returning officer for the first Waverley municipal elections. Next year he was elected to the council; he was chairman in 1861 and presided over the building of the council chambers. He was returning officer for many local government elections; in 1868 he became an alderman on Marrickville Borough Council and was mayor in 1868-69 and 1871. Author of two guides to the ambiguous 1858 Municipalities Act, in 1866 he was elected chairman of the municipal councils' conference and helped to draft the 1867 Municipalities Act which lasted until 1906. He published a handbook on *Municipal Elections* in 1867 and next year the *Municipalities Act of 1867 with notes thereon* ... which was 'regarded by every lawyer in the colony as a work of authority, being constantly cited'. In February 1870 he was gazetted a magistrate and sat regularly on the bench of the Central Police Court.

St Julian also wrote many articles for the *Herald*, notably on the supply of water to Sydney, the charitable institutions of New South Wales, and sketches of Australian society 'rapidly thrown off during his visits to circuit courts'. In 1870 he published *Pastoral Freeholds* and in 1872 *The International Status of Fiji*. Despite unfavourable reception by the Colonial Office of his suggestion of a confederation between Fiji and Hawaii, in 1871 he visited Fiji as a special commissioner of the Hawaiian government to investigate an alliance. In March

1872 he became chief justice and chancellor of the kingdom of Fiji, apparently on the recommendation of Sir Alfred Stephen [q.v.] who on 17 April told the British consul at Levuka, 'I am sure that he will be found an upright, fearless, discriminating, just, and painstaking magistrate'. He was involved in the transfer of sovereignty to Great Britain in 1874 and was recommended by Governor Sir Hercules Robinson for a pension of £600, but he died on 26 November, survived by his second wife and ten children. His portrait hangs in the Waverley Council Chambers.

B. T. Dowd and W. Foster (eds), *The history of the Waverley municipal district* (Syd, 1959); *SMH*, 7, 29 Apr 1868, 22 Dec 1874; *Brisbane Courier*, 3 May 1872; *Fiji Argus*, 4 Dec 1874; *ISN*, Jan 1875; Parkes letters *and* St Julian family papers (ML); Stephen uncat MS 211/3 (ML); Col Sec letters and Insolvency files 1862, 6001 (NSWA); Foreign Office, Executive file 1848-72 (Hawaiian Archives).

MARK LYONS
MARION NOTHLING

SALIER, GEORGE (1813-1892), merchant and politician, and JAMES EBENEZER (1819-1894), merchant, were the sons of George Cooley Salier, Congregational minister, and his wife Ann, née Hyat. James arrived in Hobart Town in 1839 in the *James* to assess the prospects for opening a drapery. His report brought George next year with a cargo of goods and they opened a store, The Gold Mine Drapery, in Elizabeth Street. Their brothers William George (1812-1899) and John Jabez (1821-1884) arrived later.

James sailed for San Francisco in 1849 with a cargo of prefabricated wooden houses for the goldfields, and his brothers visited the Victorian diggings with little success. The business expanded to New Norfolk with William as manager. The Saliers combined wholesale trade with importing consumer goods and exporting wool and oil. They also acquired a fleet of whalers, second only to A. McGregor's [q.v.]; their best-known barque was the *Offley*. They were shareholders and directors of the Bank of Van Diemen's Land, the Derwent and Tamar Fire, Life and Marine Assurance Co., the Mersey & Deloraine Tramway Co. Ltd amongst others; they were also leading members of the Hobart Chamber of Commerce. They lived in two solid town houses, George in Melbourne Lodge, and James in Sydney Lodge. John taught music, especially church music.

In the early 1850s George, not liberal enough for Hobart emancipists, was jostled in anti-transportation meetings. He became a justice of the peace in 1862 and was a member of the House of Assembly for North Hobart in 1866-69 and 1871-86 and of the Legislative Council in 1886-92. He was a humanitarian, evangelical liberal.

G. Clarke's [q.v.] Congregational Church in Davey Street was the focus of the brothers' lives. James was its deacon, treasurer, librarian, choirleader and president of the Southern Tasmanian Sunday School Union. George was on the local committee of the Colonial Missionary Society, the board of management of the Brickfields Pauper Establishment for Males and the executive committee of the Servants' Home. James became chairman of the Benevolent Society and honorary secretary of the Ragged Schools Association; he joined George on the board of management of the General Hospital, Hobart, and on the committees of the Girls' Industrial School and the Mechanics' Institute, where John organized successful music classes. All three brothers were members of the Glee Club, the Choral Society and various gardening and regatta committees.

The Salier brothers have been described as a 'conspicuous example of a philanthropic, high toned, successful merchant' family. George's first wife Anne Georgiana, née Bush, died in 1845 and on 5 March 1846 he married Harriet Mary Willis. He is said to have sired sixteen children. He died of heart failure on 11 June 1892 while walking between his warehouse and his home. His estate was valued for probate at £28,750 in Tasmania and £2596 in Victoria. Predeceased by his wife, James died of apoplexy on 17 August 1894 without issue; his estate was valued for probate at £8632.

Cyclopedia of Tasmania, 1-2 (Hob, 1900); P. Bolger, *Hobart Town* (Canberra, 1973); *Hobart Town Courier*, 18 Dec 1840, 20 Feb 1845, 8 Mar 1848, 18 Sept 1852; *Mercury*, 13 June 1892, 18 Aug 1894, 5 Sept 1904; The Hutchins School, Admission register (TA).   PETER BOLGER

SALOMONS, SIR JULIAN EMANUEL (1835-1909), barrister and politician, was born on 4 November 1835 at Edgbaston, Birmingham, Warwickshire, England, only son of Emanuel Solomons, merchant, and his wife, née Levien, whose sisters married (Sir) Saul Samuel, S. A. Joseph [qq.v.] and P. J. Cohen, a founder of Sydney's Jewish community. Privately tutored, he arrived in Sydney on 4 September 1853 in the *Atalanta* and worked as a stockbroker's clerk and in a book shop. He became a skilled debater at the Sydney Mechanics' School of Arts. Appointed secretary to the York Street Synagogue in October 1855 at a salary of £100, by 1857 he had passed with credit the preliminary examination of the

Barristers Admission Board. Assisted financially by the Jewish community, he returned to England, altered the spelling of his name to Salomons, entered Gray's Inn on 14 October 1858 and was called to the Bar on 26 January 1861. He came back to Sydney and was admitted to the colonial Bar on 8 July. He married his cousin Louisa Solomons at Lower Edmonton, Middlesex, England, on 17 December 1862.

In 1866 Salomons appeared for Henry Louis Bertrand after he had been convicted of murder. The Supreme Court ordered a new trial, but next year the Privy Council ruled that the court had acted beyond its powers. Bertrand's sentence was commuted to life imprisonment and the case reinforced Salomons's growing repute for industry and brilliance. But overwork resulted in a nervous breakdown and on 16 August he was admitted to Bay View House, a mental hospital at Tempe; he was discharged on 2 December. Working incessantly, he concentrated mainly on real property, electoral and municipal matters, bills of exchange and criminal law; every brief was treated as though worth a high fee and, if necessary, he would argue a case without charge. A certain emotional brashness and vanity did not retard his mounting eminence; he was increasingly briefed by the Crown and held a general retainer by 1884. In 1870 he had been a member of the Law Reform Commission and on 16 August 1881 he was appointed royal commissioner inquiring into the complex affairs of the Milburn Creek Copper Mining Co. Ltd. His skilful report led to E. A. Baker's [q.v.] expulsion from parliament.

Salomons was a conservative free trader but not strongly partisan in politics. Defeated for East Sydney in December 1869, he became solicitor-general from 18 December 1869 to 15 December 1870 in (Sir) John Robertson's and (Sir) Charles Cowper's [qq.v.] ministries, though he was not appointed to the Legislative Council until 11 August. He resigned from the council on 15 February 1871.

In 1886 the chief justiceship was refused by W. B. Dalley and F. M. Darley [qq.v.]. Salomons accepted the office despite a sacrifice in income, 'being assured by those most qualified to guide me ... that my appointment will be acceptable to the public and to both branches of the profession'. The *Sydney Morning Herald* and *Bulletin* were pleased but other newspapers stated that he lacked 'aristocratic position', judicial balance and dignity. Uncertain of the reaction of the puisne judges, Salomons displayed irresolution by calling on (Sir) William Windeyer [q.v.], who taunted him with being unacceptable and accused him

of 'always breaking down mentally'. It was true that Salomons's habit of working with 'frantic energy' had necessitated several health trips to Europe but he always returned restored, to be besieged with briefs. Gazetted as chief justice on 13 November, he took the unprecedented step of resigning on 19 November before being sworn in; though urged by the legal profession to reconsider, he refused. The office had been his goal 'for many years', but he decided that his 'temperament would not bear ... the strain and irritation that would be caused by unfriendly relations'.

Reappointed to the Legislative Council in 1887, Salomons became vice-president of the Executive Council and representative of the Sir Henry Parkes [q.v.] government in the Legislative Council from 7 March 1887 to 16 January 1889. On 28 August 1888 Parkes, who believed Salomons stood 'at the head of his profession at the Bar', recommended him for a knighthood and he was appointed K.B. in May 1891. He broke with Parkes over Federation, and from 23 October 1891 to 25 January 1893 was a member of Sir George Dibbs's [q.v.] protectionist cabinet as vice-president of the Executive Council and representative of the government in the Upper House. He resigned from the council on 21 February 1899.

On 6 April 1895 George Dean was convicted of attempting to poison his wife. Clamorous popular agitation resulted in a royal commission at which Salomons appeared for the Crown; its report resulted in a free pardon for Dean. On 18 July the defending lawyer R. D. Meagher, informed Salomons in chambers that Dean had confessed his guilt to him. Salomons was appalled: not only had the press and public been duped but Dean's wife and her mother had been harassed for allegedly seeking to incriminate him falsely. Salomons appealed in vain to Meagher to speak out and offered fifty sovereigns to begin a fund for Dean to leave the country and to publish a letter clearing his wife. After much soul-searching 'in an awful nightly pain', Salomons concluded that it was his duty to publish the facts as 'efficiently' as possible, even though a client relationship existed between him and Meagher. Again he was accused of mental aberration and vilified as a Jew. His emotional speech of self-defence in the Legislative Council did not fully dispose of the possibility of unprofessional conduct on his part, but it displayed great moral courage and advanced his reputation for integrity: 'They are at liberty to tear my whole life to pieces and to show to anyone anything that will make me ashamed', he said, and dwelt with pride on his Jewishness. Meagher was disbarred; Dean received fourteen years for perjury.

In 1899-1900 Salomons was agent-general for New South Wales in London. In 1899 he was elected a bencher of Gray's Inn. He had opposed Federation as faddish and inimical to the best interests of New South Wales, but after the passage in 1900 of the Commonwealth of Australia Constitution Act, he received a general retainer from the Federal government and was gracious in his address of welcome to the first judges of the High Court. He possessed the 'pluck and tenacity of a soldier-ant'; with short stature, cross-eyes and squeaky voice, he combined a caustic tongue and mordant wit and was 'quite the fastest long-distance talker of his time'. He blended benevolence with his pugnacity, was courteous to his juniors and was a very active member of the Jewish community. Broadly cultivated from his youth, he had contributed to the *Empire*, collected fine paintings and was a trustee of the National Art Gallery of New South Wales. In 1872-73 and 1889-90 he had been a member of the Barristers Admission Board and was a member of the Linnean Society of New South Wales.

Salomons retired in 1907. On the eve of a projected visit to Europe, he died of a cerebral haemorrhage on 6 April 1909 in his home, Sherbourne, Woollahra, and was buried in the Hebrew portion of Rookwood cemetery. He was survived by his devoted wife and by two married daughters. Despite recent losses from sugar investments, his estate was valued for probate at £34,813.

W. Blacket, *May it please your Honour* (Syd, 1927); A. B. Piddington, *Worshipful masters* (Syd, 1929); L. Blackwell, *Death cell at Darlinghurst* (Lond, 1970); A. M. Cohen, 'Sir Julian Emanuel Salomons . . .', *and* H. H. Glass, 'Some Australian Jews and the Federal movement', *Aust Jewish Hist Soc, J*, 2 (1944-48) *and* 3 (1949-53); J. M. Bennett, 'Sir Julian Salomons—fifth chief justice of New South Wales', *JRAHS*, 58 (1972); *Empire* (Syd), 12 Feb 1864; *Cosmos Mag*, 31 Aug 1895; *Bulletin*, 19 Feb, 19 Mar 1881, 23 Dec 1882, 13, 20 Nov 1886; *SMH*, 26 Jan 1893, 7, 8 Apr 1909; *Daily Telegraph* (Syd), 7 Apr 1909; Parkes letters (ML); Windeyer uncat MS 186 (ML); CO 201/557/46, 53, 559/527, 615, 595/379, 580, 605/297.   SUZANNE EDGAR
BEDE NAIRN

SALTER, WILLIAM (1804-1871), vigneron, was born at Exeter, Devon, England. After four years of farming near Tiverton he trained as a chemist before going into business at Devonport and later at Stonehouse; he saw little hope of a career in England and accepted an offer from King & Co.,

London merchants, to be their South Australian agent. With his wife Anne, née Shea, and their three children he sailed from Plymouth in the *Caroline* and reached Adelaide on 16 December 1839. Anne died two months later and on 19 October 1841 he **married Mary Nattle at Holy Trinity Church, Adelaide**.

With right of purchase, Salter rented a section of the Barossa surveys which he named Mamre Brook, and moved there in 1844 after King & Co. had closed their agency because of the depression; he built a six-roomed house and kitchen which still stands. First interested in cattle, he prospered when he turned to sheep. He was elected treasurer of the first Angaston District Council in 1853 and was deacon of the Angaston Congregational Church which he had helped to found. When copper was discovered on his property he opened the Crinnis Copper Mine which flourished until the late 1860s. In 1859, with his son Edward, he formed W. Salter & Son and started a vineyard by clearing ten acres and planting shiraz vines. The first vintage was in 1862 when eight pickers gathered enough grapes to keep three treaders busy crushing four hogsheads of must a day. In 1863 he continued his pastoral enterprise when, with his son William, he bought the lease of the Baroota run of sixty-five square miles from Samuel Davenport [q.v.]; when the area was revalued and the rent increased fourfold he abandoned it at great loss. He toured South Australia in 1865 and promoted Saltram wines in Melbourne, selling over £900 worth. The company bought its first grapes from other growers in 1868. Aged 67, he died on 30 July 1871 at Mamre Brook, survived by his wife, three daughters and two sons. His estate was sworn for probate at £7000.

His son EDWARD (1837-1913) was born in Exeter. He had little education and at 10 was his father's shepherd. He often spent days away from home and had a small portable box which he used as shelter for the night. After joining his father as partner in W. Salter & Son in 1859, Edward began keeping a journal in which he recorded the details of their wine-making. While his father continued his interests in sheep and cattle Edward did most of the work in the vineyard. On 7 September 1867 he married Emily Oldham of Kapunda.

W. Salter & Son were among the South Australian exhibitors who won a medal at the 1876 Philadelphia International Exhibition. In 1882-92 Edward sold his wine to Thomas Hardy [q.v.] & Son, who undertook to market all the Saltram wine and created a demand for it in London. In 1888

Edward was first chairman of the Nuriootpa District Agricultural Bureau. He became a member of the South Australian Vinegrowers' Association. When he retired from his position as justice of the peace in 1898 the attorney-general made him an honorary justice. He was also deacon and treasurer of the Angaston Congregational Church. Retiring from the family business in 1902, he died on 5 October 1913 survived by seven sons. His estate was sworn for probate at £31,361.

R. Cockburn, *Pastoral pioneers of South Australia*, 2 (Adel, 1927); W. Salter & Sons Ltd, *The Saltram vineyard 1859-1959* (Adel, 1959); Salter papers, BRG 1 (SAA).

JAKI ILBERY

SAMUEL, SIR SAUL (1820-1900), merchant and politician, was born on 2 November 1820 in London, the posthumous son of Sampson Samuel and his wife Lydia, née Lyons. In 1832 his mother decided to join her brother Samuel Lyons [q.v.] and eldest son Lewis in New South Wales and arrived with Saul in *The Brothers* on 25 August. He was educated at W. T. Cape's [q.v.] school and at his Sydney College. In 1837 he joined the Sydney counting-house of his uncles A. and S. Lyons. With his brother Lewis he later formed the mercantile firm of L. and S. Samuel with a store at Bathurst. By 1841 he had taken up 190,000 acres on the Macquarie River. He was the first Jew to become a magistrate, in 1846. Although successful, he abandoned pastoral pursuits after the discovery of gold in 1851 and became a director of several companies operating in Bathurst. In 1856 he explored the feasibility of laying an electric telegraph line to Belvoir, the northern terminus in Victoria. On 16 December 1857 he married Henrietta Matilda Goldsmith-Levien (d. 1864).

Favouring full representative government, in 1854-56 Samuel represented the Counties of Roxburgh and Wellington in the Legislative Council, and Orange in 1859-60 in the new Legislative Assembly. He was the first Jewish legislator in New South Wales. Described as a practical, independent and liberal politician, from 27 October to 8 March 1860 he was colonial treasurer under William Forster [q.v.] and the first Jew to become a minister of the Crown. In 1862-69 he represented Wellington and in 1869-72 Orange. In 1872 he held East Sydney until June when he was appointed to the Legislative Council where he sat until 1880.

In 1865 Samuel had become colonial treasurer under Charles Cowper [q.v.], but resigned in 1866 after his budget proposals for trade licences and increased duties on tea and sugar had been defeated. In 1868 Samuel became treasurer under John Robertson [q.v.] and continued under Cowper in 1870. In 1869-70 he opposed Governor Belmore's reforms of public expenditure methods, though he assisted him by reducing recommendations to the Executive Council to sanction payments in anticipation of Appropriation Acts. In 1870 he attended the Intercolonial Conference in Melbourne and proposed intercolonial free trade to settle the border customs dispute. Samuel hoped to abolish *ad valorem* duties but his plans for a tax on incomes of over £200 were bitterly contested and led to the downfall of the government in December.

In 1872-75 Samuel was postmaster-general and vice-president of the Executive Council and Henry Parkes's [q.v.] government representative in the Legislative Council; he also acted as treasurer in 1872. He was again postmaster-general and government representative under Parkes in 1877 and in 1878-80. In 1873 he visited New Zealand, the United States and England and negotiated a subsidized mail service from England to Australia via San Francisco; the tender for the service was given to H. H. Hall [q.v.] who was soon bankrupt and unfounded imputations were made against Samuel's official and personal honour. In 1874 as postmaster-general he opened the new General Post Office.

In the 1860s Samuel had been a founder of the Newcastle Wallsend Coal Co. and a director of the Wentworth Gold Field Co., Tomago Coal Mining Co., Moruya Silver Mining Co. and the Sydney Exchange Co., of which he was chairman in 1876-80. In the 1870s he was involved with the governor Sir Hercules Robinson, John Frazer, John Sutherland [qq.v.] and others in exploiting Henry Parkes's coal lands at Jamberoo. He was sometime chairman of the Australian Mutual Provident Society and the Pacific Fire and Marine Insurance Co. and in 1881 still owned the copper mine at Canobolas.

Active in the Jewish community, in the 1840s Samuel had contributed to the London *Voice of Jacob*; he was a member of the board of management of the York Street Synagogue and remained loyal to it after it divided. He was a trustee of the Jewish section of the Devonshire Street cemetery and from 1871 chairman of the Sydney Hebrew Certified Denominational School Board. On 26 January 1875 he laid the foundation stone for the Great Synagogue, Elizabeth Street, and was later its president. He was a member of the Royal Society of New South Wales and the New South Wales Academy of Art, and with his second wife Sarah Louisa, née Isaacs, whom he had married on

31 October 1877, was a founder and committee member of the Hospital for Sick Children.

On 10 August 1880 Samuel was appointed agent-general for New South Wales in London, despite the opposition of Sir Daniel Cooper [q.v.] who suspected him of being 'in favour of the Colonial Office'. An energetic, shrewd and efficient representative, he helped negotiate government loans and by 1885 claimed that he had raised £30 million. He fostered assisted immigration, negotiated with the Peninsular and Oriental and the Orient shipping companies for weekly mail services to the colony and in 1885 about the New South Wales contingent to the Sudan. He was a commissioner for New South Wales at the 1883 Amsterdam Exhibition and represented the colony at the 1887 Colonial Conference in London. In 1891 he also represented Queensland at the Postal Convention in Vienna.

Appointed C.M.G. in 1874, K.C.M.G. in 1882, C.B. in 1886 and created a baronet in 1898, Samuel was a London director of the Mercantile Bank of Sydney, a councillor of the Jews' College and of the Royal Colonial Institute, and a vice-president of the Society of Arts, London. He visited Sydney in 1888 and retired as agent-general in 1897. He died in South Kensington, London, on 29 August 1900. Survived by two sons and two daughters of his first wife and by his second wife and their son, he was succeeded by his second son, Edward Levien. His estate was sworn for probate at £17,000. His brother Lewis, who had returned to England, died on 17 February 1867.

Aust Jewish Hist Soc, J, 1-4 (1939-58), 6 (1964-69); Southern Cross (Syd), 21 Jan 1860; SMH, 30 Sept 1867, 15 May 1871, 30 Aug 1900; The Times, 30 Aug 1900; Sydney Mail, 8 Sept 1900; Parkes letters (ML); York Street and Great Synagogue minutes (Synagogue Archives, Syd); CO 201/535, 538, 548, 551-53, 557-59, 563, 570, 574, 577, 583, 585, 591-92, 601, 603-05, 608, 616, 620.

GEORGE F. J. BERGMAN

SANDFORD, DANIEL FOX (1831-1906), Anglican bishop, was born on 25 July 1831 at Jordan Hill, Shropshire, England, son of Sir Daniel Keyte Sandford, professor of Greek at the University of Glasgow, and his wife Cecilia, née Charnock. Educated at the Grange School, Bishop Wearmouth, Trinity Theological College, Glenalmond, and the University of Glasgow (LL.D., 1874), he was a lay worker at Lambeth before being made deacon in 1853. Next year he was appointed incumbent of Alyth and Insigle, Perthshire. On 30 August 1855 he married Elizabeth Barret Rae; he went to St John's, Edinburgh, was ordained priest, served as curate until 1863 and as examining chaplain to the bishop of Edinburgh until 1872. In 1864 he became a special preacher at St Paul's Cathedral, London, and at the Chapel Royal, Whitehall, and was elected a fellow of the Royal Society, Edinburgh. In 1873 he succeeded Dean Ramsay as incumbent of St John's, Edinburgh, later becoming synod clerk for the diocese and in 1878 a canon of St Mary's Cathedral; he was vice-chairman of the Poor Association, director of the Royal Maternity and Simpson Memorial Hospital and the Indigent Gentlewomen's Fund for Scotland, and in 1882 was elected to the Edinburgh School Board. He was the author of lectures on education, many printed sermons, and a noted obituary on Ramsay read before the Royal Society in 1873. Described as a decided but moderate churchman with wide philanthropic, educational and charitable interests, he was liberal in outlook and highly esteemed and loved by his parishioners.

In 1883 Sandford accepted the Tasmanian see and was consecrated at St Paul's Cathedral on 25 April. He arrived in Hobart in the Manapouri on 6 September 1883 with his wife, one son and two daughters and was enthroned on 12 September.

Sandford encouraged building and supported Church sisterhoods, particularly in nursing, education and penitentiary work, and issued a pastoral letter on the subject in 1887. A firm advocate of temperance, he favoured local option. In 1888 he resigned his see because his wife, disliking Tasmania, had returned to England. In his final address to synod he urged the preferment of local clergy, saying the Church could never become a really indigenous institution until a majority of her clergy was colonial born. With one of his daughters he left Hobart on 29 December. He became coadjutor to Bishop Lightfoot and later to Bishop Westcott of Durham, and rector of Bolden. He died at Durham on 20 August 1906 survived by his wife, two sons and a daughter; six children had predeceased him.

W. R. Barrett, History of the Church of England in Tasmania (Hob, 1942); Mercury, 3, 16 Jan, 15 Mar, 27 Apr, 3 May, 7 Sept 1883, 28 Nov, 31 Dec 1888; Australasian, 6 Jan 1883; Church News (Hob), 2 Mar 1883, 1 Feb 1884; T&CJ, 3 Mar 1883, 29 Aug 1906.

NEIL SMITH

SANDS, JOHN (1818-1873), engraver, printer and stationer, was born in Sandhurst, Berkshire, England, on 12 November 1818, son of Robert Sands and his wife

Hannah. His great-great-grandfather, Robert (b. 1729), was a noted engraver and his great-grandfather, Robert, grandfather, James, and father were all engravers and printers of distinction. His father worked with such notable craftsmen as John Le Keux and the Cruikshanks and also on *Punch*. Thomas Hood, the poet, was a cousin. In 1837, after serving his apprenticeship as an engraver and map-colourer, Sands came to Sydney for the sake of his health and with stationery valued at £500 set up a retail business in George Street. In 1848 he took over Mary Reibey's [q.v.] house and shop front and on this site, next to the General Post Office, the firm operated until 1970.

Sands formed several partnerships in Sydney and Melbourne. The first, in April 1851, was with his brother-in-law Thomas Kenny; in 1852 Sands and Kenny took over James Williams's printery in Queen Street, Melbourne, moving next year to Collins Street. In 1860 Dugald MacDougall (1834-1885) joined them as Melbourne manager and the firm there became Sands, Kenny & Co. Kenny retired from both partnerships in December 1861 and the firm became Sands and MacDougall. By 1870 as stationers, booksellers, printers and account book manufacturers the firm was one of the largest of its kind in Australia and in that year won prizes for printing and book production at the Intercolonial Exhibition in Sydney. Sands printed and published a wide variety of publications, but especially notable were his directories, almanacs, gazetteers and prints by F. C. Terry and S. T. Gill [qq.v.] depicting colonial life. In 1881 the Sydney firm, known as John Sands Ltd, offered one of the first groups of Christmas and New Year cards in Australia: the first card, at a price of 1s. 3d., was listed as 'Little girl offering a Christmas pudding to Swagsman'.

In 1864 Sands had been a member of the general purposes committee of the New South Wales Free Trade Association and in the 1860s was a director of the Phoenix Building and Investment Society. He died at his residence, Marmion, Waverley, on 16 August 1873, survived by his wife Marjory, née Moffat (d. 1904), whom he had married in Sydney on 6 December 1850, and by five sons and a daughter. He was buried in the Presbyterian section of Rookwood cemetery and in 1904 was reinterred in Waverley cemetery. His estate was sworn for probate at £20,000. His wife then separated the business, the Sands family retaining the Sydney operations as John Sands Ltd, and the MacDougall family continuing in Melbourne as Sands and MacDougall. Sands's eldest son, Robert (d. 1925), took

over the Sydney firm when he completed his apprenticeship. Another son, Herbert Guy (d. 1927), was a director of the firm for many years, a founder of Davy and Sands, engineers of Pyrmont, and later a pastoralist in the Orange district. The firm's 'hourglass' trademark is based on the old printers' tradition of punning pictorially on the logotype of the founder. John Sands Holdings Ltd was formed in 1950 to acquire all the shares in John Sands Pty Ltd.

V&P (LA NSW), 1861, 2, 83, 1875-76, 5, 631; SMH, 18 Aug 1873, 22 Oct 1881, 16 Jan 1970; *Bulletin*, 29 Oct 1881; *Daily Telegraph* (Syd), 29 Oct 1881; information from Dr John Sands, Syd.   G. P. WALSH

SANI, TOMASO (1839-1915), sculptor, was born in Florence, Italy, son of Stephen Sani, farmer, and his wife Catherine, née Falconi. He trained as a sculptor's pointing assistant and migrated to Melbourne in the late 1870s. In 1880 he exhibited a marble statue, 'Welcome', in the Italian sculpture section of the Melbourne International Exhibition. Soon afterwards he moved to Sydney.

In May 1882 Sani was engaged by the colonial architect, James Barnet [q.v.], to carve for £800 high relief figures on the spandrels of the Pitt Street façade of the new General Post Office. Barnet intended that Sani should depict contemporary types of Australian men and women in realistic form, but when completed in August 1883 they caused a public outcry and became known as 'Barnet's blot': questions were asked in parliament, and in letters to the *Sydney Morning Herald* they were castigated as 'grotesque and inartistic' and 'terrible travesties'. In October the government appointed a board comprising W. W. Wardell, H. C. Dangar and E. Du Faur [qq.v.] to report on the carvings; it unanimously recommended their replacement by blocks of stone. Barnet defended Sani's work: 'the bold and dashing stroke of the chisel ... shows the artist's power of producing a masterly effect of life and reality with a few touches', and pointed out that realism had become common in European art. The government approved the removal but in June 1884 the postmaster-general, James Norton [q.v.], suggested that they follow Barnet's plea to 'wait and see'. Despite (Sir) Frederick Darley's [q.v.] efforts in the Legislative Council and other sporadic protests for over a decade, the sculptures were left untouched. In 1886 they were pronounced works of art by the Legislative Council.

Sani sculptured other public statues, such as 'Aesculapius' for the old Medical School building, University of Sydney, and a bronze 'Mercury' for the *Evening News* building in Market Street, but his reputation suffered from the odium raised by the Post Office carvings. In 1889 he was bankrupt; with debts of £1420 his only asset was a half-share in 'Welcome' which did not realize the expenses of its removal. He then borrowed money to build a new studio at Annandale. In 1891 he was commissioned by Sir Henry Parkes [q.v.] to cast 'Footballer' in bronze for Centennial Park and the statues, at £150 each, of Allan Cunningham, W. C. Wentworth [qq.v.] and Barnet for niches on the Lands Department building; however, Sir George Dibbs [q.v.] substituted Sir John Robertson [q.v.] for Barnet.

Sani soon felt the loss of his patronage when Barnet was replaced in 1890; he apparently had no more public commissions after 1892 and was again bankrupt in 1895. Aged 76, he died of senile decay at Paddington on 28 August 1915 and was buried in the Catholic section of Rookwood cemetery. At the Registrar-General's Department, Sydney, on 16 August 1884 he had married Marie Louise Barry of Melbourne; he was survived by their daughter. 'A man of talent and cultivation, accustomed to the advanced style of architecture', Sani's sculpture was generally realistic in style with an underlying humour that contributed to his unpopularity.

PD (NSW), 1883, 1538, 1886, 1167, 1890, 6413; V&P (LA NSW), 1883-84, 9, 557, 563; SMH, 17 Dec 1890; A'*sian Art Review*, 1 July 1899; G. V. F. Mann, Controversy over the post-office carvings (1934, ML); J. Barnet papers (ML); D. I. McDonald, Barnet notes, 3149 (NL); Parkes letters (ML); Bankruptcy files, 9592/6, 1258/1 (NSWA).   NOEL S. HUTCHISON

SARGOOD, SIR FREDERICK THOMAS (1834-1903), merchant and politician, was born on 30 May 1834 at Walworth, London, son of Frederick James Sargood (d. 1873), merchant, and his wife Emma, née Rippon, daughter of a chief cashier of the Bank of England. Young Sargood, his education at 'private schools' in England presumably complete, arrived with his parents and five sisters in Melbourne in the *Clifton* on 12 February 1850. He worked briefly as a clerk in the Public Works Department before joining the wholesale softgoods business of Sargood, King & Co., which his father had already established. He spent some time on the Mount Alexander goldfields in 1852-54, and managed the firm's business in the

Bendigo-Castlemaine district. In 1858 he married Marian Australia, daughter of George Rolfe, merchant and later a member of the Legislative Council; next year he became a junior partner in the firm. His father, a radical in politics and a voluntaryist in religion, was member of the Legislative Council for Melbourne in 1853-56 and of the Legislative Assembly for St Kilda in 1856-57 before returning to England. Meanwhile the firm had prospered, extending its operations to other colonies, including New Zealand in 1863. Partners came and went, but the Sargoods remained dominant.

Sargood entered the Legislative Council in 1874 at a by-election for the Central Province, and a merger in 1879 with the firm of Martin, Butler and Nichol gave him more time for public affairs. His wife had died in childbirth on 6 January and in March 1880 he resigned from the council to take his nine children to England. On 2 December at the Independent Chapel, Ventnor, Isle of Wight, Sargood married Julia Tomlin, aged 34, and the family returned in October 1882.

Sargood held the Legislative Council seat of South Yarra in 1882-1901. On 13 November 1883 he joined the Service-Berry [qq.v.] ministry as Victoria's first minister of defence. He had long had an interest in the subject, having joined the Victorian Volunteer Artillery in 1859 as a private, rising to the rank of lieut-colonel. Described as 'one of the best shots in Victoria' he was also closely involved in the rifle club movement; he had formed the St Kilda Rifle Corps in 1859. As minister Sargood backed an energetic programme to build up the Victorian navy, local fortifications and armament supplies, especially during the Russian war scare in March-May 1885. His task of organizing the change-over from volunteer to paid militia forces involved him in controversy with the new commandant, Colonel Disney [q.v.], who believed that he should report direct to the governor. Sargood quickly disabused him and in 1885 appointed Major-General M. F. Downes [q.v.] as departmental secretary. This issue forced the Colonial Office to accept local control of defence. Many of Sargood's admirers considered the formation of the school cadet corps in 1884 his greatest monument. Commissioner of water-supply from April 1884 to 18 February 1886, he again held the defence portfolio, together with public instruction, in the Munro [q.v.] government in 1890-92 and for three months under Turner [q.v.] in 1894, when he was also vice-president of the Board of Land and Works. Created C.M.G. in 1885 he became K.C.M.G. in 1890.

In 1888 Sargood had succeeded W. E. Hearn [q.v.] as unofficial leader of the Legislative Council. Like many other free traders in Victoria he became reconciled to a lost cause, and 'did not trouble to state whether he was a Conservative or Liberal'; his opposition to 'One Man One Vote' and to land taxation reveal his conservatism. Nevertheless, when introducing the factory bill in the council in 1885, he deplored the long hours he had worked as a young man, and praised his father's part in the early closing movement. In 1895-96 he was a leader in the consensus supporting legislation to set up the first wages boards; and in 1900 he persuaded the council temporarily to accept new boards, thereby ensuring that the system would become the basis of industrial relations in Victoria. A firm believer in the role of the Upper House, Sargood was tactful and reasonable in his dealings with the assembly; indeed, by avoiding constitutional crises he consolidated the council's authority. A supporter of Federation, he was omitted from the Age list, and missed out on the 1897 Convention but, appropriately, was elected to the first Senate in 1901.

Sargood was a commissioner of savings banks in 1874-80 and of the Melbourne Harbor Trust in 1877-80, also a director of the Commercial Bank until about 1895. By the 1880s he was very wealthy, with landholdings in New South Wales including Ellerslie (Tumut) and Jerilderie (Urana). Although he has not been identified as a 'land boomer', as president of the Melbourne Chamber of Commerce in 1886-88 he did not doubt the sound basis of 'this unprecedented wave of prosperity'. His firm actually expanded in the depression of the 1890s. He was closely involved with the Melbourne Centennial International Exhibition, but his appointment as executive vice-president of the organizing commission provoked the resignation of Chief Justice Higinbotham [q.v.] from the presidency. Under Sargood the exhibition was a success but expensive.

Sargood was dapper and of medium height, with conventional beard and moustache and more than a suggestion of military style. With common sense, cool judgment and grasp of detail, he combined kindness and a sense of duty. Sidney and Beatrice Webb found him pleasant and sensible. Although a prominent supporter of the Congregational Church he refrained from joining, reputedly because he held opinions on rites and ceremonies similar to those of the Quakers. As a philanthropist he was 'not ostentatious in his charity, but large in his gifts'. He was also renowned as a generous host at his exuberant and famous mansion, Rippon Lea, designed by J. Reed [q.v.], built in 1868-69 and set in superb gardens and grounds, complete with miniature rifle range.

Sargood died suddenly on 2 January 1903, on a holiday in New Zealand. On a scorching day in Melbourne thousands watched his funeral procession, which included eight massed bands, 1200 cadets and a firing-party of 300. He was buried in St Kilda cemetery, where members of the Metropolitan Liedertafel, of which he had been president, sang Sullivan's 'The Long Day Closes'. He was survived by Lady Sargood and their daughter, and by five sons and four daughters of his first marriage. His estate was valued for probate at £680,000; he also had substantial property in New South Wales, Western Australia and New Zealand.

A. Sutherland et al, Victoria and its metropolis, 2 (Melb, 1888); B. Webb, The Webb's Australian diary, 1898, A. G. Austin ed (Melb, 1965); F. Strahan, 'Rippon Lea', National Trusts of Aust, Historic houses of Australia (Melb, 1974); PD (Vic), 1885, 2199, 1902-03, 1530; Argus, 2 Sept 1885, 24 Apr 1888, 3, 19 Jan 1903; Age, 3, 5, 19 Jan 1903; Table Talk, 8 Jan 1903; Punch (Melb), 27 Aug 1907; J. E. Parnaby, The economic and political development of Victoria, 1877-1881 (Ph.D. thesis, Univ Melb, 1951).   JOHN RICKARD

SAVAGE, ROBERT (1818-1888), agricultural writer and inventor, was born on 24 March 1818 at Cork, Ireland, son of Francis Savage, gentleman, and his wife Catherine, née Dring. Educated at The Seminary, Rutland Square, North Dublin, he entered Trinity College on 17 October 1834. Intended for the Church he was never ordained. Instead he sailed in the London and arrived in Hobart Town on 3 April 1839. In December he took sheep across Bass Strait to Portland and in 1840-45 occupied Nangeela on the Glenelg River north of Casterton, with H. E. P. Dana [q.v.] as a sleeping partner. In 1840 he was attacked by Aboriginals after he had caught them stealing sheep and shot one dead; in 1842 he wrote to Governor Gipps that it was the only time that he had ever seen 'the dead body of an Aboriginal' and added that he did not consider the state of society in his district 'in the least dreadful'. In 1848 he became clerk of Petty Sessions at the Grange (Hamilton) and in 1852 registrar of the Court of Requests for the police district of the Grange.

Remaining in touch with friends in the district, including the Winters [q.v. S. P. Winter] of Murndal, Savage moved to Melbourne in the late 1850s and was agricultural writer for the Argus. His first wife

Ann, née Wrentmore, whom he had married in Van Diemen's Land in May 1841, died at Hawthorn on 10 July 1860. After his marriage to Annie Sarah Dyer on 9 June 1864 he lived at St Kilda. About 1869 he took up farming at Northcote but lost money in a mining speculation in 1872 and was in financial difficulties. A member of the Land Tenure Reform League, in 1873 he wrote for it a closely argued pamphlet on *Political Economy*, which owed much to Ruskin; he also published a general discourse on agriculture in Victoria in the *International Exhibition Essays*, 1872-3. Associated with the National Agricultural Society of Victoria, in 1871 he was briefly its first honorary secretary.

In August 1874 Savage became inspector of stock and was made a commissioner of the Supreme Court for the Moama district. By October he had moved to Echuca, where he was still living in September 1876. He returned to Melbourne and in 1877 argued for land taxation in an article in the *Melbourne Review* on 'The Incidence of Taxation and Expenditure of Public Money'. In July 1880 he was made a temporary inspector of sheep and stock.

Savage's main interest lay in invention. In December 1846 his reaping machine, similar to Ridley's [q.v.], had been displayed in Melbourne. In March 1857 he invented improvements for stone-breaking machinery and 'a mode of working compound levers applicable to crushing, stamping, punching, and other purposes'. In 1858 he patented advances in methods of puddling and washing earth containing gold or other metals, and in October 1865 new types of cement and paint. In 1872 with J. Hicks he applied for a patent for a better sewing machine, and next year for 'improvements in reaping and binding machines'. From about 1874 he was working with F. Y. Wolseley [q.v.] and claimed a share in the invention of his shearing machine. Savage may have tested it with Wolseley in Walgett in 1876 and the two took out a patent in March 1877, but the machine failed and Wolseley continued to work on it without Savage. In 1881 Savage invented a torpedo which he hoped to sell to the Italian government. Patented in 1882, his Australian earth scoop and elevator went into production about 1884 and sold for £75. Next year he applied for a patent for his improved steam vacuum lift pump. Poor health impeded work on several projects including an electric shearing machine which he never completed; on 12 July 1888 he died of paralysis at South Melbourne. Survived by a daughter of his first marriage, by his second wife and a son and a daughter, he was buried in St Kilda cemetery with Anglican rites.

F. Wheelhouse, *Digging stick to rotary hoe* (Melb, 1966); V&P (LA Vic), 1861-62, 2 (D57); *Argus*, 16 July 1888; Savage family papers, MS 1203 (ML); MS cat (ML).   SALLY O'NEILL

SAYWELL, THOMAS (1837-1928), merchant and developer, was born on 20 February 1837 at Radford, Nottinghamshire, England, son of George Saywell, lacemaker, and his first wife Eliza Ann. When the Nottingham lace trade declined his parents moved to France and lived at Baysville, Calais and Lille, where Thomas received his early education. In 1848 the Saywells and other Protestant lacemaking families returned to England but bleak prospects led them to migrate as a group in the *Agincourt*; they reached Sydney on 6 October.

After some time on the goldfields Saywell set up as a tobacconist in Sydney in 1863. He prospered and in 1881 was managing director when Saywell's Tobacco Co. Ltd became a public company; one of his partners was (Sir) Hugh Dixson. From 1871 Saywell also invested in coal and brick production, and success persuaded him to sell his tobacco interests and invest substantially in coal-mining and real estate. He developed the Ziz-Zag Coal Co. at Lithgow and the South Bulli Colliery. He built the Bellambi jetty in 1887 at South Bulli for £40,000 and won large government contracts for coal. Later he bought and developed other south coast mines, notably the Clifton and South Clifton collieries.

In the early 1880s Saywell foresaw that the construction of the Illawarra railway would create new suburbs in the sparsely settled area south of Cook's River; he bought an estate at Lady Robinson's Beach, Botany Bay, erected the fashionable New Brighton Hotel, a public bathing enclosure described as the best in Australia', and other amenities including a race-course. He planned to create a model suburb and seaside resort for working-class families. In 1884 Saywell's Tramway Act granted him a thirty-year franchise for a private tramway from Lady Robinson's Beach to Rockdale railway station. On his suggestion the new suburb was named Brighton-le-Sands and he lived there for many years.

Saywell also had large land holdings at Alexandria and Redfern. He was a director of the Wickham and Bullock Island Coal Co. in the 1890s and invested in copper mines at Cobar. A New South Wales commissioner for the Centennial International Exhibition, Melbourne, in 1887 he also represented the colony's wine industry in North America and was a successful commercial exhibitor at the World's Columbian Exposition, Chicago, 1893.

Saywell died on 23 November 1928 at Mosman and was buried in the Congregational section of Waverley cemetery. He was survived by five sons and six daughters by his first wife Annie Ellen, née Fawcett, whom he had married on 1 November 1862; she died in 1905 and he married Rebecca Elizabeth Osborne on 31 January 1906. His estate was valued for probate at over £164,000.

W. F. Morrison, *The Aldine centennial history of New South Wales*, 2 (Syd, 1888); P. Geeves and J. Jervis, *Rockdale: its beginning and development* (Syd, 1962); *SMH*, 27 Nov 1928; *Propellor*, 28 Dec 1944, 4, 11 Jan 1945; family records (held privately).

PHILIP GEEVES

SCHIRMEISTER, CARL FRIEDRICH ALEXANDER FRANZ (1814-1887), Lutheran pastor, was born on 22 July 1814 at Eberswalde near Berlin, son of Hans Schirmeister, civil servant, and his wife Albertina, née Muszel. After graduation in theology at the University of Halle he became a tutor in the home of Baron von Puttkammer. Prompted to missionary work by the death of the baron's son, Schirmeister became clerical leader of a missionary party trained by Rev. J. E. Gossner for work 'in the South Seas, preferably New Zealand'. The five missionaries were designated at the Bethlehem Church, Berlin, on 12 June 1842 and sailed from Bremen in July. Destined for Blind Bay (Nelson), they landed at Otago Harbour. At Cloudy Bay (Blenheim) Samuel Ironside, Wesleyan minister, suggested that they should go to the Chatham Islands, and they commenced a mission to the Moriori people there on 20 February 1843.

Their isolated and difficult existence was relieved in 1846 by the arrival of three deaconesses sent out by Gossner as prospective wives. Schirmeister married Maria Alwine Gericke who bore him two daughters. Bishop G. A. Selwyn visited the mission in 1848 and failed to persuade Schirmeister to accept Anglican orders or Church control. In 1853 he removed to Pitt Island and became tutor in the family of Frederick Hunt for two years. In 1855 he became dangerously ill and was taken to Wellington by Selwyn.

In 1857 Schirmeister arrived in Sydney where J. D. Lang [q.v.], as agent for the Gossner mission, persuaded him to visit the German station at Zion's Hill near Brisbane, founded by K. W. E. Schmidt and C. Eipper [qq.v.]. Determined to set up a Lutheran ministry, especially among the German settlers, Schirmeister travelled widely preaching on many stations. Registering

himself as a Lutheran pastor, he formed the first congregation in Brisbane in 1858 and obtained grants for church sites. The Bethlehem Church (later St Andreas) was dedicated in December 1861 and a church at South Brisbane next year. Schirmeister continued to itinerate and organize in the country.

In 1863 Gossner's society sent out Rev. C. A. Anger to be Schirmeister's assistant. He settled at Toowoomba and in 1864 Schirmeister sought his de-registration. Another party of Gossner missionaries arrived in Queensland in September 1866, followed by Rev. C. Gaustadt from Gossner's Indian mission in 1869. Schirmeister's zeal for a united Lutheranism led to the Evangelical Lutheran Synod of Queensland in 1885; he remained as foundation president until his death. Although supported by other Gossner and Basle-trained men, he failed to prevent formation of the United German and Scandinavian Lutheran Synod of Queensland which remained as a separate body until 1921.

A skilled musician, Schirmeister was described as a sensitive and exemplary missionary. His stress on orthodoxy antagonized some of his Gossner colleagues, particularly J. G. Haussman, who allowed laymen to preach and ordained some of them without theological training. Without him most of the early Queensland Lutherans would probably have been absorbed in the Methodist, Presbyterian and Congregational Churches. He died of lung cancer on 8 October 1887 and was buried in the Toowong cemetery.

F. Hunt, *Twenty-five years' experience in New Zealand and the Chatham Islands* (Wellington, 1866); Th. Hebart, *The United Evangelical Lutheran Church in Australia*, J. J. Schultz ed (Adel, 1938); F. O. Theile, *One hundred years of the Lutheran Church in Queensland* (Brisb, 1938); W. Holsten, *Johannes Evangelista Gossner Glaube und Gemeinde* (Gottingen, 1949); W. N. Gunson, 'The Nundah missionaries', *JRHSQ*, 6 (1959-61); *Die Biene auf dem Missionsfelde* (Berlin), 1842-87 (microfilm, 1836-57 PMB); *Australische Christenbote*, Oct 1887; J. D. Lang papers (ML); Lutheran Church Archives (Adel).   NIEL GUNSON

SCHLEINITZ, GEORG GUSTAV, FREIHERR VON (1834-1910), hydrographer and governor, was born on 17 June 1834 at Bromberg, Prussia (Bydgocsz, Poland), son of Hans Eduard von Schleinitz, civil servant, and his wife Johanna, née Gottlieb. After a voyage as ship's boy in a trading brig, he entered the Prussian navy in 1849 and served in the *Danzig*, *Amazon* and *Gesion*. He fought in the 1856 operations against the

Riff pirates and joined the naval expedition to China in 1860-62. About 1872 he married Margot von Hippel, who had been brought up in Mexico City and Havana as daughter of a surveyor in the government of Emperor Maximilian. They had four children.

Von Schleinitz was given command of the imperial corvette *Gazelle* in 1874-76 to carry out a voyage of circumnavigation and research. He spent the summer of 1874-75 at the Kerguelen Islands where astronomers observed the transit of Venus and in mid-1875 moved to New Guinea waters. While others studied plants, animals, rocks, waters and the climate of Melanesia, he collected anthropological data and named the Gazelle Peninsula of New Britain after his ship. On the way home they visited Fiji, Tonga and Samoa. Back in Germany in 1876 he reported to Bismarck on German influence in the South Pacific. Appointed in charge of the Admiralty Hydrographical Office, he worked in 1880-86 on the publication of the expedition's research; it appeared in five gilt-edged volumes in 1889 and 1890 as *Die Forschungsreise S.M.S. 'Gazelle' in den Jahren 1874 bis 1876 unter Kommando des Kapitän zur See Freiherrn von Schleinitz*, containing unique descriptions and illustrations of contemporary Melanesian artefacts.

Described in 1886 as 'a not exactly imposing middle sized, already ageing gentleman with pince-nez who looks like a scholar. He speaks and moves just as he looks', von Schleinitz resigned from the navy in February to go to New Guinea with his family as the first governor *(Landeshauptmann)* of the protectorate of the New Guinea Co. En route he told guests at a banquet at Cooktown of Germany's endeavour to impart some of its 'high culture to the native races'; on reaching the capital Finschhafen in June he shared his employers' hopes that Germany could also make large profits in New Guinea. Visiting New Britain in November, he was impressed with the success of cotton and coconut palm plantations near Kokopo owned by Thomas Farrell and 'Queen Emma'; he became the first European to bring labourers from the New Guinea islands to work on the mainland (Kaiser Wilhelmsland): towns were built, a shipping service established and scientific expeditions were launched including one up the Sepik River in 1887. He published a number of scientific papers.

When his wife died after seven months in the colony, Schleinitz sought relief to save his children from the dangers of the wet season, but was unable to sail before March 1888. In Berlin he resigned after he had failed to convince the directors of the continuing need for heavy investment. His last twenty-two years were spent at Haus Hohenborn near Bad Pyrmont, in Saxony. He died there on 12 December 1910.

A. H. H. Schnee, *Deutsches Kolonial-Lexikon* (Leipzig, 1920); O. Schellong, *Alte Dokumente aus der Südsee* (Königsberg, 1934); *SMH*, 5 June 1886; Reichskolonialamt records (Zentrales Staatsarchiv, Potsdam, German Democratic Republic); Reichsmarinamt records (microfilm, LaT L, ML, NL).   S. FIRTH

SCHOMBURGK, MORITZ RICHARD (1811-1891), botanist, was born on 5 October 1811 at Freyburg, Saxony, son of Johann Friedrich Ludwig Schomburgk, assistant Lutheran pastor, and his wife Christiane Juliane Wilhelmine, née Krippendorf. Educated at a Freyburg primary school and by a private tutor, in 1825 he began a gardening apprenticeship at Merseburg. After his military service with the Royal Guard at Berlin in 1831-34 he worked in the garden of a Berlin shooting range and in 1835 was a gardener at Sanssouci, Frederick the Great's palace at Potsdam. He accompanied his explorer brother Robert on an expedition in 1840-44 to British Guiana, as botanist and historian. He later published his three-volume *Reisen in Britisch-Guiana in den Jahren 1840-1844* (Leipzig, 1847-48).

Unable to find suitable employment at home, Schomburgk and his brother Alfred Otto formed an emigration society and in March 1849 sailed for South Australia in the *Princess Louise*. On 24 June 1849 on board ship he married Pauline Kneip, daughter of a Potsdam timber merchant and carpenter. The passengers included C. W. L. Muecke, C. G. A. Linger and T. G. H. Buring [qq.v.]. On 30 August, three weeks after his arrival, Schomburgk was naturalized and on 19 September settled at Buchsfelde, four miles from Gawler. While his brother started the *Süd-Australische Zeitung*, Schomburgk planted a vineyard. By 1862 he had about five acres of verdelho and mataro grapevines from which he made a small quantity of wine, and also grew table grapes. In 1860-61 he was chairman of the district of Mudla Wirra; he organized the Gawler Museum.

In September 1865 Schomburgk was appointed curator of the Adelaide Botanic Gardens and soon began to transform it from 'a sterile waste' into one of the most beautiful spots in the colony. At his first board meeting he outlined a comprehensive programme of building and improvement and by 1868 the rosery and the experimental garden were open. He visited F. von Mueller [q.v.] with whom he frequently corresponded, and returned from Melbourne with a valuable collection of plants for the gardens.

Within South Australia he distributed plants and trees to public bodies and exchanged specimens with private gardeners. In 1873 he sent out a total of 18,000 trees. He was responsible for the planting of Wellington Square, North Terrace, the Government House gardens and Marble Hill in Adelaide, and of the government farm at Belair. Afforestation claimed much of his attention and he spoke and wrote widely on the importance of forests for their effect on climate as well as for their economic value. In 1867 he planted in a specially built hothouse in the gardens the first and for a long time the only *Victoria Regia* in Australia. This giant water-lily, which he had classified, brought many visitors to the gardens while its growth was reported weekly in the press. It produced leaves over 6ft. wide and flowers 13 ins. across. He also built a palm house, a museum of wood specimens, a herbarium and a museum of economic botany.

In particular Schomburgk's *Report on the Progress and Condition of the Botanic Garden and Government Plantation* of 1881 summarized his work on the introduction and acclimatization of plants and seeds of economic importance that was among his most important contributions to the colony. He corresponded with colleagues and friends, especially in California, northern Africa and Italy where the climate resembled that of South Australia, seeking seeds of grasses, fodder, cereals and other plants, with which he experimented before distributing them within the colony. He was often disheartened by a lack of response: of 100 samples sent to growers in one year he had only one reply. His efforts to encourage the planting of almond groves and flowers for perfume were unsuccessful, the farmers preferring more orthodox crops; but three of his new wheat strains became favourites in South Australia. He also introduced a phylloxera-resistant vine and some of his new grasses stood up to severe drought. He persuaded some farmers to grow wattle for tanning. He reported in 1891 that he had increased the number of known South Australian species in the Botanic Gardens from 5000 to nearly 14,000. He was frequently called upon to give evidence to select committees on subjects ranging from sanitation, education and main roads to disease in wheat, vegetable products and the alleged harmfulness of sparrows. He had been a member of the Philosophical Society of Adelaide from 1865 and read many papers to it and to other Adelaide societies. He was a member of many other learned societies in Europe, America and the Australian colonies. Honoured for his work by the kings of Prussia and Italy and by the duke of Hesse,

he was awarded an honorary D.Phil. by the Germania Academy. In 1872 he was offered, but refused, the directorship of the Melbourne Botanic Gardens.

Schomburgk died on 24 March 1891 at his house in the Adelaide Botanic Gardens and was buried in the North Road cemetery, survived by a son and four daughters. His estate was sworn for probate at £5300.

E. Ward, *The vineyards and orchards of South Australia* (Adel, 1862); H. T. Burgess (ed), *Cyclopedia of South Australia*, 1-2 (Adel, 1908-09); A. Lodewyckx, *Die Deutschen in Australien* (Stuttgart, 1932); Adelaide Botanic Garden, *Centenary volume, 1855-1955* (Adel, 1955); D. Van Abbé, 'The Germans in South Australia', *Aust Letters*, Oct 1960; *T&CJ*, 22 Mar 1873; Aust botanists biog and bibliog files (Basser Lib, Canberra); family information from Richard Schomburgk, Adel.

RAOUL F. MIDDELMANN

SCHURR, FELIX (1827-1900), missionary, was born at Dambach, Alsace-Lorraine, France, son of Joseph Schurr, vigneron, and his wife Magdalena, née Ehlinger. Educated at a Paris Catholic seminary, he volunteered for missionary work on the west coast of Africa. Soon stricken with fever, he returned to Paris where he was ordained as a priest and sent to the West Indies to work among the slaves. Again forced back to Paris by ill health, he was offered a position in Ireland by Archbishop Cullen [q.v.] of Dublin, and remained there seventeen years. Affectionately known as 'Abbé' he was already a scientist, musician and linguist, but continued his studies and became professor of languages at Maynooth and Trinity colleges, Ireland, while working among the inmates of an institution for the blind.

In 1870 he accepted a call from Bishop O'Mahony [q.v.] to work in the new see of Armidale, New South Wales, which included the valleys of the Clarence, Richmond and Tweed rivers. Arriving on the Richmond in 1872 the Abbé was in charge of the first Catholic church in Casino; in 1874 he saw the first church built at Coraki and in 1877 opened the first at Lismore. In 1880-82 he was at Rocky Mouth (Maclean) on the Clarence and assisted in building new churches at Palmer Island and Iluka.

Later, whenever a priest was needed he returned to the Clarence. He was remarkable for his long journeys by heavily laden pack-horse, by rowing-boat and later by buggy and pair. Often he carried a small organ for he believed there should be music in every home. He loved tea and children, was famous for his charity to everyone and was beloved by people of all creeds and ages. Schurr died at Casino on 17 July 1900 aged

73 and was buried there in the Catholic cemetery. His estate was valued for probate at £1456. His widowed sister Magdalene Schurr Schmidt, who in 1870 had come to Wardell, Richmond River, died in 1890.

J. Green, *The lost echo: a story of the Richmond* (Syd, 1910); L. T. Daley, *Men and a river* (Melb, 1966); R. B. Walker, *Old New England* (Syd, 1966); *Catholic Weekly* (Syd), 6 Aug 1942; *Aust Messenger of the Sacred Heart*, 4 Jan 1943; *Richmond River Express*, Apr 1873, 18 July 1900; *Northern Star* (Lismore), 5 Aug 1876, 7 July 1877, 13 Nov 1915; Richmond River Hist Soc files.   LOUISE T. DALEY

SCOTT, ALEXANDER WALKER (1800-1883), entomologist and entrepreneur, was born on 10 November 1800 in Bombay, India, son of Dr Helenus Scott and his wife Augusta Maria, née Frederick. Educated at Bath Grammar School and Peterhouse, Cambridge (B.A., 1822; M.A., 1825), he entered Lincoln's Inn but discarded a legal career for speculation as a merchant. On 17 January 1827 he arrived at Newcastle, New South Wales, in his ship *Australia*. This and voyages to the colony in 1829 and 1831 proved financially disastrous. In 1829 he took up a 2560-acre grant on Ash Island in the Hunter River and in 1831 with his mother and sister he returned as a settler. He bought land between Newcastle and Maitland. From Newcastle House, built in 1837 on the harbour front at Newcastle, he supervised the establishment of an iron-foundry, forge and patent slip at Stockton and the construction of large tanks on Moscheto Island, where sea-water was used to supply salt for Sydney. He grew tobacco and flax on the Maitland farms and oranges on Ash Island. In 1842 Ludwig Leichhardt [q.v.] visited the island, found it 'a romantic place' and noted the artesian bore. In 1844 Scott presciently financed detailed plans for a railway between Newcastle and Maitland and was undeterred by Governor Gipps's comment that 'the colony was not sufficiently advanced to entertain such important works'; he advocated a tramway to Singleton and in 1853 became a shareholder in the Hunter River Railway Co., taken over by the government in 1855. Scott's original project became part of the Great Northern Railway.

From his father, a distinguished physician and botanist, Scott had acquired a deep interest in the natural sciences, and in 1835 became the founding treasurer of the Newcastle Mechanics' Institute which had a library and museum. He was an original member of the Australian Club, a magistrate, warden of the first Newcastle District Council in 1843, a trustee of Christ Church and later a founder of the Newcastle Corps of Volunteer Rifles; in these activities he conformed to the traditional pattern of behaviour so important to his brothers Robert and Helenus [qq.v.] and their fellow exclusives, although his friends were drawn from a wider range of colonial society.

In 1856 Scott was elected to the new Legislative Assembly for Northumberland and Hunter; he held his seat in 1858, won Northumberland in 1859 and the Lower Hunter in 1860. A liberal, he favoured the secret ballot and an extension of the franchise. In 1861 he resigned from the assembly to accept nomination to the Legislative Council, where he was inactive and resigned on 1 May 1866. His appointment as a land titles commissioner on 4 June did not stave off bankruptcy in November, caused by his business incapacity and generous hospitality. He resigned as president of the Victoria Club and had to sell Ash Island, already heavily mortgaged.

Scott had given up Newcastle House and made Ash Island his home after his marriage on 29 December 1846 to Harriet Calcott (d. 1866), the mother of his daughters Harriet and Helena; he welcomed distinguished artists and scientists there and devoted his time increasingly to entomology. In 1862 he was a founding member of the Entomological Society of New South Wales, next year a councillor and president in 1866 and from 1868. He published seven papers on butterflies and moths in its *Transactions*, and the first volume of *Australian Lepidoptera and Their Transformations* ... (London, 1864), illustrated by his daughters, was followed by *Mammalia, recent and extinct* (Sydney, 1873). On the initiative of Helena the second volume of his *Lepidoptera* was completed and published in five parts, 1890-98, by the Australian Museum. An active trustee of the museum in 1864-66 and in 1867-79, he was involved in the dismissal of Gerard Krefft [q.v.]. In 1876 he became a member of the Royal Society of New South Wales.

Scott died of liver disease at Paddington on 1 November 1883 and was buried in the Anglican section of Waverley cemetery. He left his estate, valued for probate at £1602, to his daughters and step-daughter Mary Ann Calcott. Scott Street, Newcastle, was named after him and a pencil drawing of him by his friend Edwin Landseer is in the Art Gallery of New South Wales.

His daughters HARRIET (1830-1907) and HELENA (1832-1910), artists and naturalists, were born in Sydney, Helena on 11 April 1832. Educated by their father on Ash Island, they acquired a considerable knowledge of Australian plants, animals and insects. They collected for and corresponded with leading colonial scientists. Their many paintings of Australian insects earned high praise from members of the Entomological Society and after the publication of *Australian Lepidoptera* they were elected honorary members.

In 1864 Helena married Edward Forde and next year accompanied him on a survey of the Darling River between Wentworth and Bourke. She made a collection of fodder grasses and of specimens for her proposed 'Flora of the Darling', but Forde died of fever at Menindee on 20 June 1866 and she returned to Sydney, transferring her collections to Rev. William Woolls [q.v.], who used them for a section of his *Contribution to the Flora of Australia* (Sydney, 1867). Harriet and Helena received commissions from the Macleays, William Macarthur, E. P. Ramsay, and Sir Terence Murray [qq.v.] and for some years provided almost all the figures for the scientific literature produced in Sydney, notably J. C. Cox's [q.v.] *Monograph of Australian Land Shells* (1868) and Krefft's *Snakes of Australia* (1869) and *Mammals of Australia* (1871). They also designed Christmas cards with Australian themes for commercial production, while Harriet's drawings of native flowers and ferns graced the 1884 and 1886 editions of *The Railway Guide of New South Wales*.

In 1882 Harriet married Dr Cosby William Morgan but the marriage was unhappy. She died at Granville on 16 August 1907. Helena, whose letters reminded Murray of 'what letter writing was in the Augustan days of England', died at Harris Park on 24 November 1910.

M. Aurousseau (ed), *Letters of F. W. Ludwig Leichhardt*, 2-3 (Cambridge, 1968); V&P (LA NSW), 1859-60, 3, 353, 1868-69, 3, 1257, 1869, 2, 875, 1873-74, 5, 917, 1875, 4, 289; 'Presidential address', Linnean Soc of NSW, *Procs*, 36 (1911) and J. J. Fletcher, 'The Society's heritage from the Macleays', 45 (1920); W. J. Goold, 'Our pioneers', Newcastle and Hunter District Hist Soc, J, 10 (1956); *SMH*, 28 Oct 1844; Forde letters, sketches, drawings (ML); Scott collection (Aust Museum, Syd); family papers (ML).

NANCY GRAY

SCOTT, ANDREW GEORGE (1842-1880), bushranger, self-styled 'CAPTAIN MOONLITE', was born at Rathfriland, County Down, Ireland, and baptized on 5 July 1842, son of Thomas Scott, Anglican clergyman, and his wife Bessie, née Jeffares. Young Scott was described as 'dark, handsome, active and full of high spirits', but was known for impulsive acts of mischiev-

ous violence. He may have studied engineering in London, and legend has it that he served with Garibaldi in Italy in 1860.

On 22 November 1861 Scott, his parents and brother Thomas arrived at Auckland, New Zealand, in the *Black Eagle*. A fellow-passenger remembered him as 'very gentlemanly and high-spirited'. His father took charge of Christ Church, Coromandel, and his brother was ordained priest; Andrew taught school for a while but in February 1864 was commissioned in the Waikato Militia; later he transferred to the Auckland Volunteer Engineers Corps. On 6 November 1867 he was refused a post of inspector or sub-inspector in the armed constabulary, although he had been endorsed by prominent members of the Auckland community as 'a gentleman well suited for an office of command'.

Within a few months Scott had arrived in Australia, possibly first in Sydney. About April 1868 he went to Melbourne, met Bishop Perry [q.v.] and in July was appointed stipendiary lay reader of the Church of Holy Trinity, Bacchus Marsh. In November he advertised that he intended to set up as a consultant surveyor and engineer in addition to his clerical duties. However in March 1869 he was sent as lay reader to Egerton near Ballarat, where he made friends with James Simpson, the local schoolmaster, and L. J. Bruun, agent for the town's branch of the London Chartered Bank. As Bruun was returning to the bank late on 8 May, Scott, disguised in mask and cloak, attacked him and forced him to hand over the contents of the safe. He made Bruun write a note certifying his resistance to the robbery; Scott signed it himself with the deliberately mis-spelt 'Captain Moonlite'. Both Bruun and Simpson were charged with robbery but were acquitted; Scott soon left for Sydney.

For some months he lived off the proceeds of the crime, but towards the end of 1870 he began passing valueless cheques. In November he fraudulently bought the yacht, *Why-not*, arranged for a skipper and a 'young lady' to accompany him, but was arrested by water police as he tried to leave for Fiji. On 20 December he was given twelve months in Maitland gaol, some of which he spent in Parramatta Lunatic Asylum, feigning madness. While he was in prison Bruun and his friends had detectives set on his trail, and when he was released in April 1872 he was charged with the Egerton gold robbery. While on remand he escaped from Ballarat gaol but was soon recaptured, and on 24 July he appeared before Judge Barry [q.v.]. Scott conducted most of his own defence, cross-examined Bruun for seven hours with 'shrewd and pertinacious questions' and amused the crowd with his facetious remarks. He received ten years hard labour and one year for escaping.

Scott was a recalcitrant and violent prisoner in Pentridge gaol. Released in March 1879, for a while he was a speaker at open-air meetings on prison reform and kindred subjects, but on 18 November with a small band he held up Wantabadgery sheep station near Wagga Wagga for two days. He used the two children of the nearby hotelkeeper as hostages, separating them by force from their parents. Two of the gang (one a boy of 15) and one trooper were killed when the police attacked the homestead. Scott and three others were found guilty of murder and he and one of his accomplices were hanged on 20 January 1880.

Julian Thomas (J. S. James), The Vagabond papers, 3 (Melb, 1877); G. Calderwood, Captain Moonlite (Adel, 1971); W. A. Osborne, 'Andrew George Scott—Captain Moonlite', VHM, 27 (1955-57); New Zealander, 20 Nov 1861; Australasian, 3 Dec 1870, 6, 13 Apr 1872; SMH, 21 Dec 1870; Ballarat Courier, 26 July 1872; Argus, 18, 19, 24 Nov 1879; Aust and NZ Gazette, 2 Sept 1882; S. Finn scrapbook no 118 (Auckland Inst and Museum Lib); J. M. Forde newspaper cuttings (ML); Army Dept files, letter CD64/318 and A. G. Scott application CD67/3955 (NZNA).

SCOTT, EUGENE MONTAGUE (1835-1909), cartoonist and illustrator, was born in London, son of William Scott, artist, and his wife Sarah, née Myers. He migrated to Victoria in the 1850s and worked as a photographer. On 20 July 1859 in Melbourne he married Amy Johnson. In 1857-65 he contributed drawings and cartoons to the Illustrated Australian Mail, Illustrated Melbourne Post and Melbourne Punch.

In 1866 Scott moved to Sydney as chief cartoonist for the Sydney Punch, producing unexceptional material for it till 1886. In 1867 he received a princely 250 guineas commission for a portrait of the duke of Edinburgh. He was established in a photographic salon in George Street and in the 1870s his large wood-engravings and lithographs of rugged outdoor scenes, formal functions and public personalities regularly enlivened the Illustrated Sydney News. Many fine lithographs were issued as supplements including a portrait of (Sir) Henry Parkes [q.v.]. At the 1870 Intercolonial Exhibition in Sydney his 7 ft. by 3 ft. 6 ins. oil, 'A Day's Picnic on Clark Island', was criticized by the Sydney Morning Herald for its 'grotesque little figures resembling gaudily bedecked marionettes', but when given to the Mitchell Library in 1930 it was praised for its faithful depiction of the fashions of the period.

Bankrupt in June 1870, Scott was forced to sell his photographic equipment to meet his creditors. In 1871 the Sydney Mail employed him as its first artist. In 1872 he had illustrations in two publications: Our Christmas Budget by H. W. H. Stephen and G. Bunster and Punch Staff Papers; in 1877 Sydney Punch ran a fine series of his chromo-lithographs, 'Our Collection of Worthies'. The December 1878 Sydney Punch included Arthur Clint's caricature of 'Monty' in sartorial attire with 'gad sir! air'. Clint and Scott illustrated 'Ironbark's' (G. H. Gibson) Southerly Busters of that year.

From 1880 the Bulletin carried some cartoons and occasional engravings of local dignitaries by Scott. The Brisbane Boomerang, founded 1887, ran his cartoons until 1891 when he drew the first cartoons for the Queensland Worker, continuing as its chief cartoonist until 1909. In 1889 he had moved to Brisbane and on 5 December married a widow, Mary Ellen Price, née Mehan; he lived there four years. His Queensland Worker cartoons were lively and admirably attuned to its optimistic, combative tone; they were being reproduced elsewhere years later. The Worker saw Scott as 'the personification of kindness' but photography eventually replaced his work. He was paid £1 5s. a cartoon but he lived 'from hand to mouth' during his last years, painting portraits and racehorses where he could, selling work to Sydney sporting papers, the Arrow, Referee, Star and Sunday Times and assisted by friends. He had become 'one of the best of the good old sort' and by August 1908, having received no orders for the previous eighteen months, was again bankrupt. On 15 May 1909, aged 74, he died at Randwick of cystitis and was buried in the Anglican section of Waverley cemetery, survived by his wife and by two daughters and a son of his first marriage.

J. Cato, The story of the camera in Australia (Melb, 1955); M. H. Mahood, The loaded line (Melb, 1973); SMH, 1 Sept 1870, 17 May 1909, 21 Aug 1930; ISN, 18 Feb 1871; Worker (Brisb), 27 June 1891, 20 Feb 1892, 12 Mar 1904, 25 Mar 1905, 1 Feb 1908, 9 Jan, 22 May 1909; Arrow (Syd), 17 Jan, 21 Feb 1903, 20 Feb 1904, 24 Jan 1905; Bulletin, 20 May 1909; Worker (Syd), 27 May 1909; Insolvency file 10059 (NSWA).

SUZANNE EDGAR

SCOTT, HENRY JAMES HERBERT (1858-1910), cricketer and physician, was born on 26 December 1858 at Toorak, Melbourne, son of John Scott, company secretary, and his wife Elizabeth, née Miller.

From 1871 he was educated at Wesley College and was already a promising batsman. On leaving school Scott worked in the Bank of Victoria. By 1877 he had joined the St Kilda Cricket Club and in February 1878 played for Victoria against New South Wales in Sydney. He nearly won the match for Victoria when he took 6 wickets for 33 runs in the second innings. In 1879-80 he studied civil engineering at the University of Melbourne and then took up medicine.

In the summer of 1882-83 Scott played for the East Melbourne Cricket Club, scored several centuries and won the club's batting trophy and prize for the best all-rounder. By 1883 he had played in four intercolonial matches and in 1884 visited England as a member of the Australian team. With 102 against England at the Oval he finished the tour third in the batting averages with 973 runs at an average of 22.62. Back in Melbourne he completed the third year of his medical course and played in several intercolonial matches. In 1886 he captained the Australian team in England. The tour was not a great success although Scott compiled 1298 runs at 21.27, and won a match against Yorkshire by hitting three sixes and a four off one over. He remained in England and in 1888 became a licentiate of the Royal College of Physicians, London, and a member of the Royal College of Surgeons, England.

Returning to Australia Scott practised in New South Wales. In July at St Kilda, Melbourne, he married Mary Minnie Mickle. The same year he became government medical officer and vaccinator in Tuena but in March 1889 bought the practice at Scone and became government medical officer, public vaccinator and medical officer at Scone Hospital. He built up an extensive practice among country families who organized relays of horses at appropriate stages and provided escorts for flooded crossings. He often assisted at Muswellbrook Hospital particularly in surgical cases and epidemics. Kindly and generous, he attended his poorer patients without payment.

Scott was a magistrate from the early 1890s and mayor of Scone in 1893-97 and 1899-1900. He was worshipful master of Lodge Scone in 1892, 1898 and 1908. Sometime vice-president of the polo club, he was vice-president of the jockey club (for amateurs only) from 1898, an office-bearer in the Scone Cricket Club and a founder of the Robertson Electorate Cricket Association. He played in local cricket and polo teams and brought a tiller-steered motor buggy to Scone. A member of the Union Club, he visited Sydney for the race carnivals and Test matches. In the 1890s he was active in the administration of the Scone

troop of the Australian Light Horse, in 1898 vice-president of the local Federation League and a committee-man of the Sir John Robertson [q.v.] Memorial and Dreadnought funds.

Survived by his wife, a son and two daughters, Scott died at his home from enteric fever and pneumonia on 23 September 1910 and was buried in the churchyard of St Luke's Presbyterian Church. His estate was sworn for probate at £4817. In 1913 the new Scott Memorial Hospital was named in his honour.

H. S. Altham, *A history of cricket*, 1 (Lond, 1926); A. D. Mickle, *Many a mickle* (Melb, 1953); *A'sian Medical Gazette*, 29 (1910); Scone and Upper Hunter Hist Soc, *J*, 1 (1960), 122, 292; *T&CJ*, 2 Mar 1878; *Cricket; a weekly record*, May 1884; *Scone Advocate*, 27 Sept 1910; *Referee*, 28 Sept 1910; Scone municipal records (Shire Council, Scone); information from Mrs N. Gray, Scone.
BELINDA F. SCOTT

SCOTT, JAMES REID (1839-1877), explorer and politician, was born on 1 April 1839 at Earlston, Berwick, Scotland, elder son of Thomas Scott [q.v.] and his wife Ann, née Reid. Educated in Scotland, he arrived at Launceston with his younger brother in 1856 to live with his uncle James [q.v. Thomas Scott], who taught him surveying. On 26 April 1860 at St David's Cathedral, Hobart Town, he married Elizabeth Sarah Evans. He was made a justice of the peace in 1865 and in 1866-72 was a member of the House of Assembly for Selby.

Scott was a member of the 1869 royal commission on distillation which, despite opposition by the Tasmanian Temperance Alliance, advocated distillation of spirits in Tasmania to encourage the market for local grains. He was chairman of committees in 1871-72 and a member of the select committee inquiring into Port Arthur, which recommended the settlement's closure and accommodation of the prisoners at Hobart and elsewhere. He helped in the downfall of the (Sir) J. M. Wilson [q.v.] ministry in 1872 and was called on to form a new government, but declined. In 1872-77 he represented South Esk in the Legislative Council and held the portfolio of colonial secretary in 1872-73. During his parliamentary career he won repute as an honest, independent politician, courteous and unobtrusive and capable in administration, whose principal concern was the welfare of the colony.

From 1873 Scott gave much time to exploration, made several visits to lesser-known areas of the west and south-west, and prepared a number of papers for the

Royal Society of Tasmania, to which he had been elected a fellow in 1868. In 1876 he reported to the minister for lands and works on 'Exploration in the Western Country', concerned chiefly with opening access tracks in western areas to encourage prospecting and mineral development. His last trip was made in March and April 1877 to the Pieman River and other places, during which he named Mount Tyndall after the scientist, and lakes Dora and Spicer after Hobart friends. He was later described as a good botanist and a hardy and enthusiastic explorer.

Scott died suddenly of congestive apoplexy at Carolside, his New Town home, on 25 August 1877. When he was buried at old St John's Church, New Town, on 29 August all Hobart government offices closed from noon; mourners at his funeral included the premier, colonial secretary and colonial treasurer; 'His Excellency's carriage followed'. His estate was sworn for probate at £8252.

F. C. Green (ed), A century of responsible government 1856-1956 (Hob, 1956); V&P (HA Tas), 1869 (44), 1871 (127), 1876, (104), 1877 (27); Roy Soc (Tas), Papers, 1877; Examiner (Launceston), 23, 25, 27 July 1872, 31 July 1873, 28 Aug, 1 Sept 1877; Mercury, 2 Nov 1872; Correspondence file under J. R. Scott (TA).

NEIL SMITH

SCOTT, WALTER JERVOISE (1835-1890), pastoralist, was the second son of James Winter Scott, M.P., of Rotherfield Park, Alton, Hampshire, England, and his wife Lucy, née Jervoise. Educated at Eton and Oxford (B.A., 1857), he became a student of the Inner Temple and acted as private secretary to a governor of Mauritius, but had returned to England by 1862. In that year his brother Arthur (1833-1895), who had been friendly with R. G. W. Herbert [q.v.] when both were fellows of All Souls, Oxford, was persuaded by Herbert to become a partner in the Valley of Lagoons, a well situated tract of country in the newly opened upper Burdekin district of Queensland. George Dalrymple [q.v.] had interested Herbert in the property but more capital was required.

The Scott brothers and other members of their family invested heavily in the venture. Arthur and Walter Scott arrived in Queensland early in 1863; Arthur went on an unsuccessful expedition with Dalrymple to blaze a trail between the Valley of Lagoons and Rockingham Bay; Walter overlanded some of the first stock from the Darling Downs north to the property. Adapting well to the conditions, Walter became managing partner at the end of 1864, when

Arthur returned to England and Dalrymple went into politics. Except for a short holiday in England in 1888, Walter remained at the Valley of Lagoons for the rest of his life. Together with normal pioneering hazards he had to cope with Arthur's impractical schemes to remain in sheep long after the Burdekin country had been found unsuitable, and to use the property to train aristocratic English jackeroos.

The size of the Scott brothers' investment gave them repute for great wealth, although for years they were heavily in debt; but after the property went over to cattle in 1873 it soon paid its way despite the development of overlanding to markets in New South Wales and Victoria. The port of Cardwell, especially gazetted by Herbert for the firm's use, benefited considerably from Walter's work as shire councillor, justice of the peace, and patron of the local Anglican church and businesses. Aged 55, he died unmarried on the property on 29 June 1890. His brothers sent a granite obelisk to be erected over his grave, but the track pioneered by the Scotts from Cardwell was too rough for the teamsters, and it had to be left at the port; a smaller one was erected at the Valley. When Arthur died in 1895, the rest of the family lost no time in disposing of the Valley of Lagoons.

D. Jones, Cardwell Shire story (Brisb, 1961); J. Farnfield, Frontiersman (Melb, 1968); G. C. Bolton, 'The Valley of Lagoons: a study in exile', Business Archives and History, 4 (1964), no 2; Macarthur papers (ML); Colonel J. Scott papers (ANU Archives); Valley of Lagoons papers (Oxley Lib, Brisb).   G. C. BOLTON

SCOTT, WILLIAM (1825-1917), Church of England clergyman and astronomer, was born on 8 October 1825 at Hartland, Devon, England, fourth son of Thomas Scott. He was brought up at Braunton near Barnstaple, and educated at Blundell's School, Tiverton. In 1844 he went up as a scholar to Sidney Sussex College, Cambridge (B.A., 1848, third wrangler; M.A., 1851). After a college fellowship he was given the Taylor's mathematical lectureship in 1850. Made deacon in 1849, he was ordained priest in 1850 by Bishop Turton of Ely and served a curacy in the Cambridge slum district of Barnwell, but his interest remained in mathematics. On 8 November 1851 he married a widow Elizabeth Anne Yonge, née Roberts, who had three sons by her first husband. Prompted by his family responsibilities he became a mathematics coach, soon built up a good connexion at the university and in 1853 published a small textbook on plane co-ordinate geometry. He tired of coaching and in April 1856 he accepted the position of colonial astronomer in New South Wales.

Scott and his family arrived at Sydney on 31 October; he found that astronomical work had long been neglected but he superintended the erection of the observatory at Dawes Point, secured the appointment of an observatory board and instituted meteorological records throughout the colony. By 1859 he was making systematic observations; in 1861 the acquisition of an equatorial telescope enabled him to enlarge his work; he planned a magnetic survey of the colony and reported that despite the shortage of staff and equipment 'the establishment is now complete in every respect'.

On 31 October 1862 Scott officially resigned as astronomer because of ill health, but he may have become discouraged by the departure of his patron Governor Denison and public criticism of his refusal to produce 'showy results'. Impulsive and sensitive, he found it difficult to adapt to colonial life, but he became headmaster of the Cook's River collegiate school whose proprietor was Rev. W. H. Savigny. In 1865 Scott succeeded Savigny as warden of St Paul's College in the University of Sydney. His wardenship marked a quiet time at the college, with his plans hampered by the slow rate of university expansion, the competition of the new Presbyterian College of St Andrew and the Church's refusal to recognize education at St Paul's as sufficient training for the ministry. He continued as mathematical examiner for the university and twice deputized for the professor of mathematics. In 1867-74 he was honorary secretary of the Royal Society of New South Wales and treasurer in 1874-78. In 1874 he read a paper to the society on 'The transit of Venus as Observed at Eden' which was published in its Proceedings. In the 1870s he preached frequently on the relation of religion to new scientific ideas but his public activities were not matched by any considerable energy at St Paul's. In 1878 criticism by the college council caused him to resign.

Earlier Scott had professed some scepticism about revealed religion and he had criticized the Sydney clergy. He then took eagerly to a country ministry at Gunning, Bungendore and Queanbeyan; he became a canon of St Saviour's Cathedral, Goulburn, and examining chaplain for Bishop Thomas [q.v.]. He revisited England in 1888 and, apart from some teaching engagements, lived in retirement on his return. Scott died at Chatswood, Sydney, on 29 March 1917 and was buried in the Gore Hill cemetery, survived by a son and two daughters. His estate was valued for probate at almost £7500.

G. B. Airy, Autobiography, W. Airy ed (Cambridge, 1896); A. Fisher, The register of Blundell's School, 1 (Exeter, 1904); R. T. Wyatt, The history of the diocese of Goulburn (Syd, 1937); Colonial astronomer papers, V&P (LA NSW), 1856-57, 21, 1858-59, 1, 841, 843, 1859-60, 4, 1047, 1861, 2, 395, 1861-62, 2, 1371, 1865, 1, 915; Roy Soc of NSW, Procs, 51 (1917), 6; K. J. Cable, 'The founding of St Paul's College', Pauline, 1967, no 65; SMH, 31 Mar 1917; Scott letters (copies, ML); Council minutes 1865-78 (St Paul's College, Univ Syd).   K. J. CABLE

SCRATCHLEY, SIR PETER HENRY (1835-1885), military engineer and colonial administrator, was born on 24 August 1835 in Paris, thirteenth child of Dr James Scratchley, Royal Artillery, and his wife Maria, née Roberts. Educated in Paris where his father practised medicine, he became a cadet at the Royal Military Academy, Woolwich, England, under the patronage of his father's school friend Lord Palmerston. He had indifferent health, but with the help of private tutoring he passed out first in his class in February 1854. Commissioned on 21 April, he served in the Crimean war in the 4th Company, Royal Engineers, until 11 June 1856 and won the Crimean and Turkish medals. From July that year to October 1857 he was employed on engineering works at Portsmouth. He then served in the Indian mutiny, was mentioned in dispatches three times and was awarded the Indian war medal with clasp.

Promoted to captain in October 1859, Scratchley was given command of a detachment of engineers to erect in Melbourne defence works which he had designed. Arriving in the Ottawa on 13 June 1860 he reported on 21 September with detailed recommendations for the defence of Melbourne and Geelong. He considered the estimated cost of £81,200 as 'insignificant ... when compared with the revenue, wealth and security of the people of the colony', but lack of funds prevented almost all construction. He served as engineer and military storekeeper and became honorary lieut-colonel of the embryonic Victorian Artillery. He supported a delegation to form a unit of Victorian volunteer engineers and the corps was formed at a meeting on 7 November 1860. To the public regret of Victorian ministers, he returned to England late in 1863.

Scratchley commanded sappers at Portsmouth until October 1864. He had been promoted brevet major in March, then was in turn assistant inspector and inspector of works for the manufacturing department of the War Office. His experience included experiments in disposal of sewage for irrigation, improving the manufacture of hydrogen for balloons and training in assaying coins. He remained interested in Australian defences, claimed to have constantly considered Melbourne's security, and in 1865 wrote a report on South Australia's defence. He became a major on 5 July 1872, brevet lieut-colonel on 20 February 1874, lieut-colonel on 1 October 1877, and brevet colonel on 20 February 1879.

Scratchley returned to Australia on 8 March 1877 in the *Tudor* to join Sir William Jervois [q.v.] in advising the colonies on their defences. After Jervois was appointed governor of South Australia, Scratchley became commissioner of defences in 1878, covering in time all the six colonies and New Zealand. His plans were again thorough and were largely implemented, so that by 1885 he was satisfied that 'the colonies, excepting New Zealand, are fairly well prepared'. His ideas had changed little since 1860 although he was aware of technological improvements. He believed that land defence works should be near key ports, advocated torpedoes for offence and submarine mines for defence, supported the obstruction of shipping channels and argued for a limited number of paid volunteers, sufficient to repel minor invasions. At sea he favoured floating batteries and unarmoured gunboats with heavy guns, and opposed expensive ironclad vessels.

The clearest statements of Scratchley's views appear in the evidence he gave to the 1881 commission on New South Wales defences, of which he was vice-president and chairman of the military sub-committee. He retained his belief that threats to Australia were limited, because of British sea power: volunteer land forces with able officers were needed only 'to meet the contingency of the naval defences not meeting the enemy at sea'. Opposed to excessive copying of the system of training of British regulars, he argued that Australian fighting conditions would be different. Well aware of the difficulties of obtaining support for defence spending, he saw his central problem as the establishment of an effective force 'at the lowest possible cost'.

Scratchley retired from active military service on 1 October 1882 as honorary major-general, but was still employed by the Colonial Office as defence adviser for Australia. In April 1883 he visited England to consult the War Office on a general colonial defence plan and on 22 November 1884 was appointed special commissioner for the new British Protectorate of New Guinea, which was seen as an important shield for Australia. But he had little power and Sir Samuel Griffith argued that Scratchley had 'no legal jurisdiction and

authority of any kind'. With few men and limited funds, he found his short term of office marked by fruitless requests for regular contributions from disgruntled colonies.

Knighted on 6 June 1885, Scratchley reached Port Moresby on 28 August and shaped policies sympathetic to the natives. He believed that they had been maltreated and justified their murders of European adventurers. Convinced that 'New Guinea must be governed for the natives and by the natives', he planned to appoint chiefs representing British authority and tried to protect native land rights. He discouraged private exploration but on his own second official journey to the mountain camp of H. O. Forbes [q.v.], he contracted malaria and died at sea between Cooktown and Townsville on 2 December 1885. His body lay in state at his Melbourne home before being buried in St Kilda cemetery with military honours on 16 December. His remains were reinterred in the Old Charlton cemetery, Woolwich, England, on 30 April 1886.

At St John's Church, Heidelberg, Melbourne, on 13 November 1862 Scratchley had married Laura Lilias, sister of T. A. Browne [q.v.], 'Rolf Boldrewood'. Two daughters and one son survived him, eventually to share his estate sworn for probate at £14,979. Fort Scratchley at Newcastle and Mount Scratchley in the Owen Stanley Range perpetuate his name. Though reserved, Scratchley gained respect from his unusually wide experience and conscientious efforts. Despite his long, waxed military moustache, his achievements and ideas were sometimes unusual for a professional soldier who believed that 'war is a stern necessity'. He resisted the formation of a military caste in Australia, compromised with the popular wish for economy in defence expenditure and gave promise of a humanitarian attitude in New Guinea administration quite out of keeping with his orthodox image.

C. K. Cooke, *Australian defences and New Guinea* (Lond, 1887); V&P (LA Vic), 1860-61, 2 (D9), 3, 2, 1864-65, 4 (45), (HA Tas), 1878 (37), (LA NSW), 1881, 4, 624; G. S. Fort. Report on British New Guinea, V&P (LA Qld), 1886, 2, 939-983; J. E. Price, 'A history of the defences of Port Phillip Bay', *Sabretache*, Mar 1972; *Australasian*, 28 Apr 1877, 5, 12 Dec 1885, 17 July 1886; Governor's and Treasurer's papers (PRO, Vic).   R. B. JOYCE

SEARLE, HENRY ERNEST (1866-1889), sculler, was born on 14 July 1866 at Grafton, New South Wales, son of Henry Samuel

Searle. bootmaker, and his wife Mary Ann, née Brooks. The family later moved to Esk Island, lower Clarence River, where they farmed at subsistence level. Searle soon learnt to scull and rowed his brother and sisters three miles to and from school. At 18 Searle first competed in a skiff race and for three years raced with some success at local regattas. His first important victory was the defeat of a Sydney professional in an out-rigger handicap at Grafton in January 1888.

Moving to Sydney, Searle was coached by an established sculler Neil Matterson, and with the financial backing of John and Thomas Spencer, chemists and sportsmen, he began a strenuous training programme and won four matches between June and October. After failing to get a match with the former world champion Edward Hanlan, Searle challenged the current champion Peter Kemp, and on 27 October on the Parramatta River he easily won the title. Searle, Matterson and other 'cracks', including William Beach [q.v.], next competed in the 'Grand Aquatic Carnival' rowed in Brisbane between 5 and 11 December. In a heat Searle and Matterson continually and deliberately fouled Beach, for which they were disqualified from the heat but not, to the public's annoyance, from the carnival. Consequently they finished first and third in the final after Beach refused to row. In 1889 with his stocks low Searle went with Matterson to England to race the American champion William O'Connor for £1000; Searle won easily and was recognized as the world's greatest sculler.

While returning to Australia in the Austral Searle contracted typhoid fever; he left the ship at Melbourne, and died three weeks later on 10 December 1889 at the Williamstown Sanatorium, after a very public illness. The colonies plunged into mourning with editorials, poems and sermons bewailing the loss of the young hero. Thousands lined Melbourne streets to see his body pass, and in Sydney an estimated crowd of 170,000 packed the city for his memorial service. Approximately 2500 attended in stifling heat to see him buried in the Protestant section of the Maclean cemetery.

Searle was a great sculler; no stylist, he had a powerful action characterized by perfect boat control; he trained much harder than was usual and could break opponents with sudden, repeated and sustained bursts of speed. He was 5 ft. 10 ins. tall, rowed at 11 stone 9 lbs., but weighed 13 stone 3 lbs. when out of training; his measurements were: chest $41\frac{1}{2}$ ins., biceps $13\frac{1}{2}$ ins., forearm 11 ins., thigh 22 ins. and calf 16 ins. He was quiet with a genial and unassuming disposition.

A memorial stands on The Brothers rocks at the finish of the Parramatta River course.

S. C. Bennett, *The Clarence Comet* (Syd, 1973); *T&CJ*, 14 Sept, 14 Dec 1889; H. E. Searle, 'How I won the world's championship', *Leeds Times*, 5 Oct 1889; *Australasian*, 14 Dec 1889; *SMH*, 16, 17 Dec 1889.   SCOTT BENNETT

SELFE, NORMAN (1839-1911), engineer and educationist, was born on 9 December 1839 at Teddington, Middlesex, England, son of Henry Selfe, plumber, and his wife Elizabeth, née Smith. Educated at Kingston-upon-Thames, he arrived in Sydney with his parents in January 1855. At 17 he was apprenticed to P. N. Russell [q.v.] & Co., reputedly becoming chief draftsman before completing his articles; while with the firm he designed gunboats for service in the Maori wars. In 1865-68 Selfe was in partnership with James Dunlop and was responsible for designing and building major installations for the Australasian Mineral Oil Co., the Western Kerosene Oil Co. and the Australian Gaslight Co. In 1869 he became chief engineer and draftsman for Mort's [q.v.] Dock and Engineering Co., designing the machinery for the *Governor Blackall* (500 tons).

Selfe set up in private practice in 1876 and soon became known as a versatile and original engineer. He designed over fifty steamships, including two torpedo boats for the New South Wales government and the first double-ended screw ferry, *Wallaby*; he was reputed to have introduced the compound engine in Australian boats. Expert in dock design, he built the first concrete quay wall in Sydney Harbour and most of the wharves for deep-sea vessels. Skilled in refrigeration engineering, he designed the first ice-making machines in New South Wales; he also introduced the first lifts, patented an improved system of wool-pressing and carried out many other hydraulic and electric light installations in Sydney. He worked and published on compressed air and its application to railway brakes, designed many friction winches and the acetylene gas storage plant for the New South Wales railways, and planned mills, waterworks and pumping stations. He was the leading representative of the generation of 'the all-round engineer'. In 1884-85 Selfe visited seventy cities in North America and Europe, inspecting engineering works and notable bridges. A strong advocate of a 'Circular City Railway' linking Sydney's outlying suburbs to the ferries, in 1903 he largely designed a cantilever harbour bridge from Dawes Point to McMahon's Point; the plans were accepted but not proceeded with owing to a change of government.

In 1870 he had been a founder of the Engineering Association of New South Wales and president in 1877-79. Like his contemporary in Melbourne, W. C. Kernot [q.v.], Selfe had a strong sense of 'natural justice' and his spirited paper, 'Sydney and its institutions, as they are, and might be', published in the *Proceedings* of the Engineering Association in 1900, gives a clear picture of his forthright personality and his professional and social interests. An active member of the Sydney Mechanics' School of Arts and of the Royal Society of New South Wales, in 1901 he was founding vice-president of the Australian Historical Society, president in 1902 and a committee-man until 1911. He was also a prominent Anglican and a Freemason.

As early as 1865 Selfe had been teaching mechanical drawing at the School of Arts and in 1883 became a member of the Board of Technical Education. He was acting president for much of 1887-89 when the board confronted the minister of public instruction, James Inglis [q.v.], and his departmental officers. Selfe wanted an independent system of technical education, with the task of building a trained workforce. The board was abolished in 1889 and Selfe lost a contest in which he had probably gone, tactically at least, too far in expressing his contempt for the civil service and for traditional educational values, but he did see the concept of workshop training introduced into Australia.

Selfe died of heart failure at Normanhurst, the suburb named after him, on 15 October 1911 and was buried in the Gore Hill cemetery. He was survived by two daughters of his first wife Emily Anne, née Booth, whom he had married in Sydney on 10 October 1872, and by his second wife Barbara Marion, née Bolton (B.A., Sydney), whom he had married on 12 May 1906. His estate was sworn for probate at almost £5000.

L. A. Mandelson, 'Norman Selfe and the beginnings of technical education', *Pioneers of Australian education*, C. Turney ed, 2 (Syd, 1972); A. Pugh, 'One hundred years ago...' Inst of Engineers (Aust), J, July-Aug 1970; *SMH*, 16 Oct 1911; MS and printed cats under Selfe (ML).   S. MURRAY-SMITH

SELLHEIM, PHILIP FREDERIC (1832-1899), pastoralist and mining official, was born on 28 September 1832 at Konradsdorf, Hesse-Darmstadt, Germany, son of Heinrich Sellheim and his wife Marian Emma Sophia, née Schaefer. His family had been small farmers and artisans in Hesse since the tenth century. Educated by tutors and at the

Polytechnic Academy of Darmstadt, he matriculated at Giessen and Berlin, then studied sheep-breeding at the Royal Veterinary Academy of Berlin and the Agricultural Academy at Proskau in Upper Silesia.

Emigrating to Queensland in 1855, Sellheim managed Banana station on the Dawson River for four years before joining George Dalrymple's [q.v.] 1859 expedition to North Queensland. In January 1861 he and C. W. Toussaint took up Strathmore, the first pastoral lease in the Kennedy district, on which Sellheim ran sheep for five years. He was naturalized at Bowen on 19 August 1862 and on 6 June 1865, at Sydney, he married Laura Theresa Morrisset, sister of an ex-police officer settled near by; she died in 1878 leaving a daughter and two sons, the eldest of whom became a major-general.

Rachael Henning [q.v.] described Sellheim as 'rather a gentlemanly German ... [who] says "apenhalt" before every word he utters. "Do you grow any apen-apen-apenhalt apenhalt pumpkins in your garden, Miss Henning?" ' Though popular, he fared no better than most sheep-owners. In 1865 his shearers struck when he reduced wages from 5s. to 4s. a score because of hard times. The men lost when he was supported by other squatters. He and his partner William Stuart were finally forced off the run in 1866 by the difficulties of pioneering a remote region infested with spear grass, and in 1867-70 he managed Valley of Lagoons station for W. J. Scott [q.v.].

Sellheim was appointed to the Queensland public service on 22 July 1874; in October he became warden in charge of the new, remote and turbulent Palmer goldfield, which attracted at its height about 15,000 European diggers and 20,000 Chinese, with much racial and social tension. He spent much time hunting Chinese who evaded buying miners' rights; but with three assistants and a handful of police he maintained law and order. 'I suppose you think you are God Almighty' one recalcitrant miner told him. 'No, I am not that', replied Sellheim, 'but I am his first mate in these parts'.

His success on the Palmer earned him promotion to Charters Towers in June 1880, and Gympie in January 1888. These appointments coincided with the rise of the earliest trade unions, and Sellheim arbitrated successfully between employers and employees. In April 1892 he became under-secretary for mines, serving under W. O. Hodgkinson [q.v.] and Robert Philp. Both as warden and under-secretary Sellheim continually advocated more orderly and systematic development of Queensland's mining resources and abandonment of the wasteful and cut-throat practices which were all too common. In 1890 he persuaded the Gympie mine-owners to form a co-operative for the drainage of mines, the first example in Queensland of any co-ordination among managements for the common good.

Sellheim's great achievement was the 1898 Mining Act, framed from the findings of a royal commission of 1897. Besides reforming safety conditions, it improved the security of mining tenures and safeguarded the rights of both the big investor and the miner. Sellheim remained under-secretary until his death at New Farm, Brisbane, on 12 October 1899. In later life a heavily built man with an immense pair of moustaches, his deliberate manner was supplemented by his great sagacity and insight into the mining industry, and he was one of Queensland's most honest and effective civil servants in the nineteenth century.

Alcazar Press, *Queensland, 1900* (Brisb, nd); G. C. Bolton, *A thousand miles away* (Brisb, 1963); V&P (LA Qld), 1897, 4, 453-67; *Brisbane Courier*, 13 Oct 1899.   G. C. BOLTON

SELWYN, ALFRED RICHARD CECIL (1824-1902), geologist, was born on 28 July 1824 at Kilmington, Somerset, England, son of Rev. Townshend Selwyn, canon of Gloucester Cathedral, and his wife Charlotte Sophia, daughter of Lord George Murray, bishop of St David's, Wales. Educated at home by private tutors and later in Switzerland, he became interested in geology by collecting fossils as a hobby. On 1 April 1845 he joined the Geological Survey of Great Britain as assistant geologist and was promoted to geologist on 1 January 1848. He worked mainly in Shropshire and North Wales on the mapping of the Palaeozoic rocks, but was also on the British coalfields. Early in 1852 he married his cousin Matilda Charlotte Selwyn, and had to seek a higher income. His brother Arthur [q.v.] was in Queensland and in September 1851 had indicated prospects in Australia. Next year the Victorian government appealed to the Colonial Office for a 'Mineral Surveyor', and Selwyn was appointed geological surveyor (later director of the Geological Survey). He arrived in Melbourne in the *Sydney* in November.

Selwyn's salary was increased by Lieut-Governor La Trobe from £500 to £800, and soon to £900; he at first worked with only 'one assistant, one tent-keeper and a horse-keeper' and mapped more than 1000 square miles each year, though he had to spend much time in supervision and training of successive staff. In 1856 he discovered near Bendigo the first graptolites found in Australia. This important group of fossils was later used for zoning much of the Lower Palaeozoic sequence. In 1853-69 the Geological Survey issued under Selwyn's direction sixty-one geological maps and numerous reports; they were of such high standard that a writer in the *Quarterly Journal* of the Geological Society of London bracketed the survey with that of the United States of America as the best in the world. Apart from annual reports, he prepared an essay on the geology of Victoria, and expanded it in 1861 for the *Catalogue of the Victorian Exhibition*; in 1865 he put out a geological map of Victoria in eight sheets. With G. H. F. Ulrich [q.v.] in 1866 he published *Intercolonial Exhibition Essays ... Notes on the Physical Geography, Geology and Mineralogy of Victoria* for the Paris exhibition; it was translated into French.

In 1855 Selwyn had surveyed the coal measures of Tasmania, and in 1859 the eastern part of South Australia including the Flinders Range. In the Inman Valley region south of Adelaide he recognized evidence for glaciation at a site now known (and preserved) as Selwyn's Rock; later he supported this important observation by similar work in the Bacchus Marsh region of Victoria. His other duties included appointments to the Mining Commission (1856), the Board of Science (1858) and the Board of Agriculture (1859); he was a commissioner for the Victorian Exhibition (1861) and the London International Exhibition (1862) and was on the management committee of the Zoological Gardens from 1858.

In 1869, pleading lack of funds, the government abruptly terminated the Geological Survey against a background of disagreement with Selwyn about its functions, apparently instigated by R. B. Smyth [q.v.], secretary for mines. He left Melbourne for England in March, visiting Sydney on the way. Before he left he announced that he had been offered the post of director of the Geological Survey of Canada. He arrived in Canada in October, took office in December and continued a distinguished career until his retirement on 1 January 1894. After moving to Vancouver, British Columbia, in 1896 he carried out consulting work in mining geology. He retained an interest in Australian geology and corresponded with various friends, notably A. C. Macdonald, F. von Mueller and J. C. Newbery [qq.v.]. He died in Vancouver on 18 October 1902 and was buried in the Mountain View cemetery, predeceased by his wife in 1882 and by four of his nine children.

Many honours were accorded Selwyn: he became a fellow of the Royal Geographical Society in 1871 and of the Royal Society in 1874, was created C.M.G. in 1886 and was a foreign member of scientific societies in fourteen countries. He was Murchison Medallist of the Geological Society in 1876. In Melbourne he was on the councils of the Philosophical Society in 1855, and the Philosophical Institute to 1857; he was also a councillor of the Acclimatisation Society. His contributions to Australian geology were recognized in 1884 by the award of the (W. B.) Clarke [q.v.] Medal by the Royal Society of New South Wales. He was not universally liked, though he was held in respect and affection by his colleagues. Quicktempered and somewhat autocratic, he made enemies in the government and especially in mining circles, in both Australia and Canada, by his unswerving and often tactlessly outspoken devotion to accuracy and scientific truth. He was a hard taskmaster, with boundless energy that he expected his assistants to emulate; but outside his work he was an amiable companion of his younger colleagues, and he had many long-standing and firm friendships.

Selwyn's undoubted dominance in Australian geology owes something to the scientific climate of the 1850s, which was one of transition from the amateur to the professional, from occasional to systematic; but this situation does not denigrate his achievement, for he had the necessary stature to implement change. He brought a rigour to the study of geology that it never could have gained from, say, the work of Clarke. It is arguable that Selwyn's greatest achievement lay not in his own work but in his legacy to Australia of a generation of geologists imbued with his ideals. Within a few years the disbanded Victorian survey was making its influence felt over the whole of Australia: Richard Daintree [q.v.] and C. D. Aplin became government geologists of Queensland; C. S. Wilkinson [q.v.] and R. F. Pitman of New South Wales; H. Y. L. Brown of South Australia and later of Western Australia; while R. A. F. Murray [q.v.] and E. J. Dunn remained in Victoria and built up the resuscitated survey after 1872. R. Etheridge junior, in the Geological Survey of New South Wales, developed into Australia's greatest palaeontologist, and G. H. F. Ulrich founded the Otago School of Mines, New Zealand.

H. Woodward, 'Eminent living geologists', *Geological Mag*, 6 (1899); H. M. Ami, 'Memorial or sketch of the life of the late Dr. A. R. C. Selwyn', Roy Soc (Canada), *Trans*, 10 (1904); E. J. Dunn and D. J. Mahony, 'Bio-

graphical sketch of the founders of the Geological Survey of Victoria', Vic Geological Survey, *Bulletin*, 23 (1910); F. J. Alcock, 'A century in the history of the Geological Survey of Canada', *Canadian Mining J*, 68 (1947) no 6; Selwyn family papers (held at King's Ferry, Quebec, Canada).

D. F. BRANAGAN
K. A. TOWNLEY

SELWYN, ARTHUR EDWARD (1823-1899), Church of England clergyman, was born on 7 March 1823 at Kilmington rectory, Somerset, England, son of Rev. Townshend Selwyn, canon of Gloucester Cathedral, and his wife Charlotte Sophia, daughter of Lord George Murray, bishop of St David's, Wales. He was a cousin of Bishop G. A. Selwyn and brother of A. R. C. Selwyn [q.v.]. Educated at Winchester College, he arrived in Sydney in 1841 and in 1846 accompanied W. C. Mayne [q.v.] to the Liverpool Plains. When gazetted a magistrate in 1848 his address was Bucklebone, Namoi River.

Late in 1850 Bishop Tyrrell [q.v.] of Newcastle persuaded Selwyn to prepare for the ministry and in May 1851 he began training at Moreton Bay. He described the primitive conditions and onerous reading course prescribed by the bishop and complained bitterly of four months teaching at Tamworth to his fiancée Rose Elizabeth, sister of G. W. and H. K. Rusden [qq.v.], whom he married at Tamworth on 30 June 1852. In December next year he was ordained priest. In 1854-67 Selwyn was in charge of the large parish of Grafton; in July 1867 he was appointed to Christ Church, Newcastle, and was made a canon of the cathedral in 1871. Selwyn was a loyal supporter of Tyrrell's policies and worked for the development of a synodical and a more powerful provincial system of Church government. Involved in Church finances, education and many lay issues, Selwyn contributed to the press on such subjects as the liquor traffic and synodical authority; he also suggested Cambria as a new name for New South Wales. He strenuously opposed Sir Alfred Stephen's [q.v.] divorce extension bills in 1886-92, and published papers that he had read to the Newcastle Clerical Society and to church congresses. In June 1887 he showed an early ecumenical spirit when he argued that the start of any mission in New Guinea should be in the name of all Christians rather than of divided denominations.

Commissary and vicar-general in 1887-89 while Bishop Pearson [q.v.] was incapacitated in England, Selwyn coped with serious financial problems and administered the diocese quietly and confidently. He wanted promotions for clergy used to Australian conditions rather than inexperienced Englishmen and sought the election of James Chalmers [q.v.] as bishop of Goulburn and G. H. Stanton [q.v.] to Newcastle. Selwyn's appointment as dean by Bishop Stanton marked the start of fresh policy for the diocese. He was involved in disputes with J. H. Hunt and F. B. Menkens [qq.v.] over designs for the cathedral, and also in the chronic debate over the relation between cathedral and parish. He was again administrator of the diocese in 1897-98.

Selwyn died childless on 27 June 1899 of cerebral haemorrhage and was buried in the Anglican cemetery, Sandgate; his estate was valued for probate at £757. His widow published the *Letters of the late Dean Selwyn, of Newcastle, chiefly to his wife* (Sydney, 1902).

A. P. Elkin, *The diocese of Newcastle* (Syd, 1955); B. R. Davis, The Church of England in New South Wales: the beginnings and development of training men for its ministry ... 1825-1925 (M.A. thesis, Univ Newcastle, 1967); Selwyn papers (ML).   REX DAVIS

SEPPELT, JOSEPH ERNEST (1813-1868), winemaker, was born in 1813 at Wüstewaltersdorf, Lower Silesia. His father fought in Napoleon's forces in Russia, and took eleven years to find his way home after the fall of Moscow. After a liberal education in music and the arts Joseph toured Germany and Italy learning the commercial and technical aspects of tobacco, snuff and liqueur production in order to head the family business; when it declined in the 1840s he decided to migrate to South Australia. He sailed from Hamburg in the *Emmy* on 9 September 1849 with his wife Johanna Charlotte, née Held, and their three children. Through a London agent, he had bought land in Adelaide but soon sold it when he found tobacco would not grow there; he moved to Klemzig. Naturalized in 1851, next year he bought property in the Barossa district and named it Seppeltsfield. After another attempt to grow tobacco he planted corn, wheat and a small vineyard. He made his first wine in his wife's small dairy and in 1867 built the first part of the stone winery. The business expanded rapidly as he concentrated on the production of wine, much of which he sold along the Murray where it was transported by paddle-steamer. Survived by his wife, a daughter and three sons, he died suddenly of delirium tremens on 29 January 1868 and was buried at Greenock. His estate was sworn for probate at £1000.

His eldest son OSCAR BENNO PEDRO was born in 1845 in Lower Silesia. Educated at Tanunda, he later attended chemistry classes run by C. W. L. Muecke [q.v.]. When his father died he became manager of Seppeltsfield and on 23 November 1870 he married Sophie Schroeder. By 1875 he had an estate of 560 acres and had enlarged the cellars; in 1877 he built a new distillery largely of his own design. He had a flair for invention and his wine-testing laboratory was considered unusual if not unique in his day. He kept pigs, which were fed on grapeskins, and cured bacon which fetched good prices. He also bred sheep which grazed in the vineyards in the autumn and in 1883 won a silver cup for a champion merino ram. In his evidence to a select committee on vegetable products in 1887 he wanted a government-guaranteed company which would buy up young wines, mature them and export only good quality products ensuring the continuation of their high repute on the London market.

That year Seppelt grew only about one third of his 200,000 gallon output, the remainder being bought from surrounding vineyards. He won the fifty-guinea prize offered by the London merchant P. B. Burgoyne at the Adelaide Jubilee Exhibition for the best claret-type wine and received a contract for 2500 gallons. By 1900 the estate extended to 1500 acres and had subsidiary industries including vinegar, cordial, liqueur and perfume production. In 1916 he bought Chateau Tanunda and in 1918 took over the Lyndoch and the Great Western vineyards near Ararat, Victoria.

Seppelt retired in 1916 and died of broncho-pneumonia on 11 May 1931 survived by nine sons and four daughters.

J. J. Pascoe (ed), *History of Adelaide and vicinity* (Adel, 1901); M. R. A. Lamshed, *The house of Seppelt 1851-1951* (Adel, 1951); PP (SA), 1887, 3 (90) 25, 1889, 2 (25) 141; *Register* (Adel), 1 Feb 1868; *Chronicle* (Adel), 14 May 1931.   JAKI ILBERY

SERISIER, JEAN EMILE (1824-1881), storekeeper and vigneron, was born at Bordeaux, France, youngest son of Emile Alexander Serisier, shipping broker, and his wife Rose Marie, née Mavon. In 1838 as a midshipman he arrived in Sydney where on account of ill health he was placed in the care of Mr Despointes, a wealthy merchant. In 1847, backed by Despointes and accompanied by Nicholas Hyeronimus, an innkeeper from the Wellington Valley, Serisier went into the central west to set up a store on R. V. Dulhunty's [q.v.] Dubbo station. Refused permission, they travelled further west and settled on the site of the future town of Dubbo where Hyeronimus established an inn and Serisier opened a general store. After he petitioned for a site for a village, land held by George Smith was selected and surveyed. Serisier bought town blocks at the first auctions in 1851. He managed a general store for Despointes who kept close control even when he visited France in 1855, though it was thriving under Serisier.

By 1855 he was also acting as local postmaster, dealt in stock and later took out an auctioneer's licence. He found that many of his customers expected extended credit so that his activities were restricted by insufficient liquid assets. In 1873 Serisier sold the store, which he then owned, and developed a vineyard on his 4000-acre property, Emulga. He planted forty acres with vines and, after initial set-backs, within the next year produced much red wine that soon began to attract the attention of connoisseurs. His vineyard was favourably compared with that of J. T. Fallon [q.v.] at Albury.

From 1859 Serisier was returning officer for the Bogan electorate and was one of three guarantors for the extension of the telegraph to Dubbo. A magistrate from 1862, he was prominent in local affairs and for a time was visiting justice to the gaol and guardian of minors. In 1872 he was defeated for the Bogan and in 1876 failed to gain nomination. He represented the Dubbo Free Selectors' Association at the first and second Free Selectors' conferences.

On 1 March 1858 Serisier, aged 33, had married Margaret (1840-1914), youngest daughter of Thomas Humphreys of Greenwich, England, in a ceremony performed first in St Mary's Cathedral, Sydney, and repeated in St Peter's Anglican Church, Cook's River. On 10 February 1881, on a visit to France, Serisier died leaving goods valued for probate at £2370. Four sons survived him.

Country Promotion League, Dubbo: the hub of the west (Syd, 1921); B. Dulhunty, The Dulhunty papers (Syd, 1959); V&P (LA NSW), 1883-84, 11, 159; SMH, 26 Nov 1849, 2 Mar 1858; ISN, 16 Mar 1865; T&CJ, 23 Mar 1872, 8 Aug 1874.   D. I. McDonald

SERRA, JOSEPH BENEDICT (1810-1886), Catholic bishop, was born on 11 May 1810 at Mataró, Spain, youngest son of Joseph Serra Fuster, merchant, and his wife Teresa Julia. Orphaned at 11, he was educated at Barcelona and at 16 became a Benedictine monk in the monastery of St Martin of Compostela, taking the name of Benedict. Completing his education at the Benedictine colleges. Irache in Navarre, and St Vincent in Oviedo, Spain, he was ordained priest in May 1835. A few months later, when the first Spanish Republic declared religious life in common illegal, Serra left Spain and entered the abbey of La Cava near Naples. In 1844 with R. Salvado [q.v.] he offered himself for work in foreign missions. Both were accepted and were intended originally for New South Wales, but were later appointed to Bishop Brady's [q.v.] missionary party bound for Western Australia where they arrived in the Elizabeth on 8 January 1846.

After initial difficulties Serra, as superior of a community of four Benedictine monks, began missionary work among the nomadic Aboriginals of Victoria Plains where the foundation stone of the monastery of New Norcia was laid on 1 March 1847. Next year, after the first diocesan synod, he left for Europe to raise funds and recruits for the mission. In Rome he was consecrated first bishop of Port Victoria but representations from Brady changed his appointment to coadjutor of Perth. With ample funds from Italy, mainly from his many influential friends in Spain, he returned in December 1849 with forty religious and artisans for New Norcia. Sharp differences arose with Brady, who refused to accept him as coadjuter of Perth and tried to obtain control of his funds. The conflict was only resolved by legal action and the disciplinary visit of Archbishop Polding [q.v.] in 1852.

During his administration of Perth diocese in 1850-62 Serra enlarged the existing church and collected money for the erection of a new one; he also built churches in Fremantle, Guildford, Toodyay, York, Dardanup, Albany and Bunbury. He built a magnificent residence for the bishop and his priests in Perth, and provided schools and teachers for Perth and Fremantle. He also showed great interest in the welfare of prisoners at Rottnest Island and newly arrived convicts. His impetuous zeal in these and other controversial issues did not increase his popularity among many local residents.

In 1853-55 Serra visited Europe for his health and returned with more missionaries and four sisters of the French community of St Joseph. In the mid-1850s he took a firm stand against Governor Kennedy on the question of education and the rights of independent schools. He left it to Salvado to smooth the difficulties created but Serra's individualistic character and attitude caused dissension between them. Salvado resented his disregard for their common foundation of New Norcia and his concentration of attention and missionaries on the monastery he had founded at Subiaco, three miles from Perth. Salvado was dedicated to the Aboriginals at New Norcia, but Serra stressed the immediate and future needs of the diocese of Perth, of which he was now the undisputed administrator.

The monastery of New Norcia was given autonomy on 1 April 1859. Serra returned to Europe expecting that the decision would be reversed; he wanted to carry out his ambitions for Subiaco and to build a new cathedral for Perth, for which he sent a Carrara marble altar. As no change was made by 1862, he resigned from 'all the titles which bound me to the Church of Perth'. He returned via England to Spain, where he founded the Oblates of the Most Holy Redeemer, a community of nuns devoted to the care of lapsed and destitute girls and based on female social work he had observed in London; it spread rapidly through South America as well as Spain and in recent years has extended its work to Boston and New York in the United States of America.

Serra died on 8 September 1886 in a rest home in Guadalajara, Spain, and was buried at the mother house of his foundation at Ciempozuelos, Madrid. The suburb of Subiaco in Perth takes its name from his monastery.

P. F. Moran, *History of the Catholic Church in Australia* (Syd, 1895); J. T. Reilly, *Reminiscences of fifty years' residence in Western Australia* (Perth, 1903); H. N. Birt, *Benedictine pioneers in Australia*, 2 (Lond. 1911); *Centenary of the Catholic Church in Western Australia* (Perth, 1946); Serra letters and papers (New Norcia Archives and Roman Catholic Archdiocesan Archives, Perth).

E. PEREZ

SERVICE, JAMES (1823-1899), businessman and politician, was born on 27 November 1823 at Kilwinning, Ayrshire, Scotland, son of Robert Service (1799-1883), sewing agent, and his wife Agnes, née Niven. About 1838 Robert moved from Kilwinning to near-by Saltcoats and then to Glasgow; he was converted from Presbyterianism to the Churches of Christ via the Baptists, and became a rash and zealous preacher on the Glasgow Green. James was educated at Kilwinning and at Glasgow College, and was intended for the kirk. He was about to enrol at the University of Glasgow when his father was converted but, emulating his piety and devotedness, he became a schoolmaster after a brief period in a Glasgow office. James was reared on the Charter: his father was a staunch 'moral forcer' and supporter of Joseph Sturge, and his uncle William Service was a 'veteran reformer'. James opened his own

small school at Saltcoats but about 1845 he contracted tuberculosis, had to rest for twelve months and abandoned teaching. In 1846 he joined the tea and coffee business of Thomas Corbett & Co. in Glasgow, and became a partner in the early 1850s.

Possibly largely for his health, Service migrated to Victoria in 1853 in the *Abdallah*, as a representative of Corbett & Co.; he brought a 'marvellously assorted' range of goods well suited to inflated demand. His parents soon followed him, and for thirty years his father was active in the temperance movement and in radical politics; a leader of the Churches of Christ, he edited their weekly *Melbourne Medley*, preached every Sunday on the wharves and was a founder of the Sunday Free Discussion Society about 1870. James began as a general importer and indentor in Bourke Street; in 1854 his former pupil James Ormond joined him and about 1860 they moved into distribution and developed a large country business. R. J. Alcock in 1886 became the third partner in James Service & Co., which specialized in Robur tea and became agents for companies such as Bryant and May, the German Australian Steamship Co. and the Standard Oil Co. of New York. Located from 1872 on a corner of Collins and William streets, the firm rebuilt after being burned out in 1892; by this time it had opened a London branch. In the 1870s Service was also linked with another former pupil A. Currie [q.v.] in his steamship line trading with India and the East.

Service had spent his first weeks in the colony in 'Canvas Town'; he gained experience in the local politics of near-by Emerald Hill, becoming the most prominent leader in the campaign for emancipation from the Melbourne Town Council. Emerald Hill was the first to break away and he was chairman of the 'model municipality' for its first two years and of the local bench of magistrates. In 1855 the locals refused to pay Melbourne rates any longer and the Melbourne Council sent the bailiffs to remove Service's furniture; in his absence John Nimmo [q.v.] rallied a crowd with a fire-bell to repulse them. When the Hobson's Bay Railway Co. planned to by-pass Emerald Hill on its line to St Kilda, Service brought the company to terms by using regulations to place obstructions in the way and threatening to have anyone arrested who removed them. He was remembered twenty-five years later as the great local hero when he received a reception on the laying of the foundations of the new South Melbourne municipal building. In 1856 he was chairman of (Sir) Andrew Clarke's [q.v.] committee of electors, and was well known as a red-hot Chartist radical who, for example, had led the cheers for J. D. Lang [q.v.] when he spoke in Melbourne in January 1855 on the land question. In March 1857 he was elected to the Legislative Assembly for Melbourne and next month seconded the motion that defeated the first O'Shanassy [q.v.] ministry. He was prominent as an anti-Catholic in the Constitutional Association opposing the second O'Shanassy ministry, lost the contest for Emerald Hill in 1859, but was then elected for Ripon and Hampden. He had succeeded William Westgarth [q.v.] as the spokesman for advanced liberal mercantile thought, and joined William Nicholson's [q.v.] ministry in October, as president of the Board of Land and Works.

The land bill which Service introduced in January 1860 largely met the demands of the Land Convention. Its main features were sale of 80- to 320-acre blocks, after immediate survey of four million acres, at £1 an acre with deferred payments of up to three-quarters of the amount and severe penalties for non-improvement. Auction was to be retained only for town lots and country land of special value; some selection before survey was envisaged. He was sincere in his desire to wipe out the 'social evil' of land monopoly; in the meantime the squatters were to be helped to buy more of their runs as a last chance. The bill passed the assembly without difficulty, but when returned from the council it had 250 amendments. The assembly stood firm on the vital points but the council refused to budge.

Service was 'miserably disappointed': the council's behaviour had produced a 'monster grievance'. He now carried a motion that the bill be returned intact to the council, and threatened the squatters with an obscure Order in Council of 1850 by which governments could state the conditions of tenants on leaseholds. With council adamant, Service and J. G. Francis [q.v.] resigned from the ministry on 3 August knowing that their colleagues were prepared to submit. Nicholson then resigned and Duffy and Heales [qq.v.] almost succeeded in forming a ministry which Service refused to join. Nicholson returned to office, the left overplayed its hand by storming parliament on 28 August, with the result that the Nicholson Act was passed in a travesty of its original form and proved almost useless. Service had allied himself with the conventionists on the land question in an attempt to make Nicholson fight the issue out. 'Had they secured a single principle for all the fighting and blood and dirt through which they had been dragged?', he asked. He refused the lands portfolio in the Heales ministry of 1860-61,

probably because of its protectionist leanings. He also rejected a place in the O'Shanassy ministry in 1861 and fought to radicalize the Duffy Act of 1862; O'Shanassy several times urged him to join the Opposition. Service lost by only one vote an amendment to limit pastoral tenure to three years.

He proved to be an advanced liberal in several other fields. In 1858 he carried provision in the estimates for state aid to the Jewish religion. In 1862 he worked closely with Heales and Higinbotham [q.v.] in forcing through the Common Schools Act against the O'Shanassy government. With the support of the Chamber of Commerce, in the same year he carried the Torrens [q.v.] reform of land transfer as a private bill against the government and the lawyers. In 1859 he was chairman of a select committee which examined the possibility of a harbour trust for the port of Melbourne.

In August 1862 Service took the first of three breaks from politics caused by health worries. For more than two years he enjoyed himself, spending most of his time on the Continent, especially in Italy. On his return he was at odds with most of his former radical associates, deploring the McCulloch [q.v.]-Higinbotham government's protectionism and its coercion of the Legislative Council. As a fighting free trader he lost West Ballarat in 1865, Collingwood in 1868 and West Melbourne in 1871; he was active in the Constitutional Association in the late 1860s. A founder of the Commercial Bank of Australia in 1866, he was chairman of directors in 1871-81. Prominent in the foundation of the Alfred Hospital in 1868-70 he long remained a very active chairman of its board; in 1876 he had a prolonged public argument with 'The Vagabond' [q.v. J. S. James], who respected his management but considered he was far too active.

Service was returned for Maldon at the election of 1874 and in August became treasurer in G. B. Kerferd's [q.v.] ministry. He was now wealthy, more deliberate and less aggressive, but the Age still approved of him as a reformer of the most advanced type despite his free-trade views. He had to prepare a budget in three weeks and accepted protection by eliminating only a few useless duties and reducing others which only hampered trade. Denounced as a traitor, turncoat, renegade or rat, Service deplored the 'egregious folly and blundering tactics of ultramontanists of the free-trade party'. In his 1875 budget he made a far too ambitious attempt to resolve the taxation question and systematize the tariff. Some form of direct taxation was overdue and he proposed progressive land and house taxes, bank-note and stamp taxes, and increased duties on alcohol and tobacco. But many imposts on necessaries were to be abolished, and some reduced on the ground that the relevant industries were no longer 'infants'. An unholy alliance of the McCulloch faction, the liquor interest (which deplored such treachery by one who dealt in wine and spirits), and extreme protectionists and extreme free traders combined against the government. The *Age* turned and denounced him and his taxation proposals were blasphemous in the eyes of the *Argus* and pure free traders. When the government's majority was reduced to one, Kerferd was refused a dissolution by the acting governor, Sir William Stawell [q.v.]. Kerferd resigned: it is likely that Service, said to be dominant in the ministry, had most to do with the unnecessary decision.

After a brief interlude while (Sir) Graham Berry [q.v.] was premier, Service was disgusted when Kerferd and most of his former colleagues joined McCulloch in a new ministry. On 25 November 1875 he scored possibly the greatest of his few oratorical triumphs, described as a crucifixion, when in a four-hour speech he pilloried McCulloch as a man who had wrecked two ministries and wasted four months, as a 'mere pirate' with no convictions and a 'slovenly financier'. 'Is there not one voice in the Assembly to say that Sir James McCulloch was justified?', he repeatedly asked, and was met with silence. Throughout 1876 he deplored Berry's 'stonewalling' tactics and the government's 'gagging', tried to conciliate the parties and 'voted as his conscience dictated' in alliance with J. J. Casey and Angus Mackay [qq.v.]. It appeared possible that he and Higinbotham might combine and sweep all before them. but the great tribune was disillusioned and retired from politics. In 1876 Service in a private bill amended the law relating to bills of sale and fraudulent preferences to creditors, and chaired a board of inquiry into charges against R. Brough Smyth [q.v.].

In the 1877 election campaign, Service broadly supported Berry by proposing a land tax on properties of more than 300 acres. Berry delayed formation of his cabinet hoping that Service would become treasurer, but he preferred to be a friendly neutral opposing Berry only on protection and payment of members. 'Black Wednesday', which Service christened, the dismissal of the judges, magistrates and civil servants gazetted on 8 January 1878, was the parting of the ways which also marked the rebirth of the Constitutionalist party.

On 31 January, Service dissociated himself from the government, deploring its inflaming of passions and setting of class against class. When McCulloch retired from the triangular struggle for power with Service and Berry, and Francis withdrew as his health declined, Service emerged as undisputed leader of the numerically insignificant Opposition. He astutely ridiculed the excesses of Berry's lieutenants, and whittled away Berry's supporters without pandering to the Catholic vote. He soon antagonized the governor, Sir George Bowen, who reinforced his support of Berry by gossip about Service's private life. In the conflicts between the council and Berry's government over proposals for council reform, he steadily won support from the waverers for moderate compromises. Eventually, through his condemnation of Berry's proposal for an Upper House of nominees as 'a Council of crawlers', he defeated the reform bill in 1879 and the assembly was dissolved.

Service won the election of February 1880 with a nominal majority of twelve, but his six months premiership was almost unproductive. He proposed a reform bill which provided for a wider council franchise, a double dissolution if the council twice rejected a bill passed by the assembly in two consecutive sessions and then a joint sitting of the Houses. When the bill was rejected in the assembly by two votes Service was granted a dissolution, in full confidence that he would win an election; but he was defeated on 14 July largely by the Catholics who, for the first time, were organized *en bloc*, and by unscrupulous use of a garbled newspaper report that he had said that a working man could live on 5s. a day. He and (Sir) Henry Wrixon [q.v.] refused to join Berry. Service was now in bad health and resigned his seat early in 1881 in order to go overseas.

Service was consistent throughout his political career. Part of the explanation of his success in the 1870s and 1880s is that he was a free trader who did not go conservative. From at least the mid-1870s he knew the fiscal issue to be overrated; his 1889 remark that free trade produced greater wealth but protection ensured fairer distribution was like a breeze of fresh air over the swamp of political rhetoric. He was a classic, old-world advanced liberal and almost the perfect colonial liberal (protection aside). He was strongly anti-Catholic, though not a sectarian bigot; he recognized the papal encyclicals for what they were, basic attacks on liberalism. In 1871 he argued vehemently as a secularist for the separation of church and state: 'place our state education on a purely secular basis, and let the words Protestant and Catholic

be heard no more as watchwords of strife
and dissension in our political assemblies.
Let our motto be, Equal rights to all, Special
privileges to none'. He defended the Education Act against the Catholics but under-
estimated their sense of outrage; his remark
that their agitation was not a question of
conscience but a question only of cash was
long held against him. He would not submit to the Bible in Schools League, but re-
laxed the Education Act in 1883 by allowing teachers to stay after school to keep
order during voluntary religious instruction
by outsiders.

Service's taxation views reflected his
marked egalitarian tendencies. He believed
that every man should start fair and have
reasonable equality of opportunity; he deplored attempts to perpetuate social in-
equality, and sincerely asserted that 'a working man is as good as any man possessing
rank and riches'. He believed that the state's
powers should have limits: the first thing
was 'to remove from the path of honest men
all obstacles that impede their progress, and
let each one do the best he can for himself';
the state should aid the working man to
elevate and improve himself. But he was
flexible: he saw the factories bill of 1885
as interfering with the liberty of the subject, but observed that parliament was doing
it every day; still, the less it did so the
better. He materially supported the rights
of trade unions, the eight-hour movement
and early closing of shops. But he stopped
short of completely democratic views: he
rejected payment of members which, he
believed, tended to replace some of the
better, more useful men with opportunists.
He believed that every man was entitled to
the vote and detested plutocratic rule, but
considered that property was a rough index
of education and ability; hence property-
owners deserved greater political weight
than loafers, drunkards and criminals. In
his old age he supported the dual (but not
a multiple) property vote; he consistently
backed the council's right to a suspensory
check, not merely because he reverenced the
Constitution, but because he wanted sustained public demand for reform. Perhaps
his most vital liberal tenet was belief in the
mutual interests of classes. He believed that
employers had nothing to fear from employees reaching for equality and fraternity,
provided they were fair, just and honest and
observed the golden rule. To his employees
he distributed bonuses pegged to the firm's
profits. As he fairly said in his Castlemaine
speech of February 1883, he was 'a liberal
of the Gladstone stamp' and 'never was
within a thousand miles of being a conservative'.

On his return from overseas in 1882

Service was regarded very much as a
saviour. At the election in February 1883
he was returned for the two-member seat of
Castlemaine. A coalition government was
being recommended in many quarters to
replace the futile O'Loghlen [q.v.] ministry.
Service was the obvious leader, as the Constitutionalists had fared slightly better than
the Liberals in the election and his friendship with Berry had survived even the trau-
matic conflicts of the late 1870s. His three
years as premier and treasurer were a
triumph. His immediate aim was to reform
the civil service and railways and to eliminate patronage: the Public Service Board
and the Railways Commission were both
established in 1883. As treasurer in the
early prosperous years he negotiated necessary loans but, aware of the dangers of over-
borrowing, he did not allow the boom to
get out of control. He was, however, over-
optimistic about the finances of the railways, though the extensive construction of
new lines was justified. Important land
legislation, preparatory royal commissions
on agriculture and irrigation, the Factories
Act, legalization of trade unions and a mass
of long-delayed minor legislation were other
achievements. The Age conceded in 1886
that 'no parliament can show a more imposing record of great public utility'.
Deakin, a junior minister, remembered very
well the energy and accessibility of Service
as his model premier and the business-like
conduct of cabinet in which nothing was
swamped or muddled.

Service's main contribution as premier
was to drag the Australian colonies on to
the international stage and to originate the
first sustained campaign for federal union.
Possibly during his holiday in Europe in
1881-82 he had sensed the emergence of a
new imperial spirit. He backed Sir Thomas
McIlwraith's [q.v.] attempt to annex New
Guinea in 1883, and used the French threat
to annex the New Hebrides to force a federal
'convention' in Sydney in November on to
an unwilling and preoccupied New South
Wales government; he was largely responsible for the proclamation of an Australian
Monroe doctrine for the South Seas and
agreement to confederate in a Federal Council. He refused to admit that he might die
before 'the grand federation of the Australian colonies'. Appointed executive chairman of the premiers for subsequent negotiations, on return to Melbourne he criticized the apathy and timidity of New South
Wales politicians and hostile reactions followed. New South Wales and South Australia refused to join the Federal Council
which was hamstrung from the start. Meanwhile, his alarm was partially vindicated by
the German annexation of north-eastern

New Guinea and the French occupation of the New Hebrides.

Service admired W. B. Dalley's [q.v.] coup in sending a New South Wales contingent in support of the Sudan campaign. Like most other colonial liberals he deplored his idol Gladstone's imperial policies, found it intolerable that England was always yielding and feared that indecision would lead to the decline of the empire. He believed in the empire's civilizing mission and in Australia's imminent destiny as a great nation. Part of the empire's 'great and noble mission' was to elevate the South Seas' savage through its Australian colonists. But the British government had to recognize both the legitimate regional interests of the colonies and their right to consultation. The Colonial Office officials saw him as a disloyal, ignorant blunderer, until German and French actions in the Pacific induced some review. He was indeed unaware of the wider diplomatic context; but he was a harbinger both of new imperial enthusiasm and of the definition of Australian regional interests. His move towards Federation might likewise be judged to be ill-prepared and insensitive to the complexity of intercolonial hostility; yet he came close to effecting a unanimous confederation which might have proved a viable and rapid path to Federation.

In 1885 Service had decided to retire from the premiership; in the same year his doctor gave urgent warning and he resigned on 18 February 1886. He presided over the first meeting of the Federal Council in Hobart, before setting off again for Europe. His retirement was met with an outburst of popular gratitude for the political peace and prosperity to which he had made such a notable contribution. A fund was created for his portrait (now in the La Trobe Library) to be painted by G. F. Folingsby [q.v.] and he was farewelled at a public function on 16 April. Service spent fifteen of his eighteen-month tour on the Continent, but was a trenchant ally of Berry and Deakin as a delegate to the Colonial Conference of 1887 in London. He was a member of the general committee of the Imperial Federation League and later of the executive committee, but supported it for its encouragement of unity of policy rather than from conviction in any short-term chance of union. He was satisfied that the conference indicated a basic alteration in the future relations of the colonies with the mother country. Salisbury approved the offer to him of a privy councillorship; but he rejected it as he had already refused the offer of a knighthood. An enthusiastic banquet on 7 December, with the earl of Rosebery [q.v. Primrose] in the chair, farewelled him for the last time from Britain in the full conviction that he was one of the empire's leading statesmen.

Service now enjoyed a unique position as a popular elder statesman. He took little part in the management of James Service & Co. after 1881, and did not become involved in any important speculation or boom business activity, although he was a director of the City Road Property Co. Ltd and with W. C. Kernot [q.v.] and F. Pirani formed the New Australian Electricity Co. in 1882. He rejected opportunities to rejoin the assembly, but took a seat in the council in June 1888. A very useful adviser to the Gillies [q.v.]-Deakin government, by late 1889 he was issuing grave warnings about public finance. In the following years of crisis he was again and again under pressure, particularly from the Argus, to resume a leading role in politics, especially in 1892-93 when many fervently hoped that he and Berry would revive their successful coalition. In April 1893 H. Willoughby [q.v.] of the Argus praised his extraordinary role as a confidential adviser of nearly all parties and factions. In 1890 and 1891 his fellow legislative councillors had urged him to represent them at the federal conventions. He refused on health grounds; possibly he also remained convinced that the Federal Council was still viable; and he may have been unwilling to confront Sir Henry Parkes [q.v.] who had poured such scorn on the council in the mid-1880s, had attacked him so bitterly and until 1889 rejected almost every proposal for intercolonial co-operation. But he gave the first speech at the banquet to the delegates in 1890 when he described the tariff as the 'lion in the way'. Gilbert Parker, the Canadian, was correct in his prediction that although Service was the 'father of Australian Confederation' and originally 'the real leader', 'yet Sir Henry Parkes is called, and will be called, the chief maker of Australian Union'.

In 1889 Service had been mainly responsible for persuading the Melbourne Chamber of Commerce to contribute £500 to the striking London dockers. 'Perish the commerce that cannot stand without trampling underfoot our fellowman', was the conclusion of his fine emotional speech. In 1890 and 1891 he was one of the most prominent conciliators of capital and labour in Australia. On 16 September 1890 he set the tone of an unusually moderate council debate on the maritime strike when he urged the employers' organizations to meet the unions in conference. He began a nation-wide movement with a letter to the Argus of 29 June 1891, headed 'The Labour War', in which he stated that although the unions had been in the wrong and he would not waver in his belief in freedom of contract, yet the pastoralists were totally at fault in refusing to confer and were embittering class relations. He dominated the Legislative Council in the early 1890s and did much to reduce the incidence of ultra-Tory behaviour; at the same time he led it to revive dangerous claims to its rights as against the assembly.

In his last years Service devoted himself quixotically to saving the bankrupt Commercial Bank of Australia: old loyalties, sense of duty and his friendship with H. G. Turner [q.v.] had prevailed. The difficult decision to become chairman of directors was followed out with fixity of purpose, and his support probably enabled the bank to survive. His successful 1893 reconstruction proposals preceded a further scheme in 1896. His last years, which must have been agonizingly self-questioning, were typical of those of his generation who had to live through the 1890s.

Service's constant health worries were crucial in his public career. He was clearly a 'worrier', a man who fought all his fights with everything he had. After a major illness in October 1898, he died on 12 April 1899 from a general breakdown of the system. He had been the last of the first parliament to be still a member. The funeral procession from his home in Balaclava Road to the Melbourne cemetery was 1½ miles long; he was buried in his parents' grave in the Baptist section. He had been a sceptic since he was a young man, although he retained a keen intellectual interest in religious questions; he occasionally attended services conducted by the Unitarian and other leading preachers and investigated spiritualism with Turner. But he believed Sunday to be no more sacred than any other day and was occasionally denounced by the *Daily Telegraph* for his 'atheistic proclivities'. He left the residue of his estate of £284,000 to his numerous family in the belief that the 10 per cent estate duty and his frequent generous donations to charity had absolved him from further responsibility.

Jaunty and sprightly, Service was a tallish, slight and spare man, full-bearded with a crest of baldness, mild-looking but with a touch of pugnacity round his large grey eyes. Deakin summed up his appearance and character as essentially those of a 'sturdy, stiff-necked, indomitable and canny' Scot. He showed in his later days that he had learned to compromise and had become far more flexible without ever being a 'trimmer'. He rarely tried to be an orator: most of his speeches were unaffected and earnest in homely simple language, but he had a gift for lucid, logical, precise expo-

sition and for incisively striking to the heart of the matter. Traces of the former teacher and preacher remained in his analytic approach and the biblical echoes in his language. His accent was not marked, although occasionally he threw in some Scotticisms for fun or for effect. He could be a remorseless and caustic critic but his exposure of the ludicrous and absurd was usually good-humoured and did not rankle. He had a taste for epigram, often signalled by a peculiar oratorical shrug of the shoulders. After his early years in parliament, he abhorred personal invective and aimed always to be courteous. His apparent coolness and command of temper allowed him to control even the rogue politicians on the floor of the House, but the strain of damping down his highly emotional reactions was marked. As a parliamentarian he had few equals in Victoria.

Service, in B. R. Wise's words, was 'a merchant of large views and fine culture— at once a scholar and a man of business', a colonial phenomenon not so uncommon among educated Scots. He had strong interests in general philosophy, metaphysics and economic and political theory. J. A. Froude [q.v.], found that he 'talked well, like a man as much accustomed to reflect seriously as if he had been a profound philosopher or an Anglican bishop'. He raised the question whether mankind had improved morally and spiritually over 2000 years, 'argued his point very well indeed, brought out all that was to be said on either side and left the conclusion open'. As a politician, he was constructive, diligent and business-like, with the supreme virtue of common sense. There was no trace of the snob in him. He had the faculty of making men like him and his influence on younger men, like Deakin, was profound. He could play the party game with consummate skill but came to abhor it; he was primarily a moderator and conciliator and few politicians can have provoked so little party hate or have been so little maligned or misrepresented. Possibly no other Victorian politician has ever held such widespread public confidence and affection. Nevertheless, his domestic life was irregular. His early marriage to Marian Allan, by whom he had two daughters, broke up in the mid-1850s. From the early 1860s he lived with Louisa Hoseason Forty, whom he never married and by whom he had several daughters. His public reputation over a long period enabled him to live down the gossip. Serviceton, a railway hamlet, is named after him but, as one of the three or four of the great founding fathers, he has been strangely neglected in the nomenclature of Canberra.

H. G. Turner, *A history of the colony of Victoria* (Lond, 1904); G. Serle, *The rush to be rich* (Melb, 1971); *Table Talk*, 2 Sept 1892; *Review of Reviews* (A'sian ed), Nov-Dec 1892; *Argus*, 13 Apr 1899; *The Times*, 13 Apr 1899; *Australasian*, 15 Apr 1899; Service newspaper cutting books (LaT L, RHSV).

GEOFFREY SERLE

SEYMOUR, DAVID THOMPSON (1831-1916), soldier and police commissioner, was born on 5 November 1831 at Ballymore Castle, County Galway, Ireland, son of Thomas Seymour, gentleman, and his wife Matilda Margaret, née Lawrence. Educated at Ennis College, he entered the army as an ensign on 1 February 1856, was promoted to lieutenant in the 12th Regiment on 23 February 1858, and served at Limerick and Deal before he arrived in Sydney on 7 July 1859 in command of a draft. On 13 January 1861 he arrived in Brisbane in command of the first detachment in Queensland after separation. He was appointed aide-de-camp and private secretary to the governor on 11 May 1861. On 1 January 1864 he retired from the army to become acting commissioner of police under the Police Act of 1863 and was confirmed in office in July. The force consisted of 150 white officers and 137 Native Mounted Police to protect a population of 61,497. Beginning with the establishment of a detective force in 1864, he soon expanded and improved the service. A select committee of 1869 supported his complaints against the appointment of police magistrates as officers and his recommendations, based on observations during extensive travel, for improved pay and conditions. The committee also approved his new-found opposition to phasing out the Native Mounted Police. He showed his faith in the native police in 1880 by sending black trackers to Victoria to participate in rounding up the Kelly [q.v.] gang.

Seymour was never afraid to use force. In the Brisbane riot of September 1866 he ordered his men to fix bayonets and load with live ammunition to disperse a large crowd in Queen Street. Giving evidence to an 1887 board of inquiry on management of gaols, he was enthusiastic for flogging. In the 1894 pastoral strike the police were given sole power to 'preserve order and secure liberty to all alike' to avoid the expensive and controversial involvement of the military as in the 1891 strike, and he took command in Longreach, Winton, and other centres. After his request for greater legal power to compensate for limited manpower the government introduced the controversial peace preservation bill, which permitted detention without trial for periods up to two months.

On 30 June 1895 Seymour retired on a pension of £700: he had increased police strength to 907 men which still included 104 Native Mounted Police. He had given some attention to social questions: his suggested new route via the Red Sea and Torres Strait for immigrant ships reduced the time of the voyage by half, and in 1878 he advocated a reformatory for girls under fourteen years of age. But his chief private interests were horse-racing and athletics. A foundation member and a committee-man of the Queensland Turf Club for over thirty years, he was also a committee-man of the Queensland Club. He died on 31 January 1916 in London. On 28 June 1864 in Brisbane he had married Caroline Matilda (d. 1884), daughter of William Anthony Brown, sheriff of Queensland; they had six daughters. He married Sara Jane Stevenson, aged 23, on 6 June 1888; of their two sons, one became a well-known engineer in Kuala Lumpur.

Alcazar Press, *Queensland, 1900* (Brisb, nd); R. S. Browne, *A journalist's memories* (Brisb, 1927); W. H. Fysh, *Taming the north* (Syd, 1950); Qld Police Dept, *A centenary history of the Queensland Police Force 1864-1963* (Brisb, 1964); PD (LA Qld), 1894; N. S. Pixley, 'An outline of the history of the Queensland Police Force 1860-1949', *JRHSQ*, 4 (1948-52); P. D. Wilson, 'The Brisbane riot of September 1866', *Qld Heritage*, 2 (1969-74), no 4.

NEIL STEWART

SHACKELL, JAMES (1833-1899), politician, auctioneer and agent, was born on 12 January 1833 at Twerton-on-Avon near Bath, Somerset, England, son of James Shackell, farmer, and his wife Ann, née Mills. In August 1852 he migrated to Victoria in the *Winchester*, went to the Ovens goldfields and took up a claim on Woolshed Creek, but became mainly a buyer of gold and stream tin. In 1858 he sold his business to the Oriental Bank and visited England, where at Gravesend, Kent, he married Annie Susannah Littlewood; they returned to Melbourne in the *Royal Charter* on 22 July 1859 and settled at Beechworth. Elected to the Municipal Council in 1861, he was a partner in J. H. Gray & Co., agents and auctioneers, until 1862. He then went to Forbes, New South Wales, and set up his own agency.

Late in 1863 Shackell transferred to Echuca, Victoria, buying valuable business property. Vigorous and ambitious, six months later he became clerk, valuer and treasurer to the Echuca Road Board (later Shire Council). He resigned as shire clerk in 1876 but was elected a councillor in 1877-82. and was president in his first year of office. As well, he was a councillor of the Borough of Echuca, serving as mayor in 1878-82 and as president of the Echuca Water Trust.

Tall, handsome and debonair in dress, Shackell dominated most aspects of local life. Successful in amateur theatricals, he also sang in concerts; he was president of the race club, a foundation member and later president of the football, cricket and rowing clubs, organizer of a young men's social club, patron of the horticultural society and the Australian Natives Club, and a committee-man of the Agricultural and Pastoral Society and of the Chamber of Commerce. In 1876 with his brother-in-law, H. T. Littlewood, he purchased Madowla Park station, east of Echuca, and next year stood against Duncan Gillies [q.v.] for the seat of Rodney in the Legislative Assembly. Narrowly defeated he appealed, but a re-election secured Gillies's position. Suffering heavy financial losses, Shackell sold his Madowla Park interest and concentrated on his agencies. In June 1878 he gave evidence to the royal commission into the progress of settlement under the Land Act of 1869, defending his dealings under the 1865 Act and refuting accusations that he had been a 'dummy-monger'.

In February 1883 Shackell won the seat of Rodney on the retirement of (Sir) Simon Fraser [q.v.] and in 1884 was a member of the royal commission into water-supply. A. W. H. White became his partner in 1885 and three years later he left Echuca to manage the Melbourne side of Shackell, White & Co. and to pursue his parliamentary career, which included membership of the 1890-91 royal commission into the coal industry of Victoria. In 1891 he visited England and failed in launching a company to develop by irrigation the Wharparilla estate near Echuca. Made a freeman of Bath, he returned to Victoria only six weeks before the 1892 elections in which he lost his seat to a local farmer, Timothy Murphy. Appointed assignee of insolvent estates in August 1893, he combined the post with mining and general agencies. A conservative free trader in politics and an Anglican, Shackell died at his home at Armadale on 25 April 1899 of debilitation caused by gout from which he had suffered for some twenty years. He was survived by his wife, four of their six sons and three of their four daughters.

S. Priestley, *Echuca: a centenary history* (Brisb, 1965); *Riverine Herald*, 1865-99; *T&CJ*, 29 Oct 1887; *Argus*, 26 Apr 1899; information from Mrs Moira Ward, Melbourne.

SUSAN MCCARTHY

SHAW, THOMAS junior (1827-1907), pastoralist, was born on 27 August 1827 at Birstall near Leeds, Yorkshire, England, son of Thomas Shaw [q.v.], wool expert, and his wife Ann, née Turner. He came with his father to Sydney in 1843 and began his country education on Robert Campbell's [q.v.] station, Duntroon. At 20 he overlanded 700 head of cattle to Adelaide. He later joined his father who was then classing and buying sheep in the Western District of Victoria; by the early 1850s after some months on the goldfields and riding with the mails between Cressy and Mortlake, he undertook commissions for stock-owners and also handled and broke in their horses.

In February 1854 with Thomas Anderson, a partner of J. L. Currie [q.v.], Shaw bought Wooriwyrite from Ebenezer Oliphant. In March he married Catherine McLaurin, whose sisters had married Oliphant and Anderson. Because he had little capital he was to manage the station but, after Anderson was killed that year in a riding accident, he carried on alone with some financial help from Oliphant who had returned to Edinburgh. He restocked Wooriwyrite with ewes bred by the Learmonths [q.v.] on his father's advice, and rams from the original Macarthur [q.v.] flock from Camden.

By the 1860s and 1870s his sheep were constantly in the prize lists and their fine wool was fetching top prices on the London market. Like his father he wrote colourful and hard-hitting letters to the press hammering at the importance of quality in wool and 'selection' in breeding, and extolling the virtues of the 'Pure Australian Merino' bred by his neighbours at Larra and Ercildoun. Later he vehemently opposed the introduction of the Vermont strain which, he said, grew hair rather than wool. Another correspondent, 'Tom Cribb', in the Melbourne *Economist*, January 1866, described Shaw as 'pugnacious as a cock-sparrow' but conceded that 'his moral character was irreproachable, and his energy and vivacity made him an excellent colonist'. Billis and Kenyon believed that 'the consensus of opinion among breeders at that time would have placed the name of Shaw with the most honoured'.

He was active and articulate, and in 1859 founded what became the important Skipton show, and was, its honorary secretary until its decline in 1873. He was the first president of the shire of Mortlake in 1863, a councillor and several times president of the shire of Hampden, and in 1890 was a foundation councillor of what is now the Graziers' Association of Victoria. He was a justice of the peace, stood unsuccessfully for parliament, lent a useful hand in many interests of his district and of his friends, and acted widely as a judge of sheep.

Shaw built a house for his mother and sisters on his own land near Mortlake, where his sister Jemima married Rev. Dr W. H. Fitchett, helped build the Methodist church and provided its parsonage. He also presented Mortlake with a museum and a temperance hall, both of enduring bluestone like the large new homestead he built for his own family in 1885, three years before his wife's death. A two-year trip overseas is described in A *Victorian in Europe*, published in 1883. He lived simply and, unlike his father, 'signed the pledge' and remained an earnest but cheerful teetotaller. Jovial and kindly, he was sometimes more honest than tactful and prone to disconcert his household by leaving without notice on trips of undisclosed duration or destination. He died at Hawthorn on 30 July 1907 on his way home from dealing with a friend's estates in Queensland. Of his seven children his younger son Thomas was left as manager of Wooriwyrite. His estate was sworn for probate at £3651.

His elder brother Jonathan (1826-1905) came out with his mother and five sisters about 1852, settled in Geelong and joined his father as a sheep-classer. He successfully took over and extended the practice there and in the Riverina, and he also became head woolsorter to Hastings Cuningham [q.v.] & Co.

G. A. Brown, *Sheep breeding in Australia*, 2nd ed (Melb, 1890); P. L. Brown (ed), *Clyde Company papers*, 6 (Lond, 1968); Mary Turner Shaw, *On Mount Emu creek* (Melb, 1969); T. Anderson, Journal 1850-54 (LaT L); J. L. Currie, Scrap-book (LaT L); Shaw family papers (held by author).

MARY TURNER SHAW

SHAW, WILLIAM HENRY (1830-1896), engineer and ironfounder, was born on 27 July 1830 in Belfast, Northern Ireland, son of James Shaw, builder and contractor, and his wife Mary, née Hunter. After working for his father, he was apprenticed to Gray Bros' Townshend Street foundry where he learnt all branches of ironworking but specialized in the mechanical drafting that greatly advantaged his later career. In 1852 he left Belfast to work for the Cork Steamship Co. Lured by gold, Shaw arrived in Melbourne in October 1853 but had little luck at Ballarat, Daylesford and Blackwood. He opened and managed a small foundry for Frederick Moore in Geelong before returning to Ballarat early in 1856 to join the moulder Robert Holden and two Lanca-

shire-trained enginesmiths, Robert Carter and George Threlfell, in launching the Phoenix Foundry. The business prospered and by November 1861 was employing ninety-six hands on a wide range of products. Shaw was proud that the eight-hour day had been worked from c.1858 and that his employees did as much in that time as Englishmen did in ten hours.

At the time of a temporary decline in mining and an increase in protectionism, the firm became a public company in November 1870 and further diversified its output: in August 1871 it successfully tendered for the first of the Victorian government locomotive contracts. By January 1884, under Shaw's skilful and enterprising management, the company had capital in excess of £30,000 and employed over 350 hands; modernized after his visits to Britain in 1871 and 1885, it was reputedly the most advanced of its type south of the equator. He was so closely identified with the company that the celebration of the manufacture of the one-hundredth locomotive in April 1883 took the form of a public compliment to his 'energy and practical experience and indomitable perseverance'. 'Without the Phoenix Foundry', observed the *Ballarat Star*, 'Ballarat would feel insignificant among the cities of Australia'. In the 1880s dividends were declared for the first time and 200 locomotives were completed by October 1887. Thereafter the company faced difficulties. In 1889 Shaw's attempt to exclude members of the Ironworkers' Assistants' Society and to enforce a non-union shop produced a bitter conflict. Free traders' criticism of the Phoenix as a quasi-government workshop became more vocal as markets for both engines and mining equipment diminished because of depression, government manufacture at Newport and a declining rate of railway expansion; in 1906 the foundry was forced to close.

A justice of the peace, Shaw died in Ballarat on 23 August 1896, survived by his wife Annie Eliza, née Cleeland, seven sons and four daughters; he was buried in Ballarat cemetery. His estate was sworn for probate at £2250.

A. Sutherland et al, *Victoria and its metropolis*, 2 (Melb, 1888); J. L. Buckland and W. Jack, 'The locomotive builders of Ballarat', Aust Railways Hist Soc, *Bulletin*, 12 (1961); *Ballarat Star*, 27 Nov 1861, 12 Jan 1884; *Ballarat Courier*, 14 Apr 1883, 24 Aug 1896, 20 Sept 1906; G. S. Cope, Some aspects of the metal trade in Ballarat, 1851-1901 (M. A. thesis, Univ Melb, 1971).

GRAEME COPE

SHEARER, DAVID (1832-1891), teacher and Presbyterian minister, was born on 23

July 1832 at Canisbay, Caithness, Scotland, son of John Shearer, farmer, and his wife Elizabeth, née Banks. In 1847-57 he taught before enrolling at the Free Church of Scotland Normal Training College in Edinburgh. He then taught in the Free Church School at Fordyce, obtained a schoolmaster's certificate in 1860, was appointed to Canisbay Free Church School, but soon returned to Edinburgh. Granted a bursary in 1863 by the Edinburgh-Caithness Association he studied at the University of Edinburgh (M.A., 1867) while working as a city missionary. In 1871 he was licensed to preach by the Free Church Presbytery of Edinburgh and was appointed to the pastorate of the Ellison Street Presbyterian Church at Gateshead; he was ordained on 12 July 1872 by the Presbytery of Newcastle upon Tyne. In 1865 he had married Margaret Fisher, daughter of Thomas Ballantine of Edinburgh.

Through the joint action of the colonial committees of the Established and Free Churches of Scotland, Shearer was commissioned to establish the Presbyterian Church in Western Australia. He sailed from Gravesend with his wife and family in the *Charlotte Padbury*, arriving at Fremantle on 1 October 1879. His initial services were held in St George's Hall, Perth, and later in the Working Men's Institute. For the first four years his stipend was met by the colonial committees, enabling him to concentrate his efforts on acquiring land and building a church, opened in August 1882. That year he visited Sydney to attend the Third General Conference of the Presbyterian Churches of Australasia and collected nearly £600 for the Church in Western Australia. He brought Rev. Robert Hanlin from Scotland to establish Scots Church at Fremantle and pioneered Albany, Jarrahdale and Geraldton.

A leading reformer in education, Shearer was chairman of the Perth District Board of Education in 1885-89. Strongly opposed to state aid for denominational schools, he aimed to overhaul the National school system and widen its curriculum, but in 1889 the combined efforts of Catholic and Anglican clergy blocked his re-election to the board. He was chairman of a commission on education in 1887, a member of a commission on technical education in 1890, president of the Perth Literary Union from its foundation in 1885, a member of the Orange Lodge and a keen supporter of the British and Foreign Bible Society. He also wrote articles on education in the *West Australian*. After a prolonged illness attributed to overwork, Shearer died of endocarditis on 13 November 1891, survived by his wife, five daughters and three sons. The adminis-

trator, the premier and the colonial secretary were among those who attended his funeral and the pall-bearers were Protestant clergymen. The hall behind the Beaufort Street manse was named the Shearer Memorial Hall and a monument, erected by public subscription, stands outside St Andrew's Church, Perth.

In memorium, Rev. David Shearer (Perth, 1891); D. Mossenson, *State education in Western Australia, 1829-1960* (Nedlands, 1972); *Inquirer*, 8 Oct 1879, 27 Oct 1880, supp; *Western Aust Bulletin*, 13 Aug 1888; *West Australian*, 13 Apr 1889, 14, 26 Nov 1891; CSR 1879-80 (Battye Lib, Perth).   JOHN SHEARER

SHEEHY, SAMUEL JOHN AUSTIN (1827-1910), Benedictine priest, was born on 1 October 1827 in Cork, County Cork, Ireland, son of John Sheehy, carpenter and builder, and his wife Harriett, née Roche. On 19 October 1838 he reached Sydney with his parents, bounty immigrants in the *Magistrate*. He studied at St Mary's seminary and in May 1845 entered the priory attached to the cathedral. He received the Benedictine habit on 2 August 1849, made his religious profession on 5 May 1851 and was ordained by Bishop Davis [q.v.] in St Mary's Cathedral on 6 March 1852.

After his ordination Sheehy was in charge of St Mary's seminary day school where he taught W. B. Dalley [q.v.]. In 1858 he became chaplain for Darlinghurst and Cockatoo Island gaols and in 1861 president of Lyndhurst College and vicar-general in succession to Abbott Gregory [q.v.]. A fellow of St John's College within the University of Sydney, in 1864 he was named parish priest of the Sacred Heart Church, Darlinghurst, and was sometime joint treasurer of St Vincent's Hospital. In 1866 he was appointed bishop of Bethesda *in partibus infidelium* and auxiliary to Archbishop Polding [q.v.], but Cardinal Barnabò, the prefect of Propaganda College, asked Polding to defer the consecration until Sheehy had been cleared of charges of negligence, of 'having connived at the apostasies of certain monks' and of having been seen leaving his room '*valde ebria*'. Sheehy resigned 'at the first sign of any opposition', but Polding claimed that the calumniators' plans were to prevent Sheehy from succeeding him; he asked Rome to appoint him to Armidale: 'I confess that since all my suffragan bishops are Irish, it would be very pleasant for me to have at least one, who, even though he is Irish, has spent his time of education and religious life at my side and in the work of the mission'. Sheehy was not consecrated but he remained vicar-general until the arrival in

1873 of Archbishop Vaughan [q.v.]. He had been appointed at a time when discontent with the Benedictine régime was at its height, and he trod cautiously. Opposition came from his close association with the English superiors of the mission and not from any personal animosity. Consulted by Polding on the Benedictine community, in 1869 he concluded that, as there was little prospect of getting fresh subjects and great difficulty in training them, it would be better to break up the institute and get the professed religious secularized; Vaughan followed this advice in 1877.

Sheehy was appointed to Windsor in 1873 and to Wollongong in 1885. That year Cardinal Moran bestowed on him the honorary title of vicar-general. In 1888 he moved to Ryde and in 1907 to Waverley. Although he was secularized with the few remaining Benedictines, he remained faithful to his early calling and merged into the Australian scene. He died of senile decay at Randwick on 14 September 1910 and was buried in the Field of Mars cemetery. His estate was sworn for probate at £30.

H. N. Birt, *Benedictine pioneers in Australia*, 1-2 (Lond, 1911); M. Shanahan, *Out of time, out of place* (Canberra, 1970); Roman Catholic Archives (Syd). MARY SHANAHAN

SHEIL, LAURENCE BONAVENTURE (1815-1872), Catholic bishop, was born on 24 December 1815 at Wexford, Ireland. He was educated at St Peter's College, Wexford, and from 1832 at the Franciscan College of St Isidore, Rome, where he remained teaching theology and philosophy after his ordination in 1839. Returning to Ireland he became guardian of the convents of St Francis at Cork and Carrickbeg. He was recruited for the Australian mission, and arrived in Melbourne with Bishop Goold [q.v.] in the *Koh-i-noor* on 12 February 1853. He was appointed president of St Francis's seminary, later St Patrick's College, and was secretary and manager of the Catholic education board of Victoria. Because of ill health he was transferred as archdeacon to Ballarat in 1859 and remained until 1866, when he was appointed to succeed P. B. Geoghegan [q.v.] as bishop of Adelaide. Consecrated by Goold on 15 August, he was installed on 16 September.

Sheil's episcopacy was one of great expansion. By 1871 twenty-one new missions had been established, nineteen new churches built, including one of his first undertakings, St Laurence's at North Adelaide opened in January 1869, and the number of priests had increased from seventeen to thirty. Catholic education also grew rapidly.

In 1866 the teaching congregation of the Sisters of St Joseph was founded by Mother Mary McKillop and Fr J. Tenison-Woods [qq.v.], and next year Sheil appointed Tenison-Woods director general of Catholic education. By 1871 there were sixty-eight Catholic schools in the diocese; thirty-five of them conducted by Josephite nuns. He had also recruited a community of seven Irish Dominican nuns in 1868.

Despite initial high expectations, Sheil was not a success as bishop. He spent less than two years of his episcopate in Adelaide: he travelled to Rome and Ireland from April 1867 to December 1868 and from October 1869 to February 1871 to recruit clergy and to attend the Vatican Council, and carried out intercolonial visitations in 1869 and 1871. These absences and his poor health left the diocese virtually leaderless and resulted in bitter clerical administrative factionalism and lay disunity. The most serious and dramatic result was his precipitous and uncanonical excommunication of Mother McKillop, the temporary disbanding of her congregation in September 1871 and the subsequent appointment, after his death, of an Apostolic Commission to investigate diocesan affairs.

Amiable, urbane and zealous, Sheil was better suited to teaching and scholarship than to coping with the problems of the Adelaide mission. He suffered greatly from the heat and, in the last years of his life, poor health contributed much to his erratic and autocratic behaviour. He moved to Willunga, south of Adelaide, in December 1871 and died there of a carbuncle on 1 March 1872. He was buried in Adelaide's West Terrace cemetery.

P. F. Moran, *History of the Catholic Church in Australasia* (Syd, 1895); O. Thorpe, *Mary McKillop* (Lond, 1957); *Illustrated Melb Post*, 18 Feb 1866; *Freeman's J* (Syd), 6 Mar 1872; *Harp and Southern Cross*, 2 Mar 1872; Roman Catholic Archives (Adel, Syd).

IAN J. BICKERTON

SHELLSHEAR, WALTER (1856-1939), engineer, was born on 17 September 1856 in London, son of Joseph Shellshear, merchant seaman, and his wife Alicia, née Scarriott. Brought up on the Clyde, he studied mathematics at King's College, London, then was employed in the engineering works of Robert Napier and Son, Glasgow. In 1877-78 he received a certificate of proficiency in engineering science from the University of Glasgow. He returned to London and worked for George Buckley on the design of bridges and the supply of materials and surveys for the Indian government railways.

In 1879 he migrated to New South Wales and on 1 February 1880 was employed as a draftsman in the roads branch of the Department of Works. On 1 April 1882 he joined the Railways Department as a draftsman.

On 1 May 1886 Shellshear was promoted district engineer in charge of the metropolitan district, which included the tramways, the Illawarra line to Waterfall, the southern line to Picton, the western line to Springwood and the Richmond and Hornsby lines. Responsible for maintaining existing lines, he also constantly travelled on new lines in the interests of safety and found the construction of the Petersham viaduct one of his most difficult jobs. An associate member of the Institution of Civil Engineers, London, in 1882, he was president of the Engineering Association of New South Wales in 1885-86; he was a member of the Royal Society of New South Wales in 1883-1922 and in 1884 published a paper 'On the Removal of Bars from the entrances to our Rivers' in the society's Journal. He corresponded with Sir John Coode [q.v.] on the subject and in 1889 told the Parliamentary Standing Committee on Public Works that the 'question of improving these bar bound rivers is a favourite study of mine. I have taken a great deal of pains with it'. In 1884 he had prepared a paper on the 'Sydney Steam Tramways' for the Society of Civil Engineers, London. He published other short papers in the Proceedings of the Engineering Association.

Shellshear was closely associated with the design and construction of many important works such as an additional generating plant for the Ultimo Tramway Power House, station yard re-arrangement for the new Sydney station in 1906, the renewal of the steel in two miles of timber viaducts across the Murrumbidgee flats at Wagga Wagga, and the new Nepean bridge at Penrith in 1907. On 1 September 1903 he had been promoted inspecting engineer; he became deputy-engineer-in-chief and in 1905 relieved James Fraser, the engineer-in-chief. In 1912-21 he was consulting and inspecting engineer in London where he supervised all materials ordered for New South Wales government works.

Painstaking, unassuming and quietly confident, Shellshear was noted for his patience and helpfulness with his subordinates. He retired in 1921, returned to Sydney and took up his residence at Ripley, Mitchell Street, Greenwich, where he died on 11 November 1939; he was buried in the Northern Suburbs cemetery with Catholic Apostolic rites; his estate was valued for probate at £2345. He was survived by his wife Clara Mabel, née Eddis, whom he had married at the Catholic Apostolic Church, Carlton, Melbourne, on 21 April 1881, and by five sons and five daughters; his son, Lieut-Colonel Joseph Lexden, won the D.S.O. in World War I.

V&P (LA NSW), 1887 (2nd S), 2, 274, 1887-88, 6, 485, 489, 539, 1889, 5, 490, 1889 (2nd S), 2, 399; NSW Railway and Tramway Mag, 1 Dec 1920.

C. C. SINGLETON*

SHENTON, ARTHUR (1816-1871), printer and journalist, was born on 11 October 1816 at Winchester, Hampshire, England, second son of Edward Shenton and his wife Charlotte. In 1843 he sailed in the Trusty from Falmouth and arrived at Leschenault (Bunbury), Western Australia, on 22 May 1844. He settled in Perth and in December 1846 bought into the Perth Gazette and Western Australian Journal. On 1 January 1848 he became editor-owner and, to emphasize his independence, renamed the newspaper the Perth Gazette and Independent Journal of Politics and News. He also bought new printing plant to avoid reliance on the press owned by the government, which had been used by the former owner; but he was government printer in 1848-57. An excellent craftsman he was not a facile or willing writer and relied heavily on contributors. In 1864 he took over a year-old contemporary, the West Australian Times, and enlarged his publication under the title Perth Gazette and West Australian Times. He became prominent in 1865 in a renewed campaign for representative government, using his editorial column to attack his opponents.

In 1870 Shenton took up the cause of a young solicitor, S. H. Parker, in a quarrel with Chief Justice Burt [q.v.]; together with Edmund [q.v.] and John Stirling of the Inquirer, was found guilty of having published a 'gross and scandalous libel' on the Supreme Court, and was fined £100 and sentenced to two months: the Stirlings were sentenced to thirty days. The case was highly contentious and Shenton received much public support. The three journalists published abject apologies, said to have been drafted by Burt, and were soon released, but the punishment had worsened Shenton's already-failing health and he died, intestate, of apoplexy on 16 March 1871. An obituary in his own newspaper said, 'his friends have at least the consolation of knowing that he died at his post, and that almost his last act was in defence of the proper privileges of the Press, and the right to criticize the acts of public men'. The £100 fine, for which the court had badgered him, was remitted only after his death.

Shenton had married Mercy Heal, of York, on 9 November 1848; they had two children.

W. B. Kimberly, *History of West Australia* (Melb, 1897); J. T. Reilly, *Reminiscences of fifty years' residence in Western Australia* (Perth, 1903); J. S. Battye (ed), *Cyclopedia of Western Australia*, 1 (Adel, 1912); J. S. Battye, *Western Australia* (Oxford, 1924); *Inquirer*, 22 Mar 1871; *Perth Gazette*, Mar 1871; Q *Bulletin* (W. A. Newspapers Ltd), Aug 1963.

O. K. BATTYE

SHENTON, SIR GEORGE (1842-1909), merchant and politician, was born on 4 March 1842 at Perth, Western Australia, son of George Shenton [q.v.] and his wife Ann, née Cousins. In 1855 he went to England to complete his education at the Wesleyan Collegiate Institute (Queen's College), Taunton. On his return in 1858 he entered the family business and assumed control in 1867 on his father's death. In the following year he married Julia Theresa, daughter of Lieut-Colonel Eichbaum of the imperial military station in Perth.

Shenton quickly made a name as a shrewd businessman: his shop became one of Perth's biggest emporiums, with a reputation for progressive management (it was the first to use life-size models in its window displays); after 1881 he gradually handed it over to his brother Ernest. He retained control of the family import agency at Fremantle which became a major shipping and importing firm, holding the local agency for Lloyds of London, and closely involved in the trade with Singapore of which Shenton was a pioneer. In 1903 with its country affiliates the firm joined with Elder Smith [qq.v.] & Co. to form Elder Shenton & Co., of which Shenton remained chairman until 1909. He was also a member of the syndicate that organized the expedition which led to the discovery of the (L. R.) Menzies goldfield, on which the Lady Shenton was amongst the best-known mines. This project was a comparatively rare instance of local investment in gold-mining. Between 1886 and 1909 Shenton was chairman of the board of the Western Australian Bank. When the Perth Chamber of Commerce was founded in 1890, he was the logical choice as its first president.

Shenton had early made his mark in public life as a member of the Perth City Council; elected in 1867, he was chairman in 1875-77. In 1880-84 he was the first mayor of Perth and was mayor again in 1886-88. In 1870 Shenton was elected to the first Legislative Council for Greenough. Re-elected in 1872, he lost the seat on appeal when the chief justice ruled that the Elec-toral Act had been breached; it was accepted that he had been the victim of an over-zealous agent but Shenton's pride was hurt. However in 1875 he won the Toodyay seat which he retained without difficulty until 1890, aided by his close business, personal and political relationship, despite his own staunch Wesleyanism, with Bishop Salvado [q.v.]. Although finance limited the scope of 'roads and bridges' politics, he secured a railway into the heart of his electorate, and as a country member he supported tariff protection of agriculture. On the most controversial question of the period, responsible government, he was very cautious; he flirted with it in the early 1870s but thereafter opposed its introduction until 1889, by which time it was almost a foregone conclusion.

Under the new Constitution in 1890, Shenton opted for a seat in the nominated Legislative Council but, invited by John Forrest to join the colony's first cabinet as colonial secretary, he remained for a time at the centre of affairs. In October 1892 he resigned and was elected president of the Legislative Council, a position which was probably more to his liking and which he held until his retirement from politics in 1906. After 1894, when the council ceased to be nominated, he represented the Metropolitan province. In later years Shenton's services were much in demand for boards and committees, including those of the Public Library and Museum, the Central Board of Education, the King's Park and the Perth Public Hospital, of which he was the first chairman. In 1897 he became chairman of a provisional committee for the establishment of a children's hospital; after eleven years of fund-raising it opened a few days after his death. One of the most notable Wesleyans in a predominantly Anglican colony, he served his Church as Sunday school teacher, treasurer, organist and choirmaster.

Though Shenton profited from the gold rushes of the 1890s, he epitomized the old order which they overturned; he was one of the last great representatives of the 'six hungry families' who dominated the colony in the nineteenth century. Very 'English' in his attitudes and life-style, he loved the city and country of his birth, and served them unstintingly. He took great pride in the symbols of status and authority: the mayoral chain, the president's wig, and the knighthood conferred on him in 1893.

Shenton died on 29 June 1909 in London. Predeceased by his wife he was survived by six daughters. His estate was valued for probate at £186,627, much of it in the form of real estate. His riverside home, Crawley House, and more than 100 acres of land surrounding it were sold to the government and became the site of the University of Western Australia.

P. W. H. Thiel & Co., *Twentieth century impressions of Western Australia* (Perth, 1901); J. S. Battye (ed), *Cyclopedia of Western Australia*, 1-2 (Adel, 1912-13); *Possum*, 8 Oct 1887; *West Australian*, 1 July 1909; *Weekend Magazine*, 9 Sept 1967; J. A. Mackenzie, Survey of West Australian politics in the period of representative government, 1870-1890 (B.A. Hons thesis, Univ WA, 1936); W. F. P. Heseltine, The movements for self-government in Western Australia from 1882-1890 (B.A. Hons thesis, Univ WA, 1950); E. Willis, The life of Sir George Shenton, *and* Shenton-Salvado letters (Battye Lib, Perth).   B. K. DE GARIS

SHERIDAN, JOHN FELIX (1825-1897), Catholic priest, was born at Martinstown, Athboy, County Meath, Ireland, son of Philip Sheridan, farmer, and his wife Catherine, née Moore. Educated at Mr Carroll's 'classical and commercial academy' in Trim, he worked for some years with his father. Resolving to become a missionary, in 1845 he entered the Benedictine Monastery of St Lawrence at Ampleforth, Yorkshire. He joined Archbishop Polding [q.v.] in the *St Vincent* and reached Sydney on 6 February 1848. He completed his Benedictine studies at St Mary's Seminary, and was ordained by Bishop Davis [q.v.] on 3 March 1852.

In 1853 Sheridan was appointed vice-president of Lyndhurst College and to Petersham, where the Church of St Thomas was soon built. Briefly at St Benedict's, Sydney, he became parish priest of the Church of the Sacred Heart, Darlinghurst, in 1857 and built the presbytery. Bearded, stocky and radiating joviality, he delighted in youth welfare work, helped by his musical gifts (he was a good fiddler) and organizing ability. In 1857-69 he was chaplain of the Australian Holy Catholic Guild of St Mary and St Joseph. In Darlinghurst he also established a home for unemployed women, a non-denominational home for immigrant girls, a teetotal society and a reading room and library.

A fellow of St John's College, University of Sydney, from 1858, in 1864-67 he was prior of Lyndhurst and president of the school, which he reorganized and improved the buildings and grounds. In 1867 he took charge of the parish of St Francis, Haymarket, one of the poorest areas of Sydney. He soon enlarged the church and raised money by bazaars to build a temperance hall, a school and the Convent of the Good Shepherd. He also raised the money to buy Sir Charles Nicholson's [q.v.] house, Tarmons, for the Sisters of Charity.

Sheridan was a director of the Sydney Infirmary and Dispensary, and a committeeman of the Home Visiting and Relief Society, the Society for the Relief of Destitute Children and the Benevolent Society of New South Wales, and a member of the Immigration Board. In 1873 he became dean and in 1877 was appointed vicar-general by Archbishop Vaughan [q.v.]. Sheridan's dual role of Benedictine monk and parish priest symbolized the innate conflict in Polding's attempt to fashion a diocese from conventual monks who did not live in a monastery. Under Vaughan, Sheridan had to preside over the dissolution of Lyndhurst and the monastic establishment of the cathedral. He administered the diocese in 1883-84 and later visited Europe. He retired to Kincumber near Gosford, where he devoted himself to St Joseph's Orphanage. Aged 72, he died of diabetes and gangrene on 15 March 1897 at Iona Cottage, North Sydney, and was buried in the grounds of the orphanage at Kincumber. His estate was valued for probate at £1046; he left his gold presentation chalice and all his books to his nephew, Rev. John Sheridan, and the residue to St Joseph's Orphanage.

J. O'Brien, *On Darlinghurst hill* (Syd, 1952); *T&CJ*, 26 May 1877; *Sydney Mail*, 27 Mar 1897; Benedictine diary and records (Roman Catholic Archives, Syd).   C. J. DUFFY

SHERIDAN, RICHARD BINGHAM (1822-1897), public servant and politician, was born on 1 August 1822 at Castlebar, County Mayo, Ireland, son of Henry S. Sheridan of Pheasant Hill, Castlebar, and his wife Margaret, née Martin. He arrived in New South Wales in 1842 and till 1844 was farm manager for Captain William Oldrey of Broulee. On 18 November 1845 in Sydney he married Adele Eulalie Masse.

Sheridan joined the Customs Department on 7 February 1846. In February 1853 because of ill health he transferred to Moreton Bay and on 31 May became a member of the local Steam Navigation Board. He became sub-collector of customs at Maryborough on 10 December 1859, the first appointment made by a Queensland government. Later he held several related positions in the Wide Bay-Maryborough area.

Sheridan was deeply involved in the life of Maryborough and was respected for his integrity, fairness and humanity. When an explosion left many families fatherless he distributed the funds donated by the citizens. He initiated the Botanic Gardens, was involved in the foundation of the School of Arts and the hospital and was first chairman of the building society. He was active in the establishment of public (non-state) schools. In 1866 he became a partner in the Tinana Creek Sugar Plantation. He was an active officer of the Queensland Volunteer Force, being captain on 7 September 1861, major unattached on 6 November 1878 and honorary lieut-colonel on the retired list on 23 December 1884.

In 1861 Sheridan was a chief witness in an inquiry into the shooting of Aboriginals by a native police detachment stationed at Ownayilla. In 1876 he was under pressures, including a select committee, because in an official report he had allowed his opposition to the abuses of Polynesian labour to overrule his discretion. He was forced to resign as inspector of Polynesians.

Sheridan won the Maryborough seat in the Legislative Assembly on 17 August 1883 and held it till 5 May 1888. He was minister without portfolio in the Griffith ministry from 13 November 1883 until 3 January 1885 and postmaster-general from 3 January to 17 February. His efforts in parliament to reform the Polynesian labour system were commended by the press and by Governor Sir William Cairns. In 1885 he had become a trustee of the Brisbane Botanic Gardens.

Sheridan lived in retirement in Brisbane but in 1897 moved to Sydney and died at Manly on 8 June, survived by two of his three sons. He was buried in the Catholic section of Waverley cemetery.

HRA (1), 27, 510; *Returns of the colony of NSW*, 1846; G. E. Loyau, *The history of Maryborough* (Brisb, 1897); J. Lennon, *Maryborough and district . . . 1842-1924*, G. I. Roberts ed (Maryborough, 1924); V&P (LA Qld), 1877, 2, 1207; *Brisbane Courier*, 9 June 1897; *SMH*, 9 June 1897; W. Oldrey, Insolvency papers 1154 (NSWA).   DOROTHY JONES

SHERWIN, FRANCES AMY LILLIAN (1855-1935), singer, was born on 23 March 1855 near Huonville, Tasmania, daughter of George Green Sherwin, farmer, and his wife Elizabeth, née Dean, and niece of Isaac Sherwin [q.v.]. As her parents had suffered financially from droughts and fires and could not afford music tuition, she was educated at home, her mother teaching her singing and giving her lessons on a piano brought from England by Amy's grandfather William Dean. F. A. Packer [q.v.] took an interest in her and recommended that she concentrate on opera. Her career began in earnest in 1878 when she joined the touring Royal Italian Opera Company as Norina in *Don Pasquale*. She sang with the company in Melbourne, Ballarat and Sydney; by September her pure and gentle voice had persuaded critics of her ability. Next month

she went to New Zealand and on 12 December 1878 at Dunedin married Hugo Gorlitz, a German merchant and entrepreneur who had business interests in Sydney.

In February 1879 Sherwin sailed to San Francisco for a five-week season with the Strakosch Company. On 27 May, despite having just recovered from pneumonia, she sang Violetta in *La Traviata* and her voice was praised for its great range. She went to New York and Boston where, hailed as the 'Tasmanian Nightingale', she gave performances while continuing her studies. In 1882 she sailed for Europe, spending time in Italy and France. She made her English début at Drury Lane, London, on 7 April 1883 in *Maritana*, with the Carl Rosa Opera Company. In 1887 she visited Australia; her Melbourne concerts clashed with jubilee festivities and were not well attended, though her opening in August 1888 was well received. To recoup her losses she made an eight-months tour of Asia which ended in Tokyo in June 1889 and then returned to England.

Sherwin sang in Dresden, Hanover and Prague in 1890, receiving enthusiastic reviews. In Berlin she declined a three-year engagement at the Imperial Opera House for Sir Arthur Sullivan's offer of the lead in *The Gondoliers*. In August she sang at the Prince's Hall, London, and included a song composed by Governor Sir William Robinson. In 1896 she toured South Africa and next year Australia, singing in Sydney, Melbourne, Adelaide and Hobart where she was given a great reception, enthusiastic admirers unharnessing her horses and hauling her carriage through the streets. Back in London, where she was regarded 'as the wittiest of all Australian singers and the most polished and easiest of hostesses', she concentrated on concert work, realizing that her acting detracted from her operatic singing.

In 1902 and 1906 Sherwin again toured Australia. In 1907 she retired in England and turned to teaching to support herself and her invalid daughter, but she was not a good manager. Her last years were spent in poverty and sickness but not despair: 'even when her voice was only a whisper she would sit at the piano and sing with an archness and vivacity peculiarly her own'. When Hobart heard of her plight the lord mayor raised nearly £200. She died in London on 20 September 1935 and was buried in the Bromley Hill cemetery.

R. H. Todd, *Looking back* (Syd, 1938); A. Fysh, *The early days of the Sherwin family* (Hob, 1965); B. and F. Mackenzie, *Singers of Australia* (Melb, 1967); *Sydney Mail*, 28 Sept 1878, 31 May 1884; *Australasian*, 21 Dec 1878,

2 July 1887, 13 Oct 1888; *Examiner* (Launceston), 18 July 1879; *Bulletin*, 29 Feb 1880; *The Times*, 9 Apr 1883, 23 Sept 1935; *Argus*, 21, 23 June, 1, 16 August 1890. DEIRDRE MORRIS

SHILLINGLAW, JOHN JOSEPH (1831-1905), public servant and historian, was born on 30 September 1831 in London, eldest son of John Shillinglaw (d. 1862), librarian of the Royal Geographical Society, and his wife Emma Nicholas, née Taylor. At 14 he was sent to study under Captain John Washington, eminent maritime surveyor, and in 1852 he migrated with his father and brothers to Victoria, arriving in October. From November he was chief clerk of petty sessions at Williamstown, and in 1854 was appointed inspector and sometime acting superintendent of the Water Police. He was also secretary to the Steam Navigation Board until December 1857. In 1856-69 he was shipping-master for the Port of Melbourne and registrar of seamen; he helped to found the first Sailors' Home and did much to improve the working conditions of seamen. On 3 December 1857 he married Emma Mary Agnes Boyd; they had four sons and a daughter.

Retrenched from the civil service Shillinglaw struggled to support himself and his six dependants by miscellaneous journalism; there is evidence that his wife was in a lunatic asylum at this time. In 1875 he found temporary work in the Chief Secretary's Department and in February next year was a supernumerary clerk in the Chief Medical Officer's Department at a salary of £210, later £250. From January 1881 he was secretary to the Medical Board of Health; from 13 June he was acting secretary and from 14 November secretary to the Central Board of Health; he was also secretary to the Police Superannuation Board and the Police Medical Board. In 1882 he returned to the Chief Secretary's Department, and in 1885-94 was secretary to the royal commission on vegetable products. He was also secretary to the Board of Viticulture.

Shillinglaw was an enthusiast in whatever department he worked; however, he is remembered for his association with colonial literature and history. He was prominent among the lively literary coterie of Melbourne in the 1860s and 1870s, an original member of the Yorick Club, and of the short-lived literary society, the Cave of Adullam. He contributed to various colonial periodicals, and in September 1869 took over the *Colonial Monthly* magazine from Marcus Clarke [q.v.] for another two or three issues. Highly regarded as an historian, he began work on a biography of Matthew Flinders [q.v.] in the late 1870s, and received valuable source material from Flinders' family in England. He continued to amass information for his 'magnum opus', but it was never published.

Shillinglaw was elected a member of the Royal Geographical Society, London, in 1851 and in 1883 was a founder and councillor of the Victorian branch of the Geographical Society of Australasia. Generous and kindly, he 'made every acquaintance a friend' and went to great lengths to help them in every way. Long, lean and bony he was described in 1869 as 'nautical to a degree in his phraseology as well as a most "robustious" singer of "chanteys" ... He wore navy-blue habitually, a tall hat, and carried a small despatch box filled with mss. paper'. Hugh McCrae wrote, 'In his eyes shone valour, honour and romance'. He suffered for many years from 'chalky gout' and by the time of his death on 26 May 1905 could no longer write his name. Predeceased by his wife and three sons, he was buried in the St Kilda cemetery; his estate was valued for probate at £227 and included a vast collection of papers and rare books. From 1850 to 1877 he had published six books, and in 1879 he edited *Historical Records of Port Phillip: the First Annals of the Colony of Victoria*. His portrait is in the La Trobe Library, Melbourne.

H. McCrae, *Story-book only* (Syd, 1948); T. O'Callaghan, 'H.M.S. "Calcutta" in Port Phillip Bay, 1803', VHM, 10 (1924-25); G. G. McCrae, 'J. J. Shillinglaw, 1869', *Southerly*, 7 (1946) no 4; *Argus*, 27 May 1905; Shillinglaw papers (LaT L). ANN-MARI JORDENS

SHOLL, ROBERT JOHN (1819-1886), civil servant, administrator and magistrate, was born on 16 July 1819 at Southwark, London, second son of Robert Sholl, navy agent, and his wife Elizabeth, née Mutton. He abandoned his medical studies when his brother William inherited property in Western Australia on the death of their uncle Richard Sholl, who had gone to the colony in the *Sulphur* in 1829. With his mother, sister and younger brother, he arrived at Fremantle in the *Shepherd* on 19 November 1840 and settled at Bunbury.

Sholl worked as a teacher until he became a clerk in the District Magistrate's Court in 1844. On 21 September at the Anglican Church, Picton, he married Mary Ann Berckelman (d. 1889). In 1846 he became registrar for Wellington district, next year was transferred to the Postal Department, and in 1849 was a tide-waiter but resigned to join the *Inquirer*, edited by William. He became editor of the *Commercial News and*

Shipping List at Fremantle in February 1855, and joint owner with Edmund Stirling [q.v.] when the two newspapers amalgamated in July. He was secretary of the Geraldine Mining Co. and was associated with the Roebuck Bay Pastoral and Agricultural Co.

In January 1865 Governor Hampton appointed Sholl government resident of the new settlement at Camden Harbour, organized by the Camden Harbour Pastoral Co. He arrived there in February to find chaos and confusion. One ship had been wrecked, all but 1000 sheep were dead and the country was parched and dry. Some of the settlers had already gone and others were leaving. In April he set out with a well-armed party to examine the country between Camden Harbour and Roebuck Bay, hoping to find a pass through the hills to the Glenelg River. Rebuffed by rugged country at the eastern tip of the Whately Range he crossed at the western end, naming the McRae River before reaching the Glenelg. He was impressed by the excellent pastures there compared with the immediate hinterland at Camden Harbour. His account of the expedition was published in the *Journal of the Royal Geographical Society* in 1866.

Back at the settlement Sholl was continually troubled by Aboriginals pilfering government property and by administrative problems, especially those involving the truculent young surgeon Charles Smith-Bompas. A visit by proas from Macassar also caused alarm. Finally, the collapse of the company persuaded him to abandon the settlement in October; 'leaving behind wooden buildings, timber fencing and shingles to the value of £150, besides a tank and several horses', he moved south to Tien Tsin Harbour, which he found almost as discouraging. The settlers, members of the Denison Plains Co., were disgruntled, their supplies almost exhausted, with many suffering from bronchitis, rheumatism or scurvy. Sholl was appalled at the low standard of their dwellings and even more distressed by the misery at the Aboriginal camp. Apart from sharing his personal rations with them, there was little he could do to help. Gradually as the drought eased and conditions improved his optimism was renewed. The Aboriginals were the most friendly he had ever met and he granted one of them, Mullagough, a free passage to Fremantle.

In April 1866 Sholl moved to Walcott. which was gazetted as the town of Roebourne next August. His personal losses in a severe hurricane in 1872 included his library. Because of an acute shortage of building materials he was compelled to live in cramped official quarters for many years, but the district flourished until 1877 when it was again hampered by drought, a depressed wool market, scarcity of oyster pearls and the cessation of a small copper and lead-mining venture.

During his term at Roebourne, Sholl was justice of the peace, district registrar and deputy-treasurer; he was chairman of the Court of Petty Sessions and, from 1878, of Quarter Sessions. His informed submission advising on the 1873 Pearl Shell Fishery Regulation Act stressed the rights of Aboriginal employees. In 1879 he bought Mount Welcome station from J. Withnell and two years later left to become resident magistrate in the Swan district, where he died on 19 June 1886.

J. S. Battye, *The history of the north-west of Australia* (Perth, 1915), and *Western Australia* (Oxford, 1924); *Inquirer*, 4 Mar 1874, 2 June 1876; *West Australian*, 21, 22 June 1886, 9 July 1889; *Northern Times*, 28 July 1966; R. M. Crawford, The Camden Harbour settlement, *and* CSO, 1865-81 (Battye Lib, Perth).

WENDY BIRMAN

SHORT, AUGUSTUS (1802-1883), Anglican bishop, was born on 11 June 1802 at Bickham House near Exeter, Devon, England, third son of Charles Short, barrister, and his wife Grace, née Millett. Educated at Westminster and Christ Church, Oxford (B.A., 1824; M.A., 1826; D.D., 1847), he spent two years as tutor and was ordained priest in 1827. After two years as curate at Culham near Abingdon, he became tutor and lecturer at Christ Church, examiner in 1833 and censor in 1834. Next year he was appointed vicar of Ravensthorpe, Northampton, and on 10 December 1835 married Millicent Clara, daughter of John Phillips of Culham House, Oxfordshire. He became interested in the Oxford movement and wrote but did not publish an apologia in defence of Newman's Tract No. 90; in 1846 when he delivered the Bampton lectures at Oxford he steered clear of the controversy and published them as *The Witness of the Spirit with our Spirit*.

In 1845 Short was given the choice of either the Adelaide or Newcastle diocese. He chose Adelaide and on 29 June 1847 was consecrated bishop in Westminster Abbey. He arrived in the *Derwent* on 28 December. His vast diocese, which included Western Australia, had only eight clergy, four church buildings, with five under construction, one parsonage and one school but, helped by state aid, he began to build. In October 1848 with Archdeacon Hale [q.v.] he visited

Perth where he consecrated St George's Church. With help from the Society for the Propagation of Christian Knowledge and William Allen [q.v.], he transformed the school which had been started at Trinity Church in Adelaide into the Collegiate School of St Peter, and on 24 May 1849 laid its foundation stone.

As a high churchman Short frequently clashed with his predominantly Evangelical flock and with the province's Nonconformists. In 1850 at a bishops' conference in Sydney he supported the doctrine of baptismal regeneration; he provoked protest from the South Australian Church Society and the formation of a vigilant committee to petition the archbishop of Canterbury for protection from episcopal interference with doctrine. Short was unperturbed and assured his flock of his dislike of most of the Tractarian beliefs. In 1848 Governor Robe had granted land in Victoria Square as a cathedral site, but in 1855 the Supreme Court ruled the grant illegal: eventually in 1869 Short laid the foundation stone of St Peter's Cathedral in North Adelaide. In 1858 he created a furore by refusing to allow the Congregationalist divine Thomas Binney [q.v.] to preach in an Anglican church. His precedence as bishop of Adelaide was regarded by many as repugnant to the foundation principles of the colony and in 1872 Short voluntarily surrendered his claim.

Abolition of state aid in August 1851 had increased Short's financial problems and led to the independent organization of the diocese. In 1852 he replaced the Church Society by a provisional diocesan assembly of clergy and laity, and in 1853-54 on a visit to England sought ecclesiastical legal opinion on a proposed constitution for a diocesan synod. Advised that imperial legislation was not required, he called the first synod at Christ Church, Adelaide, on 16 January 1855. In October the fundamental provisions, regulations and compact were finally signed, ending satisfactorily an extended struggle about the rights of the laity in determining doctrine and discipline; but in 1862 the Legislative Council sent the Church of England incorporation bill to a select committee which declared it unnecessary. Finally in 1871 Short brought the synod under the Associations Incorporation Act.

He took an interest in Hale's Poonindie Mission to the Aboriginals at Port Lincoln and in 1853 wrote a report, Mission to the Heathen. In 1857 Short wrote a pamphlet against marriage with a deceased wife's sister and in 1869 read a paper to the Philosophical Society of Adelaide, 'On the proper relations of physical science to revealed religion'. He was actively involved in the founding of the University of Adelaide and was vice-president of the University Association. Elected vice-chancellor on 11 December 1874, he delivered the university's inaugural address on 25 April 1876 and that year succeeded Sir R. D. Hanson [q.v.] as chancellor.

In 1877 the citizens of Adelaide presented Short with an address and a testimonial to commemorate the fiftieth anniversary of his ordination. Next year he represented the diocese at the Lambeth Conference. In November 1881 failing health compelled him to resign his see, but he dedicated St Barnabas Theological College and on 6 January 1882 he celebrated his last communion service in the cathedral; he left for England that day. He lived quietly in London until his death on 5 October 1883. He was survived by his wife, three of their five sons and four of their five daughters. His estate was valued for probate at £8200.

Short successfully accomplished the immense task of building up the Church of England in South Australia. His Tractarian churchmanship was divisive, but it proved to be a firm basis for the Church and imparted to the diocese of Adelaide its distinctive character. Portraits hang in the Collegiate School of St Peter and in the Church Office and Bishop's Court, North Adelaide.

The Adelaide correspondence (Syd, 1859); F. T. Whitington, Augustus Short (Adel, 1887); E. K. Miller, Reminiscences of forty-seven years' clerical life in South Australia (Adel, 1895; F. W. Cox and L. Robjohns, Three-quarters of a century (Adel, 1912); G. H. Jose, The Church of England in South Australia, 1-2 (Adel, 1937, 1954); A. G. Price, The Collegiate School of St Peter, 1847-1947 (Adel, 1947); D. Pike, Paradise of Dissent (Melb, 1957); T. T. Reed, A history of the Cathedral Church of St Peter (Adel, 1969); Judith M. Brown, Augustus Short (Adel, 1974); N. K. Meaney, 'The Church of England in the Paradise of Dissent. A problem of assimilation', J Religious History, 3 (1964); Register (Adel), 9 Oct 1883, 16 Apr 1923; Hale-Short letters (ML); A Short, Diary and papers (SAA).   DIRK VAN DISSEL

SHORT, BENJAMIN (1833-1912), insurance salesman and lay evangelist, was born on 19 April 1833 in London, son of William Short, spice merchant, and his wife Elizabeth, née Smith. Apprenticed to a wheelwright, he later set up as a coachbuilder. He was also a life insurance agent and assisted in the evangelistic meetings of the London City Mission.

Short arrived in Sydney in March 1860 as an insurance agent and soon persuaded the Australian Mutual Provident Society to appoint him as its first canvasser. He combined his work with successful collecting for the Destitute Children's Asylum, Randwick, and quickly sold policies worth £138,000. In 1865 he worked country districts and in the 1870s lectured in New South Wales, Victoria and New Zealand on life insurance. Short applied the lay evangelist's art to his lectures. He was popular, with an easy and unpretentious style and his topics included 'Courtship and Marriage', 'Happy Homes' and 'Total Abstinence', illustrating the advantages of life insurance. In 1881 he returned to Sydney as chief metropolitan agent and was joined by his son Benjamin. He opened his office on Saturday nights for working men and often lectured to employees of large firms in the lunch hour. He retired to Bowral in 1886 having 'taken' some 12,000 'lives'.

Determined to be elected to the board of the A.M.P. Society, Short, after failing in 1887 and 1891, campaigned on a comprehensive reform platform. Elected in 1892, he achieved lower interest rates, the acceptance of female lives on equal terms with male and better terms for young lives. He retired in 1895 under the by-laws, was re-elected in May 1896 and a change of rules enabled him to remain a director until 1912.

Short, a free trader, was defeated for the Legislative Assembly seat of Petersham in 1894, but religion rather than politics was his dominant interest. With the help of J. H. Goodlet [q.v.] and others he founded the Sydney City Mission in 1862, was its joint secretary that year and secretary in 1863-68. Active in the Young Men's Christian Association, he also supported the British and Foreign Bible Society and overseas missions, especially in India. He helped to found Congregational churches in Ocean Street, Woollahra, in 1865 and later in Dunedin and Nelson, New Zealand.

In retirement Short concentrated on evangelistic work. He ordered a large and costly model of the Jewish tabernacle in the wilderness and lectured on it in Australia and in England on three visits. He often supplied vacant pulpits in Congregational churches and held annual religious conventions at his home, Fernside, Bowral. Unsophisticated and largely self-taught in theology, Short had limitations with informed congregations, but his style served him as well in offering salvation as in selling insurance.

In London on 22 July 1856 Short had married Elizabeth Thomas (d. 1887) according to the rites of the countess of Huntingdon's connexion. He died of influenza at Petersham on 10 June 1912, survived by their two sons and seven daughters and by his second wife Elizabeth Jane Cantilo, née Rivers, whom he had married at Port Adelaide on 20 January 1890. Buried in the Congregational section of Rookwood cemetery, he left an estate valued for probate at £14,667.

L. H. Hoare, *Presenting ten decades* (Syd, 1962); *Bulletin*, 18 Mar 1882; *Daily Telegraph* (Syd), 25 June 1894, 11 June 1912; *SMH*, 11 June 1912; *Aust Christian World* (Syd), 21 June 1912; *Congregationalist* (Syd), 1 July 1912; B. Dickey, Charity in New South Wales, 1850-1914 (Ph.D. thesis, ANU, 1966); AMP Soc Archives (Syd).   WALTER PHILLIPS

SIEDE, JULIUS (1825-1903), conductor and flautist, was born in Dresden, Saxony, son of August Siede, magistrate, and his wife Amalia. Showing early musical talent, he studied under the flautist A. B. Furstenau and the composers E. J. Otto and K. G. Reissiger. Making his debut at 12, Siede rapidly gained public recognition as a flautist. After touring Germany and Russia (including western Siberia) in 1846-47, he settled in Berlin but left in 1848 for a tour of the United States of America, where his playing was well received. In 1849 he was appointed musical director of the Castle Garden concerts in New York. In 1850 he travelled with Jenny Lind through the United States and Cuba. In 1851-52 Siede accompanied Madame Anna Bishop on her tour of the United States, West Indies and Mexico and he lived in New York until about 1855. He joined Anna Bishop on tour in Australia and appeared in her concerts in Melbourne, Adelaide and Sydney from October 1856 until about mid-1857.

Siede remained in Melbourne. One of his first solo performances was in July 1857, when he gave a 'Grande Soiree Musicale' at the Mechanics' Institute; in October and November he played again. From 1858 he conducted the earliest operatic performances at the Theatre Royal for G. V. Brooke [q.v.] and in November 1862 he re-orchestrated Meyerbeer's opera *The Huguenots* for W. S. Lyster's [q.v.] production; C. E. Horsley [q.v.] praised him for his high skill and extraordinary memory in working from nothing more than a pianoforte arrangement, and acclaimed him as 'one of the best flautists living'. As conductor for Lyster's opera company in 1865-71, Siede was regarded as 'a general favourite, who combines sterling ability with genuine modesty'. In 1863 he had organized the Headquarters Band, which for over a decade gave popular open-air music recitals, notably in the Fitzroy Gardens. In later years he attempted a revival of this type of performance by giving several seasons of 'continental concerts'. On 9 August 1870 he was associated with Horsley and David Lee [q.v.] as conductor at the opening of the new Town Hall. With C. G. Elsässer, J. Herz [qq.v.] and others he took part in many fund-raising concerts both as conductor and as flute soloist.

From about 1872 Siede was conductor of the Melbourne Deutsche Liedertafel, which in 1879 split into two with Siede becoming chorus master of the Melbourne Liedertafel, and conductor in 1879-89. He was president of the Melbourne Musical Association of Victoria in 1879; it later merged into the Musical Society of Victoria, of which he was a vice-president in 1896. At the International Centennial Exhibition of 1888 he was chairman of the jury judging musical instruments. His health failed in 1889 and he appears to have been short of money despite his salary, the receipts of a benefit concert and the generosity of A. Zelman [q.v.]. He resigned as conductor of the Liedertafel in January 1890 and, in an unprecedented gesture, the society raised £491 for him in tribute to his blameless professional and private life and the public respect that he commanded.

Siede was also a composer though little is known of the extent of his work. He wrote two cantatas for the Melbourne Liedertafel: 'Hymn to the Night' and an 'Occultation of Orion' as well as part-songs and arrangements. He also wrote much military band music and three concert overtures: 'Faust and Margarethe', 'Festival' and 'Anthony and Cleopatra'. Aged 78, he died on 23 April 1903 at his home in Auburn, Melbourne; he was predeceased by his wife Anna, née Holzer, whom he had married on 11 February 1858 at the German Church, Malvern, and survived by two daughters and five sons, of whom August was well known as a musician and as pianist for the Melbourne Liedertafel in 1884-1902.

H. M. Humphreys (ed), *Men of the time in Australia: Victorian series*, 2nd ed (Melb, 1882); *Argus*, 24 Nov 1862, 25 Apr 1903; *Australasian*, 31 Dec 1870; *IAN*, 1 Apr 1890; M. T. Radic, Aspects of organised amateur music in Melbourne 1836-1890 (M. Mus. thesis, Univ Melb, 1969); Minute books 1878-95, scrap-book 1887, 1890 (Melb Liedertafel Soc).   MAUREEN THERESE RADIC

SILVERLEAF, *see* LLOYD, JESSIE GEORGINA

SIMONETTI, ACHILLE (1838-1900), sculptor, was born in Rome, son of Louis Simonetti, sculptor, and his wife Rosina.

Educated at the Accademia Nazionale di San Luca, he trained under his father and visited Greece. In 1871 at the instigation of Bishop James Quinn [q.v.] he migrated to Brisbane. By 1874 he had moved to Sydney, where he set up a large studio at Balmain and worked on St John's College, within the University of Sydney. He modelled a bust of Governor Sir Hercules Robinson, and won a silver medal for 'sculpture and modelling' at the New South Wales Academy of Art's exhibition. Next year he was awarded the sculpture prize at the exhibition held by the Agricultural Society of New South Wales and a gold medal at the academy's annual exhibition; he continued to win similar awards until 1880. In May 1875 he became instructor in sculpture and modelling at the academy's new art school. Next year he showed a bust of Commodore J. G. Goodenough [q.v.] at the Royal Academy of Arts exhibition in London. At the Sydney International Exhibition in 1879 his 'Venus of the South' attracted favourable criticism. With two busts it was shown as the New South Wales sculpture exhibit at the 1880 Melbourne International Exhibition.

Befriended by (Sir) Saul Samuel [q.v.], Simonetti became the most fashionable sculptor in Sydney and modelled busts of many of the city's notables. In the 1880s he served on the committee of the Art Society of New South Wales. He was commissioned by the government to carve six allegorical figures for the niches on the building of the Colonial Secretary's Department fronting Macquarie, Bridge and Phillip streets. In 1891 he completed a marble memorial statue of Quinn, reputed to be his best work, and worked on a life-sized marble statue of J. H. Challis [q.v.] for the University of Sydney.

On 18 October 1889 Simonetti had been commissioned by Sir Henry Parkes [q.v.] to construct for £10,000 an elaborate monument to Governor Phillip, to be sited in the Botanic Gardens and completed by May 1893, but the work was later delayed for a year by Sir George Dibbs's [q.v.] 'express authority'. Further delays occurred when, at the suggestion of Sir Julian Salomons and E. L. Montefiore [qq.v.], the supporting figures were changed from realistic to classical. In November 1893 Simonetti visited Italy to supervise the bronze casting by Messrs Galli Bros, of Florence, of the fifteen-foot statue of Phillip and the base statues of Agriculture, Commerce, Neptune (navigation) and Cyclops (mining). Coriolano Fontana executed the Carrara marble pedestal and basins in Genoa. Eventually the fifty-foot high monument was completed for over £14,000 and unveiled by Governor Hampden on 22 June 1897 during Queen Victoria's Diamond Jubilee celebrations. Its eclectic combination of realistic and neo-classic styles was unfavourably received.

Aged 62, Simonetti died of heart disease on 23 March 1900 at his home in Birchgrove and was buried in the Catholic section of Rookwood cemetery. He was survived by his wife Margaret, née Doherty, and by a son and daughter; his estate was valued for probate at £529. Talented and industrious, Simonetti preferred to sculpture in the neoclassic style but his clients preferred realism. Examples of his work are owned by the Art Gallery of New South Wales, the Legislative Council and the University of Sydney.

H. E. Badham, A study of Australian art (Syd, 1949); A. McCulloch, Encyclopedia of Australian art (Lond, 1968); J. G. De Libra, 'The fine arts in Australia', A'sian Art Review, 1 July 1899; Freeman's J (Syd), 7 Nov 1891; SMH, 26 Mar 1900; S. N. Hogg, Balmain past and present (ML); Col Sec letters (NSWA).

NOEL S. HUTCHISON

SIMPSON, ALFRED (1805-1891), iron and tin manufacturer, was born on 29 August 1805 in London, son of John Simpson, Wesleyan later Unitarian clergyman, and his wife Anne, née Salter. Apprenticed in 1820 as a tin-plate worker he also found time to study science and chemistry. He was admitted to the Worshipful Company of Tinplate Workers and in 1829 became a Freeman of the City of London. After joining his brother in a tailoring firm as traveller he set up as a hatter. On 21 June 1838 he married Sarah Neighbour.

The prosperity of Simpson's business was checked by a fire and the depression following the collapse of the railway boom, and he and his family were forced to migrate. They sailed in the John Woodhall for Melbourne but disembarked at Port Adelaide on 17 January 1849. After several unsuccessful business ventures and having twice visited the goldfields while Sarah gave piano lessons, in 1853 he turned to tinsmithing, making pots and pans and supplying cans for the Glen Ewin jam factory. In 1862 he leased premises in Gawler Place, Adelaide, which later were rebuilt.

Simpson was an innovator and introduced labour-saving machinery and new products such as fire-proof safes, bedsteads, japanned ware, colonial ovens and gas stoves. He was one of the first members of the South Australian Chamber of Manufactures. Of a retiring disposition, he was esteemed for his commercial ability and consideration to employees. Survived by two of his three children, he died on 23 September 1891 and was buried in the West Terrace cemetery. A

memorial window to him and his wife (d. 1874) was installed in the Unitarian Church in Wakefield Street.

His son, ALFRED MULLER (1843-1917), was born on 4 April 1843 in London. Educated at Martin's Academy in Pirie Street, Adelaide, he learnt drawing at Mrs Hill's School of Arts in 1861 and in the same year joined the Volunteer Corps. Beginning his apprenticeship in 1857 in his father's firm, he became a partner in 1864. On 18 October 1871 he married Catherine Allen.

Simpson was an enterprising businessman with an eye for advanced mechanical techniques. At the 1878 Paris exhibition he bought from the American, E. W. Bliss, a double-action press. He was interested in the welfare of his employees and in 1872 was on a commission inquiring into legislation for the regulation of shops and factories and improvement of working conditions. Under him the firm continued to expand and prosper, in 1901 pioneering the manufacture of enamelware in Australia. Prominent in business and civic affairs, he was a promoter and director of the Adelaide and Suburban Tramway Co. from its formation in 1876 and was also associated with the Port Adelaide Dock, the Commercial Wharf and the South Australian Gas companies. He was a member of the State Board of Conciliation from 1895, president of the Royal Agricultural and Horticultural Society of South Australia in 1898-99, and a trustee of the State Bank of South Australia from 1902. As a member of the Legislative Council for Central District in 1887-94, he was known for his forthright speeches in favour of tariff protection and against payment for members of the council. His own parliamentary salary went to provide a shooting prize for the defence forces, first awarded in 1890 and still contested.

Of wide interests, Simpson held a St John Ambulance certificate and sponsored chess exhibitions; he was a prominent Freemason and a strong supporter of the Unitarian Church. His private benefactions included support for Kalyra Consumption Sanatorium, and the Blind, Deaf and Dumb Institute. He presented to the Adelaide City Council Chambers the stained glass windows commemorating the coronation of King Edward VII. After the death of his first wife in 1887, he married Violet Laura Sheridan on 23 August 1888. He died of cancer on 28 September 1917 survived by two sons and three daughters. His estate was sworn for probate in Adelaide at £207,000, in Victoria at £19,561 and in New South Wales at £3106.

Simpson & Son Ltd, 'To-day not to-morrow': a century of progress (Adel, 1954); PP (SA),

1868-69, 3 (125); *Register* (Adel), 24, 26 Sept 1891; *Advertiser* (Adel), 26 Sept 1891; letters received by A. M. Simpson *and* papers of A. M. and A. Simpson *and* Sarah Simpson diaries (SAA); newspaper cuttings relating to South Aust churches, vol 1 (SAA).

MARJORIE FINDLAY*

SIMPSON, SIR GEORGE BOWEN (1838-1915), politician and judge, was born on 22 May 1838 at Oatlands near Parramatta, New South Wales, son of Pierce (Percy) Simpson, then a police magistrate, and his wife Hester Elizabeth, sister of the celebrated engineer Sir John MacNeill. Pierce was a naval captain who became a lieutenant in the Royal Corsican Rangers. He came to Sydney in 1822 and was successively commandant of convicts at Wellington Valley, a surveyor of roads and police magistrate at Patrick's Plains. He built Oatlands on a grant at what is now Dundas, one of his many land holdings.

Educated at The King's School, Parramatta, Simpson was admitted to the colonial Bar on 8 November 1858. Because of strenuous and independent advocacy he won a large practice very rapidly. In August 1867 he became a District Court judge. The salary was only £1000 and, as he was so young, he soon found that the financial sacrifice was too much to bear. He resigned in 1874, protesting that judges were underpaid, and became a crown prosecutor instead.

Simpson was nominated to the Legislative Council on 22 December 1885 as government representative and attorney-general in Sir John Robertson's [q.v.] last ministry. By right of office he became a Q.C. in 1886, before the government fell in February. In February 1888 he succeeded B. R. Wise as attorney-general in Sir Henry Parkes's [q.v.] cabinet and was soon involved in the vexed question of how legally to exclude Chinese immigrants. In June the Supreme Court determined that Chinese paying poll tax could not be excluded under current laws. Simpson, fearing heavy claims against the government, threatened to resign unless his advice was followed to permit entry to all immigrants paying the tax. His advice was rejected, but he did not resign. In 1888-91 he again served as attorney-general under Parkes, and complained that the salary was too low. In September 1892 he resigned from the council to act as a judge of the Supreme Court; reappointed two months later, in 1894 he was attorney-general in George Reid's first ministry. He introduced major government legislation with well-prepared speeches, often spoke on law reform, but resisted proposed weakening of trial by jury and was opposed to amalgamation of the legal profession.

On 18 December 1894 Simpson became a judge of the Supreme Court. He was capable but severe. When appointed judge in Divorce in 1896 he said, 'I like to see things properly done, and when they are so done all goes merry as a marriage bell — though, perhaps, that is hardly an appropriate expression to use in this Court. When work is not conducted as it should be, I am afraid I frequently show my displeasure'. Although abhorring a jurisdiction tainted with 'tales of misery and wretchedness, which are calculated to make one feel depressed', Simpson remained there until his retirement. He dressed well, fashionably, and with great preciseness, often exhorting members of the Bar to follow his sartorial example. Likewise he maintained great form and ceremony in his court, being 'a large man of impressive appearance [who] moved with much dignity and . . . was fond of imposing attitudes and gestures'.

Knighted in 1909, Simpson acted as chief justice for a year after the retirement of Sir Frederick Darley [q.v.] until January 1910 and was twice acting governor. Retiring on 11 April, he led a withdrawn life in poor health at his home Cloncorrick, Darling Point, which, designed by J. H. Hunt [q.v.] and built in 1884, was named after Cloncorrick Castle, County Leitrim, Ireland, where his grandfather had lived. Simpson died of pneumonia on 7 September 1915 and was buried in the Anglican section of Waverley cemetery. Predeceased by his two children, he was survived by his wife Martha Margaret, née Cobcroft, whom he had married at East Maitland on 10 October 1861, and to whom he left his estate, sworn for probate at £27,423. A memorial tablet is in St Mark's Church, Darling Point.

H. Blacket, *May it please your Honour* (Syd. 1927); V&P (LA NSW), 1870-71, 1, 129, 201; 'Memoranda', *NSW Law Reports*, 1895-96; 'Memoranda', *State Reports* (NSW), 1908, 1910; H. T. E. Holt, The lives and times of the judges of the District Court of New South Wales (held by author); Parkes letters (ML); family papers (held by Mr & Mrs Philip Simpson, Bellevue Hill, Syd).

J. M. BENNETT

SIMSON, ROBERT (1819-1896), pastoralist, was born on 4 October 1819 at Coalfarm, Fife, Scotland, son of Robert Simson, farmer, and his wife Elizabeth, née Carstairs. With his cousin Philip Russell [q.v.] of Kincraig, he sailed to Van Diemen's Land; they arrived in November 1842 with £1800 between them. Three months later they crossed to Port Phillip and in April 1843 purchased Carngham station in the Western District, where they fared well;

Simson earned a reputation as a horseman. He revisited England in 1847 and returned to Carngham in 1850 with his brother John and cousin Thomas Russell [q.v.]. In April 1851 he married Catherine, sister of C. M. Officer [q.v.] and a forceful personality who, after a month of marriage, wrote to a friend, 'I have taken Simson completely under my care; reduced him to a state of subordination and content'. The marriage was childless.

In April 1853 Russell and Simson dissolved their partnership; in July Simson purchased Langi Kal Kal near Beaufort, and in time acquired the freehold. He devoted himself to the breeding of high-class merino sheep, experimenting in the 1860s with Rambouillet rams which he had sent from England, and with imported rams from the Steiger stud flock. Dissatisfied with the results, he founded a Lincoln sheep stud and with both Lincolns and merinos had great success at the Skipton, Ballarat and Melbourne shows. In 1865 he moved to Melbourne where he bought Leura in Toorak and in 1873 built a new mansion on the site. Langi Kal Kal was run by a manager and Simson continued to win prizes at shows until the late 1880s when he turned mainly to cattle-breeding.

Simson was a member of the Legislative Council for the Western Province in 1868-78. A staunch free-trade conservative, he opposed payment of members. Although not without critics, he was returned unopposed in June 1880 but in November 1882 he retired on medical advice. Simson was an active committee-man and sometime president of associations including the National Agricultural Society, the Sheepbreeders' Association, the Zoological and Acclimatisation Society and the Royal Horticultural Society of Victoria. He was on the committee of the Victorian Coursing Club, president of the Melbourne Club in 1889 and a trustee of the Victorian Asylum and School for the Blind. He was a director of the British and Australasian Trust and Loan Co. and of the Land Mortgage Bank of Victoria. In Melbourne he was a prominent member of the Scots Church congregation and a trustee of Scotch College and other church property. In 1880 he became a councillor of Ormond College and gave £500 to its fund; he also gave staunch continuing support to the Beaufort Presbyterian Church. With a lively manner and good looks, he was sometimes nicknamed 'Sir Robert' and he left a 'host of friends and acquaintances' when he died on 3 November 1896, predeceased by his wife. His estate in Victoria was valued for probate at £182,957.

Simson's family connexions spread a wide net over western Victoria and beyond. Besides his cousins, the Russells, two of his brothers became well-known pastoralists. John (1822-1896) held Trawalla near Beaufort in 1853-73 and then made his home in Melbourne, but in 1880-81 took up Gurley station near Moree, New South Wales, and Carella in Queensland. He died on 29 March 1896 at his Toorak mansion, Trawalla, survived by his wife Margaret, née Luke, of Fife, whom he had married in 1856, and by a son and four daughters. Colin William (1828-1905) reached Victoria late in 1851, failed at the gold diggings and then worked with Robert until experienced enough to take a share in and manage the Mount Ross section of Langi Kal Kal. In January 1858 he bought York Plains station near Warracknabeal. He married Marguerite Madeleine Smith in 1862 at St Peter's Church, Melbourne, reputedly with eighteen bridesmaids in attendance; that year he took up Mungadal near Hay, New South Wales. In 1877-80 he represented Balranald in the New South Wales Legislative Assembly. He acquired Trinkey station on the Liverpool Plains in 1888 but for many years lived at his Melbourne mansion, Carmyle. He died of pneumonia on 23 February 1905 at Geelong while staying at the home of his son-in-law, Thomas Fairbairn, predeceased by his wife and a son, and survived by three sons and five daughters.

T. W. H. Leavitt (ed), *Australian representative men*, (Melb, 1887); P. L. Brown (ed), *Clyde Company papers*, 3, 5 (Lond, 1958, 1963); *Warrnambool Standard*, 22 May, 3 June 1880; *Australasian*, 4 Apr 1896; *Argus*, 24 Feb 1905; Alexander Adam, Autobiography (LaT L).

J. ANN HONE

SINCLAIR, JAMES (1809-1881), landscape gardener, was born at Altyre, Forres, Morayshire, Scotland, on the estate of Sir William Gordon Gordon-Cumming (1787-1854), son of Lewis Sinclair, head steward, and his wife Elizabeth, née Hardy. Because of his drawing talent he was sent to London for training in painting and landscape gardening. He worked in Kew Gardens under T. A. Knight (1759-1838).

Sinclair's originality in design and his skill in delineating exotic plants became known through his illustrations for Knight's journal articles. In 1838 Prince Mikhail Semenovich Vorontsov of Russia invited him to plan his estate at Sebastopol in the Crimea. The quality of his work so impressed Tsar Nicholas I that he borrowed him to assist in laying out the Imperial Gardens at St Petersburg. He was honoured with the Imperial Order of St Anne, and arrangements were made for him to be granted access to all royal gardens in Europe. At 37, at Sebastopol, Sinclair married Mary Ann Cooper, governess to Prince Vorontsov's children, and they lived in a house in the palace grounds where their first child was born. At the outbreak of the Crimean war in 1853 they returned to England.

A conflict of loyalties between friendship and country soon influenced Sinclair to leave his native land and in 1854 he arrived in Melbourne with his wife and child. He began business as a seedsman and in June 1855 published the first number of *The Gardener's Magazine and Journal of Rural Economy*, a monthly that ran for twelve issues and sold for 1s. He had come at an opportune time: the Melbourne City Council was debating the disposition of Fitz Roy Square. Originally intended for land development, the scheme had been impeded by the swamps and bluestone quarries which were being used as rubbish tips. In 1856 a decision was reached to turn the sixty-four acres into gardens. A sum of £1000 was voted for the project at the February council meeting and Sinclair became the planner next year. The square was renamed Fitz Roy Gardens in August 1862.

The City Council intended a spread of formal lawns and flower beds but Sinclair remained firm in his concept of trees and shaded walks. With the co-operation of C. Hodgkinson [q.v.] he had the swamps drained and diverted to form a natural winding channel running through clumps of native tree-ferns with weeping willows planted on its banks. The replacement of many of the ferns with palm-trees later destroyed the woodland character of this area. In 1859 Sinclair planted the first twelve-year-old elms, which flourished side by side with avenues of poplars and plane trees, interspersed with massed shrubs and grassy lawns sloping towards the railway yards of Jolimont. His work contributed much to the development of Melbourne as a garden city.

Sinclair also wrote poetry. *The Australian Sacred Lyre* was published in Melbourne in 1857, while his *Original Australian Proverbs and True Love Songs* appeared in 1859.

Sinclair died of apoplexy on 29 April 1881, aged 72, and was buried in Kew cemetery. He was survived by two daughters and a son of his first marriage and by his second wife Ellen, née Roberts, whom he had married in 1860 and who had helped him to complete his drawings when rheumatism crippled his hands. A memorial tablet is set into a pathway near the house on the eastern edge of the gardens, in which he had lived from about 1872 and where he died.

H. Knight, 'James Sinclair—maker of Fitzroy Gardens', *and* E. E. Pescott, 'The pioneers of horticulture in Victoria', VHM, 18 (1940); *Argus*, 19 Feb 1856; *Herald* (Melb), 6 July 1968.

JEAN GITTINS

SINGLETON, JOHN (1808-1891), physician and philanthropist, was born on 2 January 1808 in Dublin, son of William Singleton, a prosperous merchant. and his wife Mary, née Lewis. Articled in 1823 to an apothecary in Kells, County Meath, in 1826 he was placed with a general practitioner for four years and attended medical lectures. He set up practice in Dublin in the early 1830s and received his M.D. on 15 April 1838 from the University of Glasgow. An Anglican, at 16 he had become a total abstainer and at 19 experienced an evangelistic conversion: gaol visiting, tract distribution and medical aid to the poor became part of his daily life. In 1834, after a brief courtship, he married Isabella Daunt of Cork; they had four sons and six daughters.

In 1849 Singleton's elder brother William, a clergyman, migrated to Victoria. He decided to follow, took a post as ship's surgeon in the *Harply* and arrived with his family in Melbourne on 30 January 1851. In 1851-56 he practised in Collins Street, Melbourne, supporting an Anglican association for promoting temperance, the Victorian Liquor Law League and the Melbourne Total Abstinence Society. He and wife soon began gaol visiting; he was opposed to capital punishment and interceded with Lieut-Governor La Trobe on behalf of some condemned prisoners. In January 1855 he moved to a farm at Merri Creek and started visiting near-by Pentridge gaol, whose governor, J. G. Price [q.v.], opposed his ideals of evangelism and reformation: their antagonism was noticeable in Singleton's evidence in December 1856 to the select committee of the Legislative Council on penal establishments.

Not robust, Singleton had weak eyes and suffered from severe headaches. Partly for health reasons, he practised in Warrnambool in 1860-64, Mount Gambier in South Australia in 1865 and Maryborough in 1866-67, forming total abstinence societies. His active interest in Aboriginal welfare helped lead to the establishment of the Framlingham Reserve near Warrnambool. In Maryborough and near-by goldfields he organized a Bible society, conducted prayer meetings and distributed religious tracts in various languages. In August 1867 Singleton returned to Melbourne in very poor health. Recovering, he settled in Hawthorn and had his M.D. confirmed by the University of Melbourne in 1868. In early 1869 he established the Collingwood Free Medical

Dispensary (now the Singleton Medical Welfare Centre), which had been first suggested by the Melbourne City Mission. The dispensary gave free medical attention to the poor and provided spiritual guidance from tracts. In 1876 a mission hall was established near by for prayer meetings, Bible classes, Sunday school, the annual old folks' tea and working men's meetings.

From 1869 Singleton was honorary corresponding secretary of what became after 1884 the Society for the Promotion of Morality, which was supported by prominent colonists and had been formed by Bishop Perry, Judge Pohlman, Sir W. F. Stawell [qq.v.] and others. Of the organizations commenced by the society, Singleton had most to do with the Model Lodging House for men in King Street, and the Retreat for Friendless and Fallen Women in Islington Street, Collingwood (now Singleton Lodge). In September 1870 he joined the newly established children's hospital as physician, but withdrew about a year later after religious differences with the managing committee. Singleton bought land in Little Bourke Street in 1879 to build a mission hall and in 1883 offered the use of it to the Salvation Army. Encouraging the army in its gaol visiting, he gave it the use of the Collingwood mission hall and laid the stone for their Collingwood citadel. In the 1870s he had initiated a public appeal known as the 'Singleton Bread Fund' for the unemployed; he also instituted a night shelter for destitute women, Widows' Cottages in Collingwood, a mission to the blind, the West Melbourne overnight shelters for men and the Women's Model Lodging House, Melbourne. His gaol visits continued until 1891.

Singleton supported the employment of women in medical practice. He read papers to the Medical Society of Victoria: on mortality in Victoria (1870), on the use of alcohol as medicine (1874), on phthisis (1876) and typhus fever (1878). In 1871-91 he lived at Ormiston, East Melbourne, where his daughters Elizabeth and Anna conducted a school for young ladies. His sons John Wesley, William Daunt and Robert Henry were associated with the Collingwood dispensary. Predeceased by his wife in 1886, Singleton died at Ormiston on 30 September 1891 and was buried in the Anglican section of the Melbourne general cemetery. Just before his death he had published in Melbourne his memoirs, A Narrative of Incidents in the eventful life of a Physician. Portraits of him are in the Royal Children's Hospital, Melbourne, and the Singleton Medical Welfare Centre.

T. W. H. Leavitt (ed), Australian representative men (Melb, 1887); P. Dale, Salvation chariot ... 1880-1951 (Melb, 1952); Church of England Messenger (Vic), 8 Sept, 3 Nov, 1 Dec 1871; P. Dale, 'Dr. Singleton lives on', VHM, 26 (1954-55); Age, 2 Oct 1891; Argus, 2 Oct 1891, 12 Nov 1932; A. M. Mitchell, Temperance and the liquor question in later nineteenth century Victoria (M.A. thesis, Univ Melb, 1966); Children's Hospital, Annual reports 1870-78 (Roy Children's Hospital, Melb); Collingwood Free Medical Dispensary, Minutes 1870, annual reports 1880, 1885, 1889, 1891 (Singleton Medical Welfare Centre, Collingwood, Vic).   SYLVIA MORRISSEY

SINNETT, FREDERICK (1830-1866), journalist and literary critic, was born on 8 March 1830 in Hamburg, Germany, elder son of London-born Edward William Percy Sinnett, newspaper editor, English teacher and author, and his wife Jane, née Fry. After his father's death in England in 1844 his mother supported the family by editing and translating. He probably trained in both surveying and engineering and as a newspaper reporter; through association with J. S. Mill, Harriet Taylor and others he became well versed in political economy.

Showing early signs of tuberculosis, Sinnett decided to migrate to Australia and arrived in Adelaide in May or June 1849, hoping to become a sub-engineer for the Adelaide and Port Railway Co. Instead, he joined Thomas Burr, land agent and surveyor, and in 1850 they laid out the town of Truro. In 1852 Sinnett joined a party exploring the Lake Torrens area; in 1854 he reported his 'Observations' in a paper to the Victorian Institute for the Advancement of Science. He moved to Melbourne in December 1852 as 'intended editor' of the Melbourne Morning Herald and General Daily Advertiser. He formed a company and brought new capital into the business but in September 1856 C. F. Somerton took over from him as printer and publisher, renaming the paper the Herald. Although cheerful and buoyant, he was not a good businessman and he lost heavily while with the Herald and in later ventures. He joined the Argus staff and was leader-writer in 1857-60. On 29 October 1857 at St Peter's Church of England, Melbourne, he married Jane Ann, daughter of Thomas Burr; he gave his religion as Unitarian.

Sinnett's professionalism and infectious wit guaranteed him a place among the literary and artistic circles of the young colony. He had a hand in several ventures, and with Edgar Ray had helped to found in 1855 the splendid Melbourne Punch; he was a member of the group, including James Smith, R. H. Horne, N. Chevalier [qq.v.] and James Stiffe, that met to plan its issues, and in 1856-59 he was editor. In May 1858, also with Ray, he began the *Daily News* in Geelong and was sole editor until its failure in August 1859. With his knowledge of German language and literature he had many friends among the German artists, scientists and scholars living in Melbourne. He was a member of the Philosophical Institute (formed in 1855). In December 1857 he was elected to the committee of the short-lived Society of Fine Arts. He went to Queensland in October 1858 as *Argus* correspondent to report on the gold rush to Canoona; next year he published in Geelong an account of his experiences.

Later in 1859 Sinnett returned to Adelaide and worked for a while as parliamentary shorthand writer. He also set up an ice-works and, as Sinnett & Co., in April 1860 produced the first ice blocks in the city. In a booklet *Ice, and its uses* (n.d.), he passed on instructions and recipes for his customers. In August 1862 he produced the *Daily Telegraph*, the first evening newspaper in Adelaide; he also contributed to other publications. His fluent and analytic essay, *An account of the Colony of South Australia*, was written for the 1862 International Exhibition in London.

In financial difficulties once more, Sinnett accepted a post with the *Argus*, arriving in Melbourne in August 1865. He and his wife took part again in Melbourne's literary and theatrical life, holding Saturday night readings and discussions of Shakespeare's plays. But Sinnett, so lively and versatile and with 'a husk of shyness', was now rapidly weakened by tuberculosis; on 23 November 1866 he died at his home in Kew and was buried in the Melbourne general cemetery. Predeceased by two daughters, he was survived by his wife (d. 1892) and two of his three sons; the elder, Percy, writing as 'Per Se', showed literary promise before his death at 23. Sinnett was mourned for his kindness of heart, the brilliance of his intellect and conversation and especially his humour. Of his few certain writings, the most notable is his essay in the *Journal of Australasia*, June and December 1856, 'The Fiction Fields of Australia'. In this discussion of the criteria of fiction and of several recently published novels, he raised important questions which are still relevant. The essay was republished in Brisbane in 1966 with an introduction by C. Hadcraft.

Table Talk, 17 Jan 1896; *Age*, 24 Nov 1866; *Argus*, 24 Nov 1866; *Herald* (Melb), 24 Nov 1866; James Smith papers (ML); H. G. Turner papers (LaT L).   MARJORIE J. TIPPING

SIXSMITH, WILLIAM (1815-1893), locomotive driver, was born on 18 November 1815 at Wavertree near Liverpool, Lancashire, England, son of William Sixsmith. As a boy he worked on the construction of the Liverpool–Manchester railway and joined the locomotive branch on the opening of the line. He became an engine-driver on the Liverpool–Manchester and later the Liverpool–Birmingham lines. He then drove engines on the construction line for the Paris–Rouen railway and was similarly employed under Sir John O'Neill in Ireland. He claimed to have driven trains containing the duke of Wellington and King Louis-Phillipe.

Lured by gold Sixsmith migrated to Sydney with his family and wife Maria, née Townsend, whom he had married in Birmingham in 1841. He soon travelled 'alone and on foot' to the Ovens goldfield where he had no luck. He made his way to Melbourne and worked his passage back to Sydney as a coal-trimmer on a coastal steamer. He was employed as driver on the ballast engine by William Randle, contractor, on the construction of the Sydney–Parramatta line.

On 26 September 1855 wearing a black silk top hat Sixsmith, with William Webster as fireman and Richard Darby as guard, drove the vice-regal train carrying Governor Denison and party to Parramatta to mark the opening of the first railroad in New South Wales. He was presented with a silver watch. When the government took over the railways, Sixsmith transferred to the service in September at 14s. a day and was listed as driver number one. By 1878 his salary had risen to 15s. a day. He drove trains over almost every mile of line in the colony but served chiefly on the Sydney–Goulburn and Sydney–Bathurst runs. He won repute as a skilful, safe and reliable driver. On 1 December 1885 he retired with a pension of £69 10s.

Sixsmith died at Redfern at the home of his only surviving son, George, on 24 October 1893 and was buried in the Anglican section of Rookwood cemetery. He was also survived by seven daughters.

Dept of Railways, *The railways of New South Wales 1855-1955* (Syd, 1955); V&P (LA NSW), 1872, 1, 1300, 1878-79, 5, 174; *Old Times*, June 1903.   H. Z. PALMER*

SKENE, ALEXANDER JOHN (1820-1894), government officer, was born at Aberdeen, Scotland, son of Alexander John Skene, army major, and his wife Catherine Margaret, née Auldjo. He was educated at King's College and the University, Aberdeen (M.A., 1838) and practised in surveying shortly after his arrival in Melbourne in 1839. He became official surveyor to the

Grant district council in 1843 and a government district surveyor in October 1848; for the next five years he was a leader in the first mapping and selection of town sites and major routes in the southern part of the Western District, and he demonstrated that the theodolite was more accurate and reliable than the compass techniques previously used. His pioneering work in a rapidly growing region was consolidated after he took over the district survey office in Geelong in 1853. His training in surveying was informal and rudimentary, but it was entirely practical and he followed his own inclinations and convictions with independence, energy and discipline; he emerged as one of the most respected and influential public servants in Victoria.

In 1857, against rising clamour for the 'unlocking of the land', Skene investigated the progress of current surveying and assessed local demands and the quality of the land available for settlement or still unsurveyed. The work took about eleven months because it included every survey office and field party in Victoria; the final report provided a simple but contentious regional evaluation that influenced the drafting and administration of Victoria's first selection Acts in 1860, 1862 and 1865.

In 1863 Skene was transferred to Melbourne; acting surveyor-general in 1868, he succeeded C. W. Ligar [q.v.] in September 1869. He diligently pursued and refined his early land classification and had charge of the grading of pastoral properties in terms of various land legislation, notably the 1862 and 1869 Acts. Although he was seldom active in political affairs, his administrative skills, wide experience and intimate local knowledge were regularly used by several ministries. His evidence in June 1879 before the 1878-79 royal commission on crown lands was particularly valuable, and under his guidance impressive county maps of Victoria were prepared for the detailed operation of the revised land regulations of the 1880s; these maps were intended as guides for controlled resource management. In the broader cartographic field he was a prime mover in the compilation of the first comprehensive and reliable map of Victoria, produced in 1876 on a scale of eight miles to the inch, and also one of the most accurate of the early maps of Australia, first published in 1880. In 1874 in Melbourne, with R. B. Smyth [q.v.], he published a *Report on the Physical Character and Resources of Gippsland*.

Above all an able, industrious and conscientious public servant, Skene was significant in the efficient development of responsible government in Victoria. He had the satisfaction of seeing his old ideas for prior classification and continuing supervision recognized at last in the Mallee Pastoral Leases (1883) and A. L. Tucker's [q.v.] Land (1884) Acts. He retired in 1886. First made a commissioner of land tax in 1878, he was reappointed in 1887, and that year was a member of the royal commission on the extension of Melbourne westward. In 1842 in Melbourne he had married Catherine Margaret Williamson (d. 1879). Aged 74 he died at his home Ellesmere, St Kilda, on 22 August 1894, survived by three of his four sons and one of his two daughters. His estate was valued for probate at £1770.

T. W. H. Leavitt and W. D. Lilburn (eds) *The jubilee history of Victoria and Melbourne*, 1 (Melb, 1888); A. Sutherland et al, *Victoria and its metropolis*, 2 (Melb, 1888); J. M. Powell, *The public lands of Australia Felix* (Melb, 1970), and *Yeomen and bureaucrats* (Melb, 1973); *Australasian*, 24 Apr 1886, 25 Aug, 6 Oct 1894; *Age*, 23, 24 Aug 1894; *Argus*, 23 Aug 1894.   J. M. POWELL

SKIPPER, JOHN MICHAEL (1815-1883), artist and solicitor, was born on 12 July 1815 at Norwich, Norfolk, England, eldest son of John Skipper, solicitor, and his wife Jane, sister of James Stark, a member of the Norwich school of landscape painting. Educated at Norwich Grammar School where he did well at classics and modern languages, he was intended for the law but was more interested in art in which he was encouraged by his uncle. In 1833 he abandoned his studies to become a midshipman in the East India Co.'s *Sherbourne* bound for Calcutta. On his return, deciding to migrate, he arranged to be articled to Charles Mann [q.v.], the new South Australian advocate-general, and sailed in the *Africaine*, arriving at Holdfast Bay on 6 November 1836. He sketched scenes on the voyage, and met Frances Amelia, eldest daughter of Robert Thomas [q.v.]; he married her on 28 December 1839.

Skipper was associated with Mann and E. G. Gwynne [q.v.] in 1836-43. In March 1840 he was admitted as an attorney and proctor of the South Australian Supreme Court and practised in 1843-51; he joined the rush to the Victorian goldfields and returned in 1852 with many sketches but little gold. In 1852-72 he was clerk of the court at Port Adelaide. After the death of his wife he married her younger sister Mary on 28 April 1856.

Chiefly remembered as an artist, Skipper combined a lively mind with acute observation and a natural and cultivated skill with some aesthetic sensibility. His sketches and paintings of the landscape, the flora, fauna and Aboriginals of South Australia, and of the streets, buildings, people, way of life and notable events of Adelaide are of some artistic and great historical interest. Most of his drawings and paintings are small, though his oil on canvas, 'Corroboree', painted in 1840 measures 106 by 152 cm. He illustrated records of some of Charles. Sturt's [q.v.] expeditions from descriptive notes lent him by the explorer. He also illustrated copies of journals of his voyages and of South Australian almanacs, embroidering margins with drawings of minute delicacy. Most remarkable is his illustration of his personal copy of G. B. Wilkinson's *South Australia* with about 360 tiny marginal sketches, including personal comments, reminiscences and puns.

Skipper retired in 1872 and lived on a small pension on his farm at Kent Town where he died intestate on 7 December 1883. He was survived by three sons and four daughters; his eldest son, Spencer John (1848-1903), was a journalist and satirist in Adelaide.

S. H. Skipper, *John Michael Skipper* (Adel, 1957); P. Hope (ed), *The voyage of the Africaine* (Melb, 1968); *Register* (Adel), 8 Dec 1883; Mary Thomas diary (SAA); Skipper family papers (SAA); family information.

JEAN CAMPBELL

SLADEN, SIR CHARLES (1816-1884), lawyer, pastoralist and politician, was born on 28 August 1816 at Ripple Court near Walmer, Kent, England, second son of John Baker Sladen, deputy-lieutenant of Kent, and his wife Ethelred, née St Barbe. Educated at Shrewsbury and Trinity Hall, Cambridge (B.A., 1837; LL.B., 1840; LL.D., 1867), he was articled to a solicitor in Doctors' Commons and was admitted proctor and notary public. On 11 August 1840 at Stockton-on-Tees he married Harriet Amelia Orton.

Sladen arrived in Geelong with his wife on 14 February 1842, soon succeeded to Henry Tyssen's legal business and in the next twelve years, latterly in partnership with Joseph Martyr, built up a flourishing practice. In 1854 he retired from business and took up Ripple Vale near Birregurra, where in 1863 he established Victoria's leading Leicester sheep stud. He retired to Geelong in 1876.

On 26 December 1854, through his friend and fellow church trustee W. C. Haines [q.v.], Sladen was nominated acting colonial treasurer, and on 28 November 1855 as a member of the Legislative Council he took office as treasurer in Victoria's first responsible ministry. Next year he was returned for Geelong in the new Legislative Assembly and was treasurer until March 1857. He did not contest the 1859 election, but, defeated in 1861, he was elected in July 1864 to the Legislative Council for Western Province and soon emerged as leader, with T. H. Fellows [q.v.], of its conservative majority.

In 1865-67 the two Houses clashed over the tariff 'tack' and the Governor Darling grant; Sladen strongly backed the council's claim to equality with the assembly, and on 6 May 1868, after (Sir) James McCulloch's [q.v.] resignation, formed a stop-gap ministry from conservatives in both Houses. Despite the defeat of two of his ministers in the ensuing election and a vote of no-confidence on 9 June in the assembly, he held out until 7 July. McCulloch returned to office and Sladen, whose term in the council had expired, did not renominate.

In 1876 he regained the Western Province seat. After the deadlock in 1877 over the payment of members, Sladen next year introduced proposals for reform of the council. The assembly countered with its own bill and neither House would give way. Sladen tried again in 1879 but the council so amended his bill that he renounced it. He continued his campaign and welcomed the reform bill of 1881. He resigned in December 1882 because of ill health.

Sladen was a devout and prominent Anglican layman. On arrival in the colony he had cared for the Anglican community in Geelong until the first resident minister arrived in 1846. As secretary to the trustees of Christ Church, Geelong, he had raised building funds for it in the early 1840s. He welcomed the appointment of Bishop Perry [q.v.] in 1847, but soon clashed with him over his plans to divide Christ Church parish. He led the opposition that thwarted Perry's first attempts, in 1850, to gain self-government for the Church of England in Victoria by legislative enactment. A member of the Church Assembly of both Melbourne and Ballarat dioceses, in 1861 he helped to defeat Perry's proposal to admit Presbyterians to the management of Geelong Grammar School. Next year he sponsored a new constitution to enable it to continue as an Anglican foundation; he maintained a continuing interest as adviser and confidant of the headmaster, J. B. Wilson [q.v.].

Tall, handsome and of great personal charm, Sladen associated himself with a range of public activities in Geelong and Birregurra and served two terms as a Winchelsea Shire councillor. In 1878 he became chairman of the Trustees, Executors, and Agency Co. and in 1879 a director of the Australasian Agency and Banking Corporation which in 1880 merged to form Richard Goldsbrough [q.v.] & Co. Ltd. He consistently opposed popular political programmes but his conservatism was based on conviction rather than expediency: his mentor was Wellington who had lived close to his family home. Neither a brilliant thinker nor a ready speaker, he displayed his legal training in detailed analysis of the principles and details of proposed legislation. He was admitted LL.D., *ad eundem*, to the University of Melbourne in 1868 and was created C.M.G. in 1870 and K.C.M.G. in 1875.

Sladen died at Chilwell, Geelong, on 22 February 1884, survived by his wife (d. 1887). His estate was valued for probate at £33,890. Portraits are in the City Hall, Geelong, and the La Trobe Library (by G. F. Folingsby [q.v.]), and a bust by Charles Summers [q.v.] is in the State Library, Melbourne.

A. Sutherland et al, *Victoria and its metropolis*, 2 (Melb, 1888); G. Goodman, *The church in Victoria during the episcopate of . . . Charles Perry* (Melb, 1892); B. Hoare, *Looking back gaily* (Melb, 1927); D. B. W. Sladen, *My long life* (Lond, 1939); W. R. Brownhill, *The history of Geelong and Corio Bay* (Melb, 1955); *Geelong Advertiser*, 23 Feb 1884.

JAMES GRANT

SLADEN, DOUGLAS BROOKE WHEELTON (1856-1947), author, was born on 5 February 1856 in London, son of Douglas Brooke Sladen, solicitor, and his wife Mary, née Wheelton. He received a strict Evangelical upbringing, against which he later reacted. Educated at Cheltenham College, he was a scholar of Trinity College, Oxford (B.A., 1879), played football for the university, read history instead of classics and developed his talent for friendship with interesting people. His disinclination for a settled life as a solicitor led him to Victoria where his uncle, Sir Charles Sladen [q.v.], had been premier.

Sladen was quickly accepted into upperclass Melbourne society and in 1880 married Margaret Isabella Muirhead, daughter of a Western District squatter; she bore him a son. He attended the University of Melbourne (LL.B., 1882) with a view to going to the Bar and eventually politics, but his uncle's influence was waning and he had no enthusiasm for the law. He began long friendships with G. E. Morrison and (Sir) John Monash, on whose *Australian Victories in France in 1918* (London, 1920) he did some editing. In 1883 Sladen moved to New South Wales and was appointed first lecturer in modern history at the University of Sydney. He lectured on constitutional history in the Oxford fashion but his subject

had no regular status in the curriculum and he made little impact. In 1883 he was a foundation member of the New South Wales branch of the Australasian Geographical Society. His uncle's death and a dislike of colonial academic work led him to resign and in 1884 he left Australia with his wife.

In Melbourne Sladen had contributed a long poem, 'Frithjof and Ingebjorg' to the *Victorian Review*; supplemented by shorter pieces, it was published in London in 1882. Other verses, first printed in colonial papers, were published as *Australian Lyrics* (Melbourne, 1883) and *A Poetry of Exiles, and other poems* (Sydney, 1883). Sladen's work was English in tone and undistinguished in quality, but he developed a keen interest in poetry written in Australia, and especially in Adam Lindsay Gordon's [q.v.] work. After his return to England, Sladen was commissioned to prepare an anthology, *Australian Ballads and Rhymes* (London, 1888); its popularity led to its enlargement that year as *A Century of Australian Song* and a further collection, *Australian Poets, 1788-1888*. His choice was conservative; even in ballads he preferred 'correct' verse with a modicum of Australian imagery but his anthologies, with their introductions, were important in stimulating interest in Australian work.

Sladen wrote many travel books, novels and anthologies. In 1897 he started editing *Who's Who* and broadened its coverage of prominent people. Clubbable, he was a ready host and conversationalist who moved easily in artistic and theatrical circles and travelled widely. He never revisited Australia, confessing that he 'owed everything to Australia but Australia was exile to me'. Australian connexions were preserved by his edition of W. M. Hughes's pamphlets and speeches, *From Boundary Rider to Prime Minister . . .* (London, 1916), and by two novels, *Fair Inez: A Romance of Australia* (1918), set in Australia in 2000 A.D., and *Paul's Wife: or 'The Ostriches'* (1919), which showed a fictional Alfred Deakin (whom Sladen had known in Melbourne) in retirement in England. Copyright had kept most of Gordon's poetry out of Sladen's anthologies but in 1912 he was able to publish an edition of Gordon and, with E. Humphris, *Adam Lindsay Gordon and His Friends in England and Australia* (1912), which elucidated the poet's English background. Sladen corresponded with Gordon's Australian admirers and was secretary of the memorial committee which placed his bust in Westminster Abbey in 1934. He produced *Adam Lindsay Gordon: the Life and Best Poems of the Poet of Australia* (1934) to mark the occasion.

Sladen's first wife had died on 15 June 1919 and he married Dorothea Duthie on 31 July 1930. He died at Hove on 12 February 1947. A portrait by Frank Beresford is in the National Gallery of Victoria. Biographers have relied heavily on his books, *Twenty Years of My Life* (London, 1915) and *My Long Life* (London, 1939).

The *Times*, 14 Feb 1947; Senate minutes (Univ Syd Archives).   K. J. CABLE

SLATTERY, PATRICK JOSEPH (1830-1903), Catholic priest, was born on 17 March 1830 at Nenagh, County Tipperary, Ireland. He attended Maynooth College, Kildare, and was ordained for the Cashel diocese in 1855. Early in his career he was a military chaplain at Aldershot, England, while on loan to the London Mission. He arrived in Melbourne in the *Anglesey* on 5 February 1862 and was at St Francis's Church, Melbourne, until May when he went to Daylesford. Slattery replaced the wooden parish church of St Peter with a stone edifice that was opened on 14 May 1865. He also built a mortuary chapel at the Eganstown cemetery in 1863, churches at Franklinford (1863), Glenlyon (1869) and began another at Mount Prospect in 1869; he supported Catholic schools enthusiastically. He was in turn chairman and life governor of the local hospital and by his pulpit oratory raised large sums for building. He was several times chairman of the Daylesford Mechanics' Institute. As community arbiter in the town where quarrels frequently ended in fisticuffs, he did not hesitate to use the horsewhip when the occasion warranted it.

Slattery succeeded Archdeacon Matthew Downing at Geelong in December 1870 and became the chief Catholic spokesman in the bitter controversies over the 1872 Education Act. In Geelong he inherited good school sites and reasonably sound buildings dating from the 1850s. He improved the quality of the teachers and, obtaining needed finance from his low-income congregations, he tenaciously kept eight schools open; but he had to pay low wages to his lay teachers and many soon left to go to newly opened state schools. The Mercy Sisters and Christian Brothers filled the teaching vacancies.

On 24 January 1875 Slattery delivered his rumbustious 'flashing sword' sermon. Challenging the secular aspect of the 1872 Act, it drew a leading article and virulent criticism in the *Age*; it created a public furore and embarrassment to Catholics and non-Catholics alike because his approach was over-simplistic and smacked of a grating authoritarianism. In 1883 with Thomas

Cahill he gave evidence for the Catholic Education Committee before the royal commission on education. He argued that religion was an integral part of education and claimed that Catholics were unjustly deprived of government education funds. He was willing to see the two systems working side by side provided that the state paid £2 for each child in the Catholic system.

Slattery was an energetic pastor. The Church of St Mary of the Angels had remained partly built for fourteen years, but he completed it within two years and opened it in 1873: one of the finest country churches in Victoria, St Mary's stands as his main monument. He was made doctor of divinity in 1876 and vicar-general to Archbishop Carr in 1891. He gave generously to charity and fostered the temperance cause. Devotion to his school children and constant visitation of the sick brought about sheer exhaustion in February 1900 and he lived in enforced retirement at St Mary's presbytery until his death on 26 January 1903, aged 72. He was buried in the priests' section of the East Geelong cemetery. A new mortuary chapel was later built to his memory at a cost of £800.

Argus, 27 Oct 1865; *Daylesford Mercury*, 16 Jan 1875; *Age*, 27 Jan 1875; *Geelong Advertiser*, 22 Apr 1875; *Herald* (Melb), Aug 1927; Ballarat Diocesan Archives (Presbytery, Bungaree); MDHC Archives (406 Albert Street, East Melb).   T. J. LINANE

SLEIGH, WILLIAM CAMPBELL (1818-1887), lawyer and politician, was born in Dublin, eldest son of William Willcocks Sleigh, medical practitioner, and his wife Sarah, née Campbell. Although matriculating at Oxford (1843) after private education, he entered the Middle Temple, and was called to the Bar on 30 January 1846. Aged 24, he had married Amelia Warner at Waterperry, Oxfordshire, England, on 25 January 1843. His celebrated legal career included acting briefly for Arthur Orton [q.v.], the Tichborne claimant. On 2 November 1868 Sleigh became a serjeant-at-law, then the most eminent status among common law counsel.

Suffering from sciatica, Sleigh visited Australia in 1871 for convalescence, bearing introductions from J. B. Darvall [q.v.] describing him as 'a gentleman of fortune a barrister of great reputation and a very agreeable person'. Sleigh and his wife decided to settle in Australia when, on returning to England, his health again declined. On 8 March 1877 he was admitted to the New South Wales Bar. In Sydney he found he was an unwelcome rival in the legal profession; he moved to Melbourne and was admitted to the Victorian Bar on 21 March. Being there accorded the courtesy title of serjeant he became the only serjeant-at-law to practise in Australia. A 'tall, "wiry", clean-shaven gentleman, wearing a red neck-tie—elderly in years, but young in style and spirit', he used a slight deafness to his advantage in court. Melbourne solicitors clamoured to brief him, and his success allegedly caused such resentment at the Bar that, by 1880, he moved to Launceston. Admitted to the Tasmanian Bar without the usual formality on 11 March, he opened chambers and rented an elaborate house that he filled with magnificent furniture. Again he was eagerly retained as counsel, especially for criminal defences.

Always interested in politics, he had three times failed to enter the House of Commons. But in April 1880 as an independent he won the Deloraine seat in the Tasmanian House of Assembly. Criticized by Hobart's press as being a 'bird of passage', he dubbed his narrow victory 'a grand triumph over attempted Ministerial dictation' by W. R. Giblin [q.v.] ministry. His parliamentary speeches were acclaimed but his efforts to ventilate local issues were often frustrated. He assessed parliament's performance as 'singularly abortive with regard to some measures of great public utility'.

Obliged to visit England in 1881, Sleigh tired of Tasmania and lived more frequently in Melbourne on his return. The death at sea in 1882 of his only child William, a barrister, probably influenced him to give up public life and Australia. He left that year and died at Ventnor, Isle of Wight, on 23 January 1887; his wife survived him.

J. L. Forde, *The story of the Bar of Victoria* (Melb, 1913); *Law Times*, 12 Feb 1887; *The Times*, 25 Jan 1887; Deas Thomson papers (ML); Sleigh file and Supreme Court papers (TA).   J. M. BENNETT

SLY, JOSEPH DAVID (1844-1934), headmaster and solicitor, was born on 13 October 1844 in Sydney and baptized in the Congregational Church, eldest son of Joseph Sly, cabinetmaker, and his wife Jane, née Meares. His father came to New South Wales about 1839, married on 11 June 1842 and by the 1860s had become a pawnbroker. After his wife's death he married Charlotte Sophia Pritchard in Sydney on 24 February 1862. He died on 16 June 1887 in Sydney and left an estate of almost £11,000 to his widow, his children and his brother Robert in the United States of America.

Sly had a distinguished career at the University of Sydney (B.A., 1866; LL.B., 1871; M.A., 1872; LL.D., 1873) and won a medal

for Greek iambics. In 1871-79 he was headmaster of Calder House, a school conducted from 1855 by J. F. Castle in a house on the Chisholm estate; it closed in 1879 when the government bought the ten-acre property in Redfern for railway purposes. In 1880-87 he was headmaster of Hurstville College, Goulburn, conducted under the auspices of the Church of England for boarders and day boys. Although he built up the enrolment to sixty pupils, the school closed when the trustees sold the property. In 1875-79 he was a lay representative for St Paul's, Redfern, on the Sydney Diocesan Synod.

In 1886 with Edwin Bean [q.v.], headmaster of All Saints' College, Bathurst, Sly wrote a short pamphlet, *High Schools Versus Scholarships: An Enquiry into the Merits of the Two Systems*. They argued for the abolition of state high schools and a system of scholarships to remove competition between state and established private schools, to encourage private enterprise, and to save the country 'from the monotony and uniformity of a centralised system'. Their preference for private secondary schools was shared by the various governments from the mid-1880s to 1910.

Helped by his father's legacy, Sly in 1888 opened Eton College in rented premises in Homebush, but it closed in 1892 when he voluntarily became a bankrupt. His main creditors were his brothers and sister. He attributed his failure to high rents and, ironically, competition among schools. Economic conditions may have played a part but the depression did not generally affect enrolments in private schools. He was discharged from bankruptcy in October 1892. On 24 August 1895 he was admitted as a solicitor and practised in Pitt Street until 1933. He died of heart failure and nephritis at Neutral Bay on 7 December 1934 and was buried in the Anglican section of the Northern Suburbs cemetery. He was survived by two sons and three daughters of his wife Annie, née Macalister, whom he had married at Pitt Town in 1875.

His brother George James was admitted a solicitor on 19 December 1868 and was a founder of the legal firm of Sly and Russell.

Sydney Mail, 22 Feb 1879; *T&CJ*, 28 July 1888; Bankruptcy file 5185/4 (NSWA).
                                                    BRUCE MITCHELL

SMALLEY, GEORGE ROBARTS (1822-1870), astronomer, was born in Banbury, Oxfordshire, and baptized on 18 April 1822, son of Rev. George Smalley and his wife Frances Jane, née Hay. Educated at St John's College, Cambridge (B.A., 1845), on 25 April 1846 he married Elizabeth Trigge and on 8 September took up his duties as third assistant at the Cape Observatory, South Africa, where he was in charge of magnetic observations under Sir Thomas Maclear. In October 1851 he became professor of mathematics at the South African College (later the University of Capetown). In 1854-62 he taught mathematics in King's College, London.

Appointed government astronomer at the Sydney Observatory on the recommendation of the astronomer royal, Smalley arrived in Sydney on 7 January 1864 in the *Blackwall*. He decided to begin magnetic work and systematic tidal observations and advised a trigonometrical survey. With the equatorial telescope he observed the positions of comet 1 in 1864 and of comet Enke in 1865. With the transit instrument he observed only clock stars and stars required for latitude and longitude or as reference stars in the work with the equatorial. In 1864 Smalley recommended a magnetic survey in order 'to construct a magnetic chart of this country comparable with those of most countries'. Smalley carried out this work on several inland journeys and at the observatory in 1866 erected an iron-free building in which to make periodical determination of the magnetic elements.

By August 1866 on Fort Denison Smalley had organized automatic recording of harbour tides. He extended the work in meteorology and arranged for daily telegraphic data. In 1869 he had volunteer observers to record rainfall, evaporation, maximum and minimum temperatures and a wind observation at 9 a.m. each day. Forty-three additional stations were listed in March 1870.

Smalley became an active member of the Philosophical Society of New South Wales and his suggestions led to it becoming the Royal Society of New South Wales in 1866; next year he became its vice-president. With (Sir) Charles Todd [q.v.] he fixed the boundary between South Australia and New South Wales, and in May 1867 telegraphic exchange of time signals took place between a station on that boundary and Sydney and Melbourne.

In 1865 Smalley successfully advocated for geodetic survey a network of astronomical stations and an arc of the meridian. About 1866 a base line at Lake George was proposed, but because of various problems Smalley could not complete the project and the line had to be moved to a higher level and later measured under the direction of the surveyor-general to whom the work was transferred.

Survived by three sons and a daughter, Smalley died from heart disease on 11 July 1870 and was buried in Rookwood cemetery.

His goods were valued for probate at £400. He was succeeded by H. C. Russell [q.v.].

H. W. Wood, *Sydney Observatory, 1858 to 1958* (Syd, 1958); V&P (LA NSW), 1866, 5, 796; Roy Soc NSW, *Procs*, 4 (1871), 5 (1872); Sydney Observatory records.   HARLEY WOOD

SMART, THOMAS CHRISTIE (1816-1896), surgeon, was born in Scotland. Educated at the High School, Edinburgh, in 1842 he qualified through the Extra-Academical School of Medicine and became a licentiate of the Royal College of Surgeons. He arrived in Melbourne as medical officer on an emigrant ship, and was appointed assistant surgeon to the convict probation station at Fingal, Van Diemen's Land, in 1842. In 1849 he was made a justice of the peace. Kindly and capable he served the Convict Department on various rural stations, including Maria Island, until control passed to the colonial authorities in 1856; he then entered private practice in Hobart Town.

Smart was medical officer to the Queen's Asylum for destitute children at New Town in 1862-64 and surgeon to the Volunteer Force, City Guards, in 1860-68. An honorary medical officer for the General Hospital, Hobart, from 1860, in 1875 he became F.R.C.S., Edinburgh. He gained the approval of the Royal College of Surgeons for the formation of a preparatory medical school in the care of the honoraries. During the 1870s he secured several Scottish-trained sisters, selected by his brother Andrew, to instruct the local trainee nurses and he championed them in the face of resistance to their professionalism. Elected chairman of the hospital's board of management and visiting committee in 1879, he designed modern buildings for it and improved its efficiency. A member of the Court of Medical Examiners for the colony from 1864 he became president in 1884. In 1878-84 he was on the board of commissioners for the Cascades Hospital for the Insane. He was chairman of the official visitors to the hospitals for the insane in 1886-87, a medical officer to the Hospital for Insane, Hobart, in 1892-93 and, in 1895-96, was medical officer for the Charitable Institutions for Males and Females, New Town, and also government medical officer.

Smart had been an alderman of Hobart in 1868-69 and its mayor in 1870. In 1880 he was a commissioner for Tasmania at the Melbourne exhibition. Elected to the Legislative Council in 1881, he was a minister without portfolio in the Giblin [q.v.] ministry in 1882-84. In 1886 he resigned from the council to reorganize the management and conditions of the Hospital for the Insane, New Norfolk.

Interested in cultural affairs, Smart was a trenchant and popular lecturer, and a trustee of the Tasmanian Public Library in 1871-73 and 1879-94. He had been a founding member of the Tasmanian Club in 1861. An enthusiastic amateur investor, he was on the committee of the Main Line Railway Association in 1864; a director of the Alliance Quartz Crushing Co. Ltd in 1867, he was chairman of directors of the Eldon Ranges Gold Prospecting Co.

On 20 March 1844 at Avoca Smart had married Agnes McGowan, a governess; they had no children. Aged 80, he died of syncope on 26 March 1896 and was buried in Cornelian Bay cemetery.

F. C. Green, *The Tasmanian Club, 1861-1961* (Hob, 1961); V&P (HA Tas), 1867 (38), 1887 (94); *Examiner* (Launceston), 27 Mar 1896; *Mercury*, 27 Mar 1896; E. Innes, 'Reminiscences of Thomas Christie Smart', *Tas Mail*, 2 May 1896; J. B. Walker diary, 25 June 1884 (Univ Tas Archives); T. C. Smart file (TA); CSO 22/49/110, 50/17/20-22/25.

PETER BOLGER

SMART, THOMAS WARE (1810-1881), businessman and politician, was born in Sydney, son of Thomas Smart, bootmaker, of Pitt Street, who had arrived in the *Admiral Gambier* in 1808 with a seven-year sentence. After six years as an assistant in Cooper and Levey's [qq.v.] Waterloo warehouse he joined Andrew Oliver for two years in a drapery business in Pitt Street. In 1836 he set up as an auctioneer, estate, land and commission agent in George Street. He soon acquired a large fortune and branched out into other activities, including banking and flour-milling. On 8 January 1842 at St James's Church he married Oliver's widow Mary Anne, née Kenyon. In 1845 he was appointed a magistrate and took out a depasturing licence for Cobargo in the Maneroo District. He was a committee-man of the Australasian Botanical and Horticultural Society.

Smart had numerous business and speculative connexions with his friend T. S. Mort [q.v.], but they had a serious rift over a matter of commercial honour in 1866. In the 1850s Smart had joined with Mort and others in pastoral ventures in Queensland and in the Murrumbidgee District; directors of the Sydney Railway Co., they had many shares in it and in the Hunter River Railway Co. In the long and costly action which W. C. Wentworth [q.v.] brought against J. C. Lloyd, C. W. Lloyd [q.v.] and others he was an important witness for the respondents. In 1862 with Mort, G. R. Dibbs [q.v.] and others he formed the Waratah Coal Co.

and, with Mort and J. A. Manton, the Peak Downs Copper Mining Co.: Smart was chairman of both companies. He was also a founding director of the Australian Mutual Provident Society, the Royal Exchange Co., the Hunter River Steam Navigation Co., the Australasian Steam Navigation Co., chairman of the Sydney Fire Insurance Co., the Australian Joint Stock Bank, the New South Wales Shale and Oil Co., founded in 1871, and a trustee of the Savings Bank of New South Wales. He was a supporter of the Anniversary Day regattas and joined the Union Club in 1858.

Active in the anti-transportation movement in the 1840s, Smart represented Sydney Hamlets from September 1851 to January 1855 in the Legislative Council where according to G. Eagar [q.v.] he was 'a dummy', taking no part in legislation. He was in England in 1855-59. Representing Glebe in the Legislative Assembly in 1860-69, under (Sir) Charles Cowper [q.v.] he was colonial treasurer in 1863 and 1865, and secretary for public works from October 1865 to January 1866. As treasurer in 1863 he precipitated the defeat of the government by exposing the existence of a large financial deficit. He was a liberal favouring free trade, extension of the franchise, an elective Upper House and (Sir) John Robertson's [q.v.] land bills.

Self-made, after starting life as 'a poor friendless boy', Smart lived in fine style at Mona, Darling Point, which he had built on a fifteen-acre site. His two sons were educated at Eton and his stepson Alexander Oliver [q.v.] at the universities of Sydney and Oxford. In July 1861 he opened his valuable picture gallery at Mona to the public; it had been largely purchased from Lord Northwick's collection, and the *Sydney Morning Herald* reported that it included works by Raphael, Murillo, Velasquez, Rubens and Gainsborough. Generous and respected, Smart had much business acumen: Mort asserted, 'It was nice to have him on a board of directors with you, as he always took such common-sense short cuts through any difficulty that arose'. A firm adherent of the Church of England, he was a trustee, benefactor and church warden of St Mark's, Darling Point, a committee-man of the Church Society and of the Diocesan Board of Missions and a fellow of St Paul's College, University of Sydney. Aged 71, he died at Mona on 28 May 1881 and was buried at St Jude's, Randwick. He left his estate, which included town property, several stations in the Gwydir district and a 4640-acre property near Singleton, to his sons, daughter and three stepchildren. His personalty was sworn for probate at £243,000.

In the House of Lords, between William Charles Wentworth, appellant and J. C. Lloyd . . . respondent (np, c1862, ML); T. Richards (ed), *An epitome of the official history of New South Wales* (Syd, 1883); N. Bartley, *Opals and agates* (Brisb, 1892); A. Barnard, *Visions and profits* (Melb, 1961); V&P (LA NSW), 1872-73, 3, 1627; *Syd Monitor*, 27 Jan 1836; SMH, 17, 19, 22 Sept 1851, 30 Nov, 8, 11, 13, 15 Dec 1860, 13, 17, 20, 23, 26, 30 July 1861, 8 May 1863, 29, 30 Nov 1864, 16-18 Feb 1865, 8 Mar 1872, 30 May 1881; Parkes letters (ML); CO 201/538/327, 542/345.
                                    G. P. WALSH

SMITH, ALEXANDER KENNEDY (1824-1881), engineer, was born on 7 July 1824 at Cauldmill near Hawick, Roxburghshire, Scotland, son of James Smith, engineer, and his wife Margaret, née Kennedy. Six of their eight sons were engineers and Alexander began his indentures with his father and, after completing them with a Galashiels firm, had a successful and varied career in England from 1846 when he joined the Great Western Railway Co. For some years he practised in Exeter, Devon, as a civil and practical engineer dealing with gas works, rope works, paper-making machinery and dynamometers, and then was engineer to the Bath and West of England Agricultural Society. He designed a piping system to service an entire model farm with water and liquid manure.

In 1853 Smith was engaged on a five-year contract to build and manage the works of the Melbourne Gas and Coke Co. Arriving in Melbourne in April 1854, he soon won a City Council prize of £50 for a refuse disposal plan. He completed the gas works despite flooding difficulties but did not stay with the company; instead he set up as a civil and consulting engineer with his own foundry at Carlton. He built gas works at Ballarat, Castlemaine, Sandhurst and Newcastle; he also provided plans and specifications for gas supplies for many centres both in Australia and abroad, including Sydney, Shanghai, Yokohama, Auckland, Dunedin and Nelson, and for Victorian country towns such as Portland, Warrnambool and Stawell. In rural areas he designed and built mining machinery, sawmills and waterwheels. He designed the Sydney and the Coliban water-supplies and was engineer to the South Yarra Waterworks in the 1860s. He was consulting and locomotive engineer for the Melbourne and Suburban Railway Co.

Able, vigorous and with broad interests, Smith was eager that citizens should understand the scientific and technological principles of the harnessing of the power of nature. He supported in 1854 both the Victorian Institute for the Advancement of Science and the Philosophical Society of Victoria and was a life member and office-bearer of their successor, the Royal Society; his papers to these groups are vividly expressed and of high practical value. A member of the Mining Institute of Victoria, he belonged to the Humane Society and was a prominent Freemason under the Scotch constitution. A promoter of the volunteer rifle movement in the 1850s, from 1860 he was a major in the Victorian Volunteer Artillery Regiment. For fifteen years he represented La Trobe Ward in the Melbourne City Council and was mayor in 1875-76. He stood twice for both the Legislative Council and the Assembly before becoming member for East Melbourne in the Legislative Assembly from May 1877 to January 1881. In the House he spoke infrequently but attended regularly while in good health.

Smith died of heart disease and anasarca at his home at Studley Park on 16 January 1881, survived by his wife Isobel Cochrane, née Brockie, whom he had married in Wiltshire when he was 22, and by two of their four daughters. He was buried in the Melbourne cemetery; the funeral service was conducted by a Presbyterian minister, followed by a Masonic ceremony. His estate was valued for probate at £12,537 and included shares in six Victorian gas companies.

H. M. Humphreys (ed), *Men of the time in Australia: Victorian series*, 1st ed (Melb, 1878); J. D. Keating, *The lambent flame* (Melb, 1974); Vic Inst for the Advancement of Science, *Trans*, 1 (1854-55); Roy Soc Vic, *Procs*, 17 (1881), 46 (1933-34); R. B. Alexander, 'Prominent personalities of the eighteen-fifties', VHM, 24 (1951-52).
                                    JILL EASTWOOD

SMITH, ALFRED MICA (MICAIAH) (1844-1926), chemist and teacher, was born on 21 September 1844 at Perth, Scotland, son of John Smith (1800-1871) and his wife Jane, née Napier. Educated at Perth Academy where his father was master, he was admitted to Owens College, Manchester, in 1861-62 and also studied at the universities of Heidelberg and London (B.Sc., 1867); as an associate of Owens College (1867) he was granted the B.Sc. degree of the Victoria University, Manchester, in 1882. He later became a fellow of the Institute of Chemistry of Great Britain and Ireland. Of high ability, he was accepted as a student by H. E. Roscoe, C. Schorlemmer and R. W. von Bunsen, and was later laboratory and research assistant to his uncle R. A. Smith (1817-1884) and (Lord) Lyon Playfair of the University of Edinburgh.

Early in the 1870s Smith contracted a lung infection and in 1873 decided to migrate to Australia, arriving in Melbourne on 13 December in the *Ben Cruachan*. He worked at mint assaying for some time and in 1876 joined the Bendigo School of Mines as registrar and head of the chemical section. Consulted on matriculation requirements, he gave sound advice on the role of natural science in the syllabus. In October 1881 he became superintendent of the laboratories and lecturer on chemistry, metallurgy, natural philosophy and botany at the Ballarat School of Mines. He also acted as a public analyst. In 1886 he applied for the chair of chemistry at the University of Melbourne but was not short listed. Nevertheless, he was head of the school's science section in the period of its affiliation with the university in 1887-93.

Smith gave information in 1889 and 1891 on the Ballarat School of Mines to the royal commission on gold-mining. He published *Report on the foul air in the Allendale mines* (Melbourne, 1892) and in 1898 was appointed to a board dealing with applications for a bonus for the best method of ventilating mines. From 1900 he was more active on general science matters than on research; as president in 1902 of the chemistry section of the Australasian Association for the Advancement of Science, he spoke in Hobart on the 'Study of the Chemistry of the Air and whither it has led', but said nothing new. He was a non-resident fellow of the Royal Colonial Institute from 1891, an associate of both the American and the Australasian institutes of Mining Engineers and an honorary life member of the Mine Managers Association of Australia. He was an active and constructive member of the Science Faculty of the University of Melbourne in 1903-05. Smith read papers to a number of societies including the Royal Society of Victoria and the Society of Chemical Industry of Victoria. He retired in 1922 and the mutual regard between him and his students was expressed in a school scholarship in chemistry, mining and metallurgy, funded by the Past Students' Association and established in 1924.

On 23 October 1875 at St Peter's Church, Melbourne, Smith had married a widow, 30-year-old Maria Louise Laura Weinritter, née Horne, daughter of a Shropshire gentleman and mother of three children. Predeceased by her in 1884, Smith died of cancer on 14 May 1926 at the home of a friend in Webster Street, Ballarat. He was cremated at Springvale, Melbourne. Shortly before his death Smith had presented the Ballarat Fine Art Gallery with his collection of paintings and art porcelain ware. His estate was valued for probate at £6354.

With no children of his own he left much of his estate to his step-daughter; among his legacies was a bequest of £300 to be shared between the past and present students' associations at the School of Mines. He also left money to the University of Manchester for a scholarship in sanitary science in the name of his uncle R. A. Smith; it was set up in 1928. A portrait commissioned by the school and painted by Max Meldrum in 1923 was rejected as 'too modern', and a sculptured bust was commissioned in its place; the portrait was purchased by the Ballarat gallery in 1934.

Ballarat School of Mines, *Annual report*, 1882, and *Students' Mag*, 1925-26; *Age*, 17 May 1926; *Argus*, 17 May 1926; *Ballarat Courier*, 17 May 1926; information from Ballarat Fine Art Gallery, and Miss Joan Radford, Kew, Vic.   AUSTIN DOWLING

SMITH, BERNHARD (1820-1885), sculptor and painter, was born at Greenwich, London, England, third son of Lord [Christian name] Henry Smith and his wife Jane Mary, née Voase. He joined the Antique School of the Royal Academy of Arts in 1840 and later that year enrolled at the Ecole des Beaux-Arts in Paris. His first notable sculpture (1838) was a memorial to his sister. After his return to London he wrote 'The World in Miniature' in 1842 but there is no evidence that it was published. By 1851 he had exhibited nineteen works at the Royal Academy, including an oil painting, 'Puck', the inspiration of T. Woolner's [q.v.] statuette. Smith and Woolner shared a studio in Stanhope Street and their circle included Browning, Carlyle, Lamb, Tennyson and Mary and William [q.v.] Howitt. Smith's daughter Minnie later claimed that he was one of the seven original members of the Pre-Raphaelite Brotherhood; he certainly belonged to it by 1850 when he helped D. G. Rossetti to plan the *Germ*. Both Woolner and Rossetti acknowledged Smith's influence on them.

Disillusioned with the movement, Smith planned to go to Canada, but instead he and Woolner decided to accompany E. L. Bateman [q.v.] to Melbourne. Their departure in the *Windsor* in July 1852 inspired Ford Madox Brown's painting, 'The last of England'. Arriving on 23 October, Smith and Woolner set out for the Ovens diggings and then went to Fryer's Creek and Sandhurst. Smith's brother Alexander John (1813 ?- 1872) had become a commissioner of crown lands for the goldfields; on 17 May 1854 Bernhard became assistant commissioner for the Westernport District, with salary of

£400 and allowances, and by 1857 was at Ballarat. On 8 February 1858 he became warden of the goldfields and Chinese protector. In 1860 he was transferred to Pleasant Creek (Stawell) as police magistrate, but resigned on 31 March 1861 and joined Alexander, who had taken up Langley Vale station near Kyneton and who won the Legislative Assembly seat of Castlemaine in May. Bernhard became commissioner of crown lands in August and warden for the goldfields of Victoria in September. Interested in astronomy, in the early 1860s he took meteorological observations for R. L. J. Ellery's [q.v.] geodetic survey; he was assisted by his wife Olivia Frances Josephine, née Boyes, whom he had married at St Paul's Church, Melbourne, on 12 February 1863. He was police magistrate and deputy-sheriff at Stawell from 9 October 1865. Along with many other civil servants he was dismissed on Black Wednesday in January 1878 while stationed at Smythesdale, but he was later reinstated and transferred to Alexandra.

Smith had corresponded with his English friends and continued to paint, though he was not interested in Australian subjects; he remained isolated from colonial artistic trends: 'A thorn pierced my foot in 1854', he wrote of his work for the government, 'So among Gum Trees I lived listlessly dreaming; jangling with sweet music; all out of tune'. In 1881 he dislocated his right arm, but continued his work, painting ethereal and heavenly objects in the manner of Blake and Fuseli; a recent art historian has noted that his art and prose are closer to surrealism than any of the other Pre-Raphaelites. Among his commissions were five illustrations of *Macbeth* and four of *Much Ado about Nothing* for a music hall. He wrote verse and sketched fairies and birds for his children. He sent for Rossetti's engravings, but in his isolation he feared for his perception; on seeing a picture of Woolner's statue of Captain Cook [q.v.] he commented, 'No, no, no ... Gum Trees and Kangaroos may have ruined my taste'.

W. M. Rossetti described Smith as 'six feet broad ... with a hearty English look and manner, and a clear resonant voice'. Alfred Howitt [q.v.] thought him rather fussy but 'a useful man of business'. His habits were abstemious: he customarily drank a handful of oatmeal in a jug of cold water and warned his student son in England against the evils of beer that 'bemuddles the clear brains'. Aged 64, he died of pneumonia at Alexandra on 7 October 1885 after trying to rescue two children from a flooded stream. Buried in the Alexandra cemetery, he was survived by his wife, three of their four sons and four of their five daughters; his estate was valued for probate at £1999, including a property at Elgar Park, Box Hill. Two of his portrait medallions, of Sir John Richardson and Sir James Clark Ross, are in the National Portrait Gallery, London.

M. Howitt (ed), *Mary Howitt. An Autobiography* (Lond, 1889); W. M. Rossetti (ed), *Pre-Raphaelite diaries and letters* (Lond, 1900); W. Holman Hunt, *Pre-Raphaelitism and the Pre-Raphaelite Brotherhood* (Lond, 1905); W. M. Rossetti, *Some reminiscences*, 1 (Lond, 1906); A. Graves, *The Royal Academy of Arts*, 7 (Lond, 1906); U. Thieme and F. Becker, *Allgemeines Lexikon der bildenden Künstler* (Leipzig, 1912); Bernard Smith, *Place, taste and tradition* (Syd, 1945); M. B. Smith, *Bernhard Smith and his connection with art* (Melb, 1917, copies SLV, ML); Howitt papers (LaT L); Woolner diary (copy NL); Chief Secretary, Letters (PRO, Vic).

MARJORIE J. TIPPING

SMITH, CHARLES (1816-1897), shipping merchant, was born at Kirriemuir, Forfarshire, Scotland, eldest son of John Smith of Kyeamba, and his first wife Elspit, née Milne. His father migrated to New South Wales in 1832 and became a grazier and a founder of the wine industry in the Riverina. Charles joined the merchant navy and served in the Baltic and West Indies. He reached New South Wales in 1836 and turned to whaling. In 1843-50 he was master of the colonial barque *Woodlark*. In 1850 he became manager of Flower, Salting [q.v.] & Co.'s whaling fleet.

Smith had first called at Butaritari in the Gilbert Islands in 1849; from his next voyage there he returned to Sydney in November 1850 with forty barrels of coconut oil and a hundred-weight of tortoise-shell. Until 1873 he was in partnership with Richard Randall of Butaritari; in 1851 he paid £750 for the schooner *Supply* and next year, as captain of the whaler *Chieftain*, he made his final voyage. After ventures with J. H. Challis [q.v.], Smith acquired a wharf at Millers Point, soon known as Smith's Wharf, in the early 1850s and maintained a regular service to the Gilbert Islands. Later in the decade he competed with Robert Towns [q.v.], who described him as that 'sweep of a neighbour' who 'sticks at nothing'. By 1863 with Alexander Macdonald he founded Macdonald, Smith & Co., general merchants.

In 1859-62 Smith was a member of the Pilot Board, Sydney, and in 1859-73 of the Steam Navigation Board. In the 1860s he served on the committees of the Sydney Sailors' Home and the Sydney Bethel Union, was a director of the Australian General Assurance Co., chairman of the Waratah Coal Co., an auditor of the Commercial Banking Co. of Sydney and a founding councillor of St Andrew's College, University of Sydney. In 1864 he was a committee-man of the New South Wales Free Trade Association. In 1867-68 he was a member of a commission preparing for the naval reception of the duke of Edinburgh, and in 1869 he sat on an imperial royal commission into alleged kidnapping of natives of the Loyalty Islands. He was a trustee of the Savings Bank of New South Wales and a local director of the Imperial Fire Insurance Co. of London in the 1870s. As president of the Chamber of Commerce in 1876-78 he advocated the connexion of the northern and southern railways. He was a director of the Bank of New South Wales in 1890-93 and 1894-97, a commissioner for the Calcutta Exhibition in 1883-84, and a trustee and committee-man of the Union Club.

Smith retired from active business in 1888 and, aged 80, died of embolism on 27 June 1897 at his home Goderich, King's Cross, Sydney; he was buried in the Presbyterian section of Rookwood cemetery. His first wife Elizabeth Ann, née Bennett, whom he had married at Parramatta on 2 March 1847, had predeceased him. He was survived by their two sons and by his second wife Marjory, née Houison, whom he had married on 10 August 1878, and their son and two daughters. His estate was valued for probate at £494,468. His elder daughter Winifred married (Sir) Leslie Wilson, governor of Queensland in 1932-46.

H. E. Maude, *Of islands and men* (Melb, 1968); *SMH*, 29 June 1897.   H. E. MAUDE

SMITH, SIR EDWIN THOMAS (1830-1919), brewer, philanthropist and politician, was born on 6 April 1830 at Walsall, Staffordshire, England, son of Edwin Smith. Educated at Queen Mary's School, Walsall, his early training was with an uncle who had business connexions with Australia. In 1853 he migrated to South Australia in the *California*, and on 25 June 1857 married Florence (d. 1862), daughter of Robert Stock of Clifton, England. After a few years in Adelaide as an importer, in 1860 he went into partnership with Edward Logue of the Old Kent Brewery. When Logue died in 1862 Smith successfully continued the business.

He was mayor of Kensington and Norwood in 1867-70 and 1871-73. In this time the roads were metalled, bridges were built,

gas and water-mains laid and new streets formed. Later Smith gave £2000 to secure the freehold of the Norwood Oval for the municipality and also donated the clock for the Norwood Town Hall. On 11 November 1869 he married Elizabeth, daughter of Edward Spicer, a well-to-do Adelaide merchant.

In 1875 Smith moved his business to the Kent Town Brewery, built at a cost of £17,000. In 1879-81 and 1886-87 as mayor of Adelaide he worked energetically to bring the city up to the best modern standards. The squares were enclosed with iron railings in place of dilapidated wooden fences; Victoria Square was beautified and in 1894 received his gift of the bronze statue of Queen Victoria. The Torrens River was converted into a lake, while Rotunda Lawn (Elder Park) and Victoria Drive were formed. City streets were asphalted, gas-lighting replaced kerosene lamps, deep drainage was laid and public baths were opened. He had trees planted in the Park Lands and also actively promoted the horse-drawn tramway system. As vice-president of the organizing committee and by raising large personal guarantees after the government had abandoned the project, he was mainly responsible for the success of the Jubilee International Exhibition of 1887-88. For this and his other services to the colony he was made K.C.M.G. in 1888.

In 1871-93 Smith represented East Torrens in the House of Assembly. Believing he could best serve his electors as an independent member, he served only one short term in the ministry, as minister of education in 1884. Popular because of his efficient interest in people and Adelaide, he never lost an election. His down-to-earth common sense, application, zeal and reliability were the basis of his parliamentary career rather than great erudition and oratory. In 1888 he retired from business and in 1894-1902 was a member of the Legislative Council for the Southern Districts. He made several visits to England, the last in 1913.

Smith was a trustee of the Savings Bank of South Australia, a director of the Australian Mutual Provident Society and a patron of the Commercial Travellers' and Warehousemen's Association. He was also vice-president of the South Australian Horticultural and Floricultural Society and chairman of the National Park Commission. Once a crack rifle shot, he was closely associated with many recreational organizations, including the cricket, football and chess associations, and the League of South Australian Wheelmen.

Smith was a prominent Freemason and in 1917 the Faith Lodge presented him with an illuminated address to congratulate him on attaining his Masonic jubilee. A Congregationalist, his main association was with Clayton Church, Norwood, which he supported and where he was a devout worshipper. A freeman of his native Walsall, he had donated generously to its hospital, school and other institutions. After some years of poor health the 'Grand Old Man' of South Australia died of a cerebral haemorrhage on Christmas Day 1919 at his home in Marryatville, Adelaide, survived by a son and a daughter of his first marriage. He was buried in the grounds of the Clayton Church. His estate was sworn for probate at £183,000 and £45,834 in Victoria. In his will he left £18,000 to nearly forty South Australian institutions and charities, including the Blind and Deaf and Dumb Institution, of which he had been president, and Adelaide Children's Hospital. There are portraits of Smith in the Adelaide Town Hall, the Norwood Town Hall and the Commercial Travellers' Association.

PP (SA), 1864, 2 (213); *Aust Brewer's J*, 20 Jan 1893; *Bulletin*, 9 Sept 1882, 5 Nov 1903; *Observer* (Adel), 17 Jan 1903; *Advertiser* (Adel), 27 Dec 1919; *Mail* (Adel), 27 Dec 1919; *Register* (Adel), 27 Dec 1919; H. R. Pearce, Economic development of brewing in South Australia in the nineteenth century (B.A. Hons thesis, Univ Adel, 1957).

HELEN R. PEARCE

SMITH, FRANCIS GREY (1827-1900), banker, was born on 23 February 1827 at Cambridge, England, the eldest son of John Jennings Smith and his wife Ann, née Timberlake. His father was an Anglican clergyman (M.A., Cambridge, 1831), who ran a boarding-school at Turnham Green, Middlesex, before migrating with his family to Sydney in 1839.

At 13 Grey Smith joined the Bank of Australasia; and after eight years as a clerk at Maitland and Sydney and one year as accountant at Geelong, he moved in February 1849 as teller to the bank's Melbourne office which was soon to become possibly the busiest banking chamber in Australia. Appointed accountant in 1851, assistant manager in 1853 and manager in 1863 he was one of the first colonial clerks to win a major position in banking. In 1868 he moved from Melbourne to Adelaide to join the Bank of South Australia, a London firm which dominated South Australian banking though it owned no branches elsewhere. After three years as chief officer he returned to Melbourne in July 1872 to become the chief manager of the young National Bank of Australasia, best known

for the quarrels amongst its shareholders and directors. As the bank was directed by rival and bickering boards which met in Melbourne and Adelaide, Grey Smith's experience in both cities was an asset. His reputation for caution was also valuable, for the National Bank specialized in rural business and had more farmland branches than any other Australian bank.

Grey Smith was said to have been unusually dignified and courteous when a young banker, but as he aged his dignity, presence, and facial expression became forbidding. His face was clean-shaven with narrow eyes, tight mouth and stiff jaw, and seems so ferocious in surviving photographs that one wonders how he could retain that expression for more than a few seconds. In the banking chamber he was a man of few words: 'No' was the most frequent. Privately he was affectionate, tactful, fond of news and gossip, and so conscientious that he was inclined to worry.

His favourite recreation was cricket, of which he was a dignified player when young and a courtly spectator when old. From the 1880s his business visits to Adelaide often coincided with an important cricket match, and he was proud that his bank employed two famous players, 'The Demon' Spofforth [q.v.] and Hugh Trumble. He would have been proud to know that from 1906 until the 1960s every Test innings at the Melbourne Cricket Ground began with the teams emerging from the Grey Smith grandstand.

Grey Smith's attitudes to banking and cricket were similar; both were exciting and intensely competitive games to be played according to firm rules. In both games he preferred a defensive innings to a lightning century, liked a longstop behind the wicketkeeper, and suspected that behind every clear sky were stormclouds. During the long late-century boom he differed from most Australian bankers in his firm belief that banking was hazardous, and he spied risks in odd corners. He confided in 1878 that some of the Graham Berry [q.v.] liberals were 'red-hot revolutionists and communists', and in the Russian war scare of 1885 he wondered whether his bank should accept deposits from female customers because they tended to be excitable in a banking crisis. A few years later the exclamation marks spattered on the pages of his private letters as he denounced the high prices of land and shares in Melbourne and the risky policies of rival banks. On rare occasions he was deaf to his own advice. His confidential clerk, the man 'to whom I gave my unreserved confidence', was also deaf, and by 1888 had lost nearly £40,000 of embezzled money on the share market.

The National Bank shared Grey Smith's personal prestige. He was president of the Melbourne Club for one year, of the Melbourne Cricket Club in 1886-1900, and lay canon and treasurer of St Paul's Cathedral. At the peak of the boom in 1888 he was chairman of the Associated Banks—the big ten—and to his delight he kept the banking account and guided the silver speculations of Governor Sir Henry Loch. It was a measure of his reputation that the Melbourne *Herald* should have called him 'the most trusted and cautious financier in Australia'.

Grey Smith did not deserve to be a victim of the 1893 financial disaster. When frightened depositors bled the National Bank of 45 per cent of its gold coin in April 1893, it was still solvent. Nevertheless the directors, on his advice, decided on 1 May to suspend payment and reconstruct rather than risk the loss of all their gold coin. The bank reopened after eight weeks, but Grey Smith felt humiliated. Much of his old verve vanished, his face became fiercer and his health frail. A high sense of honour made him work on beyond his seventy-third birthday in the hope of meeting all the bank's obligations. He died in his St Kilda house on 1 May 1900, on the eve of the meeting at which he was to announce formally that the bank's debts to its depositors had been repaid. His own estate was sworn for probate at £21,711.

In 1849 Grey Smith had married Susanna Amelia, daughter of a Dublin solicitor, Joseph William Belcher. They had eight sons and three daughters; a grandson, Sir Ross Grey-Smith, was chairman of the Victoria Racing Club.

G. Blainey, *Gold and paper* (Melb, 1958); K. Dunstan, *The paddock that grew* (Melb, 1962); A'sian Insurance and Banking Record, 19 May 1900; Chief manager's letter-books (National Bank of A'sia Archives, Melb).

GEOFFREY BLAINEY

SMITH, SIR FRANCIS VILLENEUVE (1819-1909), politician and chief justice, was born on 13 February 1819 at Lindfield, Sussex, England, son of Francis Smith, merchant, of London, and his wife Marie Josephine, née Villeneuve, of Santo Domingo, Dominican Republic, West Indies. He acknowledged his mother's descent from the French admiral Villeneuve by adopting that name in 1884.

The Smiths came to Van Diemen's Land in 1826 and settled at Campania near Richmond. Francis returned to London and became a student at the Middle Temple in 1838 and at University College, University

of London (B.A., 1840). After reading law under Montagu Smith and Russell Phillips, he was called to the Bar on 27 May 1842. In October 1844 he was admitted to the Tasmanian Bar. In 1848 Lieut-Governor Denison described him as 'a barrister of some standing ... whose talent and legal knowledge have obtained for him a very large amount of practice', and appointed him acting solicitor-general. Next year he was crown solicitor, often acting as solicitor-general instead of A. C. Stonor [q.v.] whom he succeeded in 1854. On 26 August 1851 at Launceston he married Sarah, daughter of Rev. George Giles; they lived at Lindfield, Hobart Town, and had two sons and two daughters.

In 1851 Smith, a government nominee, became a legislative councillor, and in 1854 attorney-general, reserving the right to oppose transportation of convicts to the colony; in 1855 he was a member of the Executive Council. A member of the House of Assembly in 1856-60, he was attorney-general in 1856-57 and premier and attorney-general in 1857-60. Ambitious and self-assertive, his ability and abrasive temper prevailed over most opponents but made him bitter enemies. His government helped the underprivileged, reformed land laws, improved government schools, established scholarships and promoted local government. His contentious attempt failed to abolish state aid to religion.

Smith was appointed to the Supreme Court bench in 1860. He helped to found the Tasmanian Club next year and was its first president. He was knighted in 1862, and on 5 February 1870 became the first Australian to hold office as a chief justice after having been a premier. His judicial career showed the extremes of legal ability and personal ineptitude. His judgments were well reasoned and backed by precedent; his sentences were moderate but he was intemperate in court, often engaging in vehement exchanges with counsel or witnesses. Where his own interests were involved, he allowed anger to overbear reason. In 1869 he sued a tenant Hollinsdale, who later claimed unfair treatment and petitioned the Colonial Office; although vindicated, Smith was embarrassed. He was humiliated in prolonged family litigation during the 1870s: his brother's wife was entitled to income from trust funds of which he and his brother were trustees; the brother made unlawful investments and his wife proceeded against the trustees. Smith was blameless and had spent time and money trying to reach a settlement; losing his temper, he wrote and published a letter defamatory of his sister-in-law. The litigation was then forced to a hearing and he had to apologize, retire from the trust, and make other reparation.

Smith was involved in a foolish controversy with Governor Weld in 1877-78. Louisa Hunt, a prisoner sentenced to seven years, was released by the Executive Council after eighteen months. The judges were not consulted and protested that the Executive Council had constituted itself a court of appeal; the governor and chief justice argued relentlessly and publicly about the consequences. The Colonial Office rebuked them and Smith felt compelled to retract. During the contest old political opponents tried in vain to have his dormant commission as lieut-governor withdrawn, and the Colonial Office noted that he was 'an excitable and injudicious man ... not specially well qualified, personally, for the temporary administration of the government'. Nevertheless, he had administered the colony in 1874-75 and did so again in 1880.

In December 1883 Smith left Tasmania on twelve months leave. He retired in 1885 and remained in England, living in London and at Heathside, Tunbridge Wells. He was a bencher of the Middle Temple (1890-98) and a member of the Conservative Club. He died of senile asthenia and pneumonia on 17 January 1909 and was cremated at Golder's Green. A plaque in the church of King Charles-the-Martyr, Tunbridge Wells, commemorates him. His estate was sworn for probate at £1390 in Tasmania and £116,470 in England.

C. I. Clark, The parliament of Tasmania (Hob, 1947); F. C. Green (ed), A century of responsible government 1856-1956 (Hob, 1956); V&P (HA Tas), 1877, 2nd S (54), 1878 (51); J. M. Bennett, 'The legal career of Sir Francis Smith', Aust Law J, Aug 1975; Mercury, 4, 7 Feb 1885, 20 Jan 1909; The Times, 17 Jan 1909; Examiner (Launceston), 20 Jan 1909; W. Wolfhagen, Some Tasmanian judges: Sir Francis Smith (TA); CSO and CSD papers (TA); Smith litigation papers (TA); CO 280/318/384/388.   J. M. BENNETT
F. C. GREEN*

SMITH, JAMES (1820-1910), journalist, was born at Loose near Maidstone, Kent, England, son of James Smith, supervisor of inland revenue, and his wife Mary. Educated first for the Church he turned to journalism and at 20 became editor of the Hertfordshire Mercury and County Press. He also contributed to London Punch, The Illuminated Magazine and other publications, and in 1845 in London published a selection of these articles as Rural Records: or, Glimpses of Village Life, which went through two editions and brought him into correspondence with Douglas Jerrold, William Howitt [q.v.], Mary Russell Mitford, and other writers of the period. He subsequently published Oracles from the British Poets (London, 1849), and Wilton and its associates (Salisbury, 1851). In 1848-54 he edited the Salisbury and Winchester Journal, and in 1852 at Salisbury organized one of the first provincial exhibitions of art and industry in England.

In 1854 Smith migrated to Melbourne where he joined the Age as leader-writer and dramatic critic. He assisted Ebenezer Syme and David Blair [qq.v.] in the weekly Melbourne Leader (issued from 5 January 1856), and became its first editor. That year he joined the staff of the Argus as leader-writer, dramatic, art and literary critic, and also contributed to journals in Victoria and other colonies. Smith was associated with F. Sinnett [q.v.] in the foundation of Melbourne Punch in 1855 and as its editor in 1859 built it into a secure and successful publication. After deciding in early 1863 to visit Europe for two years, partly to recover from overstrain due to his 'severe intellectual labours', he became instead Victorian parliamentary librarian; before the post was abolished in February 1869 he had classified and catalogued the library's 30,000 volumes. On 2 October he began the short-lived satirical magazine Touchstone. Resuming work with the Argus, he became editor of its weekly, the Australasian, in 1871. He was a founder of and frequent contributor to the Victorian Review in 1879. On 17 October 1881 he began editing a new Melbourne daily paper, the Evening Mail, which was discontinued next year when he visited Europe. Back in Victoria, he continued as a journalist with the Argus until his retirement in 1898, when he returned to the Age as literary writer and dramatic critic until 1910 : he had lost all his savings in the depression of the 1890s. A voracious and systematic reader with a retentive memory, he covered a wide range of topics in his journalism, though often in a facile and derivative manner.

Smith was a conservative in politics and espoused free trade. Although for many years one of the best lecturers in Melbourne, he was never an extempore speaker. As an advocate of the cultural and intellectual elevation of the colony, he helped to establish the Garrick Club (1855), the Melbourne Shakespeare Society (1884), the Alliance Française (1890) and the Dante Society (1896). He read French, Spanish and Italian and his library of some 6500 volumes contained a fine selection of French literature. For his work for the Alliance Française he was elected an officer of the French Academy of Paris; he was created knight of the Order of the Crown of Italy for his research into Italian literature. He had been an ardent sympathizer with Italy's nationalist movement; his play *Garibaldi* (1860) was performed at the Prince of Wales Theatre, and in June 1861 he organized a presentation to the Italian patriot.

Smith was the first to suggest the foundation of a National Gallery, and his influence on art in Melbourne was great as a critic and as trustee of the Public Library, Museums and National Gallery of Victoria in 1880-1910 and treasurer of the trustees from 1888. He helped Louis Buvelot [q.v.] to gain recognition as a professional artist, and his favourable review of the work of the then unknown artist Tom Roberts in 1881 indicated his ability to recognize potential talent. He embodied the cultural values of colonial Melbourne. Like Ruskin and the Pre-Raphaelites he wanted art to stimulate the moral and spiritual faculties; he became, especially after the 9 x 5 Impression Exhibition of 1889, an outspoken opponent of impressionism. As a drama critic Smith was diligent, prolific and able, though neither as experienced nor as competent as his fellow critic James Neild [q.v.]. He displayed only a limited understanding of stage tradition, theatrical trends and the intellectual issues raised by works of legitimate drama. He was susceptible to the personal blandishments of visiting actors, and could be more than 'a little blind' to their shortcomings on the stage. With Neild and R. H. Horne [q.v.] he was a combatant in the great 'Hamlet controversy' of 1867; their letters to the *Argus* were collected and published in Melbourne as *The Hamlet Controversy. Was Hamlet Mad?* ...

Converted to spiritualism in the 1870s he became one of its major propagandists and controversialists and some of his contemporaries lost confidence in his judgment. He corresponded with prominent European spiritualists and contributed numerous articles to the local journal, the *Harbinger of Light*. However his proclamation of the imminent destruction of the world in 1873 was condemned as heresy both on rational and theological grounds by the Victorian Association of Progressive Spiritualists, and caused the defection of a number of believers. He reputedly attempted to educate his children by magnetically transmitting to their minds the wisdom of dead scholars and artists.

Aged 89, Smith died of cystitis at his home Amwell, Hawthorn, on 19 March 1910 and was buried in the Boroondara cemetery. His estate was valued for probate at £1525. By his first wife Annie Fieldwick, née Notcutt (d. 1849), he had two sons who predeceased him. His second wife Eliza Julia, née Kelly, of Melbourne, whom he married on 11 April 1857, bore him two sons and four daughters, one of whom predeceased him. One son, Charles Lamb, became a journalist with the *Argus* and later with the *Ballarat Star*; another, Tennyson, wrote a crime novel with Percy Hulbert. Of Smith's own numerous publications the most valuable is his *Cyclopedia of Victoria*, which he edited in three volumes in 1903-05. He also wrote *From Melbourne to Melrose* (1888), *Junius Unveiled* (London, 1909), and contributed to at least eleven other books published in Melbourne between 1867 and 1909. He wrote articles for most of the important Melbourne literary journals and many of his lectures were published.

A. McCulloch, *The golden age of Australian painting* (Melb, 1969); L. B. Cox, *The National Gallery of Victoria, 1861 to 1968* (Melb, 1970); *Harbinger of Light*, 1 June 1904; *Age*, 21 Mar 1910; *Argus*, 21 Mar 1910; *Australasian*, 24 Mar 1910; *Bulletin*, 24 Mar 1910; F. B. Smith, *Religion and freethought in Melbourne, 1870 to 1890* (M.A. thesis, Univ Melb, 1960); James Smith diary and letters (ML); H. G. Turner papers (LaT L); information from Mr K. Stewart, Univ New England.

ANN-MARI JORDENS

SMITH, JAMES (1827-1897), explorer, known as 'PHILOSOPHER', was born on 1 July 1827 at George Town, Van Diemen's Land, eldest child of John Smith and his wife Mary Ann, née Grant. His father was shot when he was 5 and his mother remarried. His early education was in Launceston; in 1836 John Guillan, a shipowner and flour-miller, became his guardian. For a time he managed a flour-mill and in 1851-53 he was on the Victorian goldfields.

Returning to Tasmania, Smith took up a square mile of forest, between the Forth and Leven rivers, which he cleared and farmed. Peaceful, six feet tall and of slender build, he was a hardy bushman and a determined amateur explorer of the dense forests and difficult country of the northwest. J. W. Norton Smith [q.v.] wrote 'it is not a matter of much consequence to him if he goes a couple or three days on one meal if he finds (what he calls) something interesting'. On an expedition to the Forth River in 1859 he discovered some gold.

In October 1871 Smith arranged for provisions to be stored at a depot in the Black Bluff Highlands. He then set off to the west; travelling slowly and examining the country carefully, he crossed the Arthur

River and reached the vicinity of Mount Cleveland. Returning to the river he descended into its deep gorge, finding traces of gold. On 4 December he found the first sample of tin ore and, following a creek to its source, he located an immensely rich deposit of tin oxide near the summit of Mount Bischoff; later he smelted the sample of ore at Stanley on the north coast. He obtained two crown leases of eighty-acre mining sections on the richest of the tin ore deposits and had them surveyed, but found that he could not interest anyone in his discovery. Failing to obtain assistance in Victoria, he sold a small farm, arranged a bank overdraft and obtained sufficient capital to commence work, his manager being W. M. Crosby of Nova Scotia. Tin oxide was mined, bagged, taken along the primitive road to the coast and shipped from Penguin and Leith to England via Melbourne.

The returns from the first shipment of ore led to the formation in Launceston of a company with capital of £60,000 in 12,000 £5 shares. When it took over the mine in 1873 Smith received £1500 in cash, 4400 paid-up shares and a permanent directorship, with power to nominate another director. But he soon severed his connexion with what was destined to become the richest tin-mine in the world. The company paid its first dividend in 1878, but by then Smith is said to have given away or sold his shares at trifling prices. That year he received a public testimonial of 250 sovereigns and a silver salver and parliament voted him an annual pension of £200.

Though Smith returned to farming, increasing his land to about 1500 acres, he continued prospecting. At Launceston on 16 September 1874 he had married a widow Mary Jane Love, née Pleas. In 1886 he was elected to the Legislative Council for Mersey but resigned in 1888. He died of heart disease at Launceston on 15 June 1897, survived by his wife, three sons and three daughters. He was buried in the Congregational cemetery at Forth. The origin of the nickname 'Philosopher' by which he was widely known on the north-west Tasmanian coast is not known. A portrait by Mary Shaw is in the Queen Victoria Museum and Art Gallery, Tasmania.

G. Blainey, The peaks of Lyell (Melb, 1954), The rush that never ended, 2nd ed (Melb. 1969); Examiner (Launceston), 16 June 1897; G. Scott, 'The discoverer of Mount Bischoff', Lone Hand, 2 Dec 1907; family information.

RONALD E. SMITH*

SMITH, JAMES WILLIAM NORTON (1846-1911), manager, was born at Nailsworth, Gloucestershire, England, son of Richard Smith. After an agricultural education he managed a sheep-run in New Zealand and was appointed manager of the Van Diemen's Land Co. in July 1869; he arrived in Tasmania in October to find its land-leasing business depressed. He soon perceived the importance of Burnie on the company's north-west Emu Bay block, and advised that it join the government to develop the port facilities. This decision began a career in which he sought to attract population and capital to the company's lands and the Tasmanian north-west coast region.

Norton Smith encouraged James (Philosopher) Smith [q.v.] to prospect on the company's land about the time of his Mount Bischoff tin discovery on 4 December 1871. On 9 October 1872 Norton Smith married Fanny Eliza Ford of Stanley. With the proving of the immense potential of Mount Bischoff he supervised the construction of a forty-four mile tramway from Waratah to Emu Bay; its completion in February 1878 helped to raise dividends substantially. The tramway was converted to a railway by July 1884, a difficult feat that involved the continuation of traffic; its success was ascribed 'to the able and unremitting presence of the Manager'. By 1888 the traffic was worth £19,000 per annum.

In the early 1870s during the rural depression Norton Smith had become manager of the 100,000-acre company farm, Woolnorth, and steadily improved the production and quality of the livestock. In 1880 he became a justice of the peace and in 1885 joined the Tasmanian Club. He represented Wellington in the House of Assembly in 1885-86, and as a federationist and intercolonial free trader emerged as a 'truly independent candidate'; in 1898 he argued that the 'Federation of Australia must lead to the federation of Empire'. He also advanced the company's cause and actively served his electorate, seeking the extension of education and cheaper justice for outlying rural areas. He sat on six select committees. Speaking on the electoral reform bill, in reference to Wellington he deplored the 'amalgamation of two districts which had no community of interest' and argued that 'diverse interests should be kept separate'.

Norton Smith was a shrewd and practical manager of the Van Diemen's Land Co. and the Emu Bay and Mount Bischoff Railway Co. Ltd, and in 1898 he visited England to attend company meetings. Despite the contraction of business in the

1890s the governing court took his advice to float a new, separate company to extend the railway from Waratah to Zeehan in 1900. After disputes with the English directors, Norton Smith retired to his farm, Amberly, in 1903. He was a coroner from 1907, a director of the Blythe Tin Mine, chairman of directors of the Table Cape Butter and Bacon Factory and in 1911 a warden of Table Cape municipality. Aged 65 he died of chronic myocarditis on 20 January 1911 at Flowerdale, and was buried in Wivenhoe cemetery, survived by his wife, four daughters and two sons. His estate was sworn for probate at £8531. The 870 dispatches he wrote in 1869-1903 to the court of the Van Diemen's Land Co. are an important source for the regional economic history of the colony.

V&P (HA Tas), 1884 (118), 1885 (155); *Mercury*, 24 Feb, 11, 17, 18 Sept, 29 Oct 1885; *Tas Mail*, 22 Dec 1900, 26 Jan 1911; *Examiner* (Launceston), 23 Jan 1911; *Emu Bay Times*, 26 Jan 1911; H. J. W. Stokes, North-west Tasmania 1858-1910: the establishment of an agricultural community (Ph.D. thesis, ANU, 1969); J. W. N. Smith papers (TA); Van Diemen's Land Co. papers (TA).

G. P. R. CHAPMAN

SMITH, JOHN (1811-1895), sheepbreeder, was born on 25 May 1811 at Trelanvean, St Keverne, Cornwall, England, son of John Smith, farmer, and his wife Elizabeth, née Cock. He reached Sydney in the *Abel Gower* on 22 April 1836, became station superintendent for John Maxwell at Narroogal in the Wellington District and in 1839 for John Betts, based on the Molong run. Concurrently he acquired sheep and runs. On 12 September 1843 he took up part of the Molong run with some pure-bred descendants of Rev. S. Marsden's [q.v.] merinos, the nucleus of his famous Gamboola stud; by 1847 he had built a substantial brick house there. In 1845 he bought 3989 contiguous acres; he acquired more runs, including Gunningbland, Dovedale Park and Boree Cabonne, and by 1855 had 35,428 sheep and had developed his stud. His tenacity and knowledge of the land laws contributed to many arguments with the authorities. In 1847 he was arrested for allegedly stealing an iron pot; he was acquitted but failed in two actions against R. J. Barton who had signed the warrant. He was appointed a magistrate in 1850.

Smith evolved a large-framed, plain-bodied sheep with medium to strong wool. He adhered to Marsden's method of breeding (Bakewell's) and the Gamboola sheep became noted for their wool, constitution and carcase. In 1860 he imported from T. S. Sturgeon and Sons, Essex, six Negretti rams certified to be directly descended from the flock of George III. He acquired numerous stations on the watersheds of the Lachlan and Macquarie rivers and settled his sons on Toogong, Boree Cabonne, Boree Nyrang, Narroogal, Nandilyan and Gamboola stations. In 1872 his second son, Lance, took his portion of the Gamboola stud sheep to Boree Cabonne. These sheep became the Boree Cabonne Merino Stud, carried on by John's great-grandson, Lance Mac. Smith. In 1879 the Kater [q.v.] brothers of Mumblebone bought sheep from Smith and continued to do so for many years, building up the Mumblebone stud and later the Egelabra stud with the Gamboola blood.

Smith was one of the first to fence in the Molong district and to use wire in the western districts. Active in the town, he helped to establish a church and a school and in 1864 was president of the first show; a free trader, he was narrowly defeated in 1880 by Dr Andrew Ross [q.v.] for the local seat in the Legislative Assembly. That year he was appointed to the Legislative Council, where his knowledge of financial and pastoral matters, combined with his sound common sense and integrity, contributed to his success. In 1857 he was a foundation member of the Union Club. About 1865 he purchased another family home, Llanarth, at Bathurst.

Smith died on 1 January 1895 at Ashfield of broncho-pneumonia and was buried in the Anglican section of the Bathurst cemetery. He was survived by his wife Mary, daughter of William Tom [q.v.], whom he had married on 12 September 1842, four of his five sons and six daughters. His eldest son, Fergus Jago Smith, represented West Macquarie in the Legislative Assembly in 1887-89 and sat in the Legislative Council in 1895-1924; his eldest daughter, Emily, married Sir J. G. Long Innes [q.v.]. His estate was valued for probate at £142,600.

Bertha Mac. Smith (ed), *Quench not the spirit* (Melb, 1972); V&P (LA NSW), 1861, 1, 966, 976, 1880-81, 1, 163, 2, 353, 1883, 1, 144; *SMH*, 8 Aug 1848; *Bathurst Times*, 2 Jan, 25 March 1895; *National Advocate*, 3, 4 Jan, 25 Mar 1895; Parkes letters (ML); MS cat under Hon. John Smith (ML). BERTHA MAC. SMITH

SMITH, JOHN (1821-1885), professor of chemistry and experimental physics, was born on 12 December 1821 at Peterculter, Aberdeenshire, Scotland, son of Roderick Smith, blacksmith, and his wife Margaret, née Shier. From 1839 he studied at the Marischal College, Aberdeen (M.A., 1843; M.D., 1844). After a voyage as a surgeon to Australia for his health, in 1847 Smith became lecturer in chemistry and agriculture at Marischal where he conducted important water analyses.

As foundation professor of chemistry and experimental physics in the University of Sydney, Smith arrived on 8 September 1852 in the *Australian* and set up his laboratory at the Sydney College, Hyde Park. On 25 March 1853 he was appointed to the National Board of Education, and served conscientiously during criticism of its policies towards denominational schools. He contributed to the reforms embodied in (Sir) Henry Parkes's [q.v.] Public Schools Act of 1866, was appointed to the new Council of Education, and was president nine times before its demise in 1880. He worked long hours on educational affairs, bringing 'a cultivated intellect, extraordinary patience and industry' to the council's business. Outspoken about the intrusion of 'dogmatic theology' into university affairs, in 1862 he deprecated the 'further extension of denominational education in New South Wales' in evidence before a select committee on the Presbyterian college.

Smith's chemistry classes offered little practical teaching but gave the current elementary theories of chemical structure and reaction; each other year he taught classes in experimental physics and illustrated his lectures with examples of his own pioneer researches in water analyses and photography. Widely recognized as an analyst, he gave evidence at parliamentary select committees on the adulteration of food and the registration and preservation of records; in 1859 at the select committee on water for Melbourne from the Yan Yean reservoir, he condemned the use of lead and tin alloys in reticulation systems. In 1860 he toured auriferous quartz workings in southern New South Wales and Bendigo with E. W. Ward [q.v.], reporting on methods and machinery. Soon afterwards he left on fourteen months leave to inspect 'the principal laboratories of Europe' and secure new equipment.

In 1864 Smith advised the government to refuse development in designated water reserves at Randwick; in 1867-69 he chaired a royal commission into the water-supply of the city of Sydney and suburbs inquiring into all aspects of supplying water for a potential population of 250,000. His own analyses were competent in regard to inorganic interpretations but showed that in the understanding of organic contaminants his knowledge was outmoded. In 1871-72 he was again on leave in Europe and at Bidston,

Cheshire, England, on 11 June 1872 he married Mary (Minnie) Macleod.

In July 1874 Smith was appointed to the Legislative Council and spoke often on educational and scientific-medical matters. In July 1875 he opposed the medical bill, thereby incurring the censure of some of the profession. Fearless in his scientific opinions, the same year he strongly contested the findings of his colleague Archibald Liversidge [q.v.] on the pollution of Lachlan Swamps water. In 1876 he received an honorary LL.D. from the University of Aberdeen and in 1878 was appointed C.M.G.

Smith's commitment to chemistry decreased after the appointment of A. M. Thomson [q.v.] as assistant in 1866, and later of Liversidge to whom he relinquished the chair of chemistry in 1882, retaining responsibility for experimental physics until 1885. He was dean of the faculty of arts in 1884-85 and of the faculty of medicine until 1883, and an *ex officio* member of senate in 1861-85. He was an early member of the Australian Philosophical Society and honorary secretary of its successor, the Philosophical Society of New South Wales, in 1856-60. Between 1856 and 1864 he read five papers before the society on chemical, meteorological and other subjects. For eighteen years a councillor of the Royal Society of New South Wales, he served ten years as vice-president and two as president. His papers again dealt principally with water analysis and applied physics.

In the 1860s Smith served on the committees of several religious organizations, also as a vice-president of the Young Men's Christian Association and as honorary treasurer of the Sydney Infirmary and Dispensary in 1866-67. He was an elective trustee of the Australian Museum, vice-president of the Highland Society of New South Wales and sat on several exhibition commissions, including that of the Sydney International Exhibition of 1879-80. 'Self-sacrificing' and 'pre-eminently philanthropic', he was a director of the Australian Mutual Provident Society in 1864-72 and 1883-85 and chairman in 1873-80 and 1883-85. In January 1882 he had called at Bombay and joined the Indian section of the Theosophical Society, having been influenced by his wife's spiritualism and the lectures of the theosophist Emma Hardinge Britten in Australia in 1878-79. In Europe in 1882-83 he experimented with the occult.

Upon returning to Sydney Smith found his 'vigor of the old days lacking' and his many activities circumscribed by ill health. Survived by his wife and adopted daughter Nora, he died of pthisis on 12 October 1885 and was buried in the Presbyterian section of Waverley cemetery. His estate was sworn for probate at £19,000; in his will he provided for the annual Smith Prize in the University of Sydney for the best first-year undergraduate in experimental physics. He sacrificed his scientific advancement to devote himself unsparingly to colonial and civic affairs: during his career theoretical and practical knowledge in chemistry and physics outstripped his own reading. 'Undemonstrative' and not brilliant or successful socially, he was a lucid, influential, conscientious teacher and expert committeeman.

A. Findlay, *The teaching of chemistry in the universities of Aberdeen* (Aberdeen, 1935); R. J. W. Le Fevre, 'The establishment of chemistry within Australian science—contributions from New South Wales', Roy Soc NSW, *A century of scientific progress* (Syd, 1968); V&P (LA NSW), 1858, 2, 1258, 1860, 1, 10, 567, 1873-74, 1, 205, 5, 945, 1875-76, 5, 421, 1882, 2 804, (LA Vic), 1858-59, 1 (D27); Roy Aust Chemical Inst, Procs, 26 (1959); *Australasian*, 3 Aug 1872, 9 June 1876, 24 Oct, 12 Dec 1885; SMH, 28 Jan, 11 Feb 1876, 13 Oct 1885; J. E. Mumford, The struggle to develop and maintain National education in New South Wales, 1848-1866 (Ph.D. thesis, Univ New England, 1975); Parkes letters (ML).

MICHAEL HOARE
JOAN T. RADFORD

SMITH, JOHN THOMAS (1816-1879), publican and landowner, was born on 28 May 1816 in Sydney, son of John Smith, a Scottish shoemaker, and his wife Elizabeth, née Biggs. Educated at W. Cape's [q.v.] school, he was apprenticed at 14 to Beaver & Co., builders and joiners, but in 1833 his indentures were cancelled. After service as a bank clerk and under the colonial storekeeper, in June 1837 he sailed for Melbourne, and in September became assistant teacher to the Church of England Aboriginal Mission Station on the Yarra River at £40 a year.

Smith soon became storekeeper to J. Hodgson and husband to Ellen, daughter of Irish Catholic Michael Pender, a pioneer publican who encouraged his sons-in-law to enter the trade. In July 1841 Smith took over the Adelphi Hotel, Flinders Lane, from his brother-in-law Robert Brettagh, and in 1844 became licensee of St John's Tavern, Queen Street, in place of Brettagh. The behaviour of the Adelphi's customers aroused much criticism but Smith disclaimed responsibility: he was probably managing St John's Tavern at the time. The publicity had not prevented him from winning Bourke Ward on the first Melbourne Town Council in December 1842. He was a councillor for the rest of his life, a 'Whittington of the South',

being seven times mayor between 1851 and 1864.

In 1845 Smith built the Queen's Theatre Royal, Melbourne's first theatre, next to St John's Tavern; it held 1200 people and was the first home of George Coppin's [q.v.] professional company. Smith attempted to make it safe for gentlefolk by reserving the dress circle for them, prohibiting smoking and putting street lamps in pot-holed Queen Street. In 1854 he leased the building to Charles Young [q.v.] for £300 a week. He lived in Queen Street in the 1850s in an elegant three-storied brick house; his last home was in Mount Alexander Road, Moonee Ponds.

In the first Legislative Council elections in 1851 Smith became member for North Bourke, and from May 1853 represented Melbourne, but he failed to win Central Province in 1856. In 1856-59 he represented Melbourne in the Legislative Assembly. He sat for Creswick in 1859-61 and for West Bourke in 1861-79. He was minister for mines in J. A. MacPherson's [q.v.] ministry from September 1869 to April 1870.

As councillor, mayor and politician Smith was lampooned and criticized by the press, especially by his political opponent Lauchlan Mackinnon and by Edward Wilson [qq.v.] of the *Argus*, who preferred independents and regarded Smith as a representative of the publican interest with questionable electioneering tactics. By his marriage and business he had put himself beyond the pale of respectable society, yet he had a great desire to return. In politics he was conservative, generally supporting the government of the day and upholding 'law and order' at all times. He was one of a die-hard group that opposed reduction of the miners' licence fee in 1853; as mayor he reacted to the Eureka rising by enrolling special constables to protect Melbourne, presenting a loyal address to Governor Hotham, and calling a public meeting which was taken over by supporters of the diggers. He voted against the secret ballot, but in favour of gold being part of property freehold, for state aid to churches and for denominational education. In 1858 he went to England to present a civic address of congratulation to Queen Victoria on the marriage of the Princess Royal. He dined at Windsor Castle but was disappointed when he did not receive a knighthood, unlike many mayors of the British Isles and despite a testimonial signed by Bishop Perry [q.v.], Supreme Court judges and the Speaker among other dignitaries. Mackinnon and others had told scandalous tales to the British government, hinting that his wealth was derived from sources even less pure than the sale of intoxicating liquors.

Smith was a well-known figure in white hat, white shirt frills and smoking a cutty pipe. Despite his political conservatism, he was considered a 'man of the people'. Shrewd, energetic and able, as a magistrate he was both kind and just. His personal generosity was great, and his charity work active. He instigated in 1848 the campaign for a Benevolent Asylum and helped the Melbourne Hospital, the Central Board of Health and the Lunatic Asylum. He gave financial and moral support to the eight-hour movement in the mid-1850s. He was a prominent Freemason under the Irish Constitution and remained active in the Church of England. He died of cancer on 30 January 1879 at Flemington and was buried in the Anglican section of the Melbourne general cemeterv. His estate was valued for probate at £42,500; he owned town property and stations on the Darling River, New South Wales, and in the Warrego District, Queensland.

Garryowen (E. Finn), *The chronicles of early Melbourne* (Melb, 1888); J. Hetherington, *Witness to things past* (Melb, 1964); *Examiner* (Melb), 10 Nov 1860; *Leader* (Melb), 14 Mar 1863; *Argus*, 31 Jan 1879; *Bulletin*, 15 Apr 1915; G. R. Quaife, The nature of political conflict in Victoria 1856-57 (M.A. thesis, Univ Melb, 1964); CO 309/47, 53.

JILL EASTWOOD

SMITH, LOUIS LAWRENCE (1830-1910), medical practitioner and politician, was born on 15 May 1830 in London, son of Edward Tyrell Smith, theatrical entrepreneur, and his wife Magdelana Nannette, née Gengoult. He attended St Saviour's Grammar School, Southwark, in 1841-46 and then was apprenticed for five years to the surgeon Sir Thomas Longmore. In 1848 he studied at the Ecole de Médecine, Paris; next year he attended lectures of the London Society of Apothecaries, and in 1850 began his training at Westminster Hospital (L.S.A., 1852). For a while he practised with Dr R. J. Culverwell, proprietor of a pathological museum. In 1852 he migrated as ship's surgeon in the *Oriental*, arriving in Melbourne on 11 December.

Briefly on the goldfields, Smith opened a surgery in Bourke Street in July 1853 and by 1862 had expanded it to include a museum of anatomy and the Polytechnic Hall. He regarded his practice as a speculative venture and by 1863 was spending £3000 a year on newspaper advertisements. He began consultations by post, at a fee of £1 per prescription, and in 1860 he first published his annual *Medical Almanac* which emphasized home treatment. He also developed his popular approach through articles in the *Australian Journal* from 1865 and in cheap pamphlets produced in the 1860s.

Smith argued that advertising showed the worth of his qualifications and thus exposed quacks. He also claimed that his practice gave him an unusually wide range of experience; but his methods were opposed by many doctors and some laymen. His museum was closed in 1869 because it offended 'taste'. Notorious for his treatment of venereal disease, in 1858 he was acquitted of a charge of procuring an abortion; the reputation stuck. Undaunted he ignored the Victorian Branch of the British Medical Association when it was formed in 1879, continued advertising and was said to be making £10,000 a year by 1880.

Smith entered politics perhaps rather for prestige and influence than on principle. As 'the people's candidate' for South Bourke, from 1859 to 1865 he seems to have won Legislative Assembly elections by force of personality. His early career was marred by his assault on J. D. Wood [q.v.] in the House on 15 May 1863. He won Richmond in 1871, but lost popularity and was defeated in 1874 when he opposed Francis's [q.v.] reform proposals. In 1872 a select committee had found that he acted imprudently but without corrupt intentions in soliciting government advertisements for the *Times and Mines* in which he had had an interest; in 1873 he was accused of approaching the commissioner of railways to gain advantage.

As a supporter of Berry [q.v.] Smith again won Richmond in 1877, but in 1881 he helped O'Loghlen [q.v.] to defeat the government and in July was rewarded with a ministerial post without portfolio. But the ministry was weak and lost office in 1883; Smith was defeated. Returned for Mornington in 1886, he opposed the Gillies [q.v.]-Deakin coalition, but supported Munro [q.v.] and Shiels until January 1893, when he crossed the floor to support the scheming Patterson [q.v.]. He lost at the election in September 1894, but stood again in 1895 and 1901, and polled last of the twenty-nine candidates for the 1897 Federal Convention. In the House Smith had spoken often, especially on manufacturing and agriculture. He chaired three select committees and was a member of several others; he served on the royal commission on coal in 1889-91, and was a member of the Phylloxera Board until 1893. He was a promoter of coal exploration and in 1876 had been involved in a proposed tramway from Cloncurry to the Gulf in Queensland.

Until 1881 Smith made the Polytechnic Hall available for theatricals, especially in the 1860s, and he associated with visiting actors such as G. V. Brooke, T. B. Sullivan and the Keans [qq.v.]. In November 1867 he organized a free public open-air dinner during the duke of Edinburgh's tour; the viands were rushed when the royal visitor did not appear. He was also associated with the *Australian Journal*, the *Ballarat Sun* in 1864, the *Times and Mines* and the *Melbourne Journal* in 1894. Most of his time and at least £20,000 were devoted to his model farms at Dandenong, Narre Warren, Nunawading and Beaconsfield on which he raised pigs and sheep. From 1863 he had racehorse stables at Emerald Hill and later at Kensington; he liked acting as steward at suburban meetings and rode in his young days. He was a patron of the Richmond Football Club, was prominent in the Yarra Yarra Rowing Club, and bred bloodhounds.

Smith joined the Chamber of Manufactures in 1881, was several times vice-president and was a leading spokesman for many years. He concentrated on wines, growing the grapes on L. L. Vale at Nunawading; he won success at overseas exhibitions. President in 1883 of the Victorian Winegrowers' Association, he wanted protection against imports. In 1898 he retired as chairman of the Exhibition Trustees, but continued his medical practice and developed his extensive art collection.

By the late 1890s Smith suffered from gout. He died of pneumonia at East Melbourne on 8 July 1910. Charming and 'a thorough Bohemian at home among all classes', he was small and dressed fashionably, often sporting a diamond ring. As a conversationalist he was sparkling and witty, and noted for his gaiety and boisterous mirth. Although his success might have been won unscrupulously (the *Bulletin* dubbed him ££ Smith) it was often the result of enthusiasm and self-confidence, combined with an inherited flair for promotion. His championing of local industry, especially wines, showed an awareness of genuine colonial interests.

Smith was twice married: first about 1860 to Sarah Ann Taylor (d. 1882), by whom he had ten children; and second on 15 May 1883 to Marion Jane Higgins, who survived him and by whom he had five children. Of these Louise (1885-1962), a pianist, settled in Paris and in 1932 founded the Lyre-bird Press; Tom Roberts's portrait of her as a child is in the National Gallery of Victoria. Sir Harold Gengoult (b. 1890) was lord mayor of Melbourne in 1931-34.

W. F. Mandle, 'Games people played: cricket & football in England & Victoria in the late nineteenth century', *Hist Studies*, no 60, Apr 1973; *Argus*, 5 Dec 1891; *Australasian*, 9 July 1910; *Truth*, 22, 29 Aug 1914; A. Williams, Doctor L. L. Smith—'The enterprising L. L.' (B.A. Hons thesis, Univ Melb, 1957); MS material (Museum of Medical Soc of Vic and AMA Lib, Parkville); Col Sec register, 1876 (QA).   GUY FEATHERSTONE

SMITH, PIERCE GALLIARD (1826-1908), Church of England clergyman, was born on 27 October 1826 at Lochvale near Langholm, Dumfriesshire, Scotland, son of Eaglesfield Smith, military officer, and Judith Ann, second daughter of Sir Paulus Aemilius Irving. He was educated at Durham University (M.A., 1852), ordained in 1851 and for the next three years held a curacy and a chaplaincy in Northumberland. In 1851 he had married Emily Philippa Davies of Llangynidr, Wales.

His cousin, Bishop F. Barker [q.v.], offered Smith an appointment in New South Wales as rector of Canberra with a stipend of £200 and the Church of St John the Baptist, already built by Robert Campbell [q.v.] of Duntroon. The Smiths and their two children sailed from Liverpool with the Barkers in the *Mermaid* and reached Sydney on 25 May 1855. They stayed with the Campbells until they moved into their rectory at Acton whence, for the next eighteen years, Smith administered his large parish and school. In 1873 the family moved to the new rectory built on the glebe near St John's. At both rectories Smith made large gardens, growing fruit, vegetables and small crops such as lucerne. A countryman at heart, he noted daily in his diaries the state of the weather and many agricultural details as well as his parochial work. Until he broke his leg in a fall from his horse in July 1898, he rode on his journeys. Tall, thin and bearded, he carried seeds, seedling trees and simple medicaments in his saddlebags and often acted as physician as well as minister. Far-flung clumps of pines, elms and oaks today mark the peregrinations of 'Parson' Smith.

Smith refused all offers of promotion except a canonry of Goulburn Cathedral in 1876, but his connexion with Barker and Bishop M. Thomas [q.v.] was close. George Campbell, peppery but kindly 'squire' of Duntroon, and his wife like the Smiths, saw much of them in Canberra and corresponded with them from abroad. Reserved, touchy, Calvinistic and somewhat intolerant of those outside the Anglican pale, Smith yet had a basic goodness and simplicity that endeared him to children and his intimates. His wife was capable and practical, with a kindly sense of humour. Failing sight and hearing compelled him to retire to Queanbeyan where he died of heart failure on 18 November 1908, survived by his wife, two of his three sons and three daughters. He was buried in St John's churchyard and a memorial tablet was erected in the church by his parishioners to mark his fifty-one years ministry. Smith's second daughter Mary married George, son of L. F. D. Fane De Salis [q.v.], in 1878, and his eldest son Pierce was well known as 'Savannah' Smith, a squatter in Northern Australia from the 1880s to 1907.

F. W. Robinson, *Canberra's first hundred years*, 2nd ed (Syd, 1927); R. T. Wyatt, *The history of the diocese of Goulburn* (Syd, 1937); L. F. Fitzhardinge, *St John's Church and Canberra*, 2nd ed (Canberra, 1959); E. Lea-Scarlett, *Gundaroo* (Canberra, 1972); P. Wardle, 'Some new light on the Rev. Pierce Galliard Smith as revealed by the De Salis letters', Canberra & District Hist Soc, *Papers*, 1960.

P. WARDLE

SMITH, RICHARD (1836-1919), merchant, was born on 27 July 1836 at Brasted, Kent, England, son of William Smith and his wife Ann, née Solomon. Educated in private schools, he received commercial training in the office of a Coventry hardware merchant. At 27 he migrated to South Australia, arriving on 19 June 1863 in the *Countess of Fife*. Employed by Lanyon and Harris as a traveller on Yorke Peninsula and in the south-east of the colony, he and G. Scarfe were taken into partnership within three years, the firm then being called Geo. P. Harris Scarfe & Co. In 1873 he and Scarfe became proprietors and under them the company expanded; by 1886 it held the government contract to supply iron and had sold imported railway engines to the Holdfast Bay Railway Co. In 1889-91 he was councillor for New Glenelg Ward and in 1892-95 was mayor of Glenelg.

Smith also had pastoral interests; in 1894 he bought Kindaruar near Lake Alexandrina where he established his Shropshire stud with twenty-five pedigreed ewes, but finding the country unsuitable bought Sweetholme, a 1200-acre property at Strathalbyn; he added ewes from England and Tasmania to his flock. He also had a smallholding at Virginia for watering stock. In 1906 he bought Nomgetty station, 35,000 acres in Western Australia which he improved; he started a Shorthorn stud and also ran sheep. Smith was a director of the Mutual Life Assurance Co. and a member of the boards of the Executor, Trustee, & Agency Co. of South Australia, the Union Insurance Co.,

the Stannary Hills Mines, the Adelaide Steam Rope and Wire Nail Works and the Adelaide Chemical and Fertilizer Co. He was also a foundation and life member of the South Australian Commercial Travellers' and Warehousemen's Association. In 1899 he was appointed vice-consul for Spain.

On 20 March 1869 Smith had married Emma Law of South Australia. In 1879 he bought Woodlands at Glenelg from the trustees of the Collegiate School of St Peter and made it his home. Closely associated with St Peter's Church of England, Glenelg, he was warden in 1879-83 and was made a trustee in 1906. A tennis player and later a bowler, he took an active interest in local and sporting affairs. He was a modest, tireless man of unvarying habits and went daily to work until three months before his death on 27 March 1919. Survived by five daughters and five sons, he was buried in St Jude's cemetery, Brighton. A stained glass window was installed in St Peter's in memory of him and his wife. His estate in South Australia was sworn for probate at £600,000 and in Western Australia at £69,645. He left nearly £5000 to employees of Geo. P. Harris, Scarfe & Co. and £500 each to the Adelaide Children's Hospital and Training School for Nurses, to the Minda Home for children and to the South Australian Institution for the Blind, and Deaf and Dumb.

H. T. Burgess (ed), *Cyclopedia of South Australia*, 1 (Adel, 1908); Garden and Field Pty, *Our pastoral industry* (Adel, 1910); Mutual Life and Citizens' Assurance Co. Ltd, *The first fifty years of service, 1886-1936* (Syd, 1937); W. H. Jeanes (ed), *Glenelg: birthplace of South Australia* (Glenelg, 1955); PP (SA), 1887, 2 (27), 1888, 3 (90); Minutes (St Peter's Church, Glenelg).

MARJORIE FINDLAY*

SMITH, ROBERT BARR (1824-1915), businessman and philanthropist, was born on 4 February 1824 at Lochwinnoch, Renfrewshire, Scotland, son of Rev. Dr Robert Smith, Church of Scotland minister, and his wife Marjory, née Barr. Educated at the University of Glasgow, he worked in commerce before migrating to Melbourne in 1854 as partner in Hamilton, Smith & Co. Next year he went to Adelaide, and replaced George Elder [q.v.] in the mercantile and pastoral firm of Elder & Co. In 1856 he married Elder's sister Joanna, and in 1863 he and Thomas Elder [q.v.] became sole partners in Elder Smith & Co.

The firm pioneered the opening of outback South Australia, including the fencing of properties and sinking of bores. It also held pastoral leases in Queensland, New

South Wales and Victoria. In 1859 it financed the Wallaroo and Moonta Copper mines which, after initial loss, brought large returns. Elder Smith & Co. also had interests in the Adelaide Steamtug and Adelaide Steamship companies. It was incorporated in 1882 with a nominal capital of £200,000, Elder and Barr Smith between them holding two-thirds of the shares, and next year they established a London office. Barr Smith was a major shareholder in Elder's Trustee and Executor Co., founded in 1910. He was also director of the Beltana, Mutooroo, and Momba Pastoral companies, the Wallaroo and Moonta Mining and Smelting Co., the Adelaide Steamship Co., the South Australian Gas Co., the Mercantile Marine and Fire Insurance Co. of South Australia, the Australian Mutual Provident Society, the English Scottish and Australian Bank, the Mortgage Company of South Australia and the South Australian Co. He also helped to found the Bank of Adelaide.

Smith's philanthropic activity became a legend. A member of the Council of the University of Adelaide for nineteen years, his donations to it totalled £21,400, including £9000 to the library which subsequently bore his name. In 1900 he contributed £10,000 to the completion of the spires of St Peter's Cathedral. He gave £2000 towards the establishment of the diocese of Willochra, and £2300 to pay off the debt on the Trades Hall in 1908. He gave a number of pictures to the Art Gallery, defrayed the cost of an observatory at the summit of Mount Kosciusko for Clement Wragge, and donated a steam lifeboat to the South Australian government. During World War I, he gave two ambulances for the front and offered his home, Torrens Park, Mitcham, for a military hospital.

Modest and unassuming by nature, Smith could not be persuaded into active politics, although he supported the free-trade advocates at the time of the founding of the Commonwealth. Greatly respected, both by the business world and his friends, he was said to have refused a knighthood. A keen patron of the turf, he often attended race meetings and bred and raced his own horses. He died of senile decay at his residence in Angas Street on 20 November 1915. His estate was sworn for probate at £1,799,500, the largest in South Australia until then; of this, more than £40,000 was left to charities. His funeral, though a private one, was attended by the premier, representatives of the university, prominent citizens, and leaders of Adelaide society. He was survived by his wife, three of his seven daughters and one of his six sons.

H. T. Burgess (ed), *Cyclopedia of South Australia*, 1 (Adel, 1908); *The Wallaroo and Moonta mines . . . their history, nature and methods* (Adel, 1920); R. Cockburn, *Pastoral pioneers of South Australia*, 2 (Adel, 1927); *Elder Smith & Co. Limited: the first hundred years* (Adel, 1940); K. Sharp and B. Crump, *A history of Milo and Ambathala . . . held by Milo Pastoral Co. Ltd* (Adel, 1963); W. G. K. Duncan and R. A. Leonard, *The University of Adelaide, 1874-1974* (Adel, 1973); *Advertiser* (Adel), 22 Nov 1915, 27 Nov 1941; *Chronicle* (Adel), 27 Nov 1915; *Observer* (Adel), 27 Nov 1915.

DIRK VAN DISSEL

SMITH, ROBERT BURDETT (1837-1895), solicitor and politician, was born on 25 August 1837 in Sydney, baptized Robert Lloyd, twin son of John Lloyd Smith and his wife Mary Ann, née Salmon. John, a native of Northumberland, had been convicted of horse-stealing at Edinburgh on 8 January 1830 and sentenced to be transported for seven years, arriving in Sydney in the *York* on 7 February 1831. Mary Ann, whom he had married with the governor's permission on 2 February 1835, had come free to the colony in the *Princess Victoria* on 4 February 1834. With his brother-in-law Thomas Armitage Salmon and later on his own, John traded as a carcass butcher in 1838-43; but on 11 April, bankrupt, he was convicted in Port Phillip of forgery and sentenced to transportation for the term of his natural life.

Robert was educated at W. T. Cape's [q.v.] school, studied classics and literature under Dr D. A. McKean and J. Sheridan Moore [q.v.] and in 1858 was articled to William Roberts of Goulburn. As Robert Burdett Smith he was admitted as solicitor and attorney of the Supreme Court in October 1863; he took chambers in King Street where his practice flourished. In 1868 he spoke at a meeting of sympathy for the duke of Edinburgh, shot by H. J. O'Farrell [q.v.]. In 1869 he failed to win the Hastings seat in the Legislative Assembly but next year he was declared elected by the Elections and Qualifications Committee that unseated Horace Dean [q.v.]. He began as a supporter of Sir James Martin [q.v.] but became an independent and in 1877 refused office under (Sir) Henry Parkes [q.v.]. Successful in obtaining public works for his electorate, he was able to have the seat divided by the 1880 Electoral Act, and won the part named the Macleay. A prominent advocate of law reform, he worked to simplify equity practice and procedure, and obtained improvements to bankruptcy and probate law. To 'Flaneur' in the *Freeman's Journal*, 13 March 1886, he had 'not an abnormal amount of wit in himself, but he is often the cause of enough wit in others'. The *Bulletin* credited him with 'high professional and political status' and 'well merited pre-eminence'. Known as a 'true straight and honourable man' he was said to be 'very fond of associating himself with' the squatting class. By 1871 he had pastoral interests in the Albert and Darling districts. With J. F. Burns [q.v.] he speculated in land in the outer Sydney suburb, Hornsby. In 1885 he supported W. B. Dalley's [q.v.] dispatch of the Sudan Contingent and published his speeches on the matter. Later that year he declined Sir John Robertson's [q.v.] offer of a seat in the cabinet as representative of the government in the Legislative Council.

A commissioner for the Sydney (1879), Melbourne (1880), Amsterdam (1883) and Calcutta (1883) exhibitions, Smith visited Europe as representative commissioner for New South Wales to the Colonial and Indian Exhibition in 1886. In London he became a fellow of the Royal Colonial Institute and a member of the Imperial Federation League. That year the Elections and Qualifications Committee dismissed allegations of bribery and corruption by a defeated political opponent, O. O. Dangar. In 1887 Smith was a commissioner for the Adelaide Jubilee International Exhibition and a member of the royal commission for centennial celebrations. Executive commissioner for New South Wales at the 1888 Centennial International Exhibition, Melbourne, he again visited Europe in 1889 as royal commissioner for Victoria to the Paris Universal Exhibition. He later claimed that his visits to Europe changed him from a free trader to a moderate protectionist. Ill health forced him to resign from the assembly in 1889 and next year he was appointed to the Legislative Council and created C.M.G. In 1891-92 he was a commissioner for the World's Columbian Exposition, Chicago, 1893.

Smith had helped start the Australian Patriotic Association in 1868 and later was its president for two years. As secretary of the Captain Cook [q.v.] Statue Committee he was largely responsible for the erection of the statue in Hyde Park in 1879. A magistrate from 1878, in 1882 he became a director of Sydney Hospital. For six years he was an examiner in law for admission of attorneys and solicitors. A bachelor, he was a member of the Athenaeum, Reform and Australian clubs; in 1883 he was a founder of the local branch of the Geographical Society of Australasia and was elected to the Royal Society of New South Wales. After a lingering illness, he died of heart and kidney disease on 2 July 1895 in his home in Macquarie Street, Sydney, and was buried at St Peter's Anglican Church,

Cooks River. He left the residue of his estate, sworn for probate at £33,891, to his sister Emily. Reticent about his convict ancestry, he was a patriotic native-born Australian whose career illustrates the mobility of New South Wales society in the mid-nineteenth century. Smithtown, on the Macleay, is named after him.

E. Digby (ed), *Australian men of mark*, 2, no 4 (Syd, 1889); V&P (LA NSW), 1870-71, 1, 445, 1885-86, 2, 63, 4, 763, 1888-89, 3, 1199, 1889, 6, 601; *Port Phillip Herald*, 4, 11 Apr 1843; *SMH*, 25 Mar 1868, 6 Apr 1886, 5 July 1895; *Bulletin*, 13 Mar 1880; *Macleay Argus*, 20 Mar 1886, 10 July 1895; *T&CJ*, 30 Apr 1887, 10 May 1890, 6 July 1895; *Cumberland Argus*, 18 Dec 1897; R. Parsons, Lawyers in the New South Wales parliament, 1870-1890 (Ph.D. thesis, Macquarie Univ, 1972); list of free passengers, 1834 *and* MS cat (ML); Convict indents *and* permissions to marry (NSWA).

CHRIS CUNNEEN

SMITH, ROBERT MURRAY (1831-1921), politician and businessman, was born on 29 October 1831 at Liverpool, England, son of Alexander Smith and his wife Sophia Sherbourne, daughter of Admiral Robert Murray. His father and uncles controlled a family shipping firm with Australian connexions. Educated at Repton and a scholar of Oriel College, Oxford, he intended to read for the Bar but had to abandon his course in 1851 when his father died. He decided to migrate to Victoria where an uncle and cousin would give him a start, and arrived in the *South Carolina* in January 1854.

Murray Smith joined with John Strachan as a merchant and commission agent and by 1863 was able to spend two years in Europe combining business and travel. On his return he joined with R. Turnbull, M.L.C., but Turnbull, Smith & Co. was wound up in 1872, and he became general manager in Victoria of the New Zealand Loan and Mercantile Agency Co. Ltd until 1880. He was also a director of the National Bank in 1872-82, and of the Moama–Deniliquin private railway company.

Murray Smith was a 'free trader by conviction ever since I could think or reason', worshipped Bright and Cobden and was perhaps the most eloquent Victorian defender of *laissez-faire*. After an unsuccessful contest for the assembly seat of Williamstown in 1865 in opposition to the McCulloch [q.v.] government, he became well known as an orator and political organizer and wrote frequently for the *Spectator* and other journals. He was mayor of Prahran in 1870-72 after joining the town council in 1867. In 1873 he was elected to the Legislative Assembly for St Kilda, gave general support to the Kerferd [q.v.] and Mc-Culloch ministries, was defeated by one vote in the Berry [q.v.] landslide of 1877, but was re-elected for Boroondara late in the year. He became one of the most prominent opponents of the Berry government, but refused offers of a ministry or the Speakership from Service [q.v.] in 1880. When Service temporarily retired from politics, Murray Smith became virtual leader of the Constitutionalists. In order to form a ministry with Francis [q.v.], he plotted to support O'Loghlen [q.v.] to bring down Berry in 1881 and then to refuse to take office with him, but O'Loghlen gathered colleagues and the Constitutionalists had to tolerate him in office. In Deakin's opinion Murray Smith was 'steeped in commercialism' and 'defended the selfishnesses of the average businessman'. He was more effective as a parliamentarian than C. H. Pearson [q.v.]; but in spite of their antagonism, they 'combined to elevate the tone of the Assembly'.

Murray Smith's outstanding political success was as agent-general in London in 1882-86. His term coincided with the Service government's campaign for the right of consultation on Australian interests in the Pacific and to forestall annexation of New Guinea by Germany and of the New Hebrides by France. The government was augmenting the ambassadorial function of the agent-general at the expense of Governor Sir Henry Loch. Murray Smith lobbied the Colonial Office, mobilized the other agents-general, rallied English sympathizers like Rosebery [q.v. Primrose] and Childers [q.v.], and supplied Service with information. He set a precedent in 1884 by interviewing the French ambassador and the British ambassador to France. He maintained good relations with the Colonial Office, despite the unpopularity of Victorian policies. He refused a knighthood but accepted a C.M.G. in 1884; the University of Oxford bestowed an honorary M.A. on him. He was unhappy when recalled, but was banquetted by several hundred friends both on his departure and on his return home.

Murray Smith became a director of the Bank of Victoria, the Trustees, Executors, and Agency Co., the Australian Deposit and Mortgage Bank Ltd, the Australian Freehold Banking Corporation (Standard Bank of Australia Ltd) till 1890, L. Stevenson and Sons Ltd and the local board of the Northern Assurance Co. He was trustee for several private estates and 'perpetual' chairman of the Edward Wilson [q.v.] Trust from its foundation in 1878. Late in 1889 he made astute warnings about government financial policy. In the early 1890s he led the free-trade political revival and was prominent in the National Association and the Free Trade Democratic Association. In 1894-1900 he held the seat of Hawthorn but was so conservative as to be almost anachronistic, fighting tooth and nail against the minimum wage movement on the grounds that 'every man knows his own business a good deal better than any Government can teach it to him'. He was a member of royal commissions on charitable institutions (1890) and state banking (1895), and of the board of inquiry into unemployment (1900). He campaigned for Federation, stood for election to the 1897 Convention, and although not even included on the *Argus* ticket ran fourteenth out of twenty-nine candidates. In old age he was gloomily pessimistic about the future of Australia and the empire.

Murray Smith was president of the Melbourne Club in 1875, a member of the Council of the University of Melbourne in 1887-1900, a trustee of the Public Library, Museums and National Gallery in 1897-1921, and treasurer of the Tucker Village Settlement Association from 1892. He was a Low Churchman, but a close friend of Charles Strong [q.v.] who officiated at his funeral. A highly cultivated man who knew his Shakespeare and Walter Scott almost verbatim, read Latin and French and a wide variety of authors including 'moderns' like Arnold Bennett, he wrote on political subjects, and lectured to literary, political and self-improvement societies. 'Rolf Boldrewood' [q.v. T. A. Browne] dedicated *Robbery under Arms* to him. Rosebery thought him possibly the most interesting man in Australia; Sir Samuel Way found him 'the best talker in Melbourne' with 'a pleasant sub-acid humour'. He was a handsome man, very gallant to ladies, but a vehement opponent of female rights or exposure of women to ugly realities. Though never wealthy, he was generous to good and bad causes alike. His chivalry was outstanding: though he strongly disapproved of Gladstone's imperial policy, he led the counter-cheering at a public meeting in 1885. It was unfortunate that his early political principles became so rigid that they limited a contribution to public life which, through his ability, energy and humanity, might have been outstanding.

Murray Smith had married Jane Carmichael Strachan at Geelong in 1858; they had three daughters and one son, who died of diphtheria while a student at Oxford in 1886. Predeceased by his wife, he died at his home in Toorak on 31 August 1921 and was buried in St Kilda cemetery. His estate was valued for probate at £16,713. A portrait by J. C. Waite [q.v.] is in the Melbourne Club.

A. Deakin, *The crisis in Victorian politics,
1879-1881*, J. A. La Nauze and R. M. Crawford
eds (Melb, 1957); G. Serle, *The rush to be rich*
(Melb, 1971); Roy Colonial Inst, Procs, 1883-86;
Argus, 15 June 1886, 1 Sept 1921; Crisp letters
(NL).   GEOFFREY SERLE

SMITH, SAMUEL (1812-1889), winemaker, was born on 17 July 1812 at Ware-
ham, Dorset, England. He was a successful
brewer before he migrated to South Australia with his wife Frances and five children
in the *China* in 1847. After a time at
Klemzig near Adelaide, he moved to Angaston where he worked as a gardener for G.
F. Angas [q.v.]. In 1849 he bought thirty
acres to establish his own vineyard and
orchard which he called Yalumba, Aboriginal for 'all the country around'; he planted
at night and worked for Angas during the
day, later asserting that it was a year of
struggle, 'but God gave me wonderful
strength and my wife helped in every possible way'.

In 1852 Smith and his son joined the rush
to the Victorian goldfields. On his sixteenth
shaft he was lucky and returned after four
months to Adelaide £300 richer. He spent
£80 on eighty acres which he let out, £100
on a plough, two horses and a harness and
kept the rest for future cellars and another
house. In 1852 he made his first wine and
by 1862 had nine acres planted with shiraz.
He gave cuttings to his neighbours and
later bought their grapes to make wine; in
1863 he produced sixty hogsheads. Yalumba
wines quickly won repute for quality, gaining a bronze medal at the 1866-67 Intercolonial Exhibition, Melbourne, and a silver
medal at the 1878 Paris Universal Exhibition.

Smith was a prominent member of the
Angaston Congregational Church and was
for many years superintendent of the Sunday school. He died of chronic Bright's
disease on 15 June 1889 survived by his
wife, four daughters and a son. His estate
was sworn for probate at £11,178.

His son SIDNEY, born on 4 March 1837
in Morden, Dorset, arrived in South Australia with his parents. He accompanied his
father to Ballarat and Bendigo in 1852. On
1 October 1862 he married Eleanor Jane,
daughter of Thomas Caley. He later became
a partner in the business and on his father's
retirement in 1888 took over the management of the estate. He supervised the building of the two storey winery and clock
tower, made of blue marble. By 1900 there
were 120 acres under vines.

Sidney was chairman of the Angaston
District Council and was long associated
with the volunteer movement. He died of

chronic renal disease on 27 November 1908,
survived by five sons and three daughters.
Some years previously because of failing
health he had retired, transferring the business to two of his sons. Percival took charge
of the wine-making and cellar operations
while Walter supervised marketing and
built up exports to England and India. In
1975 Yalumba was in the hands of the fifth
generation of the family in South Australia.

E. Ward, *The vineyards and orchards of
South Australia* (Adel, 1862); J. J. Pascoe, *His-
tory of Adelaide and vicinity* (Adel, 1901); S.
Smith & Sons Ltd, *100 years in the good earth,
1849-1949* (Adel, 1949); *Register* (Adel), 17
June 1889.   JAKI ILBERY

SMITH, SHEPHERD (1835-1886), banker, was born in Durham, England, son of
Thomas Smith and his wife Isabella, née
Thompson. Educated in Durham, he became
a choir-boy at the cathedral. He worked
briefly in a London private bank, migrated
to Sydney in 1853 and joined the Bank of
New South Wales as a junior clerk. In 1856
he opened the bank's gold-buying agency at
Rocky River, also a branch at Tamworth
and early in 1858 one at Deniliquin. The
next year he became manager in Brisbane
and in 1860 was acting colonial auditor-
general for Queensland. In 1864 he went to
New Zealand as inspector for the bank but
was recalled at the end of the year to Sydney
and appointed general manager.

Under Smith's guidance the bank became
the largest in the colonies in terms of deposits and advances and won repute for stability, leadership and independence. An
administrator rather than innovator, he
stressed the necessity of large reserves, especially after some early losses in 1870.
Hard-working, with fine attention to detail
he maintained a firm central control in a
competitive era over the expanding network
of branches and all aspects of the bank's
activities. In principle Smith favoured loose
agreements regulating interest rates with
other banks, provided they were observed
in all colonies; but, too much of an individualist to tolerate breaches, he was pre
pared to play a lone but powerful hand. In
tangled negotiations in the 1870s he was at
odds with most of his fellow bankers, particularly the Associated Banks of Victoria,
and his strong personality earned him a
reputation for being uncompromising and
arrogant.

Smith developed efficient machinery for
the New South Wales government's banking operations, but the size and fluctuations
of the business created problems for the
bank which sought exclusive rights while

the treasury wanted the best terms for its funds. He failed to resolve the ensuing difficulties with successive treasurers and in 1875 clashed with William Forster [q.v.]. Smith's political ineptitude helped to make each renewal of the agreement increasingly acrimonious, until in 1885 the treasurer, G. R. Dibbs [q.v.] made other arrangements. Both the government and the bank published their correspondence and a protracted lawsuit followed; after the government's technical victory in the Privy Council in 1887, the bank paid over £25,000 to the treasury.

In Queensland Smith had been a director of the Cabulture Cotton Co. and in 1866 joined John Richardson [q.v.] in three runs on the Darling Downs and nine in the Maranoa District. In 1872 they sold four runs to John Watt [q.v.] and W. Gilchrist, and gradually disposed of the remainder but retained Gideon Land in the Darling Downs until 1883.

A formidable High Churchman, Smith was a lay member of the first Sydney diocesan synod of the Church of England in 1866, and of the first provincial and general synods of 1869 and 1872. He devoted much time to the financial affairs and the management of the property and charities of the Church, but became embroiled in political and liturgical issues. As a leading member of the Church of England Defence Association he, with (Sir) Alexander Stuart [q.v.], opposed the abolition of state aid to denominational schools. After the introduction of the 1880 Public Instruction Act he resisted the supply of religious teachers to public schools and reaffirmed that the Church should support its own schools. He withdrew from the general synod in 1881 after censure by senior clergy for outspoken criticism of some of the forms of the prayer book and for his advocacy of revision. A founder and trustee of the Clergy Widows' and Orphans' Fund, he was a committeeman of the Sydney Female Refuge Society and, in 1879, a founder of the Industrial Blind Institution. He supported the establishment of volunteer fire brigades and used the bank's services to import the latest equipment.

Beneath his uncompromising exterior Smith retained a sense of compassion and a respect for the dignity of the individual. Aged 51, he died on 13 September 1886 and was buried in the Anglican section of Rookwood cemetery. He was survived by his wife Emily, née Phillips, whom he had married at Parramatta on 11 January 1859, and by two sons and seven daughters. His estate was valued for probate at over £20,000.

R. F. Holder, *Bank of New South Wales: a*
history, 1 (Syd, 1970), and for bibliog; *V&P* (LA QLD), 1860, 425, 1864, 1311 (LA NSW), 1875, 2, 739.   R. F. HOLDER

SMITH, THOMAS (1823-1900), trade unionist, was born at Leominster, Hereford, England, son of John Smith and his wife Mary, née Harper. He learned the mason's trade at Hampton Court and worked on the construction of the Houses of Parliament in London, the Hull and Stoke-on-Trent railway stations and the Birmingham lunatic asylum. He shipped as a carpenter's mate in the *J. S. Ford* and arrived in Melbourne in 1849. He worked at his trade on the Melbourne gaol and was the first president of the Operative Masons' Society in 1850-51. In a humorous toast to 'Success to Bluestone' at the opening of the Princes Bridge in November 1850 he forecast the success of the eight-hour movement. After working in Geelong on J. F. Strachan's [q.v.] mansion he returned to Melbourne, but when gold was discovered he dug with some success at Golden Point, Mount Alexander, Bendigo and the Ovens. He returned to Melbourne and was employed as Abraham Linacre's foreman, and then with Lawrence and Cain [q.v.], working on many Melbourne buildings, including the Bank of Victoria, the Australasian Alliance Insurance Co., the Town Hall and the Melbourne Banking Co., where he lost the sight of an eye as a result of an accident.

In February 1855 the Masons' Society was revived after the disruption of the gold rush years; Smith, who had retained its early records, was re-elected president. On 5 March 1856 he attended a meeting of building operatives at the Belvidere (Eastern Hill) Hotel and became one of a committee of twelve elected to set the eight-hour idea into motion. On 26 March at a large meeting at the Queen's Theatre he moved a resolution, seconded by James Stephens [q.v.], that an eight-hour day in the building trade was desirable, and seconded J. G. Galloway's motion that it take effect from 21 April; as first treasurer of the inaugural Eight Hours' Committee he presided over the celebratory banquet held on that date at the Belvidere. He was flag-bearer for the masons in their first anniversary march in 1857. Appointed to the central committee of the society on 9 June 1859, he was secretary from 8 December to 15 March 1860.

From February 1867 Smith was a government inspector of works, supervising the construction of buildings such as the Parliament House, Government House, Law Courts and extensions to the Public Library. He invested profitably in property in South Preston (as early as 1858) and in Collingwood, and on his retirement in 1886 visited England. On 6 April 1893 he defeated Ben Douglass [q.v.] for the presidency of the Eight Hours' Pioneers Association; at the time Douglass quipped that Smith had walked in procession thirty-seven years previously and had done nothing since.

Smith, aged 28, had married Harriet Dudley at Collingwood. He died at his home Ivy Bank, Oakover Road. South Preston, on 21 December 1900, aged 77, survived by two daughters and two sons, and an only brother. He was buried in the Melbourne general cemetery with a Wesleyan minister officiating at the service. His estate was valued for probate at £4050.

A. Sutherland et al, *Victoria and its metropolis*, 2 (Melb, 1888); W. E. Murphy, *History of the Eight Hours' Movement* (Melb, 1896); *Tocsin*, 27 Dec 1900; W. E. Murphy, Formation of the pioneer unions, Hist sketches of unions and trade unionists, no 7, Trades Hall papers, item 4, letter-book (ML).   N. W. SAFFIN

SMITH, THOMAS (1829-1882), Anglican clergyman, was born on 21 December 1829 at Leominster, Herefordshire, England, son of William Smith, wool-buyer, and his wife Ann, née Cartwright. About 1854, after little education and a drunken and dissolute youth, he underwent a religious conversion and became a missioner of the Colonial and Continental Church Society. Recommended to Bishop Barker [q.v.] he arrived in Sydney probably in the *Oneida* on 23 December 1856. In December 1857 Barker licensed him as catechist at Providence Chapel, a rented shack at Blackwattle Swamp, one of the roughest areas of Sydney. On 19 December 1858 he was made deacon and was priested in June 1861. He built St Barnabas's Church, a parsonage known as 'Parson Smith's farm', and schoolrooms for a thriving denominational day school. In 1869 he claimed a congregation of 1200 and a Sunday school of 1000 pupils with 73 teachers. After preaching in England and Ireland in 1869-70, he lifted the parish debt and in 1872 was elected a canon of St Andrew's Cathedral.

Smith ignored 'the barriers which always encompass ministers of the Church of England' and preached 'like a man burning with iconoclastic zeal for the welfare of his fellow men'. In 1875 he claimed to have inspired twelve men to enter Anglican orders; but many clergy scorned this untrained 'interloper'. He supported the Sydney Female Refuge Society, the Sydney Ragged schools, the local Young Men's Christian Association and the Working Men's Book Society.

In February 1873, at the invitation of Bishop Marsden [q.v.], Smith became incumbent and canon of All Saints' Cathedral, Bathurst, and soon founded All Saints' College for boys. Next year he began extensions to the cathedral and in August 1875 opened St Barnabas's Church for the railwaymen in South Bathurst. As secretary of the diocesan Church Society, in five years he doubled its income and travelled widely.

In July 1879 Archbishop Vaughan's [q.v.] anti-public schools pastoral prompted Smith to close the Anglican school, already decimated by the opening of a public school, and to preach before his bishop and an overflow congregation a bitter anti-Catholic sermon that was repeated many times and published in Sydney. At the provincial synod in October the Bathurst delegates opposed the denominational system. Consequent accusations from outside Bathurst that Smith had ruined the Church Society and misappropriated funds, caused him to leave in December for England. After commending New South Wales to British emigrants, he returned in February 1882. Barker debarred him from the Sydney diocese, and a meeting of the Bathurst clergy in Grenfell backed Marsden's repudiation of him. James Rutherford [q.v.] accused Marsden of provoking a schism, but Smith accepted a testimonial and retired to Sydney where he died on 12 August of cirrhosis and was buried in Balmain cemetery. He was survived by his wife Maria Sarah, née Spooner, whom he had married in Worcester in 1851, four sons and five daughters. His estate was valued for probate at £3266. An obelisk to his memory was erected at St Barnabas's Church, Sydney.

W. H. Mitchell, *Sketch of the life & ministry of the Rev. Thomas Smith* (Syd, 1873); G. S. Oakes, *Jubilee of the diocese of Bathurst 1870-1920* (Bathurst, 1920); W. A. Steel and C. W. Sloman, *The history of All Saints' College, Bathurst 1873-1934* (Syd, 1936); *Aust Churchman*, 17 July 1869; *T&CJ*, 13 Aug 1870; *Bathurst Times*, 28 Aug 1875, 30 July 1879, 4, 9 Feb, 6 Mar 1882; *SMH*, 15 Aug 1882; *ISN*, 2 Sept 1882; Bishop Barker journals (ML).
                                                RUTH TEALE

SMITH, WILLIAM COLLARD (1830-1894), agent, investor and politician, was born on 19 July 1830 at Bollington, Cheshire, England, youngest son of William Smith, cotton manufacturer, and his wife Margaret, née Wright. He arrived in Melbourne in the *Birmingham* in October 1852, went to Bendigo, returned to Melbourne and was at Creswick before settling at Ballarat early in 1855. Well built, with a good voice, ready wit and genial manner, he won repute as an auctioneer and land agent in partnership with E. A. Wynne, doing a brisk trade in crown land and often acting for squatters. In 1856 he was returned to the newly formed Ballarat West Council, and became chairman in 1860. By then, with Wynne, he had founded a bank and was a leader in mobilizing the vast investment needed to develop Ballarat's mines; he was prominent in the late 1860s in companies exploring the westward extension of the field; in 1868 he visited England with limited success to raise money for The Winter's Freehold Gold Mining Co. He was also interested in mining in South Australia and joined Wynne in several pastoral ventures.

Smith was elected to the Legislative Assembly for West Ballarat in August 1861. His platform reflected concern for local water-supply, a higher gold price and democratic reforms of the Upper House, education, land and the tariff. Never a centralist, he initiated the idea of country districts collecting and spending their own revenues and proposed the payment of country members of parliament. He was a pragmatic liberal democrat, though the *Age* saw him as a pseudo-liberal because he was acting as a land shark. Opponents claimed later, and some admirers conceded, that he lacked principles, but he was no demagogue and often formed policies in advance of the mood of the electorate. His sincerity and personal disinterestedness were never in question; although wealthy and an employer, he believed in social justice. After resigning from parliament and from the Ballarat West Council through pressure of business in 1864, he returned to parliament in 1871 on a platform that included inspection of mines, the protection of miners' wages by a lien on company plant and a radical taxation policy. He wanted to abolish the Mines Department, to introduce free and compulsory education, new electoral boundaries and strictly controlled immigration. One of his meetings broke up in complete disorder on the education issue.

Smith identified the future of Ballarat with that of the colony. He opposed Melbourne 'influence' sucking up public money and forcing expensive railway construction, which put a burden on country people. He favoured single track, light lines to open up the hinterland rapidly. In 1871 he influenced legislation that stipulated that miners should not work on Saturday night. and in 1873 he brought down Australia's first Factory Act which helped to protect seamstresses and to improve conditions in factories; he chaired the 1882-84 royal commission into shops and factories and possibly wrote its scouring reports that produced the

Factory Act of 1885. He was at home with the young and in 1877 he advocated votes for 18-year-olds and a free university. In 1873 he had chaired the royal commission on local government legislation.

The support of the Orange Lodge and membership of the Loyal Liberal Organization and later the National Reform League defined Smith's connexion with Graham Berry [q.v.], under whom he served as minister of mines (1875), mines and public instruction (1877-80) and education (1880-81). As acting treasurer in 1879, he was misled into planning the expenditure of a non-existing £2 million, which caricaturists depicted as having been lost in his boots: the 'Major's boots' became famous. Later he fell out with Berry, apparently over Federation, and clearly over factory reform, and was not a member of the coalition ministries of the 1880s. His championing of Federation, however, earned him a place in the Federal Convention of 1890. Neither an orator nor a convincing debater, his ministerial strength lay in his great skill as a negotiator and energetic administrator. Yet there was a justified outcry in 1880 over his crowding of the Education Department with people from Ballarat, and anger when his influence gained a third member of parliament for Ballarat West.

Smith's pride in Ballarat was matched by the community's acceptance of him as its most popular public figure. He was a life patron of the Ballarat Imperial Football Club, an office-bearer of many other sporting clubs, prominent in the Old Colonists' Association and, from its inception, marshal of the important eight-hour procession. Commonly called 'The Major', he was a captain in the Ballarat Rifle Rangers in 1861, major in 1872 and retired in 1884 as an honorary lieut-colonel. A member of the Ballarat City Council in 1870-99, he was mayor in 1874-75 and 1887-88.

On a visit to California in 1891 Smith contracted a severe heart and liver illness from which he never fully recovered. His misgivings about his health contributed to his defeat in the 1892 election. He stood again in 1894 and was returned in September, but died on 20 October and was buried at Ballarat with public honours. In 1854 he had married Ellen Teresa Newman, a Catholic, who died on 12 March 1881, aged 41; their only son had died in 1875. In his last years Smith lived at Brunswick with Eliza Ellen Turnbull, who was referred to in his will as his housekeeper and nurse and whose daughter Mabel he had adopted: they were well provided for under the will. He had hoped even in death to serve Ballarat by a residual bequest to provide over £2000 for statuary for the Botanical Gardens or pictures for the art gallery, but his estate was sworn for probate at £19 2s. 5d.

G. Serle, *The rush to be rich* (Melb, 1971); *Ballarat Star*, 14 Sept 1860, 17 July, 8 Oct 1861, 11 Mar 1871, 22 Jan, 16 Mar 1874; *Ballarat Courier*, 16 Jan 1871, 12 Jan 1877, 12 June 1890, 22, 23, 24 Oct 1894; *Ovens & Murray Advertiser*, 19 Jan 1875; *Table Talk*, 6 Nov 1891.

WESTON BATE

SMITH, WILLIAM HOWARD (1814-1890), master mariner and ship-owner, was born at Yarmouth, Norfolk, England, son of Ormond Smith, mariner, ship-owner and mail contractor for Amsterdam and Rotterdam, Holland, and his wife Kesier, née Edmunds. At 10 Howard Smith went on his first voyage; he later studied navigation and qualified as a master. He became a partner of his father at 21 and was given command of the steamship *Adonis*. For some years he was employed by Malcolmson Bros, ship-owners, and sailed to Dutch, Spanish and Latin American ports. His first wife Anna Geil, née Hansen, died without issue; in 1854 he brought his second wife Agnes Rosa, née Allen, and their five children to Australia.

With S. P. O. Skinner, a marine engineer, Smith had bought the *Express*, a 136-ton schooner-rigged steamer, and entered the Port Phillip Bay trade between Melbourne and Geelong. After eight good years Smith sold out to his Geelong agent, T. J. Parker, later a founding partner of Huddart [q.v.], Parker & Co., and entered the intercolonial trade. In 1862 he and his family revisited Europe. He bought the steamer *Kief*, renamed it *You Yangs*, and from mid-1864 commanded it in competition with the powerful Australasian Steam Navigation Co. between Melbourne, Sydney and Newcastle. The venture was successful and two years later he bought another steamship in England, the *Dandenong*. It was his last command and he remained ashore after 1870.

Establishing himself in the Newcastle coal trade, Howard Smith formed a limited partnership with L. J. L. Burke, who had a large coal business in Melbourne in the mid-1860s; he acquired the firm in 1884 and in that decade it became one of Melbourne's largest and most efficient coal importers, constantly acquiring vessels because of the growing demand for passenger and general cargo services from Melbourne to all the eastern coast ports. In the late 1870s he had three of his sons in the partnership and they took charge of the Melbourne, Sydney

and Brisbane offices. The firm became a limited liability company in September 1883, William Howard Smith and Sons Ltd, with a nominal capital of £1 million, paid up to £500,000: all the £10 shares issued were taken up by the family. He became managing director at Melbourne and his second son, Edmund, at Sydney. Howard Smith retired from active management in 1888 and· his son Arthur Bruce succeeded him.

Smith was a justice of the peace, a director of many commercial companies, a commissioner of the Melbourne Harbor Trust in 1884 and a member of the Marine Board of Victoria in the late 1880s. He was also a committee-man of the Melbourne Sailors' Home in 1874-80 and chairman next year, and a committee-man of the Victorian Shipwreck Relief Society in 1877-80. Aged 76, he died on 22 March 1890 in Melbourne, survived by his wife and seven sons and two daughters of their twelve children. His estate was sworn for probate at £137,153. The business was reorganized under the control of four sons, Edmund (Melbourne), Walter (Geelong), Harold (Sydney), and Ormond (Brisbane) who later acquired extensive pastoral properties near Kilcoy, Queensland. · Howard Smith's great entrepreneurial ability had ensured the firm's prosperity in the 1890s.

H. M. Franklyn, *A glance at Australia in 1880* (Melb, 1881); W. H. Smith & Co., *Handbook of W. Howard Smith & Sons' line of intercolonial steamers* (Syd, 1883); Howard Smith Ltd, *The first hundred years 1854-1954* (Syd, 1954); *A'sian Insurance and Banking Record*, 10 Jan 1881, 12 Oct 1883; *J of Commerce*, 28 Apr 1891; *Argus*, 24 Mar 1890; E. H. Collis, 'Sea carriers of the colonies: growth of Howard Smith Ltd', *Today*, May 1933; *Age*, 7 Dec 1935.

G. R. HENNING

SMYTH, ROBERT BROUGH (1830-1889), civil servant and mining engineer, was born at Wallsend, Northumberland, England, son of Edward Smyth, mining engineer, and his wife Ann, née Brough, who was related to Robert B. and William Brough, well-known theatrical and miscellaneous writers. Educated at Whickham, Durham, he was instructed by his father and brothers in iron-making and mining techniques, finding some time to study chemistry, natural history and geology. He was employed in 1846 at the Derwent Iron Works and then as a clerk at the Consett Iron Works.

On 14 November 1852 Smyth arrived in Melbourne and went to the gold diggings, where he worked as a carter on the construction of roads at Sawpit Gully. Back in Melbourne, on 7 November 1853 he became a draftsman under the surveyor-general, Andrew Clarke [q.v.], and soon was acting chief draftsman. In April 1855 he took over official meteorological observations in Melbourne, the results of which were published in three comprehensive parliamentary reports in 1856-58. As a practical and theoretical meteorologist Smyth achieved wide recognition in Australia and abroad. Professionally cautious and conservative, in 1858 he warned against premature theoretical speculation about Australian conditions 'when the data are so few'.

In 1855 Smyth began to correspond with Adam Sedgwick who secured his election as a fellow of the Geological Society of London and the publication of his first geological paper in the society's Quarterly Journal (1858), and commended him to (Sir) Frederick McCoy [q.v.]. He early secured the support of (Sir) Redmond Barry [q.v.], and became the first secretary of the Board of Science in January 1858. Primarily responsible to the mining committee, he issued instructions to mining surveyors, compiled statistics and data to prevent the 'useless movements from place to place' of prospectors and obtained details of gold finds and types of digging machinery. In December 1860 he became secretary for mines at a salary of £750. His influence over official mining policy was unrivalled for more than a decade and he helped to standardize leasing regulations. In 1862 at a royal commission into the goldfields he demanded the 'doing away with all obstacles in the way of persons desiring to obtain land for mining', and trenchantly criticized A. R. C. Selwyn [q.v.] and the Government Geological Survey. Supported by McCoy, he favoured a more general geological and utilitarian survey of the colony. Some of his recommendations were adopted when the Mining Department was reorganized under a minister.

Smyth compiled numerous reports and wrote catalogues for exhibitions of minerals and fossils. In November 1869 he superintended the establishment of a museum of economic geology, mineralogy and mining and published in Melbourne The Gold Fields and Mineral Districts of Victoria . . . Covertly involved in the controversy that led to the disbanding of the Geological Survey in 1869, he became its director on its reinstatement in 1871; he increased its part in the search for and proving of economic mineral and coal deposits. In 1875 he became chief inspector of mines and published the geological reports on John Forrest's Western Australian exploration.

On 19 June 1860 Smyth had become honorary secretary to the Board for the Protection of Aborigines and in 1863 became a voting member. Zealous and determined, he assumed the role of chairman, which belonged ex officio to the chief secretary, and wielded great power, including the dubious dismissal of John Green, general inspector of Aborigines in 1861-75 with whom he had earlier collaborated. Smyth's compilation, The Aborigines of Victoria . . . (1878), arose from his efforts to gather information and artefacts of Victorian Aboriginal cultures at a time when their vestiges were fast disappearing. The work, still valuable though long since superseded, relied heavily upon others such as L. Fison, G. B. Halford, A. Howitt and J. Milligan [qq.v.].

Press reports and a petition from officers in the Mining Department accused Smyth of 'tyrannical and overbearing conduct', and in February 1876 a board of inquiry was constituted and heard evidence until April. McCoy defended 'one of the best heads of department he had ever known' but the board found the charges of 'excessive severity . . . in the main substantiated', and reported that Smyth had been irritable, lacking self-control and over-fastidious, but acknowledged his 'unremitting energy and zealous labours in the public service'. On 4 May Smyth resigned all public offices except his membership of the Aborigines' board.

In June 1878 the Indian government temporarily engaged Smyth to report on auriferous deposits at Wynaad in the Madras Presidency. On completion of the work in May 1880 he became a mining engineer with the Davala (Devalah) Moyar Gold Mining Co. At the end of the year he was in London, and when he visited Melbourne in 1881 he was reportedly earning £3000 a year. After his reports induced 'English capitalists to float companies and lose their money' in India he retired to Victoria, writing mining articles for the Argus. From February 1883 to March 1887 he was director of the Sandhurst (Bendigo) School of Mines at a salary of £600. In his last years he lectured widely on geology and ethnology; in 1889 he revived the controversy over the age of the Australian coal measures when he attacked in the Argus a report by R. A. F. Murray [q.v.] advocating the exploitation of the brown coal deposits in Gippsland.

Apart from his many official reports Smyth published several scientific papers in 1855-87, mainly on meteorology. He was an active member of the Philosophical (Royal) Society of Victoria and was secretary for four months in 1863. Elected a fellow of the Linnean Society of London in November 1874, he was a member and corresponding member of several European, United States of America and colonial learned societies. An agnostic, he was demanding and officious as an administrator but conscientious, shrewd and hard working. R. H. Horne [q.v.] called him 'the half-mad Bureaucrat . . . A damned Jack-in-Office—yet one of various attainments'.

Smyth died of cancer on 8 October 1889, aged 59, at his residence Medenia, High Street, Prahran, survived by his wife Emma Charlotte, née Hay, whom he had married on 15 August 1856 at St Paul's Church, Melbourne, and by a son and daughter. He was buried in St Kilda cemetery.

R. Etheridge and R. L. Jack (eds), *Catalogue of works . . . on the geology . . . etc of the Australian continent* (Lond, 1881); D. J. Mulvaney and J. Golson (eds), *Aboriginal man and environment in Australia* (Canberra, 1971); M. E. Hoare, 'Learned societies in Australia : the foundation years in Victoria, 1850-1860', 1 (1967) no 2, *and* '"The half-mad bureaucrat": Robert Brough Smyth', 2 (1974) no 4, Aust Academy of Science, *Records*; *Australasian*, 14 Aug 1880, 12 October 1889; *Argus*, 12 Feb-6 May 1876, 23, 25, 28 May, 6 June 1889; *Bulletin*, 21 Aug, 20 Nov 1880, 7 May 1881, 7 July 1883; R. B. Smyth papers (LaT L); personal information from Dr D. E. Barwick, Canberra, ACT.   MICHAEL HOARE

SOARES, ALBERTO DIAS (1830-1909), Church of England clergyman, was born on 26 November 1830 at Highbury, London, son of Manoel Joachim Soares, a Portuguese merchant resident in England, and his wife Camilla, daughter of Judge Ledington. Educated at Stoke Newington mercantile school and University College School, London, he worked in his father's office, spent two years in Oporto and a year each in Paris and at the Putney College for Civil Engineering. In 1852 with his brother Gualter he sailed for New South Wales in the *Formosa* to report on the feasibility of a scheme to connect Sydney, Melbourne and Adelaide with a central railway junction on the Murray River, to be named Alberto Town; it proved to be premature.

When Soares failed to find an engineering position he studied theology and supported himself as a merchant. In 1855 he became lay assistant to Rev. Robert Cartwright [q.v.], whom he succeeded the next year as deacon in charge at Collector in southern New South Wales. He was ordained priest by Bishop Barker [q.v.] in 1857 and was incumbent of Christ Church, Queanbeyan, until 1877. He was a trustee of the Quean-

beyan Penny Bank and active in founding the School of Arts. Renowned as an architect, he drew up plans for churches, parsonages, schoolhouses and halls. He designed a new stone church for Queanbeyan which was built in 1859-60, redesigned and enlarged the rectory and planned a Gothic stone church for St Philip's, Bungendore, which was opened in 1865. His other designs included Christ Church, Cooma, the Anglican churches at West Goulburn and Wentworth and the Presbyterian church in Queanbeyan. In recognition of his work Bishop Thomas [q.v.] appointed him an honorary canon of St Saviour's Cathedral, Goulburn, in 1876; he was also honorary diocesan architect. A talented water-colour artist and engraver, Soares was an enthusiastic and pugnacious Latin. As a trustee of Christ Church school, he had violent rows with its teacher, George Lane. Despite Lane's removal the school lost its certificate from the Council of Education and its reputation, which it never recovered; it was closed in 1870.

In 1877 Soares was appointed to West Goulburn and in 1877-81 was first organizing secretary of the Church Society of the diocese; he resigned in 1881 to concentrate on his parish work. While at West Goulburn he was diocesan registrar in 1884-93. Soares's most valuable work was as secretary of the Church Society in 1887-93, which enjoyed its most fruitful years under his guidance; his efforts to gain support for it took him on long and arduous journeys throughout the extensive diocese.

On his retirement in 1897 Soares settled in Sydney. In 1857 at Campbelltown he had married Catherine Tom Lane, of Orton Park, Bathurst. He died at Double Bay on 27 April 1909 and was buried in Waverley cemetery. Predeceased by two sons and a daughter, he was survived by two daughters.

W. F. Morrison, *The Aldine centennial history of New South Wales*, 2 (Syd, 1888); R. T. Wyatt, *The history of the diocese of Goulburn* (Syd, 1937); E. J. Lea-Scarlett, *Queanbeyan: district and people* (Queanbeyan, 1968); family papers held by and information from Mr E. Slater, Hughes, ACT.   IAN MATHESON

SOLOMON, EMANUEL (1800-1873), merchant, was born in London, son of Samuel Moss Solomon, pencilmaker, and his wife Elizabeth, née Moses. On 4 August 1817 he was convicted of house-breaking at the Durham Assizes and sentenced to seven years transportation. He arrived in Sydney on 1 May 1818 in the *Lady Castlereagh* with his brother Vaiben who had been convicted of larceny at the same time. Both were described as pencilmakers. On 6 November 1826 Emanuel married Mary Ann Wilson who had been convicted of larceny in April 1825 and sentenced at the Old Bailey to life imprisonment. With his brother he went into business in George Street as general merchants and auctioneers and they accumulated property and land in Sydney and Bathurst. In 1835 Emanuel bought a share in a South Australian land grant, and in 1838-44 he was resident partner in Adelaide for the Sydney enterprise: most of its trade between Sydney and Adelaide was carried in its brig *Dorset*. In 1840 he opened the Queen's Theatre, the first in Adelaide; he built city residential blocks and promoted the Burra mine. Although affected by the depression of the early 1840s, he recovered and in 1848 established Solomontown near Port Pirie, providing an endowment for religious observance. He retired in 1870.

Solomon was a member of the House of Assembly for West Adelaide in 1862-65 and of the Legislative Council in 1867-71. Conservative in politics, he nevertheless 'advocated important reforms, particularly in the interests of the working classes'. In 1871 he financed in Adelaide a pioneers' banquet for 520 people to celebrate the 35th anniversary of the foundation of the colony. His second wife Celia, née Smith, whom he had married on 12 April 1844 in Sydney, died in 1852 and he married Catherine Abrahams in the same year. One of the founders of the Adelaide Hebrew Congregation, he has been described as 'the paterfamilias of the Jewish community'. Aged 73, he died of senile decay on 3 October 1873 in Adelaide and was buried in the Jewish portion of West Terrace cemetery. Survived by his wife, four daughters and three sons, he left an estate sworn for probate at £4500.

His nephew JUDAH MOSS SOLOMON (1818-1880), merchant, was born on 21 December 1818 in London, son of Moss Solomon and his wife Betsy, née Myers. He probably arrived in Sydney in 1831 where he was educated at Sydney College. He was employed by his uncles as supercargo on board their vessels and visited Adelaide in October 1839 with a cargo of ponies from Timor. In 1842-45 he was government auctioneer at Moreton Bay but in 1846 he went to Adelaide to join Emanuel and another uncle Isaac in an auctioneering firm. In 1854-57 he was in England for his health; after his return he set up in business on his own.

Solomon was an alderman for Gawler Ward in 1852-54, a member of the House of Assembly for the City of Adelaide in 1858-60, a member of the Legislative Coun-

cil in 1861-66 and in 1871-75 he represented West Adelaide in the assembly. He was mayor of Adelaide in 1869-71, and originated the conference of mayors of various municipalities and chairmen of district councils that inquired into nuisances over which the municipalities had no control: the outcome was the Public Health Act. He participated in movements for the drainage of Adelaide, the provision of waterworks and the control of diseased meat. He became chairman of the Destitute Board in 1877 and was instrumental in arranging the boarding-out system for orphans in whom he took a personal interest.

Solomon was a firm free trader and, it was said, 'when he once formed an opinion, no consideration of party or interest could induce him to change it, indeed, he might have been more successful in his parliamentary career had he been less independent'. He acted as coroner and as auditor to public companies and was the first president of the Adelaide Hebrew Congregation. Aged 73, he died of cancer on 29 August 1880 in Adelaide; his estate was sworn for probate at £1750. He was twice married: first to Rachel Cohen on 7 August 1842, and second on 4 September 1867 to Adela Pulver (d. 1875). Seven of his sixteen children survived him; one of his sons, Vaiben Louis, was premier and treasurer of South Australia in 1899 and a member of the first Federal parliament until 1903.

H. Munz, *Jews in South Australia, 1836-1936* (Adel, 1936); J. S. Levi and G. F. J. Bergman, *Australian genesis* (Adel, 1974); PP (SA), 1877 (102); *Register* (Adel), 19 Mar 1872, 9 Oct 1873, 30 Aug 1880; 'Centenary of Adelaide Hebrew Congregation', 2 (1944-48), *and* H. H. Glass, 'Some Australian Jews and the Federal movement', 3 (1949-53), Aust Jewish Hist Soc, J; MS and newspaper indexes (ML); Col Sec land letters (NSWA); E. Solomon business letter-book (SAA); records (Adel Hebrew Congregation); HO 10/19, 26/31.   ERIC RICHARDS

SOO HOO TEN, *see* TEN, GEORGE SOO HOO.

SOUL, CALEB (1817-1894), druggist and chemist, was born in London on 13 January 1817, son of Eli Soul, commodore in the East India Co., and his wife Elizabeth, née Hodges. After a grammar school education he learned the wholesale drug trade and for about eighteen years worked in a drug manufacturing company which, among other things, supplied preparations to the British forces during the Crimean war. In 1840 in London he had married Jane Elizabeth Peters; she and their infant daughter died in 1843 and next year he married Mary Anne Handley at Islington, London.

About 1863 Soul came to New South Wales and managed a store at Morpeth before moving to Sydney where he became a country representative for the Colonial Sugar Refining Co. and Tucker [q.v.] & Co. He and his only son WASHINGTON HAND-LEY, born in London on 6 November 1845, who had been in the British mercantile marine and had arrived in the colony in 1863, also acted as mining brokers for a time. In 1872 they opened a drug store and dispensary in Pitt Street, Sydney, styled Washington H. Soul & Co.; for a time George W. Bull was a partner. Business flourished and operations were gradually extended on the manufacturing side. In 1876 Washington petitioned parliament to amend the sale and use of poisons bill. In 1887, in evidence to the select committee on the Pharmaceutical Society of New South Wales incorporation bill, he protested against the exclusiveness of the society and the Pharmacy Board which, without reason, had refused them leave to sell poisons and drugs. By 1888 they had about thirty employees and their handsome shop, featuring an American ice-fountain that dispensed ingeniously concocted and palatable drinks, had become a fashionable social resort. In sixteen years of operations Caleb claimed to have saved the public £120,000, the difference between prices formerly charged and their much cheaper prices.

Soul was interested in certain social issues: he had promoted building societies in the Morpeth and Maitland districts and held radical views on taxation. In 1886 he gave detailed advice to the premier, (Sir) P. A. Jennings [q.v.], about duties on certain chemicals and encouraged his efforts to introduce direct taxation to restore the colony's finances. He died of acute bronchial catarrh at his residence, Ardleigh, Point Piper Road, Sydney, on 31 August 1894 and was buried in the Congregational section of South Head cemetery. His estate was sworn for probate at £40,600.

Washington carried on the business and it continued to expand. It amalgamated with Pattinson & Co. and became a public company on 21 January 1903 as Washington H. Soul, Pattinson & Co.; he retired from active business after 1903 and by 1940 the firm had forty-two stores in Sydney and Newcastle and in 1974 it was one of the first hundred companies in Australia. Like his father, he was a prominent Freemason: a noted benefactor to the craft, he donated the temple in Beresford Road, Strathfield, that bears his name. He had married Charlotte Louisa Bird (d. 1923) in Sydney in

1873; survived by her and three daughters, he died of heart disease at his residence, Agincourt, Albert Road, Strathfield, on 13 December 1927 and was buried in the Congregational section of South Head cemetery. His estate was sworn for probate at £76,000.

W. F. Morrison, The Aldine centennial history of New South Wales, 2 (Syd, 1888); V&P (LA NSW), 1875-76, 1, 429, 441, 6, 829, 1887-88, 2, 1067; SMH, 3 Sept 1894, 14 Dec 1927.

G. P. WALSH

SOWERBY, WILLIAM (1799-1875), Anglican clergyman, was born on 31 August 1799 at Castle Sowerby near Penrith, Cumberland, England, son of William Sowerby, farmer. Educated by two clerical tutors, at 16 he became a schoolteacher, but in 1823 entered St Bee's College to study for the ministry. Ordained in 1826 he went as curate to Beckermet, Cumberland, where that year he married Hannah Grayson, a member of a farming family.

Sowerby was one of the first to respond to an appeal by Bishop Broughton [q.v.] for clergy to serve in New South Wales, and on 31 October 1837 he reached Sydney in the Andromache. In November he became the first Anglican clergyman at Goulburn, which had no church and only about thirty houses. His work entailed long visits over rough country. He drove bullock teams to haul timber and spent almost £1000 of his limited private means on building the original St Saviour's Church and parsonage. He ministered to the convict gangs at Towrang and had to attend executions and from 1852 was chaplain at Goulburn gaol. In 1863 he gave a lecture advocating life assurance which was published as a pamphlet for the Australian Mutual Provident Society. By then he had so developed the parish that it was chosen as the second rural diocese in the colony. In 1855 the people of the district presented him with a testimonial of £200; in 1869 Bishop Mesac Thomas [q.v.] created him dean of Goulburn and his parishioners presented him with a silver salver and tea service.

In the early 1840s Sowerby kept a school for 'the sons of highly respectable families' and took a keen interest in the institutions of the growing town. In 1850 he was active in the anti-transportation agitation. He was treasurer of the Goulburn District Hospital for many years, an agent and trustee of the Goulburn Savings Bank and succeeded the Presbyterian minister, Rev. William Ross, as president of the Mechanics' Institute. He was also an honorary member of the Strangers' Friend Lodge of the Manchester Unity Order of Oddfellows. Genial and kindly, Sowerby enjoyed attending the early race meetings, lent his paddock for cricket matches and delighted in the fine garden he had created round the deanery. He died from chronic diarrhoea on 22 November 1875 at Goulburn and was buried in the Anglican cemetery. All business premises closed an hour before his funeral which was attended by Catholic and other clergy as well as those of his own Church. Predeceased by a son, he was survived by his wife (d. 17 June 1884) and three of his four daughters; the eldest, Hannah, married F. R. L. Rossi [q.v.] and the second, Eliza, Sir William Manning [q.v.].

R. T. Wyatt, *The history of the diocese of Goulburn* (Syd, 1937), and *The history of Goulburn*, 2nd ed (Syd, 1972); *ISN*, 30 Jan 1874; *Goulburn Evening Penny Post*, 25 Nov 1875; *T&CJ*, 4 Dec 1875. IAN MATHESON

SPEIGHT, RICHARD (1838-1901), railway commissioner, was born on 2 December 1838 at Selby, Yorkshire, England, son of Richard Speight (d. 1851), railway officer, and his wife Ann, née Bray. Richard rapidly made a name for himself as an employee of the Midland Railway Co. and at 19 at Derby he married Sarah Knight. After only nine years experience he was attached to the general manager's office and in 1877 became assistant general manager. With his salary at £1500, in November 1883 he accepted an offer of £3000 to head the new three-man Board of Commissioners established under the Victorian Railways Act of 1883, which aimed to remove the railways from political influence. He arrived in Melbourne in the *Lusitania* on 10 February 1884 with his mother, five sons and five daughters. He overshadowed his fellow commissioners, A. J. Agg and R. Ford [q.v.], who were both unskilled in railway affairs.

Speight faced daily interference by politicians, problems with fledgling railway unions, public clamour for better service and government attempts to make the railways pay. Genial and gifted, he handled these pressures firmly, establishing cordial relations with his minister, the unions and the press, but inevitably he had critics. Successful in his initial aim of managing the state-owned monopoly both as a 'business speculation' and as a public service, he showed an average profit of £6548 in 1883-88. In 1889 his salary was increased and he visited England and the United States of America; but his profit balance was wiped out by the large deficit of 1889-90, partly because of the opening of many new lines that were not initially well patronized.

Speight had implemented the Railway Construction Act of 1884 which authorized fifty-nine new lines and additional works. Optimistic of future traffic growth, he favoured solidly made, durable railways built to conservative standards that avoided the high maintenance and operating costs of the cheap light lines being advocated by ex-ministers of railways T. Bent and J. Woods [qq.v.]. This policy resulted in some monumental white elephants and excessive costs. In March 1891 the *Age* attacked his administration. Duncan Gillies [q.v.], who had defended him, lost office in October 1890 and relations rapidly deteriorated between the new minister William Shiels and the commissioners. Under the influence of David Syme [q.v.] and the financial depression, Shiels demanded cost reductions, but Speight, fearing an implied censure, made only token economies. The minister's Railways Act of 1892 relieved the commissioners of railway construction and reduced much of their power. Becoming premier, Shiels suspended the commissioners on 17 March. They later resigned when the government offered liberal compensation.

Speight issued a writ for £25,000 against Syme and two libel actions ensued between June 1893 and September 1894. The *Argus* and conservative forces rallied to Speight hoping to damage Syme, who pleaded 'fair comment'; the final verdict was for Syme on nine counts and Speight on one, for which he received one farthing in damages. In the action J. L. Purves [q.v.] had accused Speight of causing the depression, and he seemed a perfect scapegoat: a stocky little Englishman heading the colony's largest public enterprise, having no personal financial power or family influence. *Table Talk*, 2 October 1891, observed that 'on railway matters he is a walking encyclopaedia, but outside his profession he is nothing more than an average citizen in the matter of shrewdness or literary and artistic tastes'.

After the litigation Speight entered business in Melbourne. He liked club life and was a member of the Athenaeum. Refused a new trial in November 1895, he rejected a Privy Council appeal as too expensive. He moved to Perth in 1898 where he became involved in arbitration cases and railway inquiry boards, and was managing director of the Jarrahdale Jarrah Forests and Railways Co. In April 1901 he was elected M.L.A. for North Perth; but he died on 19 September of cirrhosis of the liver and ascites, survived by four sons and four daughters. He was buried in the Karrakatta cemetery after a service at St Alban's Anglican Church. He left Victoria a notable legacy: most of his works, seemingly extravagant in the 1890s, became the basis for thirty years of railway expansion.

H. G. Turner, A history of the colony of Victoria, 2 (Lond, 1904); R. L. Wettenhall, Railway management and politics in Victoria, 1856-1906 (Canberra, 1961); G. Blainey, The tyranny of distance (Melb, 1966); M. Cannon, The land boomers (Melb, 1966); G. Serle, The rush to be rich (Melb, 1971); Argus, 11 Feb 1884; Morning Herald (Perth), 20, 23 Sept 1901; M. A. Venn, The octopus act and empire building by the Victorian Railways during the land boom (M.A. prelim. thesis, Univ Melb, 1973).   MICHAEL VENN

SPENCE, CATHERINE HELEN (1825-1910), writer, preacher, reformer and feminist, was born on 31 October 1825 near Melrose, Scotland, daughter of David Spence, lawyer and banker, and his wife Helen, née Brodie. In 1839 David's wheat speculations failed and Catherine could not further her education in Edinburgh. The family migrated to South Australia in the Palmyra, arriving in November. David was clerk to the first Adelaide Municipal Council in 1840-43.

In Adelaide Spence became a governess and set out to fulfil her childhood ambition to be 'a teacher first and a great writer afterwards'. The first novel about Australia written by a woman, Clara Morison: A Tale of South Australia During the Gold Fever, was published in London (1854) in 2 volumes, followed by Tender and True: A Colonial Tale in 2 volumes (1856); both were anonymous. Mr. Hogarth's Will, 3 volumes (1865) was the first to bear her name as author, then came The Author's Daughter (1868) also in 3 volumes. 'Gathered In' was serialized in the Adelaide Observer in 1881-82, and 'Handfasted', submitted for a prize offered by the Sydney Mail in about 1880, was rejected as 'calculated to loosen the marriage tie . . . too socialistic and therefore dangerous', and remains in manuscript. Though never popular, these works won respect; but she stopped writing novels because her ambition changed as she grew older. An Agnostic's Progress from the Known to the Unknown (1884) and A Week in the Future (1889) were her last major fiction.

In her Autobiography (1910) she wrote, discerningly, 'my work on newspapers and reviews is more characteristic of me, and intrinsically better work than I have done in fiction'. By 1878 she had overcome her diffidence and won repute as a literary critic

and social commentator, with articles in South Australian newspapers as well as in the Cornhill Magazine, Fortnightly Review and Melbourne Review. In becoming a regular, paid contributor of the South Australian Register she was able to express her keen interest in the colony and its future, and she obtained a ready forum for her chosen causes.

In 1872 Spence helped Caroline Emily Clark [q.v.] to found the Boarding-Out Society, to board orphaned, destitute and reformed delinquent children in the homes of families, and visit them to check on their behaviour and treatment. She was an official of the society in 1872-86 and worked strenuously as a visitor. When the State Children's Council was established in 1886 she became a member, and was later a member of the Destitute Board.

Most of her work for education was done with her pen. Spence supported the foundation of kindergartens and a government secondary school for girls. In 1877 she was appointed to the School Board for East Torrens, an ineffectual and short-lived body. Her book, The Laws we live under (1880), was the first social studies textbook used in Australian schools, and anticipated similar courses in the other colonies by twenty years.

Spence had become an enthusiast for electoral reform in 1859 when she read J. S. Mill's review of Thomas Hare's system of proportional representation. In 1861 she wrote, printed (at her brother's expense) and distributed A Plea for Pure Democracy. Mr. Hare's Reform Bill applied to South Australia, but she commented, 'it did not set the Torrens on fire'. Though she later claimed that the system had been her life's major cause, she ignored it between 1861 and 1892, except to inject a discussion of it into Mr. Hogarth's Will and visit Hare when she was holidaying in Britain in 1864-65. She had initially presented Hare's scheme as a means of ensuring representation of minorities by men of virtue, learning and intelligence, which was seen as conservative support of privilege. In 1892 she propounded the modified Hare–Spence system as the only way of attaining truly proportionate representation of political parties, an argument well suited to the current political climate of the colony.

By then Spence had acquired greater confidence and become an accomplished public speaker, a process that had begun when she read papers to the South Australian Institute, being the first woman to do so, and brought her acclaim when she addressed Australasian conferences on charity in 1891 and 1892. About 1856, after much doubt and distress over the doctrines of the

Church of Scotland in which she had been raised, she joined the Unitarian Christian Church. In 1878 she substituted for the minister by reading a published sermon, and the same year seized an opportunity to deliver one of her own. Later she frequently preached in Adelaide, and occasionally in Melbourne and Sydney.

R. Barr Smith [q.v.] gave financial backing for her campaign for proportional representation; it was supported by the nascent Labor Party and several small populist and socialist groups, and was launched with widespread public meetings in 1892-93. In 1893 Spence went to the Chicago World Fair to address the International Conference on Charities and Correction, the Proportional Representation Congress, the Single Tax Conference, the Peace Conference, and a gathering in the Women's Building. She then lectured and preached across the United States, visited Britain and Switzerland and returned to South Australia in 1894. Next year she formed the Effective Voting League of South Australia. She ran for the Federal Convention in 1897, becoming Australia's first female political candidate, and came twenty-second out of thirty-three candidates. In 1899 and 1900 she campaigned unsuccessfully for the introduction of 'effective voting' in Federal elections, and in 1902-10 her supporters introduced proportional representation bills into the South Australian parliament. The heterogeneous executive of her Effective Voting League exemplified her non-party and probably personal following. Spence was 67 when she began her campaign, white-haired, short, stout, energetic, with a 'carrying' but not strident Scot's burr, and a direct, natural, sometimes brusque manner. She aroused much enthusiasm, especially for herself as a woman transcending social restrictions on permissible activities.

Spence joined the fight for female suffrage in 1891 and became a vice-president of the Women's Suffrage League of South Australia. After South Australian women were enfranchised in 1894, she supported campaigns in New South Wales and Victoria and spoke at meetings of the Women's League, a body formed in Adelaide for the political education of women. She urged the establishment of a local organization affiliated with the International Council of Women. This work also won her acclaim; she had become a symbol of what Australian women could attempt. When she died on 3 April 1910 she was mourned as 'The Grand Old Woman of Australia'. She had lived with her parents (her father died in 1843, her mother in 1886) and had raised three families of orphaned children in succession. Her estate was sworn at £215. Her portrait hangs in the South Australian Art Gallery.

SA Public Library, *Bibliography of Catherine Helen Spence* (Adel, 1967); R. B. Walker, 'Catherine Helen Spence, Unitarian utopian', *Aust Literary Studies*, May 1971; S. Eade, A study of Catherine Helen Spence 1825-1910 (M. A. thesis, ANU, 1971); C. H. Spence papers (ML, SAA, microfilm NL).   SUSAN EADE

SPENCE, WILLIAM GUTHRIE (1846-1926), trade unionist and politician, was born on 7 August 1846 at the island of Eday, Orkney, Scotland, son of James Maxwell Spence, stonemason, and his wife Jane, née Guthrie. He came to Geelong, Victoria, with his family probably in February 1852. Next year they moved to Spring Hill near Creswick and as a small boy he reputedly observed the Eureka rebellion in 1854, later claiming that he had vivid and formative memories of it. At 13 he was a shepherd at G. Bell and P. McGuiness's station, Corong, in the Wimmera, and in 1861 he was a butcher-boy, having had a miner's right at 14. In 1912 he recalled that goldfields life had 'made such a deep impression on my youthful mind that nothing but the grave will efface it'. Spence had no formal schooling but 'at odd moments' was taught by a graduate of Trinity College, Dublin; he read 'in a curiously miscellaneous way' including, as he matured, the works of Bellamy, Blatchford, Ruskin and Morris. He became secretary and Sunday school superintendent for the Creswick Presbyterian Church and in the 1880s often preached with the Primitive Methodists and the Bible Christians. On 20 June 1871 at the Presbyterian manse, Creswick, he married Ann Jane, daughter of William Savage of Londonderry, Northern Ireland.

Spence's mining experience included work as a 'shift boss' and manager. In the Clunes district in 1874 he initiated an ephemeral trade union that was part of the process of the formation at Bendigo in the same year of the Amalgamated Miners' Association of Victoria. In 1878 as secretary of the Creswick Miners' Union, with John Sampson president, he led 600 men into the A.M.A.: both were later blackballed by the mine-owners. In 1882-91 Spence was general secretary, and under him the association 'was moderate and conciliatory but firm on fundamentals'; he claimed it never refused a conference, but it had twenty-nine strikes before 1890. A superb negotiator, he wanted a union that would cover all kinds of miners in Australia and New Zealand, and from 1884 several unions, including New South Wales coalminers, affiliated loosely and the union became the A.M.A. of Australasia.

Spence co-operated with the Melbourne Trades Hall Council but could not convince his union of the need of political organization, although in 1886 he secured several amendments to the colony's Regulation of Mines and Machinery Act. At the second Intercolonial Trades Union Congress, Melbourne, 1884, he gained unanimous approval for the establishment of an Intercolonial Federal Council of Amalgamated Trades, but nothing came of it. A teetotaller, in Creswick he became a member of the militia and a leading temperance advocate; prominent in the debating society, he was a borough councillor from 1884 and a justice of the peace from 1888: a recent historian has said of him, 'Genial and quite imperturbable, he stands out as the most remarkable man in the remarkable town of Creswick in the eighties'.

Spence's great repute as an industrial organizer of widely dispersed workers led to his appointment in 1886 as foundation president of the Amalgamated Shearers' Union of Australasia. With great skill and zeal, and against aggressive opposition from many pastoralists, by 1890 he had unionized most shearers in South Australia, Victoria and New South Wales and had gained the 'closed shop' in about 85 per cent of the shearing sheds. With main objectives of recruiting the Queensland shearers and obtaining the complete 'union shed', this work took him for the first time consistently among city unionists; in the late 1880s he encouraged his New South Wales branches to join the Trades and Labor Council in Sydney.

On 17 May 1890 he dominated a conference in Brisbane at which the owners of Jondaryan station recognized the Queensland Shearers' Union in the face of a putative united front of maritime unions which had refused to handle their wool. This victory led Spence to intensify his efforts for maximum unionism in New South Wales and Victoria. In a verbose manifesto of 12 July which put great pressure on non-union pastoralists, he claimed incorrectly that the Wharflabourers' and Seamen's unions had agreed to back his campaign with direct action. His plans excluded strikes by shearers; but he exacerbated inflamed industrial relations in the intercolonial maritime industries, especially in New South Wales and among ships' officers, and helped to precipitate the maritime strike that broke out on 15 August and ended on 2 November 1890 with the workers defeated. Against his vote on the Labor Defence Council the shearers were partially involved in September for one week.

Spence's ineptitude resulted in part from his heavy work load. In September at a critical stage of the strike he gave valuable evidence in Melbourne to the royal commission on gold-mining, but essentially his great success with bushworkers had limited his industrial understanding and enlarged his populist longings. Some of his pastoralist opponents shared his mysticism; they believed their own propaganda that somewhere in the outback 'Spence's station', allegedly acquired by levies on the workers, was the ultimate in luxury and wealth. His unique mixture of inspirational socialism and hard-headed unionism evoked a confused vision of all employees in one big union but produced little understanding of the problems of city workers. He emphasized the primacy of the A.S.U. in Labor political action, and broke with the A.M.A. in Victoria in 1891-92 when it drew up its own programme in opposition to that of the Progressive Political League; in 1892 he ran for the league at the by-election for the seat of Dundas in the Victorian Legislative Assembly but lost narrowly. At the seventh Intercolonial Trades and Labor Congress of Australasia in Ballarat in 1891, he backed the scheme for the Australasian Federation of Labour, which envisaged a firm link between industrial and political organization.

Spence took no part in the determined work of the Trades and Labor Council in Sydney in 1890-91 that produced the Labor Electoral League and spectacular success at the 1891 general elections. More than most of his contemporaries, he was muddled about the connexion between the 'New Unionism' and the old. In Sydney on 12 June 1892 his lecture on 'The Ethics of the New Unionism' (published 1892) confused its relationship with political action, but revealed his own millennialism: 'It is useless', he said, 'to go on preaching from Sabbath to Sabbath asking men to be better but ... the New Unionism is to deal with those evils in a practical manner'. In the 1891-93 conflicts in the Labor Party in New South Wales he used the Federation of Labour to oppose the 'solidarities'; when they triumphed in 1894-95 his prospects of assuming a leading political role had evaporated and he was lampooned by the bright young city Labor men, especially W. A. Holman and W. M. Hughes in the radical newspaper, the *New Order*.

Spence's industrial success continued. In 1894 he helped to combine several small bush unions with the A.S.U. and to found the Australian Workers' Union; as its secretary in 1894-98 and president 1898-1917, he saw the union as the industrial wing of the Labor Party. He held the mining-pastoralist seat of Cobar in the New South Wales Legislative Assembly in 1898-1901, but made little impression in parliament though he was accorded the deference merited by past achievement. A supporter of Federation, he pointed to the successful organization of the A.W.U. He was elected to the first Federal parliament in 1901 as member for Darling in far-west New South Wales. In Sydney in 1909, helped by his son-in-law H. Lamond, he published *Australia's Awakening*, which stated that the organization of the bushworkers and the 1890 strike marked the foundations of industrial trade unionism in Australia. The book was an effort both to disarm growing opposition in the A.W.U. to his presidency and to defend the union from the International Workers of the World, who were organizing the 'One Big Union'. In 1911 in Sydney he published the *History of the A.W.U.*; he wrote several pamphlets; he also contributed to and helped to edit the *Australian Worker*. In the 1900s he worked hard for a Labor daily under the control of the A.W.U.

In 1914-15 Spence was Commonwealth postmaster-general and in 1916-17 vice-president of the Executive Council; as a minister he was 'largely the voice of the permanent heads'. In the Labor Party crisis in 1916-17 he was ill and, according to A.W.U. officials, was tricked by Hughes and Lamond into voting for conscription. He was the one member of the union allowed to resign instead of being expelled for his action. Rejected by the Labor Party he lost his seat in 1917, but at a by-election the same year he won Darwin (Tasmania) as a Nationalist candidate. He ran for Batman (Victoria) in 1919 but lost. He died of pulmonary oedema in his son's home at Terang on 13 December 1926, survived by his wife, four daughters and three of his five sons; buried in Coburg cemetery, he left an estate valued for probate at £1200.

J. A. Graham, *Early Creswick* (Melb, 1942); G. Serle, *The rush to be rich* (Melb, 1971); B. Nairn, *Civilizing capitalism* (Canb, 1973); N. B. Nairn, 'The 1890 maritime strike in New South Wales', *Hist Studies*, no 37, Nov 1961; C. Lansbury, 'The miners' right to mateship', *Meanjin*, 25 (1966); *Worker* (Brisb), May 1890, special ed; *Punch* (Melb), 24 Aug 1904.   CORAL LANSBURY
                                  BEDE NAIRN

SPOFFORTH, FREDERICK ROBERT (1853-1926), cricketer, was born on 9 September 1853 at Balmain, Sydney, son of Edward Spofforth, bank clerk, and his wife Anna, née McDonnell. After spending his childhood at Hokianga, New Zealand, he was educated in Sydney by Rev. John Pendrill and at Eglinton College; he then became a clerk in the Bank of New South Wales. Attracted to cricket as a boy in Glebe, at first he bowled fast under-arm but became a fast over-arm after watching G. Tarrant of the 1864 English touring team, and in 1873 he learned variations in pace from the English slow bowler J. Southerton. In 1871-72 he played for the Newtown Cricket Club, then for the Albert Cricket Club with W. L. Murdoch [q.v.]. In January 1874 he played for the New South Wales 18 against W. G. Grace's team; in December his performance in the intercolonial match in Melbourne gave New South Wales its first victory for seven years.

In 1877 Spofforth refused to play in the first Test against James Lillywhite's team because J. M. Blackham [q.v.] had been selected to keep wicket instead of Murdoch. He toured England with the Australian teams of 1878, 1880, 1882, 1884 and 1886, and sprang to fame when he took 10 wickets for 20 runs in Australia's one-day victory by nine wickets over a strong Marylebone Cricket Club team at Lord's on 27 May 1878. In 1879 at Melbourne Spofforth took the first 'hat-trick' in a Test match and later twice obtained 3 wickets in 4 balls. In the Test at the Oval in 1882, England, needing 85 runs to win, reached 51 before the third wicket fell; but Spofforth declared 'This thing can be done', and Australia won by 7 runs : in a victory from which 'the Ashes' were derived, he had taken 14 wickets for 90 runs, 7 in each innings—a record that was not surpassed by an Australian in a Test match for ninety years.

In his eighteen Test matches Spofforth took 94 wickets at an average of 18.41 each, and in all first-class matches 1146 wickets for 13.55 apiece. On three of his five tours of England he took over 100 wickets and in 1884 he took 216, a feat only once surpassed by an Australian. Wiry-framed, he stood 6ft. 3ins. and weighed less than 12 stone. He could make the ball whip from the pitch and possessed an uncanny control, not only of length, pace and direction but also over the amount of break. The 'demon' bowler's aquiline nose and 'Mephistophelian cast of countenance' combined with a right-handed 'catherine wheel' action, described as 'all legs, arms and nose', generated an intense air of hostility towards batsmen. He was almost unplayable on bad wickets. Although he once rode 400 miles to play in a country match and clean bowled all 20 wickets, it was usually the great occasion which roused him to his greatest feats. Active and reliable in the field, he had a long throw and was capable of running 100 yards in under 11 seconds. He could bat effectively and in 1885 going in last he top scored with 50 in a Test.

Spofforth played for New South Wales until 1885 when he went to Melbourne as manager of the Moonee Ponds branch of the National Bank of Australasia. On 23 September 1886 at the parish church of Breadsall, Derbyshire, England, he married Phillis Marsh Cadman, daughter of a wealthy tea merchant. They returned to Melbourne but in 1888 Spofforth settled in England as Midlands representative for the Star Tea Co., of which he later became managing director. In 1889 and 1890 he played occasionally for Derbyshire and thereafter for Hampstead Cricket Club for nearly a decade. He occasionally contributed to books and periodicals: some of his reminiscences appeared in *Chats on the Cricket Field*, edited by W. A. Bettesworth (London, 1910) and in *The Memorial Biography of Dr. W. G. Grace*, edited by Lord Hawke and others (London, 1919), and he wrote an introductory essay on bowling for *Great Bowlers and Fielders: their methods at a glance* (London, 1906), by G. W. Beldam and C. B. Fry.

Hospitable, genial and an entertaining raconteur of 'tall stories', Spofforth acquired an intimate knowledge of horticulture and botany, competed in horticultural shows and planted Australian trees in his English grounds. He died on 4 June 1926 of chronic colitis at Ditton Hill Lodge, Long Ditton, Surrey, survived by two sons and two daughters. His estate was valued for probate at £164,000.

R. H. Lyttleton et al, *Giants of the game* (Lond, 1899); F. S. Ashley-Cooper, *Cricket highways and byways* (Lond, 1927); N. Cardus, *Days in the sun* (Lond, 1924); G. F. McLeary, *Cricket with the kangaroo* (Lond, 1950); A. G. Moyes, *A century of cricketers* (Lond, 1950) and *Australian bowlers* (Syd, 1953); G. D. Martineau, *They made cricket* (Lond, 1956); R. Barker, *Ten great bowlers* (Lond, 1967); *Wisden Cricketers' Almanack*, 1927; *Australasian*, 8 Oct 1892; *Punch* (Melb), 5 Feb 1925.

CHRISTOPHER MORRIS

SPRING, GERALD (1830-1888), politician, was born on 1 July 1830 at Castlemaine, County Kerry, Ireland, youngest child of Francis Spring (1780-1868), gentleman, and his wife Catherine, daughter of Tobias Fitzgerald of Rathkeale, County Limerick. He arrived in New South Wales about 1853 and after visiting the goldfields probably became a squatter. On 8 February 1862 he became chief constable at Dubbo

and on 27 January 1865 a sheep inspector for Coonabarabran at a salary of £250. He resigned in 1869.

Spring represented Wellington in the New South Wales Legislative Assembly in 1869-72: he advocated westward extension of the railway, secular education, free trade, triennial parliaments, the eight-hour day and suggested that the miners make their grievances known and 'organize themselves for that purpose'. For a short time he was a commission agent and in 1876 was returning officer for Gulgong's first municipal elections. On 2 February 1878 he was appointed inspector of conditional purchases in the Department of Lands at a salary of £350. Exchanging appointments with W. J. Barnes in November 1882, he became agent for the sale of crown lands at Goulburn. On 4 December he defeated James Watson [q.v.] for the seat of Young in the assembly; as 'a thoroughly independent member' he sat until 26 January 1887.

Spring's practical experience as a departmental official enabled him to concentrate on the land question. Critical of both Sir John Robertson's [q.v.] 1861 Acts and the Stuart [q.v.] ministry's 1883 bill, he suggested a compromise by taking the best features of each; he strongly opposed 'dummying' and the system of land auctions. Champion of the small settler, liberal, fairminded and a good speaker, Spring made a notable contribution to the 1883-84 land legislation debate and became secretary for lands in Robertson's fifth ministry from December 1885 to February 1886. He also opposed local option and advocated payment of members of parliament. In failing health, he did not contest the election of 1887. He died of consumption at his 130-acre property, Moorong near Young, on 9 November 1888, and was buried in the Church of England cemetery, Young. On 27 August 1867 at Pine Ridge station, Denison Town near Dubbo, he had married Jane, daughter of David Watt, grazier. He was survived by five sons and a daughter; his third son David Hugh (b. 1875) represented Mudgee in the Legislative Assembly in 1932-35.

Ex-M.L.A., *Our present parliament, what it is worth* (Syd, c1886); *SMH*, 2, 22, 29 Dec 1869, 3 Jan 1870, 30 Nov, 2, 5 Dec 1882, 15, 23 Oct, 23 Dec 1885, 7 Jan 1886, 12 Nov 1888; *T&CJ*, 16 Jan 1886, 17 Nov 1888.   G. P. WALSH

STACY, JOHN EDWARD (1799-1881), surgeon, was born on 9 June 1799 at Hammersmith near London, tenth child of Rev. Dr Henry Peter Stacy and his first wife Anne, née Keele. Although orphaned at 9, he received a sound education and in 1820 became a member of the Royal College of Surgeons and of the Physical Society of Guy's Hospital. He practised at Finchley and in 1823 married Jane West who brought with her a generous marriage settlement. In 1828 he was appointed surgeon to the Australian Agricultural Co. at Port Stephens. He reached Sydney on 25 October in the *Magnet* with his wife and two children, arriving at Carrington settlement, Port Stephens, while the company's affairs were in disorder.

Stacy was a keen botanist and became a member of the Ashmolean Society, Oxford; he planned experimental cultivation of drugs, but after the arrival of Sir Edward Parry [q.v.] late in 1829, in addition to normal medical and dispensary work, he became responsible for treatment of all diseased stock, acting on occasion as veterinary surgeon. In 1831 Parry reported to London that 'Mr Stacy's abilities appear to me to consist in anything rather than in medicine. His *forte* is Botany . . . But it is justice to add that he is a good-natured and obliging man'. He could not often leave Carrington as the area had long been a haven for escaping convicts and the men of the settlement were frequently away for long periods.

In 1835 Stacy was re-engaged with salary increased from £150 to £200, Henry Dumaresq [q.v.] commenting that he was 'an active, accomplished and skilful man, honourable and disinterested in all his dealings'. He made pastoral investments in the colony from time to time but not successfully. Next year Stacy resigned; he remained briefly at Port Stephens but in 1838 was practising in Elizabeth Street, Sydney.

In 1839 he took up 500 acres at Upper Rollands Plains near Port Macquarie; he built a comfortable home and started a practice, paying visits to the Liverpool Plains. In 1846 he acted as colonial surgeon for six months at Newcastle; after a brief return to Port Macquarie, he filled the post again in 1848-55. In 1854 his wife died, leaving him with seven sons and four daughters. For most of his time in Newcastle he was also magistrate, district coroner, port health and vaccine officer and helped Dr R. R. S. Bowker [q.v.] with his practice. He was also warden of the Newcastle District Council in 1854-59 when sale of company-owned land allowed the township to expand. On 4 February 1858 at Balmain he married Elicia Antonia, sister of William Beit [q.v.], by whom he had two more sons.

In 1860 Stacy set up in practice at Toowoomba, Queensland. A magistrate, he was also licensed for marriages, and in 1864-68 was visiting surgeon to the gaol. He returned to England in 1872 where he died at Finchley on 13 March 1881. He was a staunch Anglican, reserved, hospitable and upright, whose public service, especially in local government, and professional work contributed much to the localities in which he lived.

J. Gregson, *The Australian Agricultural Company, 1824-1875* (Syd, 1907); Governor Gipps, Dispatches 1838 (ML); MS cat (ML); A. A. Co. papers (ANU Archives); Stacy land file (QA); papers held by family of late Judge Stacy (NSW).   JEAN CASWELL BENSON

STANDISH, FREDERICK CHARLES (1824-1883), government officer, was born on 20 April 1824 at Standish Hall, Wigan, Lancashire, England, son of Charles Standish, one-time companion of the prince regent, and his wife Emmeline-Conradine, née de Mathiesen. He was educated at the Roman Catholic Prior Park College and at the Royal Military Academy, Woolwich, and was commissioned in the Royal Artillery (second lieutenant, January 1843; first lieutenant, April 1844; captain, August 1850). His nine years in the army included a period on the staff of the lord lieutenant of Ireland. Financed by his father he bought Cayton Hall near Harrogate, Yorkshire. From 1848 'no backer of horses was better known or more liked upon English racecourses', but despite his popularity his money losses were heavy, and in 1852 he sold his mortgaged property and left England for the colonies.

Standish worked on the gold diggings in various parts of Victoria until April 1854, when he was appointed assistant commissioner of the goldfields at Sandhurst (Bendigo) and later was also protector of the Chinese. He remained at Sandhurst until September 1858 when he was appointed chief commissioner of police in Victoria with salary of £1200 to succeed Captain (Sir Charles) MacMahon [q.v.]. Standish remained in charge of the police force until September 1880, when he retired on a pension of £468. While in the full vigour of health he was credited with considerable intellectual administrative skill, and he dealt ably with the secret conspiracies and open attacks of 1862. He inspired loyalty among his men until his later years, when his lack of firmness led to a state of disorganization, particularly noticeable in the heyday of the Kelly [q.v.] gang. Although there is no evidence to support the legend that Standish suspended the hunt for the gang when the weights for the Melbourne Cup were declared, his conduct of the police operations was, according to the 1881 royal commission on the police, 'not characterized either by good judgment, or by that zeal for the interests of the public service which should have distinguished an officer in his position'.

A prominent Freemason, in 1861 Standish was installed as provincial grand master for Victoria (English constitution). His keen interest in the turf continued and he was for many years a member and in 1881-83 chairman of the committee of the Victoria Racing Club. He was an elegant, free-and-easy personality, indolent and addicted to the delights of the sideboard, the card table and the theatre. His diary, written in the firm hand of an educated gentleman of the time, reveals an aimless pursuit of pleasure. According to John Sadleir, this hedonism led Standish to 'form intimacies with some officers of like mind, and to think less of others who were much more worthy of regard', but his 'almost pathetic' affection for Superintendent Frank Hare, notable in the period of the Kelly pursuit, was a symptom of the mental trouble under which he eventually broke down. In 1882 he was involved in what was for many years a *cause célèbre* when he was almost thrown out of the window of the Melbourne Club by one Colonel Craigie Halkett, whom he had addressed by a provocative nickname.

From about 1872 Standish lived at the Melbourne Club, where he died on 19 March 1883 of cirrhosis of the liver and fatty degeneration of the heart. He is said to have abandoned Freemasonry on his deathbed, and after a funeral service at the club was buried in the Roman Catholic section of the Melbourne general cemetery. His estate was sworn for probate at £550; unmarried, he left his two horses and his pictures to his servant. The Standish Handicap run at Flemington over six furlongs on New Year's Day is his memorial.

H. M. Humphreys (ed), Men of the time in Australia: Victorian series, 1st ed (Melb, 1878); J. Sadleir, Recollections of a Victorian police officer (Melb, 1913); E. Scott, Historical memoir of the Melbourne Club (Melb, 1936); N. A. Hudleston, Stainley and Cayton (Scarborough, 1956); V&P (LA Vic), 1881, 3 (1); Bulletin, 30 June 1883; J. A. Panton autobiography and F. C. Standish diary (LaT L).   J. S. LEGGE

STANFORD, WILLIAM WALTER TYRELL (1839-1880), sculptor, was born in London, son of Thomas Tyrell, contractor, and his wife Frances, née Trevor. He came to Australia when 13, probably as a ship's boy, and went to the gold diggings. In 1853, immediately before the official opening of the Bendigo Racecourse, he galloped down the empty track on a smart bush horse and collided with Police Magistrate Lachlan McLachlan [q.v.], almost unseating him. According to J. A. Panton [q.v.], McLachlan, not a good horseman, tried to arrest Stanford on the spot and the incident probably ensured that he was not treated with leniency next year when he was convicted for horse-stealing: he received a ten-year sentence and his bitterness and resentment led to much of it being spent in solitary confinement at Pentridge, then under the severe discipline of John Price [q.v.].

In 1860 Stanford was released on a ticket-of-leave. He lost his job on the Malmsbury Viaduct when work was suspended and made his way to Bendigo, where he was arrested and charged with horse-stealing and two robberies, one with arms and the other with violence. With McLachlan conducting committal proceedings and then assisting on the bench, Stanford was convicted and sentenced to eight years on the roads, the first two in irons, for his part in the robberies, and eight years with hard labour for the other charge. At the trials Stanford conducted his own defence with 'remarkable self-possession'; he admitted to only one of the charges, that of robbery of £17 10s.

In his prison notebook, filled with sketches and notes in exquisite handwriting, Stanford copied the motto: 'I will either find my way or make it' and he showed determination in making it against great odds. He became a difficult, intransigent prisoner, his behaviour and an escape in November 1861 alienating the prison authorities; but the chaplain discovered by chance Stanford's great talent in carving and persuaded the prison governor to allow him tools and facilities. With his behaviour transformed, he found that 'the work has engrossed the whole of my time ... so that ... the injustice of my convictions has weighed but lightly upon me'. Charles Summers [q.v.] tutored him in basic principles of design, and amongst other works Stanford planned and executed the graceful bluestone fountain now standing near Parliament House, Melbourne. A petition for his release was rejected in 1869 but the new gaol governor Claude Farie became convinced that Stanford was the victim of injustice. He promised him freedom once the fountain was finished and public pressure, including Dr L. L. Smith's [q.v.], forced the government to grant it.

Stanford was released in October 1871; he became a 'monumental mason' at Windsor and did some fine work. About 1872 at Melbourne he married Mary Ann Protty; his second wife was Mary Ann, née Bienvenu, whom he married at Prahran about 1879; she survived him with their three-month-old daughter when, aged 40, he died of 'ulceration of the stomach' on 2 June 1880 at Prahran. A novel by Mrs Katherine Andrews, *Stephen Kyrle: an Australian story* (Melbourne, 1901) is based on Stanford's life.

W. Moore, *Studio sketches* (Melb, 1906); D. Prout and F. Feely, *50 years hard* (Adel, 1967); *Bendigo Advertiser*, 9, 16, 19, 23, 30 Apr, 1-3 May 1860; J. A. Panton autobiography (LaT L); Stanford notebook (LaT L); Crown Law Office, Letters 1875/2674 (PRO, Vic).

STANTON, GEORGE HENRY (1835-1905), Anglican bishop, was born at Stratford, Essex, England, on 3 September 1835, son of William Stanton, of the Inland Revenue Department, and his wife Charlotte, née Hopkins. Educated at the Merchant Taylors' School and Magdalen Hall, later Hertford College, Oxford (B.A., 1859; M.A., 1862; D.D., 1878), he was made deacon in 1858 and ordained next year by the bishop of Winchester; in 1858-62 he was assistant curate at Christ Church, Rotherhithe, in 1862-64 at All Saints', Maidstone, and in 1864-67 at St Saviour's, Fitzroy Square, London. In 1867 he became vicar of Holy Trinity Church, St Giles-in-the-Fields. He was chosen in January 1878 as the first bishop of North Queensland. Consecrated in St Paul's Cathedral, London, on 24 June by the archbishop of Canterbury, he was enthroned in St James's Pro-cathedral, Townsville, on 21 May 1879.

By four years of perseverance and personal contacts, he largely overcame the shortage of clergy and funds, and within ten years erected ten new churches. A diocesan magazine, the *Monthly Record*, appeared in 1883 and next year Stanton summoned the first diocesan synod of clergy and lay representatives and in 1886 he set up a cathedral chapter. He travelled widely on horseback to get to know the conditions and needs of the outback and to encourage its clergy and people. He planned a permanent cathedral at Townsville and consulted Edmund Blacket [q.v.] about its design. He turned the first sod on the site on 27 June 1887, but the work lagged.

In 1890 Stanton accepted the vacant bishopric of Newcastle, New South Wales, and was enthroned in Christ Church Pro-cathedral on 12 May 1891. He consolidated the work of his predecessors and undertook the construction of a permanent cathedral; its foundations were already laid but it had been the subject of much disagreement between the architect, J. H. Hunt and Rev. A. E. Selwyn [qq.v.]; the first section was dedicated on 2 November 1902. Stanton was a meticulous administrator and pastor; he chose good staff, and several later became bishops. A scholar, he read widely in science, theology and philosophy. He detested war and spoke his mind in jingoistic days.

His friendly disposition and sincerity won an immediate response, especially from his clergy. It was said of him that 'he was a simple and deeply spiritual soul, marked by utter humility and utter devotion of the whole life to the service of God and of man for God's sake'. Unmarried, he died of heart disease at Morpeth on 4 December 1905 and was buried in the Church of England cemetery. He left £2000 to the diocese to help theological students.

J. O. Feetham and W. V. Rymer, *North Queensland jubilee book 1878-1928* (Townsville, 1929); A. P. Elkin, *The diocese of Newcastle* (Syd, 1955); E. C. Rowland, *The tropics for Christ* (Syd, 1960); J. M. Freeland, *Architect extraordinary* (Melb, 1971); *T&CJ*, 6 Dec 1905; Diocesan and cathedral records (Diocesan Registry, Townsville and Newcastle).

E. C. ROWLAND

STAWELL, SIR WILLIAM FOSTER (1815-1889), chief justice, was born on 27 June 1815 at Old Court, Mallow Parish, County Cork, Ireland, second son of ten children of Jonas Stawell, barrister and classical scholar, and his wife Anna, second daughter of William Foster, D.D., bishop of Cork, Kilmore and Clogher. Both the Stawell and Foster families were Anglo-Irish and traced their descent from Henry III. Stawell was educated at Trinity College, Dublin; with honours in classics (B.A., 1837), he read law at King's Inns, Dublin, and Lincoln's Inn, London, and was called to the Bar in England and Ireland in 1839. After travel in Europe with his friends Redmond Barry and James Moore [qq.v.], he practised in Dublin and on the Munster Circuit until 1842 when he saw 'forty hats on the Circuit and not enough work for twenty' and decided to migrate.

In July Stawell boarded the *Sarah*, chartered by his distant relation Lieutenant Pomeroy Greene, R.N., father of R. M. Greene [q.v.], and bound for Port Phillip. Wiry, with a powerful physique, Stawell was well over six feet; his 'fine figure and delightful manner' attracted Greene's daughter Mary Frances Elizabeth, his future wife. She described him then as 'ruddy and of fair countenance with wonderfully expressive eyes of bright chestnut colour'. He spent much of the voyage reading law and Shakespeare. They reached Port Phillip on 1 December and his two stud bulls were swum ashore. He engaged briefly in squatting with his cousin J. L. F. V. Foster [q.v.]; they acquired property, including Rathescar, which Stawell held until 1853, but within a few months he had moved to Little Lonsdale Street West, Melbourne.

Stawell was admitted to the Port Phillip District Bar early in 1843 and soon built up a considerable practice. He was a painstaking advocate with a sound knowledge of the law and great capacity for work. With a compelling, earnest manner, he was a tactful cross-examiner, and his knowledge of human nature enabled him to handle jurors skilfully. He was briefed in most of the important criminal cases, including many murder trials, and he was in constant demand for civil actions. On 17 April 1844 with Barry he acted for Foster in an action for assault and battery: one of the first of many civil cases, involving prominent Melbourne citizens, in which he appeared. In March 1848 he and E. E. Williams [q.v.] were briefed for Henry Moor [q.v.] in his libel suit against the Argus. This case, its sequel and the libel suit of St John v. Fawkner [q.v.] on 8 November further established his eminence and he, Barry and Williams were regarded as the leading barristers of the small local Bar.

A great advocate for separation from New South Wales, Stawell threw himself into all the movements for the progress of the district. He helped in the formation of the Anti-Transportation League in 1850 and in February next year was appointed to the committee of the Victorian branch of the Australasian League. He was also active in most sports and pastimes. The first amateur whip to sport a four-in-hand drag at Flemington Racecourse, he was a familiar figure in the hunting field, whilst his skill in riding 'buckjumpers' was common town talk. He rode in amateur steeplechases and on Master of the Rolls won a Grand National at Pomeroy Greene's Woodlands. He enhanced his reputation for courage by saving a drowning man from the Yarra and by stopping a runaway horse and cart laden with women and children at Flemington Racecourse. An agnostic, he also took part in some of the more dissolute amusements of the era, but in 1848 a sermon preached by Bishop Perry [q.v.] converted him, and next year he became a devout Anglican. He was no longer the 'blythe barrister', and his transformed behaviour produced differing reactions among his friends and associates.

By the time of separation in 1851 Stawell's all-round ability and capacity had so impressed Lieut-Governor La Trobe that he appointed him a nominee Crown member in the first Legislative Council and attorney-general at a salary of £500. He gave up his private practice at great financial sacrifice, but with much personal satisfaction he devoted himself to his huge pioneering task. He did not again appear in court except for the Crown.

As both senior member of the executive and government leader in the Legislative Council, Stawell did much of the work in setting up an administration, the public service, and the governmental machinery of the colony. His report, with Barry, in September recommended a Supreme Court consisting of a chief justice and not more than two puisne judges with a civil and criminal jurisdiction; as a result legislation in January 1852 set up the court, and subsequently the County Court; the Court of General Sessions and the Insolvency Court were also established. With Foster he also took on the heavy duty of preparing the Constitution bill of 1854 which in its final form was largely his own work. In apathetic times he was immensely interested in politics, regarded himself as a liberal and saw the reform bill of 1832 as a great victory over reaction; but he was no radical or democrat. He and Foster aimed to reproduce the leading components of the British Constitution, crown, lords and commons. Although he favoured a colonial peerage, Stawell deemed a House of Lords unsuitable for the colony; but he and Foster substituted a house elected by property owners, university graduates, lawyers, doctors, clergymen and naval and army officers. The Lower House was also to have a restricted franchise. They thus guarded conservative interests and carried the bill through the Legislative Council; with some amendments it was enacted by the British parliament in 1855. The names of the two Victorian houses, Legislative Council and Legislative Assembly, were Stawell's own choice.

As attorney-general his duties were intensified by prosecutions for murder and bushranging occurring after the gold rush. As a zealous prosecutor Stawell was described by Melbourne Punch as 'hating crooked ways' but 'ill-inclined to brook control or guidance'. He was generally recognized as the ablest and strongest of the governor's advisers; La Trobe and Sir Charles Hotham both came to rely on his advice and to be dominated by him. His strong influence on land policy favoured the squatters; to raise revenue he supported a system of miners' licensing instead of an export duty on gold, and perpetuation of the licence fee contributed to the conflict which led to the tragedy of Eureka in 1854. Referring to the miners as 'wandering vagabonds' and 'vagrants', he resolved to suppress what he regarded as their lawless and treasonable activities; in the subsequent trials he prosecuted them determinedly, even when it became apparent that juries would not convict and that public opinion supported each successive acquittal. Stawell thus gained much temporary unpopularity but he cared nothing for the opinion of the crowd. Within the executive he accepted many duties, including the planning of some inner suburbs, the setting up of 'Canvas Town' between Melbourne and St Kilda for the reception of migrants and the establishment at Yan Yean of the city's water-supply. So diverse were his activities and so great the deference of the council that more than once his absence on circuit led to suspension of its business.

On 2 January 1856 Stawell was married at Woodlands to Mary Greene. They lived for a short time in William Street before moving to St Kilda. He was invited to stand for the Legislative Assembly and, to obtain the necessary qualification, he bought a large property on the Yarra at Kew. The bluestone mansion, D'Estaville, the home of the Stawell family for many years, was completed there in 1859. When free from public duty he enjoyed the life of a country gentleman, establishing vegetable gardens, an orchard with fruit trees from all over the world, a vineyard, stables and a dairy with Irish dairymaids. In 1877 one of the first tennis courts in Victoria was built on the estate. On the inauguration of the new Constitution in 1856, Stawell began his election campaign at Astley's Theatre with a fiery meeting during which the stage collapsed; he carried on astride a window ledge and his speech, known as Stawell's 'leg out of the window oration' ended in triumph, and he won one of the five seats of the City of Melbourne in the assembly: he continued as attorney-general.

Chief Justice Sir William à Beckett [q.v.] resigned in February 1857 and Stawell replaced him after a series of political manoeuvres and considerable hesitation. Much of the political animosity of the goldfield period had now disappeared, and he received a testimonial from the citizens of Melbourne and a knighthood from the Queen on 13 July. A rift followed with Barry who had expected the office, but there is little doubt the choice of Stawell was a happy one. He was the better lawyer, with a more judicial and impartial mind; unlike Barry, he avoided florid oratory, was not sanctimonious and his private life was impeccable.

In the next twenty-nine years Stawell played an important part in establishing the Supreme Court as an honoured and respected tribunal, administering law with distinction and justice with impartiality. His integrity, industry and ability and his strong sense of justice coupled with patience and courtesy soon won him the goodwill of the Victorian Bar; his austerity was tempered with a sense of humour. Much of his time was occupied with important criminal trials in which his kindliness was often obscured by the stern sense of duty he felt as a judge in a community he considered somewhat primitive and lawless. Whilst Stawell was tenacious in exposing evil-doers he was equally insistent that the Crown should prove its case. His views on punishment tended to the simplistic; in murder trials when he deemed it appropriate he did not flinch from recommending that the death penalty be carried out. He often invoked solitary confinement against young offenders to avoid contamination by older criminals. Like Barry, however, he believed that when law and order were more firmly established lesser punishments would be appropriate.

Stawell also administered the general body of laws, much of which he had designed, prepared and carried into legislative effect. Most of the equitable jurisdiction was undertaken by Judge Molesworth [q.v.], but Stawell's contribution as a common lawyer was notable. He undertook an enormous volume of work and his dispatch was excellent. His decisions were invariably delivered extempore or within a matter of hours; they exhibited the sound grasp of common law principles of an instinctive lawyer with a pragmatic rather than philosophic mind. His reported judgments on many diverse topics are admirably succinct but did not exhibit deep learning. At times he erred; in April 1869 when Glass [q.v.] and Quarterman were imprisoned for contempt by the Legislative Assembly, he ordered their release on the basis that the assembly did not enjoy the full privileges of the House of Commons. The decision, though popular with the general public, caused grave consternation in parliament and on petition by Speaker Sir Francis Murphy [q.v.], the judgment was set aside by the Privy Council. Notable civil trials over which Stawell presided included the petition for judicial separation filed in 1864 against Judge Molesworth by his wife Henrietta on the ground of cruelty, and Molesworth's cross petition on the ground of his wife's alleged adultery with R. D. Ireland [q.v.] and also with a man unknown.

In March 1873, desirous of having his sons educated in England, Stawell took the leave to which he was entitled. He was warmly received in Ireland and Trinity College conferred on him honorary M.A. and LL.D. degrees. Late in 1874 he was recalled by Sir

George Bowen to become acting governor the following year. As governor he advised his ministers fully in writing on each measure and thereafter did not interfere. In August 1875 when the Kerferd-Service [qq.v.] government was defeated he refused to dissolve the assembly, judging that it was his first duty to exhaust the parties in parliament, and Sir James McCulloch [q.v.] became premier.

Stawell took a deep interest in the material welfare of the colony. He was president of the Philosophical Institute of Victoria (Royal Society) in 1858-59. As chairman of the Exploration Committee of the Royal Society he superintended the arrangements for the ill-fated Burke and Wills [qq.v.] expedition. Burke bequeathed his watch and his papers to Stawell who headed the mourners at the explorers' funeral. He was a trustee of the Public Library, president of the Victorian Deaf and Dumb Institution, a president of the Melbourne Hospital and the Benevolent Asylum and was connected with many charitable objectives. From its foundation he was a member of the Council of the University of Melbourne, and on the death of Barry in November 1880 was for a brief period its chancellor. He was a member of the royal commissions on penal and prison discipline (1870) and the Aborigines (1877). He also helped to form the constitution of the Anglican Church in Victoria; he favoured self-government of the Church by a democratic assembly and always took an active part in the deliberations of synod, over which he exercised considerable influence.

In August 1885 despite his still 'elastic step and active mind' Stawell had to take leave for reasons of health; after resuming office in July 1886 he resigned as chief justice on 24 September. He was created K.C.M.G. on 25 October and appointed lieut-governor. In February 1889 he sailed with his wife for England but died suddenly at Naples on 12 March and was buried in the English cemetery there. His estate was sworn for probate at £48,496.

Less conservative than many of his immediate contemporaries, Stawell outstripped nearly all of them in stature and ability. His efficiency as an administrator, his infinite capacity for hard work, and his conscientious nature were admired even by his political enemies. He never learnt the political necessity for occasional retreat and his sense of duty and unwillingness to take advice occasionally led him to serious error. There was perhaps a grain of truth in the comment of the *Argus* that 'he could ruin a country, if committed to a bad cause'. However his fine intellect and intense practicality coupled with complete integrity and other outstanding qualities enabled him to make a remarkable contribution to Victoria's early history. It is impossible not to repeat the observation so often made that it was the great good fortune of the colony to have, in its formative years, a man of Stawell's stature presiding over its highest judicial tribunal.

Stawell was survived by his wife and a distinguished family of six sons and four daughters. Lady Stawell (d. 2 February 1921) also played a prominent part in the life of Melbourne; her autobiography, *My Recollections*, published privately in London in 1911, is a valuable and interesting work. Two sons became lawyers, two were doctors and two engineers. His second son William was for a time his associate and later became a partner in the Melbourne legal firm of Stawell and Nankivell (now Mallesons). His fifth son Richard was knighted for his services to medicine, whilst his youngest daughter Melian became a noted classical scholar.

A portrait by Edward à Beckett, photographs, and other records are in the library of the Supreme Court of Victoria. Stawell, a town in western Victoria, is named after him.

Garryowen (E. Finn), *The chronicles of early Melbourne*, 1-2 (Melb, 1888); G. D. Stawell (ed), *A Quantock family* (Taunton, 1910); J. L. Forde, *The story of the Bar of Victoria* (Melb, 1913); P. A. Jacobs, *Famous Australian trials* (Melb, 1942); G. Serle, *The golden age* (Melb, 1963); A. Dean, *A multitude of counsellors* (Melb, 1968); *Argus*, 28 Mar 1856, 14 Mar 1889; *Age*, 14 Mar 1889; *Daily Telegraph* (Melb), 14 Mar 1889.   CHARLES FRANCIS

STEEL, ROBERT (1827-1893), Presbyterian minister, was born on 15 May 1827 at Pontypool, Monmouthshire, England, son of James Steel, Blaendere colliery agent, and his wife Ann, née Gillespie. His mother died in his infancy and his father took him home to Scotland at an early age. He attended the Ochiltree Parish School, the Royal Burgh Academy at Ayr, and matriculated at King's College, Aberdeen, in 1843 (M.A., 1846). He took the divinity course at New College, Edinburgh, studying under Thomas Chalmers, and was ordained by the Free Church Presbytery of Irvine. After assisting at Blairgowrie, Perthshire, in 1852 he was inducted as colleague and successor to the minister of the Free Church Parish of Millport on the Isle of Meikle Cumbrae in the Firth of Clyde. Next year at Huntly, Aberdeenshire, he married Mary Allardyce (d. 1890). He moved to Salford, Lancashire, in 1855 and to Cheltenham in 1859. Steel had already published his first book, was contributing freely to religious journals and was co-founder and joint editor of *Meliora*, a quarterly review of social science. He became interested in working-class education and his work was praised by Lord Brougham. The University of Göttingen awarded him the degree of doctor of philosophy in 1861 for his publications.

Steel was persuaded to accept a call to Sydney by Professor John Smith [q.v.] and two other commissioners from St Stephen's, the Free Church congregation in Macquarie Street. He arrived with his family in 1862. In 1873, after Adam Thomson [q.v.] had become principal of St Andrew's College, University of Sydney, his congregation joined with Steel's, and his large stone church in Phillip Street became St Stephen's, with a fine tower and spire added by William Munro. Despite increasing deafness Steel continued a brilliant and eloquent ministry there until 1893, holding a large congregation and generously serving church and community.

Steel was a man of great personal culture and dignity, described as 'liberal without being latitudinarian and conservative without being narrow'. The annual review in his last sermon of each year became a notable feature of the cultural life of Sydney. He founded a young men's society and in 1862-66 he edited the *Presbyterian Magazine* and later the *Witness* for five years. Ecumenical in outlook, he supported the union of the groups that became the Presbyterian Church of New South Wales in 1865, and was the third moderator. He collected funds for founding St Andrew's College and headed the poll of clerical candidates elected to the first council, serving until 1893. He was a foundation lecturer when the Presbyterian faculty of theology was created in 1873, and was its first president. In 1872 he had received an honorary degree of Doctor of Divinity from Lafayette College, Pennsylvania, United States of America.

On 8 May 1869 Steel had published in the *Sydney Morning Herald* a letter from Thomas Nelson, a missionary, about Captain A. R. Hovell, a blackbirder awaiting trial in Sydney for murder, later sentenced to death. Although he pleaded ignorance of Hovell's committal, two of the three judges concluded that he should have known of the proceedings and 'severely reprimanded' him. At a large public meeting presided over by (Sir) John Hay and attended by (Sir) Henry Parkes [qq.v.] he was presented with a purse of sovereigns to defray his legal costs. Steel travelled widely in Australia, visited the New Hebrides in 1874 and America, Europe and the Holy Land in 1880. That

year he published *The New Hebrides and Christian Missions, with a Sketch of the Labour Traffic*. In the 1880s he supported Sir Alfred Stephen's [q.v.] efforts to extend the grounds for divorce.

Steel died on 9 October 1893 at North Sydney and was buried in the Presbyterian section of Rookwood cemetery. He was survived by three married daughters and three sons, Rev. Robert Alexander Steel, M.A., Dr John James Steel, who died of dysentery in 1900 at Taku, China, while on active service with the New South Wales naval contingent, and Hugh Peden Steel, a solicitor. His estate was valued for probate at £2114. Memorial tablets to Steel are in St Stephen's Church, Macquarie Street, and in St Andrew's College, to which he left his books and a fine portrait in oils. The General Assembly remembers him in the Steel lectureship in pastoral theology in its theological hall.

E. Digby (ed), *Australian men of mark*, 1 (Syd, 1889); J. Cameron, *Centenary history of the Presbyterian Church in New South Wales* (Syd, 1905); *NSW Law Reports*, 1869; *SMH*, 26 June 1869; *Sydney Mail*, 14 Oct 1893; H. P. Steel papers, 1-4 (ML); Stephen uncat MS 211 (ML); General Assembly, Minutes 1894 (NSW Presbyterian Lib, Assembly Hall, Syd).

ALAN DOUGAN

STEINFELD, EMANUEL (1828-1893), furniture manufacturer and retailer, was born on 1 November 1828 at Oberglogan, Silesia, Prussia, eldest son of Hyman Steinfeld, a wealthy Jewish merchant, and his wife Ernestine, née Deutsch. Educated locally and at the College of Brieg (Silesia), he went to London in 1847 to learn the business of Krohn Bros, exporters, who sent him to represent them in Victoria in 1853. He arrived in Melbourne on 28 September in the *Ballarat*, settled at Ballarat and in 1856 opened his own furniture warehouse. Naturalized in 1857, he took a leading role in business and civic life, being significant in getting a local water-supply and in the foundation of the orphanage and public library. He was also a prominent Freemason. On 23 January 1861 at Ballarat he married Theresa Levinson (d. 1876); there were no children of the marriage.

In 1860 he was defeated for the Ballarat East Council, partly, he claimed, because of xenophobia. Next year he won, and improved the administration so firmly that ten years later a ratepayer called him 'Bismarck Steinfeld'. As mayor in 1866-69, when Ballarat East was in eclipse, he used his influence to negotiate a favourable loan, and arranged for good roads through Buninyong and Bungaree shires to tap the timber resources of the Bullarook Forest. But a public inquiry into council affairs revealed that contracts were being let on special terms to councillors, most of whom, including Steinfeld, were defeated at an extraordinary election in 1871. He was discredited, yet many remembered the distinction with which he had greeted the duke of Edinburgh in 1867, for he was a cultivated man, and his friends included Redmond Barry [q.v.] who shared his enthusiasm for libraries.

From 1871 Steinfeld was listed in Melbourne directories as agent for 'La Silencieuse' sewing machines; by 1875 he had established a furniture warehouse as well, and by 1876 had premises in Elizabeth and Lonsdale streets. That year he took his brother-in-law Hyman Levinson into partnership, trading as 'furniture merchants and importers'. Steinfeld left the Ballarat shop in the hands of two nephews and lived in Melbourne, from 1881 at St Kilda. He retired from business in 1888.

In 1871 and 1873 Steinfeld had failed at elections for the Ballarat East seat in the Legislative Assembly. His platform suggested an Australian Zollverein, a national bank of issue and technical education. He was finally elected to parliament in 1892 when he won the Legislative Council seat of Wellington Province. During four visits to Europe, which included a trip to the United States of America, Steinfeld gathered ideas and brought back books on mining and technical education, many of which he donated to the Ballarat Public Library and the School of Mines. But the Zollverein was his passion. In 1885 he became a member of the Chamber of Manufactures; as Victorian president in 1887 he initiated an intercolonial conference which was held in successive years at Adelaide, Sydney and Melbourne. The chief motion on each occasion was his: that they resolve to work for intercolonial free trade and a uniform tariff. Through the chamber he took up the subject of technical education with the government, and in September 1888 was appointed a member of the technical education board, with a special appointment to inquire into technical schools during his visit to Europe. Visiting Adelaide to speak about intercolonial free trade, he died of apoplexy on 16 April 1893. His estate was valued for probate at £22,781.

Intercolonial Free Trade Conference, *Report of the proceedings ... at Adelaide* (Melb, 1887); A. Sutherland et al, *Victoria and its metropolis*, 2 (Melb, 1888); A'sian Commercial Congress, *Report of proceedings* (Melb, 1889); G. Serle, *The rush to be rich* (Melb, 1971); *Ballarat Star*, 1 Feb 1871; *Table Talk*, 13 June 1890; *Ballarat Courier*, 17 Apr 1893.   WESTON BATE

STENHOUSE, NICOL DRYSDALE (1806-1873), lawyer and literary patron, was born on 27 June 1806 at Coldstream, Berwickshire, Scotland, son of James Stenhouse (d. Jamaica 1806), a brewer of Clockmill, and his wife Elizabeth Pringle, née Young. Educated at a grammar school in Berwick-upon-Tweed, in 1822 he entered the University of Edinburgh (M.A., 1825) with a sound knowledge of the classics and four European languages; in 1825 he enrolled as a student of divinity. Articled to J. B. Gracie in 1828, he qualified as a lawyer in 1831. Stenhouse associated with the literary coterie who wrote for *Blackwood's Edinburgh Magazine*, and in 1831-36 he assisted Thomas De Quincey with his financial affairs, becoming intimate with the family. A keen student of German literature, he was a friend of the metaphysician Sir William Hamilton and in 1835 became first clerk in his legal firm.

With opportunities limited in Edinburgh, Stenhouse migrated to Sydney, arriving on 22 October 1839 as a steerage passenger in the *Georgiana*. Admitted as a solicitor on 1 April 1840, he practised in Sydney with William Hardy until 1872: Daniel Deniehy [q.v.] was one of their articled clerks. Stenhouse's scholarship, lively literary conversation and encouragement of Deniehy's writing talent earned him repute as a literary patron. He accumulated one of the best private collections of classical, religious, British and European literature in the colony, which he lent freely. His home, Waterview House, Balmain, became in the 1850s and 1860s a centre for such colonial writers and intellectuals as Richard Rowe, Frank Fowler, Charles Harpur, Henry Kendall, J. S. Moore, J. L. Michael, Henry Halloran, W. B. Dalley, Henry Parkes and professors John Woolley and Charles Badham [qq.v.]. He had written some translations of contemporary German works and essays on literary topics for the *Quarterly Review* and the *Border Magazine*, but published nothing after migrating.

Although neither wealthy nor leisured Stenhouse was generous with his money, time and help to those with literary or personal difficulties, and he was active in colonial institutions. A committee-man of the Sydney Mechanics' School of Arts in 1855-63, he was its senior vice-president in 1863-67 and president in 1867-73. A committee-man of the Australian Library and

Literary Institution in 1857-69, he was a foundation trustee of the Free Public Library in 1869-73. He became a trustee of the Sydney Grammar School in 1866, and a law examiner of the University of Sydney and a member of the Senate in 1869. An alderman of Balmain Municipal Council, he was its chairman in 1862. A devout Presbyterian, he was a friend and sometime legal adviser of Rev. J. D. Lang [q.v.] and an elder of the Balmain congregation in 1858.

Stenhouse died of chronic nephritis on 18 February 1873 at his home and was buried in the Balmain Presbyterian cemetery. He was survived by his wife Margaretta, née Underwood, whom he had married at the Scots Church on 23 January 1846, and by two sons and five daughters. His goods were sworn for probate at £1800. His library of some 4000 titles was bought by the philanthropist Thomas Walker [q.v.] and, donated to the University of Sydney in 1878, it helped to prompt the foundation of the [Thomas] Fisher [q.v.] Library. Described by his early biographers as 'the Maecenas of Australian Literature', Stenhouse is entitled to be regarded as the colony's first, and probably foremost, nineteenth-century literary patron.

Catalogue of books in the library of the University of Sydney (Syd, 1892); D. H. Rankin, The spirit that lives (Melb, 1945); H. Bryan, 'An Australian library . . . Earlier years of the University of Sydney library', JRAHS, 55 (1969); A. M. Jordens, 'The Stenhouse collection', Aust Academic and Research Libraries, Mar 1973; SMH, 21, 24, 25 Feb, 5 Mar 1873; Daily Telegraph (Syd), 2 Feb 1899; A. M. Williams, Nicol Drysdale Stenhouse: a study of a literary patron in a colonial milieu (M.A. thesis, Univ Syd, 1963); C. Harpur papers, H. Kendall letters (ML); Stenhouse letters (ML, NL).

ANN-MARI JORDENS

STEPHEN, SIR ALFRED (1802-1894), chief justice and legislator, was born on 20 August 1802 at Basseterre, St Christopher (St Kitts), West Indies, fourth son of John Stephen [q.v.] and his wife Mary Anne, née Pasmore. He returned to England with his mother in 1804 and lived at Alphington near Exeter. In 1807 they moved to Shefford, Bedfordshire, where he attended the village school and was taught knitting to keep him quiet. In 1810 he went to Charterhouse, London, and next year to a small school kept by Rev. W. Valentine at Martock, Somerset; he completed his schooling under Dr Richard Lewis at Honiton Grammar School. In 1815 Stephen went back to Basseterre where he read Blackstone's Commentaries, acted as clerk to his father, and in 1817 was commissioned a lieutenant in the local Militia Regiment of Foot (Fusiliers). In 1818 he returned to London and entered Lincoln's Inn on 16 May where he read for the Bar under his cousins Henry Stephen, serjeant-at-law, and (Sir) James Stephen [q.v.]. Although impecunious, Alfred led a gay life, enjoying the theatre, concerts, pleasure trips, walking tours and visits to his relations on which he met prominent politicians and members of the Clapham sect. He recalled that 'Paganini on his unearthly violin, and Lindley on the violincello, were a delight to me'. On 20 November 1823 he was called to the Bar, having already joined Girdlestone and Cooper 'in Business Chambers'.

On 22 June 1824 at St George the Martyr's Church, Queen Square, Holborn, Stephen married Virginia, daughter of Matthew Consett, a merchant. On 31 July James Stephen wrote to his friend Lieut-Governor Arthur asking for his good offices towards Alfred: 'He is a pleasant, lively, talkative youth, who has neither thought nor read deeply upon any subject . . . generally well informed, though not profound in his own profession as a lawyer; . . . I am afraid he is something of a spendthrift . . . He is coming out to Van Diemen's Land to live by the Law'. The Stephens arrived at Hobart Town in the Cumberland on 24 January 1825. Arthur, assailed by R. W. F. L. Murray [q.v.] in the Hobart Town Gazette and doubting the loyalty of his attorney-general J. T. Gellibrand [q.v.], availed himself 'of the timely arrival of Mr Stephen', and on 9 May appointed him solicitor-general and ten days later crown solicitor with a salary of £300. His duties included drawing up all conveyances of government property.

Stephen soon protested against Gellibrand's intimacy with Murray and his habit of drawing pleadings for and accepting fees from both sides. In August Arthur refused to accept Stephen's resignation pending a commission of inquiry, which five months later found his charges against Gellibrand substantially proven. Stephen complained to Arthur on 3 October that he had been compelled to give up his practice, had 'been made the unceasing object of gross scurrility and invective . . . and [had] no opportunity for resorting to advice better than my own'. Arthur commended him to Lord Bathurst as he had 'done himself the most material personal injury in the cause of the Crown'.

In 1825 Stephen, having goods and cash to the value of £3000, was granted a block fronting Macquarie Street where he built a two-storied stone house with a walled garden 'studded' with the choicest fruit trees'. Founding vice-president of the Hobart Town Mechanics' Institute in 1827, he was a churchwarden of St David's in 1827-31 and registrar of the Archdeacon's Court in 1828-31 at £60 a year. Stephen was an original shareholder in the Derwent Bank until asked by the lieut-governor to sever his connexion in 1828, and was involved in speculative financial ventures. He also borrowed money from Arthur to buy real estate and to lend out on mortgages, which he believed to be 'the best mode of investing, & the most profitable'. After repeated requests in 1829 his salary was increased to £600 in lieu of extra fees.

In 1828 Stephen questioned the validity of all land titles in the colony on the grounds that grants had been made in the name of the governor rather than the sovereign. After 'laborious researches', in 1831 in four massive reports he exposed extensive land jobbery and wilful violations of conditions of grants. He argued that a royal warrant and subsequent proclamation were insufficient to validate titles, for 'to confirm grants so grossly and extensively inaccurate' would perpetuate confusion and error and involve the people in massive litigation. The lieut-governor acted upon Stephen's advice to set up a land board to issue new titles after proper description and inquiry.

By 1830 he was finding that he could not 'discharge with satisfaction to myself both my public & private professional duties'; refusing to give up his practice as his salary would not maintain his family, he asked for either a large increase in salary or higher office. Promised the attorney-generalship, on 22 January 1832 Stephen took his wife and five children to England to visit her ageing parents. In January 1833 he asked for extended leave because of illness, but he so pressed his views on the Colonial Office that he confided to 'Cousin James' that he was 'afraid of being thought rather too impertinent a person for a "Colonial Attorney-General"'. He was pleased that some of the new rules of the Supreme Court of Van Diemen's Land had been 'followed' in England, and also with the admiration accorded the two pictures of John Glover [q.v.] that he had taken with him: moreover, the Consetts had settled £5000 on Virginia and the children.

The Stephens returned to Hobart on 14 November 1833. Confirmed as attorney-general on 6 May 1832 with a salary of £900, he found great arrears of work; he was also a member of the Legislative Council ex officio and his new duties included drafting all legislation and piloting it through the council. Always a strong advocate of trial by jury, on 5 November 1834 he carried the Trial by Jury Act. He was also very proud of the Deserted Wives and Children Act of 1837 that allowed a deserting husband to be sued for maintenance. In 1836 Arthur allowed Stephen to relinquish the duties of crown prosecutor, as he still complained of overwork partly because of 'the most lucrative and extensive private practice, of any of the Barristers in the Colony'. Stephen managed to engraft 'upon the Colonial Code a large portion of those reforms in the law and in the practice of the courts which have recently received the sanction of the Imperial Legislature'. Nevertheless in the scandal-loving and backbiting society of Hobart with its scurrilous press he made many enemies, especially among opponents of Arthur's government.

On his return from England, Stephen had a misunderstanding with Arthur over the possibility of the lieut-governor's recall and replacement by James Stephen. Late in 1835 they became estranged after Alfred's brother George [q.v.] allegedly cheated while playing cards with Henry Arthur [q.v.], the lieut-governor's nephew; he intervened on his brother's behalf, feelings ran high and in a strange scene at an inn in New Norfolk in the early hours, Alfred was challenged to fight a duel by an emissary of Henry Arthur. The local police constable bound him over to keep the peace. Indignant, Stephen begged the lieut-governor to restore George 'to Society'. The affair rankled for months and led to the alienation of old friends. From July 1836 he was in conflict with Judge Montagu [q.v.] whom he accused of 'violent conduct & most improper language' on the bench. Montagu retorted that Stephen had 'attacked the Judges and had endeavoured to lower both the Government & the Court in public esteem' by disrespectful behaviour, such as 'eating sandwiches from a basket and drinking wine and water out of a flask' while sitting in court. Arthur severely admonished them.

On 23 January 1837 Virginia Stephen died in childbirth leaving two daughters and five sons; two daughters had died in infancy. Grief-stricken, and with his health impaired, Stephen resigned as attorney-general on 19 September and soon sold his house. He made £3000 a year in private practice, but a new phase of his life had begun, with sober assessment replacing his earlier carefree outlook. On 21 July 1838 at St David's Church he married Eleanor Martha Pickard (d. 1886), daughter of Rev. W. Bedford [q.v.]; with many virtues but lacking humour and an inquiring mind, she was an admirable stepmother and bore him four sons and five daughters; one son died in infancy. Next year he accepted a temporary judgeship in Sydney despite a pecuniary sacrifice.

After laudatory farewells in Hobart and Launceston, Stephen reached Sydney in the *Medway* on 7 May 1839 and took his seat on the bench on the 14th. He was soon involved in differences of opinion with Judge J. W. Willis [q.v.], particularly over equity procedure, and in 1840 corresponded with Chief Justice Dowling [q.v.] about the Supreme Court rules. Appointed a puisne judge in 1841, he gradually introduced the Westminster system of pleading at Common Law and drafted the Administration of Justice Act that provided for circuit courts. He continued to draft legislation and afforded 'great assistance' with the Insolvency Act. In 1843-45 he published a treatise on the *Constitution, Rules, and Practice of the Supreme Court of New South Wales*, which W. B. Dalley [q.v.] in 1883 asserted was still 'the best authority on the subject'.

In 1844 Dowling's fatal illness and the departure of Judge Burton [q.v.] for Madras, left Stephen the only effective judge. In October he and Attorney-General J. H. Plunkett [q.v.] claimed the vacant chief justiceship; but Stephen was appointed in an acting capacity and confirmed in office on 2 June 1845: James Stephen played no part in the decision. He was knighted in 1846 after pointing out that the two previous chief justices had been thus honoured. Presiding over his court with courtesy, he guarded its dignity and strove to appoint sufficient officials to it. A capable administrator, he protested to the government about the squalid and insanitary state of the building, suggesting improvements supported by plans drawn by the colonial architect Edmund Blacket [q.v.]. In the 1850s he made representations about the incomplete state of the Criminal Court House, Darlinghurst. Although fussy about his health, he 'possessed a robustness beyond the ordinary' to survive sitting constantly in the Sydney court-houses. In 1848 the Privy Council, upholding Stephen, had reversed the Supreme Court decision in *Bank of Australasia* v. *Briellat* [q.v.], and that year he chaired the law commission on the Supreme Court which recommended the appointment of an additional judge. He argued that the judges should have leisure for professional and general reading: 'All my own studies, and almost all my office work, have been at night'.

A prominent Anglican layman, Stephen

in the 1840s was a member of the Australian Diocesan Committee and in 1858 was a delegate to the synodical conference. He was vice-patron of the Commercial Reading Rooms and Library and a committee-man of the Temperance Society. From the 1850s he served as president of the Sydney Female Refuge Society and the Sydney Opthalmic Institution, as a director of the Society for the Relief of Destitute Children, on the committee of the Diocesan Board of Missions, as a vice-president of the Australasian Botanical and Horticultural Society and as an official trustee of the Australian Museum. In 1861 he was a founder and president of the Home Visiting and Relief Society, and in the 1860s a director of the Sydney Eye and Ear Institution and a vice-patron of the Orpheonist Society.

In 1853 Stephen published a pamphlet, *Thoughts on the Constitution of a Second Legislative Chamber for New South Wales*, in which he advocated an Upper House of twenty-five members, twelve nominated for life and twelve elected for nine years by the Legislative Assembly, with the chief justice as *ex officio* Speaker. He repudiated a wholly nominated chamber because of the danger of 'swamping', but defended the power of nomination as 'an ancient and valuable prerogative of the Crown'. On 13 May 1856 he was appointed to the new Legislative Council. Although (Sir) Edward Deas Thomson [q.v.] had refused the presidency as a political appointment, Stephen thought otherwise and accepted the office. Delighted, he carefully prepared all the rules and forms of the House and those respecting communications between both Houses. Determined not only to administer the law but also to make it as perfect as possible, Stephen made the most of his opportunities in the council. In 1856-58 he introduced fourteen law reform bills of which six were enacted. By identifying 'party' with rancour and prejudice, he could deny he was a party man and assert that his duties were 'calmly to consider, deliberately to investigate, and impartially ... to decide'. Nevertheless, he wrote confidentially to Thomson, vice-president of the Executive Council, to ask if his resignation 'would inconvenience the government'. He resigned as president on 8 January 1857 but, despite criticism from the *Empire* and attacks from the assembly, did not resign from the council until 16 November 1858. He complained to James Macarthur [q.v.] that 'there is *no man of authority, or of note*—out of N. S. Wales,—who has advanced the opinion that Judges ought not to be in the Legislature'.

Meanwhile in 1854-55 Stephen had been

president of the commission for the Paris Universal Exhibition of 1855 and conducted all the relevant correspondence. That year he was chairman of the committee to found an affiliated Anglican college within the University of Sydney. He collected for its building fund, drafted the legislation and ensured its freedom from diocesan control. In 1856 he became a founding fellow of the council of St Paul's College. He confessed to Thomson that his interest in the college 'amounts to something like mania'. When not sitting late in court he delighted to play with his children and his pets, ranging from a dog to a marmoset. By the late 1840s his sons were starting to follow him in the legal profession: Matthew Henry [q.v.] was his father's associate and M. Consett [q.v.] a newly admitted solicitor. As Eleanor told her stepdaughter Virginia, 'The law seems the easiest and most natural of the professions for our boys ... Papa's position gives him the opportunity of putting his sons forward in the Law, whereas other professions require what he has not—money'.

In 1859 the Cowper [q.v.] ministry refused Stephen's application for leave. William Forster's [q.v.] ministry granted it but his salary was dependent on a vote of the Legislative Assembly. On 7 December a motion providing for his full salary (£2600) was 'violently opposed by Mr Arnold and Mr Windeyer [qq.v.] in very offensive speeches', but carried on 25 January 1860. Stephen sailed for England on 14 February, but Forster's government fell in March before implementing the vote. On 4 April (Sir) John Robertson's [q.v.] ministry, amid angry scenes, carried a motion to pay Stephen £1400; (Sir) James Martin [q.v.] had it rescinded on 11 April and £2000 was voted. Stephen was so outraged that he applied for the chief justiceship of Madras, but was refused on the score of his age. He even contemplated retiring.

Stephen returned on 17 February 1861, restored in health but saddened by the death of his beloved 21-year-old daughter Eleanor. Attacks on him continued; in April in an acrimonious Legislative Assembly debate, he was accused by (Sir) Terence Murray [q.v.] of breaching parliamentary privilege, but was exonerated by a select committee. Stephen was having difficulty in administering the court because of greatly increased litigation, which largely comprised complicated wills and settlements and disputed land titles, 'including that most embarrassing class called squatting actions', caused by Robertson's 1861 land Acts. Lady Stephen recorded that he was often in court after 11 p.m. and on several occasions sat up all night to write judgments. At his farewell dinner in 1860 he had referred to the arrears of the Supreme Court 'which tend much to the injury of suitors there' and said it was impossible for three judges to 'deal with the admiralty business, the ecclesiastical business, the common, the equity and the criminal law'. His pleas to the government to appoint an additional judge were unavailing until after the deaths in 1865 of judges Milford and Wise [qq.v.]. However, he regarded the government's appointment of Alfred Cheeke, J. F. Hargrave and Peter Faucett [qq.v.] as infelicitous.

Every year Stephen went on circuit which involved dangerous voyages or difficult travelling over bad roads. He kept careful notes of routes and the best inns: he found the Willow Tree Inn 'Tolerable but bedrms seemed close & damp. Good Australian Wine'. At Goulburn in September 1863, despite seldom rising from court before 7 p.m., he went to a meeting of the Philharmonic Society; members of the Bar and local worthies dined with him on most days, and at the end of the sittings he visited F. R. L. Rossi [q.v.] at Rossiville. Stephen became known for his severe sentences. No case created a greater stir than that of Mary Ann Brownlow, whom he had sentenced to death at the Goulburn Circuit Court on 11 September 1855 for the murder of her wastrel husband; he repudiated 'the very dangerous idea that mere absence of a *preconceived design* to take life ... can make the act of taking life less than murder'. In November 1894 the *Bulletin* used the case as evidence of his severity.

In a memorandum to the Colonial Office dated 19 July 1864, Stephen supported the retention of hanging for attempted murder and rape; he argued that it was the only penalty dreaded by criminals, but concluded that the death sentence 'should never be pronounced ... if the Judge himself entertains a scintilla of Doubt as to the Prisoner's Guilt'. To the administrators of justice the upsurge of bushranging in the 1860s seemed like a breakdown of law and order. In 1865 the Felons Apprehension Act made it a felony to harbour or assist a bushranger, a measure he had recommended to the government in February 1863 and helped to draft. In 1864 he tried Frank Gardiner [q.v.], who had already been acquitted on a charge of attempted murder, for armed robbery and two indictments of robbery, and sentenced him to thirty-two years hard labour. In 1874 when Governor Robinson decided to pardon the bushranger on condition of his exile, Stephen submitted notes he had made on the activities of Gardiner and his family connexions with Ben Hall [q.v.], and took exception to the remarks the governor made about him in a controversial minute to the Executive Council. Robinson replied that he had 'never intended to imply, and I did not think, that in passing such a sentence you had either exceeded your legal authority or been influenced by any circumstances which you were not perfectly justified in taking into account'.

The demands of criminal sittings and of appellate hearings consumed so much of Stephen's time that he was anxious to delegate some of his other duties. He refused to be primary judge in Equity and wanted to surrender the burden of being judge commissary in Vice-Admiralty. His efforts in England in 1860 to obtain changes in the organization and practice of the Vice-Admiralty Court had been unavailing, but in 1859-65 the jurisdiction was exercised by Milford. Stephen took over the court from 1865 and had to deal with an increasing number of blackbirding cases. In 1869 after the *Daphne* had been seized by Captain Palmer, R.N., for slave-trading, he acquitted her master because he was not technically guilty of kidnapping under the legal definition of slavery. Stephen urged the British government to alter the law, and argued that if the Polynesian labour trade were not abolished it should be stringently regulated.

In 1870-72 Stephen was chairman of the Law Reform Commission. Most of the work fell to him and the first report included a draft criminal law consolidation bill of 464 clauses. Collectively his colleagues 'took rather more than their share of the credit for a work so profoundly influenced by Stephen alone and by the stimulus he had derived from reforms to the English criminal law' effected by his cousin Sir James Fitzjames Stephen. He made available to the commission a book in which for over thirty years he had noted down 'every criticism of the rules, and every flaw detected in 'them during litigation', and 'difficulties arising from the administration of law'. The commission also produced draft lunacy and Supreme Court consolidation bills and recommended reform of the insolvency laws; the Criminal Law Amendment Act was eventually carried in 1883, having been improved by Stephen during its long passage. 'In most matters of legal principle, the law retained, and has continued to retain, the shape and design fashioned for it by the hand of Sir Alfred Stephen'.

On 26 February 1872, after the departure of Governor Belmore, Stephen was called upon to administer the government. He had confessed to Belmore that Prudentia 'is the Deity I regret to say, whom I have least worshipped—& her Temple ought to be the Vice-Regal Mansion'. He was immediately confronted with problems: Judge Hargrave objected to his decision only to 'sit *in banc* and in Vice-Admiralty Cases', and before sailing the governor had dissolved parliament after supply had been refused. Stephen felt keenly the hardship of the unpaid civil servants and believed they could enforce a claim against the Crown. He therefore sanctioned an arrangement whereby the Bank of New South Wales at its own risk paid the salaries in anticipation of supply being voted. In March, in compliance with instructions from the Colonial Office and after consulting the captains of H.M.S. *Blanche* and *Basilisk*, he had accorded *de facto* recognition to Mr Woods's government under King Thakombau in Fiji and officially informed the British consul that he had done so. Martin strongly protested and disassociated his government from the action.

Martin resigned on 26 April. Stephen was not amused at (Sir) Henry Parkes's [q.v.] successful amendment to the address-in-reply which condemned his agreement with the Bank of New South Wales; but after first asking Forster, he approached Parkes to form his initial ministry; although he made some acerbic comments on the cabinet's members, he recalled his commissioning of Parkes with pride. During his self-styled administration of 'One Hundred Days', Stephen was kept busy. Typically he found time for decorating and altering the hall at Government House and laid the foundation of a portico there. At the end of his term he lamented that it 'was thus my ill fortune ... to have met with the disapproval of both the Colonial Executive and Parliamentary authority'.

Stephen was finding his confrères harder and harder to deal with: in 1869 when he judged Rev. Robert Steel [q.v.] innocent of contempt of court in *ex parte Hovell*, he was overruled. He contemplated resigning and in 1871 asked Sir John Dickinson [q.v.] if he was willing to accept the chief justiceship if he were offered it. Frequently in the minority on the bench, he found it 'little consolation' that his opinion was usually upheld by the Privy Council as he realized that litigants 'cannot always appeal to England'. He complained to Cowper in England of Hargrave's 'insolence, gross & unprovoked insults, & overbearing temper'.

On 12 June 1873 Stephen resigned as chief justice, to take effect from 5 November to allow the government to import a replacement from England if they desired. As the attorney-general E. Butler [q.v.] was a Catholic, his choice of Guy Fawkes

Day may have been mischievous, and helped to provoke a major political crisis. He was farewelled by the bench and Bar in Sydney on 26 September and went on circuit to Goulburn. He received many addresses from the magistrates and other citizens in the towns and a silver tea service from the solicitors of the Supreme Court. Wined and dined by the Victorian Bar on 14 November he praised the appointment of Martin as his successor, and claimed that 'had it not been for the fact that a gentleman was appointed to the office of judge of the Supreme Court of New South Wales from political motives purely', he might have been chief justice for the next ten years. Sir Roger Therry [q.v.] commented in 1874 that Stephen's 'acknowledgment that he was put to flight from the bench by that fellow Hargrave was an humiliating one—& his opinion as to Butler's right to the Judgeship was characteristic of his imprudence in not always saying the *right thing at the right time*'.

The Judges' Salaries Act of 1857 had reduced the scale of pensions for judges after fifteen years service and deprived the chief justice of his patronage in Supreme Court appointments. When Stephen had contemplated retiring in 1871 he asked the Martin government in vain for a pension equal to his salary; he pointed out that had he retired in 1854 as entitled to do, his pension would have been £1610 instead of £1400 and he had thereby saved the colony over £34,000. For a decade he badgered successive governments for increased salaries and pensions for judges. He owned to Thomson 'how pained I was at finding it my duty to accept the moneys raised by public subscription,—*not* for some public purpose, in memory of me, but for my wife & her daughters ... *I have never lived on my salary.*—I have expended *thousands* of pounds in the Colony above'. After the failure of the Parkes government to carry a gratuity of £7000 in 1874, nothing was done in 1875-78 despite the support of the governor. In 1879 he was voted £1140, being the £600 of salary he had been deprived of in 1860 and £540 interest. Acting governor when it was carried, he explained his reasons to the Colonial Office for assenting to a grant to himself. In 1883 the Stuart [q.v.] ministry carried the Retired Judges' Pensions Act whereby his pension in future would be calculated on his retiring salary of £2600.

Active in retirement, Stephen was a member of the Council of Education in 1873-80, was nominated to the Legislative Council in 1875 and that year appointed lieut-governor; he was acting governor from 19 March to 4 August 1879, from 9 November to 12 December 1885 and from 3 November 1890 to 5 January 1891. A fellow of the Senate of the University of Sydney in 1878-87, he was an enthusiastic trustee of the National Art Gallery of New South Wales from 1876, a trustee of Hyde, Phillip and Cook parks from 1878 and crown trustee of the Australian Museum in 1880-89. He was responsible for many improvements to Hyde Park (he lived opposite it for many years), and was quick to complain of encroachments by the Sydney Municipal Council. He was also a vice-president of the 1878 Paris Universal Exhibition and 1879 Sydney International Exhibition commissions, and president of the New South Wales commission for the 1886 Colonial and Indian Exhibition in London.

In 1870 Stephen had resigned from the council of St Paul's College with regret; he told the warden that because of circumstances connected with the administration of Church affairs in this diocese 'I cannot any longer identify myself with any Church Institution or Society whatsoever'. In the 1870s he carried on most of his good works and in addition was chairman in 1873 of the Captain Cook [q.v.] Statue Committee, president of the New South Wales Academy of Art from 1873, the Civil Service Building Society in 1875-82, the Society for the Prevention of Cruelty to Animals, the City Night Refuge and Soup Kitchen, the Charity Organization Society and the Industrial Blind Institution and a life director of the (Royal) Prince Alfred Hospital. In the 1880s he quit some organizations but joined the Primrose League. He was especially interested in the Industrial Blind Institution and was often called on for help by people in distress.

Stephen and his wife campaigned for early closing; he went on circuit to Grafton in 1875 as acting judge, took endless trouble to discover whom Port Jackson was named after, spoke at meetings for famine relief and sent the Colonial Office unsolicited advice on legal aspects of imperial legislation such as the Mutiny Act, the Fugitive Offenders Acts and guano licences. He also wrote many letters to the *Sydney Morning Herald*, often under known pseudonyms such as 'Respublica', 'Justitia' and 'Nominus Umbra'.

Stephen maintained his interest in the temperance movement although not a teetotaller himself, believing that strong drink was responsible for much crime. In 1870 he published as a pamphlet his *Address on Intemperance and the Licensing System*. He had given evidence on the subject before the Legislative Council select committee on intemperance in 1854 and the Legislative Assembly's select committee on the Sunday sale of liquors prevention bill in 1878. Unlike his contemporaries he recognized drunkenness as a disease which affected all classes of the community as early as 1854. In 1886 in evidence to the royal commission on the excessive use of intoxicating drink, he was explicit about the evils that wives suffered from drunken husbands.

In the Legislative Council Stephen introduced eighteen bills, some of them repeatedly, and many connected with law reform, of which four were enacted. He failed four times with his animals protection bill and twice with his medical bill, which had provisions against charlatans and sought a medical council to decide who was qualified to practise. In the 1879-80 clash with the assembly he played a conciliatory role and vainly sought to change the Constitution Act by removing the council's power to amend money bills. He improved legislation that came up from the assembly, acted as unofficial parliamentary draftsman for many private members' bills and served on sundry standing and select committees. He published many pamphlets, including speeches he had made in the council. His most important legal work was the *Criminal Law Manual, Comprising the Criminal Law Amendment Act of 1883* published with Alexander Oliver [q.v.] in 1883. In 1879 when called on to act as governor, Stephen failed to convince Parkes that it was unnecessary to resign from the council, and claimed that he would prefer to resign 'that barren honour' if necessary, as 'the seat in the Legislature, employing my mind, on matters familiar to me, affords me *much* pleasure—and (pardon the conceit) moreover is of service to the country'. On this occasion his term as acting governor was shadowed by his exercise of the prerogative of mercy in two rape cases. Advised by the Executive Council to allow the law to take its course, he was inundated with petitions for mercy and deputations and abused in the assembly, while 'monster meetings' took place in Sydney. After much agonizing he reprieved two of the condemned men.

Despite Stephen's earlier protests against David Buchanan's [q.v.] successful efforts to extend to women the right of divorce for simple adultery, in February 1886 he moved the first reading of a bill extending the grounds of divorce to cover desertion, habitual drunkenness, imprisonment for at least seven years and assault on the petitioner. He deliberately excluded incurable insanity as an act of God. Carried in the next session the Divorce Extension Act was refused the royal assent. It provoked violent controversy both within and without parliament. When Stephen reintroduced the bill every session until 1890 it encountered filibusters, count-outs and adjournments and so lapsed. Exasperated, he failed in 1889 to carry a bill to prevent the lapsing of bills through prorogation.

Stephen wrote nine pamphlets defending divorce extension, some reprinted from his letters to the *Sydney Morning Herald*. The most important was *The Law of Divorce: (a Reply to Mr. Gladstone)* (Sydney, 1891), reprinted from the London *Contemporary Review* (June, 1891); it cost him 'a world of trouble' to write as it required 'great care & accuracy'. Among the authorities he corresponded with on the question were Lord Carnarvon, Lord Hannen, president of the English Divorce Court, Rev. Samuel Dike in North America and D. Dudley Field, a noted New York law reformer. In 1890 the bill was carried in the council and Stephen, who was acting governor, provoked strong criticism by sending a message of thanks to his supporters from Government House. The Divorce Amendment and Extension Act was carried in the session of 1891-92; it received the royal assent on 6 August 1892. Only Stephen, with his unique prestige in the colony, could have carried such a radical measure in the conservative council.

In 1888 Stephen had caused a flurry when he had resolutions passed in the council to change the name of the colony of New South Wales to Australia. He told Parkes that if the neighbouring colonies objected he would 'adopt the East or Eastern addition'. In 1890 he introduced a labourers' protection bill to protect nonunion workers, exchanged unfriendly letters with Admiral Lord Charles Scott over precedence while acting governor, and in October offered himself as a mediator between the Trades and Labor Council and the New South Wales Employers' Union. With great regret in February 1891 he declined renomination to the council because of increasing fragility and resigned as lieut-governor on 27 April. Created a C.B. in 1862, K.C.M.G. in 1874, G.C.M.G. in 1884, he was appointed Australia's second privy councillor in 1893.

Handsome, sprightly and joyous, with wit and charm, and 'the family perception of the ridiculous and humorous side of things', Stephen greatly enjoyed social occasions all his life. In 1866 he wrote to Cowper suggesting the postponement of a ministerial trip to Bowenfels as 'a Ball is (I have just heard) to be given by Mrs

Knox on Friday'. He played the flute, frequented the theatre, dined with the Shakespeare Club and entertained most visiting dignitaries. On terms of warm friendship with the governors and their families, leading colonial families, scholars such as Thomas Woolley and Charles Badham [qq.v.] and younger colleagues such as (Sir) Frederick Darley [q.v.] and (Sir) Edmund Barton, he was probably closest to Sir William Manning [q.v.]. Stephen was no snob: above anything he loved the company of Parkes, Martin and Dalley. In 1877 he had bought a block of virgin bush adjoining Martin's Numantia in the Blue Mountains, where he built a rude wooden cottage, Alphington. 'In that valley, or at that classical retreat, I have with those men enjoyed many a pleasant intellectual and festive hour'. He went there most weekends until he found the expense too great and sold it in 1882 for £3800. He also carried on a lifelong correspondence with his godson Leslie Stephen and his other English relations. He started to write his 'Jottings from Memory', enthusiastically swopped his reminiscences with Parkes and philosophized with him over old age. In 1893 he wrote 'For many years past, I have never dared to rely on even a day's continuation of my life; and I never expected to live beyond my eightieth year'.

Stephen had faults: among them were 'his great failing in meddling in matters that did not concern him' observed by Therry, and his 'overweening vanity' noted by 'Cassius' in the Freeman's Journal; he confessed to Parkes of having 'said too many things in the excitement of debate, & speaking in Court wh: I have found to be mistaken, & which I have regretted'. Yet Therry thought Stephen 'really was a clever pains-taking judge, & ... an excellent public officer'. Martin appreciated 'the depths of his learning, the acuteness of his intellect, and his unfailing courtesy to members of the Bar'. Sir John Darvall [q.v.] discerned his kindness to the Bar, impartiality and incapability 'of nourishing the slightest feeling of resentment'. His decisions were often models of lucidity and show his versatility over the whole range of the law, but were also pragmatic, narrow in application and have not endured as precedents. As a judicial administrator of great ability, he made the law respected in New South Wales in the face of such obstacles as personal antipathies between the judges, antique procedure, excessive litigation and inadequate accommodation.

Stephen died of senile decay on 15 October 1894 in his house 24 College Street, Sydney, and was buried in St Jude's churchyard, Randwick. He was survived by two sons and a daughter of his first wife, and by three sons and four daughters of his second wife. His estate was sworn for probate at almost £12,000. His portrait, attributed to John Prescott Knight, R.A., is in the Supreme Court of New South Wales; marble busts by Simonetti [q.v.] are in the Art Gallery of New South Wales and the Legislative Council, and a bust by Allen Hutchinson is also in the Art Gallery.

HRA (1), 22-24, (3), 4-6; R. M. Bedford, Think of Stephen (Syd, 1954); J. M. Bennett, A history of the Supreme Court of New South Wales (Syd, 1974); M. Rutledge, 'Edward Butler and the chief justiceship, 1873', Hist Studies, no 50, Apr 1968; M. Rutledge, Sir Alfred Stephen and divorce law reform in New South Wales, 1886-1892 (M.A. thesis, ANU, 1966); R. Parsons, Lawyers in the New South Wales parliament, 1870-1890 (Ph.D. thesis, Macquarie Univ, 1972); N. I. Graham, The role of the governor of New South Wales under responsible government, 1861-1890 (Ph.D. thesis, Macquarie Univ, 1973); Arthur letters and papers (ML); Earl Belmore, Letters from his ministers ... 2 (ML); Bourke papers, Letters from Arthur (ML); Cowper letters (ML); S. A. Donaldson ministry letters (ML); Knox papers, uncat MS 98/9 (ML); W. M. Manning papers (ML); Sir Charles Nicholson papers in Norton Smith & Co. papers no 118 (ML); A. Oliver papers (Univ Syd Archives); Parkes letters (ML); Alfred Stephen, Diaries, letters and family papers, MS 777, uncat MS 211 (ML) and letter-books (ML, NSWA); MS, newspaper and printed cats (ML); GO dispatches and CSO records, 1825-39 (TA).   MARTHA RUTLEDGE

STEPHEN, ALFRED HAMILTON HEWLETT (1826-1884), Anglican clergyman, was born on 24 April 1826 at Hobart Town, eldest son of Sir Alfred Stephen [q.v.] and his first wife Virginia, née Consett. After his early education in Van Diemen's Land, he reached Sydney in the Medway in May 1839 with his father and stepmother. He continued his education at the Sydney College under W. T. Cape [q.v.], where he became head boy and won Sir John Jamison's [q.v.] medal for classics. In 1845 he matriculated as a pensioner at Trinity College, Cambridge (B.A., 1849; M.A., 1884). He was befriended by his father's cousin James Stephen [q.v.] and met the English branch of his family. Made deacon on 3 June 1849 by Bishop Blomfield of London, in September he returned to Sydney and acted as immigration chaplain. Bishop Broughton [q.v.] ordained him priest on 23 June 1850 and licensed him as curate of Christ Church St Laurence on 1 July.

Stephen took services in the outlying district of the parish and in 1854 began a school at Redfern. When the church of St

Paul in Cleveland Street was opened the next year he became incumbent and remained until 1884. He saw the church completed, a new school and parsonage built and the parish subdivided. It was a mixed area with substantial middle-class houses and a working-class district connected with the railway-yards. Stephen lacked oratory and sustained scholarship (he published only a few sermons), but was an effective preacher and a sound administrator; he excelled as a pastor and counsellor: the tendency to conceit that his family had noted in him as a young man gave way to great kindliness. Canon W. H. Walsh [q.v.] likened him to Nathaniel, 'in whom there was no guile'.

Stephen's university background and family connexions led him to join the movement for an Anglican college affiliated with the University of Sydney. He supported his father's policy against Bishop Tyrrell [q.v.] and became joint secretary with Robert Johnson [q.v.] of the appeal committee, secretary to the St Paul's College council and a fellow in 1855-84. In 1863 'after examination in the School of Classical Philology and History', he was awarded an M.A. by the university. He did not follow Sir Alfred's lead in other Church affairs: at the 1858 conference he had voted against his father's amendment to make the proposed bill for synodical government an enabling measure only. Stephen gradually lost sympathy with the High Churchmanship, associated with Broughton, Walsh and his father and stepmother; he moved towards a Low Church position in the episcopate of Bishop Barker [q.v.], but was not a party man. In synod he was independent, though he was chiefly notable for his championing of the autonomy of the clergy. He was a member of the editorial board of the *Australian Churchman*, rural dean of South Sydney and in 1869 a canon of St Andrew's Cathedral. In 1873 he visited England.

As befitted his personal and ecclesiastical connexions Stephen did much philanthropic work. He served on the committees of the Church of England Temperance Society, the local auxiliary of the British and Foreign Bible Society, the Sydney Ragged Schools and, from 1850, the Benevolent Society of New South Wales. A director of the Sydney Infirmary and Dispensary in 1852-54 and 1859-68, he was its honorary secretary in 1855-58 and a vice-president in 1869-84. In 1852 he was founding secretary and later president of the Society for the Relief of Destitute Children, which had 'greatly disappointed my expectations'. In April 1882 he was appointed to the Immigration Board.

Stephen suffered a stroke in December 1883. He retired from active work though not from office and died of Bright's disease at Hunters Hill on 20 July 1884. After one of the largest funerals accorded by Sydney to an Anglican clergyman he was buried at St Jude's, Randwick. He was survived by his wife Rebecca Maria (d. 1901), daughter of George Cox of Winbourne and granddaughter of William Cox [q.v.], whom he had married at Mulgoa on 5 May 1852, and by two sons and four daughters. His estate was valued for probate at £2560. Over £1000 was raised in his memory: part was spent on memorial plaques at the Randwick Asylum and St Paul's and on the improvement of his church; the balance was used for a scholarship at St Paul's College.

St Paul's Church, Redfern, *Diamond jubilee* (Syd, 1915); R. M. Bedford, *Think of Stephen* (Syd, 1954); Church of England diocese of Sydney, V&P of Synod (1866-84); *Aust Churchman* (Syd), 24 July 1884; *Church of England Record* (Syd), 1 Aug 1884; SMH, 25 Aug 1855; *Sydney Mail*, 26 July 1884; H. W. H. Huntington, Life and career of the Hon. Sir Alfred Stephen (1884, ML); Bishop's Act books and registers (Syd Diocesan Registry).

K. J. CABLE

STEPHEN, JAMES WILBERFORCE (1822-1881), politician and judge, was born on 10 April 1822 in London, son of SIR GEORGE STEPHEN and his wife Henrietta, née Ravenscroft. The family had many colonial connexions, including John Stephen, Sir James Stephen and Sir Alfred Stephen [qq.v.]. His father George was born at St Christopher, West Indies, in 1794, son of James Stephen and his first wife Anne (Anna), née Stent. Destined for a medical career he entered Magdalene College, Cambridge, in 1812 but after two years was apprenticed instead to a firm of solicitors for five years. He married in 1821 and his activity in the anti-slavery crusade from 1824 led to his knighthood in February 1838. He also turned to writing: his *Adventures of a Gentleman in search of a Horse* (London, 1837) ran into six editions. About 1847 he decided to become a barrister and on 6 June 1849 was called to the Bar at Gray's Inn. In the next few years he built up an insolvency practice in Liverpool and Manchester.

James Wilberforce was educated privately and at St John's College, Cambridge (B.A., 1844; M.A., 1847; fellow, 1848-52). From 1844 he read at Lincoln's Inn and was called to the Bar on 30 January 1849. In 1851 in London he married Katherine Rose Vernon. About 1854 he persuaded his father to migrate with him to Victoria, and on 31 July 1855 Sir George, Lady

Stephen, 'family and suite', James Wilberforce and his wife arrived in Melbourne in
the *Oliver Lang*. Father and son were admitted to the Victorian Bar on 9 August
and for the rest of their working lives shared
professional chambers. Sir George practised
mainly in the Insolvency Court and was
appointed Q.C. in 1871; James Wilberforce
soon became the acknowledged leader of
the Equity Bar, built up a 'large and highly
lucrative practice' and became a recognized
authority on conveyancing and mining
law. Sir George applied for a land grant in
1856 on the grounds that as a former
deputy-lieutenant of Buckinghamshire he
was eligible for grants given to military
persons, but the claim was disallowed.
From at least 1863 he shared a home with
James Wilberforce in Glen Eira Road, Caulfield.

In Victoria Sir George led a life which
he described variously as 'the life of a
recluse' and 'twenty years of happy existence in a small but honorable circle'. In
1856 he was a member of the Citizens'
Committee that worked for the reform of
the prison hulks. In 1857 he was a member
of the Land Convention. As one of the
colony's very few knights he was in demand as patron or president for sporting
and philanthropic societies; a keen player,
he was president of the Chess Club, founded in 1866. He dabbled in politics but failed
to gain nomination. He claimed to be an
admirer of the colony 'apart from its democratic constitution', but was very critical
of secular education. A prominent Anglican, he was a member of the Church of
England Assembly and taught a class of
young men on Sundays. He was a leading
opponent in 1857 of Bishop Perry's [q.v.]
restrictions on church music. Those outside his circle objected to his 'cantankerous
spirit' and 'dogmatic style' in his defence
of the legal profession in the press, although the *Age* admitted that 'long experience has imparted power to his pen as
a correspondent'. His nephew, Sir James
Fitzjames Stephen, son of Sir James of the
Colonial Office, described his uncle as 'a
terrible thorn in my father's side for many
years', but added that he was also 'a very
clever vigorous old creature'. In his later
years Stephen turned from legal to religious writing and published *The Life of
Christ* (Melbourne, 1870) for the 'use of
the poor and the young'. Ailing for the last
two years of his life, he died at Caulfield
on 20 June 1879, predeceased by his wife
in 1869 and survived by six of his seven
children. His estate was valued for probate
at £3722.

James Wilberforce taught the new first
year law course at the University of Melbourne from 1858 but resigned in 1860 because of ill health. In March 1865 he was
appointed to the Council of the University
of Melbourne and on 27 April 1867 was
awarded the degree of M.A. (*ad eund.*). He
was an original trustee and life member of
Trinity College, Melbourne. An active
Anglican layman, he was until 1877 chancellor of the diocese. In 1866 he stood
against G. Higinbotham [q.v.] for the
Legislative Assembly seat of Brighton. In
October 1870 he was elected unopposed for
St Kilda following the retirement of B. C.
Aspinall [q.v.]; despite his opposition to
McCulloch [q.v.] he was made chairman
of the Elections Committee. In the May
1872 election he retained his seat against
vigorous opposition from Gavan Duffy's
[q.v.] party. An accusation of venality
made by a Roman Catholic priest, although
quickly withdrawn when found to be false,
added personal bitterness to the campaign.

Stephen was appointed attorney-general
on 10 June 1872 in the Francis [q.v.] ministry. He was also placed in charge of the
important and controversial education bill.
Although admitting his hesitancy in leading the debate 'in the presence of gentlemen ... who know very much more about
it than I can claim to do', he shepherded
the bill through committee virtually unchanged. As first minister of public instruction from 2 January 1873, he vigorously brought the legislation into operation
until 1 May 1874, when he was appointed
to the Supreme Court and resigned from
parliament. As attorney-general he had
faced a censure motion against the government over the release of H. C. Mount and
W. C. Morris; his opinion that they were
wrongfully set free was upheld by the Privy
Council.

Stephen had the reputation of being a
conscientious and sound lawyer, effective
in court though somewhat given to dif-
fusiveness. Of an 'eager, nervous temperament', he also had the 'infirmity of
saying unhappy things that he afterwards
regretted'. Not long after his appointment
to the bench he became seriously ill of a
disease that baffled both local and London
specialists. On leave of absence from 1877,
he travelled in Europe with his family
before returning to the bench in early
1879. But his marasmus and anaemia had
not been cured and he died suddenly at
Fitzroy on 14 August 1881, survived by
his wife, a son and three of his five daughters. His estate was sworn for probate at
£3153.

J. L. Forde, *The story of the Bar of Victoria*
(Melb, 1913); E. Scott, *A history of the Uni-*

versity of Melbourne (Melb, 1936); A. Dean, A multitude of counsellors (Melb, 1968); D. Grundy, Secular, compulsory and free (Melb, 1972); Argus, 1 Aug 1856, 15 Aug 1881, Age, 15 Aug 1881; Australasian, 20 Aug 1881; IAN, 24 Aug 1881; A'sian Sketcher, 27 Aug 1881; E. R. Campbell, History of the Melbourne Law School (held by author).

A. THOMSON ZAIN'UDDIN

STEPHEN, SIR MATTHEW HENRY (1828-1920), barrister and judge, was born on 5 December 1828 at Hobart Town, third son of Sir Alfred Stephen [q.v.] and his first wife Virginia, née Consett. In May 1839 he reached Sydney in the Medway with the rest of his family. Stephen was educated at W. T. Cape's [q.v.] Sydney College, where he was head boy for two years. At 17 he was associate to Sir James Dowling [q.v.] and later to his own father. On 20 December 1850 he was admitted to the colonial Bar and spent 1852 in England studying under an equity draftsman and a special pleader; he returned to Sydney on 1 January 1853 in the Waterloo.

On 30 September 1854 at Christ Church St Laurence Stephen married his cousin Caroline Sibella (1833-1897), daughter of H. T. Shadforth, usher of the Black Rod, and granddaughter of Thomas Shadforth [q.v.]. He soon acquired a good general practice and the Sydney Morning Herald, 21 May 1887, reported that he had excelled in the case of Hassall v. Rodd 'in which he was opposed by three Attorneys-General (past and present)'. In 1860 Judge Dickinson [q.v.] wrote to his father, 'your son . . . does his work remarkably well. I look on him as certain for the Bench'. In the early 1860s Stephen twice refused the solicitor-generalship and again when offered the position by Edward Butler [q.v.]. On 16 December 1869 he was elected to the Legislative Assembly for Mudgee. A member of the Elections and Qualifications Committee, he was once described by Butler as a 'political baby', but he was intelligent and quickwitted in debate. He supported the 1866 Public Schools Act, immigration, legal reforms and a reduced price for land, but would not promise to urge the extension of the railway to Mudgee, for 'what was the use of running trains to carry bandicoots and kangaroos?'

Stephen acted as leading counsel for the Crown on many occasions and held a general retainer. He was a surrogate of the Vice-Admiralty Court and in the 1870s was an examiner of the University of Sydney. On 2 April 1879 he was appointed a Q.C. and in July refused appointment as a Supreme Court judge; he told Sir Henry Parkes [q.v.] that compared to the income

of a barrister in full practice, a judge's salary was inadequate for 'men whose anxieties duties and responsibilities are so arduous and unceasing'. However, from 1876 he had often acted as judge on circuit. As leading counsel he won a farthing damages, with costs, for John Davies [q.v.] in Davies v. Harris [q.v.] in 1883 and the Apollo Candle Co.'s case against the government over customs duties. In 1886 he chaired the meeting of the Bar which unanimously resolved to ask (Sir) Julian Salomons [q.v.] to withdraw his resignation as chief justice. On 23 May 1887 he was sworn in as a puisne judge of the Supreme Court. On the Bench Stephen was noted for the conscientious discharge of his duties, for 'the fearlessness with which he expressed himself on matters which he conceived to be for the public welfare', and for advocating many legal reforms. He repeatedly denounced 'hard-swearing' and perjury. His notebooks filled 125 volumes. From 16 June 1902 to 4 February 1904 he was acting chief justice during the absence of Sir Frederick Darley [q.v.]. He resigned from the Bench in 1904; knighted that year, he was known as Sir Henry Stephen.

A staunch Anglican, Stephen gave much time to charitable work. Over the years he served on the committees of the Benevolent Society of New South Wales, the Church Society, the Home Visiting and Relief Society, the Sydney Female Refuge Society, the Sydney City Mission and the National Shipwreck Relief Society of New South Wales. A director of the Sydney Infirmary and Dispensary in 1857-75 and 1908-10. he was honorary secretary in 1859-66 and 1868-73. In the 1880s he was chairman of the trustees of Sydney Grammar School and president of the Young Men's Christian Association. His wife was a committee member of the Hospital for Sick Children, Glebe. Stephen was a member of the Sydney Diocesan synods and was chancellor of the diocese of Sydney in 1886-87. A patron of cricket, he was senior vice-president of the New South Wales Cricket Association. From 1895 he was a fellow of the Royal Colonial Institute.

Though 'he practised all his life in Common Law', Stephen 'had missed a good deal about the ways of ordinary men'. Sitting on a horse-stealing case at Maitland, he asked the crown prosecutor to speed up proceedings by calling 'Mr. Brumby'; the incident was immortalized by A. B. Paterson in the ballad 'Brumby's Run': 'who is Brumby, and where is his Run?' From 1863 he lived for many years at Glen Ayr, Glenmore Road, Paddington, and had a house, Summerleas, at Sutton Forest. Later he moved to

Honiton, Victoria Road, Bellevue Hill, where he died of nephritis on 1 April 1920; he was buried in the South Head cemetery. He was survived by his second wife Florence Sophie, née Huthwaite, a distant cousin whom he had married on 20 December 1900. and by Caroline, his only daughter by his first wife; three sons had died in infancy. He left the bulk of his estate, valued for probate at almost £28,000. to his wife, his daughter already being well provided for.

A. B. Piddington, *Worshipful masters* (Syd, 1929); A. B. Paterson, *Collected verse*, 13th ed (Syd, 1945); R. M. Bedford, *Think of Stephen* (Syd, 1954); J. M. Bennett (ed), *A history of the New South Wales Bar* (Syd, 1969); V&P (LA NSW), 1873-74, 6, 114, 128, 1883-84, 1, 716, 7, 1211; SMH, 10, 16 Dec 1869, 6, 13 Mar 1871, 22 Nov 1882, 21, 24 May 1887, 2 Apr 1920; *Old Times*, May 1903; Parkes letters (ML); Stephen papers MS 777 and uncat MS 211 (ML); printed cat under M. H. Stephen (ML).

MARTHA RUTLEDGE

STEPHEN, MONTAGU CONSETT (1827-1872), and SEPTIMUS ALFRED (1842-1901), solicitors, were the second and seventh sons of Sir Alfred Stephen [q.v.]. Consett was born on 28 April 1827 in Hobart Town, son of his father's first wife Virginia, née Consett. He had his early schooling in Hobart and in May 1839 accompanied his father to Sydney in the *Medway*. He was educated at the Sydney College under W. T. Cape [q.v.], where he won several prizes for mathematics, and in 1843 at Tonbridge, England. In May 1844 he returned to Van Diemen's Land and was articled to Robert Pitcairn [q.v.]. On 13 July 1849 he was admitted as a solicitor in Hobart, worked in the office of Butler [q.v.] and Nutt and in August was back in Sydney. On 22 December he was admitted to practice by the Supreme Court of New South Wales despite an objection by William Redman that he was not properly qualified.

On 1 January 1850 Stephen set up in practice with Charles Lowe as Lowe and Stephen, and in September was a member of the managing committee of the New South Wales Association for Preventing the Revival of Transportation. In 1849-53 he was closely involved professionally with Sir Charles Nicholson [q.v.], a trustee of the £5000 Consett family trust fund, which his father wanted to lend out on mortgage. In 1850 his father told Nicholson, 'I am *sure* you may safely rely on [Consett's] caution, & knowledge of law—especially conveyancing law—in all such matters'. Lowe and Stephen were solicitors for the Australian

Mutual Provident Society from 1850 until their partnership was dissolved in March 1852; he was reappointed as the society's sole solicitor in March 1853 and in 1857 drafted its first Act of incorporation. He practised alone until 1864 when the firm became Stephen and Stephen.

On 25 May 1853 he had married Emily Clara (d. 1878), daughter of Rev. J. Jennings Smith. In 1862 he built Quambi, a large house in Woollahra. Although sociable he devoted his leisure to botany, astronomy and natural history. A committee-man of the Volunteer Club, Stephen became an alderman on the Woollahra Borough Council in 1868 and was mayor in 1868-70. He was also a trustee and director of the Perpetual Building and Investment Society and a councillor of the Law Institute of New South Wales. In the 1860s with Edward Knox [q.v.] he held one run in the Moreton and six runs in the Burnett districts of Queensland. A devout Anglican, he was a member of the first and second Sydney Diocesan synods in 1866 and 1870 and an active member of the standing committee; in 1869 he was a lay representative on the Provincial Synod.

In 1869, standing as an independent, but in favour of the 1866 Public Schools Act and 'anti-protection', Stephen was elected to the Legislative Assembly for Canterbury and was a member of the Elections and Qualifications Committee. He resigned on 13 December 1870 and, in delicate health, visited England with his family. He died in London of diseased kidneys on 19 May 1872 and was buried at St Jude's, Randwick, Sydney, in September.

Septimus Alfred was born on 8 May 1842, second son of his father's second wife Eleanor Martha Pickard, née Bedford. He was educated by Rev. T. H. Wilkinson at the Meads, Ashfield, and at Rev. W. H. Savigny's Collegiate School, Cook's River. In 1858 he was articled to his brother Consett; his admission as a solicitor to the Supreme Court was moved by Sir William Manning [q.v.] on 2 July 1864, and in November he was taken into partnership by his brother, with a fifth of the business. 'Clever, lively, energetic and handsome', Stephen married Lucy (d. 1914), daughter of Robert Campbell junior [q.v.] on 31 December; she had fifteen bridesmaids and their health was proposed by the governor, Sir John Young. They lived at Rialto Terrace, Upper William Street, until 1868 when they moved to Woodside, Enmore (Petersham).

Under Septimus the firm continued to act as confidential advisers to the A.M.P. Society; they also became solicitors for the *Sydney Morning Herald* and the Australian Joint Stock Bank. In 1868 Stephen became a notary public and in the 1870s was a director of the Perpetual Building and Investment Society. With new partners the firm had several changes of name until 1888 when it became known as Stephen, Jaques and Stephen. In 1879 in evidence before the royal commission into the working of the Real Property Acts, Stephen claimed to have 'a large amount of practice, principally in conveyancing', and criticized the long delays getting titles and simple matters through the Land Titles Office.

In 1882-87 Stephen represented Canterbury in the Legislative Assembly. An independent supporter of (Sir) Alexander Stuart's [q.v.] government, he opposed the Dibbs-Jennings [qq.v.] ministry allegedly because 'his capitalist instincts are alarmed at "The Deficit", and ... he blames the Government for keeping the House sitting so late of nights'. He carried the Settled Estates Act and three private Acts. In 1887-1900 he sat in the Legislative Council.

In 1881 with G. H. Cox, V. J. Dowling and his brother-in-law, E. W. Ward [qq.v.], Stephen invested in cattle stations on the Diamantina River in south-west Queensland; their runs were consolidated in 1899 as Connemara. They had another run, Pillicawarina near Warren, used for fattening cattle. Profitable in the 1880s, the enterprise ran into difficulties in the 1890s with the long drought and selectors on Pillicawarina. By 1901 Connemara had lost £124,000 of which Stephen's share was £74,000.

Despite his charm, he was also quick-tempered, sometimes conceited and 'dearly loved a lord': a Union Club committee-man, he enjoyed gambling and cards, and played whist at his London club. For many years a committee-man of the Australian Jockey Club, Stephen raced a number of horses but never won a big race. He owned a country house, Elvo, at Burradoo, a half-share in Elizabeth Farm and other real estate in and near Sydney. In 1888-89 he took his family on a visit to Britain. He complained to his cousin, Percy Bedford, that 'Racing here at most places isn't much fun', but he supervised the colts that James White [q.v.] had sent to England. In 1889 he hired two houseboats at Henley for the regatta and claimed that 'having made a big splash [I] shall retire into obscurity. The only thing that I can guarantee is the liquor and of that there shall be no stint'.

From 1870 Stephen had sat on the Sydney Diocesan synods and in 1896 was a lay representative to the General Synod and a lay member of St Andrew's Cathedral Chapter. He was a life member of the Royal Society of New South Wales from 1879 and a fellow of the Royal Colonial Institute from 1888. In the 1890s he was president of the Hospital for Sick Children, Glebe, a director of Sydney Hospital in 1894-95, the Seaham Colliery Co. and the Australian Mortgage and Agency Co.

In 1896 Stephen went to live in London and negotiated on the reconstruction of the Australian Joint Stock Bank. He practised in partnership with George Slade and was a London director of the Australian Mortgage, Land and Finance Co. and of the Chillagoe Railway and Mines Co. He died of a gastric ulcer at Enbridge Lodge, East Woodhay, Hampshire, on 28 August 1901, survived by his wife, five sons and two daughters. His estate was valued for probate at £104,105. His second son Colin, a partner in Stephen, Jaques and Stephen, and chairman of the Australian Jockey Club, was his only child to live in Australia.

Ex-M.L.A., *Our present parliament, what it is worth* (Syd, c1886); V&P (LA NSW), 1870-71, 4, 908, 1879-80, 5, 1110; SMH, 21 June, 16 Dec 1842, 22 Dec 1849, 1 Jan 1850, 16 Dec 1869, 3 July 1872, 10 Oct 1885, 1 Sept 1901; *Bulletin*, 30 Dec 1882; T&CJ, 7 May 1887, 7 Sept 1901; R. I. Parsons, Lawyers in the New South Wales parliament, 1870-1890 (Ph.D. thesis, Macquarie Univ, 1973); L. C. Stephen, History of the office (held by Stephen, Jaques and Stephen, Syd); Sir Charles Nicholson papers in Norton, Smith & Co. papers, vol 35 (ML); Parkes letters (ML); letter books and papers (held by Sir Alastair Stephen, Syd).   MARTHA RUTLEDGE

STEPHEN, WILLIAM WILBERFORCE (1835-1903), civil servant, was born on 24 September 1835 in Hobart Town, fifth son of Sir Alfred Stephen [q.v.] and his first wife Virginia, née Consett. In May 1839 the family moved to Sydney where William attended Rev. T. H. Wilkinson's school at the Meads, Ashfield, and Sydney College. After some experience as a voluntary clerk and passing the admission examination, on 1 July 1852 he was appointed a third-class clerk in the land and legislative branch of the Colonial Secretary's Department. On 1 November 1858 he became second clerk in the Department of Lands and Public Works; next year he remained in the Lands Department when it was separated from Public Works. He was dissuaded in 1866 by (Sir) John Robertson [q.v.] from applying for outside promotion, and on 1 October 1870 he replaced A. O. Moriarty [q.v.] as under-secretary at a salary of £700, taking over a large department with huge arrears and insufficient staff, and administering perhaps the most contentious laws of the time.

In October 1878 Stephen's work was scrutinized by the Lands and Survey Department's commission which grilled him with 2117 questions mostly put without notice or opportunity for reference; when resigning on 4 November Commissioner James Thomson said 'I also had a strong impression ... that my colleagues were inclined to hold Mr Stephen responsible for far more than his share of the alleged delays and mis-management'. The commissioners reported in February 1879 that Stephen had used his position to expedite work for friends and lacked the qualities 'essential for intelligent vigorous and upright administration'; they also uncovered a feud between him and Moriarty who constantly challenged his authority.

In a minute to the secretary for lands Stephen criticized the partial nature of the inquiry that had 'so virulently and so unfairly assailed' him. He argued that lack of staff, repeatedly reported, and inadequate and scattered accommodation made it impossible to run efficiently his enormous department. In 1872-79 land selections had risen to an average of 100,000 acres annually. Early in 1880 the *Bulletin* commended Stephen's 'perseverance', his 'genial manner and business-like attention to ... the duties of his really diplomatic office' and noted the high and just respect accorded Stephen 'by all his subordinates'.

In August 1880 an investigation into the embezzlement of £800 by James T. Evans, a junior clerk in the accounts branch, resulted in the suspension of Stephen and James P. Croft, the accountant. Robertson told Sir Henry Parkes [q.v.] that James Hoskins [q.v.], secretary for lands, had 'set his heart on taking the under-secretaryship from' Stephen, and argued that the charge of incapacity 'cannot for a moment be sustained by those who know him and the business best'; Sir Alfred Stephen tried to intercede on his son's behalf. On 22 September Governor Loftus suggested reinstatement and transferral to the Department of Justice, and on 7 November Stephen became secretary to the attorney-general at a salary of £500. He retired on a pension in 1896.

A keen cricketer, Stephen was a founding trustee of the Sydney Cricket Ground in 1876. He had joined the Volunteer Corps in 1854, in 1865 was on the committee of the Volunteer Club and in 1874 joined the Union Club; he was a committee-man of the Society for the Prevention of Cruelty to Animals. In the 1870s he was a member of the Sydney diocesan synods. Always convivial, Stephen described himself as a 'loud impulsive talker'. He grew increasingly absent-minded with age and was cared for by his niece Thea.

Unmarried, Stephen died of cirrhosis of the liver at his home, Clanricarde, Potts Point, on 25 October 1903 and was buried in the Anglican section of Waverley cemetery. His estate was valued for probate at £542.

R. M. Bedford, *Think of Stephen* (Syd, 1954); G. Buxton, *The Riverina 1861-1891* (Melb, 1967); V&P (LA NSW), 1870-71, 1, 291, 1872 1, 721, 2, 167, 1877-78, 3, 463, 1878-79, 4, 9, 152, 1882, 2, 429, 488; PD (NSW), 1879-80, 1881, 1495; *Bulletin*, 10 Apr 1880, 29 Oct 1903; *SMH*, 27 Oct 1903; *T&CJ*, 28 Oct 1903; I. M. Laszlo, Railway politics and development in northern New South Wales 1846-1889 (M.A. thesis, Univ New England, 1956); Parkes letters *and* MS cat (ML).   SUZANNE EDGAR

STEPHENS, EDWARD JAMES (1846-1931), newspaper editor and publisher, was born on 17 October 1846 in London, son of George Stephens, coachsmith, and his wife Amelia, née Ford. The family reached Melbourne in the *Result* in October 1853, revisited England in 1860, and then returned to Victoria. After a five-year apprenticeship with James Curtis, owner of Caxton Printing Works, Ballarat, Stephens began publication of a trade gazette. His friend James Merson advised that the spread of settlement in the Wimmera indicated good prospects for a newspaper in the selectors' tiny supply centre, Horsham.

In 1873 Stephens found that the town lacked rail and telegraph facilities, and that some storekeepers 'preferred the continuance of squatterdom', but he gained the support of Robert Clark, president of Horsham and Wimmera Farmers' and Selectors' Reform Association. Former pack-horse mailman, Constantine Dougherty, arranged rental of part of a log hut in Firebrace Street where, in June, Stephens installed his double demy Albion press, hauled in a wagon from Ballarat. With fellow apprentice Edwin Boase, he worked from Sunday midnight to Tuesday morning, 1 July, when the first issue of the *Horsham Times* (3d.) appeared. By 1882, with widespread selection on the plains, the paper flourished as the *Horsham Times, Dimboola, Warracknabeal, Murtoa, Natimuk, Wail, Rupanyup, Minyip, Drung Drung, Longerenong and Wimmera Advertiser*. Liberal in outlook, the editor sought 'to promote the weal of the whole community'. His paper, which helped overcome the selectors' isolation and gave them a common voice, grew into a bi-weekly with commodious quarters in Wilson Street. As one of the Horsham Railway League delegates, he had attended a Legislative Council meeting in December 1880 to urge successfully the building of the inter-colonial railway through the town.

On 6 December 1878 Stephens had help-ed Boase to establish the *Dunmunkle Stan-dard* (Murtoa) and on 1 February 1879 bought the *Dimboola Banner* from its founder Henry Barnes. In June 1883 he sold the *Times* to Fred Martin and retired to live at Finch Street, East Malvern. Losing heavily in land speculation in 1885-86, he established the *Broken Hill Times* on 21 August 1886. The *Broken Hill Argus* took over this paper on 20 February 1888. Stephens was also sometime proprietor of the *Omeo Telegraph* (established 1884), the *Warragul News* (1887) and the *Yarram Chronicle* (1886). In 1889 he bought the *Nhill Free Press* and settled with his family in Nhill, Victoria. He acquired the *Kaniva and Lillimur Courier and Serviceton Gazette* in July 1890. He incorporated both this paper and the *Nhill Mail*, bought on 4 Janu-ary 1901, in the *Free Press*: both Nhill papers had printed the poems of local farm-hand John Shaw Neilson in the early 1890s. Stephens sold out to Pharez Phillips in June 1909, and at his farewell on 12 February 1910 he was praised 'for helping to guide on a liberal basis the settlement and progress of our great Wimmera district' and for his assistance with 'patriotic and progressive town movements'. Handsome and bearded he was well known as a Presbyterian lay preacher. He loved tennis and cricket and established one of the first literary societies in the Wimmera. He contributed much to the development of the provincial press in both eastern and western Victoria.

On 12 October 1875 Stephens had mar-ried Margaret, daughter of George Lang-lands [q.v.]. In 1910 he and his sons became graziers and wheat-growers at Glen Logan, New South Wales, and in the 1920s he moved to Urana. He died of cerebral throm-bosis at Lockhart on 9 December 1931 and was buried at Urana; his wife had died at their home Nargoon on 30 April 1930, aged 84. Two sons and a daughter survived him.

J. Smith (ed), *Cyclopedia of Victoria*, 3 (Melb, 1905); L. J. Blake and K. H. Lovett, *Wimmera Shire centenary* (Horsham, 1962); *Argus*, 29 June 1909; *Nhill Free Press*, 29 June 1909; *Horsham Times*, 29 June 1923; family records.   L. J. BLAKE

STEPHENS, JAMES (1821-1889), trade unionist, was born on 8 August 1821 at Chepstow, Monmouthshire, Wales, son of James Stephens, stonemason. As a youth he moved to Newport, a stronghold of Char-tism, joined the Masons' Society in 1839 and that year was seriously injured in a fall of thirty feet. He joined the Chartist move-ment and was one of the participants in the riot at the Westgate Hotel when soldiers fired on the rebels, killing twenty. He was 'severely handled' but escaped to London. He worked as a mason at Windsor Castle but was dismissed when it became known that he was a Chartist. Working on the new Houses of Parliament he found himself among like-minded people. He was still active in Chartism but like many other sup-porters of the cause, increasingly directed his energies to craft unionism. He became a prominent leader of the masons, acquiring a wide experience as a union organizer. A zealous attender of meetings and lectures in London, he was one of the leading agitators in the four-o'clock movement.

When the gold rush created an enormous demand for tradesmen Stephens, like many other Chartists, migrated to Victoria and arrived on 17 July 1853 in the *Elizabeth*. In February 1855 the Operative Masons' Society, which had been suspended in the confusions of the time, was resuscitated, and with James Gilvray Galloway he formed a local branch on 4 February 1856 at Clark's Hotel, Collingwood. This meeting is seen as the genesis of the eight-hour movement, for a committee was set up to confer with the building contractors, most of whom proved co-operative on the introduction of the eight-hour day. Stephens, using the language of the Chartists, proposed to per-suade the recalcitrant by 'physical force' if necessary and to coerce the non-unionists; but on 26 March a mass meeting of employ-ers and operatives resolved, on the motion of Thomas Smith [q.v.] seconded by Steph-ens, that the eight-hour day must come into force in April. On the 'glorious 21st of April' he led a major demonstration, and wrote: It was a burning hot day and I thought the occasion a good one, so I called upon the men to follow me, to which they immediately consented, when I marched them ... to Parliament House, the men ... dropping their tools and joining the proces-sion'. Afterwards a banquet was held at the Belvidere (Eastern Hill) Hotel, Fitzroy.

The same year Stephens seconded the nomination of Henry Langlands [q.v.] for the Legislative Assembly seat of Melbourne. The Trades Hall Committee was set up in 1857 and Stephens was treasurer in 1859-61. On the formation of the Eight Hours' League in 1859 he became a delegate. He later claimed that he was victimized for sub-contracting, of which the unions dis-approved, and that public work was closed to him. Looking back in 1883, the Operative Masons' Society determined that Stephens had begun the eight-hour agitation but that a number of his companions were entitled to 'at least equal honour', the 'most talented and prominent of whom was James Galloway'. Meanwhile, he had been forgotten by society at large, and the Trades Hall Council issued an eloquent appeal, saying that he was now an old man, almost blind and maimed by a fall from a scaffold. wholly unable to provide for himself and his wife. Unionists subscribed the considerable sum of 'upwards of £500'. On 14 November 1889 he died of Bright's disease in his cottage at Carlton. Aged 26, he had married Eliza Cuthbert in London and was survived by one of their two sons. His estate was sworn for probate at £448.

The history of capital and labour ... (Syd. 1888); W. E. Murphy, History of the Eight Hours' Movement (Melb, 1896); Report of the committee appointed by the Victorian Operative Masons Society to inquire into the origin of the Eight Hours' Movement in Victoria ... (Melb, 1912); C. Turnbull, Bluestone (Melb, 1945).   CLIVE TURNBULL*

STEPHENS, JAMES BRUNTON (1835-1902), poet, novelist, critic, schoolteacher and public servant, was born on 17 June 1835 at Bo'ness near Edinburgh, son of John Stephens, schoolmaster, and his wife Jane, née Brunton. Educated at his father's school, then at a free boarding-school, he attended the University of Edinburgh in 1849-54 but took no degree.

As a tutor with the Massey-Dawson family he travelled widely on the Continent; with the family of Lieutenant Leyland of the 2nd Life Guards for about fifteen months he toured the Mediterranean, the Middle East and Egypt. Parts of his travel diary survive. For another year he was probably a tutor in a military garrison and a teacher in London. In 1859 he became a teacher at the Greenock Academy and then at the Kilblain Academy in Greenock where he wrote some minor verse and two short novels 'Rutson Morley' and 'Virtue Le Moyne', which were published in Sharpe's London Magazine in 1861-63.

On 28 December 1865 for obscure reasons Stephens migrated to Queensland in the Flying Cloud, which reached Moreton Bay on 28 April 1866. He taught French briefly at Tollerton House Academy, and then became a tutor with the Barker family of Tamrookum station on the Logan River. Though he admired the scenery, Stephens found bush life monotonous and the conversation boring; thrown on his inner resources, he turned to verse and composed his best-known poem, Convict Once (London, 1871).

In 1869 Stephens applied to the Board of Education and on 1 February 1870 began teaching at the Normal School in Brisbane but resigned on 9 December 1871 and spent 1872 once more on Tamrookum. Next year he returned to the Normal School, but in April again resigned and went as tutor to the family of Captain Sherwood on Unumgar station, only to return to teaching at Stanthorpe in 1874. There are suggestions that his erratic moves were caused by drink.

In 1870-74 Stephens had been writing, and in 1873 published The Godolphin Arabian, a brilliant narrative poem in the ottava rima made famous by Byron, on the life of Scham, the Barb that was the ancestor of the modern thoroughbred; it contains more ingenuity and wit than any other poem Stephens wrote. In the same year appeared a collection of his verse, The Black Gin and Other Poems. At Stanthorpe he apparently passed some of his happiest years, though he missed his friends and the stimulus of city life.

At Brisbane on 10 November 1876, while a relieving teacher at Kelvin Grove, Stephens married Rosalie Mary Donaldson. In 1877 he was headmaster at Ashgrove. These years were 'Jog-trot, jog-trot. Peaceful monotony, all the happier because it has no annals', as he wrote to W. H. Traill [q.v.]. He was one of the founders of the Johnsonian Club in 1878, attended its meetings, entertained his friends, and wrote mainly reviews and criticism. Leaving Ashgrove at the end of 1882, he was nominally headmaster at Sandgate in January 1883 and then, reputedly through the influence of the governor's daughter, was appointed to the Colonial Secretary's Office as dispatch writer.

For the next nineteen years Stephens was a devoted public servant. Though he was supposed to have some leisure for writing, he found his tasks exacting and time-consuming, but he wrote for the Brisbane Courier, the Australasian, and other newspapers, and contributed some articles to the 'Red Page' of the Bulletin. He also wrote three of his four most famous patriotic poems, 'The Dominion of Australia' (1877), 'An Australian National Anthem' (1890) and 'Fulfilment' (1901). He aspired in vain to be a dramatist, though Fayette (1892) was both published and produced.

Stephens died of angina pectoris on 29 June 1902 survived by his wife, a son and four daughters. For about twenty years after the death of Henry Kendall [q.v.] in 1882 he had been regarded as the greatest Australian poet living, even though his best work had been produced in the 1870s. This repute, which lasted for some time after his death, has decreased considerably, but there is reason for claiming that *Convict Once* does not deserve all the denigration it has received nor *The Godolphin Arabian* the neglect.

C. Hadgraft, *James Brunton Stephens* (Brisb, 1969), and for bibliog; Stephens letters to W. H. Traill and Francis Kenna (NL); Francis Kenna newspaper cuttings (ML). CECIL HADGRAFT

STEPHENS, THOMAS (1830-1913), educationist, was born on 4 October 1830 at Levens, Westmorland, England, second son of Rev. William Stephens, vicar of Levens, and his wife Alicia, née Daniell, and younger brother of W. J. Stephens [q.v.]. Educated at Marlborough College and Magdalen Hall, Oxford (B.A., 1854; M.A., 1864), he migrated to Melbourne in 1855. Next year he went to Tasmania and became sub-warden of Christ's College, Bishopsbourne, until it closed in May 1857. He was then appointed inspector for the Northern Board of Education and moved to Launceston where, in 1861-62 he also served on the Northern Board of Works, responsible for planning roads. He went to Hobart Town in 1863 as inspector of schools for the whole island under the new single Board of Education and in 1870 was promoted chief inspector.

In evidence to select committees on education Stephens advocated improvements in the training and certification of teachers by a central body, increased salaries for teachers, systematic inspections, properly arranged courses and testing of results. His enthusiasm for reform, also expressed in his annual reports and letters, led him into conflict with the board: in 1868 it thought he should include more than 'an exposition of general principles or the abstract views of the inspector'. He repeated his arguments in evidence to the 1882 select committee and the 1883 royal commission on education. Under the 1885 Act which replaced the Board of Education with a responsible minister, he became permanent head of the new department as director. He drafted the first regulations under the new Act, and administered its provisions with 'inflexible fidelity' until he retired in 1894.

Stephens never lost interest in Christ's College, worked for its re-establishment and wrote its history. He was a member of its council in 1877-1911 and president from 1891. In 1889 he was a founding member of the Council of the University of Tasmania, vice-chancellor in 1900-01 and chairman of the faculty of science in 1905. A member of the Royal Society of Tasmania from 1858, he contributed some twenty-seven papers to its *Proceedings*, most of them dealing with the geography and geology of the colony. He was a councillor of the society in 1863 and vice-president in 1880. He also contributed papers to the Linnean Society of New South Wales, to which he was elected in 1904, and to the Australasian Association for the Advancement of Science. He was a fellow of the Geological Society of London.

On 5 April 1866 at St Thomas's Church, Mulgoa, New South Wales, Stephens married Jane Maria (d. 1884), third daughter of Edward Cox of Fernhill and sister of E. K. Cox [q.v.]; on 2 May 1895 at St Peter's Church, Melbourne, he married Jane Maria, eldest daughter of John Whitefoord [q.v.] of Launceston. He died of heart failure at his home in Fitzroy Crescent, Hobart, on 25 November 1913, predeceased by his second wife, and survived by five of his seven children.

C. Reeves, *History of Tasmanian education* (Melb, 1935); V&P (HA Tas), 1861 (47), 1867 (44), 1868 (73), 1871 (21), 1876 (81), 1882 (106), 1883 (70), 1889 (145), Education Reports, 1861-94; Roy Soc Tas, *Procs*, 1913; *Mercury*, 30 Jan 1883, 26 Nov 1913. NEIL SMITH

STEPHENS, THOMAS BLACKET (1819-1877), newspaper proprietor and politician, was born at Rochdale, England, son of William Stephens, Baptist minister, and his wife Elizabeth, née Blacket, aunt of Edmund Blacket [q.v.]. Before migrating to New South Wales he owned woollen mills near his home town, and as a friend of John Bright and Richard Cobden acquired lifelong political attitudes during the anti-corn-law agitation.

Stephens reached Sydney in the *Bengal* on 12 February 1849, and became a wool-broker. Attracted by the growth of Brisbane, he went there in January 1853, and established a wool-scour and fellmongery near Cleveland. About 1863 the business was transferred nearer town to a site called by the Aboriginals Yee-keb-in, now the suburb of Ekibin. When he added a tannery the enterprise became one of the largest of its type in the colony.

Stephens's radical politics and advanced social and moral views encouraged him in May 1861 to buy the *Moreton Bay Courier*. Although he wrote little, he supervised the paper for four years in which it was enlarged and became a daily. In July 1868 he floated a company, became managing director but retired in ill health in November 1873 and the paper was auctioned.

Stephens was a fervent Primitive Baptist and a benefactor of the sect. With his radical stance, he was associated with most important political issues of the period before and after separation from New South Wales in 1859. When Brisbane was incorporated he became an alderman for South Brisbane, and advocated development of the area. He initiated the first bridge linking the north and south of the city. He served on a committee to establish waterworks and advocated building a town hall. In 1862 he became Brisbane's second mayor.

In 1860 Stephens stood unsuccessfully for Toowoomba in the first parliament but in 1863 was elected for South Brisbane. In 1867-70 he was colonial treasurer, colonial secretary, postmaster-general, and secretary for public lands in the Lilley and Macalister [qq.v.] ministries. His advocacy of a wider franchise and closer settlement measures made him unpopular with conservatives and pastoralists. In 1876-77 he was a member of the Legislative Council.

Contemporaries described Stephens as upright, enthusiastic and able. The *Week* said of him: 'If he had devoted his wonderfully keen, clear intellect, his unwearying industry and his great business tact and judgment to his private affairs instead of to the furtherance of the public interests, or what he most earnestly and heartily believed to be the public interests, he would have been, long ago, one of the wealthiest men in the colony'. The *Brisbane Courier* argued that 'Politically speaking, he was deficient in dash, but then on the other hand, he well knew how to bit and bridle coadjutors who had that quality in dangerous excess'.

On 10 July 1856 in Sydney Stephens married Anne Connah, daughter of an early love. Aged 58, he died on 26 August 1877 survived by his wife and eight children. His home, Cumbooquepa, in South Brisbane, is now the boarding section of the Somerville House School for girls.

Supreme Court reports (Qld), 1873, 98; N. Bartley, *Australian pioneers and reminiscences*, J. J. Knight ed (Brisb, 1896); Baptist Assn of Qld, *Queensland Baptist Jubilee . . . 1855-1905* (Brisb, 1906); G. Greenwood and J. Laverty, *Brisbane 1859-1959* (Brisb, 1959); Qld Women's Hist Assn, *1859 and before that — 1959 and all that* (Brisb, 1960); *Brisbane Courier*, 28 Aug 1877; *Daily Mail* (Brisb), 20 July 1907; *Week*, 20 July 1907.   ELGIN REID

STEPHENS, WILLIAM JOHN (1829-1890), teacher and scholar, was born on 16 July 1829 at Levans, Westmorland, England, son of Rev. John Stephens, vicar of Levans, and his wife Alicia, née Daniell, and elder brother of Thomas [q.v.]. William was educated at Heversham Grammar School and Marlborough College where he became school captain and won many prizes. He matriculated in 1848 and was a scholar at Queen's College, Oxford (B.A., 1852; M. A., 1855). With first-class honours in classics, in 1853-60 he was a fellow of his college, a lecturer in 1854 and a tutor in 1855-56.

Encouraged by Benjamin Jowett and Sir Charles Nicholson [q.v.], in 1856 Stephens was appointed foundation headmaster of Sydney Grammar School. With Professor Woolley [q.v.] he organized the curriculum on advanced lines but the enrolment failed to grow, mainly because of high fees; the school was criticized for being 'exclusive'. He and his mathematics master, Edward Pratt, disagreed over organization and discipline. In 1866 the trustees investigated Pratt's complaints, mainly that Stephens had banned the cane: he said that he disapproved of corporal punishment and argued that discipline must be based on equal justice between teacher and pupil else 'it degenerates into tyranny and servility'. The inquiry tended to support the allegations and the trustees accepted Stephens's resignation, ignoring his plea that it had never been formally submitted and a strong petition of protest from the 'Old Boys'. Resilient but resentful, Stephens in 1867 built and opened his own private school in Darlinghurst with fifty of his former pupils. The New School (Eaglesfield from 1879) was an immediate success; he implemented advanced educational practices and won the respect and affection of his pupils, who performed well in public examinations. He claimed that he opposed 'teaching grammar as the way to language . . . He had been equally emphatic in his claims for the teaching of science—that is, of observation of facts with their examination—as the essential basis of all intellectual progress'.

Prominent as an organizer in colonial scientific circles from his arrival, in 1857 Stephens had joined the Philosophical (Royal) Society of New South Wales and in May 1863 was elected to its council; honorary secretary in 1864-65, he edited its *Transactions* in 1866 but was an inactive member thereafter. In 1862-66 he had been a founding councillor of the Entymological Society of New South Wales and its treasurer in 1864-65. He was a foundation member of the Linnean Society of New South Wales in 1874, a councillor from 1875, vice-president in 1879-80, co-honorary secretary in 1881-84 and president in 1877-78 and

1885-90. He read seven presidential addresses and a number of papers on geology and allied subjects to the society. In 1879 he helped to found the Zoological Society of New South Wales and in 1883-85 was a founding vice-president of the New South Wales branch of the Geographical Society of Australasia. He was also examiner in classics and English language and literature for the Board of National Education in 1864-66, an elective trustee of the Australian Museum from 1862 and a trustee of the Free Public Library of New South Wales from 1870 and its president in 1885-90.

In March 1882 Stephens was privately appointed to the new chair of natural history at the University of Sydney and to the W. H. Hovell [q.v.] lectureship in geology and physical geography. His appointment was criticized as his academic qualifications were in classics and mathematics, but Alexander Oliver [q.v.] pointed out that Stephens had long and passionately pursued science as a hobby. Despite a lack of facilities and apparatus, he organized his department with characteristic speed and thoroughness. He devised a broad course and, as a member of the professorial board and the senate, worked with Professor Liversidge [q.v.] for the extension of scientific studies and the institution of a bachelor of science degree. In 1884-85 he was also acting professor of classics. He largely planned and developed the Macleay [q.v.] Museum. In 1890 the title of his chair was changed to geology and palaeontology. His academic contemporaries found him a man of 'rare candour, modest, unobtrusive, with a genial disposition'. A 'most instructive and delightful talker', his lectures were noted for 'his power of expressing his opinions'. He had also published several textbooks, two long articles in the *Sydney University Review* (1881-83) and a pamphlet *Literae Humaniores: A Letter to the Chancellor of the Sydney University concerning the literary side of the Arts Course* (Sydney, 1887).

Stephens died suddenly at his Darlinghurst home of acute nephritis on 22 November 1890 and was buried in the Anglican section of Rookwood cemetery. He was survived by his wife Anna Louise, née Daniell, whom he had married at St Mark's, Darling Point, on 8 July 1859, and by a son and a daughter Ethel, a skilful painter. His estate was sworn for probate at £14,400. In March 1891 his classical and scientific library of some 1431 books and nearly 200 pamphlets was bought by the Free Public Library. A portrait of Stephens by his daughter is owned by the University of Sydney and another by the Linnean Society in Sydney.

H. E. Barff, *A short historical account of the University of Sydney ... 1852-1902* (Syd, 1902); V&P (LA NSW), 1859-60, 4, 87, 1866, 2, 581; A. Oliver, 'On some recent appointments by the senate', *Syd Univ Review*, Apr 1882; P. J. Stanbury, Biology at the University of Sydney, 1882-1917 (held by Univ Syd Archives); W. J. Stephens testimonials (ML); One hundred years of geological science ... 1866-1966, *and* Senate and Board of Studies minutes (Univ Syd Archives).   CLIFF TURNEY

STEWART, JOHN (1810-1896), veterinary surgeon and politician, was born in October 1810 in Northumberland, England, son of Malcolm Stewart, estate agent, and his wife Elizabeth, née Scott. He graduated in veterinary science from the Royal (Dick) Veterinary College, Edinburgh, in 1827 and practised in Glasgow. In 1834-40 he was professor of veterinary medicine at the Andersonian University, Glasgow. In 1831 he published *Advice to Purchasers of Horses ...* and in 1838 *Stable Economy ...* Both ran to many editions in England and America and the latter was described a century later as 'one of the few veterinary classics'.

Leaving Glasgow in 1840 Stewart arrived in Sydney next year and set up practice. On 1 November 1842 at St James's Church he married Sarah Pringle, a native of Aberdeen, and took a fifteen-month break in 1845-46. He combined a horse bazaar with his work until 1852, when he retreated to Kiera Vale near Wollongong to provide a country upbringing for his young children. Active in local public life, he was a magistrate for a time, chairman of the Central Illawarra Municipal Council in 1860, a leader-writer for the *Illawarra Mercury* and a promoter of the Wollongong School of Arts and the Albert Memorial Hospital. A late convert to free selection before survey, in 1860 he lost the election for the Legislative Assembly seat of Illawarra. He ran again in 1864 as a supporter of (Sir) Charles Cowper [q.v.] against the conservative P. H. Osborne [q.v.]; despite support from influential townsmen he was defeated but he won a by-election in 1866. His three campaigns were marked by accusations from certain Protestant circles that he was irreligious; he had championed National schools, sought the abolition of the Upper House and of state aid to religion, and criticized the University of Sydney as impractical and a waste of money. In parliament he drew attention with attacks on its ceremony and 'wasteful' government expenditure on such things as pensions. He frequently jousted with opponents of (Sir) Henry Parkes's [q.v.] 1866 Public Schools Act. Rarely absent from debates, he possessed a dry sarcastic wit which he exercised frequently but never maliciously, and was a delight to parliamentary reporters.

In the panic after the attempted assassination of the duke of Edinburgh, Stewart was one of the few to keep his head and he opposed (Sir) James Martin's [q.v.] notorious Treason Felony Act. Nonetheless, his wit sometimes surrendered to his dislike of Roman Catholicism and he occasionally supported the Orangemen. A freethinker, he stressed the principles of moral enlightenment, backed eight-hour legislation to help self-education for working men, and supported Rev. James Greenwood's [q.v.] New South Wales Public School League. In 1869 his success as parliamentary spokesman for the ideas of the barrister T. J. Fisher, helped the setting up of the 1870 Law Reform Commission and led him to believe that he was qualified to speak on law reform, but he displayed at times 'an almost incredible ignorance' of his subject. He failed four times to carry his legal practitioners relief bill to destroy the privileges of the Bar, and also bills to reform the law on the custody of infants, married women's property, divorce and unlawful promises. His electoral popularity was precarious. Defeated in 1869, he was elected unopposed for Kiama in a by-election in 1871, holding his seat in 1872 and losing it in 1874. Despite his liberal principles he supported Martin in 1866-68 and 1870-72, but from 1872-74 he supported Parkes, with whom he was friendly. In 1879 Parkes had him appointed to the Legislative Council, where he remained until his retirement in 1895.

Stewart had removed to Sydney in 1866 and in 1872-82 practised as a veterinary surgeon in Darlinghurst Road. From 1873 he was a trustee of the Free Public Library. He died on 30 July 1896 of cerebral haemorrhage and exhaustion, and was buried in the Waverley cemetery. He was survived by his wife, three sons and a daughter. His estate was sworn for probate at £16,193.

J. F. Smithcors, *Evolution of the veterinary art* (Lond, 1958); 'Report on veterinary science and practice in Australia', *Veterinarian* (Lond), Sept 1881; *SMH*, 23 Apr 1845, 4 July 1846, 22 July, 17 Sept 1867, 19, 23 Mar, 15 Sept 1868, 22 Feb 1871; *Illawarra Mercury*, 4, 7, 12 Dec 1860, 6, 9 Dec 1864, 18 Sept 1866, 6 Aug 1896; *Protestant Standard*, 11 June, 3, 24 July 1869, 17 July, 27 Aug 1870; *Freeman's J* (Syd), 25 Feb, 4 May 1871, 26 Sept 1874; R. Parsons, Lawyers in the New South Wales parliament, 1870-1890 (Ph.D. thesis, Macquarie Univ, 1972); Parkes letters (ML).

MARK LYONS

STEWART, JOHN junior (1832-1904), veterinary surgeon, was born in Edinburgh, son of John Stewart, veterinary surgeon, and his wife Annie, née Robinson. Educated at the Royal (Dick) Veterinary College he gained the certificate of the Highland and Agricultural Society of Scotland. He became a member of the Royal College of Veterinary Surgeons and set up a 'business and practice' in Glasgow, but about 1860 migrated to New South Wales. At Campbelltown on 21 January 1862 he married Jessie, daughter of James Walker of Parramatta.

Stewart first practised at Morpeth but after a few months moved to Windsor where he established a veterinary hospital. According to his obituary in the *Hawkesbury Herald*, 26 February 1904, he was appointed an inspector of pleuro-pneumonia in cattle in 1862 and was asked by (Sir) John Robertson [q.v.] to report on the efficacy of inoculation against the disease; about 1863 during an outbreak of scab he became a sheep inspector. In 1865 he set up another veterinary hospital and a forge at Bathurst, which were at first successful but were abandoned in 1876 because of drought. About the same time his Windsor hospital was moved to Castlereagh Street, Sydney, where his eldest son John Malcolm joined him in practice. Reputedly veterinary inspector for the Agricultural Society of New South Wales, he was honorary veterinary surgeon and a committee-man of the Society for the Prevention of Cruelty to Animals. In 1877 in the Agricultural Society's *Journal* he published an article, 'Horses' Feet and Horseshoeing'. He became foundation president of the Veterinary Medical Association of New South Wales in 1894, the first successful veterinary organization in Australia and next year participated in the Department of Agriculture's conference of agricultural societies. He was an elder of the Windsor Presbyterian congregation.

Aged 72, Stewart died of diabetes at Church Street, Windsor, on 15 February 1904. Predeceased by his wife, he was survived by five sons and by three of his five daughters; his estate was valued for probate at £1952. Two of his sons became veterinary surgeons of whom the best known was James Douglas, who was lecturer in elementary science at the Sydney Technical College in the late 1890s and early 1900s, and professor of veterinary science at the University of Sydney in 1910-39.

Hawkesbury Herald, 26 Feb 1904; printed cat (ML).
J. C. BEARDWOOD
D. F. STEWART

STIRLING, EDMUND (1815-1897), printer and newspaper proprietor, was born on 19 August 1815 near Worstead, Norfolk, England, son of a naval officer who served with Nelson. According to family history, Stirling asked for his inheritance and sailed for New South Wales with a guardian in the *Edward Lombe* but was persuaded to land at Fremantle on 24 August 1830. He and his guardian helped a fellow passenger Charles Macfaull to plant the colony's first vines near Fremantle. In 1833 he, Macfaull and W. K. Shenton produced the colony's first printed newspaper, the *Fremantle Observer, Perth Gazette and Western Australian Journal*, on a tiny Ruthven press, now in the Fremantle Museum. In 1836 he married Ethel Read (d. 1887), who had reached the colony in the ill-fated *Rockingham*. They had five sons and six daughters.

In 1838 Stirling began a job printing business. In 1840, when the *Inquirer* was launched as the town's second weekly newspaper, he became principal compositor and printer, still carrying on his business. By May 1847 he had become sole owner of the *Inquirer*; his eldest son John joined him about 1863 and three other sons Horace, Frederick and Baldwin in 1878. While he was proprietor the *Inquirer* was a vigorous paper, keeping a close eye on local affairs and often clashing with authority. In January 1853 he noted in his diary, 'Another government prosecution commenced against the proprietor of the Inquirer which, after pending for several weeks, was, like a former one, abandoned'. The most important clash was that in 1870 in which he and John Stirling, with Arthur Shenton [q.v.] of the *West Australian Times*, were gaoled briefly after both papers had denounced a judgment by Chief Justice Burt [q.v.]; on publishing an abject apology they were released.

Stirling was interested in public works and was a member of the Perth Town Trust and later of the City Council. He was a director of the Geraldine Mining Co., launched in 1848, and his paper was the first to have a section devoted to mining. With Alexander Cumming, an auctioneer, he formed the West Australian Telegraph Co. in the late 1860s and in 1869 opened the first line between Perth and Fremantle, the government having supplied convict labour to erect the poles. He retired in April 1878. On 7 January 1889 he married a widow Emma Amelia Meares, née Wright, of York. He died of heart failure at York on 2 November 1897 and was buried in the Perth Anglican cemetery. His estate was sworn for probate at £2473.

Files of *Inquirer, Daily News, West Australian, Western Mail* (W.A. Newspaper Ltd, Battye Lib, Perth); family information.
O. K. BATTYE

STIRLING, Sir EDWARD CHARLES (1848-1919), surgeon, scientist and politician, and Sir JOHN LANCELOT (1849-1932), politician, were the sons of Edward Stirling (1804-1873) and his wife Harriett, née Taylor. Their father arrived in South Australia in 1839; he eventually bought the pastoral stations of Highland Valley in the Mount Lofty Ranges and Nalpa on Lake Alexandrina. In 1855-61 he was in partnership with T. Elder, R. Barr Smith [qq.v.] and John Taylor, as Elder, Stirling & Co., which financed the Wallaroo and Moonta copper mines. Appointed to the Legislative Council in 1855 he helped frame the Constitution and was a member of the new council in 1856-65. He died on 2 February 1873 in London. Two South Australian towns bear his name.

Edward Charles was born on 8 September 1848 at Strathalbyn, South Australia. Educated at the Collegiate School of St Peter and at Trinity College, Cambridge (B.A., 1870; M.A., 1873; M.B., 1874; M.D., 1880; Sc.D., 1910), he became a fellow of the Royal College of Surgeons in 1874 and was lecturer in physiology and assistant surgeon at St George's Hospital, London, and later surgeon at Belgrave Hospital for Children. Returning to South Australia in 1875 he married Jane, daughter of Joseph Gilbert [q.v.], on 27 June 1877, and took her to England for specialized medical treatment. In 1881 he settled permanently in South Australia where he became consulting surgeon to Adelaide Hospital, lecturer and later first professor of physiology at the University of Adelaide and a member of the University Council.

In 1884-87 Stirling was member for North Adelaide in the House of Assembly and in 1886 he introduced a bill to enfranchise women; but the South Australian Museum became his major life's work. He was its director in 1884-1912 and was largely responsible for its excellent collection of Aboriginal cultural specimens. In 1888 he received from central Australia a specimen of the previously unknown marsupial mole which he named, described and illustrated in the 1890-91 *Transactions and Proceedings of the Royal Society of South Australia*.

Stirling crossed the continent from Darwin to Adelaide with the earl of Kintore in 1891, collecting ethnological and zoological specimens. In 1893 he travelled to Lake Callabonna where a field party, organized by him, was excavating numerous remains of the giant marsupial Diprotodon. In the same year he was made a fellow of the Royal Society, London, and created C.M.G. He was medical officer and anthropologist with the W. A. Horn expedition which, in 1894, made a comprehensive survey of the country between Oodnadatta and the MacDonnell Ranges. He wrote the extensive anthropological section published as part of the four volumes that recorded the expedition's discoveries. His work on the Diprotodon culminated in a full description of its skeletal anatomy in the *Memoirs* of the local Royal Society in 1899, and the complete reconstruction of its skeleton in 1906. Casts of the latter are still the only articulated examples to be found in museums in Australia and abroad.

Actively associated with the Public Library, the Art Gallery, the Zoological Society, the Adelaide Hospital and the State Children's Council, Stirling was dean of the Faculty of Medicine in 1908-19 and president of the Society for the Prevention of Cruelty to Animals in South Australia. He participated in the long struggle to secure Flinders Chase on Kangaroo Island as a sanctuary. In 1917 Stirling was knighted. He died on 20 March 1919 at his home St Vigeans, Mount Lofty, where he had established a famous garden, survived by his wife and five daughters; two sons predeceased him. His estate was sworn for probate at £65,700.

John Lancelot was born on 5 November 1849 at Strathalbyn and followed his brother to St Peter's. After two years on the Continent he went up to Trinity College, Cambridge (B.A., LL.B., 1871), where he won a blue for athletics. In 1870 and 1872 he won the amateur hurdles championship of England. At 23 he was called to the Bar at the Inner Temple. He returned to South Australia in 1876, and with his brother bred merino sheep; he also bred Ayrshire cattle and horses on the family properties. On 12 December 1882 he married Florence Marion, daughter of Sir William Milne [q.v.]. He was a member of the House of Assembly for Mount Barker in 1881-87 and Gumeracha in 1888-90, and in 1891-1932 was a member for the Southern Districts in the Legislative Council and was president in 1901-32. Though an unexceptional speak-

er he was respected for his ability. He was appointed K.C.M.G. in 1909.

Stirling was director of the Beltana and Mutooroo Pastoral companies, the Australian Mutual Provident Society, the Wallaroo and Moonta Mining and Smelting Co. and the Alliance Insurance Co. He introduced polo to South Australia and captained a team that twice defeated Victoria. He was the steward of several racing clubs, and was once master of the Adelaide hounds. A member of the University of Adelaide Council, he was also president of the Royal Agricultural and Horticultural Society of South Australia, the Society for the Prevention of Cruelty to Animals, the Pastoralists' Association of South Australia, and the Zoological and Acclimatization Society. He died on 24 May 1932 at Strathalbyn, survived by his wife, three sons and two daughters.

H. T. Burgess (ed), *Cyclopedia of South Australia*, 1 (Adel, 1908); H. M. Hale, *The first hundred years of the South Australian Museum* (Adel, 1956); R. Cockburn, *Pastoral pioneers of South Australia*, 1 (Adel, 1925); *Roy Soc SA, Trans*, 43 (1919); D. Scott, 'Woman suffrage: The movement in Australia', *JRAHS*, 53 (1967); *Advertiser* (Adel), 21 Mar 1919, 25 May 1932.   HANS MINCHAM

STOW, RANDOLPH ISHAM (1828-1878), judge, JEFFERSON PICKMAN (1830-1908), editor and magistrate, and AUGUSTINE (1833-1903), public servant, were the sons of Rev. Thomas Quinton Stow [q.v.] and his wife Elizabeth, née Eppes. In 1837 the family arrived in South Australia in the *Hartley*. The brothers were educated by their father and at D. Wylie's school.

Randolph was born on 17 December 1828 at Framlingham, Suffolk, England. He was articled in Adelaide to the legal firm of Bartley and Bakewell, who later took him into partnership. In 1854 he married Frances Mary MacDermott. He went into practice on his own account in 1859 and later was a partner with T. B. Bruce and F. Ayers. He built up a large practice and for many years was regarded as the leader of the Bar. A brilliant advocate, clear-thinking and industrious, in 1865 he was one of the first three barristers appointed Q.C. in South Australia. He displayed courage and determination in brushes with Judge Boothby [q.v.], who challenged his right to appear as Q.C. and on one occasion threatened to commit him for contempt of court.

Stow was a member of the Legislative Assembly for West Torrens in 1861-62,

Victoria in 1863-65, East Torrens in 1866-68 and Light in 1873-75 and was attorney-general in three ministries. In 1864 he brought down the Ayers [q.v.] government with a no-confidence motion but was then unable to form a cabinet. In 1875 he was appointed a judge of the Supreme Court and next year he was deeply disappointed when S. J. Way was appointed chief justice to succeed Sir Richard Hanson [q.v.].

Stow died of atrophy of the liver on 17 September 1878, survived by his wife and six of their seven children. He was given a state funeral and his estate was sworn for probate at £2500. Despite his brief judicial service he was regarded by his contemporaries as a great judge. Way considered that his forensic gifts had 'never been surpassed in Australia and would have gained him distinction in any part of the world'; Sir John Downer described him as 'one of the greatest Judges Australia ever had, having a commanding presence, a striking voice, unusual swiftness in comprehension with an immense combination of eloquence and power'. After his death £500 was raised by public subscription to provide annual Stow prizes and scholarships for the LL.B. course at the University of Adelaide.

Jefferson was born on 4 September 1830 at Buntingford, Hertfordshire. In 1850 he worked on a farm near Adelaide and on 30 October 1851 married Elizabeth Manning. Widowed soon after, in 1854 he went to the Victorian gold diggings, but soon returned to South Australia and married Jourdiana Maria Brodie on 1 February 1855. In 1858, after a further short residence in Victoria, he started an auction business at Gawler in South Australia; it was not very profitable and in 1862 he tried his hand as a journalist and wrote a series of articles for the *Critic*. He went with B. T. Finniss's [q.v.] survey party to the Northern Territory in 1864 and next year embarked with W. McMinn [q.v.] and five companions at Adam Bay in a small open boat, the *Forlorn Hope*, in which they sailed to Champion Bay, Western Australia. Next year he published an account of the voyage. In September 1865 he became a reporter for the *South Australian Advertiser* and editor in 1876. At the request of the government he wrote, in 1883, *South Australia: its History, Production, and Natural Resources* for the Calcutta exhibition. Next year he was appointed a special magistrate, and served first at Naracoorte and later at Mount Gambier and Port Pirie. He retired in 1904 and died on 4 May 1908, survived by his wife, two sons and five daughters. His estate was sworn for probate at £620.

Augustine was born on 3 August 1833 at Halstead, Essex. He was a member of the Legislative Assembly for West Torrens in 1862-65 and for Flinders in 1866-68, a member of the Legislative Council in 1869-75 and chief secretary in the Strangways [q.v.] government for a few days in May 1870. He was associate to the judges of the Supreme Court in 1877-83 and registrar of probates and chief clerk of the Supreme Court in 1883-1903. He also held office as public trustee, commissioner of inland revenue, curator of convict estates and deputy registrar of companies. His main outside interest was the Congregational Church. He was a deacon of the Stow Memorial Church and in 1880 was the first lay chairman of the Congregational Union of South Australia. He was a member of the board of governors of the Public Library, Art Gallery and Museum. On 10 September 1867 he had married Elizabeth Augusta, daughter of Robert Frew of Greenhill. Stow died on 29 May 1903 and his estate was sworn for probate at £1220.

E. Ward, *The vineyards and orchards of South Australia* (Adel, 1862); G. C. Morphett, *Rev. Thos. Quinton Stow* (Adel, 1948); A. J. Hannan, *The life of Chief Justice Way* (Syd, 1960); *Public Service Review* (SA), Dec 1902; *Advertiser* (Adel), 18 Sept 1878; *Register* (Adel), 18 Sept 1878, 3 Aug 1915; *Chronicle* (Adel), 20 Oct 1906.   D. BRUCE ROSS

STRACHAN, JOHN (1846-1922), shipmaster and explorer, was born in Montrose, Scotland, son of John Strachan, engineer, and his wife Sarah, née Delarne. His family moved to England in 1853; he studied engineering but ran away to sea, served the North in the American civil war, sailed in the India-Japan trade, went whaling in the Arctic, was naval adviser to the feudal Japanese prince of Higo till 1869, and managed guano workings on Baker Island near Hawaii. As mate of the *Rita* he arrived in Tasmania on 25 April 1872 and established country lodges for the Good Templars society. He married Alice Sarah Henrietta Plummer at Launceston on 3 March 1875, and managed guano workings at Bird Island in the Coral Sea for the Anglo-Australian Guano Co. From there, he visited Torres Strait in the *Alice Maude* in September.

Strachan settled in Sydney and in 1884 replaced G. E. Morrison as correspondent for the *Age* in New Guinea. With four companions he entered the Mai Kassa River on 6 May and, after much fighting and the loss of one man, returned to Saibai Island on 3

June. His reports aroused violent criticism, especially of his use of an improvised torpedo. Supported from Sydney he sailed with eighteen men on 17 September in the *Herald*, followed the Mai Kassa again for 100 miles, returned to the coast and explored the Gulf of Papua. Back in Sydney on 20 January 1886 his claim was disallowed for 500,000 acres of the area explored. He lost on a cargo to the Kimberley goldfield, traded in the Dutch East Indies, explored round McClure's Gulf in Dutch New Guinea and returned to Cape York on 2 March 1887. He took his claim to England but was described by the Colonial Office as 'excitable and rather ignorant'. His book *Explorations and Adventures in New Guinea* (1888) was ridiculed by geographers.

Strachan returned to Sydney in 1889. In his *Envy* he traded for some years round Borneo and the Dutch East Indies. In 1896 he sued the Launceston *Daily Telegraph* because of a story it had published about his early life and won £2000. Defeated by W. M. Hughes in the New South Wales general election of 1898, he is in a chapter of Hughes's *Crust and Crusades* (Sydney, 1947) as 'Captain Alistair'. Imprisoned for debt in North Borneo in November 1902 he pleaded in vain for Commonwealth intervention in his pamphlet *Capt. John Strachan JP and the British North Borneo Company* (Sydney, 1903). He lost to Joseph Cook in the Parramatta election of that year.

Strachan lost a High Court action in 1906 against the Commonwealth for detention of his ship at Daru in Papua, and in 1909 was charged by the Germans with illegal recruiting in New Guinea. He then retired, wrote an anti-German pamphlet and in 1916 presided over an anti-German league. A last political fling for Parramatta in 1917 brought 26 votes. Survived by one son he died of chronic cystitis in Sydney on 30 August 1922, aged 76, and was buried in the Presbyterian section of Rookwood cemetery.

Strachan's long letters appear in many archive repositories. In his forty years in the news he was frequently described as an adventurer but he was no scoundrel.

Cyclopedia of N.S.W. (Syd, 1907); A. Wichmann, *Nova Guinea*, 2 (Leiden, 1910); *Petermanns Geographische Mitteilungen*, 1886-88; *Scottish Geog Mag*, 1888; W. E. L. H. Crowther, 'The development of the guano trade from Hobart Town in the fifties and sixties', Roy Soc Tas, *Procs*, 1938; *Argus*, 18 June 1884, 19 June 1885; *Queenslander*, 16 Apr 1891; *Examiner* (Launceston), 10-12 Sept 1896; *Brisbane Courier*, 11-31 May 1909; 'Adventures in Australian seas', *Lone Hand*, Feb 1913; SMH,. 8,
15 Jan 1916; Griffith papers (Dixson Lib, Syd); H. Poett diary (NL); CO 422/4/18, 39, 232, 7/645.
　　　　　　　　　　　　　　　H. J. GIBBNEY

STRAHAN, SIR GEORGE CUMINE (1838-1887), governor, was born on 9 December 1838 at Fraserburgh, Aberdeenshire, Scotland, son of Rev. W. D. Strahan. Educated at the Royal Military College, Woolwich, in 1857 he entered the Royal Artillery as a lieutenant. He was aide-de-camp in 1859-64 to Mr Gladstone, lord high commissioner of the Ionian Islands, to his successor Sir Henry Storks, and to governors in Malta in 1864-68. He acted for a time as chief secretary of Malta. was colonial secretary in the Bahamas from 1868 and acting governor in 1872-73. Promoted captain in 1871, he was administrator of Lagos in 1873-74, governor of the Gold Coast in 1874-76 and of the Windward Islands in 1876-80. He had been promoted major in 1874 and made C.M.G. in 1875. In 1877 he married Catherine Livingstone, daughter of Robert Reade of New York; she died in England without issue in less than a year.

Appointed governor of Tasmania in April 1880, Strahan was created K.C.M.G. in May. Before taking up the post he acted as administrator of the Cape of Good Hope and high commissioner of South Africa until the arrival of Sir Hercules Robinson. After much criticism of the delay, Strahan eventually arrived in Hobart in the *Southern Cross* on 7 December 1881 and was sworn in the same day. He came with the reputation of an able, far-sighted and popular colonial administrator; despite reports of indifferent health, attributed to long residence in the tropics, he quickly displayed his energy and range of interests. The day he arrived he visited the hospital, and soon after was reported at Elwick races, St David's Cathedral for divine service and the annual meeting of the Council of Education; by mid-December a country tour included Launceston and Longford.

In January 1883 Strahan authorized the establishment of a royal commission to inquire into public education in Tasmania and the neighbouring colonies; its findings led to important changes. He was also responsible for convening and formally opening the first meeting of the Federal Council of Australasia, held at Hobart in 1886. Attentive to rural industries, he was patron of the Southern Tasmanian Agricultural and Pastoral Society and travelled widely in the colony, informing himself on the welfare of the settlers and the need for public works and services to improve their lot. He was president of the Royal Society of Tasmania, but it was a traditional appointment which appears not to have attracted his active concern. Interested in hospitals and other public institutions he was described as 'generous in his time and charity'.

Before Strahan's term expired he was given leave to return to England. After a round of farewells that demonstrated his popularity, he left Launceston for Melbourne on 28 October, attended the Melbourne Cup, and sailed for England on 4 November in the *Massilia*. He died at Bournemouth on 17 February 1887 before he could take up his new office as governor of Hong Kong. A few weeks earlier he had been appointed G.C.M.G. Strahan, on the west coast of Tasmania, was named after him.

Cyclopedia of Tasmania, 1 (Hob, 1900); V&P (HA Tas), 1880, 1882, 1884, 1886, (LC Tas), 1886; *The Times*, 12-13 July 1878, 19 Feb 1887; *Mercury*, 23 Apr, 23 June 1880, 1, 7-8, 12-13, 15 Dec 1881, 13-14, 26, 29 Oct 1886, 21 Feb 1887; *Australasian*, 3 Dec 1881, 22, 29 Jan, 26 Feb 1887.   NEIL SMITH

STRANGWAYS, HENRY BULL TEMPLAR (1832-1920), lawyer and politician, was born in Shapwick, Somerset, England, eldest son of Henry Bull Strangways, military officer. As a boy he visited an uncle Thomas Bewes Strangways in South Australia. Back in England he studied law, entered the Middle Temple on 14 November 1851 and was called to the Bar on 6 June 1856. He returned to Adelaide in early 1857, practised as a solicitor and was admitted to the South Australian Bar on 8 August 1861. On 10 January he had married Maria Cordelia, daughter of Henry Wigley, stipendiary magistrate.

In March 1857 Strangways had failed to win a seat in the first elective Legislative Council. Elected to the House of Assembly for Encounter Bay in 1858, he held the seat until 1862 and was member for West Torrens in 1862-71. His first move towards office in 1859 had received a cool reception and he 'declined the call' to form a cabinet, but was a member of seven ministries in 1860-70: he was attorney-general in 1860-61, minister for crown lands and immigration in 1861-65 and premier and attorney-general in 1868-70, when much of his legislation was defeated. In February 1870 he obtained a dissolution; the elections brought sweeping changes and on 30 May his reconstructed ministry was overwhelmed.

Strangways had achieved one notable legislative success. From 1857, when the parliament had been granted control of crown lands, many attempts were made to obtain satisfactory land legislation. Strangways introduced a bill for the Act which now bears his name, and after much conflict with pastoralists in 1868, he carried it in January 1869. The legislation provided for the creation of agricultural areas and credit purchases of up to 640 acres, with a down payment of 25 per cent and four years to pay. The *South Australian Register* acclaimed him as 'St. George of Land Reformers'. He was also prominent in initiating railways in South Australia and the overland telegraph. Supporting exploration and development, he discovered and named the Gawler River. Mayor of Glenelg in 1862-66, he also continued to practise his profession.

In February 1871 Strangways returned to England on private business, formally resigning from parliament in July. On his departure the *Register* noted his arbitrary handling of the parliament. He was remembered by colleagues and the press for his 'powers of administration' and devotion to the 'work of legislation'. Criticized for his 'hostility to individuals and to the government of the day', he was praised as a 'progressive politician, a clear thinker and a man of fine judgement'.

Living in London and on the family estate in Somerset, Strangways became a justice of the peace. He appeared before the judicial committee of the Privy Council, and from 1875 until his death was a resident fellow of the Royal Colonial Institute. On 8 June 1875 he read a paper to the institute, 'Forty Years Since, and Now'; published in the *Proceedings*, it reviewed the progress of Britain's colonial empire from 1835. In 1877-87 he was a member of the council of the institute. He was also a member of the Windham Club. Survived by his wife and daughter, he died of senile decay on 10 February 1920 and was buried in the churchyard of the family chapel at Shapwick. His estate in South Australia was sworn for probate at £3527 and in England at £22,713.

His portrait is held by the Glenelg City Council; the town of Strangways, Lake Strangways and Strangways River are named after him.

J. Foster, *Men-at-the-Bar* (Lond, 1885); E. Hodder, *The history of South Australia* (Lond, 1893); J. J. Pascoe (ed), *History of Adelaide and vicinity* (Adel, 1901); K. R. Bowes, *Land settlement in South Australia 1857-1890* (Adel, 1968); PD (SA), 1871, 5; Roy Colonial Inst, *Yearbook*, 1912; *Register* (Adel), 28 Feb 1871; *Observer* (Adel), 19 Feb 1907; *The Times*, 14 Feb 1920.   DEAN JAENSCH

STRELE, ANTON (1825-1897), Jesuit priest, was born on 23 August 1825 at Nassereit, Austria. Educated at the Jesuit Gymnasium, Innsbruck, he entered the Society of Jesus at Gratz on 14 August 1845 and took his first vows in 1849. He completed his studies in France and was ordained priest at Laval on 23 September 1854. He was then appointed to the Jesuit colleges at Mariastein, Linz, and in 1859 to the College of Nobles at Kalksburg. He volunteered for the Austrian Jesuit mission in South Australia and sailed from London in April 1867. He reached Sevenhill on 22 December.

In March 1868 Strele was appointed the first Jesuit master of novices in Australia, an office he held intermittently until 1882. As superior of the mission in 1870-73 he supervised the expansion of Jesuit work in Adelaide and Sevenhill, the building of a separate residence at Georgetown and the establishment of a Polish settlement at Hill River. In 1873-80 he was rector of St Aloysius College, Sevenhill, lectured in philosophy and also undertook pastoral work around Clare, Farrell Flat and Manoora, where he built the church and presbytery. As superior again in 1880-82 he negotiated the transfer of some Jesuit parishes to local diocesan control and made arrangements to found the Northern Territory mission. To launch the mission he toured South Australia and Victoria seeking funds. With rare foresight he began to study Aboriginal lore.

On 2 October 1882 Strele and three confrères opened the first station at Rapid Creek near Palmerston (Darwin). He founded a second on the Daly River in 1886, and a third at Serpentine Lagoon in 1889. The mission was always short of money and in 1887-89 he toured the United States of America and Europe to raise funds. When Salvado [q.v.] resigned his nominal office of bishop of Port Victoria and Palmerston, Strele was appointed administrator apostolic of the diocese on 1 August 1888. He resisted the promotion in vain and moved to Palmerston where he tended the white Catholic population; he secured sites for churches and schools there as well as in Pine Creek, Burrundie and the new settlement. He remained superior to the three mission stations until 6 February 1891. The rigours of the life and his responsibilities told on Strele and he was forced to return south in October 1892, broken in health. He died at St Aloysius College on 15 December 1897, and was buried in the crypt of the church. His estate was sworn for probate at £90.

The breadth of vision of the Jesuit Aboriginal mission was due to Strele's painstaking efforts to accommodate as much of the find-ings of the early writers on Aboriginal anthropology as he could. Needing finance and deeply committed to the success of the mission, he often refused to admit failures that were obvious and maintained agricultural ventures that were patently not viable.

P. F. Moran, *History of the Catholic Church in Australasia* (Syd, 1895); *Our Australian missions* (Melb, 1899); E. Bülow, *Hundert Lebensbilder aus der Österreichisch–Ungarischen Provinz der Gesellschaft Jesu* (Vienna, 1902); Society of Jesus, *Centenary in Australia* (Norwood, 1948); G. J. O'Kelly, The Jesuit mission stations in the Northern Territory, 1882-1899 (B. A. Hons thesis, Monash Univ, 1967); Austro-Hungarian Mission in NT, Records (Jesuit Provincial Archives, Hawthorn, Vic).

G. J. O'KELLY

STREMPEL, CARL FRIEDRICH ADOLPH (1831-1908), Lutheran pastor, was born on 10 September 1831 at Posen, Prussia, third son of Carl Ferdinand Strempel, government waterways inspector, and his wife Marie, née Crzikacrzinska. Educated at a private school and then at the Friedrich Wilhelm Gymnasium in Posen, Strempel and a brother and sister migrated to South Australia with Pastor Phillipe Oster and his family, arriving in the *Gellert* on 21 December 1847. His parents and the rest of the family followed in 1851.

Strempel and his friend Phillip Jacob Oster [q.v.] enrolled at Lobethal College where, under the instruction and guidance of Pastor G. D. Fritzsche [q.v. Kavel], they passed a preliminary examination in 1851 and matriculated in 1852. They studied theology, graduated from the college and on 29 August 1855 were ordained. Strempel became pastor of the Hahndorf parish on 21 October. Next year he was elected to the Church Council and was its secretary for forty years. On 5 May 1858 he married Marie Charlotte Friederike, daughter of Rev. H. Meyer of Bethany, South Australia. For the next forty-five years he continued to serve his parish as well as the congregations on Yorke Peninsula and at Mount Gambier; he also cared for Lutherans in Melbourne and Western Australia.

In 1864 Strempel was appointed chairman of a committee to look into the establishment of a teachers' training college. He became director of the boarding section of Hahndorf College after it opened in 1876 in the buildings of Hahndorf Academy, where he had been Latin and Greek master. After the college was sold in 1883 to meet its debts he continued to train teachers for Church schools. He was co-editor of the

Lutherische Kirchenbote für Australien in 1874-80. Having been a leading member of most church boards and commissions, and naturalized by 1872, he was president of the Evangelical Lutheran Church of Australia in 1897-1903. He was a faithful and loving pastor to his parishioners and often used his wide medical knowledge for their benefit. At his jubilee in 1905 they presented him with two addresses and a purse of sovereigns. An honest and dependable counsellor, he was an able theologian and a conscientious church official and leader. He died on 20 January 1908 survived by seven of his fifteen children. He was buried in the Hahndorf cemetery.

A. Brauer, *Under the Southern Cross* (Adel, 1956); *Lutherische Kirchenbote für Australien,* 35 (1908); *Lutheran Almanac* (Adel), 1955; *Register* (Adel), 22 Jan 1908; C. F. A. Strempel papers, Church Council and other minutes (Lutheran Church Archives, Adel).

F. J. H. BLAESS*

STRETCH, THEODORE CARLOS BENONI (1817-1899), Anglican clergyman, was born on 11 February 1817 at Worcester, Worcestershire, England, elder son of John Cliffe Stretch, rector of St Swithin's, and his wife Elizabeth, née Long. Educated at Worcester College, Oxford (B.A., 1841; M.A., 1844), he was made deacon in 1841 and ordained priest next year by Bishop Henry Pepys of Worcester. After curacies in Warwickshire at Wishaw (1841-42) and Harborough Magna (1842-44), he served as vicar of Potterspury, Northamptonshire (1844-51), acting also as Midlands Association secretary of the Church Missionary Society in 1848-51.

Stretch arrived in Victoria in 1852 and in July was appointed by Bishop Perry [q.v.] to Geelong as minister, first of the suburban and district and then of the town churches and finally in 1855-63 of St Paul's alone. In 1854 he was collated as archdeacon of Geelong with responsibility for the visitation and oversight of the Ballarat goldfields. He is remembered as the principal founder of Geelong Grammar School: at his instigation in 1855 G. O. Vance [q.v.], his curate at St Paul's, opened the private school that preceded the public school and Stretch acted as chairman of its trustees. He was in England when the school had to close, but on his return in 1862 he helped collect sufficient funds to enable it to reopen under J. B. Wilson [q.v.].

Stretch transferred to Sale as incumbent and archdeacon in 1863, was then appointed archdeacon of Geelong (but resident in Ballarat) in 1866-69 and archdeacon of Ballarat and Hamilton in 1869-75. A superb horseman, Stretch covered his vast archdeaconries; he visited every house and cabin he came to, held meetings and services in stations, schoolrooms, stores and inns, and collected donations. In 1872-73 he canvassed the colony to raise the endowment for a second Victorian bishopric at Ballarat. He was well fitted to fill the position but from the first declined lest he appear to be working for his own advantage. Instead, in August 1875 he installed Samuel Thornton [q.v.] as first bishop of Ballarat.

Stretch expected to remain in the new diocese but, apart from a brief and vigorous locumcy at Hamilton where he arranged the building of the present church, no suitable work was found for him. He returned to Melbourne in March 1876 and accepted the cure of Holy Trinity, Balaclava, a rising suburb. Two years later he became administrator of James Moorhouse's [q.v.] 'Bishop of Melbourne's Fund', was assistant to the archdeacon of Melbourne in 1877-87, rural dean of Melbourne South in 1877 and canon of Melbourne in 1879. He was responsible for church extension and development in Gippsland and northern Victoria as well as in the metropolitan area. From 1887 until he retired in 1894 he was archdeacon of Melbourne and Geelong.

Although essentially a man of action, Stretch edited the *Church of England Record* in 1855-60 and maintained a lifelong interest in classical authors, especially Horace. His churchmanship was broadminded Evangelical; laity and readers responded to his positive leadership. His geniality and dry humour belied his military appearance and commended him to a large circle of friends. He delighted in playing whist, but 'his grandchildren in his old age had to stack the family cards to protect him from sleeplessness occasioned by a loss'. He died on 12 April 1899 and was buried in the Geelong eastern cemetery. On 3 February 1842 he had married Martha Butler (d. 2 May 1891). He was survived by two of his five sons and three of his four daughters. His estate was sworn for probate at £1560. There is a portrait by G. A. J. Webb in the Chapter House of St Paul's Cathedral, Melbourne. His nephew, John Francis Stretch (1855-1919), became bishop of Newcastle.

G. Goodman, *The church in Victoria during the episcopate of Charles Perry* (Melb. 1892); P. L. Brown. *Geelong Grammar School* (Geelong, 1970); *Geelong Grammar School Q,* April 1899; *Church of England Messenger* (Vic), 1 May 1899.

JAMES GRANT

STRICKLAND, SIR EDWARD (1821-1889), army officer, was born on 7 August 1821 at Loughglynn House, County Roscommon, Ireland, third son of Jarrard Edward Strickland (1782-1844) of the East India Co., and his wife Anne, née Cholmley; he was the uncle of Sir Gerald Strickland, first and last Baron Strickland of Sizergh Castle, Kendal, Westmorland, England. Educated at Stonyhurst College, Lancashire, he joined the Commissariat Department on 15 February 1838 as a clerk and served in Canada in 1838-39. From January 1840 to December 1841 he was stationed in New South Wales; on 26 December 1840 he was promoted to deputy-assistant-commissary-general; in 1842-44 he served in Van Diemen's Land, and in 1844-60 in Malta, Turkey, Greece and the Middle East. In the Crimean war he received the Crimean medal with clasp and the Turkish medal. In 1860 he wrote Note on the reorganization of the British Army (London) in which he urged certain reforms including the creation of a military board and the post of chief of staff. After acting as the British member of the Joint Financial Commission of Enquiry on Greece he published Greece: its condition, prospects, and Resources (London, 1863).

Appointed deputy-commissary-general, ranking with colonel, on 8 September 1861, Strickland was in Melbourne in 1863-64 and in New Zealand in 1864-67. In the Maori war he received the New Zealand medal and was made a C. B. After service in Nova Scotia he was in Malta in 1874-76, and the Cape of Good Hope in 1877-79. He was appointed K. C. B. for his service at the Cape and Natal during the Zulu wars. Promoted commissary-general, ranking with major-general, on 23 November 1878, he served in Ireland as senior commissariat officer in 1880-81 until he retired on 8 August.

Strickland went to live in Sydney where he published, among other papers, Lecture on our South African Colonies (1882) and Letters Embodying Suggestions for a Volunteer Force in New South Wales (1883) in which he advocated 'an Australian Wimbledon' modelled on the ancient Olympic Games. In a letter to the Sydney Morning Herald on 12 February 1885 he suggested sending a contingent to the Sudan. An intimate of W. B. Dalley [q.v.], in 1884 he had presented to Governor Loftus the thanks of Sydney Catholics for inviting Archbishop Moran to Government House. Elected a fellow of the Royal Geographic Society of London in 1860, he was vice-president of the Geographical Society of Australasia, a founder and president of the society's New South Wales branch, presi-

dent of the Australian Geographical Conference in 1884 and vice-president of the Australasian Association for the Advancement of Science. He helped promote Captain H. C. Everill's expedition to New Guinea in 1885. He died in Sydney on 18 July 1889 and was buried in the Catholic section of Gore Hill cemetery.

Strickland was twice married. First, on 18 November 1841 at St Mary's Cathedral and then at St James's, Sydney, to Georgina Frances (d. 1876), second daughter of F. A. Hely [q.v.]; second, on 29 January 1877 at The Oratory, London, to Frances Mary, only daughter of General John Tattan Brown-Grieve of Orde House, Northumberland. His only child, Fanny Cecelia (1844-1922), married Rev. Percival Fiennis Swann, rector of Brandsby, Yorkshire. The Strickland River in New Guinea is named after him.

H. Hornyold, Genealogical memoirs of the family of Strickland of Sizergh (Kendal, 1928); SMH, 19, 22 July, 31 Dec 1889; The Times, 20 July 1889; WO 25/3921.   G. P. WALSH

STRICKLAND, WILLIAM HENRY JOHN (1841-1927), hotelkeeper and businessman, was born on 6 October 1841 in Perth, Western Australia, eldest son of Henry Robert Strickland and his wife Mary Ann, née Hokin. Henry had arrived in 1830 under Thomas Peel's [q.v.] settlement scheme; after various jobs he acquired an interest in the whaling industry and in 1857 became manager of the Freemasons' Hotel, Perth.

Educated at the Perth Boys' School, Strickland was its first dux. He left at 13 and joined the large trading firm of R. Habgood. On 17 April 1862 at St George's Church of England he married Margaret Crosset. He was licensee of the Shamrock Hotel in 1863-66 and made it a fashionable meeting place for young people. For the next four years he held the licence of the Freemasons' Hotel, Albany. When his wife, who had borne him two sons, died in 1870 he returned to Perth to help his father manage the United Services Hotel, which had been left to William by H. L. Cole in 1866. On 22 September 1875 he married Henrietta Bell, daughter of Samuel Craig, licensee of the Castle Hotel, York.

In 1896 Strickland retired from the hotel trade to pursue other business interests. He was a substantial shareholder in the Stanley (Swan) Brewery, and was one of the founders as well as the chairman of directors of the Perth Gas Co. He was also a director of the Swan River Shipping Co. and was associated with insurance, trading and mining interests. Devout, he read the Bible daily but seldom attended church services. He left the colony only once for a short trip to Adelaide. He was a foundation member of the Volunteer Corps and an active Freemason, and as chairman of the West Australian Turf Club he was well known for his interest in racing, as well as in hunting, shooting and fishing. He built up his wealth by a keen business sense and by taking advantage of gold rush prosperity.

Strickland died at his residence in St George's Terrace, Perth, on 8 July 1927, survived by six sons and four daughters, and was buried in the Anglican section of the Karrakatta cemetery. His estate was sworn for probate at £11,766.

J. S. Battye (ed), *Cyclopedia of Western Australia*, 2 (Adel, 1913); *West Australian*, 9 July 1927; *Western Mail* (Perth), 14 July 1927; *Daily News*, 25 Jan 1960; information from Miss I. B. Clark, West Perth.   E. ZALUMS

STRONG, CHARLES (1844-1942), clergyman, was born on 26 September 1844 at Dailly, Ayrshire, Scotland, third son of Rev. David Strong (1803-1855) and his wife Margaret Paterson, née Roxburgh. After schooling at Ayr and Glasgow academies he studied arts and divinity at the University of Glasgow in 1859-64 (hon. LL.D., 1887) where, influenced by Rev. John Caird, he rejected the Calvinist scholasticism of his day and adopted a liberal, Broad Church theology. In 1865-66 he travelled on the Continent as a private tutor, and in 1866-68 led a mission to the Dalmellington ironworks, Ayr. He was licensed to the presbytery of Glasgow, ordained to the Old West Kirk, Greenock, in 1868 and was minister to Anderston parish church, Glasgow, in 1871-75. In 1872 he married Janet Julia Fullarton, daughter of Archibald Fairrie Denniston, a Greenock solicitor; they had three daughters and five sons.

In May 1875 Strong was chosen to replace I. Hetherington [q.v.] at Scots Church, Melbourne; he arrived with his family on 23 August. His success as pastor, preacher, liberal theological teacher and social reformer brought him prominence, but he soon aroused suspicion and hostility among a powerful section of the Presbyterian Church. His clerical opponents were alarmed by his essays that appeared between January 1878 and December 1879 in the liberal *Presbyterian Review* (edited by Rev. William Henderson [q.v.]), and by an article on the atonement in the *Victorian Review* in 1880; his worship and catechetical innovations, his advocacy of reform of the Westminster Confession, as well as his outspoken condemnation of social evils encouraged them to attack his orthodoxy at the Melbourne presbytery in March-April 1881 : as a result he was instructed to change the emphasis of his preaching. Facing continuing friction with the presbytery, aware of his intellectual isolation and desiring to avoid serious divisions in the Church, he tendered his resignation on 8 August. At the request of the church officers and congregation he agreed instead to take six months leave. However, an incautious speech by J. C. Stewart, a supporter and elder of Scots Church, rekindled attacks on him; amid the turmoil he left his family in Melbourne and visited Scotland in March-October 1882.

On his return Strong supported the opening of the Public Library and Art Gallery on Sundays and was admonished by the presbytery. In August 1883 he was attacked for failing as chairman to register dissent from G. Higinbotham's [q.v.] lecture on 'Science and Religion'. The presbytery threatened him with a libel for heresy and asked the General Assembly to intervene. He resigned from Scots Church in September and prepared to leave Victoria. The assembly delayed the case until 14 November, when Strong was being farewelled by a huge crowd at the Melbourne Town Hall and presented with a cheque for £3000; at the meeting he declined an invitation to attend the assembly and affirm his orthodoxy, and in a letter he described its proceedings as unconstitutional and illegal. He sailed on 15 November and next day the assembly declared him to be no longer a minister of the Presbyterian Church of Victoria.

In November 1884 Strong returned to Melbourne. At the Temperance Hall, Russell Street, he ministered to a congregation largely composed of religious liberals and ex-members and adherents of Scots Church. In November 1885 the Australian Church, a free religious fellowship, was founded and he was invited to be its first minister. The foundation stone of a large new church was laid in 1887.

Passionately concerned for his fellow men, Strong continued his work for the underprivileged. In 1880 he had been active in the Australian Health Society, and that year was president of the Convalescent Aid Society which was largely supported by Scots Church. He was a member of the Society for the Promotion of Morality, and with G. Coppin [q.v.] promoted model lodging-houses in 1883. Interested in education, he was a member of the council of

Scotch College and in 1880 of Ormond College. In 1886 he and members of the Australian Church established the Social Improvement Friendly Help and Children's Aid Society to carry out social and charitable work in Collingwood and Richmond. He had been a member of the council of the Working Men's College from the 1880s and helped to open a branch in Collingwood in July 1891; he founded a Working Men's Club the same year. He formed societies to discuss literature and music but his major association was the Religious Science Club. In 1892 he was involved with H. F. Tucker in the utopian Village Settlement Movement; by 1894-95 they were in debt over the scheme. He was also very active in the National Anti-Sweating League and was elected a vice-president on 12 August 1895.

Strong's earnest and strenuous advocacy of unpopular economic and social views was a factor in the decline of the Australian Church. He was active against the Boer war and imperialism, and in 1905 founded and chaired the first Melbourne Peace Society. In England in April-November 1914 he talked with prison reformers and attended a peace conference at Liverpool; on his return to Melbourne he helped to form a branch of the Women's International League for Peace and Freedom. With a son in World War I, he signed the anti-conscription manifesto in December 1917 and was attacked in the press for it; many of the best members of his Church resigned. Between the wars Strong campaigned for the relief of victims of the Spanish civil war, advocated justice to the Aboriginals, and urged prison reform and, above all, abolition of capital punishment. He also worked for the proper care of mentally defective children.

From 1913 Strong lived in Barnato Grove, Armadale. His wife died on 23 April 1919. Active to the end, he suffered a fall while on holiday at Lorne and died there on 12 February 1942. His estate was valued for probate at £8372. He had received many legacies over the years including some £20,000 from an uncle in 1938, but gave virtually all to charities. His Church continued in smaller premises in Russell Street that had been bought in 1922, but in February 1957 it was dissolved. In 1958 the Charles Strong (Australian Church) Memorial Trust was established to further the study of comparative religion.

'With a pale, thoughtful face ... tall spare figure [and a manner] charming in its mingled mildness and dignity', Strong was a gifted, profoundly religious, highly intelligent idealist; but he was seen by many contemporaries as a destructive rationalist. His teaching was defensive and apologetic: he taught that Christianity was more endangered by theological obscurantism than by critical historical investigation, natural science or biblical criticism and that failure to love one's neighbour was more serious than doctrinal doubt. He was admired and trusted by men like Charles Pearson, Bishop Moorhouse, Alfred Felton [qq.v.], George Higinbotham, Alfred Deakin, H. B. Higgins and Bernard O'Dowd. Strong kept abreast of contemporary scholarship in biblical studies and comparative religion; but he was neither a profound scholar nor a systematic thinker, and his views must be reconstructed from a profusion of writings such as sermons and lectures. Until his death he edited a publication for the Social Improvement Society known variously as *Our Good Words* (1887-89), *The Australian Herald* (1889-1908) and *The Commonweal* (1908-42).

The Scots' Church case. By the promotors of the bill (Melb, 1884); R. Hamilton, *A jubilee history of the Presbyterian Church of Victoria* (Melb, 1888); A. Macdonald, *One hundred years of Presbyterianism in Victoria* (Melb, 1937); *Australasian*, 24 Oct 1885; General Assembly minutes 1875-84, Melbourne Presbytery minutes 1874-85, Scots Church Session and Committee of Management minutes 1875-85 (Presbyterian Church Assembly Hall, Melb); Strong papers, Australian Church minutes 1904-46, sermons and lectures (NL).

C. R. BADGER

STRONG, HERBERT AUGUSTUS (1841-1918), classicist and humanist, was born on 24 November 1841 at Clyst St Mary near Exeter, Devon, England, son of Edmond Strong, Anglican clergyman, and his wife Sarah, née Forbes-Coulson. He was educated at Winchester School and Corpus Christi College, Oxford (B.A., 1863). In 1866 he became assistant to the professor of humanity, George Ramsay, and was briefly warden of University Hall at the University of Glasgow.

In 1871 Strong replaced M. H. Irving [q.v.] as professor of classical and comparative philology and logic at the University of Melbourne. He arrived in Melbourne on the *Nubia* on 31 May 1872, took up his post in June and joined four other professors and fewer than 150 full-time students. The burden of teaching and matriculation examining was heavy, but Strong's requests for the appointment of a lecturer in logic to relieve him of the teaching of rhetoric were refused. He was also anxious to promote the study of French and German. In 1881 approval was given for a lecturer in English, and in 1882 a new chair of modern languages and literature was created, and he remained professor of classical and comparative philology.

Strong entered fully into the life of the university, played in the football team and encouraged athletics among his students as well as debating and wide reading. He contributed frequently to the *Melbourne Review* and the *Victorian Review*. A witty and humorous raconteur, he was a popular public lecturer on literary subjects; from 1878 he was also a trustee of the Public Library, Museums and National Gallery of Victoria and in April 1883 successfully moved for the opening of the library and picture galleries on Sundays. In 1882 Strong received the honorary degree of LL.D. from the University of Glasgow; in recommending him, Ramsay wrote that he 'has not only been a most successful and popular teacher, but has never ceased to be [a] diligent student both of literature & language', and added that his publications were marked by 'great taste scholarship and literary power'. In ill health by September 1883, he was given leave of absence and returned to England. He was offered the chair of Latin at the newly founded University College in Liverpool and his resignation was received by the University of Melbourne in June 1884.

In Melbourne Strong had published translations from the Latin poets, notably Plautus and Catullus. With A. Leeper of Trinity College he put out *A Guide to Classical Reading intended for the Use of Australian Students* (1880) and an English translation of *Thirteen Satires of Juvenal* (1882). With his close friend C. H. Pearson [q.v.] he produced an edition of the same thirteen satires in 1887 (revised 1892); they had also published a *Student's English Grammar* and a *Student's Primer*. At the request of students of the university Strong's addresses to them in 1879 and 1881 were printed. In Liverpool he collaborated with others in several studies of language and in 1896 edited Pearson's *Reviews and Critical Essays*. His contributions to periodicals were mainly in the field of language.

Strong was a classical scholar in the best English tradition; of a broad humanistic outlook, he was deeply convinced of the value of the humanities. He knew the language and literature of France, Germany, Italy, Spain and, later in life, of Russia. His contributions to classical scholarship were not so original as those of his successor in Melbourne, T. G. Tucker, but both there and in Liverpool he devoted himself to pioneering university education; anxious to extend its benefits, he was generally on the side of reform and keen to broaden the range of traditional studies. Cheerful and warm-

hearted, he was fond of walking and golf and was a skilful angler.

Strong died at Farnham Common, Buckinghamshire, on 13 January 1918. He had married Helen Campbell Edmiston of Glasgow in January 1875 at Terang, Victoria; they had a daughter who died in infancy, and two sons who survived him together with his second wife Isobel, née White, artist and academy exhibitor. The elder son, Archibald Thomas (1876-1930), returned to Australia in 1901 and became a well-known poet and scholar. A portrait of Strong by Hall Neale is in the possession of the University of Liverpool.

G. Blainey, *A centenary history of the University of Melbourne* (Melb, 1957); Guild of Undergraduates, Univ Liverpool, *Sphinx*, 14 Feb 1918; *The Times*, 14 Jan, educational supp, 17 Jan 1918; *Liverpool Post and Mercury*, 15 Jan 1918; *Argus*, 16 Jan 1918; George Ramsay, Letter to the principal, 4 Mar 1882 (Univ Glasgow Archives); Council minutes (Univ Melb Archives).

G. R. MANTON

STRUTT, WILLIAM (1825-1915), artist, was born on 3 July 1825 at Teignmouth, Devon, England, son of William Thomas Strutt (1777-1850), a noted miniaturist, and his second wife Mary Ann Price. His grandfather was Joseph Strutt (1742-1802), social historian and artist. The family lived for a short time in Boulogne, France, when William was small and he was educated by a French tutor. Returning to France in the late 1830s, he studied in Paris in the atelier of Michel-Martin Drölling and later at the Ecole des Beaux-Arts. He spent much time at the Louvre, and Raphael remained a lifelong influence. An excellent draftsman, he received many commissions for illustrating books : but, near breakdown and fearful of losing his sight, he decided to leave Europe and on 5 July 1850 arrived in Melbourne in the *Culloden*, much restored.

Employed by the Ham brothers [q.v.], Strutt that month published engravings in the first issue of the *Illustrated Australian Magazine*. He designed, engraved or lithographed postage stamps, posters, maps, transparencies and seals and began to learn all he could about the history of the colony. His friend and patron J. P. Fawkner [q.v.] encouraged him to record important events of the ensuing years. In between sketching and painting important historical occasions, he received commissions for portraits in oil, of which his best known are of Fawkner, Sir John O'Shanassy [q.v.] and a fine equestrian portrait of Sir Edward Macarthur [q.v.]. He also painted many miniature water-colour portraits of Aboriginal troopers as well as members of the Victorian mounted police. When bushrangers held up a number of people in St Kilda Road, he produced lively sketches of the event and later a fine oil painting. But his most dramatic work, not finished until after his return to England, was 'Black Thursday' commemorating the tragic bush fires in Victoria in February 1851; it was acquired by the State Library of Victoria. In 1853 he had been a founder of the short-lived Fine Arts Society. He exhibited at the Melbourne Exhibition in 1854.

On 2 June 1852 at the Congregational church, Lonsdale Street, Melbourne, Strutt had married Sarah Agnes Hague. With her and their small daughter he went to New Zealand in February 1855 where he bought 105 acres at Mangorei, New Plymouth, and painted mountain landscapes and Maori groups. He left New Zealand for Sydney in July 1856, and returned to Melbourne to renew friendships with the artists Eugène von Guérard, Ludwig Becker, Nicholas Chevalier and the art critic James Smith [qq.v.]. Together they revived the defunct Fine Arts Society, renaming it the Victorian Society of Fine Arts and holding several conversaziones and an exhibition in December 1857 before disbanding once again for lack of support. His final major works in Victoria were the on-the-spot sketches of the preparations for the Burke and Wills [qq.v.] expedition. He carefully prepared from eye-witness description many sketches of the explorers' tragic deaths, later reproducing the sketches in oils. His full-length painting of Burke commissioned by the Melbourne Club shows a man of flesh and blood and casual air that is unique among the portraits of distinguished Australians at that time; soon after completing it he left Melbourne for London on 29 January 1862 in the *Great Britain*.

Strutt excelled as an animal painter. In England, heavily influenced by the Pre-Raphaelites, he came to regard the lion as the greatest symbol of nobility and strength. Restless again, he visited North Africa to see wild animals in their native habitat. From 1865 to 1893 he exhibited twenty-three times at the Royal Academy and twenty-seven times at Suffolk Street, London. He was elected a member of the Royal Society of British Artists.

Aged 89, Strutt died at his home at Wadhurst, Sussex, on 3 January 1915, survived by his son Alfred William, an artist, and by three daughters. Frequently described as a melancholy artist, Strutt suggests conflict in many of his works, but his sketches and water-colours indicate that he had a very good sense of humour : some are quite amusing. The journal that he kept for a greater part of his life also shows that he had considerable literary ability, if not complete historical accuracy. Although he acknowledged his indebtedness to France for his early art training, undoubtedly Australia provided the inspiration for his best paintings. His works are represented in galleries in Sydney, Melbourne, Ballarat, Adelaide and Hobart. Among European collections, le Musée de Lucerne and the Peace Palace at The Hague hold important paintings. The Dixson and Mitchell libraries, Sydney, the National Library of Australia, State Library and the Parliamentary Library, Victoria, and the Alexander Turnbull Library, Wellington, all hold extensive collections of his sketches, paintings or manuscript material.

E. J. Wivell, *William Strutt's great historical picture 'Black Thursday'* (Adel, 1883); R. M. Christy, *Joseph Strutt, author, artist . . .* (Lond, 1912); G. Mackaness (ed), *The Australian journal of William Strutt, 1850-1862* (Syd, priv print, 1958); Bernard Smith, *Australian painting 1788-1960* (Melb, 1962); A. Chester, 'The art of Mr. William Strutt', *Windsor Mag*, Nov 1912; K. Stevenson, 'William Strutt', *Art and Aust*, Mar 1969; *Examiner* (Melb), 1 Feb 1862; M. Tipping, *The world of William Strutt* (1974 presidential address, RHSV); James Strutt papers (ML); W. Strutt papers and autobiog (ML); information from Mr T. O. Fitzgibbon, Auckland, NZ, and Mr C. W. Strutt, Red Hill, ACT.

MARJORIE J. TIPPING

STUART, SIR ALEXANDER (1824-1886), merchant and politician, was born on 21 March 1824 in Edinburgh, son of Alexander Stuart, writer to the signet, and his wife Mary, née McKnight. Reared in a religious atmosphere as a member of the Episcopal Church in Scotland, he was educated in 1832-35 at the Edinburgh Academy (of which his father was an original proprietor), and at the University of Edinburgh but did not graduate; he worked in a merchant's office in Leith and Glasgow before going to Belfast as manager of the North of Ireland Linen Mills. In 1845 he joined Carr Tagore & Co., a large mercantile and banking house in Calcutta, and in 1850 moved to New Zealand. On 9 October 1851 he reached Sydney in the *Scotia*; after a few months on the Ballarat goldfield, Victoria, he went back to Otago where he failed in a sheep-run with his friend Hugh Robison, later Sir Charles Cowper's [q.v.] son-in-law, before returning to New South Wales in August 1852 in the *Louisa*. On 10 November 1853 at Cobbity in the presence of Cowper he married Christiana Eliza (d. 1889), daughter of Lieutenant John Wood, R.N.

Late in 1852 Stuart had joined the Bank of New South Wales as assistant secretary and next year was also assistant inspector. In 1854 he was promoted secretary and inspector at a salary of £1200. In December he was sent to investigate the defalcations of G. D. Lang, manager of the bank's Ballarat branch. Lang and F. L. Drake were convicted in Melbourne and the vials of Rev. J. D. Lang's [q.v.] wrath were poured on Stuart, who calmly replied to the attacks in the *Empire*. When Lang published *The Convicts' Bank; or a Plain Statement of the Case of Alleged Embezzlement* ... (Sydney, 1855) Stuart, backed by the bank, sued him for criminal libel and he was imprisoned for six months.

Stuart's efficiency and organizing ability impressed Robert Towns [q.v.]; by early 1855 he had joined R. Towns & Co. and soon became prominent in commercial circles. He was a director of the Bank of New South Wales in 1855-61, 1867-76 and 1877-79, and its president in 1861. In 1862-63 he visited England on behalf of R. Towns & Co. and saw his ageing parents. In the 1860s and 1870s he was a committee-man of the Sydney Chamber of Commerce, sometime chairman of the Australian General Assurance Co., and a trustee of the Savings Bank of New South Wales. He was a director of the Waratah Coal Co., the Trust and Agency Co. of Australia, and in the 1880s the National Mutual Life Association of Australasia Ltd and the Bowenfels Coal Mining and Copper Smelting Co., the Sydney Exchange Co. in 1882-86 and a local director of the North-British and Mercantile Insurance Co. In the 1860s he was also a director of the Sydney Sailors' Home and a committee-man of the Sydney Bethel Union.

Despite his native caution and advice to Towns against new enterprises, in the 1860s Stuart invested extensively in land in Queensland with Towns and Cowper who in 1867 joined R. Towns & Co. at his suggestion. By the end of the decade the Queensland properties were losing money and he was unable to persuade Towns that his ships were no longer profitable. After the death of Towns in 1873 Stuart was not only senior partner of the company but a trustee and guardian of Towns's children who proved very troublesome. In the early 1870s he took up extensive mining leases in the Illawarra district, some with R. Harnett.

A devout Anglican, Stuart was a vocal lay member of the Sydney diocesan synods from 1866 and was active on the standing committee; he represented Sydney on the Provincial Synod in 1874-83 and on the General Synod from 1876. He was a member of St Andrew's Cathedral Chapter from 1868, was a trustee of Church lands and of Moore Theological College, a fellow of St Paul's College, within the University of Sydney, a committee-man of the Church Society and a member of the standing committee of the Sydney Diocesan Committee and Educational and Book Society. In the 1870s Stuart battled for the continuation of state aid to denominational education and with Shepherd Smith [q.v.], manager of the Bank of New South Wales, was a founder of the Church of England Defence Association. In 1874 he was asked by Bishop Barker [q.v.] to stand for parliament.

Opposing Rev. James Greenwood's [q.v.] Public School League, Stuart upheld the 1866 Public Schools Act; a free trader he advocated the 'rapid extension' of railways and aid to municipal institutions. In December he was elected to the Legislative Assembly as third member for East Sydney, and on 8 February 1876 he succeeded William Forster [q.v.] as colonial treasurer in (Sir) John Robertson's [q.v.] cabinet and held office until 21 March 1877: Governor Robinson believed he would lend strength to the government. A capable minister, he carried the Border Duties Convention Act. In the confused politics of 1877, exacerbated by the governor's refusal to dissolve parliament without supply, he refused to join Robertson in August, and failed to form coalition ministries in September and December. He held his seat in the 1877 elections and in 1878-79 visited England. Shepherd Smith told D. Larnach [q.v.] that Stuart 'certainly would have been treasurer' in the Parkes [q.v.]-Robertson coalition 'had he been in the Colony'.

He returned from England to near bankruptcy. According to Sir Daniel Cooper [q.v.], apart from debts to the Bank of New South Wales, Stuart owed Thomas Walker [q.v.] over £30,000, the Oriental Bank in London £20,000 and R. Towns & Co. 'about the same'. He also lost heavily in the failure of his brother James's firm in London, James Barber Son & Co. In March 1879 he made an agreement with other banks behind Smith's back and was offended when not re-elected a director of the Bank of New South Wales in September. Larnach told Smith that he regarded him 'as an exceedingly sanguine and dangerous man to have anything to do with any bank'.

In November 1879 Stuart was appointed agent-general for New South Wales in London and resigned from the assembly. Smith commented, 'We dont know how he proposes to arrange his debts here before he starts ... It is rumoured that Parkes will ask Parliament to give him £2500 a year and to Parkes he is worth that purchase at present, for he is the only solid oppositionist [to] the Govt.' Cooper criticized the appointment to Parkes, 'I note what you say about Mr. Stuart who has been so clever in concealing his insolvent position ... He cannot be in a position to play the part of Agent General ... as he must pawn his salary to get away from Sydney & keep his creditors quiet ... neither he nor Mrs Stuart know anything about "entertaining"'. Unable to unravel his own and R. Towns & Co.'s difficulties, in April Stuart resigned the position, never having left Sydney. He somehow recovered his financial position: he had real estate on the North Shore, from the late 1870s was chairman and a proprietor of the Coal Cliff Coal Co. and owned two steamships built in 1879.

Stuart represented Illawarra in the assembly from 7 July 1880 to 7 October 1885. In August 1882 he was elected leader of the Opposition. On 8 November he condemned the underlying principle of Robertson's land bill and put forward his own proposals, including limited security of tenure for squatters and the abolition of indiscriminate free selection. The Parkes-Robertson coalition was defeated. Stuart won the elections and took office as premier and colonial secretary on 5 January 1883. Despite having W. B. Dalley [q.v.] as attorney-general, the ministry was regarded by the governor and the press as weak and 'a stopgap'; however, Stuart had a strong following and his 'new "Reform" cabinet [had] an outward stability and an inner coherence'.

On 8 January Stuart appointed Augustus Morris and George Ranken [qq.v.] to inquire into the land laws; their report was presented in May and J. S. Farnell [q.v.], his secretary for lands, introduced the new crown lands bill in October. Dissected in a session of thirteen months, it was enacted in October 1884 after the government had made concessions to the squatters. Stuart had established the Aborigines Protection Board in February 1883 and in September he carried the Civil Service Act; other important measures carried by the ministry were the Fire Brigades and Sydney Corporation Acts. In March he had taken over as acting secretary for public works after Henry Copeland's [q.v.] indiscretion at the St Patrick's Day picnic, and he dealt firmly with the sectarian problems raised by the visit of John and William Redmond [qq.v.]. He supported Queensland's annexation of eastern New Guinea and in November-December presided over the Intercolonial Convention held in Sydney, which planned the Federal Council of Australasia. However by 1884 the government was in financial difficulties with the virtual stopping of land auctions and unprecedented spending on railways.

Conscientious, 'imprudently industrious' and unable to delegate, Stuart did not spare himself either in his office or in tumultuous late sittings in the House. Throughout 1884 he was harassed by questions from J. McElhone, A. G. Taylor [qq.v.] and others on his extensive mineral lands in the Illawarra. Early in October he suffered a severe stroke which paralysed his left side. Dalley was acting colonial secretary while he convalesced in Tasmania and with his brother Edward, bishop of Waiapu, at Napier, New Zealand. He resumed his duties in May 1885 and was created K.C.M.G. next month; he clung to office against the advice of friends and doctors until ill health forced him to resign on 6 October. He was appointed to the Legislative Council next day.

Stuart had been a member of the Royal Society of New South Wales since 1874, a New South Wales commissioner for the 1876 Philadelphia International Exhibition, an elective trustee of the Australian Museum in 1881-82 and a vice-president of the Highland Society of New South Wales. In 1886 he went to London as New South Wales executive commissioner for the Colonial and Indian Exhibition. Soon after its opening he died of typhoid fever on 16 June at 52 Stanhope Gardens, London, and was buried at Roxeth Church near Harrow-on-the-Hill. He was survived by his wife, son and probably one of his three daughters. His estate was valued for probate at £83,600.

David Buchanan [q.v.] said that Stuart had 'total ineptitude for public speaking' and 'an utter disregard to everything in the shape of emphasis or elocution'. But the Sydney Morning Herald, 18 June 1886, maintained that 'He was slow in making up his mind, and there was a want of resolute firmness ... but ... he had a good deal of the dogged determination that belongs to the Scotch character, and a large capacity for patient endurance ... He was very friendly ... but he lacked that magnetic power which great leaders have of fascinating their comrades, and of binding them as it were by hooks of steel'.

R. F. Holder, Bank of New South Wales: a history, 1 (Syd, 1970); V&P (LA NSW), 1875-76, 1, 374, 1879-80, 1, 167, 2, 675, 4, 31, 1883, 3, 47, 1883-84, 1, 52, 58, 109, 125, 167, 331, 646, 653, 685, 1885, 1, 50; Church of England diocese of Sydney, V&P of Synod (1866-84); SMH, 4, 5 June, 17 July 1855, 18 June 1886; T&CJ, 19 Feb 1876, 19, 26 June 1886; Cowper letters (ML); letters to Lord Augustus Loftus (ML); Parkes letters (ML); Robert Towns & Co. papers (ML); Shepherd Smith-Donald Larnach letters (Bank of New South Wales Archives, Syd); Stuart family letters, MS 1279/13-15 (ML); CO 201/581, 583-84, 591, 597-603.

BEDE NAIRN
MARTHA RUTLEDGE

STUART, JOHN McDOUALL (1815-1866), explorer, was born on 7 September 1815 at Dysart, Fife, Scotland, fifth son of William Stuart, army captain, and his wife Mary, née McDouall. Educated at the Scottish Naval and Military Academy, Edinburgh, in 1838 he decided to migrate to South Australia. He arrived in the *Indus* in January 1839 and joined a surveying party. Having had a taste of the outback, in 1844 he accepted Charles Sturt's [q.v.] offer to join a party exploring the centre of the continent. The seventeen-month journey revealed only desolation, but Stuart now knew the problems of exploring waterless regions with a large expedition: he had seen fatal scurvy at close hand, had observed the Aboriginals and, having drawn many of the maps, had become familiar with the topography of the centre.

In 1846-58 Stuart practised as a surveyor, had an estate agency and spent some time at Port Lincoln. With financial help from William Finke, Stuart set out on 14 May 1858 with an assistant, an Aboriginal tracker and provisions for four weeks to explore beyond Lake Torrens and Lake Gairdner and to look for grazing land. He travelled as far as Coober Pedy before turning south and then west. The Aboriginal left them on 3 August, and with supplies and water almost exhausted and the horses lame they struggled into T. M. Gibson's outstation at Streaky Bay on 22 August. After ten days rest Stuart returned to Adelaide to an enthusiastic welcome. He had discovered 40,000 square miles of possible sheep country at minimal cost. He gave his diary and maps to the South Australian government and was granted a lease of 1000 square miles of the new country.

In 1859 Finke and James Chambers [q.v.] financed another expedition. Leaving in April with four others, Stuart travelled 500 miles blazing a trail with sufficient water for a permanent route north. On 4 November he set out on his third expedition and spent six weeks surveying new runs. In the Davenport Range he found signs of gold; after three weeks fruitless prospecting his men rebelled and the party returned to Chambers Creek where all but William Kekwick were paid off. He set off again on 2 March 1860 with two men and thirteen horses. Most of their provisions were soon spoilt by floods, and when the party reached the freshwater creek that Stuart named after Finke on 4 April, they were suffering from scurvy and he had lost the sight of his right eye. They followed the Finke to the mountains that Stuart named after Governor Macdonell and headed north again, naming Anna's Reservoir after Chambers' youngest daughter; on 22 April he camped where he calculated the centre of the continent to be. Two miles away he named Central Mount Sturt (later changed to Stuart) and planted a flag as 'a sign to the natives that the dawn of liberty, civilization and Christianity was about to break on them'.

For the next month the party tried in vain to find a route with sufficient water to take them to the north-west. When rain fell late in May they travelled 200 miles north to Tennant's Creek where they made a depot. Pressing on to Kekwick Ponds Stuart tried to penetrate the near-by scrub but on 25 June was forced back. Two months later the party staggered into Chambers Creek. On his return to Adelaide Stuart was fêted at a public banquet and at Government House; one newspaper urged that he be given the government reward for crossing the continent because Attack Creek, his furthest point, was only 200 miles from explored country in the north.

At the end of 1860 the South Australian government voted £2500 to equip a large expedition to be led by Stuart. Burke and Wills [qq.v.] had already set out to cross the continent so there was no time to lose if a South Australian party was to arrive first. On 1 January 1861 he left Chambers Creek with eleven men and reached Attack Creek late in April; with two others he discovered a way through the scrub that had defeated him before, and found Sturt's Plain. After exhausting failures to pass the plains, with their provisions low and their clothes in shreds, Stuart gave in and on 12 July turned south to reach Adelaide on 23 September. He received the 1861 gold medal of the Royal Geographical Society from the governor.

Stuart was still convinced he could cross the continent. Shopkeepers gave him supplies for a fresh party, Chambers provided the horses and saddlery, and the government gave him £200 and instructions to take a botanist F. G. Waterhouse [q.v.] with him. They left Adelaide at the end of October 1861 but Stuart was delayed for five weeks by an accident; he joined the party at Moolooloo station where one of the men left after a quarrel. The party reached the centre on 12 March 1862, Attack Creek on the 28th and Sturt's Plain on 15 April, where they were blocked and Stuart turned to the scrub. Although they only made a mile an hour and the waterbags were badly torn they arrived at Daly Waters, named after the new governor, on 28 May and made camp for two weeks. His endurance was beginning to falter, but on 24 July they forced their way through a thick belt of scrub and came upon the Indian Ocean. Many of the horses were so weak they had to be abandoned on the way back. Ill with scurvy and nearly blind, Stuart had to be carried on a stretcher slung between two horses; recovering sufficiently to ride by the time they reached Mount Margaret on 26 November, he pushed on with three of the party and arrived in Adelaide on 17 December. On a public holiday on 21 January 1863, crowds lined the streets amid banners strung from buildings. He was awarded £2000, though allowed only the interest from it, and his party received £1500 between them.

White-haired, exhausted and nearly blind, Stuart decided to visit his sister in Scotland and sailed in April 1864. He later went to London. His claims for a greater reward from the South Australian government led to another £1000, again with only the interest. His *Explorations in Australia. The Journals of John McDouall Stuart* was edited by W. Hardman and published in 1864. He died of ramollissement and cerebral effusion on 5 June 1866 in London and was buried in the Kensal Green cemetery. He has remained a controversial figure, lonely and independent, with a fierce pride. His reputation as a heavy drinker has led detractors to minimize his achievements, even to the extent of doubting that he reached the Indian Ocean in 1862, though the tree he had marked with JMDS was positively identified in 1883 and photographed in 1885.

B. Threadgill, *South Australian land exploration 1856 to 1880*, 1 (Adel, 1922); D. Pike, *John McDouall Stuart* (Melb, 1958); M. S. Webster, *John McDouall Stuart* (Melb, 1958); T. G. H. Strehlow, *Comments on the journals of John McDouall Stuart* (Adel, 1967); I. Mudie, *The heroic journey of John McDouall Stuart* (Syd, 1968); W. Hardman (ed), *The journals of John McDouall Stuart ...*, 2nd ed (Adel, 1975); PP (SA), 1858, 1, 39, 49, 2, 114, 119, 148, 1859, 1 (21), 2 (148), 1860, 2 (65), 3 (169), 1862, 2 (219), 1863, 1, 6-21, 2 (21), (HA), 1865, 98, 106; M. S. Webster, 'John McDouall Stuart: his character and personal qualities', PRGSSA, 62 (1960-61); M. Quick, 'John McDouall Stuart', JRAHS, 49 (1963); *Examiner* (Melb), 5, 19 Oct 1861, 21 Mar 1863; Governor's dispatches, 24 Oct 1863, 26 Apr, 21 June 1865, CO 13/112/117.   DEIRDRE MORRIS

STURT, EVELYN PITFIELD SHIRLEY (1816-1885), police magistrate, was born in Dorset, England, son of Thomas Lenox Napier Sturt, puisne judge in Bengal under the East India Co., and his wife Jeannette, née Wilson. His brother was the explorer Charles Sturt [q.v.]. Evelyn was educated at the Sandhurst Military College but in 1836 migrated to New South Wales, arriving in the *Hooghly* on 12 October. On 20 February 1837 he was appointed commissioner of crown lands based on Yass, and was sometimes spoken of as 'the boy commissioner'. Of an ebullient temperament, in 1853 he wrote to Lieut-Governor La Trobe : 'It has often been a source of regret to me that all the charms attending the traversing of a new country must give way to the march of civilization ... I look back to those days as to some joyous scene of school-boy holidays'.

Sturt resigned in 1839 to overland sheep and cattle from Bathurst to Adelaide. After occupying country at Willunga in the Mount Lofty Ranges, he took up Compton station in the Mount Gambier district in 1844. He encountered many difficulties and, although he did not dispose of his run until 1853, he accepted appointment as police magistrate in Melbourne in 1849. Next year he became superintendent of the Melbourne police but had to contend with 'the great inefficiency of the District (Melbourne and County of Bourke) Police Force arising from their scattered and isolated stations' and insufficient constables. His troubles were greatly intensified by the gold rushes; in December 1851 he reported that forty of his staff of fifty had resigned. When (Sir) William Mitchell [q.v.] took charge of the police early in 1853, Sturt was reappointed as magistrate for Melbourne and for the next twenty-five years presided over the city bench.

In 1854 Sturt was appointed to the commission of inquiry into the Bentley hotel affair at Ballarat. While the report by no means satisfied most of the diggers, it recommended dismissal of some corrupt government officers and compensation to some who had suffered losses. Sturt was a member of the royal commissions on the Burke and Wills [qq.v.] expedition in 1861 and on charitable institutions in 1871. For many years he was a member of the Church of England assembly. In 1852 he had married Mary Frances, daughter of Rev. J. C. Grylls; in March 1869 he took leave of absence and with his wife visited England and was present at the death of his brother Charles. In 1875 he was one of the three executors of the Victorian estate of La Trobe. Dismissed in the Black Wednesday retrenchments of January 1878, Sturt accepted a pension and in December left with his wife for England. On their return to

Victoria in April 1881 they lived at Brighton.

Sturt was described by Rolf Boldrewood [q.v. T. A. Browne] as the hero of many local legends, 'a very grand-looking fellow —aristocratic, athletic, adventurous; an explorer, a pioneer, a *preux chevalier* in every sense of the word, a leading colonist, with a strong dash of Bayard about him; popular with the men of his set, and, it is unnecessary to say, a general favourite with the women'.

On another trip to England Sturt suffered from severe bronchitis. He was returning with his wife in the *Pekin* to retire in Victoria when he died, aged 69, on 10 February 1885, a day before reaching Port Said; his body was taken back to England for burial. Childless, he was survived by his wife. In Victoria his estate was valued for probate at £17,715. Sturt Street, Ballarat, is named after him.

N. G. Sturt, *Life of Charles Sturt* (Lond, 1895); R. Boldrewood (T. A. Browne), *Old Melbourne memories*, 2nd ed (Lond, 1896); T. F. Bride (ed), *Letters from Victorian pioneers* (Melb, 1898); C. Fetherstonhaugh, *After many days* (Syd, 1918); V. S. Devenport, 'Links with Captain Charles Sturt and his family', VHM, 22 (1947-50); *Australasian*, 21 Feb, 21 Mar 1885; N. Sturt, History of the Sturt family (held by author, Storrington, Sussex, England); Kenyon papers (LaT L); information from Mr & Mrs K. T. Borrow, Erindale, SA.   ALAN GROSS*

STUTCHBURY, SAMUEL (1798-1859), geologist and biologist, was born on 15 January 1798 in London, son of Joseph Sidney Stutchbury and his wife Hannah, née Smith. After some training in medical and natural science, he was appointed on 3 January 1820 to assist William Clift, the conservator of the Hunterian museum, Royal College of Surgeons, London, at a salary of £80. He resigned on 13 July 1825 and became naturalist to the Pacific Pearl Fishery Co.'s commercial expedition to New South Wales and the Pacific islands. Sir Everard Home presented him with a list of instructions and equipped him with a diving bell.

Stutchbury reached Sydney on 17 December in the *Sir George Osborne*; he made biological and meteorological observations and collected specimens *en route*, many of which he dissected and described. In Sydney Harbour he found living specimens of the pelecypod *Trigonia*, known in Europe only from fossil remains, and other new marine organisms which he later described in English scientific publications. Although his main work was on marine biology he also engaged in geology and met most of the colonists interested in science.

Stutchbury left Sydney in the *Rolla* on 8 March 1826 for the Pacific islands. His observations, published in Bristol in 1835, were widely quoted in geological literature until superseded in 1842 by Charles Darwin's [q.v.] work. He rejoined the *Sir George Osborne* at Tahiti on 14 January 1827, returned to England and apparently worked with his brother Henry; on 26 July 1827 they held a sale of objects he had collected in the South Seas. In September 1828 he failed to obtain the curatorship of the museum of the University of London, but in August 1831 he became curator of the museum of the Bristol Philosophical Institution. His published papers reflect his broad interests and support his repute as 'a man remarkably skilled in the various branches of natural history'. He also won wide success as a coal viewer and in 1844 was one of the advisers of the government on the Haswell Colliery explosion in County Durham.

Rumours of gold finds in New South Wales led in 1849 to a successful request that a geologist be sent to the colony. At short notice Stutchbury accepted the post with salary of £600 and reached Sydney on 16 November 1850. He visited the Newcastle coalfields and his unpublished report describes the mines, methods of working and the general geology. On 18 January 1851 he set out on his geological and mineralogical survey. When E. H. Hargraves [q.v.] publicized the gold discovery at Lewis Ponds Creek, Stutchbury was at Carcoar. He confirmed the find and brought some order to the confusion on the goldfield, but received small thanks from E. D. Thomson [q.v.], the colonial secretary.

Stutchbury extended his survey northward through Mudgee and Wellington almost to Dubbo, then back to Wellington in the early part of 1852. Next year he went to the Warrumbungle Mountains and into Queensland, paying attention to the need for water on the Darling Downs and coal deposits in the Brisbane-Ipswich area. He reached Brisbane early in December 1853 and in April 1854 went north into rugged and relatively undeveloped areas, under threat of attack by Aboriginals. When his party reached Wide Bay he was in poor health; he went by ship to Port Curtis (Gladstone), and returned to Sydney early next year. In the previous November he had complained to Thomson about the treatment and slanders he had received, and aroused official ire by publishing a copy of the letter in the *Sydney Morning Herald*.

Early in 1855 at the Australian Museum Stutchbury catalogued his specimens and prepared duplicate sets. Some of his material was put on display and proved a popular attraction. In August he returned to Port Curtis and when he submitted his last report from Sydney on 20 November he had examined some 32,000 square miles of diverse and geologically complex terrain. He had supplied the colonial secretary with sixteen important tri-monthly reports with geological sketch maps; they were printed only as parliamentary papers and are still largely unknown. However his mapping was incorporated in the geological map of Australia collated by Brough Smyth [q.v.] and published in 1875. His appointment was terminated late in 1855 and he left Sydney in December virtually unnoticed. Failing to get a government post in England he carried out consulting work on the coalfields although his health was poor. He died at Bristol on 12 February 1859 of haematemesis and was buried in the Arnos Grove cemetery. About 1823 he had married and had at least one son.

Stutchbury was a conscientious scientist of considerable skill and imagination, but his official career in Australia was marred by the government's apparent demand for no more than a skilled prospector who would discover gold and other mineral deposits. W. B. Clarke's [q.v.] influence and writings in the *Sydney Morning Herald* also damaged him. He had been elected a fellow of the Geological Society, London, on 1 December 1841; he was also an associate of the Linnean Society of London, and in 1851 he became a committee-man of the Australian Society. The molluscan fossil genus *Stutchburia* was named in his honour, and a number of recent Australian and New Zealand shells bear his name.

V&P (LC NSW), 1853, 2, no 302, 1854, 2, 1855, 1, 193, 3, 936, 982; SMH, 9 May 1859; Stutchbury diaries and reports (ML, Dixson Lib, Syd, Turnbull Lib, Wellington, NZ); D. Vickery, Bristol Calendar 1858-64 (MS collection, Bristol Central Lib, Eng); family papers (held by Mr O. Stutchbury, Eastbourne, Sussex, Eng).   D. F. BRANAGAN
                                                  T. G. VALLANCE

SUFFOLK, OWEN HARGRAVES (born 1830?), convict writer, was born, according to his autobiography, at Finchley, Middlesex, England, only son of a well-to-do family. When his father suffered financial reverses, Suffolk was sent, aged 8, to an inferior boarding-school at Margate, where he learned Latin, French and book-keeping. At 12 he went to live with his parents, then virtually penniless; as cabin-boy he soon joined a ship bound for Rio de Janeiro. During the seven-month voyage Suffolk rebelled against the fierce discipline; on his return he failed to find his parents, whose letter telling him of their new address had never reached him. He led a vagabond life until sent to Coldbath-fields prison for vagrancy. There he learned the arts and rewards of crime and on his release briefly became a successful confidence trickster, spending his gains on culture and self-education. An advertisement by his father in *The Times* brought written contact with his family but both guilt and success made him refuse reunion. On 30 March 1846 he was convicted at the Central Criminal Court for 'forging an undertaking for payment of money'; next year he sailed as a chaplain's clerk in the convict ship *Joseph Somes* which arrived in Melbourne on 24 September. Prison records described him as 'age 17, reads and writes, former tailor, single'.

In the Port Phillip District Suffolk was successful in two positions as tutor-bookkeeper until information about his past brought dismissal. In 1848, attempting to escape arrest on a false accusation, he stole a horse and was sentenced to five years on the roads, but served two years and three months only; due for a ticket-of-leave he 'absconded while on pass to take up his indulgence'. On 21 June 1851 he was sentenced to ten years for robbing the Portland mail; during the trial he had 'addressed the jury in a very clear and eloquent speech, which fairly took the Court by surprise'. His help to gaol authorities, his writings and remorse appealed to Chief Justice Sir William à Beckett [q.v.], who commented in July 1852 that 'He is certainly no common criminal—and both in prose and poetry professes no mean powers of composition'.

Probably through à Beckett, Suffolk was made prisoner-clerk, and he met and fell in love with the daughter of a prisoner. He gained a ticket-of-leave and sentence remission in September 1853 and planned to marry, but in November it was discovered that he had forged an entry reducing the sentences of two prisoners from four to two months. In December he was sent to the prison hulk *President*; after fourteen months his health broke down and he was transferred to the *Success* and then to the *Sacramento*. Among his several unsuccessful petitions was a fourteen-page document of 16 January 1857, written in a distinctively neat, round hand, which described the revocation of his remission of sentence as 'a proceeding which carries with it an utter violation of faith, and which, as such must be derogatory to the essential dignity of the power by which it is enforced'. In December 1857 he was again given a ticket-of-leave; but his fiancée had died and he was soon unemployed. Again reverting to crime, in February and June 1858 he was given sentences totalling twelve years for horse-stealing; he received a ticket-of-leave on 4 July 1866, and on 1 September his application for pardon was granted. On 17 September, giving his occupation as miner, he sailed in the Norfolk for England.

Suffolk claimed to have begun his autobiography on 6 August 1858. It was bought by the Argus, possibly for the £50 that he claimed in his petition for pardon had come to him from a brother in England, and was published in the Australasian between January and October 1867. Called 'Days of Crime and Years of Suffering', it included six of his poems and a chapter, 'Thoughts on Penal Discipline', written after his release. His fate is unknown, though J. M. Forde in 1911 maintained that he again relapsed, causing trouble in a Midlands town. While regretting his criminality, Suffolk frankly enjoyed those aspects of his career which involved play-acting and fooling society. His library included works by Cowper, Byron, Moore and Scott, Bacon's Essays, and Adam Smith's Wealth of Nations; though his verse was mediocre he had an excellent prose style. The publication of his story led to the formation of a Discharged Prisoners' Aid Society.

J. Graham, Laurence Struilby (Lond, 1863); Argus, 23 June 1851; Australasian, Jan-Sept 1867; Old Chum (J. M. Forde), 'Early Melbourne', Truth, Mar-June 1911; MS collection, box 20/7 (LaT L); Chief Secretary, In-letters 1866/9027, Prisons box 302 and Inspector General of Penal Establishments, Suffolk file, 57/1 to 57/1500 box 573 (PRO, Vic).

JILL EASTWOOD

SULLIVAN, JAMES FORESTER (1817-1876), businessman and politician, was born at Waterford, Ireland, son of James Sullivan, merchant, and his wife Margaret, née Forrester. Left fatherless, he went to Liverpool about 1830 but later absconded to sea and then settled in the United States of America. He worked as a backwoodsman, timber merchant and shipping and plantation entrepreneur. In 1845 he interrupted law studies at Franklin, Indiana, to fight in the war between Mexico and the United States. He volunteered for the Louisiana Guards and later secured a commission. Gold attracted him to California in 1848, but when he heard of the Australian gold discoveries he bought the Long Island and, with cargo

and fare-paying passengers, sailed for Sydney where in April 1853 he sold the ship and goods. He was in Melbourne in June, but soon moved to Bendigo as a partner in a jewellery business. He was granted the first liquor licence in the town in May 1854 and conducted a business known as the Red Store until 1861.

Sullivan at once interested himself in local affairs. He was prominent in the formation of the first Sandhurst municipality in 1855 and was chairman twice. He also participated in the founding of the Mechanics' Institute, the Digger Defence Council, the Sandhurst Fire Brigade, the Bendigo Hospital, the Benevolent Asylum, the Bendigo Land League and the Bendigo Agricultural and Horticultural Society. In 1856 he was defeated for Sandhurst Boroughs in the Legislative Assembly, being depicted as the shopkeepers' candidate by his radical mining opponents. In the next five years Sullivan became a director or shareholder in various enterprises, including the Bendigo Mercury and the Bendigo Gas Co.

In 1861 Sullivan was elected unopposed for the seat of Mandurang and became commissioner of trade and customs in the Heales [q.v.] ministry from 10 June to 14 November. He served on the Burke and Wills [qq.v.] commission in the same year. From June 1863 to July 1866 he was minister for mines in the first (Sir) James McCulloch [q.v.] government and fought strongly and successfully for the unpopular Coliban scheme to harness water for his electorate. In 1865 he represented Victoria at the Dublin International Exhibition. He was vice-president of the Board of Land and Works and commissioner of railways and roads from 4 March 1867 to 6 May 1868, minister of mines from 11 July to 20 September 1869, vice-president of the Board of Land and Works from 1 February to 20 September, and commissioner of railways and roads from 12 April to 2 September 1869. He was on the royal commission on federal union in 1870. He did not stand for re-election in 1871 and visited America to bring back his brother's four orphaned children. A liver complaint limited his activity, but he was returned for Collingwood in 1874. In 1875 he served on the royal commission on volunteer forces.

Sullivan had married Alice, née Redpath, on 5 January 1857 according to the rites of the Wesleyan Church; they had no children. Aged 59, he died on 3 February 1876 and was buried as a Methodist. His estate was sworn for probate at £1530. An able and successful businessman, Sullivan applied his wide experience to community service. He was a forceful speaker and an honest, determined and independent politician with radical sympathies. Gentle and genial, he was generous of both his time and money. His portrait by Alice Chapman is in the Bendigo Art Gallery.

G. Mackay, *The history of Bendigo* (Melb, 1891); F. Cusack, *Bendigo: a history* (Melb, 1973); *Argus*, 4 Feb 1876.   G. R. QUAIFE

SULLIVAN, THOMAS BARRY (1821-1891), actor, was born on 5 July 1821 at Birmingham, Warwickshire, England, son of Peter Sullivan and his wife Mary, née Barry. His parents, natives of Cork, Ireland, both died when he was 8, and he was brought up by his grandfather in Bristol. Educated at a Catholic school, at 14 he entered an attorney's office but after seeing W. C. Macready's Hamlet became obsessed with the idea of becoming a great actor. Known as Barry Sullivan, he joined a strolling company and made his way to Cork in 1837 where he played minor Shakespearian parts to Charles Kean's [q.v.] lead, supported the 'divine' Ellen Tree (who later married Kean) and, having a good light tenor voice, sang occasionally in opera. In November 1840 he left Cork for Scotland and by 1844 was playing leading roles; in the next seven years he made successful tours of Scotland and England. On 7 February 1852 he was well received as Hamlet at the Haymarket Theatre in London. In 1858 he went to America for eighteen months.

On 25 July 1862 Sullivan arrived in Victoria in the *City of Melbourne* making his début as Hamlet at Melbourne's Theatre Royal on 9 August. Local audiences, particularly the 'Irish party' gave him an enthusiastic reception but the critics were less responsive. The *Argus* described his performance as 'thoughtful, earnest, easy, artistic, and elaborate, but not great', but agreed that he appeared under adverse conditions: he had followed the favourite, G. V. Brooke [q.v.], his voice had suffered from the sea voyage, and his supporting cast was very poor. Sullivan appeared as Richelieu, Richard III, Macbeth, and in alternate performances Othello and Iago, before going to Sydney where he opened at the Victoria Theatre on 29 September. Claiming later that his poor reception in Melbourne had 'induced him to stay and fight the battle out', he returned there to manage the Theatre Royal at the close of W. S. Lyster's [q.v.] opera season. He opened on 7 March 1863 with *The School for Scandal*, produced 'in a style that would do credit to any theatre in the world', and continued with a range of Shakespearian drama as well as other British masterpieces. He later asserted he had played 1200 nights in Melbourne. Cheap prices (he instituted a 'shilling pit'), an excellent company and efficient presentation contributed to his success; even bitter rivalry from the Keans who opened at the Haymarket in October under contract to G. Coppin [q.v.], did not affect his popularity.

On 16 February 1866 Sullivan played his final night at the Theatre Royal. He was banquetted by leading Melbourne citizens and soon after left for London where for two years he managed the Holborn Theatre until stopped by financial losses. He played in London and toured North America several times but was most popular in Dublin, Cork, Liverpool and Manchester. He lived frugally, and his slight, wiry, flexible figure allowed him to play relatively young parts well into late middle age. His deeply pock-marked face did not lend itself to make-up but he had very fine, expressive eyes. In failing health after 1886, he was last seen on stage as Richard III in Liverpool on 4 June 1887. He suffered a stroke in August 1888 and received last rites, but did not die until 3 May 1891, survived by his wife Mary, née Amory, whom he had married on 4 July 1842, and by his two sons and three daughters. In Melbourne his death occasioned lengthy obituaries; he was remembered as an actor and manager of 'more than ordinary talent, combined with considerable force of character, great tenacity of purpose, untiring industry, and a dogged application to the business of his profession'.

W. J. Lawrence, *Barry Sullivan: a biographical sketch* (Lond, 1893); C. J. Kean, *Emigrant in motley*, J. M. D. Hardwick ed (Lond, 1954); H. Porter, *Stars of Australian stage and screen* (Adel, 1965); *Argus*, 23 Aug 1862, 17, 19 Feb 1866, 5 May 1891; *Examiner* (Melb), 14 Mar 1863.   JEAN GITTINS

SUMMERS, CHARLES (1827-1878), sculptor, was born on 27 July 1827 at Charlton, Somerset, England, son of George Summers, builder and mason, and elder brother of Joseph [q.v.]. Charles's schooling was negligible and he worked from the age of 8. Business failure forced the family to Street near Glastonbury, Somerset, from where Charles worked in masons' yards. Known for his industry and for his skill at stone-carving, he pleased the foreman of prominent sculptor Henry Weekes and at 19 obtained work at Weekes's London studio and then with M. L. Watson. At night he practised his craft and prepared models for his entry submissions to the Royal Academy. He was admitted as a student in 1850 and next year won medals for the best model from life and for the best group of historical sculpture. Ill health forced him to migrate to Melbourne in 1852, where he built a house before taking up a claim at Tarnagulla goldfield. A week after he sold his claim and returned to Melbourne it yielded £20,000 to the buyers. Later he directed the sculpture work in the superb chamber of the Legislative Council (completed in 1856) and modelled the ceiling figures.

Summers became a central figure in local artistic circles; he arranged annual art exhibitions and was a founder of the Victorian Society of Fine Arts in October 1856. In 1863 he became a member of the commission of inquiry into the promotion of the fine arts in Victoria, and next year was made chairman of a board of examiners testing drawing instructors for Common Schools. He did many fine portraits, busts and medallions of local notables such as Charles Sturt, Sir Redmond Barry and J. P. Fawkner [qq.v.], but his finest achievement is the bronze group of Burke and Wills [qq.v.], which is made entirely of Australian materials; he lived for six weeks among Aboriginals to help him to represent their figures accurately. With great courage, patience and skill he built the furnace and did the casting himself, reputedly the first ever done in Australia, and to that time the figure of Burke was the largest ever cast in one piece. The statues were completed and the bronze bas-reliefs, depicting scenes of the expedition, were fixed into place in September 1866.

In May 1867 Summers left Melbourne in the True Briton for England and thence to Rome, where he made a successful career. He exhibited at the Royal Academy twelve times between 1849 and 1876. His last work was commissioned by (Sir) W. J. Clarke [q.v.] for the National Gallery, a marble group of Queen Victoria, her consort and the prince and princess of Wales. After an operation for acute goitre he died in Paris on 30 November 1878. Friends in Australia paid tribute to his high ideals, and the Argus obituarist described him as 'Simple in manners, frank and gentle in speech, modest and unassuming by nature, and entirely free from that self-consciousness and self-assertion which make some artists so intolerable in private life ... his opinions [were] always the fruit of independent thought and reflection'. As a sculptor Summers was dedicated to his craft and highly revered the classical form. He was 'competent in a dull and un-inspiring period'. His work is represented in the State Library and the National Gallery of Victoria, the Mitchell Library, Sydney, and the Adelaide Art Gallery. Summers married Augustine Ameot in 1851 in London. Their only son, Charles Francis (b. November 1857), joined him in Rome in 1868; he was a minor sculptor

whose work is a feature of the Ballarat Gardens.

A portrait in oils of Summers, by Margaret Thomas [q.v.], is in the La Trobe Library, Melbourne.

M. Thomas, A hero of the workshop and a Somersetshire worthy (Lond, 1879); G. Tibbits, 'Parliament House, Melbourne', Aust Council of National Trusts, Historic public buildings of Australia (Melb, 1971); Argus, 9 Dec 1878.

JILL EASTWOOD

SUMMERS, JOSEPH (1839-1917), musician, was born at Charlton, Somerset, England, youngest son of George Summers, mason. He was a chorister at Wells Cathedral and studied under H. J. Gauntlett and W. Sterndale Bennett; he fulfilled the requirements of the bachelor of music degree at the University of Oxford about 1863, but it was not conferred until April 1887. He composed many hymn tunes and anthems and was organist at St Andrew's College, Bradfield, from 1861; Holy Trinity Church, Weston-Super-Mare, in 1864; and St Peter's, Notting Hill, London, in 1865. On 21 July 1863 at the parish church of St George, Bloomsbury, he married Constance, daughter of William Henry Summers, a solicitor.

In 1865 Summers and his wife migrated to Melbourne where his brother Charles [q.v.] was making his name as a sculptor. He soon won renown both as pianist and as composer. He held posts as organist at St Peter's, Eastern Hill, in 1868-79 and at All Saints, St Kilda, until 1896; he was also organist for the Melbourne Philharmonic Society in 1869 and its conductor in 1872-74, and organist for the Metropolitan Liedertafel in 1882-83. He became an examiner of music teachers under the Board of Education in 1867. As inspector of music in the Education Department from 1878, he advocated the staff system of notation and opposed the Tonic Sol-fa method of teaching music, then being propagated by Dr S. McBurney [q.v.]. Summers visited England in 1887 and reported on music in elementary schools in London for the Education Department. In December 1887 he was admitted to the degree of Mus. Bac. (ad eund.) by the University of Melbourne and in March 1890 the degree of doctor of music was conferred on him by the archbishop of Canterbury.

A mining speculator, Summers had become insolvent in 1872 and again in 1891, when he forfeited his post as music inspector. Upon obtaining a certificate of discharge, he applied for reinstatement but was accused of misappropriation and other irregularities; after an inquiry in November, the minister of education decided not to reappoint him. In 1893 he sued the *Age* newspaper in vain for £500 for printing a satirical review of one of his musical productions. Next year he took charge of the Melbourne examination centre of Trinity College of Music, London. He was also an examiner in music for the Tasmanian Council of Education, the University of Tasmania and the University of Adelaide.

In early 1897 Summers moved to Perth, Western Australia. Late in 1899 he was commissioned by Fr James Duff to compose music for a dramatized version of Milton's poetry, to be called 'The Two Worlds'. Summers completed twenty-seven pieces of music, which he assessed at £10 10s. each, but Duff had already turned to another composer; in a court case in March 1901 Summers won public performing rights, but in August he failed to obtain payment from Duff of money which he claimed was still owing to him. He continued to compose and to teach music in Perth and under his conductorship a Philharmonic Society and a Liedertafel were established. In 1910 he published *Music and Musicians: Personal Reminiscences*. Aged 78, he died of heart failure on 10 October 1917, predeceased by his wife in April 1901 and survived by a son and a daughter. He was buried in the Anglican section of the Karrakatta cemetery.

J. T. Lightfoot, *The music of the Methodist hymn-book* (Lond, 1935); W. A. Carne, *A century of harmony* (Melb, 1954); A. H. Kornweibel, *Apollo and the pioneers* (Perth, 1973); Roy Com on education, Report, V&P (LA Vic), 1884, 3 (47); *Church of England Messenger* (Vic), 6 Jan 1880; *A'sian Schoolmaster*, Jan 1894; *Australasian*, 13 July 1872, 30 May 1891, 15, 22 July 1893; *Musical Herald*, Nov 1890; *Age*, 6, 13, 28 Nov 1891; *Morning Herald* (Perth), 2, 5 Mar, 20, 23 Aug 1901; M. T. Radic, Aspects of organised amateur music in Melbourne 1836-1890 (M. Mus. thesis, Univ Melb, 1968); Education records (PRO, Vic).   ROBIN S. STEVENS

SUPPLE, GERALD HENRY (1823-1898), Irish patriot, poet, barrister and journalist, was born in Cork, Ireland, eldest son of Thomas Supple and his wife Letitia Anne, née Sherlock, of Ballintemple, Cork, who claimed linear descent from the poet Edmund Spenser. He studied law, history and literature in Dublin; as 'Torquil' or 'G. H. S.' he contributed patriotic poetry to C. G. Duffy's [q.v.] *Nation* and *The Ballad Poetry of Ireland* and to *Bentley's Miscellany* in 1851. Some of his work was reprinted in Edward Hayes's *The Ballads of Ireland* in

1856. Supple was probably a Young Irelander and after the unsuccessful insurrection of 1848 he went to London where he associated with the radical journalist and publisher George Holyoake, writing articles for the *Reasoner*, the *Empire* and the *Morning Star*. In 1856 his *History of the Invasion of Ireland by the Anglo-Normans* was published in Dublin.

Supple migrated to Melbourne in 1857 and, with introductions to Ebenezer Syme [q.v.] of the *Age*, joined the Melbourne press and read for the Bar. He was admitted in December 1862, but defective eyesight impeded his practice and he had to continue in journalism, writing leading articles for the *Herald* and the *Australasian* and working for the *Age*. He won repute as a writer on Irish genealogies and antiquities, but his unstable nature, intense sense of honour, both national and personal, and his failing sight made him susceptible to disappointment and imagined insult. In 1862 he left the *Age*, offended by the treatment of Irish matters by the editor, George Paton Smith, a barrister, later M.L.A. and attorney-general; on 17 May 1870 the obsessed Supple shot Paton Smith in Latrobe Street, wounding him in the elbow and killing a bystander, John Sesnan Walshe.

The trial, heard in July, stirred up much interest. G. Higinbotham and F. S. Dobson [qq.v.] defended Supple voluntarily, and Higinbotham's speech for the defence on the grounds of insanity was regarded as one of his best. Supple was found guilty but the case was referred by Chief Justice Stawell [q.v.] to the Full Court on the legal point of intention to kill. The verdict was confirmed, Supple was sentenced to death and placed in irons in the condemned cell in Melbourne gaol. Public sympathy had been aroused; Duffy and other prominent men spoke or wrote in his defence and many petitions were presented. The Executive Council reprieved him pending his request to appeal to the Privy Council; but the lesser charge of attempted murder was pressed. At first the jury failed to agree, but he was again found guilty; at both trials he vehemently defended himself, denying insanity and claiming that he was undertaking a public duty in attacking the slander and vilification rife in the colony. In September 1871 the death sentence was commuted to life imprisonment and he was removed to Pentridge.

Supple suffered bad health in gaol but published what he could to support two unmarried sisters. His poem 'Voces Dulces Animae Vinci' in the *Australasian* of 15 April 1876 has a certain pathos as the cry of a prisoner envying the freedom of the winds. On 5 October 1878, after Paton

Smith's death, he was released on compassionate grounds.

The next week Supple left Melbourne to join his sisters in Auckland. Dependent on their help to earn a precarious living in journalism, he wrote articles for the *New Zealand Herald*. In January 1879 the *Melbourne Review* published his major work, 'A Dream of Dampier', a long, descriptive poem in which the buccaneer sees a vision of the future of the unknown land he has reached. In 1892 Melbourne sympathizers, hearing of his plight, arranged for publication of *Dampier's Dream: An Australasian Foreshadowing, and Some Ballads*. He died in poor circumstances in Auckland on 16 August 1898, a pathetic, even tragic, figure, who had regarded himself as the victim of moral assassins, but whose friend Henry Kendall [q.v.] regretted that 'his really great abilities had not been balanced by anything like an even temperament'.

J. F. Hogan, *The Irish in Australia* (Melb, 1888); G. J. Holyoake, *Sixty years of an agitator's life*, 2 (Lond, 1892); D. J. O'Donoghue, *The poets of Ireland* (Dublin, 1912); P. S. Cleary, *Australia's debt to Irish nationbuilders* (Syd, 1933); A. Dean, *A multitude of counsellors* (Melb, 1968); Vic Law Reports, 1870; *Age*, 18 May, 21 July, 10, 14-16 Sept, 5-8, 17, 25, 28 Oct, 5, 16, 22 Nov 1870; *Argus*, 19, 20 May, 21 July 1870; *Australasian*, 16 Sept 1871, 24 Oct 1874, 15 Apr 1876, 5, 12 Oct 1878, 30 Jan 1892, 10 Sept 1898; *Sydney Mail*, 3 May 1884; H. Kendall, Notes on men and books, no 1 (Moir collection, LaT L); G. Supple letters 1860-97 (Co-operative Union Ltd, Holyoake House, Manchester, Eng).

E. M. FINLAY

SUTHERLAND, ALEXANDER (1852-1902), journalist and schoolmaster, was born on 26 March 1852 at Glasgow, Scotland, son of George Sutherland and his wife Jane, née Smith. His father, a carver of ships' figure-heads, draftsman, talented commercial artist and teacher of drawing, brought his family to settle at Sydney in 1864 for the sake of his health. At 14 Alexander was a pupil teacher with the Council of Education. The family moved to Melbourne in 1870 and he taught at Hawthorn Grammar School. In 1871 he gained an exhibition at the matriculation examination and attended the University of Melbourne (B.A., 1874; M.A., 1875). In 1874 he shared the Shakespeare scholarship with H. B. Higgins. Next year he became mathematical master at Scotch College and in 1877 headmaster of Carlton College, making the school an immediate success. In 1879 at All Saints Church, St Kilda, he married Elizabeth Jane, daughter of Robert Ballantyne, penal superintendent in Tasmania; they had a son and three daughters.

In 1892 Sutherland retired with an apparently assured, if modest, income from the school. He aimed to devote his time to literature and scientific investigation at his retreat near Dromana, but his plans were shattered by the depression of 1892-93. He turned to journalism and in 1895-97 he wrote leaders for the *Argus* and *Australasian*, mainly on politico-economic questions. In 1897 he failed to win Williamstown in the Legislative Assembly. Next year he returned to Melbourne in order to be more active in journalism and for the higher education of his children; he became London correspondent for the South Australian *Register*, but his stay was brief and dismal and he returned to Melbourne in 1899. In 1900-01 he continued his journalism, gave occasional courses of lectures and failed to win the Federal seat of South Melbourne. In September 1901 he became registrar of the University of Melbourne at a time when it was the subject of a royal commission, and was forced to adopt stringent financial measures. After Professor E. E. Morris [q.v.] died in Europe on 1 January 1902, Sutherland combined the duties of registrar with lecturer in English language and literature.

Sutherland's devotion to scholarship and education had led him in 1883 to head the campaign for a science degree at the university. With his wife's help he gave popular lecturettes on Shakespeare and other literary subjects at Mechanics' institutes. He was honorary secretary of the Royal Society of Victoria in 1878-85 and 1892, and read diverse learned papers to it. With his brother George [q.v.] he wrote a *History of Australia . . .* (1877) for schools; it sold more than 100,000 copies and remained a standard work for decades. He wrote the first volume of *Victoria and its Metropolis* (1888), and his *The Origin and Growth of the Moral Instinct* (1898), an attempt to establish that moral development conformed to evolutionary theory, won wide international acclaim and in recent times has been regarded by Morris Ginsberg as a pioneer work in the field. He contributed many articles to the *Melbourne Review*, of which he was a founder and for a time coeditor with H. G. Turner [q.v.]. He wrote biographies of Henry Kendall and Adam Lindsay Gordon [qq.v.] for *The Development of Australian Literature* (1898), which he also edited with Turner, and memoirs of Sir Redmond Barry and his old teacher, Edward Hearn [qq.v.]. He provided the details about Victoria which Sir Charles Dilke [q.v.] used freely in his *Problems of Greater Britain* (1890).

He published *Thirty Short Poems* (1890), wrote many short stories and left manuscripts of two unpublished novels. He also had a talent for sketching, a profound knowledge of music and a good baritone voice. At Dromana he even provided valuable service as a doctor. Of medium height and dark complexion, his manner was genial and unobtrusive, his speech deliberate and judicious. He enjoyed bush-walking. Australia has been endowed with few all-round men capable of generating such cultural force.

Sutherland died suddenly of heart disease on 9 August 1902 at Adelaide and was buried in Kew cemetery with the service conducted by Rev. Charles Strong [q.v.]. His estate was valued for probate at £5959. His sister Jane (1853-1928) was a well-known artist, and his brother William (1859-1911) a prominent physicist.

H. G. Turner, *Alexander Sutherland* (Melb, 1908); G. Blainey, *A centenary history of the University of Melbourne* (Melb, 1957); *Table Talk*, 23 Dec 1892, 21 Mar, 21 Nov 1901, 14 Aug 1902; *Argus*, 13 Aug 1902; *Australasian*, 16 Aug 1902.   P. H. NORTHCOTT

SUTHERLAND, GEORGE (1855-1905), journalist, was born on 1 October 1855 at Dumbarton, Scotland, second son of George Sutherland, draftsman, and his wife Jane, née Smith. In 1864 the family, which included Alexander [q.v.], migrated to New South Wales where George attended Sydney Grammar School for five years. When the family moved to Melbourne in 1870 he went to Scotch College.

Sutherland worked briefly as a junior teacher in private secondary schools, and then read history and political economy at the University of Melbourne (B.A., 1877; M.A., 1879). He taught humanities at Carlton College where Alexander was headmaster; though fond of teaching he found the management of classes wearing. Turning to journalism, he went up the Darling River to do an assignment 'among the Riverina sheep runs'; he then took a steamer down river and visited Adelaide, where he met J. H. Finlayson [q.v.] of the *South Australian Register*. He joined the editorial staff of the *Register* in 1881 and in the next twenty years gained a reputation as a 'highly cultivated and remarkably versatile journalist' who at a moment's notice could write on almost any conceivable theme. He had already collaborated with Alexander in a lively textbook account of the *History of Australia from 1606 to 1876* (Melbourne, 1879) and had published on his own account *Tales of the Goldfields* (1880). In Adelaide he wrote further works: *Australia or England in the South* (London, 1886) was designed to give the impression of life in Australia while *The South Australian Company. A study in colonisation* (London, 1898) was his most serious work. More practical books, based on his own and others' observations, were published on vine-growing, livestock-handling and the geography of Australia. Of an experimental, inventive bent, he had from 1880 engaged in what he termed 'technological journalism', beginning with his descriptions of promising inventions displayed at various international exhibitions. His book *Twentieth Century Inventions. A Forecast* (London, 1901) included his own patented and successful photographic engraving process, rapid-printing newspaper portraits process and ore concentrators, as well as a discussion of inventions in other fields.

In 1902 Sutherland returned to Melbourne to join the editorial staff of the *Age*. Modest, cultured and urbane, with 'high integrity and exceedingly happy temperament', he died suddenly at his home at Kew on 1 December 1905 of rupture of the heart and was buried in the Boroondara cemetery, with Rev. C. Strong [q.v.] officiating. He left an estate valued for probate at £339. In Adelaide on 25 September 1882 he had married Ada Alice, daughter of R. G. Brown, and was survived by her and their two sons and three daughters, one of whom, Margaret, became a distinguished composer.

Age, 4 Dec 1905; *Argus*, 4 Dec 1905; *Register* (Adel), 4 Dec 1905; Sutherland papers (NL).   SUZANNE G. MELLOR

SUTHERLAND, JOHN (1816-1889), builder and politician, was born on 16 February 1816 near Wick, Caithness, Scotland, son of John Sutherland, crofter, and his wife Louisa, née Thompson. His formal education was slight and his native shrewdness unadorned by literary ability. Trained as a carpenter, he paid his passage to New South Wales in 1838 and, after early struggles, prospered as a builder. By the time of his retirement in 1860 his Abercrombie Street business had handled some large-scale projects, and in 1866 he successfully sued the government for £3514 for contracts carried out in 1853-54. In 1863 with John Frazer [q.v.] and William Manson he took up 287 square miles near Port Denison in the Bourke district of Queensland; he held another 250 square miles in South Kennedy, and Lindisfarne in North Gregory in the 1870s.

Sutherland took an early interest in politics, supporting (Sir) Charles Cowper [q.v.] from the 1843 Legislative Council elections. In 1857-68 and 1871-72 he represented Phillip Ward on the Sydney Municipal Council and was mayor in 1861. In 1860-80 he sat for Paddington in the Legislative Assembly. He professed himself a 'workingman's M.P.', advocated improved working conditions and wages and had cordial relations with the Trades and Labor Council; but he was more concerned with economy in public works. He supported Cowper and (Sir) John Robertson [q.v.], and by opposing overseas contracts and encouraging local manufactures he gained a 'protectionist' reputation; but his attitude was pragmatic and in October 1868 he helped to defeat the protectionist premier (Sir) James Martin [q.v.]. He was secretary for public works under Robertson and Cowper in 1868-70 and won repute, though his early attack on treasury procedures caused public alarm. In the same office in 1872-75 under (Sir) Henry Parkes [q.v.], he broke politically but not personally with Robertson. In the parliamentary confusion of 1877 he refused to serve with either Robertson or Parkes, but in December he reluctantly accepted the works portfolio in J. S. Farnell's [q.v.] ministry, and next year sought efficiency in railway contracting and planning.

Sutherland had become expert in a post that needed administrative skill and political courage and, although he debated land law reform and promoted technical education, he preferred his own field. Blunt, 'straightforward, businesslike and thoroughly honest', he was also 'warm tempered and warm hearted', happier at his desk than in the House. He accepted the popular policy of rapid railway expansion but insisted on elaborate surveys and careful planning, and argued that local iron products would encourage native industry and eventually be safer and cheaper. His attitude provoked a long controversy that was not helped by his lack of any real consistency of action or knowledge of political economy.

Between September and December 1873 Sutherland and Parkes took up 3760 acres of mineral leases near Jamberoo and held another 408 under conditional purchase; they persuaded Frazer, Governor Sir Hercules Robinson, (Sir) Saul Samuel [q.v.] and others to back them in a vain attempt to mine coal. About 1874 with James Rutherford [q.v.] he set up the Eskbank Ironworks at Lithgow and next year the firm lost over £100,000 under his management, despite the freight concessions he had arranged. In 1878 John McElhone [q.v.] questioned whether Sutherland, as a partner in the Lithgow Valley Iron Mining Co. which had govern-

ment contracts, could remain in parliament: he was cleared by the Elections and Qualifications Committee. He resigned his seat in February 1880 because his unlimited liability company had accepted a government contract for re-rolling old rails. His disabilities legally removed, he won Redfern in November but did little. In 1881 he was nominated to the Legislative Council but did not take his seat; he represented Redfern in the assembly in 1882-89. A moderate supporter of (Sir) Alexander Stuart's [q.v.] 1883-85 government, he was bewildered by the mid-1880s political confusion produced by recession and fiscalism; but he joined Parkes's 1887-89 ministry in his old portfolio, as railway administration deteriorated and the use of the unemployed on public works grew: his contracting methods proved a problem for the free-trade ministry.

From the 1860s Sutherland had been a magistrate for Sydney, a vice-president of the Sydney Mechanics' School of Arts and a committee-man of the Benevolent Society of New South Wales. He was a trustee of the Mutual Benefit building societies and chairman of the Australian Mutual Fire Insurance Society. A Freemason under the English constitution, he had a long connexion with the Oddfellows' and Foresters' friendly societies. A trustee of the Savings Bank of New South Wales and a vice-president of the Highland Society of New South Wales, he was a member of the Board of Technical Education from 1883 and of the Parliamentary Standing Committee on Public Works in 1889.

Sutherland died of diabetes at his home in Abercrombie Place, Sydney, on 23 June 1889 and was buried with Masonic rites in the Congregational section of Rookwood cemetery. He was survived by his wife Mary, daughter of Captain Ogilvie of Campbelltown, whom he had married on 2 May 1839, and by their only daughter; two sons had died young. Although his estate was valued for probate at £11,286, his liabilities necessitated a memorial fund to assist his widow, which the Trades and Labor Council supported.

Ex-M.L.A., *Our present parliament, what it is worth* (Syd, c1886); P. Loveday and A. W. Martin, *Parliament factions and parties* (Melb, 1966); V&P (LA NSW), 1866, 1, 130, 5, 803, 1875-76, 2, 973, 1878-79, 2, 63; PD (NSW), 1879-89; *Government Gazette* (Qld), 27 June 1863; K. J. Cable, 'Eastern suburbs railway: early plans and politics', *JRAHS*, 51 (1965); *SMH*, 7 Dec 1860, 19 Nov 1864, 11 Nov 1868, 6 Dec 1869, 6 Jan, 14, 22 May 1872, 11 Apr, 9 Dec 1874, 29 Dec 1877, 24 Feb, 18 Nov 1880, 2 Dec 1882, 12 Oct 1885, 30 Apr, 2 May 1887, 29 Jan, 24 June, 18 Oct 1889; *Sydney Mail*, 14 Feb 1880; *Daily Telegraph*

(Syd), 24 June 1889; Parkes letters and autograph letters (ML).   K. J. CABLE

SUTHERLAND, SULINA MURRAY
MacDONALD (1839-1909), nurse and child
welfare worker, was born on 26 December
1839 at Culgower, Sutherlandshire, Scotland, third child of Baigrie Sutherland,
crofter and road and bridge-builder, and
his wife Jane, née MacDonald. 'Sulie Baigrie' attended the Portgower school and the
Free Church of Scotland in Helmsdale, and
worked on her father's croft until she was
25. Early fired by Florence Nightingale's
example, she decided to follow her sister to
New Zealand and to become a nurse. She
left Gravesend as a 'domestic servant and
assisted emigrant' in the *Eastern Empire* on
28 August 1864, and in the Wairarapa
Valley worked for the sick and helpless
both Maoris and settlers. Stressing prevention and permanent provision for welfare, she lectured on child-rearing, advocated better care for orphans and fatherless
children and in 1879 was a principal
founder of Masterton Hospital. From early
1879 to December 1880 she was matron of
Wellington Hospital, but deep-rooted
troubles in the hospital flared up in accusations against her and the hospital dispenser. Their accusers were dismissed and
they were exonerated but given the 'privilege of resigning'. Her sense of injustice
unallayed by a presentation and much
acclaim, she left New Zealand and settled
in Melbourne in 1881.

After brief periods of nursing at the
Melbourne Lying-in and Alfred hospitals,
Sulina became captured by the plight of
destitute children. By August she was 'lady
missionary' with the Scots Church District
Association which on her advice set up in
October a Neglected Children's Aid Society.
She also superintended the Scots Church
Sunday school and, with her close friend
Mrs Maria Lord Armour, conducted a
Saturday afternoon class and savings bank
for local children. In 1885 at her suggestion
her society rented premises, which she
supervised, for children needing temporary
care. By March 1883, also at her instigation,
her association in co-operation with all
Church denominations had established the
Society in Aid of Maternity Hospital
Patients. She urged the establishment of a
skilled nursing service for the sick poor in
their own homes, and remained a lifelong
active committee member of the Melbourne District Nursing Society formed on
17 February 1885.

In May 1886 the Presbytery of Melbourne appointed Miss Sutherland missionary within their bounds. Next year her
society was the first to be approved under
the provisions of the Neglected Children's
Act, 1887, and she was 'specially authorised' to apprehend children in brothels.
By now well known and much respected,
she was fearless in her search for children
in back streets and alleyways, brothels and
gambling houses, going in perfect safety,
recognizable in her 'no-nonsense' habit of
firmly fitting coat and skirt, mannish hat
and umbrella. Although only of average
height, her dignity and confidence gave her
undeniable authority.

Convinced that, except in some cases of
severe handicap, 'family life, in however
humble a home, is far better for a child
than that in any institution, however well
regulated', she appealed through country
clergymen of all denominations for permanent foster homes for her children, while
encouraging the formation of local groups
to support the work of the society. She pronounced with conviction on all social issues,
offering strongly critical comments on all
stages of the Neglected Children's Act,
1890, and the Infant Life Protection Act,
1890. In November she gave evidence to
the royal commission on charitable institutions, advocating her foster home system
and arguing that voluntary aid alone could
not solve the problems of poverty. In 1891
she wrote an important paper on slum life
in Melbourne for the second Australasian
Conference on Charity.

By now 'Miss Sutherland's Children's
Society' was highly regarded, receiving
particular praise from the inspector of
charities who supported her call for expansion in a time of growing unemployment. However, in September 1893, fearing
financial embarrassment, the society's committee ordered limitation, and she and
fourteen committee members resigned. By
November, through her advocacy, the
Presbyterian General Assembly had set up
the wider-based Presbyterian Society for
Destitute and Neglected Children with
Miss Sutherland as agent. The society
flourished, but criticism led the General
Assembly's commission to direct that it
receive children only under legal guardianship, give preference to Presbyterian children and use only Presbyterian foster
homes. A bitter press debate on these issues
was intensified when she stated that resentment arose from her denunciation of
Church office-holders receiving rents from
houses used for immoral purposes. She was
arraigned before various Church courts and
admonished by the General Assembly on
15 November 1894. Next day she resigned
and was followed by her entire ladies' committee. On 7 December a public meeting
organized by her committee resolved to

inaugurate the Victorian Neglected Children's Aid Society with Miss Sutherland as agent, a controlling ladies' committee and an advisory council of twenty-five gentlemen.

The new society prospered. To their city receiving centre a home in Parkville was added, twice extended and in 1905 named the Sutherland Home: 'The value of Miss Sutherland's noble work', wrote Alfred Deakin in 1906, 'is simply incalculable'. From July 1895 she had been helped by Sister Ellen Sanderson and in 1899-1901, though her own salary was never more than £100 a year, she paid a second assistant from her own pocket. In 1897, impaired in health, she visited the United Kingdom during Queen Victoria's Diamond Jubilee, raising money for her society on the way. In 1904 she was severely injured in an accident, while an old New Zealand injury was worsening. In 1908 she was clearly thinking of reducing her duties but the committee, listening to complaints from domestic staff, moved into a head-on dispute with her and in May dismissed her.

Determined to carry on her work, Miss Sutherland moved to the City Receiving Home, rented in her name, and was joined by Sister Sanderson and other supporters. By June 'The Sutherland Homes for Orphans, Neglected and Destitute Children' had been formally constituted with a committee of prominent citizens, including some of her old committee. On 3 November a government inquiry into her dismissal, instigated by her critics, completely vindicated her. The new society attracted generous support. On 17 April 1909 Miss Auguste Meglin made a gift of house and property at Diamond Creek to the Sutherland Homes Trust and in July bequeathed it a substantial share of her estate. By September the trust had completed plans to remove the receiving home there while retaining the city centre as headquarters and for emergencies. But Miss Sutherland died suddenly of pneumonia in Melbourne on 8 October 1909, the day which was to take the children to Diamond Creek. Her tombstone in the Melbourne general cemetery, erected by public subscription, paid tribute to her twenty-eight years as 'an unwearying friend' of Melbourne's poor. While her brusqueness and impatience with ineptitude, her zeal and disinterested honesty in exposing social evils often ruffled the feelings of others, she gained and kept the strong loyalties of those with whom she worked closely. Her work must rank with that of Catherine Helen Spence and Caroline Chisholm [qq.v.] and, Christian rather than sectarian, is perpetuated in the continuing services of the societies she established.

J. Thomson, Rescue of neglected and destitute children. A defence of Miss Sutherland and the Rev. A. Stewart (Melb, 1894); J. C. Jessop, Selina Sutherland. Her life and work (Melb, 1958); V&P (LA Vic), 1892-93, 4 (60); Presbyterian Church of Vic, Procs of the second Australian conference on charity (1891) and of the General Assembly and the Commission of the General Assembly (1893-94); Scots Church District Assn and Neglected Children's Aid Soc, Records 1881-93 (Scots Church, Melb); Records 1885-1909 (Melb District Nursing Soc); Presbyteries of Melb, Minutes 1886 and Melb North, Minutes 1893-94 and Presbyterian Soc for Destitute and Neglected Children, Records 1893-95 (Presbyterian Church of Vic, Melb); Kirk Session minutes 1893-94 (Scots Church, Melb); Vic Neglected Children's Aid Soc, Records 1894-1909 (Vic Children's Aid Soc, Melb); Sutherland Homes for Orphans, Neglected and Destitute Children, Records 1908-09 (Sutherland Homes for Children, Melb); City Council and Hospital Committee minutes 1880-81 (Wellington City Council); Chief Sec 1908/C 7697 (PRO, Vic); papers, IMCH 4/63 (National Archives, Wellington); family papers and information.   RUTH HOBAN

SUTTON, HENRY (1856-1912). inventor, was born on 3 September 1856 at Ballarat, Victoria, son of Richard Henry Sutton and his wife Mary, née Johnson. Richard founded a music firm in a tent on the Ballarat goldfield in 1854. After a short stint as a miner he had found that playing a home-made concertina in his tent at night attracted crowds and he began to make them for his friends. Persuaded by the astute Mary to buy a dray-load of musical instruments in Melbourne, he sold them in a few days. He bought land on Plank Road and built a music warehouse of brick and wood with a plate glass window.

Henry, his three brothers Alfred, Walter and Frederick, and his two sisters, Elizabeth and Emilie, were mainly educated by their mother, and all but Henry in their younger years helped in the business. Shy and modest, Henry studied unaided from the age of 11; interested in science and engineering, he had read all the scientific books in the well-stocked Ballarat Mechanics' Institute before he was 14. Although he had little access to current literature, apart from Engineer and Engineering, his own models and machines were ingenious and his drawings revealed great talent. He won a silver medal and thirty other prizes for drawing at the Ballarat School of Design. Observations at the age of 10 of the flutter of insect wings against smoked glass led to his theory on the flight of birds which he propounded in a paper read to the Aeronautical Society of Great Britain and published in its annual report of 1878. Sutton's experimental ornithopter (c. 1870), driven by clockwork, could fly in a circumference of twelve feet and from left to right and upwards at any desired angle. His experiments with heavier-than-air materials for flight seem to be the first of their kind in Australia.

According to his friend W. B. Withers [q.v.], Sutton designed an electric continuous current dynamo with a practical ring armature as early as 1870. A similar device had been invented in 1860 by an Italian, Pacinotti, and in 1871 the Belgian Z. T. Gramme showed the French Academy of Sciences his own improved version, the Gramme Dynamo; it used the same principles as Sutton's. When it was found in 1873 that the device was reversible and could be used as an electric motor the rapid development of the electrical industry followed. Less than a year after A. G. Bell had received his patent on 7 March 1876, Sutton had devised and constructed more than twenty different telephones, sixteen of which were patented by others. Bell visited Ballarat to see a complete telephone system installed by Sutton in the family warehouse. Thomas Edison's carbon lamp was announced on 21 December 1879; Sutton had been working independently on similar lines, and on 6 January 1880 the Victorian government astronomer R. L. J. Ellery [q.v.] was aware of his successful experiments. Ellery acknowledged him as one of the best lecturers at the Ballarat School of Mines, where Sutton taught electricity and applied magnetism in 1883-87.

He worked tirelessly with 'daylight sometimes surprising him every morning for a week'; he declared that 'eight hours' work won't lift a man in this world'. Always by invitation, Sutton contributed papers to societies in Australia and abroad on topics including electricity, colour photography and the process of engraving by the aid of photography; his paper on his new electric storage battery received acclaim when it was read before the Royal Society of London in December 1881. He rarely applied for patents, partly because he spurned material gain and wanted to 'benefit fellow workers in science'. According to available records, only two patents were taken out in his name in Victoria: in 1886 for 'Improvement in electric circuits for telephonic purposes' and in 1887 for 'An improved process of converting a photographic image on a gelatine surface into a relief or intaglio printing surface ...'. Records in New South Wales include two patents: for ex-

plosion engines and 'Intaglio ... photoprinting'. His mercury air pump, of which details were published in the English Mechanic and World of Science on 21 July 1882, was recommended for the manufacture of lamp bulbs and was developed by others. A vacuum pump, worked by a water jet, was presented to the Ballarat School of Mines for use in chemistry classes. In some respects his most interesting work was in the field of what has since become television: he claimed in the late 1880s to have designed, but not constructed, an apparatus that would transmit to Ballarat the running of the Melbourne Cup.

Sutton's father had died in 1876 and the prospering business was then run by his mother and brothers, with 19-year-old Alfred as manager; Alfred opened a music store in Elizabeth Street, Melbourne, in 1884 and the firm became Sutton Bros. In 1894 the four brothers formed a private company, Suttons Pty Ltd. Henry now concentrated on business, although he experimented with radio and built a portable set with a range of 500 yards. Interested in the advent of the motor car, he designed, built and drove two efficient vehicles with carburettors of his own invention. At a meeting of fifty-five motorists held at the Port Phillip Club on 9 December 1903, Sutton moved the resolution that founded the Automobile Club of Victoria.

Aged 25, Sutton had married Elizabeth Ellen Wyatt at Ballarat. Aged 46, he married Annie May Patti at Malvern; he died of heart failure and chronic nephritis on 28 July 1912. He was buried in Brighton cemetery, survived by his second wife, their two sons, and two of the three sons of the first marriage. He died intestate but left property worth £9984. At the very least Sutton was a gifted innovator and developer over a very wide range; the isolation in which he worked underlines his remarkable talent. He was clearly in the van of several international experimental areas but precise claims to fame remain to be established.

W. B. Withers, The history of Ballarat, 2nd ed (Ballarat, 1887); G. Sutton, Richard Henry Sutton, Esq., 1830-1876 (Melb, 1954); J. Goode, Smoke, smell and clatter (Melb, 1969); R. J. Gibson, Australia and Australians in civil aviation, 1 (Syd, 1971); Ballarat School of Mines, Annual report, 1883-84; information from Mrs E. Wolf, Warrandyte, Vic.

AUSTIN McCALLUM

SUTTOR, SIR FRANCIS BATHURST (1839-1915), pastoralist and politician, was born on 30 April 1839 at Bathurst, New South Wales, son of William Henry Suttor [q.v.] and his wife Charlotte, née Francis. Educated at The King's School, Parramatta, at 19 he managed his father's properties near Bathurst. In 1863 he took up Redbank and Katella near Wellington, and later Bradwardine at Bathurst. In 1868 he bought 100 merino ewes from C. C. Cox of Brombee and the use of the sire Brombee Pet for two months. By in-breeding and rigorous culling at Katella he maintained the high standards of Mudgee sheep. In 1881, with ewes bought from James Gibson [q.v.], he founded at Bradwardine a second stud of Tasmanian merinos that proved successful in shows. In 1889 he joined a Bathurst syndicate that imported two Vermont rams and formed another stud flock of American-Australian merinos. A popular judge at agricultural shows, he also imported a Cleveland Bay sire and bred coaching horses.

In January 1875 Suttor was elected as a free trader to the Legislative Assembly for Bathurst after a bitter campaign against Edmund Webb [q.v.]. Abandoning his support for denominational education, he became minister of justice and public instruction in Sir Henry Parkes's [q.v.] 1877 ministry; he brought Parkes support in the Bathurst district. In the Parkes-John Robertson [q.v.] coalition he was successively minister of justice and public instruction, postmaster-general, acting secretary for mines, and minister of public instruction. He introduced the Public Instruction Act of 1880. Later he fell out with Parkes and turned to protection, convinced that it would arrest falling rural prices: the change maintained his cabinet potential in the confused fiscal politics of 1885-94. In 1886 he became postmaster-general under (Sir) Patrick Jennings [q.v.]. In January 1889 he was minister of public instruction under (Sir) George Dibbs [q.v.], but lost his seat at the general elections in February after intervention by Parkes and Webb; also losing East Macquarie, he offered to resign but was nominated at the request of Dibbs to the Legislative Council.

In 1891-1900 Suttor again held Bathurst and was minister of public instruction until 1894 in Dibbs's second ministry. He was acting colonial secretary for five months in 1892 and represented the government at the Colonial Conference in Ottawa in 1894. Though rejecting Parkes's federal proposals in 1891, by 1898 he had joined Edmund Barton's conservative federalists. He resigned his seat in June 1900 to become vice-president of the Executive Council and representative of the government in the council. Knighted in 1903, he was from that year

until 1915 president of the Legislative Council.

In 1907-15 as president of the Royal Agricultural Society of New South Wales Suttor revitalized the Sydney Royal Show. He was vice-president of the New South Wales Sheepbreeders' Association and its president in 1903-15; he was also president of the Stockowners' Association of New South Wales, a director of the Australian Joint Stock Bank and the Mutual Assurance Society of Victoria, president of the Council of the Royal Alexandra Hospital for Children and the Royal Life Saving Society, trustee of the Art Gallery of New South Wales and the Australian Museum, a member of the Senate of the University of Sydney, and a patron of Australian literature, especially of Miles Franklin. Long an Anglican synodsman in Bathurst, he was chairman of committees in 1903 and an episcopal elector in 1911.

Despite political differences, Suttor remained close to his brother 'Willie'. 'Dignified and splendidly courteous' with a merry twinkle in his eye, he was 'generous minded and fearless in his views'. He died on 4 April 1915 at his residence at Darling Point and after a state funeral was buried in the Anglican section of South Head cemetery. Predeceased by his wife Emily Jane (1841-1911), daughter of T. H. Hawkins of Walmer, Bathurst, whom he had married in July 1863, he was survived by three sons and five daughters. His estate was valued for probate at £34,107. His bust by Nelson Illingworth is owned by the Legislative Council, Sydney.

E. Digby (ed), Australian men of mark, 2, no 4 (Syd, 1889); C. McIvor, The history and development of sheep farming from antiquity to modern times (Syd, 1893); Bathurst Times, 2 Jan 1875, 2 May 1914, 5 Apr 1915; Bulletin, 28 Aug 1880, 6 July 1903; Bathurst Free Press, 16, 18 July 1898; Pastoral Review, 16 Apr 1910, 15 May 1915; SMH, 29 Apr 1914, 5, 6 Apr 1915; Daily Telegraph (Syd), 2 May 1914; Miles Franklin letters, Parkes letters, Suttor family papers and letters (ML); CO 201/600/58, 110, 610/41; information from R. C. Suttor, Bathurst.   RUTH TEALE

SUTTOR, WILLIAM HENRY (1805-1877), pastoralist and politician, was born on 12 December 1805 at Baulkham Hills, New South Wales, third son of George Suttor [q.v.] and his wife Sarah Maria, née Dobinson. He was educated by his parents and an assigned convict. In 1822 William became overseer of his father's 320-acre grant at Brucedale, Peel, taking it over in 1834, and by September 1838 was managing his father's 10,020 acres and occupying his

own 3344 acres. In the 1840s these properties were let to Irish tenants. In 1845 with
his father he bought Alloway Bank from
John Piper [q.v.] and in 1852 Cangoura, an
adjoining 5000 acres. In 1843 he had formed
stations at Walandra, Lachlan River, and
Beau Desert, Logan River (Moreton Bay);
by 1865 he occupied over 600.000 acres on
the lower Lachlan, Darling, Macquarie and
Bogan rivers.

In 1843-54 Suttor represented the Counties of Roxburgh, Phillip and Wellington in
the Legislative Council; he opposed the
resumption of transportation, supported
Caroline Chisholm [q.v.] and was regarded
by some Catholics as their spokesman. He
represented Bathurst (County) in the Legislative Assembly in 1856-59, East Macquarie
in 1859-64 and Bathurst in 1866-72. Independent and liberal, he supported manhood
suffrage, freehold agricultural settlement on
crown lands, local government and National
education. In Bathurst he was steward of the
turf club, patron of the agricultural show
(in 1863-64 held at Alloway Bank), benefactor of the Anglican diocese, synodsman
and warden of Holy Trinity Church, Kelso.
A founding member of the Union Club,
Sydney, in 1857, he was president in 1863-
70.

In December 1833 in Sydney, Suttor had
married Charlotte Augusta Ann Francis
(1817-1879), by whom he had ten sons and
four daughters. He died on 20 October 1877
at Alloway Bank, leaving goods valued for
probate at £107,250, and was buried in the
family vault at Holy Trinity, Kelso.

His eldest son, WILLIAM HENRY junior
(1834-1905), pastoralist and politician, was
born on 14 November 1834 at Brucedale.
Educated by Dr William Woolls [q.v.], at
16 he managed his father's runs, becoming
an excellent bushman. By 1865 he was in
partnership with his father and also occupying 64,000 acres in the Albert District. He
sold these runs in the 1880s after trouble
with selectors, and engaged in sheep-breeding on Curranyalpa, Budda, Tilpa and his
other runs on the Darling. At the same time
he entered pastoral partnerships with his
brother Walter and E. U. Bowler, and with
William Kite and T. C. Ashe. In July 1890
he was founding president of the Pastoralists' Union of New South Wales for some
months, but by 1892 all his runs were mortgaged to the Commercial Banking Co. of
Sydney.

From January 1875 to July 1879 Suttor sat
for East Macquarie in the Legislative Assembly as a free trader and in 1877-78 was
minister for mines in J. S. Farnell's [q.v.]
ministry. In December 1880 he was nominated to the Legislative Council; in 1889-91
he was vice-president of the Executive Coun-

cil and government representative in the
council in Parkes's [q.v.] last ministry: a
loyal supporter of Parkes, he never sought
office, doubting his abilities and facing
bankruptcy. In 1894-95 he held the same
offices in George Reid's first government.

Quiet, unassuming and genial, 'Willie'
Suttor often gave public readings for charities. His contributions to the *Daily Telegraph* were reprinted as *Australian Stories
Retold and Sketches of Country Life* (Bathurst, 1887); for its centenary supplement
(23 January 1888) he wrote an article on the
pastoral industry reprinted in *Centenary of
Australia* (Sydney, 1888), and for the issue
of 22 June 1889 on 'Early Christian missions
among the Aborigines' (reprinted. Sydney,
1889). He lived at Cangoura after 1873 and
until 1891 was a trustee of the Bathurst
Hospital, president of the Bathurst Agricultural, Horticultural and Pastoral Association, captain in the reserve rifle company.
president of the Bathurst Mechanics' School
of Arts, member of the public school board.
warden of Holy Trinity Church, Kelso, and
member of the Anglican diocesan council.

In March 1862 Suttor had married Adelaide Agnes Henrietta Bowler (d. 1920), who
bore him one son and six daughters. He died
in Sydney on 20 October 1905, leaving
assets valued at £8102 and debts of £118,188.

JOHN BLIGH junior (1859-1925), civil servant, nephew of William Henry senior, was
born on 10 December 1859 at Wyagdon,
Wattle Flat, fourth son of John Bligh Suttor
(1809-1886) and his wife Julia Nina Frances,
née Bowler (d. 1901). His father, a large-
scale pastoralist, represented East Macquarie
in the Legislative Assembly in 1867-72 and
was a member of the Legislative Council in
1881-86. Educated in Bathurst and Sydney,
John junior joined the Department of Public
Works on 15 December 1879 as a draftsman
and surveyor. Appointed assistant engineer,
western division, in January 1885 and later
engineer, he introduced the first day labour
system on the railways, and became an associate member of the Institution of Civil
Engineers, London. In October 1903 he was
appointed commercial commissioner in the
east for the New South Wales government,
and was stationed at Kobe, Japan. His
reports on the overseas trade of China, Man-
churia and Siberia, Japan, Korea, India and
Burma, Ceylon, the Dutch East Indies, the
Philippine Islands and the Straits Settlements were published between 1904 and
1919. His familiarity with the Japanese
language and habits rendered valuable his
reports to his premier in 1914-18. After
retiring in June 1922 he remained in Kobe,
where he died on 28 May 1925, leaving an
estate of £2431 and survived by his wife,
Emma Isabel Parker, née Bullough, whom

he had married on 13 December 1882, and by one son and two daughters.

T. L. Suttor, *Hierarchy and democracy in Australia, 1788-1870* (Melb, 1965); T&CJ, 7 Apr, 3 Nov 1877, 11 May 1889; *Bathurst Times*, 24 Oct 1877, 27 Feb 1891, 18 Feb 1914; *Pastoral Review*, 15 Apr 1891; *Bulletin*, 6 July 1903; SMH, 1 June 1925; Parkes letters, George Suttor diary, Suttor family papers and letters (ML).

RUTH TEALE

SWALLOW, THOMAS (1827-1890), manufacturer, was born at Reading, Berkshire, England, son of William Swallow, maltster, and his wife Frances, née Dodd. He migrated in 1849 to the United States of America, where he lived for four years. At 23 he married; his wife died without issue. On 16 March 1853 in New York he married Isabella Fulton, a migrant from Paisley, Scotland, and together they sailed for the Victorian goldfields, settling first at Ballarat where he sold Colt revolvers. In 1854 he set up at Sandridge (Port Melbourne) as a manufacturer and purveyor of ships' biscuits, probably using his youthful experience of the trade in Reading. In 1854 Thomas Harris Ariell (1832-1875) became his partner, followed in 1877 by F. T. Derham [q.v.], who soon became his son-in-law. After a break of a few years the firm continued to operate as Swallow & Ariell, with assets of about £40,000 and a solid reputation as biscuit manufacturers, flour-millers, and sugar refiners; it became a public company in 1888 with assets of £160,000 and liabilities of £47,000, but its growth ceased with the slump of the 1890s.

Swallow's sons were enterprising but extravagant agricultural pioneers; he substantially backed two of their projects: their attempt after 1874 to develop a large tract of the Goulburn Valley near Shepparton, where they were among the first landowners to attempt irrigation, and investment in Queensland sugar in the 1880s. Keen to obtain sugar for his firm's Melbourne industries Swallow founded the large Hambledon plantation near Cairns in 1881, and saved the district from stagnation. Other plantations followed, but the decline of prices after 1884 and the Griffith ministry's plans to end the import of Pacific island labour in 1890 jeopardized the industry. Swallow's sons ran up deficits, both through pioneering new crops such as coffee and tropical fruit, and expenditure on hospitality and horseflesh. By 1888 Hambledon was £180 000 in the red, which may explain why Swallow and Derham then each retained less than 20 per cent in their parent company. In that year R. A. Kingsford [q.v.] acquired Hambledon

and in 1897 it was taken over by the Colonial Sugar Refining Co.

Swallow was a prolific mechanical inventor, a just businessman and a kindly if paternalistic employer. A Freemason, he was a member of the first municipal council of Sandridge in 1860 and was mayor for several terms before retiring in 1875. Interested in defence, he was a good marksman and held a commission in the Volunteer Artillery, retiring with the honorary rank of major in October 1884. He was also a patron of local cricket and football teams. Aged 63, he died of pneumonia at Cairns on 26 June 1890, survived by his wife, three of his four sons and three of his four daughters. His body was brought to Victoria and buried in the Church of England section of the Melbourne general cemetery. His estate was valued for probate at £189,814.

Swallow & Ariell Ltd, *The first hundred years 1854-1954*, G. A. Derham ed (Melb, 1954); *Industrial Victoria*, Feb 1950; *Cairns Post*, 26 June 1890; *Argus*, 27 June, 14 July 1890; S. C. P. Turnbull, 'Romance of industry', 12 Feb 1930; scrapbook (Swallow & Ariell Ltd, Port Melb); Swallow and Ariell papers (Univ Melb Archives).

G. C. BOLTON

SWAN, JAMES (1811-1891), newspaper proprietor, was born in Glasgow, Scotland, son of Daniel Swan, a private in the Highland Light Infantry killed in the Peninsular war, and Jennet McLaren, a deaf mute. In August 1823, his mother was murdered by another woman in his presence in a quarrel over a man. The boy gave evidence at the trial, was taken into a foster home and later entered a lawyer's office. Leaving the law, he was apprenticed first to a carver and gilder and finally to the printing office of the *Scots Times*. In 1831 he married Christina Mackay.

Swan was offered employment in Sydney by J. D. Lang [q.v.] in 1836, his second year as a journeyman. He arrived with Lang in the *Portland* on 3 December 1837, served for three years on Lang's newspaper the *Colonist*, then undertook a brief, unsuccessful farming venture in the Illawarra district. Returning to his trade he joined the *Sydney Herald* when the *Colonist* closed in 1841 and, after a second farming failure, took employment at Brisbane in June 1846 as foreman printer for A. S. Lyon's new *Moreton Bay Courier*. Early in 1848 Lyon was in financial trouble and in July Swan bought him out. He employed William Wilkes [q.v.] as editor till 1856 then, leasing the paper to W. C. Belbridge and Charles Lilley [q.v.], visited Scotland. Swan resumed management of the *Cou-

rier in September 1858 and probably also became editor; he spoke of the liberal attitude taken by the paper in opposing convict labour and squatters, an attitude probably shared with him by Wilkes. He participated strongly in the movement to separate Queensland from New South Wales but when it was achieved in 1859 he sold the *Courier* and retired. In 1873-75 he was mayor of Brisbane when the first bridge was built over the Brisbane River and on 18 April 1878 he was appointed to the Legislative Council as a supporter of Samuel Griffith.

As an ardent Baptist, Swan had been a foundation member of the temporary united Church for Congregationalists and Baptists established in August 1855; he welcomed the first resident Baptist minister in September 1858. His extensive real estate investments included two successful suburban hotels, and he had supported the establishment of the Democratic Association.

Swan's wife died on 27 January 1888 and on 10 January 1889 he married Christina Street, aged 31. The couple sailed for Scotland in 1891 but he died in the Red Sea on 26 May and was buried near Port Said, Egypt. After legacies to friends, relations and a number of charities, the remainder of his £33,100 estate was left in trust for his widow. On her death in 1930 it passed to the Baptist Church for the support of evangelists of impeccable theological orthodoxy.

T. W. H. Leavitt (ed), *Australian representative men*, 3rd ed (Melb, 1888); J. J. Knight, *In the early days* (Brisb, 1895); Baptist Assn of Qld, *Queensland Baptist jubilee ... 1855-1905* (Brisb, 1906); F. J. Brewer and R. Dunn, *... Sixty-six years of municipal government* (Brisb, 1925); A. G. Davies, 'Queensland's pioneer journals and journalists', *JRQHS*, 3 (1937-47); *Moreton Bay Courier*, 15 July 1848, 2 Oct 1858; *Moreton Bay Free Press*, 20 Apr 1858; *Brisbane Courier*, 2 June 1891, 2 Apr 1894; *Queenslander*, 7 Aug 1909.

CLEM LACK*
A. A. MORRISON*

SWEET, SAMUEL WHITE (1825-1886), sea captain, surveyor and photographer, was born on 1 May 1825 at Portsea, Hampshire, England. He probably joined the navy in 1844, served on the China Station for five years and had several voyages to India. In 1858-62 as commander of the *Pizarro* he kept the meteorological log for the Board of Trade, and in 1861 he surveyed Pena Blanca harbour, South America. He had spent six years working for N. J. Myers Son & Co. of Liverpool as a master,

his last ship being the *Sarah Neumann*. About 1863 he spent two years in Queensland, hoping to grow cotton; in 1867 he moved to Rundle Street, Adelaide, and worked as a photographer.

In January 1869 Sweet took command of the two-masted schooner *Gulnare*, which was later bought by the South Australian government for the Northern Territory survey expedition. He sailed from Adelaide on 12 February, returning in June, and again in February 1870 to collect more supplies. He also visited Timor and returned to Palmerston (Darwin) on 15 September with eighteen buffaloes, ponies, monkeys, fruit and vegetables. In September in Darwin he photographed the official party at the ceremonial planting of the first pole of the overland telegraph; he also took pictures of the township, the men at work and forest scenery. In November he sailed to the Roper River and took part in the survey there before sailing to Normanton, Queensland, for more supplies, returning in March 1871. In October on his way back to the Roper from Darwin the *Gulnare* grounded on a reef near the Vernon Islands and by 1872 was condemned.

In January Sweet, a disciplinarian, was piloting the *Bengal* and other ships, surveying and navigating the Roper, but by the end of April he was back in Adelaide. He spent the next three years as master mariner in the Black Diamond Line of colliers but on 11 May 1875 his ship the *Wallaroo*, with his wife aboard, ran aground in a gale on Office Beach, Wallaroo. An inquiry attributed it to Sweet's error of judgment, and he was censured. He retired from the sea, opened a photographic studio in Adelaide and concentrated on landscapes. With his horse-drawn dark room he travelled through South Australia taking hundreds of skilful pictures of the outback, stations and homesteads. The colony's foremost documentary photographer of the 1870s, in the early 1880s he was one of the first to use the new dry-plate process. A large collection of his photographs is held by the South Australian Archives.

Before migrating to Australia Sweet had married Elizabeth Tilly. They had four daughters and five sons. He died suddenly of sunstroke on 4 January 1886 at Halldale near Riverton. His estate was sworn for probate at £440.

J. Cato, *The story of the camera in Australia* (Melb, 1955); M. G. Kerr, *The surveyors* (Adel, 1971); R. Parsons, 'Ships of the overland telegraph', *A'sian Shipping Record*, 30 Sept 1972; *Register* (Adel), 29 Nov 1871, 13, 17 May, 12 Aug 1875; S. W. Sweet papers and photographs (SAA).

ALLAN SIERP

SYME, DAVID (1827-1908), newspaper proprietor, was born on 2 October 1827 at North Berwick, Scotland, fourth and youngest son of George Alexander Syme (1791-1845), schoolmaster, and his wife Jean, née Mitchell. G. A. Syme was a classical scholar, radical in both church and state, who became parish schoolmaster at Montrose, his native town, and from 1822 parish schoolmaster and clerk of the kirk session of St Mary, North Berwick. Never a popular citizen, he was strong-willed, obstinate in his opinions, nervous, arrogant, shy, brusque, inarticulate and awkward with his fellows. He passed these characteristics to his sons, especially to David, who like his brothers and sister, was taught by their father in the schoolroom attached to their house, but only he failed to escape from its atmosphere of close study, severe discipline and curt control. Much of his shyness, his nervous inability to join his fellows in business or companionship, arose from complete obedience to his father, although Syme was never physically unkind to his sons. Of this David wrote in later years: 'It was difficult to understand my father's attitude to us boys. He had naturally a kind disposition; he was a devoted husband and no-one ever asked him for help that he did not freely give ... but his affection for us never found expression in words'.

His father's death left David at 17 'fairly stranded ... I had received a sound English education and a fair knowledge of Latin, but I had no training whatever to fit me for a profession or business career, and no friends or relations to help me'. He first thought of religion as a profession, but not with the Church of Scotland, which had been renounced by his brothers George and Ebenezer [q.v.]. He studied for two years under James Morrison at Kilmarnock, but lost enthusiasm for a 'doctrine of Salvation by faith in its most literal sense'. He toured Germany as a student, worked for some time as a proofreader's assistant on a Glasgow newspaper; then early in 1851, he went via Cape Horn to California seeking gold, but found little and no place for an introvert. By mid-1852 he was in Melbourne, and in the next three years prospected with some success on Ballarat, Bendigo, Castlemaine and Beechworth diggings. In 1855 he lost a possible fortune at Egerton near Ballarat when a promising claim was jumped.

Syme then turned to road contracting and was making a useful living when Ebenezer bought the insolvent Melbourne Age for £2000, and invited him to take up a share. In September 1856 Syme put up some cash and his contracting business to obtain a half-share. He helped to manage the paper but returned to contracting late in 1857. When Ebenezer retired in 1859 Syme reluctantly returned to the business, and on Ebenezer's death next year he began his fifty-year career as publisher and editor of the Age.

To the extent that he addressed the unprivileged, Syme continued his brother's policies but he was not so passionate an advocate. He had convictions, though his approach to them was opportunist: but when he adopted his beliefs as campaigns he clung to them with fewer nervous misgivings than had Ebenezer. Early in 1860 he reduced the price of the paper from 6d. to 3d., in a bid to raise the circulation of only about 2000. This essay in newspaper publicity marked him as an entrepreneur of courage and yielded immediate results. The Age had been diffuse in approach to public issues; Syme began to concentrate on three main practical policies: land for the people, protection for native industries, full rights of self-government. He fought for them ruggedly, determinedly, and as he mellowed came to believe that he was their inventor, not merely their powerful advocate. He did revivify them, especially protection, but primarily as a newspaper entrepreneur. At different periods and with varying intensity the Age suffered from their advocacy, but great persistence enriched the business and made Syme powerful and, in his heyday, feared. His land policy, selection of crown lands before survey, had been pressed by radicals even before Syme arrived in Victoria, but he saw it as a means of breaking the squatters' monopoly and creating a farming population.

Syme came slowly to accept protection as a fiscal policy. It had been debated on public platforms, and given newspaper space (notably by James Harrison [q.v.] in the Geelong Advertiser), at least nine years before Syme supported it early in 1860. By that time the agitation had spread to Melbourne; and if the Age was to sustain its tone as a radical paper it had to take some stand on the matter. Syme claimed in later years (and the claim was kept alive for him by others) that his was the first voice and the power that made protection the fiscal faith of Victoria. He did indeed foster the faith in the editorial and the news columns of the Age, and his thinking on the fiscal issue was far ahead of public opinion, but land settlement remained the first plank in his reform platform. Yet some immediate means had to be found for using idle capital, for attracting fresh funds, and for employing the workless artisan. His solution, and it was almost an expedient, was the creation of manufacturing industries. His editorial theme became during 1861: 'cheap land, abundant labour and fiscal protection must go hand in hand in this country before it attains to the prosperity of which it is so eminently capable'. Nevertheless, in 1863, when tariff reformers believed that practical protection was at hand, he was not prepared to make protection a major public issue and advised caution. James McCulloch [q.v.], although a free trader, responded to the aroused public demand, made a protective tariff a major election issue and was returned late in 1864 with 58 supporters in a House of 75 members. Willy-nilly the *Age* acclaimed the result, although warning that 'a sudden change might be productive of mischief, and bring the principle of protection into disrepute'. Thereafter Syme was the apostle of protection, preaching it in and out of season. For thirty-five years before Federation, Victoria had a high protection wall that was at Syme's bidding if not wholly of his making. This was his greatest newspaper achievement.

Syme fought for protection without thought of his own well-being once he was convinced of its rightness as a public policy. The *Age*, which was his whole life, was threatened by a constant campaign fostered by free-trade interests. His strength as a publisher grew through the late 1860s; steadily increasing circulation evidenced greater popular influence, but also caused stronger attempts to stifle the newspaper, if possible to ruin it. In the early 1860s the government and his commercial adversaries had withdrawn advertising, which fell to 12 columns of a 56 columns newspaper, an uneconomic proportion. Syme replied by reducing the price of the *Age* to 2d. in 1863 and to 1d. in 1868. Circulation increased markedly to 15,000 at the end of that year but the size of the paper dropped from 56 to 36 columns because of the shrinkage of advertising and the need to reduce expenditure to offset the price reduction. But the greater circulation brought back profitable advertising and for the first time the paper began to prosper. The business was aided by the success of the weekly *Leader* from 1856 and by taking over the morning *Herald* in 1868, converting it to an evening paper and then disposing of it.

For the next forty years, though he wrote little himself, Syme used the *Age's* power for fearless and ruthless prosecution of his public policies. Never scrupling in his methods of attack against his opponents, he used the bludgeon as his chief editorial weapon. Politicians were fair game: his method was to put a man on a public pedestal, or assist him to it, and extol his strength, with a warning about consequences should he backslide: examples were Graham Berry [q.v.] and McCulloch, who was, however, never unreservedly accepted by Syme. It was not uncommon for the public pedestal to become

a public chopping-block, with Syme sometimes a flaming accuser, sometimes a discreet defender. He never relented editorially on public men whom he regarded as enemies of his policies. John O'Shanassy [q.v.] was an example; deep personal enmity between them was aggravated by Syme's constant opposition to the Irish Roman Catholic approach to public questions, such as state aid to religion and church schools, and by his contempt for lay advocates.

The resounding electoral success of Berry's high protection liberals in 1877 brought great popularity to the *Age*. Syme felt that the time had come for a final showdown with the interests which he considered blocked the way to radical reforms and democratic needs, and which he specified as the importers and free traders who were gathering their strength to resist Berry's tariff, the squatters whose hold on arable land was checking agriculture, and the Legislative Council whose restrictive franchise and wealthy membership made it representative of both merchants and squatters. The council was cowed into passing a discriminatory land tax, but it laid aside a bill for permanent payment of members of the Legislative Assembly which had been sent up to it as a tack to the appropriation bill. After Berry had dismissed judges of the County courts, magistrates and other senior public servants, the council agreed to payment of members. But in a long conflict until 1881 over Upper House reform, the council defeated Berry and Syme for, although its constituency was widened, its powers remained intact. Throughout the 1880s the *Age* did not control governments, though it exercised powerful influence and helped to bring about the coalition of 1883.

Despite popular belief, Syme had been neither the founder nor the sole owner of the *Age*. When Ebenezer died in 1860 the business had to provide for his widow and five young children, and for David and his young wife. The loose arrangement, which had made Ebenezer and David equal partners, now became a binding partnership, with Ebenezer's widow, Jane, and David sharing the profits equally, and David in full control of the business. Jane returned to England during 1862, with an agreed weekly payment from the paper's revenues, to be offset against profits. The deed of partnership, originally for seven years, was renewed from time to time until 1877. Next year a change was made.

Syme at all times acknowledged Jane Syme his equal partner, and declined to have direct dealings with her children. A legal opinion upheld this when Jane gave a power of attorney to her eldest son, William Holden, a doctor at Stawell, Victoria. Her third son, Joseph Cowen, employed in the *Age* counting-house from late 1868, was a forceful character who felt that he and his brothers should have a share in the business, either directly or on behalf of their mother. Syme was pressed to give Joseph part of it. This was eventually arranged by Jane (who had remarried) accepting £8250 for her partnership share, her children renouncing any interest they may have had in the business under their father's intestacy, and Joseph being made a partner with a quarter-share. This partnership was announced on 22 March 1878 with a new imprint: 'Printed and published by David Syme & Co.'. Joseph's name was added on 21 October 1879: 'printed and published by David Syme and Joseph Cowen Syme under the style David Syme & Co.'. The partnership survived twelve stormy years. Uncle and nephew were long estranged, writing to each other on business matters but rarely meeting. After protracted negotiations, Syme agreed to buy Joseph out with £140,000. From 21 March 1891 the imprint read: 'Printed and published by the proprietor David Syme at the *Age* office Collins Street east, Melbourne'. In 1901 his income from the paper was about £50,000.

Syme's journalism encouraged several libel actions. *Wood* [q.v.] v. *Syme* (1865), *Langton* [q.v.] v. *Syme* (1877) and the most celebrated of them all, the great railways case of the 1890s, *Speight* [q.v.] v. *Syme*, were partly politically motivated. Richard Speight, chairman of the Victorian commissioners from 1883, inherited a lavish programme inspired by politicians. It was a period of boom in public spending. From late 1890 the *Age* strongly criticized his administration, accusing him of extravagance, incompetence, dereliction of duty, and contempt of parliament and the public. Speight and his two commission colleagues were suspended by the Shiels government in 1892, and soon issued writs against the *Age* alleging libel on eleven counts. Speight's action was heard first, over ninety-two sitting days, and ended with a verdict for him for £100 on one count, and disagreement on the other counts. A second action occupied eighty-eight sitting days and resulted in a verdict on one count for Speight, with nominal damages, and for Syme on the other counts. The case cost him an estimated £50,000 in costs, but the result brought him unprecedented popular acclaim.

Syme had few professional or social intimates. Public men were embraced within his dour favour so long as they accorded with his will, and were as easily cast out. They were to be used to espouse his policies, a not altogether selfish ambition for he be-lieved that his views were for the public good. Intimacy on that basis was not easy to make or keep. He sought no public popularity and shunned social life. Men like A. L. Windsor [q.v.] and G. F. H. Schuler, his chief editors and leader-writers, and A. B. Robinson, his financial editor and personal financial adviser, were able and loyal lieutenants, but outside the office he had little contact with them. Charles Pearson [q.v.], a treasured contributor and sought by Syme to criticize the drafts of his books, was another who was not socially encouraged. Perhaps it was not within Syme's ingrown shyness to make a move that could have led to warm relations.

An exception was Alfred Deakin. Theirs was a rare friendship, first encouraged by Syme and enjoyed by both for many years. The idealistic young Deakin and the hard-bitten middle-aged newspaper publisher were unlike each other in almost every way. Yet Syme had a genuine affection for Deakin, who became his protégé in journalism and politics and wrote, 'He was always most gracious and considerate to the very young man whose enthusiasms he criticized with a generous simplicity conveying no hint of the legitimate authority to which his age, ability and experience fully entitled him'. Deakin worked part time for the *Age* for almost five years from May 1878. In that period Syme moulded his journalistic and political thinking. Deakin's impressions of Syme (in notes made in 1881) revealed a broad sympathy with him: 'He had a fine intelligence, open, accurate and aspiring, limited in its scope but admirably thorough in all its work'. Their relations were almost breached several times, notably in the last stages of the campaign for federal union and in the early years of Federation, but their friendship survived. Deakin wrote after Syme's death: 'I saw him to the last and was one of the few whom he admitted to his intimacy in all public or political matters'.

The *Age* grew in circulation from 38,000 in 1880 to 100,000 about 1890 and to 120,000 in 1899; in proportion to population it had by far the largest circulation of any daily newspaper in the empire. Although he always distrusted Duncan Gillies [q.v.], Syme was taken in by the boom of the late 1880s, was bewildered by the collapse of Victorian prosperity in the early 1890s, and had little policy to offer except rigid retrenchment and persecution of the railways commissioners as scapegoats. Yet the 1890s was probably the period of the *Age*'s greatest political influence; it backed the successive ministries and Syme had an almost complete power of veto, at least, over appointments to them. Although he had consistently supported the growth of trade unions, he disapproved of the nascent political Labor organization and continued to the end to support Victoria's radical liberals. The ten Victorian delegates elected to the 1897 Federal Convention were the ten on the *Age* 'ticket'. In 1898 the overcoming of Syme's doubts about safeguarding Victorian and protectionist interests in the draft constitution enabled a massive favourable vote in the referendum. In 1898-99 a sustained campaign attacking the deficiencies in technical education led to the appointment of the Fink royal commission. After 1900 Syme's power to make ministries declined; although he had much to do with the dismissal of W. H. Irvine in 1904 he could not prevent the succession of his old enemy, Thomas Bent [q.v.].

Syme's undoubted power as a publicist encouraged the quicker development of things that became an accepted part of the fabric of Victoria than might otherwise have been the case. He encouraged small farming, especially dairying, irrigation and water conservation, the opening-up of mallee lands, *crédit foncier* loans for farmers. He supported the anti-sweating movement and reforms in factory and shops legislation, with wages boards an attendant instrument of better wages and working conditions. A state bank and a state note issue, and direct taxation were among other progressive causes which he did much to bring about.

Practical farming engaged much of Syme's tireless attention outside his newspaper office. On his Yarra Valley properties, on a narrow strip of flats, Syme was cultivator, grazier, dairy-farmer, stock-breeder and orchardist. He introduced to Victoria Kerry and Dexter dairy cattle from the Irish county Kerry, and experimented with pasture improvement and drainage. He poured thousands of pounds into these lands, but he was no idle rich man playing at being a farmer; everything he did had a serious purpose.

Syme won a minor international reputation as a political economist. His *Outlines of an Industrial Science* (London, 1876), a vindication of protection and state socialism, owed something to the work of Friedrich List and Carey and other American protectionists. Syme was a friend and ally of Cliffe Leslie in attacking the methodological foundations of 'English' political economy. The book was translated into German and published in an American edition, but attracted little attention in England. Syme published articles in the field of political economy in the *Westminster Review*, the *Fortnightly Review* and the *Melbourne Review*. His *Representative Government in England ...* (London, 1881), was a general attack on the

system of English parliamentary government as it had developed from Walpole's time, especially on government by party; the *Age* from time to time, finally in a sustained campaign in 1904, vainly argued the virtues of ministries directly elected by lower houses. *On the Modification of Organisms* (Melbourne, 1890) was a criticism of Darwinian theory from an evolutionist position; Syme contended that all modifications of organisms originated in the cell— 'the psychological as well as the physiological unit'. In his last book, *The Soul: a study and an argument* (London, 1903), Syme argued that matter and energy never perished; they were only transferred, and therefore the organizing power would not perish with the body that was its handiwork.

Syme was a slim six feet in height, with deep-set eyes, a thin straight mouth and iron-grey hair and beard, grim and gaunt in appearance, smiling rarely. For much of his later life, he suffered from a poor digestion. His family life made a secure retreat from the world and, though he may not have been very warm towards his children and grandchildren, he was a much better parent than his father had been.

Syme kept a close hold on his newspaper business until almost the end of his life. He was once asked why he did not get away from it again on a world tour, as he had in 1866, 1882 and 1887. He answered, 'I'm getting old and all my interests are here. It's my business interests which absorb my attention. I'm different from you; I'm a man with few friends'. He died at his home, Blythswood in Kew, on 14 February 1908. In 1859 he had married Annabella Johnson who survived him with five sons and two daughters. His estate was valued for probate at £880,000; he had contributed generously to charity and founded a prize for scientific research at the University of Melbourne in 1904. His widow and sons carried on the business as a trust; Herbert (1859-1939) was chairman and general manager, Geoffrey (1873-1942) controlled the editorial department, and the last surviving son Oswald (1878-1967) became chairman until and after 1948 when the trust was converted to a public company which still has the trade name, David Syme & Co.

GEORGE ALEXANDER (1822-1894), second son of the family, was born at Montrose and studied theology at the University of Aberdeen. Rejecting a call in the Established Church of Scotland, he was for a time incumbent of the Free Presbyterian Church at Dumfries. He broke from the Church over dogma, and fell under the influence of Morrison at Kilmarnock Academy, which he attended for some time. About 1847 he became minister of a flourishing Baptist church at Nottingham, England. He held this pulpit for fifteen years, was active in radical causes, then became a secularist after association with G. J. Holyoake. His health was bad and in 1863 he migrated to Australia, to employment on the *Age*. He had editorial charge of the paper in 1866 and later edited the *Leader* until 1885. He was afflicted with a great nervousness throughout his life; kindly, calm and considerate when unexcited, he was incoherent under stress. He died at Melbourne on 31 December 1894. Aged 31, at Lancaster, England, he had married Susannah Goodier; a daughter died but his son, Sir George Adlington Syme (1859-1929), became a world-famed surgeon.

E. E. Morris, *A memoir of George Higinbotham* (Lond, 1895); A. Pratt, *David Syme, the father of protection in Australia* (Lond, 1908); W. Murdoch, *Alfred Deakin* (Lond, 1923); B. Hoare, *Looking back gaily* (Melb, 1927); G. Cockerill, *Scribblers and statesmen* (Melb, 1944); J. A. La Nauze, *Political economy in Australia* (Melb, 1949), and *Alfred Deakin* (Melb, 1965); A. Deakin, *The crisis in Victorian politics, 1879-1881*, J. A. La Nauze and R. M. Crawford eds (Melb, 1957); A. Deakin, *The federal story*, J. A. La Nauze ed (Melb, 1963); C. E. Sayers, *David Syme; a life* (Melb, 1965); W. S. Robinson, *If I remember rightly*, G. Blainey ed (Melb, 1967); *Age*, 1854-1908, C. E. Sayers (ed), *Age* centenary supp, 16 Oct 1954; David Syme papers (LaT L).

                                              C. E. SAYERS

SYME, EBENEZER (1826-1860), journalist, was born at North Berwick, Scotland, third son of George Alexander Syme, schoolmaster, and his wife Jean, née Mitchell. Educated by his father at the parish school, he studied theology at the University of St Andrews. He was the most religious of the Syme brothers and the most troubled in conscience. As a missionary student he preached in village kirks of a Sunday, tramping from St Andrews in all weathers. In 1845 he attended classes at James Morrison's liberal Kilmarnock Academy, but soon noted in his diary, 'I can see no medium between high Calvinism and the new theology'. He went to Liverpool intending to study the Chinese language and become a missionary to the heathen. Rejecting any absolute creed, he soon became a zealous street-corner preacher in Liverpool, Manchester and other north country industrial towns and in Scotland; it was an austere life of poverty. In 1850 he became a missionary for the north of England Unitarian Christian Association, and in May was installed as pastor of a Unitarian chapel in Sunderland. But in May 1851 he noted in his diary: 'Determined at last to leave the pulpit and engage in business'.

In July Syme became assistant to John Chapman, London bookseller and proprietor of the *Westminster Review*, for which he wrote regularly: he was acquainted with Marian Evans (George Eliot), Joseph Cowen, G. J. Holyoake and Horace Greeley, and gave frequent public lectures. In April 1853, partly for health reasons, Syme, his wife Jane Hilton, née Rowan, of Manchester, whom he had married about 1848, and three young sons sailed for Australia in the *Abdalla*. They reached Melbourne in July and he soon became a regular contributor to the *Argus* and helped to launch and edit the *Diggers Advocate*, a short-lived journal which supported the most radical demands of the diggers. Edward Wilson [q.v.], owner of the *Argus*, disagreed with the manner of Syme's defence of the Eureka prisoners and lost a trenchant, if at times hysterical, editorial writer. He had drafted resolutions passed at the Melbourne public meeting of 6 December 1854 in defence of the Eureka men. Later that month he joined David Blair [q.v.] as editor of the *Age* in a co-operative attempt to keep it afloat. But the enterprise failed and in June 1856, although penniless, he bought the business with £2000 guaranteed by several mercantile and progressive friends. David Syme [q.v.] joined as partner on 27 September 1856.

Syme was a valiant fighter and an incisive journalist, but no businessman. A strong vein of radical idealism ran through his writings, but he was diffuse in argument and gave little thought to commercial results. His weapons were the bludgeon and the cutlass, never the rapier. He pitilessly attacked and scandalously libelled opponents. He supported every radical movement of the time: the eight-hour day, manhood suffrage and equal electorates, unlocking the land, abolition of state aid to religion and free and secular education. Under his uncompromising editorship the *Age* gained influence on the goldfields and in working-class areas of Melbourne, but it made little money and antagonized merchants, importers and squatters. In 1856-59 he represented the Loddon in the Legislative Assembly, but although his ability was widely respected, he was a lone wolf in politics.

Syme's health worsened under the strain of almost single-handed management and editing; he was forced to retire late in 1859 and died on 13 March 1860, aged 34. His wife, four sons and a daughter survived him and went to England, but all the children returned to Victoria.

C. E. Sayers, *David Syme; a life* (Melb, 1965); D. Elder, *Ebenezer Syme and the Westminster Review* (Melb, priv print, 1967); Ebenezer Syme papers (LaT L).   C. E. SAYERS

SYMES, JOSEPH (1841-1906), secularist and publicist, was born on 29 January 1841 at Portland, Dorset, England. His parents were devout Wesleyans. At 17 Symes underwent conversion and started as a lay preacher. In 1864, encouraged by his mother, he entered the Wesleyan college at Richmond to train for the ministry. Here the shy, weakly youth was pained by the levity he remarked in his fellow seminarians. He joined his probationary circuit in Kilmarnock, Scotland, in September 1867. In 1871 at Kilmarnock he married Matilda Wilson, née Weir, a widow.

Reports of the declaration of papal infallibility and the Franco-Prussian war first shook Symes's belief in providence. He suffered a physical and mental crisis and was ordered rest from his clerical duties. In July 1872 he refused ordination and resigned his charge. His health recovered next year when he became lecturer to the Northern Union of Mechanics' Institutes and a speaker for the National Agricultural Labourers' Union. Setbacks to the Labourers' Union in 1875 confirmed his suspicions of divine beneficence and in May 1876 he joined the National Secular Society and began contributing to Bradlaugh's *National Reformer* and the *Newcastle Weekly Chronicle*. Next year he was appointed lecturer to the N.S.S. in Newcastle upon Tyne. Symes's compelling honesty and fervent eloquence enlarged the congregation. He was now a keen astronomer and zoologist and his scientific expositions were acclaimed. In 1881 he became a vice-president of the N.S.S. and lecturer in Birmingham, where he established a secularist boarding-school. His rise was checked in 1883 when he sided with the flamboyant G. W. Foote against Bradlaugh in challenging the blasphemy laws. Symes was contemptuous of 'dilettante freethinkers' who flinched from publicizing the cruelties and lies of Christianity.

During this dispute the Victorian secularists asked Bradlaugh to send them an organizer. He nominated Symes, who arrived in Melbourne with his wife on 24 February 1884. Within the year he had bought a printing press, begun the weekly *Liberator* and provided his flock with secular meetings, sermons and Sunday schools. In October he presided at the second Australasian Freethought Conference. Aroused by the smugly parochial, wowserish society of his exile, he led agitations for free speech,

an uncensored press, excursion trains and the opening of art galleries and public libraries on Sundays. The Lord's Day Observance Society and the Victorian government retaliated with three major and some minor prosecutions in 1885-87. Unable to engage reliable counsel, Symes defended himself in the courts and routed his persecutors. These harassments worsened his health and temper. He became dictatorial with his followers and his denunciations of cant became increasingly strident and exhibitionist. The Australasian Secular Association broke up in 1888. Backed by a faithful few, Symes struggled on with the *Liberator* and the Sunday meetings.

At the Legislative Assembly elections of 1889 Symes ran for Collingwood. His programme included land nationalization, graduated income tax, abolition of colonial titles and governorships, a free Sunday, legalized contraception, the ending of discrimination against Chinese, and Home Rule for Ireland, Scotland and Wales; he came last. In 1892 he retired before the poll for want of money. His radicalism, probably the most extreme to be announced in nineteenth-century Australia, was too thorough for the Democratic Club, which thrice black-balled him; he was also excluded from the Field Naturalists' Club.

The secularist movement became quiescent in the early 1890s. Symes's wife died on 21 March 1892. Ill and impoverished he retired to Cheltenham with his second wife Agnes Taylor, née Wilson, whom he had married at Collingwood on 4 May 1893; he continued to issue the *Liberator* until 1904. He died of chronic heart disease in London on 28 December 1906 while visiting England, survived by his wife and his daughter Stella. His death passed apparently without comment in the colonies; yet he contributed much to the distinctive sharpness of argument and combative righteousness of radicalism in Victoria.

P. Coleman, *Obscenity, blasphemy, sedition* (Brisb, 1962); F. B. Smith, 'Joseph Symes and the Australasian Secular Association', *Labour Hist*, no 5, Nov 1963, *and* Religion and freethought in Melbourne, 1870 to 1890 (M.A. thesis, Univ Melb, 1960).   F. B. SMITH

SYMONS, JOHN CHRISTIAN (1820-1894), clergyman, was born in Cornwall, England, son of Mark Symons, farmer, and his wife Ann, née Christian. He was a Wesleyan local preacher and an apprentice at the drapery firm of G. Hitchcock & Co. in London in 1844 when fourteen employees formed the first Young Men's Christian

Association; he was elected secretary. In 1846 he was religious instructor aboard the convict ship *Maitland* travelling to Port Phillip. In port Symons attended the Wesleyan chapel, Collins Street; he was nominated for the ministry at a Melbourne Circuit Quarterly Meeting in July 1847, and was later approved by the British Conference.

Symons began his ministry at Kapunda, South Australia, and was assistant minister in Adelaide when Rev. J. Draper [q.v.] authorized him in February 1852 to visit the Victorian goldfields to raise money for chapel debts. One of the first resident clergymen on the goldfields, he arrived at Forest Creek in March; next year he went to the Melbourne East circuit. In 1856 he moved to Beechworth and while there a chapel was built and a Young Men's Association formed; his presidential lecture that year was published in Melbourne as *The History and Advantages of Young Men's Associations*. He was later a vice-president of the Melbourne Young Men's Christian Association. After a year at Geelong he was circuit superintendent at Carisbrook and encouraged the building of two local chapels. In 1863-77 he was editor of the *Wesleyan Chronicle* and manager of the Wesleyan Book Depot.

Symons had been a prominent member of the Victorian District Education Committee which until 1855 fostered Wesleyan schools; when they were impeded by a new method of allocating government funds, he responded with the pamphlet *What is the Best System of Education for Victoria?* (Melbourne, 1857). In 1865 he was secretary of Wesleyan Grammar School (Wesley College) which opened next year. He criticized the Education Act of 1872 which made no provision for religious teaching in state schools. Constantly opposed to spiritualism, he also publicly debated Sabbath observance and defended the literal interpretation of Scripture.

The Victorian and Tasmanian Conference of 1876 elected Symons president. After a visit to England in 1881, he was appointed by the General Wesleyan Conference of Australasia as treasurer of the Supernumerary Ministers' and Ministers' Widows' Fund. With Rev. W. P. Wells he codified the laws of the Australasian Wesleyan Church and perfected a model deed for Church ownership of property. He was elected president of the General Conference in 1888. Although he lacked formal education, Symons read widely and in 1891 was appointed a part-time lecturer in Church history at Queen's College, University of Melbourne. He was the author of many pamphlets and also published a *Life of the Rev. Daniel James Draper* ... (London,

1870). Dogmatic and outspoken, conservative in theology, in later life he proved a sound administrator of affairs which did not require a larger vision. He died on 14 February 1894 at Hawthorn survived by his wife Matilda, née Hodgson, whom he had married at the age of 27 at Truro, Cornwall, and one of their three sons. His estate was sworn for probate at £1834.

M. Dyson (ed), *Australasian Methodist ministerial general index*, 2nd ed (Melb, 1896); *Spectator and Methodist Chronicle*, 23 Feb 1894; R. Howe, *The Wesleyan Church in Victoria, 1855-1901: its ministry and membership* (M.A. thesis, Univ Melb, 1965).

RENATE HOWE

SYNNOT, MONCKTON (1826-1879), pastoralist and businessman, was born in December 1826 in County Armagh, Ireland, fifth son of Captain Walter Synnot and his second wife Elizabeth, née Houston. In 1836 Walter arrived in Van Diemen's Land with his wife and nine of their ten children. A year later two elder sons crossed to Port Phillip, followed by the next two, Albert and the 12-year-old Monckton. They brought sheep with them and became pioneer landholders at Little River near Geelong, where they remained in various partnerships for about ten years. By 1852 they had scattered and Monckton, after a brief sortie with Albert to the Californian and Victorian goldfields, was the only one left in the Little River district, as sole owner of the 26,500-acre Mowyong, later called Bareacres. On 25 February 1853 at St Kilda, Melbourne, he married Annie Emily Wedge Lawrence. He later bought the South Brighton sheep station in the Wimmera where, in 1862, he was a member of the first Horsham District Roads Board, and a councillor in 1862-63.

The prize-winning superfine merino wools of the Western District had been extolled by the Thomas Shaws, C. H. MacKnight, J. L. Currie [qq.v.] and others, but in the mid-1860s Synnot's letters to the papers queried their real value and gave rise to a drawn-out and sometimes bitter battle of words. Selling South Brighton in 1868, he bought the large Terrick Terrick station near the Murray River, and for a few years had some share with his brothers Albert, George and Nugent in Gunbar and Cowl Cowl in the Riverina. In 1873 he moved to Melbourne, bought large central city premises from the merchants and flour-millers, William Degraves [q.v.] & Co., and set up the Flinders Wool Warehouse in Flinders Lane: in this he followed the lead of his elder brother George who, opening in Geelong as a stock and station agent, had held one of the first auction sales of wool there in November 1858.

Synnot entered Melbourne wool-broking in prosperous and expansive times, when many firms were offering warehouse services, selling wool by auction or privately, or arranging and often financing its shipping for sale overseas. A pioneer of the wool trade with the East, he visited China, sent a consignment of woollen yarns to Hong Kong and arranged for silk and cotton weavers at Ning-Po to produce samples of woollen cloth, which were exhibited throughout Australia and New Zealand and at the Paris Exhibition of 1878. His efforts failed at first, but later that year when the first Japanese Trade Commission visited Australia his ideas bore some fruit.

Synnot died on 23 April 1879 at Elstern-wick, aged 52, and was buried in St Kilda general cemetery. The eldest of his seven sons, Monckton Davey Synnot, and three of the younger ones carried on as wool-brokers. Both father and his son, Monckton, were tall, handsome, genial and convivial, with the Irish tendency to enjoy a brisk argument, but the senior Monckton was the only one to take any part in public affairs.

R. V. Billis and A. S. Kenyon, *Pastoral pioneers of Port Phillip* (Melb, 1932); A. Henderson (ed), *Australian families*, 1 (Melb, 1941); W. R. Brownhill, *The history of Geelong and Corio Bay* (Melb, 1955); A. Barnard, *The Australian wool market, 1840-1900* (Melb, 1958); L. J. Blake and K. H. Lovett, *Wimmera Shire centenary* (Horsham, 1962); *Economist*, 1862, 1863, 2 Feb 1866; *Argus*, 16 Sept 1877, 8 Jan 1878, 8 Sept 1883.   MARY TURNER SHAW

T

TAIT, JAMES McALPINE (1828-1911), newspaperman, was born in Glasgow, Scotland, son of John Tait, journalist and newspaper proprietor, and his wife Margaret, née Allison. When his father died in 1836 James was adopted by George Troup, a Scottish newspaper proprietor who trained him as a compositor and reporter in Belfast, Ireland. Tait was later a compositor for Troup's Glasgow *Daily Mail*, and when it ceased in 1851 he went to the United States of America and worked on the *New York Herald*. Next year he arrived in Victoria in the *Revenue* and spent two moderately successful years on the Mount Alexander and Ovens goldfields. A compositor on the Melbourne *Argus* in 1854-55 and on the *Herald* in 1856-64, he was also the registered printer of the Melbourne evening *Daily News* and weekly *Dispatch*, both short lived. On 25 August 1854 at the home of Rev. Adam Cairns [q.v.] he married Margaret Borthwick; they had three sons and two daughters.

After his marriage Tait settled at North Fitzroy, then an outer suburb. He supported agitation to sever the Fitzroy Ward from the city of Melbourne in 1858, thereby contributing to the curtailment of the original city of Melbourne and to the development of the present pattern of independent suburban municipalities. He also instigated and financed the pressure that resulted in the Fitzroy municipal district taking in North Fitzroy.

In December 1864 with a partner, Tait bought the Collingwood-Fitzroy weekly *Observer* from Graham Berry [q.v.]. It circulated in the most populous suburbs and, with Tait as editor, often rivalled the metropolitan papers in quality and influence; contributors included J. P. Fawkner and Dr T. Embling [qq.v.]. Collingwood and Fitzroy were centres of agitation for tariff protection for local industry, and the *Observer*, under both Berry and Tait, became the leading protectionist organ in the suburbs in opposition to free trade interests in the city. In association with local parliamentarians, councillors, businessmen and workers, Tait's *Observer* championed the growth of factories, then usually of a noxious nature, along the River Yarra. Editorials predicted that Collingwood would become the Manchester of the Southern Hemisphere, with the Yarra as its canal. In 1866 after a partnership dispute, Tait sold his interest in the *Observer* (which was briefly renamed the *Manufacturer*) and struck out on his own with a new paper, the Collingwood-Fitzroy *Advertiser*. By 1870 he had regained the *Observer* cheaply; he then amalgamated the papers as the *Advertiser and Observer*, later shortening this again to the *Observer* that he operated until its last issue in 1909.

Tait was radical on certain issues: he supported land reform in the 1860s, abolition of state aid to church schools, the eight-hour movement, reduction of franchise qualifications, reform of the Upper House and payment of members. In 1868-69 he helped to expose political corruption involving C. E. Jones [q.v.]. An early propagandist for technical schools in Victoria, he helped to establish one in Collingwood in 1870. He campaigned against Federation in the 1890s and was unsympathetic to Trades Hall politics. A justice of the peace, he was connected with the management of St George's Presbyterian Church, Collingwood, for thirty years. Aged 83, he died in his home in Collingwood on 11 December 1911, and was buried in the Melbourne general cemetery, survived by a son and a daughter.

Observer (Collingwood), 1892-93, April 1897, 3 Jan 1907, 23 Dec 1909; A. H. B. Barrett, The making of an industrial environment: Collingwood, Victoria, 1851-91 (M.A. thesis, Univ Melb, 1970).   BERNARD BARRETT

TAIT, JOHN (1813-1888), racehorse owner and trainer, was born on 5 November 1813 at Melrose near Edinburgh, son of Robert Tait, jeweller and engraver, and his wife Margaret, née Maitland. Trained as a jeweller he, with his wife Janet, née Buchanan (d. 1880), and daughter, reached Hobart Town in the *Hindo* on 2 November 1837 and opened a business. He soon moved to New South Wales and in June 1843 became the licensee of the Albion Inn, Hartley, and in 1847 took over the Black Bull Inn at Bathurst. Strong and wiry, his 'great skill as a boxer' enabled him to cope with his rougher patrons.

In 1847 Tait won the New South Wales St Leger at Homebush with Whalebone. He soon acquired a string of horses from such local breeders as Thomas Icely and George Lee [qq.v.] and engaged Noah Beale as trainer and James Ashworth as rider. In 1851-54 at Bathurst, Parramatta, Homebush and Penrith he won races with stakes totalling about £2500, including two more St Legers with Cossack and Surplice and three Queen's Plates with Cossack **(twice)** and Sportsman, carrying his first colours, a black jacket and red cap. In 1854 in a match race at Homebush Sportsman defeated John Eales's [q.v.] Cooramin for £1000-a-side. Tait had probably moved to Sydney in 1853 and become licensee of the Commercial Hotel, Castlereagh Street.

In 1855 he sold his racehorses and visited England with Ashworth to choose breeding-stock. With Alfred Cheeke [q.v.] he imported **Warwick, New Warrior and Magus**, who sired Clove, winner of the first Australian Jockey Club Derby in 1865. He returned early in 1857 and was in partnership with Cheeke for several years in a stud farm at Mount Druitt and in racing some good horses. Tait adopted his famous racing colours of yellow jacket and black cap and in the early 1860s set up with stables at Byron Lodge, Randwick. In the mid-1860s he acquired the Overland Stores at Dubbo which he still owned in 1888.

Unlike his fellow sportsmen Tait 'went into racing as a business'; as his fortunes depended upon the winning of many races he closely supervised the training of his horses, which always ran in top condition. His most famous horse was The Barb, 'the black demon', among whose 17 wins in 24 starts were the A.J.C. Derby and the Melbourne Cup in 1866 and the Sydney Cup in 1868 and 1869. In 1868 The Barb won the Metropolitan and defeated E. de Mestre's [q.v.] Tim Whiffler in the Queen's Plate but weighed in 2 lb. light; Tait vainly offered £100 reward for proof of foul play. He owned two triple Derby winners: Fireworks, who won 12 of his 16 starts including the 1867 A.J.C. Derby and the Victoria Racing Club Derbys in both 1867 and 1868 (when the date for the race was changed to 1 January); and Florence who in 1870-71 won the A.J.C., V.R.C. and Queensland Turf Club Derbys and the V.R.C. Oaks Stakes. His other notable horses included three Melbourne Cup winners: Glencoe (1869) who also won the A.J.C. Derby, The Pearl (1871) and The Quack (1872). Goldsbrough won the Epsom-Metropolitan double for him in 1875 and Amendment won Tait's last big race, the 1877 Metropolitan. 'Caspian', writing in the *Australian Town and Country Journal* on 1 May 1880, estimated that between 1865 and 1880 Tait had won almost £30,000 in stakes without added money. Known as 'Honest John', he won repute for fair dealing with the press and protested only once —after the 1866 Sydney Cup when Pitsford crossed Falcon and 'hocked' him; Thompson, the offending jockey, was disqualified.

In bad health in 1880 Tait visited England and on 18 August in London he married a widow Christian Ann Swannell, née Garie, who had borne him six children. By 1883 he had moved to Toddington, The Boulevard, Petersham, where he was noted for his hospitality. A justice of the peace from 1879, he was a committee-man of the Animals Protection Society and a New South Wales commissioner for the 1887 Adelaide and 1888 Melbourne exhibitions. On 21 May 1888 he collapsed and died of heart disease; he was buried in Waverley cemetery without religious rites. Tait was survived by two sons and a daughter of his first wife, by his second wife and by two sons and two daughters of their children. His estate was valued for probate at £24,296.

D. M. Barrie, *The Australian bloodhorse* (Syd, 1956); *Australasian*, 13 June 1868, 26 May 1888; *T&CJ*, 1 May 1880, 26 May 1888; *SMH*, 22 May 1888; *Old Times*, May 1903.

MARTHA RUTLEDGE

TALBOT, JOHN RICHARD (1835-1905), trade unionist, was born at Cork, Ireland, son of Richard Talbot, naval lieutenant, and his wife Julia, née Bradley. Apprenticed to an ironmoulder at 13, in 1858 he married Catherine Finnigan in London. He was brought to Sydney in 1860 by (Sir) Peter Russell [q.v.] 'to supervise certain work requiring high-class mechanical knowledge and skill'. Active in Labour affairs in the 1860s, he was a founder of the Friendly Trade Society of Ironmoulders of New South Wales in October 1872 and became its delegate on the Trades and Labor Council of New South Wales. In 1888 he told the select committee on the trades conciliation bill that his trade union had 107 members.

Although a skilled artisan belonging to a craft union, Talbot followed F. B. Dixon [q.v.] and majority opinion on the Trades and Labor Council in accepting unskilled workers as an integral part of the Labor movement. He emerged in the 1880s as one of the outstanding leaders of the council, giving expression to a strong strand of belief that trade unions had a separate identity which would be threatened by links with other political and social groups. By 1884 he was vice-president of the council and consolidated its bias towards fiscal protectionism; in that year he represented his union and was elected vice-president at the second Intercolonial Trades Union Congress in Melbourne. In November he was a member of a deputation to the *Sydney Morning Herald* seeking 'a place in their columns for the claims of labour as well as capital'. Next year he persuaded the council to 'erase from [its] books' the Free Trade Association's request for two Labor delegates to attend its inaugural conference.

In 1888 he became president of the council. He had contributed much to its high community status with his emphasis on the primacy of trade unionism in Labor action; he believed that 'No trades-unionist is in love with strikes ... [but] if the customs of their trade are attempted to be invaded, it is as sacred a thing to fight for them as to fight for their hearths and homes'. In 1890 he assisted materially the attempts of the Mercantile Marine Officers' Association to improve their conditions and pay; when the maritime strike broke out that year he became a member of the New South Wales Labor Defence Committee and later sat on the royal commission that inquired into the strike. He was not wholly sympathetic to the council's plans for political action and when the parliamentary Labor Party was formed he objected to its 1892 conference 'dictating to the Council'.

Talbot had been a foundation trustee of the Trades Hall in 1883 and played a major role in the acquisition of a site for its building which was completed in 1895. In 1893 he became president of the Ironmoulders' Society and of the Iron Trades Conference of New South Wales. After a long illness he died of nephritis on 5 October 1905 at Surry Hills and was buried in the Catholic section of Rookwood cemetery; at his request his funeral cortège passed the Trades Hall. Predeceased by his three sons and one daughter, he was survived by his wife.

L. Frost, *Official souvenir for the 8 hour demonstration* (Syd, 1900); B. Nairn, *Civilising capitalism* (Canb, 1973); V&P (LA NSW), 1890, 8, 63; *Daily Telegraph*, 6 Oct 1905; Trades and Labor Council minutes 1881-94 (ML). BEDE NAIRN

TAPLIN, GEORGE (1831-1879), missionary and teacher, was born on 24 August 1831 at Kingston-upon-Thames, Surrey, England. At 12 he went to live with his maternal grandfather in Andover, Hampshire, and was educated there in a private school. His father died when he was 14 and in 1842 he became a solicitor's clerk at Andover. A committed Congregationalist, from the age of 15 he had desired to become an overseas missionary. He arrived in Adelaide in the *Anna Maria* on 12 October 1849 and worked as a labourer and as a lawyer's clerk.

In June 1851 Taplin was recruited for the ministry by Rev. T. Q. Stow [q.v.]. He lived with Stow, studying and working in the garden for his board and lodging. On 28 February 1853 at Payneham he married Martha Burnell, a servant of Stow's who also aspired to missionary work. In October they went to Currency Creek and later to Port Elliot where in February 1854 Taplin opened a school. The Central Board of Education took it over but he remained as teacher until 1859. That year the Aborigines Friends Association appointed him as their first missionary-teacher at a salary of £200 to work in the lower Murray districts. The site he chose for a settlement on the shores of Lake Alexandrina was a traditional camping ground called Raukkan (The Ancient Way), known to Europeans as Point McLeay.

On 4 April Taplin began his mission to the Narrinyeri (Ngarrindjeri), the confederacy of eighteen tribes that had previously owned the country around the lower Murray lakes. He met immediate opposition from John Baker [q.v.] who leased the cattle station in the area from which the mission land was cut. In 1860 Taplin and the Aborigines Friends Association faced a Legislative Council select committee which had been organized by Baker ostensibly into Aboriginal affairs, but which was heavily slanted towards the Point McLeay mission. Taplin weathered the inquiry and worked on vigorously, teaching, building, proselytising, establishing farming, dispensing government rations and acting as a mechanic and district physician. Later he acquired a teaching assistant.

Taplin was ordained by the Congregational Church in 1868 so that he could administer sacraments and solemnize marriages; next year the chapel, still in regular use, was completed and opened. Keenly interested in Ngarrindjeri culture and society, he learned their language, used it in preaching, and translated and published Bible tracts. He published invaluable anthropological studies which were much superior to contemporary work on South Australian Aboriginals. His papers on philology and ethnology were acclaimed in Australia and abroad. His most important books were: *The Narrinyeri* (Adelaide, 1874), with a second, enlarged edition in 1878 and included next year in *Native Tribes of South Australia*, edited by J. D. Woods; and *The Folklore, Manners, Customs, and Languages of the South Australian Aborigines* (1879), which he edited.

Despite his sympathy with the people and their traditions, Taplin adhered to the contemporary view that Christianity and

Europeanization should be adopted and Ngarrindjeri civilization abandoned; as a result he assisted in undermining their government and social structure, further weakened traditional discipline and morale within the confederacy and provoked strong opposition from conservative tribal members. But they had been dispossessed and persecuted before his arrival, and by helping them become literate and numerate and to acquire trades he enabled them to survive and flourish briefly in European society. Today hundreds of their descendants remain in various districts of Australia; their durability can largely be attributed to Taplin.

He was a compassionate Christian and a courageous fighter. Exhausted, he died of heart disease at Raukkan on 24 June 1879, survived by his wife and six children. He was buried in the village cemetery. Taplin's son Frederick William succeeded him as superintendent of the mission. His estate was sworn for probate at £100.

G. Rowe, *A century of service to the Aborigines at Point McLeay, South Australia* (Adel, 1960); PP (SA), 1860 (165); *Register* (Adel), 17 Oct 1849, 30 June, 12 July 1879; W. R. Bury, The foundation of the Point McLeay Aboriginal mission (B.A. Hons thesis, Univ Adel, 1964); Minute books and documents (Aborigines Friends Assn); G. Taplin, Journal and material (SAA).   G. K. JENKIN

TART, QUONG; *see* MEI QUONG TART.

TASMA; *see* COUVREUR.

TATE, RALPH (1840-1901), geologist and botanist, was born on 11 March 1840 at Alnwick, Northumberland, England, son of Thomas Turner Tate (1807-1888), teacher of mathematics and science, and his wife Frances, née Hunter. He was educated at Cheltenham College and the Royal School of Mines, London, where he was an exhibitioner in 1858. He taught at the London Polytechnic, at Bristol and in Belfast, where he founded the Belfast Naturalists' Field Club. He was appointed assistant curator to the museum of the Geological Society of London in 1864, having published work in geology, particularly palaeontology, and in botany. In 1867-68 he worked in central America and Venezuela largely on mining prospects; after returning to England he taught at mining schools in Bristol, Darlington and Redcar, and undertook a major investigation of the Yorkshire Lias. His work was recognized by the Geo-

logical Society in 1874 by the award of a moiety of the Murchison Fund.

When the University of Adelaide was founded in 1874 Tate was appointed to the Elder [q.v.] chair of natural science. His arrival in Adelaide in 1875 stimulated the small scientific community. By 1878 he had published a number of papers on local geology, and in 1880 he converted the comatose Adelaide Philosophical Society into the Royal Society of South Australia, becoming its first president. In 1877 he had founded the colony's first continuing scientific journal, which became the *Transactions and Proceedings of the Royal Society of South Australia*. In the same year he discovered at Hallett Cove impressive evidence of former glaciation. His earliest geological interest in his new homeland was in the sequences of Tertiary sediments in the coastal region south of Adelaide and in cliffs formed by the River Murray: this became the basis of his most notable work. He was also associated with the discovery and study of Cambrian rocks on Yorke Peninsula and of Mesozoic strata in the Great Artesian Basin.

The chair of natural science embraced botany and zoology as well as geology. Tate's publications on zoology as distinct from palaeontology consisted of about twenty papers, mainly on *Mollusca*. His contributions on botany, about forty, culminated in his *Handbook of the flora of extratropical South Australia* (1890) and were the foundations of the present knowledge of the plants of the colony. He persuaded the South Australian government to appoint its first permanent geologist in 1882; that year he accompanied a parliamentary party which investigated the potentialities of the Northern Territory, and was a key member of the W. Horn expedition which explored the Finke River region in 1894. He belonged to numerous learned scientific associations in Australia and overseas; a constant worker for the Australasian Association for the Advancement of Science, he was its president in 1893. That year he was awarded the [W. B.] Clarke [q.v.] memorial medal.

Tate's contribution to the growth of science in Australia, through his personal investigations and stimulation of research in natural science, can hardly be exaggerated. Only a man with an unlimited capacity for work could have accomplished so much. He was rugged and of 'marked personality', but able to induce great loyalty in friends and students; he was also a persistent and indefatigable conductor of field naturalist parties in South Australia. Although his activities provoked much controversy, all his work was marked by a fine critical sense, and this was certainly true of his work on Tertiary stratigraphy, probably his greatest legacy to Australian geology.

For many years Tate spent his leisure on a farm near Nairne, where he had a wattle plantation and a walnut grove; in later life he was an orchardist. He married twice. He died of heart disease at Buxton Street, North Adelaide, on 20 September 1901 and was buried in the North Road cemetery. He was survived by two daughters and a son of his first marriage, and by his second wife Mary and their daughter and two sons. His estate was sworn for probate at £1700. An obituary by J. F. Blake in the *Geological Magazine* (London), February 1902, lists Tate's publications.

J. J. Pascoe (ed), *History of Adelaide and vicinity* (Adel, 1901); R. S. Rogers, *An introduction to the study of South Australian orchids*, 2nd ed (Adel, 1911); W. G. K. Duncan and R. A. Leonard, *The University of Adelaide, 1874-1974* (Adel, 1973); A. R. Alderman, 'The development of geology in South Australia: a personal view', Aust Academy of Science, *Records*, 1 (1967), no 2; *Advertiser* (Adel), 21 Sept 1901; *Observer* (Adel), 28 Sept 1901.   A. R. ALDERMAN

TAYLER, LLOYD (1830-1900), architect, was born on 26 October 1830 in London, youngest son of William Tayler, tailor, and his wife Priscilla, née Lloyd. Educated 'at Mill Hill Grammar School, Hendon, and King's College, London, he is said to have been a student at the Sorbonne. In June 1851 he left England to join his brother on the land near Albury, New South Wales, but the run had been burned out and instead he tried his luck at the Mount Alexander goldfields. In 1854 he set up an architectural practice with Lewis Vieusseux, civil engineer, but by 1856 was working on his own in Melbourne and had designed premises for the Colonial Bank of Australasia. In the 1860s and 1870s he won repute by his designs for the National Bank of Australasia and rivalled Leonard Terry [q.v.] in this field: examples are at Richmond, North Fitzroy, Warrnambool and Coleraine; distinguished by a refined strength, they follow simple Renaissance revival formulae. His major design for the bank was the Melbourne head office (1867) which he described as Palladian. The whole of the framing and iron construction of the ambitious dome were made in London.

With E. W. Wright in 1874 Tayler won the competition for the South Australian Houses of Parliament (begun in 1881). They are also credited with the design of the Bank of Australia, Adelaide (1875). His impressive Australian Club, Melbourne (1878), is a fine interpretation of the Palazzo Farnese model, while the Melbourne Exchange is a modest example of his dignified urban manner. His commercial designs include works of great novelty such as the powerful warehouse and offices of the New Zealand Loan and Mercantile Agency Co., Melbourne (1880) and the delicate set of shops which included the Cafe Gunsler (1879). In all his public and commercial designs he seems to have been committed to a restrained classicism spiced with reserved mannerist details.

Tayler's domestic architecture featured similar characteristics; the finest example is the colonnaded mansion Kamesburgh, Brighton, commissioned by W. K. Thomson in 1872. Other houses include Thyra, Brighton (1883); Leighswood, Toorak, for C. E. Bright [q.v.]; Roxcraddock, Caulfield; Cherry Chase, Brighton; Blair Athol, Brighton; and a house for his son-in-law J. C. Anderson in Kew. Tayler is credited with the design of Kilwinning, East St Kilda, for James Service [q.v.]. His church work was also carried out in restrained manner but in the Gothic style. His known designs are St Mary's Church of England, Hotham (1860); St Philip's, Collingwood, and the Presbyterian Church, Punt Road, South Yarra (both 1865); Trinity Church, Bacchus Marsh (1869); and the extension to the C. Webb [q.v.] portion of St Andrew's, Brighton (1866).

In 1881 Tayler went into partnership with his pupil and assistant, Frederick A. Fitts (d. 1903). Of Tayler's other articled pupils only George Jobbins (1842-1924) and J. D. Scott are known. Tayler and Fitts seem to have resisted the architectural extravagance of the boom years and were complimented for the design of a building for Lambert and Son, Melbourne (1890), for 'avoidance of the overcrowding of ornamentation ... which forms a far too prominent feature on [many contemporary] façades'. In 1899 Tayler opposed decorative stucco work and warned against extremes in which the picturesque became the grotesque. The stylistic impetus which Fitts brought to the practice has not been established but perhaps he was responsible for the bias towards plain and decorative brick designs with stucco details which came from the office in the later 1880s.

Tayler crowned his career with an elaborate design, won in a difficult competition (1890), for the Melbourne head office of the Commercial Bank of Australia; he and Alfred Dunn (1865-1894) became joint architects. All evidence points to the finished building being based on Tayler's plan. The vast, domed banking chamber created a sensation at the time and is carefully preserved. His last important design was the

Metropolitan Fire Brigade Headquarters Station, Eastern Hill (1892).

Tayler was active in architectural affairs. He had been an inaugural member of the Victorian Institute of Architects in 1856 and helped to obtain its Royal Charter in 1890: he was president in 1886-87, 1889-90 and 1899-1900. In May 1900 he read a paper on 'Early and later Melbourne Architects' before the institute. While on a two-year visit to Europe and Britain, he was admitted a fellow of the Royal Institute of British Architects in 1874, and in 1899 contributed a paper on 'The Architecture of the Colony of Victoria' to its *Journal*. He was a 'staunch and valued supporter' of the Architectural and Engineering Association.

A justice of the peace, Tayler was a founder of the St John Ambulance Association in Victoria in June 1883 and a councillor of the Australian Health Society. A commissioner to the Melbourne International Exhibition in 1880-81, he often acted as professional adviser to the government and was a judge in 1900 of the competition plans for the new Flinders Street railway station.

Tayler had married Sarah Toller, daughter of a Congregational minister, at St Andrew's Church of England, Brighton, on 9 September 1858. They established a comfortable residence, Pen-y-Bryn, at Brighton, built from three prefabricated oak cottages originally imported from Wales. He was active in the formation of the Brighton library and was also a leading member of the Bowling Club. Tayler died of cancer of the liver at Pen-y-Bryn on 17 August 1900 survived by his wife, four daughters and a son. He was buried in the Brighton cemetery and the pallbearers included F. T. Sargood and F. S. Grimwade [qq.v.]. His obituarists referred to him as 'probably the best known figure in the architectural profession in Melbourne'. He left an estate valued for probate at £24,328.

A. Sutherland et al, *Victoria and its metropolis*, 2 (Melb, 1888); J. M. Freeland, *The making of a profession* (Syd, 1971); Roy Vic Inst of Architects, J, Mar 1905; *Building Times*, 12 Nov 1869; *Building, Engineering and Mining J*, 22 Mar 1890, 10 Jan 1891, 28 May 1892, 23 Aug 1900; *Table Talk*, 26 Mar 1891; *Argus*, 18 Aug 1900; *Australasian*, 25 Aug 1900; *Leader* (Melb), 25 Aug 1900; R. Tonkin, George Jobbins (B. Arch. research report, Univ Melb, 1971); D. J. Dunbar, Lloyd Tayler (B. Arch. research report, Univ Melb, 1969).

DONALD JAMES DUNBAR
GEORGE TIBBITS

TAYLOR, ADOLPHUS GEORGE (1857-1900), journalist and politician, was born on 14 June 1857 at Mudgee, New South Wales, son of George Taylor, gentleman, and Mrs Sarah Burton, née Shellum. Educated at the local Church of England school, he passed the Junior Public Examination in 1872 and in 1875 was teaching in Mudgee. He may have worked for the *Mudgee Independent* before joining the New South Wales Permanent Artillery as a private. Court-martialled for 'insubordination' in June 1878, he was committed to Darlinghurst Gaol and was released on 4 December. He rejoined the *Mudgee Independent* where his writing on politics attracted attention.

On 11 December 1882 Taylor was elected to the Legislative Assembly as senior member for Mudgee. In his maiden speech next year he moved an amendment to David Buchanan's [q.v.] motion advocating the teaching of history in the public schools, arguing that it should be delayed 'until the publication of an impartial and lucidly-written history of England'. On 20 February, after an exchange of personal abuse, he accepted John McElhone's [q.v.] challenge to resign his seat and contest it with him; Taylor won handsomely. When called to account by the House he admitted that his list of thirty-five members who, he alleged, had been drunk in the assembly was false and 'an electioneering dodge'.

In 1883-84 Taylor introduced nine bills, mostly on law reform and parliamentary procedure, and one to abolish flogging. He repeatedly obstructed parliament, caused disorder by his violent language, raised points of order, challenged the Speaker Edmund Barton and displayed an embarrassing knowledge of constitutional law. In December 1883 he pointed out that F. B. Suttor [q.v.] and George Reid were improperly appointed as ministers; the Committee of Elections and Qualifications reluctantly agreed and the government had to amend the Constitution Act to increase the number of ministers. When Reid stood for re-election Taylor, helped by McElhone, John Davies [q.v.] and E. W. O'Sullivan, secured victory for Sydney Burdekin [q.v.]. In 1884 he challenged the right of the governor to make appointments as commander-in-chief and accused him of interfering with the commandant.

Twice suspended for a week, Taylor successfully sued Barton for £1000 damages for illegal suspension. Re-elected in 1885 but often ill, Taylor rarely attended. On 19 January at Darlington, with Wesleyan rites, he married Rosetta Nicholls. Next year, when Barton appealed to the Privy Council, Taylor raised his fare by lecturing on 'The Iron Hand in Politics' and selling his stamp collection, took 'his wife, his mother, a cockatoo, a parrott and a magpie' to England and successfully conducted his own case. On his return he grandly refused to accept the damages.

Although returned for Mudgee in February 1887, Taylor resigned on 21 April and next month accepted Sir Henry Parkes's [q.v.] offer to become examiner of patents with a salary of £500. That year he published the *Law and Practice of New South Wales Letters Patent ...*, the copyright of which was bought by the government, and compiled a patents' index. In September he voluntarily sequestered his estate, explaining that 'long continued ill health' had caused his bankruptcy. He resigned on 13 May 1888 and published a satire, *The Marble Man* (1889). Preferred to P. J. Brennan [q.v.] by maritime unions, in 1890 Taylor won a by-election for West Sydney but was beaten in the 1891 election. In August 1894 he was defeated for Sydney-King despite the help of Sir George Dibbs [q.v.].

In 1890-91 Taylor had become first editor of the scurrilous newspaper *Truth* and in May-June 1892 conducted the *Spectator*; from the end of 1893 to June 1896 he was again editor of *Truth* and nominal proprietor from 1894. About this time he established and conducted Echo Farm Home for Male Inebriates at Middle Harbour. In 1897 he worked for the *Cumberland Free Press*, then took to freelance journalism. In 1898 he was admitted to the Hospital for the Insane, Callan Park, where he died on 18 January 1900; survived by his wife, he was buried in the Anglican section of Rookwood cemetery. A contemporary politician described Taylor as 'a smart, incisive writer, a really good speaker when he likes, and can earn a living as a journalist any day'. Tall and gangling, he was known variously as 'Giraffe', 'Doll' Taylor, 'The Mudgee pet' and the 'Mudgee camel'. Rowdy, brilliant, unstable and addicted to the bottle, he sometimes drew attention to real evils.

Ex-M.L.A., *Our present parliament, what it is worth* (Syd, c1886); C. Pearl, *Wild men of Sydney* (Lond, 1958); V&P (LA NSW), 1872-73, 3, 11, 1875-76, 5, 260, 1890, 1, 299; PD (NSW), 1883-84; NSW *Law Reports*, 6 (1885); *Barton v. Taylor* (1886) 11 App. Cas. 197 [P.C.]; *Bulletin*, 9 June 1883; *Bombala Herald*, 10 May, 6 Sept 1884; *Australasian*, 20 Dec 1884, 24 Mar 1888; T&CJ, 23 Apr 1887, 27 Jan 1900; Bankruptcy file 122831/14 (NSWA); CO 201/598, 600-602, 606, 615.

MARTHA RUTLEDGE

TAYLOR, ALFRED JOSEPH (1849-1921), librarian and publicist, was born on 24 March 1849 in Hobart Town, son of Thomas Joseph Taylor and his wife Emma. His father, son of Rev. Thomas Taylor, Witney, Oxfordshire, England, was transported from Sydney in 1842 under a life sentence for forgery; in 1849 he was a schoolteacher but from 1853 served as under-keeper at the New Norfolk Hospital for the Insane, and died in 1881 aged 69. In New Norfolk as a child Alfred suffered an accident which crippled him for life. He received little formal education but enthusiasm for books won him a post as librarian at New Norfolk in his teens. In January 1874 he became librarian of the Tasmanian Public Library which had been constituted in 1870. The appointment caused some stir, but he held it until his death.

The extreme financial stringency imposed on the library made any great success impossible, but Taylor gave of his best. A grant from Andrew Carnegie prompted the transfer of the library to a new building on the corner of Argyle and Davey streets in 1907, and a lending section then began operations. He used the new library as a centre for lectures and entertainments. 'Despite a forbidding exterior Taylor was a soft-hearted man', E. Morris Miller remembered; 'but in his control of the library he was adamant'. As early as the 1880s he had aroused hostility by insistence on determining the library's opening hours and by refusing to house an ultra-Protestant journal; but bigger controversies developed in 1914 when, as an opponent of capital punishment, he criticized the Supreme Court for sentencing J. H. Belbin to death and fought for his reprieve. The library trustees disapproved and instructed him not to express opinion on public issues. A compromise was reached but in July 1915 Taylor again commented on a court decision, to the anger of most trustees. Debate on both occasions concentrated on the right of civil servants to engage in public controversy. Labor politicians (in the second case, the Labor government) supported him with considerable vehemence and helped him win out.

Free, compulsory and secular primary education; technical training; dispensary services; land redistribution; wider franchise; workers' organization and self-betterment through trade unions; sexual purity: all these causes received support from Taylor's tongue and pen. He anchored them in a Spencerian-cum-Unitarian faith that promised no eternity for individual personality, but irrepressible betterment of all human kind. Moncure Conway, the American deist, included Taylor among 'that circle of aspiring spirits in Hobart' congenial to himself. A. I. Clark [q.v.] and R. M. Johnston were others of 'that circle'.

Science, especially medical science, was Taylor's other great interest. He claimed to have cured himself of consumption by inhaling sulphur fumes and to have anticipated the germ theory of disease. He wrote of Tasmanian fauna, flora and Aboriginals, and built up an impressive museum at his home, 28 D'Arcy Street. The *Tasmanian School Journal*, which he edited and largely wrote in 1901-03, presented these interests in their most attractive light; when more ambitious, he sometimes showed the arrogance and naivety of a self-made scholar. He early visited, publicized and invested in silver-mining on the west coast, only to lose heavily in the Van Diemen's Land Bank smash in 1891.

On 31 December 1874 at Hobart Taylor had married Mary Anne Forde (d. 1920); their only child was stillborn in 1875. Taylor travelled overseas in 1905 and suffered ill health from 1919. He died of heart disease on 9 October 1921, leaving an estate valued for probate at £3770.

M. D. Conway, *My pilgrimage* (Lond, 1906); *Library Opinion*, 2 (1954); *Tasmanian News*, 21 July 1893; *Mercury*, 10-12 Oct 1921; *Illustrated Tas Mail*, 13 Oct 1921; Tas Public Library, Scrapbook (SLT).   MICHAEL ROE

TAYLOR, HUGH (1823-1897), politician, was born on 19 March 1823 at Parramatta, New South Wales, eldest son of Hugh Taylor, general agent, and Elizabeth Brown, née O'Farrell, his housekeeper. His father had arrived in Sydney in 1815 in the *Marquis of Wellington* with a life sentence for 'larceny from a person', and had been 'in Newgate before'. Educated by Daniel Thurston and at The King's School, Taylor became a butcher. He later became agent for many of the Sydney newspapers and wrote for the *Sydney Morning Herald*. On 29 December 1846 he married Frances Eliza Connor (d. 1896) at St Patrick's Church, Parramatta, and was converted to Catholicism.

In the 1860s Taylor supported James Byrnes [q.v.] electorally and learned much about politics. He won a seat on the Parramatta Borough Council in 1865, two years after its incorporation, and remained a member until 1897. In 1869 he failed to win one of the two Parramatta seats in the Legislative Assembly; the consequent break with the Byrnes family led to fifteen years of electoral contests in Parramatta, both municipal and parliamentary, between the Taylors and the Byrneses. Each commanded large family groups and many friends, but the division was also sectarian, with the Orangemen supporting Byrnes and the Irish Catholics behind Taylor. Instinctively generous, Taylor also cultivated an image as 'the poor man's friend', selling meat and bread cheaply, particularly at election time. In 1871 he became mayor and was re-elected for the next two years—in 1873 after a long tussle with the Byrnes party, resolved only after fourteen meetings and the death of one of them. On another occasion he was unseated when Byrnes appealed to the Supreme Court.

In 1872 Taylor won Parramatta, defeating C. J. Byrnes; J. S. Farnell [q.v.] was the other representative. The election was marked by sectarian violence, largely provoked by larrikins imported by the Sydney-based Protestant Political Association, which backed Byrnes. Taylor resigned his seat before parliament met, but won the ensuing by-election. Re-elected in 1875, he resigned next year after suggestions that his contract to supply meat to government institutions made him ineligible. Returned in the subsequent by-election and again in 1877, in the assembly he supported (Sir) Henry Parkes [q.v.] with whom he formed a lasting friendship, supplying meat for his Faulconbridge home and in 1895 being best man at his third marriage. Taylor was defeated by C. J. Byrnes only once, in 1880, partly as a result of his opposition to the public instruction bill: he favoured the dual education system of 1866. The passage of time finally eroded his electoral basis and he was defeated by Dowell O'Reilly in 1894 and in 1895; he was preparing to contest the seat again when he died.

In the House Taylor won repute as a mild radical; opposed to the squatters he defended the free selectors and championed most working men's causes. Although a free trader he supported E. W. O'Sullivan's protectionist Democratic Alliance. He excelled as a local member, winning for Parramatta many improvements, such as its inclusion in the area covered by the penny post. A conscientious magistrate, he was a committee-man of the Parramatta District Hospital and of the Catholic Orphanage, also a trustee of Parramatta Park and St John's Park. For many years he was president of the Parramatta Jockey and Cricket clubs and the Liedertafel. He strongly supported the local fire brigade and Protestant orphan school.

Taylor presided over his tightly knit family as a patriarch. Survived by three sons and three daughters, he died on 13 December 1897 of syncope and cardiac disease, and was buried in his family vault in the Catholic cemetery at Parramatta. His estate was valued for probate at £563.

J. Wharton, *Jubilee history of Parramatta*

(Parramatta, 1911); J. Jervis, *The cradle city of Australia*, G. Mackaness ed (Parramatta, 1961); J. Jervis, 'A history of politics and politicians in Parramatta', *Parramatta and District Hist Soc, J*, 3 (1926); *Freeman's J* (Syd), 24 Feb 1872, 25 Dec 1897; *Cumberland Mercury*, 21 Oct 1885; *Cumberland Argus*, 18 Dec 1897; Parkes letters (ML).　　MARK LYONS

TAYLOR, JAMES (1820-1895), squatter, investor and politician, was born in 1820 in London, son of John William Taylor, merchant, and his wife Ann. He probably reached Sydney as an assisted migrant in the *James Pattison* on 2 February 1840 and in 1840-46 acquired pastoral experience. He arrived on the Darling Downs in 1848 with sheep for the Dawson River district, becoming H. S. Russell's [q.v.] head stockman at Cecil Plains, a partner in 1856 and sole proprietor in 1859. He prospered by making the station a fattening and disposal centre for western sheep. By 1880 the 147,310 acres of freehold carried nearly 100,000 sheep and was supplemented by Dunmore, Goodar and Coomrith stations on the Western Downs and Mount Marlow on the Barcoo River.

Taylor entered Queensland politics as M.L.A. for Western Downs in 1860. Although a staunch supporter of the Downs squatters he joined Sir Charles Lilley's [q.v.] administration as minister for lands on 28 January 1868 as part of the price paid by Lilley for Downs and squatting support. Taylor administered his office from Toowoomba without scrupulous regard for the public good. Huge areas of Cecil Plains were withheld from selection and suddenly sold off to Taylor himself in 1870. This action was one of the reasons for his resignation on 3 May 1870 and the subsequent fall of Lilley. Taylor lost the next election.

Elevated to the Legislative Council in November 1871, he soon proved to be one of the most vigorous and obstructive of the squatting rear-guard. His attempt to recapture Toowoomba in 1881 was defeated by the W. H. Groom [q.v.] machine and Taylor concentrated on being a director of the Queensland Brewing Co., the Queensland Mercantile and Agency Co., and the Land Bank of Queensland.

Toowoomba was virtually Taylor's creation. Perceiving advantages in the 'Swamp' with its key position he succeeded in replacing Drayton with Toowoomba as the regional centre of the Downs. Mayor of Toowoomba in 1890, he held much central real estate which was enhanced in value by judicious public works expenditure and private pressures. He was also intimately concerned with the School of Arts, the Queensland Turf Club, the Royal Agricultural Society, the Queensland Club and the Brisbane Diocesan Synod.

The onset of paralysis gradually destroyed Taylor's health, and his public activities were marked by increasing irascibility and conservatism. Survived by his wife Sarah, née Boulton, whom he had married on 16 February 1850, four of his five sons and three daughters, he died at Toowoomba on 19 October 1895 and was buried in the local cemetery.

Popularly known as the 'King of Toowoomba', Taylor was never a 'Pure Merino'. His philosophy was essentially the crude social Darwinism of his contemporary 'robber barons' in the United States of America. Though rough and ungrammatical he was a sound practical man of the frontier who boasted that he never read books. He derided all 'wild theorists', but his superb management and development of Cecil Plains, his role as the founding father of Toowoomba, and his wider impact on Queensland business rescue him from complete obloquy.

W. F. Morrison, *The Aldine history of Queensland*, 2 (Syd, 1888); O. de Satgé, *Pages from the journal of a Queensland squatter* (Lond, 1901); *Queenslander*, 30 June 1866; *Darling Downs Gazette*, 21 Oct 1895; *Week*, 25 Oct 1895; B. R. Kingston, Land legislation and administration in Queensland, 1859-1876 (Ph.D. thesis, Monash Univ, 1970); Hurd cutting book no 3 (Oxley Lib, Brisb).

D. B. WATERSON

TAYLOR, RACHEL; see HENNING.

TAYLOR, ROBERT (1834-1907), Anglican clergyman, was born on 30 April 1834 at Brighton, Sussex, England, son of Robert Taylor, contractor, and his wife Elizabeth, née Barnard. Educated at Haileybury College he became a teacher and, after marrying Elizabeth Stevenson in 1854, migrated to Australia. In Sydney he was influenced strongly by Rev. Thomas Smith [q.v.]. After training at Moore Theological College, Liverpool, he was made deacon by Bishop Barker [q.v.] on 26 June 1859 and became locum tenens for Smith at St Barnabas's Church, George Street West, which had a large working-class congregation; though less demonstrative than Smith, he carried on the same kind of vigorous ministry. Sent later to the rural district of Castle Hill, he was ordained priest on 24 February 1861. In January 1866 he returned to St Stephen's, Newtown, as curate; he became officiating minister in 1868 and incumbent in 1870.

Newtown had many wealthy parishioners but the subdivision of the large estates was providing working-class housing. To replace the overcrowded church-school, Taylor promoted the building of a new St Stephen's within Camperdown cemetery; opened in 1874 it was one of E. Blacket's [q.v.] best Gothic churches. Taylor saw the church as comprehending all classes of Anglicans while exemplifying his own strict principles. He held a high proportion of free sittings and planned to meet the cost of £12,700 by freewill donations, but they proved insufficient and land previously granted for a church had to be sold. The enabling legislation was resisted by parishioners whose landed interests made them prefer the old site and who resented his firm direction and uncompromising Evangelicalism. He prevailed in 1873 but his health suffered and he took leave in 1877 in England.

Taylor was impressed by the efforts of English Evangelical churchmen in organizing parochial life and work. He returned to the colony in 1878 determined to invigorate and unify his socially fragmented parish by religion-oriented cultural, charitable and community activities. He justified the programme by a 'holiness' doctrine that stressed Christian leadership. His theology aroused opposition (he was dubbed 'sanctification' Taylor) but his methods provoked emulation in a hitherto conservative diocese. From Newtown came a stream of ordinands and laymen who contributed especially to the 'Bible belt' of the expanding western suburbs: one local organization became the nucleus of the Church Lads' Brigade. When Moore College moved from Liverpool in 1886 to the site of old St Stephen's parsonage, his parish provided practical training for its students and he lent his house at Mount Victoria for its use. In 1884-88 he was also incumbent of the new church built in the working-class district of Erskineville. From work such as Taylor's the concept of modern parochial communal activities emerged.

He published addresses and played a large part in diocesan affairs. Taylor was rural dean of West Sydney, 1884-85, canon, of St Andrew's Cathedral, 1891-1907, and served on most synod committees. He was prominent in the Evangelical opposition both to ritualism in the diocese and the emphasis on episcopal authority made by the 1897 Lambeth Conference. His advocacy was rarely strident; he co-operated with the moderate Archbishop Saumarez Smith and, in his later years, was regarded as an elder statesman. His wife died on 19 December 1897 and at Gladesville on 28 December 1898 he married a deaconess

Mary Augusta Sophia Schleicher. He died of angina pectoris in St Stephen's rectory on 21 July 1907 and was buried in Randwick cemetery. He was survived by five sons and two daughters of his first wife and by his second wife; his estate was valued for probate at £1161. There are memorials to Taylor in St Andrew's Cathedral and at St Stephen's, where the church hall is named in his memory.

T. G. Rees, *Historic Camperdown* (Syd, nd); M. L. Loane, *A centenary history of Moore Theological College* (Syd, 1955); M. E. Herman, *The Blackets* (Syd, 1963); V&P (LA NSW), 1872, 2, 727, 1872-73, 3, 239; Church of England Hist Soc, *J*, 7 (1962), no 3; *Daily Telegraph* (Syd), 22 July 1907; Gledhill collection (Moore College).
K. J. CABLE

TAYLOR, WILLIAM (1818-1903), pastoralist, was born on 20 November 1818 in Glasgow, Scotland, son of William Taylor, merchant, and his wife Martha, née Kirkwood. He was educated at a Glasgow high school and had begun a mercantile career when he decided to migrate. He arrived in Port Phillip on 7 August 1840, and purchased a sheep-run on the Moorabool River, twenty miles from Geelong. In February 1844 he and Dugald McPherson took up 206,000 acres in the Wimmera; with 33,000 sheep, they were the first pastoralists north of Glenorchy. After trouble with Aboriginals in 1844-45 they subdivided their holding in 1848; Taylor's portion was known as Longerenong. In the winter of 1849 with Archibald Fisken [q.v.] and Robert Scott he travelled down Yarrambiak Creek to Lake Coorong in search of new land; they then went north-west to Pine Plains in the Mallee and on to the Murray River, returning below Lake Hindmarsh where they saw the tracks of E. J. Eyre's [q.v.] 1838 expedition.

Taylor bought Overnewton at Keilor in 1849 and that year married Helen Wilson Fisken, sister of Archibald. He retained the lease on Longerenong until 1856 when he sold it to (Sir) Samuel Wilson [q.v.] and returned to Britain for three years. In 1861 he bought a station on the Murray River at Euston and over the years improved and brought water to over one million acres of dry country in the Lower Darling District. His other interests included the Manfred run, a half-share in Garnpung and at one time Salisbury Downs and Ariool, and Bootra stations, all in New South Wales. He was also interested in Queensland and with A. Rowan [q.v.] and Fisken was a partner in Darr River Downs from 1888.

In 1847 Taylor was appointed a magistrate, and that year was one of a deputation which waited on Sir Charles FitzRoy to protest against the landing in Hobson's Bay of ticket-of-leave men from Pentonville (London) prison. In 1854-56 Taylor was member for the Wimmera in the Legislative Council and supported the secret ballot. He contested Creswick in the Legislative Assembly in 1859 and in 1864 was elected for Southern Province to the council; he did not seek re-election in 1866. The severe seasons of that and the preceding year affected Taylor's properties. In June 1874 he contested the seat again but was defeated by James Balfour [q.v.].

Elected to the Keilor District Road Board in 1861, Taylor was chairman in 1863 and president of the Shire Council in 1874-82 and 1884-94. He was also a member of the Stawell Shire Council. In Melbourne he was a director of the Union Mortgage and Agency Co. and owned many Melbourne and country town blocks. He was a member of the Scots Church congregation and a trustee of church property. Appointed to the Council of Ormond College in 1880, he gave the college £200 and in 1881 a scholarship, valued at £50, for three years. He died on 21 June 1903, survived by his wife, six of his seven sons and four of his six daughters. His substantial property was seriously eroded by mortgage debts and his estate was valued for probate at £117,446, with a final deficit of £12,000.

A. Sutherland et al, *Victoria and its metropolis*, 2 (Melb, 1888); J. Smith (ed), *Cyclopedia of Victoria*, 1 (Melb, 1903); *Pastoral Review*, 16 July 1903.   J. ANN HONE

TAYLOR, WILLIAM (1821-1902), evangelist, was born on 2 May 1821 near Lexington, Virginia, United States of America, son of Stuart Taylor, farmer and tanner, and his wife Martha, née Hickman. He taught school in rural Virginia before being accepted in 1843 by the Baltimore Annual Conference of the Methodist Episcopal Church as a candidate for the ministry. After appointments to rural circuits he moved to the city of Washington in 1846; in October that year he married (Isabelle) Anne Kimberlin of Fincastle, Virginia. Of their five sons and one daughter, four sons survived infancy.

In 1849 Taylor was sent as one of the first two Wesleyan missionaries to California where he became known in the frontier town of San Francisco for his forceful street preaching, in which his ringing baritone voice was used to advantage, and for his work among seamen. When a seamen's bethel, for which he was personally liable, was burned down in 1856, Taylor was given

leave by the California Conference to raise money for the building debt. In 1857-61 he conducted religious revivals in mid-west and eastern America. Whilst preaching in Canada, Taylor was told of Australia as a likely field for evangelism and, after travelling to Great Britain, Palestine and Egypt, he arrived in Melbourne in June 1863. Rev. D. Draper [q.v.] engaged him to conduct nightly revival services at Wesley Church, Lonsdale Street; large crowds attended.

Taylor also visited Geelong, Sandhurst (Bendigo), Ballarat, Beechworth and at least a dozen other Victorian towns, generating an outburst of religious exaltation in the colony. Known as 'California Taylor', he attracted many by his almost vehement nervous energy and by his informal 'Yankee' preaching which Rev. James Bickford [q.v.] found 'in forceful contrast to our prosaic and quieter style of working'. Although Taylor claimed that he never accepted gifts of money for his own cause, funds to pay his personal expenses and to meet the $23,000 bethel debt were raised by the brisk sale of his books, especially his *Seven Years' Preaching in San Francisco, California* (New York, 1856) and *California Life illustrated* (New York, 1858). In June 1864 he conducted revivals in Tasmania; in New South Wales, including Sydney, Wollongong, Mudgee, Maitland, Bathurst and Braidwood; in Queensland, including Brisbane, Maryborough, Rockhampton and Ipswich; in New Zealand and in South Australia. In November 1865 his wife and three sons, whom he had not seen for four years, arrived in Sydney. He joined them there; they returned to Adelaide early next year and on 15 February left in the *St Vincent* for missionary work in South Africa.

While Bickford and others praised Taylor's work, many Wesleyan clergymen were dissatisfied with the results of his visit. The Australasian Conference of 1864 believed that the money raised by him had hindered the payment of colonial chapel debts, although Taylor wrote later that his 'raising of money to pay for their newly built churches was a specialty in which the Lord gave great success'. His claims to have dramatically increased church membership were not verified by the figures. He returned to Australia by way of the West Indies in 1869, arriving in Melbourne from Sydney on 4 September. At Bickford's request he conducted revival services at Wesley Church, preaching there with 'wonderful power'. Invitations to other Victorian circuits followed. After visits to New South Wales and Tasmania, he returned to Melbourne to conduct street meetings before leaving for India in July 1870. His return visit was not welcomed by many clergymen and his meetings failed to arouse the religious fervour of his first tour.

Taylor won later fame for the missions he established in India, South America and Africa; the General Conference of the Methodist Episcopal Church appointed him missionary bishop to Africa in 1884. In 1896 in New York he published his autobiography, *Story of My Life*. He retired to California where he died at Palo Alto on 18 May 1902.

J. C. Symons, *Life of the Rev. Daniel James Draper* (Lond, 1870); J. Bickford, *An autobiography of Christian labour* (Lond, 1890); *Sydney Mail*, 15 July 1865.

TEBBUTT, JOHN (1834-1916), astronomer, was born on 25 May 1834 at Windsor, New South Wales, only son of John Tebbutt, farmer, and his wife Virginia, née Saunders, and grandson of John Tebbutt who had arrived free in the *Nile* in 1801 and settled in the Hawkesbury district. He was educated at the local Church of England parish school by Edward Quaife, a great lover of astronomy and to whom Tebbutt later acknowledged his debt. In 1843 he went to the Presbyterian school conducted by Rev. Matthew Adam and completed his education under Rev. H. T. Stiles [q.v.] in 1845-49. When he was 11 his father had bought a farm on land known as the Peninsula, on the Hawkesbury River, which he inherited in 1870 and improved from time to time; he also bought other land in the area.

Tebbutt bought his first instrument, a marine sextant, in 1853 and he had the use of a clock with a seconds pendulum which he regulated by celestial observation. He also had a small telescope with which he projected an image of the sun. From an early age he had taken an interest in mechanical objects and later developed his 'attention to celestial mechanism', gradually accumulating instruments and experience and winning international repute. In 1863 at the Peninsula he built with his own hands a small wooden observatory.

Tebbutt calculated the circumstances of the total eclipse of the sun of 26 March 1857 when conditions proved cloudy and made a series of measurements of the position of the comet Donati (1858 VI) for which he calculated the orbit. On 13 May 1861 he observed a faint nebulous object with his marine telescope; a few days of observation showed that it was in motion and he announced the notable discovery of the great comet of 1861 (1861 II), one of the finest comets on record—at one stage it had a tail which could be traced for over

100 degrees. The earth passed through the tail late in June. Acquiring a 3¼-in. refracting telescope, in 1862 he made his first acquaintance with Encke's comet (1862 I). That year he refused the position of government astronomer for New South Wales after W. Scott's [q.v.] resignation.

Over the years Tebbutt kept up a remarkable series of patient, reliable observations on comets, occultations of stars by the moon, eclipses and transits of Jupiter's satellites, variable stars and double stars and the position of minor planets. He observed Encke's comet on seven of its returns and discovered the great comet of 1881. He also published extensive meteorological observations made between 1863 and 1896. In 1872 he bought a 4½-in. equatorial refractor with which he observed the transit of Venus in 1874. In 1879 he erected 'a substantial observatory of brick' a few metres south of the old observatory and in 1886 he bought an 8-in. equatorial refractor by Grubb. His observations of comets and minor planets, being among the relatively few made in the southern hemisphere and of proved reliability, were much in demand by orbit computers.

A member of the Philosophical (Royal) Society of New South Wales from 1862, Tebbutt won a silver medal at the 1867 Paris Universal Exhibition for his paper 'On the Progress and Present State of Astronomical Science in New South Wales', published in Sydney in 1871. In 1873 he became a fellow of the Royal Astronomical Society, London, and in 1905 was awarded its Hannah Jackson, née Gwilt, gift and bronze medal; in 1895 he was first president of the New South Wales branch of the British Astronomical Association. In his *Astronomical Memoirs* (Sydney, 1908) Tebbutt listed his 371 publications in various learned journals, including 120 in the *Monthly Notices* of the Royal Astronomical Society and 148 in the *Astronomische Nachrichten*. He never left Australia but he taught himself to read French and German, corresponded with international colleagues and acquired a large astronomical library. When the British Association for the Advancement of Science met in Sydney in 1914 the astronomers visited him at Windsor.

Although Tebbutt devoted most of his time to astronomy he was president of the Windsor branch of the British and Foreign Bible Society; in 1877 he asked Sir Henry Parkes [q.v.] for leniency towards settlers in paying their government land dues. He died of cerebral paralysis at Windsor on 29 November 1916 and was buried in the Anglican cemetery. Predeceased by his wife Jane, née Pendergast, whom he had married at St Matthew's Church, Windsor, on 8 September 1857, he was survived by a son and three of their six daughters. His estate was valued for probate at £69,364.

J. Steele, *Early days of Windsor* (Syd, 1916); Roy Astronomical Soc, *Monthly Notices*, 33 (1873); Roy Soc NSW, *Procs*, 51 (1917); *Syd Q Mag*, June 1889; *Lone Hand*, Feb 1909; Tebbutt papers (ML); printed cat (ML); family records (held by John Tebbutt, Peninsula Farm, Windsor).   HARLEY WOOD

TEMPLETON, JOHN MONTGOMERY (1840-1908), actuary, was born on 20 May 1840 at Kilmaurs, Ayrshire, Scotland, eldest son of Hugh Templeton, schoolmaster, and his wife Margaret, née Harvie. He arrived with his parents at Melbourne in December 1852, qualified under the National Board of Education and became a schoolteacher at Fitzroy in 1857. His interest in mathematics developed and in 1868 he became an accountant with the newly formed National Insurance Co. of Australasia. He suggested radical improvements to the existing system of insurance and persuaded his directors to found the National Mutual Life Association of Australasia in 1869, which became the first Australian company to include the non-forfeiture principle in its policies. Templeton became its actuary and in 1872 its secretary. That year he qualified as a fellow of the Institute of Actuaries.

An able administrator, considerate yet strict, Templeton retained the style of the schoolmaster; he aroused ill feelings by his frequent and sometimes bitter disputations in English and Australian insurance journals, especially over the origin of the non-forfeiture concept. He was nominated by the government in 1874 to certify the insurance tables of friendly societies and in 1878 was appointed actuary under the Friendly Societies Act of 1877. In 1881 he was appointed to the royal commission on education, and as chairman in the absence of J. W. Rogers [q.v.] organized the final majority report which Rogers refused to sign.

In 1883 Templeton accepted J. Service's [q.v.] offer to become first chairman of the Public Service Board, and in February next year he resigned from the National Mutual. The board's abolition of political patronage and introduction of new salary scales earned him much resentment, and his attempts to achieve greater independence for the board by direct approach to the governor put him at odds with the ministry. When in 1888 he accepted a seat on the board of the National Mutual, his political enemies attacked him. Rather than relinquish his outside work, he resigned from the Public Service Board in February 1889.

Templeton was appointed on 9 December to investigate the Premier Permanent Building, Land, and Investment Association, one of the first casualties of the collapse of the land boom. In February 1890 he was made official liquidator for the firm and despite political opposition forced the prosecution of its directors, including J. Mirams [q.v.]. In 1891 he became official liquidator for the Anglo-Australian Bank and was also chairman of liquidators for the Mercantile Finance, Trustees, and Agency Co. Ltd. Templeton became chairman of the board of the National Mutual in 1895 and its managing director in 1897-1908. In October 1893 he had won the Legislative Assembly seat of Benalla and Yarrawonga, but the result was contested and in a new election he was defeated. In the 1903 Federal elections he stood unsuccessfully for the Senate.

Templeton took a great interest in citizen defence. At 19 he joined the volunteers as a private in the Collingwood Rifles and became a first-rate rifle shot. Lieutenant in 1864 and captain and battalion adjutant in 1867, he became major in the Second Metropolitan Victorian Battalion in 1873 and in 1883 was promoted to lieut-colonel in the reorganized defence forces. In 1895 he became a full colonel. In 1883-97 he was a member of the Victorian Council of Defence and was honorary aide-de-camp to the governor in 1885 and 1895. He captained the successful Victorian team that went to Bisley, England, in 1897 and in London he rode in the leading section of the colonial procession at Queen Victoria's Diamond Jubilee. On his return he was transferred to the Reserve Officers Militia, but in 1898 was appointed to the Local Defence Committee. He was treasurer of the Victorian Naval and Military Club in 1889-97. Vice-president from 1888 and chairman in 1899 of the Victorian Rifle Association, in 1900-02 he was officer commanding rifle clubs. He did much to promote rifle shooting in Victoria; his lecture at the Town Hall, Melbourne, on 29 July 1900 to commemorate the movement, was the basis for his *Consolidation of the British Empire, the growth of citizen soldiership, and the establishment of the Australian Commonwealth* (Melbourne, 1901). He published several other pamphlets on aspects of insurance and defence. He was created C.M.G. in 1897.

Of 'medium height, sturdily built, square-shouldered, with fine massive head and set, inscrutable face, walking always quickly with short, light step', he was indefatigable and honest, although his pugnacious self-confidence involved him in many conflicts. He had married Mary Lush of Melbourne on 20 April 1866; on 19 August 1905 at Sydney he married Carrie Taylor, 38-year-old secretary of Melbourne. He died on 10 June 1908 of pleurisy and heart failure at Kilmaurs, East Melbourne, and was buried in the Melbourne general cemetery. Childless, he was survived by his second wife and left an estate valued for probate at £22,321.

J. Smith (ed), *Cyclopedia of Victoria*, 1 (Melb, 1903); M. Cannon, *The land boomers* (Melb, 1966); National Mutual Life Assn of A'sia, *A century of life* (Melb, 1969); G. Serle, *The rush to be rich* (Melb, 1971); *A'sian Insurance and Banking Record*, 13 Mar 1884, 20 June 1908; *Table Talk*, 22 Sept 1893; *Argus*, 11 June 1908; *Aust Worker*, 9 July 1908.

ANN-MARI JORDENS

TEMPLETON, WILLIAM (1828-1890), public servant and company director, was born on 3 December 1828 in Glasgow, Scotland, son of Andrew Templeton (d. 1829), banker, and his wife Janet, née Forlonge. On 24 January 1831 William arrived at Launceston in his mother's chartered brig *Czar*; the family went to Campbell Town, Van Diemen's Land, where William Forlonge [q.v.] had land, but soon moved to Parramatta, New South Wales. William was educated at The King's School. About 1843 he joined his mother at Seven Creeks station near Euroa, Port Phillip District. In 1851 he enlisted in the gold escort corps and was in charge of the first escorts from the Mount Alexander diggings; in May next year he became an officer of the mounted police. In 1853 he transferred to the gold commissioner's office, Maryborough, and was successively sub-inspector, acting assistant and senior commissioner; next year he was commissioner and after the Eureka uprising was transferred to Ballarat. He was a witness before the select committees on police in 1852 and 1863.

Templeton was resident warden, Maryborough district, in 1855-62. A judicious administrator, who declared the miners 'a most respectable and orderly class', he insisted on a restrained police force and constantly sought its efficiency. As chairman of the local court he suggested procedural changes, and when the office of warden was abolished in 1862, he became police magistrate to the Melbourne and suburban districts. He occasionally sat on boards of inquiry appointed by the Education Board to investigate problems in Common schools. He was a member of the royal commission on penal and prison discipline; its third report in 1872 gave the results of its inquiry into the system of industrial and reformatory schools set up under the Neglected and Criminal Children's Act of 1864; he also gave evidence to the commission, which included in its report his view that children of the destitute should be boarded-out privately or provided for by government-assisted local authorities.

In Melbourne in 1870 Templeton published *A Guide to Courts of Petty Sessions in Victoria* . . . In 1874 he sold his home, Elmshurst, Brighton, to T. Bent [q.v.], moved to Windsor, and was a member of the Prahran Council in 1881-84 and mayor in 1883-84. He also supported a number of charitable institutions. Dismissed on Black Wednesday, January 1878, he decided to form a company in Victoria similar to two trustees and executors companies he had observed in South Africa. The Trustees. Executors, & Agency Co. Ltd was floated in 1878; the directors included Sir Charles Sladen, D. C. Macarthur, John Benn, J. Balfour, F. R. Godfrey and J. M. Davies [qq.v.].

Templeton was managing director until 1890. Despite the company's slow start he remained confident of its soundness and future success. His high reputation, his many business and professional friends and his legal knowledge were important in winning public confidence. The business was soon administering many valuable estates and by 1890 its original £1 shares were worth £15.

Templeton was a foundation member and first chairman of directors of the Mutual Store. Originally a member of the Church of England, he later joined Dr Strong [q.v.] in forming the Australian Church. On 6 October 1859 at Brighton he married Mary Anne Godfrey of Stanley, Tasmania, who bore him seven sons and five daughters. He died at Tarana, Lewisham Road, Windsor, on 18 September 1890; his estate was valued for probate at over £12,000.

H. M. Humphreys (ed), *Men of the time in Australia: Victorian series*, 1st ed (Melb, 1878); H. M. Franklyn, *A glance at Australia in 1880* (Melb, 1881); T. Brentnall, *My memories* (Melb, 1938); A. Henderson (ed), *Australian families*, 1 (Melb, 1941); W. Bate, *A history of Brighton* (Melb, 1962); A'sian Building Societies and Mortgage Companies, *Gazette*, 25 Sept 1890; *Argus*, 3 July 1880, 19 Sept 1890; Trustees, Executors, & Agency Co. Ltd records (Melb); Warden's reports, Maryborough mining district (PRO, Vic).

JACQUELINE TEMPLETON

TEN, GEORGE SOO HOO (1848-1934), Anglican missionary to the Chinese, left his birthplace Hoiping, Kwangtung, China, aged about 17, for San Francisco where he learned English and was converted to Christianity by a Baptist minister. In 1876 he was a tea merchant in Sydney, and in July 1879 first went among the market gardeners of Botany and Waterloo as a catechist sponsored by the Sydney Diocesan Corresponding Committee of the Australasian Board of Missions.

Despite ridicule and open opposition from many Chinese, especially gamblers and opium dealers, and bitter anti-Chinese feeling among some Europeans, Ten began Sunday afternoon services at Botany and the St Andrew's Cathedral schoolroom, as well as week-night classes in English. His first six converts were baptized in June 1882. In February 1884 he preached to the Chinese at Bathurst, and later in Sydney formed 'a Chinese YMCA' which met monthly 'for fellowship and special instruction'. In January 1885 his annual stipend was increased from £75 to £125 with house rent. On 20 December he was made deacon and licensed as 'missionary to the Chinese and to officiate at Christ Church, Botany', whose foundation stone had been laid in June.

Ten conducted missions in Brisbane in October 1887, in Melbourne in July 1888 and in Parramatta in May 1891. In February 1889 his stipend was doubled and by 1890 he was conducting 38 services a week at Botany, Waterloo, Cook's River, Canterbury, North Willoughby and at St Andrew's and St Philip's schoolrooms in the city, as well as training Chinese catechists. After 1894 he helped raise funds for land, a church and mission hall in Wexford Street, an area that was a centre of prostitution and gambling in Sydney; and in March 1898 St Luke's Church was opened there. On 24 June he was priested, his annual salary rose to £300 and he confined his ministry to the inner city; at the same time control of the mission passed to the New South Wales Church Missionary Association. By 1912 he appears to have retired to Homebush. On 24 September 1934, aged 86, he died of cancer in the Royal Prince Alfred Hospital, survived by a daughter and predeceased by his wife Elizabeth, née Lett, a dressmaker, whom he had married in Sydney on 25 April 1889. His estate was valued for probate at £4882.

A'sian Missionary News, Jan 1889; Church Missionary Assn of NSW, Annual reports 1903-04, 1912 and Diocese of Sydney, Official register and Diocesan Corresponding Cttee, A'sian Board of Missions, V&P, Synod (Syd Diocesan Registry).   RUTH TEALE

TENISON-WOODS, JULIAN EDMUND (1832-1889), Catholic priest, educationist and scientist, was born on 15 November 1832 at West Square, London, sixth son of James Dominick Woods, of the Middle Temple, who also worked on The Times, and his wife Henrietta Maria Saint-Eloy, née Tenison. Among his ancestors were several outstanding Irish Catholic and Anglican religious leaders. He attended Thomas Hunt's Catholic school, Kent House, Hammersmith, and, briefly, Newington Grammar School. In 1846 he worked for The Times then moved to Jersey with his family. In 1848 he assisted Fr Frederick Oakeley in a school at Islington and discussed the ideas of the Tractarian movement. He joined the Passionist Order but ill health obliged him to continue his studies at Marist seminaries near Toulon, France, where he taught English at a naval college. His interest in natural history and geology appears to have started at this time.

In 1854 in England Tenison-Woods met Bishop R. W. Willson [q.v.] and accompanied him to Van Diemen's Land; they arrived in the Bernicia on 30 January 1855, but he disagreed with the bishop, left after about three months and went to Adelaide. After working as sub-editor of the Adelaide Times he entered the Jesuit college at Sevenhill near Clare, was ordained as a diocesan priest on 4 January 1857 and took charge of the large parish of Penola, in southeastern South Australia. In 1862 he published his first book, Geological Observations in South Australia. With Mother Mary McKillop [q.v.] he helped to found the Sisters of St Joseph of the Sacred Heart at Penola in 1866.

Next year Tenison-Woods accepted the demanding and often controversial positions of director-general of Catholic schools and secretary and chaplain to Bishop Shiel [q.v.]. In 1867-69 he edited a religious magazine, the Southern Cross, but had to discontinue it in favour of the Irish Harp and Farmer's Herald, a more politically oriented journal, which contributed much to divisive diocesan quarrels. A believer in mystical experiences including visions, in 1870 he began editing a new, devotional magazine, The Chaplet and Southern Cross, advocate of the Children of Mary. Next year he was eased out of Adelaide and until 1883 he conducted missions and retreats in New South Wales, Tasmania and Queensland, where in Brisbane on 15 June 1874 he founded the Sisters of Perpetual Adoration. He was often at odds with his superiors, and clashed with Mother McKillop.

Tenison-Woods was an accurate observer of the physical world and made original contributions to Australian geology, palae-ontology and zoology. In 1883 Governor Sir Frederick Weld invited him to report on the geology and tin-mining resources of the Malay States. He also visited Java, Borneo, Siam and Japan, and saw some of the Kraka-toa eruptions. In 1885 he was asked to survey the mineral potential of the Indian Archipelago. He travelled widely in Aus-tralia and published over 150 papers in the journals and transactions of Australian learned societies and overseas periodicals; he contributed popular scientific articles to leading Australian newspapers. His sub-stantial reports to government departments described his geological surveys of coal resources and tin-mines in Queensland and the natural history of New South Wales; he published two accounts in 1864 and 1887 of the physical geography, mineral reserves and natural history of the Northern Territory.

Tenison-Woods's *History of the Discovery and Exploration of Australia* (London, 1865) in two volumes, and his serialized survey 'Australian bibliography' in the *Australian Monthly Magazine*, 1866-67, evidence wide scholarship. A member of the Royal Asiatic Society, he was a fellow of the Geological Society of London and the Linnean Society of London and an honorary member of the New Zealand Institute, the Royal societies of New South Wales, Victoria and Tas-mania and the Adelaide Philosophical (Royal) Society. He was a president of and contributed papers to the Linnean Society of New South Wales and was a member of the Union Club, Sydney. William III of the Netherlands gave Tenison-Woods a gold medal for his book, *Fish and Fisheries of New South Wales* (Sydney, 1883) and he was awarded the 1888 (W. B.) Clarke [q.v.] medal of the Royal Society of New South Wales for his work in natural history and the paper, 'The Natural History of the *Mollusca* of Australia'.

In 1887, his health ruined, Tenison-Woods returned from the Northern Territory to Sydney, and was looked after by a group of religious women; he dictated a partly fanciful autobiographical memoir to them. He died of paralysis on 7 October 1889 and was buried in the Roman Catholic section of Waverley cemetery. His estate, sworn for probate at £609, was left to Mary Jane O'Brien, commonly called 'Mrs Abbott', formerly a nun, who founded a refuge for unmarried mothers which later became St Margaret's Hospital.

Possessing profound, though romantic, religious convictions based on a childlike piety, Tenison-Woods was esteemed as a preacher and missionary; he was a dedicated priest, an outstanding though stubborn and individualistic religious leader and an ad-vanced educator; although his original rules for the Sisters of St Joseph were modified, they retained his single-minded dedication to the education of poor children. Professor A. Liversidge [q.v.], aware of his scientific repute, praised his 'great simplicity, cour-tesy and kindness of manner'; and J. C. Cox [q.v.], in testifying to his 'exuberant industry ... [and] extraordinary variety of attainments', published in 1889 a bibli-ography of his writings in the *Proceedings* of the Linnean Society of New South Wales.

G. O'Neill, *Life of the Reverend Julian Ed-mund Tenison Woods* (Syd, 1929); J. O'Brien, *On Darlinghurst hill* (Syd, 1952); C. Turney, *Pioneers of Australian education*, 2 (Syd, 1972); T. P. Boland, *Quiet women* (Aust, 1974); PP (SA), 1886, 3 (122); J. M. Curran, 'Julian Edmund Tenison Woods', *Centennial Mag*, 2 (1889-90); A. Liversidge, 'Anniversary address' and bibliog, Roy Soc NSW, *Procs*, 24 (1890); M. McNamara, 'Father J. E. T. Woods and the Bathurst foundation of the Sisters of St. Joseph' *and* G. O'Neill, 'Remarks', *A'sian Catholic Record*, Jan 1930; *Advertiser* (Adel), 8 Oct 1889; *T&CJ*, 12 Oct 1889; *Advocate* (Melb), 14 July 1894.   D. H. BORCHARDT

TENNANT, ANDREW (1835-1913), pas-toralist and politician, was born on 20 June 1835 at Hawick, Roxburghshire, Scotland, son of John Tennant, shepherd, and his wife Jessie Aitken; as an assisted migrant John brought his family to South Australia in the *Duchess of Northumberland* on 19 De-cember 1839; he later overlanded stock from Adelaide to Port Lincoln and bought Tallala station, fifteen miles away. Tennant Creek, Northern Territory, is named after him. Andrew was educated at E. W. Wickes's school at North Adelaide and inherited the property on his father's death. Aged 18, he took cattle west to the shores of Lake New-land near Elliston, and settled at Salt Creek. The holding had been abandoned because of the Aboriginals' hostility, but Tennant was unafraid and for seven years he controlled the natives while successfully managing his sheep and cattle station.

Later Tennant owned stations at Mount Wedge, Coffin's Bay and Streaky Bay. In 1886 he leased the large block, Baroota near Port Germein, but owing to severe droughts had to move, subsequently acquiring from Sir Thomas Elder [q.v.] the Oorama and Baratta runs. He remained there for a year or two, then sold the properties and purchased Willipia station in the same neighbourhood, Moolooloo (1800 square miles), Murapatina near Mannahill (1500), and Undoolya station near Alice Springs

(10,000). Later he established Yardea station and owned and worked Corraburra near Port Augusta until his death. Other runs held by him included Portee near Blanchetown, Princess Royal and Middle Back. In addition he owned 13,000 acres at the Hermitage near Riverton, much valuable freehold property in the city of Adelaide and held stations in New Zealand.

Tennant had large interests in the Seaham and Abermain Colliery companies in New South Wales and was the principal shareholder in the Tarcoola Blocks Gold Mine, a venture in which he lost heavily. He was a director of the China Traders Co. and of the Adelaide Steamship Co. Ltd from its inception. A justice of the peace, he was for many years a Freemason under the Grand constitution. A generous patron of the turf and lover of thoroughbreds, Tennant established a stud at Hermitage and successfully raced horses throughout South Australia. For many years president of the Port Augusta and Flinders Jockey Club, he was closely associated with all metropolitan and a number of country racing clubs.

In 1881-87 Tennant represented Flinders in the House of Assembly in South Australia. In 1898-1902 he sat in the Legislative Council for the Northern District. He was a member of the Pastoral Lands Commission in 1897-98. On 28 August 1862 in Adelaide he had married Rachael Christina Ferguson. Survived by his wife, three daughters and three of his four sons, he died of diabetes and senile dementia in his home, Essendene, Mosely Street, Glenelg, on 19 July 1913, and was buried in the Brighton cemetery. His South Australian estate was sworn for probate at £506,248.

J. J. Pascoe (ed), History of Adelaide and vicinity (Adel, 1901); H. T. Burgess (ed), Cyclopedia of South Australia, 1 (Adel, 1908); R. Cockburn, Pastoral pioneers of South Australia, 1 (Adel, 1925); Observer (Adel), 26 May 1900, 26 July 1913; Advertiser (Adel), 21 July 1913.   GORDON D. COMBE

TERRY, FREDERICK CASEMERO (CHARLES) (1825-1869), artist and engraver, was born at Great Marlow, Buckinghamshire, England, third son of Henry Terry, language teacher, of Cheshunt, Hertfordshire, and his wife Isabella, née Clark. Educated in Switzerland, he arrived in Sydney in the early 1850s: his picture, 'Point Piper, Sydney', is dated 10 April 1852. Other early works include 'Sydney from the Old Point Piper Road' (1852), 'Sydney Cove from Fort Macquarie' (1853), 'The Nobbies from Newcastle' and 'Newcastle from the Nobby' (1853). Soon accept-

ed as a thoroughly professional water-colour artist, he did some of his own engraving. In 1854 he submitted a design for a medal to the New South Wales commissioners for the 1855 Paris Universal Exhibition; he won second prize of five guineas and a five-guinea bonus was voted him 'out of regard for the exquisite finish of his design'. The same year his painting of the grave of Fr Receveur, the French naturalist with Compte Jean-François La Pérouse [q.v.], was presented to the French government by the New South Wales government. It now hangs in the Marine Museum, Paris.

Some of Terry's engravings were published by Sands [q.v.] and Kenny as the Australian Keepsake (1855). The volume contained scenes of 'Port Jackson', 'Pinch Gut', 'The Gap, South Head', Sydney's Streets, fruit markets and churches as well as country views of Richmond, Windsor and East and West Maitland; an erratum slip noted that an engraver's error had resulted in Terry's name being incorrectly recorded throughout as 'Fleury'. In 1855 he was represented at the Paris exhibition with five other Australian artists including Conrad Martens, G. F. Angas and Adelaide Ironside [qq.v.]. It was the first time Australian paintings had hung in an important overseas display. In January 1857 Terry was invited to exhibit in the Further Exhibition of the Society for the Promotion of the Fine Arts in Australia, which was presided over by Sir Charles Nicholson [q.v.] and held in the Mechanics' School of Arts, Sydney. Among the other artists showing were S. T. Gill and Marshall Claxton [qq.v.].

Terry's output was consistent and ample; by 1860 he was recognized as one of the best colonial painters. About that year another small volume appeared as The Parramatta River Illustrated with six prints. By 1861 he had become examiner of a drawing class established at the Mechanics' School of Arts in 1859 by Joseph Fowles [q.v.]. In the early 1860s he executed the covers for The Maude Waltzes, 'as played by the Band of the 77th Regiment' and The Darling Point Polka. He later collaborated with Edmund Thomas to illustrate pieces in The Australian Musical Album for 1863. His paintings were almost entirely views of Sydney and its environs and were painstaking in detail. Almost every work included people, animals, birds and some form of activity. Historically pictorial, they give an excellent record of life in the city. A contemporary, O. R. Campbell [q.v.], noted that his pictures 'are the best productions of the kind that I have seen in Sydney— clear and characteristic in drawing and beautifully composed ... they would be greatly prized in London'.

Aged 44, Terry died on 10 August 1869 of effusion of the brain and was buried in the Camperdown cemetery. He had married Margaret Jane Reynolds (d. 1866) on 14 July 1858 and was survived by their son Henry. He had found it hard to make a living and owed his landlord £65. All his 'goods chattels credits and effects', valued for probate at £45, went to a creditor. His work is represented in the Art Gallery of New South Wales, the Mitchell and Dixson libraries, Sydney, and the National Library of Australia, Canberra.

ISN, 20 May 1854; F. C. Terry acquisition file (NL); MS cat (ML); printed cat (Dixson Lib, Syd).   MERLE PETERS

TERRY, LEONARD (1825-1884), architect, was born at Scarborough, Yorkshire, England, son of Leonard Terry, timber merchant, and his wife Margaret, née Walker. He reached Melbourne in 1853 and after six months was employed by C. Laing [q.v.]. Evidence suggests that he did not, as has been alleged, acquire sole control of Laing's practice in 1855; but by the end of 1856 he had his own practice in Collins Street West; after Laing's death next year Terry succeeded him as the principal designer of banks in Victoria and of buildings for the Anglican Church, of which he was appointed diocesan architect in 1860. His first-recorded commission, late in 1856, was the design of Sands [q.v.] and Kenny's printing house in Collins Street West, which he remodelled in 1864. Other commissions included a number of bluestone warehouses in central Melbourne, especially in 1857-58; the Melbourne Club of 1858; the works of the Victoria Sugar Co., Sandridge (Port Melbourne) of 1857-59 (burnt 1874); Alfred Joyce's [q.v.] house, Norwood, near Maryborough, of 1863-64; and the large James McEwan & Co. ironmongery warehouse of 1869.

Terry's first-known bank commission was for additions to the Union Bank in Melbourne in 1857. Next year he won a competition for the Melbourne office of the London Bank, and he later designed at least fifty branches for all the major banks, mainly in Victoria, but also in Tasmania, Western Australia and New Zealand. Lloyd Tayler [q.v.] became a serious rival in the late 1860s. In all this work Terry favoured a Renaissance palazzo mode, in which he designed even his bluestone warehouses: a fine example (1858) is the Cleve Bros building, in Lonsdale Street. His banks are best illustrated in Lydiard Street East, Ballarat, where the Bank of New South Wales of 1862, the Colonial of 1860, the three-storied National of 1862, and the Australasia at the corner of Sturt Street of 1864, stand in a row and harmonize well, though varying widely in design. This group continued originally on the opposite corner of Sturt Street with his London Chartered Bank of 1866, and a little further west is his Union Bank of 1863-64.

Even within Terry's Renaissance manner some developments can be traced, such as the introduction of segmental arches in about 1870. The James McEwan building of 1869 presented new problems because it was four storeys high; his solution was developed more strikingly in his remodelling of the Monster Clothing Co.'s building in Bourke Street in 1873, where the frontage was narrow enough for one large arch at first floor level to carry across the display windows below. This treatment is important because it is the antecedent of a whole school of brick Romanesque buildings in Melbourne of about 1890-1920, in which giant order piers carry through from ground level up to major arches in the upper storeys. The McEwan building was also of technical interest for its iron roller-shutters, fire proof partitions and hydraulic goods lift.

As diocesan architect, Terry not only designed many Anglican churches but also vetted designs and sometimes, it seems, called tenders from his Melbourne office on behalf of country architects. Thus it is often difficult to determine which buildings were Terry's own, though there is certainty in the case of St Paul's, Humffray Street, Ballarat, (a rebuilt school) of 1861-64; Holy Trinity, East Melbourne, of 1864 (burnt 1905) and its associated deanery of 1864 and parsonage of 1868 and 1875; St John's, Ballarat, of 1864-65 (extended by Terry and Oakden [q.v.] 1884); Christ Church, Birregurra, of 1867; and Holy Trinity, Williamstown, of 1870-74. Stylistic evidence suggests that he was in fact responsible for many other buildings with which his name is associated. He prepared a scheme for the Church of England Theological (Trinity) College, Parkville, of which only the principal's house (Leeper Wing) was built in 1869-72, the remainder being completed between 1877 and 1891 to designs by E. Blacket, J. Reed [qq.v.] and others. Terry's churches were generally of bluestone, and in fairly austere Early English or Decorated Gothic and, with the exception of Birregurra, well composed and satisfying. In his parsonages, and at Norwood and Trinity College, he used a simple Tudor manor style with steep gables and banks of rectangular windows, generally given a sober and rugged character by the use of bluestone.

Terry also undertook commissions for the Roman Catholic Church, including major work in 1870. some of it probably in association with W. W. Wardell [q.v.]. This work occurred in a lull in Terry's practice, which seems to have begun in the late 1860s, and finished on 1 January 1874 when he took in as junior partner (with a one-third interest) the former Ballarat architect Percy Oakden, who brought in numerous Nonconformist church and school commissions: Terry continued to work for the Anglican and the Roman Catholic Churches. Generally the partners maintained distinct clienteles and distinctive styles, though Terry's output was now small. He was appointed supervising architect for St Paul's Cathedral and about 1879 visited England and consulted with the architect William Butterfield, although eventually much of the supervision was done by Oakden.

Terry was first married, at 30. on 26 June 1855 to Theodosia Mary Welch (d. 1861), by whom he had six children including Marmaduke, who trained as a surveyor and entered his father's firm in 1880. Terry's second marriage, at 41, on 29 December 1866 was to Esther Hardwick Aspinall, who bore him three children and survived him when on 23 June 1884, at the age of 59, he died of a thoracic tumor in his last home, Campbellfield Lodge, Reilly (Alexandra) Parade, Collingwood. He left no real estate but other assets that were valued for probate at £12,000, including an interest by way of goodwill in the firm of Terry and Oakden, worth £4000. Gifted but reticent, in his lifetime he had received no personal publicity and only the minimum of attention for his works: his death went unremarked in the daily, the banking and the Anglican press. He was a conservative but competent and highly sensitive designer, who produced a greater number of noble buildings than more progressive contemporaries like Reed. His work is urbane by comparison with the coarse neo-classicism and picturesque Gothic of Laing, or the fussy polychromy of Oakden; Tayler was more of a kindred spirit, and described Terry as 'a man of much more than ordinary ability, and ... modest, unassuming and gentlemanly manner'.

Terry and Oakden (firm), What to build and how to build it (Melb, 1885); A. Sutherland et al, Victoria and its metropolis, 2 (Melb, 1888); L. Tayler, 'Early and late Melbourne architects', Building, Engineering and Mining J, 5 May 1900; H. Troppe, Leonard Terry and some of his banks (B. Arch. report, Univ Melb, 1970); H. Zuzowski, The works of Leonard Terry (B. Arch. report, Univ Melb, 1971).   MILES LEWIS

TERRY, SAMUEL HENRY (1833-1887), landowner and politician, was born on 9 April 1833 at Box Hill, Pitt Town, New South Wales, eldest son of John Terry (d. 1842), landholder, and his wife Eleanor, née Rouse, and grandson of Samuel Terry and Richard Rouse [qq.v.]. Educated at John Mills's school at Parramatta and at W. T. Cape's [q.v.] Elfred House Private School in Sydney, he entered J. R. Young's Sydney counting-house. On 13 May 1856 at St James's Church he married Clementina Parker, youngest daughter of John Want.

In June 1859 Terry failed to win the Legislative Assembly seat of Canterbury, but in December won a by-election for Mudgee which he represented for ten years. A supporter of (Sir) John Robertson's [q.v.] land Acts, he proved himself to be a liberal free trader and energetic local member. 'One of the most independent laymen in the Assembly', he carried a motion for the restoration of the cross-benches, where he always sat. Determined to reform the law, he introduced seventeen public bills and eleven of them were enacted; they included the 1874 Triennial Parliaments Act, carried in spite of the opposition of the Parkes [q.v.] government, Acts for the Enforcement of Claims Against the Crown and Betting Houses Suppression, and the 1874 Suppression of Garrotting Act, which he lifted piecemeal from the criminal law amendment bill as he believed that the House would have to 'wait a month of Sundays' before the ministry carried that lengthy measure. He also advocated payment of members. Terry disliked lawyers in parliament: 'Would a lawyer', he had asked in 1864, 'vote for any motion to cheapen the law?' Members of the legal profession invariably opposed him at elections; he defeated them all, except the barrister M. H. Stephen [q.v.] in 1869.

Terry devoted himself to his business affairs until he won New England which he held from 28 August 1871 to 9 November 1880. He again represented Mudgee from 1 December 1880 until 29 December 1881 when he resigned to allow Robertson to return to the assembly. Appointed to the Legislative Council, he continued to take a special interest in matters affecting land and property. In 1879-80 he had been a member of the royal commission into the working of the real property Acts and was a commissioner for the Sydney International Exhibition. Inheriting Box Hill and 5000 acres at Yass Plains from his father, he acquired Jeremiah and Bongongo stations in the Tumut and Gundagai districts, as well as property in Queensland and New Zealand and much city and suburban real estate. A magistrate, he was a founding member of the Union Club in 1857.

Terry died of heart disease on 21 September 1887 in his residence, The Lilacs, Ashfield, and was buried there in St John's churchyard. He was survived by a son and daughter of his first wife and by two sons and a daughter of his second wife Caroline Jane, née Weaver, whom he had married at St John's, Darlinghurst, on 12 September 1863. His personal estate was sworn for probate at £125,222.

E. Digby (ed), *Australian men of mark*, 1 (Syd, 1889); *SMH*, 30 Nov, 27 Dec 1864, 9 Dec 1867, 29 Aug 1871, 6 Mar 1872, 22 Sept 1887; *ISN*, 10 Mar 1875; R. Parsons, Lawyers in the New South Wales parliament, 1870-1890 (Ph.D. thesis, Macquarie Univ, 1972).

G. P. WALSH

TERRY, WILLIAM HENRY (1836-1913), shopkeeper and spiritualist, was born at Islington, London, son of Thomas Charles Terry (d. 1876), manager of the Wood Paving Co., and his wife Martha Ann, née Smith. He came to Melbourne in 1853 with his father, a brother and a sister. In 1855 the family opened a general store at Flemington on the road to the goldfields. Terry and his father were interested in at least four drapery shops around Melbourne between 1859 and 1866, with no marked success.

Like his father, who had been a follower of W. J. Fox, Terry was a free-thinking Unitarian. In the late 1850s the Terrys took up spiritualism, and at Berigny's and Crookes's circles William discovered that he possessed mediumistic skills. When spiritualism burgeoned in Victoria, Terry and his father forsook drapery selling in 1869 for full-time mediumistic work, and early next year William set up in Russell Street, Melbourne, as spiritualist bookseller, medium, trance and magnetic healer, and clairvoyant herbalist. His busy shop became the headquarters of the movement. In September 1870 he launched under 'direct spiritual injunction' the *Harbinger of Light*, which became the Australasian organ of the faith. Terry edited the *Harbinger* until his retirement in 1905, and wrote much of its staple of reports of spiritual phenomena and advocacy of vegetarianism and temperance until he sold the paper in 1907.

Steadfast, evidently sincere, and mild in public, Terry was an ideal spokesman for his often absurd and embattled co-devotees. Within the movement he was constructive and hard working. He founded the Progressive Lyceum (children's Sunday school) in 1872 and taught there until 1889. He sponsored tours by celebrated mediums including Dr Slade and Dr Peebles. The Victorian Association of Progressive Spiritualists (later the Victorian Association of Spiritualists), which he helped establish in 1870, depended upon his administrative and financial acumen for its survival. Terry was elected an honorary member of the British National Association of Spiritualists and in March 1880 became an inaugural fellow and councillor of the Theosophical Society in Australia. In 1893-94 he visited the United States of America as representative of the Australian spiritualist movement.

Terry had married Martha Robinson on 7 December 1858. The union was unhappy and he finally obtained a judicial separation in 1874, with custody of eight of their nine children. Aged 77, he died at Malvern, Victoria, on 27 October 1913, and was buried in Melbourne cemetery.

J. Smith (ed), *Cyclopedia of Victoria*, 2 (Melb, 1904); M. K. Neff, *How Theosophy came to Australia and New Zealand* (Syd, 1943); *Australasian*, 16 May 1874; F. B. Smith, Religion and freethought in Melbourne 1870 to 1890 (M.A. thesis, Univ Melb, 1960).

F. B. SMITH

THATCHER, CHARLES ROBERT (1831-1878), goldfields entertainer, and RICHMOND (1842-1891), journalist, were the eldest and youngest sons of Charles Robert Thatcher and his wife Sophia, née Hornsby (Hossey). Charles was born in Bristol, England, but the family later moved to Brighton where Richmond was born and where their father, sometimes described as 'conchologist', owned a curio shop. As a boy, Charles was taught the flute and he later played in London theatre orchestras.

Arriving in Melbourne in November 1852 in the *Isabella*, Charles tried the Bendigo diggings but soon became an entertainer. He joined the orchestra at the Royal Victoria Theatre, Sandhurst, and filled in between plays by singing new words to popular tunes. In these songs he described the troubles of the new chums, the excitement of rushes, fisticuffs, horse-racing, cricket, the nuisance of dogs around the township and other topical events. He soon attracted large audiences and in May 1854 was given top billing at the Shamrock Hotel, which remained his base for several years; he also toured other goldfields. Big, broad-shouldered and weighing some fourteen stone, he was considered handsome with his well-cut hair, clean-shaven face and drooping moustache. With a pleasant but slight voice, he sang 'in that jolly off-handed style that suits so well a rattling, rollicking bit of comicality'. Other singers were vocally superior but none could match his ability to write catchy local songs.

Aged 30, on 8 February 1861 at Geelong, Thatcher married a widow Annie Vitelli. née Day, a singer. In December they left via Hobart Town for Dunedin, New Zealand. They stayed in various parts of New Zealand until the latter half of 1866. Back in Victoria Thatcher performed on his own, appearing at the Polytechnic in Melbourne in November-December 1867. In June 1869 he returned to New Zealand, but about May next year rejoined his wife and two daughters in Melbourne and from there they went to England. He settled in London, collecting and selling curios from Europe and Asia. He died of cholera in Shanghai, China, in September 1878.

Fourteen of Thatcher's songs were sold as broadsides, many appeared in newspapers, but most were published as collections, including the Victoria Songster (1855). Thatcher's Colonial Songster (1857) and Thatcher's Colonial Minstrel (1859). Booklets of his New Zealand songs appeared after 1862 and his Adelaide Songster was issued in 1866. A few have been collected as Australian folk songs, others have appeared in books of reminiscence; he himself wished them to be 'regarded as a popular history of the time'. Recent historians have spoken of Thatcher as the vocal equivalent of the artist S. T. Gill [q.v.].

Richmond (Dick) Thatcher was to some a 'typical Australian Bohemian' but was more generally known as a facile and forcible journalist and theatre publicity agent. As a youth he had sailed as midshipman to India, China, the Cape, and Western Australia but about 1861 he joined Charles in New Zealand. He tried the diggings but, apparently unsuccessful, he spent some years collecting shell specimens for (Sir) F. McCoy of Melbourne and Dr J. C. Cox [qq.v.] of Sydney.

Although Thatcher had contributed to Sydney Punch and other periodicals, he first gained newspaper experience as editor of the Fiji Times in 1870; from 1871 he lived in New South Wales and worked for several newspapers: he founded the Upper Hunter Courier (from Murrurundi), edited the Western Independent at Bathurst and wrote for the Empire, the Evening News, and the Town and Country Journal. Between 1875 and 1885, Richmond's publications included two anthologies, three novels, and Life and Times of Jem Punch (Sydney, 1885).

In the late 1870s he became theatrical agent for artists, including Mrs Scott Siddons and Miss Ada Ward, whom he accompanied to England, Europe and South Africa; in 1884 he went to England as advance agent for an Australian minstrel troupe. At the end of 1888 'his brain gave unmistakable signs of giving way' but he seemed to recover. Within a month of taking up a trading job in the New Hebrides in 1891 Thatcher contracted a fever and returned to Sydney where he was also found to have Bright's disease. Aged 49, he died soon after on 9 June and was buried in the Anglican section of Waverley cemetery. He had married first Maria Blunt on 4 January 1872 at St Alban's Church of England, Muswellbrook, and second, Alice Emma Smith on 29 March 1881 at Surry Hills. He was survived by his second wife and a son and a daughter of the first marriage.

G. Mackay, Annals of Bendigo (Bendigo, 1912); P. Serle, Bibliography of Australasian poetry and verse (Melb, 1925); G. H. Scholefield (ed), A dictionary of New Zealand biography (Wellington, 1940); H. Anderson, The goldrush songster (Melb, 1958) and The colonial ministrel (Melb, 1960); Australasian, 23 Nov 1867; Table Talk, 19 June 1891; NZ Graphic, 12 May 1894; Thatcher MSS (LaT L).

HUGH ANDERSON

THOMAS, JULIAN; see JAMES, JOHN STANLEY.

THOMAS, LEWIS (1832-1913), colliery proprietor and politician, was born at Tanyrallt, parish of Llanfihangel-Genau'r-Glyn, near Talybont, Cardiganshire, Wales, on 20 November 1832, son of Thomas Thomas, carrier, and his wife Mary, née Hughes, who were members of the Talybont Independent Chapel. At 9 Lewis went to work in a woollen factory, at 15 in the lead-mines of Esgair and Bwlch Gwyn and later in the coal and iron mines of South Wales. Before migrating to Australia in July 1859, he married Ann Morris; she joined him in Queensland in July 1877.

After failing on the Victorian gold diggings, Thomas moved to Queensland in April 1861. Having completed his share of a railway tunnel contract, he turned again to coal and discovered and opened up much of the West Moreton field. In 1866, while continuing the search for good quality coal, he exploited the outcrop deposits at Tivoli with J. M. Thompson [q.v.]. The partnership collapsed after quarrels in 1870. He opened the famous Aberdare Colliery at Bundamba, followed by a new mine at Dinmore in 1870, where coal chutes serviced the Ipswich to Brisbane steamers. The extension of railways in Queensland created a demand for coal that boosted Thomas's fortunes and earned him the title of 'Coal King', though a depression in 1894 caused him to convert his mine-ownership into a co-operative that lasted for a decade.

News of Thomas's success stimulated Welsh migration to Queensland. In 1891 he built Brynhyfryd, a mansion overlooking the coalfields; around it clustered a Welsh community at Blackstone, stressing Welsh life and culture in Queensland in the United Welsh Church, the Blackstone-Ipswich Cambrian Choir and the eisteddfodic movement, the last two of which Thomas founded and endowed. He established scholarships to the Ipswich grammar schools and, for students from the Talybont district, to the University College of Wales, Aberystwyth.

Later his interests expanded to dairying and politics. With Samuel Grimes, M.L.A. for Oxley, Thomas introduced the first Illawarra Shorthorn milking herd to Queensland. In 1893-99 he was M.L.A. for Bundamba. Called to the Legislative Council in 1902, he remained a member until his death on 16 February 1913. His only child Mary married Thomas Bridson Cribb, grandson of Benjamin Cribb [q.v.].

G. Harrison (ed), *Jubilee history of Ipswich* (Brisb, c1910); M. J. Fox (ed), *The history of Queensland*, 1 (Brisb, 1919); *Dictionary of Welsh Biography down to 1940* (Lond, 1959); E. Ross, *A history of the Miners' Federation of Australia* (Syd, 1970); V&P (LA Qld), 1877, 3, 59, 618; T. MacDonald, 'The Welsh boy who made good', *Coal Miner*, Nov-Dec 1959; Jack cutting book (Oxley Lib, Brisb).

MARGARET BRIDSON CRIBB

THOMAS, MARGARET (1843-1929), artist, sculptor and author, was born at Croydon, Surrey, England, daughter of Thomas Cook, a ship-owner. She came with her parents to Melbourne in 1852. Taught by C. Summers [q.v.], she was the first woman to study sculpture in Victoria and was later described by D. B. W. Sladen [q.v.] as 'the first Australian-bred sculptor of eminence'. Her work was first shown when the Victorian Society of Fine Arts held its initial exhibition in December 1857; she lived at Richmond and continued to exhibit regularly. Her oil paintings and drawings as well as her popular medallion portraits and busts were noted by Melbourne critics. She also had a bust and plaster figure accepted for the London International Exhibition, 1862. Commenting on her work shown at the Fine Arts exhibition of January 1863, James Smith [q.v.] wrote that her 'essays in sculpture betoken the diligent exercise of no ordinary plastic skill, and contain the promise of future excellence'; the *Illustrated Melbourne Post*, 3 January 1863, acknowledged her 'persever-

ing industry ... true poetic feeling ... undoubtedly spiritual element ... innate love of the beautiful ... refined delicacy of pure taste ...', but suggested that her hand required discipline.

About 1867 Thomas left for England and soon decided to continue her studies in Rome and Paris. Returning to London in 1870, she received a studentship next year at the Royal Academy of Arts, where she had the distinction of being the first woman awarded a silver medal for modelling at the academy schools. Between 1868 and 1880 she exhibited eleven times at the academy (six of her portraits were hung in 1874), seventeen times at the British Institution and five times in other galleries. She paid tribute to Summers in her monograph *A Hero of the Workshop* ... (London, 1879); her memorial bust of him for the shire hall at Taunton, Somerset, brought further commissions to commemorate famous sons of the county, including Henry Fielding.

Thomas was a colourful artist, skilled in realistic portraiture. Mainly a traditionalist, she was an admirer of Turner and was influenced by neo-classicism. According to Sladen her portraits were so successful that she was able to retire and devote the rest of her life to travel and book-writing. She had a comprehensive knowledge of the picture galleries of the Continent; she published in London in 1906 a lively dissertation on *How to judge Pictures* and in 1911 *How to Understand Sculpture*. An intrepid traveller, she wrote and illustrated *A Scamper through Spain and Tangier* (1892), *Two Years in Palestine and Syria* ... (1899) and *Denmark, past and present* (1902). She accompanied Rev. John Kelman (1864-1929) through the biblical lands and her sixty-seven coloured paintings for his book. *From Damascus to Palmyra* (London, 1908), included also scenes in Baalbek, Armenia and Lebanon.

Thomas's verse was published in English, American and Australian periodicals, including the *Australasian*; seven of her poems appeared in Sladen's *Australian Poets, 1788-1888* (London, 1888) as well as other anthologies. A volume of rather erotic love poems, *Friendship, Poems In Memoriam* (London, 1873) was dedicated to her friend Henrietta Pilkington; she published another book of verse, *A Painter's Pastime*, in 1908. She never married and for some years before her death, aged 86, on 24 December 1929 she lived at Norton near Letchworth, Hertfordshire. Among her more important works in Australia are an oil painting of Summers and a plaster medallion of Sir Redmond Barry [q.v.], both in the historical collection of the La Trobe Library, Melbourne.

D. B. W. Sladen (ed), A *century of Australian song* (Lond, 1888); H. A. (Mrs A. Patchett) Martin (ed), *Coo-ee: tales of Australian life by Australian ladies* (Lond, 1891); L. Fisher (ed), *By creek and gully* (Lond, 1899); A. Graves, *The Royal Academy of Arts*, 7 (Lond, 1906); W. Moore, *Studio sketches* (Melb, 1906); D. B. W. Sladen, *Twenty years of my life* (Lond, 1915); E. W. Syme, 'Women and art', *Centenary gift book*, F. Fraser and Nettie Palmer eds (Melb, 1934); *Argus*, 5 Jan 1863; W. Moore, 'From my scrap book', *New Triad* (Syd), 1 Nov 1927.

MARJORIE J. TIPPING

THOMAS, MESAC (1816-1892), Anglican bishop, was born on 10 May 1816 at Typorth near Aberystwyth, Cardiganshire, Wales, son of John Thomas and his wife Elizabeth, née Williams. Educated at Oswestry Grammar School and Shrewsbury School, in 1836 he matriculated at St John's College and next year moved to Trinity College, Cambridge (B.A., 1840; M.A., 1843; D.D., 1863). In 1839 he became founding secretary of the Cambridge Camden Society (Ecclesiological Society, 1841) and retained a lifelong interest in church buildings. Made deacon in 1840 he was ordained priest on 25 July 1841 by the bishop of Worcester; in 1840-43 he served as curate at Birmingham and was incumbent at Tuddenham St Martin, Suffolk, in 1843-46. He married Mary Campbell Hasluck at Aston near Birmingham on 7 November 1843. He was vicar of Attleborough, Warwickshire, until 1851 when he became clerical organizing secretary of the Colonial Church and School Society; he extended and consolidated the work of the society as he gained insight into missionary life. Living at Islington, London, he inaugurated weekly services for cab drivers at their local depot.

On 14 March 1863 Thomas was appointed first bishop of Goulburn, New South Wales. His nomination had been opposed by Charles Campbell [q.v.] and Rev. Ernest Hawkins, of the Society for the Propagation of the Gospel, because of his Evangelical churchmanship, but Bishop Barker [q.v.] recognized that he had qualities of leadership and supported him; he was consecrated in Canterbury Cathedral on 25 March. Neither Thomas nor Campbell allowed this clash to colour their future relations and Campbell became his trusted chancellor and friend.

Thomas and his wife arrived in Sydney in the *Bombay* on 13 March 1864 and at Goulburn on 8 April. With an energy that concealed his despondency, he set about the task of building up an insufficiently endowed diocese in a sparsely populated district. As he increased the number of his clergy he provided spiritual comfort for isolated settlers and many diggers on the Araluen and Lambing Flat goldfields; finding this a missionary task beyond the resources of his diocese, he turned to the S.P.G., the Colonial and Continental Church Society and the Colonial Bishoprics' Fund, stressing that the needs of their own countrymen were greater than those of the heathen. In 1874-75 he visited England seeking further financial support.

With the formation of the Goulburn Church Society in 1864, Thomas introduced the principle of the interdependence of parish and diocese; thus he ensured that all his clergy received adequate stipends and that local building efforts were assisted from diocesan funds. By far-flung visitations and through his extensive correspondence, he made personal contact with his clergy and laity and guided his vast diocese. In some ways Thomas was aloof, the 'Lord Bishop', conscious of his position and dignity; he was authoritarian, setting high standards for his clergy, but he was also humane and tender, though these qualities were often concealed under his brusque manner. He developed a passionate loyalty to his diocese and learned to love his strange adopted land.

The establishment of the diocesan synod in February 1867 extended the co-operation of the clergy and laity in Church management. Thomas insisted that legislation was necessary to validate synods and that they were the effective organs of Church government; his stance led to clashes with more liberal churchmen, particularly in the discussions about the formation of the Provincial Synod of New South Wales and the General Synod. In later years he questioned the usefulness of synods which he then saw as an interruption rather than a contribution to Church administration.

Thomas's responsibility increased with the growth of population and closer settlement in the western part of his see. The strain was eased by the formation of the diocese of the Riverina in 1884. In 1880 he supported John Gribble [q.v.] in establishing an Aboriginal mission at Warangesda on the Murrumbidgee River. For ten years he had spent much time and energy on raising funds to build the new St Saviour's Cathedral at Goulburn; designed by Edmund Blacket [q.v.] it was dedicated on 29 April 1884. His later years were saddened by disputes between himself, F. R. L. Rossi [q.v.] and Archdeacon A. T. Puddicombe about the trusteeship of the cathedral and its place as a parish church. The clash of personalities divided the Church of England in Goulburn, with the authority of the bishop questioned and the influence of the Church lessened. For Thomas there could be no compromise and the dispute dragged on with court cases.

Wracked by bouts of serious illness, Thomas lost control and the diocese foundered. He died of heart disease on 15 March 1892 and was buried in the cathedral grounds, survived by his wife to whom he left an estate valued for probate at £8226.

B. Thorn (ed), *Letters from Goulburn* (Canb, 1864); Parkes letters (ML); M. Thomas, Letterbook 1865-90 (St Mark's Lib, Canb); Diocese of Goulburn, Church Society reports 1864-92 *and* Synod reports 1866-92 (St Mark's Lib, Canb).

BARBARA THORN

THOMAS, MORGAN (1824-1903), surgeon and public benefactor, was born at Glynneath, Glamorgan, Wales, on 15 December 1824. Educated at University College, University of London, in 1847 he became a member of the Royal College of Surgeons and a licentiate of the Society of Apothecaries. He reached South Australia on 26 May 1848 in the barque *Zealous*. In May 1853 at Macclesfield he applied for registration as a medical practitioner and in the next month he was appointed medical officer at Guichen Bay at a salary of £50 with the right of private practice. In 1854 he resigned and went to Nairne where he practised; he is said to have married and possibly his wife died while he was there; the marriage was probably childless.

On 22 May 1855 Thomas was appointed house surgeon at the Adelaide Hospital and resident medical officer at the Lunatic Asylum at a salary of £225 with quarters. In 1856 he became assistant colonial surgeon, but resigned in 1858 and practised for some years in Adelaide; from 1873 he lived in Wakefield Street and until his death frequented the Adelaide Circulating Library and the magazine room of the Public Library of South Australia. He usually lunched in the Hamburg Hotel in Rundle Street; after the meal he leant against a hitching-post until exactly 2.30 p.m. when he entered a near-by chemist's shop to chat with its proprietor who witnessed two of Thomas's wills.

He made the Adelaide Hospital the chief beneficiary under his first will but he changed his mind after dissension between the medical staff and the government. In December 1901 Thomas made his last will under which, subject to certain legacies totalling £16,000, he left the residue to the Public Library, Museum and Art Gallery, which received about £65,000. That sum is now divided equally between the South Australian State Library, the South Australian Museum of Natural History and the Art Gallery of South Australia. He was reputed to have inherited money from land in Wales and to have invested wisely; he also lived frugally and had no debts. About a quarter of his estate was in British consols; most of the balance was in shares in gas, banking and tramway companies. Thomas had no relations in Australia and no close friends. There is no evidence that he was interested in the fine arts or in natural history, and he owned few books: the most plausible explanation for his choice of his residuary legatee is that he incorrectly believed that the Adelaide Circulating Library was conducted by the board of the Public Library, Museum and Art Gallery.

Thomas was a small spare man who walked with a limp. He died in his house on 8 March 1903.

PP (SA), 1866-67, 3 (150); *Register* (Adel), 27 May 1848; *Observer* (Adel), 14, 21 Mar 1903; Morgan Thomas papers (SAA); Col Sec, Index to in-letters and out-letters (SAA).

E. J. R. MORGAN

THOMAS, ROBERT (1781-1860), newspaper proprietor, was born in November 1781 on a farm, Rhantregynwen, at Llanymynech, on the border of Shropshire, England, and Montgomeryshire, Wales. At 21 he established a printing, bookselling and law stationery business in Fleet Street, London. On 18 January 1818 he married Mary Harris (1787-1875) at Southampton; they had seven children. Mary wrote poetry some of which was distributed among her friends as 'Serious Poems' in 1831.

Attracted by E. G. Wakefield's [q.v.] ideas, in 1836 Thomas bought 134 acres of land in the proposed province of South Australia for £81. On 18 June, with his friend George Stevenson [q.v.] as editor, he printed in London the first number of the *South Australian Gazette and Colonial Register*. Preceded by their eldest son Robert, who was on Colonel William Light's [q.v.] staff in the *Cygnet*, Thomas and his family embarked in the *Africaine* and reached Holdfast Bay on 10 November. He printed Governor Hindmarsh's proclamation of the province of 28 December. After living for a time in tents and a rush hut, in March 1837 he bought nine more prime town lots, moved to Hindley Street and established a general store, stationery and printing business. Using a Stanhope hand press Stevenson and the Thomas family produced on 3 June the first colonial edition of the newspaper, announcing a firmly independent policy; with much difficulty because of the death of a compositor and staff shortages, it became a weekly by

1838. Already Thomas, who was making bricks on his country sections, was 'perfectly infatuated with this country', but his wife was very homesick. They befriended the Aboriginals, witnessed a corroboree and planned to print a native dictionary. In 1838 they issued the *South Australian Church Hymn Book*, arranged by Rev. C. B. Howard [q.v.].

Still short-handed, Robert Thomas & Co. published in 1839-42 the first four copies of the *Royal South Australian Almanac*. In 1839 they announced a further newspaper, the *Port Lincoln Herald and South Australian Commercial Advertiser*, although their first venture, from 22 June called the *South Australian Register*, had not yet succeeded in paying its way. In 1840 Thomas joined the Literary & Scientific Association and Mechanics' Institute and the Association For The Prosecution of Felons. That year the paper's circulation reached 900 and Thomas, with a staff of twenty-one, bought two new Columbian presses and paid £800 for the rival *Adelaide Chronicle and South Australian Advertiser*. The *Register*, critical of Governor Gawler's economic policies, in September strongly attacked him again for ordering the execution without trial of two Aboriginals suspected of murdering some settlers. As a result, on 11 November the firm lost all government business, worth about £1650 a year, to the fiercely competitive *Southern Australian*; Thomas claimed that he had been authorized by the British government to do their printing, but he had no written proof. A visit to England to protest was unsuccessful and in 1842 he returned to Adelaide, became insolvent and sold the *Register* to James Allen for £600. In May *The Adelaide Chronicle and South Australian Literary Record* had ceased to appear. In January 1841 he had opened a new commercial exchange and reading room.

In 1845-52 Thomas was an inspector of weights and measures for the government. On 1 July 1860, aged 78, he died of congestion of the lungs in his home, Rhantregwnwyn Cottage, Hindley Street. Governor Sir George Grey had described him as an 'earnest, able, energetic pioneer ... of great natural ability and singular force of character'. He was survived by three sons and two daughters and by his wife, whose valuable account of settlement, the *Diary and Letters of Mary Thomas 1832-1866* was edited and published by her grandson E. K. Thomas in 1915. His estate was sworn for probate at £2000.

His second son WILLIAM KYFFIN was born on 4 November 1821 in London and educated at a Rickmansworth boarding-school before being apprenticed to Leighton and Murphy, Fleet Street printers, for six months. During the voyage to South Australia he had scarlet fever but reached Kangaroo Island on his fifteenth birthday and helped his father print the early issues of his newspaper. In 1837-42 as overseer of the printing office he was 'very useful and industrious'. In 1843-53 he farmed at Nailsworth, spending several months at the Victorian goldfields in 1852. On 24 May 1853 with A. Forster, E. W. Andrews and J. Fisher [qq.v.] and others he bought the daily *South Australian Register*, and its weekly counterpart, *The Adelaide Observer*. Next year the paper was moved to Grenfell Street and William resumed sole control of the printing department which was converted to steam; a four-feeder Hoe press was added in 1870. He continued as a principal proprietor of W. K. Thomas & Co. publishing the *Register*, *The Adelaide Observer* and the *Evening Journal* for the next eight years.

In 1863 William had been an elected councillor for Grey Ward and in 1864 failed to become mayor of Adelaide; he was a lieutenant in the First Adelaide Rifles and in 1866 became a justice of the peace. He was a quiet genial family man who moved to Glenelg in 1875 for his health. One of the founding members of the Flinders Street Baptist Church, he was its secretary for many years. He died of heart disease and dropsy on 5 July 1878, and was buried in the West Terrace cemetery, survived by his wife Mary Jane, née Good, six daughters and three sons. His estate was sworn for probate at £8000.

ROBERT KYFFIN, eldest son of William Kyffin and Mary Thomas, was born on 19 August 1851 at Nailsworth near Adelaide; he was educated at J. L. Young's [q.v.] Adelaide Educational Institution before joining the staff of the family paper in 1869. He worked first in the printing department and learned stenography on the reporting staff, concurrently attending Union College, which became the University of Adelaide in 1876. On 6 January he married Amelia Bowen; they had four daughters and six sons. In 1877 he became the principal joint proprietor of the *South Australian Register*, and as chief of staff he also edited the *Adelaide Observer*. A parliamentary reporter, he was in charge of the Hansard branch until 1882, when he became general manager of the *South Australian Register* which became the *Register* in 1901.

An ardent Freemason and a justice of the peace, Robert was president of the Royal Geographical Society of Australasia, South Australian Branch, in 1900-03, and of the Adelaide Chamber of Commerce in 1906-

07. He visited England in 1884, 1902 and 1909 when he was elected chairman of the overseas delegates to the Imperial Press Conference in London; on 31 January 1910 he was knighted for his work at the conference. An Anglican, he played a leading role in many charitable and cultural organizations, and was responsible for a collection in the Adelaide Art Gallery illustrating the art of newspaper sketching.

On 13 June 1910 Sir Robert died of stomach cancer in his home, Ardington, North Adelaide. He was buried in the North Road cemetery and survived by his wife (d. 1923), three sons and four daughters, one of whom, Nora, was a proficient violinist. His estate was sworn for probate at £38,202. His sons Reginald Kyffin (d. 1914) and Geoffrey Kyffin carried on their father's share in W. K. Thomas & Co. with J. H. Finlavson [q.v.], W. J. Sowden and their uncle Evan Kyffin Thomas. In 1893 the Australasian edition of the *Review of Reviews* had said 'The *Register* . . . always . . . held itself aloof from . . . political parties . . . it has given to some of the dominant politicians of the day the suggestions . . . for many of their edicts. It has ever been broadly liberal . . . a fighting paper from the beginning'.

J. Bonwick, *Early struggles of the Australian press* (Lond, 1890); H. T. Burgess (ed), *Cyclopedia of South Australia*, 1 (Adel, 1908); G. H. Pitt, *The press in South Australia 1836 to 1850* (Adel, 1946); *Register* (Adel), 18 June 1836, 3 June 1837, 11 Jan, 18 July, 12, 19, 26 Sept, 14 Nov 1840, 16 Jan 1841, 6 Aug 1842, 2 July 1860, 5 July 1878, 14 June 1910; *Advertiser* (Adel), 6 July 1878; *Observer* (Adel), 6 July 1878; *Daily Herald*, 14 June 1910; *Australasian*, 18 June 1910; W. J. Sowden, Our pioneer press . . . a history (SAA); Robert and Mary Thomas papers (SAA); Col Sec letters (SAA); Registry of insolvencies, GRG 66/1/1 (SAA).   S. COCKBURN
                          SUZANNE EDGAR

THOMPSON, JOHN LOW (1847-1900), agricultural educator and innovator, was born on 16 April 1847 at Insch, Aberdeenshire, Scotland, son of John Thompson, farmer, and his wife Jessie, née Low. After a three-year apprenticeship on the farm of William McCoombie, at 22 Thompson became land steward on a farm at Deeside. He came to Australia in 1870 in charge of a valuable shipment of stud cattle. He worked on the land at Omeo, Victoria, and then spent six years as stock-manager on Joel Horwood's property at Bridgewater-on-Loddon near Bendigo, where at 31 he married Agnes Clay Kentish.

Thompson quickly won wide repute for his knowledge of livestock and other aspects of farming and in 1878 was appointed first manager of the Victorian government experimental farm at Dookie. With fifteen pupils enrolled there two years later, it was the first farm school in Australia, but its work was hampered by financial stringency and the government's failure to appoint enough qualified staff. The scheme was discontinued when Thompson resigned in 1881 after a dispute with R. Richardson, minister of agriculture, over the conduct of the farm. He went to South Australia as manager of the Beefacres Estate near Adelaide, where he won recognition for his stock-breeding, his work in restoring fertility to exhausted soil and for championing the use of ensilage.

In 1886 Thompson was appointed farm-manager of the reconstituted Dookie Farm School, later renamed Dookie Agricultural College. Succeeding R. L. Pudney, he was principal from 1887 until 1891, when he was chosen from some fifty applicants as foundation principal of Hawkesbury Agricultural College, Richmond, New South Wales. In 1897 he was appointed travelling instructor of the New South Wales Department of Mines and Agriculture. In constant demand as a judge at country shows, he came into direct contact with landholders in most parts of the colony; as early as 1888 the *Town and Country Journal* had commented that 'Possibly there is no man better known in Australian agricultural circles'. He delighted in meeting farmers on their own ground and his 'peculiar knack of giving a canny turn to all he said seldom failed to command confidence'.

Genial and hearty, Thompson was described by one of his students as 'a 6 ft. 3 in., 18 stone, braw Scot'. His significance lies not only in the part he played in the foundation of two Australian agricultural colleges but also in his contribution to the processes of agricultural innovation and diffusion. A Presbyterian, he died of a diabetus carbuncle at Burwood on 17 January 1900 and was buried in Rookwood cemetery; he was survived by his wife, three sons and five daughters. His estate in New South Wales was valued for probate at £1152, and in Victoria at £1227. Portraits of him are at Dookie and Hawkesbury colleges.

R. N. Dart, *Hawkesbury Agricultural College* (Syd, 1941); *Agr Gazette* (NSW), 11 (1900); *T&CJ*, 4 Aug 1888, 6 Dec 1890; *SMH*, 18, 19 Jan 1900; A. W. Black, Organisational genesis and development (Ph.D. thesis, Univ of New England, 1972); Council of Agricultural Education, Minutes 1886-91 (Dept of Agr, Vic).
                          ALAN W. BLACK

THOMPSON, JOHN MALBON (1830-1908), lawyer and politician, was born in

Sydney on 24 December 1830, son of John Thompson, deputy-surveyor-general, and his wife Anne Mary, daughter of Charles Windeyer [q.v.]. Educated at Sydney College and W. T. Cape's [q.v.] school, he was trained as a solicitor, was admitted to practice in 1853 and entered a partnership with Richard H. Way.

In 1857 Thompson set up a practice at Ipswich in the Moreton Bay District where he took part in the volunteer movement and was elected to the first municipal council in April 1860. On 29 November 1863 he married Clara Georgiana Bedwell at Paterson, New South Wales. When she died soon afterwards, he married Louisa Gadsden at Ipswich in 1867. In June 1866 he joined Lewis Thomas [q.v.] in a coal-mining venture but after disputes sold out to Thomas in June 1870. Thompson continued to let coal lands to tribute miners.

In September 1868 he was elected to the Legislative Assembly for Ipswich and soon became chairman of committees. Described as 'a liberal whose moderation has been interpreted as weakness', he became secretary for lands in (Sir) Arthur Palmer's [q.v.] first ministry in May 1870. While in office he succeeded in carrying the Homestead Areas Act. He became minister for public works in July 1873 and in January 1874 went out of office with the government. He became minister for justice in the first McIlwraith [q.v.] ministry in January 1877 but because of his junior status the legal profession organized powerful opposition at the ministerial elections.

Because of his devotion to his electorate Thompson soon found himself disagreeing with his colleagues. Disillusioned by retrenchment of public servants at Ipswich in May, he resigned as minister and joined the Opposition; he was called to the Bar on 1 June 1880. When his wife's health declined he resigned his seat on 27 August 1881, sold his Queensland interests and returned to Sydney where he became a partner of J. E. V. Nott, solicitor, and indulged in dilettante writing. He married Mary Harriett Montague Russell on 9 December 1896. Survived by his only child, a daughter from his first marriage, he died in Sydney of heart disease on 30 May 1908 and was buried in the Church of England section of Waverley cemetery. He left an estate valued for probate at £4786.

R. S. Browne, A journalist's memories (Brisb, 1927); V&P (LA Qld), 1877, 3, 591; Brisbane Courier, 3, 10 Feb 1879; Queenslander, 8, 15 Feb 1879; A'sian Sketcher, 15 Mar 1879; Bulletin, 13 June 1903; Truth (Syd), 31 May 1908; Palmer-McIlwraith papers (Oxley Lib, Brisb).

H. J. GIBBNEY

THOMPSON, JOSEPH (1838-1909), bookmaker, was born on 6 March 1838 in London. Probably of Jewish parents, he is said to have exchanged his surname of Solomon(s) for Thompson when he shipped before the mast in 1854 bound for Australia. At Sandridge, Victoria, he deserted ship by hiding in an off-loaded water-cask; he went to the diggings but after a year at Ballarat went back to the sea. On returning to England he found that his parents had gone to America and he worked his way to Sydney. By 1857 he was back on the Victorian goldfields, first at Ballarat and then at Ararat and Pleasant Creek.

Thompson claimed in 1903 that he had first started to make a book at Ararat in 1857; other sources make it 1861 when he went to Beechworth races. He made a handsome profit on doubles and bought a 'flash crimean, knee boots, spanking new cabbage tree [hat], and a crimson sash around the waist with tassels hanging on each side'. After winning and losing large sums at New South Wales country meetings and in Sydney, he returned to Melbourne and at the 1862 spring meeting operated on the Flemington hill. Despite heavy losses on The Barb and Tim Whiffler in the 1860s, his shrewdness and adaptability soon made him a leader of the ring; with the encouragement of F. C. Standish [q.v.] he gained official acceptance. After winning £17,000 on Lapdog in 1870 he began to work at country meetings, always coming to town for the principal races. He also owned and had interests in horses, including King of the Ring, which was his name for himself although he was better known as 'the Leviathan'; Argus Scandal, named after the newspaper that had criticized him; Don Juan, winner of the Melbourne Cup in 1873; Romula, St Albans and Mentor. Out of his winnings on Don Juan he built Don Juan House in Albert Street, East Melbourne—its 'furniture and adjuncts came to something fabulous'—and he entertained there lavishly.

In 1884 he visited England and was 'treated like a prince'; in 1889 he decided to work there. He left Melbourne in the Arcadia on 8 March and the Australasian wrote that 'though his thatch is more snowlike than it was a few years ago, he is still possessed of wonderful energy, and has the additional advantage of more than £100.000 behind him. His mellifluous voice will be missed'. In January-February 1903 he returned to Australia aboard the Ophir and was much fêted among old racing friends. In several long interviews to the press he described his rise on the English turf: he fielded five days a week in England, went to Paris for the Sunday races and returned to London for settling on Monday. Stories about him featured huge wagers, hampers of delectable food, unlimited champagne and practical jokes.

Thompson's other sporting interests included sculling and boxing which he shared with his brother Jack, who had joined him in Australia about 1869 from the American ring. In 1879 the Thompson brothers promoted the Foley[q.v.]-Hicken fight; they also successfully lobbied the Victorian government to pass legislation enforcing glove fighting according to Queensberry Rules. Another brother Barnett (Barney) worked closely with Joseph from the late 1860s and accompanied him on both trips to England in the 1880s.

On 3 March 1909, when returning from a health trip to South Africa, Thompson died at Funchal, Madeira, leaving a widow Rose, three daughters and a son John. Accounts suggest that he had married in Melbourne on 12 February 1867 although in 1889 his family entourage included an infant. He had invested in Melbourne city property and left an estate in Victoria sworn at a gross value of £23,450.

Tip and Top, *The life of Joe Thompson* (Melb, 1877); 'Vigilant' (ed), *Australian sporting celebrities* (Melb, 1887); A. Sutherland et al, *Victoria and its metropolis*, 2 (Melb, 1888); A. Joseph, *A Bendigonian abroad* (Melb, 1892); T. Haydon, *Sporting reminiscences* (Lond, 1898); S. Griffiths, *Turf and heath* (Melb, 1906); J. M. Christie, *Reminiscences...*, related by J. B. Castieau (Melb, 1913?); J. Scobie, *My life on the Australian turf*, F. H. Hart ed (Melb, 1929); K. Roberts, *Captain of the push* (Melb, 1963); *Australasian*, 15 Nov 1873, 12, 19 Jan 1884, 2 Mar 1889, 17, 31 Jan 1903, 6, 13, 20 Mar 1909; *Table Talk*, 18 Mar 1887; *Argus*, 6 Mar 1909; *Bulletin*, 11 Mar 1909.
CLIVE TURNBULL*

THOMSON, ADAM (1813-1874), Presbyterian minister, was born on 22 February 1813 at Coldstream, Berwickshire, Scotland, son of Rev. Dr Adam Thomson and his wife Isabella, née Turnbull. His father won fame as secretary of the Free Bible Press Co. which published 50,000 Bibles in Coldstream between 1839 and 1851, before being undercut by other printers. He was the leader of the movement that abolished the Bible monopoly held by the Royal Printers and the universities.

Thomson was taught at home by private tutors and in 1824 matriculated at the University of Edinburgh (M.A., 1829). Described by Dr Thomas Chalmers as 'a model student', he completed his studies for the ministry at the United Secession Divinity Hall (later United Presbyterian

Hall), and was licensed by the Presbytery of Coldstream at 18. He declined a call to the parish of Dunoon, accepting one to be colleague and successor to the minister of East Bank, Hawick, Roxburghshire, where he was ordained and inducted on 12 June 1833. Greatly admired he ministered there for twenty-seven years. He vigorously supported the Forbes MacKenzie Act, which regulated public houses in Scotland, and with John Bright campaigned for the repeal of the Corn Laws and for educational reform. At Hawick about July 1840 he married Helen Ritchie Wilson and, after her death, a widow Margaret Smellie, née Weir, of Gibraltar.

Prone to bronchial infection, Thomson was advised to seek a warmer climate; he accepted a call to the United Presbyterian Church (later St Stephen's), Phillip Street, Sydney, and arrived with his second wife and family in the *John Banks* on 13 April 1861. He won esteem in New South Wales as an advocate of the union of the divided presbyteries and synods, acting as secretary of the Presbyterian Union Conference. He was called 'a model of Christian courtesy' by Rev. Archibald Gilchrist; his success arose from his gentleness, wisdom and integrity, and his representing of a group of Scottish Presbyterians not involved in the disputes that raged between the different Church sects. He was opposed to state aid to religion. When the Presbyterian Church of New South Wales came into being in 1865 he was unanimously elected first moderator. In 1864-74 he was a director of the Sydney Infirmary and Dispensary.

Supporting the establishment of an affiliated college within the University of Sydney, Thomson travelled extensively to collect funds. On one journey he was injured in a coach accident. When St Andrew's College was founded he was elected to the first council in November 1870. After the validity of the initial election of Rev. John Kinross [q.v.] was challenged by Rev. J. D. Lang [q.v.], Thomson was chosen first principal on 24 September 1873. While the buildings were being constructed, he organized the new college and admitted the first students to temporary accommodation at Cypress Hall, Newtown.

Thomson developed a throat infection and died at Cypress Hall on 8 November 1874. He was survived by a son and three daughters by his first wife, by his second wife and their son and daughter Annie Elizabeth, who gave long and distinguished service to the Young Women's Christian Association in New South Wales. A stone and window in St Stephen's, Macquarie Street, and a window in St Andrew's College Chapel commemorate him. A large

Polyglot Bible presented to his father is also in St Andrew's College.

D. B. Horn, A short history of the University of Edinburgh (Edinb, 1967); Australian Witness, 14, 21 Nov 1874; SMH, 19 Nov 1874; Empire (Syd), 24 Nov 1874; A. Thomson, Diary while journeying in country NSW raising funds (St Andrew's College Archives); General Assembly minutes 1861-74 (Presbyterian Lib, Assembly Hall, Syd); Thomson papers (held by Professor J. F. D. Wood, Hunters Hill, NSW).   ALAN DOUGAN

THOMSON, ALEXANDER MORRISON (1841-1871), geologist and chemist, was born on 4 February 1841 at Bartholomew Square, London, son of William Dalrymple Thomson, bookseller, and his wife Mary Ann, née Ranger. He received an elementary education in London before moving in 1853 to Aberdeen, where in 1857-59 he attended classes in arts at King's College and University, Aberdeen, spending much time on geological excursions with his schoolfriend James Campbell Brown. After returning to London, Thompson worked for Winsor and Newton, colourmakers, and in 1859-61 attended night classes at King's College, University of London (B.A., 1862; B.Sc., 1864; D.Sc., 1866), gaining the prize for natural philosophy in 1860. In 1862 he passed the Civil Service Commission examination and worked briefly with the boards of Inland Revenue and Customs. Next year he won an exhibition of £50 in chemistry and natural philosophy. In 1865-66 he worked at the Royal School of Mines.

In 1866 Thomson was appointed reader in geology and assistant in the chemical laboratory of Professor John Smith [q.v.] at the University of Sydney. He arrived in Sydney in December bringing with him new instruments and specimens. Next March he began courses in geology, physical geography and mineralogy; his lecture notes show his thoroughness and his zeal in keeping up his reading. He quickly gained the confidence and co-operation of colleagues such as Smith and Rev. W. B. Clarke [q.v.] who became a close friend. After acting as examiner in scientific subjects in 1869 he was appointed professor of geology in November at a salary of £450 'together with the fees'. He also lectured in physical and natural science at Sydney Grammar School.

Thomson's 'integrity of purpose ... singleness of mind and readiness to oblige at all times and by all means' won him many friends among the divided scientific community of New South Wales. Elected to the Royal Society of New South Wales in 1867, he served on its council in 1870-71. At the Australian Museum, where he was a trustee

from 1869-71, he did useful work in cataloguing and assaying. He worked vigorously in the field. In December 1868 at Marulan he prepared a paper on the geology of the Goulburn region which he read in August 1869 to the Royal Society. That year he published in Sydney his Guide to Mineral Explorers, in distinguishing Minerals, Ores & Gems, and in September with Gerard Krefft [q.v.] he explored the Wellington Valley caves. In May 1870 their report included Thomson's detailed summary of the geology, in which he attacked Samuel Stutchbury's [q.v.] ideas on the theory of limestone cave formations. He also geologized at Molong and Boree, visited the diamond washings on the Cudgegong River near Mudgee, and made surveys of other centres in the west.

Thomson was forced to convalesce with chronic rheumatism early in 1871. Constantly in pain, by August he was confined indoors, able only to catalogue specimens brought from the university and write to his many geological co-workers. Aged 30, he died on 16 November 1871 in his residence in Queen's Street, Newtown, and was buried in Rookwood cemetery. He was survived by his wife Lydia Martha, née Barnes, and by a son and daughter. His personal estate was valued for probate at £850.

His early death shocked Thomson's scientific colleagues and friends, and they raised money to repatriate his family to Britain. Had he lived longer he undoubtedly would have made a notable contribution to Australian chemistry, mineralogy and geology. His successor Archibald Liversidge [q.v.] built on the foundations which he and Smith had laid.

D. F. Branagan (ed), Rocks, fossils, profs (Syd, 1973); V&P (LA NSW), 1870-71, 4, 1182; SMH, 18 Nov, 1 Dec 1871; T&CJ, 2 Dec 1871; A. M. Thomson notebooks (Fisher Lib, Univ Syd); Thomson letters in W. B. Clarke papers (ML); Senate minutes (Univ Syd Archives).
                                    MICHAEL HOARE

THOMSON, GEORGE EDWARD (1826-1889), miners' leader, was born on 3 October 1826 at Coupar Angus, Perthshire, Scotland, son of Charles Pratt Thomson and his wife Jane, née Oliphant, of Gask near Perth. The family normally lived at Croydon, Surrey, England, where his father owned considerable property. Thomson was educated at Sutton Valence near Maidstone and at a grammar school at Rickmansworth, Hertfordshire. At 16 he entered a lawyer's office in London and later began and abandoned medical studies. He took part in the anticorn-law and Chartist movements and knew many of the leaders and Thomas Carlyle. He became an Owenite socialist and remained faithful throughout his life. An active member of the British Association, he worked with the Mayhews in gathering material about the London poor and was prominent in movements for taxation and patent law reform. In 1848 he presided at a meeting in the City of London which protested against legislation suppressing the right of public discussion.

Thomson developed symptoms of familial tuberculosis in 1852 and decided to migrate. Arriving in Melbourne on 19 November in the *Blorenge*, he made for the Forest Creek (Castlemaine) goldfield where he had some success; in April 1853 he went to Sandhurst (Bendigo). Prominent in the formation of the Anti-Gold-Licence Association on 6 June, at a meeting next month he presented the petition for licence fee reduction, reform of the police, land reform and enfranchisement of the diggers; he went the rounds of the diggings and took the petition to Melbourne. When La Trobe rejected the petition Thomson rallied support at meetings in Melbourne and Geelong. At Bendigo on 13 August a huge meeting adopted his recommendation of passive resistance; it was agreed to tender only 10s. instead of 30s. for the next month's licence, and the red ribbon became the movement's insignia. On 28 August Thomson and others tendered 10s. to Commissioner Panton and Chief Commissioner Wright [qq.v.] who rejected the offer and a 'courteous discussion' followed: the licence fee was soon reduced by more than one half. Thomson gave evidence to the select committee of inquiry and to the royal commission on Eureka. In 1888 he analysed the movement in his 'Leaves from the Diary of an old Bendigonian' in Leavitt and Lilburn's *Jubilee History of Victoria and Melbourne*, and revealed that an attack by troops would have been resisted. Acknowledged as the chief leader of the most efficient and popular of the diggers' movements, he had consistently advocated 'moral force' with 'physical force' only as a last resort.

Late in 1853 Thomson, with J. H. Abbott [q.v.], founded and edited the *Diggers Advocate*; Ebenezer Syme [q.v.] was a prominent contributor, but it soon failed. He agitated about 1856 for agricultural settlement in the Loddon Valley, and in 1857 represented Bendigo at the Land Convention, where his land nationalization objective had little backing and he was persuaded to support Wilson Gray [q.v.]. He prospected in the Grampians, but soon organized the registration of miners as voters in the Pleasant Creek and Ararat areas. In Maldon about 1859 he was active in the movement for local government and

refused to stand for the Legislative Assembly. Moving to Castlemaine he again took up law and formed a partnership with F. E. Paynter; he opened a branch at Daylesford where he was a borough councillor. In 1862 in evidence to the royal commission on the goldfields he advocated a general code of mining by-laws for the colony.

Thomson returned to Bendigo in 1875 to partner J. T. Saunders. He was 'Sandhurst's ripest scholar', with a phenomenal memory and learned in literature, history and science, especially geology, electricity, navigation and astronomy. He wrote often for the press, sometimes as 'Nemesis'. His socialist beliefs kept him out of colonial politics. He collapsed in his office after an overdose of chlorodyne, died in his home, Hustlers Terrace, on 17 January 1889, and was buried in Sandhurst cemetery with Anglican rites. He was survived by his wife Rosalind, née Harper, whom he had married at Daylesford on 30 May 1863, and by two sons and three daughters. He left debts amounting to £579.

G. Mackay, *The history of Bendigo* (Melb, 1891); G. Serle, *The golden age* (Melb, 1963); F. Cusack, *Bendigo: a history* (Melb, 1973); *Herald* (Melb), 9, 18, 22, 29 Aug 1853; *Bendigo Evening News*, 17 Jan 1889; *Argus*, 18 Jan 1889; *Bendigo Advertiser*, 18 Jan 1889, 25 Jan 1890; *Bendigo Independent*, 18 Jan 1889; Thomson press-cuttings (LaT L).

DOROTHY KIERS

THOMSON, ROBERT (1829-1905), actuary, was born on 25 February 1829 in Belfast, Northern Ireland, son of James Thomson, then headmaster of the Royal Academical Institution, Belfast, and his wife Margaret, née Gardiner (d. 1830). Frail as a child, he had an operation for calculus at 10 and in 1845 was very ill with scarlet fever. He was educated at home by his father who had become professor of mathematics at the University of Glasgow in 1832. He matriculated at Glasgow in 1842 in the Greek class but did not graduate. His two elder brothers had distinguished careers: James (1822-1892) became professor of engineering at Queen's College, Belfast, and later at Glasgow, and William, later Lord Kelvin (1824-1908), was appointed to the chair of natural philosophy at Glasgow when only 22.

Robert shared the family gift for mathematics. He entered the Glasgow office of the Scottish Amicable Life Assurance Society and after his father's death in 1849 migrated to Dunedin, New Zealand. About 1853 he came to Sydney, where he joined the Liverpool and London Fire and Life Insurance

Co. On 20 April 1854 he married a Catholic, Sarah Mary Murphy, at St Mary's Cathedral. On 11 July he became secretary to the Australian Mutual Provident Society, then a small and obscure organization. He supervised the expansion of the society's operations to New Zealand in 1854 and Hobart Town in 1855, and in 1860 appointed B. Short [q.v.] as the first full-time canvassing agent in Australia. In 1861-65 he was secretary and actuary to the society whose growth under his direction was shown in his last annual report of 1865. 'Whatever his shortcomings', said Professor John Smith [q.v.] in 1877, 'there can be no question that his enthusiasm in the cause of life insurance contributed much to the rapid development of our society'.

Thomson's 'shortcomings' cost him his post with the society. From July 1861 he had been in personal financial difficulties; he was also unable to account for £1500 in his reckoning of the society's funds. He strenuously denied fraud, pleading irregular book-keeping during a period of ill health and overwork as the cause of the deficiency; he claimed that one investigation alone, made gratuitously, had involved some 130,000 calculations. Dismissed but then reinstated, Thomson was helped by the directors with personal loans but by October 1864 he was still further in debt, especially to James Mitchell [q.v.], industrialist. Arrangements were made for monthly payments to a group of trustees but Thomson was unable to meet mounting bills. In October 1865 he was finally asked to resign from the society and in November he became bankrupt; he was granted a certificate of conformity in March 1866. Struggling to gain regular employment, on 17 February 1868 he was again bankrupt after losing money in attempting to promote the Aerated Bread Co., the New Guinea Co. and sundry unsuccessful mining companies.

In 1868 Thomson had left his home at St Leonards and set up as 'accountant, actuary and insurance broker' from lodgings in Pitt Street. Success came next year when he helped to establish the Mutual Life Association in Sydney, acting in association with T. Jaques Martin who was the resident agent in Victoria; until July 1870 Thomson was actuary for the Sydney branch. By May 1871 he had moved to Melbourne where he was a founder and consulting actuary to the Australian Widows' Fund Life Assurance Society. His long-lasting achievement was, however, his successful association with the Colonial Mutual Life Assurance Society Ltd, founded in 1873 with Martin as its general

manager. For many years the society's consulting actuary, Thomson gained a reputation as a man of 'genius' but erratic working habits.

He prepared actuarial tables for superannuation funds for friendly societies and, in 1870, conversion tables to help the Melbourne Chamber of Commerce to introduce the metric system into wholesaling. Thomson also early advocated the protection of life policies against the claims of creditors and favoured general legislation on life assurance. In 1880 he received formal notification of his admission to the Institute of Actuaries of Great Britain and Ireland. In December 1886 he read a paper before the Historical Society of Australasia on the development of life assurance in the southern hemisphere.

Thomson died of inflammation of the lungs and heart failure on 9 September 1905 at Strathblane, Prahran, predeceased by his wife and survived by three daughters, one of whom married W. L. Stillman. He was buried in the Kew cemetery after a Church of England service. In 1908 his daughters were remembered in the will of their uncle Lord Kelvin who left £10,000 to be divided equally amongst them.

A'sian Insurance and Banking Record, 9 July 1880, 20 Sept 1905; *Table Talk*, 1 Dec 1899; *Argus*, 12 Sept 1905; Dr J. Mitchell papers, 1824-69 (ML); AMP Society Archives (Syd); Insolvency files 7397/5, 8827/6 (NSWA); information from Mr J. T. Lloyd, Dept of Natural Philosophy, Univ Glasgow.

JILL EASTWOOD

THOMSON, WILLIAM (1819-1883), medical practitioner and epidemiologist, was born at Paisley, Renfrewshire, Scotland, in 1819, son of Thomas Thomson and his wife Agnes, née Robertson. Educated at the Andersonian School of Medicine and the University of Glasgow, he obtained prizes in medicine and anatomy, as well as the highest commendations from his teachers, two of whom he assisted in additional research in chemistry and anatomy. He probably served a clerkship at the Royal Infirmary, Glasgow, and he became a member of the Royal College of Surgeons of Edinburgh in 1843. Several voyages as ship's surgeon to Australia, America and the East led to the development of a safety rigging, a lifelong hobby of building model yachts and a pamphlet (1872) on the advantages for passengers of sail over steam for long voyages. He was surgeon to the overcrowded *Wanata* when she was quarantined in 1852 off St Kilda, Melbourne, because of typhus fever and whooping cough. In 1855 Thomson brought from

Scotland his wife Emma, née Hutchison, and a prefabricated wooden house. Admitted to the medical register the same year, he practised at first in Chapel Street and then in Punt Road, South Yarra, finally building Garnoch at the corner of Walsh Street and Gardiner's Creek (Toorak) Road. Within a year of his arrival he unsuccessfully opposed the formation of the Prahran municipality.

Thomson soon achieved prominence in the Medical Society of Victoria, and in 1856-64 he was sometime committee member and librarian, as well as secretary and editor of the society's *Australian Medical Journal*. He attempted, prematurely, to raise the status of the society and the local medical profession, by converting it to a faculty with fellows and members, and by encouraging it to take an active part in medical education; his motion in 1861 advocating the establishment of a medical faculty at the University of Melbourne is of historic significance, although he played no further role. It is a moot point whether, in 1864, he resigned on account of a heated dispute with the chair, or was expelled for returning a subsequent notice with 'Audacity—Blackguards' written across it. In any case, from the mid-1860s Thomson was no longer an acknowledged leader of his profession but rather a contumelious backbencher.

In 1863 his advocacy of Huxley's [q.v.] evolutionary views brought violent conflict with Professor G. B. Halford [q.v.], who resented Thomson's anonymous but informed criticism of his anatomical arguments to support the opposite view. This breach played a part in the rejection of Thomson's candidature for two of the first lectureships in the faculty of medicine in 1865 and 1867, and perhaps in his failure to secure election to the staff of the Melbourne Hospital. From this period dates a bitter argument, continued over twenty years, with S. D. Bird [q.v.], author of *On Australasian Climates and their influence in the prevention and arrest of Pulmonary Consumption* (London, 1863), who was supported by John Singleton [q.v.] and the Medical Society. In several publications Thomson refuted the evidence for a favourable influence of the local climate by carefully collected and collated statistical data showing, *inter alia*, that the mortality from phthisis was increasing in the Australian-born population. Thomson was later a member of the British Medical Association (London) and a 'moving spirit' in the formation of a Pathological Society in Melbourne in the 1870s. He became a fellow of the Royal College of Surgeons,

Edinburgh, in 1871 and was also a fellow of the Linnean Society.

A disciple of William Farr and William Budd, Thomson won international repute as an epidemiologist through his many publications between 1870 and 1883, chiefly on typhoid fever and tuberculosis in Australia. He was more than a verbal advocate of the contagionist doctrine, for he supported this concept by statistical study of local epidemics of several infectious diseases after their introduction by sea or from other localities, and by the analysis of changing patterns of mortality and morbidity; his detailed studies of localized milk-borne epidemics of typhoid fever are particularly notable. To control epidemics he advocated notification and isolation of the sick, followed by disinfection of all possible sources of contagion. By contrast, the more popular theory of a miasmatic basis for infectious diseases, spread by effluvia from open drains and cesspits, required adequate sewerage as the only valid preventive measure. Thus, the two theories had different practical and socio-political implications of vital interest to the community; Thomson, resentful of any criticism or opposition, put his views forcibly and all too bluntly in the lengthy public controversy.

Keenly interested in the related problems of cattle plagues, notably pleuro-pneumonia and foot and mouth disease, Thomson demanded a ban on the importation of livestock, maintaining that quarantine and disinfection were inadequate safeguards in relation to the possible economic consequences. Similarly, he would not have permitted the common practice of sending consumptive patients to Australia to 'take the cure', whether as migrants or visitors. With remarkable prescience and sound logic, if no personal experimental data, he later applied the new germ theory of disease to explain the contagious nature of tuberculosis, its spread by dried sputum particles and its divers manifestations in the body. In 1876 he clearly enunciated the principle of modern chemotherapy: the possibility of 'destroying germs [by means of chemical substances] in living tissue without at the same time destroying its integrity'. Six years later, when Robert Koch discovered the tubercle bacillus, Thomson's jubilation—for his views had been poorly received in Melbourne—led him to publish a pamphlet indicating his claims to priority and emphasizing the sheer perfection of his original hypothesis. There were mistakes in Thomson's work: he considered pleuro-pneumonia of cattle and human measles to be the same disease, and he recognized only the ambulant, not the asymptomatic, carrier of typhoid fever and diphtheria, so that he was led to exaggerate the influence of contagion. None the less, his views were scientifically based on critical analysis of carefully collected data; their lack of acceptance locally was due more to his uncompromising attitude, even to fair comment, than to errors of observation or interpretation.

Thomson's final controversy concerned the Baconian authorship of Shakespeare's plays, a cause he warmly espoused. He argued with great erudition in his two major works on this theme, *On Renascence Drama* ... (1880) and *William Shakespeare In Romance and Reality* (1881); both were published in Melbourne and widely reviewed at the time. The detail and complexity of the unconventional argument both suited and illustrated Thomson's extreme tenacity of purpose. With no little insight, he quoted Bacon on the turbulent person and innovator: 'If one or two have the boldness to use any liberty of judgment, they must undertake the task all by themselves; they can have no advantage from the company of others'.

Intellectually arrogant and condescending, Thomson was a quick, energetic, dapper little man, with bright eyes and a well-trimmed beard; according to his opponents, who granted his ability and industry, he was vain and impossibly irascible, but family tradition credits him with a dry sense of humour. Like his friend and colleague Sir Thomas Fitzgerald [q.v.] he was an enthusiastic race-goer and patron of the theatre, especially opera. His last illness, an abscess of the liver precipitated by a kick from a demented patient, lasted for nine months, but only a week before his death on 22 May 1883 did he seek professional help. He was survived by his wife, a daughter and four of his six sons, including Matthew Barclay, who graduated in medicine at Edinburgh, succeeded to his father's practice and later specialized in nose and throat surgery.

E. Ford, *A bibliography of William Thomson* (Syd, 1954); *A'sian Medical Gazette*, 1883; *Aust Medical J*, 1883; B. Gandevia, 'William Thomson and the history of the contagionist doctrine in Melbourne', *MJA*, 21 March 1953; MS material (Museum of Medical Soc of Vic and AMA Lib, Parkville).   BRYAN GANDEVIA

THORN, GEORGE (1806-1876), soldier, businessman and politician, and GEORGE HENRY (1840-1905), politician, were father and son. George was born on 11 April 1806 near Stockbridge, Hampshire, England, son of Simon Thorn, farmer, and his wife Sarah. A colour-sergeant, he arrived in Australia with the 4th (King's Own) Regiment in 1832. He served Governor Richard Bourke as an orderly, joined a detachment for service in Port Phillip in 1836, entered the Town Survey Department and was on the governor's staff at the first survey of Melbourne in March 1837. In June when his regiment left for India he bought his discharge, joined the Commissariat Department and on 2 November in Sydney he married the seventeen-year-old Jane Handcock.

In 1838 Thorn was sent to Moreton Bay and, on 20 July 1839 with salary of £60 and quarters, was put in charge of the Limestone Hill penal settlement with control of all government stock. He resigned when the establishment closed in 1839, kept the Queen's Arms Hotel and in 1847 sold it and set up a store. His purchase of Ipswich town lots at the first sale in 1843 began an accumulation of land that included Rosebrook, Nukienda and Warra Warra stations totalling 58,000 acres, and allotments in Toowoomba, Mogill and Cleveland. In 1859-60 he returned briefly to England.

Thorn was a member for West Moreton in 1860-63 in the Legislative Assembly. His main interest was in Ipswich, where he was an alderman in 1862-65 and helped establish the Anglican church, School of Arts, hospital, Grammar School, Botanic Gardens, North Australian Club, racing club and the Queensland Pastoral and Agricultural Society. When he died on 28 April 1876 he left a reputation for 'larky humour', thoroughness and integrity. Of his nine surviving children, Henry, John and William represented Dalby, Fassifern and Aubigny respectively in the Legislative Assembly, while Jane married the merchant George Harris [q.v.] and became grandmother to Governor-General Lord Casey.

George Henry, his eldest son, was born at Ipswich on 6 November 1840. Educated at The King's School, Parramatta, he attended the University of Sydney (B.A., 1858) and for the next nine years managed his father's properties on the Darling Downs. In 1867 and 1870 he topped the poll for the three-membered seat of West Moreton. When the colony was split into single-member electorates he won Fassifern, which included part of West Moreton, in November 1873, but in January he was nominated to the Legislative Council as government representative on the council and postmaster-general; he attended the 1874 intercolonial conference on cables in Sydney.

The appointment of Arthur Macalister [q.v.] as agent-general in 1876 brought Thorn to the fore. He formed a government in June but, finding it impossible to lead from the council, soon resigned his seat and won Ipswich in the assembly; remaining postmaster-general until July, he was also secretary of public works and mines, and served as premier until 8 March 1877; he resigned to become secretary for public lands and mines under John Douglas [q.v.]. Thorn's ministry was not taken seriously and Samuel Griffith was considered the power behind the throne. On 14 February 1878 at Ellengowan he married Celia, daughter of Richard Uniacke, Oxley's [q.v.] companion. He resigned his seat on 20 February and spent the rest of the year travelling in Europe and representing Queensland at the Paris Universal Exhibition. On his return he held Northern Downs from 17 April 1879 to 7 September 1883, and Fassifern from 8 August 1887 to 10 May 1888 and again from 6 May 1893 to 13 March 1902.

An Anglican and a Freemason, Thorn died at Booval on 13 January 1905, survived by his wife and one of his two sons. Of vast bulk, very popular because of his good nature, genial romancing, frivolous pranks and minimal dignity, Thorn was adept at electioneering. He was full of tricks of dubious legality, 'constantly sailing', according to C. A. Bernays [q.v. L. A. Bernays], 'before the wind raised by the breath of applause'.

W. Coote, *The history of the colony of Queensland* (Brisb, 1867); T. W. H. Leavitt (ed), *Australian representative men*, Qld ed (Melb, 1887); H. S. Russell, *The genesis of Queensland* (Syd, 1888); N. Bartley, *Australian pioneers and reminiscences*, J. J. Knight ed (Brisb, 1896); W. H. Traill, *A queenly colony* (Brisb, 1901); G. Harrison (ed), *Jubilee history of Ipswich* (Brisb, c1910); C. A. Bernays, *Queensland politics during sixty years* (Brisb, 1919); M. J. Fox (ed), *The history of Queensland*, 1 (Brisb, 1919); A. D. Gilchrist (ed), *John Dunmore Lang*, 2 (Melb, 1951); L. E. Slaughter, *Ipswich municipal centenary* (Brisb, 1960); V&P (LA Qld), 1877, 1, 738.　　　　　　　　HELEN HAENKE

THORNTON, GEORGE (1819-1901), merchant and politician, was born on 23 December 1819 in Macquarie Street, Sydney, son of Samuel Thornton (d. 1842), publican, and his wife, Sarah (alias Thorn). 'In Newgate before', Sarah had been sentenced to death at the Old Bailey on 3 November 1813 for larceny; with her sentence commuted to transportation for life she reached Sydney in the *Broxbornebury* in 1814. Samuel arrived free in the *Somersetshire* the same year. George was educated at St Phillip's primary school,

W. T. Cape's [q.v.] academy in King Street and Rev. J. D. Lang's [q.v.] Australian College. About 1836 he joined the Customs Department as a storekeeper and became a clerk. By 1840 he had set up as a Customs House agent and on 4 August he married Mary Ann Solomon (d. 1913). In February 1844 he sequestered his estate; paying 5s. in the pound, he resumed business in August and by 1850 was in partnership with Walter Church as Customs House agents and shipbrokers. He owned the schooner, *Tom Tough*.

Elected to the Sydney Municipal Council in November 1847 for Cook Ward, Thornton was mayor in 1853 and again in 1857. He successfully agitated for the removal of the stocks and pillory, and established the first public baths at Woolloomooloo. His mayoralty is recalled by an obelisk (Thornton's 'scent bottle') in Hyde Park, facing Bathurst Street. Supporting manhood suffrage, in 1858 he won the seat of Sydney in the Legislative Assembly. He carried resolutions against the government questioning the right of Governor Denison to order to India the company of Royal Artillery stationed in Sydney under the control of the New South Wales government; he chaired the subsequent select committee on privilege over the governor's reply; the artillery stayed in Sydney.

Thornton was appointed to the Legislative Council on 10 May 1861, but was prevented from taking his seat by the resignation of the president Sir William Burton [q.v.]. He was a partner in Tucker & Co. in 1859-63 and 1869. A Freemason under the Irish constitution, he was founding provincial grand master in 1857-67, and in 1860 was first chairman of the Woollahra Borough Council. Returning from England in the *Duncan Dunbar*, he was wrecked off the coast of Pernambuco on 7 October 1865; he organized the passengers and distributed rations. On 17 October they were rescued by the *Oneida* and returned to London. His fellow passengers presented him with an address of gratitude, but he calculated that his losses were £5845.

A magistrate from the 1850s, Thornton was a founding director and chairman in 1885-88 of the City Bank of Sydney, a trustee of the Savings Bank of New South Wales, chairman of the Mutual Insurance Society of Victoria, a director of two other insurance companies and a committee-man of the Victoria and Reform clubs and a member of the Union Club. In 1867 he was returned to the Legislative Assembly for Goldfields West but resigned in 1868 to revisit England where he administered the Agent-General's Office for more than a year. In 1873-86 he was a New South Wales commissioner for five international exhibitions and in 1880 sat on the royal commission into the fisheries.

Appointed to the Legislative Council in 1877 Thornton carried the Animals Protection Act, 1879, and in 1885 was secretary for mines and (Sir) George Dibbs's [q.v.] government representative in the council. A founding councillor of the New South Wales Aborigines Protection Association in 1880, on 29 December he was officially appointed protector of the Aborigines. With the assistance of Edmund Fosbery [q.v.], inspector-general of police, he organized a census of Aboriginals and recommended that those living in Sydney should be sent back to their own districts. In 1883 he was founding chairman of the Aborigines Protection Board but soon resigned. Long interested in the orthography of native place names, in 1892 with Richard Hill [q.v.] he published Notes on the Aborigines of New South Wales. Enthusiastic about cock-fighting and aquatic sports from his boyhood, Thornton was vice-commodore of the Sydney Yacht Club in 1859, a founding member of the Royal Sydney Yacht Squadron in 1862, founding president of the Sydney Rowing Club and of the New South Wales Rowing Association.

Thornton died of dysentery on 23 November 1901 in Lang Syne, the house he had built at Parramatta, and was buried in the Anglican section of Rookwood cemetery. Survived by his wife and daughter Fanny, he had been predeceased by a son and a daughter. His assets were valued for probate at £62,500 but his debts exceeded them by £5000.

K. R. Cramp and G. Mackaness, A history of the United Grand Lodge of New South Wales, 1 (Syd, 1938); J. Jervis, The history of Woollahra, V. Kelly ed (Syd, 1960); P. R. Stephensen (ed), Sydney sails (Syd, 1962); V&P (LC NSW), 1855, 3, 955, (LA NSW), Sel cttee on the Customs Dept 1856-57, 3, 23 and 1858, 3, 521, 1882, 4, 1525, 1883, 3, 891; SMH, 22 Jan 1866, 25 Nov 1901; T&CJ, 3 May 1890, 30 Nov 1901; Hassall papers (ML); G. Thornton, Diary 1865 (ML) and papers (NL); MS and newspaper cats (ML); Insolvency file 1195/2 (NSWA); CO 201/523, 317.

MARTHA RUTLEDGE

THORNTON, SAMUEL (1835-1917), Anglican bishop, was born on 16 April 1835 in London, son of Thomas Thornton, author and a writer for The Times, and his wife Elizabeth, née Robinson. Educated at the Merchant Taylors' School, in March 1852 he matriculated for The Queen's College, Oxford (B.A., 1855; M.A., 1858;

D. D., 1874). Both his brothers were graduates of Oxford; one entered the Church and the other became a judge in the Indian Civil Service. Ordained deacon in 1858, he began an impressive preaching ministry in East London as diocesan clerical missionary. In 1860 he became priest-in-charge of St Jude's, Whitechapel, and in 1864 rector of St George's, Birmingham. In 1866 he married Emily, daughter of H. T. Thornton of Devon.

On 1 May 1875 at Westminster Abbey, Thornton was consecrated first bishop of Ballarat. He arrived in Melbourne with his wife on 5 August in the Lord Warden and on the 11th was installed in Christ Church Pro-Cathedral, Ballarat, at a service conducted by Archdeacon Stretch [q.v.]. In December 1876 he was admitted M.A., (ad eund.) at the University of Melbourne. With 'conspicuous energy' and great organizing capacity, he tackled the task of bringing orderly administration to a diocese that extended to Mildura and the South Australian border. He attracted men of high calibre, one of whom described him as 'probably the best scholar on the Australian Episcopal Bench of his day'. He was a brilliant extempore preacher and speaker.

A Broad Churchman, Thornton did not belong to any ecclesiastical party and welcomed both High and Low. Before it became officially accepted, he encouraged the use of the revised version of the Bible; he suggested changes, not doctrinal, to the Book of Common Prayer. He condemned lotteries and raffles as Church fund-raising methods. Politically conservative he was active in discussion of public issues, and as a constant critic of the 1872 Education Act he wanted undenominational scripture teaching in state schools. In the 1890s he was embroiled in long newspaper debates with G. E. (Chinese) Morrison over the efficacy of missionaries in China; he advocated the adoption of partnership schemes between labour and capital, asserting that on their own the former was tyrannical and the latter selfish. On the question of Sunday trains he expressed the view that Christian principles should not upset the recreation of non-Christians. He was not conspicuous in the debate against rationalism, but affirmed that the Church would stand or fall by her care for the people. His annual presidential addresses to the diocesan Church Assembly were published from 1876 to 1899.

In 1900 Thornton resigned and returned to England via South Africa in July; he became assistant bishop of Manchester and vicar of Blackburn, retiring from active ministry in 1910. His first wife had died in 1909 and at 78 he married a widow Caroline Wakefield, née Rice. By 1915 he confessed that his 'boating, and tennis, and horseback days are over; reading is his recreation—in all departments'. He was described as a 'short portly prelate, quick in speech and movement, who had a lofty sense of the dignity of his high office'. Of sometimes hasty judgment, he was nevertheless an independent thinker with a genuine sympathy for knowledge. He died on 27 November 1917 in London, survived by his wife and by his son of his first marriage who was sometime vicar of Colac, Victoria, during his episcopacy.

G. Cockerill, *Scribblers and statesmen* (Melb, 1944); *Ballarat Church Chronicle*, 8 Dec 1917; *Punch* (Melb), 6 Nov 1913; *Argus*, 27 Nov 1917; *Ballarat Courier*, 30 Nov 1917.
R. E. NORTHEY

THUNDERBOLT; see WARD, FREDERICK.

TIETKENS, WILLIAM HARRY (1844-1933), surveyor, prospector and explorer, was born on 30 August 1844 at Ball's Pond, Islington, London, son of William Henry Tietkens, chemist, and his wife Emily, née Dovers. Educated at Christ's Hospital until June 1859, he reached Adelaide in September in the *Alma* with his mother's friend George A. T. Woods. In 1860 he went to the Castlemaine diggings, Victoria, where he worked as newsboy, shop assistant and cowherd, and came to love the bush. Soon abandoned by Woods, he moved to Melbourne and served three years as ticket clerk with the Hobson's Bay Railway. In 1865 he spent two months with Ernest Giles [q.v.] assessing the pastoral potential of the upper Darling. Apart from a droving trip to Adelaide and three months on the Gippsland goldfields, he remained in western New South Wales and northern Victoria for seven years working mainly as a stationhand. With a party from Corona station opening up new country 200 miles beyond the Darling at lakes Cobham and Yantara, he observed the Aboriginal response to the invasion of their territories. He believed that two attacks were inspired by a desire both for Western goods and for the expulsion of whites. When blacks were killed and wounded, he concluded that exploration and settlement were acts of conquest.

In 1873 and 1875 he acted as second-in-command of parties led by Giles from northern South Australia to the western coast of the continent. The second expedition succeeded, and Tietkens left it at Perth to resume studies for the South Aus-

tralian Licensed Surveyors' examination which he completed in 1878. He went to England in 1877, then worked as a surveyor at Richmond and Windsor, New South Wales. His dogged but unsuccessful attempt in 1878-80 to open country near Maralinga, South Australia, for pastoral settlement by well-sinking was motivated and financed by Louis Leisler of Glasgow, whom he had met in 1877 and after whom he named the Leisler Hills. He then returned to surveying in New South Wales. After marrying Mary Ann Long at Richmond on 14 June 1882 he worked as a station-hand and prospected for silver near the Barrier Ranges.

Unemployed in Adelaide in 1886, Tietkens gave a lecture to the South Australian branch of the Royal Geographical Society of Australasia, shrewdly calculated to secure command of an expedition to the Lake Amadeus district. He argued that the lake was bound to have a supply channel probably coming from a chain of hills that he had seen to the north-west in 1873; this might open a reliable route to the north-west coast settlements. His expedition left Alice Springs in March 1889 and returned to the overland telegraph at Charlotte Waters in July. He reported no new country suitable for settlement, but discovered Lake MacDonald, the Kintore Range, Mount Rennie, and the Cleland Hills. He defined the western borders of Lake Amadeus, photographed Ayers Rock and Mount Olga for the first time and collected plants, including seven new species; his samples enabled the South Australian government geologist to compile a 'geological sketch' of much of the country between Alice Springs and the Western Australian border. The government awarded him £250 for his services and the Royal Geographical Society elected him a fellow. He resumed surveying in 1891 with the New South Wales Department of Lands. On retiring in 1909 he lived at Eastwood; he died of cancer at Lithgow on 19 April 1933 and was buried in the Field of Mars cemetery, Ryde. His estate was sworn for probate at £1946. He was survived by a daughter Emily Mary Daniels of Lithgow.

Although Tietkens took a leading part in three major expeditions, his most useful work was probably in defining the features, establishing the worth and initiating white exploitation of the country between the tracks of the great explorers. He published numerous papers in geographical and scientific journals; his 'Experiences in the life of an Australian explorer' in the *Journal* of the Royal Australian Historical Society, 1919, is a major autobiographical source. He has been aptly described as a 'wanderer by accident' and the last of 'the old school of explorers', who wanted 'nothing so much as to settle down to a quiet life with those he loved'.

E. Giles, *Australia twice traversed* (Lond, 1889); R. Ericksen, *West of centre* (Lond, 1972); L. Green, 'A Voss among the explorers ...', *Quadrant*, 7 (1963); *Chronicle* (Adel), 27 April 1933; M. C. Hartwig, The progress of white settlement in the Alice Springs district and its effect upon the Aboriginal inhabitants, 1860-1894 (Ph.D. thesis, Univ Adel, 1965); Tietkens papers (ML).

MERVYN HARTWIG

TIGHE, ATKINSON ALFRED PATRICK (1827-1905), butcher, politician and police magistrate, was born at sea off Corfu, Greece, son of Robert Tighe (d. 1844), sergeant in the 17th Regiment. Robert probably came to New South Wales in 1830 with his regiment. By 1836 he had transferred to the 28th Regiment; in 1840 he was chief constable at Newcastle and by 1843 had bought the Union Inn.

Tighe was educated in Newcastle and established a slaughter-house. Active in public affairs by 1858, he was elected to a committee to provide relief for the sufferers of the Indian mutiny; he also petitioned for the proclamation of Newcastle as a municipality. In the 1859 and 1860 parliamentary elections he campaigned for James Hannell [q.v.]. A free trader, he supported male suffrage and (Sir) John Robertson's [q.v.] land proposals and opposed state aid to religion. In his last political campaign in 1882 he confessed that he still liked the 1861 land Acts but argued that loopholes in them had been exploited by the squatters.

In December 1862 Tighe won a Legislative Assembly by-election for Northumberland, a mining and maritime electorate. An independent, he retained the seat in December 1864 and began to attract the attention of faction leaders. In 1866 he introduced a bill to amend the Coal Fields Regulation Act by providing miners with some wage security; he later obtained the use of government dredges and was partly responsible for the removal of the hated tonnage dues at Newcastle. In January 1869 he opposed the connexion of the Sydney-Newcastle rail link with the Great Northern Railway, asserting that it would be too costly and would develop the hinterland at the expense of Newcastle. He became postmaster-general in September 1868 in the Martin [q.v.] ministry, and the *Newcastle Chronicle* predicted that he was soon to be 'one of our leading statesmen', but a month later the government fell.

On 14 July 1859 at St John's Church, Darlinghurst, Tighe had married Arabella Vine, daughter of Thomas Grove. In 1859-62 and 1871-73 he represented Honeysuckle Ward on the Newcastle Municipal Council and was mayor in 1872 and 1873. An early advocate of the gas-lighting of city streets, Tighe had helped in 1866 to steer the enabling bill through parliament. Several times he sat on committees to arbitrate in disputes between coalminers and masters and was auditor of the Waratah Coal Co. In Sydney he was a committee-man of the Benevolent Society of New South Wales.

In December 1869 Tighe did not stand in the general election owing to ill health. He aligned himself firmly with (Sir) Henry Parkes [q.v.]. His campaign for G. A. Lloyd [q.v.] in the 1869 and 1872 elections earned the gratitude of Parkes, who in 1873 appointed him coroner for Newcastle and a member of the local Marine Board. In 1874-78 he was police magistrate at Waratah at a salary of £325. He had sat regularly on the Newcastle bench as a justice of the peace from 1866 and had read for admission to the Bar in the late 1860s.

In 1877 Parkes asked Tighe to 're-enter parliamentary life', but he declined because of modest means, his 'seven little ones', and a distaste for the rough-and-tumble of political life. In 1882 he yielded to local requests and won Northumberland; he refused the portfolio of minister for justice in (Sir) Alexander Stuart's [q.v.] ministry and ill health forced him to resign in 1884. He died of heart failure at Glebe Point on 13 June 1905 and was buried in the Anglican section of Waverley cemetery, survived by his wife, three sons and four daughters; his youngest son Henry (b. 1877) achieved some notice in England as a novelist. Tighe's estate was valued for probate at £7431.

Newcastle Chronicle, 24 Dec 1862, 28 Dec 1864; *Newcastle Morning Herald*, 4 Dec 1882; Parkes letters (ML).

DAN O'DONNELL

TIMPERLEY, WILLIAM HENRY (1833-1909), policeman and civil servant, was born on 22 May 1833 at Solihull, Warwickshire, England, son of William Thomas Timperley, who was ordained in the Church of England about 1842, and his wife Elizabeth, née Bradney. William was educated at Shrewsbury School, and when his father became British chaplain at Berne, Switzerland, he enrolled in the philosophical faculty of the Berner Hochschule in 1850.

Next year Timperley arrived in Western Australia with his brother, father and a Mrs Pennefather, whose presence caused scandal. In the 1850s he joined the police force, and on 2 November 1858 when sergeant at Bunbury he married Rebecca, daughter of Charles Properjohn, a butcher. He was promoted to sub-inspector in 1860 and inspector in 1870. During a tour of duty at Champion Bay in 1877 he became foundation master of the Geraldton Masonic Lodge (in 1903 he was a past senior grand warden of the Grand Lodge of Western Australia). After lengthy leave in England he returned to Western Australia in the *Glengoil* on 11 October 1884.

In August next year Timperley was appointed superintendent of the native prison on Rottnest Island and took up duty in July 1886. Life on the island was busy but isolated; visitors needed a pass. The only communication was a daily heliograph message and a weekly boat bringing mail, stores and passengers. The governor took his holidays on the island and Timperley supervised arrangements for viceregal shooting parties. Improving conditions for prisoners, who supported themselves by a farm, he planted an experimental grove of pines and directed construction of subterranean tanks to augment inadequate rain-water. In 1890-1905 he was resident magistrate and electoral registrar for the Wellington, Blackwood and Sussex districts. Until 1901 he was also sub-collector for customs and revenue at Bunbury. On retirement to South Perth in June 1905 he was awarded the Imperial Service Order.

Timperley was described by Lady Broome [q.v.] as a genial man of imposing appearance 'six feet high, broad-shouldered and straight as a life guardsman, blue-eyed ... with white hair and a beard which looked almost ridiculous on such a young fresh merry face'. Fascinated by his stories, she persuaded him to write *Harry Treverton* ..., virtually an autobiography which she edited. He enjoyed his prestige as an author and subsequently wrote *Bush Luck*. Both were serialized in the *Boys' Own Paper* from 1887 to 1890 and later were published in London (1889 and 1892) in book form. An accomplished violinist and singer, he often performed publicly; he was a prominent lay reader in the Church of England. He died of a stroke at South Perth on 11 August 1909 and was buried in Karrakatta cemetery, survived by his wife and seven of their ten children. His estate was sworn for probate at £6763.

P. W. H. Thiel & Co., *Twentieth century impressions of Western Australia* (Perth, 1901); N. R. Collins and H. C. Foster, *Golden jubilee history ... Grand Lodge of Western Australia* (Perth, 1950); *West Australian*, 12 Aug 1909; L. C. Timperley, Notes on Rottnest Island (Battye Lib, Perth); Synod reports 1902-04 (Perth Diocesan Registry); CSO 1720/04 (Battye Lib, Perth).   RICA ERICKSON

TINDAL, CHARLES GRANT (1823-1914), cattle-breeder and canned meat manufacturer, was born on 31 July 1823 at Littleton Cottage, Honiton, Devonshire, England, eldest son of Lieutenant Charles Tindal (1786-1859), R.N. and later governor of the West End branch of the Bank of England, and his wife Anne Sarah (1794-1879), née Grant. Educated at King Edward's School, Birmingham, he spent two years farming in Norfolk which he considered a waste of time 'tho' it was useful in other ways'. In 1843 he brought out rams for his father's naval colleague William Ogilvie, arriving in Sydney on 17 December in the *Hamlet*. Unable to get work as a station superintendent he accepted Ogilvie's invitation to Merton on the Hunter River. In the next five years he accompanied the brothers W. K. and E. D. S. Ogilvie [q.v.] and others on various expeditions in northern New South Wales. Despite 'differences in temperament' he worked with E. D. S. Ogilvie at Yulgilbar until late 1849.

By September 1850 when his brother Frederick Colquhoun (1829-1855) joined him, Tindal had leased Koreelah station near the headwaters of the Clarence. They worked hard and prospered. In September 1852 he bought Ramornie at Copmanhurst which was to be the headquarters of his Australian enterprises. Early in 1855 he sailed for England and on 14 August 1856 at St Mary's Church, Turville, Buckinghamshire, he married Anne Amory Travers (1832-1901). After sight-seeing and business trips in Europe and England, they returned to New South Wales in January 1857 and work was started on a stone homestead at Ramornie that was occupied in December 1858.

Tindal had brought with him four thoroughbred stallions including Pitsford who sired Ramornie, winner of the 1863 Australian Jockey Club Derby and a great influence on Australian racing stock in the 1860s. In 1858-61 he owned Sir Hercules, who established a male line that survived until the twentieth century. In June 1858 Tindal claimed 'I have now the best English and the best Colonial bred horse in the country'. From the early 1850s Tindal was also a celebrated breeder of Suffolk Punch draughthorses; he found that they 'stood the heat much better than the Shires, [and] they did well to cross with their light horses, so as to get saleable "gunners" or artillery horses for India'. In the 1850s he ran mainly Shorthorn cattle but later set up Devon and Hereford studs.

In 1862 Tindal and his family returned to England, settling in the late 1860s at Fir Grove, Eversley, Hampshire. He made two long visits to his Australian properties in

1879-81 and 1886-89, and kept a very close scrutiny on his colonial ventures. In 1865 he launched the Australian Meat Co. in London with a capital of £100,000. Early in 1866 plant and tin-plate were shipped to Ramornie; meat extract production, which was based on Justus von Liebig's process, and canning began in September. Within a few years Ramornie brand canned meats had become well established on the English market. With some 35,000 beasts slaughtered annually, the cannery ensured a regular market to the local cattlemen and one of the largest suppliers was Tindal himself. Preserved meat, tallow, artificial manure, hides and pelts were also produced.

Tindal's income from the company ranged 'from £10 to 20,000 a year', and in 1879 he bought out the other shareholders. Next year the first consignment of frozen meat from Australia to London marked the beginning of the company's gradual decline. As the meatworks had prospered so Tindal had increased his holdings in land and stock. In 1885 he purchased the amalgamated stations of Bonshaw and Gooniam on both sides of the New South Wales-Queensland border near Texas. Later he bought the adjoining property, Trygamon, and, at the end of the century, Albany Downs in the Maranoa District, Queensland. In 1893 to evade being taxed as a non-resident he took his eldest son Charles Frederick (1857-1938) into partnership; in 1910 to avoid death duties he made over the properties to him.

Troubled by failing eyesight, Tindal died of senile decay at Fir Grove on 16 January 1914 and was buried in the Eversley churchyard. He was survived by two sons and five daughters; his English estate was sworn for probate at £224,965. Hard on himself, his family and his employees, he had great physical strength and a strong loyalty to the Crown and to old servants; above all, he remained devoted to the Australian Meat Co., even in its days of decline. It was sold to the Kensington Meat Preserving Co. in 1915.

E. J. Brady, *Australia unlimited* (Melb, 1918); D. M. Barrie, *The Australian bloodhorse* (Syd, 1956); L. T. Daley, *Men and a river* (Melb, 1966); K. T. Farrer, The beginning of the Australian canning industry (held by author); J. F. Stevens, Histories of pioneers in the Clarence, Hunter and Richmond districts (ML, Clarence River Hist Soc); Tindal letter-book (ML); Tindal papers (Univ New England Archives).

G. T. STILWELL

TINLINE, GEORGE (1815-1895), banker and pastoralist, was born on 28 October 1815 at Jedburgh, Roxburghshire, Scotland, son of John Tinline and his wife Esther, née Easton. He was 'brought up in hardship and poverty' and at 14 left school to work in the local branch of the National Bank. He migrated to Sydney to work for the Bank of Australasia in 1838, was transferred to the new Adelaide branch in 1839, but resigned the same year to become accountant for the Bank of South Australia. On 30 November 1843 at Adelaide he married Helen Madder, also of Jedburgh; they had six children.

Tinline was acting manager in the economic crisis of 1851-53 when his bank faced collapse. From December 1851 he urged the governor Sir Henry Young to exercise extraordinary powers, even to the extent of usurping imperial authority, to avert the currency crisis caused by the Victorian gold rush. His scheme for minting gold tokens was abandoned for technical reasons but he argued that Adelaide should outbid Melbourne for Victorian gold and use it to back a paper currency. The bullion Act of 1852 provided that assayed gold ingots made a basis for bank-note issue at the rate of 71s. an ounce. Confidence was restored, gold flowed from diggers and dealers to the lucrative Adelaide market, the devalued currency ensured a roaring export trade with Victoria and the Bank of South Australia boomed.

For this crucial work and for his imaginative efforts in maintaining credit throughout a difficult period 200 leading citizens honoured Tinline in 1853 with a public dinner, proclaiming him a 'faithful steward of South Australia' and giving him 2000 guineas and an inscribed silver salver; the London directors awarded him £1000. He became manager in 1855 and established the bank's first branches, but was summoned to London in 1858 and dismissed next year when a customer defaulted with much loss to the bank.

In 1852 Tinline had been appointed treasurer of the Adelaide City Council. From 1858 he began a long and successful investment in pastoral properties with W. D. Fisher and later with his brother-in-law Alexander B. Murray at Wirrabara, and with his brother John in New Zealand. In 1860 he was elected to the Legislative Council, but because of his failure to attend his seat was declared vacant and he returned to England in 1863 to educate his children. They remained 'a South Australian family living in London'. Tinline was a devout Presbyterian. He travelled extensively, revisiting the colonies several times. He died of pneumonia in Melbourne on 1 February 1895, survived by two of his six children. His body was returned to Melrose, Roxburghshire, Scotland, for burial on

30 March near his wife who had pre-deceased him. He left his inscribed salver to the Adelaide Institute; it is now in the National Gallery of South Australia. There is a bust at Jedburgh. His estate in South Australia was sworn for probate at £40,000 and in England at £19,794. In 1907 his nephew Sir George Murray donated £1000 to the University of Adelaide to found the Tinline scholarship for historical research.

S. J. Butlin, *Australia and New Zealand Bank* (Melb, 1961); G. H. Pitt, 'The bullion Act and the gold escort', PRGSSA, 28 (1926-27); S. J. Butlin, 'The South Australian devaluation of 1852', *Business Archives and History*, 3 (1963); Tinline papers (SAA).

CHRISTINE HIRST

TITHERADGE, GEORGE SUTTON (1848-1916), actor, was born on 9 December 1848 at Portsea Island near Portsmouth, Hampshire, England, son of George Robert Titheradge, accountant, and his wife Sarah, née Emblin. He made his first appearance on the stage of the Theatre Royal, Portsmouth, in December 1865. After provincial work he toured Britain and by about 1873 was leading man at the Bristol Theatre. On 27 February 1871 at Hendon, County Durham, he married Isabella Maria Murdoch, an actress. In 1876 he joined the Chippendale Classical Comedy Company and late that year he played Hamlet at the Corinthian Theatre, Calcutta. He was the herald at Lord Lytton's durbar in Delhi and on 1 January 1877 announced Queen Victoria as 'Empress of India'. After playing in Edinburgh, on 6 October he made his first London appearance as Sir Francis Marsden in *The House of Darnley* at the Royal Court Theatre.

Late in 1878 Titheradge revisited India with Miss Alma Santon, an actress, and on 23 April next year he arrived in Melbourne in the *Siam* accompanied by 'Mrs. Titheradge and infant'. He opened on 27 May as Lord Arthur Chiltern in *False Shame* at the Academy of Music and on 14 June appeared at the Theatre Royal, Sydney, as Lord Clancarty in *Clancarty, or Wedded and Wooed*. In November he returned to Melbourne for a season at The People's Theatre after supporting Miss Dargon in Tennyson's *Queen Mary*. The *Australasian* critic found him 'so intelligent, so refined, and so generally mentally cultured, that no matter what kind of a part he plays, he plays it well'. His acting was noted for its naturalness and lack of affectation. In December in Adelaide he joined Alfred Garner's London Comedy Company which in March 1880 began a long season at the Theatre Royal, Sydney.

At the end of November 1882 Titheradge left Sydney to tour the United States of America. Next year he went briefly to England where in June he was divorced for adultery and desertion; his wife was given custody of their three children. On 4 March 1884 at the Fitzroy Registry Office, Melbourne, he married Alma Maria Johanna (Santon), daughter of William Saegert, picture dealer. He had been engaged by Garner to return to Australia and on 27 October 1883 he scored a triumph as Wilfred Denver in *The Silver King*. He remained under the management of Williamson [q.v.], Garner and Musgrove [q.v.] for four years and in 1885 supported Dion Boucicault senior in his Irish plays. Unwilling to become an actor-manager, in November 1887 he joined the Brough and Boucicault [qq.v.] Comedy Company, 'the finest comedy organisation seen in Australia'; Titheradge became 'their chief ornament in a succession of 140 parts extending over ten years'. He created the role of Aubrey Tanqueray in A. W. Pinero's *The Second Mrs. Tanqueray* for Australian audiences: other successes in contemporary comedies included Colonel Lukyn in *The Magistrate*, Abbé Dubois in *A Village Priest*, Lord Illingworth in Oscar Wilde's *A Woman of No Importance*, Partridge in *Sophia* and Charles Surface in *The School for Scandal*. His only Shakespearean role was Benedick in a lavish production of *Much Ado About Nothing* in December 1892.

Titheradge returned to the London stage on 7 February 1899 and until 1907 had successful runs, interspersed with American tours, supporting Mrs Patrick Campbell, Marie Tempest and Margaret Anglin, among others. In May 1908 he returned to Australia to act with Margaret Anglin and settled with his family in Sydney in 1910. Their repertoire included *The Thief* and *Twelfth Night* in which he played Malvolio; his son Dion was in the company. His occasional appearances after 1910 included a season of revivals with Florence Brough in 1912 and as George II in *A Fair Highwayman* in 1913 with his daughter Madge in the name role. His last appearance on the stage was as Shylock to the aged Ellen Terry's Portia at her benefit in July 1914. On 30 November 1911 and 10 December 1915 J. C. Williamson Ltd tendered matinees to him as a public tribute.

'A gentleman on and off the stage', Titheradge had great charm and was a lover of shooting, fishing and playing cricket in his youth. Later 'Tith' became an enthusiastic gardener and a recognized authority on daffodils, acting as a judge at daffodil shows in England and Australia. In his last years he lived at Oak Cottage, Vaucluse,

Sydney, and was president of the Actors' Association of Australasia. He died of cancer in a private hospital at Darlinghurst on 22 January 1916 and was buried in the Anglican section of South Head cemetery. He was survived by his second wife and by their son and six daughters, to whom he left his estate valued for probate at £1623.

The Times, 6 Oct 1877, 18 June 1883, 8 Feb 1899; *Argus*, 23 Apr 1879, 20 Oct 1888; *Australasian*, 31 May, 8 Nov, 6 Dec 1879, 8 Apr, 4 Nov 1882, 3 Nov 1883, 18 July 1885, 19 Nov 1887, 4 Dec 1915, 29 Jan 1916; *SMH*, 16, 17 June 1879, 27 Nov 1892, 29 Nov 1911, 18 July 1914, 10 Dec 1915, 24 Jan 1916; *Bulletin*, 25 Nov 1882, 13 Apr, 12 Dec 1889, 2 July 1908, 18 Jan, 8 Feb, 4 July 1912, 22 May, 4 Sept 1913; *Red Funnel*, 1 Sept 1908; MS and printed cats (ML).   MARTHA RUTLEDGE

TODD, SIR CHARLES (1826-1910), astronomer, meteorologist and electrical engineer, was born on 7 July 1826 at Islington, London, eldest son of Griffith Todd, grocer and tea merchant of Greenwich. Educated locally he was appointed to the Royal Observatory, Greenwich, as a supernumerary computer in 1841; he showed ability in mathematics and potential as an observer. As junior assistant to Professor Challis at the Cambridge university observatory in 1848-54 he assisted in the determination of longitude between the Cambridge and Greenwich observatories by telegraphic means. Early in 1854 he returned to Greenwich as superintendent of the galvanic apparatus for the transmission of time signals. This involved close co-operation with the Electric Telegraph Co., and also with C. V. Walker, electrical engineer to the South Eastern Railway, who was one of the pioneer experimenters with submarine cables. Todd became fascinated with telecommunications. In 1855 the South Australian government requested Sir George Airy, the astronomer royal, to select an observer and superintendent of electric telegraph at a salary of £400; he nominated Todd, who was appointed on 10 February. He reached Port Adelaide in the *Irene* on 4 November.

Todd wanted to initiate plans for the connexion of Melbourne and Sydney by telegraph, followed by a link with England. In March 1856 he completed the first government telegraph between Adelaide and its port. He then told Governor Sir Richard MacDonnell that a line to Melbourne was of prime importance and that it should precede meteorological proposals. He went to Melbourne in July where he met Samuel W. McGowan [q.v.], the Victorian superintendent, and commenced a lifelong friendship. Both governments accepted their joint recommendation that the line should be laid down under one uniform and successful system (Morse's), that New South Wales be included and that Australia be ultimately connected by telegraph to India: they had projected the first national communications system, one of the most significant colonial decisions of the century. Todd returned to survey the route of the 300 miles section from the border to Adelaide. His success boosted his confidence and reputation and confirmed the governor's high opinion of his character, ability and vision. In 1858 the government awarded him good service pay of £1820.

Todd's meteorological plan, which he had submitted in 1856, depended on a network of observation stations which were required to report daily to the observatory. The telegraph system was the answer; he trained his own observers, including interested private individuals. Growth was slow initially and it was not until 1860 that the observatory was ready with the necessary instruments and fourteen selected stations. As the telegraph system expanded so did the meteorological stations, with a greater impetus ten years later when post offices came under Todd's control.

In England proposals for connexion with Australia by telegraph had been mooted in 1854 and the first plans were submitted to the colonies in 1858. The route was by India to Singapore and the Dutch islands to the north, by cable around the east coast to Brisbane and by landline to Sydney. The link depended on subsidies from the British and colonial governments, and involved much complex negotiation. Todd, courteous and never contentious, examined every proposal and reported simply and lucidly. J. McD. Stuart's [q.v.] crossing of the continent in 1862 proved the feasibility of the project but the discussions dragged on until 1863 and then lapsed. In Australia the line from Adelaide to Melbourne was doubled, a direct line to Sydney with Todd as the chief negotiator was completed in 1866 and a line was run to Port Augusta which could be a starting point for extension west or north. In 1863 South Australia had gained control of the Northern Territory and suitable cable landing places there.

1866 saw a resurgence of English proposals, and early in 1870 the British Australian Telegraph Co. planned to land a cable near Palmerston (Darwin) and connect to Queensland. On 1 January Todd became South Australia's postmaster-general and superintendent of telegraphs and revived an old scheme for a line to Perth and up the west coast, but received little support. Then the company sought permission to land the cable, and H. B. T. Strangways [q.v.], premier of South Australia, decided to build an overland line to Darwin, independent of other colonies, and the company accepted.

Todd now produced a detailed organization, the result of years of practical experience. He had to build a line some 1800 miles, handicapped by lack of time and inadequate survey. He had to rely on Stuart's journals and maps for the greater part. But determined and confident, he divided the work into three sections: the southern and northern were let to contractors, each with one of Todd's overseers, the central was to be done by government labour under him. Having overcome initial difficulties of the passage of the MacDonnell Ranges early in 1871, he heard of disaster in the northern part: his overseer W. McMinn [q.v.] mishandled the contractors, terminated their contract in May and returned to Adelaide. Work was practically at a standstill for five months. The government sent R. C. Patterson north with a relief party and Todd followed in January 1872. As work progressed he went south inspecting the line, which was completed on 22 August, although cable communication was not made for another two months. 'This epic construction project provided one of the greatest advances in communications between England and Australia and the enthusiastic leadership of Charles Todd ... must mark the Overland Telegraph Line as an outstanding example of engineering in Australia'. During the final difficult months he proved his acumen in dealing with the captious and dissident Patterson. He was made C.M.G. in November. These two years were the peak of Todd's career and he achieved international recognition. One line remained to be built, that to Western Australia. By 1877 he had built his portion from Port Augusta to Eucla, the connexion being made at the end of the year.

In 1864 Todd had suspected the accuracy of the fixing of the 141 meridian boundary between South Australia and New South Wales; on completion of the Sydney line in 1866 he obtained agreement to check it. In 1868 with the co-operation of the observers of New South Wales and Victoria, he worked in the Sydney and Melbourne observatories and established a transit at the border to complete the operation. The solution agreed to by all was that the 141 meridian was two and a third miles to the east of the original boundary.

The full development of Todd's beloved astronomy depended on the spread of the telegraphic network and the acquisition of modern instruments to provide a complete observatory. By the early 1880s he had organized constant general astronomical work, time services, a standard point for geodetic surveys, and gradual improvement in the accuracy of climatic statistics. Before that he had made regular observations, notably of Venus in 1874, and again in 1882 when in order to get the best possible results he established a temporary station at Wentworth, New South Wales. A long series of notes on the phenomena of Jupiter's satellites was published in the *Journal* of the Royal Astronomical Society, of which he had been made a fellow in 1864. His meteorological system spread to all colonies and New Zealand. He sought systematic interchange of information and pioneered the production of weather maps. When he retired there were 510 rainfall stations in South Australia and the Northern Territory, twenty-two of which were completely equipped for all meteorological observations.

Todd attended an International Telegraphic Conference in Berlin in 1885, and next year while in England he was made an honorary M.A. of the University of Cambridge. Professor J. C. Adams, co-discoverer of the planet Neptune, was his sponsor. In 1889 he was elected a fellow of The Royal Society, London. These two distinctions gave him great personal satisfaction and by 1889 his salary was £1000. In June 1893 he was made K.C.M.G. He was also a fellow of the Royal Astronomical Society, the Royal Meteorological Society and the Society of Electrical Engineers. In 1895 at the request of the Western Australian government, he chose a site and suggested the design and equipment for its new observatory, and his deputy was appointed government astronomer.

Todd held leading positions in numerous learned societies and educational and public institutions in the colony, and was always ready to assist and advise. After Federation in 1901 his departments were the only ones to show a profit. His designation was changed to deputy-postmaster-general but, although he was a septuagenarian, the State government deferred its retirement legislation until he retired in January 1905. In his later years he ruled his departments as a 'benevolent autocrat', trusted by employers and employees. The keynote of his life was service, and psychic experiences had led him to a firm belief in his destiny. Kindly and tolerant but never pessimistic, 'his natural impulse was to believe that the purpose of every man in his employ was as single as his own ... he rarely failed to find what he thought to see'. He was essentially happy and good humoured. His besetting 'weakness' was his constant punning of which, as a connoisseur of tea from his early days, the hackneyed example was 'I'd be odd without my T'. Much of the history of astronomy, meteorology and telegraphs in South Australia is contained in his reports to parliament between 1856 and 1900.

Prior to leaving England in 1855 Todd had married Alice Gillam Bell (d. 1898) of Cambridge. They had two sons and four daughters, a devoted family that also brought up two sons and a daughter of his eldest brother who died in 1861. One of the founders in 1859 of the Brougham Place Congregational Church, North Adelaide, and of the Stow [q.v.] Memorial Congregational Church, Adelaide, in 1865, Todd and his family were regular worshippers. He died of gangrene on 29 January 1910 at Semaphore and was buried in the North Road cemetery. He was survived by one son and four daughters; Gwendoline married Professor (Sir) William Bragg of the University of Adelaide. Todd's estate was sworn for probate at £12,876.

Aust Post Office, The centenary of the Adelaide-Darwin overland telegraph line: symposium papers (Syd, 1972, and SAA); W. L. Manser, The overland telegraph (B.A. Hons thesis, Univ Adel, 1961); Todd papers (SAA); Magnetic Telegraph Dept, Letter-book 1856-58 (G.P.O., Adel); family papers (held by Mrs A. Caroe, London, Miss P. Fisher, Hahndorf, SA, Mrs L. Smith, Amesbury, Wiltshire, England, and Mr G. W. Todd, Sidcup, Kent, England).
                                        G. W. SYMES

TOLMER, ALEXANDER (1815-1890), police officer, was born in England of French refugee parents, but spent his early childhood in France. At 8 he rejoined his widowed father, who had remarried and was a language teacher at Plymouth, England; Tolmer went to schools there and in Rouen, Maidstone and Hawkhurst, from which he ran away to sea, but did not enjoy the experience. He entered Rev. H. Boyce's school at Edgware to train as a language teacher, but enlisted in the British legion raised in 1826 to support Donna Maria's cause in Portugal. He saw much action with Colonel Bacon's lancers, being three times wounded, most seriously outside Lisbon in October 1833. He became a corporal and claimed to have obtained the Order of the Tower and Sword. He resumed his studies in France but soon entered the 16th Lancers at Maidstone, Kent. He was a good cavalryman and by 21 he was acting adjutant and drill supervisor.

Failing to get the vacant adjutancy Tolmer decided to migrate to South Australia. In 1836 at Rochester near Maidstone he was married clandestinely to Mary Carter. They arrived in Adelaide with their infant son in the Branken Moor

on 8 February 1840 and, having a letter of introduction to Governor Gawler, he became sub-inspector of police on 19 February. Gawler wanted him to organize the mounted branch, a task for which his cavalry background well prepared him. Promoted inspector almost immediately, he was also appointed captain and adjutant of cavalry in the Volunteer Militia. His years as inspector of mounted police were active and successful. Soon after his arrival he accompanied T. S. O'Halloran's [q.v.] force, which after a drumhead court martial executed two Aboriginals who had allegedly killed the survivors of the Maria. Tolmer led many expeditions to prevent trouble between settlers and Aboriginals, and he spent much time in the bush pursuing cattle thieves, murderers, smugglers and seeking illicit stills. His duties also took him to Tasmania and Victoria.

Tolmer succeeded G. F. Dashwood [q.v.] as commissioner of police on 3 January 1852; he had been acting commissioner and police magistrate in 1849-50 when he had proposed a superannuation scheme. He now decentralized the force, instituted water and native police and the detective force. As soon as the bullion Act of January 1852 was passed Tolmer suggested an overland gold escort service from Victoria to South Australia, designed to reverse the drain of currency from the colony during the gold rush. He left with the first escort on 10 February and returned a month later with gold worth £21,000. The service lasted until December 1853, a month after his supersession as commissioner.

Tolmer's dismissal arose partly from the disorganization of the police force as a result of his long absences on escort duty and partly from his character. A good leader, capable of inspiring great devotion, he was also hasty tempered, petty and suspicious, especially under criticism. He regarded any disagreement as a personal attack and became involved in demeaning disputes with his subordinates. Following the report of a board of inquiry in November 1853 he was demoted, but remained in the force as inspector and then as superintendent until the position was abolished in 1856. In 1859 he rejoined the force for nine months.

Tolmer's remaining years were active but he felt himself degraded. A trading venture on Lake Alexandrina failed, as did an attempt to cross Australia from south to north in 1859 and a grazing enterprise on Emu Springs and Reedy Well runs in the south-east. In 1862 he was appointed crown lands ranger, in 1863 inspecting ranger; in 1877 he was transferred as sub-inspector of credit lands at a salary of £330. He retired in 1885 with a gratuity of £1000 which he invested in Broken Hill mining shares. In 1882 he had published in London his *Reminiscences of an Adventurous and Chequered Career at Home and at the Antipodes*, an engaging and egotistical work in two volumes mainly devoted to his service in Portugal and with the police. In 1889 he visited England.

Tolmer's first wife had died in 1867, leaving him three children. On 14 October 1869 he married Jane Douglas at Mount Schank station; they had four daughters and two sons. He died of uraemia at Mitcham on 7 March 1890 survived by his wife and large family, and was buried in Mitcham cemetery after an Anglican service. His estate was sworn for probate at £8350.

J. W. Bull, *Early experiences of life in South Australia and an extended colonial history* (Lond, 1884); E. Hodder, *The history of South Australia* (Lond, 1893); L. J. Blake, *Gold escort* (Melb, 1971); G. H. Pitt, 'The bullion Act and the gold escort', PRGSSA, 28 (1926-27); *Observer* (Adel), 8, 15 Mar 1890; Police records (SAA).   J. MAYO

TOMKINSON, SAMUEL (1816-1900), banker, was born on 25 April 1816 at Wrexham, Denbighshire, North Wales, son of Charles Tomkinson, grocer, and his wife Elizabeth. Educated at a private boarding-school in that county, at 12 he was apprenticed for seven years to an East Indian merchant in Liverpool. From 1836 to 1850 he was employed by the North and South Wales Bank. He became involved in Liverpool politics after the death of William Huskisson and is said to have been associated with John Bright and Richard Cobden in the campaign for the repeal of the Corn Laws.

Tomkinson arrived in Sydney in 1850 as an employee of the Bank of Australasia. Within a few months he travelled to Adelaide and in March 1852 he succeeded Marshall MacDermott as manager at the height of the bullion crisis. He immediately challenged the wisdom and legality of the bullion Act of 1852, endangered the existing arrangement between the banks in South Australia and jeopardized the policy that his predecessor had created. Probably his actions in refusing to accept gold ingots as legal tender during the crisis damaged the relative business position of the Bank of Australasia in South Australia. In 1856 he was chairman of a commission into the state accounts, and was later involved in inquiries into the liquor laws, the Education Board, the Police Department and

the public service. In 1857 he inspected the Victorian goldfields. He was twice chairman of the Chamber of Commerce and held directorships in the South Australian Gas Co. and the Burra Burra mine of which he became deputy-chairman. He was also the lessee of Wilyerpa north run. When he retired as manager of the bank in 1879 he was made a local director.

Tomkinson was a member of the House of Assembly for Gumeracha in 1881-84 and of the Legislative Council in 1885-94 and 1897-1900. He was also a justice of the peace, an official visitor of the Lunatic Asylum and an alderman of the Adelaide City Council for twelve years. Known as a pessimist, he was a man of firm and frequently unpopular views. Scornful of 'experimental politics', he consistently opposed 'reckless expenditure and over hasty Socialistic legislation'. In parliament he voted against most loans on the grounds that expenditure should be kept within revenue, and that taxation was at all times excessive. He was staunchly anti-protectionist and a supporter of proportional representation. He regarded state education as extravagant, tyrannical and unnecessary. Having been a survivor of the Dee bridge disaster he held doubts about the safety of railway travel, and in 1856 he had opposed the idea of building railways on loans. A man of extreme rectitude and obstinacy he was considered a conservative also in Church affairs; he was a member of the Anglican synod.

Described by the *Bulletin* as a poor orator, 'short, spare and erect in stature, immaculately dressed', on 7 September 1853 Tomkinson had married Louisa Charlotte MacDermott at North Adelaide. He died of acute nephritis at Fitzroy, Adelaide, on 30 August 1900, survived by his wife (d. 1910), five daughters and five of his seven sons; he was buried in North Road cemetery. His estate was sworn for probate at £30,000; he stipulated that a maximum of £20 be spent on his funeral. His paper on 'Adventure in the First Steamer, "Melbourne", out of the Mouth of the River Murray on 20th August, 1854', was published in the *Proceedings* of the Royal Geographical Society of Australasia, South Australian Branch, in 1901.

A. Tolmer, *Reminiscences*, 2 (Lond, 1882); *The 'Register' guide to the parliament of South Australia* (Adel, 1887); J. J. Pascoe (ed), *History of Adelaide and vicinity* (Adel, 1901); Universal Publicity Co., *The official civic record of South Australia* (Adel, 1936); S. J. Butlin, *Australia and New Zealand Bank* (Melb, 1961); *Church News* (SA), 11 June 1897, 14 Sept 1900; *Bulletin*, 1 July 1882; *Observer* (Adel), 14 July 1883, 21 Nov 1885, 12 Nov

1887, 1 Sept 1900; *Advertiser* (Adel), 31 Aug 1900; W. R. C. Jacques, The impact of the gold rushes on South Australia 1852-1854 (B.A. thesis, Univ Adel, 1963).   ERIC RICHARDS

TOOHEY, JOHN THOMAS (1839-1903) and JAMES MATTHEW (1850-1895), brewers, were the sons of Matthew Toohey (d. 1892), businessman, and his wife Honora (d. 1878), née Hall. John Thomas was born on 26 April 1839 at Limerick, Ireland, and was taken to Melbourne by his parents in 1841. His father bought town lots and settled many Irish families in Victoria. One of the founders of the St Patrick's Society in Melbourne, he was a political ally of (Sir) John O'Shanassy and (Sir) Charles Gavan Duffy [qq.v.]. In the 1860s he was forced to sell at a loss; in 1866 he went to New South Wales and lived in virtual retirement. James Matthew was born on 18 March 1850 in Melbourne: he is said to have been named after Fr Matthew, the Irish apostle of temperance.

After unsuccessful business ventures in Victoria, New Zealand and Queensland, John settled near Lismore: later James had a property near Coonamble. About 1869 with W. G. Henfrey John set up an auctioneering agency and cordial manufacturing business in Castlereagh Street, Sydney; the next year the brothers began brewing at the Metropolitan Brewery and in 1873 they bought the Darling Brewery in Harbour Street. In 1876 they moved to new premises on the site of the old Albion Brewery in Elizabeth Street and began the Standard Brewery, employing twenty-six hands. Before 1880 imported beer was preferred to the local product, but in the 1880s Toohey's and Tooth's [q.v.] beers quickly became popular.

Vice-president of the Licensed Victuallers' Association, in 1886 James was appointed to the royal commission on the excessive use of intoxicating drink, but withdrew when he felt the balance between local and anti-local optionists was upset. In evidence to the commission he said that 'the system of shouting' was the cause of all the excessive drinking in the colony and that beer was less injurious to health than 'the ardent spirits'. He approved of the tied-house system and maintained that the 830 public houses in the Sydney metropolitan licensing district were not an excessive number, though there were a few too many in certain areas of the city.

Campaigning in 1885 for the Legislative Assembly seat of South Sydney, James claimed that the government's action in sending troops to the Sudan 'had resulted in a huge advertisement for the colony.

Favouring an elected Upper House, payment of members and the eight-hour system, he said he opposed local option and the abstinence party, as no Act of parliament could make a man sober. He represented the seat in 1885-93. A firm protectionist by 1887, he saw most free traders as 'the curled darlings of the [Potts] Point and the merchants of Sydney'. He was a good speaker, if a little impetuous at times. According to the *Sydney Morning Herald's* political correspondent in 1887, he 'rolls the letter "r" beautifully, he drops his voice down to sweet whisper, lifts it up to a palpitating splendour, and then rolls it over the solemn path of prophetic parlance'. Dissatisfied with Sir George Dibbs's [q.v.] administration, he opposed him for Tamworth in July 1894, but polled poorly. Next year he visited Ireland, England and Europe. James died at Pisa, Italy, on 25 September 1895 and was buried in the Catholic section of Rookwood cemetery, Sydney. He was survived by his wife Catherine (Kate) Magdalene (d. 1913), née Ferris, whom he had married at Parramatta on 5 June 1873; they had four sons and eight daughters. Probate of his estate was sworn at £133,623.

On James's death, John and James's eldest son, also named John Thomas, took over the brewery. John was a leading Catholic layman, benefactor to numerous Catholic charitable institutions and a financial supporter of the Irish nationalist movement. On Christmas Day 1888 Cardinal Moran invested him as a knight of the Order of St Gregory. A leader in the Home Rule movement, he was prominent in the erection of the monument over the grave of Michael Dwyer in Waverley cemetery in 1898. Well known in business circles, he was a director of several companies including the City Mutual Fire Insurance Co. Ltd. He lived first at Moira, Burwood, and later at Innisfail, Wahroonga, and assisted in the development of both suburbs. He stood for Monaro in the Legislative Assembly in 1880 but was defeated by H. S. Badgery and R. L. Tooth [qq.v.]. In April 1892 he was nominated to the Legislative Council, but he very rarely spoke. In September 1901 he gave evidence to an assembly select committee on tied houses. Next year the brewery became a public company, Toohey's Ltd, with John as chairman; the vendors received 375,000 fully paid shares and £175,000 cash. The well-known advertising slogan and symbol 'Here's to 'ee' originated in 1894.

For health reasons John went on a world tour with his family in 1902. He died suddenly in Chicago on 5 May 1903 and was buried in the Catholic section of Rookwood cemetery, Sydney. On 26 August 1871 at

St Mary's Cathedral he had married Sarah Doheny who died in 1891 survived by two sons and three daughters. Toohey was survived by his second wife, a widow Annie Mary Murphy, née Egan, whom he had married in Auckland, New Zealand. His estate was sworn for probate at £275,215.

W. F. Morrison, *The Aldine centennial history of New South Wales*, 2 (Syd, 1888); *V&P* (LA NSW), 1875-76, 5, 633, 1887-88, 7, 257, 1901, 6, 789, evidence 95, 101; *T&CJ*, 22 Nov 1879; *SMH*, 8 Dec 1880, 13, 14, 16, 17 Oct 1885, 29 Jan, 4, 7 Feb, 29 Apr 1887, 1 June 1895, 8 May 1903; *Bulletin*, 5 Jan 1889.

G. P. WALSH

TOOTH, ROBERT (1821-1893), EDWIN (1822-1858), and FREDERICK (1827-1893), merchants, pastoralists and brewers, were born on 28 May 1821, 28 August 1822 and 14 February 1827, the first, second and fourth sons of Robert Tooth (b. 1799), hop merchant of Swifts Park, Cranbrook, Kent, England, and his wife Mary Ann (d. 1845), née Reader; they were nephews of JOHN TOOTH, merchant and brewer, born in 1803 at Cranbrook, who had arrived in Sydney in the *Bencoolen* in 1828 and received a 2560-acre grant in County Durham. John acquired numerous cattle runs and set up as a general merchant and commission agent in Spring Street, Sydney. In September 1835 with Charles Newnham, an experienced brewer from Kent, he opened the Kent Brewery on a 4½-acre site on the Parramatta Road; Newnham withdrew from the partnership in 1843. John overextended his pastoral ventures and became bankrupt in 1848, paying 9d. in the pound; the brewery was mortgaged for £30,200. He died of dropsy at Irrawang near Raymond Terrace on 1 October 1857, survived by his wife Elizabeth (d. 1858), daughter of John Newnham, brewer and timber merchant, whom he had married at Cranbrook on 22 March 1830, and by four sons and five daughters.

The merchant and brewing firm of R. and E. Tooth began on 1 September 1843 when John leased the brewery to Robert and Edwin who had arrived in the *Euphrates* on 5 August 1843. On 15 April 1844 he agreed to lease it to the brothers for nine years for £4000 a year. Frederick joined the partnership about 1853 and R., E. and F. Tooth became R. and F. Tooth & Co. on 2 January 1860 when J. S. Mitchell became a partner. In 1850 Robert with T. S. Mort [q.v.] and F. Mitchell, financed C. Ledger [q.v.] to bring alpacas from Peru. In 1852 with J. E., J. A. L. and W. M. Manning [qq.v.], Mort. J. Croft and Edwin,

Robert formed the Twofold Bay Pastoral Association which acquired some 400,000 acres on the south coast and Monaro; Kameruka was the head station. Threatened by (Sir) John Robertson's [q.v.] land bills they bought as much land as possible in their own names and disbanded in 1860. Robert was in London in 1853-55; in the 1850s with Mort, Thomas Holt [q.v.] and others he speculated in buying pastoral properties. With Edwin and Mort he was a shareholder in the unsuccessful Great Nugget Vein Gold Mining Co. of Australia. In August 1857 he chaired a meeting of publicans in Sydney which raised the retail price of spirits, wines and beers; colonial ale was fixed at 4d. a pint.

In 1850 Robert was active in the anti-transportation movement. From May 1856 to February 1857 he was a member of the Legislative Council. A large squatter with about 600 employees, in January 1858 he stood for the seat of Sydney Hamlets in the Legislative Assembly, advocating free selection of land at £1 an acre without auction, tramways instead of expensive railways to bring produce to market and an elective Upper House. He lost, but represented Sydney in the assembly in 1858-59. Questionably claiming to have disposed of all his runs except one on the Queensland border and opposing Robertson's land bill, Robert stood for West Sydney in December 1860 but again was defeated.

Tooth then concentrated on his business interests in the colony and in England. Their London house, R. & F. Tooth & Mort, 155 Fenchurch Street, acted also as agents for Smyth's Sydney Marine Assurance Office and the Peak Downs Copper Mining Co. He became a committee-man of the Society for the Suppression of Cattle Stealing in 1861 and of the Agricultural Society of New South Wales. He was a partner of Robert Cran, F. F. Nixon, (Sir) Robert Lucas Tooth [q.v.] and Frederick under the style of Tooth and Cran until March 1872 at Yengarie near Maryborough, Queensland, and in the Wide Bay and Burnett districts. From 1865 they experimented with meat preserving at Yengarie and in 1870 won a prize at the Intercolonial Exhibition, Sydney. In the mid-1860s Robert still nominally held the Lachlan and Wide Bay runs he had leased in the 1850s; he had added Jondaryan and Irvingdale, almost 300 square miles on the Darling Downs and some twenty-eight runs, amounting to 700 square miles, in the Maranoa District of Queensland.

Tooth was a director of the Bank of New South Wales in the 1850s and 1860s (president in 1862-63) and a director of the Colonial Sugar Refining Co. in 1855-63; R.,

E. & F. Tooth were the second largest share-holders when the company was established in 1855. A prominent Anglican layman, he was a director of the Society for the Relief of Destitute Children, a fellow of St Paul's College within the University of Sydney and an original committee-man of the Union Club. He began building his fine residence, Cranbrook, at Rose Bay in 1859 but sold it to Robert Towns [q.v.] in 1864. Robert retired from R. and F. Tooth & Co. in April 1872 and Frederick and R. L. Tooth carried on as F. Tooth & Co. This partnership was dissolved on 31 March 1873 when Frederick retired, Mitchell and R. L. Tooth carrying on as Tooth & Co. Most of the profit from this successful business came from importing wines, spirits and beer, as colonial beer was not widely drunk until the 1880s. Leaving issue, Robert died at Bedford in the United States of America on 19 September 1893. On 1 May 1849 he had married at St Mark's Church, Pontville, Van Diemen's Land, Maria Lisle, daughter of Captain G. B. Forster, R.N.; on 24 June 1871 he married Elizabeth Mansfield.

Edwin had pastoral interests outside his partnership with Robert until 1855; he had bought J. C. Lloyd's stations and also runs in Gippsland. He was in pastoral partnership with his father, brother Robert, Holt and T. de Lacy Moffatt [q.v.], and was a director in 1855 as well as shareholder in the Colonial Sugar Refining Co. Edwin lived in Tasmania for many years, settled in Sydney in 1852 and left the colony in December 1855. In London he lived at 29 Cleveland Square, Hyde Park, and was on the London board of the Bank of New South Wales. He died at Tutbury, Staffordshire, on 29 August 1858 and was buried in St Dunstan's churchyard, Cranbrook, Kent. In February 1844 he had married Sarah, daughter of Francis Lucas of Blackheath, Kent; they had three sons and three daughters.

Frederick was a director of the Southern Insurance Co. Ltd, the Bank of New South Wales in 1857-61, 1863-69 and 1871-74 (president 1867-68), and of the Colonial Sugar Refining Co. in 1863-64. In England he was on the London board of the bank with Edwin and lived at Park Farm, Sevenoaks, Kent. He died of apoplexy in his London residence, 4 Orme Square, Bayswater, on 20 December 1893, survived by his wife, son and three daughters. Probate of his estate was sworn in London at £343,000; he bequeathed £1800 to Sydney charities, including £500 to Sydney Hospital, and smaller amounts to charities in England. He married three times: first on 22 August 1848 to Jane Jackson of Southsea, Hampshire, England; second to Susan Frances

Gosling; third to Fanny Peach on 12 June 1889 at Notting Hill, London.

The enduring legacy of this enterprising pioneer family is the Kent Brewery on its original site on the Parramatta Road, Sydney, and the famous 'Tooth's K.B.' beer. Tooth & Co. Ltd became a public company in 1888 with a capital of £900,000; in 1929 the firm took over Edmund Resch's Waverley Brewery.

HRA (1), 14; *In the House of Lords, between W. C. Wentworth ... and Robert Tooth ...* (np, c 1862, copy ML); Tooth & Co. Ltd, *The first hundred years* (Syd, 1935), and *Over a century of brewing tradition* (Syd, 1953); A. Barnard, *Visions and profits* (Melb, 1961); *Sydney Gazette*, 24 Sept 1835; *SMH*, 7 Aug, 4 Sept 1843, 2, 5 Dec 1844, 7 Aug 1857, 6, 13, 14, 16 Jan 1858, 23, 28 Nov, 8, 11-13 Dec 1860; *T&CJ*, 19 Mar 1870.   G. P. WALSH

TOOTH, SIR ROBERT LUCAS LUCAS-(1844-1915), brewer, was born on 7 December 1844 in Sydney, eldest son of Edwin Tooth [q.v.] and his wife Sarah, née Lucas. He was educated in England at Eton and in 1863 rowed in the college eight. In December he returned to Sydney, joined R. and F. Tooth [qq.v.] & Co. and became active in the management of the Kent Brewery; in 1868 he became a partner. He had bought the Kameruka estate near Bega from his uncle Frederick in 1864; between 1868 and 1871 it shrank from 75,000 acres of leasehold to 22,000 acres of freehold land. He put into practice there his own humanitarian social ideas, providing his tenant farmers with six-roomed cottages, a school, a church designed by Edmund Blacket [q.v.], a meeting-hall, store and post office. He planted English trees on a large scale, built an ornamental lake, kept an aviary of golden pheasants and liberated all kinds of game: pheasants, quails, hares and foxes. He gradually changed from grazing Durham and Shorthorn cattle to dairying, founded a fine Jersey herd from imported stock, evolved a matured cheddar cheese and was the first in the colony to make Edam cheeses. Kameruka became a 'transplanted segment of the English countryside'. With his uncles Frederick and Robert and others he was a partner in Tooth and Cran in business ventures in Queensland. In Sydney on 2 January 1873 he married his cousin Helen, daughter of Frederick Tooth.

In December 1879 Tooth contested a by-election for East Sydney. He strongly supported Denominational schools and castigated the government's new excise on colonial beer, which he believed would 'press lightly on the rich man and heavily on the labouring classes' and lead to the extinction of native industries. He was not elected, despite the support of Archbishop Vaughan and John McElhone [qq.v.] and the assistance of two bands, and free beer and transport on polling day. However, next December he won the Monaro seat in the Legislative Assembly. He rarely voted but generally supported the Parkes-Robertson [qq.v.] ministry and in 1883 served on the Elections and Qualifications Committee.

A member of the Union Club from 1867, Tooth built Eridge Park at Bowral in the late 1870s; the house was lined with barley husks; in 1883 he laid down a coursing track there and planted gorse and blackberries to protect the hares. In 1882 he built a castellated Gothic mansion at Darling Point, with a ballroom larger than that at Government House, and named it Swifts after the family home in Kent. He was awarded a silver medal for his services as a Canadian commissioner at the Sydney International Exhibition in 1879-80. In 1881-90 he was a director of the Bank of New South Wales and in 1894-1907 served on its London board and was sometime chairman. A permanent committee-man of the Industrial Blind Society in the 1880s, he was a large shareholder in the Colonial Sugar Refining Co. and a director in 1888-89. In 1888 Tooth & Co. Ltd became a public company; holding 10,000 shares he was managing director until 21 October 1889.

That year Tooth took his family to England to be educated; he settled there but paid frequent visits to Australia, particularly to Kameruka. He leased a house in Queen's Gate, London, and in 1909 bought Holme Lacy, an estate near Hereford. He was a member of the Carlton and Junior Carlton clubs and a fellow of the Royal Geographical Society. In 1895, as a Conservative, he was defeated for a Leicestershire seat in the House of Commons. In 1902 he gave £10,000 to the King Edward's Hospital Fund for London, and was a member of the management committee of King Edward's Horse (the King's Overseas Dominions Regiment). In 1904 by royal licence he took the name and arms of Lucas-Tooth and in 1906 was created a baronet in recognition of his services to the empire. Soon afterwards he gave £50,000 to promote the physical and moral training of boys, and endowed a scholarship in Sydney for Anglican theological students to attend Oxford or Cambridge universities for three years. On the outbreak of World War I he gave £10,000 to Lady Dudley's fund to set up the 'Australian Voluntary Hospital' at the front and was chairman of its London committee of management.

Lucas-Tooth died of cerebral haemorrhage at Holme Lacy on 19 February 1915. He was survived by his wife, three daughters and youngest son who succeeded him but was killed in action in 1918; his two elder sons had been killed in the war in 1914. His estate was sworn for probate at over £905,000 in New South Wales and over £276,000 in England. In 1920 King George V recreated the baronetcy for the eldest son of Lucas-Tooth's eldest daughter Beatrice, wife of Major Hugh Warrand; he became Sir Hugh Lucas-Tooth.

Tooth & Co. Ltd, *The first hundred years* (Syd, 1935); G. N. Griffiths, *Some houses and people of New South Wales* (Syd, 1949); B. Ryan, 'Kameruka Estate, New South Wales, 1864-1964', *NZ Geographer*, 20 (1964) no 2; *SMH*, 16-18 Dec 1879, 22 Feb 1915; *Bulletin*, 19 Aug 1882; *The Times*, 11 Aug 1914; *Aust Financial Review*, 31 Mar 1967.

MARTHA RUTLEDGE

TOOTH, WILLIAM BUTLER (1823-1876) and ATTICUS (1827-1915), pastoralists, were born at Cranbrook, Kent, England, sons of William Tooth, farmer, and his wife Anne, née Fulcher. They were nephews of John Tooth, founder of the Kent Brewery, Sydney, and cousins of Robert, Edwin and Frederick Tooth [qq.v.]. Part of the family, including Atticus, came to New South Wales in 1839 and settled near Camden. William reached Sydney in the *Lalla Rookh* on 26 December 1841 escorting two sisters. The brothers probably gained pastoral experience on their uncle's stations. In 1846 they overlanded a herd from the Murrumbidgee to Wide Bay, Queensland, to occupy an abandoned run, then settled on Widgie Widgie using it as a base to acquire further runs in the Wide Bay, Burnett and Darling Downs districts. In 1853 they bought Clifton station near Allora from the Gammie estate for £30,000. They travelled constantly, acquiring more stations from the Murrumbidgee and Darling rivers to the Gulf of Carpentaria. For five years they operated a boiling-down works at Ipswich.

On 15 August 1850 in Sydney William married Lucy Ann, sister of George Harris [q.v.], and in 1856 the brothers separated. William lived in Sydney, representing the United Pastoral Districts of Moreton, Wide Bay, Burnett, Maranoa, Leichhardt and Port Curtis in the New South Wales Legislative Assembly in 1858-59. A founder of the Union Club, he was a committee-man of the Sydney Club, the Society for the Suppression of Cattle Stealing and the Agricultural Society of New South Wales. He lived in fashionable suburbs and his children attended prominent schools.

William was notoriously litigious and his obvious desire to live like an English squire led to constant disputes with neighbours and workers. From 1857 to 1861 he fought a long, technical action with Joseph Fleming [q.v.] over the stock on Talavera station, Queensland, and threatened a Privy Council appeal. In 1872 his violation of traditional bush hospitality led to the burning of Clifton woolshed by a disgruntled traveller. In July 1874 he lost £500 in damages and costs to a selector who charged him with malicious prosecution and false imprisonment. In February 1876 an employee won £22 unpaid wages in court; Tooth challenged the verdict and secured a rule *nisi* against the magistrates for exceeding their jurisdiction. He began a long battle in May with a selector who challenged his right to close a road, but after he died of cirrhosis of the liver and dropsy on 5 June the case was dismissed. His widow and nine surviving children were left with a debt of £102,000, owing mainly to the Bank of New South Wales which had held title to Clifton since 1875. A select committee recommended an enabling Act in 1879 authorizing the family to break the will and disperse the estate, but most of it went eventually to a reluctant bank.

Atticus joined G. E. Dalrymple's [q.v.] expedition to Port Curtis in 1859 and settled near Bowen as a station manager. On 22 December 1869 he married Sarah Emmerson, daughter of a grazier; as a manager he rejoined William, who was then settled at Clifton. After William's death, he managed the Brisbane municipal markets but returned to Bowen just before his death on 15 January 1915. Survived by his wife and eleven children he was buried in the Church of England section of the Bowen cemetery.

W. F. Morrison, *The Aldine history of Queensland* (Syd, 1888); N. Bartley, *Opals and agates* (Brisb, 1892); D. B. Waterson, *Squatter, selector and storekeeper* (Syd, 1968); V&P (LA NSW), 1858, 1, 53, 209, 271, 903, 917, 919, 928-30, 932, 2, 880, 882 (LA Qld), 1879, 2, 1085-1102; 'Time's changes. Career of Mr. Atticus Tooth . . .', *Brisbane Courier*, 1 Oct 1910; J. J. McGinley, Cutting book no 2 and J. G. Palethorpe, Cutting book no 3 (Oxley Lib, Brisb).

NOELINE V. HALL

TOPP, ARTHUR MANING (1844-1916), journalist, and SAMUEL ST JOHN (1850-1902), barrister, were born on 7 October 1844 and 13 June 1850 at Huddersfield, Yorkshire, England, eldest and youngest sons of Samuel Topp, wool-importer and merchant, and his wife Sarah, née Clapham. Arthur Maning arrived in Melbourne with his parents and brother Charles Alfred [q.v.] on 17 March 1858 in the *Royal Charter*. Samuel St John followed in 1861.

Arthur was one of the first pupils in April 1858 at the Melbourne Church of England Grammar School before entering his father's business; in 1868-80 the firm was known as A. M. Topp & Co. In 1867 in Melbourne he published a play *Enderby; a tragedy*. He was one of the 'literary and journalistic friends' brought together by H. G. Turner [q.v.] in November 1875 to launch the *Melbourne Review*, a quarterly journal of high standard and wide coverage. Topp was on the editorial committee for its first six years. In his own contributions he used an historical approach to determine the basic socio-political forces of current European and colonial affairs. Of a speculative mind, he took 'the long view' of human society and although his generalizations could be shaken by specific analysis, he exposed in incisive prose the trends of his time. Tender spots were touched in an article in 1879 on the social role of banks in Victoria, leading to a break with Turner who resigned from the editorial committee. One of Topp's themes was the role of the Roman-Teutonic race in Western civilization; the idea led him to admiration of Bismarck's Germany, opposition to Russian expansion and, on the local scene, to polemical attacks on the Celtic Irish as 'an alien and only partially civilized race'. His *English Institutions and the Irish Race*, reprinted from the *Melbourne Review*, was published by himself in 1881. His ideas on race were linked with his study and admiration of Herbert Spencer's scientific method of philosophy, especially in analysis of religious belief.

Topp was a member of the Eclectic Association; his close friends included fellow members A. P. Martin [q.v.], Theodore Fink, Alfred Deakin and David Mickle. He became cable sub-editor for the *Argus* in 1882 and later leader-writer and reviewer for the *Argus* and the *Australasian* until his retirement in 1911. Bedridden for two years, he died at South Yarra on 17 January 1916, survived by his wife Leila Leonora, née Sanders, whom he had married at South Yarra in 1884, and by his two sons. His estate was valued for probate at £1412.

Samuel was educated at King Edward's School in Birmingham before arriving in Melbourne, where he attended the Melbourne Church of England Grammar School. He left school early to work as a legal clerk, studying at night for matriculation. He had a brilliant career at the University of Melbourne (LL.B., 1877; B.A., 1878), winning the Shakespeare scholarship in 1877. That year he was admitted to the Victorian Bar where his early practical training helped him. He made his reputation as an Equity lawyer during the winding-up proceedings of the Oriental Banking Corporation in

1884 and soon became a leading member of the Bar; he also practised in insolvency and mining matters.

Samuel Topp did not fit the Equity stereotype; he was witty, with a 'slightly audacious' manner in court. As befitted a member of the Eclectic Association he held progressive views on social and religious issues. The literary articles that he contributed to the *Melbourne Review* were scholarly and well argued. In 1879 he wrote a critique of existing marriage and divorce laws and set out a series of reforms which were substantially incorporated in Shiels's Act of 1890. As a hobby he collected snakes, which he hunted on his annual holiday at Lorne and kept pickled in spirits in his cellar. A drooping eyelid gave him a deceptively 'reposeful' look in court.

Topp had married Mary Anne Chesterton in 1876; she died on 18 May 1878 and he married Emma Dunn in 1881. His death of an internal haemorrhage at Caulfield on 1 August 1902 was much lamented; he was buried in the Brighton cemetery after a Church of England service, with leading legal men as pallbearers. He was survived by his second wife and by a daughter of his first marriage. His estate was valued for probate at £4885.

A. P. Martin, *Australia and the empire* (Edinb, 1889); A. D. Mickle, *Many a mickle* (Melb, 1953); *Table Talk*, 22 July 1892; *Australasian*, 20 Nov 1897; *Argus*, 2 Aug 1902, 19 Jan 1916; H. G. Turner, Personal memorabilia (LaT L).   JILL EASTWOOD

TOPP, CHARLES ALFRED (1847-1932), educationist and civil servant, was born on 22 March 1847 at Huddersfield, Yorkshire, England, third son of Samuel Topp, merchant, and his wife Sarah, née Clapham. He arrived in Melbourne with his parents in the *Royal Charter* on 17 March 1858. He was educated at Melbourne Church of England Grammar School and the University of Melbourne (B.A., 1867; M.A., LL.B., 1869), and admitted to the Bar in 1869 but did not practise. In September he was appointed assistant inspector of schools under the Board of Education. On 1 January 1873 at a salary of £450 he became one of the first nine inspectors for the new department under the provisions of the 1872 Education Act. By 1884 he was senior inspector of schools and that year became superintendent of the Training Institution and principal of the Training College in Spring Street, taking up his duties in March 1885. At the end of 1889 the new residential Training College in Carlton was opened under his control.

As a metropolitan district inspector Topp had given evidence to the 1882-84 royal commission on public education; like most teachers he emerged as a cautious supporter of the payment by result system, though advocating a less rigid approach. In 1888 Topp and Inspector-General John Main were asked by C. H. Pearson [q.v.] to compare the efficiency of the school systems of South Australia, New South Wales and Victoria. They reported in March 1889 in a careful, even-handed way; in Pearson's view, it was 'a most searching investigation' and he used it in explaining subsequent legislation to replace the Victorian system by fixed salaries.

In January 1890 Topp became chairman of the reconstructed Board of Public Health, and in the next two decades won distinction as a versatile and efficient departmental head. In May 1894 he became under-secretary of the Chief Secretary's Department. He supervised parliamentary elections and was also returning officer for Victoria for elections in 1897 to the Australasian Federal Convention, for the referenda on the draft Constitution bill in 1898 and 1899, and for the Commonwealth general elections in 1901. He served at various times as commissioner of audit and in 1901 was a member of the Public Service Board; under the provisions of the Audit and Public Service Acts of 1901 he became in January 1902 the first public service commissioner in Victoria. He was awarded the Imperial Service Order in 1903. After his retirement on 30 April 1908 he continued to serve until 1917 on the Indeterminate Sentences Board in Melbourne and on wages boards.

Topp was also warden of the Senate of the University of Melbourne in 1886-90 and member of council in 1890-96; he was active in the 1880s in the foundation of a chair in biology and in the establishment of degrees in science. His interest in the natural sciences was practical as well as promotional. In 1887 he was elected a fellow of the Linnean Society of London on the nomination of F. von Mueller [q.v.]. He was president of the Field Naturalists' Club of Victoria in 1889-91, gave papers on natural history subjects and was a member of the committee of the Royal Society of Victoria in 1889-92 and of its associated Port Phillip Biological Survey Committee, active in 1887. He also contributed to the *Melbourne Review*.

At South Yarra on 25 July 1877 Topp had married Euphemia Shields, and became brother-in-law to R. L. J. Ellery and P. H. MacGillivray [qq.v.]. He died at East Malvern on 13 July 1932 of cerebral thrombosis and was buried in the Boroondara cemetery, survived by his wife and a daughter and predeceased by three daughters and a son. His estate was valued for probate at £3400.

A. Sutherland et al, *Victoria and its metropolis*, 2 (Melb, 1888); E. Sweetman, *History of the Melbourne Teachers' College and its predecessors* (Melb, 1939); Education Dept (Vic), *Vision and realisation*, L. J. Blake ed (Melb, 1973); *Weekly Times* (Melb), 5 May 1894; *Australasian*, 4 Dec 1897; *Age*, 14 July 1932; *Argus*, 14 July 1932; *Bulletin*, 20 July 1932.

PETER GILL

TORPY, JAMES (1832-1903), miner and hotel-keeper, was born at Fermoy, County Cork, Ireland, son of James Torpy, miller, and his wife Jane, née Mortimer. He worked in Manchester and Liverpool before sailing for Victoria in 1853. After a time at the goldfields he went to New South Wales and mined successfully at Turon (Sofala).

Torpy was a hotel-keeper at Lambing Flat (Young) in 1861 when the anti-Chinese riots broke out. As a leader of the Miners' Protection League he addressed a meeting in March 1861 that was called to explain the miners' position to the premier (Sir) Charles Cowper [q.v.]. Stating that 'the instinct of self-preservation impels us to oppose their coming here', Torpy argued that if the Chinese were allowed to flood on to the diggings the Europeans would be forced off and the gold quickly exhausted. In July he was chosen as miners' delegate to present a petition to Governor Sir John Young, but while in Sydney was arrested on 5 August and charged with riot, unlawful assembly and wilful destruction of Chinese property on 30 June at Burrangong; denying the allegations, he was allowed bail and appeared in the Burrangong court. The charges were dismissed as the prosecution's witnesses could not be found.

At the time of Torpy's defence of miners' rights, he lost much support when a mining claim in which he was principal shareholder was sold to some Chinese. He was accused of acknowledging the right of the Chinese to work on the field. In a letter to the *Miner and General Advertiser* he asserted that he had not been inconsistent and that he 'would rather make a profit out of an enemy than a friend'.

On 3 June 1862 Torpy married Isabella Jane Walwyn at St Saviour's Church of England, Goulburn. He then lived at Forbes before going to Orange where, by 1867, he was licensee of the Commercial Hotel and later of the Wellington Inn. In 1876 he retired from the hotel business, visited Ireland and, on his return to Orange, became a wine and spirits merchant. He was elected alderman in 1878 and was mayor of Orange

in 1879 and 1880. While mayor he became acquainted with Sir Henry Parkes [q.v.] who supported his attempt in 1882 to enter the Legislative Assembly, but he was defeated by Thomas Dalton. In 1884 he became a guarantor of the *Western Daily Advocate* and proprietor in 1886. He was an active member of the Provincial Press Association.

Torpy represented Orange in 1889-94 in the Legislative Assembly as a protectionist. In 1890 he opposed Federation as unnecessary but by 1901 favoured Orange as the site for the federal capital. In July 1894 he was one of those nominated to the Legislative Council by Sir George Dibbs [q.v.] but was rejected by Governor Duff.

An original member of the Athenaeum Club, Torpy was vice-president of the Orange Jockey Club, president of the Central Western Rugby Football Union, a director of the Orange Permanent Building Society and president of the Orange Mechanics' School of Arts. He belonged to the Orange Volunteer Rifle Corps. He continued to write for his newspaper until a few days before he died in Sydney on 22 June 1903 of broncho-pneumonia. Buried in the Church of England cemetery, Orange, he was survived by his wife, four daughters and four sons.

V&P (LA NSW), 1861-62, 1, 809, 1871-72, 2, 335; P. A. Selth, 'The Burrangong (Lambing Flat) riots 1860-61: a closer look', *JRAHS*, 60 (1974), *and* 'James Torpy and the "Engine Claim"', RAHS, *Newsletter*, Jan 1975; *SMH*, 28 Oct, 1 Nov 1880, 23 June 1903; *Sydney Mail*, 30 Aug 1890; *Bulletin*, 2 July 1903; *T&CJ*, 24 June, 1 July 1903; *Central Western Daily*, 27 July 1967; G.C.J., 'Some recollections of James Torpy', newspaper cuttings (ML); Parkes letters (ML); CO 201/615.

DEIRDRE MORRIS

TORRANCE, GEORGE WILLIAM (1835-1907), clergyman, organist and composer, was born at Rathmines, Dublin, son of George Torrance, master tailor, and his wife Elizabeth, née Flinn. A chorister at Christ Church Cathedral, Dublin, he attended its grammar and music schools and studied piano and organ. As a young man he was organist at several Dublin churches and at 19 he composed his first oratorio, 'Abraham', and conducted it with great success at its first performance in Dublin in 1855. In 1856 he went to Leipzig for further musical studies and on his return wrote an opera, 'William of Normandy', and in 1859 a second oratorio, 'The Captivity'. That year he entered Trinity College, Dublin, to study for the Church of England ministry (B.A., 1864; M.A., 1867; Mus.B., Mus.D., 1879).

Ordained deacon in 1865 and priest next year, he held curacies at Shrewsbury, England, and in Dublin before deciding to join his brother in Victoria.

Torrance arrived at Williamstown in the *Thomas Stephens* on 15 December 1869. He was appointed to Christ Church, South Yarra, in February 1870 and next year became acting curate at St John's, La Trobe Street. In 1872 he was appointed acting principal of Trinity College, later affiliated with the University of Melbourne, which was opened in February. On 19 November he married Annie Julia Vaughan, daughter of a solicitor; they lived at the college until February 1876 supervising the few students then in residence. Torrance continued at St John's until 1877 when he was appointed to All Saints, Geelong. He was at Holy Trinity, Balaclava, from 1878 to 1895, when the permanent church was built to J. Reed's [q.v.] design and a fine three-manual organ, built by G. Fincham [q.v.], was installed. Torrance also acted as organist in 1880-82, donating his fee to the organ fund.

In December 1879 Torrance was admitted D.Mus. (*ad eund.*), at the University of Melbourne, the first degree in music conferred by the university. On 27 June 1882 his third oratorio, *The Revelation* (Novello & Co. Ltd, 1899), was first performed in the Melbourne Town Hall. He visited Europe with his wife and daughter in 1886-87. Appointed an examiner of music teachers to the Education Department in 1888, with Dr S. McBurney [q.v.] he became a temporary inspector of singing in February 1892 to replace Dr J. Summers [q.v.], but his services were only briefly required. Torrance was among the finest composers of the period; his works include numerous hymns and anthems, a chant book, and many songs and madrigals. In November 1880 as president of the Fine Arts section he addressed the Social Science Congress, Melbourne, on music; he was an adjudicator at musical competitions and an examiner to the Royal College of Music for the (W. J.) Clarke [q.v.] scholarships. In 1888 he formed the choir for the new St Paul's Cathedral and in 1896 was elected a fellow, *honoris causa*, of the Guild of Church Musicians, London. With Fincham he also advised on organbuilding for many churches in Victoria. In 1874 he was on the first committee of the Victorian Humane Society, and in the 1890s was prominent in the foundation of the Anti-sweating League. He was remembered as possessing 'much personal charm, and many lovable qualities'.

In 1895 Torrance returned to St John's, but in May 1897 his third and last surviving child died, aged 17, and on 12 October he and his wife left for Europe. Instead of returning as planned they settled in Ireland, where he was appointed chaplain to the bishop of Ossory and bishop's vicar choral at St Canice's Cathedral, Kilkenny; in 1900 he was made a canon, and was also cathedral librarian. Aged 72, he died at St Canice's Library on 20 August 1907, three days after his wife. A memorial service for him was held in Trinity College Chapel, Melbourne, on 29 August. There are tablets to his memory at the college and at Holy Trinity, Balaclava.

J. D. Brown and S. Stratton, *British musical biography* (Birmingham, 1879); A. Sutherland et al, *Victoria and its metropolis*, 2 (Melb, 1888); J. B. Cooper, *The history of St Kilda* (Melb, 1931); E. Blom (ed), *Grove's dictionary of music and musicians*, 5th ed (Lond, 1954); E. N. Matthews, *Colonial organs and organbuilders* (Melb, 1969); J. A. Grant (ed), *Perspective of a century ... Trinity College* (Melb, 1972); E. A. C. Farran, 'Dr George William Torrance', *VHM*, 39 (1968); *Musical Herald*, Apr 1892, May 1898; *Musical Times*, Nov 1899, Sept 1907; *Table Talk*, 8 Nov 1889; *IAN*, 1 Feb 1890.
         ROBIN S. STEVENS

TORREGGIANI, ELZEAR (ALOYSIUS) (1830-1904), Catholic bishop, was born on 28 May 1830 at Porto Recanati near Loreto, Marchian Province of Ancona, Italy, youngest son of Vincenzo Antonio Torregiani and his wife Margarita Francesca, née Osimani. Baptized Aloysius, he was educated by the Jesuits at Loreto; hoping in vain to enter their Order, on 20 October 1846 he joined the Order of St Francis at the Capuchin monastery of Camerino in Umbria. Professed on 20 October 1846, he received the name Elzear and later studied philosophy and theology at Ancona, where he was ordained priest on 23 May 1853. Volunteering for the foreign missions, he was surprised to be sent to England: 'I knew it must be the will of God, because there was none of my own in it'.

In June 1856 Torreggiani reached Peckham, London, but was soon sent to assist in founding a friary at Pantasaph, North Wales, where he helped to begin missions in Flint, Mold and Holyhead. In 1860 he took charge of the mission at Pontypool and organized the building of the monastery and a large school; in 1876-79 he was guardian of Peckham friary where his success as a missioner and as an administrator came to the notice of Archbishop Vaughan [q.v.], who wanted a replacement who was neither English nor Irish for Bishop O'Mahony [q.v.].

On 3 March 1879 Torreggiani was consecrated bishop of Armidale and after a visit to Rome reached Sydney in the *Avoca* on 8 November 1879 accompanied by five Capuchin priests. His huge diocese of some 10,000 Catholics was served by only nine priests and two schools and his first pastoral visitation of over 40,000 miles took three years. Jovial, kindly, black-bearded and weighing twenty-one stone, he became known in every hamlet. He brought harmony and organization to his diocese, but on Christmas Day 1884 as he was about to celebrate Mass, a road-worker named Mc-Cafferty tried first to stab him, then fired a revolver shot through his vestments; after falling he continued the service.

In 1881 Torreggiani established Mother Mary McKillop's [q.v.] Sisters of St Joseph at Tenterfield and successfully defended their power of central government against the Irish bishops at the 1885 Plenary Council. In 1882 he invited the Ursuline Sisters and in 1887 the Mercy nuns to start schools. By 1885 he had spent £60,000 on new buildings. Grafton became a separate diocese in 1887; by 1904 he had nineteen priests, seventeen schools, and many handsome buildings.

Torreggiani died at Armidale of pulmonary thrombosis and heart disease on 28 January 1904, and was buried in the Catholic cemetery. Dedicated to a life of poverty, his debts exceeded his assets by £130. His vicar-general and coadjutor from 1903, Patrick Joseph O'Connor, claimed that he had lived in the same house with Torreggiani for twenty-five years and had 'seen him under circumstances that would almost tempt a saint, yet I never saw him once ruffled'.

P. F. Moran, *History of the Catholic Church in Australasia* (Syd, 1895); *Analecta Ordinis Minorum Capuccinorum*, 20 (1904); *Franciscan Annals and Monthly Bulletin* (Lond), Aug 1879; *Armidale Express*, 5 May 1885; E. J. Doody, History of the diocese of Armidale (Roman Catholic Archives, Armidale); Archives, Congregation for the Propagation of the Faith (Rome); Roman Catholic Archives (Syd).   C. J. DUFFY

TORRENS, SIR ROBERT RICHARD (1814-1884), public servant, politician and land titles law reformer, was born in Cork, Ireland, son of Colonel Robert Torrens [q.v.] and his first wife Charity Herbert, née Chute. Educated at Trinity College, Dublin (B.A., 1835), in 1836 he became a landing waiter in the Port of London. In 1839 he married Barbara Ainslie, widow of George Augustus Anson and niece of Mungo Park. On 12 December 1840 in the *Brightman* they arrived in South Australia; Torrens became collector of customs, probably through his father's influence as chairman of the colonization commission for

South Australia; his salary was £350 (later £500). He lived handsomely, yet within a few years had acquired substantial assets.

Torrens soon established a pattern of unorthodoxy in his office. In his first year he was censured for reducing wharfage rates without authority, for carelessness with pay lists, for unauthorized absence and for not supporting some of Governor Grey's policies. Grey reported that Torrens had not shown that 'cheerful acquiescence in my views which I have received from the other Government officers'. In 1841 controversy surrounded Torrens's arrest of the *Ville de Bordeaux* when he became involved in an extravagant chase to prevent her escape. But he probably acted correctly, for in November the vessel was forfeited to the Crown though the Treasury later had to compensate the French owners.

Torrens was often censured for irregularities. In 1845 he was sued successfully by crew members of the *Hanseat* for false imprisonment, and in 1848 was involved indirectly in a pitched battle fought for control of the *Emma Sherratt* and directly in libel actions arising therefrom. He was reprimanded the same year for discourtesy to the advocate-general for declining the advocate's help in a legal action; the advocate-general declared that it was a pleasure to be relieved of the duty. His chief clerk Henry Watson complained about him to the English authorities but a board of inquiry neither condemned nor cleared him. George Stevenson [q.v.] lampooned this result and Torrens assaulted him in the street; lengthy civil and criminal proceedings ended with Torrens paying £250 damages, being convicted of common assault, but 'winning' a libel verdict of one farthing damages. He was appointed colonial treasurer and registrar-general in 1852, and in these offices, too, he was often censured by the governor. In 1851-57 he was a nominated member of the Legislative Council and he became a member of the Executive Council in 1855. Next year he joined in the land titles registration crusade.

The *South Australian Register* published an outline of a Torrens bill on 17 October 1856. Other bills were being publicized, indicating that the development of registration of title to land was not Torrens's achievement alone but the culmination of an evolutionary process. Intense interest was generated, for in South Australia titles were in an unsatisfactory state and, as he put it, land was no longer 'the luxury of the few', therefore 'thorough land reform ... [was] essentially "the people's question"'. He stood for Adelaide in the House of Assembly elections of 1857 and, almost entirely because of his espousal of land titles reform, topped the poll. Treasurer from 24 October 1856 to 21 August 1857, he published a further draft of his bill on 14 and 15 April and introduced it as a private member's bill in yet a third form on 4 June. He was premier from 1 to 30 September, but no action was taken on the bill until 11 November, when the second reading was carried. Despite very strong opposition, mainly from the legal profession, it passed through both Houses and was assented to on 27 January 1858.

The basic principles of what was to become known outside South Australia as the Torrens system were: land titles no longer passed by the execution of deeds but by the registration of dealings on a public register; once registered the title of a purchaser became indefeasible unless he was guilty of fraud; and innocent dealers with interests in registered land were guaranteed either their interest in the land or monetary compensation therefor. Torrens explained the system's operation in *The South Australian System of Conveyancing by Registration of Title* (1859); although he 'claimed authorship' of the system, it is clear that many people and influences helped considerably, including Ulrich Hübbe, R. B. Andrews, G. F. Angas, Anthony Forster, W. H. Burford, and, later, R. D. Hanson [qq.v.]. Torrens conceded the significance of the opportune arrival 'on the eve of the day appointed for the [bill's] second reading' of the report of the English royal commissioners, 1857, which recommended the adoption of registration of title to land in England.

Torrens resigned his seat in 1858 on becoming registrar-general under the Real Property Act at a salary of £1000. From that year to 1862 he helped to turn the Act into a workable and working system, manipulating public opinion and organizing meetings and petitions to parliament. He also travelled to other colonies successfully advocating the adoption of the system. These endeavours in 'the Cause', as Torrens so often calls it in his writings, undermined his health and amid enthusiastic farewells he sailed for England on leave without pay.

He lectured on the system in England, Scotland and Ireland in the next three years and vacillated about returning to South Australia. When nominated as a candidate for the borough of Cambridge in 1865, Torrens resigned as registrar-general; failing to be elected that year and also the next, he complained bitterly about 'intimidation practised by Heads of the Colleges' and bribery which turned voters against him. He won the seat in 1868. He had entered politics in England largely to sponsor his titles system; but despite some slight success in Ireland, the South Australian methods could not be applied because land holding was not 'the people's question' in England.

Torrens largely withdrew from public life when he was not re-elected in 1874 and, although he continued as a director of several companies, spent most of his time at his country home, Hannaford, near Ashburton. He was created K.C.M.G. for his services 'especially in connection with the Registration of Titles to Land Act' in 1872 and was made G.C.M.G. in 1884. Leaving personal estate sworn for probate at £17,292, he died of pneumonia at Falmouth on 31 August 1884, aged 70, and was buried in Leusdon churchyard on the edge of Dartmoor. His wife (d. 1899) is buried with him.

Despite his tempestuous career in South Australia Torrens was not quite the charlatan that Governor Daly called him. He had a propensity for arousing animosity and sometimes undying hatred. When the attorney-general (Sir) William Bundey [q.v.] moved in the House of Assembly in 1880 that a pension of £500 should be granted to him chaos broke out in the House. After bitter personal attacks on Torrens the proposal was dropped. He had been happy to use the full pressure of public opinion to achieve land titles reform, but he opposed an elected legislature and the secret ballot. The mainspring of the last thirty years of his life was his espousal of land titles reform. He did not acknowledge publicly the assistance that he received, but it was his dedication, bordering on zealotry, for 'the Cause' that initiated the Real Property Act in South Australia and the spread of the Torrens system to other Australasian colonies. It has sufficient identifying features to be regarded as an important legal reform that is indigenous to Australia.

There is a portrait in the National Gallery of South Australia, Adelaide, and a fine drawing by C. Hill in the South Australian State Archives.

D. J. Whalan, 'The origins of the Torrens System and its establishment in S.A.', Law Council of Aust, *Souvenir ... XIV Convention in Adelaide* (Adel, 1967); D. J. Whalan, 'The origins of the Torrens System and its introduction into New Zealand', G. W. Hinde (ed), *The New Zealand Torrens System centennial essays* (Wellington, 1971); R. Mitchell, 'The Torrens System of land titles—its development in the land of its birth', *Cwlth and Empire Law Conference Record*, 1 (1955); D. Pike, 'Introduction of the Real Property Act in South Australia', *Adelaide Law Review*, 1 (1960); D. J. Whalan, 'Immediate success of registration of title to land in Australasia and early failures in England', *NZ Universities Law Review*, 2 (1967).

DOUGLAS J. WHALAN

TOWN, ANDREW (1840-1890), stud-breeder, was born on 7 March 1840 at Richmond, New South Wales, son of William Town, squatter, and his wife Mary Ann, née Durham, both of whom were born in the colony. He was educated at the Church of England school, Richmond, and at Rev. Matthew Adam's Presbyterian school at Windsor. In the 1860s with his father he held three runs on the Liverpool Plains and one in the Bligh District. On 8 July 1863 at Richmond he married Emma Susannah Onus, a member of an old Hawkesbury family; he lived on the corner of Windsor and Paget streets, Richmond, where much of his stud was housed; he also had extensive stables at Clarendon.

Interested from an early age in racing and breeding, in 1868 Town inherited his father's sire, Tarragon, winner in 1866 of the Australasian Champion Stakes at Flemington after a dead heat with John Tait's [q.v.] Volunteer. In 1871 Rosebud carried his colours of red jacket and black cap to victory in the Metropolitan and Sir William dead-heated in the Doncaster Handicap. In 1878 he won the Australian Jockey Club St Leger Stakes with Cap-a-pie. The previous year he had bought Hobartville where he bred pedigreed Hereford, Devon and Ayrshire cattle, Berkshire pigs, draught and carriage horses, ponies and trotters as well as his celebrated thoroughbred racehorses. Without equal as a judge of horse-flesh, he had 130 blood and 40 draught mares and imported many mares and stallions. His sires included colonial-bred Maribyrnong and the unbeaten Grand Flaneur. His most successful mare was The Fawn whose yearlings sold for a total of 12,701 guineas; her colt Segenhoe by Maribyrnong was sold to James White [q.v.] for 2000 guineas. In 1882 Town imported the much-travelled American trotting stallion, Childe Harold, in whose memory Harold Park, Sydney, is named.

From 1879 he held annual yearling sales 'under the oaks' at Hobartville with T. S. Clibborn [q.v.] as auctioneer. They reached their zenith in the 1880s: special trains were run from Sydney for the racing fraternity; Governor Carrington often attended with his suite; free luncheon and liquid refreshments were provided for all in a huge marquee seating 300. In 1886 ninety-two pedigreed thoroughbreds, trotters and draughthorses realized over 13,000 guineas.

A magistrate from 1866, Town was a councillor of the Agricultural Society of New South Wales, sheep director for Windsor in 1873-89, a trustee of St Peter's Church of England, Richmond, a director of the original Richmond Bridge Co., a committeeman and judge of the Australian Jockey Club, a founder of the Hawkesbury District Agricultural Association and president in 1879-89, founding chairman of the Hawkesbury Race Club in 1882-89 and judge of the Sydney Turf Club, the Hawkesbury, Warwick Farm and Canterbury Park race clubs.

A lavish host, large-hearted with warm sympathies, Town was no businessman; late in 1889 his mortgagees W. A. Long [q.v.] and George Hill junior foreclosed. On 4 January 1890 the Hawkesbury Race Club and the A.J.C. held a complimentary race meeting for him at Randwick and £1830 was donated to his wife 'for her sole separate use'. Heart-broken at the loss of his patrimony and Hobartville, Town died of typhoid fever at Rockdale on 10 February and was buried in the family vault at St Peter's, Richmond. He was survived by his wife, four sons and six daughters. The Bulletin claimed that if 'all men connected with horse racing were as straight and true as was Andrew Town the turf would indeed be the sport of Kings and not a mere spider's web'. However, his liabilities exceeded his assets, valued for probate at £91,233, by over £15,000; £84,714 was owing to Long and Hill. Town's portrait is in the Hawkesbury Museum at Windsor.

W. F. Morrison, *The Aldine centennial history of New South Wales*, 2 (Syd, 1888); N. Gould, *The double event* (Lond, 1891); D. M. Barrie, *The Australian bloodhorse* (Syd, 1956); *SMH*, 4 Jan, 11 Feb 1890; *Windsor and Richmond Gazette*, 4 Jan, 15 Feb 1890; *Bulletin*, 15 Feb 1890; V. Cox, Hobartville, N.S.W. (ML); Newspaper cuttings, vol 92 (ML).

D. G. Bowd

TOWNS, ROBERT (1794-1873), merchant and entrepreneur, was born on 10 November 1794 in Long Horsley, Northumberland, England, son of Edward Towns and his wife Ann, née Pyle (Ryle). He had little formal education and was apprenticed to the master of a collier out of North Shields. Determined to improve his position in life, he studied navigation at night when his ship was in port. At 17 he became a mate and within two years had command of a brig in the Mediterranean trade. In 1827 he arrived in Sydney in the *Bona Vista* with a general cargo and in 1832 he brought out his own ship, the *Brothers*; in 1839 he bought the *Royal Saxon*. In 1832-42 he made a voyage to Sydney almost every year, each time staying briefly to seek profitable investments and buy property. On 28 December 1833 at St Phillip's Church, Sydney, Towns married Sophia, the 17-year-old half-sister of W. C. Wentworth [q.v.], who had arrived in the *Brothers* that year.

On 9 March 1843 Towns arrived in the

Seahorse via Launceston to settle in Sydney; his wife and son followed in the *Royal Saxon* in June 1844. He was authorized to represent Robert Brooks & Co., London, in the colony and soon established himself as a mercantile agent. He told Brooks, 'I am thinking of investing any means I have in small vessels for the Colonial Trade', and in 1844 he bought the *Elizabeth*. He sent her to the New Hebrides for sandalwood and she arrived in China with a full cargo to profit by a rise in prices. That year he bought 'Jones's wharf' and moved to Miller's Point; he worked every day from 6 a.m. to 6 or 7 p.m.—'as regular as the platipus', he said—for the next twenty years, supervising multifarious enterprises, and sending explosive letters to his captains, agents and business associates all over the world.

Towns's ships went to New Caledonia, the Loyalty Islands and the New Hebrides for sandalwood and trepang; by 1850 he had established a depot at the Isle of Pines near New Caledonia, where it was collected, prepared for the market and stored for transport to China. Anxious to reduce competition, from 1856 he combined with Captain James Paddon in a relationship of mutual respect and dislike; they also supplied the new French colony of New Caledonia and brought in settlers. In the 1850s Towns added to his stations in Melanesia and worked the Gilbert and Marshall islands for the collection of coconut-oil and turtle-shell. The high risks prevented insurance of his ships in Sydney and the market was unpredictable at the China ports; but he made his first substantial profits in the island trade and was able to invest them in more certain enterprises. By 1856 he employed ten whalers, though the industry had suffered much from the labour shortage of 'this infernal gold discovery'. He brought out labourers from England, Germany, India and China, and later Asians for other employers; he claimed that he had 'saved Moreton Bay from ruin' with Chinese.

Associated with the reorganization of the Bank of New South Wales, Towns was a director in 1850-55 and 1861-67 and its president in 1853-55 and 1866-67. By the 1850s he was a large landholder and his shipping business extended to Europe, the East and India. Agreeing that he had 'too many irons in the fire', by early 1855 he had taken (Sir) Alexander Stuart [q.v.] as a partner under the style of R. Towns & Co. He was a committee-man of the Sydney Chamber of Commerce for many years and president in 1856-57, 1863 and 1865. He was also a director of the Sydney Gold Escort Co. in the 1850s. A magistrate and member of the Pilot Board, he gave evidence to several

parliamentary select committees on marine matters and in the 1860s sat on the committee of the Sydney Bethel Union.

About 1856 Towns began a feud with W. C. Wentworth over his wife's share of the D'Arcy Wentworth [q.v.] patrimony. In 1858 the Privy Council upheld the Supreme Court's decision that her brother John's estate went to Wentworth, who refused to pay John's debts to Towns out of the disputed estate as Towns had put him to much legal expense. Towns filed a suit in chancery in 1860 on Sophia's original share of D'Arcy's estate.

In 1856 he had been one of the first (quinquennial) appointments to the Legislative Council. Towns defended the mercantile interest and was opposed to 'democracy'. On 10 May 1861 he resigned in support of the president Sir William Burton [q.v.]. In 1858-60 he visited England, and in 1859 served on a London committee to help E. C. Merewether [q.v.] negotiate a steam postal service between Sydney and England. He was reappointed to the council in 1863.

Towns dismayed Stuart with his expansion of interests, especially in Queensland. One of the subscribers to George Dalrymple's [q.v.] 1859 expedition in the far north, in the 1860s Towns took up land on the Darling Downs, along the Brisbane and Logan rivers and then vast areas in north Queensland. He foreclosed on pastoralists, often retaining them as managers, and leased properties in 'unsettled districts'. By 1867 he held 42 runs, amounting to almost 2000 square miles in the North and South Kennedy districts alone; 94 runs in partnership with Stuart, including over 1200 square miles in the Burke District, and 60 with Stuart and (Sir) Charles Cowper [q.v.], including nearly 400 square miles in the Warrego District.

In England Towns had discussed the prospects of growing cotton. On his return he undertook a project on 1280 acres on the Logan, but believed it would never pay 'with labour at the rate of Colonial Wages'. In May 1861 he gave (Sir) Henry Parkes [q.v.] letters of introduction to English cotton interests, hoping to attract immigrants. In May 1863 Towns sent the schooner *Don Juan* to get Melanesian labourers; the captain had a letter seeking the co-operation of missionaries. The first shipload of seventy-three islanders arrived in August; many of them had already worked for him in the islands. He had provided contracts for them for up to twelve months, with wages of 10s. a month with food and housing, and a provision that they should be repatriated if they wished.

Towns failed in his bid to get the support of 'the Exeter Hall Mob', but continued to import Melanesians despite an outburst in the press; he printed his instructions to the master of the *Don Juan* and his letter to the missionaries in his *South Sea Island Immigration for Cotton Culture* (Sydney, 1863). He failed to form a colony of islanders on his plantations as he could never induce married men to bring their wives. The Queensland Polynesian Labourers Act, 1868, convinced Towns that bureaucratic control had made islanders more expensive to employ than Europeans, although he was not opposed to proper safeguards. In evidence to the royal commission into the alleged kidnapping of natives of the Loyalty Islands in 1869, he advised that recruiting ships should be licensed, with 'a proper official ... duly accredited by the Government to prevent any abuses'; his suggestion was incorporated in regulations next year, and proved the most effective of the rules. Towns did not expect immediate gains from the cotton crop, but he hoped to do well by the bounty of £10 per bale payable in Queensland land orders. However, the cotton never made a profit and the bounty only saved the enterprise from ruin. In 1868 the Logan plantation showed a deficit of £5744.

At 70 Towns was urged to retire by Stuart, Brooks and other friends. But new enterprises were the stuff of life to him: in 1863 he had justified to Brooks a branch in Dunedin, New Zealand, as 'self-defence ... but you will I fear say I am *past warning*'. In partnership with J. M. Black he took up land on Cleveland Bay, Queensland, in 1865; by mid-year they had a woolstore, wharf and boiling-down works there and owned the adjoining land. Towns soon reported that the 'Government have paid me the compliment to call the town "Townsville"'. Disillusioned with cotton, he now concentrated on Townsville and his Queensland stations, envisaging his own ships carrying his own wool out of his own harbour.

With J. G. Macdonald and (Sir) John Robertson [q.v.] Towns also took up and stocked stations on the Gulf of Carpentaria. They founded Burketown on the Albert River in 1865, dreaming of a flourishing port closer to the world markets than those of the older colonies. That year Towns & Co. dispatched the first vessel from Sydney to the Albert, the *Jacmel Packet*, with a strange cargo of pigs, dogs, fowls, horses, building materials, drays, rations and rum for the founders of Burketown.

By mid-1865 Towns had conceded a little to his friends by moving to Cranbrook, Rose Bay, bought from Robert Tooth [q.v.]: he grumbled that 'I suppose I shall [settle] down to it but it is a monster effort'. That

year he was elected a member of the Union Club; an early member of the Royal Sydney Yacht Squadron, he owned the *Nautilus*, the first steam yacht on Sydney Harbour. He continued working his old ships, against the advice of Stuart, who in 1871 grimly reported to Brooks that the firm was 'steadily working down the debt ... but it is grinding work'.

Towns suffered a stroke in 1870, but recovered and continued in active business. Soon after another stroke he died at Cranbrook on 11 April 1873 and was buried in the Balmain cemetery with Anglican rites, survived by his wife, two sons and three daughters. Leaving personal estate valued for probate at £74,000 he stipulated that his son Robert should be disinherited unless he conducted himself over the next five years 'in a sober reputable proper and becoming manner'. Daughter Sarah was also to lose her inheritance if either she or her children left the Church of England.

Towns was the incarnation of the puritan virtues of thrift, sobriety, industry and 'perseverance'. Bluff and peppery, with simple habits, he was respected by all for his honesty, reliability and especially for his energy and his 'never ending speculative spirit'. By many of his employees he was known as a cheese-parer, full of furious criticism for failure but few words of praise for success. 'A hard but a just master' was about the most flattering comment to come from an employee; it was one that would have pleased him.

Roy Com on alleged kidnapping of natives of the Loyalty Islands (Syd, 1869. Microfilm under Misc. Documents ML, *and* G1819 Roy Navy Aust Station NL); D. Shineberg, *They came for sandalwood* (Melb, 1967); Sel cttees on Asiatic labour *and* the proposed Nautical School, V&P (LC NSW), 1854, 2, 1855, 2, 1079; R. Brooks and Co. papers (ML); R. Towns *and* R. Towns & Co. papers (ML); Uncat MS 307 (ML); MS and printed cats (ML).

D. SHINEBERG

TOWNSEND, WILLIAM (1821-1882), politician, was born in the Borough of Southwark, London, son of John Townsend, carriage draftsman. For a time assistant to his brother, a potato salesman, he later took a post as a clerk in a hop warehouse. On 25 December 1852 at St Pancras he married Emma Slade. As steerage passengers in the Dutch *Fop Smit*, he and his wife and child arrived in South Australia on 2 August 1853. His wife died soon after their arrival and he later married Jane Hooper. At first employed as a salesman in a boot shop, Townsend later opened a business as a bootmaker until advised to become an auctioneer by F. J. Botting, who was 'struck by his smartness and ready wit'. He learned the trade with various firms, including J. M. Solomon [q.v.] & Co., F. J. Botting, and Neales [q.v.], Wickstead & Co., and later formed his own business, Townsend and Son.

Despite lack of education (he signed his marriage certificate with a mark), Townsend was a fluent and forcible speaker and a popular public lecturer. He was involved in politics from the beginning of responsible government, having helped to frame the 1855 Constitution. He was mayor of Adelaide in 1864-66 and of Unley in 1878-81. An unsuccessful candidate for the Adelaide hills district of Onkaparinga in the colony's first election, he won the seat in a by-election on 23 December 1857 and held it until elected in 1870 for Sturt, which he represented until his death. Appointed commissioner of public works in the eleven-day F. S. Dutton [q.v.] ministry in 1863, he was commissioner of crown lands and immigration in the sixteen-day J. Hart [q.v.] ministry in 1868. That year he was called to form a government in a period of marked ministerial instability, but was unable to secure sufficient supporters. In 1870 he attended the Intercolonial Conference in Melbourne. Again holding the crown lands portfolio in the A. Blyth [q.v.] ministry of 1871-72, he initiated a survey of the Northern Territory. He was chairman of committees and acting Speaker in the assembly from 1872 until his death. A 'spirited ... advocate of Chartism in its milder form', he fought for many years for payment for members of parliament.

Townsend was a lay preacher in the Congregational Church. In 1869-71 he was a member of the board of management of Adelaide Hospital. He proposed an institution for the blind, deaf and dumb, worked for many years for its establishment in the suburb of Brighton and was chairman of its committee in 1875-82. Contemporary descriptions of him were epitomized by the view that 'he rose from humble rank to be one of the most influential and well-known men of the day'. Aged 61, he died of phthisis on 25 October 1882 at Mitcham, survived by his second wife, four daughters and three sons; his estate was valued for probate at £200. His portrait is held by the Adelaide City Council.

E. Hodder, *The history of South Australia* (Lond, 1893); PD (SA), 1882; *Observer* (Adel), 28 Oct, 4 Nov 1882.   DEAN JAENSCH

TRACY, RICHARD THOMAS (1826-1874), physician, was born on 19 September 1826 at Limerick, Ireland, son of Thomas Tracy, gentleman, and his wife Elizabeth, née Coghlan. He began his medical studies in 1845 in the Dublin School of Medicine and in 1848 graduated licentiate of the Royal College of Surgeons, Ireland. In December he was appointed to the Cholera Hospital, Glasgow, and in May 1849 took by examination the M.D., Glasgow, with honours. He practised briefly in King's County, Ireland, and at Reading, Berkshire, England, but, becoming uncertain of his future, he decided to migrate and South Australia was chosen on the toss of a coin. On 29 April 1851 he married his cousin Fanny Louisa Sibthorpe and on 16 May they left England in the *Ballangeich*, to which he was surgeon. They reached Melbourne on 20 August and soon sailed for Adelaide.

Tracy began practice in North Adelaide and befriended a schoolteacher James Bonwick [q.v.]. On news of the discovery of gold in Victoria, they formed a small party and left for Melbourne in February 1852. They first went to Forest Creek (Castlemaine) and then to Bendigo and had some success. Quickly tiring of the life, Tracy went back to Adelaide in June but soon returned to Melbourne with his wife and infant daughter; until 1864 he practised in Fitzroy, becoming its first health officer, a magistrate, and a trustee of St Mark's Church of England. Moving to Collins Street East, he became assistant surgeon to the East Melbourne Corps of Artillery, Victorian Volunteer Force, with the relative rank of lieutenant, captain in 1867.

An original and active member of the Victorian Medical Association, Tracy later joined the rival Medico Chirurgical Society of Victoria, and helped to unite these two bodies as the Medical Society of Victoria, of which he was president in 1860. He was one of the original committee that first published in 1856 the *Australian Medical Journal*. He was rapidly successful in his practice and with John Maund [q.v.] was medical co-founder in 1856 of the Melbourne Lying-in Hospital and Infirmary for Diseases of Women and Children (later the Royal Women's Hospital), to which he was appointed honorary physician for life. His work was more and more directed to obstetrics and gynaecology, and he became one of the outstanding figures in these specialities in Australia in the nineteenth century. He was admitted to the University of Melbourne (M.D. *ad eund.*, 1857) and in 1864 was appointed first lecturer in obstetric medicine and diseases of women and children at the university, at a salary of £100 with fees. He performed the first successful ovariotomy in Victoria in 1864 and quickly established an international reputation as a pioneer gynaecological surgeon. In 1871 he was elected an honorary fellow of the Obstetrical Society of London, a very great distinction, and two years later became a fellow of the Medico-Chirurgical Society of London. He visited Britain in 1873 and spent much time in London with the eminent surgeon Thomas Spencer Wells, whom he greatly admired.

Tracy's health, however, was deteriorating and returning to Melbourne in April 1874 he died on 7 November from an abdominal malignancy. He was survived by his wife and six of his seven daughters. He left an estate valued for probate at £24,000, including a valuable collection of books on medical and general subjects which was auctioned soon after his death. A marble bust of Tracy by Charles Summers [q.v.] is at the Royal Women's Hospital, Melbourne.

C. E. Sayers, *The Women's* (Melb, 1956); F. M. C. Forster, 'Richard Thomas Tracy and his part in the history of ovariotomy', *Aust and NZ J of Obstetrics and Gynaecology*, 4 (1964), no 3.   FRANK M. C. FORSTER

TRAILL, WILLIAM HENRY (1843-1902), public servant, journalist and politician, was born on 7 May 1843 in London, son of John Heddle Traill (1819-1847), customs clerk and Orkney islander, and his wife Eliza Dunbar, née Heddle. Educated for the Indian army in Edinburgh and London, he had by 1861 arrived in Queensland, where he was employed as a station-hand at Dalby. Two years later he visited the Westove (Westeve) estate in the Orkneys that he had inherited from his grandfather Thomas Traill (1790-1859), but it was so heavily encumbered that he returned to Queensland to manage Maroon station near Beaudesert. He moved to Ipswich and on 23 April 1866 at Brisbane he married Jessie, daughter of James Lewis. In 1866-67 he was a draftsman in the Victorian Department of Mines and in 1869-73 a clerk in the Queensland Department of Public Lands, where he worked under Gresley Lukin [q.v.].

Traill's real interest lay in journalism. While a public servant he contributed a column, 'Passing Thoughts', to the *Queensland Express*, which led to an appointment, again under Lukin, on the *Brisbane Courier* and the *Queenslander*, investigating 'dummying' on the Darling Downs. His interest in land administration was enduring: in 1877 his explanatory digest of the 1876 Lands Alienation Act was published by the Queensland government, and in New South Wales he was a member of the board of inquiry which in 1887 recommended re-

organization of the Lands Department. Briefly proprietor of the *Darling Downs Gazette*, he returned to the *Courier* and *Queenslander* until 1878, when he moved to Sydney to become editor of the *Sydney Mail* and began contributing to the *Sydney Morning Herald* and the *Echo*.

In 1880 Traill, now Reuter's agent in Sydney, became a leader-writer on the radical *Bulletin*. On 8 January 1881 its founders J. F. Archibald and John Haynes [qq.v.] published 'The Larrikin Residuum', Traill's sober attack on the behaviour of 'satyrs and bacchantes in soiled tweed suits and squalid finery' at Clontarf on New Year's Day. The proprietors of the picnic grounds wrote protesting their innocence, Haynes composed a cheeky rejoinder ('The Bulletin's Home Thrusts', 15 January) and thus ensued the Clontarf libel action and the imprisonment of Archibald and Haynes for failing to pay legal costs. Well before their incarceration in March 1882, Archibald and Haynes had handed over control to Traill and become salaried sub-editors. Appointed editor in June 1881, Traill by August was also proprietor and publisher; although he allowed Archibald and Haynes to purchase a quarter-share in the business when the Bulletin Newspaper Co. was constituted in 1883, he remained firmly in charge until he sold out in April 1886.

The Traill régime was a period of consolidation for the *Bulletin*. In the first year the task was mainly one of survival: Traill continued to write the editorials, churned out most of the pars that were packed into the 'Plain English' and other columns he instituted, and helped repair and run the machinery he bought and had installed at new premises in Pitt Street. As circulation slowly improved he guided the *Bulletin* in new directions, developing its nationalist and protectionist themes and giving it a slogan, 'Australia for the Australians', and a distinctive red cover. On trips to the United States of America and England he secured the services of its most famous black and white artists, Livingston Hopkins and Philip May [qq.v.]. Inevitably there were set-backs: sales fell for a time when the price was increased to 6d. Haynes left after disputes with Traill over economic policy, and Hopkins more than once threatened resignation when Traill tried to 'improve' the new processes of reproducing illustrations that he had brought back from America. But by the time he left to go into politics, his boundless energy had saved the *Bulletin*: he had changed it from a smart Sydney weekly into a magazine with broad national appeal and set it on its way to becoming the legendary 'Bushman's Bible'. Without minimizing the contribution of

Archibald, A. G. Stephens and James Edmond to the phenomenal success of the *Bulletin* in subsequent decades, it was Traill, Stephens claimed, who 'made the paper' by turning 'an insolvent concern into a thriving business'. Traill also introduced into the management William Macleod, another sober Scot whose heavy ballast helped sustain and restrain Archibald.

Traill's subsequent career was something of an anti-climax. After two failures to enter parliament he topped the poll in South Sydney in 1889. Although a committed protectionist he took an independent and idealistic line on most other questions and never achieved ministerial rank. Defeated in 1894, he failed in various farming and mining ventures and was declared bankrupt in April 1896: his creditors included Archibald and Macleod. On his discharge in August he returned to Queensland and worked on a variety of journalistic assignments; among other commissions he prepared *A Queenly Colony: Pen Sketches and Camera Glimpses* (Brisbane, 1901). He died of heart disease in Brisbane on 21 May 1902 and was buried in the South Brisbane cemetery. On 11 March 1871 at Brisbane he had married Agnes Lewis, half-sister of his first wife; she survived him, together with their four sons and two daughters, and the daughter of his first marriage.

As a leader-writer Traill was able but ponderous; his prose exhibited the fundamental seriousness of his character and suited his imposing manner. He gave an impression of largeness: ruggedly built, with enormous eyebrows and a black beard, he habitually wore a tam-o-shanter perched precariously on his head as he hurled 'Jovian thunderbolts' through teeth clenched around a coarse cigar. Although he struck terror into the hearts of flippant poets scrounging a handout from the *Bulletin*, he was warm and generous towards those whom he trusted. His *Bulletin* friends remembered him with affection and his parliamentary colleagues respected him as a man of principle—a 'model of propriety', as Sir Henry Parkes [q.v.] put it, 'in language and the graces of oratory'.

W. Traill, *A genealogical account of the Traills of Orkney* (Kirkwall, 1883); D. J. Hopkins, *Hop of the 'Bulletin'* (Syd, 1929); A. C. Macleod, *Macleod of 'The Bulletin'* (Syd, 1931); V&P (LA Vic), 1868, 2, 51 (LA Qld), 1871, 513, 1874, 2, 250 (LA NSW), 1887, 2, 57; A. G. Thomson, 'The early history of the *Bulletin*', *Hist Studies*, no 22, May 1954; *Bulletin*, 1880-86, 31 May 1902, 29 Jan 1930; *Sydney Mail*, 10 Jan 1880, 31 May 1902; *Daily Telegraph* (Syd), 14 June 1894; *Newsletter* (Syd), 15 Apr-16 Dec 1905; 'The genesis of the *Bulletin*', *Lone Hand*, May-Dec 1907; MS cat under Traill (ML); Bankruptcy papers 10,787/7 (NSWA).

                     B. G. ANDREWS

TRAIN, GEORGE FRANCIS (1829-1904), merchant and entrepreneur, was born on 24 March 1829 at Boston, Massachusetts, United States of America, son of Oliver Train and his wife Maria, née Pickering. His parents and three sisters died in a yellow fever epidemic in New Orleans in 1833 and he was raised in Waltham, Massachusetts, by his maternal grandparents, who were staunch Methodists. Train remained a lifelong total abstainer from alcohol and tobacco. From the age of 16 he worked in Boston and Liverpool with the White Diamond Line of Enoch Train, his father's cousin, and gained experience of both American and English commerce. On 5 October 1851 he married a Southern belle Wilhelmina Wilkinson Davis; on 23 May 1853 they arrived in Melbourne in the *Bavaria*.

The flamboyant Train was representative in many ways of the scores of American merchants attracted to Australia by the gold rushes. Melbourne partly owes its nineteenth-century reputation for being Americanized to men like him and his partner Ebenezer Caldwell, a respectable New England sea captain. As few left any account of their experiences, the letters that Train wrote to American newspapers are of much value, revealing the refreshingly different reactions of an American republican to Australian conditions. He and Caldwell generated enthusiasm for the Melbourne Chamber of Commerce and the Exchange and continually stressed the need for more public and private enterprise. Train wrote several reports for the chamber; he drafted its motion in favour of the unrestricted entry of Chinese; and with other Americans he promoted a land policy modelled on United States principles. He usually eschewed politics and, despite persistent rumours to the contrary, his eloquent advocacy of the virtues of republicanism was reserved for Independence Day speeches and for his American readers.

By putting substantial warehouses at each end of the new railway from Sandridge to Flinders Street, Caldwell, Train & Co. made it easier for passengers of the White Star Line of Liverpool, for which they were agents, to transfer themselves and their luggage from port to city. The partners were prominent in organizing a volunteer fire brigade; they imported clothing, guns, flour, building materials, patent medicines, mining tools, coaches and carts, wagons and buggies. After Caldwell left Melbourne in the *Red Jacket* in August 1854 the firm, now G. F. Train & Co., continued to make money and traded until 1858. The *Argus* credited Train's 'energy, spirit and restless activity' with 'stirring up a spirit of emulation' among Victorian merchants and so succeeding in 'vitalising our whole commercial system'. C. S. Ross remembered him in those days as 'full of indomitable energy, faultlessly dressed, always swinging an elegant cane in his hand; his jaunty air, breezy manner, and genial volubility made him a general favorite'.

Train's wife returned to Boston in 1854 and gave birth to a daughter. He decided to rejoin her and left Melbourne in early November next year, travelling by way of the Orient and the Middle East. His accounts of the trip were sent to the New York *Herald*, were published in 1857 with his Australian letters as *An American Merchant in Europe, Asia, and Australia . . .*, and were so well received that Freeman Hunt of the *Merchants' Magazine* sent him to Europe to report on economic and social conditions. In 1859 in New York he published *Spread-Eagleism*, which included speeches he had made at banquets in Melbourne. In the next few years Train established horse-drawn tramways in Birkenhead and London and played an elusive role in the financing of the Atlantic and Great Western Railroad and the Union Pacific in the United States. His noisy support of the American Union harmed his English enterprises. In 1870 he went on a second world trip which he claimed gave Jules Verne the model for *Around the World in Eighty Days*. Insolvent at 47 and his presidential ambitions unsupported, he turned to lecturing as his main source of income.

Train's enthusiastic pursuit of 'causes', ranging from Fenianism to women's suffrage, resulted in several imprisonments in Britain and America. 'Ubiquitous and irrepressible' he toured the world again in 1890 and 1892. His wife, from whom he had lived apart since 1872, predeceased him in 1879. He died in New York on 18 January 1904, two years after publishing *My Life in Many States and in Foreign Lands*. He was survived by three of his four children.

W. Thornton, *The nine lives of Citizen Train* (New York, 1948); G. F. Train, *A Yankee merchant in goldrush Australia: the letters of George Francis Train 1853-55*, E. D. and A. Potts eds (Melb, 1970); C. S. Ross, 'Two American types that left their stamp on Victorian history', VHM, 7 (1919); *Argus*, 6 Nov 1855.

E. DANIEL POTTS

TREACY, PATRICK AMBROSE (1834-1912), Catholic educationist, was born on 31 August 1834 at Thurles, County Tipperary, Ireland. Educated at an academy and the local Christian Brothers' school at Thurles, he excelled in mathematics. In February 1852 he joined the Congregation of Christian Brothers, Waterford. After a rigorous course he was posted to various local schools for experience and also continued his studies, including part-time courses under the aegis of the Science Museum, South Kensington. After eight years of teaching at Wexford schools he became headmaster of the Christian Brothers' schools at Carlow. Showing administrative skill he achieved high teaching efficiency and improved school buildings and equipment.

In 1868 Bishop Goold [q.v.] asked for a community of Christian Brothers to establish schools in Victoria. Treacy was chosen as leader, and with three confrères arrived in Melbourne in the *Donald McKay* in November to find the Catholic school system receiving some state aid, but in a parlous condition under the control of local parish priests. Treacy opened a primary school in Lonsdale Street in 1869. When the Education Act of 1872 set up a system of 'free, compulsory and secular' education, controlled by a state department, the Catholic hierarchy determined to retain and pay for their own school system. Undaunted by lack of money, Treacy initiated a colony-wide campaign to finance land and buildings. With generous help from colonists of all creeds a college was erected in Victoria Parade on Eastern Hill, Melbourne; opened in January 1871, its final cost was about £12,000. Having observed the deplorable state of diocesan schools during his collecting tours, Treacy advocated to the Catholic Education Committee a rise in teachers' salaries and a training college. He offered in the meantime to train as teachers senior boys selected from his own system. There were no funds for a teachers' college but his further offer to inspect metropolitan schools was accepted.

Treacy's report on the condition of the system resulted in up-to-date equipment, and under him the Brothers organized a training scheme for their aspirants. At first they were trained in the schools, but in 1897 Treacy decided to use a recent foundation at Lewisham, New South Wales, as a training centre under a qualified master of method. He also arranged for several trained Irish Brothers to migrate each year.

Treacy decided to extend the studies of the more talented of his pupils beyond the primary level and to present them for the civil service and the matriculation examinations. Small classes at Victoria Parade College and St Patrick's, Ballarat, taught by

Brothers Nugent and Kennedy respectively, achieved eminent success in these examinations. In the early days not many boys sat for matriculation, but many entered both the civil service and commerce. At this time there were no Irish secondary schools; it was Treacy's initiative and dedication that shaped the pattern of the Australian Christian Brothers' higher education without regard to pupils' social or financial standing.

Gifted with great prudence and business acumen, Treacy also acceded to the requests of the hierarchy to open in many parts of Australia. By 1900, when he retired after thirty years as a provincial superior, he had established twenty-seven schools in the principal cities of Australia, and one in New Zealand. He was recalled to Ireland in 1900 as an assistant to the superior-general, and returned to the Australian province in 1910. Although retired, he insisted on working and was sent to Brisbane in a bid to prolong his years in a warm climate. He died at St Joseph's College, Gregory Terrace, on 2 October 1912.

R. Fogarty, *Catholic education in Australia 1806-1950*, 2 (Melb, 1959); Christian Brothers (Dublin), *Educational Record*, 1913-14, 1965-66; Christian Brothers, Centenary book, 1868-1968 (Parade College, Bundoora, Vic); P. A. Treacy letters (Christian Brothers Archives, Rome); Catholic Education Cttee minute books 1875, 1877 (Roman Catholic Archives, Melb).

A. I. KEENAN

TRICKETT, EDWARD (1851-1916), sculler, was born on 12 September 1851 at Greenwich, on the Lane Cove River, New South Wales, son of George Trickett, bootmaker, and his wife Mary, née Evans. He worked as a quarryman and in 1868 with C. Bullivant won the under-18 double skiffs at the Anniversary Day Regatta; next year he won the under-21 skiffs. He rowed little in 1871-73. At the 1874 Balmain Regatta he won the outrigger race and was in the winning whale-boat crew. In October he was second to Michael Rush in the £200 'Clarence River Champion Outrigger Race'. At the 1875 Anniversary Regatta he won the light skiffs race, although it had been made a handicap as he was now much the best sculler in the colony.

After wins in 1875-76, Trickett was taken to England by James Punch, a Sydney innkeeper and former sculler, to challenge for the world championship. On 27 June 1876 he defeated James H. Sadler on the Thames on the Putney-Mortlake course in 24 mins. 36 secs. and became the first Australian to win a world championship in any sport. Trickett was 6 ft. 4 ins. tall and weighed 12 stone 1½ lbs. for this race. He returned to Sydney on 9 November and was greeted by 25,000 people. At the 1877 Anniversary Regatta, after winning outrigger and skiffs races, he was presented with a cheque for nearly £900 by (Sir) John Robertson [q.v.].

Trickett became licensee of Trickett's Hotel and later proprietor of the International Hotel on the corner of Pitt and King streets, Sydney. On 30 June he defeated Rush in a £200-a-side challenge for the world championship, having trained daily for a month. Next year a rolling keg crushed his hand; the self-amputation of fingers affected the balance of his stroke, but in August 1879 he defeated Elias Laycock in a £200-a-side championship contest. In June 1880 he went to England but lost his world title to the Canadian Ned Hanlan on the Thames on 15 November and was also defeated in a match race by Wallace Ross. Losing in Ottawa, Canada, on 4 July 1881 he failed in a challenge to Hanlan on the Thames on 1 May 1882. On his return to Australia he rowed against William Beach [q.v.] on the Parramatta in 1883-84, but was troubled by using narrow-rigged boats.

In May 1884 Trickett moved to Rockhampton, Queensland, where he had apparently been given a hotel by an admirer. He came out of retirement to race against Hanlan on the Fitzroy River, Rockhampton, on 14 June 1888. He invested in a worthless mining venture and returned to Sydney in dire straits. On 17 September 1893 he became a tide-waiter at a salary of £120 with the New South Wales Customs Department and in 1896 was a bridge watchman at Moama on the Murray River. In 1901 he was transferred to the New South Wales branch of the Commonwealth Department of Trade and Customs. He retired as a customs assistant in the shipping branch on 11 September 1916.

An envoy of the Salvation Army and reputedly a teetotaller, he had reformed his ways after duck-shooting on the Sabbath at Rockhampton. On 28 November 1916 in the home of his son Frederick at Uralla, New South Wales, he died of injuries and shock received when the walls of a gold-mine shaft collapsed. Buried in the Salvation Army section of the Uralla cemetery, he was survived by six of his eight sons and two of his three daughters by his wife Maria Frances, née Silva, daughter of the South Head lighthouse-keeper, whom he had married at North Sydney on 20 January 1874. His estate was sworn for probate at £163.

Winner of over 150 trophies, Trickett was one of the most versatile rowers of his time. His prowess was recorded in ballad and verse and his portrait in rowing colours was featured on cigarette cards for many years. A memorial to him was erected by public subscription at Uralla in 1918.

J. E. Tonkin (ed), *The English, Australian & American sporting calendar* (Syd, 1884); E. O. Knee, *An Australian athlete* (Ballarat, 1899); G. Cockerill, *Scribblers and statesmen* (Melb, 1944); *SMH*, 26, 28 Jan 1867, 27, 28 Jan 1868, 26, 27 Jan 1869, 26, 27 Jan 1870, 19 July 1876, 27 Jan 1877; *Referee*, 6 Dec 1916; information from Miss J. Trickett (Lavender Bay, NSW).

J. L. STEWART

TRICKETT, WILLIAM JOSEPH (1843-1916), solicitor and politician, was born on 2 September 1843 at Gibraltar, only son of Joseph Trickett, civil engineer, and his wife Elizabeth, née Backshall. The family arrived in Sydney on 14 March 1854 in the *Maid of Judah*. After supervising construction at the Sydney branch of the Royal Mint, his father became second officer there; he was a magistrate and an alderman, sometime chairman, of Woollahra Borough Council. Educated at St Philip's school and Sydney Grammar School, Trickett studied law, was articled to Rowley, Holdsworth and Garrick and admitted as solicitor in 1866. He practised in King Street from 1868 to 1883 in partnership with W. H. Pigott; the *Bulletin* later described his professional position as 'deservedly high'. In 1878 he had inherited his father's personal estate sworn at £8000.

An alderman on the Woollahra Borough Council in 1873-1908, Trickett was mayor in 1879-81 and 1886-88. In 1880 he was elected to represent Paddington in the Legislative Assembly. A keen law reformer, his pressure was responsible for the passage of the 1881 Metropolitan Magistrates Act. Though he described himself as a free-trade independent, in parliament he was non-partisan: 'It is immaterial to me', he said in 1883, 'what government is in power ... I have always supported measures, not men'. He held generally liberal views, especially on education, but opposed payment for members of parliament. A 'painstaking and hardworking' postmaster-general in Sir Alexander Stuart's [q.v.] ministry in 1883-84, he abolished the fixed subsidy for mail matter shipped to and from England; he secured regular weekly mail services on the route by negotiating a contract with the Orient Steam Navigation Co. to supplement the service of the Peninsular and Oriental Steam Navigation Co. He also improved local telegram services and extended the penny postage system to Parramatta.

Although less successful as minister for public instruction in 1884-85, Trickett started work on the new National Art Gallery of New South Wales, of which he was appointed a trustee in 1886. Chairman of committees from March to July, next year he resigned from the assembly and was appointed to the Legislative Council, where he was a member, sometime chairman, of the Parliamentary Standing Committee on Public Works in 1889-1900 and chairman of committees in 1900-12. Although a die-hard opponent of provisions in the Commonwealth of Australia bill which he judged unfair to New South Wales, he was a member of the organizing committee for the inaugural celebrations.

A commissioner for the Calcutta (1883), Colonial and Indian (1886), Adelaide (1887), and Melbourne (1888) exhibitions, Trickett was also a member of the State Children's Relief Board, and of the South Head Roads Trust from 1886, chairman of the Metropolitan Transit Commission in 1890 and member of the Dental Board of New South Wales from 1900. He was solicitor for several building societies and a director of the Mutual Life Association of Australasia and the Mercantile Mutual Insurance Co. A keen and successful yachtsman, he was on the committee of the Royal Sydney Yacht Squadron. He was also president of the New South Wales Cricket Association, a trustee of the Sydney Cricket Ground and member of the Australian Club. He visited Europe and America in 1882, and China and Japan in 1892; details of the latter trip were published in the *Sydney Mail* in July to October and then as a book, *Notes of a Trip to China and Japan* (Sydney). On 23 January 1869 at St Thomas's, Enfield, he had married Charlotte Louisa Ashdown (d. 1932). Survived by his wife, two sons and four daughters, he died of heart disease on 4 July 1916 in his home, Shorewell, Woollahra, and was buried in the Anglican section of Waverley cemetery. His estate was sworn for probate at £23,406.

Cyclopedia of N.S.W. (Syd, 1907); J. Jervis, *The history of Woollahra*, V. Kelly ed (Syd, 1960); Postmaster-General, Annual report 1883, *V&P* (LA NSW), 1883-84, 9, 443; *SMH*, 15 Mar 1854, 5 Oct 1885, 5 July 1916; *Bulletin*, 16 July 1881, 3 Nov 1883; *T&CJ*, 12 May 1883, 26 Feb, 10 Sept 1887; *Daily Telegraph* (Syd), 3 Oct 1885; R. Parsons, Lawyers in the New South Wales parliament, 1870-1890 (Ph.D. thesis, Macquarie Univ, 1972).

CHRIS CUNNEEN

TROEDEL, JOHANNES THEODOR CHARLES, known as CHARLES (1836-1906), lithographic printer, was born at Hamburg, Germany, son of Carl Auguste Troedel (Trödel) and his wife Maria, née Buck. Apprenticed to his father in Denmark, at 23 he went for further experience to Norway, where he came to the notice of

A. W. Schuhkrafft, a Melbourne printer who was visiting Europe seeking craftsmen; he engaged Troedel and Robert Wendel, a brilliant lithographic artist and draftsman. They arrived in Melbourne in the *Great Britain* on 5 February 1860 and served Schuhkrafft for a three-year term.

In 1863 Troedel rented a very small shop in Collins Street and set up on his own account. On a press brought from Europe (and still preserved) he produced *The Melbourne Album*, employing various artists, notably the otherwise-unknown F. Cogné. Wendel did much admirable work for Troedel; the best was probably his magnificent coloured plates, many from drawings by Baldwin Spencer, which illustrate the zoological section of Spencer's *Report on ... the Horn Expedition to Central Australia* (1896).

Aged 32, Troedel was naturalized on 19 March 1869. He had turned 33 when he married Julia Sarah Glover, daughter of a contractor, on 29 June at St Paul's Church of England, Melbourne; they had five sons and three daughters. He was a member of the Victorian Master Printers' Association from the early 1880s and was a member of the wages board for the printing industry about 1900. A prominent figure in musical and artistic circles, he was associated with many distinguished people, including N. Chevalier [q.v.] who worked on his lithographic stones, and young Arthur Streeton who was apprenticed to Troedel when he was 'discovered' by Tom Roberts and Fred McCubbin; Streeton had his indentures cancelled, and looked back on Troedel with affection. Other painters associated with his firm were W. Blamire Young, Charles A. Wheeler, Lionel Lindsay and Percy Leason. Randolph Bedford, for whom Troedel printed, remembered him as 'a charming old man'.

By 1877 he was trading in Sydney as C. Troedel & Co.; in 1891 he formed a partnership in Sydney with Edward Cooper, who had joined him at 13, but Cooper soon returned to the Melbourne business. Troedel died of cancer on 31 October 1906 at St Kilda Road, Prahran, survived by his wife, two daughters and four sons, of whom Walter, Rudolph and Ferdinand joined their father's business. His estate was valued for probate at £8044. Although not the first of Melbourne's lithographers, Troedel was the most distinguished, and the work produced under his direction is of the highest quality, ranging from the twenty-four prints of the Victorian scene in the *Album* through a very large range of theatrical and other posters, labels and book illustrations. In 1968 the firm of Troedel & Cooper Ltd (formed in 1910) presented to the Library Council of Victoria its remarkable collection of lithographs of all kinds; now housed in the La Trobe Library, they are a social record of great value.

R. Bedford, *Naught to thirty-three* (Syd, 1944); C. Troedel, *The Melbourne Album*, C. Turnbull ed (Melb, 1961); Troedel collection exhibition notes (LaT L). CLIVE TURNBULL*

TROLLOPE, ANTHONY (1815-1882), novelist and civil servant, was born on 21 April 1815 at Russell Square, London, son of Thomas Anthony Trollope, lawyer, and his wife Frances, née Milton, novelist. Educated at Winchester College and Harrow School, he became a clerk in the Post Office in 1834 and was transferred to Ireland as a post-office surveyor in 1841. On 11 June 1844 at Rotherham, Yorkshire, he married Rose Heseltine. In 1843 he began writing novels to supplement his income; he retired from the Post Office in 1868.

On 27 May 1871 the Trollopes left Liverpool in the *Great Britain* to visit their son Frederick who had settled on a sheep station, Mortray, near Grenfell, New South Wales. Interested in the problems facing the British empire, Trollope had a contract with his publishers for a book on the Australian colonies. On the two-month voyage he wrote the novel *Lady Anna* (London, 1874) which was serialized in the *Australasian* from May 1873. A welcome celebrity, he arrived in Melbourne on 27 July 1871 and embarked on a years intensive travelling. In August he went to Queensland and in October visited Gulgong and Bathurst in New South Wales. In Sydney he attended parliament and on 7 December, in evidence to the Legislative Assembly select committee on the civil service, he opposed the patronage system and urged entry to the service by examination. In Melbourne he lectured to an admiring audience of 3000 on 'English Prose Fiction as a Rational Amusement'.

Meanwhile, in snatches between numerous public engagements and effusive hospitality and 'on the road', he began writing. On 23 December his comments on the colonies began in a series of letters published in the London *Daily Telegraph*, under the thinly disguised pseudonym 'Antipodean'. In Tasmania in January 1872 he commented on the amenities for convicts at Port Arthur for the government. He visited Gippsland, Victoria, in February, then Western Australia and South Australia in April-May. He sent one of his hostesses, Mrs E. Landor of Perth, a specially bound and inscribed copy of *The Claverings* (London, 1867). In July he left in the *Macedon* for two months in New Zealand.

When he reached London Trollope was able to give Chapman and Hall 1100 handwritten sheets, and his *Australia and New Zealand* appeared in 1873; George Robertson [q.v.] brought out an Australian edition; the book was also published in separate sections. Serialized in the *Australasian* it received a mixed reception. Trollope himself believed it 'must be inaccurate ... as the rapid work of a traveller'. W. B. Dalley [q.v.] admiringly reviewed the second division on New South Wales in the *Sydney Morning Herald* on 31 March 1873: 'he sees among us nothing but beauty everywhere'. Dalley was 'startled' that 'the delicate delineator of sweet female character, who could follow even the musings of a young girl ... was passionately fond of all sport, fishing, hunting, clambering over rocks only to see the fish-spearing of our aboriginals (as the writer of this notice saw him last year)'.

Trollope revisited Australia in 1875 and wrote twenty letters for the *Liverpool Mercury*, which were republished in B. A. Booth's *The Tireless Traveller* (Berkeley, 1941). He directly used his Australian experiences in two novels: *Harry Heathcote of Gangoil* (1874) and *John Caldigate* (London, 1879), a better literary work which contains a deeper analysis of the moral values of colonial life than in his travel book. He died of a paralytic stroke on 6 December 1882 in London and was buried in Kensal Green cemetery, survived by his wife and two sons. His *Autobiography* was published in 1883.

M. Muir, *Anthony Trollope in Australia* (Adel, 1949); B. A. Booth (ed), *The letters of Anthony Trollope* (Lond, 1951); A. Trollope, *Australia*, P. D. Edwards and R. B. Joyce eds (Brisb, 1968); A. Trollope, *South Africa*, J. H. Davidson ed (Cape Town, 1973); A. Trollope, *Australia and New Zealand* (MS NL).

R. B. JOYCE

TROUTON, FREDERICK HENRY (1826-1896), master mariner and company manager, was born at Chester, Cheshire, England, son of Charles Robert Trouton, merchant, and his wife Mary Ann, née Creek. Educated at Dr Sargent's school in Dublin, at 17 he joined the *Ballantyne* and in 1851 he became captain of the *Zenobia*. Attracted by the gold discoveries he arrived in Melbourne in the *Sarah Sands* on 16 December 1852 and prospected without success at Forest Creek. In 1853 he was in command of the coastal ship, *East of Dalhousie*, and in November sailed the *Elizabeth* from Melbourne to London; her cargo included gold which stowaway convicts attempted to steal, but Trouton subdued them. He bought the *Osprey*, returned in it to Melbourne in 1855 and successfully carried gold and merchandise from Port Phillip Bay. He sold the ship in 1857 and settled at Geelong; when the town's trade declined because of Melbourne's growth he partnered Captain Thomas Robertson in transporting livestock to New Zealand in 1860. Next year he was part-owner and captain of the *Balclutha* and on 23 April at St Paul's, Geelong, he married Harriette Smith, who had been born in Dublin in 1837.

Trouton joined the Australasian Steam Navigation Co. in 1862 in Sydney and became general manager in 1866. His enterprise and skill stimulated the firm's complex growth and rationalized its competitive position; by 1868 it had taken over the Queensland Steam Navigation Co.; next year it began trade with Fiji via Auckland, and in 1870 it was carrying the San Francisco mail. In 1877 the company entered the China trade and in November next year its employment of Chinese at wages less than the rates of the Federated Seamen's Union of Australasia led to a strike; Trouton argued that the high price of white labour and excessive competition had forced the company to employ Chinese. The strike ended in a compromise in January 1879, and the last of the Chinese crews was discharged in 1883. In 1881 Trouton went to England to arrange for the construction of eleven new steamers, but intense competition affected the company and in 1886 it was bought out by the Queensland Steamship Co. Trouton stayed on until 1888 when the Australasian United Steam Navigation Co. took over. He was chairman of the Steamship Owners' Association of Australasia in the 1880s.

Trouton was a prominent figure in Balmain, where he lived and the A.S.N. Co. operated. He was president of the Balmain and District Hospital and the Bowling Club, and a committee-man of the School of Arts; in the 1870s he was an alderman of the Borough Council. A magistrate of the city of Sydney in 1880, he was a member of the commission that prepared for the naval reception of the duke of Edinburgh in 1867, and of the commission for the Centennial International Exhibition, Melbourne, in 1888. He was appointed to the royal commission on strikes, Sydney, in 1890 and his expert questioning helped to expose the policy errors and the dissimulation of the shearers' union leader W. G. Spence [q.v.]. A keen harbour yachtsman he skippered Alfred Fairfax's *Magic* in many duels with the *Mistral*.

Trouton, aged 70, died of a cerebral haemorrhage on 19 September 1896 and was buried in the Anglican section of Balmain cemetery. He was survived by his wife, four of his seven sons and three daughters. His estate was sworn for probate at £7388.

Report of the Royal Commission on strikes (Syd, 1891); T&CJ, 8 Dec 1877; SMH, 21 Sept 1896.   BEDE NAIRN

TRUGERNANNER   (TRUGANINI) (1812?-1876), Tasmanian Aboriginal, was born in Van Diemen's Land on the western side of the D'Entrecasteaux Channel, in the territory of the south-east tribe. Her father was Mangerner, leader of one of the tribe's bands, and in her adolescence she was associated with its traditional culture, making occasional visits to Port Davey. The tribe was disrupted by European sealers, whalers and timber-getters; by March 1829, when she and her father met G. A. Robinson [q.v.] at Bruny Island, her mother had been killed by sailors, her uncle shot by a soldier, her sister abducted by sealers, and Paraweena, a young man who was to have been her husband, murdered by timber-getters. At Bruny Island mission in 1829 she 'married' Woorraddy, from Bruny. They were associated with all the missions that Robinson and his sons conducted around Tasmania in 1830-35; they acted as guides and as instructors in their languages and customs, which were recorded by Robinson in his journal, the best ethnographic record now available of traditional Tasmanian Aboriginal society.

Trugernanner, Woorraddy and other Aboriginals from Robinson's mission arrived at the Flinders Island settlement in November 1835. With the hundred or so captured Aboriginals still alive they were to be 'christianized and europeanized' and taught to be farmers. She was renamed Lallah Rookh by Robinson, but held to her traditional ways. In March 1836 she and Woorraddy returned to Tasmania to search in vain for the one family remaining in the north-west. By July 1837 when they went back to Flinders Island, many had died there and Robinson's programme had proved unsuccessful. Trugernanner told him that all the Aboriginals would be dead before the houses being constructed for them were completed.

In February 1839, with Woorraddy and fourteen other Aboriginals, she accompanied Robinson to Port Phillip. She and four others, without Woorraddy, later joined a party of whalers near Portland Bay. In 1841 all five Aboriginals were charged with the murder of two whalers and in January 1842 the two men were hanged. In July Trugernanner and two other

women, Fanny and Matilda, were sent back to Flinders Island with Woorraddy who, however, died en route. She lived with the Aboriginal Alphonso until October 1847 when, with forty-six others, she moved to a new establishment at Oyster Cove, in her traditional territory. She resumed much of her earlier life-style, diving for shellfish, visiting Bruny Island by catamaran, and hunting in the near-by bush. By 1869 she and William Lanney were the only full bloods alive. The mutilation of Lanney's body after his death in March led Trugernanner to express concern; she told Rev. H. D. Atkinson, 'I know that when I die the Museum wants my body'.

In 1874 she moved to Hobart Town with her guardians, the Dandridge family, and died in Mrs Dandridge's house in Macquarie Street on 8 May 1876, aged 64. She was buried at the old female penitentiary at the Cascades at midnight on 10 May. Her body was exhumed in December 1878 by the Royal Society of Tasmania, authorized by the government to take possession of her skeleton on condition that it be not exposed to public view but 'decently deposited in a secure resting place accessible by special permission to scientific men for scientific purposes'. But it was placed in the Tasmanian Museum where it was on public display in 1904-51. Trugernanner was the most famous of the Aboriginal Tasmanians, but her life is shrouded in myth and legend. As the faithful companion of Robinson in 1829-35, she assisted in bringing in her compatriots because she wanted to save them from European guns. The establishment at Flinders Island was a grave disappointment to her. Small in stature, forceful, gifted and courageous, she held European society in contempt and made her own adjustment on her own terms.

N. J. B. Plomley (ed), Friendly mission. The Tasmanian journals and papers of G. A. Robinson 1829-1834 (Hob, 1966); G. A. Robinson papers (ML); CSO, Records, registers and indexes, 1824-76 (TA); correspondence file under Trucanini (TA).   LYNDALL RYAN
                                          NEIL SMITH

TRYON, SIR GEORGE (1832-1893), naval officer, was born on 4 January 1832 at Bulwick Park, Northamptonshire, England, son of Thomas Tryon and his wife Anne, daughter of Sir John Trollope, Bart. Educated at Eton, he entered the navy as a cadet in H.M.S. Wellesley in 1848 and passed his midshipman's examination at 18, gaining the high regard of his superiors for his intellect and disposition.

Tryon served with distinction in the Crimean war; promoted acting lieutenant he was confirmed in that rank in 1855. He served in the Black Sea before being posted in 1858 to the Queen's escort to Cherbourg, which resulted in an appointment to the royal yacht. Thereafter his career was closely associated with innovation and improvement of several aspects of the service. Promoted commander in 1860, next year he was appointed to H.M.S. *Warrior*, the first British sea-going ironclad. He received his own command in 1864, became a captain in 1866 and attended the Royal Naval College, Portsmouth. Next year he was appointed director of transports at Annesley Bay in the Red Sea, landing troops and supplies for the Abyssinian expedition, work that gained him the C.B. in 1868. On 5 April 1869 in London he married the Honourable Clementina Charlotte, daughter of Gilbert John Heathcote, first Lord Aveland.

In 1871 Tryon was made private secretary to G. J. Goschen, first lord of the Admiralty. In 1874 he was given command of H.M.S. *Raleigh*, another experimental warship, and in 1877, by reason of his reputation as a tactician, was appointed to committees for revision of the signal book and manual of fleet evolutions. Following command of the prestigious H.M.S. *Monarch*, in 1882 he became secretary to the Admiralty, the last naval officer to hold that post; he established a department of naval intelligence and contributed to the bluewater versus bricks and mortar debate which resulted in the navy regaining ascendancy over the army.

A rear-admiral in April 1884, Tryon was influential in the establishment of the Australian Station and in December was appointed its first commander-in-chief; he arrived in Sydney on 22 January 1885 in the *Indus*. His wife did not accompany him but he entertained Sydney society at Admiralty House with long-remembered hospitality. His handsome presence and robust, cheery personality combined with high professional ability made him the confidant of many important people in Australia. Among his first duties was an inquiry into the native labour trade between Queensland and the Pacific islands; it led to his inclusion in discussions regarding the annexation of New Guinea. The heightened colonial consciousness of defence following the Russian scare of early 1885 gained Tryon much publicity which he used to urge increased naval effort. He proposed greater colonial participation in defence of the general Australian area by an auxiliary squadron not limited to the Australian coast; an integral part of his concept was his opposition to payment to Britain in return for protection. But Admiralty policy was opposed to a colonial blue-water cap-

ability and a policy of monetary contribution was accepted by colonial leaders at the 1887 Imperial Conference in London, to which Tryon had not been invited. As a result, Tryon asked to be relieved of his command and left Australia in the *Ballaarat* on 19 April 1887. He had filled the Victorian naval forces with his nominees, but failed to forge a coherent Australian unit or effect involvement in defence beyond coastal waters. Nevertheless, he stimulated a school of thought which eventually produced the Royal Australian Navy.

On his return to Britain Tryon was created K.C.B. and appointed superintendent of reserves, which allowed him to pursue his interests in tactics and other matters. In 1889 he was promoted vice-admiral and in 1891 became commander-in-chief, Mediterranean Station, where he implemented many of his ideas on training, including the introduction of a greater sense of realism into fleet manoeuvres. He was drowned following a collision on 22 June 1893 between his flagship, H.M.S. *Victoria*, and a consort, H.M.S. *Camperdown*, in a manoeuvre ordered by him and generally regarded as a lapse of judgment. His body was not recovered. Subsequent controversy concentrated on the risks inherent in his methods and tended to obscure his great contribution to naval development. His estate was sworn for probate at £34,794, and in New South Wales at £2064. He was survived by his wife (d. 1922) and son George Clement, later a major in the 3rd Grenadier Guards and Conservative M.P. for Brighton in the House of Commons.

C. C. P. Fitzgerald, *Vice Admiral Sir George Tryon, K.C.B.* (Edinb, 1897); H. J. Feakes, *White ensign—southern cross* (Syd, 1951); Court martial procs . . . loss of HMS *Victoria*, PP (GB), 1893 (Cmd 7120 and 7178); *Naval Annual*, 1894; *The Times*, 17 May 1871, 24, 30 June 1893; *Sydney Mail*, 23 Aug, 1 Nov 1884; *SMH*, 11 Nov 1884, 23 Jan 1885, 22 June 1887; *Australasian*, 24 Jan 1885, 18 June 1887, 21 Jan 1888, 28 Jan, 1 July 1893; *ISN*, 30 Apr 1887.
                                        B. N. PRIMROSE

TUCKER. ALBERT EDWIN ELWORTHY LEE (1843-1902), parliamentarian, was born on 16 March 1843 at Fitzroy, Melbourne, son of John Lee Tucker, farm-servant and later contractor, who had migrated from Devon, England, in 1842, and his wife Elizabeth Grace, née Elworthy. Educated at St Mark's Church of England School where he became an assistant teacher, he briefly studied law, travelled widely in Australia and New Zealand as a softgoods salesman, and in 1870-71 was an insurance agent in Fitzroy. A member of the Fitzroy Council in 1870-79, he was mayor in 1871-72 and 1879; in 1872 he floated the first municipal loan to finance road improvements and the construction of a town hall. In 1871 he failed to win the Collingwood seat in the Legislative Assembly, but won it in 1874. When the electorate was divided in 1877 he gained the Fitzroy seat, which he held until 1900.

Tucker became president of the Board of Land and Works and commissioner of crown lands and survey in the Service-Berry [qq.v.] ministry of 1883-86. He was equipped for this position by his experience as chairman of the 1878 royal commission on closed roads and member of the 1878 commission of inquiry into crown lands. His principal achievements as minister were the Mallee pastoral leases bill of 1883 and the Land Act of 1884, which introduced systematic classification, and provisions for leasing potentially rich swamplands. He declined the Speakership in 1887 when Lalor [q.v.] resigned. He was valued for his 'practical common sense and straightforwardness' as a member and chairman of many inquiries: among those he chaired were the royal commission on the extension of Melbourne westward in 1887, the railways standing committee in 1890, the inquiry into the Factory and Shops Act in 1893, the board of inquiry into the fiscal system of Victoria in 1894, and the royal commissions on the Mildura settlement in 1896 and on state forests and timber reserves in 1897.

A prominent civic leader, Tucker was a director of the Melbourne Permanent Mutual Benefit Building Society, a Freemason, a member of the Ancient Order of Foresters, and a police magistrate from 1875. In 1871 he was a founding member of the Australian Natives' Association. Originally a free trader, he later espoused protection and became known as a radical liberal. In 1888 he urged direct taxation, the reduction of probate duty on small estates and, in order to check unscrupulous land speculators, the establishment of a commission to investigate and reform the company laws. Although always a reliable party man he retained his independence of judgment and earned respect as an able, resourceful and hard-working politician.

Tucker married Elizabeth Isabella Payne on 20 July 1865 and had twelve children. He died of apoplexy on 8 May 1902 at his home, Colebrooke, North Fitzroy, and was buried in the Anglican section of the Melbourne general cemetery, survived by his wife, six sons and four daughters. He died intestate and his estate was valued for administration at £5438.

A. Sutherland et al, *Victoria and its metropolis*, 2 (Melb, 1888); G. Serle, *The rush to be rich* (Melb, 1971); *Observer* (Collingwood), 28 Mar 1889; *Age*, 9 May 1902; *Argus*, 9 May 1902; *Australasian,* 10 May 1902; *Bulletin*, 17 May 1902.   ANN-MARI JORDENS

TUFNELL, EDWARD WYNDHAM (1814-1896), Church of England bishop, was born on 3 October 1814 at Bath, Somerset, England, son of John Charles Tufnell, army officer, and his wife Uliana Margaret, daughter of Rev. John Fowell, of Bishopsbourne, Kent. Educated at Eton and at Wadham College, Oxford (B.A., 1837; M.A., 1842; Hon. D.D., 1859), where he became a fellow; he was made deacon, ordained priest in 1839 and served as curate of Broadwindsor, Dorset, in 1837-40 and Broadhinton, Wiltshire, in 1840-46. He was rector of Beechingstoke, Wiltshire, in 1846-57 and of St Peter and St Paul, Marlborough, in 1857-59. In 1850-59 he was a prebendary of Salisbury Cathedral.

Tufnell was consecrated first bishop of Brisbane in Westminster Abbey by J. B. Sumner, archbishop of Canterbury, on 14 June 1859. Though an honorary secretary of the Society for the Propagation of the Gospel, his mild, cultured manner and restricted rural experience made him an unlikely candidate for the bishopric. He sailed in the *Vimiera* on 5 May 1860 with five priests, two deacons, four laymen, £7000 in donations and the promise of further annual contributions. He reached Brisbane in September. Tufnell expected to find the Church in Queensland 'in an exceedingly languid state' and was not disappointed. The new diocese included all Queensland south of the twenty-first parallel; its five parishes had a scattered population of 25,000 who were served by three clergymen including Benjamin Glennie [q.v.]. State aid to religion had been abolished during Tufnell's journey.

At his enthronement on 4 September 1860, Tufnell said that he sought the people's acceptance of the doctrines and precepts of the Church of England; he also desired the conversion of the Aboriginals but was never able to begin it. His new priests filled vacancies and he arranged a further supply from England; though the flow diminished he had twenty-five clergymen by 1874. He set up new parishes, encouraged building and visited the chief centres of population seeking increased financial support. Church attendances increased and the Church became a more effective force.

Initially, with no constitution, Tufnell wielded sole authority over appointments, finance and property. Glennie's promotion as archdeacon in 1863 made no significant difference. Some of the laity resented this autocratic rule and critics questioned the bishop's financial competence. Tufnell projected synodical government in 1864, but neither clergy nor laity seemed enthusiastic; nevertheless, next year an attempt was made by disaffected laymen to pass ill-conceived legislation regulating the Church. The example of the southern dioceses, and the recognition by the mid-1860s of legal deficiencies in the letters patent establishing the bishop's temporal authority changed the climate. In 1867 Tufnell convened a conference which accepted synodical government based on consensual compact, and a committee including Judge Lutwyche [q.v.] prepared a constitution that was approved by the first synod in 1868, thus reducing the bishop's burden. But Tufnell did not manage his synod and council skilfully and was too ready to expect the synod to take responsibilities that were still his own.

From the six weak schools that he had inherited Tufnell wanted to develop a comprehensive and efficient system of Church education. Needing government subsidies, he announced on arrival strong opposition to the abolition of state aid. Opposed by powerful secularist and non-conformist forces, Tufnell organized meetings and petitions and even joined Bishop J. Quinn [q.v.] in a wide campaign. His cause was weakened by the opposition of many of his laymen and, though by 1871 he had succeeded in securing payment of teachers, the secularist victory in the 1875 Education Act signalled defeat and presaged the collapse of the Anglican school system.

In 1865-67 Tufnell sought funds in England but illness and other factors prolonged the visit, reducing his already slender popularity. He seemed unable to identify with the crudity of colonial life. Though dignified, devout and high principled, and a good administrator with sound policies, he had not related well to his flock. His moderate High Churchmanship widened the gap. His stipend was modest and he used private means generously for diocesan purposes, but he was criticized for devoting money to the see endowment and to Bishopsbourne, the gracious episcopal residence which he erected. His weaknesses were real, but his pioneering achievements were significant though not recognized at the time. His resignation came after he had sailed for England in February 1874 and was received in Brisbane without surprise or regret.

Tufnell returned to the kind of English country ministry that he had known before he became a bishop. He was curate of Char-

ing, Kent, in 1877-79, vicar and rural dean of Croydon, Surrey, in 1879-82, and vicar of Felpham and residentiary canon of Chichester Cathedral in 1882-96. Survived by his wife Laura, née Tufnell, a cousin whom he had married in England on 12 February 1867, and by a son and daughter, he died on 3 December 1896 at Chichester and was buried in Felpham churchyard. His widow made a gift to the Society of the Sacred Advent towards the establishment of an orphanage, the Tufnell Home, in Brisbane. There is a portrait of him at Bishopsbourne.

E. B. Tufnell, The family of Tufnell (Guildford, 1924); Moreton Bay Courier, 6 Sept, 4 Oct, 3 Nov 1860; Qld Daily Guardian, 28 Apr 1863, 11, 21 Oct, 9 Nov 1864; Brisbane Courier, 23 July, 20 Aug 1864, 17, 24 May, 8 July 1865, 16 Feb, 14, 16 May, 20 Aug, 4 Sept 1867, 22 July 1874; Week, 15, 22, 29 Sept, 6, 13, 20, 27 Oct 1877; K. Rayner, The history of the Church of England in Queensland (Ph.D. thesis, Univ Qld, 1962); Diocese of Brisbane, Diocesan Conference procs 1867, Synod procs 1868-73, Council minutes 1868-74 (Diocesan Registry, Brisb); letters, 'D' MSS (SPG Archives, Westminster).

K. RAYNER

TULK, AUGUSTUS HENRY (1810-1873), librarian, was born at Richmond, Surrey, England, son of Charles Augustus Tulk (1786-1849), and his wife Susannah, née Hart. His father was a Swedenborgian who owned property in Leicester Square and represented Sudbury and later Poole in the House of Commons. Augustus attended Winchester School and received a good classical education. Later he studied at Heidelberg and elsewhere on the Continent, and gained fluency in German, French, Russian and Italian. Like many other young Englishmen of his class and time, he was brought up as a 'gentleman' with no particular calling or profession. In 1838 at Newcastle upon Tyne he married Jane Augusta Browne.

For health reasons Tulk was advised to live in a warm, dry climate. At the suggestion of J. J. E. von Guerard [q.v.], his son's former tutor then in Australia, Tulk decided to migrate. He bought the schooner Guyon and, with his wife and family, sailed from London in March 1854, reaching Melbourne on 13 July. Optimistically, he had loaded his vessel with mining machinery and goods likely to be in demand on the goldfields; a few months experience proved that he lacked business aptitude and, after heavy losses, he sought a more congenial occupation. Learning of the establishment of a public library in Melbourne, he applied for the position of librarian and was selected from forty-eight applicants; he took up his post on 5 May 1856 at a salary of £600.

Tulk was soon on excellent terms with the library's president (Sir) Redmond Barry [q.v.] with whom he had much in common. Both worked indefatigably in gathering a notable collection of 80,000 volumes, Tulk contributing his first-hand knowledge of most of the great book shops of Europe. In 1863 he was appointed a member of the commission of inquiry into the promotion of the fine arts in Victoria, and he worked assiduously for the establishment of an art gallery. Next year he was given leave of absence to visit England and to collect the donations that Barry's representations abroad had produced. While there Tulk proposed a novel, but unsuccessful scheme by which a copy of every book published in England would be sent to Victoria in exchange for local copyright protection. Back in the colony, he introduced an unusually advanced system of book classification according to subjects.

Tulk's success in building up the Melbourne library led to offers of appointments from Sydney and overseas, but he could not bring himself to leave his 'own' library. Grave, courteous and dignified, he had a high reputation both as bookman and linguist. His knowledge of literature both ancient and modern was extensive and he loved books. In Victoria he added a study of Fijian and Australian native dialects to his repertoire of languages. In later life he suffered from diabetes. Aged 63, he died in his home in St Kilda on 1 September 1873 and after a Church of England service was buried in the general cemetery at Carlton. Survived by his wife, three of his four sons and his two daughters, he left debts amounting to some £600. His portrait by Philip Lindo is held in the State Library of Victoria.

E. LaT. Armstrong, *The book of the Public Library . . . 1856-1906* (Melb, 1906); D. McVilly, 'Augustus Henry Tulk', *Aust Lib J*, Feb 1975; *Age*, 2 Sept 1873; *A'sian Sketcher*, 4 Oct 1873.   C. A. McCALLUM

TULLY, WILLIAM ALCOCK (1830-1905), surveyor, was born on 14 March 1830 in Dublin, son of William Tully, captain R.N., and his wife Mary, née Alcock. Educated privately, in 1846 he matriculated at Trinity College, Dublin (B.A., 1852). He arrived at Hobart Town as religious instructor in the convict ship *Lord Dalhousie* on 14 August 1852.

Tully entered the public service as a road surveyor on 1 May 1853 and became a third-class surveyor on 1 May 1854. In July 1856 he resigned and became a contract surveyor until 31 December 1858 when he was appointed inspecting surveyor. He also acted for a time as a gold commissioner and in 1859 led a party of twelve to the west coast in a vain search for gold. He was a foundation member of the Tasmanian Club and in 1860 at Hobart married Louisa (d. 26 February 1866), granddaughter of Simeon Lord [q.v.].

With a glowing reference from Surveyor-General J. E. Calder [q.v.], Tully arrived in Queensland in October 1863 as a commissioner of crown lands in the Kennedy and Warrego pastoral districts. On 1 December 1864 he was appointed deputy-chief commissioner of lands and on 16 August 1866 under-secretary for public lands and chief commissioner of crown lands. He soon clashed with A. C. Gregory [q.v.], surveyor-general; on 12 March 1875 he became acting surveyor-general in place of Gregory. On Tully's advice the offices of surveyor-general and under-secretary for lands were divided in 1880; he was made surveyor-general on 9 July and E. Deshon became under-secretary for lands.

Tully had helped to draft the Lands Alienation Act of 1868 which began a comprehensive closer settlement policy, and the Consolidating Crown Lands Alienation Act of 1876. As surveyor-general he directed a wide expansion of activities and strove to make standards better. He also initiated improved reproduction of Survey Office maps. On 4 December 1889 he was appointed to the Land Board under the Crown Lands Act of 1884; when the 1897 Land Act replaced the board with a court the members continued in office. Tully retired on 31 December 1900.

His determination, education and wide experience in surveying, mining and land settlement made Tully an effective administrator. He probably exerted more influence on the land laws, procedures and practices of Queensland than any other person. He died of heart disease in his home, Luciani, Bayswater Road, Sydney, on 26 April 1905 and was buried at St Anne's Church of England, Ryde. On 27 May 1868 at Ryde he had married Sarah Anne Darvall. Their four children and two of his first marriage survived him. The town of Tully and the Tully River in North Queensland are named after him.

C. A. Bernays, *Queensland politics during sixty years* (Brisb, 1919); V&P (HA Tas), 1863 (63), 1866 (52), 24; *Mercury*, 25 May 1859, 23 Mar 1866; *Examiner* (Melb), 3 May 1862; *Brisbane Courier*, 31 Mar 1875; *T&CJ*, 3 May 1905; CSD 4/47/690 (TA).   L. J. DUFFY*

TURNER, ALFRED ALLATSON (1826-1895), explorer and civil servant, was born on 21 November 1826 at Calais, France, son of Lieutenant Frederick Turner, R.N., and his wife Sarah, née Allatson. On 5 March 1831 he arrived with his parents at Perth in the *Eliza*. After his father's death his mother moved to Sydney about 1840; he spent three years at Lindenow, Gippsland, Victoria, gaining farming and grazing experience.

Late in 1846 Turner was living in Sydney where he became a friend of Edmund Kennedy [q.v.]. Next year as second-in-command, he joined Kennedy's expedition to the Gulf of Carpentaria. Instead of being led north-west by the mythical 'Victoria River', they found themselves going south-west, following what proved to be the Barcoo River into Cooper's Creek; forced by drought to retreat, they went down the Warrego River until it dissipated itself. Finding the distance across to the Culgoa River greater than he had calculated, Kennedy left Turner in charge of a base where the carts remained. For a week Turner and his companions had practically no water and were forced to drink their own urine until rescued. He was 'reduced to jockey weight' but, small and wiry, he soon recovered and helped to bring the abandoned carts to the Culgoa. The expedition returned to Sydney in February 1848 and Kennedy praised Turner; but he found work scarce. An ungrateful government refused him a tracing of Kennedy's maps, although he was later permitted to copy them; he used the material to prepare a lively unpublished record of his exploit.

On 23 May 1848 Turner became a temporary clerk in the Colonial Secretary's Department at 5s. a day and by 1850 was an extra clerk. On 19 June at Wollongong he married Maria Rebecca (d. 1921), daughter of Charles Throsby Smith, a local pioneer; on 1 January 1853 he became clerk of Petty Sessions there at a salary of £175. In 1857 he also became local agent for the sale of crown lands and in 1859 registrar of the District Court and, until 1862, clerk of the peace. He became registrar for births, deaths and marriages in 1869 and was mining registrar in 1875-78. He was promoted police magistrate in 1876 and retained his other offices. Appointed an officer to issue miners' rights and licences and a collector of revenue in 1883, two years later he ceased to be clerk of Petty Sessions and on 1 January 1888 retired on a pension of £277 2s.; he was then a guardian of minors.

Turner led a quiet but active life, his offices keeping him aloof from the 'commotion of public affairs'. He was closely connected with the Anglican Church, the Wollongong Agricultural and Horticultural Association, the Wollongong Benevolent Society and the Wollongong Harbour Trust League. A keen angler all his life, he visited New Zealand, North Queensland and Tasmania in the 1880s. When the barque *Queen of Nations* was wrecked near Corrimal in 1881 he saved the life of the drunken and rampageous captain by knocking him out with a cudgel.

Turner was noted for unswerving and equal justice to all, administered with patience and kindness. He was known to uphold the law by fining decent 'old hands' who had misbehaved a little, but paid their fines for them if they had no money. Aged 68, he died of cancer of the liver on 3 August 1895 and was buried in the Anglican section of Wollongong cemetery; he was survived by his wife, two sons and two daughters, to whom he left an estate valued for probate at £5244.

E. Beale, *Kennedy of Cape York* (Adel, 1970); *Illawarra Mercury*, 6 Aug 1895; Col Sec miscellaneous letters 1848, and in-letters 1849-52 (NSWA); family papers (held by author).

EDGAR BEALE

TURNER, CHARLES THOMAS BIASS (1862-1944), cricketer, was born on 16 November 1862 at Bathurst, New South Wales, son of Charles Biass Turner, innkeeper, and his wife Mary Ann, née Pye. Educated at the Bathurst Grammar and Commercial School, where he failed to get into the cricket team, he worked for Cobb [q.v.] & Co. and practised bowling on a variety of prepared wickets after dispatching the morning coaches. In December 1881 playing for the Bathurst 22 against A. Shaw's England XI, he took 17 wickets for 69 runs, including 10 for 36 in the second innings. In 1882-83 he made his début for New South Wales against Ivo Bligh's Englishmen and at the end of that season moved to Sydney, where he played for the Carlton Cricket Club. On 19 July 1882 at Christ Church, Enmore, he married Sarah Emily Matthews.

In January 1887 at Sydney, playing for a combined New South Wales and Victorian XI, Turner took 6 for 15 against Shaw's English XI, which was dismissed for the record low score of 45. In 1887-88, when two English sides visited the colonies, he took 8 for 39 and 8 for 40 in the same match for New South Wales against A. Shrewsbury's XI; 5 for 44 and 7 for 43 in the only Test played against the combined sides, and became the first and only bowler to amass 100 wickets in an Australian season.

An automatic choice for the 1888 tour of England, he formed, during a summer of 'indescribable' conditions, a formidable partnership with J. J. Ferris (1867-1900). The left-arm spin of the 'Fiend' Ferris was a perfect foil for the right-arm medium pace of the 'Terror' Turner. Bowling virtually unchanged throughout the tour, they exploited each other's footmarks, took 534 of the 663 wickets to fall to the Australians and were named among *Wisden's* cricketers of the year. Turner's share in all matches was 314 wickets at 11, including 9 for 15, 8 for 13 and 9 for 37 in the same match at Hastings, and 5 wickets in each of the Test innings in which he bowled. The partnership was resumed on the 1890 tour of England, when they each took 215 wickets. Turner toured England again in 1893 and although his opportunities were limited by influenza and the presence of George Giffen [q.v.] and Hugh Trumble, he headed the bowling averages with 149 wickets at 14 in the eleven-a-side matches. In his last series in 1894-95 in Australia, he was dropped from the team that narrowly lost the deciding Test. He refused a last minute invitation to tour England in 1896.

Quiet, gentle and dignified, Turner stood just under 5 ft. 9 in. and was sturdily built. His appearance, demeanour and action belied his nickname; 'with a sudden swing around', wrote the English captain A. C. Maclaren, 'he would come tripping up to the wicket in the most cheery and at the same time graceful manner imaginable'. He stood squarer to the batsman at the moment of delivery than most classical bowlers, relying on accuracy and change of pace. His stock ball was a medium-paced sharply turning off-break which he mixed with yorkers, leg-cutters and top-spinners; his lift and pace from the pitch were renowned. A courageous and tireless mainstay of the Australian attack at a time when the batting was weak, he was the first of the great modern medium-pacers, and one of the best bowlers of all time on helpful wickets. In 17 Test matches against England he took 101 wickets at 16, including 5 or more wickets in an innings 11 times; in all first-class matches he took 992 wickets at 14. His average of 7.68 in 1886-87 and aggregate of 106 in 1887-88 are Australian records that have seldom been approached. A free-hitting batsman, he scored a century against Surrey in 1888 that lived in the memory of Ranjitsinhji, and twice opened the innings in the 1890 Tests.

A bank manager in 1891, Turner worked briefly for some English merchants and as editor of a cricket magazine in the 1890s. His first-class career ended in 1897 when he moved to Gympie, Queensland, although in 1910 he returned to the Sydney Cricket Ground to open the bowling in his testi-monial match which raised over £534. By 1917 he was a teller in the Government Savings Bank of New South Wales, and in 1926 the loss of the Ashes led him to publish an instruction manual, *The Quest for Bowlers* (Sydney). Turner died of senile decay on 1 January 1944 and was cremated at the Northern Suburbs crematorium. He was survived by a daughter of his second wife Harriett Emily, née Goldman, whom he had married at the Registrar-General's Department, Sydney, on 28 October 1891, and by his third wife Edith Rebecca Susan, née Sargent, who inherited his estate valued for probate at £202. In 1972 his ashes were returned to Bathurst.

J. N. Pentelow, *England v. Australia* (Bristol, 1904); F. Lillywhite, *M.C.C. cricket scores and biographies*, 15 (Lond, 1925); B. Frindall, *The Kaye book of cricket records* (Lond, 1968); *Cricket* (Lond), 5 May 1887, 20 Apr 1893, 24 Feb 1910; *Wisden's Cricketers' Almanack*, 1889, 1891, 1893, 1911, 1944, 1945, 1974; *World of Cricket*, 21 Mar 1914; *Advocate* (Melb), 31 Oct 1963; *Western Advocate* (Bathurst), 10, 15 Mar, 7, 8 Dec 1972; information from Messrs I. Rosenwater and D. Frith (London) and J. Gunning (Bathurst, NSW).   B. G. ANDREWS

TURNER, HENRY GYLES (1831-1920), banker, historian and littérateur, was born on 12 December 1831 at Kensington, London, son of William Turner, tailor of Worcester, and his wife Caroline, née Gyles. Turner spent four years at the Poland Street Boys' Academy, revealing an early love of literature and history in his capture of several school prizes, extensive reading and attempts at historical narrative and verse composition. However, in 1845 his father apprenticed him to Aldine publisher-bookseller William Pickering preparatory to a business career. Turner enjoyed the chance to browse and meet notables like Charles Dickens [q.v.] and Archbishop Manning; but in 1849 he learned that his mother's legacy had been squandered by her husband and a dishonest trustee.

Next year Turner began work with the London Joint-Stock Bank as a clerk, the low pay, limited prospects and mediocre status being viewed with disfavour by his prospective mother-in-law. An attempt to ease the monotony by forming a reading club amongst his colleagues back-fired after their first publication satirized a senior bank officer. Failing to obtain promotion in 1854, he decided to try 'another hopeful land where wealth might wait on honest work and will'. With the help of a family friend he left Southampton for Melbourne in the *Argo* on 4 October 1854 to work for the Bank of Australasia. He arrived on 6 December amidst the furore of Eureka. His fiancée Helen Ramsay followed him and on 28 September 1855 at Prahran they were married according to the rites of the Church of Scotland; their association was to be saddened only by childlessness.

After tedious clerical work Turner became chief accountant in 1864, but he had pursued a wide range of cultural and recreational interests. On the voyage out he had befriended George Coppin [q.v.] and he later performed for the Melbourne Histrionic Club in city theatres and country towns. In 1856-57 Sydney Gibbons, an aspiring journalist, offered Turner space in the *Illustrated Journal of Australasia and Monthly Magazine* and introduced him to Melbourne's literati, including James Smith, A. Michie, G. G. McCrae, N. Chevalier and fellow bank employee Marcus Clarke [qq.v.]. With their encouragement he helped to launch the short-lived *Australian Monthly Magazine* on 1 September 1865, and contributed articles to weekly periodicals such as the Melbourne *Spectator*, Clarke's *Colonial Monthly* and James Smith's satirical *Touchstone*. He was also a founder, leading contributor and first president in 1868-70 of the Eclectic Association.

Turner was tall and muscular, with a great love of the outdoors: he initiated the Banks Rowing Club and helped to defend their annual trophy in the 1860s, later serving for many years as president of the Victorian Rowing Association. On holidays he explored the Victorian countryside, climbed the You Yangs, tramped eighty-five miles in three days along the Mornington peninsula and rode on horseback up to the Murray River and into New South Wales. His social and sporting interests influenced him to decline three managerial transfers in the 1860s, but his patience was rewarded in June 1870 when the Commercial Bank of Australia offered him the general managership in Melbourne.

The bank was on the edge of ruin, but fifteen years later Turner could boast deposits of £2,250,000, a reserve fund of £120,000, a 10 per cent dividend, and new branches throughout the Mallee, Goulburn Valley and the Western District, and in London, Sydney, Adelaide and Brisbane. No financial genius, Turner rescued the bank through hard and conscientious work, wooing mercantile and farming interests and distributing shareholders' profits with caution. But as Victoria prospered in the aftermath of the gold boom, he advanced easy credit on the basis of land securities, a practice which stimulated the bank's expansion and which he justified as essential for the colony's growth. By the late 1880s his success and impressive articles in financial journals had made Turner one of Melbourne's most influential bankers. Elected a fellow of the Bankers' Institute, London, in 1880, he was asked by the Victorian government in 1882 to help to negotiate a £4 million loan in England and to serve as commissioner to the Bordeaux Wine Exhibition. In July 1886 he became a founder and first president of the Bankers' Institute of Victoria, and next year honorary treasurer of the Queen's Fund and sole banking appointee to the royal commission on banking. He also served as president of the Chamber of Commerce in 1889-92 and chairman of the Associated Banks three times between 1875 and 1900.

Turner's literary achievements were equally remarkable. While trustee-treasurer of the Yorick Club and founder-president of the Kew Literary Institute and Free Library in the early 1870s, he became aware of Melbourne's need for a 'high class literary magazine'; in November 1875 a dozen friends, including Alexander Sutherland, A. P. Martin and A. M. Topp [qq.v.], gathered at his Albert Street home to launch the *Melbourne Review*. Its reputation as Australia's first successful quality review, acquired in a decade of production, owed much to Turner's efforts as contributor, editorial committee chairman, and editor in 1881-85. He became a trustee of the Public Library, Museums, and National Gallery in April 1884, and commissioner of the Centennial International Exhibition in 1887-88.

Turner was also involved with the Melbourne Unitarian Church, of which he had been secretary in 1860 and one of six elected lay preachers in 1870. His talented younger sister Martha [q.v.] arrived for a visit on 11 October 1870 and was persuaded by the congregation to take over the pastorate. Her decision to marry and settle in the colony and news of his mother's death in 1876 weakened Turner's attachment to England; after a trip to London next year he returned convinced of Melbourne's superiority in living conditions, life-style and public entertainments. After a further visit in 1882 work began on his permanent home, Bundalohn, a stately St Kilda mansion completed in 1886, where he entertained with a lavishness typical of the decade.

In Rome in 1889, Turner learned that 'the boom has bust'. A steady loss of deposits swelled to a rush in 1893 when the bank announced the sale of shares at half-price, culminating in suspension of trading on 7 April 1893. But for a scheme that lowered interest and delayed repayment to creditors, the bank would have collapsed. Turner blamed the disaster on dishonest finance companies, government ineptitude, and the reckless policies of his locum in 1888, but he was equally culpable through injudicious backing of land speculators; and he suffered by remaining in an uncongenial post, from which he had twice tried to resign, until satisfied in 1901 that reconstruction was complete.

Turner welcomed his retirement at 70 with undisguised relief. Having joined with Sutherland to produce *The Development of Australian Literature* in 1898, he was impatient to begin on a book first mooted in August 1856. In 1904 his two-volume *A History of the Colony of Victoria from its discovery to its absorption into the Commonwealth of Australia* was published in London, followed in 1911 by *The First Decade of the Australian Commonwealth*, and two years later by *Our Own Little Rebellion: the story of the Eureka Stockade*, both published in Melbourne. Thereafter he continued to foster a high culture and a community of letters in Melbourne.

Turner was a paradoxical figure. Renowned for his humanity, he was interested in a wide range of community bodies, including hospitals, schools and charities; yet he was an extreme Spencerean individualist, notorious for advocating eugenics for pauperism and crime. A banker who attacked socialism, trade unionism and economic protection, he presented an easy target for the labour press; but his denunciations of capital punishment, British imperialism, Aboriginal murders and White Australia led Bernard O'Dowd to suggest playfully in 1911 that he was an 'anarchist-communist'. He was certainly a libertarian in theology, inclining towards naturalistic Theism. Hatred of ecclesiastical tyranny moved him to support G. Higinbotham and Charles Strong [qq.v.] in the Scots Church conflict in 1883, to become a committee-man of the anti-Sabbatarian Sunday Liberation Society the same year and in 1907 president of the Education Act Defence League. He was prominent in the early years of the Victorian Historical Society.

Much of Turner's journalism is laboured and unoriginal, particularly the literary criticism which is strongly prejudiced against the 'Bulletin school': but it has flashes of wit and insight. His history is uneven; most of the post-1860 material is marred by excessive personal bias and lack of affinity with 'records of conventional politics and ... prosaic competition for place and power'. Yet in his writings on early Victoria Turner produced history of outstanding quality and lasting value. Few possessed better qualifications: active personal experience, an intimate knowledge of the Victorian countryside, half a century of observation and notation, empathy with the themes and skills of the great romantic literary historians and a compelling moral purpose—his wish to revive the spirit of Victoria's pioneers and indigenous people. Predeceased by his wife on 30 May 1914, he died on 30 November 1920 at Bundalohn and was buried in the St Kilda cemetery. His estate was valued for probate at £29,233, and in his will Turner left the charge of his household to Sutherland's widow Elizabeth, a close family friend. Apart from legacies to friends and relations, his bequests included £1000 to the University of Melbourne for a scholarship encouraging the scientific study of agriculture and he also directed that the chief librarian of the Melbourne Public Library choose books on Australian subjects from his personal library.

Apart from his four monographs Turner published some dozen pamphlets, including in Melbourne, *The Aims and Objects of a Literature Society* (1903) and *The War; with some thoughts on its aftermath in Australia* (1916), and over forty essays and reviews in journals and newspapers. His papers contain a number of unpublished literary works and an early monograph on the history of the Delaware Indians. An oil portrait by E. Phillips Fox was presented to the Victorian National Gallery in 1914.

M. Cannon, *The land boomers* (Melb, 1966); G. Serle, *The rush to be rich* (Melb, 1971); Bankers' Inst of A'sia, J, Oct 1887, Dec 1889; J of A'sia, Aug 1856; *Melbourne Review*, 1 (1876), 10 (1885); *Argus*, 5 Nov 1890, 3 Dec 1910, 1 Dec 1920; A'sian Insurance and Banking Record, June 1901; *Age*, 3 Dec 1904, 1 Dec 1920; *Punch* (Melb), 28 July 1904; R. Kugler, Henry Gyles Turner (B.A. Hons thesis, Univ Melb, 1971); H. G. Turner papers (La TL) and MS material in pamphlet collection (SLV).

IAIN McCALMAN

TURNER, JAMES FRANCIS (1829-1893), Anglican bishop, was born at Yarmouth, Norfolk, England, son of Sir George James Turner, a lord justice of appeal in Chancery, and his wife Louisa, née Jones. Educated at Charterhouse in 1838-44, he was apprenticed for four years in an architect's office in London. In 1848 he matriculated at University College, Durham (B.A., 1851; M.A., 1854; D.D., 1868). Made deacon in 1851 and ordained priest in 1853 by Bishop Maltby, Turner was chaplain and censor at Bishop Cosin's Hall in the university in 1852-54. Honorary secretary of the Architectural and Archaeological Society of Durham and Northumberland, he designed the chapel of Bishop Hatfield's Hall. He became curate of Walton, Somerset, in 1857 and was rector of North Tidworth, Wiltshire, from 1858; he was appointed rural dean of Amesbury in 1868.

Turner was nominated to the new see of Grafton and Armidale, New South Wales, and was consecrated in Westminster Abbey on 24 February 1869. With his wife Mary, née Sorsbie, he arrived in Sydney on 13 August in the *Commissary* and was installed at Armidale on 10 September. His see, equal in area to England and Wales, had a nominal Anglican population of about 25,000 and ten clergymen, mostly itinerant. In forming new parishes and providing new clergy, he found himself hampered by lack of financial aid from any of the British missionary societies. Letters in the *Sydney Morning Herald* accused him of ritualism before and after his arrival, and he suffered pain when the Irby family of Tenterfield took up the cry and stirred up animosity. He convened the first diocesan synod in May 1873 and in 1881 divided his diocese into two archdeaconries. The decision enabled the Grafton section to deal with some of its own affairs, but the duality expressed in the title of his diocese constituted a major problem throughout his episcopate.

Because of failing health Turner was unable to make extensive visitations in the 1880s, but diocesan growth continued. By 1892 the original ten clergy and parishes had increased to twenty-eight and the number of churches from twenty-one to fifty-eight. St Peter's Cathedral, Armidale (1875) and Christ Church Cathedral, Grafton (1884) owe much to Turner's continuing interest in architecture, his opposition to pretentiousness and regard for 'fitness and goodness' in church building.

Clearly High Church in outlook, Turner insisted on the Catholic rather than the Protestant character of the Church of England, but he was consistent in advocating less party spirit within the Church. Pessimistic on the question of Christian unity, he strongly defended the Church's role and attitude to marriage and outspokenly criticized Sir Alfred Stephen's [q.v.] divorce extension bill of 1887. While he supported the temperance cause he advocated moderation rather than total abstinence. He reaffirmed the traditional standpoint of the Church on education, but in practice was forced to acquiesce in the closure of denominational schools except on a proprietary basis; he urged his clergy to take full advantage of religious instruction in public schools. His *Letter to the Members of . . . the diocese of Grafton and Armidale* (1883) was commended by the *Church Quarterly Review*. He was a vice-president of the English Church Union.

Turner resigned his see in 1892; on his way to England he died, aged 64, in Rome,

on 27 April 1893 and was buried there in the English cemetery. Predeceased by his wife in 1879, he left his estate, valued for probate at £1766, to their adopted child Emily Harriett, daughter of Robert Issel Perrott of Haroldston near Armidale. His portrait is in St Peter's Cathedral, Armidale.

J. T. Fowler, *Durham University* (Lond, 1904); *Durham Univ J*, May 1893, 146; K. H. Aubrey, The Church of England . . . in the diocese of Grafton and Armidale 1867-1892 (M.A. thesis, Univ New England, 1964); Bishop Turner letters 1869-73, 1884-92 *and* Diocesan Synod reports 1873-92 (Diocesan Registry, Armidale); Bishop Turner letters (SPG Archives, Lond); information from Mrs J. Newall (archivist, Diocese of Armidale).

KEITH H. AUBREY

TURNER, MARTHA (1839-1915), Unitarian preacher, was born in London, daughter of William Turner and his wife Caroline, née Gyles. She was educated for three years at a high school at Dijon, France, where according to her brother H. G. Turner [q.v.] she 'early developed high intellectual qualities'. She arrived in Melbourne in the *Dallam Tower* on 11 October 1870 on what was intended to be a visit to her brother; in 1872 he preached several times to the Melbourne Unitarian congregation but found it 'a great labour' because of limited time and 'severe self-criticism'. 'Happily my sister came to my assistance' late in the year.

On 26 October 1873 a special meeting of the congregation elected Martha as third regular minister. During her formal inauguration on 23 November she read for the second lesson from I Corinthians XIV, including the verse: 'Let your women keep silence in the churches'. The novelty attracted large audiences; several journalists inevitably quoted Dr Johnson on woman preachers. Martha Turner dressed in ordinary costume and wore no badge of office; she sat on a small raised platform before a desk, spoke with 'clear and crystal intonation' and 'displayed a plain undemonstrative demeanour'; she had a 'rather abstract, colourless style' but a lucid liberal intelligence. She had feared that 'the natural conservative instincts of women would lead the ladies of the congregation to discountenance or forsake me', but was quickly reassured. Her exacting congregation was well pleased. She performed marriages and three of her early sermons were published.

On 22 August 1878 at the office of the Registrar-General, Melbourne, Martha married John Webster (d. 1920), a bank officer. She had intended to resign her pastorate but was persuaded to continue until a successor W. E. Mellone was appointed from England in 1880. When he resigned after three months, she resumed until 1883 when she retired and was succeeded by Rev. George T. Walters. The Websters then visited Britain and Martha preached to Unitarian congregations in London, Birmingham and Scottish cities. After two years they returned to live at Boolarra, Gippsland. Martha spent long periods in Melbourne for, although said to be reserved in temperament, she greatly enjoyed intellectual society; she was reported to be a humorous and sarcastic but nevertheless kindly conversationalist.

From October 1914, needing medical treatment, she lived with her brother at Bundalohn, St Kilda, where she died on 11 August 1915 aged 76 and was cremated at her express desire. The *Woman Voter* predicted that 'in relation to the Woman Movement ... Martha Webster's name will be associated with those of Catherine Helen Spence [q.v.] and Vida Goldstein, as pioneers in Australia'.

Argus, 12 Aug 1915; *Woman Voter*, 2 Sept 1915; H. G. Turner papers (LaT L).

GEOFFREY SERLE

TURNER, WILLIAM (1837-1916), miner, politician and florist, was born at Wickham, Durham, England, son of William Turner, bootmaker, and his wife Ann, née White. In 1857 Turner migrated to the Victorian goldfields; later he became a temperance lecturer and Methodist preacher in Ballarat and at Scarsdale where he lived. On 15 February 1861 at Fitzroy, Melbourne, he married Margaret Elliott. In the Legislative Assembly elections of February 1871 he stood as an anti-ministerial liberal for the seat of North Grenville, defeating the Speaker Sir Francis Murphy [q.v.] but missing election by thirteen votes. About 1873 he moved to Wallsend near Newcastle, New South Wales, and worked as a mine foreman and as a reporter on the *Miner's Advocate and Northumberland Recorder* (*Newcastle Morning Herald and Miner's Advocate* from 1876).

Turner promoted the incorporation of Wallsend, which was achieved in 1874, supported the local literary institute and was prominent in Rev. James Greenwood's [q.v.] Public School League. A founding member of the New South Wales Political Reform League and secretary of Lambton branch, he was selected by Wallsend branch in July 1877 to stand for election as 'a working man to represent working men'. His platform included opposition to assisted immigration and support for electoral and land law reform, land taxation, payment of members, abolition of the property qualification and plural voting, fiscal protection and free, compulsory and secular education. Guaranteed £300 a year, made up of 1s. 6d. a quarter from each member of the league's branches, he was returned for Northumberland at the by-election on 20 July. Four hundred well-wishers cheered as he left for Sydney.

Initially diffident in parliament, Turner was received cordially and soon adapted to the situation. He joined J. S. Farnell's [q.v.] 'third party' of seven who held the balance of power and whose policy was similar to the league's. The group arranged for Farnell to move a vote of no confidence and (Sir) John Robertson's [q.v.] government fell on 12 October. In the ensuing elections Turner was again endorsed for Northumberland by the league, despite being discarded by his influential press supporters for his part in the fall of Robertson; he was narrowly defeated. He blamed plural voting, money spent on drink, and cajolery by his opponent. On 4 December he petitioned against the return of Thomas Hungerford [q.v.] but withdrew.

In November 1880 Turner stood again for Northumberland with a similar platform, including advocacy of arbitration. He was returned with Ninian Melville [q.v.], the other workers' candidate, and became an acknowledged debater and assiduous local member. By November 1881 both were in financial difficulties and a committee was belatedly formed to raise funds for their support; it failed and Turner was forced to resign on 20 December. He denied that the miners had reneged on their financial support which had not been mooted at the 1880 election.

Turner was a school attendance and payments officer with salary of £200 from 10 March 1882 until 1887; he later took up land at Belmore where he was a horticulturist and florist until he retired in 1903. While living there he contested the seat of Hunter. Aged 81, he died of uraemia at Hurstville on 24 April 1916, survived by his wife, two daughters and three sons. He was buried in the Anglican section of the Sutherland cemetery.

V&P (LA NSW), 1877-78, 1, 60; *Age*, 14 Jan, 6, 13, 15, 16 Feb 1871; *Newcastle Morning Herald*, 6, 12, 13, 16, 19, 24, 25, 27, 28, 30 July, 15, 18, 20, 22, 25, 27, 30 Oct, 7 Dec 1877, 17, 24, 27 Nov, 25 Dec 1880, 25 Oct, 3 Nov, 24 Dec 1881, 13 Jan 1882, 26 Apr 1916; *SMH*, 20, 25 July 1877, 25 Apr 1916.   SUZANNE EDGAR

TURRIFF, HALDANE COLQUHOUN (1834-1922), hospital nurse, was born on 12

January 1834 at Paisley. Renfrewshire, Scotland, eldest child of Alexander Turriff, ironfounder and engineer, and his wife Janet, née Hardie. In August 1866 she entered the Nightingale Training School attached to St Thomas's Hospital, London, and was selected as one of the five nurses to accompany Lucy Osburn [q.v.] to the Sydney Infirmary and Dispensary in December 1867. Her arrival in Sydney on 5 March 1868 in the *Dunbar Castle* was enlivened the next week by the attempted assassination of the duke of Edinburgh and she was one of the two nurses who cared for him.

The Nightingale nurses were engaged on a three-year contract. When their performances were reviewed in 1870 Lucy Osburn would not recommend the reappointment of Sister Haldane, who then resigned. She had made no secret of her dissatisfaction with her working conditions and with most of her colleagues, and especially resented attacks made on the status of the sisters. Observant, shrewd and caustic of tongue, she had considerable powers of expression. She alienated both Lucy Osburn and Miss Nightingale, who tried in vain to convince her of the necessity for tolerance. To Miss Nightingale she replied, 'I am sure that it is not your wish that anyone should call evil good or good evil. But it may be expedient to refrain from saying that evil is evil and it is without doubt prudent to withhold censure where censure is considered a worse offence than the evil committed'. She was blind to reason when she considered herself to be a victim of injustice. Her superiors finally concluded that she was a bad nurse and unsuited to hospital work, but in December 1870 she was appointed as first matron of the Alfred Hospital in Melbourne. The rumour that she owed this to Prince Alfred's favour was denied.

The Alfred Hospital's progressive administrators had ensured the autonomy of their nursing establishment by writing it into the hospital constitution. But they could not anticipate the unyielding nature of their prized Nightingale matron, nor the prejudices of doctors who adhered to the concept of nurses as degenerate housemaids. Assisted by brilliant journalism in the *Argus* by 'The Vagabond' [q.v. J. S. James], complaints about Miss Turriff's ill temper, her alleged usurpation of authority and her command of female staff exploded in 1876. Control of the hospital was the issue at stake but this was obscured by personal differences. However, the matron had a champion in the hospital president James Service [q.v.] whose influence outweighed all protest. Most of the plaintiffs resigned or were dismissed. The matron suffered a slight diminution of her authority.

The rest of Miss Turriff's tenure was uneventful. That she failed her duty as a Nightingale graduate and did not establish a training school was probably due to her lack of talent as a formal teacher. In spite of this, even her critics agreed that her nurses were the best in Melbourne. Two women who had started nursing under her were given charge of the training school when it was established late in 1880. She gave notice in January 1880 and on 6 March married a widower William Gilmour Murray, who was a respected senior member of the shipping firm of Gibbs, Bright [q.v.] & Co., and opened its Sydney office in 1875. He had arrived in Melbourne in 1853 and was the first honorary auditor of the Alfred Hospital.

After Murray's death on 6 May 1888 his widow remained in Sydney until about 1894 when, financially secure but not rich, she appears to have returned to Scotland, where she died at Catrine, Ayrshire, on 5 February 1922. She was handsome with a beautiful speaking voice, and dressed well; a Presbyterian, she turned to Anglicanism in her colonial years. Outside the hospital milieu she rarely alluded to the fact that she had been one of Miss Nightingale's pioneers.

M. P. Susman, 'Lucy Osburn and her five Nightingale nurses', *MJA*, 1 May 1965; A. M. Mitchell, The hospital south of the Yarra (Ph.D. thesis, Univ Melb, 1972); Nightingale papers (BM).   ANN M. MITCHELL

TWOPENY, RICHARD ERNEST NOWELL (1857-1915), journalist and author, was born on 1 August 1857 at Little Casterton rectory, Rutland, England, son of Rev. Thomas Nowell Twopeny (d. 1869) and his wife Mathilde, née Lewis. His father migrated to South Australia in 1860 but Twopeny spent part of his childhood in France and was educated at Marlborough College, England, until 1875 and the Ruprecht-Karl-Universität, Heidelberg, Germany. With tact, energy, wide interests and some literary ability, he made journalism his profession. He arrived in Melbourne in the *Northumberland* on 15 May 1876 and soon moved to Adelaide where he worked on the *South Australian Register* in 1876-77.

Twopeny's organizing ability, economic interests and gift for publicity won him many special appointments: he was secretary for the South Australian royal commissions for the exhibitions in Paris (1878), Sydney (1879) and Melbourne (1880). He spent nine months in Paris where he met Jules Joubert [q.v.] and in 1879 was created an officer of the French Academy of Paris. In 1881-82 he edited the *Telegraph* in Christchurch, New Zealand, and the *Otago Daily Times* in 1882-90. Meanwhile with Joubert he managed private-venture exhibitions in Adelaide and Perth in 1881 and Christchurch in 1882. Next year he tried to organize an Australasian exhibition in London and published his proposals in a pamphlet. He was commissioner for New Zealand at the 1888 Centennial International Exhibition in Melbourne and executive commissioner for the New Zealand and South Seas Exhibition, in Dunedin in 1889-90.

Twopeny resigned from the *Otago Daily Times* in 1890 after a disagreement with the directors. When the Australian pastoralists decided during the 1891 shearers' strike to have their own paper, he was chosen with Captain A. W. Pearse to found and edit the *Australasian Pastoralists' Review*; he was senior proprietor until 1915. In 1896-97 he visited Liverpool and Manchester in England as representative of the Australian Frozen Meat Export Association to study the Argentine meat trade. At his suggestion a meat marketing committee was formed to represent colonial freezing companies in England. He went to Europe in 1907 apparently for relaxation and visited Egypt, Italy, Germany, France and England. On his return to Melbourne in 1910 he wrote four articles for the *Pastoralists' Review* on his travels in Germany, Austria and Switzerland. Childless, he died suddenly of heart disease and pneumonia in London on 2 September 1915. He was survived by his wife Mary Josephine, daughter of Rev. A. H. Wretislaw, vicar of Manorbier, Pembrokeshire, Wales, whom he had married on 4 December 1879 at St John's Church of England, Darlinghurst, Sydney. He was attached to two nephews living in South Australia.

Twopeny impressed contemporaries as a man of charm, humour and executive talents. A fluent speaker and writer both of English and French, he had a perennial freshness of approach that matched his clear-eyed, open expression and alert, square-cut face, with trim moustache and goatee beard. Posterity has known him as the author of *Town Life in Australia* (London, 1883), an excellent, witty and sophisticated guide to Sydney, Melbourne and Adelaide about 1880. He was one of the first to note the predominance of lower middle-class models in English influence on Australian society, the derivative character of most political thought in Australia and the special characteristics derived from the

assimilation of English, Scots and Irish in proportions that existed nowhere else in the world. Originally the book appears to have been written as letters for publication in an English periodical; neither the letters nor their place of publication, if any, has been found. The book, published by Elliot Stock, bears no editor's name and was carried through the press anonymously 'without communication with the writer, who is in New Zealand'. It was reprinted in Sydney in 1973.

R. E. N. Twopeny, *Town life in Australia*, introduction by J. M. Ward (Syd, 1973); PP (SA), 1880, 4 (102), 15; G. Davison, 'R. E. N. Twopeny and town life in Australia', *Hist Studies*, no 63, Oct 1974; *Pastoral Review*, 15 Feb 1897, 15 Mar 1907.　　JOHN M. WARD

TYAS, JOHN WALTER (1833-1903), linguist, bibliophile and university registrar, was born on 26 November 1833 at Brixton, London, son of John Tyas, classical scholar and member of the literary staff of *The Times*. Educated in France and at King's College School, he became tutor to the grandsons of the chief proprietor of *The Times*, John Walter, after whom he was named. Tyas was admitted to the Inner Temple on 31 March 1855 but for some years travelled widely with his pupils on the Continent before he was called to the Bar on 26 January 1861. He then served on the staff of *The Times*.

Tyas's uncle Charles John Leaf was a silk manufacturer whose London home adjoined that of Matthew Arnold. With help from him Tyas sailed for South Australia, arrived on 22 February 1868 in the *Coorona* and opened a softgoods warehouse. Unsuited for commerce, he soon moved to Western Australia, hired a schooner and for three years searched with some success for pearl-shell on the north coast of Australia, in New Guinea and the Aru Islands. In 1873 he returned to England where he became very friendly with his cousin Walter Leaf, who was beginning to win repute as a Greek scholar. For some years Tyas roved the Continent collecting bric-à-brac, pieces of art and books on antiquity. In 1878 he was appointed Reuter's agent in Adelaide arriving there on 18 September, and in 1882 became registrar of the University of Adelaide.

Tyas also acted as examiner in modern languages, especially in French. A natural conversationalist and an entertaining host, he was envied for his library and his knowledge of literature. He made many friends, among them the chief justice and chancellor S. J. Way. The council of the university deeply regretted his loss when he resigned in ill health in January 1892. He left Adelaide next year and returned to London, making his home at Campayne Gardens, South Hampstead. His visits to the Continent became fewer and his library was his main solace. Tyas had married Jane Turner on 11 September 1879 at St Paul's Anglican Church, Adelaide; they had four daughters. He died of heart disease and chronic bronchitis in his home on 18 December 1903.

J. Foster, Men-at-the-Bar (Lond, 1885); Register (Adel), 22 Feb 1868, 29 Dec 1903; Observer (Adel), 6 Feb 1892; Bulletin, 7 Jan 1904.

TYRRELL, WILLIAM (1807-1879), Anglican bishop, was born on 31 January 1807 at the Guildhall, London, tenth and youngest child of Timothy Tyrrell, remembrancer of the City of London, and his wife Elizabeth, née Dollond, granddaughter of the optician John Dollond. Educated at St Paul's School, London, Reading Grammar School and Charterhouse, in 1827 he entered St John's College, Cambridge (B.A., 1831; M.A., 1834; D.D., 1847) and rowed in the same boat as George Augustus Selwyn, later bishop of New Zealand and of Lichfield, England. Made deacon in 1832 and ordained priest on 22 September 1833, he became successively curate of Aylestone near Leicester and Burnham near Maidenhead. In 1839 he was presented by the duke of Buccleuch to the Beaulieu donative living in Hampshire. In 1841 he declined to accompany Bishop Selwyn to New Zealand as archdeacon, but in March 1847 reluctantly accepted nomination to the new diocese of Newcastle, New South Wales. On 29 June, in Westminster Abbey, he was consecrated by Archbishop Howley with A. Short, C. Perry [qq.v.] and Robert Gray (for Cape Town).

On 16 January 1848 Tyrrell reached Sydney in the Medway accompanied by two ordained clergymen, seven candidates for orders whom he had rigorously instructed on the voyage, a schoolmaster and mistress, his gardener and groom from Beaulieu and his housekeeper. On 26 January he was installed in St Andrew's Cathedral and on 31 January at the Newcastle Pro-Cathedral. During his entire episcopate he resided at Closebourne, renamed Bishopscourt, Morpeth, which he bought privately from E. C. Close [q.v.] in 1849. His diocese stretched from the Hawkesbury River north to Wide Bay, and from the Pacific coast west to the South Australian border. It then contained seventeen parishes; some had parsonages and schoolhouses, and nine had consecrated churches. The modest endowment was contributed by the Colonial Bishoprics' Fund.

In his early years, with his well-bred horses, groom and saddle-bags, Tyrrell enjoyed travelling throughout his diocese, confirming, encouraging his clergy, lifting parochial debts and opening bush churches and schools. He helped form dioceses at Brisbane (1859) and Grafton and Armidale (1867); yet in 1879 the diocese of Newcastle still contained twenty-four parishes, all staffed and with parsonages, many with substantial churches. Failing health alone caused him to appoint an archdeacon in December 1878. Despite offers of handsome livings in England from Selwyn, Tyrrell refused to leave Newcastle and was notable among colonial bishops for never visiting England. He was not, he claimed, 'an exciting preacher ... encouraging itching ears ... instead of being the Bishop of this vast Diocese'.

In asserting that education without religion was anathema, Tyrrell took little stock of colonial opinion. In his own diocese he fought for 'full complete religious Teaching' in Denominational schools and often required candidates for ordination to supply his chronic shortage of schoolmasters. He encouraged parochial Sunday schools, in 1852-53 established a book depository at Morpeth and supported moves to establish a Church of England grammar school at Newcastle and other secondary schools. In 1852 as the only Anglican bishop after Bishop Broughton's [q.v.] departure, he entered the controversy surrounding the establishment of a university, whose 'evil principle ... is that its course of instruction is totally devoid of religious teaching'. In a newspaper war with Vice-Provost Sir Charles Nicholson [q.v.], Tyrrell fought for an autonomous Anglican college with religious as well as secular teaching. He refused to send students to Moore Theological College near Liverpool; instead, candidates for orders were inadequately trained as catechists within the diocese.

In November 1850 Tyrrell attended the Australasian episcopal conference in Sydney which determined to revive synodical church government; he was the only bishop not to have trouble with his laity after it. In April 1851 he convened the first meeting of the Newcastle Church Society, and assembled his first synod in August 1865 without the parliamentary sanction he had earlier supported. He contended that the authority of a synod rested in the voluntary compact made by its members to respect its decisions. Bishop Barker [q.v.] disagreed and the unilateral determination of Sydney churchmen again to approach the legislature began diocesan divergence. Tyrrell argued against those clauses in the Church of England Property Management Act of 1866 that gave autonomy to diocesan synods. However he fostered the Australasian Board of Missions, visited Selwyn in New Zealand in May to September 1851 and was a founder of the mission to the Melanesian Islands. He later sponsored sporadic missions among Aboriginals.

After the loss of £13,000 of his private funds in the collapse of a gas company in England and foreseeing the withdrawal of state aid, Tyrrell drew up an elaborate scheme to provide an episcopal endowment and clergy stipend and superannuation funds. He invested his own and diocesan moneys in runs in the New England and Clarence districts, where in 1866 he held 106,000 acres, and on the Culgoa in Queensland. A man of fine physique, Tyrrell lived simply, his habits methodical and painstaking. Retiring by temperament, his manner was stiff, even austere. A High Churchman of the old school, he taught the Apostolic succession and exalted the duties and dignity of the episcopal office. In 1861-66 his autocratic interference in parochial wrangles at the Newcastle Cathedral alienated its laity. In August 1877 a stroke left him partially paralysed and he consulted Selwyn about appointing a coadjutor.

On 24 March 1879 Tyrrell died at Morpeth after an operation without chloroform for a strangulated hernia and was buried in St James's churchyard, Morpeth. By his wish his funeral service was that read for Selwyn. Unmarried, his diocese had become his family and he was so closely identified with it that on his death Newcastle was spoken of as 'the widowed Diocese'. In 1879 after poor seasons, Brenda station near Angledool was almost insolvent and his estate, valued for probate at £41,200, seemed unlikely to realize bequests of £250,000. His successor Bishop Pearson [q.v.] in 1882 claimed that Tyrrell's powers as a financier were 'very much over-rated' and it took thirty years to implement the bequests, reduced and amended by a private Act of parliament in December 1910.

The Church of England and the Sydney University: documents and correspondence (Syd, 1852); R. G. Boodle, The life and labours of ... William Tyrrell (Lond, 1881); A. P. Elkin, The diocese of Newcastle (Syd, 1955); D. O'Donnell, The Christ Church Cathedral controversy, 1861-1866 (Newcastle, 1967); Aust Churchman (Syd), 27 Mar 1879; A'sian Missionary News, Aug-Oct 1889; SMH, 25, 26 Mar 1879; B. R. Davis, The Church of England in New South Wales: the beginnings and development of training men for its ministry ... 1825-1925 (M.A. thesis, Univ Newcastle, 1966); Selwyn papers and SPG papers (ML); W. Tyrrell diary (Diocesan Registry, Newcastle).   RUTH TEALE

TYSON, JAMES (1819-1898), pastoralist, was born on 8 April 1819 near Narellan, New South Wales, third son of William Tyson and his wife Isabella, née Coulson, who had arrived in the colony on 19 August 1809 in the *Indispensable* with a seven-year sentence for theft in Yorkshire. Her husband and son William came free in the same transport; by 1819 William senior had a 40-acre grant at Narellan. James started work about 1833 as a farm-hand for the Vine brothers near Appin and spent a short time in Sydney in 1837 apprenticed to a bootmaker; he then worked as a pastoral labourer for Henry O'Brien [q.v.] at Douro near Yass. Later he took up Barwigery (Barwidgee) on the Ovens River for John Buckland.

James was unsuccessful with his brother William on Bundoolah (Goonambil) in 1845, and next year with his brothers William and John he moved to Tyson's run (Toorong) on the west bank of the Lachlan near its junction with the Murrumbidgee: this holding became the nucleus of his Tupra-Juanbung complex. Early in 1852 James and William arrived at the Bendigo goldfield with a small mob of cattle, set up a slaughter-yard and butcher's shop and in three years established a business which was sold late in 1855 for an estimated £80,000. James and John bought three sheep stations, South Deniliquin, Conargo and Deniliquin, which they improved with fencing and earth tanks. James made important experiments in digging channels for water, and was interested in the Deniliquin-Moama rail link, the Deniliquin and Echuca Electric Telegraph Co. and the Riverina separatist movement as well as local matters. John died at Deniliquin on 3 June 1860 leaving his estate to James who, in 1862, sold most of his Deniliquin holdings and moved back to the Lachlan and began the aggregation of leasehold pastoral land. In 1864 when James McEvoy refused to pay his share of costs of arbitration in their dispute over a boundary, Tyson successfully sued him in the Supreme Court but McEvoy appealed to the Privy Council.

By 1898 Tyson held 5,329,214 acres including 352,332 acres freehold. His stations included Tupra, Juanbung, Bangate, Goondublui and Mooroonowa in New South Wales; Heyfield in Victoria; and Glenormiston, Swanvale, Meteor Downs and Albinia Downs, Babbiloora, Carnarvon, Tully, Wyobie, Felton, Mount Russell and Tinnenburra in Queensland. He held other runs as mortgagee. Uninterested in stud-breeding he bred and fattened stock for the metropolitan markets. At Tully his nephews tried to grow sugar on his behalf as well as run cattle. Tyson also owned some land in Toowoomba, Hay and Brisbane and made two abortive visits to New Zealand to investigate the possibility of land investment.

Tyson was a member of the Queensland Legislative Council in 1893-98 but made only one short speech. He was a magistrate on the Maude, New South Wales, and Jondaryan, Queensland, benches, and a prominent lobbyist against the building of the Queensland transcontinental railway line by overseas capitalists on the land grant system; he opposed the Victorian border stock tax and campaigned actively for the land tenure reforms embodied in the Crown Lands Acts of 1884 in New South Wales and 1885 in Queensland. Generous to a wide range of charities, he contributed £1000 to the New South Wales Sudan Contingent and variously to the building funds of the Women's College, University of Sydney, and the Church of England at Leyburn.

Unmarried and intestate, Tyson died 'apparently [of] inflammation of the lungs' at Felton near Cambooya, on 4 December 1898. He was buried in the Toowoomba cemetery, but his remains were moved to the family vault at St Peter's Church of England, Campbelltown, New South Wales. His estate, realizing £2 million, was divided among his next of kin after an extended series of court cases involving the question of his domicile. A byword for wealth and a legend in his own lifetime, Tyson was usually called 'Hungry' by the *Bulletin* and was commemorated by A. B. Paterson in 'T.Y.S.O.N.'. Frugal, he was never known to drink, smoke or swear.

Z. Denholm, 'James Tyson, employer', *Wealth & Progress*, A. Birch and D. S. Macmillan eds (Syd, 1967); T. M. Z. Denholm, James Tyson 1819-1898: a man in his environment (M.A. thesis, Univ Qld, 1969); Tyson papers (NL, Oxley Lib, Brisb); *Regina* v. *Queensland Trustees*, CRS/85-98, SCT/514A, 228/1898 (QA).   ZITA DENHOLM

U

UHR, WENTWORTH D'ARCY (1845-1907), overlander and prospector, was born on 31 October 1845 at Wivenhoe station, Moreton Bay District, son of Edmund Blucher Uhr, grazier, and his wife Amy, née Kemp. He joined the Queensland police about 1866 and by 1867 was acting sub-inspector at Burketown, a tough and law-less settlement; from May that year to March 1868, via Palmerston (Darwin), Perth and Brisbane, he escorted to Rock-hampton a prisoner who was later dis-charged. Reputed to have allied himself with the rougher element of Burketown, he was refused promotion and left the force, probably in 1869. In 1872 he drove 400 head of Dillon Cox's cattle from Charters Towers to Darwin, pioneering the Gulf-McArthur-Katherine route. Late in 1872 he found the first gold at Pine Creek; a monu-ment there records his find.

For the next seven years Uhr worked across north Queensland and the Northern Territory with various partners, procuring cattle for the Palmer goldfield and droving into the Thompson River country; he finally returned to the Territory about 1880. For a time he managed Florida station, formed on the Goyder River, Arnhem Land, by J. A. Macartney [q.v.]. Hostile Aborig-inals, distance and poor country doomed the venture, but Uhr became known as a fearless and competent bushman who had little sympathy for natives. In 1881 he ran a hotel at Yam Creek and was secretary of a prospectors' association. In 1883 droving with Nat Buchanan for J. A. Panton [qq.v.] and W. H. S. Osmand, he organized repri-sals for the Aboriginal murder of a stock-man. Later that year C. B. Fisher [q.v.] and J. C. Lyon charged him with cattle-stealing; found not guilty, he sued for unlawful arrest, won damages of £3000 in 1885 and took up the Exchange Hotel in Darwin. In 1886 he was at the Halls Creek, Western Australia, gold rush and then left northern Australia.

Uhr maintained his interest in both gold and cattle. He was at Coolgardie in 1894, too late for the gold rush but in time to form the D'Arcy Uhr Goldmining Co. in 1895 with a capital of £6000; probably a speculation, it was registered in New South Wales. He settled down to become a popular pillar of Coolgardie society; he had interests in several meat supply firms, including Butcher and Uhr, and was elected to the Municipal Council and the Roads Board despite possible association with the hated meat ring.

Uhr had married Jane Haves on 2 May 1872 at Norman, Queensland; on 4 March 1885 at Darwin he married Myra Essie Thompson. He had four sons (all of whom died in infancy) and a daughter Gladys Vivien. He died in Coolgardie on 18 Feb-ruary 1907, apparently of natural causes, and was given a large public funeral.

G. Buchanan, *Packhorse and waterhole* (Syd, 1933); V&P (LA Qld), 1869, 1, 691; A. Laurie, 'The Kimberleys, Western Australia ...', *JRHSQ*, 6 (1960-61); NT *Times and Gazette*, 6 Feb 1874, 4, 18 Dec 1880, 23 Apr, 21 May, 11 June, 10, 12 Sept 1881, 29 Apr, 10 June 1882, 5 Apr, 27 Dec 1884, 14 Feb 1885; *Advertiser* (Adel), 1, 2 Apr 1885; *Coolgardie Miner*, 6 Feb 1898, 19, 20 Feb 1907.   F. H. BAUER

ULRICH, GEORG HEINRICH FRIED-RICH (1830-1900), geologist and mineral-ogist, was born on 7 July 1830 at Zellerfeld, Upper Harz, Germany, son of Friedrich Engelhard Ulrich, engineer, and his wife Catherine Elisabeth, née Herstall. He was educated at Clausthal at the Königliches Gymnasium, and from 1847 at the König-liche Preussische Bergakademie, graduating 'with distinction' in September 1851. He worked for a short time for the Prussian mines service and, after an attempt to go to Bolivia as a mining superintendent, migrat-ed to Melbourne, arriving in the *Wilhelms-burg* on 3 August 1853.

Ulrich went to the diggings and pros-pected at Forest Creek, Daisy Hill, Tarran-gower, Bendigo and other fields until 1857 when, through the good offices of L. Becker and F. McCoy [qq.v.] he became assistant secretary and draftsman to the royal mining commission. Next year he became field geologist and surveyor to the expanded government Geological Survey. He was naturalized on 29 July 1858 and anglicized his forenames. A meticulous geologist and painstaking cartographer he prepared plans and reports on the goldfields. His quarter sheets, some of them published with Chris-topher Aplin and Henry Lyell Brown, were among the most accurate work of A. R. C. Selwyn's [q.v.] staff. In 1864 he was pro-moted to senior field geologist; in November all his 'moveable property' was destroyed in a bush fire near Maldon.

On leave in 1867-68, Ulrich studied the

most recent techniques of ore treatment in central Europe and visited the Paris Universal Exhibition to gather specimens for the proposed Industrial and Technological Museum in Melbourne. Back in Victoria he published a short work on the occurrence and treatment of auriferous lead and silver ores at Chemnitz (Karl-Marx-Stadt). After the disbanding of the Geological Survey in 1869, he was appointed curator of the mineral collection and lecturer in mineralogy at the Industrial and Technological Museum in June next year under J. C. Newbery [q.v.]. He prepared detailed catalogues of the museum's rock and mineralogical specimens. He also became lecturer in mining at the University of Melbourne and continued in private practice as a consulting mining expert. On 31 July 1871 at Christ Church, South Yarra, he married Catherine Sarah Spence of Belfast, Northern Ireland; they had four daughters and three sons, one of whom, Frank Ferdinand Aplin, became a well-known New Zealand surgeon and another, George Henry Roemer, a prominent lawyer.

In 1872 Ulrich published a report for the South Australian government on mineral resources near Port Augusta; he later reported on the Mount Bischoff tin and the Mount Ramsay bismuth mines in Tasmania. In 1875 he visited New Zealand and published, with Professor F. W. Hutton, Report on the geology & goldfields of Otago. Ulrich was now one of the foremost petrologists, crystallographers and mineralogists in Australasia. In 1864 he named Maldonite and later, in New Zealand, identified Awaruite. In 1877 he became foundation director of the School of Mines and professor of mining and mineralogy at the University of Otago. He contributed much to New Zealand geology and mineralogy and did valuable work as Hutton's successor in 1878-80 at the Otago Museum.

Ulrich, a Freemason and accomplished amateur singer and musician, was modest and kindly, highly respected throughout Australasia by colleagues and students alike as an industrious, enthusiastic teacher and accurate scientist. He was a fellow of the Geological Society of London, an original member of the Australian Institute of Mining Engineers and a corresponding member of several other colonial learned and Royal societies. Examining rock specimens on Flagstaff Hill, Port Chalmers near Dunedin, on 26 May 1900 he fell 100 feet and died later that day. He was buried in the Northern cemetery, Dunedin.

W. Perry, The Science Museum of Victoria (Melb, 1972); V&P (LC Vic), 1874 (C14); E. J. Dunn and D. J. Mahony, 'Biographical sketch of the founders of the Geological Survey of Victoria', Vic Geological Survey, Bulletin, 23 (1910); Otago Daily Times, 11 June 1880, 28, 29 May, 5 June 1900; A. D. McRobie, An administrative history of the Otago Museum (M.A. thesis, Otago, 1966); Ulrich papers (Hocken Lib, Dunedin); Otago Univ Archives (Dunedin); private papers (held by Ulrich family, Timaru, NZ).   MICHAEL HOARE

USING DAENG RANGKA (1845?-1927), a captain in the Macassan trepanging industry of northern Australia, was born at Labbakang in south Celebes, the son of a Bugis father and a Macassarese mother. Using first came to Australia with the annual fleet as a small boy. In December 1883 he was the first captain to purchase, most unwillingly, a South Australian government trepanging licence for the proa under his command, Bondeng Patola. In the 1886-87 season, in the Erang Poleang, he was wrecked on Melville Island, Northern Territory; with an old carbine he kept off an attack by Aboriginals until four dug-out canoes were launched; three weeks later three of the canoes arrived 'in a very sorry condition' at Bowen Strait revenue station, where they were given rice to continue eastward.

From 1887 Using commanded a new and larger Bondeng Patola. In March 1895 he was again wrecked, on the western coast of the Gulf of Carpentaria. With another crew wrecked in the same storm, in three weeks Using made a 400-mile trip in canoes to Bowen Strait. In an unsuccessful application for the refund of £47 paid by the wrecked proa, Alfred Searcy, sub-collector of customs for the Northern Territory, described Using as 'honest and always willing to pay [his] duties'. In 1899 Using was by chance discovered in Melville Bay by a government party; he insisted that the loss of his mainmast had kept him from Bowen Strait but paid the greater part of his licence fee and duty.

From the late 1890s Using seems to have regularly commanded the Bunga Ejaya. In 1906 the sudden decision to prohibit the Macassans in favour of local enterprise prompted the entrepreneur Puddu Daeng Tompo to choose him to check the truth of the report. Using thus saw the decline of the 200-year-old industry and was the last of the trepanging captains from Macassar to visit Australia. His signature in Macassarese script preserved on a proa's manifest shows that he was literate, and he was undoubtedly aware of the relevant government regulations. The loss of two vessels and the final problems of the industry make it unlikely that he earned much money from his voyages. After his return from Australia in 1907 he completed one further voyage to the Lesser Sunda Islands and then retired to Kampong Maloku in Macassar.

Using's first marriage to a Macassarese woman named Basse' was childless; his second wife Daeng Tanang, also Macassarese, bore him eleven children. A son Mangngellai Daeng Maro accompanied his father to Australia on his two last voyages. Using is also said to have had two daughters and a son by an Aboriginal woman in eastern Arnhem Land. His name is still remembered by Aboriginals in that area. He died at Kampong Maloku in 1927.

C. C. Macknight, *The voyage to Marege': Macassan trepangers in northern Australia* (Melb, 1976); in-letters, NT govt resident *and* minister controlling NT (SAA); information from Mangngellai Daeng Maro, Ujung Pandang, Indonesia.   C. C. MACKNIGHT

V

VAGABOND, THE, *see* JAMES, JOHN STANLEY.

VALE, WILLIAM MOUNTFORD KINSEY (1833-1895), and RICHARD TAYLER (1836-1916), politicians and booksellers, were born on 10 August 1833 and 30 August 1836 in London, sons of John Vale, bookseller, and his wife Elizabeth, née Tayler (Taylor). Richard was educated at Cowper Street school and worked for two years with a wholesale stationer. In March 1853 they arrived with their parents and sisters in Melbourne in the *Blackheath*. The family settled at Castlemaine where the brothers set up in partnership as booksellers and newsagents in 1854. Richard soon went to Beechworth and William moved to Ballarat.

In 1859 at Hackney, London, William married Rachel Lennox. They returned to Victoria and, as a liberal with a keen interest in protection, Vale represented Ballarat West in the Legislative Assembly from November 1864 to August 1865 and from September 1865 to April 1869. He was vice-president of the Board of Land and Works and commissioner of public works from July 1866 to May 1868 and commissioner of trade and customs from July 1868 to May 1869, when he resigned on principle in an attempt to prevent the return of C. E. Jones [q.v.]. Unsuccessful in the May by-election, in October he won Collingwood which he represented until March 1874 when he did not stand for re-election. In 1870 he was a member of the royal commission on the civil service, and from November 1871 to June 1872 he was commissioner of trade and customs in the Duffy [q.v.] ministry; but his fighting spirit did not allay the fear and distrust stirred up by the Irish Catholic leadership and the policy of the ministry. About 1872 he sold his business in Ballarat to his brother and moved to Melbourne.

In 1874 Vale went to England where he was a member of the Board of Advice to the agent-general. He qualified as a barrister in 1878, returned to Melbourne and next year was admitted to the Victorian Supreme Court. He set up in Temple Court, sharing a room with Alfred Deakin who described him as 'renowned for his democratic proclivities, his strict adherence to total abstinence and its platform, and for his ever bitter tongue'. Vale was prominent in the fight between manufacturers, miners and selectors and the landed and mercantile groups which climaxed at the end of the 1870s; but by the time he had returned to the assembly much of the heat had gone and he was too late to persuade Berry [q.v.] to accept his extreme ideas. In May 1880 he won Fitzroy and from August until July 1881 he was attorney-general and minister of justice in the Berry ministry, effecting what the *Age* described as 'very necessary' reforms in the Titles Office. He was reputedly a land speculator, and in 1883 the Collingwood *Observer* attributed his defeat at Emerald Hill to his attendance at a land sale on election day. He was defeated in 1889 as a candidate for Collingwood.

In the 1860s Vale had been interested in the early-closing movement: he felt it was a mockery to have mechanics' institutes and the public library only for the leisured few. He was a trustee of the Public Library, Museums, and National Gallery in 1872-95 and was a foundation member of the board of the Young Men's Christian Association. As an active Congregationalist he believed that 'the state has nothing to do with religion', but as a member of the Independent Order of Good Templars he was keen to use the state in the temperance cause. In November 1880 at an international temperance conference in Melbourne he moved the resolution which founded the Victorian Alliance.

Vale early advocated protection as the basis of social progress. The tariff was to assist the growth of industry, but the workers must be given technical training. In 1869-70 he was a member of the commission 'upon the promotion of technological and industrial instruction . . . among the working classes of Victoria'. In the late 1880s he was a founder of the Working Men's College. An enthusiastic treasurer of the 1880-81 Melbourne Exhibition he was chairman of its manufacturers' committee. He was a commissioner of the Centennial International Exhibition in 1887 but had to resign because of ill health. After a visit to England in 1888 he lived quietly until his death from Bright's disease at Collingwood on 23 October 1895. Buried in St Kilda cemetery, he was survived by five of his six daughters and three of his five sons; his daughter Grace graduated in medicine from the University of Melbourne and practised in Ballarat in 1896-1915. Deakin described Vale as handsome, 'well-featured, with fine eyes and a ringing mellow voice, abounding in energy, voluble, fairly well-read and a strict Puritan in life and ideals, strong in domestic affections ... His faults were an egotism which made him envious and suspicious, a biliousness which made him intolerant and vindictive and a vocabulary which made him a master of personal abuse'.

Richard Tayler Vale visited England in 1860-62 and after his return was a bookseller and newsagent in Smythesdale until 1869. On 7 October 1865 at Newtown near Scarsdale, he married Gertrude Campbell according to the rites of the Wesleyan Church. In 1869 he moved to Ballarat; some three years later he bought his brother's business which he carried on until about 1900. A 'radical of the old school', drawn to political activity but unable to enter parliament before payment of members, he advocated protection. A Congregationalist and a temperance worker, in 1871 with Henry Bell he organized the Ballarat Liberal Association and in 1875 the first National Reform League. He represented Ballarat West in 1886-89 and in 1892-1902 and was minister without office under (Sir) George Turner from September 1894 to August 1896, when he resigned from the government on issues arising from his membership of the sub-committee of cabinet inquiring into possible retrenchments. He was a vehement advocate of White Australia.

Strongly interested in mining, Vale held shares in most of the Sebastopol mines. He was on the council and for some years was vice-president of the Ballarat School of Mines. He took a course in assay and metallurgy, and from May 1911 was librarian for the Geological Survey, Department of Mines and Forests, in Melbourne. He did much for Ballarat and was keen for it to be the centre of a network of railway extensions. He was at one time deputymaster of the Loyal Orange Lodge, and in 1911 won a plebiscite conducted by the *Ballarat Courier* to determine the 'grand old man of Ballarat'. On 18 June 1916 he died of bronchitis and heart failure at Ballarat North; survived by three of his five sons and four of his five daughters, he was buried in the Ballarat new cemetery.

A. Deakin, *The crisis in Victorian politics, 1879-1881*, J. A. La Nauze and R. M. Crawford eds (Melb, 1957); *Age, Argus, Ballarat Courier, Ballarat Star*, 24 Oct 1895, 19 June 1916; *Observer* (Collingwood), 31 Oct 1895; *Table Talk*, 31 May 1895; A. M. Mitchell, Temperance and the liquor question in later nineteenth century Victoria (M.A. thesis, Univ Melb, 1966).

JOY E. PARNABY

VANCE, GEORGE OAKLEY (1828-1910), Anglican clergyman, was born on 25 May 1828 in London, son of Rev. William Ford Vance, vicar of Coseley, Staffordshire, and his wife Ann Arabella Atterbury, née Oakley. He was educated first at the Islington proprietary school under Rev. John Jackson (later bishop of London), then at St Paul's School, Southsea, and at King's College School, London. In 1846 he headed the open scholarships to Lincoln College, Oxford (B.A., 1850; M.A. (Melbourne), 1856; D.D., 1886).

After eighteen months as a schoolmaster at Exmouth and probably Birmingham, Vance sailed for Australia in the *Orestes*, arriving in Melbourne on 5 December 1852. In October 1853 he was appointed a lay reader and on Christmas Day was ordained deacon by Bishop Charles Perry [q.v.]. Appointed as curate to Dean H. B. Macartney [q.v.] at St James's, Melbourne, he was responsible for the erection of temporary churches at Philipstown (Brunswick), Flemington and North Melbourne. In July 1854 he was transferred to St Paul's, Geelong, as curate to Archdeacon T. C. B. Stretch [q.v.] and on 31 December was ordained priest. On 6 March 1855 at Philipstown schoolhouse, he married Harriett Catherine Cresswell, daughter of a Melbourne solicitor.

In August 1855 Stretch proposed the establishment of a 'really good Grammar School in Geelong'; with his support Vance opened a school two months later which flourished so well that it was soon transformed into a 'Public School'. Trustees were elected, a portion of the government grant allocated for Church of England schools was obtained through Perry, and Vance appointed headmaster. The school took possession of its new buildings in April 1858, but a large debt remained. The opening of the Flinders National Grammar School in Geelong and economic depression precluded the increased enrolments necessary to service the debt, and creditors began to press. Vance tendered his resignation on 19 June 1860, and the school soon closed.

Vance moved to Castlemaine and conducted a school for a year. In January 1862 he was appointed to the charge of the parish of Chewton and in December was nominated incumbent of St Paul's, Kyneton, including Blackwood and Woodend. From January 1869 he acted as locum tenens for C. T. Perks at St Stephen's, Richmond, until nominated as vicar of Holy Trinity, Kew, in March 1870. Elected by one vote over H. H. P. Handfield [q.v.], he was installed as dean of Melbourne and incumbent of St James's in December 1894, and continued in office until 1910.

As headmaster, Vance's deficiencies as an

organizer had contributed to his school's collapse, but as cleric he was more successful. Perry appointed him to the Diocesan Council in 1869, and he was one of the three Melbourne clerical representatives to the first General Synod of the Church of England in Australia, held in Sydney in October 1872. In 1874 he was proposed for election by the Brisbane Synod to succeed Bishop Tufnell [q.v.] but, while the clergy favoured the election of a colonial clergyman, the laity favoured delegation to England and the matter was resolved by the Australian bishops translating Bishop Hale [q.v.] from Perth. Vance was elected a canon of St Paul's Cathedral in 1879 and appointed rural dean of East Melbourne in 1894.

Vance had proved a stimulating teacher at Geelong and maintained his literary and scholastic interests as editor of the *Church of England Messenger* in 1877-1900, and as matriculation classical examiner for the University of Melbourne. To promote local theological education he acted as registrar in Australia for the University of Trinity College, Toronto, and in 1891 helped to found the Australian College of Theology. Other interests included the presidency of the Christian Social Union and of the Guild of Church Musicians. In 1896 he was described as 'solidly built, broad as his views, with a thorough English face and good-humoured and pleasant manner'. He died of heart failure at the deanery, East Melbourne, on 25 August 1910, survived by his wife and eleven of his fifteen children. He was buried in the Boroondara cemetery.

Geelong Grammar School, *History and register . . .* (Geelong, 1907); P. L. Brown, *Geelong Grammar School* (Geelong, 1970); *Church of England Messenger* (Vic), 2 Sept 1910; Geelong Grammar School, *Corian*, June 1971, Apr 1974; *Australasian*, 16 May 1896.   JAMES GRANT

VAUGHAN, EDMUND (1827-1908), Catholic priest, was born at Courtfield, Herefordshire, England, son of William Vaughan and his wife Theresa, daughter of Thomas Weld of Lulworth Castle, Dorset. He was the uncle of Archbishop Vaughan [q.v.] and related to Governor Sir Frederick Weld. Educated at Stonyhurst College, he taught science for a few years at St Mary's College, Oscott near Birmingham, before preparing for the priesthood. He was in deacon's orders when he applied for admission to the Congregation of the Most Holy Redeemer, known as the Redemptorists, and spent his year of initiation at St Trond near Liège, Belgium; in 1852 he took his religious vows and was ordained priest. He devoted himself to popular preaching, the principal work for which St Alphonsus Liguori had founded the Order. Quickly showing his aptitude for work among all classes and as a kindly superior, in 1867 he introduced the Redemptorists into Scotland, his foundation at Perth being the first Catholic monastery there since the Reformation.

Bishop James Murray [q.v.] of Maitland, New South Wales, arranged for a Redemptorist community in his diocese, and in 1882 Vaughan, as superior, with four priests and two Brothers took up residence at Singleton. They used the summer for campaigns in New Zealand, leaving the preachers free for the rest of the year to meet the requests that came from all the eastern colonies. The inconvenience of Singleton and the burden of parish duties led in 1887 to the community being established at Waratah near Newcastle. Next year a new foundation was made at Ballarat; by 1894 the Redemptorists had conducted missions in every diocese from Cooktown to Adelaide.

When Archbishop Vaughan died suddenly in 1883, Fr Edmund was told confidentially that cardinals Manning and Howard were negotiating to have him named archbishop of Sydney. Although his candidature remained unknown, expressions of partisanship in the Australian press and strong feeling against English superiors made Vaughan's position uncomfortable. His letters showed his awareness of the intensely Irish sentiment of most Australian Catholics. Although he rarely experienced any personal animosity, he insisted that it seemed necessary that ecclesiastical offices in Australia be held by Irishmen; but he readily encouraged Australian candidates for the priesthood and urged his superiors to disregard the contrary arguments of the Irish bishops.

Recalled to England in 1894, Vaughan became English provincial, the major superior of Redemptorists in England, Ireland and Australia. He negotiated the establishment of a separate province in Ireland to assume responsibility for the Australian houses. Aged 80 he died of heart disease and congestion of the liver on 1 July 1908 at Bishop Eton, Liverpool.

J. Lemire, *Le Catholicisme en Australie* (Paris, 1894); R. Mageean, *The Redemptorists, their life and work* (Syd, 1922); S. J. Boland, Very Rev. Edmund Vaughan and the foundation of the Redemptorists in Australia (Ph.D. thesis, Pontifical Gregorian Univ, Rome, 1958); Manning papers (Oblates of St Charles, Bayswater, Lond); Maitland Diocesan Archives; Vaughan papers (Redemptorist Archives, Provincial House, Pennant Hills, NSW).   S. J. BOLAND

VAUGHAN, ROGER WILLIAM BEDE (1834-1883), Catholic archbishop, was born on 9 January 1834 at Courtfield, Ross, Herefordshire, England, second son of the fourteen children of Lieut-Colonel John Francis Vaughan, a leading county figure, and his first wife, Louisa Eliza, daughter of John Rolls of The Hendre, Monmouthshire. The Vaughans were recusant gentry who had survived in possession of the Courtfield estate; the growth of religious toleration allowed them to resume a long tradition of leadership in church and state. Vaughan was status conscious: his great-uncle Thomas Weld was the first English cardinal since the Reformation, several uncles and cousins were priests and bishops, and his cousin Sir Frederick Weld was governor of Western Australia and Tasmania. Of his five brothers who were priests, Herbert, the eldest, became a cardinal and archbishop of Westminster and John, the youngest, auxiliary bishop of Salford; another brother, Reginald, married Julia Shanahan, sister-in-law of Sir Patrick Jennings [q.v.]. Four of his five sisters became nuns.

Vaughan was probably afflicted with congenital heart disease. At 7 he was sent briefly to a local school, but his mother worried over his health and he was educated at home in a religious atmosphere. In 1850 he was sent to St Gregory's College at Downside near Bath. His mother's death in 1853 prompted serious thoughts of a religious vocation and on 12 September he took the Benedictine habit as Brother Bede. In 1855 at his father's request and expense, he was sent to Rome for further study under the guidance of the Italian scholar and reformer, Angelo Zelli-Jacobuzzi. He was ordained priest by Cardinal Patrizi in the basilica of St John Lateran on 9 April 1859.

Even before going to Rome Vaughan had considered English Benedictinism too lax and he returned to England in August eager for reform. After parish work and school-teaching at Downside, in 1861 he was appointed professor of philosophy at the new St Michael's Cathedral Monastery near Hereford, known as Belmont, and in 1861-72 he strove to make it the basis of a reformed monasticism. In 1862 he was elected superior as cathedral prior of the diocesan chapter of Newport and Menevia and was re-elected in 1866 and 1870. Vaughan's Belmont was distinguished by 'the enthusiasm and fervour of both staff and students'; he had a profound influence on a generation of monks, though he complained of lack of financial support from the major monasteries and of their recalling of 'half formed monks' to be schoolteachers. By 1872 he was tiring of the personal 'begging' by which he had raised £5000 to keep Belmont solvent.

Vaughan's intellectual development had been stimulated by his years in Rome where he was influenced by the revival of Thomistic philosophy, but he distrusted the main trends in German philosophy and theology. In the early 1860s he was in contact with Liberal Catholics, such as Lord Acton, associated with the *Home and Foreign Review*, and he contributed to the *Dublin Review*. He opposed the attendance of Catholics at the universities of Oxford and Cambridge as he feared it would destroy the English Catholic tradition. Convinced that Thomism was Christianity 'in its scientific form', he published the first English biography of Aquinas as *The Life and Labours of S. Thomas of Aquin* in two volumes (1871-72). As prior of Belmont he won repute as a scholar and preacher but never again had time for major scholarly work. A tall, impressive figure, he seemed completely self assured but his brother Herbert believed he was 'so very impressionable, of such strong feelings [and] of such little knowledge of the world'. In 1867 Herbert feared that Vaughan was in danger of losing control of 'his immensely strong feelings' in his friendship with the widowed Lady Herbert of Lea, who resembled his mother; but he emerged from this emotional crisis stronger, wiser and more mature.

In 1866 Archbishop Polding [q.v.] failed to get Vaughan as his coadjutor in Sydney; but he renewed his plea in 1871 and 1872 and gained the support of Cardinal Manning, who shared the British government's desire to have an Englishman appointed. Vaughan's reluctance was also weakened by his discontent at Belmont and on 28 February 1873 he was appointed titular archbishop of Nazianzus *in partibus infidelium*, with the right of succession to Polding, and was consecrated at Liverpool by Manning on 19 March. He arrived in Sydney in the *Nubia* on 16 December. The Irish suffragan bishops in New South Wales had failed to prevent 'the calamity' of another English appointment, and their protest to Rome was unavailing. In fact they had much in common with him in attitudes to Church government and discipline and to education. To Vaughan, Polding was a relic and symbol of the old Benedictinism he had tried to reform. Quickly concluding that the colonial Benedictines based on St Mary's College, Lyndhurst, were 'rotten dead' and that the only hope was for a new foundation from Belmont, he recommended secularization in a scathing report to Rome. He closed Lyndhurst in 1877.

Vaughan found that Polding had 'let things run terribly to seed and disorder', both financially and in the condition of the clergy. He demanded full powers as administrator and sole vicar-general, but Polding impeded relations with the suffragans and the planning of major initiatives. In 1874 Vaughan adroitly arranged his election as rector of St John's College, in the University of Sydney, and resided there. Finding it 'a ruin without a student', he hoped to make it the centre for educating both a lay elite and a native clergy; he introduced regular part-time theological training for the clergy, who were mainly Irish. He revelled in public controversy, beginning in 1876 with a strong retort to Bishop Barker [q.v.] in four 'Advent Conferences' that drew thousands to St Mary's Pro-Cathedral. Believing the colonies no place for 'polished frigidity' and that colonial audiences were 'a regular lot of rhinoceroses', he consciously adapted his style but too often the result was verbosity and over-reliance on 'resonant phrases, ridicule and humour', though he was a popular preacher. At his worst he could descend to irrational fantasy as in *Hidden Springs* (1876); at his best he could popularize a rational defence as in *Arguments for Christianity* (1879). He succeeded Polding as archbishop of Sydney on 16 March 1877.

In 1874-75 Vaughan had investigated the alleged indiscretions of Bishop O'Mahony [q.v.] and reported that he should resign. Bishop James Quinn [q.v.] intervened and the case embittered episcopal relations; it also undermined Vaughan's ability to concert an education policy and plan a reforming synod; but his judgment was upheld by Rome despite opposition from (Cardinal) P. F. Moran. Determined to break 'the Irish masonry', he influenced the appointment of E. Torreggiani [q.v.] as O'Mahony's successor. In 1878-79 Vaughan administered the diocese of Armidale and was given 'the hateful task' of investigating complaints against Quinn; he recommended the appointment of a coadjutor with succession rights, but Quinn died in 1881 and his brother Bishop Matthew Quinn [q.v.] accused Vaughan of persecuting him to the grave.

He found New South Wales Denominational education on the defensive and concluded there would be 'godless' secular education 'in the end', so Catholics must prepare to organize their own system from their own resources. Ready to take the initiative in rousing Catholics with 'a small earthquake', Vaughan was handicapped by the distrustful suffragans. Faced with plans for state grammar schools and the formation of the strong Parkes-Robertson [qq.v.] coalition ministry, he was delighted when Matthew Quinn offered in April 1879 to co-

operate. A bishops' meeting in May left Vaughan to draft a joint pastoral; published in July as *Catholic Education*, it condemned schools founded on 'secularist' principles as 'seedplots of future immorality, infidelity and lawlessness', and precipitated fierce sectarian conflict which helped Parkes to abolish state aid. Vaughan rightly believed that the pastoral was the occasion not the cause of the 1880 Public Instruction Act.

He issued five more pastorals in the next six months, spoke constantly in defence of Catholic rights and, enjoying 'real stand up public fighting', provoked Parkes to brand him as 'seditious'. In 1880 Vaughan bought the *Catholic Times* from J. G. O'Connor [q.v.] and published it as the *Express* to personally 'red pepper' his opponents. In organizing an education system he could build on the sound financial administration he had introduced, but religious teachers were essential. He had early established good relations with the Marist Brothers and in 1877 he invited the Jesuits to open secondary schools; from 1878 he provided welcome patronage for Mother Mary Mc-Killop's [q.v.] Sisters of St Joseph in their troubles with the Quinn brothers. In 1873-83 the number of schools and pupils more than doubled; by 1883 12,500 of Sydney's 15,200 Catholic children were in the system.

Realizing that education would now dominate Church finance, Vaughan made a major effort to build a usable section of the new St Mary's Cathedral before all state aid ended in 1882. To complete a plan by William Wardell [q.v.], he raised almost £30,000 in two and a half years by writing about 3000 personal letters. He dedicated the new cathedral in September, but under the physical strain of incessant work his health was rapidly deteriorating. He had travelled constantly throughout the archdiocese as far as Brisbane in episcopal visitations. Late in 1882 he announced that he would make an *ad limina* visit to Rome intending to recruit religious teachers and plan for a synod late in 1883. He left Sydney on 19 April 1883 and travelled slowly to Europe via North America. At Liverpool he went to the near-by home of Weld relations, Ince Blundell Hall, and on 18 August he died of heart disease in his sleep. He was buried there in the family vault but his remains were moved to Belmont in 1887 and finally reburied in the crypt of St Mary's Cathedral in August 1946. Vaughan left almost all of his estate, valued for probate at £61,828, to his successor.

J. T. Donovan, *The Most Rev. Roger Bede Vaughan ... life and labours* (Syd, 1883); H. N. Birt, *Benedictine pioneers in Australia* (Lond, 1911); S. Leslie (ed), *Letters of Herbert Cardinal Vaughan to Lady Herbert of Lea*

(Lond, 1942); C. B. Whelan, *The history of Belmont Abbey* (Lond, 1959); A. G. Austin, *Australian education, 1788-1900* (Melb, 1961); P. J. O'Farrell, *The Catholic Church in Australia, 1788-1967* (Melb, 1968); *Downside Review*, Jan 1884; Courtfield papers (National Lib of Wales); Vaughan family papers (held privately); Abbey Archives (Downside, Belmont, Ampleforth, Eng); Irish College Archives (Rome); Propaganda Congregation Archives, Vatican Secret Archives (Rome); Roman Catholic Archives (Sydney, Maitland, Bathurst, Goulburn).   A. E. CAHILL

VAUGHN, ROBERT MATTERSON (1833-1908), building contractor and politician, was born in Ohio, United States of America, son of Jesse Vaughn, farmer, and his wife Betsy, née Matterson. Educated at the Baptist Geauga Seminary, Chester, Ohio, in 1852 he sought his fortune on the Californian goldfields. Arriving in Sydney in 1853, he became a professional goldminer on the major diggings in New South Wales and Victoria.

On 12 February 1864 he married Sarah Anne, daughter of Thomas Colls [q.v.], in St Clement's Anglican Church, Yass, New South Wales, and in 1867 settled in the gold-mining town of Grenfell where he became a partner in a company operating a steam-driven quartz-crushing machine. By 1875 he was proprietor of several steam sawmills and later set up an iron-foundry. Involved deeply in the local community, he was appointed magistrate on 16 February 1870, became president of the School of Arts next year and of the hospital in 1872, and on 10 June 1873 was appointed coroner for the district. By 1879 he was chairman of the Public School Board, a committeeman of the Pastoral, Agricultural, Horticultural and Industrial Association and of the Prospecting Association, a leading Anglican layman, steward for the races and from May 1879 commissioner of insolvent estates for the district. As chairman of the Railway League, with James Watson [q.v.] he led a deputation to the secretary for public works in a vain attempt to get the southern and western railways connected from Murrumburrah to Orange via Young, Grenfell and Forbes. He also owned land in Grenfell, was local agent for the Australian Mutual Fire Insurance Society and operated as a building contractor, successfully tendering to construct the Forbes post office. Later he set up business as a civil engineer in Sydney in partnership with J. H. May and became a director of the Illawarra Harbour and Land Corporation, acquiring large land holdings in the Lake Illawarra area.

In 1880 Vaughn was elected to the Legis-lative Assembly for Grenfell and was secretary for mines in Sir John Robertson's [q.v.] 1885-86 ministry. A staunch protectionist, he was returned at every election until 1889 when he was defeated by the free-trade candidate G. H. Greene. He was re-elected in 1891 as the oldest of thirty-five members of the new Labor Party, twenty-one of whom were under 40; he could not conform to the 'solidarity' discipline of the party and was defeated in 1894 by M. J. Loughnane, a young Grenfell solicitor who had gained the support of the local Labor Electoral League. Able and energetic, Vaughn represented country interests, especially those of the selectors. His speeches show liberal-democratic sympathies, wide practical experience and sound common sense.

Vaughn became a member of the Grenfell Municipal Council in 1898-99; chairman of the progress committee, he was a trustee of the Show and Recreation Grounds in 1900. He moved to Sydney in 1903 and, aged 75, died of chronic endocarditis at his home in Paddington on 14 April 1908. Survived by his wife, five daughters and three sons, he was buried in the Anglican section of Rookwood cemetery. Vaughn Park in Grenfell is named after him.

B. Nairn, *Civilising capitalism* (Canb, 1973); PD (LA NSW), 1883, 2nd S, 1149; V&P (LA NSW), 1889, 2, 57, 1898, 2nd S, 3, 777; SMH, 11 Oct 1879; T&CJ, 16 Jan 1886, 5 Mar 1887; *Daily Telegraph* (Syd), 6 July 1894; *Grenfell Record*, 18 Apr 1908.   ANN-MARI JORDENS

VEKEY, ZSIGMOND; *see* WEKEY.

VENABLES, HENRY PARES (1830-1890), educationist, was born in London, second son of Thomas Venables, private secretary to Lord Sidmouth and Sir Robert Peel, and his second wife Jane Elizabeth, née Sturt, sister of Charles and E. P. S. Sturt [qq.v.]. He was educated at Eton and matriculated to Exeter College, Oxford, on 3 May 1849 (B.A., 1853). Attracted by the goldfields, he arrived in Melbourne in the *Gauntlet* with Henry Kingsley [q.v.] on 3 December 1853 but, like Kingsley, little is known of his activities for the next few years.

In March 1858 Venables became sub-inspector under the Board of National Education in Victoria at a salary of £550 and, recommended for his 'quiet and unobtrusive manner and active habits', was promoted to the rank of inspector in October 1860. In September 1862 he became first-class inspector of schools for the Western District under the Common Schools Board set up by Heales's [q.v.] Education Act; based on

Warrnambool, he took up duties on 14 April 1863. He had been admitted to the degree of B.A. (*ad eund.*) by the University of Melbourne on 1 April.

His appointment as examiner under the board in April 1866 made Venables directly accountable to the secretary B. F. Kane [q.v.] : his duty was to deal with the professional work of the office. After Kane's death in December 1872, he became secretary on 2 January to the new department set up under the 1872 Education Act. However, with many other public servants he was dismissed on Black Wednesday, January 1878; instead of being reinstated he was replaced in March by G. B. Brown [q.v.]. The decision excited much comment: the *Age* alleged that he could not cope with an enlarged department and argued that he should not have been appointed in the first place. But the *Argus* concluded that Venables had been a laudable success and pointed out that the (C. H.) Pearson [q.v.] report on public education had vindicated him; the real fault lay with the Act itself.

In August 1878 Venables was appointed an examiner in English for matriculation to the University of Melbourne. As well, in June 1881 he became referee for geography and in 1882 examiner in history. In 1884-89 he was examiner in English language and literature and served as assistant librarian from 1884. In 1875 he had bought land at Gembrook as a retreat from work, but he reportedly lost money in gold speculations at the end of the 1880s. He enjoyed rowing and was an avid reader, especially of travel, history and poetry. His published works include *Outline of the Geography of Victoria, for the use of schools* (1861), *Syllabus of parsing and analysis ... for the pass examination at Matriculation* (1882, 1885, 1887, 1890), and maps of Australasia, Malaysia and Western Polynesia (1870, 1874), and New Zealand (1870). Photographs of three of his sketches are in the university archives, Melbourne.

Venables had married Christina Mary Burke on 27 June 1867 at All Saints Church, St Kilda. He never fully recovered from the shock of her death on 15 November 1885 and on 4 February 1889 he resigned his university appointments because of ill health. On 26 March Venables left Melbourne with his two sons in the *Waihora* and returned via New Zealand to live in England. He died at his sister Anne's home at Bowerwood, Fordingbridge near Bournemouth, on 31 December 1890, survived by his sons; a daughter had died in infancy.

D. H. Rankin, *The history of the development of education in Victoria, 1836-1936* (Melb, 1939); V&P (LA Vic), 1867, 1st S, 4 (27),

1877-78, 3 (105); *Argus*, 26 Jan. 27 Apr, 1-4. 8, 13, 16 May, 6 Aug 1878, 5 Feb 1889, 6 Jan 1891; *Age*, 29 Apr 1878; Victorian Survey maps index (LaT L); Board of National Education, Inspectors' reports 1858-62, *and* Board of Education, In-letter register 1862-73 *and* Education Dept, Professional record books, index of special cases and file 382 (PRO, Vic); Univ Melb Archives; information from Mrs E. Venables, and R. E. C. Venables, Penzance, Cornwall.
                                        PETER M. COWAN

VERDON, SIR GEORGE FREDERIC (1834-1896), politician and banker, was born on 21 January 1834 near Bury, Lancashire, England, son of a Dubliner, Rev. Edward Verdon, vicar of St Anne's, Tottington, Lancashire, and his wife Jane, née Hobson, daughter of a London doctor. At 12 he went to Rossall School and at 17 he sailed for Melbourne with a letter of introduction to (Sir) James Palmer [q.v.]. He was distantly related to Lieut-Governor La Trobe.

Verdon made a brief and unsuccessful visit to the diggings at Campbell's Creek, Mount Alexander; back in Melbourne La Trobe offered him a government post but he preferred to 'chance his arm' in business. Through R. W. Pohlman [q.v.] Verdon joined the firm of Heape and Grice [q.v.], later Grice, Sumner & Co., and in 1853 he went to New Zealand to manage their business for a year. On his return he obtained a sub-agency of the Northern Assurance Co., and set up as a ship-chandler in Nelson Place, Williamstown; styled in 1856 Probert, Verdon & Co., merchants and sailmakers, Flinders Lane, it failed with 'losses great' and 'prospects dubious' in 1858. Meanwhile he had joined the volunteer force in 1854 and in 1857 commanded the Williamstown Company which was ordered out after the killing of J. G. Price [q.v.]. Interested in astronomy, in 1858 he was appointed honorary assistant in the observatory. He was elected to the committee of the Mechanics' Institute, and in 1856 to the Williamstown Municipal Council; two years later he chaired a conference on municipal institutions and wrote a pamphlet, *The Present and Future of Municipal Government in Victoria*, urging greater powers for local councils. In July 1857 he was elected to the Land Convention and in December contested a by-election in Williamstown as a radical candidate; he was beaten—in his view because of Catholic opposition to his objections to Denominational schools—but won the seat in 1859.

Verdon became treasurer in the R. Heales [q.v.] ministry in 1860; next year his slightly protectionist budget led to the government's defeat. On 28 March he married

Anne Armstrong, daughter of a Melbourne solicitor, and while out of office he studied for the Bar; he was admitted in April 1863, though he never practised. In June he became treasurer in (Sir) James McCulloch's [q.v.] ministry. As public opinion changed from free trade Verdon resubmitted another mildly protective budget in 1864; to overcome probable opposition from the Legislative Council the ministry tacked the tariff to the general appropriation bill. When the council deferred it, Verdon supported collection of the unauthorized duties and co-operated in the doubtfully legal procedure by which the London Chartered Bank lent money to the government. He strongly criticized a petition to the Queen by former ministers who opposed the government's actions, and in September 1865 was cited with the attorney-general G. Higinbotham [q.v.] in an action for conspiracy. Next year Verdon was equally active in renewed disputes with the council over the Darling grant.

He successfully advocated a new building and new instruments for the observatory, an increase in the salaries of the astronomer and his staff, assistance to Professor McCoy [q.v.] in establishing a national museum, and to (Sir) Ferdinand Mueller [q.v.] in his botanical research. Verdon was a member of the royal commission on fine arts. He was also concerned about the defencelessness of Port Phillip. He went to London in 1866 and obtained from the earl of Carnarvon, colonial secretary, the H.M.S. *Nelson* as a training ship, and £100,000 towards the cost of the armour-plated monitor *Cerberus*. He 'acquired the esteem and respect of everyone', got agreement for a Melbourne branch of the Royal Mint and negotiated a loan. Awarded a C.B., he remained treasurer until March 1868 and in August sailed for London as Victoria's first agent-general. His report on the Darling grant controversy led to Higinbotham's vigorous denunciation of Sir Frederic Rogers, permanent undersecretary in the Colonial Office. Verdon was elected a member of the Athenaeum Club and, in 1870, a fellow of the Royal Society. He went 'everywhere', revelling in the social prestige derived from an 'honorable and significant post'. He was created K.C.M.G. in 1872.

In April 1867 Verdon had been appointed to the Victorian board of the English, Scottish and Australian Chartered Bank; in 1869 be became a director in London, and Australian manager in May 1872. His appointment was twice renewed and his salary raised to £3500 a year in March 1885. He was chairman of the Associated Banks in 1889. He harmonized interest rates with the Bank of New South Wales, and his directors noted the advantages accruing from 'his former position in the government' when it was necessary to negotiate on any matter with the authorities. But in 1887 the London board sent out C. J. Hegen, a director, whose report was not wholly favourable to him. Criticism continued, and Verdon's comments on various accounts suggest that he authorized some unwise advances; although the bank's failure in 1893 was not his fault alone, he had allowed liquidity standards and coin and bullion ratios to fall. When he retired in May 1891 his management had not been an unmitigated success, but he received a substantial testimonial which he used to found a scholarship for art education at the Working Men's College.

Verdon always maintained his interest in the arts. As bank manager, a friend of Pugin and of William Wardell [q.v.], he was largely instrumental in building, at a cost of £50,000, the magnificent banking chamber on the corner of Collins and Queen streets. He had a 'handsome summer mansion' on Mount Macedon. He was an active trustee of the Public Library, Museums, and National Gallery from 1872, becoming vice-president in 1880 and president in 1883-96, though described as 'pompous and over-bearing'. The most important event during his presidency was the opening of the new Verdon Gallery in 1886, and he helped to arrange for purchases from continental schools. He was also president of the Philharmonic Society, and of the Victorian Institute of Architects, for which he helped to obtain the 'Royal' patronage; he was one of the Board of Visitors to the Observatory, a royal commissioner for the Centennial International Exhibition of 1888-89, a member of the Shakespeare Society, and only ill health prevented him being vice-president of the literary section of the Australasian Association for the Advancement of Science. A sufferer from gout, he died of diabetes at the Melbourne Club on 13 September 1896, predeceased by his wife in 1889 and one of his four sons. He was commemorated at the old National Gallery and by the Verdon Library (1897) in the Janet Clarke [q.v.] Hostel.

Verdon was representative of the 'better' class of unassisted Victorian immigrants of the gold rush period, well educated, energetic, responsible, high minded. He sought a better Britain in the antipodes; when the radical objectives of his youth had been achieved, he was reluctant to 'advance' further politically; but he remained devoted to impartial public service, and made a substantial contribution to the artistic, intellectual and political development of Victoria.

B. A. Knox, 'Colonial influence on imperial policy, 1858-1866', *Hist Studies*, no 41, Nov 1963; A. G. L. Shaw, 'Sir George Frederick Verdon, a forgotten Victorian', *VHM*, 43 (1972); Carnarvon papers (PRO, Lond); Verdon letter-books (LaT L, RHSV, E.S.&A. Bank, Melb); CO 309/67-68, 82, 88, 102.

A. G. L. SHAW

VERJUS, HENRI STANISLAS (1860-1892), missionary, was born on 26 May 1860 at Oleggio, Piedmont, Italy, younger son of Philippe Verjus, a Savoyard soldier in the Sardinian army, and his wife Laura, née Massara. Precociously devout he enrolled in 1872 in the Petit-Oeuvre of the Missionaries of the Sacred Heart at Chezal-Benôit. After he had been threatened with expulsion in 1876 for levity, academic failure and other misdemeanours, his superiors had to restrain him from mortifications including eating inedible scraps and self-flagellation with wire-tipped twine. In 1878 he took his first vows and was teaching at Petit-Oeuvre when the Ferry Laws closed all Catholic teaching institutions in France. He took his final vows in exile at Barcelona, Spain, in 1881 and was ordained in Rome in November 1883.

Appointed to New Guinea under Fr Navarre, Verjus left Marseilles in November 1884 and arrived at Thursday Island on 24 February 1885. He was obstructed by magistrate H. M. Chester [q.v.] until the piratical 'Yankee Ned' Mosby, discharging obligations to the bishop of Cooktown, brought him and two Italian religious Brothers to Yule Island, Gulf of Papua, on 30 June. He named Port Leo after the reigning Pope, said the first Mass on 4 July and bought land, but was asked by Sir Peter Scratchley [q.v.] to leave in September to avoid possible conflict with the London Missionary Society.

After Scratchley's death, Verjus returned to Yule Island in February 1886. The Polynesian catechist of the LMS withdrew but Verjus and his companions suffered badly from famine, fever and overwork. With Fr Louis Couppé he explored the Roro and Mekeo hinterland in 1886-87, named the St Joseph River and explored as far as Rarai. In September 1889 he was consecrated bishop in a hut at Yule Island by Archbishop Navarre. Intended as vicar apostolic of New Britain, at his own and Navarre's requests he was made coadjutor for British New Guinea in 1890. Although Navarre saw him as 'my best missionary, my right arm', Verjus opposed the archbishop's policy of consolidation on the island before working on the mainland and won his point: eight stations were established by 1891. The first Papuan baby was baptized in 1886, the first male in 1889 and the 250 people of Yule Island at Christmas 1891.

Verjus single-handedly conciliated and overawed warring tribes and baffled the sorcerers, not all of whom he thought were satanic. Although abhorring heresy, he was tolerant in practice of Protestant teachers. He co-operated amiably with Sir William MacGregor and guided him through the Mekeo. MacGregor admired him, praised his 'rare liberality' and lack of sectarianism, and extolled his progressive methods of pacification. Ill health sent him to Europe in April 1892. In October he presented to the Pope, with other symbolic objects, a triple tiara of bird-of-paradise head-dresses from converted chiefs, an address of submission, and religious and other books in the Roro language. He died of pneumonia at Issoudoun, France, on 13 November 1892, 'martyred by regret at not being a martyr'. When Verjus first landed natives had accepted 'Missionary' as his name. In village tradition, he is still 'Mitsinari'.

British New Guinea, *Annual reports* 1889-93; J. Vaudon, *Monseigneur Henri Verjus M.S.C.* (Paris, 1913); A. T. Cadoux, *L'Apôtre des Papous: Mgr Henri Verjus* (Lyon, 1931); A. Dupeyrat, *Papouasie: histoire de la mission, 1885-1935* (Paris, 1935); P. L. T. G. Goyau, *Le Christ chez les Papous* (Paris, 1938); R. B. Joyce, *Sir William MacGregor* (Melb, 1971); *Annales de Notre Dame du Sacré-Coeur*, 1887-95; *Vox Missionum* (Croydon), 1943; *Catholic Missions*, June 1945; Protectorate letter-books (PNGA); notes de Mgr Navarre sur sa vie (R.C. Mission Archives, Yule Island and microfilm PMB 654).

JAMES GRIFFIN

VICARS, JOHN (1821-1894), manufacturer, was born in Dunblane, Perthshire, Scotland, son of John Vicars, butcher, and his wife Helen, née Archibold. He managed Dickson and Laing's tweed-mill at Hawick, Roxburghshire, and about 1863 migrated to Australia. After some years on the Queensland goldfields near Rockhampton he went to Sydney and in 1871-73 managed Thomas Barker's [q.v.] tweed-mill in Sussex Street. When it was extensively rebuilt in 1873 after a fire Vicars took it over and began to expand it. In March 1876 his evidence to the select committee on the employment of children disclosed that while wages were higher than in England and Scotland, children worked a twelve-hour day and many were illiterate and unhealthy. There was no factory Act in New South Wales, but Vicars favoured legislation as in England where working children were compelled to go to school and those under 8 were restricted to a six-hour day. At the time he employed 100 persons, including 50 children, some as young as 10.

Vicars was actively interested in politics and in 1867 had published an open letter to (Sir) Henry Parkes [q.v.] on *The Chinese Question*. He often criticized Parkes's and (Sir) John Robertson's [q.v.] policies and in the 1870s sent long letters to the *Sydney Morning Herald* on immigration, the labour question and protection of secondary industry, on which he wrote in 1877, 'There is really nothing to prevent this, which would soon bring plenty of people to our shores, and that, too, without money and price. In this colony we want but little that nature has not provided us with, for the best iron ore, the best coal, the best limestone, the best clay we are blest with'. That year he published a pamphlet, *The Tariff, Immigration and The Labour Question;* expanded in 1879, it later ran to a third edition. He was chairman of the protectionist, anti-assisted immigration and somewhat radical Political Reform League in 1878; next year he addressed the first Intercolonial Trades Union Congress in Sydney on the need to foster local industries.

A skilled and experienced craftsman, Vicars won many first prizes for tweeds and woollens at both colonial and international exhibitions in the 1870s and 1880s. He retired in 1887 and the business was taken over by his sons William and John who moved the factory to Marrickville in 1894. In 1914 John Vicars & Co. bought all the shares in Sydney Woollen Mills Ltd which then operated in Parramatta.

Aged 73, Vicars died of paralysis at his residence, Palace Street, Ashfield, on 8 September 1894, and was buried in the Presbyterian section of Rookwood cemetery. He was survived by his wife Ann, née Moor, whom he had married at Rothbury, Northumberland, England, on 25 March 1855, and by five sons and two daughters. His estate was sworn for probate at £10,313.

W. F. Morrison, *The Aldine centennial history of New South Wales*, 2 (Syd, 1888); V&P (LA NSW), 1875-76, 5, 619, 6, 903; SMH, 7 July, 23 Aug 1877; Echo (Syd), 17 Jan 1878; Bulletin, 5 Nov 1881; T&CJ, 12 Aug 1899.

G. P. WALSH

VICKERY, EBENEZER (1827-1906), merchant, manufacturer and philanthropist, was born on 1 March 1827 in Oxford Street, London, son of Joseph Vickery (d. 1892), boot and shoe manufacturer, and his wife Mary, née Burgess. The family arrived in Sydney in the *Richard Reynolds* on 14 August 1833. Educated at W. T. Cape's [q.v.] Sydney College, Ebenezer left school

at 16 and was apprenticed to T. Bowden, ironmonger. In 1849 he joined the mercantile firm of Richard Fawcett. His father concentrated on squatting in 1851 and Ebenezer took over the boot factory in George Street. On 28 February he married Jane Begg (d. 1904).

In 1860 Vickery moved to larger premises in Pitt Street, adding general trading and importing. He became chairman of the Fitzroy Ironworks Co. in 1864 and though he reorganized the company financially, it failed for other reasons: this was Vickery's only business set-back. Fitzroy iron was used the same year in the construction of his new chambers in Pitt Street, the first building in the colony to utilize structural iron. Next year his Sydney factory, associated with J. E. Begg's Glenmore tannery, employed twenty-five persons on the premises and about seventy-five outworkers. He visited England in 1866 and became interested in the shipping trade; he had the *Parramatta* built there and became part-owner of the *Sobroan, Hawkesbury* and *La Hague.* He was executive commissioner for Fiji at the 1879 Sydney International Exhibition.

Vickery gradually built up a vast empire by hard work and sound business acumen. He acquired an interest in seven coal-mines; he owned two collieries and a colliery at Mount Keira, was chairman of the South Greta Coal Co. and of the Mount Kembla Coal and Oil Co., and in 1896 took over the Coal Cliff Coal Co. from the estate of Sir Alexander Stuart [q.v.]. He was one of the largest station-owners and property speculators in the colony: among the runs he held was Munyer near Moree, which in 1884 covered 170,000 acres and carried 2800 cattle and 9600 sheep. He had much real estate in Sydney and Waverley and was a director of the City Bank of Sydney, the Pacific Fire and Marine Insurance Co., the Perpetual Trustee Co. and the Mutual Assurance Society of Victoria. He also was a member of the general committee of the New South Wales Free Trade Association and chairman of the New South Wales Trade Protection Society. In 1881 he took his sons Ebenezer and Joseph into partnership and on 31 January 1902 his entire business was incorporated as a public company under the style of E. Vickery and Sons Ltd; it became a proprietary company in May 1937.

Appointed to the Legislative Council of New South Wales in 1887, he confined his speeches to social and mining matters. He opposed the cremation bill but supported Sir Alfred Stephen's [q.v.] radical divorce bill in April; speaking on the coal-mines regulation bill in October 1894 he strongly defended capitalism, attacked 'union leaders and socialistic agitators' and opposed the eight-hour clause and the proposed minimum age of 14 for boys in mines.

A staunch Methodist, Vickery made lavish donations to the Church. In 1901-02 he spent £10,000 on tent missions throughout New South Wales. He bought the Lyceum Theatre in Pitt Street in 1905, spent £27,000 on alterations and gave it to the Church: it was opened in September 1908 as 'The Vickery Mission Settlement'. A founder and honorary treasurer of the Sydney Young Men's Christian Association, he also gave money and help to the Young Women's Christian Association and was a benefactor to Sydney public charitable institutions. Self made and self contained, Vickery cared little about society or culture: his business, his family, his Church and his philanthropic work were his absorbing interests.

On 5 May 1905 at Camden Park, Menangle, Vickery married Deborah Louise Ellis, a teacher, with Church of England rites; they visited the United States of America and England for him to study modern evangelistic methods. He survived the great Californian earthquake, but died after an operation at Leeds, England, on 20 August 1906. He was buried in Waverley cemetery, Sydney, not far from his fine residence, Edina, now the War Memorial Hospital. His estate was sworn for probate at £483,354, of which £11,000 was willed mainly to Methodist charities.

W. F. Morrison, *The Aldine centennial history of New South Wales*, 2 (Syd, 1888); E. Digby (ed), *Australian men of mark*, 2 (Syd, 1889); W. G. Taylor, *The life-story of an Australian evangelist* (Lond, 1920); V&P (LA NSW), 1883-84, 11, 223; *Sydney Mail*, 1 Apr 1865; SMH, 22, 23 Aug 1906; *The Times*, 22, 24 Aug 1906; T&CJ, 29 Aug 1906; J. Colwell, *The passing of a great philanthropist* (ML).

G. P. WALSH

VINCENT, MOTHER MARY; *see* WHITTY.

VOGEL, SIR JULIUS (1835-1899), journalist and premier, was born on 24 February 1835 in London, son of Albert Leopold Vogel, a Jew of Dutch origin, and his wife Phoebe, née Isaac. Educated at home and at the University College School, London, at 16, on the death of both parents, he was employed by his grandfather, a merchant trading with South America and the West Indies. Attracted to Australia by the gold rush, he studied chemistry and metallurgy

at the Royal School of Mines; he arrived in Victoria in late 1852.

In partnership with a London friend A. S. Grant he opened an assaying agency in Flinders Lane, but after a business depression moved to Maryborough as the rush began there late in 1854. He sold wine and spirits before setting up as an apothecary in a small canvas den complete with 'large, colored bottles, a number of empty boxes and a stuffed iguana'. Turning to journalism, as correspondent for the *Argus* in 1856 he reported the Dunolly rush and from that year to 1859 edited the *Maryborough and Dunolly Advertiser*. He was also associated with the *Talbot Leader* in 1860-61 and owned and edited the *Inglewood Advertiser* from 1859 to February 1861. His sparkling leading articles, although disparaged for their 'low and vulgar style', identified with local needs and interests. He speculated in mining and was for a time director of a gold reef company. He was also a cricketer, an inveterate gambler and an aspiring bon vivant.

In the Legislative Assembly elections of August 1861 Vogel stood for the mining seat of Avoca. While largely agreeing with the Heales [q.v.] ministry, he attacked its Melbourne-based protectionism and supported free trade and the abolition of the export duty on gold. He also wanted a Bendigo-Ballarat railway, to be financed either by land grants or by government guarantee. He lost to J. M. Grant [q.v.] and B. G. Davies, both of whom had ignored protection.

This set-back and declining opportunities caused Vogel to move in October 1861 to Dunedin, New Zealand, which was booming as a result of the Otago gold rush. While editor of the *Otago Daily Times* he was returned to the Otago Provincial Council in 1863 and in September entered the House of Representatives. He led the Provincial Council from February 1867. His success was based at first on his opposition to the expensive Maori wars fought on behalf of the North Island, but from 1869 as colonial treasurer in William Fox's ministry in Wellington, he initiated a national policy of 'public works, in the shape of roads and railways and immigration'. Vogel not only launched the massive, developmental programme of the 1870s but also went to England to float two of the required loans. His public life oscillated between the fashionable world of London and New Zealand, and his close British links may have been the basis of his commitment to imperial federation.

As premier intermittently from 1873 Vogel was also one of the first Australasian statesmen to see the Pacific as an area for

British expansion. He failed to persuade the Colonial Office to annex Fiji and Samoa and turned to the idea of informal empire—the creation of a joint stock company with a monopoly of trade with Polynesia. He welcomed the occupation of Fiji by Britain in 1874 and the annexation of eastern New Guinea by Queensland in 1883, and was prepared to contribute over £2500 for three years towards the administration in New Guinea.

Created K.C.M.G. in 1875, Vogel became agent-general in London in 1876-81. His period of greatest influence in London and in New Zealand coincided with Disraeli's conversion to imperialism, and in 1880 Vogel stood unsuccessfully as the Conservative candidate for Falmouth. Returning to New Zealand in 1884, he formed a ministry with Robert Stout from that year to 1887. He opposed moves towards Australasian Federation and the Federal Council on the grounds that they would deflect attention from imperial federation, an attitude bequeathed to later New Zealand politicians. He returned to London early in 1888 suffering from gout and deafness, and lived in comparative poverty at East Molesey where he died on 12 March 1899.

At Dunedin on 19 March 1867 Vogel had married Mary, eldest daughter of William Henry Clayton, an architect; she survived him with two of their three sons and a daughter.

R. M. Burdon, *The life and times of Sir Julius Vogel* (Christchurch, 1948); J. Flett, *Dunolly* (Melb, 1956); A. Ross, *New Zealand aspirations in the Pacific in the nineteenth century* (Oxford, 1964); R. Blackstock, 'Sir Julius Vogel, 1876-1880: from politics to business', *New Zealand J of History*, Oct 1971.

B. E. KENNEDY

VON SCHLEINITZ, *see* SCHLEINITZ.

VOSZ, HEINRICH LUDWIG (1812-1886), hardware merchant and paint manufacturer, was born on 3 May 1812 at Bodenwerder, Hanover, Germany, of poor parents who a few years later moved to a village near Hamburg. From the age of 12 Vosz worked for local farmers, but at 15 he was apprenticed to a carpenter. After careful saving he set up as a carpenter and builder in Hamburg and was successful until, apparently engulfed in the turmoil of 1848,

his business collapsed. Leaving debts behind him he migrated to South Australia. With his wife Friederike Dorothea Sophie (1810-1875) and their two sons, Vosz arrived in Adelaide in the *Alfred* on 6 December 1848, reputedly with a few sheets of window glass and little else.

Vosz was naturalized on 9 August 1849 and set up as a cabinetmaker and joiner. After a period on the Victorian diggings, he established himself at 82 Rundle Street, Adelaide, as a painter, paper-hanger and glazier. Assisted by his sons he developed a flourishing business in the import and sale of glass and as a house decorator and plumber. In 1860 he had the great satisfaction of repaying all his Hamburg debts, including interest at ten per cent. He became an expert in artesian wells and specialized in importing and installing pumping machinery when the city of Adelaide was starting a water-supply and drainage system. Although influential in the economy and society of South Australia Vosz held aloof from politics, but was an Adelaide City councillor for Hindmarsh Ward in 1860-62 and a justice of the peace.

Self effacing, Vosz nevertheless was widely known for his generosity and charity and his kindly paternalism as an employer. Born in 1842, his younger son Adolph Frederick Emil died in 1868; his elder son Wilhelm Hartwig Edward (1840-1883) also predeceased him, but left a considerable part of his estate of £155,591 to his father. For many years Vosz had suffered from severe neuralgia and visited Germany for treatment and an operation. He died of old age at North Terrace, Adelaide, on 10 March 1886 and was buried in West Terrace cemetery. His estate, sworn for probate at £73,947, was distributed among local charities, relatives in Germany and many former employees. His business, said to have been the first to manufacture paint in Australia (originally in a backyard workshop), became a limited liability company, H. L. Vosz Ltd, in 1904 and in 1915 changed its name to Clarkson Ltd.

F. E. H. W. Krichauff, *Water supply by artesian and tube wells* (Adel, 1879); H. T. Burgess (ed), *Cyclopedia of South Australia*, 1 (Adel, 1908); Clarkson Ltd, *The romance of a great business* (Adel, nd), and *Seventy-fifth birthday, 1848-1923* (Adel, 1923); *Observer* (Adel), 13 Mar, 3 Apr 1886; *Pictorial Aust*, May 1886; *Progress in Aust*, June 1933.

ERIC RICHARDS

W

WAITE, JAMES CLARKE (1832-1920), artist, was born at Whitehaven, Cumberland, England, son of John Waite, schoolteacher, and his wife Isabella, née Clarke. He studied at the Government School of Design, Newcastle upon Tyne; the Scottish Institute, Edinburgh; the Royal Academy School, London; and for a year in Paris. He trained as an art instructor at South Kensington, became a certificated master, and in the 1860s taught at his old school in Newcastle. He first exhibited at the Royal Academy in 1863. After becoming well known in the north of England as a genre painter, he settled in London in 1869-85, exhibiting over the period 25 works at the Royal Academy, and 117 at Sussex Street. He was elected a member of the Royal Society of British Artists in 1873.

Waite's work was first displayed in Australia with four paintings at the Sydney International Exhibition, 1879-80. He arrived in 1886 in Melbourne, held his first exhibition, of thirty works, in November and became a leading portrait painter. Among his early commissions were portraits of the architect Joseph Reed, Sir William Clarke and M. Lang [qq.v.]. His portrait of A. Felton [q.v.] hangs in the National Gallery of Victoria. Waite was an early member of the Australian Artists' Association and joined the Victorian Artists' Society at its inception in 1888, being elected to the council for one year in 1894. He exhibited regularly at the Victorian Artists' Society and was represented in both the British and Australian galleries at Melbourne's Centennial International Exhibition of 1888. After G. Folingsby's [q.v.] death in 1891, he applied unsuccessfully for the position of art director of the Victorian National Gallery.

Waite's work was characterized by great detail and high finish; he was well known for his ability to render domestic animals. His paintings commanded high prices in the 1880s and 1890s when he was noted for his 'conscientious work and quiet style'; at least one critic, in 1891, considered his portrait of Lang to have been one of the best painted in Melbourne at that time. Waite made several trips to Tasmania and he had a special affection for the Ovens District, Victoria. At his last exhibition, held at the Athenaeum Gallery, Melbourne, it was noted that he had been more successful in his paintings in England than in his renderings of Australian life and landscapes. On 8 August 1920, aged 88, while staying with his sister-in-law at Woollahra, Sydney, Waite died of bronchitis and was buried in the Anglican section of Waverley cemetery. He was not married. The National Gallery of Victoria, Bendigo Art Gallery, Footscray Historical Society and Manly Art Gallery, New South Wales, hold examples of his work.

Argus, 11 Nov 1886, 18 Aug 1920; *Table Talk*, 21 Dec 1888; Fine Arts pamphlets, vol 52 (SLV); application, National Gallery of Vic file 283, miscellaneous letters, Public Lib of Vic (PRO, Vic).
J. H. HOLMES

WAITE, PETER (1834-1922), pastoralist and benefactor, was born on 9 May 1834 at Pitcairn near Kirkcaldy, Fife, Scotland, son of James Waite, farmer, and his wife Elizabeth, née Stocks. Left fatherless, Waite trained and worked as an ironmonger in Edinburgh and Aberdeen. On 8 June 1859 he arrived in Melbourne in the *British Trident* and went to his brother James's station, Pandappa, near Terowie, South Australia. In 1862 with (Sir) Thomas Elder [q.v.] Waite bought the adjoining Paratoo run, and he took over Pandappa's lease when his brother died in 1863. On 21 November 1864 Waite married his first cousin Matilda Methuen (d. 1922) at Woodville; they had eight children.

Drought beset the north in 1864-66 but from 1869 Elder, Waite and N. E. Phillipson accumulated sheep and cattle runs from Beltana to the Queensland border, though after 1880 resumptions caused some loss of profits. In 1883 Waite became chairman of Elder's Wool & Produce Co. Ltd, a subsidiary of Elder Smith [q.v.] & Co.; in 1888 they were amalgamated and he became chairman of directors of Elder Smith & Co. Ltd, displaying remarkable ingenuity and initiative. After Elder's death in 1897 his interests and those of Waite and Phillipson were merged in the Beltana Pastoral Co. Ltd; Waite was its managing director, and also of the Mutooroo Pastoral Co. Ltd, in 1898-1911. He had directorships in the Commercial Union Assurance Co. Ltd, the British Broken Hill Co. Ltd, and the S.A. Woollen Co. Ltd. He held Momba station in New South Wales.

Waite gave leads to pastoralists with his improvement and management of semi-arid salt bush country. By poisoning vermin, fencing paddocks and providing permanent water he achieved larger sheep numbers; he

336

emphasized breeding, flexible stock movement and the rotation of paddocks. A member of a railway extension committee, in 1874 he had pressed for a northern rail link with Adelaide. He advocated large leases of long tenure and close personal supervision, and he gave useful evidence to the 1897-98 pastoral lands commission. An exacting, energetic employer, Waite lived at Paratoo until he bought Urrbrae, near Adelaide, in 1874. He was a member and vice-president of the Pastoralists' Association of South Australia and West Darling and the Federated Employers' Council of South Australia. In 1875 he was chairman of the Stockbreeders' Association.

In the 1870s Waite was a patron of the arts and later became a benefactor to the pastoral and agricultural industry, donating Urrbrae Estate to the University of Adelaide in 1913, subject to life tenancy for himself and his wife; half was to be for agricultural studies and the rest for a park. A further 114-acre site nearby was given to the South Australian government for an agricultural high school. In 1915 Claremont and part of Netherby, also near Urrbrae, were bought and given to the university, followed in 1918 by 5880 shares in Elder Smith & Co. Ltd to enable the land to be used as intended. The total value of his gifts to the university was estimated at £100,000; in 1923 the Waite Agricultural Research Institute was established.

Waite retired in 1921 and died of heart failure on 4 April 1922 at Victor Harbor; he was survived by his wife and four children and a memorial service was held at St Michael's Anglican Church, Mitcham. His estate was sworn for probate at £160,000. His family continued the tradition of generous gifts to the university and the institute.

Elder Smith & Co. Limited: the first hundred years (Adel, 1940); The Mutooroo Pastoral Company Limited after fifty years (Adel, 1951); PP (SA), 1898-99, 3 (77); Register (Adel), 15 Dec 1874, 5 Apr 1922; Observer (Adel), 15 Apr 1922; information from Sir Edward Morgan, North Adelaide, and The Waite Agricultural Research Inst, Urrbrae, SA.

MARJORIE FINDLAY*

WALCH, CHARLES EDWARD (1830-1915), bookseller and lay preacher, was born on 8 May 1830 at Cannanore, Kerala, India, son of Major James William Henry Walch, 54th Regiment, and Eliza, née Nash. The family returned from India to England in 1837 but, probably influenced by Henry Hopkins [q.v.], they migrated to Van Diemen's Land in 1842 in the Royal Saxon and were granted 300 acres in the West-

bury district. About three years later they moved to Hobart Town, where Walch's father bought the bookselling business of S. Tegg [q.v.]; with his eldest son James Henry Brett he traded as J. Walch and Son; another son was G. Walch [q.v.].

In 1845 Walch was apprenticed for five years to Captain William Crosby [q.v.] in the barque Jane Francis, trading between Hobart and London. He spent two more years as an able-seaman and second officer but, soon after his father's death in 1852, went to the Victorian gold diggings. Unsuccessful, he returned to Tasmania intending to go back to sea. But J. Walch and Son had prospered and his brother offered him a partnership and position as buyer in London, where he worked in 1854-58. Growth of business in Tasmania led to his recall, but he returned to London in 1861 to buy stock and printing machinery and engage tradesmen. Walch's Literary Intelligencer, first produced in 1859 and edited by him for some fifty years, and Walch's Tasmanian Almanack became standard references.

In England Walch had joined the Young Men's Christian Association and the King's Weigh-House Chapel, in Eastcheap, under Rev. Thomas Binney [q.v.]. Back in Tasmania he took charge of a Sunday school held in the Ragged School building, Collins Street, Hobart; later he became a regular teacher and was superintendent for thirty-five years of the Davey Street Congregational Church Sunday School. He sought new and improved teaching methods on which he gave lectures and published pamphlets. In 1868 he led 516 teachers and 4618 children in an ode of welcome to the duke of Edinburgh. He became a well-known Congregational lay preacher and an advocate of the principles of competitive business.

In 1874 Walch opposed plans to build showgrounds and buildings on the Queen's Domain and later became chairman of a committee to advise on its use. He was a member and sometime chairman of the Central School (Bathurst Street) Board in Hobart and campaigned successfully for new buildings. In evidence to the 1882 select committee on education he criticized the Board of Education for 'the want of a head to the department'. He moved resolutions at a Town Hall meeting in 1875 supporting the public works proposals of the Kennerley [q.v.] government, and again in 1876 protesting against the proposed closure of the Hobart-Launceston railway line. He was a director of the Commercial Bank and other companies, and a foundation member of the Society for Prevention of Cruelty to Animals.

Among Walch's many writings was The

Story of the Life of Charles Edward Walch, with a selection of his writings, printed in 1908 for private circulation. He was married twice; first at Halstead, Kent, England, on 27 February 1861 to Emma Elizabeth (d. 1863), youngest daughter of Henry Stoe Man, R.N.; their daughter died in 1864; next year he married Fanny Eugenia Clara, daughter of George Birch; they had four sons and six daughters. He died at his home in Davey Street, Hobart, on 25 March 1915 survived by his wife and five daughters. His estate was sworn for probate at £42,855.

Cyclopedia of Tasmania, 1 (Hob, 1900); P. Bolger, *Hobart Town* (Canb, 1973); *V&P* (HA Tas), 1882 (106); *Mercury*, 26 Mar 1915; indexes and correspondence file under C. E. Walch (TA).   NEIL SMITH

WALCH, GARNET (1843-1913), author and dramatist, was born on 1 October 1843 at Broadmarsh, Van Diemen's Land, son of Major James William Henry Walch of the 54th Regiment, and his wife Eliza, née Nash. C. E. Walch [q.v.] was his brother. Major Walch had arrived in Van Diemen's Land in 1842 and settled in Hobart Town about 1845, where he purchased a bookselling and publishing business. He died in 1852 and Garnet was sent in the care of a relation to England, where he was educated at Denmark Hill Grammar School, near Camberwell, London, and then at a private college at Hameln on the River Weser, Germany. He returned to Tasmania in 1860 and drifted into journalism, after deciding that commerce, banking or law did not appeal to him. He went to Sydney, where his first full-time job as a journalist was with the *Sydney Punch*. In 1867 at Parramatta he started his own newspaper, the *Cumberland Times*, and on 9 March at Scots Church, Sydney, he married Ada Kate Sophia Mullen.

George Darrell [q.v.] introduced Walch to the theatre, engaging him to write the pantomime *Trookulentos, the Tempter: or, Harlequin Cockatoo*, which was produced at Sydney's Royal Victoria Theatre at Christmas 1871. After moving to Melbourne next year he wrote a steady stream of pantomimes, burlesques, comedies and comediettas; he published about thirty works. Titles such as *Australia Felix*, considered his best pantomime, and *Pygmalion and His Gal (a Dear!)* (both Melbourne, 1873) suggest the themes and flavour of his work. The pantomimes, full of local allusions and atrocious puns, were especially significant for helping to introduce a range of stock Australian characters, many of whom were incorporated in the tradition of local melodrama. Later Walch worked with Alfred

Dampier [q.v.]; they adapted Rolf Boldrewood's [q.v. T. A. Browne] *Robbery Under Arms* which, produced in 1889, was acclaimed as a major contribution to the development of a native drama and was repeated many times in following years. Much of his writing, however, was hack work, the colonial stage requiring continual adaptations or 'localisations' of overseas pieces.

Walch produced two books of verse (1874, 1881), a number of miscellanies, popular annuals which included works by leading writers of the day, and books about Tasmania. On the recommendation of (Sir) Henry Parkes [q.v.], he was made secretary of the Melbourne Athenaeum in 1873, resigning in 1879 to devote his energies to the preparation of *Victoria in 1880*. Despite his insolvency in October 1880 caused by difficulties in his publishing business and family sickness, the book appeared in Melbourne next year. In August 1883 he went to Madagascar as special correspondent for the *Argus* and the *Australasian*. His *Life of General Gordon* was published in Melbourne in 1885.

Walch seems to have enjoyed a somewhat raffish reputation. He was a member of a bohemian circle in Melbourne which included Marcus Clarke [q.v.], while Hugh McCrae recalled him as a tremendous talker, 'shabbily dressed and distracted looking'. For many years he lived in retirement at his home in Surrey Hills, Melbourne, where he died of heart failure on 3 January 1913. Survived by his wife, two of his four sons and three of his four daughters, he was buried according to Anglican rites in the Box Hill cemetery.

H. M. Humphreys (ed), *Men of the time in Australia: Victorian series* (Melb, 1882); H. McCrae, *My father and my father's friends* (Syd, 1935); *Table Talk*, 14 Mar 1890; *Argus*, 4 Jan 1913; M. Williams, Nimble naiad, lonely squatter and lively Aboriginal. Dramatic convention and national image in Australian drama (Ph.D. thesis, Monash Univ, 1973).

JOHN RICKARD

WALKER, FREDERICK (1820 ?-1866), pastoral superintendent, police officer and squatter, was born probably at Dawlish, Devon, England. His widowed mother reared six children in genteel poverty, one invalided and one mentally retarded. Soon after his arrival in New South Wales in the *Ceylon* in August 1844, Frederick became superintendent on W. C. Wentworth's [q.v] Tala station on the Murrumbidgee River. He was big and commanding; his fine singing, heavy drinking, courage and easy acceptance of Aboriginals soon made him popular.

Walker became clerk of Petty Sessions at Tumut on 12 April 1847 and at Wagga Wagga on 12 June. His views on racial harmony won him command of the native police force. He recruited and trained Aboriginals, and in May 1848 led them to the disturbed Macintyre River district. Based first at Boggabri and then at Callandoon, the force soon impressed warlike tribes and some squatters, two of whom enlisted as senior subalterns; another, Augustus Morris [q.v.], supported and advised Walker. Despite government objection to 'the Battle of Carbucky' in 1849 and his outspoken criticism of many squatters, the force was widely acclaimed in 1848-49. He declared that if white settlers broke the law protecting Aboriginals, the latter had a reciprocal 'right'. He even proposed that protection be denied to settlers who took the law into their own hands.

In 1851 Walker's men were welcomed in Wide Bay and the Burnett. He stayed at Callandoon but some Burnett squatters joined William Forster and W. H. Walsh [qq.v.] to denigrate and oppose him. When he began to drink to excess in 1852 his incapacity seemed proven to all but close friends. Factions accentuated discipline problems in the force. Money was short and distance made it difficult to obtain authority for payments. He muddled through 1852 and 1853 by withholding some or all of his officers' salaries, but angry victims found the sympathetic ears of his critics, and he was accused of defalcations. Humanitarians like the missionary William Ridley [q.v.], noting Walker's intemperance, began to accept hearsay reports of native police outrages; his view of race relations became discredited. The government supported him and rejected demands that control of the police be handed over to local benches of squatter magistrates. At Christmas 1854 Walker arrived drunk at a Brisbane Court of Inquiry. Summarily dismissed, he was vilified for two more years by Forster and Walsh.

In mid-1857, seeking self-respect, he joined Arthur Wiggins and two ex-troopers in search of new pastoral land. On the night of 27-28 October some of the Aboriginals responsible for the Hornetbank massacre attacked the party. An Aboriginal trooper saved them but Walker and Wiggins were injured. He soon recovered and raised a force of ex-troopers; probably paid by squatters, it patrolled the disturbed Dawson River area until disbanded on instructions from Sydney. The new commandant of the native police, Edric Morisset, complained to the government that Walker was calling him 'the boy Commandant'. With peace restored and his ego on the mend, Walker joined in speculative tenders for thirty-one runs, comprising almost 800 square miles. Most were soon sold.

Walker's protests against the methods of the new native police were disregarded, but he remained a respected bushman, commissioned in 1861 to search for Burke and Wills [qq.v.], and in 1866 to find a route for a telegraph line from Cardwell to the Gulf of Carpentaria. He arrived at the Gulf ill, and on the return journey on 19 November 1866 he died at Floraville on the Leichhardt River, and was buried there. The calumnies of Walsh and Forster obliterated all memory of his dream.

J. E. Murphy, *Frederick Walker's expedition in 1866* (Brisb, 1953); V&P (LC NSW), 1848, 315, (LA NSW), 1856-57, 1, 1157, 1858, 2, 843, (LA Vic), 1861-62 (108), (LA Qld), 1867, 2, 1015; 'Journal of Mr Walker', *JRGS*, 33 (1863); *SMH*, 16, 23 June 1852, 31 Oct 1854; *Brisbane Courier*, 28 Jan 1867; *Cummins & Campbell's Mthly Mag*, May 1934; J. H. Watson, Scrapbook, 1 (ML); F. Walker journal (Oxley Lib, Brisb); MS cat (ML); Col Sec, Special bundles 4/719.2, 7/2697b (NSWA); Native Mounted Police, Special bundles RES 2 (QA).

DAVID DENHOLM

WALKER, HENRY (1821-1900), industrialist, was born on 24 December 1821 near Wakefield, West Yorkshire, England, son of Robert Walker, land bailiff, and his wife Hannah, née Cudworth. Educated from the age of 10 at the Quaker school at Ackworth, Yorkshire, he left at 14 to learn from an uncle in Leeds the merchandizing of tea, coffee and hops. He then travelled for a tea firm in London, Liverpool and Belfast. In 1849 at Leeds he married Elizabeth Lee and in 1852 they left England in the *Cleopatra*, arriving in Melbourne on Christmas Day. They went to Sydney and conducted a profitable confectionary shop. Revisiting England in 1854, they returned to settle permanently in Melbourne next year.

Walker was a book-keeper and salesman for several Melbourne merchants before managing a soap and candle factory by the River Yarra at Collingwood; in 1863 he bought it. He soon opened another works near by where he also produced wax matches and smelted antimony. In 1868-88 he owned and operated the Hobson's Bay soap and candle works at West Melbourne. With other industrialists he was continually criticized for causing air and river pollution, but a royal commission in 1870 reported that he was less negligent than most others. He upheld the local council's view, however, that the benefits of local prosperity outweighed complaints about pollution. In 1874 he became a shareholder in a company which proposed to distil the contents of Collingwood's cesspits into a concentrated fertilizer. Although the company failed after a year because of engineering difficulties, it encouraged many householders to substitute portable pans. In 1881 he was a founding director of the Victorian Tramway Co.

For twelve years between 1872 and 1894 Walker was a member of the Collingwood Council, and was mayor in 1872-73, 1874-75, 1878-79, 1880-81 and 1887-88, visiting England twice. He helped to introduce into Collingwood some of Australia's first underground storm-water drains and was a pioneer advocate of asphalt paving. In the early 1880s he was instrumental in having the Victoria Street bridge built over the Yarra near his factories; he subscribed £100 to the building fund. He encouraged spectacular mayoral and municipal festivities and was a supporter or patron of many community and sporting organizations, especially bowling, racing, cricket and football. A justice of the peace, he was for many years chairman of the local bench. He was originally a free trader but became a protectionist; although regarded as 'very passive' in political matters, in February 1880 he contested the seat of Collingwood in the Legislative Assembly, but was defeated.

Walker died of chronic cystitis at Collingwood on 3 December 1900, survived by his only child, a daughter. He was buried in the Boroondara cemetery. A mayoral portrait, by Tom Roberts in 1889, is held by the Collingwood City Council.

Our local men of the times, reprint from Collingwood Observer (Melb, 1889); B. Barrett, The inner suburbs (Melb, 1971); V&P (LA Vic), 1870, 2nd S, 1 (22); Advertiser and Observer (Collingwood), 1 July 1875, 15 Mar 1888, 4 Apr 1889; Argus, 4 Dec 1900; A. H. B. Barrett, The making of an industrial environment: Collingwood, Victoria, 1851-91 (M.A. thesis, Univ Melb, 1970). BERNARD BARRETT

WALKER, JAMES BACKHOUSE (1841-1899), solicitor and historian, was born on 14 October 1841 in Hobart Town, son of George Washington Walker [q.v.], shopkeeper, and his wife Sarah Benson, daughter of Robert Mather [q.v.]. Educated at the High School, Government Domain, Hobart, and at the Friends School, York, England, he was first employed as junior clerk in the office of T. D. Chapman [q.v.] and later in his father's Hobart Savings Bank. But in 1872 he took articles and on 7 July 1876 was admitted as barrister, solicitor and proctor of the Supreme Court of Tasmania. Senior partner in the firm J. B. Walker and

Wolfhagen he was also an active councillor of the Southern Law Society. From 1877 he was a member of the Tasmanian Club.

Of advanced liberal views, socially committed, Walker was a member of the Bathurst Street school board and the Tasmanian Board of Education. In evidence before the royal commission on education in 1883 he favoured the appointment of a director of education as permanent professional head, but feared political patronage in the appointment of teachers. In 1889 he proposed an examining university with affiliated colleges, as a first step towards a teaching university. Next year he was appointed member of the first council of the new university, and in 1898 became its second vice-chancellor.

As a trustee of the Tasmanian Public Library Walker did much to establish its collection of manuscripts and books. He was credited with having one of the finest collections of Australiana. Elected to the council of the Royal Society of Tasmania in 1888, he was a regular contributor to its proceedings. Most of his papers on the discovery, early settlement and Aboriginal inhabitants of Tasmania were tabled in parliament and printed; they were collected and published posthumously in 1902 as Early Tasmania: Papers read before the Royal Society of Tasmania between 1888 and 1899. Reprinted in 1914 it remained a standard work for many years. In 1892 he read a paper on 'Old and New Hobart' to delegates to the Hobart conference of the Australasian Association for the Advancement of Science. He was also a fellow of the Royal Geographical Society, London.

Walker attributed his 'wider views of God and religion' to the teachings of his friend Rev. G. Clarke [q.v.]. A member of the Society of Friends, he was also for many years a Sunday school teacher in the Davey Street Congregational Church. An active supporter and sometime secretary of the Hobart Working Men's Club, he sought improved conditions for workers and better attitudes to work. Later, disenchanted with militants in the labour movement, he wrote, 'the tyranny of the Trade Unions in Australia has been quickly growing unbearable'.

A bachelor, Walker died of pneumonia at his home in Davey Street on 4 November 1899. His estate was sworn for probate at £1106. The J. B. Walker Memorial Prize commemorates him in the Law School of the University of Tasmania.

Cyclopedia of Tasmania (Hob, 1900); P. B. Walker (ed), All that we inherit (Hob, 1968); P. Bolger, Hobart Town (Canb, 1973); J. N. D. Harrison (ed), Court in the colony (Hob, 1974);

Roy Soc Tas, *Papers and Procs*, 1899; *Advertiser* (Hob), 5 Feb 1859; *Mercury*, 23 Oct 1882, 6 Nov 1899.   NEIL SMITH

WALKER, RICHARD CORNELIUS CRITCHETT (1841-1903), civil servant, was born on 28 June 1841 at sea, son of Rev. James Walker, Anglican minister, and his wife Fanny, née Billingsley. His family reached Launceston, Van Diemen's Land, on 27 August 1841 in the *Arabian*. Appointed to George Town, James later went to Sydney in 1843 and became headmaster of The King's School, Parramatta. Critchett was educated at St James's Grammar School, Sydney, and in October 1856 joined the civil service as a sessional clerk in the Legislative Assembly. In 1857 he became a clerk in the Executive Council office and from 1858 undertook personal duties for several ministers. On 1 March 1862 he became an inspector of police under the new Police Regulation Act but resigned in July 1863 to enter the Bank of New South Wales.

On 1 April 1865 Walker rejoined the civil service as a clerk in the Colonial Secretary's Department and was private secretary to (Sir) Charles Cowper [q.v.]. He was promoted to second clerk in 1869 and first clerk in 1878; next year he became principal under-secretary of the colony on the recommendation of Sir Henry Parkes [q.v.]. His unassuming manner, tact and knowledge enabled him to earn the confidence of no less than 13 colonial secretaries and 3 acting colonial secretaries in 24 years. He had a special affection for Parkes and in October 1891 thanked him for his 'great kindness and consideration' during his eight years as colonial secretary. His greatest administrative and political pressures probably occurred when W. B. Dalley [q.v.], acting colonial secretary in 1885, dispatched the Sudan Contingent.

As principal under-secretary Walker had to supervise not only the ministerial branch of the department, but eight sub-departments and also the government statistician, lunacy matters, hospitals for the insane and the charitable institutions. In evidence to the 1895 royal commission into the civil service, Walker claimed he had 3752 persons under his control and an additional 5782 partially-paid military and naval personnel, but he did not see how any substantial economies could be effected in his department. The royal commission reported that the chief secretary's 'office premises are so constructed that a proper supervision is impossible'.

A magistrate from 1884, Walker was a member of the Civil Service Board in 1887-95. He was an honorary member of the United Service Institution, a committee-man of the Civil Service Club and a founding member of the Australasian Geographical Society in 1883; he was also a New South Wales commissioner for the 1886 Colonial and Indian Exhibition, the 1887 Adelaide Jubilee International Exhibition and the 1888 Centennial International Exhibition in Melbourne. From 1889 he was a trustee of the National Park, where 'he invariably spent his Sundays'. Walker was returning officer for the 1897 Australasian Federal Convention, for the two referenda on the Constitution and for the first Federal elections in 1901. Appointed C.M.G. that year, Walker died unmarried of diabetes and pneumonia at Bligh Street, Sydney, on 13 June 1903 and was buried in the Anglican section of Waverley cemetery. His estate was sworn for probate at £4885. His brother R. C. Walker [q.v.] was the principal librarian at the Free Public Library and another brother, Colonel Philip Billingsley Walker, was chief electrician and engineer-in-chief for electric telegraphs, Sydney, and a member of the Institution of Civil Engineers, London.

A. G. Kingsmill, *Witness to history* (Syd, 1972); *ISN*, 17 Jan 1891; *Daily Telegraph* (Syd), 15 June 1903; *SMH*, 15 June 1903; *T&CJ*, 11 Aug 1900, 17 June 1903; Parkes letters (ML); Col Sec, General records and special bundles 2/8020.10 (NSWA).   A. G. KINGSMILL

WALKER, ROBERT COOPER (1833-1897), librarian, was baptized on 17 August 1833 at St Mary's, Charlton Kings, Gloucestershire, England, fourth son of Rev. James Walker and his wife Fanny, née Billingsley. He arrived at Launceston, Van Diemen's Land, with his family in the *Arabian* on 27 August 1841 and moved to New South Wales in 1843. He was educated at The King's School, Parramatta, where his father was headmaster. After office experience in Sydney, Walker became a clerk in the colonial architect's branch of the Department of Lands and Public Works on 1 April 1855, transferring to the roads branch in 1857 where he was promoted chief clerk in 1860. In 1861-67 he was accountant in the railway branch of the Department of Public Works. Despite no evidence of inefficiency, he was charged with neglect of duty over the defalcations of a subordinate and was required to resign on 31 May 1867.

Walker was selected as parliamentary librarian but the colonial secretary (Sir) Henry Parkes [q.v.] demurred at his lack of literary attainments and knowledge of books and provoked a debate on parliamentary privilege. Disappointed, Walker wrote to Parkes on 11 April 1868, stressing his business habits and knowledge of official duties and asked for the new position of inspector of public charities; appointed on 17 April, at his former salary of £500 a year, he held the position until 30 September 1869. One of his duties was to approve the books ordered on a government grant by free libraries under the Municipalities Act of 1867, which he did with some discernment.

In 1869 the government bought the Australian Library and Literary Institution and reopened it on 30 September as the Free Public Library, Sydney. Walker was appointed librarian on 1 October, with a salary of £400 and free quarters, fuel and light. With characteristic energy he immediately began the pioneering work of systematic organization and management, including cataloguing and classifying, acquiring new stock, drafting regulations and devising statistical records for what became the State Library of New South Wales in 1975. The first trustees, led by Professor Badham [q.v.] until 1883, recognized Walker's capacity and worked harmoniously with him in transforming 16,057 mixed volumes into a substantial reference library, with strong emphasis on its educational role as a 'storehouse of learning' and on ready access to its resources.

Walker showed considerable ingenuity, judgment and administrative skill in overcoming the library's problems of lack of statutory foundation, meagre funds and an inadequate building. His enthusiasm, kindliness, and urbanity helped. A lending branch, which later became the Sydney Municipal Library, was opened in 1877 and Walker became principal librarian. A service for country libraries followed in 1883, while the dilapidated building was added to and substantially rebuilt in the succeeding years, necessitating a rearrangement and relabelling of most of the reference library. Meanwhile, Walker strove to make effective the deposit provisions of the Copyright Act, 1879, and served as a member and from 1890 as chairman of the Board of International Exchanges. In twenty-four years he fostered the library to its first 100,000 volumes and to 200,000 visitors a year. He produced the printed catalogues and developed the Australasian collection, compiling periodic lists that led to the delayed publication in 1893 of a full catalogue to 1888, under the title *Australasian Bibliography in three parts...* This remained the greatest work of its kind for many years, while the strength of the collection was one of the influences in the bequest to the library by D. S. Mitchell [q.v.].

Walker retired on 31 August 1893 on a pension of £587 and was appointed a trustee on 7 October. He acted as honorary principal librarian when his successor H. C. L. Anderson was abroad. He died of chronic disease of the bladder at Guildford, New South Wales, on 25 July 1897 and was buried in the Anglican section of Waverley cemetery. He was survived by his wife Grace (d. 1931), née Brown, two sons and three daughters, to whom he left an estate valued for probate at £3407.

V&P (LA NSW), 1867-68, 1, 949, 3, 807, 829, Roy Com on public charities, 2nd Report, 1873-74, 2, 244; F. M. Bladen, 'Biographical and historical notes', JRAHS, 2 (1907-08); Sydney Mail, 28 Aug 1897; Col Sec letters (NSWA).

G. D. RICHARDSON

WALKER, THOMAS (1858-1932), lecturer, journalist and politician, was born on 5 February 1858 at Preston, Lancashire, England, son of Thomas Walker, flour-mill operative, and his wife Ellen, née Eccles. Precociously exhibiting his quick memory and histrionic bent, Walker became a child preacher in the local Wesleyan circuit and then a pupil-teacher at St Thomas's school. In the early 1870s he migrated with his family to Canada, where they worked as labourers in villages near Toronto.

In 1874 Walker set up in Toronto as a materializing spiritual medium. During a seance with a believer, John Saunders, Walker burned himself with the phosphorus he used to make 'illuminated writing' and 'spiritual lights'. Saunders helped extinguish the fire and received burns on his hands and left foot. He died from tetanus three weeks later. A coroner's jury found that Walker had 'feloniously' caused Saunders' death: but Walker had left Canada the morning following the accident and was never indicted. Subsequently he claimed that he had bought his ticket to England before the mishap.

On returning to Lancashire Walker wrote for the *Preston Herald* and other local newspapers. He later asserted that he had returned to Canada in 1875 and offered to stand trial for Saunders' death, but this has not been verified. Around 1876 Walker turned up in Toledo, Ohio, United States of America, as a journalist. In the same year, dressed as a frontiersman, he made a triumphant début at the Michigan state spiritualist congress. He then joined the entourage of Dr James Peebles, the itinerant spiritualist healer, who commended Walker to Australian spiritualists; apparently at their invitation he arrived in Sydney from San Francisco in the *Zealandia* on 3 March 1877. His first lecture in Melbourne, delivered in a trance under the 'control' of Giordano Bruno, was chaired by Alfred Deakin.

Walker's racy flow of invocations to the spirits, plagiarized from A. J. Davis, geology plagiarized from Lyell, and anti-orthodoxy plagiarized from Voltaire and Volney, won him enthusiastic audiences. But his sponsors tired of his vulgarities and in August 1879 he left for Britain, where he lectured for the National Reform Union in Lancashire, Wales and Scotland. In March 1880 he sailed for South Africa and resumed spiritual preaching. At Graaff-Reinet on 19 May 1881 he was licensed to marry Andretta Marie Somers, niece of the lieutenant-governor of Cape Colony. He also published his first volume of poems there. After attacks on the genuineness of his mediumship he accepted an invitation from Victorian spiritualists to return. He recommenced trance lecturing, now with eyes open, to a full Temperance Hall on 27 November. His preoccupation with 'iconoclastic' subjects, linked with his 'independent protectionist' candidature for the Richmond seat in the Legislative Assembly, estranged him from respectable spiritualists; he was not elected.

Early in 1882 Walker broke with the spiritualists, denounced the phenomena as fraudulent and proclaimed himself a materialist. He founded the Australasian Secular Association in July with himself as salaried president and lecturer. In 1883 he allied himself with the agitation to open the Public Library, Museums, and National Gallery of Victoria on Sundays, but the leaders disowned him, thereby heightening his popularity. His advance as people's champion halted in September when the spiritualists released details of his adventures in Toronto. He removed to Sydney, briefly returning to Melbourne for a three-day debate with David Blair [q.v.] in January 1884.

Walker established himself in Sydney as secularist spokesman and larrikin populist campaigner. He opposed the Sudan Contingent, imperial federation, Australian intervention in Papua and the Pacific islands and proposed giving to the poor the funds raised for the Queen's jubilee. In 1885 he was convicted for exhibiting obscene pictures while advocating birth control. He conducted his own appeal and won. He was prominent in the agitation to save the bushranger Frank Johns, who had been sentenced to death after a doubtful trial. Johns was hanged, but Walker was acclaimed for his humanity. The same year his second volume of poems, *Bush Pilgrims and other Poems*, appeared and his dramatization of *His Natural Life* was the hit of the season. He also acted in his own play, *Marmondelle the Moor*.

In February 1887 Walker was elected to the Legislative Assembly as a 'protectionist, democratic republican' for Northumberland. In parliament he emerged as an indefatigable troublemaker on points of procedure, on which he usually proved correct. He advocated reform of the legal profession, reduction of legal costs, easier divorce, abolition of distress for rent, capital punishment and the Legislative Council, and the establishment of a national bank. His parliamentary career was damaged in mid-1892 when he inadvertently shot and wounded a clergyman. He was convicted of being drunk and disorderly, though acquitted of criminal negligence. He immediately set up as a temperance lecturer. He did not stand when his constituency was redistributed in 1894.

Walker arrived in Western Australia in 1899, after a time in New Zealand as a temperance and elocution exponent. In Perth, in addition to temperance work, he wrote for and eventually edited F. C. B. Vosper's *West Australian Sunday Times*, after an interlude in Kalgoorlie with the *Sun* and the *Kalgoorlie Miner*. In 1903 he became editor and part-owner of the *Sunday Press*, but soon returned to Kalgoorlie to edit the *Sun* and to win the Kanowna parliamentary seat in October 1905 which he represented until 1932. Walker now ceased newspaper work and began to farm and to study law. As a Labor back-bencher he spoke long and often on extending country libraries and irrigation, creating a central bank and, almost alone, he defended the Aboriginals. He regularly dissented from the Speaker's rulings, lectured the House on British constitutional history and on 5 October 1909 passionately defended Martha Rendall, who was accused of murdering her three stepchildren. In October 1911 he became minister for justice and education in John Scaddan's cabinet and on 22 November, the day he was admitted as a barrister and solicitor, was sworn as attorney-general, a post he held until July 1916. As attorney-general he intermitted capital punishment, promoted education, reformed the criminal law and local courts, and legislated against cruelty to animals.

In February 1912 he joined the Senate of the University of Western Australia and until his term ended in 1916 he was a courageous advocate of its spending money to secure first-rate scholars and build the highest standards. In 1924-30 he was Speaker of the Legislative Assembly. Survived by his wife Andretta, a daughter and two sons, Walker died on 10 May 1932 at Inglewood, Perth, and was buried in the Anglican section of Karrakatta cemetery. His favourite saying was, 'Charity never faileth'.

J. S. Battye (ed), *Cyclopedia of Western Australia*, 1 (Perth, 1912); V&P (LA NSW), 1889, 1, 681; *Liberator* (Melb), 5 June 1887; F. B. Smith, Religion and freethought in Melbourne, 1870 to 1890 (M.A. thesis, Univ Melb, 1960); printed cat (ML).   F. B. SMITH

WALKER, WILLIAM (1828-1908), solicitor and politician, was born on 26 February 1828 in Glasgow, Scotland, son of George Walker, schoolteacher, and his wife Elizabeth, née Ferguson. His father was recruited by Rev. J. D. Lang [q.v.], reached Sydney in the *Portland* with his family on 4 December 1837 and opened a Presbyterian school at Windsor. William was educated there and by Rev. Matthew Adam, and was articled to Francis Beddek, a local solicitor, in 1841. Admitted as a solicitor on 30 October 1852 he practised successfully in Windsor until 1908. On 29 March 1853 at near-by South Creek he married Mary Cover Hassall, granddaughter of Rev. Rowland Hassall and Richard Rouse [qq.v.]; she died in childbirth on 13 July 1858 after bearing two sons who died in infancy.

Walker was a member of the Anti-transportation League, although he found Lang too advanced in political ideas. He acted as election agent in Windsor for (Sir) John Darvall [q.v.] in 1856 and successfully canvassed for T. W. Smith against (Sir) Henry Parkes [qq.v.] in 1857. On 12 March 1860 he won a Legislative Assembly by-election for Windsor; he became a loyal supporter of (Sir) James Martin [q.v.] and a friend of Parkes. He favoured *ad valorem* duties for revenue, supported the 1866 Public Schools Act and wanted to make the Legislative Council elective. Without losing sight of wider political issues he proved an energetic and effective local member, agitating for the railway to Richmond and Windsor, opened in 1864, and for a bridge across the Hawkesbury River at Windsor, built in 1874. He acted as an unpaid assistant whip for Martin, who rarely went to an important division without consulting him 'to ascertain if all was right', but his support of Martin's unpopular land legislation offended his squatting friends and led to his defeat in 1869. In November 1880 Walker asked Parkes to recommend him for a seat in the Legislative Council: he believed he was 'sufficiently independent to sustain the dignity', as he had 'a private income of £500 a year and £500 from my profession', and

explained that he 'might' support Parkes's government. However, he was not appointed to the council until 1887.

An elder of the Presbyterian Church and for many years a representative on its General Assembly, Walker was secretary of the Hawkesbury Benevolent Society and Hospital and founding president of the Windsor School of Arts in 1861-77. Long an advocate of the town's incorporation, he was an alderman on the first Windsor Borough Council from 1871 and mayor in 1878. He contributed articles to the press on the Windsor floods and published a collection of lectures, speeches and articles as *Miscellanies* (1884, 1887) as well as a volume of *Poems, written in youth* (1884), a *History of the Hawkesbury Benevolent Society* (1887), *Recollections of Sir Henry Parkes* (1896) and *Reminiscences...* (1906).

Walker died of influenza at Windsor on 12 June 1908 and was buried in the Presbyterian cemetery. He was survived by four sons and three daughters by his second wife Henrietta Medora, daughter of Robert Cooper [q.v.], whom he had married at Paddington on 24 August 1859; and by two sons and two daughters of his third wife Jessy, née Wood, whom he had married at Windsor on 20 April 1876. His estate was valued for probate at £1380; he carefully divided his extensive library among his children.

J. Steele, *Early days of Windsor* (Syd, 1916); P. Loveday and A. W. Martin, *Parliament factions and parties* (Melb, 1966); D. G. Bowd, *Macquarie country* (Melb, 1969); *Daily Telegraph* (Syd), 12 June 1908; *SMH*, 13 June 1908; J. D. Lang papers (ML); Parkes letters (ML); W. Walker papers (ML).   VERNON CREW

WALLACE, DONALD SMITH (1844-1900), pastoralist, racehorse owner and parliamentarian, was born at Ballark station near Morrisons, Victoria, on 10 August 1844, eldest son of John Wallace, squatter, and his wife Elizabeth, née Smith. He was educated at Charles Goslett's Academy in Melbourne. After pastoral experience at Alexander Wilson's property, Vectis, he went to Queensland about 1870 to a series of sheep station partnerships, including large ventures with (Sir) Samuel Wilson [q.v.]. He returned to Victoria in 1878, and in 1880 failed to win the seat of Grant in the Victorian Legislative Assembly. Next year he headed a syndicate that sought to establish an agricultural college on crown land at Dookie, and in December an authorizing bill was introduced. David Syme [q.v.] did not doubt Wallace's integrity, but questioned the site and doubted the wisdom of the proposed terms and conditions; the bill was discharged.

He inherited his father's pre-emptive rights to the Ballark estate in 1882; he also bought Terrick Terrick, a 535,000-acre station in Queensland, and Mewburn Park, Gippsland, Victoria. In 1883-88 Wallace represented Clermont in the Queensland Legislative Assembly, but spent much time out of the colony, leaving his brother-in-law R. G. Casey [q.v.] as managing partner of his four properties; they covered 1,387,000 acres, were valued at £412,000 and mortgaged for £350,000.

Wallace raced several horses. Calma won the Caulfield Cup for him in 1883 and Mentor the Melbourne Cup in 1888. His most famous horse, the great Carbine, won thirty-three races out of forty-three starts, including the Sydney Cup in 1889 and both the Sydney and Melbourne cups in 1890. He is reported to have said to Lady Hopetoun at a dinner: 'I love you because you love old Carbine'. His pastoral enterprises were less successful. Bad seasons, together with falling wool prices, made it difficult for him to meet capital repayments and interest charges; by 1890 the debt on his Queensland stations had reached £650,000. The partnership with Casey was dissolved in 1893 and the properties realized little more than their liabilities.

Casey complained that Wallace disregarded the properties and seldom answered letters. In parliament he was equally casual. He spoke three sentences in four years in the Queensland Legislative Assembly and one in five years in the Victorian Legislative Council, where he represented South-Western Province in 1889-94. Described by many as a genial sportsman, Wallace served, with a years break, on the committee of the Victoria Racing Club in 1881-98 but gradually had to sell most of his property including his stud. At his death at Ballark station on 27 May 1900, he had been a councillor of the Ballan Shire since 1889. A Presbyterian, he had one son John Vivian from his marriage to Ida Australia, daughter of George Thorn [q.v.].

Lord Casey, *Australian father and son* (Lond, 1966); R. Mortimer and P. Willett, *Great racehorses of the world* (Lond, 1969); *Leader* (Melb), 10 Dec 1881; *Australasian*, 1 Nov 1890, 2 June 1900; *Ballan Times*, 31 May, 28 June 1900.   ALAN W. BLACK

WALLACE, JOHN ALSTON (1824-1901), mining entrepreneur and politician, was born on 15 December 1824 at Rutherglen, Lanarkshire, Scotland, son of James Wallace, draper, town councillor and magistrate, and his wife Jean, née Miller. Educated locally, he entered his father's store and later worked in a Glasgow drapery for a year and engaged in a coal-mining venture near Airdrie. After the death of his young wife Anne, née Hall, whom he had married about 1846, and hearing of the Victorian gold rushes, he decided to follow his brother Peter (1831-1886) to Victoria; he arrived in Melbourne in the *Southampton* in 1852.

Wallace went to the Ovens goldfield and with the proceeds of a find at Spring Creek opened stores in 1853 at Robinson Crusoe Gully and Myer's Flat, Bendigo. Back at the Ovens in 1854 he opened a store at Snake Valley (Stanley) and in 1855 the first of a chain of Star hotels in the north-east: with help from Peter, these enterprises were extended throughout the Ovens field; Wallace often rode through the night to supervise ventures as far away as Bright. Portly, with genial features, he delighted miners with his enthusiasm, spirited action, generosity and occasional madcap stunts. He backed small mining concerns, encouraged prospecting and, as initiator and a director of the Ovens Gold Fields Water Co. (1860), promoted a bold though abortive project of water conservation for sluicing. He bought the Beechworth Hotel in 1855 and transformed it into a popular Star hotel under the management of Peter; in 1859 he extended his interests to the new Indigo goldfield near Chiltern. In 1860 Rutherglen was named after his home town.

Wallace sold his stores and hotels in 1862-64 and turned more to mining. In the 1870s he formed the Chiltern Valley Gold Mines Co. and later acquired interests in other major Chiltern and Rutherglen deep lead companies. He invested heavily in the 1860s and 1880s in the quest for deep leads near Bright. The Rose, Thistle and Shamrock reef near Harrietville was the most celebrated of his quartz-mining projects in the Bright-Myrtleford area, and he had similar interests in the Upper Goulburn district. He made a major breakthrough in the separation of refractory ores at Bethanga and, after trying unsuccessfully to use non-union labour in the mid-1880s, employed about 150 men there. He revived the Yackandandah field in the 1890s by pioneering steam-driven sluicing and dredging and he also introduced dredging at the Woolshed diggings near Beechworth. His enterprise gave employment to hundreds of miners and appreciative banquets were held for him at Chiltern in 1880, Beechworth in 1884 and Yackandandah in 1888. He also had mining interests in New South Wales and Queensland.

Wallace visited Britain in 1872. In November 1873 he was returned unopposed to the Victorian Legislative Council for the Eastern Province, and moved to Melbourne. In 1882-1901 he represented the North-Eastern Province. Conservative in his political views, he exerted much influence over mining legislation. Although requisitioned by 3000 Victorian electors, Wallace failed to win a Federal Senate seat in 1901.

A liberal benefactor of the Ovens district hospitals, Wallace donated regularly to the Melbourne poor and the Salvation Army. In November 1865 he had married Theresa (d. 1882), daughter of T. Monahan [q.v.] who later gave him several properties including Quat Quatta station near Corowa and the London Hotel in Port Melbourne. Theresa bore six sons and three daughters. In 1898 Wallace was estranged from his four surviving sons after they challenged his trusteeship of the Monahan estate. He later disinherited them and at the same time curtailed the inheritance of his only surviving daughter should she marry, to ensure that she did not 'endure the anxieties and sufferings caused by children'. He lost heavily in the 1890s depression; but moved to Quat Quatta, a gracious mansion in Elsternwick, and on 11 September 1895 married Ada Rona Reid, aged 25; they had no children. He died of heart disease on 16 October 1901 and was buried in the St Kilda cemetery. His estate was valued at £121,350.

Ovens and Murray Advertiser, 20 Sept 1884, 11 Jan 1890, 19 Oct 1901; *Argus*, 13-20 Sept 1898; C. Woods, The early history of Beechworth (M.A. thesis, Monash Univ, 1970).

CAROLE WOODS

WALLEN, ROBERT ELIAS (1831-1893), stockbroker and journalist, was born on 5 June 1831 at Port of Spain, Trinidad, West Indies, son of Francis Robertson Wallen, of Donegal, Ireland, and his wife Catherine, née Hobson. He was educated at Foyle College, Londonderry, Ireland, and in 1848 joined a firm of American merchants in Liverpool, England.

On news of gold discoveries in Victoria, the Wallen family decided to migrate. Robert arrived in Melbourne in 1852 in the *Rip Van Winkle*, the cargo of which was consigned to him, while the rest of the family came in the *Great Britain*. He set up in business for a few years with his father and brother, trading as F. R. Wallen and Sons, merchants, but by 1860 he had joined William Clarke and Sons, gold-dealers and brokers. In 1860-61 he edited a stock and share journal, which was published by major stockbroking firms in Melbourne to give a record of share prices and to provide

informed comment for investors. In 1861 he was secretary and member of the short-lived Stock Exchange. William Clarke and Sons was dissolved in May 1867 and Wallen became a partner with Alfred, one of the sons, in the firm of Clarke & Co. (which still survives). Wallen was the first secretary and later several times chairman of the Melbourne Stock Exchange set up in 1865. On the formation of the new Stock Exchange in 1884 he became its first chairman for two years; later a committee-man, he was a member of a subcommittee in 1889 which initiated the first major redrafting of the rules. Over thirty years he thus played a leading part in stock exchange affairs.

For many years Wallen was also a part-time journalist. Working from 7 or 8 p.m. to 2 a.m. most evenings, he contributed to the *Age*, the *Leader* and the *Argus*; and in 1870-87 as 'Aegles' wrote the shrewd and genial column 'Talk on Change' for the *Australasian*. He later claimed that his writing had earned him some 12,000 guineas. As well, he edited the *Australasian Insurance and Banking Record* from its first issue in 1877 until its one-hundredth in mid-1885 when he resigned because of expanding business. His wide financial knowledge and experience, his undoubted journalistic ability and his careful handling of statistics established the *Record* as a financial journal of the highest quality. In recognition of his standing among professional statisticians and bankers, he was elected a fellow of the Institute of Bankers, London, and of the (Royal) Statistical Society of London.

Wallen was active in civic affairs and in 1877-83 was a member of the Hawthorn Borough (later Municipal) Council and mayor in 1878 and 1879. Keenly interested in art, he was president in 1882 of the Art Union of Victoria and for some ten years thereafter held the posts of president or vice-president. In 1889-93 he was a trustee of the National Gallery, Museums, and Public Library of Victoria. Described as 'Full of tact, considerate in his views, urbane in his manner', Wallen was an active layman of St Columb's Church of England, Hawthorn.

On 21 May 1863 Wallen had married Marian May Pitman (d. 1887), the 17-year-old daughter of a solicitor; they had eight daughters and three sons. From about 1892 his health was impaired by his anxiety over the prevailing financial crisis. He embarked on a long sea voyage in 1893, but on 1 October, just out of Auckland, New Zealand, he died of a paralytic seizure. His body was brought back for burial in the Boroondara cemetery. He was survived by seven daughters and three sons of whom Frank (b. 1870) joined Clarke & Co. in 1890, purchased his father's seat on the Stock Exchange of Melbourne in 1895 and was a member until 1929.

James Smith (ed), *Cyclopedia of Victoria*, 1 (Melb, 1903); A. R. Hall, *The Stock Exchange of Melbourne and the Victorian economy 1852-1900* (Canb, 1968); *A'sian Insurance and Banking Record*, 14 July 1885, 19 Oct 1893; *Australasian*, 19 Feb 1887; *Argus*, 4 Oct 1893; records (Stock Exchange of Melbourne).

A. R. HALL

WALSH, JOHN JOSEPH (1819-1895), land reformer, journalist and political agitator, was born on 24 June 1819 at Langhill, East Galway, Ireland, son of Patrick John Walsh, farmer, and his wife Catherine, née Callogy. Migrating to New South Wales in the late 1830s, Walsh moved to Singleton on the Hunter River in 1841 where he was secretary to the local total abstinence society. He met Charles Harpur [q.v.] whose poetry he admired and encouraged. Returning to Sydney in 1844 he joined J. J. Moore, Dublin-born bookseller in George Street, and supported the local protest and petition against the exclusion of Catholic jurors from the 1843 Dublin state trials of Irish nationalist leaders. On 18 June 1849 at St Patrick's Church, Parramatta, he married Sarah Ellen, third daughter of James P. Russell of Glashare Castle, Kilkenny, Ireland. He moved to Melbourne in June 1852 and, closely associated with J. P. Fawkner [q.v.], managed a newsagency at 239 Elizabeth Street in 1853-59; they were also involved in the *Diggers Advocate* campaign in 1854 for a miner's vote and in the Victorian Liquor Law League Council, 1855-56. Fawkner cared for Walsh's children following Sarah's death in September 1855. On 17 September 1857 at St Francis's Church Walsh married Anne O'Shea, aged 24, daughter of a farmer.

As secretary of the Victoria Land League, which he had begun in December 1856 with Thomas Loader [q.v.], Walsh invited 'a Congressional Assembly of Delegates' on 20 June 1857 to formulate a programme of constitutional and land reform. The response, especially from the goldfields, vindicated his initiative. Secretary to the subsequent Victorian Convention (July-August) and its standing council, he published *Resolutions, Proceedings, and Documents of the Victorian Convention* in Melbourne that year and sent 400 copies to the New South Wales Land League in Sydney; he also edited single issues of the *Freesoil Papers for the People* (1857) and *The Freeholder and Convention Expositor* (1858),

and published and edited *The Convention and True Colonizer*, February-June, 1859. When an attempt to convene a second convention failed that year he organized the Land Bill Central Committee's support in 1860 for the 'Convention Corner' members of the Victorian Legislative Assembly.

Failing to win the seats of West Bourke in 1860 and Castlemaine in 1861, Walsh moved to Fitzroy where he worked as a law clerk, supported protection for local industry and published parliamentary voting lists; as 'Agricola' he produced in Melbourne in 1864 the *Elector's Hand-book & Guide* ... and in 1868 *The Black and White List; or, Electors' Handbook & Guide*; new editions appeared under his own name in 1871 and 1877. On 13 December 1870 at both Holy Trinity Church, Kew, and St Ignatius's Church, Richmond, he married Fawkner's widow Eliza, aged 53; her estate enabled him to continue reading for the Bar, to which he was called in 1873, and to resume his political activities.

Standing for East Melbourne in 1871, Walsh favoured an Australian protective policy, a land system based on the United States of America's Homestead Act, equal electoral districts, payment of members, Upper House reform, non-sectarian public education, mining on private property, the eight-hour system, and absentee income and property taxes. Defeated again, he revived his tactics of the 1850s, initiating the Constitution Reform League in January 1874, and the Progressive Land Tax League in April 1875, supported by old convention associates and younger urban radicals. With F. Longmore and J. Mirams [qq.v.] he drafted petitions and organized demonstrations on behalf of the Victorian Protection League in July-December and the National Reform League in January-June 1876 to unite popular support behind (Sir) Graham Berry's [q.v.] opposition to Sir James McCulloch's [q.v.] ministry. A committee-man of the National Reform and Protection League (February 1877), he was a vice-president in 1878-80, and chairman of the executive committee in 1879, publishing his proposed *Amended Programme. The Policy of the future* for league delegates to a Melbourne conference in the same year.

More concerned with drafting political briefs Walsh did not follow his profession. In 1876 he drew up an abortive workman's and miner's lien bill for W. C. Smith and James Munro [qq.v.]. He was appointed a magistrate for the Central District in 1878. He was ignored by Irish Catholic political leaders and his studied platform manner discouraged the electors of Rodney in 1874, North Melbourne in 1877, Dalhousie in

1880, Richmond in 1880 and 1883, and West Gippsland in 1889. Too jealous of his own contributions to reform, he alienated those whose support might have realized his political ambitions. In 1886 he retired to his Drouin property, Walshvale, in Gippsland. His last political gesture shortly before his death there on 15 October 1895 was a five-guinea donation to the Irish Parliamentary Fund.

After his third wife's death on 8 July 1879, Walsh had married on 9 October 1884 at the Church of the Immaculate Conception, Hawthorn, Elizabeth Anne Lucas, aged 39, Fawkner's grand-niece. He was survived by her and a son and a daughter of his first marriage, a son and a daughter of his second and two sons of his fourth. He was buried in Drouin cemetery.

Age, 7 Aug 1857, 28 Aug 1860, 2 Oct 1866, 7 May 1874, 7 May 1875, 9 Aug, 27 Dec 1878, 10 Nov 1879, 18 Apr 1882, 11 Feb 1885, 16 Oct 1895; *Herald* (Melb), 9 Nov 1870; *Daily Telegraph* (Melb), 13, 21 July 1874, 25 Dec 1875, 28 Apr 1876; *Argus*, 22 June 1875, 22, 27 Jan 1876; *Warrnambool Examiner*, 3 May 1876; *Bendigo Advertiser*, 23 Sept 1876; *Geelong Advertiser*, 29 June 1888; *Advocate* (Melb), 13, 27 Apr 1889, 19 Oct 1895; *Gippsland Independent* and *South Gippsland Express*, 16 Oct 1895; G. R. Bartlett, Political organization and society in Victoria 1864-1883 (Ph.D. thesis, ANU, 1964); Fawkner papers *and* J. J. Walsh papers (LaT L).

J. H. RUNDLE

WALSH, WILLIAM HENRY (1823-1888), squatter and politician, was born probably on 18 December 1823 at Milton, Berkshire, England, son of Charles Walsh, and his wife Elizabeth. He reached Sydney in the *Mary Sharp* on 11 June 1844, gained colonial experience with David Perrier of Bathurst and in 1847 opened a station for him on the Macintyre River, Moreton Bay. He took a Perrier flock through floods to open another station on the Burnett River, then took up Degilbo near Gayndah for (G. R.) Griffiths, (W.) Fanning & Co. [qq.v.] of Sydney. He later acquired the property himself. In August 1850 Walsh joined M. C. O'Connell, W. Forster [qq.v.] and others in punishing Aboriginals for the murder of Gregory Blaxland junior. A subsequent bitter feud led to the dismissal of native police commandant F. Walker [q.v.] and was followed by public quarrels with Edward Deas Thomson, A. G. Maclean [qq.v.], Sir George Bowen and A. E. Halloran; the conflict revealed Walsh as gauche, nasty, devious, highly egocentric and prone to strident appeals to English tradition. On 20 February 1857 at Paterson he married Eliza Brown.

He sat in the New South Wales Legislative Assembly in 1859. Believing that separation would leave him stranded 'among pigmies', Walsh declined any part in the Queensland parliament but tried to keep in touch with New South Wales. He soon relented, failed to win Leichhardt in 1863 but won Maryborough in 1865. Accused of monomania about maltreatment of Aboriginals, with little help he continued an eloquent fight for the rights of Aboriginals, Kanakas and Chinese for the rest of his life: he was governed by genuine Christian charity and by a distaste for working-class prejudice.

Despite early attacks on railway construction Walsh joined the Palmer government in 1870 as secretary for public works in charge of railways. The 'Demon of discord' had found a satisfying occupation and he emerged as a creditable administrator. He had opposed payment of members and the abolition of non-vested schools; when the ministry sponsored legislation for them he resigned his office on 10 July 1873. On 7 November he lost Maryborough to B. B. Moreton [q.v.] but managed to win Warrego on 1 December. He was manoeuvred into the Speakership on 6 January 1874 but was never happy in a role that silenced him; unable to secure proper respect, he resigned suddenly on 20 July 1876. He was defeated again in December 1878, failed to win Logan and on 20 February 1879 was appointed to the Legislative Council.

Two years in London in 1885-86 as an executive commissioner to the Colonial and Indian Exhibition almost ruined Walsh; relatively poor, he died on 4 April 1888 leaving four sons and three daughters. Bernays claims that much of Walsh's prickly pugnacity was a conscious pose which amused him, but he was probably one of the most hated men of his time. Sir Robert Herbert [q.v.] described him as 'a horrible new member of Parliament called Walsh who makes endless speeches and bores me to death. He is rather mad'. W. H. Wiseman was probably fairer when in 1852 he described him as 'The deceiver who first deceived himself!'

G. E. Loyau, *The history of Maryborough* (Brisb, 1897); C. A. Bernays, *Queensland politics during sixty years* (Brisb, 1919); D. Dignan, *The story of Kolan* (Brisb, 1964); P. Bell, 'The Walshs of Degilbo', Qld Women's Hist Assn, *1859 and before that—1959 and all that* (Brisb, 1960); V&P (LA Qld), 1861, 75, 1864, 347, 1865, 395, 1875, 2, 437, 1876, 1, 62; PD (Qld), 1867, 1877, 1878; *Moreton Bay Free Press*, 17 Jan 1854, 22 Nov 1859; Archer papers (ML); Griffith papers (Dixson Lib, Syd); Herbert letters *and* Palmer-McIlwraith papers

(Oxley Lib, Brisb); Parkes letters (ML); Col Sec files 60/512, 61/290 (QA); CO 234/18/24.

DAVID DENHOLM
H. J. GIBBNEY

WALSTAB, GEORGE ARTHUR (1834-1909), writer and journalist, was born on 31 December 1834 at Tottenham, London, eldest son of Arend John George Walstab, former planter at Demerara, West Indies, and his wife Georgina Frances, née Steele. He was educated at Merchant Taylors' School, London, and was in France at the time of the *coup d'état* of December 1851.

In 1852 Walstab migrated with his parents to Victoria, arriving in Melbourne on 18 November in the *Dinapore*. His father set up as an auctioneer and estate agent. Walstab became a cadet in the Mounted Police until after the Eureka incident in 1854. He then saw further service in India and, as a subaltern in the latter part of the mutiny (1857-58), he received a leg wound which troubled him for the rest of his life. In 1860 he turned to journalism, becoming sub-editor and in 1862 editor of the Calcutta *Englishman*. His novel *Looking Back, or, pique, repique and capot* ... was published in Calcutta in 1864 and was well received in London.

In 1865 Walstab returned to Melbourne with his wife Mary Anne, née Nolan, whom he had married in Calcutta in 1861. He began writing for the *Age* and the *Herald* and in September 1865 became first editor of A. H. Massina's [q.v.] *Australian Journal*. In 1866 he edited the *Australasian Monthly Review*.

A close friend of Marcus Clarke [q.v.] Walstab was a founding member of the bohemian Yorick Club. He was associated with Clarke when the latter took over the *Colonial Monthly* in 1868, but with J. J. Shillinglaw [q.v.] he lost money on the venture when it passed out of Clarke's hands about a year later. Walstab also collaborated with Clarke in supplying news items to Victorian country papers and was with him when he died in 1881. They shared an interest in the theatre; after a much-acclaimed amateur performance in 1866 Walstab appeared briefly as a professional actor at the Theatre Royal. He also had a hand in Clarke's first novel, *Long Odds*: when it was being serialized in the *Colonial Monthly* in 1868, Walstab wrote what became chapters XV-XVIII while the author was incapacitated. Clarke incorporated these chapters, somewhat pruned and polished, in the published book.

In 1867-69 Walstab's own novels appeared in serial form. The *Australian Journal* published *Looking Back* as 'Harcourt Darrell or,

Pique, Repique, and Capot' in 1867, and 'Confessed at Last' and 'The Bushranger' in 1868. The *Colonial Monthly* published 'Double Harness; or, Pierce Charlton's Wives' in 1869-70 and his short stories and sketches appeared in various anthologies. He was a scholarly writer and some of his works show genuine feeling for colonial life despite their hackneyed titles.

By the end of 1869 Walstab was bankrupt, partly because family illness had prevented him from gaining regular employment. He went to Castlemaine where for about a year he edited the *Castlemaine Representative and Chronicle*. In December 1873, as a protégé of J. J. Casey [q.v.], he was appointed to the Department of Lands and Survey at a salary of £315; by 1880 he was the highest-paid clerk in the department at a salary of £400. According to a contemporary his ability was undeniable, but the effect of his 'highly efficient military Walstabian swank' was like 'boiling water on an anthill' and his retrenchment in 1880 provided mutual relief.

Walstab returned to the *Herald* as leader-writer and, briefly in 1882, editor. He was described as a striking figure in his prime, paying considerable attention to his dress. A good swordsman, in his younger days he often gave exhibitions of fencing. He contributed to the *Herald* until his death of chronic ulceration of the legs on 8 February 1909 at his home at Elsternwick. After an Anglican service he was buried in Brighton cemetery, survived by two daughters and predeceased by two daughters and a son.

T. Carrington, *The Yorick Club, its origin and development* (Melb, 1909); H. McCrae, *My father and my father's friends* (Syd, 1935); S. R. Simmons, *Marcus Clarke and the writing of 'Long odds'* (Melb, 1946); R. G. Campbell, *The first ninety years* (Melb, 1949); B. Elliott, *Marcus Clarke* (Oxford, 1969); P. M. Kirk, 'Colonial literature for colonial readers!', *Aust Literary Studies*, Oct 1971; G. A. Walstab letter, *Lone Hand*, Aug 1907; *Age*, 9 Feb 1909; *Weekly Times* (Melb), 9, 10 Feb 1909; *Bulletin*, 13 Feb 1909.   E. M. FINLAY

WANT, RANDOLPH JOHN (1811-1869), solicitor, was born in London, eldest son of John Want, surgeon and co-editor of *The Medical and Physical Journal*, and his wife Mary, née Nott. He arrived in Sydney on 8 May 1829 in the *Swiftsure* and received a grant in the County of Camden. Articled to F. W. Unwin he was admitted as a solicitor on 25 February 1837. In 1841 he took over Unwin's practice and became an examiner for aspirants to law. Among his clients were the wealthy emancipists S. Lyons and S. Terry [qq.v.]. Acting for merchants seeking an equitable distribution of a bankrupt's assets, he was consulted about a new insolvency Act and in 1843 gave evidence about it to a Legislative Council select committee. He also appeared before select committees on Supreme Court rules and orders (1845), the Preferable Lien on Wool Act (1845) and the division of the legal profession abolition bill (1846).

In 1843 Want acted for the Bank of Australia when it met difficulties; he briefed counsel in the two famous trials, *Bank of Australasia* v. *Breillat* [q.v.], and assisted the select committee that inquired into the proposed lottery to dispose of its assets. He became secretary of the Sydney Law Library Society which developed as a forum for professional discussion. When it was reconstituted in 1862 as the Law Institute of New South Wales, he became its second president; he drafted a bill of incorporation but it was not enacted for fifteen years. In the 1850s Want was a member of the Australian Philosophical Society, a committeeman of the Australasian Botanical and Horticultural Society, an elective trustee of the Australian Museum, a councillor of the Philosophical Society of New South Wales and later a fellow of St Paul's College within the University of Sydney. A committeeman of the Union Club and a member of the Australian Yacht Club, in 1862 he was a founding member of the Royal Sydney Yacht Squadron.

Want was appointed in 1856 for five years to the new Legislative Council and in its first year sat on ten select committees; on 10 May 1861 he resigned with the president Sir William Burton [q.v.] to prevent the 'swamping' of the council to pass (Sir) John Robertson's [q.v.] land bills. In 1860 he was a member of the general committee of the New South Wales Constitutional Association. Interested in mining and mining law, he was a pioneer of shale-mining and in the 1860s was chairman of the Ophir Copper Mining Co., the Moruya Silver Mining Co. and the Hartley Kerosene Oil and Paraffin Co., and solicitor for the Commercial Banking Co. of Sydney and the Peak Downs Copper Mining Co. Aged 57, Want died of haemorrhage of the stomach on 28 June 1869 and was buried in Ashfield cemetery. He was survived by his wife Harriette, née Lister, whom he had married at Christ Church St Laurence on 28 September 1839, and by five sons and four daughters. His son John Henry, Q.C., was attorney-general of New South Wales in 1885, 1886-87 and 1894-99.

S. E. Napier and E. N. Daly, *The genesis and growth of solicitors' associations in New South Wales* (Syd, 1937); V&P (LC NSW), 1843, 15, 1845, 727, 853, 1846, 2, 383; J. M.

Bennett, 'The Law Institute of N.S.W. 1862-1884', *Sydney Law Review*, Mar 1960; Deane papers (Fisher Lib, Univ Syd); Minter, Simpson & Co. papers (ML).   RICHARD WANT

WARBURTON, PETER EGERTON (1813-1889), explorer, was born on 16 August 1813 at Arley Hall, Northwich, Cheshire, England, fourth son of Rev. Rowland Egerton Warburton and his wife Emma, née Croxton. Educated at home and by tutors in France, he entered the navy at 12 and served as midshipman in the *Windsor Castle*. Between 1829 and 1831 he was at the Royal Indian Military College, Addiscombe, Surrey, before joining the 13th Native Infantry Battalion, Bombay army, where he served until 1853, retiring as assistant adjutant-general with the rank of major. On 8 October 1838 he had married Alicia Mant of Bath.

In 1853 Warburton visited his brother George at Albany, Western Australia, before going to Adelaide where he replaced A. Tolmer [q.v.] as commissioner of police on 8 December, and was made a justice of the peace. In 1857 he visited the area of Lake Gairdner and the Gawler Ranges; and in 1858 the government sent him north to recall and supersede B. H. Babbage's [q.v.] exploring party. Warburton continued with a companion towards Mount Serle, finding a way through Lake Eyre and South Lake Torrens. He discovered groups of springs, grazing land and the ranges he named after (Sir) Samuel Davenport [q.v.]. While the government disapproved of Warburton's criticism of Babbage, it praised his skill and granted him £100 for his achievements. Next year however £100 per annum was taken off his salary, and he continued to receive this reduced rate.

In 1860 with three mounted police he explored north-west of Streaky Bay; he covered about two hundred miles of barren country and reported unfavourably on it. In November 1864 Warburton was defeated by inhospitable country north-west of Mount Margaret and in 1866 he examined the area around the northern shores of Lake Eyre. He searched unsuccessfully for Sturt's [q.v.] Cooper's Creek, but found a large river, since named after him, which he traced to near the Queensland border. He returned in October.

After a secret court of inquiry into the police force, the government suggested 'that other employment more congenial to his habits and tastes should be found' for Warburton, but they refused to show him the evidence. He declined to resign and was dismissed early in 1867. A subsequent Legislative Council select committee on the police force failed to reveal why Warburton had been victimized, deplored his unfair treatment and vainly recommended reinstatement. On 24 March 1869 he accepted the lower salary of chief staff officer and colonel of the Volunteer Military Force of South Australia.

In 1872 Warburton left South Australia as leader of an expedition that included his son Richard and J. Lewis. It was financed and provided with seventeen camels and six months supplies by (Sir) Walter Hughes and (Sir) Thomas Elder [qq.v.], and sought to link the province with Western Australia. After leaving Alice Springs in April 1873, they endured long periods of extreme heat with little water, and survived only by killing the camels for meat. They reached the Oakover River with Warburton strapped to a camel. On 11 January 1874 they were brought to Charles Harper's [q.v.] de Grey station in northern Western Australia. They had conquered the formidable Great Sandy Desert to become the first to cross the continent from the centre to the west. Warburton was emaciated and blind in one eye; at a public banquet in Adelaide later he attributed their survival to his Aboriginal companion Charley.

Warburton was awarded the patron's medal of the Royal Geographical Society, London, and in 1874 he visited England for six weeks. He received the C.M.G. and the South Australian government granted him £1000. He had contributed much useful information to the colony and to later explorers about some of the driest and most difficult areas of the continent; his journal was published as *Journey Across the Western Interior of Australia* (London, 1875).

In 1877 Warburton resigned from the volunteer force. He had been an honorary fellow since 1858 of the Adelaide Philosophical (Royal) Society and lived at his property and vineyard, Norley Bank, Beaumont near Adelaide, where he died on 5 November 1889. He was buried in the churchyard of St Matthew's, Kensington, and was survived by his wife (d. 1892), two sons and a daughter; his estate was sworn for probate at £5000.

B. Threadgill, *South Australian land exploration 1856 to 1880* (Adel, 1922); PP (SA), 1858, 1859, 2 (37), 1867, 3 (120), 1868-69, 3 (77), 1874, 1, 25, 27, 28; Roy Geog Soc, *Procs*, 44 (1874); E. C. Black, 'The Lake Torrens hoodoo', PRGSSA, 64 (1963); *Australasian*, 6 Mar 1875; *Register* (Adel), 6 Nov 1889; *The Times*, 17 Dec 1889; Addiscombe College cadet records, and Bombay army service records 1831-53 (India House, Lond).   DENISON DEASEY

WARD, EBENEZER (1837-1917), journalist and politician, was born at Westminster, London, on 4 September 1837, son of Joseph Ward, oil and colour merchant, later a Baptist minister, and his wife Grace, née Guy. Educated at the Baptist Dumpton Hall School, Ramsgate, he went to London at 12 to avoid becoming a clergyman. He joined the *Morning Post* as a proofreader's boy, learned shorthand and became a junior reporter.

Arriving in Melbourne in 1859 Ward became theatre critic on the *Melbourne Herald*. In August 1860 he accompanied G. V. Brooke [q.v.] to Adelaide, appearing briefly at the Victoria Theatre before returning to Melbourne and journalism. In 1861 he joined the *South Australian Advertiser* and wrote a series of articles, published in 1862 as *The Vineyards and Orchards of South Australia*. In August he joined Frederick Sinnett [q.v.] as sub-editor of the *Daily Telegraph* until 1863 when he went back to Melbourne to write for the *Age*. In 1864 he was clerk-in-charge, accountant and postmaster in the first South Australian government expedition to the Northern Territory but was dismissed by B. T. Finniss [q.v.] for insubordination. Rejoining the *Daily Telegraph* he became its editor in August 1865. He was secretary to the South Australian Agricultural and Horticultural Society in 1866-68. He published *The south-eastern district of South Australia: its resources and requirements* in 1869.

In 1861 Ward had eloped with Matilda Ann Simmons, aged 17, whom he married on 19 December. Two sons were born before 1866 when she sued for divorce, charging adultery and cruelty. Ward counter-petitioned alleging adultery, and was granted a divorce in June 1870. On 12 December he married Lucy Johnson of Willaston. They had four sons and five daughters.

Unsuccessful in 1868, Ward was elected to the House of Assembly for Gumeracha in 1870 as a radical land reformer. In 1871 he won repute with a campaign that persuaded the government to suspend auction sales pending a more liberal credit selection law; in 1872-75 he criticized land administration effectively and advocated more generous terms for farmers. His own newspapers, the *Northern Guardian* and the *Farmers Weekly Messenger*, gained him influence and notoriety. In 1875-76 Ward was minister of agriculture and education, a minor portfolio which J. P. Boucaut [q.v.] created to keep him from land administration. He introduced the compulsory and secular education bill of 1875 and chaired the commission on agricultural and technical education. In 1876-77 he held the same office in J. Colton's [q.v.] ministry.

Bankrupt in 1880, Ward resigned from parliament and unsuccessfully sued E. H. Derrington [q.v.] of the *Port Adelaide News, Shipping and Commercial Advertiser* for libel. The six-day trial resurrected past scandals but did not prevent his re-election for Burra in 1881-84 and Frome in 1884-90, when he was chairman of committees. He represented the Northern District in the Legislative Council in 1891-1900. He was a consistent advocate of Federation and of railway-building to the eastern colonies and the Northern Territory, but in the 1880s he led opposition to South Australia joining the Federal Council, which he saw as a hindrance to genuine Federation. He criticized the 1891 draft Federal constitution on states-rights grounds and in 1897 advocated unification. He ran unsuccessfully for the Federal Convention.

Ward was regarded as the most eloquent man in parliament, but his indolence when in office and his contrariness limited his effectiveness, even apart from the scandal of his private life. His need was for individual display and assertiveness. Out of parliament from 1900, he was again in financial difficulties. In 1911 he moved to Perth and resumed his old trade, writing for the *Western Mail*. Survived by six sons and five daughters, he died in Perth on 8 October 1917 and was buried in the Anglican section of the Karrakatta cemetery.

J. B. Hirst, *Adelaide and the country 1870-1917* (Melb, 1973); *Register* (Adel), 28 Apr-6 May 1880; *Advertiser* (Adel), 9 Oct 1917; Matrimonial causes jurisdiction no 92, 102, 130 (Supreme Court records, SA).

J. B. HIRST

WARD, SIR EDWARD WOLSTEN-HOLME (1823-1890), military engineer and deputy-master of the Royal Mint, was born on 17 August 1823 in Calcutta, India, son of John Petty Ward, Bengal civil service, and his wife Elinor, née Erskine. Educated at the Royal Military Academy, Woolwich, from 6 May 1839, he was commissioned into the Royal Engineers on 19 June 1841. He studied engineering and architecture at Chatham, then served in Bermuda and in Britain. A student at the Royal School of Mines, London, he worked at the Royal Mint and was promoted captain in 1852.

The Treasury appointed Ward on 26 April 1853 to report on colonial proposals to mint gold. His report of 23 May was accepted and he became deputy-master of the Sydney branch of the Royal Mint—its first overseas branch. He arrived in the *Calcutta* on 22 October 1854. The mint began operations in Macquarie Street on 14 May next year; in 1857 its coins became legal tender in all the Australasian colonies and in 1863 throughout the British empire. Ward proved a capable administrator, and chose a wide library on classical and current economic thought, banking and cambistry as well as technical books on coining. His assayer W. S. Jevons [q.v.] complained of Ward's utter dedication, 'a military man, very determined and arbitrary', but admitted that he was 'generally civil and attentive, but very distant'. In the 1860s he repeatedly advised the opening of a branch of the Royal Mint in Melbourne and a government bank of issue.

In 1855-56 Ward was a nominated member of the Legislative Council and in 1855 a member of the select committee on Circular Quay. That year he was also briefly chief commissioner of railways and served as a commissioner under B. H. Martindale [q.v.] in 1857-58. He lived at Dawes Battery and on 21 November 1857 at Holy Trinity (Garrison) Church married Anne Sophia (d. 1923), daughter of Robert Campbell junior [q.v.]. He was the first round-arm bowler in intercolonial cricket and played in the first match in Melbourne and the return in the Sydney Domain on 14-16 January 1857; in four matches he took 27 wickets at 7.62 runs.

Ward was a councillor, sometime honorary secretary and later a corresponding member of the Philosophical (Royal) Society of New South Wales and published three papers in its *Transactions*. He was also an elective trustee of the Australian Museum, a committee-man of the Church Society, a trustee of the Savings Bank of New South Wales, a local director of the European Assurance Society, a superannuation fund commissioner in 1864-65 and a member of the Government Asylums Board for the Infirm and Destitute. A member of the Legislative Council in 1861-65 he wrote regularly about politics to his friend James Macarthur [q.v.]. In 1863 he published his report for Major-General Sir Thomas Pratt [q.v.] on the *Defences of the City of Sydney*.

Promoted lieut-colonel in 1864, Ward was on leave in 1866 on half-pay and did not return to the Sydney mint. In 1869 he became a colonel and on 13 October arrived in Victoria from England to take up duty as deputy-master of the Melbourne branch of the Royal Mint. He supervised its design, construction and setting up, and it was opened on 12 June 1872 on the site of the original Exhibition building. In 1870 he was appointed to the Board of Defence, and in 1872 chaired the board of inquiry into the condition of the existing powder magazines. A member of the 1874 royal commission on volunteer forces, with Sir George Verdon [q.v.] and G. V. Smith he disagreed with most of the commission's recommendations. On 10 June 1876 he went to England on leave with his family and from 1 August 1877 received a pension of £217 from the New South Wales government. From the 1870s he invested in cattle stations in Queensland, first with Langloh Parker in Retreat on the Barcoo River and in the 1880s with his brother-in-law S. A. Stephen, G. H. Cox and V. J. Dowling [qq.v.] in Connemara on the Diamantina.

Ward was promoted major-general in 1877 and was created C.M.G. in 1874 and K.C.M.G. in 1879. He lived at 14 Lowndes Square, London, and in 1880 bought the Villa La Garde in Cannes, France, where he died on 5 February 1890. He was survived by his wife, three sons and three daughters. His Australian estate was valued for probate at £16,890.

W. Westgarth, *Remarks upon the proposed branch of the Royal Mint ... Sydney ...* (Melb, 1854); R. Chalmers, *A history of currency in the British colonies* (Lond, 1893); A. G. Moyes, *Australian cricket: a history* (Syd, 1959); C. D. W. Goodwin, *Economic enquiry in Australia* (Durham, N.C., 1966); W. S. Jevons, *Papers and correspondence...*, R. D. C. Black ed, 1-2 (Lond, 1972); V&P (LA NSW), 1858, 3, 471, 1056, 1861, 2, 1032, 1863-64, 1, 75, 733, 2, 1057, (LA Vic), 1871, 2 (D7); NSW Railway and Tramway Mag, 1 Dec 1920; Australasian, 15 Feb 1890; SMH, 22 Mar 1923; Macarthur papers (ML); CO 201/53.

P. J. GREVILLE

WARD, FREDERICK (1835-1870), bushranger, alias 'CAPTAIN THUNDERBOLT', was born at Windsor, New South Wales. He was working as a drover and horsebreaker at Tocal station on the Paterson River when arrested with James Garbutt for receiving seventy-five stolen horses at Maitland on 21 April 1856; they were sentenced to ten years hard labour on 13 August.

Released conditionally from Cockatoo Island on 31 July 1860, Ward worked as a horse-breaker at Cooyal near Mudgee until his ticket-of-leave was cancelled on 17 September 1861 for 'absence from Muster' and he was tried on 3 October for horse-stealing. Returned to Cockatoo Island to complete his original sentence with an additional three years, Ward escaped with Frederick Brittain about 11 September 1863, probably assisted by his wife Mary Ann (née Bugg?), a half-caste Aboriginal. She and Ward lived quietly on the Culgoa River near Bourke with two children until he adopted the name 'Captain Thunderbolt' in February 1865. He carried out a series of armed robberies near Bourke with three associates, including a 16-year-old boy John Thomson, who was shot and captured by the police at Millie near Moree. Ward and two others robbed inns and mail-coaches in the Liverpool Plains District; in December 1865 at Caroll near Gunnedah they held up an inn and danced and drank until the police arrived. They wounded a policeman and escaped, abandoning three pack-horses. Ward separated from his companions and never again made a stand when the police approached.

Alone, with a reward of £200 on his head, Ward held up mailmen and on 3 February 1867 was almost captured while drunk near Manilla. He took an accomplice Thomas Mason, a 16-year-old orphan, with whom he robbed the mails in the New England and Upper Hunter areas as well as the Liverpool Plains District. While hiding out in the Borah ranges they became separated, Mason was captured in August and convicted of highway robbery. Mary Ann followed Ward whenever possible; at Stroud in March 1866 she had been sentenced to six months for vagrancy but was released in April, probably because she was pregnant. Her health was undermined by her rigorous life and, aged 28, she reputedly died of pneumonia on 24 November 1867 in a settler's home near Muswellbrook where Ward had taken her.

Ward's next companion was William Monckton, a 13-year-old runaway, with whom he robbed travellers and the mails in the New England area. In October 1868 Monckton abandoned Ward who then worked alone and less actively; on 25 May 1870 he was surprised while testing an inferior horse and was chased and shot by Constable Alexander Binney Walker at Kentucky Creek near Uralla. A Protestant, he was buried in Uralla cemetery without religious rites.

Ward was 5 ft. 8¼ ins. tall, slight, and of sallow complexion with hazel-grey eyes and light-brown curly hair. He undoubtedly had great nerve, endurance and unusual self-reliance and his success as a bushranger can be largely attributed to his horsemanship and splendid mounts, to popular sympathy inspired by his agreeable appearance and conversation, and to his gentlemanly behaviour and avoidance of violence; he also showed prudence in not robbing armed coaches, or towns where a policeman was stationed. The last of the professional bushrangers in New South Wales, Ward was the most successful.

A. R. Macleod, *The transformation of Manellae* (Manilla, 1949); R. B. Walker, 'Captain Thunderbolt, bushranger', JRAHS, 43 (1957);

Maitland Mercury, 22 May, 14 Aug 1856, 11 Feb 1868; *Mudgee Liberal*, 27 Sept, 11 Oct 1861; *SMH*, 16 Sept 1863, 3 May, 28 Dec 1865, 1 June 1870, 1 Apr 1929; *Armidale Express*, 16 Feb 1867; *T&CJ*, 4 June 1870; information from NSWA.   VICTOR CRITTENDEN

WARDELL, WILLIAM WILKINSON (1823-1899), architect and civil servant, was born at Poplar, London, and baptized on 3 March 1824 at All Saints Church of England, son of Thomas Wardell, baker, and his wife Mary. Educated as an engineer he served articles in London, then spent a short time at sea before practising in London. He worked for the commissioners of sewers for Westminster and part of Middlesex, and for W. F. East, an architect. His interest in Gothic Revival architecture was stimulated by his friends Augustus Pugin and (Cardinal) John Henry Newman, who encouraged him to become a Roman Catholic. While employed on railway surveys in the early 1840s he studied near-by churches. In 1846-57 he designed some thirty Catholic churches, including the Redemptorist Church of Our Immaculate Lady of Victories on Clapham Common, and the vast Church of Saints Mary and Michael, Commercial Road, Whitechapel. At St Mary's Chapel, Moorfields, in the City of London, he married Lucy Ann (d. 1888), daughter of William Henry Butler, an Oxfordshire wine merchant.

Ill health led Wardell to migrate and he reached Melbourne in September 1858 in the *Swiftsure*. On 7 March 1859 he was appointed inspecting clerk of works and chief architect in the Department of Works and Buildings and on 7 January 1861 was promoted inspector-general of public works, with the right of private practice. He was responsible for the construction of all public buildings in Victoria; some, such as Government House, Melbourne (1872), are attributed to him. All drawings and plans were probably prepared to his specifications and submitted to him for approval.

Wardell directed works on the Gippsland lakes, harbour works at Warrnambool, and the completion of the reconstruction of the foreshores of the lower Yarra River. He was a member of the Central Board of Health from 1860, a trustee of the proposed zoological gardens, Royal Park, a member of the Board of Land and Works and of the Board of Examiners for the Civil Service from 1862, and was a commissioner for the 1865 Dublin and 1873 London international exhibitions. He was a member of some eleven boards of inquiry and royal commissions, including the 1863-65 royal commission on the fine arts, chaired by (Sir) Redmond Barry [q.v.], and the board of inquiry into the state forests in 1867.

The 1873 royal commission on the Public Works Department upheld complaints by Joseph Reed [q.v.] that private architects' designs for public buildings had been accepted and then ignored, and that funds had been wasted by the unnecessary use of expensive materials. The Old Custom House buildings were described as 'monuments of utter waste and extravagance'. Reed also asserted that Wardell took the credit for work of his subordinates, but the commission found Wardell overworked because of his control of both administrative and professional departments. In 1874 a board inquired into charges published in a pamphlet by Thomas Eaton, a disaffected superintendent of works, who claimed to have been victimized as an Orangeman and refused promotion; Wardell countered that Eaton's work was unsatisfactory. The board dismissed Eaton's charges, but censured Wardell for poor administration and for allowing an inefficient officer 'to draw his salary without giving an adequate return to the state'; two years later a Legislative Assembly select committee recommended Eaton's reinstatement, or compensation. In 1875 Wardell examined plans for the Western Australian government, reported on Fremantle harbour and suggested King George Sound as the overseas terminal.

Before entering the civil service, Wardell had contracted to design and supervise the construction of St Patrick's Cathedral, Melbourne, one of his greatest works; he prepared plans in 1858 for St John's College, within the University of Sydney; he also designed St Mary's Cathedral, Hobart Town, but was not responsible for faults in its construction involving H. Hunter [q.v.] in 1876. Soon after his appointment, professional colleagues alleged that Wardell used his official position to boost his private practice and passed work to other architects willing to share the fee. Other critics, jealous of his monopoly of Catholic work, believed he also tried to cajole the Protestant clergy as he had prepared plans and specifications without fee for St John's Church of England, Toorak. His private practice flourished in the 1860s as he designed Gothic Revival churches in Melbourne and its suburbs and St Mary's Cathedral, Sydney.

Dismissed with other civil servants by the Victorian government on 8 January 1878, Wardell was influenced by Archbishop Polding [q.v.] to settle in Sydney; he took W. L. Vernon as a partner in 1884 and practised with his son Herbert in the 1890s. Eschewing ecclesiastical works, he indulged 'his newly discovered love for Italianate, Palladian and Venetian architecture' in such buildings as the Union Club, the New South Wales Club, and Cliveden, East Melbourne, completed in 1888 for Sir William Clarke [q.v.]. He acted as consulting architect to banks and other commercial firms, for which he designed offices, notably the English, Scottish and Australian Chartered Bank's head office in Melbourne, which has been acclaimed as 'the most distinguished building of the whole Australian Gothic-Revival era'. He also prepared plans for St Mary's School, North Sydney, and Gidleigh, Bungendore, New South Wales, for William Forster Rutledge. However the two cathedrals gave him most satisfaction and took up more and more of his time as he sketched altars and church furniture, including pews, which he thought should not be too comfortable; he sought skilled artisans to execute his designs.

In 1883 Wardell was a member of the board which vainly recommended the removal of T. Sani's [q.v.] carvings on the General Post Office, Sydney; and, as consulting engineer, he reported on proposed dock improvements for the Auckland Harbour Board, New Zealand, but was strongly criticized by the board's engineer. In 1890 he was a member of the royal commission on defence works which found the colonial architect J. Barnet [q.v.] guilty of negligence in his supervision of works on Bare Island, La Perouse; next year he was an assessor to examine entries submitted for the construction of a bridge across Darling Harbour. A fellow of the Royal Institute of British Architects (1849) and a member of the Institution of Civil Engineers, London (1857), he was a member of the Australian Club; in 1883 he became a member of the Royal Society of New South Wales and was a founder of the New South Wales branch of the (Royal) Geographical Society of Australasia. He several times arbitrated in disputes over fees between J. Horbury Hunt [q.v.] and his clients and was a member, off and on, of the Institute of Architects of New South Wales during Hunt's stormy presidency.

Wardell died of heart failure and pleurisy on 19 November 1899 in his home, Upton Grange, North Sydney, and was buried in the Catholic section of the Gore Hill cemetery. He was survived by three of his six sons and by four daughters; his daughter Mary was the mother of John Joseph Wardell Power (1881-1943) who left a large sum to the University of Sydney for the promotion of the fine arts. Wardell's estate was valued for probate at £12,919.

Critics have varied in their assessment of his ability: W. B. Dalley [q.v.] referred to him as 'the most thoroughly cultivated member of his profession' and A. G.

Stephens acclaimed him as 'by far the most eminent architect who has lived in Australia'. In achievement he ranks with E. Blacket [q.v.], Barnet and Reed, and was unsurpassed as a sensitive and scholarly interpreter of Gothic Revival : his cathedrals and churches, notable for purity of expression and richness of symbolism, rank among the greatest buildings constructed anywhere in that style.

Testimonials to W. W. Wardell (Lond, 1858); H. R. Hitchcock, *Early Victorian architecture in Britain* (Lond, 1954); M. Herman, *The architecture of Victorian Sydney* (Syd, 1956); J. M. Freeland, *Melbourne churches, 1836-1851* (Melb, 1963); B. Little, *Catholic churches since 1623* (Lond, 1966); V&P (LA NSW), 1894, 3, 693, (LC NSW), 1891-92, pt 1; D. I. McDonald, 'William W. Wardell, architect and engineer', *VHM*, 41 (1970), *and* '"A Gross Want of Knowledge". W. W. Wardell, inspector general of public works, 1861-78', *VHM*, 43 (1972); Public Works Dept (NSW), Proposed bridge across Darling Harbour to Pyrmont, 1892 (ML); V. A. Wardell, A review of the architectural and engineering works of W. W. Wardell (ML); Parkes letters (ML); W. W. Wardell papers (ML, *and* Roman Catholic Archives, Syd, *and* MDHC Archives, East Melb, *and* Univ Melb Archives); letters (St John's College Archives, Syd).   D. I. McDonald

WARDILL, RICHARD WILSON (1835-1873), cricketer, was born near Liverpool, Lancashire, England, son of Joseph Wilson Wardill, stockbroker, and his wife Mary, née Briddon. He migrated to Melbourne about 1858 and began his cricketing career. In the 1858-59 season he topped the aggregate of the Richmond Cricket Club second XI with 108 runs. Next year he transferred to the Melbourne Cricket Club and was its honorary secretary until 1863. He excelled as an opening batsman and in 1862 was selected to play for Victoria against New South Wales. The same year he played for the combined Victoria-New South Wales team against Stephenson's first All England XI in Melbourne. He soon won repute as a cricketer and all-round sportsman; in 1866 he was a delegate at a conference to formulate the rules of Australian Football. He captained the Melbourne Cricket Club against the Edenhope Aboriginal Team on Boxing Day 1866 when about 11,000 saw his team have a hard fight to win.

Wardill was also a capable administrator. In 1864 he suggested in a letter to the press the formation of a central organization to arrange intercolonial matches and also administer the game. He became honorary secretary of a provisional committee, and the Victorian Cricket Association was formed at a meeting in the Clarence Hotel on 10 October with W. C. Haines [q.v.] as first president. In 1867 it was forced into recess and intercolonial matches were arranged by the Melbourne Cricket Club until the association was reorganized in 1875.

In 1872-73 Wardill had serious personal problems probably because of speculation in mining shares; he embezzled £7000 from his employers, the Victoria Sugar Co. On 17 August 1873, aged 38, he committed suicide by jumping into the Yarra River; he left a note saying that his defalcations had taken place over two years. Many adverse statements were made against him in the press, but the cricketing fraternity rallied to his defence, and W. J. Hammersley of the *Australasian* wrote, 'Amongst cricketers there will be one feeling, that of sorrow; for, great as Mr. Wardill's crime must now be regarded, it is but doing him bare justice to state that cricket in Victoria is greatly indebted to him for its present position'.

Wardill was one of the finest cricketers to play in the colonies prior to the commencement of the Anglo-Australian Tests in 1877. For Victoria he made 348 runs for an average of 31. He also made over 400 runs a year in club cricket in Melbourne during the 1860s. He was survived by his wife, Eliza Helma Lovett, née Cameron, whom he had married at Richmond in 1871, and by his son.

His brother, BENJAMIN JOHNSTON (1842-1917), cricket administrator, was born on 15 October 1842 at Everton, Liverpool, Lancashire, and was educated at the Collegiate Institute at Liverpool. He migrated to Melbourne in 1861 and worked for several years with Richard at the office of the Victoria Sugar Co. Joining the garrison artillery soon after his arrival, he rose to the rank of major in the Harbor Trust Garrison Battery in 1885. Secretary of the Melbourne Cricket Club from 30 April 1878 to February 1911, he retired owing to ill health; the membership had increased from 572 to 5353. He organized and managed the 1886 Australian tour of England which was arranged by the club and later managed the tours of 1899 and 1902. Wardill was largely successful in his aim to make the Melbourne Cricket Club the Australian counterpart of the famous Marylebone Cricket Club in England, and his influence on Charles Bannerman, F. R. Spofforth [qq.v.], Clem Hill, Victor Trumper and others helped them lay the foundations of the Anglo-Australian Test cricket series.

Wardill was also a capable all-round sportsman; as a cricketer he was a solid batsman and a useful round-arm bowler, playing once for Victoria in 1866. He also excelled as a rifleman and in 1876 was a member of an Australian team which toured the United States of America and shot at the Philadelphia International Exhibition. He died of heart disease on 15 October 1917 and was buried in the Anglican section of St Kilda cemetery; he was survived by his wife Elizabeth Mary, née King; a daughter had died in infancy.

F. J. Ironside, *50 years of cricket*, 3rd ed (Syd, 1895); K. Dunstan, *The paddock that grew* (Melb, 1962); *Argus*, 18 Aug–6 Sept 1873, 16 Oct 1917; *Herald* (Melb), 18 Aug–6 Sept 1873; *Australasian*, 23 Aug 1873; *Punch* (Melb), 11 Nov 1909; *T&CJ*, 24 Oct 1917.

LOUIS R. CRANFIELD

WARREN, WILLIAM HENRY (1852-1926), engineer and educationist, was born on 2 February 1852 at Bristol, Somerset, England, son of William Henry Warren, railway guard, and his wife Catherine Ann, née Abrams. Educated at Rev. Trevelyan's school, in 1865-72 he was an apprentice in the London and North-Western Railway locomotive works, Wolverhampton. A student at the Dublin Royal College of Science in 1872-74, he was awarded a (Sir Joseph) Whitworth scholarship in 1873. He obtained further practical experience in engineering construction in 1874-81, and studied part time at Owens College, Manchester, where he absorbed the German idea of investigation by experiment. He was admitted to the Institution of Civil Engineers, London, in 1877. On 27 July 1875 at St Pancras, London, he married Albertine King with Church of England rites.

In 1881 Warren migrated with his family to Sydney where on 9 May he began work in the roads and bridges branch of the Department of Public Works; he taught applied mechanics at Sydney Technical College in the evenings. Next year he was appointed lecturer in engineering in the Department of Physics at the University of Sydney with salary of £500; in 1884 he became professor of engineering and in 1890 (J. H.) Challis [q.v.] professor with salary of £900.

Supported by W. C. Kernot [q.v.] in Melbourne, Warren worked to gain recognition for the place of engineering in universities. Popular, but not an outstanding lecturer, he required students to work from technical papers and textbooks, developing their abilities by personal guidance and example. At Sydney he built up a great engineering school. In 1900 senate approved the first four-year engineering course, and later introduced a requirement of practical experience during the third year. By 1910 courses in the three major branches of engineering were established in a form that remained essentially unchanged until the 1950s. He had visited England and the United States of America in 1895 and met Sir Peter Russell [q.v.] whose gifts to the university led to the foundation of the school of engineering named after him, with facilities unmatched in Australia. In 1908 Warren became dean of the faculty of science and later of engineering, and chairman of the professorial board.

Warren published *Australian Timbers* (1892) and an important textbook, *Engineering Construction in Iron, Steel and Timber* (1894, 2nd ed 1910). In 1921 a third edition included a second volume, *Engineering Construction in Masonry and Concrete*. In 1911 he published *The ... properties of New South Wales Hardwood Timbers*. He also contributed over fifty papers to learned societies including the Royal Society of New South Wales, to which he had been elected in 1883 and of which he was sometime honorary secretary, and president in 1892 and 1902. As president of section J of the Australasian Association for the Advancement of Science in 1887, his published address was a history of civil engineering in New South Wales.

For many years Warren was consulting engineer to the New South Wales government; his designs included the first suspension bridge at Northbridge. He served on royal commissions into railway bridges (1885-86) and Baldwin locomotives (1892-93) and for the Adelaide (1887) and Melbourne (1888) exhibitions. In 1901-03 he was on the Sydney harbour bridge advisory board. He was also on the council of an international society for the testing of materials, and was associated with the 1910 report on dams for irrigation for the Indian government, and the 1912 report on the Aswan dam for the Egyptian government.

At a time when little was known in Britain of reinforced concrete, Warren developed the theory in papers to the local Royal Society in 1902, 1904 and 1905, and taught European and American methods of design and construction. In World War I Warren was associated with the manufacture of munitions, the calibration of testing machines and the certification of steel. In 1916 he became chairman of a committee responsible for the New South Wales Aviation School at Richmond and he tested Australian timber for aeroplane construction.

The acknowledged leader of his profession, with a reputation extending beyond Australia, in 1919 Warren was the unanimous choice as first president of the new Institution of Engineers, Australia. His retiring address next year stressed restrictions on the use of the word 'engineer', registration of engineers with the institution as a qualifying body, a code of ethics and the engineer's duty to his profession. He emphasized that the University of Sydney's courses, more like those of the United States of America than those of Britain, met Australia's needs. Possessing clear insight, depth of knowledge, wide experience and mental ability, he had the gift of delegating work and authority. One of his major achievements was to convince the engineering industry by his personal example that graduate engineers were a sound investment.

A member of the Union Club from 1913, a keen golfer and the owner of prize-winning bulldogs, Warren was also passionately fond of music and had a fine tenor voice, trained by an Italian master. He was a member of the American Society of Civil Engineers and honorary LL.D., University of Glasgow, 1913. Survived by two sons, he died of chronic myocarditis in his home at Elizabeth Bay on 9 January 1926 and was buried in the Anglican section of Waverley cemetery. His estate was sworn for probate at £48,474. A portrait of him by J. S. Watkins is held by the University of Sydney.

A. H. Corbett, *The Institution of Engineers, Australia: a history...* (Syd, 1973); V&P (LA NSW), 1903, 6, 913-980; Inst of Engineers (Aust), *Trans, 7* (1926); Roy Soc NSW, *Procs*, 60 (1926); A. H. Corbett, 'The first hundred years of Australian engineering education, 1861-1961', Inst of Engineers (Aust), *J*, 33 (1961); *Sydney Mail*, 23 Aug 1890; SMH, 11 Jan 1926; Warren papers (Univ Syd Archives).

ARTHUR CORBETT
ANN PUGH

WARUNG, PRICE, *see* ASTLEY.

WATERHOUSE, FREDERICK GEORGE (1815-1898), naturalist and museum curator, was born on 25 August 1815 near London, son of James Edward Waterhouse, a notary public, and his wife Mary, née Newman. He worked at the British Museum with his elder brother George, an eminent entomologist and zoologist. On 7 July 1852 he married Fanny Shepherd Abbott (d. 1875) of London and soon sailed for South Australia in the *Sydney*. He made an unsuccessful visit to the Victorian goldfields and worked with C. T. Hargrave surveying the Adelaide hills. In October 1860 he became curator of the South Australian Institute Museum which opened in January 1862.

On 5 December 1861 Waterhouse accompanied J. McD. Stuart [q.v.] on his expedition across the continent. His enthusiasm and scientific zeal irritated Stuart but other members of the group found him congenial and praised his unselfishness. Several of his instruments and best specimens were lost or destroyed, but he returned to Adelaide on 21 January 1863 with a fine series of bird and mammal skins, insects and plants, including the first collection of the rare Princess Alexandra Parrot, Polytelis alexandrae. He received a government bonus of £100 and reported his observations to the commissioner of crown lands.

Waterhouse was a corresponding member of the Zoological Society of London. From 1859 a member of the Adelaide Philosophical (Royal) Society, he was its vice-president in 1869 and read two papers to it, 'On a remarkable insect Stylops' and 'Observations on the Palaeontology of Australia'; his article 'Entomology' is in the society's 1866-67 annual report. He contributed the fifteen-page 'Fauna of South Australia' for William Harcus's [q.v.] South Australia: its history, resources, and productions. About 1872, with his friend Albert Molineaux [q.v.], he found forty species of fish previously unknown in South Australian waters, later described by François Laporte [q.v.] in Melbourne.

Waterhouse was one of the foremost naturalists of his era; he gained much repute for his 'labour of love' in building up the early collections at the South Australian Museum. He has been criticized for exchanging a great variety of material with overseas museums, and the loss of many valuable Australian collections must be regretted; but in the nineteenth century exotic material was normal in museums. In 1874 a commission inquiring into the institute and museum praised his zeal and ability despite 'a very low salary [£220] and insufficient space'.

In February 1882 Waterhouse resigned and took eight months leave in England; he returned to live at Wandean, Burnside, until 1897 when he moved to Jamestown to live with a son Edward George. He died of senile decay at Mannahill on 7 September 1898 and was buried in St George's Anglican cemetery, Magill. His family included five sons and one daughter and his estate was sworn for probate at £346. His name is commemorated by a river in the Northern Territory and several natural history species.

H. M. Whittell, The literature of Australian birds (Perth, 1954); PP (SA), 1863 (125), 1874, 2 (23); R. Tate, 'Anniversary address', Roy Soc SA, Trans, 1877-78, 1882-83; J. H. Maiden, Presidential address Section D, Report 11th Meeting, A'sian Assn Advancement of Science, 2 (Adel, 1907); SA Museum, Records, 12 (1956); Register (Adel), 24, 25 Feb 1863, 15 Apr 1872, 12 Aug 1875, 9 Sept 1898; Evening Journal, 25 June 1898; Observer (Adel), 16 July, 10 Sept 1898; L. A. Gilbert, A naturalist and his diaries, relating to F. G. Waterhouse, MS 41/2 and Aust botanists, biog and bibliog files (Basser Lib, Canb).

DARRELL N. KRAEHENBUEHL

WATERHOUSE, GEORGE MARSDEN (1824-1906), merchant, pastoralist and politician, was born on 6 April 1824 at Penzance, Cornwall, England, sixth surviving son of Rev. John Waterhouse and his wife Jane Beadnell, née Skipsey. He was a brother of Jabez Waterhouse [q.v.]. Educated at Kingswood School, a Wesleyan college near Bristol, he accompanied his family to Hobart Town in the James, arriving on 1 February 1839. After working for a brother in Manchester House, Hobart, he moved to Adelaide in 1843 and soon prospered as a merchant. On 5 July 1848 he married Lydia, daughter of William Giles [q.v.].

Elected member for East Torrens in the Legislative Council in 1851 on a liberal platform, Waterhouse resigned in 1854 because of ill health and visited England. On his return in 1856 he was appointed to the Adelaide Water-Works Commission. Next year he was elected member for East Torrens in the new House of Assembly; in August the first ministry under responsible government resigned and the governor sent for him, but he declined office and resigned from the assembly next month. In 1860 he won a seat in the Legislative Council, insisting that tariff duties be 'repealed on unenumerated articles to allow traders to compete on equal terms'. From 10 May to 5 February 1861 he held office as chief secretary and in March became honorary chairman of a commission on the Real Property Act. Convinced that Judge Benjamin Boothby [q.v.] was unjustified in his refusal to recognize the validity of this and other Acts, Waterhouse proposed and then chaired a select committee of the Legislative Council on the matter. In the council debate on the committee's report he seconded a successful motion that the House should submit an address to the Crown seeking the judge's amoval; he warned that Boothby 'with one fell swoop would clear away the legislation of ten years'.

On the resignation of the premier T. Reynolds [q.v.], a Boothby supporter, Waterhouse reluctantly formed a government specifically for transmitting the address and a similar one from the assembly; he recruited his attorney-general from outside parliament. Nine days later he was persuaded to form a new ministry on a wider basis 'to carry out those [measures] which had already been introduced'; it lasted from 17 October 1861 to 4 July 1863, when he resigned after his treasurer (Sir) Arthur Blyth [q.v.] had been attacked in the assembly for alleged misappropriation of the immigration fund. In the previous month his own interest in the Tipara (Moonta) mine had come under the scrutiny of an assembly select committee that concluded that the Tipara company, of which Waterhouse had been an original director, had no legal right to the mine. He was evasive in replying to some questions and had probably made the large personal profits alleged by F. S. Dutton [q.v.], but no clear evidence emerged for Dutton's further claim that Waterhouse had been bribed with shares. He did not scruple to resume his directorship after it was clear that the assembly would take no action on the mine's ownership.

After another visit to England Waterhouse migrated to New Zealand in January 1869 and purchased for £21,000 cash the original Huangarua station, together with 18,000 sheep. Member for Wellington in the Legislative Council in 1870-90, he was minister without portfolio in the Fox ministry in 1871, premier in 1872-73, and Speaker of the Legislative Council in 1887. He visited England several times before retiring to Torquay, Devon. Survived by his wife and two adopted daughters, he died at his home on 6 August 1906, leaving an estate sworn for probate at £69,000.

A successful capitalist with a variety of investments in several countries, Waterhouse was interested above all in economic development and the freeing of trade; these objectives led him to advocate a uniform tariff for Australia and shaped his views of Judge Boothby. Although reluctant to hold office he proved a lucid exponent of legislation and a capable administrator. His portrait is in Parliament House, Wellington, New Zealand.

G. H. Scholefield (ed), A dictionary of New Zealand biography, 2 (Wellington, 1940); D. Pike, Paradise of Dissent (Melb, 1957); PD (SA), 1861-63; PP (SA), 1863, 2 (51); SA Almanack, 1844-63; S. M. K. Churchwood, Wheels within wheels (NL); Moonta Mines, Deed and settlement, and Proprietors' minutes (SAA); letter, F. S. to F. H. Dutton, A740/A2, and research notes no 16 (SAA).

JEAN F. TREGENZA

WATERHOUSE, JABEZ BUNTING (1821-1891), JOSEPH (1828-1881), and SAMUEL (1830-1918), Wesleyan ministers, were the fifth, ninth and tenth children of Rev. John Waterhouse (d. 1842) and his wife Jane Beadnell, née Skipsey. In 1838 their father, a prominent Yorkshire Meth-

odist, was appointed general superintendent of the Wesleyan Methodist Mission in Australia and Polynesia with a roving commission. With his wife, seven sons and three daughters, he reached Hobart Town in the James on 1 February 1839.

Jabez was born in London on 19 April 1821, educated at Kingswood School in 1832-35 and apprenticed to a printer. In Hobart A. Bent's [q.v.] printing premises were purchased and worked by Jabez. In 1840 he became a local preacher extending his ministry to convict road menders. Received as a probationer in 1842, he returned to England to enter Richmond (Theological) College and in 1845 was appointed to Windsor circuit. After his ordination at the Methodist chapel, Spitalfields, he was sent to Van Diemen's Land in 1847, and ministered successively in the Hobart, Westbury, Campbell Town and Longford circuits. In 1855 the first conference of the Wesleyan Church in Australia appointed him to South Australia; he served at Kapunda, Willunga and Adelaide, his ministry marked by his business acumen and his role as secretary of the Australasian Conference at Adelaide in 1862.

In 1864 Waterhouse was transferred to New South Wales and was appointed successively to Maitland, Goulburn, Orange, Waverley, Parramatta, Newcastle and Glebe. In 1874-75 he was secretary of the New South Wales and Queensland Annual Conference and president in 1876; he was elected secretary of the first three general conferences of the Australasian Wesleyan Methodist Church: in Melbourne 1875, Sydney 1878 and Adelaide 1881. In 1882 he retired as a supernumerary, but remained on committees such as those of the Sustentation and Extension Society and the Missionary Society, frequently looking after missionary interests during the absence of George Brown [q.v.]. He supported the Wesleyan Church in Tonga in the dispute with S. W. Baker [q.v.], and published The Secession and Persecution in Tonga ... (Sydney, 1886). Regarded as a gifted preacher by his denomination and as the architect of most of the conference legislation, he died of heart disease and dropsy at Randwick on 18 January 1891 and was buried in the Wesleyan section of Rookwood cemetery. He was survived by his wife Maria Augusta, née Bode, whom he had married at Windsor, England, on 13 August 1847, and by seven sons; his second son John was headmaster of Sydney High School.

Joseph was born at Halifax, Yorkshire, England, in February 1828 and educated at Kingswood School in 1832-36, and St Andrew's Presbyterian school, Hobart; he became a member of the Methodist society at 14. In 1846 he joined his brother George Marsden [q.v.] in Adelaide. After serving as a local preacher for a year, in 1849 he was recommended for the ministry by Rev. D. J. Draper [q.v.] and volunteered as a missionary to Fiji. He worked in the group from 1850-57 when he returned to Australia on deputation for two years. He went back to Fiji in 1859 and, as chairman of the district, accompanied Colonel W. J. Smythe on his tour of the islands, and influenced him against their cession to Britain. Forced by ill health to leave Fiji in 1864, next year he was appointed to New Norfolk and served in Tasmania until 1870 when he moved to Victoria, ministering at Beechworth and Ballarat. In 1874, after its annexation to Britain, he returned to Fiji at the request of the Sydney Conference and took charge of the Training Institution at Navuloa until 1878 when he returned to Australia. He was drowned in the wreck of the *Tararua* off Dunedin on 29 April 1881 after visiting New Zealand.

Regarded as a great missionary, Joseph championed the system of indigenous teachers in Fiji against the policy of F. Langham [q.v.], and was credited with the conversion of Cakobau, chief of Bau and afterwards King of Fiji. A man of forceful personality he believed in 'a Methodism startling *hell* itself by its aggressive movements', and was described as 'a splendid man, inclined to hardness, but just'. He published in London *Vah-tah-ah, the Feejeean Princess* (1857), *The Native Minister ...* (1858), *The King and People of Fiji* (1866) and *The ocean child... a memoir of Mrs. Anna M. Rooney* (1868). By his wife Elizabeth, née Watson, whom he married on 26 March 1850, he had ten children.

Samuel was educated at St Andrew's school, Hobart. In 1850 he was appointed to the Melbourne circuit as a 'bush missionary' with a commission to itinerate around Kilmore, Bacchus Marsh and Mount Macedon and was the first minister to preach at the Mount Alexander goldfields. In 1851 he became a missionary to Fiji, but was forced by ill health to return to Victoria in 1857. Stationed successively at Warrnambool, Kyneton and Amherst, he became a supernumerary in 1865. Next year he moved to Hobart but was confined in the Hospital for the Insane, New Norfolk, from 1870 until he died on 19 November 1918. He was described by his family as 'a real genius, fiery, eloquent, affectionate, generous'. He had one son George Wilson Waterhouse, a celebrated lawyer, by his first wife Esther Day, née Wilson, whom he married on 27 January 1852; she died in Fiji on 17 April 1856. On

9 February 1858 he married Eleanor Watson, sister of Joseph's wife, who bore him three sons and a daughter.

S. Dunn, *The missionary of Australasia and Polynesia* (Lond, 1842); R. Young, *The southern world* (Lond, 1854); Mrs W. J. Smythe, *Ten months in the Fiji Islands* (Oxford, 1864); J. Colwell, *The illustrated history of Methodism* (Syd, 1904); G. C. Henderson, *Fiji and the Fijians, 1835-1856* (Syd, 1931); C. Irving Benson (ed), *A century of Victorian Methodism* (Melb, 1935); G. J. Waterhouse et al, *A brief account of the life ... of Rev. John Waterhouse* (Syd, 1937); *Wesleyan Missionary Notices* (Lond), 1838-65, *and* (A'sia) 1857-81; T&CJ, 4 Mar 1876; *Weekly Advocate*, 7, 17 May 1881, 24 Jan, 7 Feb 1891; Methodist overseas mission papers (ML); Waterhouse papers (Trinity College, Auckland, NZ); family papers (copies held by author); MS and printed cats (ML).

NIEL GUNSON

WATERS, EDWARD ERNEST (1853-1881), journalist, was born in February 1853 at Richmond Terrace, Stretford, Lancashire, England, son of Joseph Hughes Waters, cotton manufacturer, and his wife Eliza Maria, née Hill. He matriculated at Owens College, Manchester, in 1870 and passed examinations in 1872 but did not graduate. He migrated to New South Wales in 1877 to improve his health. In October he began contributing 'Notes on Current Events', first a column then a page, in the *Australian Town and Country Journal*. His 'pithy and often scathing comments' impressed Samuel Bennett [q.v.] who engaged him to write also for the *Evening News*. As its editor after September 1878, he was liberal 'in politics, in religion, and in every department of social life ... [with] a strong sense of justice, a strong belief in the essential dignity of human nature, and a thorough detestation of shams'. As a journalist he was esteemed by the contemporary press, including the *Freeman's Journal*.

From his Manchester experience he advised on founding the Sydney Technical College in 1879 and delivered its inaugural address. His lecture course in English literature and history, well attended by public school teachers, displayed 'a great breadth of view, deep political insight and extensive historical research'. In 1880 he also delivered a modified series of popular lectures at metropolitan and suburban schools of arts. Financially secure, on 11 April 1879 at Ashfield he had married a widow Jane Kirby, née Green. He died of typhoid fever on 13 January 1881 at his residence at St Leonards after accidentally slashing his wrist while pruning roses, and was buried in the Congregational section of the Gore

Hill cemetery. He was survived by his wife and daughter and by two children of his wife's first marriage.

Evening News (Syd), 13 Jan 1881; SMH, 14 Jan 1881; Freeman's J (Syd), 15 Jan 1881; T&CJ, 15 Jan 1881.　　　　RUTH TEALE

WATSFORD, JOHN (1820-1907), Wesleyan minister, was born on 5 December 1820 at Parramatta, New South Wales, son of James Watsford and his wife Jane, née Johns. James had arrived in the colony in the Guildford in 1812, transported for life for horse-stealing; converted to Wesleyanism by Rev. S. Leigh [q.v.], he was pardoned in 1826 and became coachman to H. H. Macarthur [q.v.], but set up on his own as one of the first royal mail coachmen in New South Wales. John was educated at The King's School, Parramatta, and later taught there. He was converted in 1838 at a prayer meeting conducted by Rev. D. Draper [q.v.], and in 1841 was accepted by the British Wesleyan Conference as a probationer for the ministry. Because of lack of facilities he received no formal theological education, but at his ordination he was the first Australian-born minister of the conference. On 8 February 1844 he married Elizabeth Jones at Windsor; they had seven sons and seven daughters, of whom James and Frederick became Wesleyan ministers and Emma married Rev. Benjamin Danks, pioneer missionary in New Britain.

Appointed to the Wesleyan Mission in Fiji, Watsford left Sydney with his wife in the Triton on 2 March 1844. Taking two years to learn the language, he was stationed at Viwa, Lakeba and Nadi, where he established and taught in schools, held revival meetings, and dispensed medical aid. Because of illness among his family he returned to Australia to circuit work in the Moreton Bay District in 1850, but at the request of the Missionary Committee went back to Fiji in 1851 and with Rev. J. Calvert [q.v.] spent three years translating the New Testament into Fijian.

Returning to Sydney in December 1853, Watsford was appointed to circuits at Surry Hills (1854-57), Goulburn (1857-60) and Maitland (1860-62), before going to South Adelaide where he was chairman of the South Australian district and was active in moves to set up a Wesleyan college (later Prince Alfred College). In April 1868 he moved to Ballarat, Victoria, to the Lydiard Street circuit and in 1869 was elected district chairman. In 1871 he was elected president of the Conference of the Australasian Wesleyan Church and was appointed superintendent of the circuit at Brunswick Street, Fitzroy. His emotional, articulate preaching and missionary lectures drew large crowds. An able administrator, in 1875 he was appointed general secretary of the newly formed Wesleyan Home Mission, of which he had been a chief founder, and he traversed Victoria raising funds to set up churches in the remote south-east and north-west. His election as president of the General Conference of the Australasian Wesleyan Methodist Church in 1878 reflected the wide respect he commanded. He was influential at this conference in opposing moves to liberalize membership regulations. In 1883 he retired from his strenuous Home Mission work to return to the Brunswick Street circuit, and that year was a founder of the Voluntary Instruction Association which favoured religious instruction in state schools by voluntary teachers.

In 1881 Watsford visited Europe and Great Britain and was an official Australasian representative at the first Ecumenical Council of Methodism in London. In 1884 he became a member of a deputation which visited Tonga to investigate dissension between S. W. Baker [q.v.] and the Wesleyan Church and he revisited Fiji. He was secretary of the Jubilee Thanksgiving Fund in 1886 and after superintending circuits at Brighton and Richmond, retired in 1891. That year he organized an interdenominational convention at Geelong. In retirement he devoted himself to evangelical and mission work. He died at Kew on 24 July 1907, predeceased by his wife and survived by six sons and four daughters; he was buried in the Boroondara cemetery. Watsford's conservative evangelical beliefs are well displayed in his autobiography, Glorious Gospel Triumphs (London, 1900).

HRA (1), 12; A. Sutherland et al, Victoria and its metropolis, 2 (Melb, 1888); Spectator (Melb), 2 Aug 1907; T&CJ, 19 June 1912; R. Howe, The Wesleyan Church in Victoria, 1855-1901: its ministry and membership (M.A. thesis, Univ Melb, 1965); MS cat (ML), HO 27/6.　　　　RENATE HOWE

WATSON, GEORGE JOHN (1829-1906), racing entrepreneur, was born at Ballydarton, County Carlow, Ireland, son of John Watson, gentleman, justice of the peace and master of foxhounds. George was schooled at Kilkenny College and brought up amongst hounds and horses. Although intended for the army, he decided to make his way in Australia and arrived in Melbourne in March 1850. On 20 August at St James's Church, Melbourne, he married Sarah Jane Townsend.

In 1851 Watson became lessee of Kirk's Bazaar, the leading colonial horse sale-yard;

his gentlemanly demeanour, business skill and honesty made it a lucrative concern and a headquarters for sportsmen. In November 1857, with Cyrus Hewitt, he won the mail contracts between Melbourne and Sandhurst (Bendigo) and Melbourne and Ballarat, and bought the two operating Cobb [q.v.] & Co. coachlines. In December they won the Beechworth mail contract which had a £10,000 government subsidy; their purchase of the Beechworth coachline was financed by the sale of their other lines. For some six months their manager on the run was J. Rutherford [q.v.] who, with his American drivers, kept the tight contract schedule of 200 miles in 26 hours.

On forfeiting the Beechworth contract in 1860, Watson and Hewitt sold the line and repurchased the Sandhurst line in June, only to lose its contract and sell the line to (A. W.) Robertson [q.v.] and Britton next year. Watson's partnership with Hewitt was dissolved in October 1862. In the 1860s and 1870s Watson retained an interest in the coaching business and was a partner until July 1880 in A. W. Robertson's firm of Robertson & Co.; in 1868 he made news by driving one of the Beechworth coaches all the way from Wangaratta to Melbourne in fifteen hours, including a 'far from hasty dinner' at Avenel. He also bred, trained and spelled horses on a large scale on Riverina properties, which he leased with Hewitt until 1862, and at I.Y.U., near Pakenham. He owned 4779 acres of I.Y.U. in 1872-84.

Watson was a member of the first committee of the Victoria Racing Club in March 1864 and was an owner, committeeman and starter into his old age. His main interest was steeplechasing in which he was an outstanding amateur rider and successful owner. His colours of cerise and black won on the flat also; his horse Flying Colours took out the Derby in 1860 and he won the first Oaks Stakes at Flemington in 1861 with Palestine. His great skill, harsh discipline and forceful language as starter brought him world fame and the nickname 'Prince of Starters'; once, after the splendid start of a large Melbourne Cup field, the enormous crowd cheered him again and again. His superb horsemanship, ability and integrity made him one of the most respected men in Victorian racing.

Watson had brought several couples from the famous Carlow pack to Melbourne and when in 1853 he bought the pick of local hounds, he founded the Melbourne Hunt Club and developed the fastest and best pack in the colony. In the 1850s they chased kangaroo and emu and later red deer imported by Thomas Chirnside [q.v.]. He hunted until 1895 when his son Godfrey became deputy-master. Watson carried the tradi-

tions of an old Irish hunting family to Australia. His face, 'well-cut and cleanshaven', often reminded people of pictures of Wellington; his courage, judgment and straightforward dealing made him one of the best known and most popular men of his time. He died, aged 80, at his home in St Kilda on 11 July 1906 and was buried in the St Kilda cemetery. He was survived by six sons and a daughter.

H. M. Humphreys (ed), *Men of the time in Australia: Victorian series*, 1st ed (Melb, 1878); T. W. H. Leavitt and W. D. Lilburn (eds), *The jubilee history of Victoria and Melbourne* (Melb, 1888); A. Sutherland et al, *Victoria and its metropolis*, 2 (Melb, 1888); K. A. Austin, *The lights of Cobb and Co.* (Adel, 1967); H. B. Ronald, *Hounds are running* (Kilmore, 1970); *A'sian Sketcher*, 24 Nov 1877; *Australasian*, 31 Oct 1891, 27 May 1899; *Argus*, 11 July 1906; *Aust sporting celebrities*, 9 (LaT L).

JILL EASTWOOD

WATSON, JAMES (1837-1907), merchant and politician, was born on 17 December 1837 at Portadown, County Armagh, Ireland, second son of James Watson (d. 1847), farmer, and his wife Sarah, née Maclean. Educated at the parish school, Richhill, in 1853 he entered the office of Thomas Carleton, a solicitor in Portadown. He followed his brothers George and William John (d. 1886) to Victoria, arriving in Melbourne on 1 June 1856 in the *Champion of the Seas* with his youngest brother Thomas and £100. They went from rush to rush at Pleasant Creek (Stawell), Dunolly, Mountain Hut and other Victorian goldfields with little success.

In 1861 they moved to Lambing Flat (Young) and next year opened a store, Watson Bros, which was provisioned by John Frazer [q.v.]; in 1866 a flour-mill was added. James became a trustee of the School of Arts and a church warden of St John's Church of England. In January 1869 he bought a quarter-share in John Frazer & Co. and moved to Sydney, while William continued to run the firm in Young.

On 28 December 1869 Watson was elected to the Legislative Assembly for the Lachlan, defeating W. B. Dalley [q.v.]; he represented the seat until it was divided in 1880 when he won Young. At first he supported (Sir) James Martin's [q.v.] ministry and in 1872 became an independent supporter of (Sir) Henry Parkes [q.v.], although in November 1873 he harassed G. A. Lloyd [q.v.], the treasurer, with questions about his interest in the Circular Quay lease; and he voted against Parkes on the release of the bushranger Frank Gardiner [q.v.]. In August 1877 he refused office under (Sir) John Robertson [q.v.].

On 8 April 1871 in Sydney Watson had married Margaret Salmon, sister of his partner James Ewan [q.v.] and sister-in-law of Frazer; they lived at Glanworth, Darling Point. Watson became prominent in Sydney commercial circles: a justice of the peace, chairman of the City Bank of Sydney in 1874-85, a director and sometime chairman of the Pacific Fire and Marine Insurance Co. of Sydney, the Australian General Assurance Co. and a committee-man and vice-president of the Sydney Chamber of Commerce. A New South Wales commissioner for the exhibitions in Philadelphia (1876) and Melbourne (1888), he was also a trustee of the Sydney Bethel Union, and a councillor of the New South Wales Academy of Art in the 1880s. In 1877 with William he invested in two cattle stations near Young.

Watson became a close friend and creditor of Parkes (in 1879 he lent him £1000), and from 21 December 1878 to 4 January 1883 served in the Parkes-Robertson coalition as colonial treasurer. Lloyd warned Parkes not to 'allow yourself to be influenced too much by Watson on questions of Finance as he is very self willed'. In July 1879 Watson came into conflict, over the government's account, with Shepherd Smith [q.v.], the tactless manager of the Bank of New South Wales, who was suspicious of Watson's refusal to resign as chairman of the City Bank. Parkes had to intervene, but he defended Watson to D. Larnach [q.v.] on 11 September: 'our Treasurer too is in the heyday of his physical strength full of confidence in his own resources; and he is not a man to be played with in any sense'.

At the end of 1879 Watson had a Treasury deficit of £468,250: although early next year he reintroduced stamp duty and increased the duty on spirits, the House rejected his excise on colonial beer, and he withdrew proposed duties on tobacco and later was forced to abandon export duties. However revenue improved and he had no need to impose additional taxes. At the Intercolonial Conference in January 1881 he proposed a commission of all Australian colonies to consider and construct a common tariff; only Victoria opposed it. Advised by G. Eagar [q.v.], he floated a new loan in London in June on very favourable terms for the colony, and in December announced a large surplus. On the question of amending the land Acts, he strongly advocated fixity of tenure and higher rents for squatters and came into conflict with Robertson. In January 1882 he intended to resign as treasurer because of Ewan's ill health, and after the defeat of Robertson's land bill in November he again tendered his resignation, but Parkes refused to accept it;

in December he was defeated for the seats of Young and Illawarra. However in April 1884 he won a by-election for Gundagai, which he held until October 1885, and was highly critical of (Sir) Alexander Stuart [q.v.] as premier.

That year Watson took his ailing wife on a visit to Britain; she died soon after their return in 1886. He was appointed to the Legislative Council on 15 February 1887, served on the royal commission into the civil service from December to August 1888 and on the Parliamentary Standing Committee on Public Works in 1888-89, and as chairman in 1890-92. In March 1889, although pressed by Parkes, he refused the vice-presidency of the Executive Council, 'in the interests of my children'. In the 1890s with Ewan he incurred heavy losses on two cattle stations in Queensland. He became a director of the Australian Joint Stock Bank in 1897.

A lavish host, Watson collected pictures and furniture. He suffered for ten years from chronic nephritis and uraemia and died at Glanworth on 30 October 1907; he was buried in the Anglican section of Rookwood cemetery. He divided his estate, valued for probate at almost £65,000, equally among his two sons and four daughters who survived him.

SMH, 22 Dec 1869, 8 Oct 1885, 31 Oct 1907; ISN, 30 May 1874; T&CJ, 11 Jan 1878; Bulletin, 14 Aug 1880; Freeman's J (Syd), 8 July 1882; G. C. Morey, The Parkes-Robertson coalition government, 1878-1883 (B.A. Hons thesis, ANU, 1968); Parkes letters (ML); Bank of NSW Archives (Syd); CO 201/591/36, 592/50, 595/73, 114, 587, 597/463; information from Miss P. Watson, Syd.   MARTHA RUTLEDGE

WATSON, JOHN BOYD (1828-1889), mining magnate and investor, was born in September 1828 at Paisley, Scotland, son of James Watson, cabinetmaker, and his wife Margaret, née Boyd. He received little schooling and on 14 March 1841 arrived in Sydney in the Orestes with his parents, four brothers and two sisters. They settled at Windsor where Watson became a currier. He moved to Sydney but in 1850 left for the Californian diggings. On his return, he set off for the Victorian rushes and in late 1852 reached Bendigo Creek, where he took up a highly profitable claim at the Fifth White Hill. Quick to realize the potential richness of the Bendigo reefs, he was amongst the first to erect a crushing battery.

Watson's initial quartz-mining venture was the Old Chum Claim on New Chum Hill. Next, with a partner he bought a claim in Paddy's Gully from which he derived the sobriquet of 'Paddy' and the nucleus of his fortune. With others he floated the Cornish United Co. and in the late 1860s secured an interest in the adjoining Golden Fleece, Kent and Garden Gully claims, later buying and amalgamating them under one lease as the Kentish Mine which he owned until 1889. It produced huge amounts of gold in 1871-80, one reef alone yielding about thirteen tons of gold valued at some £1,500,000.

Watson had interests in other Sandhurst (Bendigo) mines but generally invested in real estate and commercial ventures. He owned much property in Sandhurst and his extensive Melbourne holdings included the freehold of some of the most valuable inner-city properties. He was a founder, director and principal shareholder of the Federal Bank and a large shareholder in the Melbourne Tramways Co., the Deniliquin and Moama Railway Co. and a Sydney steamship company. He had mining and pastoral interests in Queensland, owned wharves in Sydney and in 1879, with a group of Sandhurst investors, launched the Sydney *Daily Telegraph*.

On 6 August 1861 at All Saints Anglican Church, Sandhurst, Watson had married Mary Ann Covell, who bore him four sons and five daughters. One daughter married W. L. Murdoch [q.v.], another married Malcolm Donald McEacharn, co-founder of the shipping company, McIlwraith and McEacharn. The pioneer aviator Basil George Watson was a grandson. In the mid-1870s the family moved to Melbourne but retained close links with Sandhurst. Predeceased by two sons, Watson died of phthisis in Sydney on 4 June 1889 on his return from a visit to San Francisco. He was buried in the Presbyterian section of the Back Creek cemetery, Sandhurst. Under the terms of his will, which was subject to much litigation to resolve legal technicalities, almost all his fortune of between £1 million and £2 million was left to his children and grandchildren. His Victorian assets were valued for probate at £976,549.

Retiring in manner, he was described by his obituarist in the *Bendigo Advertiser* as 'a close and plodding sort of man'. None, however, could deny his business astuteness. Generous when occasion demanded, he did not parade his affluence and sought no public role in the community. He contributed to the fund enabling E. Giles [q.v.] to explore central Australia in 1873-74; Glen Watson in the Musgrave Ranges is named after him. The Watson Sustentation Fund, providing assistance for permanently invalided local miners, was instituted by his son John Boyd on his father's death.

G. Mackay, *The history of Bendigo* (Melb, 1891), and *Annals of Bendigo* (Bendigo, nd); G. Meudell, *The pleasant career of a spendthrift* (Lond, 1929); F. Cusack, *Bendigo: a history* (Melb, 1973); *Bulletin*, 3 Apr 1880; *Argus*, 5, 10 June, 4 July 1889, 22 Aug 1890; *Bendigo Advertiser*, 5, 10 June 1889, 22 Aug 1890, 8 Nov 1911, 9 Feb 1915; *Bendigo Independent*, 5, 6, 10, 17 June 1889; *Australasian*, 8 June, 5 Oct, 14 Dec 1889, 22 Feb 1890, 10 Jan 1891.
                                    FRANK CUSACK

WATSON, MARY BEATRICE PHILLIPS (1860-1881), heroine, was born on 17 January 1860 at Fiddler's Green, Cornwall, England, eldest child of Thomas Oxnam, butcher and cattle-dealer, and his wife Mary, née Phillips. She was well educated but in 1877 the family was compelled by financial loss to migrate and settled at Maryborough, Queensland. Mary established a private school there to augment the family finances but gave it up for a position as governess. Dissatisfied with the conditions she resigned and opened a private school in Cooktown.

Mary was reserved, nervous and delicate but her ability as a pianist attracted many friends and on 30 May 1880 at Christ Church, Cooktown, she married Captain Robert E. Watson, a Scots seaman who shared a bêche-de-mer station on Lizard Island with P. C. Fuller. On 3 June 1881 a son Thomas Ferrier was born at Cooktown: Mary returned to the island with her baby at the end of the month.

In October, when Captain Watson and his partner were two hundred miles away, Lizard Island was invaded by mainland Aboriginals. They killed the Chinese gardener, wounded the Chinese house-boy Ah Sam and threatened Mrs Watson. She defended herself with a rifle but realized it would be unsafe to stay on the island. As no boat was available she collected provisions and equipment and left with her baby and the wounded Chinaman in a square ship's tank used for boiling bêche-de-mer. The Aboriginals, probably satisfied with removing her from a ceremonial ground on the island, did not interfere.

From 2 to 7 October the tank alternately drifted and was stranded on reefs or pulled into islands; the presence of Aboriginals prevented the replenishment of dwindling water supplies. On 7 October they reached a small waterless island, No 5 Howick. A few days later a passing ship missed their signals and in five days all three had perished from thirst. Their remains were discovered in January 1882 by the crew of the *Kate Kearney* and soon after were brought to Cooktown by the Water Police magistrate for a large public funeral.

Mary Watson's diary of the ordeal demonstrated more than ordinary intelligence, self-reliance and imagination. Her courage and initiative in planning and executing the escape emphasized her final misfortune. Her tender care, both of her baby and the wounded Chinaman, has helped to make the story an Australian legend and the tank is preserved in the Queensland Museum.

Mrs Watson, a Cooktown heroine (Port Douglas, c1891), also published as The heroine of Lizard Island (Cairns, nd); R. S. Browne, A journalist's memories (Brisb, 1927); Coroner's inquest no 373, 1882 (Cooktown Court records); M. B. P. Watson diary (Oxley Lib, Brisb).   S. E. STEPHENS

WATT, JOHN BROWN (1826-1897), merchant, businessman and politician, was born on 16 May 1826 in Edinburgh, eldest son of Alexander Hamilton Watt and his wife Margaret, née Gilchrist. He matriculated at the University of Edinburgh in 1840, but a severe pulmonary illness led him to migrate to Australia. He arrived in Sydney in the Benares on 6 December 1842 and became a clerk in the mercantile and shipping firm of (John) Gilchrist [q.v.] (his uncle) and Alexander.

Watt's journal and letters to his father in 1845-58 reveal him as an introspective and intensely religious Calvinist. Almost a recluse, enduring a clerk's soulless life for less than £50 a year, he immersed himself in business but often thought of going to the bush; in 1848 he spent a year travelling in the interior and North Queensland. He went to England in 1850 and, on hearing of the discovery of gold, he obtained a diploma as an assayer of precious metals. On his return he induced Gilchrist to enter the lucrative gold-buying business. His perseverance and foresight were rewarded when he was made a partner in 1852. When John Alexander retired in 1853, the firm became Gilchrist, Watt & Co. and on the death of his uncle in 1863 Watt became the senior partner.

With a branch in London in 1860, the business continued to flourish and Watt began to rise in society, gaining respect for his probity and judgment. In 1861 he was appointed to the Legislative Council and next year to a board of inquiry into the Post Office Department. On 30 July at St Paul's Church, Canterbury, Sydney, he married Mary Jane (d. 1879), daughter of G. K. Holden [q.v.]. In 1866, in bad health, he resigned from the council and left for a long holiday, returning to Sydney late in 1868. Involved in the Pacific islands trade, he headed a deputation of Sydney merchants and others to (Sir) Henry Parkes [q.v.] in 1873 seeking the British annexation of Fiji.

Watt was a director of the New South Wales Marine Assurance Co., the Liverpool & London & Globe Insurance Co., the Union Bank of Australia, the Australasian Steam Navigation Co., the Clarence and Richmond River Steam Navigation Co., the Pyrmont Bridge Co., the Australian Gaslight Co., the Sydney Meat Preserving Co., the Colonial Sugar Refining Co. (in 1880-84, 1886-88), and of the Sydney Exchange Co. He was chairman of the Newcastle Coal and Copper Co., and the Mutual Life Association of Australasia; president of the Commercial, Pastoral and Agricultural Association and of the Sydney Chamber of Commerce in 1870-71 and 1879-83. With Robert Towns and J. L. Montefiore [qq.v.], Watt had helped to revive the chamber in 1865. An ardent free trader, he was also vice-president of the Marine Board of New South Wales in 1872-83. He invested in pastoral property in New South Wales and Queensland.

In 1876 Watt visited England, and was involved in an experiment with charter steamers via the Cape of Good Hope that led to the formation of the Orient Steam Navigation Co.; Gilchrist, Watt & Co. acted as its general agents in Australia. The firm also acted for other shipping companies, including Lund's Blue Anchor Line in which Watt was a shareholder. In 1901 the Sydney maritime business was converted into a public company under the style of Gilchrist, Watt & Sanderson Ltd, while the pastoral and financial aspects were carried on by the firm Gilchrist, Watt & Co. both in Sydney and London.

In 1874-90 Watt was again a member of the Legislative Council; active in debate, he was regarded by Lord Carrington as 'one of its most valuable members'. His political interests reflected his diverse business connexions, though he favoured payment of members. In 1881 he sat on the royal commission on military defences. He was a commissioner for New South Wales at the exhibitions at Philadelphia (1876), Paris (1878), Sydney (1879), Amsterdam (1883) and at Calcutta (1883-84). Interested in education, he was on the committee to examine the possibility of a Presbyterian college within the University of Sydney in 1858, and in 1877 gave £1000 to the university to found an exhibition for students from public schools. He was also a director of the Sydney Infirmary and Dispensary in 1869-73 and the Prince Alfred Hospital and a founder of the Hospital for Sick Children, Glebe. In England in 1884 Watt was on the executive committee of the Imperial Federation League.

Watt was independent, broadminded, kind and generous. R. D. Adams commended him as a possible investment adviser to

Robert Browning at the Athenaeum Club in 1889 and described him as 'a man of cultured taste' who could appreciate the poet's 'genius'. Watt's intimate friends included Sir Alexander Stuart, Sir John Robertson, W. B. Dalley, Archbishop Vaughan [qq.v.], E. W. Knox and Parkes. He was a member of both the Union and Australian clubs and for many years president of the Mercantile Rowing Club. He had gone back to England in 1888 and his second daughter's marriage and the education of his sons delayed his return to Sydney for two years; by this time his health rendered a voyage risky. He died of paralysis agitans and pneumonia at Brunstath House, Grove Road, Bournemouth, Hampshire, England, on 28 September 1897 and was buried in St Jude's churchyard, Randwick, Sydney. He was survived by three of his five sons and five daughters; his youngest son Walter Oswald (1878-1921) was a noted pioneer aviator. His estate in New South Wales was sworn for probate at £196,386 and in England at £33,125. He willed £2000 to public charities in Sydney and smaller amounts to charities in England.

E. Digby, Australian men of mark, 1 (Syd, 1889); E. A. S. Watt, A few records of the life of John Brown Watt (Syd, priv print, nd); V&P (LA NSW), 1863-64, 3, 1254, 1881, 4, 581; SMH, 30 Jan, 6 Apr 1858, 14 Oct 1873, 2 May 1876, 19 Mar 1881; ISN, 22 July 1876; Bulletin, 21 Jan 1882; Parkes letters and J. B. Watt papers (ML); Gilchrist, Watt & Sanderson Pty Ltd records (Univ Syd Archives).

G. P. WALSH

WAUGH, JAMES SWANTON (1822-1898), Wesleyan clergyman, was born on 22 March 1822 at Newtownbarry, County Wexford, Ireland, son of Rev. John Waugh, of the Irish Wesleyan Conference, and his wife Sarah, née Swanton. He was educated at private schools and at the Royal School, Dungannon. In 1837 he was indentured to a physician and surgeon in Dublin but decided to prepare for the ministry and went to the Wesleyan Theological Institution at Hoxton near London. Ordained in 1840 he was appointed to Dublin circuits, but poor health, his father's death and depression in Ireland led him to volunteer to serve on the goldfields in Victoria. On arrival in the Beulah in Melbourne on 8 February 1854 he was appointed superintendent of the St Kilda circuit. In 1858 he returned to Ireland and married Olivia Eleanor Fayle of Parson's Town, King's County (Offaly); they had five sons and five daughters.

Waugh returned to Victoria and a year later was assigned to the newly built Wesley Church, Melbourne; he also edited the Wesleyan Chronicle and, despite conference threats to close it down, he improved its quality and increased its circulation before going to the Lydiard Street circuit, Ballarat, in March 1862. His election as president of the Australasian Conference in 1865 indicated his influence among the Wesleyans. As treasurer of the Chapel and Building Fund, he was associated with Rev. D. Draper [q.v.] in obtaining sites for chapels and distributing money for buildings; and as chairman of the conference educational committee he wanted a single board which would allow local school committees to provide undenominational religious teaching. He maintained this policy after the 1872 Education Act and was later elected vice-president of the National Instruction League, an interdenominational organization formed to introduce religious teaching into state schools.

As president until 1883 of Wesley College (founded 1866), Waugh sought a 'liberal and pious' education grounded in Scripture. He was also tutor of the Theological Institution attached to the college although he advocated a separate school under an English theologian. Waugh was also custodian of Church deeds, the Church's appointee in its dealings with the Victorian government, and president of the General Conference of Australasia in 1881. After spending 1884 in the Richmond circuit he retired to Hawthorn.

Waugh was traditionalist in conference debates and opposed lay participation in the appointment and discipline of ministers. He also opposed union with the minor Methodist Churches because he feared the greater power of their laymen. He contributed more to Wesleyanism as an administrator rather than as a theologian and educationist. Although reputedly scholarly he wrote little outside the denominational magazine. In 1879 the degree of Doctor of Divinity was simultaneously conferred on him by Albion College, Michigan, and Indiana (de Pauw) University, Asbury. Predeceased by three daughters, he died of heart disease at Hawthorn on 6 November 1898 and was buried in Boroondara cemetery.

IAN, 14 May 1884; Weekly Times (Melb), 19 Nov 1898; R. Howe, The Wesleyan Church in Victoria, 1855-1901: its ministry and membership (M.A. thesis, Univ Melb, 1965).

RENATE HOWE

WAWN, WILLIAM TWIZELL (1837-1901), mariner, cartographer, artist and author, was born on 6 January 1837 at

Boldon, County Durham, England, eldest son of John Twizell Wawn, banker and M.P., and his wife Mary, née Matterson, of York. After a sound education he entered a York architect's office which suited his talents with a pencil but not his wider vision, and he abandoned the drafting board for the deck probably before he was 20.

As a young man he served in sailing ships trading between India and England. He became a second mate in 1861, a first mate next year and in 1863 he shipped aboard the *New Great Britain* from London to New Zealand. In November or December he left the ship at Twofold Bay, New South Wales, to begin his long association with Australia and the Pacific islands. He visited England in 1865 to get his master's certificate.

In 1867 Wawn gathered bêche-de-mer off Queensland, and next year he made his first visit to the islands, probably to Samoa. In 1870 he took command of the *Mary Ira* and began five years trading, salvaging and beach-combing among the islands of the western Pacific. He returned to Sydney in January 1875 and later that year made his first voyage in the island labour trade in which, off and on, he spent the next twenty years. Wawn met all the typical troubles of a labour trade skipper. He was also ship-wrecked and accidentally shot a recruit; his vessel's government agent was murdered. He recruited for Queensland and for Fiji, under sail and under steam. Something of a misanthropist, Wawn was intensely critical of his fellow Europeans, and never concealed his disapproval of the manners of the Pacific islands people but he did not deny their intelligence and resourcefulness. His book, *The South Sea Islanders and the Queensland Labour Trade* (London, 1893), is a valuable, sensitive and subtle account of the nature of the trade.

Wawn made his last recruiting voyage in 1894 and in 1895-1900 mined, commanded a vessel trading between Sydney and the Gilbert Islands and managed a copra hulk in Levuka Harbour. In 1901 he retired to Sydney with 'a fair competence'. He frequented the National Art Gallery and probably painted and drew. Collections of his drawings of islanders and fish are preserved in the Mitchell Library, Sydney, and some are still owned by the Wawn family in Durham, England.

Late in June he was knocked down by a cab and blood poisoning set in. He died on 5 July and was buried in Rookwood cemetery. There is a sketched self-portrait of Wawn in his manuscript, 'Amongst the Pacific Islands' (Alexander Turnbull Library, Wellington, New Zealand), and a photograph of him taken in his thirties is in the Fiji Museum, Suva.

W. T. Wawn, *The South Sea islanders and the Queensland labour trade*, P. Corris ed (Canb, 1973); Wawn private logs, 1888-1900 (ML).

PETER CORRIS

WAY, ARTHUR SANDERS (1847-1930), headmaster and translator, was born on 13 February 1847 at Dorking, Surrey, England, son of William Way, Wesleyan Methodist minister, and his wife Matilda, née Francis. He was educated at the new Kingswood School, Bath, at the Wesleyan Collegiate Institution, Taunton, and the University of London (B.A., 1870; M.A., 1873). In 1870 he returned to Queen's College as classical master and in 1876 to Kingswood School as vice-headmaster.

In September 1881 Way was appointed headmaster of Wesley College, Melbourne. He arrived in the *Mirzapore* with his wife Rubena Blanche, née Barnicott, and a daughter on 25 January 1882 and began duty in February. Way is spoken of affectionately by those who knew him well, and he seems to have enjoyed pleasant relationships with both boys and masters, but his term at Wesley was not happy. Economic depression had already depleted the number of pupils and he lacked the personality that might have attracted either fresh pupils or contributions of money to the school. Although the curriculum favoured natural science and commerce in the hope of attracting numbers, there was no appreciable rise. In the late 1880s other schools were growing fast, but not Wesley. When the boom burst, the school debt mounted and in 1890 the presidency of the school was abolished; in 1892 salaries, including Way's, were cut and he resigned at the end of the year. He returned to England and there lived on the royalties of his classical translations which continued to appear every few years. In 1913 he served as acting headmaster at Mill Hill School.

Way had been president of the Melbourne Shakespeare Society and a councillor of the Royal Society of Victoria but he moved about little in the community. He had a holiday house at Lorne, and spent much of his leisure time in writing, the activity for which he is remembered. In later life he wrote two novels with ancient settings and produced versions of the 'Song of Roland', the 'Nibelungenlied', St Paul's Epistles and the Psalms. But his reputation was made by his translations of Greek and Latin poetry. In 1876 in London he had published *The Odes of Horace ... translated in metre* and, under the pseudonym 'Avia', produced *The*

Odyssey of Homer. Done into English verse
(1880). During his years at Wesley *The
Iliad of Homer...* appeared in three parts.
In retirement he produced translations of
the works of some twenty Latin and Greek
writers.

Way was called by one reviewer the
'translator-general of his time', but even in
his own day his work received a mixed
reception. He brought to translating much
rhythmic flexibility and the capacity to
render meaning, despite the demands of
rhythm and rhyme, with a crib-like
accuracy. But the total effect rarely does
credit to the originals. His vocabulary is
quaint and stilted. The jaunty anapaestic
metre which he used for the translations of
Homer, and which owed something to William Morris and Swinburne, was reviewed
by a contemporary as 'neither flowing, glid-
ing, rushing, nor leaping, but mere bounc-
ing'. His translations into iambic verse were
more successful and are still published in
the Loeb Classical Library editions of Euri-
pides and Quintus Smyrnaeus.

Way died at Ventnor, Isle of Wight, on
25 September 1930.

G. Blainey et al, *Wesley College. The first
hundred years* (Melb, 1967); *Table Talk*, 8 July
1892; *The Times*, 26 Sept 1930.

G. H. GELLIE

WAYLEN, ALFRED ROBERT (1833-
1901), medical practitioner and vigneron,
was born at Point Walter, Western Australia, son of Alfred Waylen and his wife,
née Bailey, who had arrived in the *Skerne*
in 1830. He was taken to England for education in 1841 and in 1856 qualified as
licentiate of the Society of Apothecaries
and as member and licentiate in midwifery
of the Royal College of Surgeons. After a
brief return to Perth in 1857, he went to St
Andrews University in Scotland. His
doctorate in medicine (1858) was the first
medical degree granted to a native West
Australian.

In 1859 Waylen began practice at Guildford as colonial medical officer for the Swan
District and as surgeon to the convict
establishment. He was registered on 30
December 1869 under the Act passed in
July and on 11 January 1870 was appointed
to the medical board. In 1872 he succeeded
Dr John Ferguson [q.v.] as colonial
surgeon, *ex officio* director of the colonial
hospital, medical officer of the Perth Prison
and superintendent of vaccination. In 1884-
85 he chaired a royal commission on metropolitan water-supply and sanitation and
implemented its findings as president of a
new central Board of Health. In 1883-84 he

chaired a royal commission into the welfare
and conditions of native prisoners on Rottnest Island. When the Aborigines Protection Board was formed in 1886 during
the negotiations for responsible government, he was appointed chairman, responsible directly to the imperial government.

Waylen was an amateur vigneron exhibiting at international exhibitions from 1866.
In 1886 he was a commissioner for the
Colonial and Indian Exhibition of London.
He was president of the Agricultural
Society and of the Horticultural Society in
1894, and after he retired in 1895 he joined
J. G. Amherst to establish the Darlington
vineyards which won a diploma in Sydney
for the best Australian raisins. He was also
at various times chairman of the Guildford
Town Council, churchwarden of St Matthew's Church, a founder of the Guildford
Mechanics' Institute, a governor of the
Perth High School (now Hale School), a
racehorse owner and a committee-man of
the West Australian Turf Club.

On 20 November 1862, Waylen married
Elizabeth Louisa, daughter of John Wall
Hardey, M.L.C. On 2 June 1887 he married
Louisa, daughter of Rev. Thomas Walpole
and widow of Sir Luke Leake, M.L.C.,
Speaker of the Legislative Council. He died
childless at Guildford on 10 January 1901
and was buried in the Church of England
cemetery. His estate, valued for probate at
£11,751, was left to his widow and
relations. He was not a highly scientific
practitioner but his enthusiastic advocacy
of public health measures led to useful
reforms.

W. B. Kimberly, *History of West Australia*
(Melb, 1897); J. H. L. Cumpston, 'A public
health pioneer in Western Australia', *Health*,
July 1923; *Civil Service J* (WA), centenary no,
July 1929; *Swan Express*, Jan 1901; *West Aus-
tralian*, 12 Jan 1901.   B. C. COHEN*

WEARING, WILLIAM ALFRED (1816-
1875), judge, was born on 12 November
1816 at St Paul's Churchyard, London,
eldest son of Christopher Hammond Wearing, merchant, and his wife Elizabeth
Augusta, née Soulsby. Educated at St John's
College, Cambridge, from 1837 (B.A., 1843),
he was admitted to Lincoln's Inn on 30
December 1841 and called to the Bar on 4
May 1847. Wearing arrived in Adelaide in
the *Sibella* on 2 February 1850 to rejoin his
family who had preceded him in the
Recovery in 1839. Admitted to the colonial
Bar in April, he went into private practice
with Charles Fenn. In 1856 he was appointed crown solicitor and public prosecutor at
a salary of £600, but also continued private

practice. On 4 October 1860 he married Jessie Clark of Adelaide.

Appointed a Q.C. on 13 March 1865, next year Wearing served on the secret court of inquiry which recommended the resignation of P. E. Warburton [q.v.] as commissioner of police. He took an active part in the amoval from the bench of Mr Justice Boothby [q.v.] and in 1867 became third judge of the Supreme Court and judge of the District Courts at Mount Gambier and Robe at a salary of £1300. It was claimed in parliament in 1869 that he 'was so mixed up with so many companies', that 'he seldom could sit in matters of the greatest importance'. But J. P. Boucaut [q.v.] retorted that Wearing had shown 'extraordinary delicacy in not sitting where interested' and that company shares had come to him through his wife's marriage settlement.

Wearing was described by Governor Fergusson as a 'somewhat impetuous and obstinate, though a useful and estimable' judge, and there were complaints that he was too lenient; but others found him unassuming with a vivacious and spontaneous wit both on and off the bench. These qualities, coupled with a considerable fluency, led him to contribute numerous anonymous articles and letters to the editor in the *South Australian Register*. An Anglican, he was a Freemason and member of the Provincial Grand Lodge of South Australia; he was also a justice of the peace.

Early in 1875 Wearing was asked by the government to open the first sessions of the Circuit Court at Palmerston (Darwin). Offered a bonus he declined it but asked that the extra payment on his insurance policy be made good. In Darwin he stayed with the government resident George Byng Scott; when he was returning to Adelaide in the *Gothenberg* with his staff, the ship was wrecked on the Great Barrier Reef, Torres Straits, on or about 25 February and Wearing was drowned. He was survived by his wife, three daughters and two sons. His estate was sworn for probate at £6500 and the government voted £4000 to his widow who moved with her children to London.

D. Lockwood, *The front door; Darwin 1869-1969* (Adel, 1968); PP (SA), 1866-67, 3 (191), 1867, 2 (22), 1870-71, 3, 82-82b (159), 1875 (14); PD (SA), 1868-69, 1414, 1875, 214-221; *Solicitors' J* (Lond), 15 May 1875; *Register* (Adel), 2 Feb 1850, 8 Mar 1875; Appointments to public office, GRG 24/91/2 (SAA); family information from A. S. Wearing, Weetulta, SA; CO 13/125/404.

WEARNE, JOSEPH (1832-1884), flour-miller and politician, was born on 19 August 1832 at St Levan, Cornwall, England, eldest son of Joseph Wearne (d. 1856), a miller of yeoman stock, and his wife Susannah, née Rogers. On 12 February 1849 the family arrived in Sydney as bounty immigrants in the *Harbinger*. After digging on various Victorian goldfields they settled about 1853 at Liverpool, New South Wales, where Joseph senior leased the Collingwood Flour Mill and ran a bakery; in 1854 he acquired Bossley's mill.

On 21 January 1857 at Parramatta Joseph junior married Isabella Caldwell and had moved to Sydney by 1860. He soon joined John Pemmell, flour-miller, and about 1864 opened the steam-operated Anchor Flour Mills at the foot of Bathurst Street. A kind and conscientious employer, he installed hot showers and a Turkish bath for his workmen. A prominent Methodist, a Freemason and an office-bearer in the Order of the Sons of Temperance, although not a teetotaller, in 1868 Wearne ran unsuccessfully for the Sydney Municipal Council. The same year he failed in a parliamentary by-election for West Sydney, and attributed his defeat to his opponents' improper electoral practices. Wearne favoured free trade, triennial parliaments, extension of municipal government, National schools and competitive selection for the civil service, and opposed state aid to religion. At a time of intense sectarianism he helped to organize testimonials in March 1869 for (Sir) Henry Parkes [q.v.].

Wearne supported the Protestant Political Association and in 1869 joined the Loyal Orange Institution. With their aid he topped the poll for West Sydney in the 1869 general elections and again in 1872. Yet he did not publicly attack Catholicism and the *Freeman's Journal* admitted that many Catholics voted for him as a liberal. Although he never sought office, his membership, and that of Protestants like him, helped clear the Loyal Orange Institution of its Irish taint and contributed to its remarkable growth in the 1870s.

Wearne supported the Martin [q.v.]-Parkes opposition, but became an independent in 1870 when Parkes retired and Martin joined (Sir) John Robertson [q.v.] in government. Late next year he worked hard and gave generously to have Parkes returned for Mudgee and, despite doubts about Parkes's choice of E. Butler [q.v.] as his attorney-general, he generally supported the ministry Parkes formed in 1872. Unimpressive as a parliamentarian, he vainly introduced the permissive liquor bill which included a local option clause. In 1874 he lost West Sydney, blaming the over-confidence of his friends, but won Central Cumberland. His business had continued to prosper and by then he was a trustee of several building societies, part-owner of a paper manufacturing business at Holsworthy, a director of the Protestant Hall and a committee-man of the Benevolent Society of New South Wales. In 1873 he was a member of the royal commission on public charities.

In the early 1870s, apparently influenced by John Hurley [q.v.], Wearne had speculated in mining shares, losing some £27,000, much of it borrowed; in June 1875 he became bankrupt with debts of almost £25,000 and resigned from parliament. Discharged nine months later, he stayed in Sydney a few more years, remaining active in the Church and in contact with Parkes. In the early 1880s he returned to Liverpool. On 8 June 1884 after a long illness he died of Bright's disease at Collingwood House and was buried in Parramatta cemetery. He was survived by his wife, three sons and three daughters; his wife inherited his estate valued for probate at £1800.

His brother THOMAS (1835-1914), engineer, set up in Sydney as an ironmonger in 1865. Gaining many government contracts he expanded into the manufacture of safes. In 1878 at the Glebe Foundry he made railway and tramway rolling-stock, locomotives and bridge components. In 1885 he was a foundation member of the New South Wales Chamber of Manufactures and in 1886 of the Protection Union of New South Wales. An original alderman on the Liverpool Municipal Council in 1872, Wearne was a member of Glebe Borough Council in the 1880s. Indebted to the English, Scottish and Australian Chartered Bank from 1881, he was forced into bankruptcy in December 1889 after a dispute with government officials over the specifications of a large contract for goods locomotives. He retained an active interest in a safe manufacturing business with his nephew W. H. Breakspear(e). He died of bronchitis and old age on 30 May 1914 at Bonnyrigg, Liverpool. He was survived by his wife Janet Ewing, née Jeffrey, whom he had married at Liverpool on 15 December 1855, and by five sons and six daughters; his estate was valued for probate at £664.

SMH, 7 Dec 1868, 13 Jan 1869, 27 Apr 1871; Empire, 15 Feb, 8 Dec 1869, 14 Feb 1872; Protestant Standard, 1 May 1869, 22 Apr 1871; Freeman's J, 18 Dec 1869; T&CJ, 3 June 1914; Methodist (Syd), 13 June 1914; Parkes letters (ML); Insolvency files 2300, 12,412/8, 1595 (NSWA); information from Dr H. Shuhevych, Liverpool, and Major R. H. Wearne, Bexley North, NSW.   MARK LYONS

WEBB, CHARLES (1821-1898), architect, was born on 26 November 1821 at Sudbury, Suffolk, England, son of William Webb, builder, and his wife Elizabeth, née Hayward. The youngest of nine children, he attended Sudbury Academy and was later apprenticed to a London architect. In 1847 he was secretary of a short-lived London Architectural Students' Society. His brother JAMES (1808-1870) had migrated to Van Diemen's Land in 1830, married Susannah Wellard at Hobart Town in 1833 and crossed to Port Phillip in 1839 where he set up as a builder in partnership with John Allee; in 1848 he bought Brighton Park, Brighton, from Henry Dendy. Charles decided to join James and on 2 June 1849, with his sister and her husband and family, arrived at Melbourne in the *Spartan*. Another brother Richard followed later and became a timber merchant in Brighton.

Charles lived with James at Brighton and in August they went into partnership as architects and surveyors. Their most important early commission was in 1850 for St Paul's Church, Swanston Street; its construction was disrupted by the gold rush, and in December 1851 Webb briefly and unsuccessfully joined the rush near Bendigo. On 1 November 1853 at St Paul's Church he married Emma Bridges; her father had been chief cashier at the Bank of England and after his death the rest of the family had migrated to Melbourne. The couple lived at Chilton, Brighton.

Charles and James built many warehouses and private homes, a synagogue in the city and the galleries in John Knox Presbyterian Church, and continued the design of St Stephen's, Richmond. They built many shops and houses at Brighton. James went to England in 1854-56 and Webb practised for four years in partnership with Thomas Taylor, designing St Andrew's Church, Brighton, and receiving an important commission for Melbourne Church of England Grammar School in 1855. In 1857 he added a tower and a slender spire to Scots Church, which James had built in 1841. Webb practised on his own from 1858 until 1888 when two of his sons joined him. He designed Wesley College in 1864, the Alfred Hospital and the Royal Arcade in 1869, the South Melbourne Town Hall and the Melbourne Orphan Asylum in 1878 and the Grand Hotel (now the Windsor) in 1884. In 1865 he had designed his own home, Farleigh, in Park Street, Brighton, and in 1875 Mount Noorat for Niel Black [q.v.]. Webb worked with systematic neatness and painstaking care and his designs in general were serious and dignified.

He was a founding member of the Victorian Institute of Architects in 1856 and was president in 1882-83. He joined the Brighton Volunteer Rifle Corps in September 1860 and helped to found the Boating Club (now the Royal Brighton Yacht Club) in 1875; he was a member of both the Melbourne Club and the Melbourne Cricket Club. For many years Webb was secretary of the local branch of the Bible Society, which James had helped to found. Although he was an Anglican and for many years an active member of Brighton's St Andrew's Church, three of his children became members of the Plymouth Brethren sect. Webb owned real estate in Brighton and held shares in many public companies. Serious, retiring and introspective, he spent long hours reading in his study. Photos of him in later life show him to be tall, immaculate in dress, with smooth hair and a fluffy white beard framing a serene face. As a young man he kept diaries, some of which survive. His death at Farleigh on 23 January 1898 was hastened by 'nervous exhaustion from excessive heat'. Predeceased by his wife in 1893 and survived by five sons and three daughters, he was buried in Brighton cemetery.

James was a devout Wesleyan. Known as 'King Webb' and 'The Lion', he was active, if somewhat cantankerous, in local affairs; he was a councillor in 1859-61 and 1867-70 and mayor in 1867 and 1868. He died suddenly, aged 63, on 9 August 1870, survived by his wife, one of his three sons and six of his nine daughters.

W. Bate, A *history of Brighton* (Melb, 1962); C. Bridges-Webb, 'Charles Webb (1821-98): an early Melbourne architect', VHM, 41 (1970); J. Denton and B. Marshall, Charles Webb, early Melbourne architect (Architecture history report, Univ Melb, 1967).

CHARLES BRIDGES-WEBB

WEBB, EDMUND (1830-1899), storekeeper and politician, was born on 4 September 1830 at Liskeard, Cornwall, England, younger son of Thomas Webb, farmer, and his wife Catherine, née Geake. Educated at Saltash, after his father's death he was advised to seek a better climate and with his mother and sisters reached Sydney in the *Penyard Park* on 13 September 1847. Refusing to be tied to an apprenticeship which would last beyond his majority, he found work with a draper at Bathurst; three years later, having saved £200 and being refused a partnership, he accepted a loan from a friend and opened his own business in November 1851. On 18 January 1854 at Springfield near Bathurst he married Selina Jane Jones (d. 1929), daughter of William Tom [q.v.].

After initial difficulties Webb prospered; he moved to larger premises in 1856 and to his own building in 1862, which he enlarged ten years later. In January 1866 he took William Ross as a partner under the style of Edmund Webb & Co. He retired from active business in 1880, leaving in charge his son Edmund Tom, and his nephew, son of his brother Thomas. Webb & Co. manufactured their own clothing, millinery and footwear, and supplied a large part of the west; in 1881 they started their own free, monthly newspaper, the *Bathurst Post*. Over the years Webb acquired much property in and around Bathurst.

A Freemason and a dedicated Wesleyan Methodist, he was a trustee of the local church, chaired Bathurst circuit meetings and was a member of the Australasian Wesleyan Methodist annual conferences in the 1860s. Webb was a generous benefactor, founder and councillor in 1879-97 of Newington College, and a councillor of the Methodist Ladies' College, Burwood, in 1890-97. Involved in town affairs, he was a founding member and later trustee of the Bathurst Mechanics' School of Arts in the mid-1850s; a member of the first Borough Council in 1863 and mayor in 1866, part of 1868 and in 1875-77; and a member of the building committee of the District Hospital in 1876, and treasurer in 1882-93. He was also a magistrate, a vice-president of the Bathurst Agricultural, Horticultural and Pastoral Association, a commissioner for the Sydney International Exhibition (1879), and deputy-licensing magistrate in 1891. He was a great supporter of cricket and football.

An upholder of free selection before survey, Webb was very interested in politics and represented West Macquarie in the Legislative Assembly in 1869-74. Described by the *Freeman's Journal* on 8 November 1873 as a 'rabid Orangeman', he approved the appointment of Sir James Martin [q.v.] as chief justice in 1873, but told (Sir) Henry Parkes [q.v.], 'I do not think you acted towards Mr Butler [q.v.] in a way in which you would like to be treated yourself'. Webb won a by-election for East Macquarie in February 1878 but resigned on 29 December 1881 when he was appointed to the Legislative Council. He opposed the Jennings [q.v.] government's fiscal policy in 1886 and Federation. He was a vice-president of the Free Trade Association of New South Wales when it was formed in 1885, and a committee-member after it was reconstituted as the Free Trade and Liberal Association of New South Wales in 1889, and a vice-president of the Local Option League when it was reformed in 1890.

In the 1860s Webb had built a fine home, Hathrop, on Vale Creek. Long a sufferer from bronchitis and asthma, he died suddenly of heart failure at Parkes on 24 June

1899, survived by his wife, two of his three sons and two daughters. He was buried in the Wesleyan section of Bathurst cemetery after a public funeral. His estate was valued for probate at £95,305.

E. Webb & Co., 1851-1937 and 1851-1951 (np, nd); D. S. Macmillan, Newington College 1863-1963 (Syd, 1963); A'sian Wesleyan Methodist Church, Minutes of NSW and Qld conference (1875-1899); ISN, 30 May 1874; Sydney Mail, 1 July 1899; Bathurst Times and National Advocate and Free Press and Mining Journal, 24, 26-28 June 1899; Western Times, 12, 16 Apr 1951; Parkes letters (ML); family information.

J. E. L. RUTHERFORD

WEBB, GEORGE HENRY FREDERICK (1828-1891), judge, was born at Lambeth, Surrey, England, son of Samuel Ody Webb, naval officer, and his wife Isabella, née Sweet. Although educated for the navy, he joined the staff of W. B. Gurney, the well-known parliamentary shorthand writer. About 1849 he married Matilda Field (d. 1860).

In poor health, Webb sought a warmer climate and in 1852 arrived in Melbourne with his wife. He planned a twelve-month visit but liked the colony and decided to stay. He became a reporter on the Melbourne Argus but on 14 December 1853 joined the civil service as a stenographer. Next year on 12 October he was appointed government shorthand worker at £610 a year. He organized a staff of shorthand writers for both the government and the Supreme Court and in 1855 reported the proceedings of the Eureka treason trials. In 1858 he attended the course for articled clerks at the University of Melbourne and won the Chancellor's Exhibition at the end of his first year; he was admitted to the Bar on 6 December 1860. In 1862 he applied for a readership in the university's Law School and was appointed on 3 February; eighteen days later he yielded to pressure to resign, ostensibly because his admission to the Bar was so recent. His application for the same post in March 1864 was rejected.

With Alfred Wyatt, Webb had published in 1861 the first of a series of Reports of Cases in the Supreme Court of Victoria; they were joined by (Sir) Thomas à Beckett [q.v.] in 1864. In 1866 Webb resigned from his government post to work as a barrister; he built up a successful equity practice although he also appeared in a number of notable divorce cases. So high was his income that in 1874 he declined the Supreme Court judgeship left vacant by (Sir) Edward Williams [q.v.]. On 14 January 1879 Webb was appointed a Q.C. In 1881 he was one of ten original share-

holders in a company formed to finance the building of Selborne Chambers to house members of the Bar. Always interested in matters relating to his profession, he won certain privileges for Victorian barristers which allowed them to be called to the English Bar. Defeated by (Sir) Hartley Williams and J. W. Stephen [qq.v.] in 1874 for the Legislative Assembly seat of St Kilda, he failed again in 1883 and 1886 to enter parliament.

On 4 May 1886 on the retirement of Sir Robert Molesworth [q.v.], he agreed to take over the vacancy on the Supreme Court; the first locally trained barrister to reach the bench, his appointment was popular. His clear and concise grasp of the law and especially of facts and figures made him an exceptionally rapid worker in court, and he was remembered as 'invariably kind and courteous', especially to junior members of the Bar. With an ironical sense of humour, he was a bright and at times brilliant conversationalist and a logical and trenchant arguer.

Shortly before his appointment Webb and his family had taken a trip to Europe via India; while away his daughter died, and he contracted smallpox and suffered an attack of bronchitis from which he never fully recovered. Ill health plagued him and he was given twelve months leave in March 1889. He resumed his work but on 26 September 1891, aged 63, he died of influenza and chronic bronchitis at his home at Caulfield; he was buried in the Melbourne general cemetery. A Congregationalist, on 16 April 1862 at Elsternwick he had married Sophia Sarah Agg who survived him with a daughter; a son and two daughters of his first marriage had predeceased him. His estate, valued for probate at £49,691, was left to his wife and daughter, with legacies to his nieces in the colony.

J. L. Forde, The story of the Bar of Victoria (Melb, 1913); A. Dean, A multitude of counsellors (Melb, 1968); Argus, 12 Nov 1883, 5 May 1886, 28, 29, 30 Sept 1891; IAN, 26 May 1886, 1 June 1891; A'sian Sketcher, 1 June 1886; Age, 28 Sept 1891; information from Ruth Campbell, Law School, Univ Melb.

ROBERT MILLER

WEBB, THOMAS PROUT (1845-1916), lawyer, was born on 22 January 1845 at Newtown (Fitzroy), Port Phillip District, son of Robert Saunders Webb, the first commissioner of customs and treasurer of the district, and his wife Ann, née Fisher. In September 1836 Webb's parents had come to Melbourne from Sydney, and his sister Ann (b. December 1836) is claimed to be the first white girl born in Melbourne.

Webb was a pupil at Melbourne Church of England Grammar School on its opening day 7 April 1858 and retained a close interest in the school. In 1863 he entered the University of Melbourne where under Professor W. E. Hearn [q.v.] he studied arts and law (B.A., 1867). He went on to study at King's College, London (B.A., 1867), read law at Lincoln's Inn from November 1867 and in 1869 gained the Inns of Court scholarship in constitutional law and legal history. He was called to the Bar on 10 June 1870.

Webb returned to Melbourne in 1872 and was admitted to the Victorian Bar. In 1874 he published the first edition of his most notable work, *Compendium of the Imperial law and statutes in force in the colony of Victoria...*, a useful and scholarly analysis of the origin of the various jurisdictions of the Victorian Supreme Court, of the extent to which the principles of English common law governed Victorians, and of the applicability of imperial statutes to the colony. On 29 July 1875 at St James's Church, Melbourne, he married Katherine, daughter of J. T. Smith [q.v.] and established a home, Bronte, in Dendy Street, Brighton. He practised in Equity until 1884, edited a collection of Victorian statutes and was also chief collaborator with Hearn in preparing an immense code of Victorian law based on a Benthamite-Austinian view of jurisprudence.

On 6 October 1884 Webb became master in equity and lunacy of the Supreme Court of Victoria and successively acting-commissioner of titles (1885), commissioner of patents (1890), commissioner of trade marks (1891), commissioner of taxes (1895) and registrar of land tax (1903). As master he was confronted with intricate probate problems, and as commissioner of taxes with both income and land pressure groups. With income tax in its infancy he helped significantly in its development, assisting in the drafting of many bills. As a public official he was able and hard working, firm but tactful, endeavouring as far as possible 'to make the unpleasant duty of taxpaying as little irksome as possible'. He was appointed a Q.C. on 12 March 1900.

Of deep learning, much charm and wide interests, Webb attracted many friends. He had inherited his mother's artistic talents and was a noted amateur artist who exhibited water-colours at the Victorian Academy of Arts for some years. In 1901 he was president of the Old Melburnians' Society. When he died of heart disease on 22 November 1916, handsome tributes were paid to his great abilities. Buried in the Anglican section of Melbourne cemetery, he was predeceased by a son and survived by his wife,

a son Keith Esmond, who became a metallurgical and mining engineer, and by a daughter, both of whom died without issue. Family papers and letters and Webb's mother's sketch-book are in the hands of his descendants.

J. Smith (ed), *Cyclopedia of Victoria*, 1 (Melb, 1903); *Australasian*, 4 May 1867, 23 Feb 1895; *Punch* (Melb), 4 Aug 1904, 2 Feb 1911; *Argus*, 23 Nov 1916.   CHARLES FRANCIS

WEBB, WILLIAM TELFORD (1842-1911), farmer and politician, was born on 28 July 1842 at Tullamore, King's County (Offaly), Ireland, son of Richard Webb, farmer, and his wife Maria, née Telford. His parents and their six children arrived in Melbourne in the *Black Eagle* on 28 January 1859 and settled at Tylden near Kyneton, but in 1863 William went to the Dunstan goldfields near Otago, New Zealand. He was moderately successful but returned after surviving a severe snowstorm in Gabriel's Gully in which three hundred people died. In 1868 he selected land at Nanneella near Rochester. By 1878 he, his mother and his uncle William Telford owned 900 acres. He was an enthusiastic supporter of McColl's [q.v.] northwest Victorian canal and irrigation scheme, first proposed in 1871, and became a commissioner of the United Echuca and Waranga Waterworks Trust from its inception in October 1882. He was chairman of the Campaspe Water Trust in 1889-1903.

Elected in 1873 as the first farming representative to the Echuca (later Rochester) Shire Council, Webb was a councillor until 1892 and president in 1877-79. In May 1879 he was active in refounding the Rochester branch of the National Reform and Protection League, whose aims were to seek reform of the Legislative Council and to secure direct representation of farmers in parliament. He also represented the shire at meetings of the Decentralization League. In 1883 he unsuccessfully contested the seat of Rodney in the Legislative Assembly but was elected in April 1889 when James Shackell [q.v.] and soon became a powerful advocate of farming and irrigation interests. He held the seat until September 1897; he was commissioner of public works and minister for agriculture from January 1893 to September 1894 and vice-president of the Board of Lands and Works from February 1893 to September 1894 in the Patterson [q.v.] ministry.

By 1889 Webb had given up active farming and lived in Rochester, where he set up as an agent and grain-buyer for farmers, ran a milling and butchering business, and was a founder of the Yeomanry stores in Mackie Street. He was also a promoter in 1889 and chief shareholder of the Fresh Food and Frozen Storage Co. Ltd which operated creameries, butter factories and cool stores throughout Victoria until its voluntary liquidation in 1902. It was one of the companies investigated and censured by the 1905 royal commission on the butter industry. Webb's belief in the worth and wealth of farming industries was the rock on which he stood in the gloom and instability of Victorian politics in the 1890s. In December 1903 he won the seat of Mandurang in a by-election but lost in the general elections of 1904.

On 24 October 1883 at St Matthew's Church, Prahran, he had married Elizabeth Alice Everitt, a 21-year-old milliner. In 1909 a stroke partially paralysed him, but he remained fairly active in Rochester until his sudden death from heart failure while on holiday at St Kilda on 17 January 1911. He was survived by his wife and three of their five daughters.

Roy Com on water supply, V&P (LA Vic), 1885, 2 (19), 3 (53); *Riverine Herald*, Aug-Oct 1881, Feb-Apr 1889, 7 Nov 1891, 20 Jan 1911; *Rochester Express*, 21 Jan 1911; G. R. Bartlett, Political organization and society in Victoria 1864-1883 (Ph.D. thesis, ANU, 1964); information from Mrs E. Kidman and Mrs L. Daunt, Naracoorte, SA.   SUSAN MCCARTHY

WEBSTER, ALEXANDER GEORGE (1830-1914), merchant, was born on 3 December 1830 in London. He spent two years at Cape of Good Hope with his mother and sister before they sailed to Sydney in the *Roxburgh Castle*; they arrived in Van Diemen's Land in 1840. Educated at the Melville Street school in Hobart Town and at a private boarding-school at Kempton, he was also a pupil of the artist T. E. Chapman [q.v.]. Later, as an amateur he exhibited both water-colours and pencil drawings of the Tasmanian landscape.

At 14 Webster began work with T. Y. Lowes [q.v.], the Hobart auctioneer. He moved to Degraves [q.v.] Bros, who then combined sawmilling with the proprietorship of the Cascade Brewery, and in 1850 he joined the wool and grain store of C. T. Smith, his uncle. After Smith retired in 1856 Webster ran the business in partnership with his relation John Tabart, trading as Tabart and Webster. At St David's Anglican Cathedral, Hobart, on 30 November 1859 he married Louisa Harriett Turnley; they had eight children.

On the retirement of Tabart in 1879, Webster retained the sole interest in the firm but immediately brought his son Charles into the business which became known as A. G. Webster & Son Ltd. From 1888 it published the colony's first agricultural journal, the monthly *Webster's Tasmanian Agriculturist and Machinery Gazette*, which contained reprints from various journals, including reports of Lawes's Rothamstead experiments, extracts from the *Scientific American* and informed articles on Tasmanian farming. By 1906 the firm had grown from a small wool and grain store on Hobart's Old Wharf to a large business employing over 100 men, with branch offices in Launceston, Devonport, Huonville and Burnie. Initiating wool auctions in Tasmania, the company handled most of the Tasmanian clip for the London market. It also imported a large range of agricultural implements and steam-motors. The name was changed again when the firm was registered as an incorporated company in 1910, and his other sons Edwin and Arthur became directors.

Webster was elected a fellow of the Royal Society of Tasmania in 1865 and a member of its council in 1871; in 1905, as chairman, he read an address of welcome to the new governor Sir Gerald Strickland. He was also a justice of the peace, chairman of directors of the Tasmanian Steam Navigation Co. and the South British Fire and Marine Insurance Co. of New Zealand, and chairman of the Perpetual Trustees Co. State trustee of the Tasmanian Museum and Botanical Gardens, Webster was also a master warden of the Marine Board, Hobart, and American consul in 1877-1907. He was a commissioner of fisheries; as chairman in 1903 he visited the Baird Hatchery in California, from where he successfully supervised the dispatch to Tasmania of some 500,000 Quinnat salmon ova. He was congratulated by Robert Mackenzie Johnstone for his 'unremitting attention' to this task.

In the 1850s Webster had been well known as an oarsman and yachtsman and on one occasion with Mathew Seal, Henry Smith, John Swan and Henry Boar, rowed a five-oared whale-boat through D'Entrecasteaux Channel and across Storm Bay. He maintained his connexion with yachting and in 1890 was commodore of the newly formed Derwent Sailing Boat Club.

Predeceased by his wife and survived by three sons and two daughters, Webster died of chronic bronchitis on 4 December 1914. His estate was valued for probate at £24,427. His son Charles E. (1861-1936) became a vigorous managing director of the company which continued to expand until the present day when it is one of the largest in the state, with a variety of interests. Webster's grandson G. F. T. Webster is one of its directors.

Cyclopedia of Tasmania, 1 (Hob, 1900); H. Allport, Early art in Tasmania (Hob, 1931); E. H. Webster and L. Norman, A hundred years of yachting (Hob, 1936); P. Bolger, Hobart Town (Canb, 1973); Hobart Town Courier, 28 Jan 1857; Tas Mail, 24 Jan 1903, 4 Aug 1910, 10 Dec 1914; Mercury, 8 Sept 1908, 13 Jan 1911, 10 Feb 1922, 23 Sept 1936, 31 July 1947; A. G. Webster papers (Univ Tas Archives).　　　　　　　　G. P. R. CHAPMAN

WEBSTER, MARTHA, see TURNER, MARTHA.

WEEKES, ELIAS CARPENTER (1809-1881), ironmonger and politician, was born on 13 July 1809 in London, youngest son of John Weekes, naval shipwright at Chatham dockyard, and his wife Elizabeth, née Orton. After a commercial career in England he migrated about 1837 to New South Wales with his wife Margaret (d. 1839), daughter of Dr W. F. Wye, whom he had married at Newington Butts, London, probably in 1830. After working for a Sydney merchant, in 1842 he acquired the Travellers' Rest Inn on the Murrumbidgee. From 1844 he was in partnership, importing wines, with John Holdsworth. In 1850 he was an ironmonger and wine merchant and by 1855 had formed E. C. Weekes & Co., ironmongers, with his son Charles and a partner in London. In the 1850s he was a committee-man of the Sydney Mechanics' School of Arts.

Active in radical politics with his friend (Sir) Henry Parkes [q.v.], Weekes was a member of the Australasian League for the Abolition of Transportation. In June 1848 he seconded Robert Lowe's [q.v.] nomination for the City of Sydney seat in the Legislative Council. He opposed W. C. Wentworth's [q.v.] draft constitution but on 23 September 1853 wrote to W. R. Piddington [q.v.] denying that he was a member of the Constitutional Committee and complaining of 'the unworthy imputations, which ... you see fit to cast on those who declined to be manoeuvred into the body'. He was a member of the Sydney Municipal Council in 1850-57.

At the first elections after responsible government in 1856 Weekes stood for the Northumberland Boroughs. He told his constituents that the new Constitution was 'radically bad' and strongly attacked the 'two thirds clause'. He opposed state aid to religion, favoured the encouragement of native industries and rural libraries and advocated 'a federal government for all the Australasian colonies'. Defeated by six votes, he was elected second member for the South Riding of Cumberland. However, he was awarded the Northumberland seat in August by the Elections and Qualifications Committee and represented it until April 1859. In 1859-64 he sat for West Maitland. Vigorous and firm, he spoke with considerable fluency and force and in 1857-58 he was a member of the Elections and Qualifications Committee.

From April until October 1859 Weekes was colonial treasurer in (Sir) Charles Cowper's [q.v.] second ministry and held the same office from March 1860 under (Sir) John Robertson [q.v.] and Cowper. He strongly supported Cowper's 1861 bill to restrict Chinese immigration but resigned from the ministry on 20 March 1863 because constant work was weakening his remaining eye; he had lost the other in an accident two years before. In October the government was defeated after attempts to conceal a large budget deficit and some of the odium fell on Weekes, who did not contest the general election of 1864. He was appointed to the Legislative Council on 10 July 1865. In the council he carried the Dog and Goat Act of 1866 and two private company Acts in 1867 and 1870. In 1873 he took over J. G. L. Innes's [q.v.] duties as Parkes's government representative in the council for a fortnight, but complained of his own impaired health.

An auditor of the Bank of New South Wales in the 1850s, he was a director in 1863, 1866-68 and 1869-75. In the 1860s and 1870s he was also a director and sometime chairman of the United Insurance Co. Ltd, a trustee of the Savings Bank of New South Wales, a vice-president of the Australian Library and Literary Institution, and a member of the Hyde Park Improvement Committee; in 1867-68 he was a member of the commission to make arrangements for the public reception of the duke of Edinburgh. He suffered from softening of the brain for eight years before he died of apoplexy at 24 College Street on 5 August 1881; he was buried in Rookwood cemetery. Survived by two sons and three daughters, he left them personalty valued for probate at £12,241.

V&P (LA NSW), 1856-57, 1, 801, 1861, 2, 1343, 1862, 2, 939; SMH, 8 June 1842, 6 Nov 1844, 24, 27, 28, 31 Mar 1856; Empire, 23 Apr 1856; T&CJ, 13 Aug 1881; Cowper letters and Parkes letters (ML); newspaper indexes (ML); CO 201/518/298, 526/333, 570/174.

　　　　　　　　　　　　　　　R. W. RATHBONE

WEIGALL, ALBERT BYTHESEA (1840-1912), schoolmaster, was born on 16 February 1840 at Nantes, Normandy, France, fourth son of Edward Weigall, vicar of

Hurdsfield and rural dean of Buxton, Derbyshire, England, and his wife Cecilia Bythesea, née Brome. His godfather and great-uncle was Admiral Bythesea. He was educated at Macclesfield Grammar School and won a scholarship to Brasenose College, Oxford (B.A., 1862; M.A., Sydney, 1869). In need of a job and a sea voyage for his health he accepted a post teaching classics at Scotch College, Melbourne. He arrived in Victoria in the *Alfred* in October 1863 and taught under A. Morrison [q.v.] until he succeeded W. J. Stephens [q.v.] as headmaster of Sydney Grammar School in January 1867.

When Weigall took over, the school had only 53 boys and 9 masters; he was told by the trustees that it would probably be closed, but by 1912 he had built it up to 696 boys, with 26 talented staff dedicated to the school. He encouraged and often initiated activities which developed *esprit de corps* and loyalty to the school, and allowed contact with individual boys outside the classroom. He formed the Sydney Grammar School Cadet Corps and became its captain in 1871. He fostered sport, introduced school colours and a uniform cap and instituted a prefect system; he also supported the publication of the first *Sydneian* in 1875 and debating, music and drama clubs. Through these activities he acquired knowledge of all the boys at the school and retained it long after they had left. He took pride in their successes in public examinations and in distinctions gained by old boys in academic, professional and public life. He was created C.M.G. in 1909.

Weigall taught Greek at the Sydney Mechanics' School of Arts in 1867-68 and was a member of the Royal Society of New South Wales from 1867. He was a prominent founder of the Headmasters' Association in 1880 and in 1892 of the Teachers' Association, New South Wales, of which he was many times president. He was a fellow of St Paul's College in 1887 and in 1891-93 a councillor of the Women's College within the University of Sydney, but failed to win election to the university senate. He criticized excessive public examinations as 'unnecessarily harassing to teachers and to pupils and ... injurious to the progressive continuity of school work'; he also disliked the low standards of examinations, lack of social recognition for teachers and parents' indulgent submission to their children. He suggested a scheme of inspection of secondary schools as an alternative to the public examinations as a measure of a school's merit. Although an admitted conservative when discussing reforms in education, he upgraded the modern or commercial side of his curriculum and expanded science teach-ing. A devout Anglican, he was a member of St Andrew's Cathedral Chapter in 1876-1912 and a member of Sydney Diocesan synods in 1884-97; but he was well aware that the school, by its foundation Act, was for 'all classes and denominations'.

Weigall died of heart and gall bladder disease on 20 February 1912 in a private hospital at Darlinghurst and was buried in the Anglican section of South Head cemetery. He was survived by his wife Ada Frances, née Raymond, whom he had married at St Philip's, Sydney, on 24 September 1868, and by four sons and four daughters. His estate was valued for probate at £13,856. After his death many distinguished old boys paid tribute to his abilities as a headmaster, and the school trustees said that he had won 'for the School the first place of the Public Schools of Australia, and for himself a name worthy to rank among the foremost in the muster roll of famous Headmasters of the Empire'. His portrait hangs in the school; the Weigall Ground, Rushcutters Bay, is named after him.

M. W. MacCallum, *In memory of Albert Bythesea Weigall* (Syd, 1913); C. E. W. Bean, *Here, my son* (Syd, 1950); C. Turney (ed), *Pioneers of Australian education* (Syd, 1969); *Sydneian*, 1875-1912; Teachers' Assn of NSW, *Aust Teacher*, 1893-1909.   J. B. WINDEYER

WEKEY (VEKEY), SIGISMUND (ZSIGMOND) (1825?-1889), solicitor, pamphleteer and man of affairs, was born in Hungary, son of Paul Vékey and his wife Pauline, née Szilvasy. His father's family were landed gentry in the famous vine-growing area of Tokaj. He was admitted to the Bar in 1847, became attorney of the County of Sáros, and later a solicitor of Eperjes, where he was known as a speaker at liberal political rallies. At the outbreak of the Hungarian revolution in 1848 Vékey joined the insurgents as a first lieutenant. Promoted to captain, he was wounded at the battle of Rákosmezö in April 1849 and, on recovery, was aide-de-camp to Lajos Kossuth. After the defeat of the revolutionary forces Vékey escaped to Hamburg. He arrived in London in 1851 where he became an active member of the Committee of Emigrants and, after Kossuth's arrival, its secretary. He also completed a volume of Hungarian grammar (1852), styling his name as Sigismund Wekey.

As an assisted migrant Wekey arrived in Melbourne in the *Midas* early in 1854. He went to the diggings where it is said he dug alone for gold, but he soon returned to Melbourne. As 'A Hungarian', from 22 April he wrote a series of articles in the *Argus* on the advantages of the cultivation of vines in

Australia, soon revised and published under his own name as *The Land, importance of its culture to the general prosperity of Victoria*... In it a prospectus announced the formation of the Victoria Vineyard and Fruit Growing Co. with Wekey as a provisional director; the trustees included J. P. Fawkner [q.v.]. Financial support proved insufficient and the company was wound up on 29 January 1856.

In 1854 at the second meeting of the Philosophical Society in Melbourne, Wekey was appointed its honorary secretary. When it amalgamated with the Victorian Institute for the Advancement of Science to become the Philosophical Institute of Victoria, Wekey became secretary of the new body. As funds were unavailable, Wekey had published the transactions of the Philosophical Society at his own expense for two years. The question of whether the new institute should pay the debt was debated bitterly and resulted in Wekey's resignation on 19 June 1856.

Wekey later lived at Sandhurst (Bendigo) where on 23 September 1861 he married the 16-year-old Agnes Florence Warden at All Saints Church. About July next year the couple visited New Zealand where he was a correspondent for the *Otago Times*; he wrote *Otago; Its Gold-fields & Resources* (Melbourne, 1862). Returning to Victoria in 1863 he lived in 1866 at Lauraville, at the mining town, Gaffney's Creek, in the Mansfield district, where he was deputy-registrar of the Mansfield electoral division, and of births and deaths for Gaffney's Creek, as well as postmaster. In 1859 and 1864 he had applied for patents for mining machinery, and in 1869 he applied again for his velox-ore-crusher and amalgamator. He became manager and a director of the Aladdin and Try-Again United Gold Mining Co. but by 1870 wrangles culminated in criminal proceedings against Wekey and two of his co-directors on a charge of conspiracy. With one of his partners he was convicted and sentenced to a years gaol. Irregularities in the prosecution prompted Wekey to attack colonial justice in a pamphlet entitled *The Institutions of the Land we Live in...* (1870).

After serving his sentence Wekey left Australia with his wife, daughter and four sons, visiting America before arriving in Europe in 1876. They travelled several times between London and Budapest before settling in Hungary. He lectured on his voyages and in 1885 published a volume of his travels in which he impartially praised Australian administrators and the spirit of development in Victoria, and extolled the charitable institutions of the Australian colonies. He died in Budapest on 23 March 1889. Agile, acute and active, Wekey was essentially a convincing purveyor of ideas, well versed in two cultures. Although overbearing and opportunist he contributed to the emergence of a colourful intellectual life in Melbourne.

E. F. Kunz, *Blood and gold: Hungarians in Australia* (Melb, 1969); *Examiner* (Melb), 5 July 1862; *Argus*, 23 July 1869; *Australasian*, 24 Sept 1870.
         E. F. KUNZ

WELD, Sir FREDERICK ALOYSIUS (1823-1891), governor, was born on 9 May 1823 at Chideock, Dorset, England, third son of Humphrey Weld of Chideock Manor, and his wife Christina Maria, daughter of Lord Clifford of Chudleigh. The Weld, or Wylde, family was one of the leading Roman Catholic families of England; his uncle Thomas Weld was the first Englishman to be created a cardinal after the Reformation. A second cousin Roger Vaughan [q.v.] became archbishop of Sydney.

Weld was educated at Stonyhurst, a Jesuit school founded by his grandfather, and at the University of Fribourg, Switzerland, where he studied philosophy, chemistry and law. In November 1843 he sailed for New Zealand to join two cousins Charles Clifford and William Vavasour; he had a modest sum of sovereigns and orders for town and country land. He assisted his cousins to drive 500 sheep to a 30,000-acre lease at Wharekaka, east of the Ruamahanga River near present-day Martinborough. None of the partners knew how to manage sheep, but Clifford engaged a border Scot with experience in New South Wales who saved Wharekaka from disaster and gradually transformed Weld into a first-rate sheep-farmer. Impressed by his enthusiasm and energy, Clifford offered Weld a quarter-share in the venture; he later managed the property. The partners eventually transferred their interests to two South Island stations, Flaxbourne near Blenheim, Marlborough, and Stonyhurst near Cheviot, Canterbury. In London in 1852 Weld published his *Hints to intending sheep farmers in New Zealand*.

He was very sensitive about political privilege. In 1848 Weld joined the Wellington Settlers' Constitutional Association, and in 1852 won Wairau in the Legislative Assembly. He was appointed to the Executive Council in the first session but the fiasco of the attempt to obtain responsible government left him disillusioned and restless.

With J. F. S. Wortley he explored the interior of the North Island in October

1854. In August next year they sailed for England via America and stopped at the Sandwich Islands to observe the eruption of the volcano, Mauna Loa. They climbed the crater and returned to New Zealand in November; Weld's account was published in the *Journal* of the Geological Society of London, December 1856. In England on 10 March 1859 he married a distant cousin Filumena Mary, daughter of Ambrose Phillips of Grace-Dieu Manor, Leicestershire, who later added de Lisle to his name. They reached New Zealand in February 1860 and he became minister for native affairs in the Stafford ministry (1860-61). In November 1864 Weld accepted Governor Grey's invitation to form a ministry, on condition that the British troops engaged in the Maori war be withdrawn and replaced by local militia. After raising a small force of white settlers and friendly Maoris which routed the insurgents, he carried the Native Rights Act, 1865, which removed many Maori grievances. In October, upset at parliamentary quibbling about defence, he resigned for medical reasons and in 1867 returned to England.

In December 1868 he was appointed governor of Western Australia and with his wife and six children arrived there in September 1869. The free settlers welcomed him as a family man with practical experience of pioneer farming. In his first six months of office he travelled 1200 miles on horseback, and visited every district of importance except the far north. He enjoyed getting about and seeing the country. In 1871 he rode to Albany and, with two white men and a native, made his way through partly unexplored country to Cape Leeuwin and back to Perth. Later that year he went by sea to inspect the pearling fleets at Nickol Bay (Roebourne) and the sheep stations inland; in 1873 he travelled 1000 miles in the Geraldton district. A keen observer and an accomplished correspondent, his letters and dispatches vividly depicted life in the colony. One of his first acts was to send John Forrest to find a possible route for a telegraph line to Adelaide. He also ordered the installation of 900 miles of internal line.

In April 1870 Weld considered a petition for representative government which had been presented to his predecessor. He realized that the main obstacle was the predominance of ex-convicts. Among the free settlers there were some educated men of substance who could be trusted to govern, but Weld doubted the next generation. In an oddly worded dispatch he saw no reason to suppose that the colonists would ever become more fitted for self-government, and that if its introduction was deferred they would become less fitted; he then introduced a bill for twelve elected members to sit in the Legislative Council with the official and nominated members; it was passed on 1 June 1870.

The new council met in December and the elected members soon asserted themselves. They passed legislation establishing municipalities and road boards; but they objected to Weld's education bill, which was inopportune, as bigoted Protestants had been disturbed by the Vatican Council and detected a Popish plot in every clause. A modified bill was passed but Weld was soon at odds with the Catholic clergy. He suspected that Irish clergy and Irish police were plotting the escape of Fenian prisoners held in Fremantle gaol, and remonstrated with them. The priests complained to the Vatican that at an official dinner party Weld had asked the Anglican bishop to say grace. After hearing his version of the story, the Pope made him a Knight of St Pius. He again clashed with the Legislative Council in August 1871 when he vetoed a protective tariff on flour and meal. He dissolved the council but gave way when the election showed a substantial majority for the duties.

Weld annoyed the convict community by revoking a ticket-of-leave, and thereafter suffered constant ribald attacks by the *Herald*. Some would have smiled on reading 'Poor dear cigar-lovin, claret-sippin, long-letter-writin Weld', but he was not amused. In 1871 the Colonial Office sought files of the local newspapers but he refused to supply the *Herald*. The contents of his dispatch leaked and to Weld's mortification he was directed by the Colonial Office to apologize to the owners of the paper. In 1872 he refused to commute the five-year sentence of the son of a leading colonist who had been convicted of the manslaughter of an Aboriginal. The Colonial Office reduced it to one year. Weld's correspondence shows how deeply distressed he was by these humiliations, and it was small consolation when Secretary of State Kimberley commended him privately on his solicitude for the welfare of the natives. His reaction was typical: 'How I wish that I could have a day with the hounds, or after partridges', he wrote to his brother; but instead he took a holiday at Rottnest Island with 'Mr. Howard—a Lincolnshire parson —one of the good old school', where they shot quail and pigeons in the mornings, went sea fishing later in the day, and had 'a very jolly week'.

Weld's last two years in Perth, 1873-74, were happier; people were ready to give him credit for his able administration and good qualities. The Constitution was again under consideration, and in August 1874 the Legislative Council asked him to bring down a bill for responsible government. True to his belief that this was the only satisfactory form of government, he complied and it passed easily. He then dissolved the council so that everyone, including the secretary of state, might have time for consideration. He was later rebuked in a dispatch to his successor, for having moved in the matter without first referring it to London, and the bill was shelved.

Early in 1874 Weld had been offered the governorship of Tasmania. Although the salary was lower, he consoled himself with the thought that Government House at Hobart Town was larger and better suited for his increasing family. Mrs Weld was expecting another child, and did not accompany her husband in January 1875. She was to follow in a suitable ship, but it was sold before she was ready. Without consulting him she chartered a vessel to convey her to Hobart with nine children and their nurses. The passage was rough and the deck cabin was constantly flooded. Weld wrote: 'The captain turned out to be an ex-convict who drank like a fish, and knew so little about his work that Mena had to give directions to the crew when to reef the sails'.

Weld's term in Tasmania, 1875-80, was a quiet interlude. The colony had had responsible government for twenty years; his main duty was to chair the weekly Executive Council but he travelled widely, performed his social duties and advocated the formation of rifle clubs and militia units for defence. War with Russia was thought to be imminent, and he feared invasion at either Albany, Western Australia, or Hobart. His efforts led later to the fortification of these ports. After a change of government in 1877 Weld wrote to his brother that he was no longer a *roi fainéant* and had been able by his advice to help the new and politically inexperienced cabinet. He said that if his late ministers had taken the hints he had given them, they might still have been in office. There was some excitement over his remission of the sentence on a woman convicted of arson in 1873, but he had no differences with the Colonial Office and at the end of 1879 was appointed governor of the Straits Settlements.

Weld went to Singapore in April 1880 and with his wealth of experience found the fullest scope for his talents. For seven years he ruled directly and, by quasi-diplomatic activities among the still-independent Malay States, succeeded in extending British influence. His work was done through a hand-picked group of young men, the most notable of whom was Sir Frank Swettenham.

When Weld's health broke down he retired in 1887 and returned to Chideock. He made a short pilgrimage to the Holy Land, provided advice and support for the Western Australian constitutional delegation of 1890 and died at Chideock on 20 July 1891. He was survived by six sons and six daughters. After his death his widow withdrew to a convent of which her daughter Edith Mary was prioress, and died there on 9 April 1903. Weld was devoted to his wife and children, and spent much time with them and members of his personal staff, who were usually relations. He was honourable and an able administrator, but lacked the common touch and did not make friends easily except amongst people of his own class. Though wedded to democratic principles he was inclined to be autocratic. His portrait hangs in the hall of the Weld Club, founded in Perth in 1871, to which he gave his name and of which he was the first patron. He was appointed C.M.G. in 1875, K.C.M.G. in 1880, and G.C.M.G. in 1885.

A. M. Fraser (Lady Lovat), *The life of Sir Frederick Weld* (Lond, 1914); T. S. Louch, *The first fifty years ... the Weld Club 1871-1921* (Perth, 1964); K. G. Tregonning, 'Frederick Weld's place in Australian and Malaysian history', *Hemisphere*, Feb 1965; *Herald* (Fremantle), 4 Feb 1871; *West Australian*, 25 June 1889, 24 July 1891; J. Williams, Frederick Weld: a political biography (Ph.D. thesis, Univ Waikato, NZ, 1973); Weld papers (Battye Lib, Perth).

T. S. LOUCH

WESTGARTH, WILLIAM (1815-1889), merchant, financier, politician and historian, was born on 15 June 1815 in Edinburgh, son of John Westgarth, a surveyor-general of customs for Scotland, and his wife Christian, née Thomson. The Westgarths were a Durham, England, landed family. William was educated at high schools at Leith and Edinburgh and at Dr Bruce's academy at Newcastle upon Tyne. He then worked with the mercantile firm of G. Young & Co. of Leith, which had Australian interests. Attracted by business opportunities, Westgarth left Leith on 11 July 1840 and arrived in Melbourne on 13 December. On Christmas Eve he wrote to his mother, 'the grand bent of all is the making of money, and I do think some is to be made here'. Within two years, however, he was caught in the economic crisis and made a settlement with his creditors. But he soon flourished as a general import merchant, in partnership with Alfred Ross from 1845; James Spowers joined the firm in 1858.

Always an 'improver' determined to promote the diffusion of knowledge, Westgarth was prominent in the Melbourne Mechanics' Institute and in founding the Benevolent Society. In 1844 he began his prolific career as an author with *Observations on the present commercial, agricultural, and civil condition of the Australian colonies*, published in Leith, and the first of his commercial, statistical and general half-yearly reports (which continued until 1848) on Port Phillip. This pre-governmental statistical service 'afforded some agreeable and improving exercise for leisure time'. In 1846 he published in Melbourne a 40-page *Report on the condition, capabilities and prospects of the Australian Aborigines*, which is notable for its sympathy and insight. He had also been prominent in the campaign for the separation of the Port Phillip District from New South Wales and suggested that the boundary would be best settled by the direction of the tracks of bullock-teams. Westgarth left the colony on business in January 1847 and on the voyage home wrote much of *Australia Felix; or, a historical and descriptive account of the Settlement of Port Phillip...* (Edinburgh, 1848). Impressed by the success of German migration to South Australia, he persuaded the colonial land and emigration commissioners to subsidize the emigration of German 'vine dressers, agricultural labourers and shepherds' to Port Phillip, and made the recruiting arrangements in Germany. Many difficulties had to be overcome but in 1848 and 1849 migrant parties arrived in Melbourne and formed settlements at Thomastown, Doncaster and elsewhere.

Soon after his return in mid-1849 Westgarth quickly became one of the two or three most respected public men in the infant colony and a spokesman for the broad radical front, including many Scottish businessmen, which opposed the conservative, largely Anglican, official class. Encouraged by W. Kerr [q.v.], Westgarth was elected unopposed in November 1850 to the New South Wales Legislative Council in succession to Earl Grey, and fought vainly for the secret ballot and a democratic new Victorian Legislative Council. At the first election in September 1851 he topped the poll as one of three members for Melbourne. In January-February 1851 he had been one of three Victorian delegates to the conference which formed the Australasian League for the Abolition of Transportation. Westgarth then became secretary of the Victorian branch, subscribed 100 guineas to the cause, and in 1852 was a delegate to a conference in Adelaide and on a mission to rally enthusiasm in Van Diemen's Land. In July at a time of public outrage over the goldfields depredations of emancipists and escaped convicts from Van Diemen's Land, Westgarth successfully introduced the Convicts Prevention Act which had been drafted by Kerr. Intent on mobilizing the mercantile community as an enlightened political force, he formed the Melbourne Chamber of Commerce almost off his own bat and became its first president in July 1851. The chamber collaborated with J. H. N. Cassell [q.v.], the collector of customs, in drawing up the straightforward free-trade tariff of 1852 which wiped out the intricate system inherited from New South Wales. At his instigation in 1853 the government opened unsuccessful negotiations with the other colonies to unify tariffs. Westgarth was prominent in the foundation of the first gas company and the Bank of Victoria (of which he was briefly a director), encouraged promoters of railways, and was the almost automatic choice as chairman of public functions such as the 'breakfast' in honour of E. Hargraves [q.v.] in December 1852.

Westgarth had few of the qualities of a popular political leader, but he carried much more authority in the Legislative Council than the eccentric J. P. Fawkner or the demagogic J. S. Johnston [qq.v.]. In his consistent support of manhood suffrage, abolition of property qualifications, the ballot, state education, abolition of state aid to religion and even direct taxation of wealth, he was probably more radical than any other member of the council. Broadly, he gave moderate expression to the vitriolic campaigns of his friend Edward Wilson [q.v.] in the *Argus* against La Trobe's administration. 'Garryowen' [q.v. E. Finn] refers to his 'plodding consistency' as a popular leader. As a voluntaryist, he unsuccessfully supported abolition of state aid and, failing that, state support for the Jewish religion. He took his full part in the 1852 campaign for unlocking of the lands. During that year he was overwhelmed by the 'vast incessant tide' of public and private business. His only leisure was a half-hour walk and thought early in the morning; the rest of the day was a succession of private business, public meetings and deputations, and council meetings and committees.

In April 1853 Westgarth again left the colony for Britain and did not return for eighteen months. Perhaps one leading motive was to 'run home for a wife': early in 1854 he married Ellison Macfie, by whom he had three daughters. His absence when the new Constitution was being drafted lost him the chance of greater historical fame, for he was fitted to provide the coherent radical critique which in the event was conspicuously lacking. On his return he was soon appointed by Lieut-Governor Hotham to the commission of inquiry into the gold-fields of Victoria and was a natural choice as chairman. Backed by strong-minded colleagues like Fawkner and O'Shanassy [q.v.], Westgarth led the commission in refusing to comply with Hotham's order not to investigate the immediate causes of Eureka. In January 1855 they recommended a general amnesty—but Hotham pressed on with the treason trials. On the other hand, the commission avoided public investigation of some of the more inflammable features of the conflict. After three months work they presented a statesmanlike report which abounded in generalizations bearing the mark of Westgarth's pen. The major recommendations—an export duty in place of the licence fee, a miner's right which gave legal rights and the vote, and the creation of local courts—were adopted, and brought peace to the goldfields. Westgarth and his fellow commissioners, who were amazed by the extent of resistance to capitalist organization, also paved the way for legislation enabling the formation of limited liability mining companies.

Westgarth did not return to the Legislative Council and refused an offer by W. Nicholson [q.v.] late in 1855 to join the ministry he was attempting to form. He remained active in politics, however: in 1856 he helped to shape the democratic 'people's programme' before the election, was working on a plan for free selection of land and supported the movement for election of governors. He vehemently resisted a proposal that the government should take over the issue of bank-notes.

'Regretfully, under the calls of business', Westgarth left the colony for London in 1857 and established a sharebroking firm; he retired from Westgarth, Ross and Spowers about 1863. From the early 1860s he 'became the centre of the syndicates of speculators who have chiefly controlled Australian loans'. In his regular business circulars and privately with colonial politicians, he encouraged consolidation of the wide variety of colonial stocks whose varying particulars made negotiability, and even quotation on the Stock Exchange, difficult. In the late 1880s he was trying to persuade the Australasian colonies to confederate, if only for joint guarantee of colonial debts; thereby he was certain that they could borrow as much as they wanted for as little as 3 per cent interest. Over the years he carried out innumerable minor diplomatic tasks and odd jobs for the Victorian and other colonial governments.

In 1853 on the voyage to Britain Westgarth had written Victoria: late Australia Felix (Edinburgh, 1853). In 1856 he revised James Bonwick's [q.v.] Discovery and settle-ment of Port Phillip (Melbourne, 1856) for publication, and produced Commerce and Statistics of Victoria, From the Commencement of the Colony (Melbourne, 1856). In 1857, again on board ship, he wrote Victoria and the Australian Gold Mines in 1857 (London, 1857). In London he continued to write. His contributions to the Encyclopaedia Britannica on 'Australia' and 'Australasia' were revised and expanded into Australia: its rise, progress, and present condition (Edinburgh, 1861); other articles for the Britannica included those on the goldfields of Australia, Melbourne, Sydney and Tasmania. He contributed to Chambers' Encyclopaedia on Australia. In 1863 he edited John Davis's Tracks of McKinlay and party across Australia (London, 1863), and followed it with The Colony of Victoria ... down to the end of 1863 (London, 1864).

Westgarth quickly became prominent in London as an old colonial hand. In 1860 he was a Victorian representative in the General Association for the Australian Colonies and at an International Statistical Congress. He joined with Edward Wilson and H. Childers [q.v.] in 1862-64 in the campaign against continuation of transportation to Western Australia. He was active among the group of Australians who largely contributed to the foundation of the (Royal) Colonial Institute in 1869, presented the first paper to the first ordinary meeting 'On the Relations of the Colonies to the Mother Country', gave papers annually for several years, and was the society's auditor from its foundation until his death. Working closely still with Wilson, he drew up the resolutions for the Cannon Street meetings of 1869-70. He professed himself to be a thorough disciple of the Manchester school except for his conviction that trade followed the flag, deplored the loss of the old imperial outlook, and in 1872 or earlier was recommending annexation and colonization of New Guinea. In 1870 he and others in the Colonial Institute discussed the need for imperial federation, but roused little support. In 1884, together with F. T. Labilliere [q.v.], he was one of the preliminary committee of six which founded the Imperial Federation League. He was so struck with reverence for the Queen and the overriding requirement of imperial unity for defence that in this area alone, perhaps, he was totally at odds with prevailing colonial opinion. His solution to the problem of colonial representation, which he consistently put forward as an intermediate step, was representation of the colonies in the imperial cabinet as a rudimentary federal chamber—either formally, or as a council of ten colonials resident in Britain nominated by the Queen sitting with the cabinet of sixteen as a council of advice on imperial questions.

In the 1870s and 1880s Westgarth gave frequent papers to the British Association and the Social Science Congress and wrote several articles and pamphlets on general economic matters. He considered the case for bimetallism, and argued for land taxation as he had in the 1850s. In 1883 in 'Practical Commerce versus Theoretical Political Economy: Crises', *Chamber of Commerce Journal*, he propounded a 'detailed trade cycle hypothesis based on assumed changes in expectations but embodying also descriptions of over-production and inventory oscillations'. In a pamphlet published in London in 1887 he attempted a *Sketch of the nature and limits of a science of Economics*. He persistently defended free-trade philosophy with hoary arguments, praising the wisdom of New South Wales and conceding protectionist measures only in the case of 'very clearly demonstrable social or political necessity'. In 1881, at last, he had succeeded in founding a Chamber of Commerce in London. At this time, also, he was preoccupied with the problem of poverty—the inadequacy of wages over a wide field of employment to provide a healthful, let alone a cheerful or respectable life. He planned a London reconstruction trust, using unearned increment of site value as the basis of a self-remunerative means of reconstructing central London, but had to abandon the massive enterprise as impracticable. In 1883 he gave £1200 to the Society of Arts as prize-money for essays on the best means of providing dwellings for the London poor and replanning the city. The essays were published in 1886, with an introduction by Westgarth, as *Essays on the street re-alignment, reconstruction, and sanitation of Central London, and on the rehousing of the poorer classes*, as a contribution to combating 'the absolute despair which seizes upon many minds at the inequalities of the country's socio-economic condition, and the drastic measures that are often proposed for its cure'.

In 1888 Westgarth paid a last visit to Australia which he saw as still far more advanced in progress than Britain. On the voyage out he wrote his *Personal Recollections of Early Melbourne & Victoria* (Melbourne, 1888), one of the very best of Australian pioneer reminiscences, a happy and lively recreation of arcadian Victoria with many vivid but charitable sketches of his contemporaries. In the opening procession of the Centennial International Exhibition he was specially honoured as a pioneer, together with Francis Henty [q.v.]; the Chamber of Commerce fêted him and he rejoiced in meeting so many surviving old friends. On the voyage back to Britain he wrote *Half a Century of Australasian Progress, a personal retrospect* (London, 1889).

After his return Westgarth had a serious bout of pleurisy, and was in feeble health when he retired in July 1889, taking £100,000 from the business. The firm of Westgarth & Co. was carried on by W. Devon Astle, but it failed late in 1890, partly because too many Victorian commitments were being carried. Westgarth had not lived to see such a sad day. On 28 October 1889 he fell from an attic window of his South Kensington home and died; a verdict of accidental death was found at the inquest when it was suggested that in a weakened physical state and being a fanatic for ventilation he had probably climbed up and forced open the window. The funeral was held in Edinburgh. Westgarth left a considerable estate. He had been a member of the Church of Scotland and held regular morning prayers in his household.

'Serious Mr. Westgarth', Hugh McCrae remembered as his father's [q.v. G. G. McCrae] description: this unobtrusive, unostentatious, methodical, indefatigable supporter of all good causes was the type of conscientious citizen Victoria desperately needed in the period of gold-rush opportunism. The most earnest of improvers, he would take the trouble to write to his temperance friends to report on the success of public drinking-fountains in Liverpool. A prolix speaker, though mellow and wise, he could be something of a bore, but he was by no means incapable of humorous repartee. Most genial and conciliatory, a natural peacemaker, he was convivial, too—a vigorous man who delighted in his trips to the pastoral interior and the goldfields, and one whose curiosity about men and nature produced continual enjoyment. Westgarth was almost infinitely tolerant and understanding of the follies and foibles of mankind. He remained a businessman almost in spite of himself; his scholarly and cultural inclinations constantly distracted him. Few men in Australian history can have led more useful lives.

Three modern historians have described Westgarth as 'the John Stuart Mill of Victoria', 'the outstanding sociological thinker of the colonies', and 'the most perceptive of early Australian historians'. His four major books on Victoria, each of which were fresh treatments, were written primarily to provide accurate information on the colony and also to advertise it. For the most part, they are unpretentious, simply written narratives. However, Westgarth is distinctive in his period for his efforts to explain the course of historical events and to seek reasons for change, and for his occasional generalizations about the nature of colonial society. In particular, he developed discussion about the relation of wide distribution of property and assumptions of social equality to political democracy, and stressed the fundamentally conservative nature of democracy in such circumstances. His pioneering statistical work was an aspect of his modern approach to the conduct of business and government. But his practical work as one of the most advanced radical liberals of his day ranks equally with his intellectual and literary achievement.

Garryowen (E. Finn), *The chronicles of early Melbourne* (Melb, 1888); G. Serle, *The golden age* (Melb, 1963); C. D. W. Goodwin, *Economic enquiry in Australia* (Durham, N.C., 1966); *Argus*, 30 Oct, 2 Dec 1889; G. H. Nadel, Mid-nineteenth century political thought in Australia (M.A. thesis, Univ Melb, 1950).

GEOFFREY SERLE

WETTENHALL, HOLFORD HIGH-LORD (1840-1920), pastoralist, was born on 17 October 1840 in the Carlton River area near Sorell, Van Diemen's Land, fourth son of Robert Horatio Wettenhall, R.N., and his wife Mary Burgess, née Bussell. Educated at Launceston Church of England Grammar School, he joined his father at Queechy, near Launceston, and later his brother-in-law Dr O. V. Lawrence, son of W. E. Lawrence [q.v.], at Penquite. In 1859 he worked with his relation Alexander Dennis [q.v.] at Carr's Plains in the Wimmera district of Victoria and in 1862 took over management of the run. For the next few years he contended with selectors and succeeded in acquiring freehold of 30,000 acres for the Dennis brothers. He later leased the property from Alexander Dennis and eventually bought the homestead and some 15,000 acres. On 21 November 1866 Wettenhall married Dennis's daughter Mary Burgess; she was a great horsewoman all her life, an accomplished musician, a crayon artist and a passionate gardener. They had seven sons and two daughters.

A breeder of pure merino sheep, Wettenhall had formed his flock in 1863 with Ercildoun rams and the American ram Old Grimes, and later used rams from the stud flocks of T. Dowling, T. F. Cumming [qq.v.] and W. Cumming. In the 1880s he was associated with the Dennis brothers in developing a specially adapted breed of sheep; his stock was named the Ideal and formed part of the Polwarth breed. He also developed the Carrsdale, a first cross between Lincoln and merino. In 1890 Wettenhall retired from active management of Carr's Plains. He bought 400 acres on the north

slopes of the Grampians near Pomonal, built his home, Glen Holford, and was one of the first in the district to grow fruit, especially apples for export. By 1907 his son Marcus managed the orchard and Wettenhall divided his time between the homes of his sons: the merino flock was kept at Bretton, a 4000-acre property near Glenorchy managed by Milton; Carr's Plains was managed by Herbert and Allan farmed parts of it; and Arthur managed the Lake Wallace property (bought 1909). The droughts of the 1890s had forced Wettenhall to dispose of Wirchilliba station near Hillston in New South Wales, which he had earlier held with Ernest Johnson.

Interested in the development of the Wimmera, Wettenhall was elected in 1861 to the Kara Kara and the St Arnaud road boards. In 1869 he began his thirty-year association with the Stawell Shire Council, of which he was president several times. He was chairman of the Shire of Stawell Waterworks Trust in 1885 and a founder and first president of the Australian Natives' Association at Stawell. In November 1882 he contested Nelson Province in the Legislative Council and after a by-election in December became the first native-born member of the council; he held the seat until September 1886. He contested the Legislative Assembly seat of Stawell in 1889 and 1892.

Wettenhall's first wife died on 5 July 1917; on 4 February 1919 at All Saints, St Kilda, he married Laura, daughter of C. J. Dennys [q.v.]. An Anglican, he died on 29 October 1920 in the Toorak home of his son Dr Roland Wettenhall, and was buried in Stawell cemetery.

Pastoral Review Pty Ltd, *The pastoral homes of Australia—Victoria* (Melb, 1910); A. Henderson (ed), *Early pioneer families of Victoria and Riverina* (Melb, 1936); *Pastoral Review*, 15 Aug, 15 Oct 1907.

J. ANN HONE

WHEELWRIGHT, HORACE (HORATIO) WILLIAM (1815-1865), hunter, naturalist and writer, was born on 5 January 1815 at Tansor, Northamptonshire, England, second son of Rev. Charles Apthorp Wheelwright and his wife Ann. Educated at Reading Grammar School, he later studied law, practising in 1843-46 as an attorney at Thrapston, Northamptonshire, but his great interest was field sports. After failing in his profession he moved to Kent and later spent some years 'rambling over the forests and fells of Northern Europe', especially Norway and Sweden.

About 1852 Wheelwright migrated to Australia, probably attracted by the Victorian gold rushes. Unsuccessful on the diggings, he decided to 'face the bush on his own account' rather than seek work on a station; although impressed by Melbourne he had no desire to live there. He became a professional shooter of game and, as he described later, luckily fell in with a mate in the same circumstances as himself, with similar education, training and tastes; together they 'roughed it' under the same canvas for some four years. Camping within a radius of forty miles of Melbourne, they shot duck, quail, pigeon and kangaroo for the city market. Occasionally they were joined on expeditions by sporting friends from Melbourne, and Wheelwright also spent some time alone in the bush. In 1859, according to his own account, although some sources say 1856, he returned to Europe.

Wheelwright's years as a shooter in the Victorian bush would have remained obscure but for the publication of his *Bush Wanderings of a Naturalist; or, notes on the field sports and fauna of Australia Felix* (London, 1861, 1862, 1864), written under the pseudonym of 'An Old Bushman'. A handbook for the rambler, it is regarded now as one of the most informative and readable narratives of early bush life in the colony. In it he details information on local animals, birds, reptiles, insects and fish, ranging from minute observations of their appearance and habits to practical notes on how to catch joeys for pets, make possum rugs or platypus tobacco pouches, cure kangaroo hams and choose suitable guns and ammunition for hunting purposes. Although he was himself a strong advocate of regulations to protect animals and birds during their breeding seasons, his book reveals how widespread was the slaughter of wildlife by the mid-1850s.

After leaving Australia Wheelwright lived in Sweden and devoted himself to natural history. But he was not so much a scientific naturalist as a pioneer who solved mysteries of nature by adventure and daring. In 1859 he published in Carlstadt, Sweden, a comparative list of birds in Scandinavia and Great Britain; from 1860 he contributed articles to *The Field*. In 1864 he published a book on his experiences in Lapland and in 1865 his *Ten Years in Sweden* appeared. His *Sporting Sketches. Home and Abroad. . .* (London, 1866) contains reprints of articles from English journals and two are based on his Australian experiences.

A fall in a slippery London street aggravated a hernia condition from which Wheelwright had suffered for years. He was taken to his brother's house at Crowhurst Parsonage, Surrey, but died on 16 November 1865 after an operation. He was buried in Crowhurst cemetery. In a preface to *Sporting Sketches* his publishers described him as an apt observer with great powers of description; though not an accomplished scholar, he was 'a kind-hearted, highly principled, honourable, manly fellow'. His writings on birds retain their value.

H. M. Whittell, *The literature of Australian birds* (Perth, 1954).   A. H. CHISHOLM

WHINHAM, JOHN (1803-1886), educationist, was born on 3 August 1803 at Sharperton, Northumberland, England, son of Robert Whinham, farmer, and his wife Jane, née Arkle. At Holystone school he favoured classics and mathematics; self taught from 14, with the help of a Catholic priest he matriculated to the University of Dublin at 19 but was unable to attend it. He taught for twenty-five years in an elementary school at Ovingham near Newcastle upon Tyne, where he enjoyed the simple village life and married Mary, a gifted elocutionist; they had six daughters and two sons.

Whinham's capital was lost in the depression of 1848-49 but he later saved enough to migrate with his family to Australia. On 1 April 1852 they arrived in Adelaide in the *Athenian*; Whinham intended to farm, but he settled in Waymouth Street, later moving to Margaret Street where he began a school with three pupils. On 25 July 1853 he became assistant master at the Collegiate School of St Peter and considered starting a secondary school of his own. Next year his North Adelaide Grammar School opened in a one storey slate building in Ward Street, with one pupil. The numbers increased rapidly and without patronage or endowments he competed successfully with older foundations; annual fees were 55 guineas for boarders and 8-12 guineas for day pupils.

Whinham achieved repute for his school and made it one of the best known in Australia. It flourished until the 1870s when the attendance fluctuated between 200 and 300. He retired in 1873, handing over to his son Robert who built a new, larger college, costing £6000, on the corner of Jeffcott and Ward streets; it was opened as Whinham College on 22 September 1882.

Robert was killed by a fall from a horse on 10 October 1884 and John resumed the headmastership, but the shock of his son's death and ensuing heavy responsibilities hastened his own death from pulmonary phthisis on 13 March 1886 at North Adelaide. An Anglican, Whinham was buried in the North Road cemetery survived by his wife (d. 1891), one son and four daughters. For many years he had prepared the astronomical calculations for local newspapers. He was also a distinguished president of the Preceptors' Association in South Australia, which promoted teachers' professional status. After his death the school, which had made an outstanding contribution to the educational and cultural life of South Australia, declined in prestige and finally closed in 1898.

Register (Adel), 15 Mar 1886, 19 Oct 1928; *Advertiser* (Adel), 20 Mar 1886; R. J. Nicholas, Private and Denominational secondary schools of South Australia: their growth and development (M.Ed. thesis, Univ Melb, 1953).

R. J. NICHOLAS

WHISH, CLAUDIUS BUCHANAN (1827-1890), sugar-planter and civil servant, was born on 5 January 1827 in London, son of General Sir William Whish, Royal Artillery, and his wife Mary, née Hardwicke. In 1851 he gained a commission in the 14th Light Dragoons, served in India, where he had family connexions, and was interpreter and bazaar master for the regiment, officer in charge of public works in one of the native states, and assistant-quartermaster-general of cavalry on General Jacob's staff during the Persian campaign of 1856. He became a captain and in 1857 visited New South Wales and South Australia to buy cavalry remounts for the Indian army.

Australia must have impressed him for on 15 August 1862 he arrived in Queensland in the *Young Australia* and established the Oaklands sugar plantation at Caboolture. Though Whish was not the pioneer of the industry in Queensland, he raised a better crop than his main competitor, Louis Hope [q.v.], becoming the first sugar-planter to market commercial quantities and to produce high-quality rum. He was chairman of the local planters' association and, as he was experienced in non-European labour, he hired Pacific islanders. This made him unpopular among near-by townspeople and selectors, though after 1865 it helped to preserve his £5000 investment.

In 1867 Whish failed to win East Moreton in the Legislative Assembly, and in 1869 a select committee on Pacific island labour was told of whippings on his estate. This evidence gained little credence among the respectable. A justice of the peace and for many years an Anglican synodsman and diocesan councillor, he accepted a seat in the Legislative Council in June 1870. Though he was believed to be the first successful sugar-producer in Queensland, his estate lost money steadily and he resigned from the council in March 1872, sold his machinery and took a government position as surveyor of roads. Bankrupted in September 1873 with a deficiency of £5598, he was promoted inspector of road surveys for the southern division in 1875 and for the whole colony in 1880.

Late in 1889 Whish left for England on leave. He sailed in the *Quetta* which sank in Torres Strait on the night of 28 February 1890. His wife Anne, née Ker, whom he had married in Bombay about 1858, perished with him; they were survived by two sons and four daughters. He was one of the small but influential group of gentleman immigrants, such as George Dalrymple, H. M. Chester [qq.v.] and Hope, who left India after the mutiny to seek their fortunes in the newly separated tropical colony of Queensland.

E. Thorne, *The queen of the colonies* (Lond, 1876); *V&P* (LA Qld), 1869, 2, 60; C. T. Wood, 'Hope, Buhot, Whish', *Producers' Review* (Brisb), 15 July 1964, and 'The sugar industry as depicted in the Whish and Davidson diaries', *JRHSQ*, 3 (1965); Whish diaries (Oxley Lib, Brisb).

G. C. BOLTON

WHITE, CHARLES (1845-1922), editor and author, was born at Bathurst, New South Wales, eldest son of John Charles White, bank clerk and Methodist lay preacher, and his wife Myra, née Oakey, of Demerara, West Indies. In October 1859 his father bought the *Bathurst Free Press and Mining Journal* which the family owned until 1904.

Interested in writing, Charles taught himself shorthand while an apprentice on his father's paper; he was also a keen billiards player and became a champion in later life. As police roundsman for the *Free Press*, he reported the activities of the bushrangers John Gilbert, Ben Hall, Frank Gardiner [qq.v.] and John Vane, and began to collect 'oldest inhabitant (and convict) stories'. When he married Sarah Beattie at Young on 3 May 1871 he gave his occupation as printer; her younger sister Mary became the mother of Dame Mary Gilmore. On the death of their father in 1884, he became editor of the *Free Press*; his brother Gloster became business manager.

As editor White used the *Free Press* to support free trade and Federation. In 1896 during the People's Federal Convention at Bathurst he opened the paper to any pro-Federation advocate, including 'Price Warung' [q.v. William Astley]. In 1901 the *Free Press* became so critical of leading protectionists and the movement that it stirred much local antagonism to White; as a result in 1902 he sold his share of the paper to Gloster and moved to Randwick. In 1906 he became first editor of the *Farmer and Settler*, a rural paper published in Sydney and founded that year by his son Percy.

An historian at heart, White meticulously collected material for future use: he discussed the bushranging days at length with Nat Gould in Bathurst, and later was visited by Vane who gave him first-hand information of the hold-ups he had participated in. Under his pseudonym, 'The Chatterer', White compiled full-scale histories of the Aboriginals, convicts, bushrangers and early governors which were serialized in the *Free Press* in 1888-93. In Bathurst in 1889 he published *Early Australian History. Convict Life in New South Wales and Van Diemen's Land*, Parts I & II, and in 1891 Part IV, *The Story of the Bushrangers*. He later published various parts of his *Early Australian History* separately and under different titles, including a *History of Australian Bushranging* (1900-1903). He also edited *John Vane, bushranger: [an autobiography]*. 'The Story of the Blacks' was not published although it reached galley-proofs. In 1917-19 'The Rise & Progress of the West' (sometimes called 'The Story of Wheat') was serialized in the *Farmer and Settler*. His work shows painstaking scholarship and a fluent, uncluttered style free of romanticism. He supervised the Bathurst editions of his books which were printed on his own presses.

White suffered the tragic loss of all his records in a fire at his Randwick home and soon after moved to Springwood. Aged 77, he died of pernicious anaemia on 22 December 1922 at his home in Mosman; survived by his wife, a son and two daughters, he was buried in the Methodist cemetery, Gore Hill. His estate was valued for probate at £618.

M. Gilmore, *Old days, old ways* (Syd, 1934); *Biblionews*, Apr 1966; *Bathurst Times*, 5 Apr 1917; Bathurst Hist Soc Archives.

THEO BARKER

WHITE, FRANCIS MALONEY (1819-1888), architect, was born in December 1819 in London, eldest son of John Charles White, merchant. Educated at King's College, London, and in Rouen, France, he served articles with S. W. Dawkes and then worked under the London architect Charles Fowler for a year before touring Europe. After a brief return to England he migrated to Australia, arriving in Adelaide in 1848. In 1849 he rode to Melbourne, visited Hobart Town and then went to New South Wales where he settled for a short time on the Edward River. Early in 1851 he overlanded his stock to Melbourne, sold it, and commenced architectural practice. His first

work in Melbourne was the Tudor style Scots Church manse in Collins Street. In 1852 he was architect for the National Model and Training School, but he was replaced next year on the grounds of dilatoriness.

In 1853 White won second prize in the competition for the proposed Legislative Council Chamber. Next year the commission for the new University of Melbourne building made his reputation; he was remembered for it long after his other work was forgotten. His plan provided for a quadrangle with cloisters and an ornamental front, all in the Tudor style; at first only two sides were erected and the impressive north side was completed in 1857—the south side was not built. The original portions of the building are adorned with the coats of arms of the members of the Buildings Committee of 1856.

White designed several flour-mills including the bluestone section of Dight's Mill on the Yarra River (1855) and at least one of W. Degraves's [q.v.] mills in the Kyneton district (1856). His commercial work included the Melbourne office of William Degraves & Co., Flinders Lane (1860), F. A. Clough & Co. woolstores and the Australian Mutual Provident Society Building, both in Collins Street, and the Colonial Bank of Australasia, Camperdown (1869). His Renaissance revival warehouse in Flinders Lane for L. Stevenson and Sons (1865) is the finest example of his known designs in the classical manner, while his Bank of New Zealand in Collins Street shows his design at its most extravagant. His domestic work included mansions for the wife of S. H. Officer [q.v.], for C. W. Simson (Carmyle, Toorak) and for F. W. Prell (Iona, Toorak). His most important public position was as architect to the Melbourne Hospital, Lonsdale Street, where a range of sober buildings in the Tudor style attested to his competence in that mode. His only known church design is St Luke's, South Melbourne (Emerald Hill), where the foundation stone was laid in 1857.

A foundation member of the Victorian Institute of Architects, in 1859 White contributed a two-part paper 'On Ventilation' to its monthly meetings. His office was at 10 Elizabeth Street. Two younger architects are known to have served their articles with him: J. A. B. Koch, and his son Alfred (b. 1862) who became his partner in 1884 and continued the practice when White died. Shy and retiring, White was a capable architect seeking to integrate the new developments in building technology and services into his restrained conservative style. Within the profession he was affectionately called 'the Field Marshal', and Lloyd Tayler [q.v.]

remembered him in 1900 as 'a warm generous friend, and an unassuming, though able and honourable professional brother'.

A member of the Melbourne Club, White died of heart disease on 14 September 1888 at his residence, William Street, St Kilda. Buried in the Baptist section of St Kilda cemetery he was survived by his son and five daughters—their mother was Harriett Broddell (d. 1914) with whom White had lived from about 1859 and whom he acknowledged in his will as guardian of their children. His estate was valued for probate at £32,081.

A. Sutherland et al, *Victoria and its metropolis*, 2 (Melb, 1888); J. Smith (ed), *Cyclopedia of Victoria*, 1 (Melb, 1903); J. A. Allan, *The old Model School ... 1852-1904* (Melb, 1934); E. Scott, *A history of the University of Melbourne* (Melb, 1936); G. Blainey, *A centenary history of the University of Melbourne* (Melb, 1957); *A'sian Builder and Contractor's News*, 29 Jan, 23 Apr 1859; *Argus*, 15 Sept 1888; *Building, Engineering and Mining J*, 5 May 1900.   GEORGE TIBBITS

WHITE, GEORGE BOYLE (1802-1876), surveyor and diarist, was born on 24 August 1802 at Bantry, Cork, Ireland, elder son of Boyle White, R.N., and his wife Honoria, née O'Sullivan. His father, reputedly a cousin of the earl of Bantry, died in 1806 and in 1814 his mother married George Henry Green, paymaster in the 57th Regiment. He left Croydon School in 1814 and was at Startforth Hall School near Barnard Castle, Yorkshire, from 1815; he had some skill in navigation and probably went to sea, visiting Sydney in 1819 and China in 1821-22. He returned to Sydney in the *Cawdrey* on 7 January 1826; his family had arrived the day before.

A month later White was appointed a third-class clerk in the Colonial Secretary's Office at a salary of £100 but resigned when he saw no prospect of advancement; his letter of 30 December to the colonial secretary showed his abrasive style and resentment of his reduced social position and lack of influence, characteristics which later hardened into paranoid misanthropy. On 1 February 1827 he was appointed assistant surveyor in the Surveyor-General's Department and worked in the Hunter River district; he farmed and ran stock at Singleton, Maitland and Raymond Terrace at various times, uniformly without success. On 17 June 1830 at St Phillip's, Sydney, he married Maria Greig (d. 1856), daughter of James Mudie [q.v.].

As a surveyor White impressed (Sir) Thomas Mitchell [q.v.] who chose him for his expedition in 1831-32 to the Barwon

River. He kept a detailed journal, the earliest surviving substantial fragment of the diary which he wrote for at least fifty years. The journal, often libellous, sometimes scurrilous, is a daily commentary on life, personalities and events in the colony in general and the Hunter Valley in particular from 1843 to 1875 (with some gaps). White surveyed much of the Hunter Valley and in 1844-45 the river itself. He continued until mid-1853, being promoted surveyor in 1838; he suffered a lean period in 1844-46 as a licensed surveyor, but survived with his job intact despite financial difficulties in the mid-1840s which led to his first insolvency in 1847. On 1 July 1853 he retired and after two years was granted a pension. A magistrate, in 1846 he was auditor of the Australian Union Benefit Society.

In 1858-59 White represented Northumberland and Hunter in the Legislative Assembly; as chairman of a select committee to inquire into the management of the Survey Department he elicited evidence central to any study of the department or land settlement in New South Wales in the first half of the century. His last years were spent in increasing ill health and declining fortune at Raymond Terrace. Again insolvent in 1867, in 1873 he made an offer of 6d. in the pound. He died of 'disease of stomach etc' at the home of his son Timothy at Double Bay, Sydney, on 25 May 1876 and was buried in Rookwood cemetery without religious rites. He was survived by two sons and a daughter.

V&P (LA NSW), 1858, 1, 937, 3, 759; White papers (ML); Insolvency files 1691/2, 8045/6 (NSWA).   M. J. SACLIER

WHITE, JAMES (1828-1890), pastoralist and racehorse owner and breeder, was born on 19 July 1828 at Stroud, New South Wales, eldest son of James White and his wife Sarah, née Crossman. His father had arrived in Sydney on 24 July 1826 in the *Fairfield* as an overseer for the Australian Agricultural Co., and acquired land in the Hunter River district including Edinglassie, near Muswellbrook. James was educated at The King's School, Parramatta, and by Rev. John Gregor [q.v.] at West Maitland. In 1842 his father died leaving goods valued for probate at £15,000 and real estate, to be divided equally among his seven sons and two daughters. James returned home to manage Edinglassie, Timor, and Boorrooma on the Barwon River.

In partnership with his brothers Francis and George, James leased Belltrees, near Scone, from W. C. Wentworth [q.v.] in

1848, bought it in 1853 and later added the adjoining Waverley station. From 1848 they acquired other freehold property in the Hunter River district including Merton and Dalswinton. About 1860 White bought the freehold estate, Martindale, near Muswellbrook, where he lived in the 1860s and made well known for fattening cattle. He was a magistrate and in 1864 a sheep director for Merriwa.

In December White was elected by a large majority to the Legislative Assembly for the Upper Hunter, despite abuse from his opponent Thomas Dangar. In favour of free selection, railway expansion and taxes on luxuries, he confessed himself 'not quite equal to grapple' with the education question. On 8 May 1868 he resigned from parliament and visited England and the United States of America; while in England he and his brothers bought Segenhoe in the Hunter Valley. Soon after his return, he was defeated for the Upper Hunter by J. M. Creed [q.v.].

About 1873 White bought Cranbrook, Rose Bay, from the estate of R. Towns [q.v.] and engaged J. Horbury Hunt [q.v.] to carry out large extensions. He filled it with 'costly art treasures': European porcelain and pictures by Italian, German and English artists.

In 1875 he sold Martindale to his brother Edward in consideration of an annuity of £5000 to himself and £2500 to his wife. On 14 July 1874 he was appointed to the Legislative Council; next year he was elected to the local Royal Society and became a founding member of the Linnean Society of New South Wales. A representative commissioner for New South Wales at the Philadelphia International Exhibition in 1876, he was also a commissioner for the exhibitions in Paris (1878) and Melbourne (1880) and the Colonial and Indian Exhibition, London (1886). In the 1880s he was a vice-president of the Agricultural Society of New South Wales, the Horticultural Society of New South Wales and the Union Club, a committee-man of the Animals' Protection Society of New South Wales, a member of the Warrigal Club and a director and sometime chairman of the Mercantile Bank of Sydney.

A long-time committee-man of the Australian Jockey Club, White was chairman in 1880 and 1883-90 and did much to promote racing. His first two horses were Goulburn and Hotspur, steeplechasers which won many cross-country races. In the mid-1870s he bought Kirkham, near Camden, where Hunt built him two houses, one a 'French inspired fairy castle'. Kirkham became his main horse-stud, although he also bred horses at Segenhoe and paid high prices for promising youngsters, such as 1200 guineas for Martini-Henri. He also built the lavish Newmarket Stables at Randwick where his horses were trained by Michael Fennelly (d. 1887) and later by Tom Payten. In 1876 White bought Chester from E. K. Cox [q.v.] and next year began a sensational twelve-year career on the turf when Chester won the Victoria Racing Club's Derby-Melbourne Cup double; the stallion had 19 wins from 29 starts and was only 3 times unplaced before becoming top sire. White won five A.J.C. Derbys in 1884-89, five A.J.C. Sires' Produce Stakes in 1885-90, five V.R.C. St Legers in 1886-90 and six V.R.C. Derbys in 1877-90, among most other important races. Out of 302 rides for him T. Hales [q.v.] rode 137 winners. White's other great horses included Martini-Henry, winner of the Victoria Derby-Melbourne Cup double; Abercorn, who raced against Carbine and whose wins included the A.J.C. Sires' Produce Stakes and the A.J.C. Derby (1887), the Australasian Champion Stakes and A.J.C. St Leger (1888) and the Metropolitan (1889); Democrat, winner of the Sydney Cup-Metropolitan double (1878); and Derby winners Nordenfeldt, Trident, Ensign, Dreadnought and Singapore. Possessed of 'the most consummate judgment in all matters of breeding, training, and racing thoroughbred horses', he was reputed to have collected over £121,000 in stakes from 66 horses winning 252 races. White was also a heavy punter and reputedly won £25,000 on Martini-Henry's double, but was popular with the racing public as he never tried to bluff them. He planned to win the Epsom Derby and bred three colts by Chester to English time. In England they were supervised by S. A. Stephen [q.v.] but only Kirkham carried White's pale blue and white colours in Sainfoin's Derby in 1890 and was unplaced. He sent another contingent to England next year.

Early in 1890 White retired as chairman of the A.J.C. and in April sold most of his racehorses for some 16,745 guineas, Titan bringing the record price of 4600 guineas. In 1889 he had given twenty blood mares to his nephews at Belltrees. He died of heart disease at Cranbrook on 13 July 1890 and was buried in the Anglican section of Waverley cemetery. He was survived by his wife Emily Elizabeth, daughter of James Arndell, whom he had married at Merton, New South Wales, on 9 July 1856; she shared his love of racing. His estate was valued for probate at almost £350,000 and willed to his brothers, nephews, and his wife who inherited Cranbrook, Kirkham, £5000 and an annuity of £2500. On 4 August 1896 at the Woollahra Presbyterian Church Emily White married Captain William

Scott, M.R.C.V.S., aged 37 and principal veterinary surgeon in the New South Wales Defence Forces; she died on 28 October 1897 at Melrose, Roxburghshire, Scotland.

White's brother FRANCIS (1830-1875) was born at Ravensworth, New South Wales, on 21 April 1830. Educated at Maitland by Gregor and Rev. Thomas Aitken he qualified as a surveyor before returning to Edinglassie. On 6 July 1853 he married Mary Hannah Cobb of Anambah, and lived at Belltrees for ten years before settling at Edinglassie, his share of his father's estate. Genial and generous he was 'a principal mover in all public matters' in Muswellbrook, where he was chairman of the bench of magistrates and president of the hospital board and the agricultural society. In 1875 he was elected to the Legislative Assembly for the Upper Hunter but died suddenly of fever at Edinglassie on 4 May. He was survived by his wife, a daughter and six sons, of whom the most notable were James Cobb of Edinglassie, a well-known breeder of Aberdeen Angus cattle, and Henry Luke of Belltrees.

E. Digby (ed), *Australian men of mark*, 1 (Syd, 1889); *Beautiful Sydney* (Syd, 1896); G. N. Griffiths, *Some northern homes of N.S.W.* (Syd, 1954); D. M. Barrie, *The Australian bloodhorse* (Syd, 1956); M. Cavanough and M. Davies, *Cup Day* (Melb, 1960); *Maitland Mercury*, 9 July 1853, 18 Aug 1860, 6, 15, 20 Dec 1864; *SMH*, 6 May 1875, 12 Apr, 14 July 1890; *T&CJ*, 6 May 1875, 19 July 1890; *Bulletin*, 30 Apr 1881, 10 Nov 1883; *Argus*, 7 Feb, 14 July 1890; *Australasian*, 19 July 1890.

MARTHA RUTLEDGE

WHITE, JAMES CHARLES (1809-1894), pastoral superintendent, was born on 28 October 1809 at Jaffna, Ceylon, son of Abraham White, military surgeon, and Theodora Elizabeth Rodolphina, daughter of Commander Frederick Willem von Drieberg. Failing to obtain a commission in the British army, White accompanied C. D. Riddell [q.v.] to New South Wales, arriving in Sydney on 15 August 1830 in the *Ceylon*. He joined the Van Diemen's Land Co. and soon became superintendent of stock to the Australian Agricultural Co. at Port Stephens. On 13 May 1837 he married Sarah Elizabeth, only child of Robert Hoddle [q.v.]. Her death in childbirth on 3 October 1841 left three sons, the eldest of whom was Robert Hoddle Drieberg White [q.v.]. In 1848 he married Ann, sister of J. D. Macansh [q.v.]. They had three sons and one daughter.

In December 1841 White became superintendent of Glanmire station at Bathurst and a magistrate on 10 September 1844.

Later he was associated with T. S. Mort [q.v.], and about 1850 rejoined the A.A. Co. In 1858 he managed Robert Tooth's [q.v.] Queensland stations, Jondaryan, Goomburra, Callandoon and Pikedale. Resident at Jondaryan where he built a famous woolshed, he joined the Drayton bench. Seeking independence he bought Widgee from Tooth in November 1862, but lost £5000 and all his stock through disease. Later he was appointed police magistrate at Warwick, Dalby and Drayton-Toowoomba in turn; he retired on 16 October 1867. Apart from an overseas trip in 1870 sponsored by a group of pastoralists, his working days were over.

White was stern, imperious and unyielding; he attracted controversy. In a duel with a bench colleague at Bathurst, White declined to return his opponent's fire because he had been drinking all night and was not 'fair game'. His report in 1854 on the use of the Port Stephens estate was partly responsible for an unfair view of P. P. King [q.v.] as the A.A. Co.'s commissioner. He was also said to have falsely accused Arthur Hannibal Macarthur of theft at Goomburra in the late 1850s. In 1862, in the suit *Beit v. Zahn*, White's alleged packing of the Drayton-Toowoomba bench to secure Zahn's conviction angered many. His posting at Warwick in 1866 was probably terminated by the political infighting of squatter-politicians.

In 1867-94 White was supported by his eldest son and visited his children in New South Wales, Queensland and New Zealand. He died as imperiously as he had lived; on 28 October 1894 he was lost with 124 others when the New Zealand-bound *Wairarapa* struck Great Barrier Island. He was said to have given up his chance of rescue for someone 'who still had their life to live'.

PD (LA Qld), 1866; R. H. Pocock, 'James Charles White', *Descent*, 5 (1971), pt 2; *Darling Downs Gazette*, 6, 27 Mar, 10 Apr, 1, 15, 22, 29 May, 12 June 1862; *Australasian*, 19 Jan 1895; A.A. Co. papers (ANU Archives).

DAVID DENHOLM

WHITE, ROBERT HODDLE DRIBERG (1838-1900), bank manager and politician, was born on 19 May 1838 at Stroud, New South Wales, elder son of James Charles White [q.v.] and his wife Sarah Elizabeth (d. 1843), only child of Robert Hoddle [q.v.] and his first wife Mary (d. 1862), née Staton. He spent 1846-49 with his Hoddle grandparents in Melbourne before going to school in Sydney.

In 1857 White became a junior clerk at £120 a year in the Bank of New South

Wales, Sydney. While accountant at the Deniliquin branch in March 1859 he pursued bushrangers who had stolen some £8000 from it; he recovered some of the money and acquired information which led to the arrest of William Lee, the leader. In 1860 White became agent for the bank at Toowoomba, Queensland, and in February 1862 was manager of the branch. On 2 May 1863 at St Philip's Church, Sydney, he married Eliza Jane, daughter of Rev. W. M. Cowper [q.v.].

A magistrate for Queensland from 1861, White became manager of the Rockhampton branch of the bank in April 1864. His spirited defence against five armed men at the Currie Hotel on the Gympie road on 19 April 1868 won him rewards from the Queensland government and townspeople. He became captain of the Rockhampton company of the Queensland Volunteer Rifle Brigade from September 1864. After conflict with some of his junior officers in May 1868, he reported the company for insubordination and tried to disband it; as a result Acting Surgeon Robertson challenged him to a duel; White resigned on 28 October. In March next year he returned to New South Wales as manager of the Mudgee branch of the bank. He was briefly relieving manager at Kyneton, Victoria, in 1874-75 and in 1877 opened the branch at Coonamble, New South Wales.

Living on expectations of inheriting his grandmother's property, White had run into debt through speculating; in 1869 he quarrelled with his grandfather after asking him for assistance. Learning of a deed of settlement, in August 1880 he sued Hoddle for his share of the property in Elizabeth Street, Melbourne, valued at £250,000 and settled originally on Hoddle's first wife and her children but later on his second wife Fanny. White accepted a compromise of £49,000 (half the accrued rent) and half the property.

He resigned from the Bank of New South Wales on 31 December, took his wife on a visit to England and later bought Tahlee House and estate, Port Stephens, from the Australian Agricultural Co. White represented Gloucester in the Legislative Assembly in 1882-87, supporting Sir Alexander Stuart's [q.v.] government. A New South Wales commissioner for the exhibitions in Melbourne (1880 and 1888), Calcutta (1883) and Adelaide (1887), he was a representative commissioner for the colony at the Colonial and Indian Exhibition, London, in 1886. He was appointed to the Legislative Council on 30 December 1887, was a member of the Aborigines Protection Board from 16 February 1893 and sat on the royal commission on fisheries in 1894-95.

White was popular with miners, selectors and graziers. He was a fellow of the Royal Colonial Institute and a foundation life member of the New South Wales branch of the Royal Geographical Society of Australasia. A member of the Union Club, he lived flamboyantly and his steam yacht *Kingfisher* graced Port Stephens and Port Jackson. He died in the Hospital for the Insane, Callan Park, Sydney, on 20 October 1900 and was buried in the Anglican section of South Head cemetery. He was survived by his wife, two sons and two daughters; his eldest daughter Lily married (Sir) William Portus Cullen. His estate was valued for probate at over £20,000.

E. Digby (ed), *Australian men of mark* (Syd, 1889); J. L. Chadban, *Stroud and the A.A. Co.* (Stroud, 1970); D. H. Johnson, *Volunteers at heart* (Brisb, 1975); R. H. Pocock, 'James Charles White', *Descent*, 5 (1971) pt 2; *Argus*, 3-7 Aug 1880; *Australasian*, 7, 14 Aug 1880; *T&CJ*, 5 Mar 1881, 17 Mar 1888; *Bulletin*, 9 Dec 1882, 25 June 1892; *SMH*, 30 Oct 1900; *Truth* (Syd), 28 Nov 1926; Board minutes 1857-68, and staff registers 1868-80 (Bank of NSW Archives, Syd).   JOHN ATCHISON

WHITE, SAMUEL (1835-1880), ornithologist, was born on 15 June 1835 at St John's Wood, London, son of John White, building contractor and Barbara, née Willingale. His father and uncle George migrated to South Australia, arriving at Holdfast Bay on 14 December 1836 in the *Tam O'Shanter*. John had chartered more than half the cargo space for his building materials and other provisions and had brought out as employees nine men, some with their families. Settling at Reed Beds, Fulham, at the mouth of the Torrens River, he prospered as a builder, farmer and station-owner. His wife and sons Samuel and William arrived in the *Taglioni* on 13 October 1842.

As a youth Samuel began observing, collecting and sketching birds. In the 1850s he managed his father's station, Tatiara, in the south-east. Able to pursue his ornithological interests after his father's death in 1860, next year he began a series of collecting expeditions. In 1863 he collected along the Murray River, and later in the area north of Lake Eyre; though forced to abandon a dray with his specimens, he brought back a wood swallow, *artamus cinereus* (*melanops*). In 1865 he was again seeking bird and insect specimens along the Murray. Later that year on an expedition west of Spencer Gulf, he found a new blue wren, *malurus callainus*, but lost all except two male specimens when a boat capsized. He forwarded the new *malurus* to John Gould [q.v.] in London. In 1867-68 he spent eighteen months with his brother William collecting in Queensland, New South Wales and Victoria. On 5 April 1869 at St Mary's Church, Morphett Vale, he married Martha Elsea Taylor and in July they sailed for England, where he met Gould. Next year he returned to Adelaide and presented to the South Australian Museum a collection of bird-skins from North Queensland, which he again visited in 1871 and in 1878-79, when he also cruised among the Torres Straits islands procuring specimens.

In April 1880 White sailed in his own vessel, the Elsea, to Sydney, where he left his family. He then sailed up the eastern coast. In the Aru Islands, Arafura Sea, he obtained species of birds of paradise; he traded guns, shot, powder, axes and other goods with the natives, but banned spirits. After collecting 800 to 1000 birds, trouble broke out with the crew. Ill, and with arsenic-damaged hands, he returned to Thursday Island, where he left the Elsea. His expedition, which he intended to resume, had cost him £5000. A few days after his return to Sydney, he died of pneumonia on 16 November, and was buried in Waverley cemetery. He was survived by his wife, two sons and a daughter and his estate was sworn for probate at £500.

White was intelligent and highly cultured, but bad luck had dogged him; he published nothing and made no lasting contribution to ornithology. Despite instructions in his will, the collection at his home, Wetunga, at Fulham, Adelaide, was dispersed after his death. He requested his executors to have his children educated in 'the protestant faith, and on no account have them sent to schools or churches where the Romish faith is taught'. A portrait of White in the uniform of a trumpeter in the Reed Beds Cavalry (c. 1860) is at Wetunga. His eldest son Samuel Albert (1870-1954) was a distinguished naturalist.

S. A. White, The life of Samuel White (Adel, 1920); R. Cockburn, Pastoral pioneers of South Australia, 2 (Adel, 1927); H. M. Whittell, The literature of Australian birds (Perth, 1954); Pioneers Assn of SA, The White collection (Adel, 1960); H. J. Finnis, Before the 'Buffalo' (Adel, 1964); E. P. Ramsay letters and papers (ML).   CHRIS CUNNEEN

WHITE, WILLIAM DUCKETT (1807-1893), pastoralist and politician, was born on 5 October 1807 at Moate Castle, County Westmeath, Ireland, son of William White, miller, and his wife Sarah, née Clibborn. He was related to T. S. Clibborn [q.v.]. Educated at Cork, he annoyed his Quaker parents by enlisting briefly in the army. He

joined Pikes Bank in Dublin, owned by an uncle, and in 1834 married Jane Simpson, daughter of a landowner from Cork. With financial help from his uncle he decided to migrate, and as an assisted migrant he reached Sydney with his wife and two children in the Royal Consort in November 1840. From January to March 1843 he taught in the Church of England school at Mangrove Creek near Gosford.

White bought land on the Richmond River but late in 1844 was forced out by flood losses. In 1844-48 he managed Beaudesert station, Moreton Bay District, for his cousin J. P. Robinson. With another cousin George Robinson, who later withdrew, he accumulated funds in 1849-50 to buy Beaudesert in 1851. By 1869 he held Tubber, Pimpama, Murryjerry, Beaudesert, Nindooinbah, Tweed Heads and Moreton, as well as town lands in Southport and Beenleigh. In 1855 he began building a house at Manly, Moreton Bay, called Lota after his wife's home in Ireland, and settled there in 1863.

White gave the freehold property Nindooinbah to his eldest son Ernest on his marriage to Annie Barker in 1867. In 1872 with Ernest and his second son Albert William (1847-1914) as partners, he took over the lease of Bluff Downs near Charters Towers, abandoned by William Hann as a sheep property. On the 400-square-mile block, expanded by subsequent leases, Albert as managing partner introduced Shorthorn cows in 1874 and Devon bulls in 1876. The cross proved particularly suitable to the rough, often dry, tropical basalt country and set the pattern for most of the herds in the region.

White had been a foundation member of the Queensland Club. After first declining, on 26 April 1861 he accepted appointment to the Legislative Council, but he was not interested in politics; he resigned in August 1880 and remained in public life only as a foundation member of the Bulimba Divisional Board and as a leading parishioner of Christ Church Anglican Church, Tingalpa. In retirement he remained the dominant partner in a family company, W. D. White and Sons, but began to lose heart when his wife died on 2 August 1887. He died on 11 August 1893 and was buried in Tingalpa cemetery.

Telegraph (Brisb), 12 Aug 1893; N. S. Pixley, William Duckett White of 'Beau Desert' and 'Lota' (RHSQ); G. E. Mylne reminiscences (Fryer Lib, Univ Qld).   E. M. ALLINGHAM
                                S. D. BASSINGTHWAIGHTE

WHITEHEAD, CHARLES (1804-1862), novelist, was born in London, eldest son of a well-to-do wine merchant. He was first employed as a clerk in a commercial house but determined to become a man of letters. In 1831 he received favourable notice for his poem, *The Solitary*, which was later re-published in a collection that included his fine sonnet 'As Yonder Lamp in My vacated Room'. In 1833 he married Mary Ann Loomes. He gained a precarious living by recounting the lives of English highwaymen, contributing to periodicals and editing *The Library of Fiction* (1836) for the publishers Chapman and Hall. The success of his biography of the hangman Jack Ketch led to the offer of a commission to write a serial with illustrations by Robert Seymour; he declined and suggested instead his young friend Charles Dickens [q.v.] who went ahead to write the *Pickwick Papers*. His play, *The Cavalier* (1825), was first performed in 1836 but his masterpiece was *Richard Savage, a romance of real life* (1831, 1842), a bitter novel which its admirers maintain has been consistently underrated.

Whitehead had been a member of the Mulberry Club and knew Douglas Jerrold, Charles Lamb, Thackeray and many other writers of the day. But despite his prolific output he led an increasingly miserable life. Drinking heavily, he became tiresome to some of his friends and was treated coldly by Dickens. His decision to migrate to Victoria was presumably a desperate throw. Described as a 'clerk', he arrived with his wife in the *Diana* at Melbourne on 17 March 1857. He already knew R. H. Horne [q.v.] and was befriended also by James Smith and Dr J. E. Neild [qq.v.] and others, who later recalled his 'pale face, attenuated figure, melancholy expression . . . and stooping gait'. His handwriting, minute but 'beautifully legible' and his scrupulous punctuation, revealed to them an 'almost morbid sensitiveness'. Gentle, nervous and very shy, 'the presence of even a stranger-child would embarrass him'.

Whitehead took lodgings in Melbourne and wrote for the *Examiner* and *Melbourne Punch*. He also became a leading contributor of articles and theatrical notices for *My Note Book*, which published 'Confessions of James Wilson', an episode from his book on Jack Ketch, and from 13 February 1858 'Emma Latham or Right at Last', a new work of considerable quality. His 'Spanish Marriage', a verse drama, appeared in the *Victorian Monthly Magazine* in July 1859.

Whitehead's small successes were not enough to keep him from poverty. Although very proud, he was forced to ask his friends for money but was elusive when they offered him shelter. His wife had become mentally deranged and died of pulmonary consumption on 21 August 1860 in the Yarra Bend Asylum. Whitehead was still writing comic verse for *Melbourne Punch* but turned increasingly to alcohol as a solace. Described as a 'respectable old man' (he was 56) he appeared in court charged with 'lunacy, caused through drink'. On meeting him in the street, Horne advised him to seek refuge in the Benevolent Asylum and told him that he had written an article for Thackeray's *Cornhill Magazine* setting out his sad circumstances; Whitehead was left with an 'agonizing sense of shame and humiliation'.

In early 1862 Whitehead applied vainly for admission to the asylum. Unbeknown to his friends, he was picked up exhausted in the street and taken to Melbourne Hospital where on 5 July 1862 he died, aged 58, of hepatitis and bronchitis. He was buried in a pauper's grave. Some weeks later his friends discovered his death but their efforts failed to have his body exhumed and reburied.

H. T. M. Bell, *A forgotten genius; Charles Whitehead* (Lond, 1894); J. Forster, *The life of Charles Dickens*, J. W. T. Ley ed (Lond, 1928); C. Turnbull, *Australian lives* (Melb, 1965); *My Note Book*, 3 (1858); *Examiner* (Melb), 23 Aug 1862; *Australasian*, 17 Nov 1866, 24 Sept 1870, 18 May 1889, 28 July 1894.

CLIVE TURNBULL*

WHITFIELD, GEORGE (1808-1864), gunsmith and taxidermist, was born in Belfast, Northern Ireland. He arrived in Sydney in the *Princess Victoria* on 4 February 1834 and was briefly in partnership with John Samuel Lambard in King Street. From October Whitfield advertised as a gunmaker and taxidermist at 3 King Street; he also made repairs on 'scientific principles, with despatch'. In 1839 he advertised 'G. Whitfield's Gun Manufactory and Repository of Stuffed Birds', and hoped to attract the attention of new migrants to his 'magnificent collection'. He had 'Flint Double Barrelled Guns' made to order for the brisk New Zealand trade.

After a heated public meeting in February 1842 demanding representative government, Whitfield advertised duelling pistols, being 'fearful that the gentlemen may not be in possession of the above very requisite articles to settle all differences of opinion'. In 1847 'The Old Rifleman', a noted firearms expert, recommended Whitfield's specially ordered 'Bush Carbines'; that year he supplied the ill-fated explorer E. B. C. Kennedy [q.v.]. His shop was illustrated in J. Fowles's [q.v.] *Sydney in 1848*.

With the increased demand for guns brought about by the gold rush, Whitfield, by then the largest firearms dealer in New

South Wales, advertised in April 1852 that he had various types of American revolvers for sale 'without which neither their lives or gold can be called safe' on the diggings. In 1854 he denied a rumour that he was going to retire from business. About 1858 he moved to 69 King Street, which became known as Cannon House.

In 1841 Whitfield had joined other sportsmen to form the Sydney Union Club of Australia for pigeon-shooting. An accomplished shot, he won a handsome pigeon gun at a match in 1842 and a silver cup valued at twenty guineas at the 1843 Anniversary Day shoot. In the 1860s he held shooting matches at his home, Ormeau View, now part of St Ignatius's College, Riverview. In 1862 he became armourer to the New South Wales Volunteers but his appointment was cancelled next year.

On 4 November 1864 Whitfield, aged 56, was shot dead at the door of his shop by a dismissed employee Patrick McGlinn. With George Hill [q.v.] as a witness, he was buried in the Anglican section of Camperdown cemetery. On 30 May 1853 at St Philip's Church, Sydney, he had married a widow Marianne Yeates, née Warman; she predeceased him on 11 April 1864. He was survived by two daughters of his first wife Margaret (d. 1851), and his business was carried on until 1866 by his nephew William John Whitfield, who was granted administration of his personalty, valued at £3000.

McGlinn was tried before Sir Alfred Stephen [q.v.] on 20 December; despite medical suggestions that he was insane, the jury found him guilty and he received sentence of death, but it was commuted to life imprisonment.

R. B. Shannon, *Colonial Australian gunsmiths* (Syd, 1967); *Syd Monitor*, 21 May, 18 Oct 1834, 9 Oct, 27 Dec 1839; *Australian*, 6 July 1841, 14 May 1842; *A'sian Chronicle*, 1 Mar 1842, 28 Jan 1843; *Bell's Life in Sydney*, 19 June 1847, 3 Apr 1852, 10 June 1854, 9 Oct 1858, 1 Sept 1860; *SMH*, 16 Feb 1861, 10 Jan, 8 Apr 1865; *Empire* (Syd), 5, 7, 8 Nov, 21 Dec 1864; *ISN*, 16 Nov 1864; Surveyor-general, Miscellaneous papers 7/2720 *and* Col Sec letters 1863, no 5120, 7138, 1864, no 128 (NSWA).

R. B. SHANNON

WHITTON, JOHN (1820-1898), engineer, was born near Wakefield, Yorkshire, England, son of James Whitton, land agent, and his wife Elizabeth, née Billington. Articled for seven years to John Billington, of Wakefield, he gained engineering and architectural experience preparing plans and tenders for railway construction and waterworks. In 1847 he was engineer for the Manchester, Sheffield and Lincoln railway, and in 1852-56 supervised the building of the Oxford, Worcester and Wolverhampton line. In 1854 he was elected a member of the Institution of Civil Engineers, London, and on 27 March 1856 was appointed engineer-in-chief at a salary of £1500 to lay out and superintend the construction of railways in New South Wales. With his wife Elizabeth, née Fowler, whom he had married about 1856 at Ecclesfield Church, Yorkshire, he arrived in Melbourne in the *Royal Charter* in December and reached Sydney on the fourteenth.

Whitton found in New South Wales 23 miles of 4 ft. 8½ ins. gauge railway, 4 locomotives, 12 passenger carriages and 40 trucks. In January 1857 before the Legislative Assembly select committee on the sole commissioner of railways incorporation bill, he vainly advocated conversion to the 5 ft. 3 ins. gauge adopted in Victoria and South Australia, and the extension of the railway from Redfern to Hyde Park in the city. He reorganized accounting and costing and took charge of the rolling stock, line maintenance and workshop departments. He resisted Governor Denison's proposal to construct 4000 miles of light, narrow-gauge tramways to be worked by horses and in the 1860s was constantly hampered by the government's uncritical acceptance of the lowest tenders for railway construction.

In April 1865 allegations of fraud were made against Whitton and his brother-in-law Sir John Fowler, an engineer and inspector of railway materials bought in England by the New South Wales government; the charges were proved groundless by W. C. Mayne [q.v.], agent-general for New South Wales. The 1870 select committee on railway extension chaired by (Sir) William Macleay [q.v.] recommended the construction of cheap narrow-gauge railways, necessitating a break of gauge within the colony, as well as at the border; estimates were prepared but Whitton, determined to sabotage the committee's recommendation, suspended all surveys and new work.

With the aid of E. C. Cracknell [q.v.] he overcame the engineering problems, partly caused by the government's cheese-paring, in building the Blue Mountains line; it included two great zigzags and was opened on 4 April 1876. In 1880-85 the unprecedented growth in railways, one thousand miles of new track and nine million more passengers, exposed existing inadequacies in administration and exacerbated the friction between Whitton and Commissioner C. A. Goodchap [q.v.]. The 1884 royal commission into railway bridges exonerated Whitton of the charges of faulty design and of using inferior materials. In 1888 Sir Henry Parkes's [q.v.] Government Railways Act reorganized the department and Goodchap's subsequent resignation made Whitton's position easier.

In 1886 and 1887 he had submitted drawings for a proposed suspension bridge across Sydney Harbour from Dawes Battery to Milson's Point. On 1 May 1889 the Hawkesbury River bridge was opened; it was the final link in the railway system from Brisbane through Sydney to Melbourne and Adelaide and Whitton had fought for adequate finance for it. He was a member of the Hunter River floods commission 1869-70, the Sydney, City and Suburban Sewage and Health Board 1875-77, and the Board for Opening Tenders for Public Works 1875-87; he was a New South Wales commissioner for the Melbourne International Exhibition in 1880.

Granted a years leave on 29 May 1889, Whitton retired on 31 May 1890 with a pension of £675, and visited England in 1892. He had supervised the laying of 2171 miles of track on which no accident had occurred attributable to defective design or construction. Parkes regarded him as 'a man of such rigid and unswerving integrity, a man of such vast grasp, that however his faults may occasionally project themselves into prominence, it would be difficult to replace him by a man of equal qualifications'. Survived by his wife, one son and two daughters, he died of cardiac disease on 20 February 1898 at Mittagong, and was buried in the cemetery of St Thomas's Church of England, North Sydney. His estate was valued for probate at £10,396.

J. Rae, Thirty-five years on the New South Wales railways (Syd, 1898); Dept of Railways, The railways of New South Wales 1855-1955 (Syd, 1955); V&P (LA NSW), 1859-60, 3, 239, 1892-93, 3, 77; PD (NSW), 1887, 1890; NSW Railway and Tramway Mag, 1 Dec 1920; R. L. Wettenhall, 'Early railway management legislation in New South Wales', Tas Univ Law Review, July 1960; T&CJ, 14 Sept 1878; Bulletin, 1 Sept 1883; Sydney Mail, 26 Feb 1898; Australasian, 5 Apr 1890; Old Times, July 1903; I. M. Laszlo, Railway policies and development in northern New South Wales 1846-1889 (M.A. thesis, Univ New England, 1956); Parkes letters (ML).   C. C. SINGLETON*

WHITTY, ELLEN (1819-1892), best known as Mother Vincent, Mercy Sister, was born on 3 March 1819 near Oilgate in County Wexford, Ireland, daughter of William Whitty and his wife Johanna, née Murphy. At 19 Ellen joined the Sisters of Mercy, a Roman Catholic Order founded in 1831 for education and social work. Influenced by the foundress Catherine McAuley who prepared her for religious profession, she was intelligent, quick and sure in judgment and within a decade was elected to the highest post in the Order as Reverend Mother of the Dublin Headhouse. She coped with the burden of social work resulting from the famine of the 1840s and organized the preparation of Sisters to go with the flood of emigrants. In 1854 Fr Robert Whitty, her brother, was vicar-general to Cardinal Wiseman at Westminster, and through him and Fr (later Cardinal) Manning, the British government invited her to send Sisters to nurse the wounded in the Crimea. After the war she established homes for neglected children and for unmarried mothers.

In 1860 Mother Vincent and five Sisters were invited by Bishop James Quinn [q.v.] to become the first women religious in the newly formed diocese of Queensland. She looked forward to this missionary venture, and the reluctance of her community to free her was overcome by the command of Archbishop Cullen [q.v.]. They arrived in Australia in the Donald Mackay in April 1861. Mother Vincent's problems in Queensland stemmed partly from the trend towards centralized and secular state education, but more from the bishop's autocracy. She wanted to have her schools independent yet adapted to a pluralist society and so open to all creeds; but Quinn, unlike other bishops, wished her to graft the convent schools on to the state system, preserving the right to choose teachers and texts. She eventually agreed.

Mother Vincent was unable to tolerate the degree of control which the bishop sought over purely conventual matters. The tension resulting when he demoted her to the ranks in 1865 could have wrecked her foundation or forced her to withdraw but for her profound spirituality. In 1870 on Quinn's instructions she returned to Ireland to recruit nuns and he appointed her assistant to the Queensland head of the Order, an office which she retained until her death.

Her schools flourished though some of her projects did not, notably a hospital and work with Aboriginals. At her death, twenty-six Mercy schools, mainly along the coastline to Townsville, had 222 Sisters with 7000 pupils. At Nudgee there was a Mercy Training College for teachers. Mother Vincent had commenced a secondary school (All Hallows') many years before the state entered this field. She duplicated in Brisbane the types of social work she had pioneered in Dublin, and provided a link between all forms of service in regular home visitation. She died in Brisbane on 9 March 1892 and was buried in Nudgee cemetery. Her work has stood the test of a century of change.

M. T. A. Carroll, *Leaves from the annals of the Sisters of Mercy*, 1-4 (New York, 1881-88); M. X. O'Donoghue, *Mother Vincent Whitty* (Melb, 1972).   EILEEN M. O'DONOGHUE

WHITWORTH, ROBERT PERCY (1831-1901), journalist and author, was born at Torquay, Devonshire, England, son of John Whitworth, engineer, and his wife Ann, née Dawson. He was brought up in Lancashire and Cheshire and was a barrister's clerk when he married Margaret Rivers Smith on 9 September 1854 at Manchester Cathedral. Next year they migrated to Sydney where, according to his own account, his activities included acting—he reputedly played Laertes to G. V. Brooke's [q.v.] Hamlet—and horse-breaking in the Hunter River district. He joined the staff of the *Empire* in Sydney and later began several short-lived magazines. He became a riding-master but returned to journalism after a severe fall.

In 1864 Whitworth arrived in Melbourne after some time in Queensland, and with F. F. Bailliere began a series of gazetteers of various Australian colonies. In Melbourne he worked with the *Age*, the *Argus* and the *Daily Telegraph* and for a time edited the *Australian Journal*. He was a proprietor and editor of *Town Talk* in the late 1870s and contributed to *Melbourne Punch* and other magazines. He wrote several plays, one of the most successful being the farce, 'Catching a Conspirator', in 1867. For many years he was one of Marcus Clarke's [q.v.] boon companions and in 1880 was closely involved with him in the adaptation of a political farce, 'The Happy Land', which satirized the government of (Sir) Graham Berry [q.v.]. The only surviving manuscript of the text is in Clarke's handwriting but bears both his name and Whitworth's. They also combined in 'Reverses', a comedy of manners which was never performed. Whitworth was a pallbearer at Clarke's funeral.

He spent at least four years in New Zealand and was living in Dunedin in 1870. He was a reporter for the *Otago Daily Times* and as 'The Literary Bohemian' contributed 'clever and witty' pieces to the *Otago Witness*. Whitworth's pamphlet, published in Dunedin in 1870, describing the possibilities of the Martin's Bay settlement on the west coast of Otago, earned him a bonus of £50 from the Otago Provincial Council. He later used his knowledge of the Maoris to write *Hine-Ra, or The Maori Scout...* (Melbourne, 1887).

Whitworth was a prolific miscellaneous writer. He published successful collections of his short stories: in 1872 *Spangles and Sawdust* and *Australian Stories Round the* Camp Fire, and in 1893, with W. A. Windus, *Shimmer of Silk: A Volume of Melbourne Cup Stories*. He wrote several novels and edited collections of stories. He compiled a *Popular Handbook of the Land Acts of Victoria, New South Wales, South Australia, and Queensland* (1872), *The Official Handbook & Guide to Melbourne...* (1880) and the second (biographical) volume of *Victoria and its Metropolis: past and present* (1888). He wrote a cantata, *Under the Holly* (1865), and *A Short History of The Eureka Stockade* (1891), and edited and contributed to several miscellanies. His wide knowledge of life in the city, bush, goldfields and theatre is reflected in his work.

A very well-known Melbourne journalist in his prime, he was described by Randolph Bedford in his later years as a 'faded Apollo'. He died of apoplexy at Prahran on 31 March 1901, aged 69 and 14 weeks, almost forgotten as a writer but lamented by a few as a 'Bohemian of the spontaneous type—not the factitious'. Buried in the Melbourne cemetery, he was survived by two sons and a daughter, all born after 1867.

R. Bedford, *Naught to thirty-three* (Syd, 1944); B. Elliott, *Marcus Clarke* (Oxford, 1958); *Argus*, 1 Apr 1901; *Table Talk*, 4 Apr 1901; *Otago Daily Times*, 11 Apr 1901; *Bulletin*, 13 Apr 1901.   HELEN K. ALMANZI

WHYTE, JAMES (1820-1882), pastoralist, politician and civil servant, was born on 30 March 1820 near Greenlaw, Edinburgh, son of George Whyte (d. 1836), captain in the Yeomanry, and his wife Jessie, née Walker. In June 1832 the family arrived in Van Diemen's Land in the *Rubicon* and settled at Kelvin Grove, Cross Marsh. In 1837-52 Whyte was in Victoria and with his brothers was a pioneer of Coleraine. Later he became a partner in a large property at Clunes on which gold was discovered. He returned to Tasmania enriched by gold royalties.

In Hobart Town Whyte failed to win the seat of Brighton in 1854 but in 1856 was elected to the Legislative Council for Pembroke. He served on a number of parliamentary committees and in 1857 became a member without portfolio of the short-lived T. G. Gregson [q.v.] ministry. On 20 January 1863 he became premier. His government was noted for its road and bridge-building, authorizing the formation of a company to construct and operate a railway from Launceston to Deloraine, reforms in the public service and courage in pursuing unpopular financial policies. It fell in November 1866 when his fiscal proposals, which included a property and income tax, were thrown out. Despite his failure to solve the financial difficulties of the colony, Whyte's term as premier had been the longest since self-government. He was chairman of committees in 1868-75. Tall and with a large black beard, he has been described as 'a public man possessing a strong reformist urge rather than an ambitious politician or careerist'.

Whyte contributed notably to the welfare of the colony with his work for the eradication of scab in sheep. Drawing heavily on his Victorian experience, he gave evidence in 1869 before a select committee; against much opposition he helped to frame and introduce a bill to enforce preventive measures. Chief inspector of sheep in 1870-82, he clung to the position despite the 1870 Act precluding holders of offices of profit under the Crown from election to either House. In 1876 he retired from parliament. In 1880 he reported that scab was 'extinct amongst Tasmanian sheep'.

Whyte represented Tasmania at a conference of inspectors of stock in Sydney in 1874, and another in 1877, to consider improving telegraphic communications with England. He was appointed a magistrate in 1857, a member of the Tasmanian Council of Education in 1870 and of the Board of Education in 1876; he was also a fellow of the Royal Society of Tasmania. An active Presbyterian, he was a trustee of Church property and a generous benefactor of the Church and charities. He was one of the original proprietors of the *Tasmanian Daily News*.

Whyte married three times: first on 3 January 1852 to Sarah, only daughter of Thomas Wilkinson of Bothwell, who died in childbirth in November; second in May 1857 to Elizabeth (d. 1865), eldest daughter of T. G. Gregson, and third on 25 June 1868 to Elizabeth, daughter of Dr John Coverdale [q.v.] of New Town. Aged 62, he died in his home in Runnymede Street, Hobart, on 20 August 1882, survived by his only son James Wilkinson. His estate was sworn for probate at £386. A river on the western Tasmanian coast commemorates him.

J. Fenton, A *history of Tasmania* (Hob, 1884); *Cyclopedia of Tasmania*, 1 (Hob, 1900); F. C. Green (ed), A *century of responsible government 1856-1956* (Hob, 1956); V&P (HA Tas), 1869 (96), 1870 (31, 43), 1875 (25), 1877 (26, 28), 1880 (106), 1882 (81); *Examiner* (Launc), 5 Aug 1856; *Mercury*, 8 Sept 1866, 27 Mar 1876, 22 Aug 1882; correspondence file under James Whyte (TA).   NEIL SMITH

WHYTE, PATRICK (1820-1893), headmaster, was born at Mallow, County Cork,

Ireland, son of Patrick Tabernarius Whyte, baker and draper, and his wife Margaret, née Hogan. He entered Trinity College, Dublin, in 1840 as a sizar and later worked as a government civil engineer, an instructor in the school of civil engineering at the college and as head of a private school.

In 1853 Whyte migrated to Victoria and worked as a land surveyor for eighteen months. After a brief period at St Patrick's College, East Melbourne, in March 1855 he began, as an assistant teacher, his long association with the state education system's Model Schools. Lacking a teaching qualification, he was required by Arthur Davitt [q.v.], principal of the Model and Normal schools, to enter teacher training in May 1855. Whyte topped the first examination for classification in January 1856 and established himself as an outstanding member of the National school system. He survived the retrenchment that followed the financial recession at the end of the 1850s, and in 1863 was appointed headmaster of the Central Common School, Spring Street, in succession to T. H. Smith. On 1 November 1853 Whyte had married Catherine Frances McMullin; she died on 3 June 1865, and on 10 July 1866 at Brunswick he married Jane Pullar (d. 1916), a Model School teacher in charge of the girls' and infants' schools; she continued teaching until his death; they had six daughters and two sons.

Whyte promoted classical studies and in a letter to the Board of Education in 1864 'regretted that after taking several promising lads through ... our programme we were unable to conduct them further by preparing them for the University'. He thought that 'they should have the facility of completing their education at the best of the Common Schools'. In 1869, assisted by a scholarship, the first pupil from his school entered the University of Melbourne as a graduating student. The state school curriculum was attacked in the minister's 1876 report, in which he deplored that 'any school situated in a populous and thriving locality should restrict the subjects taught' and cited Whyte's school as one of two notable exceptions.

From 1870 until 1893 a stream of ambitious and talented pupils from the 'Old Model School' entered the professions and business, justifying the faith of Whyte and his predecessors in the quality of the Common School product. He retired in 1886, ending an era which had firmly established the reputation of the Spring Street school. In 1891 his daughter Margaret was one of the first two female graduates in medicine at the University of Melbourne. Frank Tate, an ex-pupil, helped to obtain the 1899 royal commission on technical education, the re-opening of the Training College for State School Teachers and, in 1905, the beginnings of the state secondary system. The Model School was widely respected for its scholarship and as the Continuation School became the first state high school. This later became Melbourne High School.

Whyte died of a heart attack at Victoria Parade, East Melbourne, on 18 July 1893, aged 73. He was buried in the Catholic section of the New Cemetery, Melbourne; his estate was sworn for probate at £629.

E. Sweetman, C. R. Long and J. Smyth, *A history of state education in Victoria* (Melb, 1922); J. A. Allan, *The old Model School ... 1852-1904* (Melb, 1934); V&P (LA Vic), 1867, 1st S, 4 (27); National Board of Education, Letters and papers 1855-62 *and* Board of Education, Letters and papers 1863-72 (PRO, Vic).

WARWICK EUNSON

WIENHOLT, ARNOLD (1826-1895) and EDWARD (1833-1904), pastoralists and politicians, were sons of John Birkett Wienholt (1775-1852), merchant, and his second wife Sarah, née Hill. Arnold was born on 22 January 1826 and Edward on 28 March 1833 at Laugharne, Carmarthenshire, Wales, the setting for Dylan Thomas's poem *Under Milk Wood*. Two other brothers, Daniel (1822-1865) and Arthur (1835-1892), were also prominent Queensland pioneers. The family, originally Winholdt, originated at Wiemsdorf, Oldenburg, Germany, in the sixteenth century.

Educated privately and at Eton, Arnold arrived at Sydney about 1847. He purchased Maryvale in 1849 and Gladfield in 1852, both on the Darling Downs, Queensland; they became two of the finest Clydesdale studs in Australia. In 1860 he failed to win Warwick in the Legislative Assembly, but held the seat in 1863-67; he ran for Maranoa in 1871 but lost. His assembly career was unspectacular and characteristically silent. Politics for him was an onerous obligation to his fellow 'Pure Merinos', neither a pleasure nor a pursuit of intrinsic satisfaction; his importance lies in his practical abilities as a stock-breeder and pastoralist and his partnership in the family pastoral empire. At the end of the 1870s he retired to Locarno, Switzerland, where he died unmarried in the Grand Hotel on 16 January 1895.

His more complex and influential brother Edward, also Eton-educated and an Anglican, arrived in Queensland in 1853. With William Kent he acquired Fassifern, Jondaryan and Goomburra stations in the 1870s in the south-east and several large runs in the interior. His 'dash and self-reliance ... tempered by a native shrewdness which caused him seldom to make a mistake' was combined with an advantageous marriage on 14 December 1874 to Ellen (1856-1898), daughter of Daniel Williams, railway contractor and entrepreneur. They had three sons and three daughters, including Arnold (1877-1940).

Wienholt and his partners rapidly built up one of Australia's largest and initially most profitable pastoral empires. In 1888 they held 289,966 acres of freehold land in the Moreton and Darling Downs districts; next year the Wienholt Pastoral Estates Co. was formed. Believing that 'it was necessary for those who had a stake in the country to take part in its Government [to] protect themselves from great and unnecessary liabilities', Wienholt was M.L.A. for Western Downs in 1870-73 and Darling Downs in 1873-75. A strong adherent of Sir Arthur Palmer [q.v.], he favoured drastic retrenchment, complete free trade in imports and land, restricted education for the masses and the continuation of the threatened pastoral hegemony. In 1875 the Privy Council in *Regina* v. *Edward Wienholt* reversed a Supreme Court decision and found for him in a ruling that gave freehold titles to all selectors, genuine or otherwise, whose rents had previously been collected by the Crown—this was a valuable victory. In May 1890 Brisbane waterside workers refused to load non-union-shorn wool from Jondaryan. This incident, an important event in the struggle between the new mass unions and the pastoralists, hastened the end of the old traditional Queensland pastoral ascendancy.

Wienholt retired to Rocklands, Ross-on-Wye, Herefordshire, England, in 1880. He died in Melbourne on 14 January 1904 on one of his frequent trips to Australia. He was regarded as 'a fine specimen of colonial Toryism', who never concealed his fundamental views. His social and political positions were eventually eroded, but his convictions, courteous deportment and correct if frigid public manners, together with his territorial acquisitions, place him above his more pedestrian fellows. A Petty Sessions district at Murgon and a parish near Dalby are named after him. His estate was valued for probate at £9144 in New South Wales and at £57,000 in Queensland.

M. J. Fox (ed), *The history of Queensland*, 2 (Brisb, 1921); D. B. Waterson, *Squatter, selector and storekeeper* (Syd, 1968); *Toowoomba Chronicle*, 20 Aug 1870, 13 Mar 1875; *Brisbane Courier*, 8 July 1871, 16 Jan 1894, 18 Jan 1895; *Queenslander*, 13, 27 Feb 1904; pedigree, compiled by G. H. Lawrence, and family information (from R. C. Foot, Clearview Beach, NSW).

D. B. WATERSON

WIGHT, GEORGE (1817-1900), Congregational minister and journalist, was born at Haddington, East Lothian, Scotland, son of James Wight, gentleman, and his wife Marian, née Brock. Trained for the ministry of the United Secession Church he chose to be ordained a Congregationalist and served at Doune (1843-47), Haddington (1847-54) and Portobello (1855-57), where he edited *Hogg's Instructor* and published *Geology and Genesis: a reconciliation* ... (London, 1857). With Moreton Bay about to become Queensland he accepted the task of establishing a church in Brisbane. Wight reached Sydney on 4 February 1858, supplied the Balmain pulpit temporarily and arrived in Brisbane on 15 May. He immediately gathered a congregation, prepared people for communicant membership, formed a church on 6 July 1859, and opened the substantial Wharf Street chapel on 10 June next year. Convinced that the colony should be inaugurated without state aid to religion and with a National rather than a Denominational education system, he campaigned successfully to have those principles enacted in the first parliament.

Believing that his Church was firmly established he resigned on 29 July 1860 and returned to his family in Scotland. His wife died and, after his remarriage, the family settled in Brisbane in 1863. While Wight undertook no formal pastorate he built a chapel on his Eildon Hill property, and maintained services there until its removal to O'Connelltown (Windsor) in 1879 for use by a new Congregational church. He remained active in Church affairs and was twice chairman of the Queensland Congregational Union (1864-65, 1886-87).

To support the secular education campaign, Wight founded the *Queensland Guardian* in May 1860 and maintained his interest in it until it ceased publication in the bank crisis of 1869; his own influential articles appeared over the pen-name, 'Willinghood'. He also published *Queensland, the field for British Labour and Enterprise* ... (London, 1861), *The Old Faiths of India and Christianity* ... (Brisbane, 1886), and *Congregational Independency: its introduction to Queensland* ... (Brisbane, 1887). His interest in science made him a foundation member (in 1859) and committeeman of the Queensland Philosophical (Royal) Society. Until 1867 papers presented to the society, including three of his own, were published in the *Guardian*.

In 1874 Wight became the colony's immigration lecturer in Scotland, and distributed 50,000 copies of his pamphlet, *Queensland, the Colony for Working Men*. He returned to Brisbane in 1877 to expressions of government gratitude for effective work. In failing health he moved to Melbourne in 1888 and, aged 83, died there on 25 October 1900. He had first married Jessie Clapperton, née Chapman, possibly in 1843. She died in the late 1850s and on 24 December 1860 he married Mary Ann Laing, at Burntisland, Fifeshire, Scotland; she died in Brisbane on 14 August 1868. In Melbourne on 19 September 1889 he married Ellen Penketh Brown. There were five children of the first marriage, and four of the second of whom two daughters drowned in the wreck of the *Quetta* in Torres Strait on 28 February 1890.

W. Mackelvie, *Annals and statistics of the United Presbyterian Church* (Edinb, 1873); H. Escott, *A history of Scottish Congregationalism* (Glasgow, 1960); E. N. Marks, 'A history of the Queensland Philosophical Society and the Royal Society of Queensland from 1859 to 1911', Roy Soc Qld, *Procs*, 71 (1959); *Vic Independent*, Nov 1900; Colonial Missionary Soc, Minutes and reports (Lond).

G. L. LOCKLEY

WILKES, WILLIAM CHARLES (1816?-1873), journalist and editor, was probably born in Surrey, England, son of Andrew Robertson Wilkes, reputedly a captain in the East India Co., and his wife Mary Christmas, née Burt. In 1833 while employed as an assistant clerk he was convicted at the Old Bailey of stealing £11 12s. 'from a dwelling house' and sentenced to transportation for life. He arrived in Sydney in the *Neva* on 21 November 1833 and probably worked as messenger at the Police Office there. In 1839 he gave evidence against Colonel H. C. Wilson [q.v.], accused of employing police for private profit. In 1841 Wilkes was assigned to J. C. Burnett's [q.v.] expedition to trace the Dividing Range north and proceed to Moreton Bay. He became overseer for Burnett, was commended for his service and, after receiving his ticket-of-leave on 3 February 1843, stayed with him on his survey of the Richmond and Clarence rivers. He then worked for James Canning Pearce at Helidon station; a skirmish there with Aboriginals led him to write a mock epic poem, 'The Raid of the Aboriginals', under the pseudonym 'James Arrowsmith Cordwainee'. It cleverly satirized the behaviour of the local squatters and is the earliest evidence of Wilkes's liberal politics and lively sense of humour. In Brisbane on 17 December 1846 he married Catherine Connolly.

While employed as a storekeeper by G. S. le Breton, Wilkes wrote for the *Moreton Bay Courier* and in 1848-56 was editor. He became a respected member of the community and proved to be a journalist of great ability and integrity. Opposing the re- introduction of convict labour to Moreton Bay, he worked for improved public education and fought for separation. Involved in the movement, he devoted the *Courier* to it, prepared estimates of revenue and expenditure of Moreton Bay if separated from the parent colony and showed that it would be financially viable. The accuracy of his figures was later praised by William Coote [q.v.]. The *Sydney Morning Herald* opposed separation for Moreton Bay and Wilkes maintained a running battle with it. In 1864 when he revisited Brisbane, the Ipswich *Queensland Times* commented, 'there is a gentleman now in Brisbane who probably did more for the cause in the days of its apparent hopelessness than Dr. Lang [q.v.], with all his boasting, ever accomplished'. Leading citizens and parliamentarians of Brisbane presented Wilkes with a testimonial of a silver cup and a hundred guineas, after which the party retired to McAdam's Sovereign Hotel to celebrate.

Popular and convivial, with an astringent sense of humour, Wilkes was only 5 ft. 3 ins.; his nature seems to have been in no way soured by his early misfortunes. When he left the *Courier* in 1856 he came to Sydney and joined the literary set of Frank Fowler, Richard Rowe (Peter Possum), J. L. Michael and J. S. Moore [qq.v.]. He contributed a serial, 'Charles Wotton, or, Bush Life in Australia', to the *Month* (then edited by Moore), but it was hastily concluded after six chapters when the magazine ceased publication. After Wilkes's death Moore published these chapters in a much longer version of the tale under his own name in the *Tamworth News*, of which he was editor. In 1878 he printed the story in the *Sydney University Magazine*. Accused by the Sydney *Evening News* of plagiarism, Moore claimed entire authorship, but published his refutation in the advertising pages of the magazine so that it would not be preserved with bound copies.

In 1857 Wilkes had become editor of Sydney *Punch* but, though praised by G. B. Barton [q.v.], it ran only four issues. He wrote also for the *Australian Era* and in 1858 for the *Sydney Dispatch*. In 1859 he joined S. Bennett's [q.v.] *Empire* and remained with it until 1873. He reputedly edited it for some of that time, and in 1872-73 wrote a weekly column, 'The Flaneur in Sydney': a lively commentary on local and foreign current events and a good vehicle for his wit and broad humanitarian interests. He contributed also to Bennett's other publications, the *Australian Town and Country Journal* and the *Evening*

News. Imprisoned in Darlinghurst Gaol for failing to pay his rent in 1865, he voluntarily sequestered his estate; he claimed bouts of severe illness had prevented him earning in his 'precarious occupation'. Wilkes died of softening of the brain in St Vincent's Hospital on 13 May 1873 and was buried in Camperdown cemetery without religious rites. He was survived by his wife and by three daughters of their five children.

G. B. Barton, *Literature in New South Wales* (Syd, 1866); W. Coote, *The history of the colony of Queensland* (Brisb, 1867); J. Campbell, *The early settlement of Queensland* (Ipswich, 1875); *Moreton Bay Courier*, 19 Feb 1853; *Brisbane Courier*, 15, 22, 24 June 1864, 16 May 1873, 22 June 1926; *T&CJ*, 17 May 1873; *Evening News* (Syd), 12 Apr 1878; Insolvency file 7065/5 (NSWA).

ROSILYN BAXTER

WILKIE, DAVID ELLIOT (1815-1885), physician, was born on 14 August 1815 at Rathobyres, in Haddington near Edinburgh, third son of Rev. Daniel Wilkie (1782-1838) and his wife Jane Clerk, née Elliot. Educated at the University of Edinburgh (M.D., 1836), he studied for two years in Paris, and in 1838 was admitted to the Royal College of Surgeons, Edinburgh, after presenting a thesis 'On Acute Pericarditis'. Attracted by the ideals of the founders of South Australia he arrived in Adelaide late in 1838 as surgeon-superintendent of the *Lloyds*. Disappointed by the state of the colony, he moved to Melbourne in March 1839 and from June practised in partnership with David Patrick, becoming an honorary of the first public hospital in 1840. Wilkie became a manager of the church and of Scots School, and on 20 October 1842 married Mary Elizabeth, daughter of Rev. James Clow [q.v.]. In December he became an elder of Scots Church and remained a member in the period of disruption.

Soon successful, Wilkie specialized in diseases of women and children, and was an honorary physician to the Melbourne Hospital for many years. His address on the alleviation of foetal distress on 1 December 1846 was the first-recorded scientific paper in Port Phillip. Earlier that year he was chairman of the committee which drew up the rules and regulations of the Port Phillip Medical Association of which he became first secretary. He was first president in 1852 of its successor, the Victoria Medical Society, and president in 1858 of the subsequent Medical Society of Victoria. From 1846 he had campaigned for rigorous academic qualifications for admission to medical practice; the Acts of 1854 and 1862 owed much to him. A pioneer of preventive medicine, he was a vigorous critic of the Yan Yean water-supply scheme and active in combating such diseases as cholera, diphtheria and smallpox. He published several medical and scientific papers, was editor of the *Australian Medical Journal* in 1858 and a member of the Medical Board of Victoria in 1874-78.

After two failures Wilkie was elected to the Legislative Council for North Western Province in 1858 but was defeated when his ten-year term expired. He was minister without office in the Heales [q.v.] government from November 1860 to November 1861 and chairman of committees in the council in 1864-68. Though regular in attendance, he rarely spoke. He had been prominent in 1839 in founding the Melbourne Mechanics' Institute (from 1873 the Melbourne Athenaeum) of which he was treasurer in 1856-78. An inveterate collector and classifier of specimens of natural history, he and his friends Sir Ferdinand Mueller and J. Macadam [qq.v.] helped Andrew Clarke [q.v.] to form a national collection initially under the charge of the Philosophical Society of Victoria (1854). He was later a council member of the Philosophical Institute of Victoria (Royal Society from 1860), and was a leading executive member and treasurer of the Exploration Committee which sponsored the Burke and Wills [qq.v.] expedition; with Mueller and Macadam he jointly published seven reports between 1857 and 1863.

Wilkie took little part in public affairs after 1870 but was in excellent health when he retired in 1881. He was a director of the Australian Alliance Assurance Co. from 1862 and of the Land Mortgage Bank of Victoria, and a member of the Port Phillip Club and later of the Melbourne Club. He visited Europe in 1884 and died unexpectedly in Paris on 2 April 1885, survived by his wife, four of his five sons and five daughters. Two sons became solicitors, one a doctor and one a sharebroker. Wilkie was buried in Greyfriars cemetery, Edinburgh. A man of integrity and versatility, he was an ornament to the medical profession.

H. B. Graham, *The Honourable David Elliot Wilkie M.D.: a pioneer of Melbourne* (Syd, 1956), and for bibliog; *MJA*, 7 Apr 1956.

WILKINS, WILLIAM (1827-1892), teacher and civil servant, was born on 16 January 1827 in the Workhouse Infirmary, Parish of St Mary, Lambeth, London, son of William Wilkins (d. 1830), parish beadle, and his wife Sarah, née Noice. Educated at Norwood School of Industry for pauper children, he attended Battersea Training School for teachers where he was strongly influenced by the work of Dr J. P. Kay (Sir James Kay-Shuttleworth) and E. C. Tufnell. After a torrid time as assistant teacher at Parkhurst prison, Isle of Wight, he was first-master to the new Swinton School of Industry, near Manchester, and in 1847 became headmaster of St Thomas's National School, Charter-House, London. In 1848, at the first annual examinations of masters of Church of England schools, he was awarded certificates of merit by the committee of the Privy Council on education. On 30 March 1850 he married Ann Sheppard. Advised to seek a warmer, drier climate because of his chronic bronchitis, Wilkins and his wife accepted the positions of headmaster and mistress of the new Fort Street Model School, Sydney, hoping to return to England after a few years 'in health and wealth'. Following an arduous voyage, during which his wife died in childbirth (the baby also died), Wilkins took up his appointment in Sydney on 23 January 1851. On 21 May next year, in York Street Wesleyan chapel, he married Harriett Bartlett.

An efficient administrator, who concentrated power in his own hands, Wilkins organized the Fort Street school on Battersea lines, based on the Dutch pupil-teacher system of training. He classified pupils according to their age, ability and sex. The work of each class was regulated by a carefully devised timetable and monitorial instruction was replaced by 'simultaneous' class teaching. Moral suasion rather than corporal punishment became a feature of school discipline. The course of study was extended to drawing, music, geography, scripture, drill and gymnastics. All his reforms spread to the other National schools. In 1853 he wrote 'Art of Teaching'; no copy survives, but an outline indicates how heavily he drew upon the work of Kay-Shuttleworth and the Swiss, Pestalozzi.

Wilkins undertook several important tours of school inspection for the Board of National Education. Impressed by his suggestions, on 1 July 1854 the board appointed him inspector and superintendent of National schools. He headed a three-man inquiry into the colony's education. The final report of December 1855 condemned schooling under the dual boards of National and Denominational education, advocated the establishment of a unified, co-ordinated system of state schools, supervised by professional district inspectors, and recommended the extension of the pupil-teacher system and the improvement of school buildings. While producing no immediate change, these proposals gave direction to the movement which urged the extension of state education, achieved in (Sir) Henry Parkes's [q.v.] 1866 and 1880 legislation.

Wilkins vigorously performed his inspectorial duties, and the system gradually grew in size and complexity. In 1863 he became acting secretary and from 1 January 1865 secretary to the Board of National Education. On several occasions he came close to total breakdown because of the job's pressure and his recurring bronchitis. His public lectures on the extension of the school system were published in 1865 as *National Education*. Concerned that textbooks be suited to the needs of colonial children, he had taken the lead by writing *The Geography of New South Wales...* (1863) and helped to prepare *The Australian Reading Books* for colonial schools. He privately urged the extension of National schools and criticized Denominational schools.

As secretary of the new Council of Education from 1867, Wilkins continued to develop the inspectorate, improve teacher-training, and advocate Pestalozzian-type pedagogy. He introduced rigid courses of study and standards of proficiency: teachers' promotion depended both on how well their pupils handled an examination by the inspector, and on formal examinations designed by Wilkins. The result was that initiative was stifled, as teachers worked for their own examinations and prepared their charges for inspectorial visits.

Wilkins encouraged teachers to improve themselves and formed an institute of teachers in 1858. In the 1860s he supported the establishment of mutual improvement societies and was behind the Teachers Metropolitan Association of 1870. In 1879 he launched another short-lived institute. He also supervised and partly edited two successful monthly publications, *Australian Journal of Education*, 1868-70, and *Journal of Primary Education*, 1871-73. But he would not permit teachers to be too critical or to adopt a trade union style of behaviour. In 1874 he and the council virtually extinguished staff organizations for twenty years when they over-reacted in punishing the president and secretary of the Teachers' Association of New South Wales, Frederick Bridges and William Matthews [qq.v.].

Wilkins created a highly centralized administrative system with himself at the centre, dispensing autocratic advice and instructions to the rapidly increasing numbers of inspectors, teachers and schools. Seriously ill in 1869, next year he took leave in England, where he inquired into educational developments. His reports on his observations reveal excessive confidence in the public school system of New South

Wales and a growing complacency. Returning to Australia, he extended and refined his earlier innovations, but changed little. Under the Public Instruction Act of 1880, he became first under-secretary in the new Department of Public Instruction. The strain of administering the expanded system and recurrence of a lung disorder forced him to retire in January 1884.

After a time at Armidale and partially restored to health, Wilkins returned to Sydney, where he taught English language and literature for the Sydney Mechanics' School of Arts, and a class for pupil-teachers in English grammar. In 1886, with his wife and daughters, he failed with the Manor House school for girls at Mount Victoria, and was all but ruined financially. He published *The Principles that underlie the Art of Teaching* (1886), a series of lectures for the Board of Technical Education, and *Australasia: a Descriptive and Pictorial Account ...* (1888). Secretary to the New South Wales commissions for the 1888 Melbourne and the 1889-90 Dunedin exhibitions, in July 1890 he was appointed to the royal commission into the civil service. His pamphlet, *Agriculture in New South Wales*, was published in connexion with the World's Columbian Exposition, Chicago, 1893. At the time of his death he was said to have been working on a major history of education in New South Wales.

Wilkins was also an executive member of the Sydney Mechanics' School of Arts in the 1850s. He was an active member of the Wesleyan York Street chapel and choirmaster until 1869. Interested in music and a talented singer, in 1854 he was a member of the Sydney Philharmonic Society. A prominent Freemason under the English constitution, he joined the Cambrian Lodge in 1855 and became master in 1864. Next year he was deputy provincial grand master and also a committee-man of the Australasian Freemasons' Orphan and Destitute Children's Society. He helped found the Victoria Lodge and became its master in 1879. In 1872-79 he was an officer in the New South Wales Volunteer Infantry.

After a long illness, Wilkins died at his Guildford home on 10 November 1892 and was buried in the Anglican section of Rookwood cemetery; he was survived by his wife, two sons and three daughters. His estate was sworn for probate at £1083.

C. Turney (ed), *Pioneers of Australian education*, 1 (Syd, 1969); Final report of the school commissioners, V&P (LA NSW), 1856-57, 2, 87; Wilkins family letters (ML); MS cat under W. Wilkins (ML); Board of National Education, Minutes and letter-books *and* annual reports,

1848-65 (NSWA); Council of Education, Annual reports 1866-79 (NSWA).   CLIFF TURNEY

WILKINSON, CHARLES SMITH (1843-1891), geologist, was born on 22 August 1843 at Potterspury, Northamptonshire, England, fourth son of David Wilkinson, a civil engineer associated with George Stephenson, and his wife Elizabeth, née Bliss. He was educated at Elby near Stroud, Gloucestershire, until his family migrated to Melbourne, arriving in the *Marlborough* in November 1852. Charles attended Rev. T. P. Fenner's Collegiate School, Prahran, and in December 1859 began work with the Victorian Geological Survey under A. R. C. Selwyn [q.v.], becoming in 1861 field assistant to R. Daintree [q.v.]. In 1863 he accompanied R. A. F. Murray [q.v.] to the Otway Ranges and became field geologist in 1866. That year he contributed an important paper on the formation and deposition of gold nuggets in drift to the Royal Society of Victoria, of which he was a member. In February 1868 while working with Selwyn in the Grampians, he became acutely ill with a lung inflammation and returned to Melbourne where he resigned from the survey.

Wilkinson moved to Wagga Wagga, New South Wales, to take up pastoral pursuits, but occasionally did some private surveying. In October 1870 in evidence before the gold fields royal commission he warned against dividing the interests and claims of geology and mining, and argued for a department of mines. After passing his surveyor's licence on 16 August 1871 he worked in the Surveyor-General's Department, then as a geological surveyor from 16 July 1874 in the Department of Lands until he became geological surveyor in charge in the Department of Mines in 1875.

In 1874 Wilkinson began the systematic geological survey of New South Wales. In 1876 he reported on the specimens collected by (Sir) William Macleay's [q.v.] expedition to New Guinea, and later announced the discovery of Miocene fossils and described the gold specimens found by Andrew Goldie and W. G. Lawes [qq.v.] in New Guinea. Although much of his work was the routine survey of coal and goldfields, Wilkinson brought to his department the diligence and dedication of his old master Selwyn. From October 1882 to March 1883 he acted as chief mining surveyor. He persuaded the government to support the search for subterranean water in the western districts, giving detailed hydrological evidence in August 1884 before the royal commission on the conservation of water. He travelled widely throughout New South Wales as a member of the Prospecting Board from 1888, gaining an intimate knowledge of its mineralogical and palaeontological wealth.

In 1882 Wilkinson was joined by T. W. Edgeworth David, to whom he delegated much responsibility. He brought together the extensive collection for the Mining and Geological Museum, Sydney, and served on every major New South Wales exhibition commission from 1875; in 1890 he visited London as the colony's representative at the International Exhibition of Mining and Metallurgy. He contributed notes on the geology to the two departmental editions of *Mineral Products of New South Wales...* (1882 and 1887), launched and gained contributors for the first *Memoirs* of the New South Wales Geological Survey, and in 1889 started its *Records* to provide more scope for research publications and exchanges. An 'unostentatious but enthusiastic' worker, he won great respect among scientific contemporaries and colleagues both as a geologist and chief.

Despite long absences from Sydney Wilkinson was active in the colony's corporate scientific life: a member of the local Royal Society from 1874, he was its president in 1887-88; a member of the Linnean Society of New South Wales from 1880 and president in 1883-84, he contributed five papers on anthropology, geology and the general progress of colonial science. He was elected a fellow of the Geological Society, London, in 1876, the Linnean Society of London in 1881 and the Victoria Institute, London, in 1885 and was a member of the New South Wales branch of the Geographical Society of Australasia. He made over ninety contributions to science in lectures, articles, maps and official reports. A member of the Engineering Association of New South Wales, Wilkinson also served on the Board of Technical Education and as a trustee of the Australian Museum. He lectured widely on religion and science, defending Charles Darwin [q.v.] as 'one of the greatest apostles of Truth'.

Wilkinson died of carcinoma at Burwood, Sydney, on 26 August 1891 and was buried in the Anglican cemetery at Enfield. He was survived by his wife Eliza Jane, née Leitch, whom he had married at Berry Jerry station, Wagga Wagga, on 4 May 1887, and by their two sons. His estate was valued for probate at £3338. Sir Frederick McCoy [q.v.] commemorated his Victorian work in the fossils *Squaladon wilkinsoni* and *Trigonograptus wilkinsoni*; his palaeontological investigations in New South Wales were acknowledged in one new genus and four new species of fossils bearing his name. His brother Robert Bliss (1838-1928), grazier and stock and station agent, represented Balranald in the Legislative Assembly in 1880-94.

V&P (LA Vic), 1868, 2 (15), (LA NSW), 1871-72, 2, 305; Engineering Assn of NSW, Procs, 6 (1890-91); Linnean Soc NSW, Procs, 16 (1891); Mining J (Lond), 17 Oct 1891; Roy Soc NSW, Procs, 26 (1892); E. J. Dunn and D. J. Mahony, 'Biographical sketch of the founders of the Geological Survey of Victoria', Vic Geological Survey, Bulletin, 23 (1910); T&CJ, 16 Feb 1889, 29 Aug, 5 Sept 1891; Australasian, 13 Sept 1890, 29 Aug 1891.　　MICHAEL HOARE

WILLIAMS, SIR EDWARD EYRE (1813-1880), judge, was born in England, sixth son of Burton Williams, a planter of Trinidad, West Indies, and his wife Jane, née Hartley. He was educated in England and called to the Bar of the Inner Temple in November 1833. On 13 March 1841 in London he married Jessie, daughter of Rev. Charles Gibbon of Lonmay, Aberdeenshire, Scotland. Next year on 13 February they arrived in the Port Phillip District in the Andromache.

Williams toyed with the idea of taking up squatting but was persuaded to practise his profession. On 30 March he was admitted to the colonial Bar and made his initial court appearance on 7 April, when he 'acquitted himself in a manner to establish his credit as a quick examiner and a self-possessed speaker'. He first lived at Brunswick Street, Fitzroy, but in 1846-52 owned Como Estate before moving to South Yarra and later St Kilda. Early in his career he appeared for the defendant in several libel cases, notably with (Sir) William Stawell for H. Moor [qq.v.] in his actions against W. Kerr [q.v.] in 1848, and against E. Wilson and J. S. Johnston [qq.v.] of the Argus in 1851. Williams became known for 'a spasmodic style of address—something of a melodious bark', which earned him the title of the 'Boanerges of the Melbourne Bar'.

Williams was active in community affairs in the 1840s and 'his portly figure was frequently to be seen ... whenever any question affecting the public welfare required a strong helping push'. In May 1844 he was appointed a member of the Bourke District Council and was made a trustee of the Port Phillip Savings Bank. He was on the committee of the Mechanics' Institute and, prominent in moves to set up the Melbourne Hospital in 1845-46, was a member of its first committee of management in 1847. Williams was a founding member of the St George's Club in April 1846. He spoke against transportation at a public meeting in March 1847. A keen Anglican, he was a founding member of the Diocesan Society in September 1848 and later supported the establishment of a Sabbath observance association.

On 1 April 1851 Williams was appointed chief commissioner of insolvent estates. In mid-July he announced his intention to stand for the Legislative Council seat of Loddon in the first elections after Victoria's separation from New South Wales; but he withdrew when later that month he was appointed commissioner of the Court of Requests for the City of Melbourne and County of Bourke; he also became chairman of Quarter Sessions. In April 1852 he was appointed solicitor-general, entitled to a non-elective seat in the Legislative Council; but on 21 July he became second puisne judge of the Supreme Court.

Not so colourful as his colleagues Stawell and (Sir) Redmond Barry [q.v.], Williams nevertheless proved both capable and reliable. Much of his time was spent on circuit and he gained a reputation for disposing of his work speedily to maintain a tight schedule of travel, sometimes keeping the court sitting until 2 a.m. Accused by some of lacking the industry of his colleagues, Williams was for many years in delicate health and from April 1859 took two years leave of absence in England. In early April 1874 he resigned on medical advice, taking only Criminal Court business in his final weeks of office to 30 April. On 28 May with his wife he left the colony in the City of Melbourne, bound for England via Sydney.

Williams was knighted on 28 May 1878. He retired to Bath where he died, aged 66, on 30 April 1880 survived by his wife, a daughter and two sons, of whom the younger was Sir Hartley [q.v.]. His other daughter had been killed in 1872 while mountaineering in Switzerland. His Victorian estate was valued for probate at £6650.

Garryowen (E. Finn), The chronicles of early Melbourne (Melb, 1888); H. McCrae (ed), Georgiana's journal (Syd, 1934); Aust Jurist, 19 May 1874; I. F. McLaren, ' "Como", an historic Melbourne home', VHM, 28 (1957-58); Port Phillip Gazette, 13 Apr 1842; The Times, 5 May 1880; Argus, 6 May 1880; P. Street, Legal history essay (Law School, Univ Melb).

ROBERT MILLER

WILLIAMS, SIR HARTLEY (1843-1929), judge, was born on 15 October 1843 at Brunswick Street, Fitzroy, Port Phillip District, second son of Sir Edward Eyre Williams [q.v.] and his wife Jessie, née Gibbon. Williams was educated in England at Repton School from the age of 9, matriculating in 1862 to Trinity College, Oxford (B.A., 1866). He was called to the Bar of the Inner Temple on 30 April 1867. He had some experience in the offices of two London solicitors before returning to Victoria, arriving in Melbourne on 29 October in the *Superb*. Admitted to the colonial Bar in April next year he began an extensive and successful common law practice. He was also a law reporter for some years. On 24 December 1870 at All Saints Church, Hobart Town, he married Edith Ellen, daughter of George Horne; they returned to Melbourne on 15 January 1871.

Williams was a member of the Education League in 1872. Next year he was appointed examiner in law at the University of Melbourne but in 1879 resigned after a disagreement with the council over an examination result. In 1874 he twice stood in vain for the Legislative Assembly seat of St Kilda, as a 'free and independent' candidate. After his defeats he concentrated on his lucrative law practice and by 1880 had an income of £6000 a year.

On Sir Redmond Barry's [q.v.] death in 1881, Williams was nominated to succeed him on the bench of the Supreme Court; when sworn in on 4 July, he was the youngest judge in the colony. He became well known and respected for the common sense of his summings-up and judgments. Most at home in common law, he showed considerable aptitude in the work of the Criminal Court but was sometimes 'frankly embarrassed' in dealing with equity. In 1889 he drew cheers from the courtroom during his sentencing of a bank embezzler, when he stated that much of the blame for such crimes rested with the banks, which were careless in supervising clerks and paid them 'starvation wages'. In 1894 his summing-up in *Speight* v. *Syme* [qq.v.] extended over seven days. His severity in dealing with the 'larrikin element' brought praise in the 1880s but by 1903 he had come to believe that first offenders should not be sent to prison.

In 1893 Williams's reputation suffered when he wrote a letter to the *Argus* on 7 January protesting over the appointment of (Sir) John Madden as chief justice—he had expected to succeed to the post himself. He added that in future he would do no more than his 'bare duty'. The letter caused a sensation at the time, but in later years Williams spoke most warmly of Madden's work as chief justice. Despite the incident he was knighted in 1894.

Williams was often criticized for his unorthodox views on politics and religion. On returning from a visit to England in July 1884 he declared that England would eventually become a republic as the 'Queen is not liked ... people think she does not do her duty and is rather niggardly'. In 1888

at a meeting of the Melbourne branch of the Australian Natives' Association he advocated the separation of Australia from Britain. He favoured Federation which would give the colonies full power to govern themselves, and wanted a federal court of appeal to assimilate the statutes of the various colonies and to deal with cases involving amounts too small to concern the Privy Council. In Melbourne in February 1885 he published a pamphlet, *Religion without Superstition*. which quickly went into three editions and provoked a strong reply from Bishop Moorhouse [q.v.]. Popular as a lecturer, he spoke in Melbourne and country towns on subjects such as 'Death and Immortality', 'Moral Courage' and 'Forward Religious Thought'; three of these addresses were published in book form in Melbourne in 1896 and others appeared in 1902. His article on anti-sweating legislation was published in the *Westminster Review* in 1908.

Known as the 'athlete judge', Williams was a great one for cycling. He was for some years an active member and executive committee-man of Victorian cycling, cricket and rowing associations and he also enjoyed boxing. In 1897 he injured his knee while walking in the Buffalo Ranges and for a time there was doubt that he would be able to resume his duties on the bench.

In May 1903 Williams announced his resignation from the bench. On 9 June he left Melbourne in the *Omrah* to retire to England on a pension of £1500. He had a small property at Staunton near Monmouth, Gloucestershire, and he also lived in London where he died on 12 July 1929. His first wife had died at their home. Flete, Malvern, Victoria, on 11 August 1885 leaving four sons and two daughters. On 4 January 1887 at Malvern he married his cousin Jessie Bruce Lawford. There were at least a son and a daughter of the second marriage.

J. L. Forde, *The story of the Bar of Victoria* (Melb, 1913); M. Cannon, *The land boomers* (Melb, 1966); A. Dean. A *multitude of counsellors* (Melb, 1968); G. Serle, *The rush to be rich* (Melb, 1971); *IAN*. 27 June 1881; *Argus*, 8 July 1884, 5 June, 14 Sept 1888, 15 Feb 1889, 7 Jan 1893, 23 May 1903, 16 July 1929; *Bulletin*, 19 July 1885; *A'sian Sketcher*, 30 June 1887; *Weekly Times* (Melb), 14 Jan 1893; *Australasian*, 23 May 1903; P. Street, Legal history essay (Law School, Univ Melb).

ROBERT MILLER

WILLIAMS, JAMES HARTWELL (1809-1881), consul and merchant, was born on 22 June 1809 at Augusta, Maine, United States of America, only son of Hartwell Williams, master mariner, and his wife Sarah, née Bridge. After the death of his father he was cared for by his uncle Reuel Williams, an influential lawyer and United States senator in 1837-43; at 14 he began his mercantile career, and late in 1834 left Boston for Sydney to act as a commission agent. In 1836 his uncle secured his appointment as the first United States consul to an Australian colony. His exequatur from the British government was delayed, partly due to a change in American presidents, and he returned from a visit to the United States on 15 January 1839 in the *Tartar* to open the consulate.

Williams's duties involved recording American shipping in Australian waters for Washington and acting as arbitrator in disputes on American ships. In 1842 he pointed out to the British government the advantages to Sydney trade if American whalers could bring in oil free of duty. Conditions which made it costly for foreign vessels to refit and victual in Sydney were alleviated. With the discovery of gold in California in 1848 relations were strained by the treatment of some Australians at the hands of the Committee of Vigilance in San Francisco; when Williams denounced the 'wholesale slanders of the Sydney people by the Californian press', he was regarded by some of his countrymen as 'to all interests and purposes an Australian'.

Connexions with the Sydney Banking Co. and James Kenworthy & Co. ended in the depressed 1840s but Williams's fortunes revived after he joined the Boston firm of Wilkinson Bros & Co., at whose premises in Macquarie Place the American consulate was housed in 1850. Active in the Sydney community, he represented his country on important social occasions in a manner applauded in the press; by 1844 he was a member of the Australian Club. On 10 December 1850 he married Helen Mary, daughter of Prosper de Mestre [q.v.], at Terara on the Shoalhaven and spent much time there. The American Whigs supplanted him as consul with Frederick W. Clarke for about six months in 1853-54, the ascent of a Democrat to the American presidency resulting in his reinstatement. In 1857 he bought 250 certified merino ewes and 14 rams from James Macarthur [q.v.] for shipment to California on his own behalf.

On 1 January 1858 Williams resigned: recent Acts of congress had modified consular powers, colonial courts were intervening too much in American shipboard disputes and the cost of the office was not being met. Unlike James M. Tarleton, consul in Melbourne from 1854, he was unpaid. By 1860 Wilkinson Bros & Co. had set up steam sawmills in Liverpool Street, as well as the 'American Warehouse' in Hunter Street; on 11 November 1861 he was natur-

alized as he was 'desirous of holding land and ships in his own name'. His partnership with W. H. Wilkinson declared insolvent in 1866, by 1870 he was trading as J. H. Williams & Co. In 1874 he took over the United States commercial agency in Sydney after H. H. Hall [q.v.] had decamped. Downgraded for a number of years due to the stagnant state of Australian-American trade, the agency became a consulate again in 1876. According to Williams, for his naturalization he 'was not required to foreswear allegiance to my own Government but simply to render allegiance to the Queen'.

He died in office of heart disease on 31 December 1881 at St Leonards, Sydney; buried in the local Anglican cemetery, he was survived by his wife and two sons. The *Sydney Morning Herald* observed that he had 'oratorial powers of no mean order' and 'considerable literary attainments'. Intestate, his personalty was valued at £81.

J. W. North, *The history of Augusta* (Augusta, Maine, 1870); Sel cttee on intemperance, V&P (LC NSW), 1854, 2, 53, 1855, 2, 1081; E. D. & A. Potts, 'The first American consul to the Australian colonies. Some unpublished letters of James Hartwell Williams', *JRAHS*, 61 (1975); *SMH*, 5 Jan 1882; Macarthur papers (ML); Reuel Williams papers (Maine Hist Soc); MS cat (ML); Sydney consular dispatches, Applications and recommendations for office (U.S.A. National Archives, Washington).   ANNETTE POTTS

WILLIAMS, THOMAS (1815-1891), Wesleyan missionary, was born on 20 January 1815 at Horncastle, Lincolnshire, England, son of John Williams, architect and builder, and his wife Jane, née Hollinshed. Bereft of his mother in 1817, reared by a strict father and educated at a private academy in Lincoln, Williams became clerk in his father's office, joined the Wesleyan society at 19, taught Sunday school and became a local preacher. He was third preacher in the Horncastle circuit when he volunteered as a missionary to Fiji in 1839; on 20 August he married Mary, daughter of a farmer John Cottingham of West Barking, and they sailed for the South Seas in September. From July 1840 to July 1853 Williams served successively at Lakeba, Somosomo and Bua. He was ordained on 10 October 1847.

Disillusioned by wars, cannibalism, widow-strangling and general opposition Williams broke down and left the mission, reaching Sydney with Rev. W. Lawry [q.v.] in December 1853 after several months in New Zealand. While in Fiji Williams developed an interest in ethnography, illustrating his material with detailed sketches. His manuscript 'The Islands and their Inhabitants' was taken to London in 1856 by his colleague James Calvert [q.v.] and edited by G. S. Rowe as *Fiji and the Fijians*, 1 (London, 1858), which is accepted as a classic account of Fijian society before the conversion of Cakobau, chief of Bau, in 1854. He also published *Memoir of the late Rev. John Hunt, Feejee* (np, nd).

On 23 March 1854 Williams arrived in Adelaide as superintendent of the circuit. In 1857 he was transferred to Victoria as minister of the Brunswick Street church in Melbourne. After a years leave in England in 1860, he returned to Victoria, serving successively at Brighton, Creswick, Colac, Ballarat, Castlemaine and South Melbourne before becoming a supernumerary in 1878. He was chairman of the Geelong and Ballarat district in 1871, of the Castlemaine and Sandhurst district in 1872, and was president of the last Australasian Wesleyan Methodist Conference in 1873. In his retirement at Ballarat he devoted his time to writing pious biographies: *Triumph in suffering: memorials of Elizabeth Ann Bennett* (Melbourne, 1879), *Memoir of Mr. James Wood* (Geelong, 1883) and *Assiduity: being a Memoir of the late Mr. Richard H. Hart, of Stawell* (Ballarat, 1886).

In 1881 Williams visited England again and in 1885 attended the jubilee celebrations of the mission in Fiji. His unpublished journal is a perceptive record of the changes in the mission. On 4 July 1891 he died at his residence and was buried in the Creswick cemetery. Three sons and three daughters of his thirteen children survived him; his eldest daughter Jane Elizabeth (1848-1932) married Robert Charles Alexander Lindsay, medical practitioner at Creswick—several of their children, Percy, Lionel, Norman, Daryl and Ruby related their artistic expression to their grandfather's ability and encouragement.

Regarded as a good preacher Williams was somewhat of a perfectionist. His more generous side was balanced by his quick temper, sarcasm and contempt for pretension. He was a devoted patron of cultural institutions and an avid collector of books and drawings. His reputation as an ethnographer was further enhanced by the publication in Sydney of his *Journal of Thomas Williams, missionary in Fiji, 1840-1853*, edited by G. C. Henderson in 1931. The *Journal* has as its frontispiece a portrait etching by Lionel Lindsay. His Fijian sketchbook and diaries are in the Mitchell Library.

J. Watsford, *Glorious gospel triumphs* ... (Lond, 1900); B. Thomson, *The Fijians: a study of the decay of custom* (Lond, 1908); M. Dyson (ed), *Australasian Methodist ministerial general index*, 2nd ed (Melb, 1896); G. C. Henderson, *Fiji and the Fijians, 1835-1856* (Syd, 1931); D. Lindsay, *The leafy tree* (Melb, 1965); *Spectator and Methodist Chronicle*, 10, 17, 24 July 1891; *Argus*, 6 July 1891; *T&CJ*, 15 Feb 1873; *A'sian Sketcher*, 14 June 1873; Aust Methodist Church, Overseas mission records (ML); MS and printed cats (ML).   NIEL GUNSON

WILLIAMSON, JAMES CASSIUS (1845-1913), actor and theatrical manager, was born on 26 August 1845 in Mercer, Pennsylvania, United States of America, son of James Hezlep Williamson (1820-1857), physician, and his wife Selina, née Campbell (d. 1878). About 1856 the family moved to Milwaukee, Wisconsin, where James was educated and made a clandestine theatrical début in 1857. In 1861 he worked for the theatrical company of 'Messres. Hurd and Perkins' as call-boy, general assistant and maker of scenery and props; next year he joined the Royal Lyceum Theatre, Toronto, Canada, and then went to New York. He became known as a dialect comedian. In 1871 he moved to San Francisco and met comedienne Margaret Virginia Sullivan [q.v. Maggie Moore], whom he married at St Mary's Cathedral, San Francisco, on 2 February 1873. On 23 February they starred in *Struck Oil*, a sketchy script bought for $100 and rewritten by his friend Clay M. Greene, and delighted audiences in Salt Lake City, Utah.

The Williamsons visited Australia under contract to George Coppin [q.v.]. On 1 August 1874 *Struck Oil* opened at the Theatre Royal, Melbourne; having taken £7000, they moved on to the Queen's Theatre, Sydney. After revisiting Melbourne and touring Adelaide they left in October 1875 wealthy and famous, to tour England, Europe and the United States until 1879.

In July, with the Australasian rights to *H.M.S. Pinafore* purchased from W. S. Gilbert for £300, the Williamsons left again for Australia. They opened on 23 August 1879 under Coppin's management at the Theatre Royal, Melbourne. A successful Sydney season followed, after which Williamson took out injunctions against illicit performances of *Pinafore*. In 1880 he formed his (Royal) Comic Opera Company and on 8 September next year became sole lessee of the Theatre Royal, Melbourne, introducing enormous technical facilities and lavish sets. After a tour of New Zealand, in 1882 he entered into partnership with Arthur Garner and George Musgrove [q.v.]. Coppin believed that both Williamson and Garner were too ill-tempered to agree. The 'Triumvirate' was often criticized for creating a monopoly, crushing the old repertory system and discouraging local actors, but it brought to Australia such artists as G. R. Rignold [q.v.] and Dion Boucicault senior [q.v. D. G. Boucicault], as well as training new talent such as Nellie Stewart. In December 1886 they opened the luxurious (New) Princess's Theatre in Melbourne with *The Mikado*.

Professional rivalry over Nellie Stewart caused Musgrove to secede from 'the Firm' in 1890, but Williamson, Garner & Co. triumphed when they brought Sarah Bernhardt to Australia in 1891, giving their business stroke the look of artistry. At the end of the year Williamson bought Garner out, but Maggie Moore left him for the actor Harry Roberts, making extensive financial claims upon Williamson. Despite his assertion that he would 'rather go to jail than pay for her debts', she persisted and in March 1894 successfully appealed against an injunction by his solicitors against her performing *Struck Oil*. Divorced by his wife for adultery in June 1899, he married his paramour Mary Alice Weir, a dancer, on 15 August in Sydney at the Registrar-General's Department.

Musgrove had rejoined Williamson in 1892, and in January 1896 they broke records with an original Australian pantomime, *Djin Djin*. Musgrove later went to London as the firm's agent, but fell out with 'cautious Jimmy', over some risky London ventures. The dissolution of their partnership in 1899 caused animosity, and Williamson continued as sole lessee of the Princess's Theatre until May 1900. He renovated the old Alexandra Theatre, Melbourne, renaming it Her Majesty's and filling it with imported stars. He also leased the Sydney Her Majesty's, and in February 1902 mounted *Ben Hur* at a cost of £14,000. A bubonic plague outbreak temporarily closed the theatre and it was burnt down on 23 March with huge losses; but Williamson organized a Shakespearian company at the Theatre Royal, and rebuilt the theatre by August 1903. Next year he entered partnership with George Tallis, his Melbourne manager, and with Gustav Ramaciotti as legal adviser. Visually sensational shows were now 'the Firm's' speciality, and 650 people were on the permanent payroll.

From 1907 Williamson withdrew from some managerial work into private life at Tudor, Elizabeth Bay, with his wife and their daughters Marjorie and Aimée. That year Ramaciotti sold out, Williamson sold half his share to Tallis, and they merged with Sir Rupert Clarke and Clyde Meynell, in a proprietary company, J. C. Williamson Ltd; Williamson was governing director.

They achieved outstanding successes with tours by H. B. Irving and (Dame) Nellie Melba. Williamson, with much to gain from protecting his right to import stars, successfully opposed an application by Australian actors to the Commonwealth Court of Conciliation and Arbitration to form a union in 1913.

In his latter years Williamson took a great interest in racehorses; his Blue Book dead-heated in the Caulfield Cup of 1909, and Cadonia won the Australian Jockey Club St Leger in 1911. He spent most of his time in Europe but in February 1913 he performed in a benefit in Sydney for the widows of Captain Robert Scott's Antarctic expedition. Returning to his family in France via the United States his heart condition worsened; he died in Paris on 6 July 1913, attended by his wife and daughters. He was buried, contrary to his wishes, in the Williamson section of Oak Woods cemetery, Chicago, Illinois. He left an elaborately divided estate, valued for probate at £193,010.

Williamson was Australia's most successful theatrical entrepreneur. His non-theatrical middle-class background gave him an understanding of what the public wanted to see, and he retained a child's 'fairy-tale' view of the theatre's magic; nevertheless, his distaste for the *avant-garde* and his consolidation of the long-run and starring system have often been criticized. Possibly an authoritarian manager, and temperamental in his youth, he still earned the adulation of his employees.

J. C. Williamson's life-story told in his own words, A. G. Stephens ed (Syd, 1913); N. Stewart, *My life's story* (Syd, 1923); G. B. Shaw, *A letter . . . to J. C. Williamson* (Cremorne, 1955); G. Lauri, *The Australian theatre story* (Syd, priv print, 1960); H. Porter, *Stars of Australian stage and screen* (Adel, 1965); V. Tait, *A family of brothers* (Melb, 1971); I. G. Dicker, *J. C. W.: a short biography* (Rose Bay, 1974); *Argus*, 3 Aug 1874; *Australasian*, 12 Dec 1891, 23 Mar 1895, 18 Mar 1899, 7 May 1904; MS and printed cats under J. C. Williamson (ML).

HELEN M. VAN DER POORTEN

WILLIS, EDWARD (1816-1895), pastoralist, was born on 12 September 1816 at Hornsby, Cumberland, England, son of Richard Willis [q.v.] and his wife Anne, née Harper. On 21 December 1823 he arrived in Van Diemen's Land with his parents in the *Courier*. Until he was 21 he worked on his father's property, Wanstead, near Campbell Town. In 1837 with his brother William he crossed to Port Phillip, taking 500 ewes and several rams from his father's pure-bred merino stud. In April the brothers took up a run at the junction of the

Plenty and Yarra rivers. At the end of the decade Edward returned to Wanstead and on 12 September 1840 at Hobart Town he married Catherine, daughter of Captain Charles Swanston [q.v.] whose enthusiasm for Port Phillip rekindled Willis's interest. In 1844 Willis joined Swanston and, later, his son Charles Lambert in their Geelong firm, living in Barwon Terrace. They acquired Kout Narin station near Harrow in 1846 and later subdivided it; Willis and Swanston retained a part known as Koolomurt. G. A. Stephen joined the firm, which traded for many years as Swanston, Willis and Stephen. Their land in the Geelong district included a run known as Native Creek No. 3 and a freehold property in the Barrabool hills.

Of tremendous energy, Willis took an active part in Geelong's development. In the 1840s he was a member of the Geelong Literary Association, a trustee for the Savings Bank, a committee-man of the Geelong and Portland Bay Immigration Society and of the Botanical Gardens; he was a vociferous supporter of local government for Geelong and an opponent of transportation. In 1845 he became a trustee of the Port Phillip Savings Bank. He was a zealous Anglican and a trustee of St Paul's Church. Until the late 1850s he continued to be active in Geelong's development although spending much time at Koolomurt. He was a member of the provisional committee of the Geelong and Melbourne Railway Co., chairman of directors of the Geelong and Western District Fire and Marine Insurance Co., a trustee in 1856-57 of the Geelong Grammar School and a promoter of the Board of Commissioners of Waterworks.

At Koolomurt Willis formed one of the finest merino studs in Victoria. In the mid-1840s he secured some of the Forlonge [q.v.] Saxon merinos and guided by Thomas Shaw senior [q.v.] he used rams from William Campbell's [q.v.] Camden flock. In 1860 Willis visited Germany and brought back selected rams. In later years he reflected with pride on his stud's purity of blood. He prepared diligently the clip for the London market and characteristically urged his agents to take care in selling it. In the early 1870s he made efforts to acquire the freehold of his runs, often going beyond the upset price to obtain vital lots. In August 1871 he wrote forcefully to J. G. Francis [q.v.] criticizing J. M. Grant's [q.v.] treatment of the squatters in throwing open reserves on which were homesteads, woolsheds, dams and other improvements. Willis felt the squatters were being persecuted. Despite these difficulties and a long illness in the second half of 1871, he had secure tenure of Koolomurt by 1872.

Willis extended his care to the Aboriginals, especially to the last members of the Glenelg River tribe who looked on Koolomurt as their home and Willis as their protector. He was a member of the Board of Advice for the Coleraine District under the 1870 Scab Act. His association with scab-control stemmed from charges brought against him and many others in the 1840s for selling scabby sheep. Willis was an early member of the Melbourne Club and president in 1881. On one of his trips overseas he bought Courteen Hall in Hampshire. In 1894 he returned to England and lived on his property, Seven Oaks, in Kent. He died at Goring near Reading on 9 August 1895, predeceased by his wife and survived by two sons and three daughters.

A. Henderson (ed), Australian families, 1 (Melb, 1941); P. L. Brown (ed), Clyde Company papers, 2-4 (Melb, 1952-59); W. R. Brownhill, The history of Geelong and Corio Bay (Melb, 1955); Willis papers (LaT L).   J. ANN HONE

WILLIS, JOSEPH SCAIFE (1808-1897), merchant and businessman, was born in Kirkoswald, Ayrshire, Scotland, on 10 May 1808, son of Thomas Willis and his wife Nancy, née Lumley. He arrived in Sydney on 7 January 1840 in the Alfred on work for an uncle, and decided to remain. He and William L. Merry began business as merchants and shipping agents under the style of Willis, Merry & Co., with offices in Pitt Street and a wharf at Woolloomooloo. George Lloyd later joined the firm and after Merry retired on 30 June 1870 it became Willis, Lloyd & Co.

Prominent in Sydney commercial circles, Willis was a committee-man and in 1853-54 and 1858 president of the Sydney Chamber of Commerce, a founding director of the Sydney Exchange Co. in 1851-71, and a director of the local branch of the Liverpool & London Fire & Life Insurance Co., the Australian General Assurance Co., the Southern Insurance Co., the Waratah Coal Co., the Trust & Agency Co. of Australia and the Northern Rivers' Sugar Co. Among other shipping agencies, he was Sydney agent for the Tasmanian Steam Navigation Co. A director of the Bank of New South Wales in 1852-56, 1858-62 and 1865, he was chairman in 1861-62. In 1864 he was a member of the general purposes committee of the New South Wales Free Trade Association. In the 1860s he lived at Greycliffe, Shark Bay (Vaucluse).

In 1874 Willis, Lloyd & Co. became insolvent with liabilities of £39,293 and assets of £10,947, and Willis retired. He died at his residence, Kirkoswald, Middle Harbour, on 15 July 1897 and was buried in St Jude's churchyard, Randwick.

At Johnstone, Renfrewshire, Scotland, he had married Janet Speir (d. 1863), who followed him to Sydney in the *Stratheden* on 5 June 1843. His eldest son Robert was one of the first graduates of the University of Sydney and became a clergyman; his other surviving sons Thomas and William established the firm of T. and W. Willis, merchants and insurance agents. His daughters Mary, Annette and Edith married respectively Archdeacon Gunther [q.v.], F. C. Griffiths and E. W. Knox.

V&P (LC NSW), 1852, 1, 867; *SMH*, 16, 23 Feb 1875; Insolvency file 12102/5 (NSWA).

G. P. WALSH

WILLOUGHBY, HOWARD (1839-1908), journalist, was born on 19 June 1839 at Birmingham, England, son of Benjamin Willoughby, accountant, and his wife Jane Georgiana, née Maddox. Educated at Birmingham and London, he arrived in Melbourne in 1857. He joined the *Age* in 1861 as a junior reporter, transferring next year to the *Argus*, where he first became known as an imaginative journalist by his dispatches from the Maori wars. His second major work was to study the convict system in Western Australia: his conclusions argued forcefully against the system and appeared in the *Argus* and as a pamphlet, *Transportation. The British Convict in Western Australia* (London, 1865).

In 1866 Willoughby left the *Argus* to be one of the three original Hansard staff, where he learned much of politics and continued to write for the press. In 1869-77, as first editor of the Melbourne *Daily Telegraph*, his style became distinctively crisp and pithy. However, he returned to the *Argus* where his career and abilities broadened. As chief of the news department and leader-writer, he developed his own and the paper's political power. A conservative free trader, Willoughby opposed the Berry [q.v.] ministry, constantly berating its actions. His weekly column, 'Above the Speaker' by 'Timotheus', which Alfred Deakin considered 'masterpieces of consistent and deliberate misrepresentation', enlivened politics and created interest by its aptness of phrase and anecdotes. He was a consistent enthusiast for Federation, and was sometimes consulted by the drafters of the constitution bills. In 1891 in Melbourne he published *Australian Federation its aims and its possibilities*. Politicians and the public were cajoled and advised by him, especially in the Federal Convention and referenda periods.

Succeeding F. W. Haddon [q.v.] as editor of the *Argus* on 1 March 1898, Willoughby gave invaluable service with his 'long experience, ripe judgment, clear-sightedness, and fine sense of form'. Walter Murdoch described him as perhaps the best editor the *Argus* ever had, but found him 'stately, august, remote'. His handwriting used to drive compositors frantic but he treasured their most amusing mistakes. In 1903 he had to resign because of a paralytic stroke and was able to write only occasionally until his death at St Kilda on 19 March 1908. At St Mary's Church of England, Hotham, on 5 March 1870 he had married Emily Frances Elizabeth Jones; she survived him with one of their two sons and two of their three daughters. He was buried in the Melbourne general cemetery.

Willoughby's appetite for work was insatiable. As well as a pamphlet on spiritualism, he published *The Critic in Church* anonymously in 1872 and, in 1886, *Australian Pictures Drawn with Pen and Pencil*, in which he described the development and distinctiveness of Australian life in the style which had long before earned him the nickname 'Cock Robin'. A characteristic, stressed in the *Argus* obituary and echoed elsewhere, was that he rarely lost the respect of his opponents and even from them he was able to extract news copy. The *Age* reported his death 'with unfeigned regret'.

Walter Murdoch and Alfred Deakin on 'Books and men', J. A. La Nauze and E. Mercer eds (Melb, 1974); *Age, Argus, SMH*, 20 Mar 1908.

SUZANNE G. MELLOR

WILLS, THOMAS WENTWORTH SPENCER (1835-1880), cricketer and footballer, was born on 19 August 1835 at Molonglo Plains, New South Wales, eldest son of Horatio Spencer Howe Wills [q.v.] and his wife Elizabeth, née McGuire. He was educated in Melbourne until 1852 when he went to Rugby School where he played football and captained the cricket XI. Intended for Magdalene College, Cambridge, in 1856, he did not matriculate but he was included, by Oxford's permission, in the Cambridge XI in the inter-university match of that year. In 1853-56 he became a notable amateur cricketer in England, playing mainly for the gentlemen of Kent, but also for the Marylebone Club and on one occasion for United Ireland.

Wills returned to Melbourne late in 1856 and played twelve games for Victoria against New South Wales in 1857-76, scoring 319 runs at an average of 21.27 and taking 72 wickets at 10.23. He played for several teams, but mainly for Richmond and for the Melbourne Club, of which he was secretary in 1857-58. Although articled to a Collingwood solicitor in 1859 he seems never to have practised. In 1861 he accompanied his father and others overland to take up a property at Cullinlaringo, Queensland; in October all but Wills and two others who were absent from the camp were killed by Aboriginals. After helping his brother to run the property he returned to Melbourne in 1864.

Wills then became a cricket coach and trained the Lake Wallace region Aboriginal side that toured England in 1867. As a batsman he could be crudely effective, 'He uses a three pound bat and hits terrific' said James Lillywhite, but he was noted more as a bowler. Wills introduced round-arm and over-arm bowling into Victoria and was constantly accused of throwing, especially his faster deliveries. But fast or slow, thrower or bowler, he returned some devastating analyses at all levels of cricket.

A frequent and cantankerous letter-writer to the sporting press, Wills's most famous letter was in Bell's Life in Victoria, 10 July 1858, calling for cricketers to take up a winter sport for fitness' sake. The response to this letter enabled him, his brother-in-law H. C. A. Harrison [q.v.], and others to meet and draw up rules for a football game later to be known as Victorian or Australian Rules. Wills played over 210 games, mainly for Geelong, until he retired in 1876.

The indulgence in drink that seemed inseparable from the cricket of those days found a too-eager practitioner in Wills. As early as 1873 there were thinly veiled public accusations that colonial beer was affecting his cricket and in later years he had to be put under restraint. On 2 May 1880 at his Heidelberg home he eluded the vigilance of a man set to watch over him and stabbed himself to death with a pair of scissors. The inquest returned a verdict of suicide while of unsound mind caused by excessive drinking. For one who had been called 'the Grace of Australia' and 'a model of muscular Christianity' it was a sad end. He was buried in the Heidelberg cemetery after an Anglican service, survived by his wife Sarah Teresa, née Barber, whom he had married at Castlemaine, aged 32. Only one Melbourne paper, the Argus, acknowledged her existence and she finds no mention in Henderson's chapter on the Wills family. There were no children of the marriage.

F. Lillywhite, A. Haygarth, Cricket scores and biographies, 4-5 (Lond. 1863, 1876); A. Henderson (ed), Early pioneer families of Victoria and Riverina (Melb, 1936); D. J. Mulvaney, Cricket walkabout (Melb, 1967); Bell's

Life in Victoria, 1857-68; Australasian, 8 May 1869, 8 May 1880; Age, 3 May 1880; Argus, 4 May 1880; Leader (Melb), 8 May 1880.

W. F. MANDLE

WILLS, WILLIAM JOHN (1834-1861), explorer, was born on 5 January 1834 at Totnes, Devon, England, son of Dr William Wills and his wife Sarah Mary Elizabeth, née Calley (Kelley). His father had studied medicine at Grainger's anatomical school, Guy's Hospital and St Thomas's, and became a member of the Royal College of Surgeons in 1827. As a youth William John, known as Jack, suffered a fever which left him with a 'slow and hesitating speech'. He was tutored by his father, and then attended St Andrew's Grammar School, Ashburton, in 1845-50. Articled to his father on 30 May 1850, he undertook courses at Guy's and St Bartholomew's hospitals, London.

Interested in Australia, Dr Wills bought a share in a Melbourne gold-mining company in 1852, but cancelled passages to Australia for himself and his sons William John and Thomas after objections from his wife. However, the brothers left Dartmouth in the Janet Mitchell, arriving at Williamstown, Port Phillip, on 3 January 1853. They became shepherds at Deniliquin, New South Wales, where they were joined by their father in October. They went to Ballarat, Victoria, where Dr Wills began to practise, assisted by William, who later worked in the River Wannon district, studied surveying and became an assistant at the astronomical and magnetical observatories at Melbourne under Professor G. B. Neumayer [q.v.].

Wills's extensive correspondence shows an examining and factual mind, with an interest in natural phenomena, literature and exploration. Described as having a 'clear ... complexion, an expressive eye that always outstripped his tongue ... golden hair, a thick tawny beard, a smile at once intellectual and sympathising, a light, clean, agile frame', Wills had a keen sense of the ridiculous. He was encouraged by Neumayer who was a member of the exploration committee of the Royal Society of Victoria which organized the government expedition to cross Australia to the Gulf of Carpentaria. When Robert O'Hara Burke [q.v.] was made leader, he chose Wills as surveyor, astronomer and third-in-command.

The well-equipped expedition left Melbourne on 20 August 1860 but after a dispute at Menindee, George James Landells was dismissed and Wills became Burke's lieutenant. The party arrived at Cooper's

Creek on 11 November and William Brahe was placed in charge of the depot. Burke, with Wills, J. King [q.v.] and Gray, six camels, one horse and three months provisions, left for the Gulf of Carpentaria on 16 December and reached it on 11 February 1861. Wills's diary of the journey evidences his own physical toughness in the tribulations of rough terrain, tropical rains, hostile Aboriginals, shortage of rations and illness; it describes Gray's death on 17 April and the return to Cooper's Creek on 21 April, only to find that Brahe had left that morning for Menindee, leaving a small cache of supplies. Against Wills's personal judgment the three survivors moved down Cooper's Creek towards Adelaide. Had they followed the route back to Menindee, they could have met Brahe returning to look for them.

After their supplies failed the trio lived precariously on fish and nardoo. Wills was left in camp whilst Burke and King sought Aboriginals to replenish their supplies of nardoo. Burke died on 28 June and King returned to find Wills dead in the camp. He had written a farewell letter dated 27 June to his father, and the last entry in his diary dated 29 June stated 'weaker than ever ... my legs and arms are nearly skin and bone'. Relieving expeditions under A. W. Howitt, Landsborough, McKinlay [qq.v.] and others were searching for the party. Howitt found King with friendly Aboriginals on 15 September, and buried Wills on 18 September; later he returned the remains of Burke and Wills to Melbourne and they were accorded a public funeral on 21 January 1863.

The government's inquiry into the tragedy criticized Burke's leadership and decisions, the appointment of Landells and William Wright, the unsuitability of Brahe, and the errors and delays of the exploration committee; but there was little or no criticism of Wills, who was a faithful second-in-command, subjugating personal doubts on Burke's decisions: it was natural that at 27 he should have deferred to the 40-year-old leader. As Dr Wills stated 'he fell a victim to errors not originating with himself'. Memorials to the expedition have been erected in Melbourne and many Victorian towns. A memorial to Wills was placed at Totnes, Devon, England, in August 1864.

W. J. Wills, A *successful exploration through the interior of Australia*, W. Wills ed (Lond. 1863); A. M. Moorehead, *Cooper's Creek* (Lond, 1963); I. F. McLaren, 'The Victorian exploring expedition and relieving expeditions', VHM, 29 (1959), and for bibliog;

I. F. McLaren, 'William John Wills', VHM, 33 (1962-63); *Australasian*, 13 Mar 1886.

IAN F. MCLAREN

WILSHIRE, JAMES ROBERT (1809-1860), manufacturer and politician, was born on 29 July 1809 in Sydney, second son of James Wilshire [q.v.] and his wife Esther, née Pitt. Educated at Dr L. H. Halloran's [q.v.] school, in 1840 he and his brother Austin Forrest (1811-1889) took over his father's large tannery on Brickfield Hill, which also included fellmongering and the making of soap, candles, glue and parchment. Gradually the ancillary operations were discontinued because of lack of skilled workmen; but tanning and currying continued until 1860 when legislation forbade such trades in the city. In the depressed 1840s the Wilshires were obliged to call their creditors together, but later fully met their liabilities. In the 1850s 'when the tannery was not half worked' it showed an average profit of £1700 a year.

Politically active, Wilshire was elected to the Sydney Municipal Council for Phillip Ward in 1842 and was mayor in 1844. Defeated for the Counties of Cook and Westmoreland seat in the Legislative Council in 1843 he joined with J. K. Heydon and (Sir) Henry Parkes [qq.v.] to canvass for Robert Lowe [q.v.] for Sydney in 1848. On Lowe's resignation in 1849 Wilshire lost the seat to Dr W. Bland [q.v.] despite the support of the Constitutional Association. With Parkes, A. Michie [q.v.] and other radicals he helped Rev. J. D. Lang [q.v.] begin the Australian League dedicated to land reform and the abolition of transportation and imperial patronage. Though 'not a fluent or effective public speaker' he was conspicuous in the anti-transportation movement and the agitation for responsible government. In 1850 he was chairman of a committee to set up a newspaper edited by Lang. He represented the City of Sydney in the Legislative Council in 1855-56, and was one of the 'bunch' that defeated J. H. Plunkett [q.v.] for the Sydney (City) seat in the new Legislative Assembly in 1856. One of sixteen native-born members in a House of fifty-four, he represented the seat until December 1857, supporting (Sir) Charles Cowper [q.v.]. Defeated at the next general election he was appointed to the Legislative Council in March 1858.

A magistrate from 1844, Wilshire was a committee-man of the Benevolent Society of New South Wales and a trustee of the Savings Bank of New South Wales. Intestate, he died of paralytic neuralgia at Darlinghurst on 30 August 1860; he was buried in the Church of England section of the Devonshire Street cemetery and re-interred in 1901 in the Gore Hill cemetery. He was survived by two sons and three daughters of his first wife Elizabeth (d. 1846), daughter of Joseph Thompson, whom he had married at St James's Anglican Church on 13 August 1836; and by his second wife Sarah (d. 1912), her sister, whom he married on 29 May 1847 with Congregational rites, and by their two sons and four daughters. His eldest son James Thompson (1837-1909) represented Canterbury in the New South Wales Legislative Assembly in 1889-91. His intestate personalty was valued at £3000.

M. Roe, *Quest for authority in eastern Australia 1835-1851* (Melb, 1965); J. N. Molony, *An architect of freedom* (Canb, 1973); V&P (LA NSW), 1862, 5, 1121, 1865, 2, 843; SMH, 10, 13 May, 10, 13 Aug 1850, 31 Aug 1860; T&CJ, 23 Nov 1889; G. P. Walsh, A history of manufacturing in Sydney, 1788-1950 (M.A. thesis, ANU, 1969).   G. P. Walsh

WILSON, EDWARD (1813-1878), journalist and philanthropist, was born on 3 November 1813 at Covent Garden, London, third son of John Wilson and his wife Mary. His father, son of a small Nottinghamshire farmer, was apprenticed to a linen-draper and became a partner in a firm of linen merchants. The business prospered and was transferred to Bond Street and the family moved from Hampstead to a Surrey estate. Educated at a Hampstead school Edward left at 16 to enter the business. At 21, after his father's death, he moved to Manchester which he believed to be 'a better field for exertion and enterprise', worked in a large firm, dabbled in journalism, studied French, read widely and, to the regret of his family, became keenly involved in radical politics. Early in 1840 he helped to launch a calico-printing firm near Manchester; it failed after a year and Wilson found that his two partners had not told him that they had borrowed their capital. He lost his inheritance and savings.

In a miserable frame of mind, Wilson decided to migrate to try sheep-farming, and sailed for Sydney in August 1841. He soon moved to Melbourne and took up a small farm on the Merri Creek near Brunswick. In 1842 he leased the Eumemmering cattle-run at Doveton near Dandenong with J. S. Johnston [q.v.], but they did not prosper and sold out in 1846. For the next eighteen months Wilson dabbled in various activities; letters to the *Argus* over the signature of 'Iota' attracted attention. In 1848 he visited South Australia on horseback and was delighted by Wakefieldianism and the success of small-scale agriculture. 'It is Eng-land', he wrote, 'with a finer climate, with a virgin soil, with freedom from antiquated abuses, with more liberal institutions, with a happier people; and this is what I always thought and hoped Australia would become'. Later that year Johnston persuaded him to buy the *Argus* from William Kerr [q.v.] for £300; Wilson had to borrow money and Johnston became joint-proprietor in 1849. The issue of 15 September 1848 was Wilson's first; from 18 June 1849 the paper became a daily. Circulation declined to about 250, but by the close of 1850 equalled the combined circulation of rivals and by late 1851 had risen to 1500. Wilson successfully met the challenge of the gold rushes. The *Argus* absorbed the *Melbourne Daily News* from 1 January 1852 and only the *Herald* and the *Geelong Advertiser* survived as competitors for the goldfield market. He brought out forty compositors from England and in mid-1852 doubled the paper's size and reduced its price from 3d. to 2d. Circulation rose from 5000 in May 1852 to almost 20,000 late in 1853, advertisements snow-balled and the number of employees grew to about 140. But costs were outrageous and Wilson was almost ruined. He was saved by Lauchlan Mackinnon [q.v.], who late in 1852 bought the partnership which Johnston had sold to James Gill in January. Mackinnon took over the management, raised the price to 4d. and increased advertising rates, thus ensuring the journal's prosperity. Wilson and Mackinnon were regarded by their printing employees as hard but fair employers, even when in 1857 they effectively reduced wages by introducing another contingent of migrant compositors.

For over five years Wilson provided the most influential opposition to the government of C. J. La Trobe and the Colonial Office. G. W. Rusden [q.v.] remarked that 'he lent his great energy to the disastrous task of lowering respect for lawful authority'. Wilson won strength and support from his prominence in the 1849 campaign to prevent the landing of convicts. The upright La Trobe was christened 'The Hat and Feathers', pilloried often for his 'sneaking treacherous course', libelled as a tool of the squatters and accused of nepotism and corruption. No allowances were made for the emergencies of 1851 and 1852, and the diggers were inflamed by exaggerated reports of the venality and inefficiency of the goldfields administration. The climax in April-May 1853 was the standing advertisement in the paper: 'Wanted a Governor. Apply to the People of Victoria'. In a dispatch of 3 May La Trobe condemned the 'studied and systematic incitement to disorder' by the *Argus*. His friends had rallied to his support and in April 1849 Wilson had been committed for libel against (Sir) William à Beckett [q.v.], but the charge was withdrawn probably because à Beckett was the only judge available; in March 1851 Henry Moor [q.v.] won a farthing from Wilson for libel; (Sir) William Stawell, T. T. à Beckett [qq.v.] and others took over the *Herald* in order to fight the *Argus* but could not compete financially.

With the influential slogan, 'Unlock the Lands', Wilson's other main offensive was on the pastoralists' 'ruinous monopoly'; he continued to classify members of the Legislative Council as squatters or liberals long after the squatters had lost their dominance. His attacks on the council and the Melbourne Town Council were unrelenting; William Westgarth [q.v.], an ally, frequently wished he could be saved from his friend. The propagandist tone of the *Argus* was extreme; yet it was not untypical of the English press of the day, even of *The Times* which was Wilson's ultimate model. He believed in the virtue of controversy for its own sake; he desired above all to stir the colonists from their apathy and to promote political consciousness; he carried his dogmatic belief in the independence of the press to the extreme of shunning personal contact with politicians and government officers. He was incorruptible, and fearless in making enemies; his desire for commercial success was far less important than pursuit of truth and justice as he saw them. Though frequently mistaken and unfair, he exposed many governmental inefficiencies and scandals. His columns were open to any radical group or charitable movement.

Wilson's appearance matched his public role: a tall, swarthy, sombre man, a commanding figure with dark penetrating eyes behind spectacles, looking like a well-to-do tradesman rather than a gentleman. Yet even the most unlikely contemporaries such as Rusden contrasted his fierce and intolerant public role with his personal charm, geniality and generosity. He drove himself unremittingly as editor, writing much and keeping very long hours. 'Get a rough trotting horse and do your ten or twelve miles a day', he advised a successor. ' "Cold bathing" and horse-exercise were my solutions in time of greatest pressure'.

Late in 1853 Wilson began to have doubts about his policy; the *Argus* was toned down and veered and wavered as the democratic movement it had helped to create gathered strength. There is much to be said for David Blair's [q.v.] attack in 1854 ('Caustic', *The Anatomy of the Argus*, Melbourne): 'The diggers showed signs of revolt; the government yielded . . . You have systematically shelved the diggers' interests ever since'. Governor Hotham was treated lightly by

the *Argus*, and Wilson grew to regret many of his early excesses. By early 1855, he was looking for a successor as editor; he retired in September but did not find a replacement till August 1856 when George Higinbotham [q.v.] was appointed. Meanwhile he had set up as a model gentleman-farmer near Keilor and enjoyed the relaxation. He had shown 'signs of being overfagged, and thought it better to stop in time', he told (Sir) Henry Parkes [q.v.] and warned him against overworking and burning out. Parkes thought Wilson 'a Radical of the Radicals' when they met in Sydney; Wilson was captivated by Parkes and looked forward to working together, 'hunting sycophancy, and corruption, . . . and unpatriotic selfishness to their kennels . . . There is so much of similarity in our positions; so much resemblance in the kind of work we have to do, and I believe, in the sincerity of spirit and purity of purpose with which we have entered upon its performance . . .'

Wilson welcomed the arrival of (Sir) Charles Gavan Duffy [q.v.] in 1856 and promised him a list of fifty desirable reforms, of which he produced twenty-six: the first was 'Justice to the Aborigines'. Later, in 1874, he shocked members of the Royal Colonial Institute by his vigorous condemnation of British treatment of aboriginal peoples. He spent time investigating the penal systems of Victoria and Tasmania and had presented radical evidence to the select committee on penal discipline in 1857: the whole system was erroneous, criminals should be treated 'to a great extent as lunatics', and capital punishment should be abolished. He also founded a ragged school for the gutter-children of Melbourne. But his chief interest early in his retirement was the introduction of European birds, fish and animals; in February 1861 he formed the Acclimatisation Society, as an offshoot of the Victorian Zoological Society, and was largely responsible for the foundation of parallel societies in the other colonies and of nine Victorian branches.

Despite his radical views, Wilson became alarmed at the speed of democratic advance. Victoria, he wrote to Parkes in April 1858, needed 'an adult population born upon the soil to keep in check the evil and restless designs of the hungry adventurers with us. I fear the game is up . . . It is a bitter pill for me and particularly as the *Argus* is an aider and abettor. Higinbotham is a most estimable man, but occasionally wild in his opinions'. In December 1856, May 1857 and April 1858 the *Argus* included a civilized series of exchanges between proprietor and editor on the subject of democracy, part of which was republished as *Enquiry into*

the Principles of Representation, the most
important contribution to the contemporary
debate. Wilson still called himself a 'staunch
democrat', supported direct taxation, and
approved of manhood suffrage; but he believed that equal representation would give
the working class perpetual power, and
tyranny and class legislation would be in-
evitable. The problem of the day was 'con-
servatising democracy', property had to be
protected, the best solution would be to
represent equally the eight major economic
interests of society. In *Principles of Representation* (London, 1866), which was written
with the help of his old friend Catherine
Spence [q.v.] and reprinted from the *Fortnightly Review*, Wilson proposed a House of
Commons composed of 180 local members
and 25 representatives of each of 19 interests
(of whom unskilled labourers and women
were two).

Wilson always allowed his editors a free
hand on policy; the precise circumstances of
Higinbotham's resignation as editor in 1859
are not known. H. E. Watts and Gurney
Patmore were appointed as editors and the
Argus began its ninety-year run of unmitigated Toryism. Wilson was no more content: he later referred to Watts so infuriat-
ing him 'with his Tory articles, that really
one felt almost impelled to head a mob to go
and break one's own office windows'.

In the late 1850s Wilson travelled widely
among the Australasian colonies. His travel-
jottings were published as *Rambles at the
Antipodes* (Melbourne, 1859). His sight was
now beginning to fail and in 1859-60 he
visited England for advice, travelled on the
Continent and served on the committee of
the General Association for the Australian
Colonies. In 1862 he again went to England;
on the homeward voyage his sight deteriorated so badly that he returned immediately,
and late in 1864 he had an operation for
cataract; he regained good vision in one eye,
but decided to remain in England close to
the best medical aid. He lived at Addiscombe near Croydon, but in 1867 bought
Hayes Place, Kent, the eighteenth-century
home of the Pitts. Surrounded by nephews
and nieces, he dispensed endless hospitality
aided by a small army of servants; the amenities included a small zoo which contained
emus, kangaroos and monkeys. Colonial
visitors were always welcome; he was on
close terms with the Darwins, Archbishop
Tait, Edward Lear and Hugh Childers
[q.v.]; children adored him.

Wilson continued to be very active in
public affairs, and used the National Liberal
Club as his London headquarters. In 1863
and 1864 he led the protest against the continuation of transportation of convicts to
Western Australia, especially when a

British royal commission reported in June
1863 in favour of it: 'In the first place Sir'
(he asked the editor of *The Times* on 1
August), 'will you allow me to observe that
we colonists claim to be the equals of you
Englishmen—in no sense whatever your inferiors?'. Concurrent letters from him to the
Argus helped to persuade the Victorian
government to organize the eventually
successful resistance.

In 1864 Wilson was active in the formation of a society to promote assisted migration, and in 1869 read a paper to the Society
of Arts on 'A Scheme of Emigration on a
National Scale'. In 1870 he gave another
paper to the National Association for the
Promotion of Social Science 'On Colonies as
fields of experiment in Government', and
recommended observation of the 'intensely
interesting experiments' proceeding in 'so
vast and varied a laboratory'. He was a
founder of the (Royal) Colonial Institute in
1868, and a member of its council until 1875;
when he then was appointed a vice-
president, he was the only councillor who
was neither titled nor a privy councillor. He
often spoke in discussions, gave several
papers and was a pioneer imperial federationist who looked forward to direct representation of the colonies in the House of
Commons. He was a member of the institute's committee formed in August 1869,
which proposed an imperial conference and
a standing committee to advise the imperial
government, and which was the proximate
cause of the Higinbotham resolutions. Wilson's letter to *The Times* headed 'National
Disintegration', on 10 November 1869
rallied support for the subsequent 'Cannon
Street meetings'.

The *Argus* continued to prosper: all
debts were cleared by the early 1860s and
the annual net profits rose to about £22,000
in 1872. Wilson and Mackinnon had taken
in Allan Spowers as a junior partner in
1857. All three proprietors remained in England and control of the *Argus* was given
entirely to the local board except when the
proprietors jointly issued instructions,
which rarely occurred; Wilson's representative on the board was Gowan Evans whom
he paid £1000 a year. After a disturbed
period of editorship, Wilson's protégé F. W.
Haddon [q.v.], who had been his private
secretary, was appointed in 1867 after a
period as editor of the *Australasian*. Wilson
remained interested in developments in
journalism, read all the London papers every
day and looked forward eagerly to the penny
illustrated daily. He held to his view that a
newspaper should be as cheap as possible
and that all profits should come from advertisements. He looked back with pride to the
period when John Bright displayed the

Argus as an example of what a newspaper could be in the absence of stamp and paper duties.

But Wilson was entirely frustrated in his plans for the *Argus*—'the great work of my life'—for he had lost control. Although he held a majority interest, Mackinnon and Spowers took a purely business-like view and under the terms of the partnership agreement regularly combined against him to resist any change, especially the price reduction from 3d. to 2d. for which he constantly agitated. The circulation of a few thousand barely increased with the years, while the *Age* sold four or five times more; Wilson fumed at the growing influence of his 'arch-enemy . . . that wretched beast and impostor', David Syme [q.v.]. Wilson deeply feared that Syme might wreck the *Argus* and issued frequent warnings and exhortations. His partners saw no reason to disturb such a profitable enterprise and Mackinnon, though fond of Wilson, came increasingly to refer to his timidity, morbid depression, inclination to panic and the total lack of business capacity of the 'poor man'. Each side offered to buy the other out.

There were added depths of irony which increased Wilson's distress. His determination that his editors must have a free hand came under increasing strain as Haddon, in his view, followed a militant and offensively expressed ultra-conservative policy. Wilson welcomed his profits, for he had plans for their ultimate use, but held firm to his radical views. In 1877 he wrote to his old friend Johnston, who was Mackinnon's representative on the board, berating him for abandoning his liberal ideals: 'I feel just as much . . . identified with the cause of the people at large as ever I did in our old days of '48 and '50, when we fought such sturdy battles against La Trobe and his pack of parasites. It seems all very well to rave about the vices of universal suffrage and the rest; but . . . we must manage to get along with [it]'. He was sick and tired of the *Argus's* 'meanness of spirit' and 'old-womanish Toryism'.

After several heart attacks, Wilson died peacefully on 10 January 1878. His remains were taken to Melbourne and interred on 7 July according to the rites of the Church of England. He was unmarried. In his will he made twenty-six legacies of £100 a year to old female friends in the colonies, but the bulk of his estate was used to form the Edward Wilson Trust which since his death has distributed several million dollars to Victorian charities, especially hospitals. A bust by T. Woolner [q.v.] is in the State Library of Victoria.

Wilson was an outstanding journalist who was briefly of crucial importance and commanding influence. A vivid and vigorous writer, he had the great journalist's qualities of high moral conscience, absolute honesty, intolerance of hypocrisy and disregard of self-interest; his emotions, however, sometimes led him into indefensible positions. His radicalism was standard English of his time, but was strengthened by marked independence of thought and intellectual curiosity in diverse fields. Always humane, he lost much of his early shyness and awkwardness and mellowed into a convivial man of considerable charm.

A. S. W[ilson], *John Wilson: Edward Wilson* (Lond, priv print, 1884); W. Westgarth, *Personal recollections of early Melbourne and Victoria* (Melb, 1888); J. Bonwick, *Early struggles of the Australian press* (Lond, 1890); G. Serle, *The golden age* (Melb, 1963); *Argus*, 14 Jan, 8 July 1878, 30 Dec 1911; Haddon papers (LaT L); Parkes letters (ML); Wilson papers (LaT L); J. S. Johnston letters (Univ Melb Archives).   GEOFFREY SERLE

WILSON, SIR JAMES MILNE (1812-1880), politician, brewer and landowner, was born at Banff, Scotland, son of John Wilson, shipowner. In 1829 he migrated to Van Diemen's Land to join his brother Captain William Wilson. He worked in engineering and the merchant marine and reputedly became a successful navigator. In 1836 he was honorary secretary to shareholders in the Theatre Royal at Hobart Town, and honorary treasurer of the first Hobart Annual Regatta in 1838. On 15 December 1847 with Anglican rites he married Deborah Hope, daughter of P. Degraves [q.v.]. Wilson's land interests in the 1840s in the Port Phillip District led to his appointment to the commission of the peace in Melbourne and, later, as territorial magistrate. From 1851, with his brother-in-law W. Degraves [q.v.], he ran sheep on 200 square miles near Mount Gambier, South Australia. Later Wilson leased the Cascade Brewery from the Degraveses for fourteen years. The *Mercury* claimed that the fame of Wilson's ale extended beyond the Australian colonies; it was commended at the 1866-67 Intercolonial Exhibition, Melbourne, and the *Cornwall Chronicle* described it as 'smooth as oil, sweet as milk, clear as amber, and strong as brandy'. In evidence before a select parliamentary committee in 1858 he supported repeal of legislation prohibiting distillation, and claimed he could produce whisky and gin equal to the world's best.

On 18 October 1859 Wilson was elected for Hobart to the Legislative Council and held the seat till his death. Minister without portfolio in the J. Whyte [q.v.] government in 1863-66, he supported its policies on free trade and direct taxation. In 1863 he served on a joint select committee of inquiry into the Launceston-Deloraine railway and next year attended in Melbourne the inter-colonial conference on coastal lighthouses. In 1868 he was a member of the royal commission on the main line railway between Hobart and Launceston which reported in favour of a 4 ft. 8½ ins. gauge.

Wilson became premier and colonial secretary on 4 August 1869 at 'some sacrifice of party predelictions and personal feelings'. Described as 'traitor' and 'renegade' by some Hobart electors, he barely won the subsequent elections. Among his achievements was the Hobart-Launceston main line railway Act and the 1871 contract for its construction with a 3 ft. 6 ins. gauge; legislation for prevention of scab in sheep and to provide for the distillation of spirits from colonial products; and amendments to the Constitution and the electoral Acts. But an 1870 law on intercolonial free trade did not receive royal assent. Defeated on property and income tax proposals, he resigned on 1 November 1872 and on 4 November was elected president of the Legislative Council. Wilson continued to represent Tasmania at intercolonial conferences. To Anthony Trollope [q.v.] he seemed 'to have clearer and juster views on the future political necessities of the colonies than any other Australian statesman'.

Mayor of Hobart in 1868-69 Wilson cut an impressive, clean-shaven figure in mayoral robes when welcoming the duke of Edinburgh in 1868. He actively supported volunteer military movements in the colony, and was sometime president of the Southern Tasmanian Rifle Association. In 1860 he had raised and led the City Guards, and in 1863 commanded the First Administrative Regiment, Southern Division Tasmanian Volunteers.

Wilson was chairman of directors of the Bank of Van Diemen's Land, a director of the Derwent and Tamar Fire, Life, and Marine Assurance Society and president of the Tasmanian Agricultural and Pastoral Society. He was foundation vice-president and chairman of the committee of the Tasmanian Racing Club (Jockey Club), supported it financially, and was prime mover in securing the Elwick race-course. A member and trustee of the Tasmanian Club, he was president of the royal commissions for the Philadelphia (1876), Sydney (1879) and Melbourne (1880) exhibitions.

Wilson was knighted in 1873 and created K.C.M.G. in 1878. He died of heart disease at his home, Melrose, Hampden Road, Hobart, on 29 February 1880 and was buried in Cornelian Bay cemetery. His estate was sworn for probate at £29,883.

J. Fenton, A history of Tasmania (Hob, 1884); Cyclopedia of Tasmania, 1 (Hob, 1900); F. C. Green (ed), A century of responsible government 1856-1956 (Hob, 1956); V&P (HA Tas), 1869, 135, 136 (44, 64), 1870, 122, 123 (23, 24), 1871 (28), 1872 (20, 21), 1873 (2); Hobart Town Courier, 10 June, 19 Aug 1836; Hobarton Guardian, 5 Feb 1851; Mercury, 15, 17 Oct 1859, 5, 7, 10, 13 Aug, 8 Dec 1869, 20 June, 2, 5 Nov 1872, 27 May 1878, 1, 3 Mar 1880; Cornwall Chronicle, 29 June 1867; Examiner (Launceston), 1, 3 Mar 1880; Australasian, 6 Mar 1880; indexes and correspondence file under J. M. Wilson (TA).

NEIL SMITH

WILSON, JOHN BOWIE (1820-1883), politician and free-thinker, was born on 17 June 1820 at Irvine, Ayrshire, Scotland, son of Rev. John Wilson, D.D. Educated at Irvine, he migrated to Australia, arriving in Sydney in the North Briton on 18 July 1840. After eight years in squatting, mostly on the Monaro, he returned to Scotland. Restless, he soon joined his brother, a medical practitioner in the United States of America, and assisted him for three years. Estranged from his father's religion in adolescence, he developed a lifelong interest in spiritualism and dabbled in phrenology. In 1854 he re-emigrated to Australia. Unsuccessful as a gold digger at Araluen, he practised hydropathy and began to call himself doctor. On 9 July 1859 at Braidwood he married Julia, daughter of Thomas Bell. That year he won the Goldfields South seat for the Legislative Assembly and was re-elected in 1860.

An ultra-radical, Wilson soon became obsessed by a desire to abolish all state aid to religion. In 1861, during the debate on (Sir) John Robertson's [q.v.] land bills, he moved to have the Church and school lands declared waste lands to ensure that any money raised from them went to consolidated revenue; but Robertson suspected the move as a plot to defeat his legislation. In 1862 he voted against (Sir) Charles Cowper's [q.v.] successful bill to abolish state aid to religion, arguing that it did not go far enough. Although calling himself a liberal, he opposed the Cowper-Robertson government at every opportunity and late in 1863 joined the conservative (Sir) James Martin's [q.v.] ministry as secretary for lands. In the 1864 general elections he won the rural seat of Patrick Plains despite being accused in verse of putting place before principle by (Sir) Henry Parkes [q.v.]; however, the government was defeated.

Again secretary for lands in the Martin-Parkes coalition in 1866-68, Wilson tried to rectify some of the anomalies of Robertson's land laws, but was popularly believed to favour the squatters in whose social milieu he sometimes moved. He was active in improving the city's recreation areas. In the 1869 elections he was defeated in two country electorates, but in 1870 won a by-election for East Sydney in a campaign organized by John Davies [q.v.] and the Protestant Political Association. In 1868 he was granted the right to retain the title honourable and wear the uniform of an executive councillor after he ceased to hold office, but was chided by the secretary of state for the colonies for his over-eagerness in applying for the honour while in office.

Despite his taste for the trappings of place, Wilson maintained radical connexions, advising the eight-hour movement on tactics in 1870. Active in the temperance movement, he was in 1868 president of the Excelsior division of the Order of the Sons of Temperance and in 1869 an executive member of the New South Wales Alliance for the Suppression of Intemperance. In 1869-70 he twice failed to amend the Sale of Liquors Licensing Act of 1862 to eliminate all but the largest hotels, and later presented a petition containing over 15,000 signatures 'of the mothers and daughters of Sydney' praying for the outlawing of dancing and music in public houses. Wilson was again secretary for lands in the 1870-72 Martin-Robertson ministry. Defeated in the 1872 elections, he withdrew from politics and put his experience to good use as a land agent with George Ranken [q.v.]. He also had interests in mining ventures. In 1875-77 he conscientiously attended meetings of the Sydney, City and Suburban Sewage and Health Board and in 1876-77 was a member of the royal commission on oyster culture.

In 1882, although in ill health, Wilson headed a commission to report on Lord Howe Island; he strongly criticized Captain Richard Armstrong [q.v.], the government resident. Two parliamentary select committees of inquiry into Armstrong's dismissal criticized posthumously Wilson's methods and report, but he was strongly defended by Robertson. He died of dilatation of the heart on 30 April 1883, survived by his second wife Elizabeth, née Gowing, whom he had married on 5 July 1873 at Strathbogie, New England, by their son and daughter and by four daughters by his first wife. An active free-thinker in his later years, in 1882 he was the first president of the Liberal Association of New South Wales. He was buried without religious rites in the Unitarian section of Rookwood cemetery: Rev. Charles Bright [q.v.] delivered the panegyric. His estate was valued for probate at £15,088.

D. Buchanan, *Political portraits of some of the members of the parliament of New South Wales* (Syd, 1863); R. R. Armstrong, *Capt. Armstrong, R.N.* (Syd, 1885); N. Turner, *Sinews of sectarian warfare?* (Canb, 1972); *Empire* (Syd), 6 Dec 1864, 30 Sept 1869; *ISN*, 16 Aug 1867; *SMH*. 23 Jan 1869; *Sydney Mail* and *T&CJ*, 5 May 1883; *Liberal* (Syd), 12 May 1883; P. Loveday, The development of parliamentary government in New South Wales, 1856-1870 (Ph.D. thesis, Univ Syd, 1962); CO 201/543/241.

MARK LYONS

WILSON, JOHN BRACEBRIDGE (1828-1895), headmaster and naturalist, was born on 13 September 1828, only son of Rev. Edward Wilson, rector and artist, of Topcroft, Norfolk, England, and his wife Lucretia, née King. His uncle was Lieut-General Sir Archdale Wilson (1803-1874). His schooling was certified by Rev. W. E. Scudamore, rector of near-by Ditchingham, and he matriculated in 1848 to St John's College, Cambridge (B.A., 1852). After graduating he apparently spent several years in painting, journalism, research and travel. Finally, at Toulouse, he faced 'the grand question—what is to be done?' With a friend Rugeley Collyer, he decided to sail for Melbourne to establish a school or, if disappointed, to open a store at the diggings. 'Once in Australia I will amass an adequate fortune, or I will never return'.

Wilson reached Melbourne on 24 November 1857 in the *Guy Mannering*. By April 1858, after three months service, he was third master, under Rev. G. O. Vance [q.v.], of Geelong Church of England Grammar School when it moved into its first proper quarters. A year later he was second in a staff of ten. In February 1860 he wrote to his mother: 'I shall I think be wise to make it the chief object of my ambition to take a prominent position in the Educational progress of this country'. Next June the school collapsed financially, but helped by a colleague Thomas Hutton, Wilson kept some forty boys together by renting three weatherboard cottages. He conducted this 'High School' so well that, after a necessary reconstitution managed by (Sir) Charles Sladen [q.v.], he was appointed headmaster of a renewed Geelong Grammar School. In February 1863 he returned to its bluestone buildings with some fifty-eight day-boys and two boarders. On 7 April at Geelong he married Oriana Maria (d. 1911), daughter of Horatio Nelson Rowcroft (1806-1878), a Geelong newspaper editor and brother of Charles Rowcroft [q.v.].

Wilson's headmastership coincided with a revival and expansion of the English public school system. His first speech-day report announced his principles: teaching to university standards; religion with toleration; athletics for enjoyment and character-building; discipline, based upon trust, justice and kindness, expectant of truth and obedience. He was, he wrote, 'convinced that the majority of boys are not naturally inclined to be idle, when properly handled and properly taught'. At first, although well supported by Sladen and by Rev. G. Goodman [q.v.], Wilson laboured largely alone. His letter-books show his problems and reveal his vigour of mind and body, vision, determination, integrity, sympathy, justice, common sense, care for detail, and controlled, explosive wrath. Wrongdoing, real or imagined, lit the fuse, when Wilson's exclamatory beard, kindling blue eyes and slightly shaken head presaged a detonation which scorched offenders. But he was always fair, would apologize when mistaken, and soon forgot simple transgressions, even later when gout distressed him. He was well set up in his prime, just under 6 ft. tall, and usually wore a frock coat with a dark-flowered vest. Although, unlike J. L. Cuthbertson [q.v.], he did not make chums of his boys, he was their loved and respected 'Chief' and watchful, unselfish guardian.

A sound classical scholar, mathematician and linguist, Wilson had a natural taste for natural science and practical affairs. Like other contemporary headmasters, he aimed at Arnold's ideal of the Christian gentleman. He echoed the fifteenth Psalm, but moved easily in the world of facts, and knew the real from the fanciful. As his staff became more reliable, and he became older, he was seen less about the school. But he still held it together, knew every boy, and was ready to help, without condescension, any who brought him a problem in natural history.

Wilson developed strong links with the University of Melbourne and its M.A. was conferred on him in 1876. He became well known as a marine biologist, and in 1882 was elected a fellow of the Linnean Society, London. He rejoiced in a succession of yachts and usually spent the school vacations in pioneer dredging about Port Phillip Heads for shellfish, seaweeds, sponges, and similar marine life, which were preserved and examined in the large well-arranged aquarium at his Sorrento cottage, Atherstone, and distributed to naturalists for further study. The Royal Society of Victoria, and museums in Australia and Britain received valuable collections from him. As scientist, Wilson was chiefly an exact collector and broad classifier, but he associated easily with men such as Sir Frederick McCoy, Sir Ferdinand Mueller [qq.v.], Arthur Dendy, A. H. S. Lucas and (Sir) Baldwin Spencer. He published several articles in scientific journals. As naturalist, his lasting bequest to the school was the Saturday ramble.

Wilson died of gout on 22 October 1895 at Geelong, survived by his wife and two of his three daughters. He was buried in the Eastern cemetery, Geelong.

Corian, Sept 1971; Wilson letter-books *and* school records (Geelong Grammar School); family information.   P. L. BROWN

WILSON, SIR SAMUEL (1832-1895), pastoralist and politician, was born on 7 February 1832 at Ballycloughan, County Antrim, Ireland, son of Samuel Wilson, farmer and landowner, and his wife Mary, née Singley. Educated at Ballymena, he had an aptitude for mathematics; although inclined toward a career as a civil engineer he spent three years as a linen manufacturer and farmer.

In May 1852 Wilson reached Victoria with his brother John who, with other brothers Charles and Alexander, had already established squatting runs in the Wimmera region. Samuel, after some success as a miner at Ballarat, Fryer's Creek, Ovens and Bendigo goldfields, prospered as a carrier of supplies from Melbourne to Ballarat and Pleasant Creek (Stawell) diggings, where he earned the sobriquet 'Bullocky Sam'. After managing Kewell station, which had been taken up by Alexander and John in 1845, Wilson sold his property in Ireland; with his brothers' help he bought from William Taylor [q.v.] Longerenong station at the junction of the Wimmera River and Yarriambiack Creek. There he created a system of dams and channels that foreshadowed the vast Mallee-Wimmera water gravitation scheme of today.

Wilson revisited Ireland in 1859. On 10 December 1861 in Melbourne, in a ceremony performed by Rev. I. Hetherington [q.v.], he married Jean, daughter of William Campbell [q.v.]; they had four sons and three daughters. The building of Longerenong homestead began next year and the property was subdivided into Longerenong, St Helens, Marma Downs, Green Hills and Kirkwood stations. The Wilson brothers, who had other extensive Wimmera holdings including Ashens, Vectis, Walmer and Talgany runs, acquired also Yanco on the Murrumbidgee River, New South Wales. Expert management enabled Wilson to gain sole ownership of Longerenong in four years and, in 1869 when the partnership was dissolved, to buy out his brothers; land values at the time were very low because of drought, but in the good seasons that followed he was able to complete most purchases by 1871.

Wilson supported the work of the Acclimatisation Society by experimenting with ostrich farming and with the breeding of Angora goats. In 1873, from T. and S. Learmonth [qq.v.] and for the record price of £236,000, he bought the graceful homestead of Ercildoune near Burrumbeet with its famous merino stud. He bought freehold estates in the Western District at Mount Bute, Marathon and Corangamite to replace the Wimmera holdings that he sold to Albert Austin [q.v.] and W. H. Bullivant in 1874, and the New South Wales leases of Coree and Goolgumbla. By 1879 he held 117,452 acres freehold in Victoria, 150,000 acres freehold in New South Wales where he had Toorale and Dunlop stations on the Darling, as well as 2,500,000 acres leased in New South Wales and Queensland where he held runs along the Diamantina and Bogan rivers. At Ercildoune he established breeding ponds for English trout. He also spent £1000 in importing salmon ova for release in Victorian streams.

Wilson represented the Wimmera in the Legislative Assembly in 1861-64 and the Western Province in the Legislative Council from 1875 until his resignation in May 1881; according to Deakin he was 'ridiculed ... and never attained any political influence'. His gift in 1874 of £30,000 to build a hall at the University of Melbourne was realized in October 1879 when he set the foundation stone for the Gothic Wilson Hall. He made many other donations to charitable and religious bodies. Governor Sir George Bowen, in recommending him for a baronetcy in 1874, estimated Wilson's average annual income as almost £100,000, stated that he owned 600,000 sheep, possibly more than anyone else in the world, and described his position and style of living as similar to an 'opulent country gentleman' in England. He was knighted in 1875.

In 1881 Wilson retired to England where he bought Hughenden Manor. Prominent in the imperial federation movement, he contributed articles to the *National Review*, September 1884, and the *Nineteenth Century*, April 1885. He was unsuccessful at an election in Buckinghamshire that year, but he represented Portsmouth in 1886-92. After visiting Australia in 1893-94 Wilson returned to England where he died at his residence in Grosvenor Square, London, on 11 June 1895. The rebuilt Wilson Hall is his chief memorial. A son Captain Gordon Chesney Wilson married Lady Sarah Churchill, aunt of Sir Winston; a daughter married the earl of Huntingdon. Two sons were living at Ercildoune at the time of his death.

Fisken, Gibson & Co., *Catalogue of ... Sir Samuel Wilson's merino ewes and rams ... Ercildoune* (Melb, 1879); A. Sutherland et al, *Victoria and its metropolis*, 2 (Melb, 1888); R. V. Billis and A. S. Kenyon, *Pastoral pioneers of Port Phillip* (Melb, 1932); P. Mc-Caughey, *Samuel McCaughey* (Syd, 1955); M. L. Kiddle, *Men of yesterday* (Melb, 1961); T. Young, 'Pioneer station owners', *Dennys, Lascelles' annual* (Melb, 1926); *Australasian* and *Weekly Times* (Melb), 22 June 1895; *ISN*, 1 July 1895; Deakin letter, May 1889, Dilke papers, 4 (BM); CO 448/113/50.   L. J. BLAKE

WILSON, WILLIAM PARKINSON (1826?-1874), professor of mathematics, was born at Peterborough, Northamptonshire, England, and baptized on 1 February 1826, son of John Wilson, silversmith, and his wife Elizabeth, née Parkinson. Educated at the Cathedral Grammar School, Peterborough, he won a sizarship at St John's College, Cambridge, and was admitted in February 1843 (B.A., 1847; M.A., 1850); senior wrangler, first Smith's prizeman, and fellow of St John's in 1847-57, in August 1849 he became founding professor of mathematics at Queen's College, Belfast. In 1850 he published *A Treatise on Dynamics*.

In 1854 Wilson was chosen as professor of mathematics, pure and mixed, at the newly established University of Melbourne; he had weighed prospects of a greater personal influence and a trebled salary against academic exile. One of the four foundation professors, he arrived in Melbourne on 31 January 1855 and gave the university's first lecture on 13 April. Students were few. Three days later an apprehensive Wilson and his colleague W. E. Hearn [q.v.] issued a pamphlet, which rejected the 'Oxford model' held responsible for the University of Sydney's 'want of success', and urged that the study of classics be optional. The university council rejected the scheme and a similar proposal in 1857. Besides Euclid, trigonometry, algebra, analytical geometry and calculus, Wilson taught in the B.A. course natural philosophy 'illustrated by models and experiments'; he spent £500 on apparatus in the first year. In a two-year course he lectured on mechanics, hydrostatics, pneumatics, heat, meteorology, optics, astronomy, electricity and magnetism. He also set and corrected the matriculation papers in mathematics. In 1858 he devised the first engineering course at an Australian university and the three-year course leading to a certificate of civil engineering was begun in 1861. Two of his students were W. C. Kernot and H. M. Andrew [qq.v.].

Wilson deplored what he termed an 'incomplete' university without residential colleges to provide moral and religious education, the encouragement of study after graduation, tutorial teaching, training for the clergy, and the cultivation of 'university spirit and feeling'. In September 1865 he became secretary of a committee set up to found an Anglican college at the university. In 1872 Trinity College was opened and he was a trustee from November 1871 and secretary of its first council.

With an extensive knowledge of architecture and the arts, Wilson served on the royal commission on fine arts in 1863-64. He was a member and a vice-president of the Philosophical Institute (founded 1855) and was active in the affairs of its successor, the Royal Society of Victoria. He was keenly interested in astronomy and in Belfast had founded and directed an observatory. In November 1856 in a paper read before the Philosophical Institute he advocated Melbourne as the site for the southern hemisphere observatory so long planned by the Royal Society, London; a committee was formed to induce the government to achieve Wilson's 'noble object'. In June 1858 he demonstrated a model of a 4-ft. reflector for the proposed Melbourne observatory, which opened in 1863. Wilson had been its secretary from 1860 and was a most active member of its Board of Visitors. In December 1871 he had charge of the small equatorial telescope of the expedition which set out to observe the eclipse of the sun off Cape Sidmouth, Queensland. At Mornington, south of Melbourne, he established an observatory as part of the transit of Venus observations on 9 December 1874. He had written a report of his findings to his friend R. L. J. Ellery [q.v.] when on 11 December he died of apoplexy, aged 48. He was buried in the Moorooduc cemetery. A bachelor, he had lived in the university's quadrangle apartments; at the time of his death his two nephews were being educated under his care.

A little man of fiery temperament, Wilson was at times outspoken and punctilious but was never factious. His ready analysis of issues, his constancy, correctness and unremitting industry made him most effective in the advocacy of causes. He was a thorough and lucid teacher.

A. Sutherland et al, Victoria and its metropolis, 2 (Melb, 1888); E. Scott, A history of the University of Melbourne (Melb, 1936); G. Blainey, A centenary history of the University of Melbourne (Melb, 1957); T. W. Moody and J. C. Beckett, Queen's, Belfast 1845-1949 (Lond, 1959); Age, 12, 29 Dec 1874; Argus, 12 Dec 1874; Daily Telegraph (Melb), 14 Dec 1874; Australasian and Weekly Times (Melb), 19 Dec 1874.

WINDEYER, Sir WILLIAM CHARLES (1834-1897), politician and judge, was born at Westminster, London, on 29 September 1834, only child of Richard Windeyer [q.v.] and his wife Maria, née Camfield. He arrived in Sydney with his parents in the Medway on 28 November 1835. His father died in 1847; his mother, with help from friends and relations, managed to retrieve the house and part of the land at Tomago from the insolvent estate. William's letters to her reveal the strong influence of her affectionate, God-fearing character and methodical good sense. All his life he liked to return to Tomago and work in the garden.

Windeyer was educated at W. T. Cape's [q.v.] Elfred House Private School and in 1850-52 at The King's School, Parramatta, partly with the help of (Sir) Charles Nicholson and Robert Lowe [qq.v.]. In October 1852 he gained a scholarship and was among the first undergraduates at the University of Sydney (B.A., 1856; M.A., 1859). An admirer of Professor Woolley [q.v.], he was strongly influenced by his liberal outlook. Windeyer ran the Sydney University Magazine. His uncle John Thompson described him at this time as 'rather a favourite with us all—very impulsive, original & independent'.

Windeyer read in the chambers of E. Broadhurst [q.v.] and was admitted to the colonial Bar on 7 March 1857; on 31 December at Hexham he married Mary Elizabeth (1836-1912), daughter of Rev. R. T. Bolton. As a law reporter on (Sir) Henry Parkes's [q.v.] Empire, he came into contact with 'the first distinct party with a Liberal creed and the means of vigorous action'. He also wrote articles for the Empire and was fostered in politics by Parkes. In January 1859 he became crown prosecutor for the northern districts but resigned in May. Defeated that year by (Sir) Daniel Cooper [q.v.] for Paddington, he was returned to the Legislative Assembly for the Lower Hunter and from 1860 represented West Sydney. In 1859 he attacked Sir Alfred Stephen [q.v.] and opposed the motion granting him full salary when on leave, but his apology in August 1863 began warm relations with the chief justice. While Parkes was in England in 1861 Windeyer corresponded with him and (Sir) Charles Duffy [q.v.] about Federation and tried to keep together Parkes's political supporters.

In 1860 Windeyer had been the main mover in the revival of the Volunteer Force; on 4 December he was commissioned captain of the No. 2 company of the Sydney Battalion of the Volunteer Rifles and in 1868 was promoted major. He was a member of the winning New South Wales rifle team in the match against Victoria in Melbourne in 1862. On the return voyage the *City of Sydney* was wrecked off Green Cape; no one was lost but Windeyer suffered shock and ill health and resigned from parliament on 22 December.

On 17 January 1866 during an absence from Sydney he was nominated, through the machinations of Parkes, and defeated (Sir) John Robertson [q.v.] at a ministerial election for West Sydney. Two years later he complained to Parkes: 'From the part I took towards you I know that I lost the favour of many who had it in their power to help a young and struggling professional man and that to this day in my private life and prospects I feel the effects of my staunch adherence to you . . . I think that you who pulled the strings in that election took an unwarrantable liberty with my name'. He was solicitor-general in the Martin [q.v.]-Robertson coalition in 1870-72 and was defeated in the 1872 general election.

On 8 September 1876 Windeyer returned to the assembly as first member for the University of Sydney and next March became attorney-general in Parkes's ministry. On 4 August he offered to resign after a political crisis caused by his legal opinion that 'five miles square' in the land Acts was equivalent to twenty-five square miles; however Parkes supported him and the ministry left office on 16 August. In 1878-79 he was attorney-general in the Parkes-Robertson coalition. A law reformer, Windeyer introduced eighteen bills as a private member and carried eight; the most important were the Patents Act and the Married Women's Property Act of 1879 which gave women control of property which was theirs by their own right or exertions; he also carried six private Acts. In 1871-72 he was a member of the Law Reform Commission and was thanked by Stephen for his help; in 1893-94 he sat on the Statute-Law Consolidation Commission.

Windeyer had an abiding interest in education. In 1855-65 he was esquire bedell at the University of Sydney, a member of its senate in 1866-97, an examiner in law, vice-chancellor in 1883-86 and chancellor in 1895-96. He advocated the extension of free and secular elementary education, supported the 1866 Public Schools Act and advocated the establishment of country high schools for both girls and boys. He was a trustee of Sydney Grammar School from the 1860s and of the Free Public Library in 1884-86 and 1888-97, and a member of the Board of Technical Education in 1883-86. He taught Latin and Greek in the 1860s at the Sydney Mechanics' School of Arts and was sometime president. He believed in higher education for women and in 1891 was founding

chairman of the Women's College, within the University of Sydney.

An advocate of social reform, Windeyer was president of the 1873 royal commission on public charities, and strongly vindicated Lucy Osburn [q.v.] in the report, which he wrote himself. Next year he was foundation president of the Discharged Prisoners' Aid Society and in the 1870s was a vice-president of the City Night Refuge and Soup Kitchen. He was also a member of the commissions to make arrangements for the public reception of the duke of Edinburgh, and for the Philadelphia International Exhibition, and a director of the Hunter River Steam Navigation Co. His efforts helped to preserve Clarke Island in Port Jackson, Belmore Park and reserves on Observatory Hill and Church Hill for public recreation.

On 10 August 1879 Windeyer resigned from parliament; next day he was appointed a temporary puisne judge of the Supreme Court and two years later became permanent. He sat mainly in common and criminal law, as judge in Divorce and as deputy-judge in the Vice-Admiralty Court. His written judgments were notable for competent and careful legal learning, literary quality and clarity of expression. As judge in Divorce he administered the law with compassion and understanding, supporting Stephen's reform efforts in the columns of the *Sydney Morning Herald* and in his judgments in both divorce and criminal jurisdiction. In 1888 in *Ex parte Collins* he upheld an appeal against a conviction for obscenity for selling Mrs Besant's *The Law of Population*.

Windeyer proved controversial in criminal cases. With a rigorous and unrelenting sense of the retribution that he believed criminal justice demanded, he had a sympathy verging on the emotional for the victims of crime, especially women. In 1886 he played a contentious part in the resignation of (Sir) Julian Salomons [q.v.] as chief justice and caused a public outcry by sentencing to death nine young men in the notorious Mount Rennie rape case. In May 1889 150 jurors and residents of Deniliquin petitioned parliament for an inquiry into Windeyer's unjust remarks and 'hurried manner'; in August he was criticized in the House for imprisoning intoxicated witnesses, but Chief Justice Darley [q.v.] pointed out to Parkes that the men 'had been imprisoned for deliberately getting drunk or feigning drunkenness . . . Mr Justice Windeyer is to be highly commended for what he did in vindication of Justice'. Hostility to Windeyer reached a climax in 1895 when he imposed the death penalty on George Dean for poisoning his wife. Despite such contentious episodes his eminence as a judge was widely recognized by those qualified to assess it. At the instigation of Sir Samuel Griffith in 1892, he was appointed a temporary judge in Queensland to preside over the Full Court to hear a case which the chief justice was disqualified from hearing.

Windeyer had visited England for Queen Victoria's Golden Jubilee celebrations in 1887 and was made an honorary doctor of laws by the University of Cambridge; he was knighted in 1891. Although outwardly unmoved and altogether unyielding, he was grieved by the clamour and obloquy aroused by the Dean case and in 1896 visited England for a rest. He retired from the bench and in 1897 accepted a temporary judgeship in Newfoundland but died of paralysis of the heart on 12 September at Bologna, Italy. He was survived by his wife, three sons and five daughters. His estate was valued for probate at £18,733. Described by Darley as 'singularly able, conscientious, zealous and hardworking ... in some respects he was much misunderstood, for those who knew him best know what a tender heart he had and what a depth of sympathy he possessed for all those in distress and misery'. Parkes, in his *Fifty Years in the Making of Australian History* (1892), wrote 'My friend Windeyer was a young man of high spirit, bold and decisive in the common incidents of life, with a strong capacity for public affairs. He would have made as good a soldier as he has made a sound Judge'.

Encouraged by her husband, Lady Windeyer was a leader of charitable organizations and a pioneer of women's rights, especially their claim to be enfranchised. In 1895 she was a founder and first president of the Women's Hospital, Crown Street, and president of the Womanhood Suffrage League of New South Wales. She was also prominent in the organization of the Women's Industrial Exhibition in 1888 and in the Woman's Christian Temperance Union of New South Wales.

Portraits of Windeyer are held by the University of Sydney, The King's School, Parramatta, and some descendants.

Cyclopedia of N.S.W. (Syd, 1907); PD (NSW), 4 Sept 1889; V&P (LA NSW), 1889, 2, 1063; NSW Law Reports, 9 (1888), 505; Qld Law J Reports, 1893 supp; SMH, 21 Apr, 9 Sept 1886, 4 Sept 1889, 18 Nov 1891, 15 Sept 1897, 5 Dec 1912; *Brisbane Courier*, 15 Sept 1892; *Australasian*, 21 Aug 1897; M. Rutledge, Sir Alfred Stephen and divorce law reform in New South Wales, 1886-1892 (M.A. thesis, ANU, 1966); R. Parsons, Lawyers in the New South Wales parliament, 1870-1890 (Ph.D. thesis, Macquarie Univ, 1972); Parkes letters (ML); Windeyer papers (ML, and Univ Syd Archives, and held by Sir Victor Windeyer, Turramurra, NSW).

WINDICH (WINDIITJ), TOMMY (1840-1876), Aboriginal tracker and explorer, was born near Mount Stirling, south of Kellerberrin, Western Australia. He belonged to the Kokar people who spoke the Njaggi Njaggi tongue but was probably also fluent in the inland lingua franca, Kalarmai. Probably detribalized when young through an epidemic, he was brought up in the recently settled Bunbury district. Without formal education, he was well trained by elders in bushcraft and by white settlers in horsemanship. He was a great help to early land seekers and government surveyors, and accompanied C. C. Hunt [q.v.] on his expedition into the country east of York in 1866. As a police tracker and native constable he helped in the arrest of the murderers of Edward Clarkson in January.

Windich was on good terms with the Forrest family, who had settled at Picton in 1851, and especially with John and Alexander, sons of William. Both led important expeditions into the interior of Western Australia and both owed much of their success to the assistance of native trackers. John took Windich on three expeditions; first into the north-eastern districts in April-August 1869, next around the Great Australian Bight to Adelaide in March-August 1870, and finally from Champion Bay to the Peake Station on the overland telegraph line and thence to Adelaide in March-November 1874. Alexander also took him on his expedition to the Hampton Plains in August-November 1871. As both John and Alexander Forrest were surveyors accustomed to navigate by astronomical observation they were never in danger of being lost in the inland deserts, but they relied heavily on their Aboriginal trackers in the daily search for drinking-water and for horse feed. Windich usually acted as the scout and was adept at finding either native wells or waterholes in the rocky outcrops. He was an expert rifleman and hunter, but in public ceremonies celebrating the end of expeditions his inarticulate reserve was in marked contrast to the expansive garrulity of his compatriot Tommy Pierre.

Windich received several small gifts from the government for his services and frequent expressions of gratitude from the Forrest brothers. They erected a tombstone over his grave after he died of pneumonia while working with a construction party on the overland telegraph at Esperance Bay in February 1876. On it they inscribed: 'He was an aboriginal native of Western Australia, of great intelligence and fidelity, who accompanied them on exploring expeditions into the interior of Australia, two of which were from Perth to Adelaide. Be Ye Also Ready'. His name is perpetuated by Windich Springs, north-west of the Frere Range, discovered and named by John Forrest on 27 May 1874.

J. Forrest, Explorations in Australia (Lond, 1875); Lord Forrest centenary booklet, 1847-1947 (Perth, 1947); G. C. Bolton, Alexander Forrest (Melb, 1958); F. K. Crowley, Forrest: 1847-1918, 1 (Brisb, 1971); West Australian Times, 17 Mar 1876; information from Dr C. G. von Brandenstein, Inst of Aboriginal Studies, Canb.   F. K. CROWLEY

WINDSOR, ARTHUR LLOYD (1833-1913), journalist, was born at sea on a voyage to Barbados, West Indies, son of Henry George Windsor, R.N.; his father's family owned sugar plantations in the West Indies. When Windsor was 5 his father died, and three years later he was sent to school at Ottery St Mary, Devon, England. He left school at 17 and lived at Clifton, Bristol, writing occasional articles for English periodicals such as the London Spectator. A few years later he went back to Barbados and taught at Codrington College. About the end of 1855 he visited Canada before returning to England. His income from inherited sugar estates diminishing, he coached young relations for the army, wrote for the Quarterly Review and taught classics at Clifton College. His collection of essays, published in London in 1860 as Ethica; or, Characteristics of Men, Manners, and Books, evidenced his wide reading and confidence in handling his subjects.

Soon afterwards Windsor was appointed editor of the Melbourne Argus. With his wife Elizabeth Jenkins, née Hucker, whom he had married at Clifton on 3 July 1861, he arrived in Melbourne in the Great Britain on 3 April 1863. He stayed with the Argus until 1865 but its political conservatism and managerial control irked him. He moved to Castlemaine and edited the Mount Alexander Mail; his 3-month-old son died there in May 1867. In 1869 he returned to Melbourne and in 1872 became editor of the Age.

Windsor worked in great harmony with its proprietor, David Syme [q.v.]. Conferring almost daily, they thrashed out the paper's attitude on matters of the day, and Windsor adapted the decisions to the editorial and news columns. He was the first editorial writer whom Syme really trusted and they became close friends. Comparing them, Alfred Deakin wrote that Windsor was more classically trained than Syme, far quicker and more adaptable . . . a far readier, more copious and polished writer and speaker. . . . He had many enthusiasms but

they were all short-lived, a fine literary taste and style, and a rich endowment of humour, insight and original speculation'. More bluntly, a colleague writing in 1913 said Windsor always passed for 'a sort of Tory, but nobody could nail him to anything . . . His forte, in which he was beyond rivalry, was the bitter satiric political or social article'. Absorbed in his work, he did not seek friends but he was not a misanthrope.

President of the Australian Institute of Journalists in 1892, Windsor was described as a scholarly looking man, with a small, straight nose, keen blue eyes and particularly fine, sensitive hands; not tall, he had a sturdy, well-knit frame. He retired in late 1900 and in March next year went to London but was not happy there and returned to Melbourne in ill health. Aged 79, he died of chronic nephritis at his home at Brunswick on 20 January 1913 and was buried in the Coburg cemetery.

B. Hoare, Looking back gaily (Melb, 1927); A. Deakin, The crisis in Victorian politics, 1879-1881, J. A. La Nauze and R. M. Crawford eds (Melb, 1957); C. E. Sayers, David Syme, a life (Melb, 1965); W. S. Robinson, If I remember rightly, G. Blainey ed (Melb, 1967); Bulletin, 5 Jan, 9 Mar 1901, 30 Jan 1913; Aust Worker, 2 Apr 1908; Age, 22 Jan 1913.

C. E. SAYERS

WINTER, JAMES (1834-1885) and WINTER-IRVING, WILLIAM IRVING (1840-1901), pastoralists, were born in Edinburgh, the sons of John Winter and his wife Janet Margaret, née Irving, of Lauder, Berwickshire, Scotland. In 1841 John brought his family to Australia in the William Mitchell and, settling near Ballarat, acquired Bonshaw estate and in 1850, Junction station. His sons were educated in Melbourne, William attending Scotch College. In 1857 John moved into the Waranga district, lower Goulburn Valley, where by the late 1860s he and his sons had acquired over a quarter of a million acres, either freehold or leasehold: their properties later included Corop, Caragarac, Toolamba, Colbinabbin, Stanhope and Dhurringile.

On the dissolution of the family partnership in 1868 James retained Toolamba and built a 68-room mansion at Dhurringile. He vastly improved the carrying capacity of his land, breeding prize-winning Lincoln, Leicester and crossbred sheep. In 1874 he helped to found the North-Eastern Pastoral and Agricultural Society and was its president; he was patron of the Murchison Agricultural Society, a magistrate, and a member and in 1873-75 president of the Waranga Shire Council. He actively supported the local Anglican church, the Mechanics' Institute and sports associations. As president of the railway league formed in 1873 he worked hard but in vain to bring the line down the Goulburn Valley; he was praised for helping Toolamba selectors in the 1873 drought.

On 27 April 1871, aged 36, Winter married Caroline, daughter of W. H. Pettett. In 1883 he took his family to England, travelling by way of the United States of America. About to return to Victoria, he died of inflammation of the lungs at Norwood near London on 3 February 1885; he was survived by his wife and children.

William Winter-Irving retained Stanhope on which he spent about £40,000 in improvements, and he had an interest in Colbinabbin. In 1869 he bought a property near Murchison on which he later built the homestead Noorilim and he also acquired Tirrengower near Colac. He later held Wealwandangie cattle station with James Alison and was part-owner of Rocklands, both in Queensland. Besides breeding cattle and sheep, he developed a famous English hackney stud. He shared the family passion for building. Noorilim, built with the help of specially imported Italian craftsmen, cost £72,000 to erect in 1877.

William was keenly interested in local affairs and was a magistrate from 1868 and licensing magistrate for Rushworth from 1885. He was a member of the Waranga Shire Council between 1865 and 1874 and president in 1868-71. A member of several deputations, in 1870 with his brother he used his influence to secure a government grant of £4000 for two bridges over the Campaspe and Goulburn rivers. He gave generously to agricultural societies at Murchison and Tatura, to the Rushworth Anglican church and to local institutions. He was a large shareholder in the Rushworth butter factory; a life governor of the Bendigo hospital and asylum; a member of the Agricultural and Horticultural Society and of the Bendigo art gallery to which he gave many paintings and collector's items. He lent his paddocks for the Colbinabbin farmers' annual picnics and for use by the local coursing club; he kept large kennels.

In 1871 he stood for the Eastern Province of the Legislative Council but retired in favour of Sir Francis Murphy [q.v.]. In 1874 he visited England and successfully conducted the Privy Council appeal against the Crown on the 5s. an acre penalty sought to be enforced against the holders of certificated lands. In 1884 he was returned unopposed to the Legislative Council for Northern Province; he held the seat until 1901. Unobtrusive and rather silent in the House, he was respected for his shrewdness,

sound judgment, straightforward manner and attention to the needs of his constituents.

In 1887 William sold Colbinabbin to David Mitchell [q.v.], installed a manager at Stanhope and moved to Melbourne. In 1888 he changed his surname by royal letters patent to Winter-Irving. Next year he was a government commissioner to the Paris Universal Exhibition. In 1893 he bought Noorilim in Dandenong Road and housed his fine art collection there. He was a fellow of the Royal Colonial Institute (life member, 1886) and of the Imperial Institute; a life member of the Royal Geographical Society of Australasia (Victorian Branch) and of the Australian Club and active in Old Scotch Collegians' affairs. He was managing director of the National Trustees, Executors, and Agency Co. of Australasia, and a director of companies including, in 1891-93, Goldsbrough Mort [qq.v.] & Co.

On 30 June 1868 he had married with Presbyterian rites Frances Amelia, daughter of William Drayton Taylor of Noorilum, Goulburn River. In poor health in his last years Winter-Irving died of cirrhosis of the liver on 28 June 1901, aged 61, at Noorilim, Prahran. He was survived by his wife, five sons and six daughters.

H. M. Humphreys (ed), *Men of the time in Australia: Victorian series*, 1st ed (Melb, 1878); A. Sutherland et al, *Victoria and its metropolis*, 2 (Melb, 1888); J. Smith (ed), *Cyclopedia of Victoria*, 1 (Melb, 1903); H. W. Forster, *Waranga, 1865-1965* (Melb, 1965); *Shepparton Chronicle*, 7 Feb 1885; *Goulburn Advertiser*, 13 Feb 1885, 5 July 1901; *Argus*, 29 June 1901; *Pastoral Review*, 15 July 1901.

J. ANN HONE

WINTER, SAMUEL PRATT (1816-1878), pastoralist, was born on 17 July 1816 at Agher, County Meath, Ireland, son of Samuel Pratt Winter and his wife Frances Rose, née Bomford. He was educated at a school at Dewsbury Moor, Yorkshire, and on his parents' death in 1831 his uncle Rev. Francis Pratt Winter became his guardian. In 1833 worsening conditions in Ireland caused Samuel to be sent to a friend W. Bryan [q.v.] in Van Diemen's Land; arriving in the *Cleopatra* on 14 June 1834 Samuel joined him at Glenore near Carrick, south of Launceston; when Bryan left the colony Samuel remained in the Carrick area and acted as his attorney. Samuel's brother Trevor (b. 1822) joined him about three years later and George (b. 1815) arrived in April 1839, together with his sister Arbella [q.v. C. P. Cooke].

Francis Winter had raised £1300 for the brothers and in 1837 Samuel crossed to the mainland and took up Tahara and Spring Valley (Murndal) on the Wannon River in the Western District of Port Phillip. In March 1838 Samuel and Trevor moved stock to the Wannon. Trevor settled in the area but Samuel divided his time between the Wannon runs and Carrick. In 1841-43 he visited Ireland. In January 1845 he made Murndal his home at a site chosen by his manager Thomas Murphy, but still spent much time in Van Diemen's Land. George took over Tahara. In 1851 Samuel travelled through South America and Panama, where he caught yellow fever, and visited the United States of America and Canada. In England he began his collection of paintings, many of them copies of famous works, and seventeenth and eighteenth-century books which in later years added much distinction to the Murndal homestead—he eventually built up a library of over one thousand volumes. Arbella, who watched over his affairs at Murndal, advised him to sell it and told him of the troubled times facing squatters, but Winter intended to return. He warned Trevor that the squatters must be ready with 'the necessary funds for the contest'. But he did not reach Murndal until late in 1854.

For the next ten years Winter remained on the Wannon, generally prospering although burnt out in 1860. An astute businessman, he had a gift for getting people to work for him and his fortune built up even in his long absences. He acquired freehold of his run, owning 19,000 acres by 1861 and was licensee of another 12,480 acres; he was still consolidating in the early 1870s. In the 1860s he added to the original stone house until Murndal became a huge rambling building; he planted acres of trees, mainly English, though he had brought seeds from Michelangelo's cypresses from Italy. C. Fetherstonhaugh [q.v.] described Murndal as one of the most beautiful places in the Western District.

To Margaret Kiddle, Winter was 'something of an enigma, this man of personal beauty and charm who never married and in his solitary wanderings left no story of a lost love behind him'. It was his custom to have a black boy in livery mounted on his horse's croup on his visits to the Melbourne Club. He introduced Pyrenean sheep dogs to guard his flocks and wrote a poem in 1874 commemorating his invention of a swing gate for drafting sheep. His undoubted intellectual loneliness at Murndal was tempered by his friendship with Dr F. T. C. Russell [q.v.], the local Anglican clergyman. Although an agnostic who very early adopted Darwinian teaching, Winter gave the money for the parsonage at Coleraine and supported the church and school. His literary appreciation was wide and his notebooks were filled with quotations from de Quincey, Arnold, Palmerston, King James I, W. E. Gladstone and James Mill.

In 1865-70 Winter again visited England. After his return his health deteriorated and he lived in various parts of Victoria and New South Wales. In 1878 he bought Fern Lodge, Mount Macedon, and died there of fibroid phthisis on 25 December. He had instructed his brother to bury him at Murndal where the Aboriginals lay, with nothing but a large stone cairn over the grave. The shocked reaction of the community caused Trevor Winter to modify this last request. He left an estate sworn for probate at £68,000; Samuel Winter Cooke, Arbella's eldest son, inherited Murndal.

A. Henderson (ed), *Early pioneer families of Victoria and Riverina* (Melb, 1936); M. L. Kiddle, *Men of yesterday* (Melb, 1961); Kiddle papers and notes from Winter Cooke collection (Univ Melb Archives).   J. ANN HONE

WINTER, SAMUEL VINCENT (1843-1904) and **JOSEPH** (1844-1915), journalists, were born on 23 March 1843 in the Goulburn Valley, Port Phillip District, and on 26 October 1844 in Melbourne, elder children of Samuel Winter, corn-dealer, an English Protestant, and his wife Alice, née Sullivan, an Irish Catholic, both of whom had arrived as assisted migrants in 1841. The family settled in Richmond near Melbourne, where the boys attended St James's Catholic School. Their father died and about 1856 the boys were apprenticed to W. H. Williams, a West Melbourne printer.

Within a few years Samuel was foreman of the works. For seven years he was secretary of the St Patrick's Society, and later president; in 1869 he was secretary of a committee to enable the Fenian prisoners released in Western Australia to migrate elsewhere. In 1868, on the advice of Michael O'Grady, C. G. Duffy and Joseph Dalton [qq.v.], he founded the *Advocate* as a Catholic weekly, managed it for about three years and handed it over to Joseph. In 1871 Samuel purchased the ailing evening *Herald* in partnership with John Halfey [q.v.] and others; by 1874 he had taken over the editorship and was building up its circulation which rose to about 20,000 in 1880 and 40,000 in 1890. Inevitably the *Herald* was reputed to be Irish Catholic in outlook, but Winter judiciously tempered his sympathies. In 1871 he was an enthusiastic founding member of the Australian

Natives' Association. He was a member of the Richmond Council in 1875-83 and a successful mayor in 1877 and 1882; he was prominent in negotiations to establish the suburban tramway system and became a justice of the peace. A staunch 'Berryite' [q.v. G. Berry] protectionist, he failed to win the Legislative Assembly seat of Richmond in 1877 and 1883. He now had a reputation for splendid elocution and wit, but he renounced political ambition to retain independence as an editor.

In 1881 Samuel founded the *Sportsman*, which later became the *Herald's* property and in 1896 was sold to A. H. Massina [q.v.], its printer. Prospering, Winter moved from his home at Albert Park to South Yarra, with a retreat at Lilydale. After Halfey's death in 1889 he arranged for G. A. Walstab [q.v.], Donald Munro, Massina, Theodore Fink and W. L. Baillieu to buy Halfey's half-share in the *Herald*. In 1891, however, the paper was in financial trouble and was sold to the City Newspaper Co., which also acquired the *Weekly Times* when the *Daily Telegraph* closed down in May 1892. Winter retired from the *Herald* in August 1891 but continued to edit the *Sportsman*. When the purchasers failed to meet payments, Massina and Fink forced the company into liquidation and the *Herald's* former proprietorship was restored, Winter resumed the managing editorship, and the *Weekly Times* was acquired by the way. In 1894 the rival *Evening Standard* was bought out and next year Winter installed linotype machines. By 1900 the *Herald*, with a stable circulation of about 50,000, was paying handsome dividends.

At least in comparison with the other Melbourne newspaper proprietors, Samuel was a generous employer. Nicknamed 'Stormy' Winter, impetuous in decision and rapid in speech, he drove his men hard in competition with rivals; a great swearer, he was described by J. F. Archibald [q.v.] as an 'incomparable artist in blasphemy' but a kind and loveable man always good for a handout. Randolph Bedford found him 'irritable', obituarists described him as generous with praise, and noted his brusqueness disguising essential tenderness and shyness. Cycling and motoring were hobbies late in life. He had been president of the Master Printers' Association in 1889, a committee-man of the Charity Organisation Society, a trustee of the Toorak and South Yarra Try Society and was a life governor of the Melbourne and Alfred hospitals. He went overseas in 1898 and 1903. He died on 16 October 1904 of peritonitis, leaving an estate valued for probate at £31,000. His wife Lucy Helen, née Stodart, whom he had married about 1862 and by whom he had five sons and two daughters, predeceased him in 1882, aged 35.

Joseph Winter was a more resolute ideologue. He had been an altar boy and Sunday school teacher, was a founding member in 1865 of the St Francis Benefit Society (forerunner of the Hibernian-Australasian Catholic Benefit Society) and was prominent in the Catholic Young Men's Society. When Samuel passed over ownership of the *Advocate* Joseph managed it for the rest of his life with W. H. Gunson [q.v. J. M. Gunson] as editor from 1868 to 1902. The chief vehicle of Church propaganda until the *Tribune* was founded in 1900, it was read widely by the faithful but had little broad impact.

One of those Australians who were 'more Irish than the Irish themselves', Winter was for thirty years the heart and soul of the Home Rule movement in Victoria. In the late 1870s he raised money for famine relief in Ireland. He became treasurer of the Melbourne branch of the Irish National Land League in 1880 and then national treasurer, and was later almost constantly president, secretary or treasurer of the Irish National League and the United Irish League. He was the chief fund-raiser for the cause; in 1887 an anonymous correspondent in the *Age* accused him of failing to account for £1000 and he sued and the *Age* settled. He was the main organizer of the frequent tours of Irish fund-raisers with whom he had close relations; he was groomsman at John E. Redmond's [q.v.] marriage in Sydney in 1883 and Michael Davitt stayed at his Hawthorn home. He bore the brunt of the fanatical hostility to the Home Rule cause led by the *Age* and *Argus*, and had the satisfaction over the years of seeing opinion change. From 1870 he published the annual *Irish-Australian Almanac and Directory*. He imported type to enable Dr N. M. O'Donnell to conduct his *Advocate* column in Gaelic. Winter's support for the Redmonds' attitude to World War I was characteristic of his generation in Australia.

He did not seek the limelight or speak often from the platform. Serious, sensible and solid, never frivolous or flippant, of 'childlike simplicity', Winter was not easy in his social relations. He became something of a recluse in his later years. He died suddenly of a heart attack on 10 December 1915, 'honoured and respected by our race and creed' as O'Donnell cabled John Redmond. In 1885 he had married Delia Euphrasia Dargan who survived him with three daughters and a son. The Catholic Church bought the *Advocate*.

J. Smith (ed), *Cyclopedia of Victoria*, 1 (Melb, 1903); W. H. K. Redmond, *Through the new Commonwealth* (Dublin, 1906); *A'sian Typographical J*, Dec 1904; *Austral Light*, 17 (1916); *Table Talk*, 6 Sept 1889, 20 Oct 1904; *Life* (Melb), 27 Nov 1890; *Herald* (Melb), 17, 18 Oct 1904, 3 Jan 1940; *Advocate* (Melb), 22 Oct 1904, 11 Dec 1915; *Lone Hand*, June 1907; G. M. Tobin, The sea-divided Gael … the Irish Home Rule movement in Victoria and New South Wales, 1880-1916 (M.A. thesis, ANU, 1969); T. Fink papers (Faculty of Education, Univ Melb); Joseph Winter papers (LaT L).   GEOFFREY SERLE

WISDOM, SIR ROBERT (1830-1888), barrister and politician, was born on 31 January 1830 at Blackburn, Lancashire, England, son of John Wisdom, collector of customs, and his wife Alice, née McGuinness. In August 1834 in the *Arab* he arrived in Sydney with his parents who soon moved to Morpeth. Educated at Maitland and at the Sydney College, he returned to Morpeth and embarked on a literary career. He wrote political articles and much indifferent poetry, some of which was published in the *Empire*. On 23 August 1855 at Hexham he married Elizabeth Avard. He became a shareholder and one of four managers of the *Northern Times and Maitland Advertiser*, established in Maitland in August 1856, and quickly won repute as a 'trenchant and graceful writer'; but he left the newspaper in January 1858 after Dr H. G. Douglass [q.v.] had sued him for libel, although the attorney-general (Sir) James Martin [q.v.] refused to prosecute.

Wisdom's literary and political activities attracted the attention of Rev. J. D. Lang, (Sir) Henry Parkes and (Sir) John Robertson [qq.v.]. Clerk of Petty Sessions at Stony Creek from 30 November 1858 he became a magistrate in 1859. In June with Parkes's support he was elected unopposed to the Legislative Assembly for the Goldfields West which he represented until November 1864; he was chairman of committees in 1861-64 with a salary of £500. He was admitted to the colonial Bar on 26 October 1861 and practised in Sydney. In 1862 he refused to be solicitor-general under (Sir) Charles Cowper [q.v.] and next year declined the public works portfolio in a proposed ministry of W. Forster [q.v.]. He represented the Lower Hunter in 1864-72, and Morpeth in 1874-87. He was defeated by one vote by (Sir) George Allen [q.v.] for the Speakership in 1875.

Noted in the 1870s for his 'equable temperament and well-governed temper', he refused office under Robertson, J. S. Farnell and (Sir) Alexander Stuart [qq.v.] in 1877 and Parkes's offer of the Treasury next year. However on 13 August 1879 he became attorney-general in the Parkes-Robertson coalition and was made a Q.C.; he was complimented by the *Bulletin* (30 October 1880) for his prosecution in the previous December of the Wantabadgery bushrangers led by A. G. Scott [q.v.]. Wisdom quit office on 4 January 1883.

He became testy in Opposition, and was disorderly in the House: in February 1884 his 'habit of persistently cheering' enraged David Buchanan [q.v.], who called him 'a d—d liar', with the result that Wisdom 'violently assaulted' him within the precincts of Parliament House. In August he challenged the right of twenty members, either squatters or land agents, to vote on the crown lands bill; and in July 1886 after repeated obstruction he was removed by the serjeant-at-arms, despite his protest that it was unlawful without a vote of the assembly. He did not contest the 1887 general election and on 2 February was appointed to the Legislative Council but never took his seat.

Wisdom visited England that year and with (Sir) Patrick Jennings [q.v.] represented New South Wales at the Colonial Conference in London; created K.C.M.G. he returned to Sydney in December. In the 1880s he was a director of the Civil Service Co-operative and the Civil Service Permanent Building societies, the City Bank of Sydney, the Mercantile Building, Land, and Investment Co. Ltd and the Colonial Mutual Life Assurance Society Ltd. He was also a commissioner for the 1876 Philadelphia International Exhibition, a member of the Council of Education in 1879-81 and a trustee of the National Park.

Weighing 18 stone, Wisdom died of cirrhosis of the liver and kidneys at his home, 7 Richmond Terrace, Domain, on 16 March 1888 and was buried in the Anglican section of Waverley cemetery. Predeceased by a son and two daughters, he was survived by his wife, two sons and a daughter. Over the years he had amassed a considerable fortune by land speculations and his estate was valued for probate at £37,921.

Ex-M.L.A., *Our present parliament, what it is worth* (Syd, c1886); V&P (LA NSW), 1885-86, 1, 379-402; PD (NSW), 1884, 1596, 1601-05; *Maitland Mercury*, 15 Dec 1857, 20 Mar 1888; ISN, 29 May 1875; SMH, 4 Dec 1879, 20 Apr 1887, 17, 19 Mar 1888; R. Parsons, Lawyers in the New South Wales parliament, 1870-1890 (Ph.D. thesis, Macquarie Univ, 1972); Parkes letters *and* MS cat (ML); CO 201/583/560, 588/116, 600/112, 601/284, 606/66.

                                        ELIZABETH GUILFORD

WISE, EDWARD (1818-1865), politician and judge, was born on 13 August 1818 at Carisbrooke, Isle of Wight, England, second son of Edward Wise, of Bembridge, and his wife Amelia, née Wilson. He entered Rugby School in 1831 under Dr Thomas Arnold and became a private tutor before entering the Middle Temple, London. Sustained by the affectionate interest and advice of Arnold, he was called to the Bar on 22 November 1844.

While working as a barrister on the Western Circuit and in London, he published six volumes, with D. T. Evans, of *The Law Digest: a general index to the reports (and statutes)* (1846-56); *The Law relating to Riots and Unlawful Assemblies*...(1848), and *The Bankrupt Law Consolidation Act, 1849* (1849). He also helped to edit *Reports of Cases in the Law of Real Property* . . . *Court of Queen's Bench* (1843-48). Associated with Lord Shaftesbury, (Sir) Edwin Chadwick and Dr John Sutherland in investigating slum housing, he observed the relation of crime to social distress.

Wise decided to join his brother George [q.v.] and brother-in-law (Sir) William Manning [q.v.] in Australia and reached Sydney on 26 February 1855 in the *Pacific*. He was admitted to the colonial Bar on 16 June, living first at Enmore, then at Edgecliffe House, Woollahra. He soon represented the Bar on the Barristers Admission Board. On 1 January 1856 at Kyneton, Victoria, he married Maria Bate, sister of Bernhard Smith [q.v.]. Wise's experience and legal talents were soon recognized, and on 19 February 1857 he was appointed to the Legislative Council; from May to September he was solicitor-general in (Sir) H. Watson Parker's [q.v.] ministry. His ability, capacity for hard work, and character soon dispelled criticism of his appointment and he became attorney-general in W. Forster's [q.v.] government on 27 October 1859.

Wise devoted himself to the welfare of his adopted land, advocating state responsibility for the moral and social condition of the people; as attorney-general he introduced legislation on district courts which would bring justice 'as near as possible to every man's home'. Anxious to establish a proper system of court reporting and recording, he offered to find and train reporters and to locate a publisher. In December 1859 in evidence to a Legislative Assembly select committee on the condition of the working classes of the metropolis, he presented cases and facts gathered from slum inspections with a police officer, and described his lectures on basic hygiene, sanitary reform and domestic economy. He emphasized that a fruitful source of crime and demoralization was the lack of adequate housing.

Wise saw education as a means of uplifting the underprivileged. In 1861 he was a founder and committee-man of the Sydney Ragged Schools and the Working Men's Book Society and Book-Hawking Society. To further his project he went on poetry-reading tours to country towns. He also served on the committees of the Sydney Mechanics' School of Arts, the Union Club and the Home Visiting and Relief Society and was a councillor of the Australian Horticultural and Agricultural Society and the Philosophical Society of New South Wales. He was also a patron of art and literature. A liberal, devout Low Church Anglican, Wise was a member of the Church Society and of the 1859 Church of England Conference to re-define the Church's government and constitutional committee. He advocated that the Church should not be too dependent on the state and urged a wider role for the laity.

Wise resigned from Forster's ministry and was appointed a puisne judge of the Supreme Court on 13 February 1860. He took part on the Full Court in two important cases involving the legal position of church and state in the colony. In (J. L.) *Purves* [q.v.] v. *Attorney-General* he concurred with Judge Milford [q.v.] in dismissing Rev. J. D. Lang's [q.v.] appeal against exclusion from the Scots Church; however, their decision was reversed by the Privy Council. In January 1861 with Judge Dickinson [q.v.], in *Ex parte the Revd. George King* [q.v.], he upheld King's general challenge to Bishop Barker's [q.v.] ecclesiastical authority but ruled that the bishop could solely hear his case. In his judgment Wise defined how the legal position of the Church of England in the colony differed from its position in England and Ireland.

In September at the Goulburn Circuit Court Wise tried the anti-Chinese Burrangong rioters amid scenes of great excitement. His summing-up was strongly against the accused and led David Buchanan [q.v.] to move for a select committee to inquire into his conduct. Buchanan compared him to Judge Jefferies, but the motion was defeated, as was his attempt soon after to have Wise removed.

In 1865 overwork led to a breakdown, and on a visit to Melbourne Wise died suddenly of softening of the brain and apoplexy on 28 September and was buried in St Kilda cemetery. Manning ascribed his death to 'overtaxation of the brain in the performance of his duties', and the *Sydney Morning Herald* spoke of his 'scrupulous integrity and uprightness'. Wise was survived by his wife and four young sons, one of whom was Bernhard Ringrose (1858-1916). His personalty was valued for probate at £3000 and the New South Wales government granted his wife a pension of £200 a year. A memorial stained glass window placed in St Andrew's Cathedral, Sydney, by the New South Wales Bar Association commemorates him and Judge Milford. Wise was the first to collect Australiana systematically. His widow gave part of his library to the people of New South Wales; it is now in the Mitchell Library, Sydney.

J. G. Legge (ed), A selection of Supreme Court cases in New South Wales, 2 (Syd, 1896); V&P (LA NSW), 1859-60, 4, 1263, 1861-62, 1, 131, 206, 1866, 4, 915, 1900, 4, 591ff, (LC NSW), 1859-60, 1, 735; R. Border, Church and state in Australia 1788-1872 (Lond, 1962); J. A. Dowling, 'The judiciary', JRAHS, 2 (1906-09); G. D. Richardson, 'The colony's quest for a national library', and R. Withycombe, 'Church of England attitudes to the social question in the Diocese of Sydney, c. 1856-66', JRAHS, 47 (1961); SMH, 22 July 1858, 20, 21, 30 Sept, 10, 20 Oct 1861, 30 Sept 1865; Empire, 28 Sept 1861; B. R. Wise letters, and E. Wise uncat MS, and MS cat (ML).   J. A. RYAN

WISE, GEORGE FOSTER (1814-1897), immigration agent, was baptized on 18 August 1814 at Carisbrooke, Isle of Wight, England, eldest son of Edward Wise, brewer, and his wife Amelia, née Wilson. He was well educated, but failing family fortunes probably decided him to migrate and he reached Sydney in the Alfred on 15 January 1839. On the voyage he became friendly with Sir Francis [q.v.] and Lady Forbes and their niece Frances Lucy Mary Ann Marsh, whom he married at Muswellbrook on 21 June 1842; they had no children.

Wise was secretary of the General Steam Navigation Co. until 1842 and then engaged in land dealing in Camden, Kiama and Moreton Bay where he set up as a land agent; he returned to Sydney in 1844 and became a magistrate in 1846. With his brother-in-law J. Milbourne Marsh, he invested briefly and unprofitably in pastoral runs in the Lachlan District of New South Wales—Demondrille followed by Moombooldool, North Bolero and Binga. He apparently possessed in full measure 'the family propensity for not making money'.

One of the 'original founders and old members' of the Australian Club, Wise was appointed agent for immigration and a member of the Immigration Board on 1 November 1862. He implemented government policy of sponsored, assisted immigration, supervised standards and conditions in migrant vessels, received newly arrived migrants, and reported to parliament. His long tenure of office met little serious criticism except in times of unemployment; his annual reports showed little innovation or reforming tendencies in his work. In 1886 he had to dissuade Lady Carrington, wife of the governor, from witnessing the hiring of female migrants at the Immigration Depot which had become rather unseemly and chaotic. He was acting sheriff and acting inspector of prisons in 1869-70 and compiler of census in 1870-73. Sincere and conscientious, he was not a notable administrator but he exerted himself to find work for migrants.

A devout Anglican, Wise was a member of Sydney Diocesan synods in 1870-91. He shared his brother Edward's [q.v.] deep interest in social humanitarian work, and was a committee-man and office-bearer of the Home Visiting and Relief Society (1862-87), the Society for the Relief of Destitute Children (1865-91), the New South Wales Institution for the Deaf and Dumb and the Blind (1866-91) and a director of the Sydney Infirmary and Dispensary (1871-81). His wife Fanny (d. 1889) earned great respect and affection for her activity in the Sydney Foundling Hospital, the Society for the Relief of Destitute Children and the Sydney Female Refuge Society, as well as her work as a lady visitor in the homes of destitute and handicapped children. In the 1870s Wise was a director of the Illawarra Steam Navigation Co. but resigned after a question in parliament in 1879.

Wise retired on a pension of £272 14s. on 31 December 1891. He returned to the Isle of Wight, where he died of syncope on 14 August 1897 at Bembridge House, George Street, Ryde.

In memoriam. Mrs George F. Wise (Syd, 1889); Macarthur papers (ML); Parkes letters (ML); E. Wise papers (ML); newspaper indexes (ML); Col Sec papers (NSWA); CO 201/527/304, 310.   J. A. RYAN

WITHERS, WILLIAM BRAMWELL (1823-1913), journalist and historian, was born on 27 July 1823 at Whitchurch, Hampshire, England, youngest son of Jason Withers (d. 1846), tenant farmer and Wesleyan lay preacher, and his second wife Elizabeth, née Hendy (d. 1829). Educated at a grammar school until 13, he was apprenticed to an uncle, a general storekeeper at Winchester. From 1843 he was a lifelong opponent of capital punishment and in 1846 wrote articles for temperance and vegetarian journals. With a legacy of £300 in 1846 he bought 300 acres of land in Natal, South Africa, and went there in 1849. He later bought a 6000-acre farm with James Ellis but, affected by the solitude, sold out to him and went to Pietermaritzburg, where he wrote for newspapers and learned to set type in Dutch and English.

Attracted by the Australian gold discoveries, Withers reached Melbourne in the *Hannah* in November 1852. He walked to Ballarat but failed as a prospector and soon returned to Melbourne where he found shelter at Canvas Town and worked as a roadmaker; he was later a dray driver and a clerk on the wharves. In 1854 he joined the *Argus* as a reader and then as a reporter, but soon transferred to the *Herald*. By June 1855 he was back in Ballarat, but still could not find gold and worked as a reporter and part-time compositor on the *Ballarat Times*; on 22 September 1855 he joined the newly founded (Ballarat) *Star*.

Withers proved a fluent and scholarly journalist, and often spiced his reporting, leaders and literary articles with appealing humour. As mining correspondent for both the *Star* and the *Miner and Weekly Star* he documented business and investment in the booming township. He had little time for outside activities, but he was elected to the first committee of the Ballarat Mechanics' Institute in 1859 and was a founder and first champion bowler in 1865 of the Ballarat Bowling Club. Sharing a comfortable home in Lyons Street with Mrs Mary Ann Dusatoy, Withers resolved to write a history of the town; for five years he corresponded with goldfield pioneers, participants and eye-witnesses of the Eureka affair and the surviving local squatters. The *Ballarat Star* published his *History of Ballarat* in twelve weekly parts, beginning on 11 June 1870; bound volumes were sold from 9 August and there were two other editions.

Reviewers praised Withers for his thorough research, literary style and objectivity, and his reputation in his beloved Ballarat reached its peak. He flourished with the city and was briefly co-proprietor of the *Ballarat Star* with H. R. Nicholls [q.v.] and E. E. Campbell. His two novels were widely serialized: 'Eustace Hopkins' (1882), which won second prize in a competition sponsored by the *Age*, and 'The Westons' (1883). After the sale of the *Ballarat Star* Withers was engaged by the *Ballarat Courier* to write leading articles and literary pieces as he desired. The reminiscences he published in *Austral Light* in December 1895 to November 1896 were a revelation of his writing talent, tolerance and gentle character.

In 1887 a second and revised edition of the history was published in Ballarat by F. W. Niven with a printing of 10,200 copies at a price of one guinea. The book was elegantly and extravagantly produced but sales were slow; remainder tables in Ballarat bookshops insulted the short, bristly whiskered, long-striding, frock-coated historian

as he walked from his home in Lyons Street, always umbrella under arm, down Sturt Street past a half-dozen bookshops.

In 1901 Withers left Ballarat for Sydney, where by 1907 he was living at Dulwich Hill with Mrs Dusatoy and her son William Leslie Withers Dusatoy; he continued to write for the *Ballarat Courier*. He left Australia to visit England on 19 March 1903 and from September to December the *Ballarat Star* published 'A Pilgrim Pioneer', which described his return to Winchester and his memories of a long life, but his writing had become pedantic. He died of a cerebral haemorrhage at Dulwich Hill, Sydney, on 14 July 1913 and was buried in the Anglican section of Rookwood cemetery. He left his estate, valued at £90, to Mary Ann Dusatoy.

T. W. H. Leavitt (ed), *Australian representative men*, 1st ed (Melb, 1887); R. Gay, *Some Ballarat pioneers* (Mentone, 1935); information from Mr R. W. P. Ashley, Mr J. A. Chisholm and Ms M. Sandow-Quirk, Ballarat.

AUSTIN MCCALLUM

WITHNELL, EMMA MARY (1842-1928), pioneer, was born on 19 December 1842 at Guildford, Western Australia, daughter of George Hancock, farmer, and his wife Sophia, née Gregory. She was tutored on a farm near Beverley by her university-educated father and was later to do the same for her own eleven children. On 10 May 1859 at York she married John, son of William Withnell, a stonemason who had migrated in 1830.

Attracted by the discovery of good pastoral land in the north-west, Withnell sailed for Port Walcott in 1864 in the chartered *Sea Ripple* with Emma, two children and her sister Frances. All of their livestock except eighty-six sheep was lost when the ship ran aground. Camped at Nickol Bay, they lost more equipment but were saved from death by thirst by a settler. Wearing makeshift clogs of wood and sheep-skin, the family walked to the Harding River and settled near Mount Welcome where Emma soon bore her third child.

They first sheared in September but for the next few years they were forced by low prices to diversify. Leaving Emma to manage the station, Withnell went pearling and, after Roebourne was founded in 1866, he acquired a lighter to convey passengers and stores from the port to the settlement. With his wife's assistance he ran a butcher's shop, on the outskirts of Roebourne, but he lost financially when the *Emma* foundered in 1867. Bad droughts in 1870 and 1872 were followed by a cyclone which destroyed their home and killed much stock. In 1878 a fire destroyed most of the buildings on their property. Next year Withnell sold Mount Welcome station to R. J. Sholl [q.v.] and moved to Sherlock station; with Emma he retired to Guildford in 1890. Their sons retained substantial holdings in the north and one, James, found the gold-bearing stone which started the Pilbara goldfields in 1887.

Widely known as the 'Mother of the north-west', Emma looked after the sick, delivered babies and regularly conducted religious services in her home. The Aboriginals trusted and respected her; she nursed and vaccinated many in a smallpox epidemic in 1866. She and John were honoured by being made a 'Boorong' and a 'Banaker', which enabled them to move freely amongst the tribes. 'The awful loneliness' was her greatest burden as she affirmed when sympathizing with new arrivals in the north, 'for the work is hard and the lonesomeness at times unbearable'.

John Withnell died on 15 May 1898 leaving an estate valued for probate at £5895. Survived by nine of her eleven children, Emma died of cholecystitis on 16 May 1928 at Mount Lawley, and was buried in the Anglican cemetery at Guildford. Her portrait hangs in the 'Hall of Pioneers' in the Baandi rest house at the National Trust property at Mangowine. In 1961 the Country Women's Association erected a memorial of Nickol Bay stone on the site of her Roebourne home.

A. R. Richardson, *Early memories of the great nor'-west* (Perth, 1914); J. S. Battye (ed), *The history of the north-west of Australia* (Perth, 1915); J. P. Stokes, *The western state* (Perth, 1958); E. Pownall, *Mary of Maranoa* (Syd, 1959); V. H. Ferguson, 'The late Mrs John Withnell', JRWAHS, 1 (1928); *Perth Gazette*, 7 Mar, 6 May 1864; *West Australian*, 18, 19 May 1898, 10, 19 Aug 1961, 11 Dec 1965; *Western Mail*, 24 May 1928; Richardson papers *and* R. J. Sholl journal, 1866 (Battye Lib, Perth).

DOUGLAS STURKEY

WOLSELEY, FREDERICK YORK (1837-1899), inventor, was born at Kingstown, County Dublin, Ireland, on 16 March 1837, second son of Major Garnet Joseph Wolseley and his wife Frances Anne, née Smith; his elder brother Garnet became Field Marshal Viscount Wolseley. He arrived in Melbourne in July 1854 in the *Norwood* and went to Thule sheep station on the Murray River. Here he worked for his brother-in-law Ralston Caldwell for five years before acquiring an interest in Thule and Cobram stations; by 1871 he had Toolong in the Murrumbidgee District. Financed by Garnet, about 1868 he began experiments on a machine for shearing sheep and by 1872 had evolved a working model which

removed at least part of a fleece. He then visited England, Ireland, and possibly the United States of America, and on his return in 1874 resumed experiments in Melbourne with R. P. Park.

In 1876 Wolseley bought Euroka station, near Walgett in New South Wales; next year he joined the Union Club in Sydney. In the 1880s he was a sheep director for Walgett and in 1883 was involved in litigation over the ownership of Rosebank station. He continued testing his machine at Euroka and on 28 March 1877 he and R. Savage [q.v.] were granted a patent for a shearing device driven by horse power. A second patent was granted in December, but there were serious problems with the drive mechanism and physical limitations on the shearer's movements. On 13 December 1884 he and Park patented an 'Improved Shearing Apparatus' which included a cog-gear universal joint. In 1885 Wolseley bought the rights of John Howard's horse-clipper and engaged him as a mechanic at Euroka at £3 per week. Howard made several improved machines which worked so well during the 1885 season that Wolseley went to Melbourne to form a manufacturing company and to arrange for public demonstrations, pitting the machine against the blades. Similar displays took place at Sydney and Euroka in 1886: Hassan Ali, a Khartoum native, used the appliance and Dave Brown was the blade-shearer. It proved superior and after William Ryley's suggestions for improving the hand-piece were adopted, the Wolseley machine was widely demonstrated in eastern Australia and New Zealand in 1887-88. In 1888 (Sir) Samuel McCaughey's [q.v.] shed at Dunlop, Louth, New South Wales, was the first to complete a shearing with machines. That year eighteen other woolsheds were fitted with the invention.

In 1889 Wolseley went to England and set up the Wolseley Sheep Shearing Machine Co. Pty Ltd in Birmingham and engaged Herbert (later Baron) Austin as foreman in his workshops at Goldsbrough, Mort [qq.v.] & Co. Ltd, in Melbourne. Austin improved the overhead gear and in 1893 went to Birmingham as production manager. Wolseley resigned the managing-directorship for health reasons in 1894, and next year Austin designed and made the first Wolseley motor car.

Handsome, likeable and well built, Wolseley lacked practical mechanical experience and had to rely on others, but he was inventive and, above all, persevering; he has the honour of inventing the shearing machine which revolutionized the wool industry in Australia. He died of cancer at 20 Belvedere Road, Penge, London, on 8

January 1899 and was buried in Elmers End cemetery, Norwood, London. He left a widow but no family.

In 1901 Vickers Sons and Maxim Ltd took over the machine tool and motor side of the Wolseley works trading as the Wolseley Tool & Motor Car Co. Ltd. Austin was general manager until 1905 when he started the Austin Motor Co.

A. D. Fraser (ed), *This century of ours* (Syd, 1938); F. Wheelhouse, *Digging stick to rotary hoe* (Melb, 1966); V&P (LA NSW), 1885-86, 6, 727; *Australasian*, 4 Dec 1886, 12 Mar, 11 June 1887; *Pastoral Review*, 15 May 1893, 16 Jan, 15 Mar 1899; *Sydney Mail*, 21 Jan 1899.

G. P. WALSH

WOOD, ESTHER see JENNINGS, ELIZABETH

WOOD, HARRIE (1831-1917), miner and civil servant, was born on 12 February 1831 at Kensington, London, son of William Alexander Wood, imperial public servant, and his wife Margaret Eleanor, née Hall. He arrived in Melbourne in the *Admiral* in November 1852, declined a position offered by Lieut-Governor La Trobe, and became a miner on various alluvial goldfields. In 1855-57 he worked in the Ballarat mines, and on 15 April 1858 he was appointed clerk of the new Ballarat Mining Board with salary of £150. In June 1861 he proposed to J. B. Humffray [q.v.], commissioner of mines, a new system for administering surveys and claim registration and on 23 September 1861 he became district mining registrar for Ballarat. His recommendations on administrative reforms were almost wholly supported by the report of the 1862 royal commission on the gold fields. Wood was a founder of the Ballarat School of Mines in 1870 and was secretary of its first council and an honorary councillor. He also actively worked for the district hospital and the benevolent asylum.

On 27 October 1873 Wood was appointed to the New South Wales new Department of Mines with a roving commission to organize its administration. His reports of 1873 and 1874 criticized the procedures for surveying and registration of claims, and he made detailed suggestions for conducting the department and a school of mines. He was also anxious to amend the law to facilitate co-operation between capital and labour ventures unsuited to either individual miners or large companies; he hoped to remove existing antagonism between these groups. Helped by a private letter to (Sir) Henry Parkes [q.v.] from his friend Angus

Mackay [q.v.], Victorian minister of mines, Wood was appointed under-secretary for mines on 1 September 1874. Some politicians and civil servants alleged that the appointment of this 'new chum' was a 'scandalous abuse' by the government and would demoralize the civil service, but his capable and innovatory work soon silenced his critics. Wood's department grew steadily and acquired wider responsibilities in the next twenty years, with sheep and stock affairs, forests, rabbit extermination and public parks being added at various times. In 1891 it was reorganized as the Department of Mines and Agriculture and his responsibilities covered agricultural matters and the new Hawkesbury Agricultural College; in 1894 water conservation, irrigation and drainage were included.

Wood served under twenty ministries and was untouched by recurring mining investigations and scandals. He was sympathetic, perhaps over generous, to his staff and protected them against outside pressure; his resulting lax control was criticized by the 1889 and 1895 royal commissions into the civil service. Opposed to an independent public service board, he told the 1895 commission that 'so-called political patronage' was not a problem, claiming that his ministers had never failed to adopt his staff recommendations. He retired on 5 March 1896 and set up in Sydney as a mining agent until 1909.

Wood was a member of the board for opening tenders for runs from 1880, a New South Wales commissioner for the Colonial and Indian Exhibition, London, 1886, and for the exhibitions in Adelaide in 1887 and Melbourne in 1888, and was chairman of the Prospecting Board. He had been a member of the Royal Society of New South Wales from 1873 and a foundation member in 1883 of the New South Wales branch of the Geographical Society of Australasia. He wrote on gold-mining in Victoria and New South Wales, revealing a fine grasp of detail and an independence of judgment on technical, legal and administrative matters; he contributed a major appendix, 'Notes on the Ballarat Goldfield' for R. Brough Smyth's [q.v.] *The Gold Fields and Mineral Districts of Victoria* (1869); and wrote two reports on gold-mining leases in New South Wales, 1873 and 1874; and *Mines and Mineral Statistics of New South Wales*, prepared for the Philadelphia Centennial Exhibition, 1876.

Wood suffered from arteriosclerosis for ten years: he died of heart failure on 18 September 1917 at Cremorne, and was buried in the Presbyterian section of Gore Hill cemetery. He was survived by four sons and two daughters by his wife Ellen (Helen)

Dalrymple, née Beattie, whom he had married at Carlton, Victoria, on 1 July 1868.

W. B. Withers, *The history of Ballarat*, 1st ed (Ballarat, 1870); *V&P (LA Vic)*, 1862-63, 3 (10), 1871, 1 (10), (LA NSW), 1874, 1, 869, 1891-92, 4, 1055, 1894-95, 3, 55; *SMH*, 23 June 1874; *ISN*, 14 Nov 1874; *T&CJ*, 26 May 1888, 21 Mar 1896; Parkes letters (ML). BRUCE MITCHELL

WOOD, JOHN DENNISTOUN (1829-1914), barrister and politician, was born on 4 July 1829 at Dennistoun near Bothwell, Van Diemen's Land, eldest son of Captain Patrick Wood and his wife Jane, née Patterson. Patrick, of Elie, Fifeshire, Scotland, was a retired officer of the East India Co.'s Madras army; he arrived in Van Diemen's Land on 1 March 1822 in the *Castle Forbes*: fellow-passengers included Myles Patterson and his daughters, Jamima who married (Sir) Robert Officer [q.v.] in 1823, and Jane who married Patrick on 1 October 1828. Patrick was an original partner with Philip Russell senior [q.v.] in the Clyde Company and they established the Dennistoun estate.

After his mother's death in 1837 John Dennistoun was sent to Scotland and attended the Edinburgh Academy and the University of Edinburgh. A student at the Inner Temple, London, from 3 November 1845, he was called to the Bar on 3 January 1852 and, on returning to Victoria, was admitted to the colonial Bar in 1853. Described as 'a sound little lawyer', he soon built up a good practice. An unsuccessful candidate for Brighton at the first Legislative Assembly elections in 1856, he was solicitor-general in (Sir) John O'Shanassy's [q.v.] ministry from 11 March to 29 April 1857, when he won The Ovens at a Legislative Assembly by-election. He retained that seat until July 1861 and then was member for Warrnambool from December 1861 until defeated in 1864. He was attorney-general from October 1859 to November 1860 in W. Nicholson's [q.v.] ministry and the first minister of justice from November 1861 to June 1863.

Regarded as something of a radical among his relations, Wood at first expressed an opportunist liberal philosophy, including a national secular education system, abolition of state aid to religion, and mining on private property. In October 1858, however, he moved destructive amendments to the electoral reform bill, asserting that 'the theory of representation based on population had to be modified': as a result the goldfields and towns lost fourteen representatives. He opposed the commonage and ballot provisions of the original Nicholson land bill and voted for it only to calm the demagogues outside.

In the 1865 constitutional crisis Wood was an active member of the conservative group opposing (Sir) James McCulloch's [q.v.] government. His legal advice to the banks had political overtones, and in 1865-66 he pursued a vindictive libel action against David Syme [q.v.] who had named him in the *Age* as an author of a plot to overthrow the government. He was a clear and forceful speaker, but a bitter tongue and spiteful temper harmed his reputation. After unsuccessful attempts to return to parliament in 1865 and 1866 he left Victoria for eighteen months travel in China, Java, India and the Middle East.

In 1870 in London Wood married 22-year-old Frances Jane Potts, daughter of a gaoler and born at New Norfolk, Tasmania. For twenty years he practised law in London, appearing mainly before the Privy Council in colonial appeal cases; and he may have practised for a while in New York in the early 1870s. A consistent supporter of imperial federation, from 1873 he was a member of the (Royal) Colonial Institute. In 1884 he was an inaugural member and honorary treasurer of the Imperial Federation League but resigned on the election of Lord Rosebery [q.v. A. P. Primrose] as chairman in 1886: he found the financial provisions of the Irish Home Rule bill incompatible with imperial federation and opposed Rosebery's stand on it.

In 1889 Wood returned to Victoria, practising there until 1898 when he retired to Tasmania to manage Dennistoun. At Bothwell he soon became a leader in local affairs and later warden of the municipality. In 1903-08 he held the seat of Cumberland in the House of Assembly, and in 1904 refused offers to act either as attorney-general or premier. His publications included two legal treatises, two pamphlets on imperial federation, and in 1903 a volume of poetry; and he collected a fine library, which was burnt with his house in January 1909. The last survivor of the first Victorian parliament, he died, aged 85 at Dennistoun on 23 October 1914, survived by his wife (d. 1917), three of his four sons, and four daughters. His estate was valued for probate at £46,205.

C. G. Duffy, *My life in two hemispheres* (Lond, 1898); J. L. Forde, *The story of the Bar of Victoria* (Melb, 1913); C. A. Bodelsen, *Studies in mid-Victorian imperialism* (Köbenhavn, 1924); H. L. Hall, *Australia and England* (Lond, 1934); P. L. Brown, *Clyde Company papers*, 1, 2, 7 (Lond, 1941, 1952, 1971); G. Serle, *The golden age* (Melb, 1963); C. E. Sayers, *David Syme; a life* (Melb, 1965); *Argus*, 2 Dec 1859, 22 July 1886, 24 Oct 1914; *Truth* (Melb), 22 Aug, 31 Nov 1914; *Mercury*, 24 Oct 1914; F. K. Crowley, Aspects of the constitutional conflicts ... Victorian legislature, 1864-1868 (M.A. thesis, Univ Melb, 1947).

JILL EASTWOOD

WOODS, JOHN (1822-1892), engineer, politician and inventor, was born on 5 November 1822 at Liverpool, England, son of Richard Woods, railwayman, and his wife Mary, née Cave. Educated locally, he trained as a locomotive engineer in Liverpool and then on the Leipzig and Dresden railway. He worked in North America and held positions in railway and iron works in Staffordshire and Lancashire, where he was active in anti-corn-law agitation. He won first prize for railway axles at the 1851 Great Exhibition. At Liverpool, aged 21, he married Sarah Gibbons.

With his wife Woods arrived in Victoria in 1852 and went to the goldfields. He first 'mounted the stump' at the Goulburn diggings to lead passive resistance to the licence fee. He became president of the Ararat branch of the Land Convention and was active in the registration of electors and in obtaining sufficient ballot papers for the 1858 election. At Ararat he was elected to the local court and then to the Mining Board and was a delegate to the 1859 Mining Board Conference. Partnership in a deep wet claim left him penniless; he took employment at Stawell, building the St George's crushing plant.

From October 1859 until his defeat in 1864 Woods was member for the Legislative Assembly seat of Crowlands. On 30 October 1865 he was appointed engineer and surveyor for the Victorian Water Supply at a salary of £300. He worked on the Malmesbury reservoir until summarily dismissed by (Sir) James McCulloch's [q.v.] government on a charge of knowingly accepting faulty pipes and tarring over the cracks. The accusation and dismissal were later privately acknowledged as unfair. Woods represented Crowlands again in 1871-77 and in 1877-92 the new electorate of Stawell. He was commissioner of railways and roads and vice-president of the Board of Lands and Works in (Sir) Graham Berry's [q.v.] governments of 1875 and 1877-80. He sat on many select committees, mainly about railways, and was also a member of several royal commissions including those on the tariff (1881-83), employees in shops (1882-84) and coal (1889-91). He was a commissioner for the 1880 Melbourne International Exhibition and an honorary commissioner to the 1883-84 Calcutta Exhibition; from 1890 he was a member of the Parliamentary Standing Committee on Railways.

A consistent, active proponent of democratic and radical principles and a staunch local member, Woods worked hard for the interests of miners and small settlers. He advocated a non-legalistic approach to mining on private property and a sliding scale of gold royalties to replace rents for mining land. He steadfastly put forward the Land Convention programme, always opposing permanent alienation of crown land and sale by auction, and proposing, in 1859, 1864 and 1873, a progressive land tax to 'burst up the great estates'; he published pamphlets on the subject in 1873 and 1880. As minister, his overriding interest was to reduce costs to small farmers, a political priority opposed by senior officials. He initiated great railway activity: a major branch line along the Goulburn Valley, the Melbourne-Oakleigh connexion and two north-western extensions into the Wimmera. He reformed the goods tariff to reduce freight charges and levelled and reorganized the Spencer Street yards; but his plans to build a block of grain and wool sheds and a new dock to reduce farmers' storage and cartage costs were cancelled by the next government.

A strong protectionist, Woods championed local industry, thereby opposing T. Higinbotham [q.v.], on the use of Victorian-built locomotives. Among his several inventions were a fast stone-breaking machine (patented 1860) and an important and successful hydraulic railway brake (1882) which was used on many Victorian lines. He had set up a company in December 1877 to register the patent and manufacture his invention but air-powered brakes dominated eventually.

Although a member of the Chamber of Manufactures, Woods was always proud of his artisan background and claimed to be a representative of labour: 'I graduated in a hard school ... I had to work my ten hours a day in England for very little money, and I know exactly what it means; and I know the advantages which have been obtained in this colony by labour in combination'. However he opposed political representation of trade unionists as such. He fought for the eight-hour principle and argued for unemployment relief and old-age pensions. In a major article, 'Wages', in the *Victorian Review* (1880), he raised the problem of ensuring for a worker a fair share in the profits of industry, not merely a days pay. After 1880 he became a liberal oppositionist to the James Service [q.v.]-Berry coalition and subsequent ministries.

Deakin first met Woods in 1879, 'his rotund form, snub nose, glistening eyes and spiky hair rendering him a rather Socrates-Silenus appearance'; he described him as a serious reader and a man of original mind and initiative. However Woods never attained high parliamentary stature. His radical ideas, heterodox opinions and abrasive approach offended the community's respectable conformism. Impetuous and unconventional in his actions, he sometimes had to apologize for 'taking intoxicants too freely' and wrote amorous doggerel which *Punch* would not publish. He was a vigorous speaker with a gift for phrase-making. Deakin, however, claimed that he lacked industry and self-control. He lent his name to some of James Munro's [q.v.] more questionable promotions and with L. L. Smith [q.v.] 'puffed' a tin mine on the London market. Attacked by the conservative press, the nickname 'Tarbrush' followed him everywhere.

Woods's first wife died, aged 74, on 12 January 1888 and on 23 September 1891 he married a divorcee, Jessica Muir, née Whitley. He died of heart disease, dropsy and gangrene on 2 April 1892 at Brighton. Survived by his second wife and two of his four daughters, and predeceased by his two sons, he was buried in the Boroondara cemetery according to the rites of the Anglican Church.

A. Sutherland et al, *Victoria and its metropolis*, 2 (Melb, 1888); A. Deakin, *The crisis in Victorian politics, 1879-1881*, J. A. La Nauze and R. M. Crawford eds (Melb, 1957); C. E. Sayers, *Shanty at the bridge* (Donald, 1963), and *Shepherd's gold* (Melb, 1966); M. Cannon, *The land boomers* (Melb, 1966); PD (Vic), 1873, 1883, 1886, 1887; *Argus*, 2 Dec 1859, 2 Oct, 23 Oct 1883, 24 Mar 1887, 4 Apr 1892; *Australasian*, 31 Aug 1878; *Table Talk*, 11 Nov 1886; *Pleasant Creek News*, 5 Apr 1892; *Leader* (Melb), 9 Apr 1892; S. M. Ingham, Some aspects of Victorian liberalism 1880-1900 (M.A. thesis, Univ Melb, 1950); J. E. Parnaby, The economic and political development of Victoria, 1877-1881 (Ph.D. thesis, Univ Melb, 1951).   JILL EASTWOOD

WOODS, JULIAN EDWARD TENISON-, *see* TENISON-WOODS

WOOLLEY, JOHN (1816-1866), professor and clergyman, was born on 28 February 1816 at Petersfield, Hampshire, England, second son of George Woolley, physician, and his wife Charlotte, née Gell. His father transferred to the Royal Humane Society, London, and John went to the Western Grammar School, Brompton, and in 1830 to University College, London. He won a scholarship to Exeter College, Oxford (B.A., 1836; M.A., 1839; D.C.L., 1844) and in 1840 became a fellow of University College. Made deacon by Bishop Bagot of

Oxford on 14 June he was priested by Bishop Musgrave of Hereford on 4 July 1841. In July 1842 in Germany he married Mary Margaret (d. 1886), daughter of Major William Turner, thereby forfeiting his fellowship; he became headmaster of Hereford Cathedral School.

Woolley became foundation headmaster of Rossall School, Lancashire, in 1844. He promoted the educational methods of Dr Thomas Arnold, whose views on both pedagogy and theology he admired. He got on well with staff and pupils but could not manage his council or cope with a falling enrolment. He failed to secure appointment to the Birmingham grammar school and to Bishop's College, Calcutta, and his nomination as rector of the Ionian University at Corfu was frustrated by the opposition of the Greek clergy. In 1849 he became headmaster of Norwich Grammar School on the nomination of Bishop Stanley, father of his Oxford friend Arthur (later Dean) Stanley. But the bishop died and Woolley, despite a good income and the opportunity to work for the local 'People's College', found Norwich too narrow a field. He had published an Oxford textbook on logic which had won Sir William Hamilton's acclaim, and he gained some reputation with his *Sermons preached in the Chapel of Rossall College* (London, 1847) and *Religious Education the Safeguard of the State* (London, 1850). They marked Woolley as a scholar of liberal opinions.

Despite his clerical status, in 1852 Woolley obtained the position of principal and professor of classics at the new University of Sydney; he arrived with his wife and five daughters on 9 July in the *Mary Ann*. At once he took the lead in pressing for a professorial monopoly of general undergraduate teaching, arguing forcibly that the proposed Church colleges be restricted to an ancillary role. He reluctantly agreed to a compromise arranged in 1854 by Vice-Provost Sir Charles Nicholson [q.v.] and Bishop Selwyn of New Zealand: resident students at state-aided Church colleges were obliged to attend the professors' lectures; in return, ethics, metaphysics and modern history would be optional and college heads were to certify the religious competence of all students. Despite his misgivings, it was a victory for the secular, professorial university, reflecting current liberal Oxford opinion with which A. P. Stanley and, through him, Woolley were identified. Sydney became the model for all Australian universities.

Woolley's insistence on the supremacy of the professoriate rested on his belief in the value of the liberal arts curriculum. This formed the core of university studies; it not only trained the intellect but promoted perception of moral and social values. To Woolley, a Platonist, the 'social sympathy' thus engendered was essential to a growing colony. He followed W. C. Wentworth [q.v.] in stressing the function of the university in educating a colonial governing class of the future, freeing the community from any reliance on either imported rulers or radical demagogues. So emphatic was Woolley on the need to raise up, through the university, a responsible group of local gentlemen that he was prepared to forego the training of professional men: law and medicine had to function under mere examining boards.

Woolley mistrusted the policies of the Churches in education. He believed that they tended to disrupt the social unity that education should promote, and considered that religious teaching belonged properly to the home and should not be accorded a major place in school and university curricula. Moving beyond the position on church and state that, under Arnold's influence, he had adopted in England, he supported the National schools, resented the university colleges and helped to secure the abolition of religious certification at the university in 1858. Similarly, his theological opinions, originally those of the Broad Church school, shifted in the direction of deism. He became critical of the new Anglican bishop, Frederic Barker [q.v.], whose evangelical policies he considered unscholarly and restrictive. Although licensed to preach in 1852 and active for some years at St Peter's, Cook's River, Woolley confined his clerical friendships to younger clergy, such as G. F. Macarthur [q.v.], on whom he had a liberalizing influence. His isolation was reinforced by his failure to gain membership of the Sydney constitutional convention and by his opposition to the new diocesan arrangements in an 1859 petition to parliament against the Church of England synods bill. An active Freemason, he was chaplain to lodges of the English and Scottish constitutions. A promoter of general religious knowledge, he joined the committees of the New South Wales Auxilliary of the British and Foreign Bible Society and the New South Wales Religious Tract and Book Society. But to orthodox churchmen, he came to appear as a religious radical with a suspect faith.

Woolley was an eloquent orator and an inspiring teacher. On younger radical politicians, such as (Sir) Henry Parkes [q.v.] and on his brighter students, such as (Sir) William Windeyer [q.v.], he exercised a profound influence. In 1855 he helped some undergraduates produce the short-lived Sydney University Magazine, which echoed his opinions. His optional lectures on political economy and constitutional history were stimulating but some university senators viewed them with suspicion. Woolley's scholarship was generally admired but his teaching, like his religion, aroused a mixed response.

The University of Sydney was only a partial success: in 1857, it moved from temporary quarters in the former Sydney College (to make way for the undenominational Sydney Grammar School that Woolley had helped to promote) to a splendid Gothic pile at Grose Farm. The building remained half empty, for he clung to a classical arts curriculum that practical men thought inappropriate. He resisted efforts to abolish compulsory lectures and allow the colleges to teach; and classes for non-matriculated students were only a partial solution. He contrived a parliamentary select committee on the university in 1859, to gain membership of the senate for the senior professors; but the committee criticized the ostentation of the building and the irrevelance of the curriculum.

Woolley's creed of 'social sympathy' through a liberal education extended beyond the university. Influenced by English developments, he believed that academics should take their learning to the wider community, which was the more necessary because the impact of graduates would take time. His positions as elective trustee of the Australian Museum and councillor of the Philosophical Society of New South Wales followed naturally from his professorship, but he went beyond the call of duty in helping to revive the Sydney Mechanics' School of Arts in 1853 (vice-president 1855; president 1866) and in lecturing widely for it. He remained critical of disorder in the School of Arts but he believed it was the most effective instrument for cultural dissemination.

By 1864 Woolley was becoming oppressed by a sense of failure. He had grown querulous under opposition and his critics, academic and ecclesiastical, were gathering. He felt he had lost touch with British scholarship; his work on logic, begun when he was Stowell scholar at Oxford and elaborated into a critique of Mill's pragmatism, had not found a publisher. Lectures delivered in Australia, seen through the press in 1862 by A. P. Stanley, was a fine collection of occasional addresses but did not measure up to Woolley's conception of scholarly production. Granted leave, he left for England on 26 December 1864 in H.M.S. Miranda, without his family. He revisited friends and relations and spoke at the commemoration of University College, London. But he could get no promise of an English post and he sailed for Australia depressed in spirit.

Woolley was drowned in the Bay of Biscay on 11 January 1866, when the *London* foundered in a storm. He was survived by his wife, who is semi-fictionally represented in E. Maitland's [q.v.] *The Pilgrim and the Shrine* (1867), by four daughters and two sons. His eldest daughter Emmeline was a prominent Sydney musician and Blanche married F. E. du Faur [q.v.]. Always imprudent in money matters, despite a large professorial income, he left an estate valued for probate at £500. A public meeting on 26 March raised £2000 to provide for his family. The tragedy of the *London* foundering, wherein several prominent people died, aroused much comment and many tributes, in which Woolley figured. H. Halloran [q.v.] in a memorial poem, called him 'The Poet's comforter, and poor man's guide'. There are two portraits of Woolley in Sydney, one by William Menzies Tweedie, at the University of Sydney and another at St Paul's College. The Woolley scholarship commemorates him.

G. H. Nadel, *Australia's colonial culture* (Melb, 1957); C. Turney (ed), *Pioneers of Australian education*, 1 (Syd, 1969); Sel cttee on the University of Sydney, V&P (LA NSW), 1859-60, 4, 204, 300, (LC NSW), 1859-60, 1, 667, 5; S. Neil, 'The late John Woolley of Oxford', *British Controversialist*, 24 (1866); K. J. Cable, 'The University of Sydney and its affiliated colleges, 1850-1880', *Aust Univ*, 2 (1964) *and* 'John Woolley, Australia's first professor', *Arts* (Syd), 5 (1968); R. J. Burns, Secondary education and social change in New South Wales and Queensland before 1914 (Ph.D. thesis, Univ Syd, 1966); J. D. Lang, Macarthur, Parkes and Deas Thomson papers (ML); Bishop's register of Acts and Procs, 1852-66 (Syd Diocesan Registry); Council minutes, 1844-49 (Rossall School Archives); Nicholson, Stenhouse, Windeyer and Woolley papers *and* Senate 1851-66 and Professorial Board 1852-61 minutes (Univ Syd Archives).   K. J. CABLE

WOOLLS, WILLIAM (1814-1893), Church of England clergyman, schoolmaster and botanist, was born on 30 March 1814 at Winchester, Hampshire, England, nineteenth child of Edward Woolls (d. 1830), wholesaler, and his wife Sarah. He was educated by Rev. Thomas Scard at Bishop's Waltham Grammar School and encouraged as a classicist and versifier by his godfather, Canon Westcombe of Winchester College. At 16 he migrated to Australia with a commendation from Lord Goderich, reaching Sydney on 16 April 1832 in the *Grecian*. Archdeacon Broughton [q.v.], impressed by his shipboard verse, found him a position at The King's

School, Parramatta, where he taught until moving to W. T. Cape's [q.v.] Sydney College. On 28 June 1838 at St John's Church, Parramatta, he married Dinah Catherine Hall; she bore him a son and daughter and died in childbirth on 12 July 1844. On 16 July 1845 he married a widow Ann Boag.

At intervals Woolls contributed to the *Colonist*, the *Atlas* and other periodicals. In 1841 he set up his own school at Parramatta, first in Harrisford and then at Broughton House. Able and sympathetic, for twenty-five years he educated the sons of many prominent colonists, endeavouring to instil a strong sense of colonial pride. He was president of the Cumberland Mutual Improvement Society, tried to found a society to promote geographical discovery, wrote a laudatory account of the pioneer clergyman Samuel Marsden [q.v.] and celebrated in verse such notable events as the founding of the University of Sydney.

A staunch Anglican and a trustee of All Saints' Church, North Parramatta, Woolls twice refused ordination but on 8 June 1873 he was made deacon by Bishop Barker [q.v.]; ordained priest on 21 December he was appointed incumbent of Richmond, becoming rural dean in 1877. Familiar with his flock and region, he exercised a vigorous ministry and retired with a general licence in 1883.

Woolls's interest in his colonial surroundings had manifested itself in his study of the local botany and 'vegetable resources'. Under the tutelage of Rev. James Walker of The King's School and Marsfield, he contributed articles to the *Horticultural Magazine*, the *Victorian Naturalist*, and the *Proceedings* of the Linnean Society of London—papers that were published in Sydney in 1867 as A *Contribution to the Flora of Australia* and earned him a fellowship of the society in 1865: he was awarded a Ph.D. of the University of Göttingen in 1871 for a dissertation on the botany of the Parramatta region. Woolls's other works included *Lectures on the Vegetable Kingdom, with special reference to the Flora of Australia* (1879), *The Plants of New South Wales ...* (1885) and *Plants Indigenous in the Neighbourhood of Sydney ...* (1880).

One of the most distinguished of a group of clergyman-botanists in the colony, Woolls was best known for his promotion of Australian botany and his assistance to other scholars rather than for large-scale systematic work. He gave many popular lectures, wrote countless letters on native flora to local newspapers and advised on the horticultural and agricultural sections of colonial exhibitions. He corresponded with fellow botanists, including Caroline Atkinson [q.v.], and wrote over a thousand letters to Sir Ferdinand Mueller [q.v.]; his assistance was acknowledged by the British botanists Robert Brown and George Bentham [qq.v.]. J. H. Maiden, later government botanist, noted that 'only his friends and pupils ... had any idea either of the depth of his knowledge or the readiness with which he communicated it to enquirers'. He is commemorated in the genus Woollsia (Epacridaceae) and in the names of six species.

Woolls died of paraplegia at Burwood on 14 March 1893 and was buried in St John's cemetery, Parramatta; a memorial window is in the church. He was survived by his third wife Sarah Elizabeth (d. 1909), daughter of Robert Lowe of Bringelly, whom he had married at St Paul's Church, Narellan, on 25 June 1862. His estate was valued for probate at £2446.

HRA (1), 17; S. M. Johnstone, The history of The King's School, Parramatta (Syd, 1932); Vic Naturalist, 9 (1893); J. H. Maiden, 'Records of Australian botanists', Roy Soc NSW, Procs, 42 (1908); J. Jervis, 'William Woolls', Parramatta Hist Soc, J, 3 (1926); Cumberland Times, 30 Sept 1871; SMH, 15 Mar 1893; Sydney Mail, 18 Mar 1893; Calvert papers and Parkes letters (ML); Ordination papers (Syd Diocesan Registry).

K. J. CABLE

WOOLNER, THOMAS (1825-1892), sculptor and poet, was born on 1 December 1825 at Hadleigh, Suffolk, England, son of Thomas Woolner, post office sorter, and his first wife Rebecca, née Leeks. He received some education at Ipswich. His father took no interest in the boy's early efforts at clay modelling, carving and drawing, but a sympathetic stepmother paid for his training at the studio of William Behnes, sculptor, where he worked for six years. In 1842 he gained admission as a student at the Royal Academy and received some minor commissions. In the next decade he exhibited works regularly at the academy, including his bronze figure of Puck.

In 1847 Woolner met D. G. Rossetti and, according to art critic F. G. Stephens, was then 'encamped in a huge, dusty, barnlike studio like a Bedouin in a desert'—probably the studio Woolner shared in Stanhope Street with Bernhard Smith [q.v.]. He became an original member of the Pre-Raphaelite Brotherhood and with Smith helped to produce its short-lived journal, The Germ, in 1850. The first issue included his poems 'My Beautiful Lady' and 'Of My Lady in Death', illustrated by W. Holman Hunt. Woolner's attempts, however, to convey the principles of the Brotherhood through his sculpture produced few commissions and when Smith and E. La T. Bateman [q.v.] decided to visit the Australian gold diggings, he joined them.

Arriving in Melbourne in the Windsor on 23 October 1852, Woolner and Smith first stayed with Dr Godfrey Howitt [q.v.] before going on to the diggings in the Ovens valley and in the Fryer's Creek, Castlemaine and Sandhurst areas. Woolner found some gold but after six months sold his tools and returned to Melbourne. He began to model medallions but had to dig the local clay, grind his own gypsum and make his own tools. He then modelled relievo in bronze of well-known citizens, charging twenty-five guineas each, and their influence and the patronage of Lieut-Governor La Trobe brought him several commissions. In 1853 some of his work was included in the exhibition of the newly formed Victorian Society of Fine Arts at the Mechanics' Institute.

Woolner then spent six months in Sydney; later writing that the lovely scenery, the 'divine air' and the great amiability of every one towards him made it one of the most enjoyable periods of his life. Many leading citizens commissioned portrait medallions from him. He hoped to gain the commission for a statue of W. C. Wentworth [q.v.] and he decided to return to England to press his case. Too late the Melbourne Argus mourned that 'the neglect which he experienced compared with his ready appreciation in Sydney remains a sort of blot on our national character'.

Alfred Howitt [q.v.] had at first found Woolner's 'variations of character' delightful, but soon found him aggressive, meddlesome, impertinent, full of 'self-esteem, [and] short temper[ed], officious, and in spite of his noisy volubility, very shy and nervous'. The other Howitts did not share Alfred's views and Woolner became engaged to Godfrey's daughter Edith. After their broken engagement, Woolner sailed for England in July 1854 in the Queen of the South, intending to return if he received the Wentworth commission. Instead he became one of the leading sculptors of his day as well as a poet of distinction. In 1871 he was an associate member and in 1875 a member of the Royal Academy, where he was appointed professor of sculpture; he resigned in 1879 before delivering any discourses. In all, he exhibited 120 works at the academy as well as at the British Institution and elsewhere. Among his best-known statues are those of J. S. Mill on the Thames Embankment, the Prince Consort and Bacon statues at Oxford, and Sir Stamford Raffles in Singapore. Among Australians whose likenesses he modelled were Lieut-Governor La Trobe, Sir Charles FitzRoy, Sir Charles Nicholson, Sir Redmond Barry, Admiral P. P. King [qq.v.] and several members of the G. W. Cole, Macarthur [qq.v.] and Howitt families.

In Sydney in 1854 Woolner had met (Sir) Henry Parkes [q.v.]; they continued to correspond and Parkes saw him in England in 1861 and in 1882, when he took Parkes to visit Tennyson. Through Parkes he was commissioned in 1874 to execute the colossal bronze statue of Captain Cook [q.v.] for Sydney's Hyde Park. The commission was the subject of acrimonious correspondence between Woolner and W. Forster [q.v.] who favoured the sculptor Charles Summers [q.v.]. In 1878 he claimed that the statue had cost him £2000 more than the 'dishonest' contract of £4000 that Forster had made him sign. Parkes had arranged for him to execute statues of Sir Charles Cowper, Sir James Martin [qq.v.] and Wentworth, but in late 1891 the new government of (Sir) George Dibbs [q.v.] cancelled the commission.

On 6 September 1864 Woolner had married Alice Gertrude Waugh at St James's Church, Paddington, England; they had two sons and four daughters. He died on 7 October 1892 from an internal disorder after a short illness and was buried at St Mary's, Hendon. The *Saturday Review* obituary stated that 'few men of his generation had a greater fund of talk or a more telling delivery ... he had, at one time or another, been the friend of almost every artist or every writer of his age'. In the print room of the British Museum there is a portrait of Woolner engraved from a photograph and also a likeness sketched in his studio after T. Blake Wirgman.

W. B. Scott, *Autobiographical notes ...*, W. Minto ed (Lond, 1892); H. Parkes, *Fifty years in the making of Australian history* (Lond, 1892); W. Moore, *Studio sketches* (Melb, 1906); A. Woolner, *Thomas Woolner ... his life in letters* (Lond, 1917); F. G. Stephens, 'Thomas Woolner, R.A.', *Art J* (Lond), 1894; A. Clyne, 'Thomas Woolner, 1825-1892', *Bookman* (Lond), Jan 1926; K. R. Cramp, 'Some historical memorials and buildings', *JRAHS*, 19 (1933); *Argus*, 6 July 1853, 25 Apr, 14 July, 28 Aug 1854; *T&CJ*, 22 Feb, 1, 15 Mar 1879; *Saturday Review* (Lond), 15 Oct 1892; G. Long, 'Thomas Woolner. Pre-Raphaelite in Sydney', *SMH*, 13 Jan 1934; M. B. Smith, *Bernhard Smith and his connection with art* (Melb, 1917, copies SLV, ML); Howitt papers (LaT L); Parkes letters (ML); T. Woolner diary (copy NL).   MARJORIE J. TIPPING

WOORE, THOMAS (1804-1878), naval officer, surveyor and pastoralist, was born on 29 January 1804 at Londonderry, Ire-

land, eldest son of Thomas Woore, army captain, and his wife Catherine Anne, née Darcus. Educated at Foyle College, Londonderry, he disappointed family hopes of an army career for him by joining the navy as a midshipman in December 1819. He served on ships suppressing smuggling along the south coast of England until April 1823 when, using family connexions, he transferred to the *Thetis*. He resigned his commission in February 1826 to settle his father's estate in Ireland but rejoined later that year. Posted to the *Alligator*, he was engaged in hydrographic experiments off the east coast of North America. He acquired skill as a surveyor and in 1828 was offered a post in the hydrography section of the Admiralty; he took command of *The Woodlark*.

In 1829 Woore joined the *Zebra*, based in India, in which he first visited Sydney. In the *Crocodile* in 1831, he was promoted to lieutenant and joined the *Alligator* which was operating out of Sydney in 1832. At the end of 1834 he resigned because of ill health. On 1 January 1835 in the Scots Church, Sydney, he married Mary, daughter of John Dickson [q.v.] and in February they left for Britain. Woore returned to New South Wales in 1839, was made a magistrate and bought a station, Pomeroy near Goulburn, where he built a charming house and became a leading pastoralist.

In May 1846 the government refused to have a survey made of the proposed railway line and Woore, on his own initiative and at his own expense, examined possible routes. He reported the results to a public meeting in Sydney in August. Insufficient funds were raised for a detailed survey, so he volunteered to do it on condition that his expenses be met and that any company subsequently formed should pay him 'proper remuneration'. He completed the work by 1848, but it was criticized and his efforts were deprecated in many quarters. When the Sydney Railway Co. was formed Woore vainly applied for the post of engineer and was refused payment for his preliminary work. He accepted the harsh treatment stoically and in 1849 prevented a group of Goulburn people from forming a rival company. In 1858 Woore asked the government, which was using his plan, for compensation but although the select committee on his railway services recommended an award of £1500 it was not accepted by the Legislative Assembly; in 1866 he petitioned parliament and in 1871 £1500 on the estimates was reduced to £1.

In 1867-69 Woore was a member of the commission on the water-supply of Sydney and its suburbs and in his minority report vainly suggested building a dam at Warragamba. In the 1870s he pressed for the scheme in two pamphlets and published *Errors in the Great Western Railroad New South Wales* ... (Goulburn, 1876). He was also a talented artist. About 1875 he advertised Pomeroy for sale and went to live with his only daughter Catherine Anne, wife of William Busby [q.v.], at Redleaf, Double Bay, where he died of chronic diarrhoea on 21 June 1878. Buried in Randwick cemetery with Anglican rites, he was survived by his wife and daughter to whom he left personalty valued for probate at £500.

G. N. Griffiths, *Some houses and people of New South Wales* (Syd, 1949), and *Some southern homes of New South Wales* (Syd, 1952); V&P (LA NSW), 1858, 3, 1037, 1858-59, 1, 207, 228, 1866, 5, 715, 1870, 2, 485, 1878-79, 7, 66; Busby family papers (ML); T. Woore, Diary and family papers (ML); MS cat (ML).

G. J. ABBOTT

WORSNOP, THOMAS (1821-1898), town clerk and author, was born on 2 February 1821 at Wortley, Leeds, Yorkshire, England. He first worked for W. Bruce, a wool manufacturer of Leeds, and reputedly studied arts and law at Cambridge but does not appear in the university's records. He taught for a time, probably at a college in Yorkshire, but ill health led him to migrate to South Australia. He arrived in Adelaide in the *China* on 12 November 1852 with his wife Mary Ann, née Kenyon (d. 1905), and their three children. Settling at Port Elliot, he later worked as a storeman for seven years for Elder, Stirling [qq.v.] & Co. In 1859 he was appointed a sergeant in the South Australian Volunteers. After an unsuccessful period on the land, from 1863 he was lessee of the Globe Inn, Rundle Street, Adelaide, but was declared bankrupt with debts of £5000 on 16 May 1864 (annulled 1884). He then worked as a teamster, servicing many of the far northern stations and suffering severe privation in the great drought of 1865-66.

In September 1866 Worsnop was appointed clerk in the town clerk's department of Adelaide City Council; in 1868 he was city treasurer and assistant town clerk, and on 11 January 1869 he became acting town clerk, taking over permanently later that year. The council had a large debt and its affairs were in arrears; but Worsnop quickly proved an efficient and conscientious administrator, reducing the debt by £3000 in a year and erasing it by 1877. He formulated many schemes for improving and enhancing Adelaide and was especially interested in developing and protecting the Park Lands. His 1885 report to the council detailed the controversy surrounding their original purchase in 1839.

In 1879 Worsnop helped to set up the Municipal Corporations Association of South Australia and was its secretary until his death. He was regularly asked to provide expert evidence on civic affairs to government select committees. A justice of the peace, a Freemason and member of the Old Colonists' Association, he was a fervent admirer of South Australia and published numerous booklets on municipal affairs, in many of which he eulogized Adelaide as a model city.

Worsnop is particularly remembered for the excellent, detailed *History of the City of Adelaide* (1878); its original is in the Adelaide City Council Archives. He also left a useful manuscript, 'The Historical Record of South Australia 1512-1854', which is in the South Australian State Archives. In 1897 he published *The Prehistoric Arts, Manufactures, Works, Weapons, etc., of the Aborigines of Australia*, consisting of material from two papers he had read to the Royal Geographical Society of Australasia, South Australian Branch, and to the ethnology and anthropology sections of the Australasian Association for the Advancement of Science in Brisbane in 1895. He was a fellow of the Royal Historical Society, London.

In 1890 Worsnop's portrait had been presented to him by the council in whose chambers it now hangs. He was 'Jealous to a fault of the citizens' privileges' and 'strong in large matters, careful over small things'. In 1898 he took sick leave but died of diabetes and gall-stones on 24 January at his home in Barnard Street, North Adelaide, aged 76. He was buried in the Anglican North Road cemetery, survived by his wife, three daughters and two sons. His estate was sworn for probate at £400.

J. J. Pascoe (ed), *History of Adelaide and vicinity* (Adel, 1901); *ISN*, 19 July 1890; *Observer* (Adel), 21 Feb 1891, 29 Jan 1898; *Register* (Adel), 25 Jan 1898; *Chronicle* (Adel), 29 Jan 1898; *T&CJ*, 12 Feb 1898; Adelaide City Council Archives; Insolvency register and papers (SAA); passenger lists 1852 (SAA).

HELEN R. MULLINS

WRENFORDSLEY, SIR HENRY THOMAS (1825-1908), judge, was born in Middlesex, England, son of Joseph Wrenfordsley, an Irish solicitor, and his wife Louisa, née Bywater. His father was known also as Wrendfordsley, Wransfordsley and Wrenford Sly. Educated privately in France, he entered Trinity College, Dublin, in March

1841 as Henry Wransfordsly but took no degree. Qualifying as a solicitor after serving articles in Dublin to his father and wealthy legal friends, he advertised as an independent practitioner from 1849. In 1854 he published a legal text and in 1859 a translation of a French evangelical sermon by Adolph Monod. In June 1860 he entered the Middle Temple and was called to the Bar on 30 April 1863.

Wrenfordsley was junior counsel in 1868 for the Privy Council office in House of Commons inquiries into the foreign cattle market. He stood unsuccessfully for Peterborough in 1868 and 1874. In 1876 he became a deputy-judge of County courts at Marylebone, Brompton and Brentford and in 1877 was appointed as puisne judge in Mauritius. In September 1878 he exchanged into the office of procurer-general where he was commended for his labour code and his review of Supreme Court procedure. Disappointed by failing to become chief justice of Mauritius he was appointed attorney-general of Jamaica but on the death of Sir Archibald Burt [q.v.] he was made chief justice of Western Australia; he arrived there in the *Bangalore* on 5 March 1880 accompanied by a lady, probably his sister. He represented the colony at the Intercolonial Conference in 1881. Next year he was appointed chief justice of Fiji but remained in Western Australia as administrator until June 1883 when he was knighted.

In Fiji he sought a specious popularity by siding with the planter community against the government defence of native rights. Admirers asserted that his judicial virtues had enhanced property values by 25 per cent. Plagued by his creditors, the Colonial Office thought his vanity and his debts were 'not a credit to us', and considered his speech attacking government policy at a valedictory banquet 'injudicious to say the least'. He left Fiji early in 1884 on sick leave, alleged to be spurious, and was acting judge in Tasmania from March 1885 to February 1887. Going to Melbourne he took silk, accepted a temporary seat on the bench and was described by Victorian barristers as 'a journeyman judge who went about with robes in his carpet bag'.

In 1891 Wrenfordsley returned temporarily to Western Australia. Chief Justice Onslow [q.v.], at loggerheads with Governor Broome, had been given leave till the end of Broome's term. Wrenfordsley acted until Onslow's return then went as chief justice to the Leeward Islands. In all his judicial appointments he was uniformly undistinguished as a lawyer. He retired to the south of France in 1901 and, aged 81, died unmarried at Antibes on 2 June 1908.

J. Foster, *Men-at-the-Bar* (Lond, 1885); *Dictionnaire de biographie mauricienne*, 2 (Port Louis, 1945-52); A. Dean, *A multitude of counsellors* (Melb, 1968); *Law Times*, 12 Feb 1887; *Inquirer*, 10 Jan 1883; *Australasian*, 17 May 1884, 2 Apr 1887; *The Times*, 10 June 1908; CO 18/200/143-146, 224, 83/36/393, 37/13, 304; information from King's Inns Lib, Dublin, and Middle Temple Lib, Lond.

T. S. LOUCH

WRIGHT, FRANCIS AUGUSTUS (1835-1903), carrier and politician, was born in August 1835 in London, son of Captain Francis Augustus Wright, R.N., and his wife Eliza, daughter of Robert Lunn, archivist and librarian of the Society of Arts, London. He probably arrived in New South Wales on 30 October 1836 in the *Jess* with his parents, who settled at Parramatta. He was educated there by W. Breathom and S. Owens and briefly at The King's School. At 9 he went to sea as an apprentice. Finding himself in London when his articles ended, he joined the office of Laugher, Dwyer & Co., architects, in Poland Street.

Learning of the discovery of gold, Wright sailed for Melbourne and arrived in the *Kent* in September 1852. He worked on the Victorian and New South Wales goldfields until 1855, when he went to sea in the service of the Australasian Steam Navigation Co. and became a first officer. In 1859 he joined the ill-fated Port Curtis, Queensland, gold rush. He returned destitute and worked as a labourer in (Sir) Peter Russell's [q.v.] foundry, before returning to the New South Wales goldfields. On 19 December 1864 in Sydney he married Alice Marcia Williams, daughter of a goldminer.

In January 1865 he began a carrying business with Edward Barber, styled Wright, Barber & Co. In 1868-72 Wright was in partnership with David MacNeill. In 1875, when Edward Heaton (d. 1894) joined them, the firm became Wright Heaton Barber & Co., general carriers and forwarding and commission agents, with capital of £14,000. The business expanded rapidly and the firm moved to a new office in Pitt Street designed by T. Rowe [q.v.] and shifted their stables to Redfern near Wright's home, Carisbrooke. In 1878 they won a five-year contract to carry all the copper from the Great Cobar Copper Mining Co. to the railhead; and in 1880 they handled 120,000 bales of wool. Wright managed the Sydney office and dealt with the Department of Railways. In February Wright Heaton & Co. Ltd was incorporated with Wright as chairman and managing director.

He represented Belmore Ward on the Redfern Borough Council in 1873-87 and was mayor in 1882-84. An avowed free trader and friend of H. Copeland [q.v.], he was elected to the Legislative Assembly for Redfern on 11 January 1882 and later modified his free-trade principles 'as revenue must be raised'. In January 1883 Wright became postmaster-general in (Sir) Alexander Stuart's [q.v.] ministry; to enable him to take office, Wright Heaton & Co. was turned into a public company with twenty-three shareholders, achieved by giving ten clerks ten shares each. On 28 May he took over as secretary for public works at a time of rapid railway expansion. In March 1885 he enthusiastically managed the dispatch of the Sudan Contingent. On 30 September J. P. Garvan [q.v.] failed with a motion disapproving of Wright as secretary for works owing to his connexion with Wright Heaton & Co., the 'most extensive carrying firm in the Colony'. On 5 October the *Sydney Morning Herald* commented that he 'had been the best-abused man on the Ministerial side. But it is admitted on all hands that as a Minister he has been capable, independent and straightforward'. After the resignation of the Stuart government he became secretary for mines in (Sir) George Dibbs's [q.v.] ministry but had to resign ten days later when he lost his seat.

In the 1880s Wright Heaton & Co. recklessly expanded into Queensland; by 1886 it had fifty-nine branches and total overdrafts of £92,000. After allegations made by F. Abigail [q.v.], Wright, with Heaton and others, was committed for trial for conspiring 'to cheat and defraud the Commissioner for Railways ... of divers large sums of money' since 1880. Committed for trial at the Water Police Court on 3 August 1886, Wright was released on bail of £500. He claimed that his trial was 'a persecution of a political character' and that the 'system of averaging wool has grown up, and if not expressly permitted by the railway officials has been known to them and tacitly acquiesced in for many years', and was used by every carrying firm in the colony. The trial was delayed by the illness of a juror, the death of Chief Justice Sir James Martin [q.v.] and the appointment of Wright's counsel (Sir) Frederick Darley [q.v.] as his successor, an appeal against a new trial, and the Crown's 'search for its wandering witnesses'. On 22 June 1887 Mr Justice M. H. Stephen [q.v.] refused another adjournment and the defendants were discharged. In 1889 the scandal was revived by the royal commission inquiring into the alleged unfitness of W. M. Fehon for appointment as a commissioner of railways because of his connexion with Wright Heaton & Co.

Wright took over total management of the New South Wales business in 1887, and by selling land and buildings, retrenching employees and reducing salaries, managed to reduce the overdraft and slowly to restore profits: in 1894 the firm again paid a dividend and in 1898 took over the McCulloch [q.v. James and William] Carrying Co. Ltd. He became chairman of directors in 1895. In 1889-1903 he represented Glen Innes in the Legislative Assembly as a protectionist.

In 1873 Wright had been commissioned as an ensign in the Sydney Battalion of the Volunteer Infantry and was promoted lieutenant next year, major in 1885 and lieut-colonel in 1898. In evidence to the 1892 royal commission into the military service of New South Wales he recommended stricter discipline, less drilling and more practical training for the volunteers, and dismissed the rifle clubs as useless. In 1897 he was responsible for establishing the 6th Volunteer Infantry Regiment, Australian Rifles. He retired in 1902 with the honorary rank of colonel. A magistrate, Wright was a trustee of the Savings Bank of New South Wales and of Ku-ring-gai Chase, Hawkesbury River, and a New South Wales commissioner for the Colonial and Indian Exhibition, London 1886, and for the World's Columbian Exposition, Chicago 1893. He was a prominent Freemason and deputy district grand master under the English constitution.

Survived by his wife, two of their five sons and three of their five daughters, Wright died of diabetes and apoplexy at his house, Putney, near Ryde, on 1 October 1903 and was buried with military honours in the Anglican section of Rookwood cemetery. His intestate estate was valued at £39,463.

E. Digby (ed), *Australian men of mark*, 2 (Syd, 1889); Wright Heaton & Co. Ltd, A *history* ... 1862-1962 (Syd, 1962); V&P (LA NSW), 1883-84, 5, 707, 1889, 5, 131, 1892-93, 5, 1159ff, 7, 568ff, 1896, 4, 427ff, 1900, 5, 600ff; PD, 1885, 1st s, 503-551, 578-627; SMH, 6 Jan 1882, 5 Oct 1885, 24, 27-31 July, 4 Aug, 6-9, 12-15, 27 Oct 1886, 23 June 1887, 3 Oct 1903; *Daily Telegraph* (Syd), 26 July 1894; CO 201/603/467.

MARTHA RUTLEDGE

WRIGHT, HORATIO GEORGE ANTHONY (1827-1901), medical practitioner, was born at Maidstone, Kent, England, son of Robert Wright and his wife Caroline, née Caldicott. Educated at Huntingdon, he studied medicine under James Paget and William Lawrence at St Bartholomew's Hospital, London (M.R.C.S., 1850; L.S.A., 1851). He arrived in Sydney on 10 December 1853 in the *Dominion* with his wife Ellen, née Hunter, whom he had married at Clapham Independent Chapel on 28 August 1848. Registered by the Medical Board in February 1854, he set up practice in Hunter Street. In March 1868 he was one of the first surgeons to attend the duke of Edinburgh after he was shot by H. J. O'Farrell [q.v.] at Clontarf.

Elected to the Royal Society of New South Wales in 1872 Wright became a councillor next year; he was honorary treasurer in 1879-85 and 1893-1901 and a vice-president in 1885-86 and 1891-92. His principal scientific contributions to the society were as a microscopist when a member and sometime chairman of Section E (microscopy), on which he served from 1877-92. He often exhibited examples of the latest techniques and of his own high skills in micro-photography. In 1885 he presented a Ross-Zentmeyer binocular microscope to the society. Chairman of the medical section in 1878, he served at various times on the astronomy and physics and sanitary science sections. In December 1874 he had been an astronomical assistant to H. C. Russell [q.v.], taking observations for the transit of Venus with an 8½-in. Browning telescope. Wright's influence on the Royal Society was 'unobtrusive' at a time of marked improvements in its scientific standards and prestige under A. Liversidge [q.v.] and others. Although frequently approached he refused to become president.

For forty-eight years Wright was one of the best-known doctors in inner Sydney, conducting his flourishing practice from his residence in Wynyard Square and supervising 'the births of many thousands of Australians'. He was consulting surgeon at St Vincent's Hospital and highly esteemed for his 'quiet genial manner' by patients and colleagues who, when he was the innocent victim of a blackmail conspiracy for alleged misconduct with a female patient, gave him a 'handsome' monetary 'solatium'.

Early in 1880 Wright was a founder and first honorary treasurer of the New South Wales branch of the British Medical Association and often took part in professional discussions. He was appointed to the Medical Board in April 1886, where he served conscientiously, sometimes as chairman, until 1901. 'Quiet and courtly in demeanour', he was benevolent and civically minded, and 'only his immediate colleagues were fully aware of the loyal service he rendered to the cause of science in Australia'. A director of the Mutual Assurance Society of Victoria and a founding member of the Australasian Association for the Advancement of Science (1887-88), he served as the Royal Society's member on the organ-

izing council for the second Sydney meeting in 1891.

Aged 74, Wright died of angina pectoris at 15 York Street, Sydney, on 14 September 1901 and was buried in the Anglican section of Waverley cemetery. He was survived by one of his three sons and one of his five daughters of his first wife, and by his second wife Augusta Lucy, née Barber, whom he had married in Sydney on 19 August 1890. His estate was valued for probate at £1417.

H. C. Russell (ed), *Observation of the transit of Venus... 1874* (Syd, 1892); British Medical Assn (NSW), *Procs*, 1880; *A'sian Medical Gazette*, 20 (1901); *Bulletin*, 21 Sept 1901; *T&CJ*, 28 Sept 1901; 'Old Sydney', *Truth* (Syd), 2 Jan 1910; Medical Board, Minute books 1854, 1886-1901 (NSWA).   MICHAEL HOARE

WRIGHT, JOHN JAMES (1821-1904), storekeeper, was born on 20 February 1821 at Ballina, County Mayo, Ireland, son of John Wright. After a childhood visit to Australia he migrated to New South Wales about 1837; in December 1842 he became poundkeeper at Queanbeyan; postmaster in February 1844, he opened the Post Office Store in 1849. On 30 September next year at St Andrew's Presbyterian Church, Sydney, he married Mary Anne Clarke. His store prospered and in 1856 he opened a second shop in Queanbeyan, part of a chain that expanded briefly into near-by towns and numbered thirteen during the Kiandra gold rush in 1859-60. He leased the Dodsworth Mill in 1858 and acquired the modern and efficient Severne Mill in November. A founding member of the Queanbeyan Parochial Association in 1848, he was an office-bearer in the Oddfellows' Happy Home Lodge and Literary Institute and president of the District Hospital.

Wright supported (Sir) John Robertson's [q.v.] 1859-61 land bills but declined to run for parliament until 1874, pleading the demands of his store. In December he defeated William Forster [q.v.] for the Queanbeyan seat in the Legislative Assembly and was the first townsman to occupy it. Although elected as a friend of (Sir) Henry Parkes [q.v.] and 'the bitterest of orangemen', he was passive in parliament and by supporting Robertson's ministry obtained amenities for the town, notably a permanent Post and Telegraph Office. But he was arrogant, choleric and spiteful, and his popularity began to wane after his eviction of the public school from his rented premises in September 1875, and his prosecution of Rev. A. D. Soares [q.v.] in January 1876 for the return of four pigeons which had nested in the church spire. He withdrew from the 1877 election according to L. F. de Salis [q.v.] because he had 'no one to whom he can confide the management of his peculiar complicated store', and from a by-election in 1881; in 1885 he was defeated by E. W. O'Sullivan.

In 1877 with William Affleck of Gundaroo Wright founded the Queanbeyan Free Selectors' Association, and in 1879-82 led the agitation which brought the railway through the town, of which he was first mayor in 1885-88. His career on the council was marked by inaction and unconcern. He controlled several important stations in the district and in 1880 was a sheep director but there was a steady decline in his affairs after the death of his eldest son James in 1886; in 1891 the store was sold and the Severne Mill failed. His wife and daughters soon quit Queanbeyan and he was left only with his son Douglas.

Wright continued to act as a justice of the peace, a member of the local Land Board, a guardian of minors and as returning officer for Queanbeyan from 1890; but he drank heavily, became an eccentric and was often seen with a rifle driving pedestrians from the vicinity of his home. He died of apoplexy on 22 October 1904 and was buried in the Anglican section of the Queanbeyan Riverside cemetery with his two sons, who are alone commemorated on the monument above the grave. He was survived by three of his five sons and four daughters. His intestate estate was valued at £48. Self made, an opportunist, an egocentric bigot and a misfit, Wright nevertheless contributed substantially to the development of Queanbeyan.

A. M. Fallick & Sons, *The story of Queanbeyan 1838-1938* (Queanbeyan, 1938); E. J. Lea-Scarlett, *Queanbeyan: district and people* (Queanbeyan, 1968); A. W. Martin, 'Electoral contests in Yass and Queanbeyan in the 'seventies and 'eighties', *JRAHS*, 43 (1957); *Queanbeyan Age*, 25 Oct 1904; Parkes letters (ML).

E. J. LEA-SCARLETT

WRIGHT, WILLIAM HENRY (1816-1877), gold commissioner and public servant, was born at Sandhurst, Berkshire, England, son of Charles Wright, army officer, and his wife Harriet, née Frere. Educated at the Royal Military College, Sandhurst, he joined the 50th Regiment in January 1833 and served in New Zealand and under Major Joseph Anderson [q.v.] at Norfolk Island. In 1838 he sold out of the service, qualified as a surveyor in New South Wales and on 27 July joined the Survey Department under Major T. L. Mitchell [q.v.]. On 13 June 1843 he became commissioner of crown lands for Welling-

ton District. At the end of 1846 he became commissioner of crown lands for the Wimmera in the Port Phillip District.

In 1852 Wright took charge of Mount Alexander goldfield at a salary of £900 and set up Central Camp near Castlemaine to control a population of some 25,000. His staff was inexperienced and his duties 'onerous and varied' with the 'most inadequate means either in material or men', but he worked so tirelessly and effectively that Lieut-Governor La Trobe appointed him chief commissioner of the goldfields on 1 May. He warned La Trobe of the defects of the 1851 licence system and opposed the compulsory licence hunts which were provocative to the diggers; however, his flexibility kept the situation under control.

Wright was instructed to make his headquarters in Melbourne in March 1853 and he was a non-elective member of the Legislative Council from August that year until March 1856. Goldfields unrest continued in 1853, with political activists talking of revolution, but Wright, with such commissioners as J. E. N. Bull and J. A. Panton [qq.v.], kept protest meetings in hand. On 13 September 1854 Lieut-Governor Hotham ordered twice-weekly licence hunts despite Wright's advice that 'extreme forbearance and conciliation' were essential. As troubles mounted at Ballarat, he warned Hotham on 2 December that 'two thousand miners have offered to defend the Camp should their services be required', but the governor bypassed Wright for Commissioner Rede [q.v.]. The military attack on the Eureka Stockade occurred on 3 December 1854.

In November Wright had been appointed a member of the commission of inquiry into the goldfields. He defended his staff but his department was abolished, and on 1 July 1855 he became secretary of the Gold Department, which he described as a 'subordinate post'. In the same month he obtained one farthing damages in a libel case against (Sir) John O'Shanassy [q.v.] who had referred to his 'habitual insolence as a corrupt official', but the court decided that the phrase had no direct personal link. In 1856 he was president of the Melbourne Club and on 15 March he received £1800 as compensation for loss of position as chief commissioner; on 1 May he was reappointed commissioner of crown lands for the Wimmera. In June 1860 his post was abolished; he was granted £1500 in compensation in 1862 and in July he became secretary for railways at a salary of £800. At his own request he was appointed sheriff of Victoria in 1871, and in December 1876 he became chairman of the Tender Board. In January 1877 he was also gazetted acting inspector-general of penal establishments.

On 28 August 1866 at St John's Church, Heidelberg, Wright had married Mary Meek. In 1876 three of his four children died of scarlet fever. On 31 January next year he dined with George Higinbotham [q.v.] at Brighton and stayed the night. Next morning he was found dead. An inquest attributed his death to 'coma caused by the pressure of a bony growth upon the brain'. Aged 61, he was buried after an Anglican service in St Kilda cemetery, survived by his wife and a son. The *Argus* commented on his 'strict conscientiousness in the discharge of his duties [and his] frank open manner [which] greatly endeared him to those placed under him'; he was 'greatly esteemed by a very large circle of private friends'.

W. Howitt, *Land, labour, and gold* (Lond, 1855); E. Scott, *Historical memoir of the Melbourne Club* (Melb, 1936); H. Anderson, *Eureka: Victorian parliamentary papers ...* (Melb, 1969); L. J. Blake, *Gold escort* (Melb, 1971); V&P (LC Vic), 1852-53, 2, 27, 1853-54, 3, (8), 1855-56, 2 (A111), (LA Vic), 1861-62, 2 (62), 1867, 1st S, 2 (D18), 1873, 2 (10); *Age*, 8 Dec 1855; *Argus*, 2 Feb 1877; diary of James Richardson of Gorinn (copy held by LaT L).

L. J. BLAKE

WRIXON, SIR HENRY JOHN (1839-1913), barrister and politician, was born on 18 October 1839 in Dublin, Ireland, son of Arthur Nicholas Wrixon, lawyer, and his wife Maria (Charlotte Matilda), née Bace. The family arrived in Melbourne in 1850. Arthur was appointed the second County Court judge in 1853 and worked mainly in the Western District. Henry was educated at Portland and entered the University of Melbourne in 1855, its first year, but left for Trinity College, Dublin, in 1857 (B.A., 1861), where he became a noted debater. He was called to the Irish Bar in 1861 but found little work, and in 1863 returned to Victoria.

After four years at the Bar and an election attempt in 1864, in February 1868 Wrixon won the seat of Belfast in the Legislative Assembly as a radical reformer of the land laws and the Legislative Council. In his election address, published in Melbourne in 1868 as *Democracy in Australia*, he remarked that 'Wealth is the only badge of our aristocracy, but it confers a nobility neither exclusive nor enduring'. He became solicitor-general in (Sir) James McCulloch's [q.v.] ministry from April 1870 to June 1871. On 17 December 1872 he married the wealthy widow Charlotte Anderson, daughter of Henry 'Money' Miller [q.v.], and bought Raheen, a great house with lands stretching to the Yarra River at Kew.

Wrixon did not contest the 1877 election but toured Europe. He became member for Portland in May 1880 and soon came close to forming, with (Sir) Graham Berry [q.v.], the coalition between 'Conservatives' and Liberals which he supported when Berry and James Service [q.v.] achieved it in 1883. In 1886 he became attorney-general in the D. Gillies [q.v.]-Deakin ministry. A disciple of George Higinbotham [q.v.], Wrixon was delighted to appoint him chief justice. He led for the Crown in the Ah Toy case in 1888 but lost on a majority judgment. Made Q.C. in 1890, Wrixon left for London to appeal to the Privy Council which reversed the decision but left unexplored the constitutional issue of the colonial government's power to exclude aliens. Wrixon returned a hero, was a delegate to the Federal Convention in 1891 and was created K.C.M.G. in 1892.

In May 1892 Wrixon was defeated narrowly by (Sir) Thomas Bent [q.v.] for the Speakership—a perfect example of the standards of Victorian politics of the time. He made a bid for the premiership in August but his no confidence motion on the Shiels ministry's budget ended in fiasco. He was appointed a delegate to the Colonial Conference in Canada in 1894 with the additional commission of investigating socialist movements, which resulted in *Socialism, being Notes on a Political Tour* (London, 1896). He had resigned from the assembly in July 1894, became a member of the Legislative Council in 1896 for the South-Western Province, and was president of the council from 1901 until his retirement in June 1910. Vice-chancellor of the University of Melbourne in 1897-1910, he was a trustee of the Public Library, Museums, and National Gallery from 1902 (vice-president from 1905), and in 1906 president of the Melbourne Club.

As a member of the 1891 National Australasian [Federation] Convention, Wrixon tried to define clear relations between the two Houses; Quick and Garran describe his comments on the draft bill as remarkable for their 'almost prophetic insight into the modifications that would be necessary before the Bill could be wholly acceptable'. In 1897, not on the *Age* ticket, he missed election to the Federal Convention by one place; H. B. Higgins, who ran tenth, was distressed at having excluded 'a man of such culture and courtesy' and so well qualified as a candidate.

Wrixon's most admired characteristics were his sincerity and eloquence. Deakin described him as 'loveable and entirely trustworthy ... animated by the sincerest and most unselfish desire to serve his country'. He never quite reached the top in politics, partly because he refused to lobby and partly because he lacked driving will-power and the vigour of dogmatism. Although a prominent leader of the 'Conservatives' in the 1880s and early 1890s, he differed from most of his colleagues on issues of class privilege. His most significant independent decision was to uphold the constitutional principle that an Upper House should not have financial powers. In consequence the Service reform bill of 1880 was defeated by two votes in the assembly and Service resigned.

Wrixon consistently stood for political equality: he supported the Hare system of proportional representation as early as 1873, advocated female suffrage, strongly supported abolition of plural voting, and condemned the class basis of the council, but he did not support payment of members. Similar principles of justice and fair-dealing led him to argue for the Saturday half-holiday in 1869 and attempts to compensate workers for injuries caused by the negligence of others. He introduced a moderate employers' liability bill in 1883, fought weakening amendments and tried to extend its provisions to seamen; it became law in 1886 and in 1899 Wrixon vainly introduced to the council a more extensive workmen's compensation bill. As president of the council, he did much to restrain its naked defence of property. Opposition to class privilege was the driving force behind his attacks on the denominational system of education which left the poor untaught. He was founding president of the Education League in 1872 in support of the principles of the Education Act. Yet, as a leading High Churchman, he was a vigorous Sabbatarian and chief opponent of Shiels's divorce reform, and earned the *Bulletin's* nickname 'Righteous'.

Wrixon's wealth, social position and religion were threads weaving him into the conservative 'establishment'. He was progressive in abstract principles, but the gulf between his life and that of the everyday world led him to harsh incomprehension in practical dealings with the poor. His criminal law amendment bill of 1871 not only introduced flogging for criminal attacks on women and children, but also whipping for boys who threw stones, broke windows or extinguished lamps. In the depression of the 1890s he condemned the unemployed for holding street-meetings to demand public works. He followed the rigid distinction between deserving and undeserving poor made by the Charity Organisation Society of which he was a committee-man; and dissented from the recommendations of the royal commission on old-age pensions (1897) by claiming that only those who could con-

tribute to their upkeep should be eligible for assistance. His party colleagues, however, opposed all pension schemes.

Wrixon's fear of socialism is expressed in his later writings, *The Pattern Nation* (London, 1906) and *Religion of the common man* (London, 1909). He also published a laborious, highly autobiographical, political novel, *Jacob Shumate; or The People's March, a voice from the ranks* (London, 1903) which was recast as *Edward Fairlie Frankfort; or, Politics among the people* (London, 1912). In 1895 he had remarked to his old student friend W. E. H. Lecky on his *History of the rise and influence of the Spirit of Rationalism in Europe*, 'I fear you will only reach mankind to set them adrift', and implored him to examine the great political question of the day, universal suffrage, which nothing could prevent but whose consequences were likely to be 'gloomy, almost fatal'.

An asthmatic, Wrixon died of heart failure on 9 April 1913, survived by his wife, two sons and a daughter, and was buried in Boroondara cemetery. He left an estate valued for probate at £20,519. A fascinating mixture of radical and conservative, he had contributed much to the tone of Victorian public life.

J. Quick and R. R. Garran, *The annotated constitution of the Australian commonwealth* (Syd, 1901); A. Deakin, *The crisis in Victorian politics, 1879-1881*, J. A. La Nauze and R. M. Crawford eds (Melb, 1957); A. Deakin, *The federal story*, J. A. La Nauze ed (Melb, 1963); B. Webb, *The Webbs' Australian diary, 1898*, A. G. Austin ed (Melb, 1965); *Ovens and Murray Advertiser*, 1 Oct 1874; *Table Talk*, 20 Nov 1891, 4 July 1901; *Punch* (Melb), 27 Aug 1903, 1 Sept 1904, 7 July 1910; *Argus*, 10 Apr 1913; L. Re, Sir Henry Wrixon (essay, Law School, Univ Melb, 1974); C. H. Pearson papers (LaT L).   JILL EASTWOOD

WYSELASKIE, JOHN DICKSON (1818-1883), pastoralist and philanthropist, was born on 25 June 1818 at Sanquhar, Dumfriesshire, Scotland, son of Louis Wyselaskie, army officer, and his wife Elizabeth, née Kerr. In 1837 he joined his uncle Robert Kerr in Van Diemen's Land and was soon sent to Port Phillip to find land for the firm of Kerr and (John) Bogle of Hobart Town and Launceston.

Wyselaskie explored north to the Mallee and then took up a run near Buninyong. In 1840 he left to take up Narrapumelap, 40,000 acres on the Hopkins River. His first years were difficult and the Aboriginals troublesome; however, the 1850s brought prosperity and enabled him to buy out Kerr and Bogle and to acquire the freehold of

24,000 acres. He formed a merino flock with sheep from the studs of J. A. Gibson [q.v.] in Tasmania and John Taylor, and the Narrapumelap merino became noted for its fine quality wool. He made extensive improvements and in 1873 employed fifty stonemasons to build a fine bluestone mansion, finished with a tower and approached by a mile-long, tree-lined avenue.

Wyselaskie was a member of the Geelong and Portland Bay Immigration Society in the late 1840s. He was active in the establishment of a school at the near-by township of Wickliffe and in obtaining occasional visits by a clergyman. He donated the church's tower and spire in the 1870s. With his wife Mary Jane Austin, née Farrell, he visited Europe in 1874-76. They moved to Melbourne in 1878 and he built Wickliffe House, St Kilda, where he lived in retirement and poor health until his death of apoplexy on 4 May 1883; he was buried in the Boroondara cemetery.

Wyselaskie left an estate valued at £72,337 realty and £28,063 personalty. An ardent Presbyterian and childless he gave most of his wealth to the Church. He had already given £30,000 to Ormond College, and he left £10,000 for the Presbyterian (now Wyselaskie) Theological Hall, attached to the college, and £20,000 to pay its professors and teachers; £5000 for the Presbyterian Ladies' College which went to build its Wyselaskie Hall; £2000 to the Wickliffe Presbyterian Church and £5000 to his old church in Sanquhar; and £12,000 to be invested for the endowment of scholarships in six different disciplines at the University of Melbourne. Several charities also benefited. Narrapumelap was bought by G. N. Buckley, son of Mars Buckley [q.v.].

A. Sutherland et al, *Victoria and its metropolis*, 2 (Melb, 1888); Pastoral Review Pty Ltd, *Pastoral homes of Australia*, 3 (Melb, 1931); L. L. Banfield, *Shire of Ararat ... 1864-1964* (Ararat, 1964); *Ararat Advertiser*, 8 May 1883.

J. ANN HONE

Y

YABSLEY, WILLIAM (1812-1880), ship-wright, ship-owner and pastoralist, was born on 2 February 1812 at Plympton, St Maurice, Plymouth, Devonshire, England, eldest son of John Yabsley, an agricultural worker, and his wife Agnes, née Elliott. William was probably apprenticed to a farmer in his youth. In 1833 he enlisted as a shipwright at the Royal Dockyard, Devonport. In the same year he married Magdalen, daughter of John and Bridget Ryder. He entered the navy on 16 February 1837 as carpenter's mate in the *Beagle* and sailed on 4 July for Australia under Captain J. C. Wickham. On 31 August 1838, after the *Beagle* had arrived in Sydney, he ran from the ship.

To escape from the Sydney police Yabsley sailed in the *John* for the Clarence River in search of a job as cedar-getter or ship-wright. When his wife joined him in 1840 he started to build his first ship, the *Providence*, but sold it before he moved with his bullocks to the Richmond River in 1843. At Ballina he built the *Pelican*, launched in 1848 and wrecked in June 1852 at Terrigal.

In 1850, as the timber trade increased, Yabsley took over the lease of Brook station and built a dealer's store and timber-yard at Coraki. Here he built the 80-ton *Coraki* in 1858, followed by the 160-ton *Schoolboy*, launched in August 1864. In the 1860s as the number of workers at Coraki increased, he turned to farming, taking up selections for his four sons and helping his employees to do the same by advancing them the first deposit. He bought cattle and in 1865 built a slaughter-house and store, followed by a training yard for the bullocks. He enlisted many young boys as apprentices.

When Yabsley's largest ship, the 265-ton *Examiner*, was launched at Coraki on 25 July 1870, he was well known to shipping interests in Brisbane, Sydney and Melbourne. The *Examiner* was the pride of the river; when she ran aground on 1 May 1872 at the entrance of the Clarence River, few people thought she could be saved but she was lifted a mile across the sand and launched into the river again—significant proof of Yabsley's skill and determination.

On 1 May 1874 the steam tug, *Index*, was launched to assist the *Schoolboy* and *Examiner* on the long trip from Ballina to Coraki. Under Captain Lachlan McKinnon she also earned good money towing sailing ships up and down the river and served as a general carrier. Yabsley's last vessel, the *Beagle*, was launched at Coraki on 16 December 1876, fitted with a new type of engine. He was drowned on 21 January 1880 when returning from Casino in the river steamer *Vesta* and was buried with Anglican rites in Coraki cemetery. He was survived by his wife, three sons and four daughters. His personalty was valued for probate at £9000.

L. T. Daley, *Men and a river* (Melb, 1966); R. Parsons, *Australian shipowners and their fleets*, 2 (Lobethal, 1973); C. Yabsley reminiscences, *Northern Star* (Lismore), 1926-27; Yabsley family records (Univ New England, and Richmond River Hist Soc); HMS *Beagle*, Adm 54/24, reel 1610; Adm 38-7618 (PRO, Lond); information from Captain E. N. R. Fletcher, R.N. (deceased) and Captain J. C. Wickham, Hydrographic Dept, Ministry of Defence, Taunton, Somerset, Eng.

LOUISE T. DALEY

YELVERTON, HENRY (1821-1880), timber merchant, was born in London, son of Edward Yelverton, jeweller. He intended to study medicine, but at 18 visited America and then joined a whaler which reached the Swan River, Western Australia, in 1845. By 1849 he employed sawyers near Perth and was a cooper in 1853. That year in partnership with Cornish, a Fremantle entrepreneur, he bought the brig *Hamlet* to transport timber to the eastern colonies. At St George's Anglican Church, Perth, on 7 June he married Mary, daughter of John Marshall, a clerk; they had two sons and nine daughters.

In 1855 Yelverton settled in the Vasse River area near Busselton. At Quindalup in 1858 he built a steam sawmill and developed a trade in ships timbers, railway sleepers, shingles, laths and paving blocks, cut from both jarrah and tuart for export to the eastern colonies, India and Ceylon. He was also interested in a whaling station at near-by Castle Rock, was licensee of the Race Horse Inn at Fremantle, and smuggled tobacco as a side-line. When customs officials interfered he lost heavily, but his local standing was not lowered and 'general commiseration' was expressed for him; the locals stoutly contended that he had done much more for the district than the government ever had. He built his own jetty, roads, bridges and a horse tramway and employed up to 120 ex-convicts in the late

1850s. His fortunes fluctuated rapidly. Bankrupt in September 1862 and in May 1866, he recovered both times and operated until 1880, apparently with slack periods in 1868 and 1872-73.

In 1860, in answer to a government questionnaire, Yelverton stated that his timber operations were on a scale at least ten times greater than any other in the trade. In 1865, when all timber exported from the colony was worth £15,693, the quantity shipped by Yelverton was valued at almost £11,000 and three years later the *Perth Gazette* called him 'the oldest and most experienced timber merchant in the colony'. In January 1880 he was seriously injured when a huge log fell on him; because of the risk of moving him a hut was built over him. He gradually recovered and was able to walk on crutches but, aged 58, he died suddenly on 1 April.

His son HENRY JOHN, born on 6 April 1854 at Fremantle, took over the Quindalup mill. In 1898 when British financiers were showing a keen interest in the Western Australian timber industry, he was bought out by the Imperial Jarrah Wood Corporation, later absorbed into Millars' Karri and Jarrah Co. (1902) Ltd. He remained as manager for a time. From 1901 to 1904 he was M.L.A. for the Sussex electorate, supporting the Liberal government. He died on 14 January 1906 when he was mill-manager at Dardanup.

Inquirer, 15 June 1853, 30 Dec 1857, 20 Jan 1858, 30 Nov 1859, 24 Sept 1862, 26 Aug 1863; *Perth Gazette*, 30 Dec 1853, 4 May 1866, 11 Sept 1868; *West Australian*, 13 Apr 1880; R. Jennings, The story of Henry Yelverton of Quindalup, *and* CSO records (Battye Lib, Perth).   J. R. ROBERTSON

YOUL, SIR JAMES ARNDELL (1811-1904), pastoralist, was born on 28 December 1811 at Parramatta, New South Wales, son of Rev. John Youl [q.v.] and his wife Jane, née Loder. He was a brother of Richard Youl [q.v.]. The family moved to Van Diemen's Land in 1819. Educated in England, on his return to Tasmania Youl worked the Symmons Plains property and enlarged the pastoral interests left by his father in 1827. He was appointed justice of the peace in 1837, and in July 1839 at Clarendon he married Eliza (d. 1881), daughter of William Cox [q.v.].

In 1854 Youl and his wife left to live in England at Clapham Park, Surrey. There he undertook many services for the colony over some fifty years. He visited Tasmania in 1860 and next year the government appointed him their accredited agent in London without salary. A commissioner for the 1862 London International Exhibition, he reported on the display of Tasmanian timbers overseas and on remedial measures to overcome prejudice against their use (especially for ship-building). For seven years he was honorary secretary and treasurer of the Australian Association which persuaded the British government to improve mail services to Australia and to accept Australian sovereigns as legal tender in Britain. In 1868 he was a founder and vice-president of the Colonial Society (Royal Colonial Institute), London, and from February to October 1888 acted as agent-general for Tasmania.

Youl is best remembered for the introduction of trout and salmon to Australasian waters. Earlier attempts in 1841 and 1852 had failed because of the difficulty of keeping ova alive under artificial conditions *en route* to Tasmania. His shipments on the *Curling* in 1860 and *Beautiful Star* in 1862 failed, and next year he directed experiments involving the use of moss in ice-vaults. On 21 January 1864 the *Norfolk* left England carrying more than 100,000 salmon and trout ova packed in moss in the ship's ice-house. Ninety-one days later the first successful delivery of living ova was made into Tasmanian hatcheries on the River Plenty. Victoria and New Zealand had supported the Tasmanian ventures and their rivers were soon stocked also.

The Tasmanian commissioners investigating the problem reported in 1864 that 'The untiring zeal and indefatigable exertions of Mr. Youl stand forth conspicuous, and have been mainly instrumental in bringing the present experiment to a successful issue'; they described the results of experiments that he had directed in 1863 as 'one of the most valuable discoveries ever yet made in the art of pisciculture'. Youl claimed no credit for the idea which he said was first mentioned to him in Paris. But P. S. Seager attributes to him 'the first practical attempt to test what had previously been many times suggested'. New Zealand presented a silver cup to him and in 1866 he received the gold medal of La Société d'Acclimatisation. He was created C.M.G. in 1874 and K.C.M.G. in 1891.

Youl was a shareholder in the English Scottish and Australian Bank Ltd and a director of the Commercial Banking Co. of Sydney. On 30 September 1882 he had married a widow Charlotte Robinson, née Williams; survived by her he died at Clapham of senile decay and bronchitis on 5 June 1904. His estate was valued for probate at £161,820.

P. S. Seager, *Concise history of the acclimatisation of the salmonidae in Tasmania* (np,

1888?); *Cyclopedia of Tasmania*, 1 (Hob, 1900);
V&P (HA Tas), 1862 (73), 1863 (101), 1864 (41),
1889 (109); *Examiner* (Launceston), 5 Oct 1860,
8 June 1904; indexes and correspondence file
under J. A. Youl (TA).   NEIL SMITH

YOUL, RICHARD (1821-1897), medical
practitioner and coroner, was born on 3
December 1821 at George Town, Van
Diemen's Land, son of Rev. John Youl [q.v.]
and his wife Jane, née Loder. Sir James
Arndell Youl [q.v.] was his brother. Educated in England from an early age, he
qualified M.R.C.S. 1842, M.D. (St Andrews)
1844. He studied in Paris for six months,
gained experience in Edinburgh and London
and in 1850 settled in Melbourne. He was
founder-member in 1852 and for a time
secretary of the Victoria Medical Association. In 1853 he was appointed colonial
assistant surgeon to the gaol and penal
establishments in Melbourne, a magistrate,
and district coroner for Bourke. In April
1854 he became acting coroner for
Melbourne in the absence of Dr W. B.
Wilmot; and also visiting justice to penal
establishments, a post he held until 1867
when the government redistributed the
duties between two police magistrates.
After the murder of John Price [q.v.] Youl
declined to preside at the inquest because of
his friendship with the dead man. Dr J.
Singleton [q.v.] and others on the Citizens'
Committee accused him of helping Price to
conceal the injury and death of convicts
arising from maltreatment. At two parliamentary committees of inquiry in 1857,
Youl showed himself to be a disciplinarian
in strict accordance with the penal code.

Succeeding Wilmot as city coroner in
August, Youl lost office temporarily in 1878
during (Sir) Graham Berry's [q.v.] 'Black
Wednesday' purge and was threatened with
compulsory retirement in 1892, having
passed the statutory age. Reputed to have
conducted over 12,000 inquests, he introduced formal medico-legal procedure including a post-mortem in every case. His interest
in the circumstances of accidental death led
to safer working conditions on building
sites, nets under ships' gangways, and
sanitary improvements in public institutions. He featured at most government
inquiries dealing with the medical profession, public health and prison discipline.
A member of the Central Board of Health
in 1855-84, he was president in 1879-84; a
member of the Medical Board of Victoria
from 1858, he was president in 1885-97. He
was chairman of the Police Medical Board
in 1892, founder and physician of the Victorian Infant Asylum and official visitor to
industrial schools, lunatic asylums and the

inebriates' retreat, Northcote. He kept up
his private practice for years, starting in
Flinders Street and moving to Collins Street
in 1860.

Youl favoured flogging. He considered the
death penalty a kindness in days when a
life sentence was interpreted literally, that
prostitution should be legalized to keep it
in bounds, that parents should be punished
for failing to control their children and that
the majority of mothers were unfit for their
role. He deplored the custom of locking up
lunatics, juvenile offenders and the children
of convicts indiscriminately with criminals.
He performed many private kindnesses for
released prisoners. Given to sardonic over-
statement, which made him popular with
the press, his reputation for disinterested
public service was unrivalled.

On 15 September 1855 Youl had married
Sarah Ann Jane (Annie), daughter of Dr
Robert Martin of Heidelberg. They had
eleven children of whom five daughters and
four sons survived both parents. Mrs Youl
died on 8 January 1881 of Bright's disease.
Youl was gout stricken and in poor health
with heart disease throughout the 1890s but
continued to fulfil his duties as coroner until
a few days before his death, precipitated by
bronchitis, on 6 August 1897. He was
buried beside his wife in the Anglican
section of the Heidelberg cemetery.

V&P (LC Vic), 1856-57 (D13), (LA Vic), 1856-
57, 3 (D48), 1870, 2nd S, 2 (18), 1871, 3 (31),
1872, 3 (55); *Intercolonial Medical J of A'sia*,
1897; *Argus*, 24 Feb 1855, 30 Dec 1856, 30 Mar
1857, 8 Mar 1867, 7 Aug 1897; *Australasian*,
25 Apr 1891.   ANN M. MITCHELL

YOUNG,   CHARLES   FREDERICK
HORACE FRISBY (1819-1874), comedian,
was born on 5 April 1819 at Doncaster,
Yorkshire, England, eldest son of Charles
Young, actor, and his wife Isabella, née
Frisby. Brought up in the theatre, he
graduated from his father's company and
played in London, scoring a success as Noah
Claypole in a dramatized version of *Oliver
Twist* at the Royal Surrey Theatre in 1838.
Inspired by nautical dramas, he spent about
five years in the navy and the merchant
service. In 1843 as a second officer he arrived
in Van Diemen's Land, where he met his
sister Emma, first wife of actor George Herbert Rogers, who persuaded him to return to
the stage.

Young appeared as Michael in *William
Tell* with Francis Nesbitt [q.v. McCrone]
at the Victoria Theatre, Hobart Town,
under Mrs Clarke's management; in 1845 he
played in George Coppin's [q.v.] company

at Launceston. At Holy Trinity Church he married Jane Elizabeth (Eliza) Thomson with banns and Church of England rites on 6 June 1845; she bore him at least two children. Tasmanian born, ELIZA was a 16-year-old dancer in the company, which included her mother Martha Mary Thomson. Young opened for Coppin in Melbourne on 21 June as Claude Melnotte in the *Lady of Lyons* at the Queen's Theatre Royal. Coppin described him as 'a very versatile actor; in his early days equally good in tragedy, comedy, burlesque, and could sing and dance well'.

In October the Youngs left Coppin because Mrs Thomson considered she was underpaid; they returned to Hobart where they kept a hotel and Eliza taught dancing. From 1849 he managed the Queen's Theatre, Melbourne, for John Thomas Smith [q.v.]; his company was joined by J. P. Hydes and in 1850 they became joint lessees. As Pizarro in W. M. Akhurst's *Rolla of Ours*, Young established his reputation as 'a perfect burlesque actor'. In 1854 he took over as sole lessee of the theatre, paying £300 a year. Next year he joined G. V. Brooke's [q.v.] company and opened on 26 February as Rodrigo in *Othello*; Eliza played Emilia. On 6 November they began a season of their own at the Prince of Wales Theatre.

In 1857 Young with Eliza and their daughter returned to England; he became 'a great favourite in London [in] low comedy and burlesque', playing at the Strand, Sadler's Wells, the Royal Lyceum and Royal St James's theatres. Eliza by 'study' had become a beguiling actress and on 15 September made a success as Julia in J. Sheridan Knowles's *The Hunchback* at the Sadler's Wells Theatre; she made more money than her husband. Violent tempered and often intoxicated, Young maltreated his wife and in 1860 lived with a dancer Miss Soward, who bore him a child; in May 1862 Eliza divorced him.

Meanwhile Young had returned to Melbourne in the *Empress of the Seas* on 11 August 1861. He appeared at the Theatre Royal as Squire Wannop in *A Friend in Need*, written expressly for him by Sydney French and William Sorell. His Dido, Queen of Carthage, 'was full of the richest and most diversified humour . . . untinctured by vulgarity'. In 1863, he supported T. Barry Sullivan [q.v.] at the Theatre Royal, Melbourne, but later left the company after a disagreement. In 1869 he acted with Walter Montgomery [q.v.] in Sydney. Celebrated for his grave-digger in *Hamlet*, Touchstone in *As You Like It*, Stephano in the *Tempest* and Launcelot Gobbo in *The Merchant of Venice*, he was congratulated by the duke of Edinburgh for his performance as Dog-

berry in *Much Ado About Nothing* on 22 March 1869.

In Sydney in 1870 Young played in the *Corsican Brothers*, and in January 1871 he supported Charles Matthews at the Prince of Wales Opera House, and was the theatre's leading comedian when it was burnt down on 6 January next year. His health was undermined by his 'exceedingly sanguine, nervous temperament, and the professional slights he experienced preyed upon his mind'. After suffering from epilepsy for eighteen months, he died on 29 January 1874 at William Street, Woolloomooloo, and was buried in the Balmain cemetery. He was survived by his second wife Ellen, née Curby, whom he had married in Melbourne, and by their son and two daughters. An obituarist claimed that Young's 'nautical training made him almost unequalled in that *rôle* of the drama; while, his excellent voice, musical knowledge, and masterly and artistic dancing, combined with much natural wit, and a keen appreciation of the ludicrous, made him unapproachable in burlesque'.

In 1863 Eliza had married Herman Vezin, an American actor. As Eliza Vezin she was successful on the London stage in many plays with her husband but refused to return to Australia for Coppin. She died at Margate, Kent, England, on 17 April 1902.

P. McGuire et al, *The Australian theatre* (Melb, 1948); A. Bagot, *Coppin the great* (Melb, 1965); *Argus*, 28 Oct 1850, 2, 3 Sept 1861; *The Times*, 16 Sept 1857, 15 May 1862; *SMH*, 22, 23 Mar 1869; *ISN*, 28 Feb 1874.

MARTHA RUTLEDGE

YOUNG, EDMUND (EDMOND) MAC-KENZIE (1838-1897), financier, was born in Coleraine, Londonderry, Ireland, fifth son of William Mackenzie Young, a banker. He became a clerk in the Coleraine branch of the Belfast Banking Co. Ltd in 1853 and accountant in 1856. He arrived in Melbourne in June 1857 in the *War Spirit* and joined the Union Bank of Australia Ltd, transferring to the National Bank of Australasia as assistant accountant in February 1859. Acting manager in 1860, he was accountant till 1863 when he became manager of the South Australian branch. On 10 October 1864 in Trinity Church, Adelaide, he married Fanny Elizabeth Colley.

In 1866 Young and his board financed pioneer farmers through a period of drought and depressed prices, at serious risk to the bank and in defiance of repeated instructions from Frederick Wright, the Melbourne general manager. Young returned to Melbourne in 1870 to replace Wright who had been sent back to London over a minor indiscretion. He returned to Australia next year and published a vindication in which he attacked Young, who was then dismissed, but who refused to go. Supported by the South Australian shareholders in February 1872 Young negotiated a resignation with compensation of £2400. He spent the next year in Europe.

In 1874 he returned to Melbourne as colonial manager of the Australian Mortgage (Mercantile), Land, and Finance Co. In the next few years he expanded the company's business into the Riverina, financing pastoralists' stock expansion, fencing and freehold purchase to confound selectors. In September 1880 Young was appointed resident London manager of the company, but returned to Australia on inspection tours in 1885-86, 1888, 1890-91, 1892-93 and 1896-97. He dominated the company's policies and management, insisting that it rely on British finance only and refusing to accept customers' deposits; it thus became independent of local money shortages and fluctuating interest rates.

From 1880 Young was reluctant to finance pioneering ventures: he lent only to men of proven ability, watched weak accounts closely and tried to force the Melbourne management into a more restrictive credit policy. As early as 1884 he had noted the effects of the rabbit plague, and from 1890 he forced many pastoralists to accept company controls and economies in their personal and business expenditure. His policies helped to lower the standard of living of many pastoralists and rural workers; by 1892-93 an 8 per cent interest rate on loans had become general, and wages and labour force reduced. In 1890 the A.M.L. and F. was the largest lessee in the Western Division of New South Wales, and Young's conservative and shrewd financing enabled it to survive the pastoral crisis of the decade.

Optimistic and speculative in his personal investments, in 1888 Young was the lessee of Cocopara station, near Narrandera, and he was associated with the Drysdale brothers [q.v.] in the Riverina property, Bynya, and the Pioneer sugar plantation on the Burdekin River, Queensland. Perceiving the need for wider employers' organization, he was influential in the foundation of the Pastoralists' Union of Victoria and at a public meeting in May 1890 he was elected chairman of its first committee. He was a strong critic of W. G. Spence [q.v.], secretary of the Amalgamated Shearers' Union, but looked forward to 'special legislation, whereby rights would be defined, and disputes arising [between capital and labour] would be finally settled by a court of conciliation'. He was later a member of the union's council and helped to establish the federation of similar employers' bodies. He resigned in February 1891 on his return to England.

Young was a friend of Sir George Dibbs [q.v.], but his forthright self-confidence made many enemies, especially Sir James MacBain [q.v.], who queried his policies in 1891. He became 'more suave' with the years, was well liked by his staff and was recognized as 'almost the beau ideal of a powerful and sagacious financier'. Aged 59, he died of pneumonia in Sydney on 23 April 1897 and was buried in the Church of England section of Waverley cemetery. He was survived by his wife, then in London, and by two daughters and two sons.

H. M. Humphreys (ed), Men of the time in Australia: Victorian series, 2nd ed (Melb, 1882); G. Blainey, Gold and paper (Melb, 1958); R. Connolly, John Drysdale and the Burdekin (Syd, 1964); J. D. Bailey, A hundred years of pastoral banking (Oxford, 1966); Australasian, 10 Feb 1872; Argus, 21 May, 21 Aug 1890; Pastoral Review, 16 Mar 1891, 15 May 1897; A'sian Insurance and Banking Record, 19 May 1897.
                                                      JILL EASTWOOD

YOUNG, Sir HENRY EDWARD FOX (1803-1870), colonial administrator, was born on 23 April 1803 at Bradborne, Kent, England, third son of (Sir) Aretas William Young (1778?-1835), sometime governor of Prince Edward Island, and his wife Sarah, née Cox, of Coolcliffe, Wexford, Ireland. He was named after his godfather General Henry Edward Fox, brother of the Whig statesman. Educated at Dean's School, Bromley, in July 1827 he was entered as a student at the Inner Temple, but probably was not admitted for he joined his father in Trinidad. By 1830 Young had moved to Demerara, British Guiana, where he became a confidential clerk in the colonial secretary's office, aide-de-camp to the governor and acting recorder of the Orphan Chamber. Next year he deputized as protector of slaves while his father was on leave. In November 1833 Young was appointed treasurer at St Lucia and arrived there next March. He served as a member of the council, as acting colonial secretary and puisne judge. In March 1835 he was promoted government secretary in British Guiana. In 1846 he returned to England, and in February 1847 was knighted and appointed lieut-governor of the eastern districts of the Cape Colony, but transferred in June to South Australia. He returned to England, where on 15th April 1848 he married Augusta Sophia (d. 1913), daughter of Charles Marryat of Park Field, Potters

Bar, Middlesex. They had two sons and five daughters.

On 1 August 1848 in the *Forfarshire* the Youngs arrived in Adelaide, where his courtesy and professed liberalism made him popular. He was fortunate in being authorized to suspend the hated mineral royalties but made some enemies by his neutrality over state aid to Churches. In 1852 he alleviated the economic crisis caused by the Victorian gold discoveries, and risked an invasion of the royal prerogative by assenting to a bill for a limited local use of gold ingots as currency. Also, the assay office in Adelaide was authorized to pay more than the prevailing Victorian rate for gold dust; this policy, backed by a police escort, ensured that most South Australians' gold earnings were brought to Adelaide. In 1850 Young examined the lower reaches of the Murray River and in 1853 accompanied Francis Cadell [q.v.] on the voyage of his steamer, *Lady Augusta*, sending a glowing dispatch to the Colonial Office from Swan Hill. His eagerness for the development of the Murray trade led in 1854 to the building of a railway from Goolwa to the coast but the choice of Port Elliot as a terminal later proved mistaken.

In 1853 the part-elective Legislative Council drafted a bill for a constitution for responsible government. Young manoeuvred to secure a nominated Upper House. Relevant dispatches were withheld from the council, and the bill was passed as he wished. London returned it in 1854 in response to a monster petition, and Young went to Van Diemen's Land as governor.

He reached Hobart Town in the *City of Hobart* with his family on 6 January 1855 to find the colonists resentful of limits to their self-government. In July the *Tasmanian Daily News* alleged corruption in the Convict Department. The Executive Council investigated and censured the comptroller Dr J. S. Hampton [q.v.] so mildly that Legislative Council radicals set up a select committee to probe further. Young denied the council's right to review the executive's decisions on an imperially controlled department. The committee summoned Hampton and when he refused to appear the Speaker issued a warrant for his arrest and insisted he appear at the bar of the House. On Executive Council advice Young prorogued the Legislative Council on 18 September on the grounds that its refusal to test its case in the Supreme Court constituted 'the supremacy of tyranny over law'. The Colonial Office upheld the prorogation but criticized Young for restricting the council's right of inquiry; the Supreme Court and the Privy Council both decided in Hampton's favour.

At the opening of the first session under the new Constitution Young attempted conciliation with a bill to grant the rights claimed in the Hampton case, but was rebuffed. He withdrew from politics, content to be a figurehead and to complete Government House at a cost of £120,000. He resigned in 1861 and returned to London, where he had many interests in the city and was an original director, and chairman in 1866-68, of the Australian Mercantile Land & Finance Co. An Anglican, he died of albuminuria on 18 September 1870, and his estate was sworn for probate at £7000.

Young was an efficient civil servant, trusted by the Colonial Office and very friendly with its senior permanent staff. Although opposed by turbulent local politicians in South Australia and Tasmania he was always able to command support. His readiness to lean on others and his enthusiasm for favourite projects sometimes provoked trouble, but he regained popularity by completing desirable measures initiated by others.

W. A. Townsley, *The struggle for self-government in Tasmania 1842-1856* (Hob, 1951); J. D. Bailey, *A hundred years of pastoral banking* (Oxford, 1966); D. Pike, *Paradise of Dissent*, 2nd ed (Melb, 1967); S. J. Butlin, 'The South Australian devaluation of 1852', *Business Archives and History*, 3 (1963); *Register* (Adel), 2 Aug 1848; *Observer* (Adel), 2 Dec 1854; *Examiner* (L'ceston), 9 Jan 1855; E. R. Denehey, The development of responsible government in Van Diemen's Land (B.A. Hons thesis, Univ Tas, 1961); CO 13/60-88, 111/70-72, 253/46-47, 280/325-353.   H. J. GIBBNEY

YOUNG, JAMES HENRY (1834-1908), businessman and politician, was born on 15 May 1834 at Moorcourt near Romsey, Hampshire, England, son of James Young, farmer, and his wife Martha, née Druce. Educated at Winchester and in London, he went to sea with the Peninsular and Oriental Steam Navigation Co. He arrived in Sydney in the *Chusan* on 3 August 1852, spent two unprofitable years on the goldfields, then returned to the sea with the Sydney & Melbourne Steam Packet Co. in 1854. In the late 1850s he settled at Port Macquarie where he became a harbour pilot and then opened a store at near-by Hursley. On 21 July 1859 at Port Macquarie he married Ellen (d. 1928), daughter of Major William Kemp, 80th Regiment.

In the late 1860s Young was also postmaster at Hursley and agent for the Clarence & Richmond River Steam Navigation Co. An active magistrate from 1870, he was also deputy-sheriff in 1873-74. About 1876 he moved to Sydney where he set up as a wholesale produce merchant, developed coastal shipping interests and retained business connexions at Port Macquarie. In the 1880s he was a director of the Australian Prudential and Medical Assurance Society Ltd.

Young represented the Hastings and Manning in the Legislative Assembly in 1890-94, the Manning in 1894-1901 and Gloucester in 1904-07. A free trader he was prominent in the Opposition to (Sir) Alexander Stuart's [q.v.] government and in 1885-86 was minister of public instruction in Sir John Robertson's [q.v.] last cabinet. As Speaker in 1887-90, he had difficulty in dealing with the scenes of 'gross disorder' provoked by such parliamentary rowdies as J. McElhone, A. G. Taylor [qq.v.], W. P. Crick and W. N. Willis. In financial difficulties in 1890, he was forced to make a composition with his creditors, although he was not declared bankrupt. He handled with remarkable coolness the debates on his position; the motion for his removal was defeated on party lines, but he resigned the Speakership on 21 October, thereby forfeiting his salary of £1500. He had been a New South Wales commissioner for the exhibitions in Adelaide (1887) and Melbourne (1888).

Quickly recovering his financial position, Young was secretary for public works from August to October 1891 in Sir Henry Parkes's [q.v.] last ministry and held the same portfolio under (Sir) George Reid in 1894-99. His department's provision of work for the unemployed raised frequent complaints of favouritism: although his own probity was not questioned, in 1896 he seriously mishandled allegations of corruption against some of his senior staff and was rescued by Reid. Over the years he won repute as a local member; in the early 1880s he had urged, not entirely disinterestedly, the improvement of the north coast bar harbours. As secretary for public works he initiated large-scale projects of dubious value at the mouths of the Tweed, Bellinger, Nambucca, Macleay, Hastings and Manning rivers. His scheme to develop a deep-water harbour at Port Kembla, begun in 1896, was of more real use. He was also responsible for extending the railway from Maitland to Taree, but (Sir) William Lyne complained that Young's impracticable dependence on coastal shipping prevented him from pushing it further north.

In 1898 a royal commissioner, William Owen, cleared him of allegations of corruptly influencing the electors, and of abusing the powers of his office when he had assisted Sydney Smith against (Sir) Edmund Barton in the 1897 by-election for the Hastings; but he rebuked Young for speaking indiscreetly at the twelve meetings he addressed. On 3 July 1899 he became sec-

retary for lands in a cabinet reshuffle. Survived by his wife, two sons and six daughters, he died of heart failure at his home, Devonia, Archer Street, Chatswood, on 9 May 1908 and was buried in the Anglican section of Gore Hill cemetery. His estate was valued for probate at £1955.

Ex-M.L.A., *Our present parliament, what it is worth* (Syd, c 1886); G. H. Reid, *My reminiscences* (Lond, 1917); PD (NSW), 1890, 4533-47, 4622, 1896, 178-204; V&P (LA NSW), 1890, 1, 375, 799, (LC NSW), 1898, pt 1, 1155; T&CJ, 16 Jan 1886, 7 Nov 1891; *Sydney Mail*, 3 Mar 1888, 25 Oct 1890; SMH, 11 May 1908; Parkes letters (ML); Commissioner's notebook, 2/6402 (NSWA); CO 201/598/154.   W. G. McMINN

YOUNG, JOHN (1827-1907), building contractor, was born at Foot's Cray, Kent, England, son of John Young, builder. While articled to Garland and Christopher, architects and surveyors, he attended lectures at King's College, London. After engineering and architectural experience in London and Yorkshire, in 1851 he was superintendent and draftsman for the Crystal Palace under Sir Joseph Paxton. In London in 1853 he married Eleanor Southernwood.

In May 1855 Young migrated to Victoria and soon prospered; he constructed many metropolitan churches, the interior of the Bourke Street Synagogue, and the Ballarat gaol and powder magazine. His most important building was St Patrick's Cathedral, designed by W. W. Wardell [q.v.]. Over eleven years his contracts in Victoria totalled some £680,000. From the late 1850s he had simultaneous commitments in Victoria, Tasmania, New Zealand and Sydney, but was over-extended and was badly served by two of his clerks of works. The construction of St Mary's Cathedral, supervised by H. Hunter [q.v.], in Hobart Town was unsound and required demolition after only twelve years. More immediately damaging was his faulty work on the Hospital for the Insane, Kew, Victoria, in 1865; he offered to replace the bad work but his contract was cancelled and he successfully sued the government.

In 1866 Young moved to Sydney, where he had already built St John's College within the University of Sydney. He undertook many of the largest jobs in Sydney until about 1890, some concurrently. His contracts included substantial sections of St Mary's Cathedral, the Department of Lands building and the General Post Office; the old Redfern railway terminus, the Exhibition Building in Prince Alfred Park, and the Garden Palace for the Sydney International Exhibition 1879; and commercial buildings such as Farmer [q.v.] & Co.'s store, Dalton's [q.v.] Building and the head office of the Australian Joint Stock Bank; engineering works, such as Fig Tree Bridge; and, in a lighter vein, 'The Abbey' and the 'Witches' Houses', Johnston Street, Annandale. Known for 'extraordinary energy' and sound work completed ahead of schedule, he deployed his men and resources 'like a general'. He adopted the latest overseas technological innovations such as the overhead travelling crane, the use of arc-lights for night shifts, and reinforced concrete; he invented an improved form of scaffolding.

An early advocate of the eight-hour day, Young respected his men; nevertheless there was constant agitation for higher pay and strikes played havoc with deadlines. In 1873 he was founding president of the Builders' and Contractors' Association of New South Wales. He invested in quarries in Melbourne and Sydney and exported Lane Cove sandstone to Melbourne and Adelaide. He mined marble at Marulan and granite at Moruya, cutting and polishing it at Woolloomooloo; but, lacking protection against imports, the enterprise failed and he lost £10,000.

In 1873-94 Young stood unsuccessfully for parliament several times, changing from a moderate free trader to a strong protectionist. He represented Bourke Ward on the Sydney Municipal Council in 1876-87. He was interested in public health and persuaded the council to wood-block some streets. Mayor in 1886, he held lavish entertainments, but the brilliance of his term was tarnished towards its close with bitter attacks by the opposing factions. He bought Annandale as a real estate speculation in 1877 and was prominent in its development. An alderman on the Leichhardt Borough Council from 1879, he was mayor that year and in 1884-85. Returning in 1891 from travels in Europe and Asia, Young led a secession movement resulting in the incorporation of the Annandale Borough Council in 1894; he was foundation mayor until 1896. A member of the Royal Society of New South Wales from 1879, he was a commissioner for the exhibitions in Sydney (1879), Melbourne (1880), and Amsterdam (1883), the Colonial and Indian Exhibition, London (1886), and the World's Columbian Exposition, Chicago (1893). He was also a member of the Board of Technical Education in 1883-89 and sat on the royal commission into charges against E. M. G. Eddy, chief commissioner of railways. He published Ye Ancient games of bowls (1899) and The proposed Federal City for the Commonwealth of Australia ... (n.d.).

Young lived at Kentville, Annandale, where he cultivated a fine garden, laid down a bowling green and provided facilities for

archery, billiards and skittles. He imbued bowls with the spirit of gentlemanly conduct, and initiated regular intercolonial matches with Victoria; the first was played at Kentville in 1880. He was foundation president of the New South Wales Bowling Association in 1880-1907 and led an Australian team to Britain in 1901. In the 1880s he was also president of the Annandale Skittle Club. In 1887 he bought Burrawong, near Cumnock, where he settled three of his children; with his family he developed the property and installed a fruit cannery.

Large framed and with a goatee beard, Young was hospitable and courteous even under stress, but he could be blunt when the occasion warranted. His ability, practical experience, energy and lucidity made him a commanding figure. After the death of his first wife, he married a divorcee Elizabeth Susan Ovenden, née Russell, on 23 December 1886 with Congregational rites. Survived by his wife, two sons and two daughters of his first marriage, he died, aged 80, of cancer at Kentville on 27 February 1907 and was buried in Waverley cemetery with Anglican and Masonic rites. A marble bust of Young is owned by the Royal New South Wales Bowling Association, and portraits by W. Reynolds Stephens and John Lamb Lyon by the Sydney City Council and the City Bowling Club, Sydney.

E. Lincoln (ed), *New South Wales Bowlers' annual* (Syd, 1906); A. Roberts, *Burrawong & John Young* (Syd, 1972); V&P (LA NSW), 1891-92, 5, 57; H. C. Kent, 'Reminiscences of building methods in the seventies under John Young', *Architecture* (Aust), 13 (1924); A. Roberts, 'Relics of John Young', *Leichhardt Hist J*, July 1973; *ISN*, June 1877 and supp; *T&CJ*, 6 Sept 1879; *SMH*, 27 May 1880, 6 Feb, 28 Oct 1882; *Evening News* (Syd), 2 July 1880, 28 Jan 1902; *Bulletin*, 20 Nov 1880; G. A. Gerathy, The role played by the Sydney City Council in the development of the metropolitan area, 1842-1912 (M.A. thesis, Univ Syd, 1970); A. Roberts, The development of the suburb of Annandale, 1876-1899 (B.A. Hons thesis, Univ Syd, 1970); printed cat (ML).

ROBERT JOHNSON
ALAN ROBERTS

YOUNG, SIR JOHN, 1st BARON LISGAR (1807-1876), governor, was born on 31 August 1807 in Bombay, India, eldest son of Sir William Young, 1st baronet and East India Co. director, and his wife Lucy, daughter of Lieut-Colonel Charles Frederick. Educated at Eton and Corpus Christi College, Oxford (B.A., 1829), he was admitted to Lincoln's Inn in January 1829 and called to the Bar in 1834. On 8 April 1835 at Kells Church, Dublin, he married Adelaide Annabella Tuite Dalton, stepdaughter of the marquess of Headfort. He represented County Cavan in the House of Commons in 1831-55, generally supporting Sir Robert Peel and in touch with W. E. Gladstone and the fifth duke of Newcastle. A lord of the treasury in 1841-44 and secretary of the treasury in 1844-46, he was chief secretary for Ireland in 1852-55.

In March 1855 Young was appointed lord high commissioner of the Ionian Islands and created G.C.M.G. The post was difficult because the representative assembly demanded union with Greece. In 1858 secret dispatches, in which he recommended that Corfu and Paxo be converted into British colonies, were published in the London *Daily News*, embarrassing the government, which had just arranged for Gladstone to report on the problem. Though recalled in January 1859, he was created K.C.B. and his administration was publicly praised.

On 18 January 1861 Young was appointed to succeed Sir William Denison as governor of New South Wales; because of intercolonial jealousy he was not given the title governor-general, borne by his two predecessors. With his wife, in the *Northam*, he arrived in Sydney on 21 March and immediately plunged into an angry and complicated political crisis. With the five-year term of the Legislative Council members due to expire on 13 May, the council disapproved of (Sir) Charles Cowper's [q.v.] proposal, accepted by the Legislative Assembly, that the council should be made elective. It also rejected two government bills and vital clauses in (Sir) John Robertson's [q.v.] land bills. Though Denison had advised against 'swamping' the council, Young conditionally approved Cowper's nomination of twenty-one new members to pass the land bills. But they were never sworn in because President Sir William Burton [q.v.] and nineteen other members resigned, and the council, deprived of a quorum, adjourned. The secretary of state for the colonies, Newcastle, disapproved of Young's action, believing that he had involved the vice-regal office in politics and encouraged the 'democratic cause'. Young considered that he had preserved the conservative character of the council, and he balanced his concessions to Cowper with an agreement for the satisfactory reconstruction of the council.

Young had to face other problems affecting the relations between his office and the cabinet. In January 1865 (Sir) James Martin [q.v.], whose ministry was tottering, advised him to appoint two more legislative councillors. Young declined the request, insisting that he had a discretion to exercise and that the conditions agreed to in 1861 had not been met. The colonial secretary William Forster [q.v.], who had already told his friends they should be appointed, resigned and accused Young of partiality, declaring that the 1861 agreement relating to the council could not be binding on succeeding ministries. Martin continued in office and the Colonial Office considered the governor 'quite right to resist'.

In September 1865, with Cowper again premier, Young helped to find an attorney-general to replace (Sir) John Darvall [q.v.], who had resigned. Most of the colony's senior barristers were too conservative to serve with Cowper, but Young persuaded J. H. Plunkett [q.v.], with whom Cowper had quarrelled, to accept the position. Next year, when Cowper requested a dissolution, Young refused and pointed out that elections had been held only a year before and that the Opposition was capable of forming a ministry. He had shrewdly perceived that elections would not help Cowper, who was publicly blamed for the consequences of drought and depression and for unpopular import duties.

Unlike some of his successors, Young had little trouble over his exercise of the royal prerogative of pardon. Except in capital cases, he dealt with pardons without reference to his ministers; most of the colony's leading men preferred the prerogative to be beyond the reach of political influence. In 1863 he overruled his Executive Council and commuted the bushranger John Bow's sentence to life imprisonment.

Reflecting the active role which an able governor retained in the early years of responsible government, Young gave frequent advice on policy, making it a practice to see one of his ministers each day. But he missed the excitement of the House of Commons, found colonial politics tiresome and complained to Newcastle that a colonial governor was a mere 'cipher' under responsible government. His correspondence reveals close knowledge of (Sir) Henry Parkes's [q.v.] 1866 education reforms before they were submitted to parliament. Parkes wrote of him: 'Fully informed on political subjects, he was frank and modest in communicating to others the lessons of his experience ... in intercourse with him one received instruction unawares'.

Unwilling to leave his ministers in Sydney unsupervised, Young did not travel widely or frequently in the colony, but he and his wife were keenly aware of the social responsibilities of Government House and were active in good causes. He worked diligently for the Sydney Ragged Schools, the Society for the Relief of Destitute Children, the Sydney Female Refuge Society, the Female

School of Industry and the House of the Good Shepherd. A devout Evangelical Anglican, he appealed for nonsectarian sympathy and tolerance, raising the ire of some Protestants when he chaired a meeting in 1865 to organize the rebuilding of the burned St Mary's Cathedral.

Young was erect and clean-shaven, with long side-burns. He possessed an easy charm of manner and was an able public speaker; (Sir) William Windeyer [q.v.] described him as 'a gentleman & a scholar'. The Youngs left Sydney in the *Geelong* on 24 December 1867 and on his return to England he thought of re-entering politics. In February 1869 he became governor-general of Canada. Though it was a post in which he had less personal influence, his term of office was successful; Prime Minister John A. Macdonald regarded him as the ablest governor-general under whom he had served. In November 1870 he was created baron Lisgar of Lisgar and Bailieborough, County Cavan. Ill health forced him to resign in June 1872 and he died on 6 October 1876 at Lisgar House, Bailieborough, Ireland, without issue. The barony became extinct and the baronetcy descended to a nephew. Lambing Flat, a town in New South Wales, was renamed Young after him. On 3 August 1878 Lady Young married Sir Francis Turville; she died on 19 July 1895.

H. Parkes, *Fifty years in the making of Australian history* (Lond, 1892); P. Loveday and A. W. Martin, *Parliament factions and parties* (Melb, 1966); F. G. Halpenny (gen ed), *Dictionary of Canadian biography*, M. La Terreur ed, 10 (Toronto, 1972); P. Loveday, 'The Legislative Council in New South Wales, 1856-1870', *Hist Studies*, no 44, Apr 1965; *Freeman's J* (Dublin), 13 April 1835; *Sydney Mail*, 8 July 1865; N. I. Graham, The role of the governor of New South Wales under responsible government 1861-1890 (Ph.D. thesis, Macquarie Univ, 1973); Cowper papers *and* Macarthur papers, (ML); Newcastle papers (Univ Nottingham Archives, England); CO 201/517/20, 30, 522/23, 526/40, 542/44.   JOHN M. WARD

YOUNG, JOHN LORENZO (1826-1881), engineer and schoolmaster, was born on 30 May 1826 in London, son of a Cornish building contractor. He was educated at the Communal College of Boulogne, France, and later under a very liberal Lutheran, Professor Opel, at Wiesbaden, Germany; in 1842 he attended the College of Civil Engineers, Putney, and in 1843-46 he studied at King's College, University of London. He then acquired engineering experience in railway construction and mining in Cornwall.

On 31 October 1850 Young arrived at Adelaide in the *Panama* and joined C. G. Feinagle as assistant teacher in the South Australian High School. The Victorian goldfields drew them both, but Young returned and in 1852 opened a school in the Ebenezer Chapel off Rundle Street with six pupils. One of a small group who founded the Adelaide Philosophical (Royal) Society, from 1853 he was an honorary member until his death. On 24 October 1855 at St Mary's Church, Sturt, he married Martha Paynter Young (d. 1887) and in 1860-61 they visited England with their two children.

Young's non-denominational Adelaide Educational Institution flourished. His brother Oliver joined the staff, pupils increased and larger accommodation was acquired in Stephens Place and in 1867 in Freeman Street. Biannual prize-givings were held at White's Rooms where work was displayed and Young reported on the school's progress. With several hundred boarders and day-boys it became the largest private independent school in South Australia. In 1872 new premises were built at Parkside in Young Street, named after the headmaster. An exceptionally progressive teacher, Young avoided rote learning, punishment and religious instruction. On week-ends he taught surveying on field trips and his courses included moral philosophy, physiology, political economy and mechanical drawing as well as the usual subjects. Intellectual stimulus and acute observation were encouraged and boys could choose their own curriculum. Young's teaching emphasized morality, justice and freedom; his goal was to 'root out the seeds of selfishness' and 'enkindle . . . generous sentiments'. He opposed compulsory education and state aid or interference.

Many of Young's pupils later attained positions of public and professional importance in the province and attested the value of the inspiration he had given. Ex-scholars included Caleb Peacock, William Bickford, Walter Samson, Charles Babbage, Elias Solomon, W. P. Auld [q.v.] and C. C. Kingston, premier and federationist. An Old Scholars' Association was formed and when the school closed in 1880 on Young's retirement, he was presented with 336 gold sovereigns and many grateful testimonials to his genial, sympathetic counselling.

Young planned to join his wife and the large family of sons and daughters who had preceded him to Veryan, Cornwall, where his father still lived. He prepared a lecture urging English workers and farmers to migrate to South Australia where he hoped to return himself, believing that it enjoyed the freest institutions in the world. He embarked on the *John Elder* in 1881 but became depressed and ill from sciatica during the voyage. On 26 July he died of apoplexy and was buried at sea. His estate was sworn for probate at £3953. He is commemorated by scholarships at the University of Adelaide for research in political economy and for general research.

G. E. Loyau, *The representative men of South Australia* (Adel, 1883); H. T. Burgess (ed), *Cyclopedia of South Australia*, 2 (Adel, 1909); PP (SA), 1861 (131), 1868 (56); 'Annual Report', Roy Soc SA, *Trans*, 4 (1880-81); Register (Adel), 1 Nov 1850, 25 Feb 1863, 29 Apr 1867, 18 Dec 1880, 6 Sept 1881, 9 July, 11 Oct 1912, 25 Nov 1915; *Observer* (Adel), 25 Dec 1880; R. J. Nicholas, Private and denominational secondary schools of South Australia: their growth and development (M.Ed. thesis, Univ Melb, 1953); Verco papers (SAA).

B. K. HYAMS

YOUNG, ROBERT (1796-1865), Wesleyan minister, was born on 14 November 1796 near Ryton, County Durham, England, son of practising Methodists. Early in 1820 he was received by the British Conference of the Wesleyans as a missionary candidate. He was ordained on 9 November and appointed to Kingston, Jamaica, where he showed preaching and administrative abilities. One of his sermons, *A View of Slavery in connection with Christianity*, was published in Jamaica in 1824. He was in Nova Scotia in 1826-29 and visited the United States of America, but returned to England in 1830. In 1837-44 he published a series of religious tracts and ministered until 1852 in British circuits, 'where his zeal was tempered by sound judgement and unusual self-control'.

In 1852 the British Conference appointed Young and Rev. John Kirk as a deputation to visit Australasia to examine the feasibility of uniting the missions of New Zealand and Polynesia with the Australian Conference as a separate, self-supporting body. Unseaworthy ships separated them and Kirk returned to England. Young went on alone and after a voyage marked by delays, gales and fire, he arrived at Port Adelaide in the *Adelaide* on 4 May 1853. He preached in the Pirie Street Methodist Chapel and continued to Melbourne where he took notice of 'the substantial edifices of worship' and immigrants at the Wesleyan Home in Drummond Street. Amazed by the spread of Methodism in the colony, he preached several times in the Collins Street chapel to over 1000 people, three-fourths of whom 'were interesting young men'.

On 11 June Young arrived in Sydney where he was met by Wesleyan ministers and Rev. W. B. Boyce [q.v.]. At a tea meeting in the York Street chapel solidarity between Methodists in Britain and Australia was affirmed and he found support for the deputation's objects. On 20 July he attended a meeting of the Australasian Board of Missions and later spoke at Windsor, Richmond and Parramatta, everywhere collecting statistics. At the District Meeting on 29 July the New South Wales Wesleyan ministers approved the constitution of the Australasian Conference proposed by Young.

In September he left for investigation and talks with Methodists in New Zealand, Tonga and Fiji. Young returned to Sydney and Melbourne, spent Christmas Day on the Victorian gold diggings and travelled to Van Diemen's Land before returning to England in 1854, well satisfied with the Australasian Conference's ability to be financially independent. In eighteen months he had travelled 40,000 miles. On 3 April Young reported favourably to the British Conference at Birmingham on his assignment and on 9 August the plan for a 'distinct and affiliated connexion' for Australasian Methodism was signed. He published a record of his travels, *The Southern World* (London, 1854), and two years later the conference elected him as its president. For the next six years he ministered in London and Newcastle.

In 1860 paralysis forced Young to become a supernumerary; with his large family he retired to Truro, Cornwall, where he died of exhaustion on 16 November 1865.

J. Colwell, *The illustrated history of Methodism* (Syd, 1904); E. G. Clancy, ' "Christianity in aggressive action" ', A'sian Methodist Hist Soc, J, Dec 1969; Register (Adel), 2 Mar, 5 May 1853; Nathaniel Turner journal (ML); Wesleyan Methodist Australian District, Minutes 1851-54 (ML); notes from Methodist Archives and Research Centre, Lond.

S. G. CLAUGHTON*

YOUNGER, MONTAGUE THOMAS ROBSON (1836-1899), church musician, was born in Sydney on 25 June 1836, third son of Charles Younger, ironmonger, and his wife Harriett, née Mills. His father was a talented amateur musician who helped found the Sydney Philharmonic Society in 1854. He attended a private school at Surry Hills conducted by Rev. Thomas L. Dodd and at 12 was appointed organist of St Thomas's Church, North Sydney, as successor to his father. He took music lessons at first from S. H. A. Marsh and later from C. S. Packer [qq.v.].

A partner in his father's firm, Younger and Son, ironmongers, until 1865, he was also organist at St Peter's Church, Cook's

River. On 26 October at St Peter's he married Anna Maria Reilly. That year he took up music professionally and moved to Ipswich, Queensland, where he was appointed organist of St Paul's Church and director of the local Philharmonic Society. On his return to Sydney in 1868 he became the first organist at St Andrew's Cathedral where a large organ had been installed. He also developed a profitable teaching connexion and became vice-warden of the Sydney College of Music. Among his pupils was Arthur Mason, Sydney city organist in 1901-07. He was one of the judges at the Sydney International Exhibition in 1879-80 and chairman of the committee which approved specifications for the organ in the Sydney Town Hall.

As a teacher Younger influenced the development of music in the colony, but it is doubtful whether he did anything to uplift currently debased tastes in church music. His published work betrays little conceptual talent, but he was a polished performer, the first native of Sydney to reach eminence as an organist.

He died of broncho-pneumonia at Ashfield on 26 December 1899 and was buried in the cemetery of St Thomas's Church of England, North Sydney. A memorial plaque was placed in St Andrew's Cathedral, Sydney. He was survived by three sons and his intestate estate was valued at £179.

[A. Wiegand], *The largest organ in the world and the musical artists of Sydney* (Syd, 1892); *Australasian*, 6 Jan 1900; *SMH*, 17 Dec 1932.

                             E. J. LEA-SCARLETT

YUILLE, WILLIAM CROSS (1819-1894), pastoralist, was born on 28 March 1819 at Cardross, Dumbartonshire, Scotland, son of Robert Yuille and his wife Anne, née Cross. Educated in Glasgow, he was apprenticed there for three years in the West India House of Messrs Ewing & Co. In 1836 he sailed to Van Diemen's Land arriving in December. In February he crossed to Point Henry near Geelong, Port Phillip District, with his cousin Archibald Yuille and a flock of merinos; they took up a run at Murgheballoak on the Barwon River. William joined the search-party for J. T. Gellibrand [q.v.] and G. B. L. Hesse, presumed killed by Aboriginals, and during the quest new country was opened up. With John Aitken, T. Learmonth [qq.v.] and H. Anderson he explored north of Mount Macedon to Mount Alexander, and from there to the Loddon Plains, Mount Misery, Lake Burrumbeet, the Grampian Range to Mount Emu and back to the Barwon—a journey that verified Sir Thomas Mitchell's [q.v.] state-

ments about the potential of Australia Felix.

In 1838 Yuille left the Barwon as the Aboriginals were very troublesome. He took up 10,000 acres at Ballarat and for a time Lake Wendouree was known as Yuille's swamp. In 1840 he went to New Zealand where he acquired large tracts of land from the Maoris (though his claim was not officially recognized), attended the ceremony at which the British took posssssion of the islands, fought against the Maoris and after nine months returned to Victoria. He visited England and on his return joined James Oliphant Denny in forming the mercantile firm of Denny and Yuille. In 1842 he married Denny's daughter Mary (d. 1889). The firm took up the Rockbank run in the Werribee Plains and in 1846 Yuille became sole lessee, holding it until the early 1850s when he sold out to W. J. T. Clarke [q.v.]. In 1851 Yuille acquired Barwidgee station from W. Forlonge [q.v.] and Ballanrong, near Hastings, where he built the first Anglican church on the Mornington peninsula. He became known as one of the main ram-breeders in the colony. Also at this time he bought Kirk's Bazaar and leased it to G. J. Watson [q.v.]. In 1852 and 1853 Yuille sold his stations, his cousin Archibald buying Ballanrong, and took his family to England.

He remained overseas until 1858 but sent back some thoroughbred horses, including the famous Warhawk and Gaslight. On his return he lived at Williamstown and set up a large stable. Horse-racing had always been his great interest and in 1839, at the second race meeting held in Melbourne, he rode his own horse and won easily. From 1842 he was actively identified with racing and in 1849 began to make a name on the turf with Jim Crow, Dinah, General Tom Thumb and others. From 1858 his success caused a sensation in racing circles and his tall, upright figure, with hat fitted jauntily to one side, was a familiar sight at Flemington. With Flying Buck in October 1859 he won the first Australian Champion Sweepstakes, for which five colonies entered, and in November the Victoria Turf Club Oaks with Birdswing; Flying Buck won the 1860 St Leger and was then sold. He also owned Carisbrook and Toryboy, who won the Melbourne Cup in 1865. He closed his racing establishment in 1866 and, as 'Peeping Tom' and 'Playboy', became the main sportswriter for the *Australasian*. In 1872 he founded the bloodstock auctioneering firm, W. C. Yuille & Co.; one of his biggest transactions was the sale of C. B. Fisher's [q.v.] Maribyrnong stud in 1878 for £84,000. Yuille compiled the *Australian Stud Book*, first published in 1877.

He was steward of the Victoria Jockey

Club for many years, handicapper to the Victoria Racing Club and a leading member of Tattersall's committee until 1881. In the 1870s he was one of the best amateur billiard players in Melbourne. In old age Yuille sported a waist-length white beard and still cherished a Scottish accent. He died in Melbourne on 19 July 1894 survived by four of his seven sons and three of his four daughters. Two sons Archie and Albert carried on W. C. Yuille & Co.

A. Sutherland et al, *Victoria and its metropolis*, 2 (Melb, 1888); A. Henderson (ed), *Australian families*, 1 (Melb, 1941); *Australasian*, 20 June 1891, 21 July 1894; *Argus*, 20 July 1894.

J. ANN HONE

Z

ZELMAN, ALBERTO (1832-1907), musician, was born in Trieste, Austria, son of Samuel Victor Zelman, linguist, and his wife Bunina, née Cologna. He received a thorough musical education in Trieste, studying composition with Luigi Ricci (1805-1859), musical director of Trieste Cathedral and conductor of the opera. In 1852 he collaborated with Alberto Randegger (1832-1911) in composing the opera *Il Lazzarone*. He toured northern Italy as an operatic conductor and had already written several suites of ballet music before leaving Italy for India.

On 28 August 1871 Zelman arrived in Sydney in the *Rangoon* from Calcutta. He joined the Cagli-Pompei Royal Italian Opera Company as conductor and made his début on 4 September. After a season in Sydney the company toured New Zealand, returning to Melbourne from Dunedin on 16 February 1872 in the *Rangitoto*. They went on to Adelaide and after a successful season returned to Melbourne in the *Coorong* on 18 April, where the company came under the entrepreneurial wing of W. S. Lyster [q.v.]. Zelman's first appearance in Melbourne was on 6 May as associate conductor at a benefit concert held at the Town Hall for the Melbourne Hospital; he also made his début as both pianist and composer, playing his own 'Scherzo Fantastica'. He first conducted opera in Melbourne on 13 May at the Princess Theatre for the performance of *Lucia di Lammermoor* in the Cagli-Lyster Italian opera season. On 6 December 1873 at the Fitzroy Registry Office he married Harriott Eliza Hodgkinson, a 22-year-old musician.

Zelman remained in Melbourne for many years as a conductor for Lyster's opera seasons. He was also a teacher of piano and an organist of some repute, and in 1884 he was vice-president of the Musical Artists' Society of Victoria. During the 1888 Centennial International Exhibition he helped to organize the exhibition's chorus and orchestra, and acted as conductor whenever Sir Frederick Cowen [q.v.] was absent. In 1887, during J. Siede's [q.v.] illness, he conducted the Melbourne Liedertafel and took over the post when Siede died in 1889; because of his own ill health he resigned in 1890, but after resuming temporarily he quit next year. As conductor of the Australian Military Band for nearly twenty-five years he was a familiar figure at Victoria Racing Club meetings at Flemington.

Zelman was a notable linguist, a voracious reader and a British patriot. Contemporaries hailed his versatility as a musician when, in an emergency, he created an orchestration from a piano score for an advertised performance of *Lohengrin*: recently this *tour de force* has been decried as musical sacrilege but it was probably a workmanlike response to a need to keep faith with the public. He conducted the choirs of several Catholic churches in Melbourne, his last post being at St Ignatius's Church in Richmond. He formed a long association with George Curtis and Alfred Montague in chamber music performances. As a composer he was best known for his offertories: 'Coronation March', 'Salve Regina', 'Legend of the Cross-Bill' and 'There is a Green Hill'.

Zelman died of heart failure, aged 75, on 28 December 1907 at his home in Albert Street, Auburn, survived by his wife and four sons. The funeral was conducted by Rev. Charles Strong [q.v.] and he was buried in Boroondara cemetery, Kew. His eldest son Alberto Victor was also a well-known musician.

G. R. Davies, *Music makers of the sunny south* (Malvern, 1932); W. A. Orchard, *Music in Australia* (Melb, 1952); *Age*, 19 Apr, 2, 4, 14 May 1872, 30 Dec 1907; *Argus*, 10, 14 May 1872, 30 Dec 1907, 3 May 1930; *Herald* (Melb), 28 Dec 1907; *Australasian, Leader* (Melb), *Weekly Times* (Melb), 4 Jan 1908; M. T. Radic, Aspects of organised amateur music in Melbourne 1836-1890 (M. Mus. thesis, Univ Melb, 1968); Minute books 1878-95 *and* Scrapbook 1887 (Melb Liedertafel Soc); hist press cuttings 2 and 5b (LaT L). MAUREEN THERESE RADIC

ZOUCH, HENRY (1811-1883), soldier, pastoralist, gold commissioner and superintendent of police, was born on 18 August 1811 at Quebec, Canada, eldest son of Lieut-Colonel Henry Zouch (d. 1818), 10th Royal Veteran Battalion, and his second wife Ann, née Ritchie. Educated in 1826-28 at the Royal Military College, Sandhurst, he was commissioned ensign, by purchase, in the 4th (King's Own) Regiment on 10 November 1829 and reached Sydney in the *Asia* on 2 December 1831. He was promoted lieutenant on 1 July 1833 and, from 1 October next year, he commanded the first division of the Mounted Police at Bathurst.

In 1835 with a party of troopers Zouch established that the botanist Richard Cunningham [q.v.] had been murdered by Aboriginals. He was appointed a magistrate on 7 October 1835; at Holy Trinity Church,

Kelso near Bathurst, on 29 December 1836 he married Maria (d. 1885), youngest daughter of Captain Richard Brooks [q.v.]. He was involved in business dealings with his friend Captain Piper [q.v.], who had lent his home, Alloway Bank, for Zouch's wedding reception. In 1837 his regiment was posted to India and he sold his commission and retired from the police. Next year he bought land on the Bell River near Wellington but lived at his wife's house, Ashby, at Bungendore near Lake George in the 1840s. A great horseman, he reputedly spent much of his time breeding and racing horses.

In 1851-53 Zouch was assistant commissioner of crown lands for the gold districts, based on the Lower Turon. His prudent administration of the hated Goldfields Management Act contributed much towards the public peace. He returned to Goulburn in 1853 when appointed superintendent of police, Mounted Patrol, southern districts, including the Gundagai and Braidwood gold escorts. He coped fearlessly with the anti-Chinese riots at Lambing Flat in 1860 and 1861. On 30 June, when the miners tried to storm the police quarters to release three arrested men, Zouch ordered his troopers to charge and in the mêlée one miner was killed and many injured. That night he ordered the withdrawal of the commissioners and police to Yass to avoid further bloodshed.

In March 1862, under the new Police Regulation Act, Zouch was appointed superintendent of police for the south-eastern district at a salary of £500. In the next three years bushrangers, especially Ben Hall's [q.v.] gang, were active in his region; but, through his discretion, courage and horsemanship, Zouch won praise in parliament, at a time when the police were proving generally ineffective. Gentlemanly and quiet in manner, he was one of the most efficient officers in the public service. He was an early member of the Australian Club, founding president of the Goulburn Rifle Club in 1865 and a member of the local Public School Board.

Zouch died of sunstroke on 28 October 1883 at Goulburn, where he was buried with Anglican rites. He was survived by his wife, four sons and three daughters. His eldest son Henry married Adelaide, sister of Major-General Sir William Throsby Bridges, his daughter Marcia married Nicholas Herbert Throsby and his son Richard Essington married Mary Emily Throsby. His personalty was valued for probate at £4057.

HRA (1), 18; *Returns of the colony of NSW*, 1834; R. T. Wyatt, *The history of Goulburn*, 2nd ed (Syd, 1972); D. L. Carrington, 'Riots at Lambing Flat, 1860-1861', Canberra and District Hist Soc, *Papers*, 1960; P. Selth, 'The

Burrangong (Lambing Flat) riots ... a closer look', *JRAHS*, 60 (1974); *Sydney Herald*, 12 Dec 1833, 29 Dec 1836; *Australian*, 7 Oct 1835; *Bathurst Free Press*, 2 Apr 1853; *SMH*, 6 Aug 1861, 16 July 1863; *Goulburn Evening Penny Post* and *Goulburn Herald*, 30 Oct 1883; Col Sec land letters (NSWA); WO 42/51, 99/17.

HAROLD ROYLE

ZOX, EPHRAIM LAMAN (LAMEN) (1837-1899), financier and politician, was born on 22 October 1837 at Liverpool (some sources say London), England, son of Eliazer Laman Zox (d. 1882), proprietor of a large cap-making business. He was educated at home by his mother who had reputedly been a governess for one of the Rothschilds. He arrived in Melbourne in December 1852 and worked as an assistant to his cousin Lewis Myer Myers in a softgoods firm. By 1857 he was listed as a clothier at 235 Elizabeth Street. In 1858 he visited England, returning to Melbourne in the *Yorkshire* on 8 April 1860. From 1863 he partnered Myers in a warehouse business and for about five years from 1866 his brother Joseph joined him in Melbourne. On 15 May 1879 his partnership with Myers was dissolved and next year he set up on his own as 'financial agent and arbitrator', Collins Street West.

After the death of E. Cohen [q.v.] in 1877 Zox represented the Legislative Assembly seat of East Melbourne until 1899. A conservative, he opposed payment of members and protection amid the bitter party strife which accompanied (Sir) Graham Berry's [q.v.] second government, and such measures as income tax and female suffrage in the 1890s. A supporter of the coalitions of the 1880s and of Sir James Patterson's [q.v.] ministry, he was more consistent and predictable than many of his contemporaries. Good natured, genial and popular, he spoke in parliament in a typically bantering style, and his puns were a byword, but he was less at ease on serious subjects. He was a 'useful and painstaking' chairman of the royal commissions on asylums for the insane and inebriate (reported 1884-86), on banking laws (1887) and on charitable institutions (1890, 1891, 1895); he was also a member of the commissions on the working of the Friendly Societies Statute (1875-77) and the tariff (1881-83).

Zox was president of the Melbourne Hebrew congregation in 1883-85, treasurer of the Melbourne Hebrew School in 1883 and president of the Melbourne Jewish Club in 1885. In 1890 he chaired a meeting of the Melbourne branch of the Anglo-Jewish Association of London which protested against Jewish persecution in Russia. He was vice-president of the Discharged Prisoners' Aid Society from 1885 and chairman in 1898-99, a director of the Royal Humane Society of Australasia and a board member of several hospitals. Prominent in the Manchester Unity Order of Oddfellows, he was a justice of the peace from May 1874.

Zox suffered financial reverses in the early 1890s, but was still known for his earnest devotion to charitable movements and for his ready assistance to 'forlorn wayfarers'. He was a keen student of Shakespeare and stories were told of his remarkable aptitude for arithmetic. With bell-topper, white waistcoat and mutton-chop whiskers, he was one of the best-known figures along 'The Block'. A bachelor, he was frequently seen with D. Gillies and R. Speight [qq.v.] at the Athenaeum Club.

Aged 62, he died on 23 October 1899 in a private hospital at St Kilda of pneumonia brought on by influenza. He was buried in the Melbourne general cemetery. His estate, valued for probate at £4400, was left to his two brothers and two sisters in London and a sister in Cape Town, South Africa.

J. B. Cooper, The history of St Kilda, 2 (Melb, 1931); L. M. Goldman, The Jews in Victoria in the nineteenth century (Melb, 1954); PD (Vic), 24 Oct 1899; L. E. Fredman, 'Some Victorian Jewish politicians', Aust Jewish Hist Soc, J, 4 (1954-58); Argus, 16 Aug 1890, 24 Oct 1899, R. W. E. Wilmot, 'The Block revisited', 3 May 1930, camera supp; Australasian, 28 Oct, 2 Dec 1899; Age, 24 Oct 1899; Table Talk, 1 Jan 1892; Melb Hebrew Congregation, Annual reports (Synagogue Archives). L. E. FREDMAN